Academic Writing

CONCEPTS AND CONNECTIONS

with Readings

Teresa Thonney
Columbia Basin College

OXFORD UNIVERSITY PRESS
New York | Oxford

Oxford University Press is a department of the University of Oxford.
It furthers the University's objective of excellence in research,
scholarship, and education by publishing worldwide.

Oxford New York
Auckland Cape Town Dar es Salaam Hong Kong Karachi
Kuala Lumpur Madrid Melbourne Mexico City Nairobi
New Delhi Shanghai Taipei Toronto

With offices in
Argentina Austria Brazil Chile Czech Republic France Greece
Guatemala Hungary Italy Japan Poland Portugal Singapore
South Korea Switzerland Thailand Turkey Ukraine Vietnam

For titles covered by Section 112 of the US Higher Education Opportunity Act, please visit www.oup.com/us/he for the latest information about pricing and alternate formats.

Published by Oxford University Press
198 Madison Avenue
New York, New York 10016
http://www.oup.com

Library of Congress Cataloging-in-Publication Data
Thonney, Teresa.
Academic writing : concepts and connections, with readings / Teresa Thonney. Columbia Basin College.
p. cm
ISBN 978-0-19-994743-0
1. English language—Rhetoric—Problems, exercises, etc. 2. Academic writing—Problems, exercises, etc. 3. Report writing—Problems, exercises, etc. 4. College readers. 5. Interdisciplinary approach in education. I. Title.
PE1408.T444 2015
808'.0427--dc23

2014034342

Printing number: 9 8 7 6 5 4 3 2 1

Printed in the United States of America
on acid-free paper

Brief Contents

Contents

Chapter 10: Conducting Primary Research 397

Chapter 11: Revising and Editing Academic Writing 439

Chapter 17: Conservation and the Environment 801

Preface for Instructors

In first-year composition courses, we are tasked with teaching students to produce academic writing. However, the kinds of academic writing our students will eventually produce in their majors will vary. The biology major's report will seem to bear little resemblance to the business major's proposal, which in turn will look very different from the English major's essay. What can we teach that has value and relevance to all of our students, no matter their intended major? This book attempts to answer this question by introducing students to academic writing concepts and demonstrating how they connect to writing practices across the disciplines.

Concepts in Academic Writing

Academic Writing: Concepts and Connections is an interdisciplinary rhetoric that focuses on common features of academic texts. A few of these features are:

- **reviewing** what others have written about a topic by summarizing and paraphrasing,
- **stating** the purpose and value of one's paper,
- **preparing** readers for what's ahead,
- **making** claims and supporting claims,
- **analyzing** and interpreting evidence,
- **qualifying** claims and anticipating objections,
- **acknowledging** other viewpoints,
- **crediting** others for borrowed ideas, and
- **creating** an ethos of expertise.

This book will help students to recognize these features in their reading and include them in their writing.

Familiarity with these core concepts increases the chances that students will make connections between what they learn in their composition classes and what they read and write in whatever field they choose as a major. In fact, research into how we transfer what we have learned to new situations indicates that if we first discover general concepts that unite situations, we then will be better able to distinguish how those situations differ and appropriately apply knowledge learned in one context to another. Once students discover that there are core concepts that connect the reading and writing they do in college, they are more likely to recognize the relevance and value of the skills they are learning in their composition course.

Connections across Contexts

In addition to teaching core concepts of academic writing, this book will broaden your students' understanding of the types of audiences academic writers write for and the kinds of writing they produce. The book includes original research reports, literature reviews, and essays written for other scholars, as well as magazine and newspaper articles, websites, and blogs written for broader audiences. Students will also see that academics often describe their work in more than one venue and for more than one audience.

The **paired readings**, found in every chapter, teach students that purpose, audience, genre, and venue will shape the way an academic writer writes about a topic. In most cases, the first reading in the pair is an interview or a newspaper, magazine, or blog article describing academic research in general terms. The second text is written by the *same scholarly author* but is intended for a different and often more specialized audience. The paired readings provide examples of how writers adjust their message to meet the expectations of different audiences and genres.

The paired readings serve another important pedagogical purpose. The first reading works as a sort of building block, a point of entry into the second, usually more difficult, text. After reading about research explained in general terms, your students will be better prepared to read the more specialized text. We want students to read authentic "academic" texts, but they need our help. The paired readings provide that help.

To recognize how common concepts are employed and connect across disciplines, students need to see a wide variety of academic writing. The reading selections in this book highlight the diversity of forms, voices, and disciplines that comprise academic writing. The book features:

1. **A broad picture of academic writing.** In many composition textbooks, students get little exposure to non-humanities writing. Math professor Patrick Bahls, along with coauthors Amy Mecklenburg-Faenger, Meg Scott-Copses, and Chris Warnick, identify a common problem:

   > Academic writing textbooks tend to avoid actual disciplinary writing in math and sciences, including instead materials written about math or science topics for a popular audience or essays written about math or science education. Since these essays reflect a disciplinary style more like that used in the humanities, students are not typically exposed to disciplinary writing. . . .

This book includes full-length readings from a wide range of disciplinary perspectives, including education, business, psychology, computer science, environmental science, rhetoric and composition, economics, media studies, and biological science. These readings are used *not* to illustrate what business or psychology or computer science writing is like, but to demonstrate how the concepts and connections discussed throughout the book appear in the writing of every discipline. Seeing concepts demonstrated in multiple contexts promotes transfer and fosters the flexibility students will need when they encounter new writing challenges. Seeing how writing concepts get applied in numerous disciplines also decreases the likelihood of students mistakenly thinking that features such as documentation and source citation are the same in all disciplines or that they matter only to English teachers.

2. **Examples of how academics write for others in their discipline.** Each chapter of the book includes an example of an original research report, written by professors in the disciplines. These texts demonstrate how experts write to other experts in their disciplines, and they illustrate various inquiry methods, including fieldwork and observation, interviews, case studies, surveys, textual analysis, and scientific experiments.
3. **Examples of how academics write for academic readers outside of their discipline.** In addition to discipline-specific writing, the book includes selections written by professors for broader academic or college-educated audiences, from such publications as *Nature* and the *Chronicle of Higher Education.*
4. **Examples of how academics write for nonacademic readers.** To get others to care about the issues they study, academics also write to those with little or no knowledge of their disciplines. This book includes writing that scholars have done for *Scientific American, New Scientist, Discover,* the *Seattle Times,* the *Wall Street Journal,* blogs, and books written for a general audience, thus providing students with a complete picture of the kinds of writing academics do.

Research-Based Rationale

Perhaps most important in a book that teaches students about academic writing is that the book itself practices what it preaches. *Academic Writing: Concepts and Connections* models the kind of research-based writing students are expected to produce in their composition courses. Throughout the book, claims about the conventions of academic writing are supported with research from the fields of rhetoric and composition, communications, and applied linguistics. Rather than merely reading a set of guidelines, students learn that the strategies taught in this book are grounded in current research. The guidelines in two chapters (4 and 6) are based on my own analysis of writing prompts and academic journal articles. These references to primary and secondary research help students understand *why* particular conventions of academic writing are so common, while at the same time explicitly demonstrating features of academic writing, including the use of documented evidence. In this way, the rhetoric enacts the principles it outlines.

This is not, however, a Writing about Writing textbook. It is research based but not limited to writing-studies research. Nor is this a book about Writing in the Disciplines. The emphasis of this book is on what's *common* in writing across disciplines, not what's different. While students will learn in this book that the writing of one discipline can vary from that of another, the focus is on teaching concepts and foundational skills they can transfer and use when asked to read and write in all of their other college courses.

After reading this book, your students will no longer be intimidated by the different terminology, citation styles, and genres they'll encounter in their course readings. They'll come to realize that even when they cannot understand everything in a text, they can recognize patterns that unite all academic writing and use their knowledge of these connections to make meaning out of their reading.

About the Book's Organization

This book emphasizes critical reading, research, and writing strategies used across a variety of academic disciplines. Each chapter reinforces the connection between the writing skills students learn in their composition course to the writing they do in their other courses. The book begins with the foundational skills of reading and analyzing the arguments of others, moves students to the more complex skills of researching and composing their own arguments, and ends with revising and collaborating with others.

Chapter 1 introduces genre theory, which explains that the features of any type of writing, including academic writing, are closely tied to audience, purpose, and situation. Chapter 1 teaches an important principle: What constitutes "good writing" varies.

Chapter 2 teaches strategies for reading challenging academic texts, such as understanding the context and purpose of the text; annotating and making connections while reading; and adjusting reading strategies according to your reasons for reading. The chapter also gives tips for reading online and onscreen documents. **Chapter 3** continues to emphasize the importance of reading skills but specifically teaches how to evaluate the evidence in an argument, an important skill for success in college and in life.

Chapters 4 to 6 move students from reading the scholarly work of others toward crafting their own arguments and analysis papers. **Chapter 4** introduces types of arguments and analysis and demonstrates how to read and respond to some common types of college writing assignments. **Chapter 5** explains how to analyze and use figures and visual evidence in academic papers. **Chapter 6** continues to address the topic of how to respond to college writing assignments by introducing ways students can imitate the patterns and conventions important for establishing their own academic voice.

Chapters 7 to 9 describe how to plan and write a multi-source researched essay. **Chapter 7** describes how to search for a research topic and how to locate the kinds of sources expected in academic papers. **Chapter 8** explains why academic writers summarize, paraphrase, and quote what they've read and demonstrates responsible use of source material. **Chapter 9** teaches students how to assess multiple viewpoints and synthesize information from sources to support the claims in their own arguments.

Chapter 10 includes advice for conducting four types of original research—observational research, interviews, surveys, and textual analysis—and provides an opportunity for students to "create knowledge." **Chapter 11** includes techniques for revising and editing one's writing. **Chapter 12** concludes the rhetoric with a discussion of collaborating with others to compose papers and revise writing.

Combined, these 12 chapters demonstrate and describe the shared practices and conventions found in all kinds of academic writing. In short, *Academic Writing: Concepts and Connections* teaches skills commonly identified in composition course syllabi, including how to:

1. **read** academic texts more efficiently and critically;
2. **analyze** and evaluate academic arguments and evidence;
3. **summarize**, paraphrase, quote, and synthesize information from sources;
4. **read and use** visual evidence in academic arguments;
5. **recognize and use** academic writing conventions;
6. **transfer** common academic writing conventions and patterns to writing assignments in other disciplines;
7. **conduct** both secondary and primary research; and
8. **revise** alone and in collaborative environments.

To give students further practice in making connections and joining academic conversations, this book includes an anthology of 42 additional readings, each written by a college or university professor. The readings are organized by five themes: Social Networks (**chapter 13**); Perceptions and Perspectives (**chapter 14**); Language, Literacy, and Technology (**chapter 15**); Violence and Justice (**chapter 16**); and Conservation and the Environment (**chapter 17**). Each of these anthology chapters contains seven to nine readings drawn from various disciplines and genres. Each chapter includes an introduction to the overarching theme, and each reading is preceded by a contextual headnote and followed by discussion and writing prompts.

Features of the Book

Several pedagogical features will help students to understand the core concepts introduced in this book:

- The *Concept in Practice* and *Applying the Concepts* features move the student from analysis to production. **Concept in Practice** activities occur throughout chapters. They ask students to analyze how concepts taught in the chapter appear in practice in disciplinary writing (Concept *in* Practice). The capstone **Applying the Concepts** features give students the opportunity to apply each chapter's concepts to their own reading analysis and writing practice.
- The **paired readings** demonstrate how academic writers match the language and presentation of texts to the intended audience. The readings show students the importance of considering audience, purpose, context, and medium when reading and writing.
- The **readings** are followed by three types of inquiry-based questions:

  » *Questions about Meaning.* These questions assess students' understanding of the reading.
  » *Questions for Rhetorical Analysis.* These questions ask students to analyze the writing to determine the rhetorical effectiveness.
  » *Questions for Discussion and Writing.* These questions ask students to respond to the reading by making connections to other readings or thinking further about the issues.

- **Marginal annotations** draw attention to rhetorical features that help writers accomplish their purposes and help students recognize features found in writing from across the curriculum. These annotations, many written as focused queries related to the rhetorical feature at hand, also provide students with active learning opportunities.

Together, these features introduce students to core academic writing concepts and demonstrate how these concepts connect to writing practices across the disciplines.

The first-year student in your class who will major in biology will eventually need to know how to write like a biologist, but she first needs to know how to read and write papers in Psychology 101, Geology 101, History 101, Music Appreciation 101, and a host of other 101s. With its emphasis on transferable skills and shared writing conventions, *Academic Writing: Concepts and Connections* will help your students anticipate and adapt to the many new contexts, purposes, and audiences they'll write for as undergraduates.

Online Resources

An instructor's manual for *Academic Writing: Concepts and Connections*, which includes additional class exercises, assignments, and recommended readings, is available for digital download on a password-protected portion of the book's Companion Website: http://www.oup.com/us/thonney. E-book versions of *Academic Writing: Concepts and Connections* are available through www.CourseSmart.com.

Acknowledgments

I want to thank the many reviewers who commented on the manuscript for this book at every stage of and whose suggestions have improved the book in countless ways: Susan Adams Delaney, Ithaca College; Chad Barbour, Lake Superior State University; Virginia Brackett, Park University; Polly Buckingham, Eastern Washington University; Alissa Buckley, City College of San Francisco; Mary Cote, Marylhurst University and Clark College; Sarah Dangelantonio, Franklin Pierce University; Douglas Dowland, Ohio Northern University; Dr. Hannah Furrow, University of Michigan-Flint; Christine A. Geyer, Cazenovia College; Susan Giesemann North, The University of Tennessee at Chattanooga; Dale Grauman, Washington State University; Jackie Grutsch McKinney, Ball State University; Mark L. Hama, Angelo State University; Barbara A. Heifferon, Louisiana State University; Sara Hillin, Lamar University; Lindsay Illich, Curry College; Ronald R. Janssen, Hofstra University; Alice Johnston Myatt, The University of Mississippi; Ethan T. Jordan, Bowling Green State University; Tom Jordan, Eastern New Mexico University – Roswell; Lynn Kilpatrick, Salt Lake Community College; Dana Lynn Driscoll, Oakland University; Jill LeRoy-Frazier, East Tennessee State University; Susan Lowther, Washington University in St. Louis; Amy Mecklenburg-Faenger, The College of Charleston; Holly Middleton, High Point University; Cynthia Miecznikowski, University of North Carolina at Pembroke; Shannon Mondor, College of the Redwoods; Osayimwense Osa, Virginia State University; Paul J. Patterson, Saint Joseph's University; Erin Phillippi, James Madison University; Laura Poladian, Loyola Marymount University; Bed Prasad Giri, Dartmouth College; Heather E. Pristash, Western Wyoming Community College; Morgan Reitmeyer, Regis University; Catherine E. Ross, The University of Texas at Tyler; Kathy L. Rowley, Eastern Washington University; Catherine A. Rusco, Muskegon Community College; Charlene Schauffler, Kent State University; Roxana Spano, Cazenovia College; Rod B. Spellman, Guilford College; Annie Rose Stathes, Fort Lewis College; Ellyn Stepanek, Cleveland State University; Brittany Stephenson, Salt Lake Community

College; Eleanor Sumpter-Latham, Central Oregon Community College; Jefferey H. Taylor, Metropolitan State College of Denver; Chris Tonelli, North Carolina State University; Dr. Tammy Trucks-Bordeaux, Peru State College; Amy Vidali, University of Colorado Denver; Steven M. Werkmeister, Johnson County Community College; Jackie K. White, Lewis University.

I am also grateful to the many students and colleagues whose contributions have enriched this book. I am especially grateful to Randy Becker—for listening.

Finally, I want to thank development editor Lai Moy, whose vision helped to shape this book, and I am most grateful to Frederick Speers, acquisitions editor for Oxford University Press, without whom this book would not exist.

WORK CITED

Bahls, Patrick, et al. "Proofs and Persuasion: A Cross-Disciplinary Analysis of Math Students' Writing." *Across the Disciplines* 18.1 (2011). Web. 28 September 2011.

CHAPTER 1

Academic Writing across the Disciplines

Let's begin with a quiz. Displayed in Figures A to F, which follow, are examples of six different kinds of documents. How many types can you identify? (Don't worry; there's an answer key after the images.)

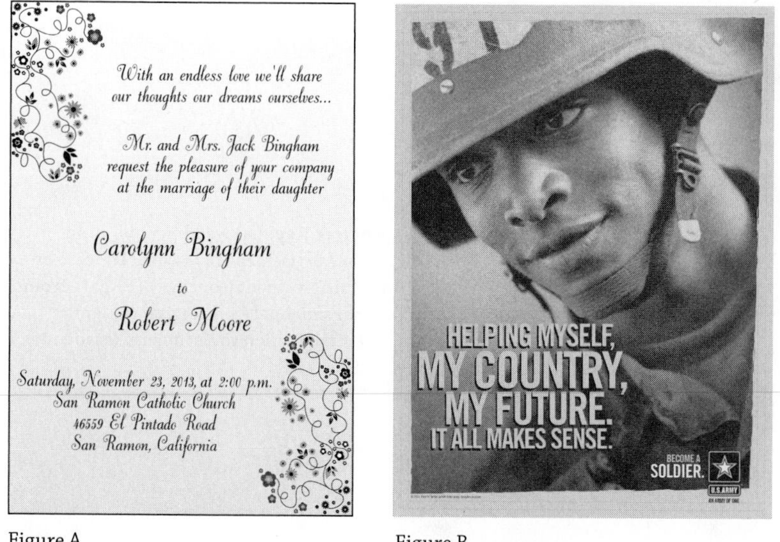

With an endless love we'll share our thoughts our dreams ourselves...

Mr. and Mrs. Jack Bingham request the pleasure of your company at the marriage of their daughter

Carolynn Bingham

to

Robert Moore

Saturday, November 23, 2013, at 2:00 p.m.
San Ramon Catholic Church
46559 El Pintado Road
San Ramon, California

Figure A __________

Figure B __________

Stephen Colbert @StephenAtHome 23 Apr

2NITE: "Thanx 2 the sequester, if you've flown in the last couple days, U may have noticed U didn't fly in the last couple days."TCR, 11:30

Expand

Figure C __________

This Rental Agreement or Residential Lease shall evidence the complete terms and conditions under which the parties whose signatures appear below have agreed. Landlord/Lessor/Agent, ____________________, shall be referred to as "OWNER" and Tenant(s)/Lessee, ____________________, shall be referred to as "RESIDENT." As consideration for this agreement, OWNER agrees to rent/lease to RESIDENT and RESIDENT agrees to rent/lease from OWNER for use solely as a private residence, the premises located at ____________________ ____________ in the city of ____________________.

1. **TERM:** RESIDENT agrees to pay in advance $ ________ per month on the _______day of each month. This agreement shall commence on ______,______ and continue; (check one)

A. ___ until ____,___ as a leasehold. Thereafter it shall become a month-to-month tenancy. If RESIDENT should move from the premises prior to the expiration of this time period, he shall be liable for all rent due until such time that the Residence is occupied by an OWNER approved paying RESIDENT and/or expiration of said time period, whichever is shorter.

Figure D __________

First Steps

Inserting the Batteries

1 Open the battery-chamber/memory card slot cover.

- Before opening the battery-chamber/memory card slot cover, hold the camera upside down to prevent the batteries from falling out.

2 Insert the Batteries

- Confirm that the positive (+) and negative (–) terminals are oriented correctly as desoribed on the label at the entrance of the battery chamber, and insert the batteries.

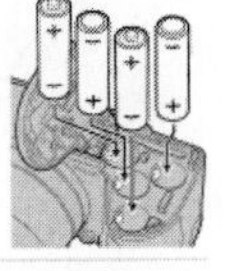

3 Close the battery-chamber/memory card slot cover.

Figure E __________

Answer Key: (A) wedding invitation **(B)** advertisement **(C)** tweet **(D)** lease or rental agreement (contract) **(E)** page from a user's manual (for a digital camera) **(F)** introduction to a scholarly (academic) article

1. Introduction

Automation has brought revolution in industry and provides cost-effective and more flexible capability in controlling of machining systems [1]. It helps companies in economic enterprise improvement and replacement of human in heavy physical and dangerous working environment [2]. The fully automated machinery systems bring higher quality, better consistency, reduced lead times, simplified manufacturing processes, less product handling, and improved work flow in manufacturing and production lines.

Automated and high-speed mechanical system is a field of engineering dealing with different machine tool development integration of machinery systems and production equipment. It has been applied to manufacturing processes to perform many dangerous, heavy labor-related, and repetitive tasks [3].

Figure F __________

The computer-aided design and modeling technology allows mechanical design teams to quickly and cost-effectively iterate the design process with better quality and reliable function. Through this technology, multiple design concepts can be reviewed and evaluated with no real prototype required until the product design is completed [4]. This paper introduces a new fully automated and high-speed gas filling mechanical system based on computer-aided simulation, analysis, and prototype testing.

2. Automated and High-Speed Gas Filling System

One critical feature in this automated mechanical system is to quickly and reliably seal high-pressure gas chamber during high-speed gas filling process. The normal sealing technologies include injecting gel into cartridge to seal gas chamber, shown in Figure 1, but it shows the poor sealing capacity in gas charging process.

In the newly developed gas filling and plug sealing mechanism, the plug is inserted into a cartridge while gas is being charged into the gas chamber, otherwise, gas will leak from chamber if cartridge is not being sealed simultaneously.

Figure F (*Continued*)

Chances are you correctly identified many of the document types because, as a college student, you already have experience with reading many kinds of texts. Different types or categories of writing are sometimes referred to as **genres**, and there are of course *many* genres. Here are only a few genres you may have read or even written:

- blog posts
- e-mails
- college websites
- science fiction novels
- bumper stickers
- song lyrics
- Facebook profiles
- newspaper articles

Distinguishing a tweet from a rental contract and a user's manual from a wedding invitation is easy because these genres (and all genres) have distinctive features. You wouldn't expect a user's manual to read like a science fiction novel, nor do you expect the writing in this textbook to resemble that of a text message. The features of genres vary because the *audiences* (readers) and *purposes* (goals) vary. For example, the purpose of the user's manual shown in Figure E is to explain how to insert a battery into a digital camera. Because people who read this user's manual are assumed to have never completed this process before, the instructions are broken down into steps, each numbered and accompanied with images. These helpful features enable the intended audience (new camera owners) to achieve the intended purpose (to insert a battery).

Every genre of writing has features that reflect how the genre is created, who reads it, how it's read, and why it's read. Writing experts refer to this concept as **genre theory**. But a genre's features aren't static. When the needs of the readers change, features of a genre will change. Consider the genre you are currently reading: the college textbook. A traditional textbook contains such standard features as a table of contents, an index, chapter summaries, and highlighted key terms. But because today's students are so visually and digitally oriented, these features have changed over time. The once one-color, all-text table of contents may now boast four colors and photographs that help distinguish one chapter from another. Data once explained textually may now be presented graphically. Some print books may come accompanied with e-books containing pop-up boxes for key terms and links to other digital resources. While the textbook genre is still recognizable as a textbook, its familiar features have changed in response to how the needs of the intended audience have changed.

Describing the features of **academic writing** (Figure F) and explaining *why* those features are so common across different fields of study are the goals of this book. By way of introduction, a few important features of academic writing are described in the following sections.

Recognizing Common Features of Academic Writing

As noted earlier, a key principle of genre theory is that different kinds of writing (genres) have different kinds of features, many of them related to why the document was written and for whom. How the features of academic writing are realized in different fields of study—or **disciplines**—can vary, as examples in this chapter and the rest of this book illustrate; but all academic writing shares many features, features you'll encounter many times in this textbook and in your other college reading assignments.

Specialized Audiences

Many genres, such as popular magazines, novels, or greeting cards, are written for a general audience. Reading them requires no specialized knowledge. For instance, consider this message from a greeting card for a person who has just moved into a new home:

> May love and laughter
> move in with you today
> and fill your home
> with happiness
> and sunshine every day!

Now compare the language of this greeting card message to that of a passage from an article about student sleep patterns:

> Fifty-four percent of students reported currently living with parents, comparable with the 52% figure for Canadian university students (Kuo et al.,

> 2002). Barker and Galambos (2007) reported that social and academic adjustment scores for this sample were in line with results from the U.S. samples. . . .
>
> (Galambos, Dalton, and Maggs 745)

This passage is from an article written for a scholarly journal on education. Because articles in academic journals are written by scholars for other scholars in a particular discipline, fully understanding the language, content, and style requires some specialized knowledge. For example, 2002 and 2007 (in parentheses) in the passage refer to the year of publication for articles written by authors Kuo and Barker and Galambos.

Contextualized Writing

Kuo and *Barker and Galambos*, referred to in the education passage, are researchers who have written about the same topic as the author of the passage. This is just one of the ways that academic writers put their writing in context. By referring to what's already been written about the topic, writers show that they are joining others who have been discussing the issue. Providing an informative title and a statement of purpose early in their papers are additional ways academic writers establish the context for readers. Here, for example, is the statement of purpose found at the end of the introduction in Figure F: "This paper introduces a new fully automated and high-speed gas filling mechanical system based on computer-aided simulation, analysis, and prototype testing." Once readers have a framework into which to put the information they are about to read, they can better understand what it means.

Specialized Vocabulary

The vocabulary in most academic writing is another indication that it is intended for readers with some knowledge about the subject matter. The courses you take in college will require that you learn specialized vocabulary so that you can participate in conversations about the discipline and precisely convey your ideas. Students learn as many new words in an introductory biology course, for instance, as they learn in a foreign language course (Langer 75).

Sometimes what you'll learn will be new definitions for familiar words. Students familiar with the nonmathematical definition of *association, average,* or *random*, for example, may struggle in a statistics course until they learn the mathematical meaning of these words (Kaplan, Fisher, and Rogness). Many words are "shared" but used in different ways by several disciplines. In statistics, *regression analysis* refers to measuring the association between variables. But in medicine, *regression* refers to the shrinking of a tumor, and in learning theory, it refers to the tendency to temporarily forget skills while learning new material. In computer programming, biology, psychology, and optometry, *regression* has different meanings still.

More often, the vocabulary you learn will be different from vocabulary you encounter in other disciplines. Each discipline has its own academic phrasing or *specialized vocabulary* that has developed over years of study and research. Consider the following passages from works of neuroscience and literature:

EXAMPLE 1.1: FROM NEUROSCIENCE

This effect contrasts sharply with observations I made recently on two patients with small paracentral scotomas caused by damage to the visual cortex. If the arc of a circle or the corner of a square fell on the scotoma, the figure was completed perceptually, although the process usually took 7 or 8 s to occur.

(Ramachandran 202)

Specialized vocabulary *such as this is common in academic writing; each discipline has its own specialized vocabulary. Compare this vocabulary to the specialized vocabulary in Example 1.2 from literature.*

EXAMPLE 1.2: FROM LITERATURE

There are other such vivid metaphoric images in Glaspell's fiction that could be cited, such as the rigidly manicured garden at the opening of *Ambrose Holt and Family* that symbolizes the constricted existence of the main character (fittingly named Blossom), and the decaying ancestral house next to the graveyard in *The Morning Is Near Us* that expresses the protagonist's yearning for her lost family.

(Carpentier 92)

Here are examples of ***specialized vocabulary*** *in literature. It differs from the specialized vocabulary in Example 1.1, which is from neuroscience, yet it is an element common to writing in both disciplines.*

While academic phrasing such as *paracentral scotomas* and *metaphoric images* may seem difficult, in both passages it serves a practical purpose. Mark Williams, a geography professor, explains: "Much of the so-called 'technical jargon' are simply code words for subjects, processes, etc., that we all agree on. If we had to define each of these words in every article, it would increase the length of the article by many pages, and for most of us, be very boring, because we already know these terms" (Williams e-mail).

Disciplinary Perspectives and Modes of Inquiry

Perspective and methods of inquiry also vary according to discipline. Many issues—for example, mental illness, racism, and crime—are studied in more than one discipline. But disciplines differ in the perspective from which they address the issue, in their reasons for studying it, and in their ways of understanding it. In other words, disciplines differ in their ways of knowing what they know.

To create knowledge, academic writers ask questions and conduct research. Disciplines in the natural sciences and mathematics might emphasize the following in their research:

- Counting and measuring of data
- Using a system of formal rules to interpret a problem
- Applying statistical or mathematical models to the analysis of problems

In other disciplines, including many in the humanities, the methods of inquiry emphasize types of interpretation, creative theory, or aesthetic appreciation, including:

- Analyzing the stories, performances, and art of societies
- Interpreting historical events and cultural practices
- Examining societal factors that play a part in the development of institutions, cultures, or organizations

Different ways of knowing result in different ways of approaching and looking at the same problem. The following responses are from a professor of wildlife ecology and a professor of English who were asked, "What questions would researchers in your discipline ask about world overpopulation?" Notice the difference in their approaches:

From my perspective, I would be interested in how world overpopulation affects the natural environment. Specifically, how does it affect wildlife species and ecosystem function? What impacts will the global economy (which is going to be the foundation for sustaining our growing human population) continue to have on native species and ecosystems with regards to introduction of nonnative wildlife and plant species?

—Stephen Ditchkoff, Professor of Wildlife Ecology

Textual analysis often deals with representation. As such we might easily explore a theme such as world overpopulation and ask questions such as "How is it represented differently by different authors for different audiences?" We may compare and contrast a fictional account, a memoir, an article in a news magazine, and a documentary. We would ask, "What were the goals of the genre?" "How did the genre influence the rhetorical choices made?" "How did these choices affect us as readers?" and "How well did each example succeed?"

—Mary Bendel-Simso, Professor of English

As these examples demonstrate, researchers from two different disciplines studying the same issue see the issue through different "lenses." One professor focused on how overpopulation affects the natural environment (e.g., wildlife species and ecosystems); the other professor focused on how the subject of overpopulation might be represented in different types of literature and by different authors. Both professors study the effects of overpopulation, but they look for evidence of those effects in different places—in the physical world and in the textual world.

Emphasis on Research and Evidence

All disciplines value concrete and specific evidence obtained by conducting research. Different perspectives and approaches to problems, however, require different types of research methods. In the natural sciences, researchers plan in advance how to gather and measure data and then carefully follow their experimental protocol. The experimental research of many social scientists involves studying people; as a result, they may be less able to control variables or objectively measure findings. Scholars in both the natural and social sciences value observable and replicable evidence. Scholars in the humanities, on the other hand, conduct a different type of research. Rather than conduct controlled experiments, they are more apt to study words, images, or artifacts. Their evidence includes such things as quotations and description that support interpretations. But make no mistake: Research in *every* discipline is based on interpretation. How we "see" and explain a subject depends on our assumptions. Our assumptions in turn influence what questions we ask and how we interpret the answers we find.

The research method will determine the kinds of evidence a researcher uncovers. Let's look again at our earlier examples from neuroscience and literature.

EXAMPLE 1.1: FROM NEUROSCIENCE

This effect contrasts sharply with observations I made recently on two patients with small paracentral scotomas caused by damage to the visual cortex. If the arc of a circle or the corner of a square fell on the scotoma, the figure was completed per-
5 ceptually, although the process usually took 7 or 8 s to occur.
(Ramachandran 202)

*Like specialized vocabulary, **concrete and specific evidence** is also common in academic writing. Here, the neuroscience researcher describes his **observations**: ". . . the figure was completed perceptually, although the process usually took 7 or 8 s to occur."*

EXAMPLE 1.2: FROM LITERATURE

There are other such vivid metaphoric images in Glaspell's fiction that could be cited, such as the rigidly manicured garden at the opening of *Ambrose Holt and Family* that symbolizes the constricted existence of the main character
5 (fittingly named Blossom), and the decaying ancestral

*In this passage from literature, the **evidence** is **textual** and **anecdotal**: "the rigidly manicured garden . . . symbolizes the constricted existence of the main character. . . ."*

> house next to the graveyard in *The Morning is Near Us* that expresses the protagonist's yearning for her lost family.
>
> (Carpentier 92)

Both passages include concrete evidence—a feature of all academic writing. However, since one example is from neuroscience and the other is from literature, the *type* of evidence differs.

Transitioning to Reading and Writing in the Disciplines

As a college student, you will take introductory courses in many disciplines. Colleges and universities require this to ensure that when you graduate, you are not just trained in your major; you are "educated." Taking courses in a variety of disciplines gives you a broad foundation of knowledge and introduces you to different ways of making sense of the world. By taking courses across the disciplines, you learn to see through different lenses and apply different modes of inquiry. These courses also help you to develop skills needed in every career. In fact, one reason some employers will hire a college graduate whose major is unrelated to the job is that general education courses hone important job skills: writing, reading, researching, critical thinking, computer, and interpersonal skills, to name a few.

You will discover that learning about various disciplines has many benefits, but you may also find that learning about several disciplines simultaneously can be daunting. The authors of the report *A Review of the Proficiencies Required by Students Entering First Year Post-Secondary English Courses* compare experiencing the first year of college to arriving in a new country:

> Students who make the transition between high school and post-secondary institutions engage, sometimes literally, but always metaphorically, in a journey: the academy is a domain of language use, and students come in as foreigners to the academy. . . . New immigrants to the academy often grossly underestimate the time required to learn the language and the customs. (1)

Even *professors* who take introductory classes in fields new to them find the adjustment challenging, as you'll learn in the end-of-chapter readings.

As an undergraduate, you may be asked to write papers in Psychology 101, Geology 101, History 101, Music Appreciation 101, and a host of other 101s. There will be differences between these assignments and differences in terminology. What one professor calls a *critical review* may or may not be the same as what another calls a *critical analysis*. The definition of words like *evidence* and *argument* will vary, so will the definition of *documentation*. It may also occasionally seem that what one instructor praises about your writing, another criticizes. Rather than interpreting these differences as your professors' idiosyncratic whims, it's best to regard them as demonstrations of how in writing, *context is everything.*

This book will help you discover connections that will smooth your transition from one context to another. It will help you transfer and apply the writing, reading, and research knowledge you learn in this course to the writing, reading, and research required in your other courses, regardless of the discipline. You'll see how these writing practices converge as well as where they diverge—and how to manage that divergence.

This book will also raise your *rhetorical awareness.* When you carefully consider the audience, the purpose, the discipline, the genre, *and* the parameters of your college writing assignments, you are demonstrating **rhetorical awareness**. Being rhetorically aware will help you determine what features are appropriate in a given writing context; many of those same features may be inappropriate in another context. In short, applying the same model to all writing contexts won't work in college. You will need to adjust the way you write from context to context.

Consider Your Study Habits and Learning Preferences

In college, you will need to adjust the way you write from context to context. Many students may also need to adjust their ideas about how to learn, as education professor Rebecca Cox discovered after interviewing more than 120 students at 34 community colleges. Some of the students interviewed thought that if the instructor didn't tell them what they needed to know (preferably in PowerPoint slides!) and then test them on what they had been told, the instructor was not "teaching us anything" (92). This mindset won't serve a student well in college, as many studies have demonstrated. In one study, 308 students enrolled in introductory courses completed a standardized assessment of study approaches. The students who said they preferred that teachers tell them exactly what to write in their notes were the same students who received significantly lower grades and were most likely to identify themselves as struggling in their classes (Stevens and Carbary). And in another study, first-year students in writing courses who were motivated only by grades tended to make fewer substantial revisions to their writing than the students motivated by a desire to master skills or effectively communicate ideas to their reader (Kodman). These studies indicate how important it is for you to have personal, or intrinsic, motives for learning rather than extrinsic motives (like good grades) alone.

The best advice to bear in mind as you begin navigating the world of academic writing: Be willing to adopt new strategies and habits. While it may not always seem that you are being "taught" anything in classes where the instructor chooses discussion, critiquing models, and hands-on learning over telling you what you need to know, a wealth of research indicates that activities like these promote real learning.

Consider Your Prior Writing Knowledge and Beliefs about Learning

Most students enter a college course with some knowledge of the subject matter. The prior knowledge about a subject—those facts, assumptions, attitudes, and related experiences that we bring into a class—usually works to our advantage, unless what we've learned is inaccurate or only partially correct. When what students know or think they know about a subject matter is incorrect, those misconceptions can be hard to correct, something mathematics professor Clifford Konold witnesses when he tries to get students to overcome the incorrect "intuitions" they have about statistical probability.

Students who do well in their courses are able to correct any misconceptions they initially had about the subject matter (Gutman 161). This may include *unlearning* some half-truths or misconceptions about writing. *Never begin a sentence with "because"; don't use contractions in academic papers; make essays five paragraphs in length*—these are only a few of the writing "rules" you may have heard that are routinely broken by many published academic writers. Context and audience determine when a writing feature is appropriate or not, and being able to adjust according to the writing situation is crucial. When writing professors Nancy Sommers and Laura Saltz tracked the progress of more than 400 Harvard University students, they discovered that those who held on to the same ideas about writing that they had when they entered college progressed at a slower rate than those who recognized that they were novices to academic writing and were open to learning how to write at the college level (134). One obvious first step to making your transition into college writing easier, then, is to accept that some of the techniques you used when writing in high school may need to be revised.

Students who are open to learning new techniques will see their writing skills improve with practice and hard work. English professors Paul J. Johnson and Ethan Krase saw this when they tracked the development of writing skills among a sample of first-year composition students. Two-thirds of these students performed below "acceptable" levels on their first essay; yet, within a single term, they showed significant improvement in their academic writing, especially in the ability to develop arguments with evidence, write appropriately for an audience, and document information from sources. Most of these students also succeeded in the writing they later did in their majors, despite the variety of majors they entered and the range of instructors, genres, and writing tasks they encountered. What did the successful students have in common? Motivation. The researchers concluded that "learning to write well is dependent neither solely on ability nor on a given professor, course, or program. Rather, becoming a competent writer depends upon a particular student's motivation to put forth the requisite effort" (Johnson and Krase). Practicing your writing, getting feedback, and revising are essential habits for you to develop in this course.

Understanding Concepts and Connections in Academic Writing

In this book, you'll learn what it means to be an academic writer. You'll learn about practices that academic writers have in common, and you'll begin to connect the writing concepts you learn in this course to the writing assignments you'll complete in your other courses. Here are a few of those concepts:

- *Academic writers respond to what others have written.* Academic writing is not done in a vacuum. Writers read what others have written about their topics, and when they write they show that they are joining an ongoing conversation by referring to what others have written. For this reason, most academic writing begins with reading.
- *Academic writers state the purpose and value of their writing.* Academic writers do more than report what others have written; they make a contribution to the conversation, one that will benefit those who read their take on the issue. To ensure they have an audience, academic writers explain the importance of their topics and how they will add to what others have written about it.
- *Academic writers make reasonable claims and support claims with evidence.* Academic writing is *evidence-based.* Claims are supported with credible evidence obtained from the writer's own research or experience or that of others. To make their claims accurate and convincing, academic writers often allow for exceptions by using qualifying words like *often, usually,* or *sometimes.*
- *Academic writers acknowledge other viewpoints.* There are always multiple ways to look at an issue. We all see things from a different perspective based on our vantage point and background. Academic writers acknowledge reasons others might disagree with their position and respond to those counterarguments.
- *Academic writers write with authority.* Academic writers convey their expertise in a number of ways. A few of the most common are announcing the value of their research for readers, using specialized vocabulary and academic phrasing, being precise when making claims and providing evidence, and establishing their first-hand knowledge.
- *Academic writers recognize that the conversation will continue.* No matter the topic, there is more to be written about it. There are additional viewpoints to consider. There is additional evidence to analyze and new ways

to understand existing evidence. Because few issues can be settled conclusively, academic writers often close their papers with a call for further research or further discussion. No writer has the final word. The conversation is ongoing.

You'll begin to notice these connections as you read in different disciplines throughout college, and you'll learn in this book how to exhibit them in the writing you do for this course and for other courses.

Over the next few years, the improvement you see in your writing may not always be consistent, and occasionally you might even feel like your writing skills are declining as you struggle to master complex material. But if you want to learn and are willing to put forth the effort necessary to learn, your writing and thinking will progress in ways single instructors, including your composition instructor, won't get to witness. By learning about the characteristics of academic writing—both those that connect and differentiate the disciplines—you will advance your ability to read and write texts for any undergraduate course. With this knowledge, you'll begin to approach college writing assignments with confidence.

Applying the Concepts to Reading: *Reading Academic Writing*

The following passage is from an article titled "Understanding the College First-year Experience," written by Kirk S. Kidwell and originally published in *The Clearing House*, a journal that publishes articles for educators. As the assistant director of the Center for Integrative Studies in the Arts and Humanities at Michigan State University and as a professor of film studies and composition, Kidwell has worked with many students. In this excerpt, Kidwell describes an important transition he has observed many students make in their first year of college.

After reading the passage, answer the following questions:

1. Kidwell is primarily addressing high school and college teachers. How and where is this target audience made clear? Consider, for example, when he uses first- and third-person pronouns (*we* and *they*).
2. According to Kidwell, "The vast majority of first-year students enter college as dualists." What does this mean? During the first year of college, what kinds of changes occur in the way many students experience learning? What brings about this change? What other changes or

challenges can a typical first-year college student expect? What advice does Kidwell offer for students and their teachers?

3. On what evidence are Kidwell's claims based? How does he establish himself as an expert on the topic?
4. Where and how does Kidwell show that he is writing about a topic that others have written about? That is, how does he show that he is joining a conversation?
5. How does Kidwell indicate that he expects more to be learned about his subject? That is, how does he show that he expects the conversation to continue?
6. Does Kidwell break any writing "rules" you have previously learned? If so, where?
7. Three features in Kidwell's essay can be found in many academic articles:

   » Numbers in parentheses throughout the text
   » "Notes" after the article
   » References listed at the end

   In a paragraph or two, identify what you understand about each feature:

   » What do the numbers in parentheses refer to?
   » What are the purposes of the Notes? (The first note from the article has been omitted here.)
   » What kinds of references are listed: Books? Articles? Websites? Interviews? Other?

   If you don't know the answer to any of these questions, indicate what you think *may* be the answer and explain your thinking. In short, identify what you understand and identify what you are not sure about.

FROM "UNDERSTANDING THE COLLEGE FIRST-YEAR EXPERIENCE," *Kirk S. Kidwell*

For the vast majority of students I have taught, the problem they face in the purgatory of the first-year is the product of neither lack of intelligence nor of aptitude (as I try to reassure my students repeatedly throughout the first semester). Instead, the difficulty they encounter arises from the workload that each course expects of them—what students learn—as well as a transformation in the students' styles of learning—*how* they learn. On the one hand, rarely have they had to read so many pages or worked so many problems in such a short amount of time, only to complete the assignments and realize that yet more is 5 due the next week in addition to a paper or exam on the material covered in the previous weeks. And the pace never seems to let up but, rather, intensifies during the last weeks of the semester, leading up to the dreaded Finals Week. But, somewhere along the way, the students learn to hone their academic skills—time management, note taking, test preparation, essay writing, and so on—and to adapt to the expectation of the college course workload. And, in this, their high-school experience often serves them well.

On the other hand, the purgatory of the first year results from the challenge posed by adopting new styles of learning that are less a matter of skills and more a matter of the student's relation with him- or herself as a learner, with instructors serving not so much as authorities but rather as facilitators, colearners with the students. And, in this, the high-school experience seems to be more a part of the problem than the solution. "Among the many changes students undergo during the college years," Bette LaSere Erickson and Diane Weltner Strommer observe in *Teaching College Freshman* [sic], "one of the most significant is the change in their perceptions of learning" (1991, 47). Erickson and Strommer suggest that the scheme of intellectual and ethical development first proposed by William G. Perry (1970, 1981) and later supplemented by Mary F. Belenky et al. (1986) and others[2] provides a productive model for understanding the rather purgatorial transformation of student learning styles that commences during the first semester of the freshman year. In brief, the transformation in learning styles occurs in four phases, often characterized as dualism, multiplicity, relativism, and commitment in relativism.

The vast majority of first-year students enter college as dualists. For them, knowledge is a matter of truth, answers are right or wrong, and positions are good and bad. Professors know the truth, which they impart in their courses and test for in examinations and essays. Learning is simply a matter of absorbing as much of the professor's knowledge as possible and producing the correct answers in exams and essays. At this phase, the student regards him- or herself as an entirely passive recipient of the professor's knowledge; like empty vessels, students attend classes to be filled with the elixir of knowledge, which they store within themselves until it is time to return that knowledge in an exam or essay.

By the end of the first year, these same students will, quite often, emerge as multiplists or, ideally, will be transitioning toward relativism and commitment in relativism.[3] At the stage of multiplicity, knowledge is no longer truth but only opinion, answers are no longer right or wrong but better or worse, and positions are simply a matter of theory, tantamount to mere beliefs. Professors simply hold privileged opinions and learning becomes a game in which students tell their professors what they think their professors want them to say. But the student is now no longer passive; instead, he or she strives to learn the rules of the academic game to win the best grade possible. Although, by the end of the freshman year, students may seem jaded and cynical on the surface, a more profound transformation is beginning to happen within as they realize that, since opinions must be backed with reasons and evidence and contrary opinions must be fairly analyzed and evaluated, they must be prepared to support their opinions as well as to be open to alternatives. At this point, the student has shifted from passivity to activity; college is no longer an environment in which professors have the sole responsibility to teach but, rather, one in which the student has an equal responsibility to learn. They are now well on the way to becoming critical thinkers who are, in the words of Richard Paul and Linda Elder, "self-directed, self-disciplined, self-monitored, and self-corrective" (in Reimers and Roberson 2004).

What happens during the nine months between when the students first arrive on campus in the fall as dualists and when they return home in the spring as multiplists? During their freshman year, students are exposed to a variety of concepts and theories, none of which are inherently right or wrong. A student in an introductory psychology course, for example, learns that there is no one agreed-on theory of personality but, rather, a series of competing models, all of which seem to be well-supported and equally viable. In a literature class, a student is informed about a number of possible readings of William Faulkner's "A Rose for Emily," none of which is presented as the definitive, authoritative interpretation of the story. Or a student is assigned to write an essay analyzing and evaluating a text, a concept, a theory, without the professor stating in advance what answer is the right one or whether there even is a "right" answer. And then the essay, which the student feels is the best he or she could possibly have written, is returned not only with errors in grammar or punctuation marked but also with observations that the essay lacks a unified focus or that certain paragraphs need to be developed more fully and coherently. In other words, first-year students are repeatedly confronted with learning situations in which there is no right or wrong answer and in which seemingly every question they ask is answered with yet another question: "What do you think?" or "Why do you think that?"

And that is what makes the first year in college so aggravating, so purgatorial, for the typical student: thinking. Students seem to be consistently amazed when they discover that they are not expected simply to recite the correct answer but to think, and to think for themselves. Merely providing the right answer is no longer sufficient; instead, students must think why an answer may or may not be right, what makes one answer better than another, and they must also be prepared to explain what they think and why.

High school teachers and college professors can help their students through this transition but not by offering the easy way out by a return to the naïve comfort of dualist thinking. To the contrary, teachers and professors should work to gain a better understanding of the process of
100 transformation induced by the freshman-year experience. As William Perry has remarked, we need to hear "where students are speaking from" as much as what they are saying (in Erickson and Strommer 1991, 54). We, too, need to change, to stop regarding ourselves as the authority-who-knows and to become facilitators of student-directed
105 learning, realizing that we, like our students, are learners as well.

NOTES

...

2. See Kurflss (1988) for a fuller discussion.

3. In my experience, very few freshman students move much beyond multiplicity, and so I limit my discussion in this article to dualism and multiplicity. Briefly, however, relativism builds on multiplicity as the students come to understand that knowledge is contextual and learning is a process, inflected by the student's background of assumptions, values, and expectations, whereby knowledge is constructed on the basis of sound reasons and evidence. The professor is now a facilitator for the student's active construction of knowledge. At the phase of commitment in relativism, the student has made an affirmation or choice based on the self-constructed knowledge developed during the phase of relativism. Learning is now wholly active as the student takes responsibility not only for his or her knowledge, values, or beliefs but also for the choices and actions that proceed from that knowledge, values, and beliefs.

REFERENCES

Belenky, M. E, B. M. Clinchy, N. R. Goldberger, and J. M. Tarule. 1986. *Women's ways of knowing: The development of self, voice, and mind.* New York: Basic.

Erickson, B. L., and D. W. Strommer. 1991. *Teaching college freshmen.* San Francisco: Jossey-Bass.

Kurflss, J. G. 1988. *Critical thinking: Theory, research, practice, and possibilities.* ASHE-ERIC Higher Education Report No. 2. Washington, DC: Association for the Study of Higher Education.

Perry, W. G., Jr. 1970. *Forms of intellectual and ethical development in the college years.* New York: Holt, Rinehart, and Winston.

———. 1981. Cognitive and ethical growth: The making of meaning. In *The American college,* ed. A. W. Chickering and Associates, 76–116. San Francisco: Jossey-Bass.

Reimers, T., and B. Roberson. 2004. Thinking critically about the teaching of critical thinking. Lilly Seminar, Michigan State University, East Lansing, Michigan, October 29.

Applying the Concepts to Writing: *Considering Your Learning Preferences*

The different vocabularies, different perspectives, and different methods of inquiry you'll experience as you move from course to course and discipline to discipline will require you to adapt to different styles of presentations and different kinds of reading, a point illustrated in the two reading selections ahead, by Sheila Tobias. Students who respond well to a particular presentation style can find it frustrating when new material is not presented in their preferred style.

Reflect on your own learning style preferences by completing a learning style inventory. (There's an online version available at http://www.personal.psu.edu/bxb11/LSI/LSI.htm or you can find other inventories online by searching for "Learning Style Preference Inventory" or "Learning Styles Inventory.")

What methods of presentation and learning do you prefer? What do you anticipate will be, or what have you found to be, most challenging about learning in college and how can you address those challenges? For instance, what study techniques can you apply to increase your learning potential? Address these questions in a "reflective essay."

Paired Readings from Interdisciplinary Studies

"Disciplinary Cultures and General Education," *Essays on Teaching Excellence,* SHEILA TOBIAS

Sheila Tobias has devoted much of her academic career to understanding teaching and learning across disciplines. She is perhaps most famous for writing and speaking about math and science anxiety, and she has written several books on the topic, including *Overcoming Math Anxiety, They're Not Dumb, They're Different,* and *Breaking the Science Barrier.* Her essay included here, "Disciplinary Cultures and General Education," was originally published in 1992 in *Essays on Teaching Excellence*, a series of scholarly essays about college teaching and learning published each year by the POD Network (the Professional and Organizational Development Network in Higher Education). In this essay, Tobias argues that it's not the content as much as it is the method of presentation that makes some courses difficult for some students.

For some years, I have been exploring the response of otherwise intelligent students to the prevailing discourse of disciplinary instruction. Note that I do not speak of the prevailing discourse of the disciplines. For while we claim to be introducing our beginning students to the disciplines we teach, the way we structure courses and measure performance often distorts or leaves unexplored the way our discipline is actually practiced. It is not surprising, therefore, that many intelligent and hard-working newcomers to our fields find them to be disciplines outside of what I call their "comfort zone," disciplines which do not "play" to their strengths. An underlying theme of any discussion of general education should be that there are a variety of "disciplinary cultures," and that it is a particularly harrowing challenge for students to cross from one to another.

As I discovered while studying "math anxiety," for anxious and avoidant students, mathematics is never just a subject but a relationship between themselves, the subject, and all who are better at it than they. Such relationships are as much influenced by teacher expectations, pace, exams, and style of presentation as by pedagogy and course content. In short, I believe students bring a "cognitive self-image" that bears on their approach to general education, their willingness to study and their capacity to succeed. For many students, a course in a discipline not their own is "hard" not because its content is too difficult for them, but because it is "packaged" and "purveyed" in unfamiliar ways.

To get a closer look at how subjects are "enculturated," and how that affects students, I placed three artificial populations of intelligent, accomplished outsiders in short and semester-long introductory courses in disciplines very different from their own.

The first were professors in fields other than science and mathematics, whose ability to think and to reason abstractly were indisputable, whose focus and concentration more than adequate. Placed in introductory science classes, they were to behave as undergraduate students, but also to keep a more sophisticated record of the teaching style and their response as learners. Second[,] I invited a certain number of distinguished science and engineering professors to commit to studying Chaucer and Wordsworth in a junior-level five-day summer poetry seminar. The third group I called "second tier" students based on my hypothesis that a good many students are rejecting science even before it rejects them. These were nonscience graduate students who would devote semester-long study to introductory physics and chemistry and share with me both daily logs and a final essay about their experience.

The reactions to the disciplines of poetry and science from these "outsiders" suggest that it is the habits of learning, the new relationships that have to be constructed between learner and subject, and the packaging of courses that are highly problematic for these students. My conclusion at this point is: Students who may be fearful, avoidant, and even hostile to courses that we think are "good" for them to take, are not dumb; they are different. Theirs is not a failure of intellect, but a failure of fit.

A few examples of the problems they experienced help us think about what might serve to make the next generation of general education courses succeed.

THE MISSING OVERVIEW

When non-science faculty were exposed to two days of "waves in elastic media," a number revealed they had trouble "following the lecture," both because there was no "overview" and because their traditional note-taking did not clarify the matters at hand. Active learners seek to translate new material into language they can understand, to hang topical detail on some overarching structure. But this is difficult when one is new to a field and not told where one is heading. One professor wrote:

> Two things struck me about this mini-course. First, how interesting the material was and, second, how when I did not understand something immediately, my mind locked and I felt helpless. It seemed to me during these lectures that I lacked any framework of prior knowledge, experience or intuition that could have helped me order the information I was receiving. I had no way of telling what was important and what was not. I had difficulty distinguishing between what was being communicated to me merely for purpose of illustration or analogy. I could not tell whether I understood or not. Nothing cohered.

Scientists expect students to write down what they do not understand in order to grapple with it later. But students in other fields are not comfortable with this. From another professor, coping with the calculus, came the following insight:

> I simply cannot write down what I do not understand. . . . I just can't put it into my notes if I cannot put it into my own words.

PROBLEM SOLVING

Our extremely intelligent learners in science grew, in time, to like problem solving, especially the setting up of the problem. They understood that "the physics is in the diagram." But in general, they found introductory physical science to be mired in a "tyranny of technique." And that teaching in science was little more than "doing problems."

Michele, a graduate student in philosophy, felt that the excessive focus on problem solving robbed her of the opportunity to "creatively interact with the material." She wanted something other than problem solving. She wrote:

> My curiosity simply was not satisfied by the simple quantitative solution. I was more interested in "how" and "why" questions than in "how much." I wanted verbal explanations, with formulae and computations only as a secondary aid. Becoming capable at problem solving was not my major goal. But it was the major goal of this course.

"SIMPLIFY AND SOLVE"

Jacki was distracted by the deeper questions that the material suggested and found it limiting to merely "simplify and solve" her physics problems. Coming out of English and creative writing, she was used to putting a premium on finding complexity in issues that might seem simple. Studying physics required her to reverse her normal strategy. The deeper questions she was asking were important, and she wrote about these in her journal. She thought at first that the students sitting next to her were also engaged in these deeper questions, but, as she wrote:

> Under time pressure and because the only feedback we get is on the homework assignments which are all problem-solving, I think the students around me are not pursuing these questions and eventually they will learn to disregard them as "extraneous" not just to this course, but to physics as well.

EXAMINATIONS

The problem of tyranny of technique is further exacerbated by narrow skills-testing on examinations. In some situations, although concepts were presented, even expanded upon, none of this material found its way onto homework assignments or examinations. As a result students learned to disregard these as "diversions." One of our visiting faculty made this observation:

> The way an instructor operationalizes the goals for the course is not simply to speak them or to put them in a handout, but to incorporate them onto his exams. While the professor was talking concepts, his exams were testing numerical solutions. And he probably never realized what the students discovered early, namely that the concepts and the history didn't really count.

More significantly, our outsiders did not find their exams in physics and chemistry to be "stretch experiences" for them. One wrote:

> The problems on exams seldom required the use of more than one concept or physical principle. Only once were we asked to explain

> or comment on something rather than complete a calculation. The final asked the most primary, basic questions about only the most important laws of physics. I had woefully over prepared. We were not required at any time to interrelate concepts or to try and understand the "bigger picture."

ABSTRACTIONS AND DEMONSTRATIONS

Many science professors believe that students who have trouble with their courses may be intelligent but not as capable of abstract thinking as they need to be to study science. None of the participants in these experiments had trouble with abstract concepts per se. They had, in fact, more trouble with the concrete than the abstract. A biologist wrote of the demonstrations:

> There were times when Isaac's demonstration just didn't make the point, but when he put it into words, I understood. And then I wished he would do the demonstration one more time because I thought that then I would see what we were supposed to have seen.

A more profound criticism of demonstrations came from a professor of philosophy:

> There were two types of demonstrations for us—at least I think there were. The first is what I would call a "clarifying demonstration," such as the passing of a wave along a slinky, and the second, what I would call a "confirming demonstration," one that made a difference in the history of science but one that required us to follow something that was either moving too fast or that required a level of understanding we did not yet have.

Since it was sometimes not quite clear what one should be looking for, the demonstrations became for him "just one more subject to learn."

Here is a clear case of miscommunication. The professor of science relies on his demonstrations to clarify complex material, but to the uninitiated these were barriers to understanding.

LANGUAGE

The issue of language was for both our scientists studying poetry and for our nonscientists studying science a barrier. Our nonscientists were aware that science and mathematics use language sparely and very precisely, also that "ordinary" words have particular meanings in science and that these meanings may be quite different from what they are in other contexts. As a result, however, they wondered about all expressions. One commented that he found the language comprehensible except for some words that were used in several different ways at once. He gave some examples that made him realize he was in "unfamiliar territory."

> The idea of zero or zero-ness. Unless a non-physicist deliberately thinks about it, zero is the absence of anything, the absolute bottom or "start." But to the physicist, zero is actually in the middle with plus and minus quantities on either side.

SCIENTISTS STUDYING POETRY

Since I realized that my student stand-ins brought to courses in other fields, even brief ones, something of the cognitive self-image I spoke of earlier: non-rational expectations as to what would be "hard" and what would be "easy" and how they would do, I instructed the 14 science and engineering faculty to begin to keep a journal record of all their thoughts and feelings even before their poetry seminar began. One chemist offered the following description of his state of mind. Prior to the arrival of the books, he had fully expected to have a very hard time with Chaucer—after all a very distant poet and one whose works would be dealt with in part in Middle English. He was sure that Chaucer would be more difficult than Wordsworth, 19th century poet who shared the chemist's fascination with Nature. But when the books arrived, the chemist changed his mind.

> The Chaucer looked like, weighed in like and was organized like a chemistry text. There was a table of contents, notes and help items, and the first assignment was on page 1. But the Wordsworth was just two bare volumes of poetry with no annotations in no particular order and the first assignment was on p. 127.

How was he going to deal with a subject that was not vertical?

TALK, TALK, TALK

Not just the material, but the "features of the delivery system" were a problem. As another engineer wrote after the first day:

> The mode of presentation—start talking and keep talking—was certainly "different" (I almost said "disconcerting"). Engineers tend to think graphically and to seek structural models for everything, and so my notes have lots of graphic doodles in the

> margins: a time line for Chaucer with the Great Vowel Shift marked in color (He brought his colored pencils to the seminar.) and abortive directed-graph taxonomy for Wordsworth, trying to connect his odes, sonnets, elegies and preludes, with arrow. (vectors)

The science and engineering professors were distressed that there was:

> Nothing on the blackboard, no diagrams, no key words, no outline, no nothing. I found it very hard to follow a lecture that was just words and more words. What was most important? What was not? And the furious writing going on around me. What the hell did they find to write down that was so interesting?

When, well into the late morning of the first day, the Wordsworth instructor finally did write something on the blackboard, everyone cheered.

MEANDER AND GROPE

The scientists had trouble particularly with the lack of "linearity" of the seminar. The problem to them seemed to be one of sequence.

> In science and engineering, we claim to build multi-story edifices starting from strong but simple foundations, with the elegance and subtlety of the principles and relations growing as one ascends. By contrast, the making and assessment of literature seems akin to building and visiting suburban subdivisions: just drop in anywhere and chat with the neighbors; no neckties needed. Some of the neighbors may talk in code, but if that gets heavy, just move on down the block.

They found it difficult to write papers when the assignments were elliptical, such as "How seriously does Chaucer take the Prioress (a character in the Prologue) and how does he take her seriously?"

One engineering professor, struggling with that assignment, said he'd fully expected to have trouble finding the answer to questions in the humanities, but not that he would not be able to understand the question. Another wrote what he thought dealt with the question and when he showed it to his wife, a graduate in English, for her approval, she told him it was "too short." "Too short?" he wailed. "I wrote enough to answer the question." Yet, when he got his paper returned, the instructor's comment was that it was "too short." Which means there are conventions in literary analysis for how much is enough to answer a question that outsiders to literature aren't explicitly told.

INTERPRETATION

The scientists and engineers were skeptical about interpretation more generally. Most of all they were put off by the "ambiguities" both in poetry and in its interpretation. One said, at the end:

> I am used to reading for what is on the surface, not for what is hidden. Poetry seems to favor the expression of ideas in purposefully complex and equivocal language.

CONCLUSIONS

What conclusions for General Education can we draw from these experiments? One conclusion, not mine, might be that disciplinary cultures are so different that it is likely scientists and literary critics are born and not made. Best for students to find the subjects that are intellectually and temperamentally suited to them, and leave other disciplines to those who find them more to their taste. Another conclusion for general education courses to explore, however, might be this one: I think we college educators owe our students an education that leads them not just out of their ignorance but very intentionally enlarges their comfort zones as well. And those who teach in college owe ourselves the experience of being on the boundaries of other disciplines, too.

QUESTIONS ABOUT MEANING

1. For some students, the way content is presented can make challenging classes more challenging, argues Tobias. To test this hypothesis, Tobias asked three groups of expert learners to attend classes in fields not their own. Describe these groups of learners and the tasks they were assigned.
2. Describe some of the frustrations the non-science students had with how material was presented in the science classes. Conversely, what did the scientists find unfamiliar and frustrating about studying poetry?
3. Although coming from different backgrounds and studying different topics, the three groups of learners shared some of the same kinds of frustrations. What were they?

QUESTIONS FOR RHETORICAL ANALYSIS

4. To whom is Tobias writing? How is this made clear in the final paragraph?
5. Important clues to understanding texts can be inferred from reading the titles and headings. What does the series title *Essays on Teaching*

Excellence: Toward the Best in the Academy suggest about the purpose and audience of the essays in the series? Based on the title of Tobias's essay ("Disciplinary Cultures and General Education"), what would you guess the article will be about? How do the bolded section headings further aid your understanding of the article?

6. Although Tobias quotes extensively from the students she interviewed, many of the quoted passages are not enclosed in quotation marks. How does Tobias signal that she is quoting? In what way(s) is this format better than integrating the quotations into paragraphs?

"Why Poets Just Don't Get It in the Physics Classroom: Stalking the Second Tier in the Sciences," *NACADA Journal* SHEILA TOBIAS

Sheila Tobias studies math and science anxiety among college students, a topic she has spoken about at many professional conferences, including the NACADA National Conference on Academic Advising. NACADA—or the National Academic Advising Association—is a professional organization for academic advisors and counselors working in higher education. In the following article Tobias writes about the topic of her address at the NACADA conference: why so many students who enter college intending to become science majors fail to graduate with science degrees. The article was originally published in 1993 in the *NACADA Journal*, which publishes research of interest to academic advisers.

Sheila Tobias, the Journal's featured speaker at the 1993 NACADA National Conference on Academic Advising, addresses here the topic of her keynote presentation in Detroit. In her investigations into student attrition in the sciences, Tobias has identified fundamental differences in the way students in the physical sciences are taught, and consequently expected to learn, and the way students in, say, the humanities or the social sciences are. Here she sketches the broad outlines of her findings and the evidence upon which they rest, with provocative implications and possibilities for academic advisors.

In 1984 I began a series of studies to ascertain the causes for the hemorrhaging of college students from the science pipeline (Tobias, 1986, 1988). I chose to focus on the first-year course in physical science because the data indicate that some 40% of students who start college with a declared interest in science do not persist to graduation in the sciences (Green, 1989). Soft figures suggest that as many as 500,000 undergraduates enroll in first-year chemistry and physics courses—some on their way to an applied science major (e.g., nutrition, agriculture, or nursing) and some on their way to meet general education requirements.

Whatever their intent, these students are potentially recruitable to a science major. Why do they not continue? And what can college educators—advisors included—do about this?

My research employed an unusual design. Instead of asking science professors what makes their courses hard and off-putting for otherwise able college students, I set up artificially constructed unit lessons in science, taught by master teachers in a variety of institutions, where the "learners" would be their faculty peers. My purpose was to tease out the one variable that might make science hard, namely newness to the field, from other variables that might intrude, such as newness to college learning altogether, lack of self-confidence, inadequate preparation, and unwillingness to work hard. My faculty surrogates were simply too intelligent, too focused, too expert at learning to be dismissed by science faculty. Yet they, too, found science hard and off-putting, not because of content per se but because of certain features of the delivery system (Tobias & Hake, 1988).

In time, after publishing my findings, I was made to realize that the entire experience of learning science—including labs, homework assignments, examinations, and continuous exposure—was not within the scrutiny of my occasional learners. And so, with funding from Research Corporation, I extended the model to full-semester courses in chemistry and physics at large state universities, this time employing graduate students in fields other than science (Tobias, 1990). My surrogate learners, whom I came to call "the second tier," had all taken high school science and liked it, were free of mathophobia (having studied calculus somewhere along the way), and were good writers. Hence, from their journal records of how they grappled with the new material and from their observations of the "delivery features," my readers and I were able to glean insights into the barriers to learning physical science that probably affect undergraduates, less confident and less articulate than these students.

My second-tier students would have met any educator's criteria for "able." They had done well in some other major—English, classics, anthropology, American studies, creative writing, or the like. They were currently in good standing in graduate school. Paid $1,000 each for their participation in the study, they were willing to devote as many as 16 hours per week to their work (including journal writing) and to present me with pages and pages of findings.

Finally, in order to triangulate my results, I engaged 14 physical science and engineering faculty at Cornell University in a week-long literary criticism seminar on Chaucer and Wordsworth, during which they could experience and react (again in writing) to the features of the delivery system in the humanities, as contrasted with their preferred ways of learning in science and engineering (Tobias & Abel, 1988, 1990).

The upshot of my work has been to rattle the cages of science faculty, many of them convinced that students who *could* do science *would* do science. My surrogates, who did for the most part outstandingly in their courses, demonstrated the obverse: some students who could do science choose not to.

Students who are able in one set of subjects are often mired in a comfort zone of learning. Not that they cannot transfer their successful learning strategies in one family of disciplines to another. But their instructors do not take the time to show them how. What they experience, painfully and without adequate explanation from professionals, is that their preferred learning styles do not serve them well when they cross certain disciplinary boundaries. Students from the humanities, for example, found themselves having difficulty following a lecture that required them to write down material they did not know; "You'll understand all this later," their professors would say, "once you get to the problem sets." Unable to translate the new material into their own language, however, they found they "could not take notes that made any sense" to them later on.

Science faculty, on the other hand, found it difficult to follow lectures that were "just words and more words." They missed the outline on the blackboard, the visuals, and the demonstrations that ordinarily pepper a science lecture. Humanists and social scientists, meanwhile, found the demonstrations difficult to follow and wanted formulas and concepts expressed in language as well as in code.

Examinations and the primary focus on problem solving also came in for criticism among the outsiders to science. Without exception, my surrogates found their exams disappointing in that the big picture was never called for, and the endless (and to them repetitive) plug-and-chug required of undergraduates in physical science was intellectually barren. "Only once was I asked to comment on or explain something on an exam," wailed one of my surrogates, now a third-year graduate student in American literature at Stanford. "I was generally asked only to complete a calculation." "This course," said another, the one surrogate who did not do as well as the others, "did not play to my strengths."

Further, they were frustrated by the lack of community in their science classes. Those who had majored in literature or creative writing noticed in particular that, given the difficulty of the material, the professor seemed the only one who could claim ownership. Students were obliged only to "mimic the professor's approach." Therefore there was little discussion in science class, almost never any debate. And the end result was that the students never learned to talk in the language of the science they were learning. That there were few questions raised by students, despite professors' willingness to answer them, was attributed by my surrogate learners to the students' lack of fluency in the language of the discipline.

My major finding (taken from theirs) was that the physical sciences are presented in too narrow a teaching and learning mode and that students with other strengths find little opportunity to use the skills they learn elsewhere, particularly their verbal skills, in making sense of the material (Rigden & Tobias, 1991a, 1991b). "I am used to getting information on the backs of little words," commented a professor attempting chemistry. "Here the definitions do not help much. I find I do not really understand the concept even when I have mastered the words."

Mine was by no means a flawless experiment. Faculty and graduate students in other fields cannot be said to be perfect stand-ins for naive undergraduates. But they were able to provide some sense of what goes on in these courses that might be putting off students similar to themselves in intelligence, motivation, and curiosity. Also the experiment managed to dispel some commonly held prejudices among science faculty. For one, that their subjects are more abstract than topics in the humanities and social sciences. My faculty and graduate students were quite able to deal with abstractions, even to follow a mathematical derivation without knowing the advanced mathematics on which it is based. They had difficulty, rather, as one faculty member put it, "moving back and forth rapidly and without adequate guideposts from the concrete to the abstract and then back again to the concrete." Nothing in their previous experience had prepared them for that.

Nor for the vertical structure of their subjects. Similarly, the outsiders to poetry characterized the pattern and sequence of the presentations as "meander and grope." Clearly there was a logical sequence, but they could not figure out what it was. Part of this was because students on both sides of the two cultures were stumped trying to figure out what was important and what was not. Instructors were sending out clues, but to the newcomers the clues were opaque. Worst of all, for the outsiders to science, was the atavism of the grading practices. "I have never before been in a class," commented the Stanford graduate student, "where my grade had any effect, real or perceived, on anyone else's."

All this leaves us, particularly counselors and advisors, with much to do. So long as science and mathematics instructors direct their presentations to the first tier of students (my designation for students who are younger versions of themselves), the critical mass of students with different learning styles and different—and in some cases inadequate—preparation will continue to shrink. Advisors are in a unique position to interface the two populations—students and instructors—in a variety of proactive ways. First, by engaging in short-term (if not long-term) experiments of the sort I have been describing, where an advisor, provided release time, would be asked by instructors to seriously audit certain difficult courses or units in standard courses to help the instructors better serve a wider variety of learners.

Providing feedback to instructors, in my view, may be as important a component of academic advising as directly assisting students. Few instructors in the physical sciences are aware of learning style research; the findings of cognitive science; or the immediate impact of certain tried-and-true habits of teaching, examining, and grading in introductory science courses. Academic advisors and counselors, as certain university teaching and learning center staff have discovered, have much to bring to the teaching enterprise itself.

It is not as though everyone can or should become a scientist. But more than the first tier can be brought to an appreciation and some mastery of fundamental concepts in physics and chemistry. How we manage this may determine whether there will be a voice for science in other professional fields and whether our economy remains competitive. Those who are lost to science in that first year suffer a downgrading of their aspirations, loss of self-esteem, and loss of direction. But science loses, too. If we can make the case that the majority of students in a first-year science course are not divided simply into those who can and those who can't but rather need to be approached as differently abled learners, we might be able to extend the attractiveness—and therewith the reach—of science to all.

REFERENCES

Green, K. C. (1989). A profile of undergraduates in the sciences. *American Scientist, 77,* 476.

Rigden, J., & Tobias, S. (1991, January/February). Tune in, turn off, drop out. *The Sciences* (published by the New York Academy of Sciences), p. 16.

Rigden, J., & Tobias, S. (1991, March 27). Too often college-level science is dull as well as difficult. *The Chronicle of Higher Education,* p. A52.

Tobias, S. (1986, Spring). Peer perspectives on teaching. *Change Magazine.*

Tobias, S. (1988). Peer perspectives on physics. *The Physics Teacher, 26*(2), 77–80.

Tobias, S. (1990). *They're not dumb, they're different: Stalking the second tier.* Tucson, AZ: Research Corporation.

Tobias, S., & Abel, L. (1988). Peer perspectives on the teaching of poetry. *American Council of Learned Societies Newsletter, 1*(4).

Tobias, S., & Abel, L. (1990). Poetry for physicists. *American Journal of Physics, 58*(9), 816.

Tobias, S., & Hake, R. R. (1988). Professors as physics students: What can they teach us? *American Journal of Physics, 56*(9), 786–794.

QUESTIONS ABOUT MEANING

1. In this article, Tobias "reframes" the research described in the previous article ("Disciplinary Cultures and General Education") for a more

specific audience: academic advisors. In what ways does she make her research relevant for this target audience?

2. What does the "Second Tier" in the article title refer to? How are "second tier" students different from "first tier" students?
3. In what ways is the initial study design—having "master" teachers teach science lessons to non-science teachers—an improvement over having first-year students describe why they find science courses difficult? On the other hand, how was Tobias's initial study design insufficient for explaining why students struggle in science courses? What additional research study design addressed the shortcomings of the first study?
4. What did the graduate students in this study find difficult or frustrating about the class presentations, class activities, and grading systems in science courses?

QUESTIONS FOR RHETORICAL ANALYSIS

5. Many research reports in academic journals begin with a one-paragraph summary called the *abstract* that identifies the purpose of the research. Sometimes the abstract is written by the author; other times it is written by a journal editor, but it is always set off in different type or with different margins. How is the abstract of this article set apart for readers? Does it appear that Tobias or someone else wrote the abstract? How can you tell? What sentence or two in the abstract identifies the purpose of the article?
6. It is standard in reports of academic research for the author to provide specific details about who or what was studied (sometimes called the *sample*). What details about the sample and study procedure are mentioned in this article but not mentioned in the more-general essay preceding this article? Which details seem especially important to consider for readers wanting to evaluate the study procedure?
7. Successful academic writers answer the "so what?" question. That is, they identify the value or importance of their topics to the intended audience. Why does Tobias believe the loss of science majors is an important problem to address? Do you think schools and society have begun to recognize and address the problem since 1993, when this essay was written? If so, how?

THINKING AND WRITING ABOUT THE TOPIC

Whether you have been a college student for a few days or a few years, you have likely experienced differences in how material is presented and in how you are asked to learn in your courses. In an essay, describe some of the differences. You might describe differences in how your professors present material, how your textbooks present material, or how course content is arranged. Or you might describe differences in how you are asked to participate in class or how you must demonstrate your learning. Reflect on the meaning of the differences you identify: In what ways do the differences appear to you to be related to the subject matter or discipline? Explain.

WORKS CITED

Bendel-Simso, Mary. "Interview Request." Message to the author. 2 Sept. 2008. E-mail.

Carpentier, Martha C. "Susan Glaspell's Fiction: *Fidelity* as American Romance." *Twentieth Century Literature* 40.1 (1994): 92–113. Print.

Cox, Rebecca D. *The College Fear Factor: How Students and Professors Misunderstand One Another.* Cambridge: Harvard University Press, 2009. Print.

Ditchkoff, Stephen. "Interview Request." Message to the author. 25 May 2007. E-mail.

Galambos, Nancy L., Andrea L. Dalton, and Jennifer L. Maggs. "Losing Sleep over It: Daily Variation in Sleep Quantity and Quality in Canadian Students' First Semester of University." *Journal of Research on Adolescence* 19.4 (2009): 741–61. Print.

Gutman, Arthur. "Misconceptions of Psychology and Performance in the Introductory Course." *Teaching of Psychology* 6.3 (1979): 159–61. Print.

Johnson, J. Paul, and Ethan Krase. "Coming to Learn: From First-Year Composition to Writing in the Disciplines." *Across the Disciplines* 9.2 (2012): n. pag. Web. 16 Nov. 2012.

Kaplan, Jennifer J., Diane G. Fisher, and Neal T. Rogness. "Lexical Ambiguity in Statistics: What Do Students Know about the Words Association, Average, Confidence, Random and Spread?" *Journal of Statistics Education* 17.3 (2009): n. pag. Web. 24 July 2013.

Kodman, Annalee. *How Undergraduate First-Year Composition Students Revise in Relationship to Their Learning Goal Orientations.* Diss. University of Delaware, 2013. Ann Arbor: UMI, 2013. AAT 3598679. Print.

Konold, Clifford. "Issues in Assessing Conceptual Understanding in Probability and Statistics." *Journal of Statistics Education* 3.1 (1995): n. pag. Web. 24 July 2013.

Langer, Judith A. "Speaking of Knowing: Conceptions of Understanding in Academic Disciplines." *Writing, Teaching, and Learning in the Disciplines.* Ed. Anne Herrington and Charles Moran. New York: MLA, 1992. 69–85. Print.

Ramachandran, V. S. "Filling in Gaps in Perception: Part 1." *Current Directions in Psychological Science* 1.6 (1992): 199–205. Print.

A Review of the Proficiencies Required by Students Entering First Year Post-Secondary English Courses. Prepared by Virginia Cooke, University College of the Fraser Valley, in collaboration with Ruth Derksen, Centre for Research in Professional and Academic Writing, Simon Fraser University, 1999. Print.

Sommers, Nancy, and Laura Saltz. "The Novice as Expert: Writing the Freshman Year." *College Composition and Communication* 56.1 (2004): 124–49. Print.

Stevens, Kay Lynn, and Kathleen Carbary. "See How They Learn: A Descriptive Assessment of the Study Skills of Psychology, Sociology, and Anthropology Students." Columbia Basin College, Pasco, WA. 21 Sept. 2012. Presentation.

Williams, Mark. "Interview Request." Message to the author. 15 May 2007. E-mail.

CHAPTER 2

Strategies for Reading Academic Writing

Our digital world inundates us with information: pop-up ads, tweets, text messages, instant messages, e-mails, hyperlinks . . . the list goes on. As a result, we become adept at transitioning quickly from one byte of information to another, but we become less adept at reading closely and critically for extended periods of time. Nicholas Carr, the author of "Is Google Making Us Stupid?" describes the changes he's seen in his own ability to stay focused when reading: "Immersing myself in a book or a lengthy article used to be easy. . . . Now my concentration often starts to drift after two or three pages. I get fidgety, lose the thread, begin looking for something else to do. I feel as if I'm always dragging my wayward brain back to the text." If you've experienced what Carr has experienced, clearly you are not alone.

The transition from reading the stream of information bytes you encounter daily to reading the texts you encounter in college can be jarring. Unlike text messages or tweets, college reading assignments demand focus, attention, and time. Many will include references to people and concepts new to you. Most will be multiple pages in length. This chapter describes strategies that will help you read and understand your assignments. The strategies include:

- understanding the context of your reading;
- making predictions about what's ahead;
- reading actively to make connections;
- adjusting how you read according to your reasons for reading.

These strategies have been found to be related to academic success among first-year students (Taraban, Rynearson, and Kerr). If you apply these reading strategies, you will enhance your comprehension of academic writing and increase your overall success in college.

Strategy 1: Understanding the Context

The first step to honing close-reading skills is to consider the context, or circumstances, of your reading before you read—both the original context of the publication and your own context for reading the text. Following are strategies for identifying and understanding that **rhetorical context**.

Analyze the Rhetorical Situation

To determine the original context of a text, you'll need to collect some information, or *rhetorical knowledge*, before you read. The rhetorical components of a text include the writer, the audience, the situation and purpose, and the genre (shown in Figure 2.1). Combined, these elements explain why a text is written the way it is and help you correctly interpret what you're reading. Considering these aspects of the original context is sometimes called **rhetorical reading**.

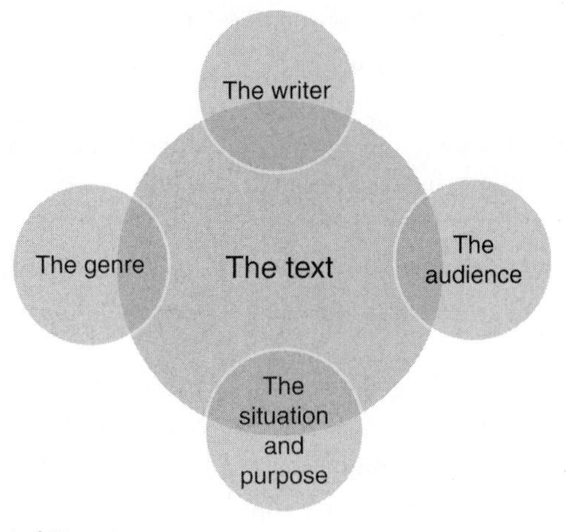

Figure 2.1 The Rhetorical Situation

The Writer. One key piece of information to determine *before* you read is the author and the author's perspective on the topic. If the author is identified as being affiliated with a college or university, for example, this tells you the writer is seeing the topic from an academic perspective. Information about the author appears at the beginning or end of articles or books. If you're reading online, you can click "About Us" or the author's name itself for further information.

The Audience. Next, determine the writer's audience. One way to do this is to identify who published the text. If a well-known publisher such as the New York Times Company or Random House published the piece, then the work is likely intended for a broad, general audience. If, however, the piece was published by a university press, such as Yale University Press, then the work is likely intended for a specialized or academic audience.

The title can provide another clue to the intended audience. Specialized or "academic" vocabulary (like "self-affirmation") in a title generally indicates a specialized audience. Such is the case in Figure 2.2. In contrast, attention-getting titles and "conversational" titles, such as the one shown in Figure 2.3, typically indicate a more general audience.

Self-Affirmation Underlies Facebook Use

Catalina L. Toma[1] and Jeffrey T. Hancock[2]

Social network sites, such as Facebook, have acquired an unprecedented following, yet it is unknown what makes them so attractive to users. Here we propose that these sites' popularity can be understood through the fulfillment of ego needs. We use self-affirmation theory to hypothesize why and when people spend time on their online profiles. Study 1 shows that Facebook profiles are self-affirming in the sense of satisfying users' need for self-worth and self-integrity. Study 2 shows that Facebook users gravitate toward their online profiles after receiving a blow to the ego, in an unconscious effort to repair their perceptions of self-worth. In addition to illuminating some of the psychological factors that underlie Facebook use, the results provide an important extension to self-affirmation theory by clarifying how self-affirmation operates in people's everyday environments.

Figure 2.2 From an Academic Journal Article

Other elements to consider when determining the audience are the paragraph length and the author(s)' affiliations. In Figure 2.2, the first paragraph is long and the authors' university affiliations (University of Wisconsin–Madison and Cornell University) appear in footnotes (not shown here). These indicators point to a specialized, academic audience. Additional clues about the intended audience, including formatting style and visual elements, are listed in Table 2.1.

TABLE 2.1

Elements to Analyze When Determining a Text's Intended Audience

	Academic Audience	Nonacademic or General Audience
Author	Usually affiliated with a college or university	Job title may or may not be related to topic or author may not be identified
Vocabulary	Specialized and technical vocabulary	Nonspecialized vocabulary and perhaps colloquial expressions
Style and Format	Usually black and white text in standard font; relatively long paragraphs; sources are identified in the text and in a bibliography	May include color or nontraditional font styles; short paragraphs; sources may be identified in text but not listed in a bibliography
Visual Elements	Tables, graphs, and charts; also images used as evidence	Photos used to capture attention or explain a concept

The Situation, Genre, and Purpose. Further insights into the audience and context come from considering the situation, genre, and purpose of a text.

Let's compare Figure 2.2 to Figure 2.3. In Figure 2.3, the image, the attention-getting title, the brief opening paragraph, the familiar, colloquial language, and the incomplete sentences (e.g., "As in not hate yourself. Weird.") all suggest the article is intended for a broad, nonspecialized audience. The context or *situation* provides further clues to confirm this first impression. The article appeared online at *CafeMom.com*, described as a "meeting place for moms," where visitors are invited to "Come in. Check out the conversations. Join a group. Ask a question. Have some fun!" The *genre*, then, is an article posted to a social network site. The author's initial *purpose* is to report on the publication of a recent study about Facebook use. The author also wants to share her opinion of the

Looking at Your Facebook Profile Makes You Like Yourself More? Wait, That Doesn't Seem Right

by Nicole Fabian-Weber June 25, 2013 at 3:03 PM

A new study has come out and pretty much negated every other Facebook study that's ever been done. Kind of. This new research shows that Facebook actually makes you like yourself better. And we're not talking silly thumbs-up like here; we're talking actually like. As in not hate yourself. Weird.

Catalina Toma, who led the team for the study, which is called "Self-Affirmation Underlies Facebook Use," said: "Most have a very large audience of friends and they selectively present the best version of self, but they do so in an accurate manner. We had people **look at their own profiles for five minutes** and found that they **experienced a boost in self-esteem** in a deep, unconscious level."

I guess when you think about it that way – people post awesome photos of themselves doing awesome things onto Facebook and their "friends" like it – it makes sense. If you take a step back and look at your profile and your network for a study, it's almost as if you're **looking at someone else's life,** no? You're perusing a "best version of yourself" reel and, at the same time, seeing your friends build you up. What's not to love?

Figure 2.3 From a Social Network Site

study. Combined, these elements make up the original *rhetorical context* of the *CafeMom* article.

The rhetorical situation of Toma and Hancock's article (Figure 2.2), on the other hand, is very different. It appeared in a **peer-reviewed journal** (or *scholarly* journal), where scholars publish the results of their research for other scholars to read. Most articles appearing in these academic journals go through a peer review process, meaning other experts in the field (peers) ensure that the discipline's standards for research are upheld. This process of peer review ensures that only high-quality research is published.

Every discipline has numerous journals, which periodically publish new issues. For example, *The Quarterly Journal of Economics* (Figure 2.4) publishes a new issue four times a year. Combined, the four issues make up a single volume. Each issue includes original research reports from the field of economics. Like articles posted on social network sites, research articles published in academic journals have distinctive genre features, which will be described in this chapter and throughout this book.

Know What to Expect *While* You Read

Information about the writer, audience, publisher, and genre can tell you what to expect while reading. Compare, for instance, the following passages, both describing the *same* scientific study. Which passage would you guess is from an Associated Press newspaper report, intended for the general public, and which is from an academic journal, intended for scientists?

EXAMPLE 2.1

Scientists have found a way to cut dads out of the picture, at least among rodents: They have produced mice with two genetic moms—and no father. . . .

5 [The scientists] say they produced two mice, one of which grew to maturity and gave birth. . . . .

For the study . . . the researchers got around the need for male-derived DNA by turning to mutant mice. The female mice were missing a chunk of DNA, and as a result, two of their genes would behave in an embryo as if they

10 had come from a male.

What's more, the scientists took this mutated DNA from the egg cells of newborns, because at such a young age the DNA has not yet taken on the full "female" imprinting seen in mature eggs.

That DNA was combined with genes from ordinary female mice to make reconstructed eggs.

(Ritter)

THE
QUARTERLY
JOURNAL OF
ECONOMICS

FOUNDED 1886

Volume 129 August 2014 Issue 3

ARTICLES

CHANG-TAI HSIEH AND PETER J. KLENOW
The Life Cycle of Plants in India and Mexico 1035

TREB ALLEN AND COSTAS ARKOLAKIS
Trade and the Topography of the Spatial Economy 1085

RAJ CHETTY, JOHN N. FRIEDMAN, SØREN LETH-PETERSEN, TORBEN HEIEN NIELSEN, AND TORE OLSEN
Active vs. Passive Decisions and Crowd-Out in Retirement Savings Accounts: Evidence from Denmark 1141

NICOLA GENNAIOLI, ANDREI SHLEIFER, AND ROBERT VISHNY
Finance and the Preservation of Wealth 1221

THOMAS PIKETTY AND GABRIEL ZUCMAN
Capital is Back: Wealth-Income Ratios in Rich Countries 1700–2010 1255

REMA HANNA, SENDHIL MULLAINATHAN, AND JOSHUA SCHWARTZSTEIN
Learning Through Noticing: Theory and Evidence from a Field Experiment 1311

ROLAND G. FRYER, JR.
Injecting Charter School Best Practices into Traditional Public Schools: Evidence from Field Experiments 1355

THOMAS BUSER, MURIEL NIEDERLE, AND HESSEL OOSTERBEEK
Gender, Competitiveness, and Career Choices 1409

JOSÉ LUIS MONTIEL OLEA AND TOMASZ STRZALECKI
Axiomatization and Measurement of Quasi-Hyperbolic Discounting 1449

JUSTIN CARON, THIBAULT FALLY, AND JAMES R. MARKUSEN
International Trade Puzzles: A Solution Linking Production and Preferences 1501

OXFORD
UNIVERSITY PRESS

QJE 129(3) 1035–1552 (2014)
Print ISSN 0033-5533; Online ISSN 1531-4650 No. 519

Figure 2.4 The Cover of a Sample Scholarly Journal

EXAMPLE 2.2

We show the development of a viable parthenogenetic mouse individual from a reconstructed oocyte containing two haploid sets of maternal genome, derived from non-growing and fully grown oocytes. This development was made possible by the appropriate expression of the *Igf2* and *H19* genes with other imprinted genes, using mutant mice with a 13-kilobase deletion in the *H19* gene as non-growing oocytes donors. This full-term development is associated with a marked reduction in aberrantly expressed genes. The parthenote developed to adulthood with the ability to reproduce offspring.

(Kono et al. 860)

Example 2.1 is written for the general public and Example 2.2 is written for scientists. As a result, you should expect these passages to differ in vocabulary (*dads* vs. *paternal imprinting*), specificity (*DNA* vs. *Igf2* and *H19* genes), and tone ("*Scientists have found a way to cut dads out of the picture*" vs. "*We show the development of a viable parthenogenetic mouse. . .*").

Concept in Practice 2.1: Considering Context Clues

Let's look more closely at the first paragraph of the article "Self-Affirmation Underlies Facebook Use," written by Catalina Toma and Jeffrey Hancock, professors of communication. An early clue to the *genre* we are reading is the word "Abstract." An **abstract** is a one-paragraph summary commonly found at the beginning of academic research studies. As you read, notice the clues to the writers' subject, audience, purpose, and stance.

Self-Affirmation Underlies Facebook Use

Personality and Social Psychology Bulletin
39(3) 321–331

DOI: 10.1177/0146167212474694
http://pspb.sagepub.com
SAGE

Catalina L. Toma[1] and Jeffrey T. Hancock[2]

Abstract

Social network sites, such as Facebook, have acquired an unprecedented following, yet it is unknown what makes them so attractive to users. Here we propose that these sites' popularity can be understood through the fulfillment of ego needs. We use self-affirmation theory to hypothesize why and when people spend time on their online profiles. Study 1 shows that Facebook profiles are self-affirming in the sense of satisfying users' need for self-worth and self-integrity. Study 2 shows that Facebook users gravitate toward their online profiles after receiving a blow to the ego, in an unconscious effort to repair their perceptions of self-worth. In addition to illuminating some of the psychological factors that underlie Facebook use, the results provide an important extension to self-affirmation theory by clarifying how self-affirmation operates in people's everyday environments.

The article appears in the Personality and Social Psychology Bulletin, *a peer-reviewed journal that publishes research of interest to social science professors.*

What did Toma and Hancock study and what did they learn in their two studies?

Use Genre Knowledge to Understand What You're Reading

Once you determine what type of genre you are reading, you can use your knowledge of the conventions and patterns of that genre to improve your reading comprehension.

You've already seen one convention of the academic research report: the article begins with a one-paragraph summary of the research. There are other standard features or conventions found in the research report genre. In the Introduction, for instance, appearing immediately after the abstract, writers state the purpose or goal of their study. But before stating their purpose, they usually will summarize what other researchers have already learned about the subject. You'll recognize this convention—called the **literature review**—by the many citations (in parentheses or superscript numbers) referring to other sources. We can see these conventions in the first two paragraphs of Toma and Hancock's Introduction:

> Social network sites (SNSs) have taken the world by storm. Facebook, for instance, counts more than one billion active users who spend nearly an hour online every day (Facebook Statistics, 2012). Even older adults are tuning in, with almost half of Americans above the age of 50 currently registered as SNS users—a 100% increase from the previous year (Pew Research Center, 2010). A fundamental question, then, is what makes these sites so universally appealing. Why do people gravitate toward them in such large numbers and with such dedication?

The first paragraph introduces the general question of study: "Why do people gravitate toward them [social network sites] in such large numbers and with such dedication?"

> The media and public opinion are ripe with speculations on this issue, most of them pessimistic: SNSs are viewed as a convenient tool for procrastinating, gossiping, relieving boredom, or expressing narcissistic drives (see also Buffardi & Campbell, 2008). Academic research has begun examining subscribers' self-reported motivations for SNS use and revealed that relational needs, such as keeping tabs on one's social network and maintaining relationships, are frequently cited (see Wilson, Gosling, & Graham, 2012, for a review). Yet more basic, and less consciously available, ego needs may also provide a compelling account of why and when people gravitate toward these sites.

What explanations for the popularity of social network sites have been proposed by the media and the public?

In parentheses, the authors refer readers to an article by Wilson, Gosling, and Graham, who have reviewed some of the academic research on social network sites.

The citations in parentheses establish the importance of the topic (others have studied it) and allow readers to locate additional sources on the topic, but when your immediate goal is to understand the report at hand, you can ignore these citations and focus on the meaning of the sentences preceding them.

After summarizing what other researchers have learned about why people use social network sites, Toma and Hancock introduce their own hypothesis:

> In the present article we argue that self-affirmation theory (Steele, 1988) can serve as a cohesive theoretical narrative for understanding important aspects of SNSs appeal. We propose that SNSs that allow users to (a) craft self-presentations that reveal core aspects of their self-concept, such as social affiliations and treasured characteristics, and (b) highlight social connections with friends and family, satisfy fundamental ego needs regarding desired self-images. In turn, these ego needs motivate SNS use. We focus our analyses on Facebook, currently the world's

The words "we propose" introduce the authors' hypothesis. Why do Toma and Hancock think people use social network sites?

most popular SNS and one that encapsulates the quintessential features of SNSs (Boyd & Ellison, 2007).

Statements announcing the purpose of an academic research report commonly appear at the end of the introduction, often preceded with signal phrases such as "In this study, we analyzed . . ." or "This article argues. . . ." Once you know this convention, determining the purpose of a particular study becomes much easier.

Recognize the Vocabulary of the Genre or Discipline

Knowing the vocabulary that is standard for a genre or discipline is often crucial to recognizing the context and may be necessary to understand certain types of documents. Consider this passage from the sports page of a newspaper, describing the Master's Golf Tournament:

> **From an article written for golf enthusiasts:**
>
> Both [players] found the trees right. From there, [Louis] Oosthuizen ended up short of the green. [Bubba] Watson, who somehow was left with an opening, hooked a wedge from 155 yards off the pine needles to about 10 feet. Oosthuizen's chip went long to the back fringe. And when his par try again barely missed to the right, all Watson needed to do was leave himself a gimme.
>
> (Herrmann C4)

Making sense of this passage requires knowledge of golf terminology (e.g., *green, hooked, wedge, chip, par*) and familiarity with the tournament's tree-lined course in Augusta, Georgia (*hooked a wedge from 155 yards off the pine needles*). In fact, understanding the passage would be difficult for someone with no knowledge of golf terminology.

Specialized language is commonplace in many genres, including academic research reports. In the case of research reports, comprehension requires some basic knowledge of research terminology. To illustrate, let's return to Toma and Hancock's report. Here, first, is a summary of their two studies. In the first study, they asked college students to spend five minutes online. Some participants viewed their own Facebook page; others viewed the Facebook profile of a stranger. Then, all of the students delivered short speeches, after which each student received a negative performance evaluation, even if they had performed well. Toma and Hancock found that students who had viewed their own Facebook page before receiving feedback took the criticism better than students who had viewed a stranger's page. In the second study, a different group of students gave speeches and received either neutral or negative feedback. After hearing the feedback, participants could visit either their Facebook page or one of several other online sites. Those who had received negative feedback were more likely to visit their own Facebook page than were those who received neutral feedback.

The researchers concluded that one reason people visit their own Facebook pages is that it makes them feel better about themselves.

Toma and Hancock describe their research procedure in a section of their report titled "Methods." As is common in Methods sections, many elements of their research are conveyed in a sort of shorthand, illustrated here in the first paragraph from the Methods section of their first study:

Method

Participants. Participants were undergraduates at a Northeastern university who received course extra-credit ($N = 98$, 68% women; M *age* = 19.81). Ten participants were excluded because they were suspicious ($n = 5$) or because they were not Facebook users ($n = 5$), reducing the effective sample size to $N = 88$.

An upper case N *refers to the total number of participants; a lower case* n *is used to refer to a subsample or segment of the entire sample of 88.*

M *refers to the mean or average.*

Abbreviations such as *N*, *n*, and *M* make reading efficient for those familiar with research vocabulary. As you begin to study in different disciplines and enter into the conversations of those disciplines, part of your role as a participant is to learn the textual conventions used by members of those communities.

Concept in Practice 2.2:
Considering the Vocabulary of Research Studies

In many experiments, such as the two studies Toma and Hancock conducted, the researchers manipulate or create different *conditions* or situations for different groups of participants: a comparison group and a treatment group. This allows researchers to compare one group to another. Here is Toma and Hancock's description of the conditions for Study 1:

In both Facebook conditions, participants were told they would take part in a "website evaluation study," which involved spending 5 min on a website and then answering questions about it. In the Facebook self-affirmation condition ($n = 21$), this website was participants' *own Facebook profile*. Participants were told they could view any element of their profile (e.g., photographs, wall, list of friends), but could not navigate to someone else's profile. At the end of the study, participants in this condition were asked to temporarily "friend" the experimenter on Facebook, so we could have access to their profile information. All participants agreed.

In the Facebook control condition ($n = 24$), participants were asked to examine a *stranger's Facebook profile*. This stranger was in fact the previous participant in the Facebook self-affirmation condition. Thus, participants were yoked such that each participant

Participants are unaware of the researchers' goals so their responses aren't influenced.

Some participants spent five minutes looking at their own Facebook page. How many participants were in this "condition"?

in the control condition viewed the profile of a participant in the Facebook self-affirmation condition. Care was taken that participants in the Facebook control condition not be acquainted with the people whose profile they were viewing. The yoking procedure ensured that, as a group, participants in these two conditions examined the exact some profiles.

In the values essay self-affirmation condition (n = 22), participants ranked six values in order of personal importance (business, art-music-theater, social life-relationships, science–pursuit of knowledge, religion–morality, government–politics) and then wrote for 5 min about why their highest ranked value was important to them. In the values essay control condition (n = 21), participants wrote about why their lowest ranked value was important to the average college student. This value-affirmation procedure is the single most widely used self-affirmation manipulation (McQueen & Klein, 2006).

Some participants spent five minutes looking at the Facebook page of a stranger. How many participants were in this group? Whose profiles did they view?

In yet another condition, participants ranked their personal values. How many participants were in this condition? What did participants in the final condition do?

Keep Your Reason for Reading in Mind

Your knowledge about the genre as well as what you know about the author's audience and intent should shape your expectations for what you read. But your own goals should also influence how you read. *Why* are you reading the text? English professors Linda Adler-Kassner and Heidi Estrem describe three common purposes for reading texts assigned in college. When students do *content-based reading*, they read in order to summarize, analyze, and synthesize what they've read. When students do *process-based reading*, they read texts as examples or templates for conducting their own writing or research. When students do *structure-based reading*, they focus on the form or genre conventions (40). Each type of reading involves noticing distinct elements about the text.

So if, for example, you were asked to summarize the *CafeMom* article we saw earlier in this chapter, you would do *content-based reading*, and your summary would describe *what* the document says. Your paper might include statements like "The author describes a recent study about why we use social network sites like Facebook." If, however, you were asked to describe the *rhetorical features* of articles posted on sites like *CafeMom*, you're being asked to do *structure-based* reading. Your paper might include statements like "The writer creates a casual tone by using informal phrasing."

The notes you take as you read the article will vary according to the purpose of your assignment, as shown in Table 2.2.

These steps toward understanding context—determining the author's original purpose and audience, using that knowledge and knowledge of the genre to guide your expectations while reading, and remembering your own reasons for reading—will improve your success as a reader.

TABLE 2.2
Note Types Based on Assignment Purpose

Content-based Reading Notes (to describe the *content* of the *CafeMom* article)	**Structure-based Reading Notes (to describe the *form* and *genre conventions* of the *CafeMom* article)**
Researchers have found that looking at your Facebook page makes you feel better about yourself.	The image and title pique interest.
But the writer wonders if in real life Facebook isn't just as likely to make people feel bad about themselves.	Colloquial language (". . . pretty much negated . . . Kind of") creates an informal tone.
	Quotations allow readers to hear directly from the researcher who conducted the study.
	Paragraphs are short: usu. 2-4 sentences each.

Strategy 2: Making Predictions

Another way to improve your reading skills is to make predictions about a text before you read and as you read. Discussions of common strategies for making predictions follow.

Preview the Entire Text

Previewing a text allows you to make predictions as well as improve your reading comprehension and speed. It's like driving a new road or skiing a new course: You make better time if you've already seen the route. When previewing a text, consider the following elements:

- *Title.* Most titles do more than announce the subject of a document. Many convey the author's purpose and whether the text is intended for an academic or general audience.
- *Abstract or introduction.* The abstract found in academic articles and the introduction in most articles, chapters, and books provide a roadmap to what's ahead.
- *Section headings, lists, or boxed material.* Many texts are divided into sections with titles that indicate what's coming. Many academic research reports, for example, have these section headings: Introduction, Methods, Results, and Discussion. Bulleted lists or boxed information also identify key points.
- *Conclusion.* Main ideas are often reiterated in the final section or paragraph(s) of a text. In addition, writers use the conclusion to explain why their argument matters. Previewing the author's conclusion can help you determine what sections of a text to read carefully.

Notice Signal Words and Transitions

Noticing textual clues while you read can also help you make predictions about what's coming within a document. Table 2.3 includes examples of signal words and their functions.

TABLE 2.3
Signal Words and Their Functions

Rhetorical Function	Examples of Signal Words
To introduce an example	*for example, for instance, such as, like, to illustrate, specifically*
To introduce repetition or clarification of an idea	*in other words, i.e., that is, to be clear, namely, put another way*
To introduce a contrasting or contradictory point	*on the other hand, in contrast, yet, conversely, but, however, nonetheless, despite this, still, whereas, alternatively*
To show a cause/effect relationship	*because, due to the fact that, as a result of, consequently, for this reason, thus, therefore*
To emphasize a point	*most important, especially, above all, indeed, even more important*

Signal words help you to determine the meaning and significance of sentences in a text. An attentive reader will recognize that an idea introduced with *most importantly* is more essential than one introduced with *incidentally.* Signal words can also help you understand new vocabulary and references to events or people unfamiliar to you, and how they fit into the larger argument.

Concept in Practice 2.3: Considering Linguistic Clues

Headings are among the most important textual clues to comprehension. Take a look at the next excerpt from Toma and Hancock's Methods section for Study 1. The passage has the one-word heading *Procedure,* which prepares readers for a list of steps. Notice how key word repetition (like *participants*), past tense verbs, and prepositions denoting time (*while, then*) help readers follow the chronological relating of events.

Procedure. Because self-affirmation occurs nonconsciously, participants were given a cover story about the purpose of the study (adapted from Swann, De La Ronde, & Hixon, 1994). Participants were asked to pilot the viability of a distance-learning Public Speaking course. To this end, they would prepare a short (3–5 min) speech on the legality of abortion,

The word "Procedure" prepares readers for a list of steps.

a common topic in such classes, and deliver it through an ostensibly live camera to an evaluator, who would provide written feedback on the speech. Participants' main task would then be to rate the fairness and usefulness of the feedback: Was it accurate? Was the evaluator able to form a good impression of the participants' public speaking abilities? Participants were observed through a one-way mirror to ensure that they delivered the speech.

Past tense verbs (e.g., "participants were observed") make clear the events occurred in the past.

While waiting for the evaluator to write the speech feedback, participants were invited to complete an additional study to double their extra-credit points. All participants agreed. This ostensibly unrelated study was in fact the self-affirmation manipulation, and it was run by a different experimenter to enhance credibility.

The first experimenter then returned with a sealed envelope containing the speech feedback. All participants were given the same generic negative feedback. A manipulation check confirmed that the feedback was perceived as negative, regardless of whether participants were affirmed (M = 3.12, SD = 1.55, on a scale from 1 = *not at all positive* to 9 = *a great deal positive*) or not (M = 2.78, SD = 1.46). Participants then filled out a "confidential" questionnaire about the validity of the feedback. This allowed them to express defensive responses to the ego threat. The self-affirmation exercise was thus completed *prior* to the ego threat, consistent with research demonstrating that timing is critical in effectively reducing defensiveness (Critcher, Dunning, & Armor, 2010).

Italics ensure readers notice an important time element.

Debriefing was done through a funneled procedure, which identified suspicious participants.

In this passage, the references to Critcher, Dunning, and Armor (in parentheses) and "funneled procedure" (in the final sentence) illustrate a sometimes frustrating aspect of scholarly texts: Many include vocabulary and references you won't understand. Rather than being distracted by the unfamiliar words, focus on following the writer's argument, and notice the signal words that indicate the relative importance and meaning of sentences, paragraphs, and sections of a text within that main argument. You've already learned to ignore citations in parentheses when your goal is to understand the writer's meaning. What about the "funneled procedure"? The sentence context indicates the purpose of the procedure is to identify "suspicious participants" (i.e., participants who would be biased because they have determined the researchers' actual goal). Once you determine the purpose of the funneled procedure, understanding the procedure itself is not necessary to understanding the authors' meaning.

Strategy 3: Reading Actively

A third strategy for becoming a more effective reader of academic texts is to read *actively* and pause occasionally to think about what you've just read. Strategies that foster active reading include highlighting, annotating, drawing concept maps, and making connections.

Highlight, Annotate, or Create Graphical Depictions as You Read

Highlighting is a close-reading technique that many students already use. But how do you decide what information to highlight? Some students highlight every sentence that includes new information; others highlight the first sentence of every paragraph thinking it must be that paragraph's topic sentence. This kind of highlighting, however, defeats the purpose—and the value—of highlighting.

After examining the way students marked texts read for history, political science, and sociology courses, researchers Sherrie Nist and Katie Kirby concluded that instead of paying attention to the author's cues, students often mark statements of fact and "random information that probably should not have been marked in the first place" (335). It's difficult to know what's worth highlighting when you first read a text. So mark only those sentences that contain signal words that suggest they are important, or wait until you've read an entire section and then determine what's worth highlighting. Also, when determining what to highlight, remember *why* you are reading. As we saw earlier, content-based reading is different from structure-based reading. Are you reading to evaluate the author's argument? Looking for evidence to use in your own paper? Reading to answer assigned questions or to prepare for an exam? Your purpose for reading should determine what's worth highlighting and what's not.

Sometimes textual clues make it easy to determine what sentences are worth highlighting in a text; just as often, however, when first reading a text it may seem like every sentence adds new information. If you begin highlighting such a passage, you may end up with a passage that is entirely highlighted. A better approach for marking most texts is to use strategies that promote understanding. Annotating is one such strategy.

When you write **annotations**, you write comments on the text. Many experienced readers have their own system of annotation, replete with checkmarks, squiggly lines, circles, arrows, and abbreviations that may make little sense to others, but these markings help a reader slow down and *think* about what he or she is reading.

Many annotations consist of phrases and short sentences that summarize the gist of paragraphs or sections. Summarizing ideas in your own words, rather than highlighting or copying sentences from the text, aids in both comprehension and memory. In one large-scale study demonstrating this, students in introductory psychology courses were directed to summarize some course material and copy other material directly from slides. When later tested over the material, students scored significantly higher on the concepts they had summarized in their own words (Brown, Roediger, and McDaniel 89–90). Summarizing while reading keeps you engaged with the text, helps you remember what you've read, and alerts you to sections that you do not understand. (If you can't summarize the point, you may need to reread.) In addition, if you condense a text in the margins, you can review it by rereading your annotations. An annotation can also classify a paragraph according to purpose: Is it an example, a summary, or a key point? Even a question mark in the margin can remind you later that you found a passage confusing or problematic.

Concept in Practice 2.4: Making Annotations

The following passage comes from an early section in Toma and Hancock's article where the authors define self-affirmation theory, the theory they set out to test in their two studies. After the initial topic sentence (highlighted), additional sentences clarify or expand on the highlighted sentence. Rather than highlight the entire passage, the reader uses selective highlighting and annotations to convey the point of the passage in a sentence or two.

Facebook and Ego Needs

The primary premise of self-affirmation theory is that people have a fundamental need to see themselves as valuable, worthy, and good. This need for a positive self-image is an important motivator of behavior. People routinely dismiss, distort, or avoid information that threatens their self-worth. Conversely, they value, cultivate, and gravitate toward information that reinforces it.

Self-affirmation = People need to feel good about themselves. When my self-esteem is threatened I'll look for ways to restore my self-worth.

One strategy for satisfying the fundamental need for self-worth is self-affirmation, defined as the process of bringing to awareness essential aspects of the self-concept, such as values, meaningful relationships, and cherished personal characteristics (Sherman & Cohen, 2006; Steele, 1988). According to self-affirmation theory, people are generally motivated to seek such information in the environment, and this need becomes particularly salient after an ego threat, as people unconsciously attempt to repair their sense of self-worth. Another key proposition of self-affirmation theory is that after attending to self-affirming information, individuals' tendency to engage in defensive processes, such as dismissal or distortion, is reduced or eliminated. This is the case because self-affirmation has already secured individuals' sense of self-worth and self-integrity, rendering these other defense mechanisms unnecessary. Consequently, self-affirmation has the salutary effect of making people more open-minded and secure toward threatening events (Steele, 1988).

Then I can be less defensive about an ego threat.

Annotations can do more than summarize the point of a paragraph or section. They can include your comments, questions, counter-examples, and objections. They may also contain your answers to such questions as:

- What underlying assumptions or biases does the author have about this topic?
- What reasons or evidence supports this point?
- How does this part of the text relate to others?
- What is the purpose of paragraphs that seem unrelated to the author's central point?
- Does my experience confirm or contradict what the author is saying?

These questions help you to think critically about an author's argument.

Some research suggests that inventing and answering your own questions as you read aids comprehension. Reading researchers Harry Singer and Dan Donlan found that when high school students created and answered their own comprehension questions while reading complex short stories, their comprehension improved. The researchers speculate that creating questions while reading helped the students to see relationships among different parts of the story (183).

Another close-reading technique is to draw a graphical depiction of the material. By visually depicting the relative importance or relationship of ideas—creating a flow chart to represent a chain of events, for instance, or a "concept map" to show how ideas relate to each other—you enhance your ability to understand and remember the material (Nilson 244). You will have a mental "picture" of the information. Figure 2.5, for example, is a graphical illustration of self-affirmation theory.

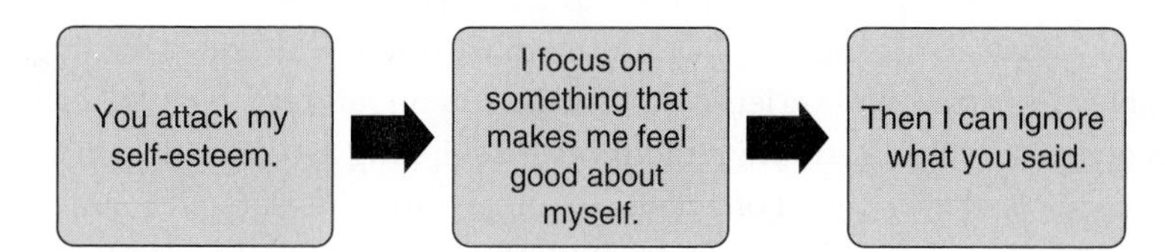

Figure 2.5 Graphical Illustration of Self-Affirmation Theory

In Figure 2.5, the cause-effect relationship implicit in self-affirmation theory is reflected in the arrows connecting the boxes. If you can convert ideas into images, you will remember those ideas longer.

Make Connections as You Read

We all have difficulty remembering random bits of information. To give the new information meaning we must connect it to what we already know. Connecting what you read to what you already know is another active reading technique.

Particularly meaningful for students is making connections between a new text and other texts they've read.

When associating the new material with what you've already read, don't just look for similarities between texts; look for points of divergence. If you're like many first-year students, you may not always be comfortable with discovering that your sources disagree. This is something that English professors Ann Penrose and Cheryl Geisler noticed while observing a first-year student and graduate student read assigned sources for a research paper. The first-year student decided to write her paper using only sources who agreed with each other and with whom she agreed, assuming the other sources must be "wrong" (511–12); but the graduate student referred to the divergent views in his paper, using the disagreement as an opportunity to raise questions and topics he could address (511).

Whether you agree or disagree with the texts you read, "talk back" to them in the margins. Note why you agree or disagree with what they say. Engage the sources in a "conversation." For example, you might write in the margins of a text, "Source X would disagree with this point" or "Source Y gives an example of this." Making connections in your annotations is an excellent way to address what many students say are their reading weaknesses: getting distracted, losing interest, and remembering little of what they've read (Roberts and Roberts 131). These "conversations" that begin in the margins between you and the text, or between one text and another, often spark the ideas you eventually develop in your writing assignments.

Strategy 4: Adjusting How You Read

One of the most important strategies toward becoming a more efficient reader involves adjusting how you read according to what and why you're reading. You probably already have experience doing this. You might, for example, read only parts of a newspaper, scanning headlines and skipping articles that don't interest you, but read every word of a novel to understand the plot and character relationships. You probably click from one link to another when reading online, and when it comes to reading textbook chapters, you might go first to the key objectives, summary, or table of contents. Your reading strategies should vary according to the genre and your purpose for reading.

Learn to Adjust Your Reading Rate

Should you read carefully or superficially? Comprehensively or selectively? Slowly or quickly? Skilled readers are self-monitors. They adjust how they read according to their comprehension level and purposes, investing more time on the more complex material in a text. This self-monitoring seems to be key to comprehension (Dole et al. 248–49).

When you understand why you are reading a text—what you want to get out of it—you know what parts you can skim and what parts to read slowly and carefully, and you understand what you read better (McCrudden, Schraw, and Hartley 305).

Concept in Practice 2.5: Adjusting How You Read

The Results section of an academic research report is where the researchers describe their findings in detail. It can be a particularly daunting section because it often includes statistical analyses difficult for lay readers to understand, but by using your knowledge of the genre and by keeping your reason for reading in mind, you can adjust the way you read accordingly.

In the Results section of their report, Toma and Hancock include the statistical analysis they conducted to determine if the difference between the groups of students studied was statistically "significant," meaning the difference was unlikely to be due to chance. If your goal is to determine what the researchers learned, you need not attend to every word equally. You can instead skim over the numerical data and focus on determining what the researchers learned. Consider, for example, this paragraph from the Results section for Study 1.

Simple effects tests confirmed that (a) participants who examined their own Facebook profiles (M = 5.91, SD = 1.10) were more accepting of the feedback than participants who examined a stranger's profile (M = 4.31, SD = 1.57), $t(43)$ = 3.90 p < .001, Cohen's d = 1.19, and (b) participants who were affirmed on Facebook (M = 5.91, SD = 1.10) were equally accepting of the feedback as those affirmed through the values essay (M = 5.53, SD = 1.31), $t(41)$ = 1.01, p = .32. Together, these results provide evidence that Facebook profile exposure is a self-affirming activity and that the self-affirmation earned from Facebook does not differ from that earned from the classic values essay manipulation.

One key finding is highlighted but not the statistical details.

What did the researchers learn?

Learn to Read Critically

In the previous *Concept in Practice*, you skipped over the statistical analysis to get to the research findings. This kind of adjustment makes sense if your only goal is to learn what the researchers concluded (rather than to determine how they reached their conclusions).

Many times, however, the adjustment an academic reader needs to make is to *slow down* and analyze the writer's claims—not because they are difficult to comprehend but because they are claims a reader should not accept at face value. This is sometimes called *reading critically*, and it's a skill highly valued in academic contexts. Your professors expect you to read critically whenever they ask you to *analyze, interpret, evaluate, assess, examine,* or *judge* the merits of an argument.

Reading critically involves reading with a healthy dose of skepticism. Consider the following sentence, used to credit a college recruitment campaign for an increase in Hispanic student enrollment:

> Since implementing the recruitment campaign in 2010, the college has seen its Hispanic enrollment increase 15%.

The claim sounds impressive, if you don't know that other schools in the same state, some without recruitment campaigns, boasted even larger increases in Hispanic student populations during the same period. Attributing the increase at one school to recruitment measures alone misrepresents the larger context (Hispanic enrollment was rising statewide) and illustrates the importance of critically reading arguments.

A critical reader is persuaded by sound reasoning and evidence rather than by impressive numbers and a writer's rhetorical skill. An experienced writer might warn that "there is a one-in-fifty chance that a bad event will happen"; but a critical reader will recognize that this means "there is a 98 percent chance that everything will be okay" (Wolfe 455). Critical reading is so important to academic success that it is the focus of a full chapter: chapter 3.

Alter Your Reading Style When Reading Onscreen

Most of us are used to reading selectively online. We look for answers to specific questions and stop reading once we've found those answers. Because the Internet contains so much information, skimming, scanning, and looking for headlines and key phrases are necessary skills. This way of reading is made possible by the conventions of writing found on most websites—including bullets, bold print, short paragraphs, and boxed information.

Many college assignments are also read onscreen, but they are documents available through library databases or print-based documents made available in digitized format through your school's course management system. Many of these assigned readings shouldn't be skimmed but read carefully.

Although digitized course materials and library resources available online don't include the ads that websites include, reading onscreen is not distraction free, as education professor Ellen Rose learned when she talked with Canadian university students about their experiences reading digitized course materials. (Rose's study appears at the end of this chapter.) Some of those distractions come from your computer. With Facebook, Twitter, and e-mail a click away, reading online course assignments requires discipline.

Several strategies can improve your ability to read assignments onscreen. For example, read when you can devote at least a half hour to long texts rather than reading piecemeal, but take short breaks during extended reading sessions to alleviate eyestrain and fatigue. Rose describes some additional strategies she uses to limit distractions while reading onscreen:

> I turn off my email. I listen to music or the white noise of talk radio to block out the conversations of those around me. When the software allows it, I use the mouse to highlight the paragraph I am reading; I enlarge the page so that what I am reading becomes the centre of both the screen and my attention and when I am alone, I read aloud. (522)

Strategies such as these can help you stay focused when reading.

In addition to mitigating the drawbacks of reading onscreen, use the digital reading skills you already have to your advantage. For example, you can quickly find specific information in a website or in an onscreen document by using the "find" function of the software. If you encounter a word you're unfamiliar with, you can hover over it, right- or left-click, and search for a definition or synonym. If you are reading several sources for a research project, you can have each source open in its own window; you can also copy and paste relevant sections of sources into a Word document to compare them side by side.

Reading on a computer screen does not mean you must read in the same superficial way you do when searching online for the best airfare. Don't skim and scan reading assignments when full comprehension is called for; instead slow down, focus, and read documents in their entirety. By applying traditional strategies for reading print texts (e.g., paying attention to structural clues and taking notes) and onscreen reading strategies (e.g., taking more frequent breaks and limiting distractions), you can read online and onscreen content as closely as you read offline and offscreen content—and save a few trees in the process.

Applying the Concepts to Reading: *Considering the IMRAD Report*

As you've learned in this chapter, many academic reports are divided into these sections:

Abstract
Introduction
Methods
Results
Discussion (or Conclusion).

The first letter of the major sections (Introduction, Methods, Results, Discussion) combine to create the acronym IMRAD, with an "a" added for easier pronunciation. The **IMRAD structure** is widely used in the physical, applied, and social sciences. Here is a review of some strategies that can help you understand the research described in an IMRAD report:

1. *Survey the report to get oriented.* In what journal or book is the report published? When was it published? What is the author's name and academic affiliation? Scientific research reports often have many authors who were involved in the research, but the name of the principal contributor appears first. Notice the title. Even the most technical-sounding titles help get you oriented.
2. *Read the Abstract.* It identifies the purpose of the study, the research methods, and the results.
3. *Read the Introduction.* Look for the statement of purpose, usually appearing after a summary of what previous researchers have learned about the topic.
4. *Skim the Methods section.* Identify who or what was studied and how.
5. *Read the Results section selectively.* If this section includes statistical analysis you do not understand, keep in mind the main objectives or hypothesis and just look for sentences that identify what the researchers learned.
6. *Read the Discussion section.* Identify the important findings. Were there any surprises? How do the results of this study compare to those of earlier studies?

An IMRAD-style report from *The Journal of Social Psychology* appears next. This article, published in 1990, is being considered as one of the sources for a paper about how our definition of "sexist" behavior has changed steadily since 1950. The article is brief and doesn't include an abstract or section headings, but headings have been inserted in brackets and aspects of the article are explained in annotations. Answer the following questions about the article's content and rhetorical context:

- What do the authors' affiliations indicate about the authors' credibility?
- Based on the title, what would you predict the authors will demonstrate exactly?
- What do the publication site (*The Journal of Social Psychology*) and the writing style tell you about the intended audience?
- What are the first textual clues in the article indicating that this is a report of original research (i.e., a primary source)? That is, how do the authors indicate they will describe research they conducted themselves?

- What was the purpose of this study? In what way does this study fill a "gap" left by previous research?
- How many people were in the sample and what was each subgroup asked to do?
- What did the researchers learn?

It's important to remember when reading an original research report that *you won't understand everything you read—especially the first time you read the article.* Even experts struggle when reading research outside of their area of expertise. But knowledge of the IMRAD report structure will help you follow the main argument. Trust that more details will become clear after you read further into the document, after you re-read sections, and after you read more within the discipline.

CULTURAL INSENSITIVITY TO SEXIST LANGUAGE TOWARD MEN

Ray Hale (Department of Psychology, Spalding University)
Robert M. Nevels and Criss Lott (Mississippi State Hospital)
Thomas Titus (Department of Psychology, Spalding University)

The name of the lead author appears first. The university affiliations for all authors appear in parentheses.

[*Introduction*]

5 Numerous studies over the past two decades have examined the perpetuation of sex bias through the use of sexist language. Although such language has been conceptually linked to sexist behavior (Blaubergs, 1978; Bodine, 1975), controversy remains regarding the effect of sexist lan-
10 guage on social behavior. Much of the research has demonstrated the deleterious effects of sexist language toward women, but little has examined the impact of sexist language on men.

In the Introduction, the subject of research is identified, the findings of previous related studies are summarized, and the need for this new study is established.

The present study investigated in 1988 the impact that
15 sexist language had on the sensitivity of American students' views toward men. **[Methods]** Subjects were 60 undergraduate students who were randomly assigned to three groups of 20. Each group responded to a neutral, a sexist-toward-women, or a sexist-toward-men statement
20 on a 5-item Likert-type scale. The stimulus question read, "How many of you have followed through with those New Year's resolutions: Started that diet, gotten rid of your (boyfriend/girlfriend/dating partner), and begun your exercise program?" In the sexist-toward-men condition, *boyfriend* was used in the sentence, *girlfriend* was
25 used in the sexist-toward-women condition, and *dating partner* was used in the neutral condition. Respondents were asked to rate the statement, "The above question is sexist," on a 5-point Likert-type scale ranging from *strongly*

In this paper, the statement of purpose appears at the beginning of the section describing the Methods, but the statement of purpose is more commonly found at the end of the Introduction.

The ***research methods*** *are described in the Methods section.*

agree to *strongly disagree*. Other statements about the question were included to camouflage the primary research interest and reduce the possibility
30 of the influence of experimenter bias.

Data were analyzed by a univariate analysis of variance, and post-hoc testing was performed with Tukey's least significant difference test. **[Results]** There was a significant *F* ratio ($p < .001$), and post-hoc testing revealed significant
35 differences between the neutral and sexist-toward-women conditions ($p < .001$) and between the sexist-toward-men and sexist-toward-women conditions ($p < .001$). In both cases, the sexist-toward-women statement was perceived as more sexist. There was no significant difference between
40 the neutral and sexist-toward-men conditions.

The results of the study are reported. Results sections often include technical terms (e.g., F ratio [p < .001], post-hoc testing). Don't get bogged down by the technical explanation. Just focus on determining the researchers' finding: "The sexist-toward-women statement was perceived [by subjects] as more sexist."

[Discussion]

The results of this study show that subjects were not sensitive to sexism in language toward men but that they were sensitive to sexist language toward women. Only two participants indicated that they saw the sexist-toward-men statement as sexist,
45 and 13 respondents strongly disagreed that the statement was sexist. Although progress has been made in the elimination of language that is sexist toward women (Percival, 1984; Pingree, 1978), this study found no support for parallel progress regarding men. Sexism in language has been
50 linked to unfair sexist behavior toward women (Bem & Bem, 1973); this and similar studies may promote greater awareness of sexism in language—and sexism—toward men.

The importance of the findings and how they compare to previous related research are summarized in the Discussion section. This section or an additional section titled "Conclusion" usually suggests areas for future research.

REFERENCES

A **list of sources** *cited in the paper appears after the report. This paper's bibliography is in what's called APA style, but formats vary depending on the journal.*

Bem, S. L., & Bem, D. J. (1973). Does sex-biased advertising "aid and abet" sex discrimination? *Journal of Applied Social Psychology, 3*, 6–18.

Blaubergs, M. S. (1978). Changing sexist language: The theory behind the practice. *Psychology of Women Quarterly, 2*, 244–261.

Bodine, A. (1975). Androcentrism in prescriptive grammar: Singular "they," sex-indefinitive "he," and "he or she." *Language in Society, 4*, 129–146.

Percival, E. (1984). Sex bias in introductory psychology textbooks: Five years later. *Canadian Psychology, 25*, 35–42.

Pingree, S. (1978). The effects of nonsexist television commercials and perceptions of reality on children's attitudes about women. *Psychology of Women Quarterly, 2*, 262–275.

Applying the Concepts to Writing: *Why Read Original Research Reports?*

We've seen in this chapter that reports of original research—sometimes called *primary sources*—can be challenging reading for those new to the discipline or genre. Given the difficulty of reading some original research reports and the ease with which you can often find summaries of that research written by others—sometimes called *secondary sources*—a natural question is: Why not just read the secondary sources?

The short answer is that when you read another person's summary of a text, you are getting that writer's interpretation of the original—or primary—text. That writer has made decisions about what to include and what to leave out of the summary; he or she has also made decisions about how to interpret the meaning of the original text. The secondary sources included in this *Applying the Concepts* section demonstrate this for you.

The two articles that follow were among the results in a Google search for "Self-Affirmation Underlies Facebook Use" (the title of Toma and Hancock's article). They both appear to summarize Toma and Hancock's studies, but the articles differ in details, tone, and interpretation. They also vary in accuracy. As you read, highlight some of the differences you notice. Then, analyze the two sources in a paper, using quotations from the articles to illustrate the limitations of secondary sources. Margin notes draw your attention to a few key details in the articles.

Article 1 (from the *Los Angeles Times*, an online edition of a newspaper)

http://articles.latimes.com/2013/feb/07/business/la-fi-tn-facebook-study-growth-fueled-by-desire-for-selfaffirmation-20130207

Facebook study: Growth fueled by desire for self-affirmation

This brief summary is generally accurate. Is there any additional information that you think should be conveyed to give readers a better understanding of what Toma and Hancock concluded or how they came to their conclusions?

February 07, 2013 | By Jessica Guynn

SAN FRANCISCO -- If he were on Facebook, Stuart Smalley would probably update his status: "I'm good enough, I'm smart enough, and doggone it, people like me!"

Turns out that Smalley, played by Al Franken in the "Saturday Night Live" skit, knew a thing or two about human nature. One of the main reasons people turn to Facebook? Daily affirmations of their self-worth.

That's according to a new study from University of Wisconsin-Madison professor Catalina Toma and Cornell University professor Jeffrey Hancock.

The pair are taking the lead in applying "self-affirmation theory" to social networks. They say Facebook is not just about checking out photos and updates from friends. It's about checking up on how others view you.

Facebook is a pick-me-up that helps people feel better about themselves, especially when they feel down or have been dealt a blow to the ego, according to the study, which is slated for the March issue of Personality and Social Psychology Bulletin.

Toma and Hancock theorize that self-affirmation is an important underlying psychological factor propelling the growth of Facebook, the world's largest social network with more than 1 billion users.

Somewhere Smalley is smiling.

Article 2 (from *YourGadgetGuide*, a technology website)

http://www.yourgadgetguide.net/want-to-feel-good-about-yourself-then-check-out-your-facebook-profile/

"Want to feel good about yourself? . . . then check out your Facebook profile"

If you want to feel a bit better about yourself then checking out your Facebook profile could be just the pick-me-up you need.

A new study has found that by spending just five minutes a day on their profile, Facebook users can dramatically boost their self-esteem.

The findings titled, "Self-affirmation underlies Facebook use," also revealed the social networking site can reduce users' ambition to excel . . . perhaps because they already feel good about themselves.

Assistant Professor Catalina Toma, who led the University of Wisconsin-Madison research team, said: "Facebook gives you a real good image of yourself, but you then don't have to look for that in other ways.

"Your motivation to perform well might be reduced because you already feel really good (about yourself)."

The findings were published in the June issue of the Journal of Media Psychology.

"Self-affirmation Underlies Facebook Use" was published in the Personality and Social Psychology Bulletin. *The study described here is a different study, published in the* Journal of Media Psychology, *titled "Feeling Better But Doing Worse: Effects of Facebook Self-Presentation on Implicit Self-Esteem and Cognitive Task Performance." It's a related study, written by Toma alone.*

Consider a few more facts as you write: The first result in our Google search for "Self-Affirmation Underlies Facebook Use" links to the actual study. But no accurate secondary sources appeared on the first page of search results. How should all of this knowledge inform the research you do for college writing assignments?

Paired Readings from Reading Studies

Excerpt from "Interview with Ellen Rose," conducted by Laureano Ralón for *Figure/Ground Communication*

The following reading is from an interview with Ellen Rose, an education professor at the University of New Brunswick, whose area of expertise is Instructional Design. Instructional Design is the study of how the method of teaching—or *pedagogy*—influences the way students learn. Instructional design experts believe that the manner of presentation—whether it be textbook, lecture, PowerPoint slide, or YouTube video—shapes how much and how well students learn.

The interview first appeared in 2011 in *Figure/Ground Communication*, a website that features conversations with professors and scholars from all disciplines talking about a variety of academic issues. In the excerpts included here, Rose discusses two topics: (1) how we read digital texts (a topic discussed further in the upcoming article, "The Phenomenology of On-Screen Reading") and (2) how presentation (such as PowerPoint) shapes the way we learn.

Because the original context is an academic forum, Rose uses academic vocabulary, such as *phenomenology* (the study of how we interpret or perceive phenomena, including texts and media) and *media ecology* (the study of how technology influences our perceptions and understanding of the world). Don't be intimidated by the unfamiliar terms and names. Focus instead on following the gist of the conversation—a task made easier by the question-answer format.

[Ralón] What makes a good teacher today? How do you manage to command attention in an age of interruption characterized by attention deficit and information overflow?

[Rose] I never think of it as "commanding" attention; attention is something that I want my students to give freely. The best I can do is "encourage" it by engaging learners in conversations about interesting, relevant ideas. But I've been doing a lot of research on the phenomenon of "continuous partial attention" in the past year or two that has made me think quite differently about the question of attention. Continuous partial attention is a term recently coined by Linda Stone, a former Microsoft and Apple executive, to describe the continually fractured state of attention—or inattention—that came into being with the computer, internet, and what Sherry Turkle calls "always-on, always-on-you" devices, such as cell phones. Say you're writing a paper, or reading a book—on- or offline; you're constantly breaking away from your primary task, drawn by the irresistible urge to send or check for incoming messages, surf for information, and so forth. That's the essence of continuous partial attention, and it certainly poses some interesting challenges for educators. Sure, students have been staring out classroom windows for years, but what seems to be happening now is that this state of perpetual distraction is becoming the new normal. I did some research recently in which I discovered, unexpectedly, that university students are actually in the process of redefining *attention* and *focus*. Students who admitted, in a survey, to often breaking away from online learning activities, sometimes for five minutes or more each time, described themselves as "very focused."

And distraction is also being reconceptualised—not as a hindrance to learning but a necessary diversion. Many students told me that they *needed* the distraction of incoming messages, etc., in order to sustain interest in their academic work.

So what can a teacher do with this new normal? There's a lot of debate at my university right now about the possibility of banning laptops in class. I don't see this as a viable option; there's no point in trying to plug the dike when we're already swimming in the ocean! In my opinion, it's much more important to involve students in the conversation, talk with them about these kinds of media effects—the ways new modes of communication structure information, thought, and language. I find that those are actually discussions they very much *want* to engage in. Beyond that, I don't pretend to have any answers.

. . .

[Ralón] One of your forthcoming papers is entitled "The Phenomenology of Onscreen Reading: University Students' Lived Experience of Digitised Text." Would you give us a sneak peek?

[Rose] I'm an avid reader, but I find it—not difficult, but different, reading on the screen. I'm much less inclined to linger over a text, more likely to scan it, search it for keywords. And yet there's the convenience trade-off (so much of our use of technology these days seems to be motivated by convenience, as though it's a miracle that we ever managed to exist without cellphones and laptops), as well as the fact that reading onscreen is more environmentally friendly. For whatever reason, there's no doubt that more and more of university students' reading for classes and research is taking place onscreen, in the form of e-books and PDF files that were originally meant for the page, but then digitized. So I wondered what the experience of *onscreen* reading (as opposed to *online* reading of hypertext) was like for students.

I did discover some interesting things about the experience of onscreen reading. For example, it appears that in screen space, as opposed to what Ong called typographic space, the page either disappears as a unit of text (to be replaced by a fraction, such as 2/21, or the scroll bar), or it becomes a source of frustration that actually impairs reading, because pages rarely fit neatly onto screens. I also found, perhaps not surprisingly, that onscreen readers are very aware of the screen "glaring in my face," as one person put it. It's often a challenge to look beyond the reflective surface, where images of oneself, nearby objects, and the glare from windows and light sources, are superimposed upon the text. Most interesting to me, however, was the whole issue of focus—or the lack thereof; in fact, it was this research that led me to an exploration of the phenomenon of continuous partial attention. Ong observes that "Print . . . situates utterance and thought on a surface disengaged from everything else," but in screen space reading takes place on a surface cluttered with endless fascinating distractions that diffuse focus. Here's how one of the students I interviewed put it: "I'm wasting more time not reading than reading, you know, with e-mail and talking to other people. If it was a book I would read more than if it was online because there are more distractions, easier ways to, oh, I'm just going to check this, and totally forget that you're reading, and then an hour or two goes by and you're like, I guess I should go back." But it was also very interesting to me to learn that students are coming up with some creative strategies for finding focus. For example, they might enlarge the text they're reading, so that it becomes the center of both the screen and their attention, or they might read aloud, when alone. And several spoke about using music to drown out other sounds; it would appear that music is becoming the new silence.

[Ralón] Toward the end of his life, McLuhan declared: "Phenomenology [is] that which I have been presenting for many years in non-technical terms." Do you think there is an affinity between media ecology and phenomenology?

[Rose] I'd like to know the source of that quote—very interesting! In fact, this is a question I'm in the midst of sorting out, because I'm currently working on a research project with Catherine Adams at the University of Alberta that is based on the assumption that there is indeed an affinity between these two perspectives. Cathy and I first connected because of our shared interest in the way PowerPoint structures pedagogy; she was looking at it as a hermeneutic phenomenologist and I was looking at it as a media ecologist. Yet it was clear to us very early in our communications that there were some strong similarities and points of connection between our two perspectives on the topic of PowerPoint and pedagogy.

So we've set out to formally examine those similarities and points of connection in a SSHRC-funded study of teachers' and students' lived experience of learning management systems, such as Blackboard. The research is now in its early stages, so I have nothing earth-shattering to share with you. But my new awareness of phenomenology has certainly caused me to read key media ecology texts in a different way. For example, McLuhan's work comes into a new focus when you look at it through the lens of phenomenology. Implicit in his biological metaphors of media as environments and extensions of the human body is a phenomenology of media—an awareness that communication technologies alter the nature of human consciousness and the texture of lived experience. Ultimately, both media ecologist and phenomenologist are concerned with understanding the interplay and intertwining of media and human being-in-the-world. Both recognize that media and technologies touch us in ways that fundamentally alter our life-worlds. As Don Ihde says, both phenomenology and ecology study the interaction of the figure (organism) with its ground (environment). Ihde suggests that the key difference may be where we position ourselves with respect to that investigation: phenomenologists try to get inside the organism, whereas media ecologists tend to be positioned outside or above it, in order to get a broader view of the kinds of interactions and interconnections taking place in the environment.

[Ralón] So how *does* PowerPoint structure pedagogy? What were some of the findings of that early study?
[Rose] My interest was not only in how PowerPoint structures pedagogy but, more fundamentally, how it structures thought. Because before we use it to present, we spend hours creating the slides, so PowerPoint is increasingly also the means by which we marshal and organize our thoughts. I could go on at length about this (and often do, as my students could tell you), but let's just say that a lot gets lost, in the way of ideas and arguments, when we are compelled to conceptualize topics in terms of efficient bulleted points. And a lot gets added that really doesn't need to be there: elaborate backgrounds, clipart, screen transitions. These not only distract from but begin to take precedence over the verbal content—because increasingly, it is the technological virtuosity of the PowerPoint display, rather than one's contributions to a body of knowledge, that give the presenter the authority to speak. And, of course this is not just in the classroom: increasingly, PowerPoint also mediates academic dialogue. This was driven home for me six or seven years ago, when I attended a conference on educational technology. In one session, titters broke out among the audience members as a speaker put an acetate sheet on an overhead projector. In another session, a

speaker apologized profusely for not having a PowerPoint presentation, and begged us not to leave, before beginning to read aloud from his paper. And in a third session, the topic of using instructional technologies in a humanizing way was presented with slide after slide of bulleted lists. When I pointed out afterwards the contradiction between medium and message, the presenters were dumbfounded: they simply hadn't considered *not* using PowerPoint in this way. It worries me that, as slideware becomes de rigueur at conferences and in classrooms, people are using it in this unreflective way, without considering how it shapes their thinking or their messages.

QUESTIONS ABOUT MEANING

1. What is "continuous partial attention"?
2. What motivated Rose to research the "phenomenology of on-screen reading"? What did she learn from the students she interviewed?
3. How does Rose feel about PowerPoint presentations in the classroom? Explain.

QUESTIONS FOR RHETORICAL ANALYSIS

4. Various linguistic clues in the interview help those unfamiliar with the people named or academic terms used to follow the conversation. Consider the following paragraph. Rose was asked what she learned by interviewing students about their online reading experiences. Several transitions and explicit linguistic cues help readers follow the discussion; a few of the early cues are highlighted for you. Read the paragraph and highlight additional examples of linguistic cues that you think help readers follow the conversation.

I did discover some interesting things about the experience of on-screen reading. For example, it appears that in screen space, as opposed to what Ong called typographic space, the page either disappears as a unit of text (to be replaced by a fraction, such as 2/21, or the scroll bar), or it becomes a source of frustration that actually impairs reading, because pages rarely fit neatly onto screens. I also found, perhaps not surprisingly, that onscreen readers are very aware of the screen "glaring in my face," as one person put it. It's often a challenge to look beyond the reflective surface, where images of oneself, nearby objects, and the glare from windows and light sources, are superimposed upon the text. Most interesting to me, however, was the whole issue of focus—or the lack thereof; in fact, it was this research that led me to an exploration of the phenomenon of continuous partial attention. Ong observes that "Print . . . situates utterance and thought on a surface disengaged from everything else," but in screen space reading takes place on a surface cluttered with endless fascinating distractions that diffuse focus. Here's how one of the students I interviewed put it: "I'm wasting more time not reading than reading, you know, with e-mail and talking to other people. If it was a book I would read more than if it was online because there are more distractions, easier ways to, oh, I'm just going to check this, and totally forget that you're reading, and then an hour or two goes by and you're like, I guess I should go back." But it was also very interesting to me to learn that students are coming up with some creative strategies for finding focus. For example, they might enlarge the text they're reading, so that it becomes the center of both the screen and their attention, or they might read aloud, when alone. And several spoke about using music to drown out other sounds; it would appear that music is becoming the new silence.

5. In the preceding passage, Rose introduces two speakers for the first time in the interview: one is media scholar Walter Ong and the other is a student Rose interviewed. What does each quotation contribute to Rose's response? Why do you think Rose names Ong but not the student? Notice the way Rose refers to Ong. How do you think she might have referred to Ong if she were responding to an interview question from a *New York Times* journalist?

"The Phenomenology of On-Screen Reading: University Students' Lived Experience of Digitised Text," *British Journal of Educational Technology* ELLEN ROSE

The following article describes research Ellen Rose conducted to learn how students experience onscreen reading. Rose is an education professor and instructional design expert who teaches at the University of New Brunswick in Canada. Her research involved interviewing students, many of them quoted in the article. The article appeared in 2011 in the *British Journal of Educational Technology*, a peer-reviewed journal that publishes research about technology for educators in all disciplines.

ABSTRACT

As reading shifts from the page to the screen, research focuses primarily upon the nature and effects of hypertextual reading. However, many of the texts that university students read for academic purposes are digitised texts that begin life as paper-based books and papers and are read on-screen. Applying the principles and practices of hermeneutic phenomenology, this study sought to gain insight into university students' experiences of reading digitised texts such as e-books and Portable Document Format files. Open-ended interviews were conducted with 10 students. A thematic analysis of the interviews revealed six main themes: the disappearing page, to have but not to hold, the ever present screen, getting in focus, the disciplined body and finding what I need.

In 1979, Christopher Evans lamented that with the rise of electronic text, "the 1980s will see the book as we know it, and as our ancestors created and cherished it, begin a slow but steady slide into oblivion" (p. 106). More recently, futurist Kevin Kelly (2006) claimed that the digital format is the book's "next stage of evolution" (p. 42) and enthusiastically anticipated a time in the near future when "[a]ll new works will be born digital" (p. 43). Despite such predictions, both dire and hopeful, rumours about the death of the paper-based publication are probably greatly exaggerated. Nevertheless, it is true that more and more of what we read is digital text. This is particularly the case in universities, where—as libraries turn to e-books and online journals, as e-books make inroads into the textbook industry (Hanson, 2008) and as professors distribute course materials as Portable Document Format (PDF) files via learning management systems—the materials that university students are required to read are increasingly found online.

As a result of the societal shift from the page to the screen, a growing body of research addresses the nature and effects of online reading. Much of this research (eg, Landow, 1991; Rouet, Dillon, Levonen & Spiro, 1996; Shapiro & Niederhauser, 2004) focuses specifically on how readers encounter the Web's hypertext. According to Carusi (2006), the gist of these studies is "that the reading practices of hypertext readers become increasingly fragmentary, that they are easily distracted by surface features; their response to the text is more general, less specific and emotionally engaged than that of linear readers" (p. 171). Jakob Nielsen, who has been studying online reading habits for two decades, goes so far as to assert that "'Reading' is not even the right word" (quoted in Bauerlein, 2008, p. B7) to describe how we process online, hypertextual information.

Complementing this empirical research is what Rich (2008) describes as "a passionate debate about just what it means to read in the digital age" (n.p.). The debate is largely fuelled by the seemingly irreconcilable differences of opinion between critics such as Sven Birkerts (1994) and Barry Sanders (1994), who believe that electronic text ultimately diminishes both the personal growth of individuals and the stability of our society, and advocates such as Rand Spiro, who believes that navigating online texts can build cognitive flexibility (eg, Spiro & Jehng, 1990).

Parties in the former camp are at pains to emphasise the haphazard, unfocused nature of screen reading, which, they insist, simply "doesn't translate into academic reading" (Bauerlein, 2008, p. B7). The proponents of digital text reply that the move from the page to the screen is evolutionary and inevitable. Moreover, according to Marc Prensky (2001), the changing propensities and cognitive abilities of young people, or "digital natives," lend themselves to engagements with the screen rather than to lengthy perusals of static texts.

As a teacher attempting to make sound pedagogical decisions about the use of digital texts, I find two big pieces missing from both the research and the debate. First, there is little consideration of digital texts that are not necessarily hypertextual, such as PDF documents and e-books. In contrast to online hypertexts, which are written for the Web, many of the texts that university students peruse for academic purposes begin life as paper-based books and papers, are digitised and are then read on-screen. Second, both the research and the debate give little consideration to the experience of online or on-screen reading. The empirical research offers some insight, but because such studies tend to be highly focused investigations into, for example, how students read digital texts (eg, Burke & Rowsell, 2008; Monk, 2004) or the effects of digital texts on reading comprehension (eg, Rodrigues & Martins, 2008), they pre-empt a holistic understanding of the experience. As I and my colleagues increasingly provide our undergraduate and graduate students with digitised course materials, it becomes clear that in order to make appropriate, pedagogically sound decisions about the use of such materials, we need to move beyond making summary judgments to seek insight into what it is like for students to read digitised texts.

My purpose in this study was to gain such insight through the use of hermeneutic phenomenology, which "aims to describe our prereflective experiences—here, with the technological things of our teaching and learning lifeworlds" (Adams, 2008, p. 167). The phenomenologist's goal is to reconnect with the lifeworld—"the world of our immediately lived experience, prior to all our thoughts about it" (Abram, 1996, p. 40)—in order to capture the pre-reflective essence of an experience. As James Heap (1977) writes of his phenomenological explorations into the experience of reading, "My interest is not in reading as a momentary event sliced from life and mounted on the slide of science. Instead, reading is understood as a course of sense making within daily life" (p. 104). It is important to emphasise that no researcher who undertakes a phenomenological inquiry expects or wishes to produce generalisable findings. Rather, the expectation is that we will gain rich insight into the essence of experiences that "can develop as researchers build on each other's work" (Polkinghorne, 1983, p. 46).

There is no step-by-step procedure for doing hermeneutic phenomenology. In fact, Max van Manen (1990) insists that it "is decidedly unmethodological in a purely prescriptive or technocratic sense" (p. 3), "more a carefully cultivated thoughtfulness than a technique" (p. 131). Yet, he adds, it definitely has "a certain *methodos*—a way" (p. 29). That way consists, in brief, of the following: collecting lived experience descriptions; conducting a thematic analysis of those descriptions in order to capture the essence, or *eidos,* of the experience—those distinctive qualities *"that make a phenomenon what it is and without which the phenomenon could not be what it is"* (van Manen, p. 106, emphasis in original); and finally, presenting that essence in a vibrant language that "reawakens or shows us the lived quality and significance of the experience in a fuller, deeper manner" (p. 10).

I gathered lived experience descriptions of on-screen reading from 10 students, the only respondents to a request for volunteer participants that I placed in my university's daily e-news bulletin for students and in the graduate students' list serve for my faculty (Education). Table 1 shows who the participants in my study were, demographically and academically.

I conducted an open-ended interview with each participant, asking them to recall a particular, recent instance when they read something substantial online—the kind of text with which they typically engaged, whether an e-book, chapter, or scholarly paper—and then to tell me in detail what they remembered about the experience. To stimulate the students' recall at a detailed level, I offered a series of probes about the space in which they read, their mood, their posture, their approach to the text and so forth.

Thematic analysis consisted of a process of reading and rereading the interview transcripts until "units of meaning" (Groenewald, 2004, p. 50) began to emerge, grouping those units into clusters and then identifying, for each cluster, a theme "which expresses the essence of these clusters" (Hycner, 1999, p. 153). As I sought to extract from the interview transcripts, and the diversity of experiences that the students had shared with me, the essence of the experience of on-screen reading, six themes emerged. According to Donald Polkinghorne (1983), the validity of a phenomenological account owes much to how vividly and elegantly it represents an experience: "If the insight is communicated well, then others will also recognize the description as a statement of the essence of the phenomenon for themselves" (p. 45). Therefore, in the following elaborations of the six emergent themes, I use a first person narrative to represent them in a way that is both clear and evocative of the lived experience. Unless otherwise indicated, the quotations are drawn directly from the interviews.

Table 1
Demographic and Academic Breakdown of Research Participants

Who the participants were, by:	
Gender	
Male	2
Female	8
Age (ages range roughly from 20–55)	
<30	6
>30	4
Programme of study	
Undergraduate	3
Graduate	7 (3 Masters, 4 Doctoral)
Discipline	
Business Administration	1
Chemistry	1
Computer Science	1
Education	3
Engineering	1
Interdisciplinary	1
Kinesiology	1
Sociology	1

THE DISAPPEARING PAGE

Reading a scholarly paper on the printed page, I enter what Walter Ong (1982) calls "typographic space" (p. 128), a realm as familiar and comfortable as a dog-eared book. Typographic space is composed less of words than of pages, "visual surface[s]" that "become charged with imposed meaning" (Ong, p. 128). I always turn a page with a frisson of anticipation, even when I am reading the driest of academic prose.

When I read a scholarly paper on-screen, however, the familiar turning of pages from left to right gives way to the march of text from the top of the screen to the bottom. Here, in "screen space," the advancement from page to page becomes immaterial, almost unnoticeable, and the page as a content structure tends to disappear. Sometimes, it is merely represented by a fraction (eg, 2/21), in which case, it becomes a temporal rather than a spatial construct, indicating how long I can expect to take perusing the text. However, generally, I ignore page numbers—especially when there are two discrepant numbers, those printed on the page and those assigned by the software—and watch the scroll bar. Using it as a visual gauge of my progress through a document is similar, in its imprecision, to holding up a book in progress to assess the thickness of the unread pages.

Sometimes, the page, or rather, the windowed page, appears to me foremost as a source of frustration, an irritation that inhibits my reading of the digitised text. This is chiefly because pages rarely fit neatly on screens, given their different aspect ratios—and especially when I "zoom in" or increase the font size in order to read more easily. In screen space, the transition from one page to the next, the dependable rhythm of typographic space, becomes a disruption in the continuity of my reading:

> You have to scroll down, okay. I can't see the whole thing and find the flow of the sentence if I haven't scrolled to the end of the sentence, you know, I get confused because then I'm scrolling down. Or sometimes if I scroll too far and then I've got to scroll back up to find what I was reading.

One of the conventions of typographic space that is particularly troublesome is the two-column display. While I tend to read the two columns on a printed page almost simultaneously, my eyes darting between them, this casual, taken-for-granted practice becomes problematic on-screen:

> I have to roll the screen, especially if I've increased the font size or the size of the page to make it easier to read, so then I have to leave the line here and quite often when I get to the bottom of the left column it will automatically take me to the next page which means I've got to back up a whole page and then go to the top of the right column.
>
> You know, it's like what did I just read? And I have to go back down and read it again and go back up.

My encounter with the digitised text is impeded by the fact that it was designed to be read on the printed page.

The page is sensuous—I can touch it, smell it and hear it rustling when I turn it. Without the materiality of the page, I am left with only the text qua text. Printing documents is one way to regain that sensuous page, but in the interests of saving money and trees, I usually resist the temptation to do so. In fact, I am learning to appreciate the elegant simplicity of digital text, which is more absence than presence—the absence of pages that accumulate, in unruly drifts, upon my desk, bookcase and floor.

TO HAVE BUT NOT TO HOLD

I am learning, but there are still times when I feel the need to physically possess the document. To comprehend something fully is to "take ownership" of it, and in order to own a text, I must hold it in my hands, scribble notes in the margins, underline, highlight, and star important bits:

> I find it's just the tactile that I can't, you know, touch it, and that's the problem I find with online reading, is that I don't physically have it. I can't make notes on it, it doesn't feel as here as, you know, it's kind of there, it's on the computer.

In the absence of the ability to make the text mine in this way, I make my own text by taking extensive notes as I read, sometimes copying and pasting important passages into a Word document or even when the format of the file prevents copying, taking a screen shot of the lines I want. However, thorough as they are, my notes have only a provisional utility. Over time, their usefulness erodes:

> So I'll find even sometimes the notes I've made, they made sense at the time, but now out of context I'm thinking, what was I talking about? But I can't go back to the document and easily find, like, with the hard copy, I'll see those yellow highlights, right, with maybe a little star. . . .

My need to have the text is only partially fulfilled by possession of the digital file, which has no material existence. True, PDF files are marvelously compact and easy to organise. I can easily slot them into my online filing system or carry them with me on my laptop or universal serial bus key. "So I would have a copy, not necessarily a physical copy, but at least a copy, so I could read it anywhere." However, these texts seem to wear protective shells that make them tamper-proof, preventing me from personalising or amending them in any way. I have them, but I cannot own them.

Still, having is good. When it comes to researching a topic, I am willing to settle for the convenience of having. In the contest between materiality and convenience, my wish to hold the text in my hands crumbles before my ability to call up what I need at any time, from any place:

> I think my preference would still be to be able to actually hold the book in my hand. . . . Although the advantage is that you don't have to leave your house, you don't have to worry about the book being signed out, you don't have to worry about getting it back to the library, so the convenience is there.

THE EVER PRESENT SCREEN

In their phenomenological account of "screenness," Introna and Ilharco (2006) assert that it is in the nature of a screen to recede beneath the content it presents:

> [W]e never seem to look at a screen, as a "screen." We rather tend to look at screens in attending to that which appears on them. What seems most evident when looking at a screen is the content being presented on that screen—the text, images, colors, graphics, and so on—not the screen itself. (p. 62).

Perhaps this is true of television. However, when I read digitised texts, I am continually aware of the presence of the screen, its flat expanse imposing itself between me and the text. In fact, I tend to refer to on-screen reading as "reading the screen" or even "staring at the screen."

My strong awareness of the screen might have something to do with the fact that it is a reflective surface, "glaring in my face all day." Unlike the page, the screen mirrors the world around it: "It can reflect sometimes, depending on where the sun is, and you can't quite see very well, so I've got to manage with that. . . ." Try as I might to look beyond the reflective surface, images of myself, nearby objects and the glare from windows and light sources are superimposed upon the words I want to read.

Even when I carefully set up my workspace and computer options to minimise such issues, I find it difficult to ignore the screen's presence: "You're focused on the screen. And that's the only thing that's going on, really, in my mind is to be able to focus on the screen."

GETTING IN FOCUS

According to Heap (1977), "The activity of reading (anything?) requires as an essential procedure a focal shift of attention, and the maintenance of that directed attention" (p. 105). When I read the printed page, that focus often simply happens without conscious effort: I slide quite naturally into another space, my physical surroundings becoming dimmed, less immediate. Not so, when I read on-screen:

> I find reading online I get distracted quite easily. When I read a book I can zone in and I don't know what's going on around me. But when I'm reading online the littlest thing can sort of distract me. . . .

Here, before the flickering screen, it takes a deliberate act of will and a consciously enacted set of strategies to achieve the necessary level of concentration.

One reason for this is that the act of on-screen reading requires that I use not only my eyes but my hands to scroll through the text, a coordinated activity that takes some of my attention from the text itself as I grapple with the mouse. My focus is further diverted from the text when every few lines, I must search to relocate myself on the scrolling screen:

> It's hard to either scroll or hit page down and get in the exact place that you were reading. So your eyes have to kind of find where you were. It's not a smooth transition between, you know, going from the one line to the next line on the screen. You need to page down and you get a whole chunk of new information or you do the scrolling and then you've gotta keep waiting, you know, hitting every time you want the line to go down, but then you still have to find out where you were before.
>
> When you're scrolling at times what you do is, okay, I was here on this line, and then you try to remember this is the line and until this spot, if I scroll it all the way up to this screen then I'll be able to see a lot of or more . . . of the page. So it's kind of, you know, diverting you from what you were doing. . . .

Focus is also an issue because it is often difficult for me to retreat to a private space when my reading takes place on a computer. When I read in public places—libraries, computer labs, shared offices and living rooms, beside family televisions—"'bracketing' the scenic environment" (Heap, 1977, p. 105) becomes a challenge, particularly because those around me are less hesitant to interrupt when I am reading on-screen than when I am reading a printed text:

> Sometimes I need the printer so I use my desktop and there'll be another TV in front of me where my grandparents watch their TV. So I'll have two TVs in front of me and sometimes I'll have my laptop because the desktop's old and can't open stuff, so I'll have to switch everything over to my laptop. So I'll have my laptop, desktop and a TV on, and it just gets—you know, you got twenty conversations going, you've got homework and news on the TV.

But the distractions in the room around me are nothing compared with those that reside on the screen itself. Ong (1982) observes that "Print . . . situates utterance and thought on a surface disengaged from everything else" (p. 132). In screen space, however, my reading takes place on a surface cluttered with endless fascinating distractions, giving rise to the phenomenon of continuous partial attention, a term popularised by Microsoft executive Linda Stone to describe minds always alert to the possibility of incoming email or instant messages:

> The computer is right there, if I have MSN on and somebody goes dadoop there's a message. Sometimes I'll try to ignore it to get to the end of the paragraph, but often times even though I'm reading I'm still thinking in my head, I wonder what they want?
>
> I'm wasting more time not reading than reading, you know, with e-mail and talking to other people. If it was a book I would read more than if it was online because there are more distractions, easier ways to, oh, I'm just going to check this, and totally forget that you're reading, and then an hour or two goes by and you're like, I guess I should go back.

Tempted as I am by Facebook, Twitter and the other online distractions that are just a mouse click away, I have not succumbed completely to the lures of this stimulating screen space. On the contrary, I have developed numerous creative strategies for finding focus. I turn off my email. I listen to music or the white noise of talk radio to block out the conversations of those around me. When the software allows it, I use the mouse to highlight the paragraph I am reading; I enlarge the page so that what I am reading becomes the centre of both the screen and my attention and when I am alone, I read aloud. On-screen reading is something I must plan for, in order to minimise ahead of time the likelihood of distractions:

> When I decide that I am going to start and read online I know that I'm going to have a hard time with it so I try to make sure that everything is done and that I'm not going to have to interrupt myself and get up, because I would hate to do that and have to come back to it. So I find that I will try to sit down and have my coffee or tea with me or whatever and just be able to read straight through for two or three hours.

THE DISCIPLINED BODY

When I read a novel, my body wants to recline and curl: that relaxed posture in a comfortable chair is integral to the immersive, leisurely moments of ludic, or pleasure, reading. That is why I never read fiction online. If my readings for courses and research were printed, I would likely gravitate to a comfortable chair or sofa because "I feel much more comfortable when I'm just lying down and going through the book. It's kind of more a leisurely activity that really gives me a better mind set for reading." However, when I read these texts on-screen, my body must be straightened up, fixed in its place before the computer:

> I can't change my posture all that much because I'm at a desk and that's where it is.
>
> You can't curl up on the couch with a blanket and a book. You can't sit in front of the fireplace, you can't be in the bathtub, you know. You can't enjoy a book and the surroundings because you're focused on the screen.

I do what I can to be comfortable. I set up my desk at home so that the relationship between my body and the computer is correct according to the disciplinary science of ergonomics, or defying the recommendations of ergonomics experts, I find ways to recline, by leaning back in my chair or putting my keyboard in my lap and my feet on the desk. Sometimes, I read from my laptop rather than my desktop computer:

> With a laptop I do have more freedom but a smaller screen, so it's a trade-off there, too—if you want to use . . . the bigger screen, then you're stationary. If you want to have more freedom in the positions that you can get into to read, then you have to use the laptop and a smaller screen.

However, even when I read from a laptop, comfort, the kind of comfort that I need for immersive, ludic reading is elusive, "because as comfortable as I can be in my reading station it's maybe not as comfortable as snuggling up in the LazyBoy." When I read on-screen, my shoulders tense, my neck and head sometimes ache, but I read on, disciplining my body, in the sense that Foucault (1979) uses the term—compelling my body to resist its natural inclinations and to sit in a strained posture of attention.

FINDING WHAT I NEED

When I read on-screen, focus is essential because I am on a quest for something very particular. The on-screen text is a pit stop in that quest; I am not interested in following mazy paths that take off in different directions, leading who knows where. Reading the printed page, I might be drawn by interesting tangents; I might linger to appreciate a thought-provoking insight or a striking turn of phrase, even one that bears no immediate relationship to my research. However, in screen space, my reading is very goal-directed and strategic. I know what I need, what I am looking for and "if I don't have to read the whole thing, I tend not to." Blinkered by the single purpose that brought me to this particular text, "I just sort of get to the point. I'm always just stuck in the facts rather than the big picture."

Because my purpose is not to reflect upon what I am reading but to find what I need, I have developed some efficient strategies for doing so. For example, I never read an e-book in its entirety but use the table of contents, index and keyword searches to locate the information I need as quickly as possible. My on-screen reading is efficient and strategic:

> Manage it well, so know what you're going in to look at. Go right to that specific area. If there's something that you think would be of interest then read it, but just sort of game plan the book before you go in. Don't read the whole thing if you don't have to. It's not really worth the time and energy.

Of course, if a text is a required reading for a course or very pertinent to my research, I will read it in its entirety. However, in the back of my mind, I am always wondering, "how can I do this faster, and how much time do I have?"

CONCLUDING THOUGHTS

In conducting this research, I struggled with the need to be impartial—or, in van Manen's (1990) terms, "presuppositionless" (p. 29). Since my instinct and inclination has always been to question rather than champion the educational use of computer technology, it was necessary for me to bracket my negative preconceptions. I consider it a sign of my success in doing so that some of those preconceptions have now been overturned. Contrary to what the critics suggest, on-screen reading is not necessarily a frenetic process of skimming and rushing from one thing to another. Students are consciously and conscientiously making an effort to adapt to the new reading conditions by developing strategies for maintaining focus, and they are successfully disciplining their minds and bodies to read digitised papers in their entirety, when necessary.

However, my research was also foregrounded by the participants' lack of impartiality on the subject of on-screen reading, such that a primary challenge in conducting this study was obtaining lived experience descriptions that were truly pre-reflective. Many of the students who responded to my call for participants admitted that they did so because they hoped to have the opportunity to describe some of their difficulties or successes with on-screen reading; all were inclined to make judgments for and against as they described their experiences. This evaluative stance may be understood as inherent to the experience of information technology in our society. The debate about online reading described earlier in this paper is characteristic: one may be either a cheerleader or a naysayer. Impartiality is not an option because the role of new technologies in our lives is rarely experienced as neutral.

However, Heidegger's (1962) notion of ready-to-hand and unready-to-hand entities suggests another possibility: that the students' awareness of their experiences reading e-books and PDF files may in fact be a reflection of the *obstinacy* of on-screen text. Most of the objects that we encounter in the world are ready-to-hand: as we seize them to perform a task, our attention is focused less upon the object itself than the activity we are performing with it. Printed texts clearly fall into this category: when we read them, we rarely give thought to the objects—the pages, the bound books—upon and in which the words are printed. The only time we concern ourselves with objects is when they are "met as something unusable, not properly adapted for the use we have decided upon. . . . When its unusability is thus discovered, equipment becomes conspicuous" (p. 102), a hindrance in pursuing our work, and thus, in Heidegger's terms, obstinate. From this perspective, if students are conscious of their experiences with reading on-screen text, it is because its fundamental obstinacy breaks the momentum of their reading, allowing them to become somewhat disengaged from the reading itself as they focus on the unready-to-hand entity: the computer used to display on-screen text.

What I am talking about here is not the occasional glitch—although several of the students I interviewed did mention technical difficulties that sometimes impeded their on-screen reading experience. Rather, the possibility Heidegger's phenomenological perspective suggests is a lack of "fit" that may prevent students from engaging fully with the content of the e-books and PDF files they read for courses and research.

Of course, this must remain pure conjecture until we have further phenomenological studies with larger, purposefully selected and perhaps less idiosyncratic, groups of students. Such studies might also begin to capture not only the essence of the on-screen reading experience but also some of the important points of difference—for example, how reading experiences vary according to the purpose and style of the text.

In the meantime, what are the implications of this research for university teachers? As new technologies enlarge the possibilities of human action, they also increase what Don Ihde (1990) calls, our "decisional burden" (p. 177). Only a decade ago, higher education without printed books and papers would have been inconceivable. Today, both teachers and students may choose to circumvent them—and in doing so, alter not only their experience of reading but perhaps the nature of higher education itself. It is now possible to foresee a time when, having grown accustomed to accessing texts instantly and scanning them for keywords, we will regard the printed books and papers that defy such possibilities as obstinate, ill-suited to the task of academic research.

Of course, we may also choose to resist a trend that is accelerated by the proliferation of devices such as Amazon's Kindle and Sony's Reader, which promise to make digitised text even more accessible and ordinary. However, I prefer a third option that is grounded in the principles and practices of hermeneutic phenomenology: it involves continuing to encourage students to articulate and share their experiences of the on-screen reading of books and papers, in the conviction that remaining attuned to students' lived experience and fostering their sensitivity to the nature of that experience is essential in achieving a sound pedagogical response to emergent technologies.

REFERENCES

Abram, D. (1996). *The spell of the sensuous.* New York: Vintage Books.

Adams, C. A. (2008). *PowerPoint and the pedagogy of digital media technology.* Unpublished doctoral dissertation, University of Alberta.

Bauerlein, M. (2008, September 19). Online literacy is a lesser kind. *The Chronicle of Higher Education, 54,* 31, p. B7.

Birkerts, S. (1994). *The Gutenberg elegies: the fate of reading in an electronic age.* New York: Fawcett Columbine.

Burke, A. & Rowsell, J. (2008). Screen pedagogy: challenging perceptions of digital reading practice. *Changing English, 15,* 4, 445–456.

Carusi, A. (2006). Textual practitioners: a comparison of hypertext theory and phenomenology of reading. *Arts and Humanities in Higher Education, 5,* 2, 163–180.

Evans, C. (1979). *The micro millennium.* New York: Viking Press.

Foucault, M. (1979). *Discipline and punish: the birth of the prison.* New York: Vintage Books.

Groenewald, T. (2004). A phenomenological research design illustrated. *International Journal of Qualitative Methods, 3,* 1, 42–55.

Hanson, C. (2008, November). E-books go to college. *Quill & Quire, 75,* 9, p. 25.

Heap, J. L. (1977). Toward a phenomenology of reading. *Journal of Phenomenological Psychology, 8,* 1, 103–114.

Heidegger, M. (1962). *Being and time* (J. Macquarrie & E. Robinson, Trans.). New York: Harper & Row. Original work published in 1927.

Hycner, R. H. (1999). Some guidelines for the phenomenological analysis of interview data. In A. Bryman & R. G. Burgess (Eds), *Qualitative research* Vol. 3 (pp. 143–164). London: Sage.

Ihde, D. (1990). *Technology and the lifeworld: from garden to earth.* Bloomington, IN: Indiana University Press.

Introna, L. D. & Ilharco, F. M. (2006). On the meaning of screens: towards a phenomenological account of screenness. *Human Studies*, 29, 57–76.

Kelly, K. (2006, May 14). Scan this book! *New York Times Magazine*, Section 6, 42–43.

Landow, G. P. (1991). *Hypertext: the convergence of contemporary critical theory and technology.* Baltimore, MD: Johns Hopkins University Press.

Monk, D. (2004). A study of e-learners use of online materials. In Proceedings of the *Third European Conference on e-Learning* (pp. 239–256). Paris: Université Paris-Dauphine.

Ong, W. (1982). *Orality and literacy: the technologizing of the word.* London: Routledge.

Polkinghorne, D. (1983). *Methodology for the human sciences: systems of inquiry.* Albany: SUNY Press.

Prensky, M. (2001). *Digital natives, digital immigrants.* Retrieved July 4, 2007, from http://www.marcprensky.com/writing/Prensky%20-%20Digital%20Natives,%20Digital%20Immigrants%20-%20Part1.pdf

Rich, M. (2008). Literacy debate: online, r u really reading? *The New York Times.* Retrieved July 27, 2008, from http://www.nytimes.com/2008/07/27/books/27reading.html

Rodrigues, M. C. A. & Martins, R. X. (2008). Digital media performance and reading comprehension: a correlational study with Brazilian students. *International Journal of Web-Based Learning and Teaching Technologies*, 3, 1, 33–42.

Rouet, J. F., Dillon, A., Levonen, J. J. & Spiro, R. J. (Eds) (1996). *Hypertext and cognition.* Mahwah, NJ: Lawrence Erlbaum Associates.

Sanders, B. (1994). *A is for ox: the collapse of literacy and the rise of violence in an electronic age.* New York: Vintage.

Shapiro, A. & Niederhauser, D. (2004). Learning from hypertext: research issues and findings. In D. H. Jonassen (Ed.), *Handbook of research on educational communications and technology* (pp. 605–620). Mahwah, NJ: Lawrence Erlbaum Associates.

Spiro, R. J. & Jehng, J. C. (1990). Cognitive flexibility and hypertext: theory and technology for the nonlinear and multidimensional traversal of complex subject matter. In D. Nix & R. Spiro (Eds), *Cognition, education, and multimedia: exploring ideas in high technology* (pp. 163–205). Hillsdale, NJ: Lawrence Erlbaum Associates.

van Manen, M. (1990). *Researching lived experience: human science for an action sensitive pedagogy.* London, ON: Althouse Press and SUNY.

Ellen Rose is a Professor of Education at the University of New Brunswick in Canada. Address for correspondence: Ellen Rose, University of New Brunswick, PO Box 4400, Fredericton, NB E3B 5A3, Canada. Email: erose@unb.ca

QUESTIONS ABOUT MEANING

1. What is the purpose or goal of Rose's study? Where does she first state her purpose in the article (outside of the abstract)? How is Rose's research focus different from that of the research she reviews (summarizes) in the opening paragraphs?
2. Describe Rose's research methods. Who participated in the study? How did Rose go about achieving her purpose? How is research like hers (sometimes called *phenomenological* research) different from the research a scientist might conduct?
3. Summarize (in your own words) the six "themes" Rose found in the interview transcripts.
4. Study Table 1. What ages and level of education are represented among participants? What biases about the subject matter do some of the participants admit to having (late in the article)? In what other ways is the sample of students studied limited? Given the limitations of this study, what future research does Rose recommend?

QUESTIONS FOR RHETORICAL ANALYSIS

5. Although Rose does not use the headings found in IMRAD-formatted articles, her article follows IMRAD organization. Draw lines to divide the article into sections and label the following parts:

   » Introduction
   » Methods
   » Results
   » Discussion (and Conclusion)

   Be prepared to justify your answers in class.
6. Throughout the article, Rose combines her own observations about reading onscreen with those of the students she interviewed. How does Rose distinguish her ideas from the student quotations? What punctuation introduces the quotations?

THINKING AND WRITING ABOUT THE TOPIC

Imagine that you were among the students who answered Rose's call for study participants and write your own response to her prompt:

> Recall a particular, recent instance when [you] read something substantial online—the kind of text with which [you would be] typically engaged, whether an e-book, chapter, or scholarly paper.

Describe what you remember, including details such as where you read, your mood while reading, your posture, or your method of approaching the text.

Come to class prepared to compare your response to those of others in class in order to conduct your own "thematic analysis" of students' on-screen reading experiences.

WORKS CITED

Adler-Kassner, Linda, and Heidi Estrem. "Reading Practices in the Writing Classroom." *WPA: Writing Program Administration* 31.1–2 (2007): 35–47. Print.

Brown, Peter C., Henry L. Roediger III, and Mark A. McDaniel. *Make It Stick: The Science of Successful Learning.* Cambridge, MA: Harvard University Press, 2014. Print.

Carr, Nicholas, "Is Google Making Us Stupid?" *Atlantic* 301.6 (2008). Web. 12 Dec. 2012.

Dole, Janice A., et al. "Moving from the Old to the New: Research on Reading Comprehension Instruction." *Review of Educational Research* 61.2 (1991): 239–64. Print.

Hale, Ray, et al. "Cultural Insensitivity to Sexist Language toward Men." *The Journal of Social Psychology* 130.5 (1990): 697–98. Print.

Herrmann, Mark. "Oosthuizen's 'Albatross' Relegated to Footnote." *Tri-City Herald* (15 Apr. 2012): C1, C4. Print.

Kono, Tomohiro, et al. "Birth of Parthenogenetic Mice That Can Develop to Adulthood." *Nature* 428 (2004): 860–64. Print.

McCrudden, Matthew T., Gregory Schraw, and Kendall Hartley. "The Effect of General Relevance Instructions on Shallow and Deeper Learning and Reading Time." *Journal of Experimental Education* 74.4 (2006): 293–310. Print.

Nilson, Linda B. *Teaching at Its Best: A Research-Based Resource for College Instructors.* 3rd ed. San Francisco: Jossey-Bass, 2010. Print.

Nist, Sherrie L., and Katie Kirby. "The Text Marking Patterns of College Students." *Reading Psychology: An International Quarterly* 10 (1989): 321–38. Print.

Penrose, Ann M., and Cheryl Geisler. "Reading and Writing without Authority." *College Composition and Communication* 45.5 (1994): 505–20. Print.

Ritter, Malcolm. "Mice Created with 2 Genetic Moms, No Dad." *Pittsburgh Post-Gazette* (22 Apr. 2004): A3. Web. 21 Aug. 2013.

Roberts, Judith C., and Keith A. Roberts. "Deep Reading, Cost/Benefit, and the Construction of Meaning: Enhancing Reading Comprehension and Deep Learning in Sociology Courses." *Teaching Sociology* 36.2 (2008): 125–40. Print.

Rose, Ellen. "The Phenomenology of On-Screen Reading: University Students' Lived Experience of Digitised Text." *British Journal of Educational Technology* 42.3 (2011): 515–26. Print.

Singer, Harry, and Dan Donlan. "Active Comprehension: Problem-solving Schema with Question Generation for Comprehension of Complex Short Stories." *Reading Research Quarterly* 17.2 (1982): 166–86. Print.

Taraban, Roman, Kimberly Rynearson, and Marcel Satsky Kerr. "Metacognition and Freshman Academic Performance." *Journal of Developmental Education* 24.1 (2000): 12–20. Print.

Toma, Catalina L., and Jeffrey T. Hancock. "Self-Affirmation Underlies Facebook Use." *Personality and Social Psychology Bulletin* 39.3 (2013): 321–31. Print.

Wolfe, Joanna. "Rhetorical Numbers: A Case for Quantitative Writing in the Composition Classroom." *College Composition and Communication* 61.3 (2010): 452–75. Print.

CHAPTER 3

Reading Academic Arguments

In chapter 2, you learned several strategies for reading academic writing—identifying and understanding context, making predictions about what's ahead, and reading actively through highlighting and annotating text. These same reading strategies will help you when you are asked to analyze an academic argument. When you analyze an argument, you evaluate, assess, or judge the merits of the writer's claims and evidence. It requires critical thinking skills.

"Critical thinking" is a term with which you are likely familiar. In a recent survey, 91% of first-year college composition students could define the term, and 87% could provide specific examples from their lives. Finding patterns in data and transferring knowledge learned in one context to another context are examples of critical thinking. So is reading critically.

A **critical reader** doesn't accept all claims at face value. For example, a critical reader would not simply accept as fact the claim that *91% of first-year composition students can define critical thinking* without first asking questions about who determined that 91% of first-year composition students can define critical thinking. More importantly, *how* did they reach this conclusion? In this chapter you will learn about techniques that writers across the disciplines use to persuade readers, and you'll learn how to analyze and assess these techniques in academic arguments.

Defining Academic Arguments

Outside the academy, the word *argument* brings to mind heated, verbal exchanges. Within the academy, however, *argument* has a different meaning. An **academic argument** is usually a written document, not a verbal encounter, and can be any text that develops a central claim (or claims) with evidence. A **central claim** is also known as the argument's **thesis (statement)**, which is the main assertion the writer wants readers to accept or understand. Some examples of claims taken from academic arguments follow. For convenience, they are grouped in categories, but the categories are arbitrary and overlapping. One could argue, for example, that all of these claims are claims of observation and interpretation.

Claims of Observation

Some claims *summarize* what the writer has learned through reading, observation, or research. Here are two examples:

> *From Psychology*: Various factors [in the published research] relate to the accuracy of eyewitness identification. These factors include characteristics of the witness, characteristics of the witnessed event, characteristics of testimony, lineup content, lineup instructions, and methods of testing. (Wells and Olson 277)
>
> *From Education*: My research identified a number of . . . forces that had transforming effects on [students'] lives. . . . These forces included parental attitudes toward knowledge; prementoring or preparing children to accept the education-related mentors who would later enter their lives; the role of home, school, and community in student success; the role of high school and peer counselors; the importance of a sense of belonging; and the role of the informal and formal curriculum. (Rodriguez 22)

Claims of Interpretation of Evidence or Research

Some claims *interpret* what the writer has studied or observed.

> *From History*: The rooms in the house [of the Barnes Home in Piketon, Ohio] have been arranged to tell a narrative, or rather to tell a succession of narratives that weave in and out of historical time and in and out of one another. The narratives add up. Their central themes are extinction and genocide. (O'Brian 193)
>
> *From Literature*: I will argue . . . that women writers produced some of the nineteenth century's most intellectually serious, politically radical, and artistically innovative prose. (Karcher 782)
>
> *From Mathematics*: Numerical simulations indicate that reducing current biting rate of female Anopheles mosquitoes by 1/16 could assist Ghana to achieve malaria free status by the year 2037. (Oduro, Okyere, and Azu-Tungmah 22)

Claims of Opinion or Value

Similar to claims of interpretation are claims that express an *opinion* or *judgment* of worth.

> *From Environmental Science*: In this paper I will illustrate how environmental policies deal inadequately with the complexity of species extinction because they fail to account for the dynamics of our social and cultural character. (Mazur 25)

From Political Science: I argue that how journalists *now* cover elections has helped fuel the rise of attack politics in presidential campaigns. (Geer 422, original emphasis)

Claims That Call for Action

Some claims state the writer's opinion *and* call on readers to take action.

From Engineering: Major investment in our infrastructure is essential if the United States is to maintain our way of life and our leading position in the global economy. (Herrmann 14)

From Biology: Science would be better served if we gave more opportunity and power to the gentle, the reflective, and the creative individuals of both sexes. And if we did, more women would be selected, more would choose to stay in science, and more would get to the top. (Lawrence 13)

You might have noticed that some of these claims aren't particularly argumentative. A claim can be a statement of belief, interpretation, value, or opinion; a claim can also be a statement of fact summarizing what the writer will describe or explain. But all claims are supportable—meaning the writer can provide examples or other types of evidence to illustrate, explain, or defend them. A successful writer persuades the intended audience to understand and accept his or her claims; but a critical reader will first judge the merits of those claims.

The Intended Audience

When you are asked to evaluate an argument, it's important to do so with the intended audience in mind because that audience will influence how the argument is written—the claims, the evidence, and the vocabulary. Let's consider an argument written in 2011 by Stephanie Wear for Conservancy Talk!, the Nature Conservancy's blog. Wear is a member of the Biology Department at the University of Florida and lead scientist for coral reef conservation at the Nature Conservancy, a not-for-profit organization dedicated to the conservation of biological diversity. Wear is writing for a general audience—meaning, the reader does not need any specific background knowledge to understand the argument. Her argument has three claims:

1. Overfishing harms the coral reefs.
2. Overfishing harms the people who depend on the reefs for their livelihood.
3. We can all take steps to help protect the reefs.

Because Wear is writing to a general audience, the claims are nontechnical. Her evidence for these points, as well, is decidedly "nonscientific." Here for example is an excerpt from the discussion of the preceding point 1, arguing that overfishing harms the coral reefs.

EXAMPLE 3.1: FROM A CONSERVATION BLOG

Overfishing has become a major problem for coral reefs. For a coral reef ecosystem to function properly, it depends on the presence of the wild diversity that it attracts and is home to.

From the predator to the grazer (herbivore) to the very picky eaters (specialists), each fish plays an important part in the coral reef "city." What has happened in the Caribbean and in many other parts of the world is that people have essentially fished down the food chain so that the reef city is out of balance and in some cases, basic functions come to a screeching halt. Think New York City with no garbage pick-up in the summertime—a big stinking mess!

The author uses nontechnical vocabulary.

The author also uses a metaphor to connect to a general audience.

In the case of coral reefs, the fish that are now landing on the dinner plate, the grazers, are extremely important for keeping coral competitors in check (namely, seaweed). If the seaweed doesn't get mowed down by herbivores like queen parrotfish or spiny urchins, they overgrow the corals and the corals disappear. Fish need corals too, so this becomes a vicious cycle if something isn't done to help fish populations recover. (Wear)

By avoiding an overly scientific explanation of the food chain being disrupted and by using a comparison most readers would understand (New York City with no garbage pickup in the summer), Wear makes her point—that just as New York City can't function without garbage pickup, the "reef city" can't function without the diversity that keeps the ecosystem healthy. If Wear were writing to other scientists about the issue of overfishing, she would likely develop an argument using different reasons and different kinds of evidence, but given the general audience, Wear's argument is written at the appropriate level.

Recognizing Persuasive Appeals

Writing at a level that is appropriate for the audience is one way academic writers make their arguments persuasive. Additional techniques for persuading audiences are used by writers across disciplines. The Greek philosopher Aristotle labeled these persuasive appeals *pathos, ethos,* and *logos*, terms still used today to describe how writers attempt to sway readers. Recognizing these appeals can help you better understand why you may or may not find a writer's argument convincing.

Pathos

Many arguments include appeals to the reader's emotions, such as pity or fear, or appeals to the reader's basic desires, such as the desire to be safe, healthy, prosperous, accepted, and respected. Collectively, these appeals to emotions and desires are called appeals to **pathos**. Imagery, figurative language, and images are among the features writers commonly employ to persuade through emotion.

Consider Imagery and Concrete Details. One way writers can evoke an emotional response is by providing images or painting a picture with words. The following passage is from a medicine journal written for health care professionals. In it, Sondra Crosby, a physician who interviews people seeking asylum in the United States, uses imagery and emotionally laden language to evoke compassion (and perhaps anger) in readers:

EXAMPLE 3.2: FROM AN ACADEMIC JOURNAL IN MEDICINE

The woman had been kept as a sex slave for so long that it was difficult for her to understand that she was a free person, deserving of human compassion and dignity. She was raped, shackled, beaten, burned, forced to drink human blood and eat human flesh. I had many sleepless nights while I was documenting her story for a medical affidavit as part of her political asylum application. Because of her fragility, the attorney had asked special permission for me to attend the affirmative asylum interview. Sitting in the small, cramped room, she had to relive her horror one more time. The interpreter cried. The officer was visibly shaken. I sat with clenched hands, sweat dampening my dress. (Crosby 431)

Sample of concrete imagery appealing to the reader's emotions.

More concrete imagery and emotionally laden language evoke compassion in the reader.

Concrete details about the woman's story and its effect on those in the room create an image intended to get a response from readers. The emotional associations of the words also create that response. "Clenched hands," in the last sentence, for example, suggests anxiety or anger. "Clasped hands" (associated with prayer or friendship) would not have had the same effect.

Consider Figurative Language. Figurative language is another device writers use to evoke an emotional response. Emotionally charged metaphors open and close the next passage, written by the editors of *Black Scholar* after Hurricane Katrina:

EXAMPLE 3.3: FROM AN ACADEMIC JOURNAL ON BLACK STUDIES

"This is the hull of a slave ship." In this sentence, Rev. Jesse Jackson summed up the significance of the Hurricane Katrina, as he visited the Louisiana Superdome teeming with the waste, filth, despair of thousands of black people. The plight of black survivors offered a grim epiphany of US

The writer quotes Rev. Jackson comparing the Louisiana Superdome, which served as shelter to thousands of victims of Hurricane Katrina, to a slave ship.

race relations today. A majority black city, 38 percent of New Orleans' citizens are below poverty level, and 27 percent, some 120,000[,] were without privately owned transportation. Some 1,836 people died. FEMA would not provide efficient social organization and the mobilization of
10 available transportation. It became apparent to the millions of US and world-wide television viewers who watched the unbearable broadcasts, day and night, that structural racism implemented through militarism, had reduced blacks to the desperate status of penned up animals. ("Hurricane
15 Katrina" 1)

By comparing the victims of Hurricane Katrina to "desperate, penned-up animals," the writers emphasize their point that these people were treated with little regard or concern.

Appeals to basic human emotions engage readers and get them to care about issues. For this reason, appeals to pathos are found in many academic arguments.

Consider Appeals to Shared Values. Responses to emotional appeals are influenced by the readers' backgrounds, interests, and previous experiences. Researchers at the University of Illinois have found that cultural backgrounds literally influence what people notice as well as how people interpret what they see. Lead researcher Denise C. Park offers this example: "An Asian would see a jungle that happened to have an elephant in it," but "a Westerner would see the elephant and might notice the jungle" (qtd. in Binns 9). Successful writers, therefore, are careful to tailor emotional appeals to the audience and context.

Concept in Practice 3.1: Appealing to Shared Cultural Values

Because members of the same country, community, or discipline have many values in common, pathos appeals often achieve their effect by appealing to these shared cultural values. Consider, for example, Figure 3.1. The men pushing passengers into the train are called *oshiya*, literally translated "train pushers." In some train stations in Japan, oshiya are paid to squeeze as many people as possible into subway cars already filled with commuters during rush hour.

For Japanese readers, the image depicts an everyday occurrence. For U.S. readers, the image of humans being pushed into cars while others passively watch and wait their turn may be unsettling. What aspects of U.S. culture and values explain why U.S. viewers might respond to this image in a way that Japanese viewers do not?

Figure 3.1 Train Pushers in Japan

Ethos

Although you will find appeals to pathos in many academic arguments, they are not nearly as prevalent as appeals to ethos. **Ethos** refers to the image or persona a writer creates for him- or herself. In general, when academic writers appeal to ethos they try to establish themselves as credible and trustworthy. Discussed in the sections that follow are various ways you might see academic writers attempt to create an ethos that lends credibility to their arguments.

Consider the Author's Experience or Qualifications. Just as we are more likely to buy a product that has been recommended by a trustworthy friend, so we are more likely to believe writers when we believe they are trustworthy. Writers who identify their experience or qualifications in the subjects they write about give us reason to trust what they say. In the following passage from the article "Doing Fieldwork in the Mud," Kathy Whitlock, a professor of geography, conveys her credentials while explaining an important point about sampling methods in geography research:

EXAMPLE 3.4: FROM AN ACADEMIC JOURNAL IN GEOGRAPHY

Whitlock establishes her credentials and expertise by citing research she presented to a group of wildlife biologists.

How do we decide which lakes to study? I once presented my research to a group of wildlife biologists who were interested in prehistory. At the end of the talk, a statistician asked me what sampling design I had used. Why were so many of my lakes in the Cascade Range, and why were so few in eastern Oregon and Washington? The question took me by surprise, because we don't usually have the luxury of developing a sampling scheme before we begin our research. (Whitlock 20–21)

Although an expert, Whitlock also demonstrates a sense of modesty and humility in her expression of surprise.

Whitlock establishes herself as an expert (why else would she be invited to present her research to wildlife biologists?), but she also conveys honesty and modesty. If a writer comes across as arrogant, she is unlikely to persuade readers, no matter how knowledgeable she may be. In fact, when a writer admits that he does not know everything, he actually helps to create a favorable persona. This is what Whitlock does when she states, "The question took me by surprise."

Consider the Author's Concern for Others. Another way authors appeal to ethos is by showing readers that they care about others and about issues that affect others. In the final paragraph of her essay, "What Helps Some First-Generation Students Succeed?" Sandria Rodriguez, Dean of the Communication Arts, Humanities & Fine Arts Division at the College of Lake County in Illinois, addresses other college teachers and administrators. She calls on them to do more to help students from poverty graduate from college:

EXAMPLE 3.5: FROM A MAGAZINE FOR COLLEGE ADMINISTRATORS AND TEACHERS

I contend that we can do much by design to influence the metamorphosis of students from poor, uneducated backgrounds into college-educated, activist members of the middle class. The benefits to the nation and to the world would certainly be great. . . . But of course the first and best reason for aiding first-generation students is that it is simply the right thing to do. (Rodriguez 22)

In this passage, Rodriguez appeals to both ethos and pathos—revealing that she knows of these students' struggles, emphasizing that they deserve aid, and stating that helping them is "the right thing to do."

In this conclusion, Rodriguez appeals to both pathos (by calling on readers to do the right thing) and ethos (by showing herself to be a person who cares about others).

Consider How the Author Acknowledges Opposing Views. Unlike people in a conversation who can express their reasons for disagreeing with one another, readers cannot "talk back" to writers. Writers must acknowledge the opposing views or risk readers thinking either that they don't understand the issue fully (making them seem uninformed) or that they are purposely ignoring counterarguments (making them seem untrustworthy). Writers who acknowledge other viewpoints and who try to find common ground with readers show that they understand the issue and respect those who disagree. In the following excerpt, the authors argue that the skills and talents that many people attribute to "innate talent are actually the result of intense practice. . . ." (Ericsson, Krampe, and Tesch-Romer 363); but they also recognize what most people assume about experts:

EXAMPLE 3.6: FROM AN ACADEMIC JOURNAL IN PSYCHOLOGY

People believe that because expert performance is qualitatively different from normal performance the expert performer must be endowed with characteristics qualitatively different from those of normal adults. This view has discouraged scientists from systematically examining expert performers and 5 accounting for their performance in terms of the laws and principles of general psychology. We agree that expert performance is qualitatively different from normal performance and even that expert performers have characteristics and abilities that are qualitatively different from or at least 10 outside the range of those of normal adults. However, we deny that these differences are immutable, that is, due to innate talent. Only a few exceptions, most notably height, are genetically prescribed. Instead, we argue that the differences between expert performers and normal adults 15 reflect a life-long period of deliberate effort to improve performance in a specific domain. (Ericsson, Krampe, and Tesch-Romer 400–01)

The authors find common ground with those who think experts are born different from "normal adults."

The authors also concede that some advantages, such as height among professional basketball players, are genetic. But after conceding these points the authors argue that experts are experts because of hard work.

By recognizing why some disagree with their premise, the authors show that they listen to other viewpoints.

Acknowledging opposing arguments is one way a writer can acknowledge other viewpoints. Using **qualifiers** (words like *usually* or *sometimes*) is another way writers can recognize that others may take exception to their claims. Notice how Wei-Cheng Mau and Richard Lynn, professors of education and psychology, respectively, qualify their explanation for the correlation they found between how much time high-school students spend on homework and how well they do on tests. Examples of qualifiers appear italicized in the passage (Example 3.7) that follows.

EXAMPLE 3.7: FROM AN ACADEMIC JOURNAL IN PSYCHOLOGY

There are two *most probable* explanations for this association. *Perhaps* the most straightforward is that doing more homework is causal to obtaining

> higher test scores. This seems *probable* because it is reasonable to expect that the amount of homework done will have a positive effect on test scores. How-
> 5 ever, an alternative explanation is that those who obtain higher test scores, *possibly* because they have higher intelligence or aptitude, have more positive attitudes to school and as a consequence do more homework. This hypothesis also seems *plausible* as a contributory factor in the positive associations between homework and test scores. (Mau and Lynn 123)

By showing that they have considered various interpretations and by recognizing that causation cannot be proven conclusively, the writers come across as reasoned and reflective. Acknowledging other viewpoints is among the most common types of ethos appeals in academic writing—found in the writing of every discipline.

Concept in Practice 3.2: Qualifying Conclusions

In chapter 2, you read several excerpts from the research report "Self-Affirmation Underlies Facebook Use," by Catalina Toma and Jeffrey Hancock. As you'll recall, Toma and Hancock conducted two studies. In the first study, students who had spent time viewing their own Facebook page before receiving criticism were less defensive than students who had viewed the Facebook page of a stranger before receiving criticism. The second study indicated that people view their own Facebook pages to mitigate a threat to their self-esteem.

In the conclusion to their article, Toma and Hancock make claims about the potential value of their research—an important ethos move for researchers. But they are also careful to qualify their claims. Their conclusion illustrates how writers can establish the importance of their research while still being careful to make reasonable claims.

> Conclusion
>
> Everyday life is rife with threats to the ego, ranging from the trivial (e.g., being treated rudely by a clerk, being ignored by a friend) to the consequential (e.g., failing an exam, getting into an argument with a spouse). These setbacks are both common and unavoidable, raising the question of how individuals manage to maintain a sense of self-worth and avoid being plagued by anxiety and self-doubt. This research shows that, just as setbacks and challenges are pervasive in everyday life, so too are opportunities to offset their effects.

In this conclusion, the researchers establish that their research has practical relevance to everyday life.

Facebook, an SNS that is ubiquitously available, has the ability to repair the damage caused by ego threats and it is actively sought after by users for the purpose of soothing a wounded ego. The availability of everyday sources of self-affirmation, such as Facebook, appears to be a useful instrument in individuals' efforts to preserve self-worth and self-integrity. (Toma and Hancock 329)

But they also use qualified language. For example, they state that Facebook "has the ability to repair the damage caused by ego threats" (rather than stating, "Facebook repairs the damage caused by ego threats").

Similarly, the researchers say that Facebook "appears to be" a way to preserve self-esteem.

Consider the Credentials and Reputations of Sources Cited. When a writer establishes that his sources are qualified to speak on the issue, he shows that he listens to those who are knowledgeable. That is what writer and activist Jonathan Rauch does in the following passage from his article published in the *National Journal*, a political publication intended for a general audience. Rauch is making the point that global warming is too large of a problem to fix quickly.

EXAMPLE 3.8: FROM A NON-PARTISAN JOURNAL ON U.S. POLITICS AND POLICY

In testimony last month before a House of Representatives panel, Kevin Trenberth of the National Center for Atmospheric Research said, "The 2007 IPCC [Intergovernmental Panel on Climate Change] report makes clear that even aggressive mitigation would yield benefits many decades in the future, and that no amount
5 of mitigation can avoid significant climate change." (Rauch 17)

Several details suggest Trenberth's opinion about global warming warrants consideration: his credentials, his reference to an official government report, and his appearance before members of the House of Representatives. By mentioning these details, Rauch establishes that he got his information from an expert. When reading arguments, consider whether or not the author has consulted trustworthy sources. If so, you know the writer has done his or her homework.

Consider the Tone and Writing Style. We've seen how writers can create a favorable ethos by establishing their qualifications, showing concern for others, acknowledging other viewpoints, and establishing the credentials and reputations of their sources. Tone and writing style also help to create the writer's persona. Using the specialized language of a discipline, for example, creates a scholarly image.

The following passage is from an article by Lauren Shapiro-Miller and fellow researchers who studied fire scars on trees in the Northwest to estimate the frequency of fires in past centuries. The research enabled Shapiro-Miller et al. to determine how changes in climate and land use have affected the size, location, and frequency of wildfires—research with obvious relevance to land developers. They describe their work in an article published in the *Canadian Journal of Forest Research*:

EXAMPLE 3.9: FROM AN ACADEMIC JOURNAL IN FOREST SCIENCE

We hand-planed and then sanded all samples until we could discern cell structure under a binocular microscope. To assign the exact calendar year to each tree ring, we visually cross dated tree rings using a master ring-width chronology generated from our sample and checked against regional chronologies. . . . We verified the quality of our cross dating using cross-correlation of measured ring-width series . . . and by having two dendrochronologists review the dating of each sample. . . . We determined the exact calendar year of each fire scar by noting the date of the annual ring in which it occurred. (Shapiro-Miller et al. 1935)

The writers establish that they conducted the kind of research common in the discipline.

Using the jargon of the discipline is another way the authors show that they are experts.

By using specialized terms and phrasing, Shapiro-Miller et al. reveal themselves to be experts in their discipline. They show their audience (other experts) that they "speak their language." Chapters 5 and 6 discuss additional ways that academic writers can create a professional and expert ethos.

Logos

"In God we trust. Everyone else must show data." So reads a plaque at the National Institutes of Health. The same sentiment applies to academic arguments: Evidence is required. Unsupported generalities about groups of people or things are insufficient proof in an academic argument. Instead, writers are expected to cite more credible and objective evidence.

When writers appeal to **logos**, they appeal to the reader's logic and reason. Writers appeal to logos when they give readers reasons to accept their claims. They also appeal to logos when they cite evidence, such as studies, surveys, expert opinion, and testimonials. The rest of this chapter offers advice for assessing the kinds of *quantitative* and *qualitative* evidence commonly found in academic arguments.

Look for Indicators of Trustworthy Quantitative Research. Quantitative research is systematic and methodical. Researchers plan in advance how to gather data and then follow the rules they've developed for conducting experiments or recording observations. Quantitative research often results in numerical estimates, or *statistics*.

When researchers want to learn about a given population, they do not poll or observe everyone in that population. They instead survey or observe a representative group from the population, called a **sample**. Researchers use information obtained from a sample to make conclusions or predictions about the larger population. The goal in quantitative research is to produce findings that are both *reliable* (meaning the observations or findings can be replicated) and *generalizable* (meaning that what is true for those in the sample studied is also true for others like them). This goal is not easily reached. In fact, researchers can sometimes come to widely divergent conclusions about a population. Consider the results of two studies reported in *Community College Week*:

> Nationally, about 43 percent of entering community college students require [sic] one or more remedial courses, according to the National Center for Education Statistics. Using different methodology, Bob McCabe, executive director of the National Alliance of Community and Technical Colleges, suggests that the actual figure is closer to 80 percent. (Pulley)

Two studies—both from reputable sources—produced two very different findings. To determine which is closer to the truth, you must assess a number of variables.

Assess the Reliability of Studies and Surveys. Among the most common types of quantitative evidence found in academic arguments are study and survey results, but as we saw in the passage quoted earlier, there can be great disparity in what researchers studying the same topic conclude. Which research should you trust? Following are four factors to consider when evaluating surveys or studies used as evidence in an academic argument.

Factor #1: The sample studied must be representative of the population. If a sample is representative, the makeup reflects the makeup of the population being studied. Two methods used to select a representative sample are *randomization* and *stratification*. To select a sample randomly, a researcher begins with a list of everyone in the population—for instance, all 5,000 students enrolled at a college. A name (or student number) might be randomly selected from the first 10 listed, and then every 10th (or 50th or 100th, etc.) student listed after that might be chosen to make up the sample. **Sampling bias** occurs when a segment of the population has no chance of being selected for the sample. An example of sampling bias would be selecting our sample from a list limited to students who attend day classes on campus and omitting students who take online or night classes. Students in some segments of the population have no chance of being selected for the sample, and students in another segment have a greater chance than others.

True random sampling is not always practical. Instead, pollsters might divide a population into non-overlapping segments called strata, making sure that all members of each stratum have something in common (such as age) and that all members of the population fall into only one stratum. This process is called *stratification*. For instance, a pollster doing a national survey might divide the country into counties. After ensuring that both rural and urban counties are adequately represented, she might then randomly choose people from a sample of counties. In this case, the pollster is selecting a *random stratified sample*—using the techniques of both stratification (when dividing the population into counties) and randomization (when selecting people from those counties).

Other samples are selected simply because they are convenient. An example would be if a psychology professor were to survey the graduate students in his or her advanced psychology course. Studying such a sample might tell the researcher something about psychology graduate students, but the results could not be generalized to *all* college students. When evaluating survey results used as evidence, think about the makeup of the sample. Are there indications that the sample represents the population being studied?

Factor #2: The measurement instrument must be reliable. A reliable method of measurement consistently produces similar results when reapplied over time. This seems easy enough but gets complicated when human interpretation is involved (we tend to see what we want or expect to see) or when trying to measure intangibles such as self-discipline or motivation. Results of surveys can be skewed because of leading questions, ambiguous questions, and variations in how questions are asked. (See chapter 10 for more on this topic.) Problems also result from questions that prevent respondents from providing accurate information. For instance, estimating how many minutes each day are spent social networking and listening to music online is difficult for those who do both activities simultaneously.

Many studies require isolating what the researchers want to measure (Factor A) to ensure any changes observed in participants are the result of Factor A and not other variables. If subjects take a drug for depression, for instance, researchers must ensure other factors are not responsible for any changes in participants. For these kinds of studies, researchers often use a comparison and control group, making sure that the two groups are similar in every important way (such as in age, place of residence, diet, ethnicity) except in their exposure to the factor being studied. Recall that researchers Toma and Hancock (chapter 2) asked some students in their sample to spend five minutes viewing their own Facebook page and asked other students to view the Facebook profile of a stranger. By altering only one element of the study design (the profile viewed), the researchers could infer that viewing one's own Facebook pages was what caused participants in one group to take criticism better than participants in the other.

Factor #3: Honest data must be obtained from the sample. Even if the sample is representative and the research methods sound, the results of a study won't be reliable unless the sample provides reliable data. Trustworthy information can be difficult to obtain when asking participants about personal information (such as weight or sexual history), illegal activity (such as drug use), or unethical behavior (such as cheating). It's also difficult to get reliable information when asking participants to remember past behavior or asking them to predict future behavior (such as asking, "Whom will you vote for next fall?"). Research that involves observing people poses another difficulty: Participants who know they are part of a study may change their behavior.

Factor #4: The sample must be large enough. There must be a sufficient number of people studied to give researchers confidence that what's true for the sample is likely true for others like them. In surveys, this requires a statistically meaningful number of people in the sample. The minimum typically used in national surveys by pollsters like Gallup and the National Opinion Research Center (NORC) is 1,500 people. Studies about smaller populations will have smaller samples, but, everything else being equal, a study with 300 participants is more desirable than one with 30 participants. That said, if the sample was inappropriately chosen, the number of participants doesn't matter; conclusions about the population cannot be made.

Concept in Practice 3.3: Evaluating Research Methods

For an illustration of what to look for when assessing a study, let's consider the methods used by Wei-Cheng Mau and Richard Lynn, the education and psychology professors cited earlier. They wanted to determine whether or not the amount of time high-school students spend on homework affects their test scores. In the following paragraph, Mau and Lynn describe the study from which they obtained their data. Notice the indicators of reliability. Can you think of any limitations to how data for this study was obtained?

The data for this study have been obtained from the American National Educational Longitudinal study (NELS) of 1988. This study consists of a nationally representative sample of tenth-grade school students tested in 1990 on math, reading and science and retested at twelfth grade in 1992. The school students were asked to provide an estimate of the number of hours per week of homework they did out of school. The sampling of the NELS was carried out by the selection of a stratified sample of 1,052 schools and selecting random samples of twenty-five students from each school. The school sample was stratified by size, urban versus rural, region and percentage of minority students. The numbers in the

Data came from two different years.

Sample size was large and . . .

. . . the sample included various ethnicities.

> sample consist of 1,406 Asians, 14,024 whites, 2,922 Hispanics and 2,260 African-Americans. The sampling procedures are described in detail in the report of the National Center for Educational Statistics (1991).
>
> (Mau and Lynn 121)

Data came from a random and stratified sample, including 1,052 schools of various sizes and in all regions of the country.

Detailed description of the sampling procedure is available by consulting the source listed in the bibliography.

There are several indicators of reliability in this passage, including the large and representative sample of schools and students. There is, however, one limitation to the data from this sample: Students self-reported time spent on homework. People often either overestimate or underestimate (whichever makes them look better!) past behavior. Mau and Lynn later acknowledge this problem with self-reported data: "It is possible that those who do well on tests claim to do more homework but do not in fact do so." After admitting there is no way of knowing whether or not this is the case, the authors "proceed on the assumption that the self-reported" data is accurate (123). By providing details about how the sample was selected and by recognizing the limitations of the methods, Mau and Lynn give readers reason to trust them and their research.

Evaluate the Visual Evidence. Many academic arguments present quantitative evidence in visual form, such as in graphs or charts. The graph in Figure 3.2, from a study of student research reports, illustrates the importance of critically reading visual data just as you should critically read the results of any study or survey used as evidence in an argument. The graph compares how often graduate students and undergraduates included images in their reports. What does Figure 3.2 suggest about the prevalence of images in graduate and undergraduate papers? What information do we need to better understand the data?

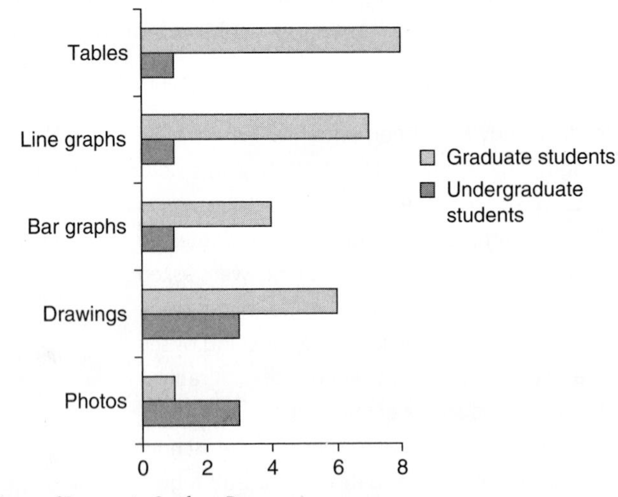

Figure 3.2 Types of Images in Student Papers

The message conveyed in Figure 3.2 is that graduate students are far more likely than undergraduates to include tables and graphs in their papers. On closer inspection, however, we can't determine just how great the disparity is or if the comparison is even a fair comparison. For example, it's unclear how many student papers included photos. Do the numbers appearing on the horizontal axis represent actual numbers or percentages? If they are raw numbers, what is the sample size? Did eight out of eight graduate papers include tables or eight out of a thousand? More importantly, did the sample include an equal number of graduate and undergraduate papers and were all of the papers of the same type? Answers to questions like these may be provided in surrounding text, but the graph illustrates the importance of reading visual data critically. Although no ethical writer would distort a figure to purposely mislead readers, the presentation can influence the way readers interpret data, so it's important to critically analyze evidence presented in graphs and charts. This is a topic we'll take up in more detail in chapter 5.

"Facts" and statistics derived from quantitative research are nothing more than educated guesses, some more reliable than others (a point well illustrated by sociology professor Joel Best in the articles found at the end of this chapter). Now that you understand this, consider again two claims found at the beginning of this chapter: 91% of first-year composition students can define the term *critical thinking* and 87% can provide specific examples of critical thinking. What kinds of questions should you ask before accepting these claims?

A few of the most obvious questions might include:

1. How many students were in the sample?
2. What was the sample makeup?
3. At what schools were these students enrolled?
4. What did the researchers count as correct definitions for *critical thinking*?
5. What did the researchers consider to be examples of critical thinking?

The researchers who originally made the claims about critical thinking, incidentally, surveyed 249 first-year composition students at Widener University. In other words this research could not be used to argue that 91% of *all* first-year composition students can define critical thinking skills, *a point with which the researchers—Patricia Dyer and Tara Friedman—would be quick to concur.* (Their research was designed to answer questions about students at Widener University *only*.) If you asked the kinds of questions in the preceding list, count yourself among those who practice critical thinking!

Look for Indicators of Trustworthy Qualitative Evidence. Quantitative research involves countable data and usually involves studying or polling numerous subjects. (Associate the word *quantity* with quantitative research.) But quantitative research can be ill equipped to capture nuance, and much of what humans consider to be most important can't be counted. **Qualitative**

research typically involves fewer subjects. The detailed description of a few representative cases is what makes qualitative evidence convincing, not the large number of instances. Testimonials, anecdotes, analogies, and expert opinion are among some of the most common types of qualitative evidence found in academic arguments.

Testimonials and Anecdotes. Testimonials or anecdotes recount the experience of individuals. They allow readers to better understand the importance of issues and they often appeal to our emotions. In "Fostering Personal and Social Responsibility," an article published in an education journal, educators Richard Hersh and Carol Geary Schneider relate an anecdote to help make the argument that colleges should teach social responsibility. The story is about Louis Slotin, a nuclear physicist who helped develop the atomic bomb. Slotin was assembling plutonium pieces in a lab experiment, directing the pieces with a screwdriver, when "the screwdriver stopped, and the pieces of plutonium came a fraction too close together. Immediately, the instruments everyone was watching registered a great upsurge of neutrons, which was the sign that a chain reaction had begun. Radioactivity was filling the room" (8). Slotin pulled the pieces of plutonium apart, exposing himself to deadly doses of radioactivity, then calmly instructed others working in the lab to mark their locations so that each one's relative degree of exposure could later be determined. After calling for medical assistance, "Slotin apologized to his companions and said what turned out to be exactly true: he would die, and they would recover" (8). Slotin's act, the authors go on to explain, exemplifies the kind of behavior colleges should foster. Here is how they analyze the events:

EXAMPLE 3.10: FROM AN ACADEMIC JOURNAL IN EDUCATION

We see, first, an uncompromising sense that other people matter, an unconditional concern for preserving individual life and welfare. We see, too, a finely honed ability to size up a situation comprehensively and accurately; a tested capacity for systematic thought. Finally, we witness the courage to act. Slotin
5 did not merely feel compassion and think efficiently, he separated the plutonium. (Hersh and Schneider 8)

This anecdote is only one piece of evidence Hersh and Schneider cite, but a well-told story tends to be remembered long after readers have forgotten other aspects of an argument.

Analogies. Another type of qualitative evidence is analogies. In an **analogy**, a writer compares two situations, different in many ways but similar enough to suggest that what's true in one situation is true in another. James Garland, who was President of Miami University when he wrote the following passage, uses an analogy to argue that forcing tuition caps on public colleges is not the way to solve the problem of escalating tuition rates:

EXAMPLE 3.11: FROM A DAILY NEWSPAPER

Part of the problem [with tuition caps] is that state higher-education budgets are not efficiently targeted. By way of comparison, consider the food stamp program, which in 2004 paid out $27 billion directly to 24 million low-income Americans. Imagine if there were, in its place, 5 a food subsidy program by which the government paid that $27 billion directly to supermarkets. Under such a program needy families would benefit little, because most of the savings would be passed on to customers who didn't need help. That would be an inefficient use of public money. (Garland A9)

The author uses an analogy to argue against tuition caps: Tuition assistance must be targeted to those in need in the same way that food stamps are available only to those in need.

Analogies, like Garland's, make an argument memorable by making it concrete, but the two situations compared must be similar enough for readers to see the comparison as valid. Consider this ad for a local nightly newscast:

> When selecting a doctor, which do you want: someone who's seen a few patients or someone who's saved thousands of lives? The same holds true for selecting a news source. Experience matters.

The ad suggests viewers should watch the news team with the most experience, but the skills required for performing medicine and reporting the news are not similar enough for the analogy to be effective.

Expert Opinion. Another type of qualitative evidence common in academic arguments is expert opinion. Most people defer to experts, but only if the credentials and background of the "expert" establish that he or she is qualified. In the following sentence, relevant credentials for the source are not established:

> According to Kathy Hampton, Ph.D., the financial benefits gained by communities who employ illegal immigrants outweigh the costs incurred when the immigrants use a community's social services.

Having a Ph.D. in one area does not make a person an expert in all areas. (The same principle applies for the title "Dr.") To be convincing, the writer should establish that Hampton's work experience or college degree qualifies her to speak on the issue:

> According to Kathy Hampton, a professor of economics, the financial benefits gained by communities who employ illegal immigrants outweigh the costs incurred when the immigrants use a community's social services.

One more note about establishing credentials: In this day of desktop publishing, mentioning that someone wrote an article or book does not in itself establish that the individual has relevant qualifications. An exception is when the article appears in *a peer-reviewed* scholarly journal or when the book is published by an academic press. In these instances, the writer's work has been scrutinized by other experts within the field.

Applying the Concepts to Reading: *Critically Reading Arguments*

As we've seen in this chapter, many aspects of an argument work together to sway a reader. We can see this illustrated in the following article, which originally appeared in *The Chronicle of Higher Education*, a news magazine reporting on issues in higher education.

The article summarizes information from a 2013 report titled "Federal Student Loan Debt Burden of Noncompleters," published by the US Department of Education. The author, Ann Schnoebelen, wrote the article while an editorial intern at *The Chronicle of Higher Education*. On the surface, the article might not seem to be an "argument," but remember that an academic argument is any text that has a central claim supported with evidence. As you read, highlight and annotate appeals to pathos, ethos, or logos.

REPORT EXAMINES LEVELS OF DEBT FOR COLLEGE DROPOUTS ACROSS SECTORS, *Ann Schnoebelen*

MANY STUDENTS who leave college without a diploma still have something to show for their time in higher education: debt. Students who first enrolled in college in 2003–4 and had dropped out six years later were saddled with federal student-loan debt equal to 35 percent of their annual income, according to a report released last week by the U.S. Department of Education.

In a breakout of noncompleters' debt by type of institution, the median ratio was highest for students who started at four-year private nonprofit institutions: Their federal student-loan debt amounted to 51 percent of their annual income. Onetime students at for-profit institutions had debt equal to 43 percent of their annual income. At public four-year institutions, the figure was 34 percent, and at public two-year colleges, it was 26 percent.

Across all sectors, the ratio of federal student-loan debt to annual income has gone up over time, most significantly for students who started at for-profit institutions.

The Education Department's report, "Federal Student Loan Debt Burden of Noncompleters," examines two cohorts of students who first enrolled in the 1995–96 and 2003–4 academic years and who had not completed a postsecondary degree six years later. Those are the two most recent cohorts of beginning postsecondary students surveyed over time by the department's National Center for Education Statistics. The report uses data from the two longitudinal studies, along with federal financial-aid information and self-reported income figures.

The debt of students who drop out of college in different sectors isn't widely known, said Pauline Abernathy, vice president of the Institute for College Access & Success. "It confirms that the only thing worse than graduating with debt is not graduating and having debt," she said.

According to the report, in 2009, noncompleters represented 19 percent of students who had started six years before at private, nonprofit four-year institutions; 22 percent of those who enrolled at public four-year institutions; 46 percent of students once at public two-year colleges; and 46 percent of students who started at for-profit institutions. The for-profit sector was the only one in which noncompletion increased over time, from 35 percent for the first cohort.

Among the more recent students, those who left for-profit institutions without degrees owed $350 per credit earned, compared with $80 to $190 per credit for students in the other sectors. Former students at for-profit institutions also had the highest federal borrowing rate, 86 percent. That compares with a quarter of students at public two-year colleges, 54 percent at four-year public institutions, and 66 percent at four-year private nonprofit colleges.

It is well established that people without college degrees earn less money than those with degrees, which compounds the financial burden of noncompleters. Even if they have less debt than do their counterparts who finished college, it can be harder for them to pay it off.

Although the report's findings are important, they are also dated, Ms. Abernathy said. "It shows how limited our federal collected data are," she said, "that the federal government is issuing the first report on this subject based on data on students who first enrolled 10 years ago."

Even so, the report reinforces what more recent data have shown, Ms. Abernathy said. "Where you go to college and how you go to college and how you pay for college all affect your chance of completing and having burdensome debt."

Burden of Debt Grows for College Dropouts

Students who first enrolled in college in 2003–4 and had dropped out six years later had higher federal student-loan debt relative to their income than did noncompleters who first enrolled in 1995–96. Over time, the ratio went up most significantly for students who started at for-profit institutions.

Median cumulative federal loan debt as a percentage of annual income, by type of first institution attended

	2001	2009
Public 4-year	26%	34%
Private nonprofit 4-year	35%	51%
Public 2-year	22%	26%
For-profit	20%	43%
All	25%	35%

Note: The for-profit category includes less-than-two-year, two-year, and four-year institutions. Federal student loans include Stafford and Perkins loans, not Parent PLUS loans. Annual income is the 2009 income of the former student, not including any income from a spouse. The debt-to-income ratio of subjects unemployed in 2009 was set to 100.

Source: National Center For Education Statistics, "Federal Student Loan Debt Burden of Noncompleters"

Applying the Concepts to Writing: *Writing a Critical Analysis*

In a critical analysis of a text (sometimes called a *rhetorical analysis*), you analyze and evaluate the way the text is written. The following questions are typical of those addressed in a rhetorical analysis:

- What is the author's purpose and how well does the author achieve that purpose?
- Who is the intended audience? Is the text appropriate for this audience?
- How does the author present himself or herself (e.g., as an expert, a peer, a concerned citizen)? How is this persona created?
- What reasons or evidence does the author provide? What kinds of sources are cited? Is the evidence appropriate, convincing, and sufficient?
- Are the author's appeals to readers' emotions or reason effective?
- In what ways does the author's writing style and word choice enhance or detract from the argument?
- How do any visual elements (such as photos, figures, tables) influence readers' responses?

These are only sample questions. Any aspect of a text might be analyzed in a rhetorical analysis.

Write a critical analysis essay for Frans de Waal's article "The Brains of the Animal Kingdom; New Research Shows That We Have Grossly Underestimated Both the Scope and the Scale of Animal Intelligence" (found at the end of chapter 12), or analyze an article assigned by your instructor. Focus your analysis on how the writer uses appeals to pathos, ethos, and logos. Here are some specific questions to get you started:

1. What is the central claim in the argument? How does the writer attempt to get the audience to see the importance of this issue?
2. Where does the author use concrete details, analogies, or words with strong connotations to evoke the reader's emotions? Are these appeals effective?
3. Identify appeals to ethos. In what ways does the writer establish himself as credible, trustworthy, or likable? Quote examples of ethos appeals and comment on their effectiveness.
4. Identify appeals to logos. What kinds of evidence support the writer's claims? What kinds of details make the evidence convincing or what details about the evidence are needed to make it convincing?
5. In general, did you find the argument effective? Why or why not?

Provide enough context to allow those who have not read the article to understand your paper, but your paper should be primarily an analysis of *how* the article is written, not a summary of what it says. Support your claims with evidence from the text—usually quotations and discussion of the quotations. In the introduction, name the author and article title and identify the elements of the text you will analyze in your paper.

Paired Readings from Sociology

"Promoting Bad Statistics," *Society* JOEL BEST

This chapter features two articles by sociology professor Joel Best, well known for his writing about flawed statistics and author of the book *Damned Lies and Statistics*. Flawed statistics and how they get used by members of the media and social and political activists is the subject of the first article, from the journal *Society*. *Society* publishes general-interest articles and research from the social sciences about social and political issues. Each issue features a special symposium, like the one Best wrote in 2001 titled "Promoting Bad Statistics." In the article, Best describes what he calls "guidelines" that some people follow when using statistics to draw attention to social causes.

In contemporary society, social problems must compete for attention. To the degree that one problem gains media coverage, moves to the top of politicians' agendas, or becomes the subject of public concern, others will be neglected. Advocates find it necessary to make compelling cases for the importance of particular social problems. They choose persuasive wording and point to disturbing examples, and they usually bolster their case with dramatic statistics.

Statistics have a fetish-like power in contemporary discussions about social problems. We pride ourselves on rational policy making, and expertise and evidence guide our rationality. Statistics become central to the process: numbers evoke science and precision; they seem to be nodules of truth, facts that distill the simple essence of apparently complex social processes. In a culture that treats facts and opinions as dichotomous terms, numbers signify truth—what we call "hard facts." In virtually every debate about social problems, statistics trump "mere opinion."

Yet social problems statistics often involve dubious data. While critics occasionally call some numbers into question, it generally is not necessary for a statistic to be accurate—or even plausible—in order to achieve widespread acceptance. Advocates seeking to promote social problems often worry more about the processes by which policy makers, the press, and the public come to focus on particular problems, than about the quality of their figures. I seek here to identify some principles that govern this process. They are, if you will, guidelines for creating and disseminating dubious social problems statistics.

Although we talk about facts as though they exist independently of people, patiently awaiting discovery, someone has to produce—or construct—all that we know. Every social statistic reflects the choices that go into producing it. The key choices involve definition and methodology: Whenever we count something, we must first define what it is we hope to count, and then choose the methods by which we will go about counting. In general, the press regards statistics as facts, little bits of truth. The human choices behind every number are forgotten; the very presentation of a number gives each claim credibility. In this sense, statistics are like fetishes.

ANY NUMBER IS BETTER THAN NO NUMBER

By this generous standard, a number need not bear close inspection, or even be remotely plausible. To choose an example first brought to light by Christina Hoff Sommers, a number of recent books, both popular and scholarly, have repeated the garbled claim that anorexia kills 150,000 women annually. (The figure seems to have originated from an estimate for the total number of women who are anorexic; only about 70 die each year from the disease.) It should have been obvious that something was wrong with this figure. Anorexia typically affects *young* women. Each year, roughly 8,500 females aged 15–24 die from all causes; another 47,000 women aged 25–44 also die. What are the chances, then, that there could be 150,000 deaths from anorexia each year? But, of course, most of us have no idea how many young women die each year—("It must be a lot. . . ."). When we hear that anorexia kills 150,000 young women per year, we assume that whoever cites the number must know that it is true. It is, after all, a number and therefore presumably factual.

Oftentimes, social problems statistics exist in splendid isolation. When there is only one number, that number has the weight of authority. It is accepted and repeated. People treat the statistic as authoritative because it is a statistic. Often, these lone numbers come from activists seeking to draw attention to neglected social phenomena. One symptom of societal neglect is that no one has bothered to do much research or compile careful records; there often are no official statistics or other sources for more accurate numbers. When reporters cover the story, they want to report facts. When activists have the only available figures, their numbers look like facts, so, in the absence of other numbers, the media simply report the activists' statistics.

Once a number appears in one news report, that story becomes a potential source for everyone seeking information about the social problem; officials, experts, activists, and other reporters routinely repeat figures that appear in press reports.

NUMBERS TAKE ON LIVES OF THEIR OWN

David Luckenbill has referred to this as "number laundering." A statistic's origin—perhaps simply as someone's best guess—is soon forgotten, and through repetition, the figure comes to be treated as a straightforward fact—accurate and authoritative. The trail becomes muddy, and people lose track of the estimate's original source, but they become confident that the number must be correct because it appears everywhere.

It barely matters if critics challenge a number, and expose it as erroneous. Once a number is in circulation, it can live on, regardless of how thoroughly it may have been discredited. Today's improved methods of information retrieval—electronic indexes, full-text databases, and the Internet—make it easier than ever to locate statistics. Anyone who locates a number can, and quite possibly will, repeat it. That annual toll of 150,000 anorexia deaths has been thoroughly debunked, yet the figure continues to appear in occasional newspaper stories. Electronic storage has given us astonishing, unprecedented access to information, but many people have terrible difficulty sorting through what's available and distinguishing good information from bad. Standards for comparing and evaluating claims seem to be wanting. This is particularly true for statistics that are, after all, numbers and therefore factual, requiring no critical evaluation. Why not believe and repeat a number that everyone else uses? Still, some numbers do have advantages.

BIG NUMBERS ARE BETTER THAN LITTLE NUMBERS

Remember: social problems claims must compete for attention; there are many causes and a limited amount of space on the front page of the *New York Times*. Advocates must find ways to make their claims compelling; they favor melodrama—terrible villains, sympathetic, vulnerable victims, and big numbers. Big numbers suggest that there is a big problem, and big problems demand attention, concern, action. They must not be ignored.

Advocates seeking to attract attention to a social problem soon find themselves pressed for numbers. Press and policy makers demand facts ("You say it's a problem? Well, how big a problem is it?"). Activists believe in the problem's seriousness, and they often spend much of their time talking to others who share that belief. They know that the problem is much more serious, much more common than generally recognized ("The cases we know about are only the tip of the iceberg."). When asked for figures, they thus offer their best estimates, educated guesses, guesstimates, ballpark figures, or stabs in the dark. Mitch Snyder, the most visible spokesperson for the homeless in the early 1980s, explained on ABC's "Nightline" how activists arrived at the figure of three million homeless: "Everybody demanded it. Everybody said we want a number. . . . We got on the phone, we made a lot of calls, we talked to a lot of people, and we said, 'Okay, here are some numbers.' They have no meaning, no value." Because activists sincerely believe that the new problem is big and important, and because they suspect that there is a very large dark figure of unreported or unrecorded cases, activists' estimates tend to be high, and to err on the side of exaggeration.

This helps explain the tendency to estimate the scope of social problems in large, suspiciously round figures. There are, we are told, one million victims of elder abuse each year, two million missing children, three million homeless, 60 million functionally illiterate Americans; child pornography may be, depending on your source, a $1 billion or $46 billion industry, and so on. Often, these estimates are the only available numbers.

The mathematician John Allen Paulos argues that innumeracy—the mathematical counterpart to illiteracy—is widespread and consequential.

He suggests that innumeracy particularly shapes the way we deal with large numbers. Most of us understand hundreds, even thousands, but soon the orders of magnitude blur into a single category: "It's a lot." Even the most implausible figures can gain widespread acceptance. When missing-children advocates charged that nearly two million children are missing each year, anyone might have done the basic math: there are about 60 million children under 18; if two million are missing, that would be one in 30; that is, every year, the equivalent of one child in every American schoolroom would be missing. A 900-student school would have 30 children missing from its student body each year. To be sure, the press debunked this statistic in 1985, but only four years after missing children became a highly publicized issue and the two-million estimate gained wide circulation. And, of course, having been discredited, the number survives and can still be encountered on occasion.

It is remarkable how often contemporary discussions of social problems make no effort to define what is at issue. Often, we're given a dramatic, compelling example, perhaps a tortured, murdered child, then told that this terrible case is an example of a social problem—in this case, child abuse—and finally given a statistic: "There are more than three million reports of child abuse each year." The example, coupled with the problem's name, seems sufficient to make the definition self-evident. However, definitions cannot always be avoided.

DEFINITIONS: BETTER BROAD THAN NARROW

Because broad definitions encompass more kinds of cases, they justify bigger numbers, and we have already noted the advantages of big numbers. No definition is perfect; there are two principal ways definitions of social problems can be flawed. On the one hand, a definition might be too broad and encompass more than it ought to include. That is, broad definitions tend to identify what methodologists call false positives; they include some cases that arguably ought not to be included as part of the problem. On the other hand, a definition that is too narrow may exclude false negatives, cases that perhaps ought to be included as part of the problem.

In general, activists trying to promote a new social problem view false negatives as more troubling than false positives. Activists often feel frustrated trying to get people concerned about some social condition that has been ignored. The general failure to recognize and acknowledge that something is wrong is part of what the activists want to correct; therefore, they may be especially careful not to make things worse by defining the problem too narrowly. A definition that is too narrow fails to recognize a problem's full extent; in doing so, it helps perpetuate the history of neglecting the problem. Some activists favor definitions broad enough to encompass every case that ought to be included; that is, they promote broad definitions in hopes of eliminating all false negatives.

However, broad definitions may invite criticism. They include cases that not everyone considers instances of social problems; that is, while they minimize false negatives, they do so at the cost of maximizing cases that critics may see as false positives. The rejoinder to this critique returns us to the idea of neglect and the harm it causes. Perhaps, advocates acknowledge, their definitions may seem to be too broad, to encompass cases that seem too trivial to be counted as instances of the social problem. But how can we make that judgment? Here advocates are fond of pointing to terrible examples, to the victim whose one, brief, comparatively mild experience had terrible personal consequences; to the child who, having been exposed to a flasher, suffers a lifetime of devastating psychological consequences. Perhaps, advocates say, other victims with similar experiences suffer less or at least seem to suffer less. But is it fair to define a problem too narrowly to include everyone who suffers? Shouldn't our statistics measure the problem's full extent? While social problems statistics often go unchallenged, critics occasionally suggest that some number is implausibly large, or that a definition is too broad.

DEFENDING NUMBERS BY ATTACKING CRITICS

When activists have generated a statistic as part of a campaign to arouse concern about some social problem, there is a tendency for them to conflate the number with the cause. Therefore, anyone who questions a statistic can be suspected of being unsympathetic to the larger claims, indifferent to the victims' suffering, and so on. *Ad hominem* attack on the motives of individuals challenging numbers is a standard response to statistical confrontations. These attacks allow advocates to refuse to budge; making *ad hominem* arguments lets them imply that their opponents don't want to acknowledge the truth, that their statistics are derived from ideology, rather than methodology. If the advocates' campaign has been reasonably successful, they can argue that there is now widespread appreciation that this is a big, serious problem; after all, the advocates' number has been widely accepted and repeated, surely it must be correct. A fallback stance—useful in those rare cases where public scrutiny leaves one's own numbers completely discredited—is to treat the challenge as meaningless nitpicking. Perhaps our statistics were flawed, the advocates acknowledge, but the precise number hardly makes a difference ("After all, even one victim is too many.").

Similarly, criticizing definitions for being too broad can provoke angry reactions. For advocates, such criticisms seem to deny victim's suffering, minimize the extent of the problem, and by extension endorse the status quo. If broader definitions reflect progress, more sensitive appreciation of the true scope of social problems, then calls for narrowing definitions are retrograde, insensitive refusals to confront society's flaws.

Of course, definitions must be operationalized if they are to lead to statistics. It is necessary to specify how the problem will be measured and the statistic produced. If there is to be a survey, who will be sampled? And how will the questions be worded? In what order will they be asked? How will the responses be coded? Most of what we call social-scientific methodology requires choosing how to measure social phenomena. Every statistic depends upon these choices. Just as advocates' preference for large numbers leads them to favor broad definitions, the desirability of broad definitions shapes measurement choices.

MEASURES: BETTER INCLUSIVE THAN EXCLUSIVE

Most contemporary advocates have enough sociological sophistication to allude to the dark figure—that share of a social problem that goes unreported and unrecorded. Official statistics, they warn, inevitably underestimate the size of social problems. This undercounting helps justify advocates' generous estimates (recall all those references to "the tip of the iceberg"). Awareness of the dark figure also justifies measurement decisions that maximize researchers' prospects for discovering and counting as many cases as possible.

Consider the first federally sponsored National Incidence Studies of Missing, Abducted, Runaway, and Thrownaway Children (NISMART). This was an attempt to produce an accurate estimate for the numbers of missing children. To estimate family abductions (in which a family member kidnaps a child) researchers conducted a telephone survey of households. The researchers made a variety of inclusive measurement decisions: an abduction could involve moving a child as little as 20 feet; it could involve the child's complete cooperation; there was no minimum time that the abduction had to last; those involved may not have considered what happened an abduction; and there was no need that the child's whereabouts be unknown (in most family abductions identified by NISMART, the child was not with someone who had legal custody, but everyone knew where the child was). Using these methods of measurement, a non-custodial parent who took a child for an unauthorized visit, or who extended an authorized visit for an extra night, was counted as having committed a "family abduction." If the same parent tried to conceal the taking or to prevent the custodial parent's contact with the child, the abduction was classified in the most serious ("policy-focal") category. The NISMART researchers concluded that there were 163,200 of these more serious family abductions each year, although evidence from states with the most thorough missing-children reporting systems suggests that only about 9,000 cases per year come to police attention. In other words, the researchers' inclusive measurement choices led to a remarkably high estimate. Media coverage of the family-abduction problem coupled this high figure with horrible examples—cases of abductions lasting years, involving long-term sexual abuse, ending in homicide, and so on. Although most of the episodes identified by NISMART's methods were relatively minor, the press implied that very serious cases were very common ("It's a big number!").

There is nothing atypical about the NISMART example. Advocacy research has become an important source of social problems statistics. Advocates hope research will produce large numbers, and they tend to believe that broad definitions are justified. They deliberately adopt inclusive research measurements that promise to minimize false negatives and generate large numbers. These measurement decisions almost always occur outside public scrutiny and only rarely attract attention. When the media report numbers, percentages, and rates, they almost never explain the definitions and measurements used to produce those statistics.

While many statistics seem to stand alone, occasions do arise when there are competing numbers or contradictory statistical answers to what seems to be the same question. In general, the media tend to treat such competing numbers with a sort of even-handedness.

COMPETING NUMBERS ARE EQUALLY GOOD

Because the media tend to treat numbers as factual, and to ignore definitions and measurement choices, inconsistent numbers pose a problem. Clearly, both numbers cannot be correct. Where a methodologist might try to ask how different advocates arrived at different numbers (in hopes of showing that one figure is more accurate than another, or at least of understanding how the different numbers might be products of different methods), the press is more likely to account for any difference in terms of the competitors' conflicting ideologies or agendas.

Consider the case of the estimates for the crowd size at the 1995 Million Man March. The event's very name set a standard for its success: as the date for the March approached, its organizers insisted that it would attract a million people, while their critics predicted that the crowd would never reach that size. On the day of the march, the organizers announced success: there were, they said, 1.5 to 2 million people present. Alas, the National Park Service Park Police, charged by Congress with estimating the size of demonstrations on the Capitol Mall, calculated that the march drew only 400,000 people (still more than any previous civil rights demonstration). The Park Police knew the Mall's dimensions, took aerial photos, and multiplied the area covered by the crowd by a multiplier based on typical crowd densities. The organizers, like the organizers of many previous demonstrations on the Mall, insisted that the Park Police estimate was far too low. Enter a team of aerial photo analysts from Boston University who eventually calculated that the crowd numbered 837,000 plus or minus 25 percent (i.e., they suggested there might have been a million people in the crowd).

The press covered these competing estimates in standard "he said-she said" style. Few reporters bothered to ask why the two estimates were different. The answer was simple: the BU researchers used a different multiplier. Where the Park Police estimated that there was one demonstrator per 3.6 square feet (actually a fairly densely-packed crowd), the BU researchers calculated that there was a person for every 1.8 square feet (the equivalent of being packed in a crowded elevator). But rather than trying to compare or evaluate the processes by which people arrived at the different estimates, most press reports treated the numbers as equally valid, and implied that the explanation for the difference lay in the motives of those making the estimates.

The March organizers (who wanted to argue that the demonstration had been successful) produced a high number; the Park Police (who, the March organizers insisted, were biased against the March) produced a low one, and the BU scientists (presumably impartial and authoritative) found something in between. The BU estimate quickly found favor in the media: it let the organizers save face (because the BU team conceded the crowd might have reached one million); it seemed to split the difference between the high and low estimates; and it apparently came from experts. There was no effort to judge the competing methods and assumptions behind the different numbers, for example, to ask whether it was likely that hundreds of thousands of men stood packed as close together as the BU researchers imagined for the hours the demonstration lasted.

This example, like those discussed earlier, reveals that public discussions of social statistics are remarkably unsophisticated. Social scientists advance their careers by using arcane inferential statistics to interpret data. The standard introductory undergraduate statistics textbook tends to zip through descriptive statistics on the way to inferential statistics. But it is descriptive statistics—simple counts, averages, percentages, rates, and the like—that play the key role is public discussions over social problems and social policy. And the level of those discussions is not terribly advanced. There is too little critical thinking about social statistics. People manufacture, and other people repeat, dubious figures. While this can involve deliberate attempts to deceive and manipulate, this need not be the case. Often, the people who create the numbers—who, as it were, make all those millions—believe in them. Neither the advocates who create statistics, nor the reporters who repeat them, nor the larger public questions the figures.

What Paulos calls innumeracy is partly to blame— many people aren't comfortable with basic ideas of numbers and calculations. But there is an even more fundamental issue: many of us do not appreciate that every number is a social construction, produced by particular people using particular methods. The naïve, but widespread, tendency is to treat statistics as fetishes, that is, as almost magical nuggets of fact, rather than as someone's efforts to summarize, to simplify complexity. If we accept the statistic as a fetish, then several of the guidelines I have outlined make perfect sense. Any number is better than no number, because the number represents truth. Numbers take on lives of their own because they are true, and their truth justifies their survival. The best way to defend a number is to attack its critics' motives, because anyone who questions a presumably true number must have dubious reasons for doing so. And, when we are confronted with competing numbers, those numbers are equally good, because, after all, they are somehow equivalent bits of truth. At the same time, the guidelines offer those who must produce numbers justifications for favoring big numbers, broad definitions, and inclusive methods. Again, this need not be cynical. Often, advocates are confident that they know the truth, and they approach collecting statistics as a straightforward effort to generate the numbers needed to document what they, after all, know to be true.

Any effort to improve the quality of public discussion of social statistics needs to begin with the understanding that numbers are socially constructed. Statistics are not nuggets of objective fact that we discover; rather, they are people's creations. Every statistic reflects people's decisions to count, their choices of what to count and how to go about counting it, and so on. These choices inevitably shape the resulting numbers.

Public discussions of social statistics need to chart a middle path between naivete (the assumption that numbers are simply true) and cynicism (the suspicion that figures are outright lies told by people with bad motives). This middle path needs to be critical. It needs to recognize that every statistic has to be created, to acknowledge that every statistic is imperfect, yet to appreciate that statistics still offer an essential way of summarizing complex information. Social scientists have a responsibility to promote this critical stance in the public, within the press, and among advocates.

QUESTIONS ABOUT MEANING

1. Best explains that every statistic is a "social construction," a result of "choices that go into producing it." Sometimes statistics are the result of bad choices. Illustrate what Best means by using the examples of statistics about homeless people, missing children, and deaths attributed to anorexia.
2. What are *ad hominem* attacks? How are they used by some social-issue activists to silence those who question their statistics?
3. How do the varying estimates related to the Million Man March demonstrate the importance of questioning statistics? According to Best, what kinds of questions should readers ask before accepting statistics derived from surveys?
4. What is innumeracy?

QUESTIONS FOR RHETORICAL ANALYSIS

5. To whom is Best writing? How does the concluding paragraph make clear at least one group Best is addressing?
6. Instead of identifying types of *mistakes* responsible for bad statistics, Best identifies *principles* and *guidelines* for creating and reporting bad numbers. Why do you think Best presents the problem with words like *principles* and *guidelines* instead of with words like *problems* or *errors*?
7. In the conclusion to an academic paper, you're likely to find the author doing at least some of the following:

    - reviewing what was discussed (the main idea);
    - reestablishing the importance of the topic;
    - reminding readers about other people in the ongoing "conversation"; and
    - looking to the future.

    The appearance of these familiar practices or "moves" signals the conclusion of an academic article. Where would you say Best's conclusion begins? Which of the listed moves do you see in his conclusion?

"Birds—Dead and Deadly: Why Numeracy Needs to Address Social Construction," *Numeracy* JOEL BEST

Many readers are inclined to accept a statistic as "factual" proof, but critical readers are not so easily swayed. That's because they know statistics and other statements presented as "facts" are merely claims that may or may not be accurate. In "Birds—Dead and Deadly: Why Numeracy Needs to Address Social Construction," sociology professor Joel Best argues that numeracy skills—the ability to assess statistics, graphs, and other kinds of quantitative evidence—involve critical evaluation of the "social processes that produce those figures." His article was originally published in 2008 in *Numeracy*, a peer-reviewed journal devoted to the teaching of quantitative skills across disciplines.

ABSTRACT

Sociologists use the term social construction to refer to the processes by which people assign meaning to their world. This paper argues that numeracy education needs to address social construction. In particular, thinking critically about the statistics the news media report regarding social issues requires understanding the competitive nature of the social problems marketplace, and the social forces that allow questionable numbers to receive widespread public attention. Such critiques must incorporate more than assessing how the numbers were calculated; they must consider the social construction of particular statistics. Two recent examples—claims about the number of birds killed flying into windows, and warnings about the threat of an avian flu pandemic—are presented to illustrate the need to incorporate social construction into numeracy education.

KEYWORDS

social construction, numeracy, bird collisions, avian flu

INTRODUCTION

Although the people promoting numeracy (a.k.a. quantitative literacy, quantitative reasoning, statistical literacy) come from a range of disciplines, they share a sense of disappointment with many students' limited abilities to apply quantitative concepts in practical situations. Today's students spend more years studying mathematics than their counterparts in the past, yet critics argue that innumeracy remains a serious problem, that students have difficulty applying their math training to real-world situations. In response, instruction in numeracy seeks to help students apply their quantitative skills to reading graphs, understanding interest rates on home loans and credit cards, and other practical situations.

I am tangentially involved with—rather than part of—the numeracy movement. My training is in sociology, but I do not teach courses in statistics or research methods, nor do I do much in the way of quantitative analysis. Most of my work concerns the sociology of social problems. That is, I try to understand how and why particular issues come to public attention. Most often, when people are trying to arouse concern about some social problem, they incorporate statistics in their claims. Many of these numbers have serious flaws, and thinking about those flaws brought me into contact with numeracy's advocates.

In 2001, I published a short book, *Damned Lies and Statistics: Untangling Numbers from the Media, Politicians, and Activists* (Best 2001). I wanted to write a more sociologically sophisticated version of Huff's (1954) classic, *How to Lie with Statistics*; that is, I viewed my book as a guide to thinking critically about the sorts of figures used to convince people that they ought to worry about social problems. A sequel, *More Damned Lies and Statistics: How Numbers Confuse Public Issues* followed (Best 2004). As people in the numeracy movement became aware of my books, I began to receive invitations to attend their conferences (and to write this essay). In this paper, I want to summarize the social constructionist approach taken in my books—maintaining my customary focus on statistics used to promote social problems claims—and to suggest what I see as its relevance for those concerned about numeracy. However, my perspective remains that of someone outside the movement, and insiders will have to judge for themselves whether my ideas are useful.

WHAT SOCIOLOGISTS MEAN BY SOCIAL CONSTRUCTION

The term *social construction* flourished briefly as a trendy bit of academic lingo during the 1990s. After originating within sociology (Berger and Luckmann 1966), it spread, first to the other social sciences, and then to the humanities. Soon all manner of intellectuals claimed to be studying the social construction of this or that, although what they meant when they invoked the term varied a great deal (Best 2008). Many in the sciences—and, I presume, mathematics—came to associate the term with postmodernism, or with postures of extreme relativism (e.g., Boghossian 2006). It is important to understand that that is not what sociologists mean by social construction.

When sociologists speak of social construction, they are referring to the process by which people assign meaning to the world. Human beings depend upon language; they must learn their vocabularies from—and use those words to communicate with—other people. This is a social process through which all knowledge is generated. (To be clear, sociologists use the term "social" very broadly, as encompassing all of the ways people interact. Thus, they understand politics, economics, and so on to be forms of social activity.) We cannot reason without resorting to language; thus, all that we know is embedded in social life.

In particular, it is important to appreciate that numbers are social constructions. This makes some people nervous; they prefer to think that "the truth is out there," that science or mathematics merely discover the universe's secrets. I am not interested in such philosophical issues. Sociologists, however, view science and mathematics as having histories, in which individual people add to the edifice of what is known. Those histories are not always straightforward; they feature debates and occasional backtracking, until consensus emerges regarding how much confidence we should have in the knowledge being produced. That intellectual building project—enlarging our body of knowledge—is a form of social construction.

The significance of these rather abstract claims for numeracy can be better understood if we examine how numbers are used to understand social problems. Within our culture, there is a tendency to assume that statistics are factual, that statistical evidence is more than mere opinion. After all, numbers suggest that someone must have counted something. But that's the point: statistics do not exist in nature; they are always produced by people. People have to decide whether to count, what to count, how to go about counting, and how to summarize the results of that counting process. (Here, and throughout this paper, I use "counting" in a general, non-technical sense; I mean it to encompass the full range of quantitative maneuvers. All numbers—tallies, but also rates, inferential statistics, and all other figures—are the results of people's activities.) This process—this *social* process—is what sociologists mean when they say that statistics are socially constructed.

It is important to be clear about this: when sociologists say that a statistic is socially constructed, they are not claiming that the number is false, bogus, generated through bad quantitative practices, or otherwise flawed. They do not draw a distinction between socially constructed numbers and good numbers. Rather, they view all numbers as socially constructed; every number is a product of people's choices. To be sure, some of those choices may be wiser and more defensible, so that we can have great confidence in the accuracy of the figures. But other numbers may be the results of flawed methods of counting, and we ought to treat those figures with considerable caution. Social arrangements provide the context within which social problems statistics emerge and shape what sorts of numbers gain attention. In my view, any serious effort to make students more numerate about those statistics requires coming to terms with this process of social construction.

STATISTICS AND THE SOCIAL CONSTRUCTION OF SOCIAL PROBLEMS

Sociologists who study the social construction of social problems ask how and why particular issues come to public attention: how is it that, at one time or another, toxic breast implants, or road rage, or identity theft come to be seen as important, troubling topics, the focus of considerable public attention. The answer is that people—social activists, experts, media figures, politicians, or whoever—must make claims arguing that something is an important issue, one that requires action. (We can, for instance, see the numeracy movement as constructing innumeracy as an educational problem that needs to be addressed through numeracy education.)

It helps to think about these various claims as competitors in a social problems marketplace (Hilgartner and Bosk 1988). That is, there are advocates promoting many causes, trying to capture the attention of—and arouse concern among—the press, the public, and policymakers. This competition encourages advocates to present the most compelling case possible, in order to grab and hold the audience. Thus, when campaigns illustrate social problems with examples, they choose especially disturbing instances: a child beaten to death may be used to illustrate the problem of child abuse (even though cases of nonviolent neglect far outnumber cases of physical abuse, and even among children who suffer physical abuse, fatalities are rare [Johnson 1995]); and so on.

Similarly, campaigns to arouse concern about social problems often present statistical evidence. Once again, there are competitive advantages to presenting the most compelling numbers. In most cases, this means introducing big numbers. Put simply: a big number suggests there is a big problem. If we can say that a social problem occurs many times each year, or that it affects many people, or that it costs lots of money, we have a stronger case that our problem deserves attention—that people ought to worry about it, that they ought to be willing to do something about it.

It is important to appreciate that the advocates seeking to call attention to different social problems are often perfectly sincere: they believe that the problem is important and merits concern. They are also likely to spend time among like-minded individuals, so that a sort of hothouse atmosphere develops around their particular issue. Such people may not be especially critical of numbers that seem to support their claims: they think this is a big problem, so a big number sounds about right.

In addition, of course, advocates often have an interest in their claims' successes. Once people start to take a problem seriously, good things—money, status, and so on—can begin to flow to its promoters. It is quite easy for someone to sincerely believe that some problem demands attention, and for that person to also have a vested interest in that problem gaining attention. Neither characteristic does much to encourage critical thinking about statistics about the problem—at least not regarding those numbers that seem to confirm the problem's importance. (Of course, people often become analytic tigers when confronted with figures that challenge their positions; they start criticizing samples, measurements, etc.)

In order to illustrate these processes, let's examine two avian examples—claims about bird deaths due to collisions with windows, and about the avian flu.

DEAD BIRDS: ESTIMATES FOR DEATHS FROM WINDOW STRIKES

When birds fly into windows, the collisions are often fatal. How often does this happen? It is impossible to count every fatal window-strike but, in recent years, the media have reported an impressively large, albeit suspiciously round estimate for the number of fatal bird collisions each year. For instance, an architecture professor interviewed on National Public Radio in 2005 put the annual number of fatal bird strikes at one billion. The reporter conducting the interview expressed skepticism: "How accurate is that number do you think? How would you ever calculate something like that?" The professor offered reassurance, insisting that the one-billion figure was "based on very careful data" ("A Major Risk Factor" 2005).

Tracing the origins of the one-billion statistic proves interesting. The previous best estimate for annual bird deaths due to fatal window collisions in the continental United States was 3.5 million (Banks 1979). This estimate simply assumed that there were about 3.5 million square miles in the continental U.S., and that, on average, one bird died after striking a window per square mile. In other words, the 3.5 million figure wasn't much more than a guess.

Convinced that that number was too low, an ornithologist decided to do some research. He arranged to have residents at *two* houses keep careful track of bird collisions at their homes; one house was in southern Illinois, the other in a suburb in New York. By bizarre coincidence, I happen to have known the people who lived in the Illinois house; they were former neighbors of ours, an older couple who loved birds, and who built a custom home with lots of windows, surrounded by trees, bushes, bird feeders, and so on. Their house was a bird magnet. Over a one-year period, our neighbors observed 33 fatal bird strikes at their home (Klem 1990). (In contrast, we lived for eight years in a house a few hundred yards away; however, most of our windows were screened, and, so far as we knew, no birds died striking our house during those years[.])

But how do we get to that one-billion estimate? The ornithologist found government estimates for the numbers of housing units, commercial buildings, and schools in the U.S.—a total of 97.6 million structures (Klem 1990). He then estimated that, on average, between one and ten birds would die from flying into each building's windows. Thus, he concluded that between 97.6 million and 975.6 million fatal bird strikes occurred each year. Although some reporters carefully acknowledged the range of estimates (Malakoff 2004), other advocates seized on the larger figure, rounded up and—voila!—concluded that "very careful data" demonstrated that one billion birds die each year from window collisions.

Clearly, some large number of birds dies this way. There is no way to accurately measure this number, and we have to make guesses. If we assume one death per square mile, we get 3.5 million deaths; one death per building gets us about 100 million; ten deaths per building a billion. Certainly a billion is a more arresting figure, and it is the one that has received the most media coverage.

However, not everyone agrees. One bird-death website suggests that only 80 million birds die from window strikes annually (it offers no basis for that figure). However, it states that: "Pet cats that are allowed to roam free account for some 4 MILLION bird deaths EACH DAY in North America, or over 1 BILLION songbirds each year. This figure does not include the losses resulting from feral cats or wild populations of cats" ("Modern Threats to Bird Populations" 2005—emphasis in original). Just to put that number in perspective, the federal government estimates that there [are] about 71 million pet cats (including, of course, some who are restricted to an indoor lifestyle) (American Veterinary Medical Association 2002). To kill a billion birds, each of those cats would have to average 14 bird kills annually.

In sum, the estimate that each year a billion birds die in window collisions is a widely disseminated statistic. This example illustrates one of the most common ways statistics are used to discuss social problems: someone gives an estimate for the problem's scope. Such big, round-number estimates pop up frequently: someone claims that there are a million cases of elder abuse each year, or two million missing children, or three million homeless persons, or a billion birds killed in window collisions.

I am not sure whether people in the numeracy movement would find such figures particularly interesting. Such numbers do not claim to be the result of complex quantitative reasoning; rather, they are presented as estimates of counts. That is, we are asked to believe that if someone were to simply count the number of cases of the phenomenon in question (e.g., bird deaths from window collisions), the result would be more-or-less the number being claimed. Do such simple numbers offer any useful lessons in numeracy?

In my view, there are at least two important lessons to be learned from examining the billion bird-death figure. The first is that every number is indeed socially constructed, and that we need to understand the process that produced the number. In this case, the ornithologist arrived at the number through a two-stage process. First, he arranged to have the people who lived in the two houses count the number of fatal bird-strikes at their homes. Second, he proposed that 1–10 birds suffered fatal collisions per building, and multiplied an estimate for the total number of buildings by 1 and 10, thereby generating a range for total bird deaths. There is nothing difficult about understanding the calculations that produced the final number, but neither is it difficult imagining that there might be critics who would find the result of this process less than convincing.

The second lesson is that statistics can have a life of their own. That is, once someone has produced a number, others are likely to latch onto the figure and repeat it. When people talk about social issues, they like to have facts to support their arguments and numbers tend to be treated as facts in our culture. Numbers that cannot bear even the most minimal inspection, that may be acknowledged to be nothing more than someone's best guess when they originate, are seized by others because they are the only—and therefore the best—statistics available. Those folks repeat the figure, and with each repetition, there seems to be broader consensus about the number's accuracy. Often, people begin to improve upon the figure.

We see these processes in our bird-death example. The initial estimated range (between 97.6 million and 975.6 million fatal bird strikes annually) was soon forgotten, in favor of the higher figure, which was then rounded up to the more impressive one billion. Thus, "97.6–975.6 million" becomes "as many as one billion," which in turn becomes "a billion." Similarly, expressions of confidence in the figure's accuracy become more robust. What was once a rough estimate becomes "very careful data." Others may even argue that the number understates the problem: thus, an Audubon Society official suggests: "I think [the ornithologist who made the original estimate has] been very conservative in his calculations" (Malakoff 2004, 66).

Estimates of a social problem's scope are extremely common. When advocates are trying to draw attention to some issue, they often seek media coverage, and reporters are likely to press for facts—numbers—that can give a sense of just how large the problem is. No matter how carefully the people offering the original figures may be to qualify their claims, there is an excellent chance that those qualifications will soon be lost. This is a very common way for dubious data to enter policy debates.

In my view, advocates of improving numeracy should find such figures worthy of attention, even though they involve rather simple mathematics. Virtually all statistics classes teach students to master a series of increasingly sophisticated concepts and the procedures necessary to conduct the attendant calculations. In general, the more sophisticated the concepts and procedures being taught, the more prestige there is in teaching the material. Choosing to focus on teaching numeracy is risky, in the sense that the skills taught in numeracy education are relatively simple—they don't seem to involve much "real math." And learning to think critically about estimates for the number of birds killed in window collisions (or the numbers of missing children, or homeless people, or whatever) involves minimal mathematical sophistication. These numbers are really just counts (or, rather, estimates of what a more-or-less accurate count would show), and counting seems to be the very simplest mathematical skill. Thinking critically about these numbers directs attention away from more complex, more mathematically interesting forms of reasoning; it requires understanding less about math than about the nature of social construction, the ways that different parties become invested in producing and promoting particular estimates.

My point is not that some numbers are based on poor data analysis. Numeracy requires more than understanding sound analytic practices. To be sure, we might quibble about the ornithologist's methods—the small and apparently unrepresentative sample of houses, the casual guesses about the limits of the range for deaths per building, and so on. But such critiques ignore much larger issues, such as the rhetorical role statistics play in promoting social problems claims, or the way claims must compete for public attention. The example is intended to suggest that numerate thinking about social statistics requires understanding that these numbers are produced and disseminated in a social context, that is, understanding the social construction of those numbers. This becomes even more evident in our second example.

DEADLY BIRDS: CONSTRUCTING THE MENACE OF AVIAN FLU

During the fall of 2005, and into the early months of 2006, the threat of an epidemic of bird flu became the subject of considerable media attention. There were already doubts about officials' ability to prevent an epidemic. The previous year, contaminated production methods had spoiled a substantial portion of the 2004 flu vaccines, so that many people who ordinarily received flu shots had to go without; then, in August, 2005, Hurricane Katrina raised questions about the competence of those responsible for emergency management. Now, there were warnings that avian flu had broken out in Southeast Asia, and that it might spread into a global pandemic.

Two sorts of numbers in particular helped give this problem shape. The first was the claim that the current strain of flu was extremely virulent, as evidenced by claims that half the known cases had ended in death. If the disease spread widely, and if it killed half the people who contracted it, the consequences would be catastrophic. How catastrophic? Various commentators who speculated on the possible death toll produced an extraordinary range of figures. Thus, *The Bird Flu Preparedness Planner* warned: ". . . this is no ordinary flu virus; this new strain is highly lethal, with a death rate of fifty percent, 80 times the normal flu, with the potential to kill hundreds of millions given the right conditions" (Woodson 2005, vii). At the upper end of the range, we find claims that "the true worst-case scenario . . . [is] in the range of *1 billion* deaths" (Davis 2005, 126; emphasis in original).

Of course, flu epidemics can be serious. The 1918 pandemic that spread in the aftermath of World War I killed millions of people, perhaps 100 million worldwide. But is that the reasonable basis for comparison? After all, the Great War created crowded, unsanitary conditions that made it particularly easy for disease to spread, and standards for medical care have improved significantly over the intervening decades. Wouldn't contemporary society be better able to manage a flu outbreak?

In fact, commentary on the flu risk presented a broad spectrum of views, from doomsday scenarios to dismissive skepticism. Not surprisingly, warnings that the flu posed a dire threat made for more compelling media coverage. These claims sketched a nightmarish sequence of events: what if a particularly deadly strain of bird flu emerged, and what if humans proved susceptible to that particular strain, and what if—once people became infected—the flu organisms mutated so that they could be transmitted directly from one person to another? Skeptics argued that the H5N1 virus had been around for decades without having morphed into a form capable of transmitting lethal infections among large numbers of people, and that this very failure suggested that a deadly pandemic was an unlikely outcome. Still, the prospect of global devastation made for better sound bites and more alarming headlines. One list of "practical pre-pandemic preparations for individuals" began: "Get your will in order" (Woodson 2005, 22).

While the worst-case scenarios depended largely upon speculation, numbers did play a role in the alarmed commentary. What about those claims that H5N1 infections had a "death rate of fifty percent"? Commentators noted that half of the people who had been treated had died, and that this demonstrated that the new strain of flu was particularly deadly. But most of these deaths occurred in Vietnam and other Asian countries, and many of those who died had worked with poultry (so they had direct exposure to infected birds). More importantly, the fifty percent death-toll seems to have been calculated using the number of people hospitalized with flu symptoms. In other words, it did not take into account the possibility that some—quite possibly a large majority—of those who became sick with flu stayed home, rather than entering a hospital for treatment. We can suspect that hospitalization is a last resort for low-paid workers in Third World countries, that only the sickest patients would come to official notice. Extrapolating the death rate among the minority of patients who received hospital treatment to the entire population of people who came down with flu created an exaggerated perception of the threat.

Similarly, the wildly varied projections of possible death tolls for a pandemic—figures that ranged from less than one million to one billion—depended upon all manner of assumptions—how far and how widely might the disease spread, how fast might it spread, how effective might medical treatments be for those infected, what might the death rate among the infected be, and so on. Obviously, there were few limits on such speculation. In retrospect, knowing that the actual worldwide death toll was far less than one thousand, the more extravagant claims now seem fantastic—akin to those doomsday predictions for the civilization-ending possibilities of computer software failing to handle the arrival of Y2K. (Some critics noted that this was by no means the first set of warnings to exaggerate the threat of a devastating H5N1 flu pandemic [Fumento 2005].) Attaching numbers—even numbers based on guesses and pessimistic assumptions—to worst-case scenarios seems to make those projections seem more plausible, because figures, even if they are grounded in little more than fantasy, demand to be treated as facts. Somebody must have calculated something, right?

Once again, I am not sure how neatly these statistics—both the 50 percent death rate, and the projections for a death toll of up to a billion people—fit within the domain of numeracy education. To be sure, it is easy to criticize the basis for those numbers—the failure to appreciate that the number of people sick enough to be hospitalized is not the best basis for calculating death rates, the readiness to string together a series of extremely pessimistic assumptions to arrive at a worst-case guess for how high the final death toll might be. But understanding warnings about the flu epidemic really requires understanding how claims regarding different social problems compete for media attention, and how coverage depends upon constructing an issue in compelling terms—which often means in the most frightening terms—that will allow it to elbow aside rival concerns.

CRITICAL THINKING ABOUT NUMERACY CANNOT BE DIVORCED FROM SOCIAL CONTEXT

Any number can be understood as the result of some set of calculations—or more sophisticated quantitative procedures—that produced it. Because many numeracy advocates seem to either be mathematicians, or to teach statistics or research methods in other disciplines, there may be a natural tendency to think of numeracy in those terms. That is, they may focus on the quantitative reasoning and methodological choices used to produce numbers, rather than the broader social context within which that reasoning occurs.

But, when we try to think critically about many of the numbers we encounter in discussions of social or political issues, coming to terms with the actual quantitative methods used to produce those figures is only part—and often a relatively uninteresting part—of the story. How did advocates arrive at the claim that a billion birds die in window collisions, or that bird flu might kill a billion people worldwide? These were little more than guesses, ballpark figures. In the 1980s, when a leading activist was asked to explain the basis for the widely circulated estimate that there were three million homeless Americans, he responded: "Everybody demanded it. Everybody said we want a number. . . . We got on the phone, we made a lot of calls, we talked to a lot of people, and we said, 'Okay, here are some numbers.' They have no meaning, no value" (Mitch Snyder quoted in Jencks 1994, 2). Not surprisingly, such casually produced estimates can prove to be off by one or more (in the case of the worst-case scenarios for avian flu, several) orders of magnitude. Still, the mathematical, quantitative-reasoning lesson illustrated by such examples is pretty basic: guessing is often inaccurate.

To fully understand the sorts of numbers that tend to appear in media reports, we need go beyond examining calculations, to explore the social processes that produce those figures, the ways people go about socially constructing statistics. Here, I should emphasize, I am referring not just to activists' estimates for the scope of social problems, but also to press coverage of government agency announcements, research results, and other seemingly authoritative figures (e.g., shifts in the crime rate, evidence of some health hazard reported in a medical journal, rankings of colleges, and so on). Within sociology, economics, and political science, for instance, there are whole literatures discussing the problems with how the federal government measures the population, crime, poverty, unemployment, productivity, and on and on. Even the most familiar social statistics are products of choices that can be questioned. Moreover, one needs to think critically about social construction at two different levels.

The first of these levels concerns the social processes—the decisions and procedures that lead to the production of the specific numbers in question. Thus, we can unpack the billion bird-deaths figure to identify the ornithologist who produced it, the calculations he used to estimate a range of bird deaths, and the ways other people improved the number (by focusing on the upper range, rounding up, and characterizing the statistic as the product of careful research). It is possible to discover analogous information for any figure. Sometimes, such information is readily available: If we read a news story reporting on a recent piece of medical research, we should be able to locate the journal where the article appeared and discover the information in the methods section. In other cases, of course, determining how people arrived at a number may require more detective work. But we can at least try to discover the process by which numbers are produced.

The second level seems further from the traditional concerns of numeracy's advocates, but it strikes me as nonetheless important. This involves teaching students to understand the larger social context within which numbers emerge. Causes compete for our attention and concern, and statistics play an important rhetorical role in social problems construction. This has various consequences, including creating a marketplace where the most compelling claims win, and less persuasive arguments get pushed aside. Thus, advocates prefer dramatic statistics, and this preference usually translates into big numbers. Big numbers make claims more attractive to the various media that showcase claims—not just newspapers or TV news shows but presumably more selective venues, such as medical journals that use press releases to maintain a public profile (Shell 1998). It is no accident that the claims about both dead and deadly birds fixed on the same figure—one billion. A billion is a big, round, impressive number. If a billion birds die flying into windows, or if bird flu might kill a billion people, we can recognize that we're talking about big, troubling problems. The persuasive appeal of such alarming statistics is to give those claims that incorporate them a competitive advantage in the social problems marketplace, no matter how dubious the assumptions that underpin the calculations that led to those figures. Trying to deal one-by-one with examples of bad numbers risks overlooking the larger social context that shapes the choices made by the people who produce and repeat the dubious figures that appear in nearly every newscast or newspaper.

IMPLICATIONS FOR TEACHING NUMERACY: A NON-AVIAN EXAMPLE

What does this mean for those directly engaged in numeracy education? Because I don't teach courses in quantitative literacy, I am ill-qualified to suggest how instruction might be improved. But let me offer a non-avian example of the sort of topic I think might warrant classroom attention.

The U.S. Census Bureau (2007) recently announced that: "The non-Hispanic, single-race white population [is] 66 percent of the total population." News reports interpreted this as a milestone: for the first time in U.S. history, over a third of Americans were minority group members.

Racial and ethnic classifications are always messy, as the press release's awkward phrasing suggests. What does it mean to say that someone is a "non-Hispanic, single-race white"? First, the federal government does not consider "Hispanic" a race; Hispanics are of different races, including many who consider themselves white. Second, thanks to recent changes in census questions, respondents are now invited to declare themselves to be of more than one race. In particular, Native American activists have urged individuals with some American Indian ancestry to acknowledge this. In its press release, the bureau classified all Hispanics and anyone who acknowledged any non-white ancestry as minority group members; that is, they classified people so as to maximize the non-white population. Very likely, a good many of the people counted as minority group members for this purpose consider themselves—and are considered by others—to be white in everyday life. As recently as the 1990 census, the bureau used a different scheme in which many of these individuals would have been classified as part of the white population.

Still, we can understand the broad appeal of the statistical milestone produced through the new classification scheme. It seemed newsworthy—minorities now account for more than a third of the population. It also advanced the political interests of activists on both the left (who could call for greater appreciation of diversity, and so on) and on the right (who could, for instance, point with alarm to the impact of immigration). There were reasons why this particular news release attracted considerable attention, but fully understanding this requires understanding both how government agencies classify race (what strikes me as a more traditional topic for numeracy education), and the political interests various groups have in those classifications (which would require thinking more about the process of social construction). In my view, teaching students about such examples requires addressing both topics.

THE BOTTOM LINE

I have tried to argue that social construction poses a challenge for those interested in promoting numeracy. Once we acknowledge that all numbers are products of social activity, we must confront the nature of the social environment in which numbers emerge and circulate. And that means moving numeracy education beyond the confines of teaching calculation and statistical concepts, to address matters of social construction.

ACKNOWLEDGMENT

Several reviewers offered helpful suggestions for improving this paper.

REFERENCES

American Veterinary Medical Association. 2002. *U.S. Pet Ownership & Demographics Sourcebook*. Schaumburg, IL: AVMA.

Banks, R. C. 1979. "Human related mortality of birds in the United States." *U.S. Fish and Wildlife Service Special Scientific Report*, Wildlife No. 215.

Berger, P. L., and T. Luckmann. 1966. *The Social Construction of Reality: A Treatise in the Sociology of Knowledge*. Garden City, NY: Doubleday.

Best, J. 2001. *Damned Lies and Statistics: Untangling Numbers from the Media, Politicians, and Activists*. Berkeley: University of California Press.

———. 2004. *More Damned Lies and Statistics: How Numbers Confuse Public Issues*. Berkeley: University of California Press.

———. 2008. Historical development and defining issues of constructionist inquiry. In *Handbook of Constructionist Research*, ed. J. A. Holstein and J. F. Gubrium, 41–64. New York: Guilford.

Boghossian, P. 2006. *Fear of Knowledge: Against Relativism and Constructivism*. Oxford: Clarendon Press.

Davis, M. 2005. *The Monster at Our Door: The Global Threat of Avian Flu*. New York: New Press.

Fumento, M. 2005. Fuss and feathers: Pandemic panic over the avian flu. *Weekly Standard* 11 (November 21)

Hilgartner, S., and C. L. Bosk. 1988. The rise and fall of social problems. *American Journal of Sociology* 94: 53–78. http://dx.doi.org/10.1086/228951

Huff, D. 1954. *How to Lie with Statistics*. New York: Norton.

Jencks, C. 1994. *The Homeless*. Cambridge, MA: Harvard University Press.

Johnson, J. M. 1995. Horror stories and the construction of child abuse. In *Images of Issues*, 2nd ed., ed. J. Best, 17–31. Hawthorne, NY: Aldine de Gruyter.

Klem, D., Jr. 1990. Collisions between birds and windows: Mortality and prevention. *Journal of Field Ornithology* 61: 120–128.

"A Major Risk Factor for Birds: Building Collisions." 2005. *All Things Considered* (March 11). http://www.npr.org

Malakoff, D. 2004. Clear and Present Danger. *Audubon Magazine* 106 (March): 65–68.

"Modern Threats to Bird Populations." 2005. Chipper Woods Bird Observatory. http://www.wbu.com/chipperwoods/photos/threats.htm

Shell, E. R. 1998. The Hippocratic Wars. *New York Times Magazine* (June 28): 34–38.

U. S. Census Bureau. 2007. Minority population tops 100 million, news release, May 17. http://www.census.gov/newsroom/releases/archives/population/cb07-70.html

Woodson, Grattan. 2005. *The Bird Flu Preparedness Planner.* Deerfield Beach, FL: Health Communications.

Joel Best, University of Delaware, joelbest@udel.edu

QUESTIONS ABOUT MEANING

1. What does Best mean when he says that statistics are "socially constructed"?
2. What are factors that determine why some issues become more prominent in the media than others and why some statistics become more repeated than others?
3. Summarize the steps taken by the ornithologist and others to attribute a billion bird deaths to window strikes.
4. What was wrong with the sampling methods used to estimate the number of deaths caused by the H5N1 virus?

QUESTIONS FOR RHETORICAL ANALYSIS

5. Who is the intended audience for this article? Cite evidence in the article that supports your answer.
6. This chapter introduces various ways authors appeal to ethos. Quote and analyze examples of ethos appeals in Best's article.

THINKING AND WRITING ABOUT THE TOPIC

Do an online search for statistics about any topic, such as the percentage of the U.S. population with tattoos, with a bachelor's degree, without health insurance, or who divorce, cheat on their tax returns, and the like. Search until you find two or more conflicting estimates about the same topic from different sources. Copy and paste the statistics and the surrounding text into a new document and identify your sources. Then, in an essay written for other students, analyze the statistics. Here are a few questions to get you started:

- What factors can explain the differences in the statistics? (Different definition of terms? Different sampling methods? Motivations of the authors?)
- What information is given in the sources about *who* determined the estimates (statistics)?
- *How* were the statistics determined and *when* were they determined?
- What additional information about the methods do you need before you can assess the statistics?
- Are there red flags that indicate you should be cautious about believing any of the statistics you found (e.g., an unreliable publication site; big

round numbers; undefined terms; numbers that you find hard to believe)?

- Which statistic appears to be most reliable? What makes it most trustworthy?

WORKS CITED

Binns, Corey. "The Hidden Power of Culture." *Scientific American Mind* 18.4 (2007): 9. Print.

Crosby, Sondra. "Seeking Asylum from Torture: A Doctor's View." *Annals of Internal Medicine* 147.6 (2007): 431. Print.

Dyer, Patricia, and Tara Friedman. "Gateway to Critical Thinking in Other Disciplines: A Study of Perceptions of First-Year Composition Students." Conference on College Composition and Communication Presentation. 23 March 2012. St. Louis, MO.

Ericsson, K. Anders, Ralf Th. Krampe, and Clemens Tesch-Romer. "The Role of Deliberate Practice in the Acquisition of Expert Performance." *Psychological Review* 100.3 (2003): 363–406. Print.

Garland, James C. "Here's How We Can Put College Back within Reach." *Tri-City Herald* 3 Jan. 2006: A9. Print.

Geer, John G. "The News Media and the Rise of Negativity in Presidential Campaigns." *PS, Political Science & Politics* 45.3 (2012): 422–27. Print.

Herrmann, Andrew W. "Continuing to Make the Case for Infrastructure Investment." *Civil Engineering* (2012): 14. Print.

Hersh, Richard H., and Carol Geary Schneider. "Fostering Personal and Social Responsibility on College and University Campuses." *Liberal Education* 91.3 (2005): 6–13. Print.

"Hurricane Katrina: Empower Black People to Rebuild New Orleans." *Black Scholar* 36.4 (2006): 1. Print.

Karcher, Carolyn L. "Reconceiving Nineteenth-Century American Literature: The Challenge of Women Writers." *American Literature* 66.4 (1994): 781–93. Print.

Lawrence, Peter A. "Men, Women, and Ghosts in Science." *PLoS Biology* 4.1 (2006): 13–15. Print.

Mau, Wei-Cheng, and Richard Lynn. "Gender Differences in Homework and Test Scores in Mathematics, Reading and Science at Tenth and Twelfth Grade." *Psychology, Evolution & Gender* 2.2 (2000): 119–25. Print.

Mazur, Nicole. "Putting the 'Social' Back into 'Science': A Policy Approach to Endangered Species Conservation." *Social Alternatives* 17.1 (1998): 25–28. Print.

O'Brian, John. "Another Report on the Age of Extinction." *Canadian Review of American Studies* 38.1 (2008): 191–97. Print.

Oduro, Francis T, Gabriel A. Okyere, and George Theodore Azu-Tungmah. "Transmission Dynamics of Malaria in Ghana." *Journal of Mathematics Research* 4.6 (2012): 22–33. Print.

Pulley, John L. "In Need of Remediation." *Community College Week* 20.16 (8 Apr. 2008). Web. 22 Aug. 2010.

Rauch, Jonathan. "Global Warming: The Convenient Truth." *National Journal* 39.10 (2007): 17–18. Print.

Rodriguez, Sandria. "What Helps Some First-Generation Students Succeed?" *About Campus* (Sept.–Oct. 2003): 17–22. Print.

Schnoebelen, Ann. "Report Examines Levels of Debt for College Dropouts across Sectors." *Chronicle of Higher Education* 59.32 (19 Apr. 2013). Web. 27 Apr. 2013.

Shapiro-Miller, Lauren B., Emily K. Heyerdahl, and Penelope Morgan. "Comparison of Fire Scars, Fire Atlases, and Satellite Data in the Northwestern United States." *Canadian Journal of Forest Research* 37 (2007): 1933–43. Print.

Stephanie Wear. "Finding Nemo on Your Plate." *The Nature Conservancy Blog.* 21 Mar. 2011. Web. 28 Apr. 2014.

Wells, Gary L., and Elizabeth A. Olson. "Eyewitness Testimony." *Annual Review of Psychology* 54 (2003): 277–95. Print.

Whitlock, Cathy. "Doing Fieldwork in the Mud." *Geographical Review* 91.1-2 (2001): 19–25. Print.

CHAPTER 4

Writing Academic Arguments

Most of the extended writing you do in college will be in response to *writing prompts*. Writing prompts answer important questions, such as, "What can I write about?" and "What is my purpose?" But these prompts do more. They also answer questions like, "What kind of reader should I imagine?" and "What role should I assume when writing?" In his book, *Genre and the Invention of the Writer*, English Professor Anis Bawarshi explains that the writing prompt "invents" a persona the student is expected to adopt while writing. Students must play the role assigned to them in the prompt; yet at the same time students are expected to respond in a way that makes it seem "that somehow their writing is self-prompted" (133–34). In other words, you are expected to write as though you are doing so for your own reasons rather than in response to an assignment prompt. You are expected to write with authority.

In this chapter, we'll consider how to respond to the complex rhetorical situations found in writing prompts across the disciplines. You'll learn techniques for deferring to the requirements of your professors, while at the same time establishing your authority as a writer. We'll also take a close look at two tasks implicit in many writing assignments: analyzing a situation and making an argument.

Understanding the Writer-Reader Relationship in College Writing

Sometimes the writer-reader relationship in college writing may seem contradictory. For example, you may wonder why your history professor asks, "What is the significance of this historical document?" when you know that your instructor already knows the answer. Such writing prompts seem to ask you to write to an *uninformed* reader, but, really, your goal is to convince a *more-informed* one that you have come to understand what the reader already knows—in this case, the significance of a historical document. This is no easy task. You are, after all, writing to an imaginary audience, while pretending not to write to the real audience (your instructor). In this section, we'll look at the ways writing prompts direct students to both surrender and claim their authority as authors. For illustrations, we will draw from a sample of 20 writing prompts taken from introductory courses across the curriculum. Together, they reveal that instructors expect students to analyze, argue, and write as an expert, all while deferring to the specifications of the prompt.

Deferring Authority in College Papers

In many ways, when you write for college you are expected to defer your authority as author. You must usually discuss an assigned subject or select from a list of topic choices. Many writing prompts explicitly determine the scope of your document, as seen in these examples:

> You must identify at least three of the four major kinds of irony in Saunders' story. (Introduction to Literature)

> You are required to analyze two different works, sections, or movements. (Music Appreciation)

These requirements determine *what* will be written about. Other requirements specify *how* the paper should be written:

> The body of the paper should be presented in a *narrative format.*

> [The paper] should be written as an *informative paper* and should contain the following three components. . . .

In these examples, the style ("narrative") and the purpose ("informative") of the writing are stipulated. Other prompts specify where students can obtain information for their papers:

> YOU CANNOT USE OUR TEXT AS A SOURCE OR A STANDARD ENCYCLOPEDIA, including Wikipedia or any other on-line encyclopedias. (Art History, original emphasis)

Words such as *cannot*, *should*, *make sure*, and *you must* are ubiquitous in writing prompts. The number of sources and the number of words are additional aspects of student papers often dictated by the reader (instructor) rather than determined by the writer. Specifications such as these benefit both student and instructor. Requiring you to use specialized vocabulary or a specific documentation style, for example, teaches you about the expectations of the discipline. Requirements about document length or source type make grading more consistent and fair, and of course such requirements help you to know "what the instructor wants." These specifications also demonstrate how the instructor can play a role in "inventing" a student's writing.

Concept in Practice 4.1: Analyzing the Rhetorical Situation in a Biology Writing Prompt

To see how a writing prompt shapes the student's writing, let's look at an assignment for microbiology from Professor Kristy Henscheid. Prior to writing this assignment, students completed a lab experiment in which they were asked to identify an "unknown organism." As you read, notice the various ways the writing prompt specifies the content and the organization of the student's report. A few key features are identified for you.

MICROBIOLOGY: UNKNOWN LAB REPORT

After you've completed the unknown project, you will write a report about how you identified your organisms. Being able to clearly communicate results is actually a key part of science!

The instructor explains the value of the assignment: communicating results of experiments is an important part of science.

I don't want this to be a stressful technical paper; think of this more as "tell me a story about your lab project (with science to prove your conclusions)." Think back to yourself at the beginning of the term: that's your audience. Use a level of detail you would have understood before you did this project. (*In other words: explain your project thoroughly, but overly scientific jargon should be kept to a minimum.*)

The "audience" is identified. In what ways should this audience influence the way the report is written?

You may be used to including quotations from your references in essays you've written in the past. In science writing, direct quotations are avoided. Instead, *paraphrase* information from your reference (rewrite it in your own words). Check out http://owl.english.purdue.edu/owl/resource/619/01 at Purdue University's Online Writing Lab.

Emphasis draws attention to important expectations related to writing in the discipline.

Layout / format:

- Type in a standard 12 pt font.
- Double space.
- I am not looking for a specific length (typically these reports end up about 6–10 pages).
- Figures (pictures, tables, flow chart) should be inserted in the report as close as possible to the related text. Do not just tack them on at the end!

Include the following sections. (You may want to add other information!)

Introduction (15 pts)
Briefly explain the project and its goals. A good introduction tells the reader:

The purpose of each section is explained.

- What you are doing, and
- Why it is interesting or important.
- Other possible introductory material to put your project in context:
- What's the scientific and/or clinical importance of identifying microbes?
- What do biochemical tests tell you about bacteria? Why/how are they used in identification?
- Where did we get our database of known results for comparison?

Questions help prompt ideas for how to write the introduction.

Results (25 pts)
Talk about how YOUR results led you to identify your organisms.

- There should be some prose in this section explaining your results.
  Don't just rattle off a list of results like "The phenol red glucose test was positive. The nitrate test was negative." (yawn!) Better: "This organism ferments A and B but not C or D, as shown by tests x, y, and z."

A warning is included, with illustration.

- Give brief explanations of what each test result tells you about the organism.
  You do not need to be as detailed about the biochemistry as the lab manual is! Remember your intended audience: you, two months ago. For example: say your organism gives you a positive result in the urea test. In explaining what that result means, saying "this organism makes urease" would probably have been confusing to you before. (It may be confusing to you now!) If you're just writing what the book says and you don't understand what that means, you should step back. (And ask me for clarification if you don't know!!) Instead, give a short *interpretation* of what urease does; e.g., "this organism is able to break down urea."
- Include your *complete* (revised?) flow chart.
  Yes, the whole thing (not just the branches with your organisms)!
- At least one microscope photo, taken by you, of each organism is required.
  This can be two photos (or more!) of each individually, or a single photo of the mixture. If the mixture, both organisms should be distinguishable from each other.
  I do not care what stain is used for these photos, but you should have a caption telling me what stain it is.

Underlining and repetition tell students that this requirement is important!

Consider: what other information should be included with a microscopic observation?

- Pictures might be useful. Refer to any figures and tables in your text when appropriate.
- Example: "A spore stain clearly showed that this organism formed endospores (Figure 1)."

  If you use photos not taken by you, make sure you credit your source.

  Pictures should have descriptive captions!

  You do not need to include methods or materials.

Students are given an illustration they can use as a model.

Discussion (25 pts)

First, tell me about your organisms. You'll need to do some research for this; your textbook is a good resource, and I've posted a few trustworthy online sites on [the course webpage]. Your research about both organisms should total at least **1 full page**. Things you might want to talk about:

Signal words ("First, Finally") indicate the order in which information should appear in this section. A minimum length is provided.

- Where are your organisms usually found?
- Can either one cause disease?
- Is either useful to humans in some way?
- Note that scientific names are *italicized* (e.g., *E. coli, Klebsiella pneumoniae*).

Another note about writing in the discipline.

Finally, discuss your project in general.

- How easy was it to identify your organisms?
- Were there any key results?
- Were there any places where you had problems? What might have caused those problems? How did you solve them?
- Any final conclusions / thoughts?

References (10 pts)

A bibliographic list of references you used for the project AND the paper.

Throughout the prompt, students are provided with resources to consult for help. Those resources include the professor!

- I don't require a particular format for the bibliography. Use what you're most familiar / comfortable with. (I can point you toward some guidelines if you're totally lost.)
- Each reference should be listed with enough information so that I can tell what it is without having to go look at it! At minimum:
  - Author

  - Title
  - Date
- DO NOT just list web addresses!
- Be careful using the Internet! If you do read something on the Web, *make sure you verify it somewhere else.* Links to trustworthy websites can be found on [the course webpage].
- Internal citations would be nice but are not required.
  If you'd like to learn / refresh how to do these, let me know!

Please be aware of what plagiarism is, and avoid it!
***Any** instance of plagiarism will result in a **grade of 0** for the assignment.*

We see here that many decisions are made for the student. The prompt specifies the organization, the sections, and the content for each section of the lab report. This information is helpful for students who have never written a lab report.

Claiming Authority in College Papers

Some writing prompts, in their specificity, may seem to limit your ability to exert your authority as author. However, most assignments actually encourage you to play the role of expert. We saw in chapter 1 that the goal of academic writers is to create knowledge; this same purpose is conveyed throughout our sample of 20 writing prompts. Business management students, for instance, propose a new business; nursing students create a way to teach patients about common health topics; and statistics students collect and interpret data about a population. In each case, students are directed to analyze and evaluate data to discover answers for themselves.

When your professors ask you to conduct original research, analyze data, make arguments, and use discipline-specific vocabulary and genres, they are asking you to "invent" yourself as a writer with authority. The lab report assignment provided earlier stipulates many required elements to help students who have never written a lab report, but it also makes clear that the student should assume the role of science researcher/writer:

> Include the following sections. (You may want to add other information!)
>
> Talk about how YOUR results led you to identify your organisms.
>
> Consider: what other information should be included with a microscopic observation?
>
> *Paraphrase* information from your reference (rewrite it in your own words).

Sentences such as these indicate that students should adopt the persona of a scientist, rather than that of a student completing an exercise designed by the instructor. The student should sometimes go beyond including the required elements and make judgments about what additional information to include.

In fact, when you refer explicitly to the assignment prompt or classroom discussions in your writing, you fracture "the illusion of autonomy" (Bawarshi 136). That is what happens in the following passage from a student's communications behavior paper. The writer's persona is one of a student writing for an assignment rather than an expert writing for his own reasons:

> As defined in Chapter 4, perception is "the process of collecting information and giving it meaning." For this assignment, we were asked to determine how other people perceive us.

The phrase "for this assignment, we were asked" shatters "the illusion of autonomy" that is crucial to establishing a voice of authority. Conversely, notice how the following passage from a student's history paper appears to be "self-prompted":

> With this Supreme Court opinion as the firm root of many segregation laws, it is clear that this document is very important in how America defined its race relations for the century following its creation. It reflects that, even after the conclusion of a war which eventually was focused on the destruction of forced human bondage, many still did not believe the two races were equal enough to be given equal protection under the law.

The writer is responding to two assigned questions (*What is the significance of the document? What insights does the document shed on the time period/topic?*), but the writing never betrays this fact. The writing appears to be self-generated.

Recognizing Analysis

National surveys of writing prompts indicate that most papers you write in college will involve analysis and argument (Head and Eisenberg, "Assigning"; Melzer; Wolfe). **Analysis** involves breaking down a subject—whether a poem, a dynasty, or an internal combustion engine—to determine how the parts are related or how they combine to achieve some purpose. Writing prompts that call for analysis might ask you to:

- discover how things are similar or different (e.g., *compare two forms of government*);
- explain how specific examples demonstrate a larger principle (e.g., *make a diagnosis based on a patient's symptoms*);
- describe how elements combine to make something work (e.g., *describe how various poetic elements achieve a poet's purpose*);
- determine which of two options is better (e.g., *argue for which approach you think is better for teaching arithmetic*).

Analysis involves looking past the surface and examining something deeply in order to discover a significance, meaning, or understanding that can't be gained otherwise.

Types of Analysis

Many college writing prompts call for one of the following types of analysis.

Find or Delineate a Recurring Pattern. Inferring patterns from raw data—such as seismograph activity, artwork, or economic data—is one type of analysis called for across disciplines. The following assignment from a sociology course illustrates this kind of analysis:

> Analyze the characters in the film that best portray the themes of racism, poverty, oppression, or discrimination. You should analyze and evaluate, not just report and describe their behavior.

This assignment is similar to most college writing assignments in that it asks you to do more than describe what you observe. You must "analyze" and "evaluate." In other words, you must make an argument for what your observations mean—what pattern or generality do the details reveal and why is the pattern important?

One way to avoid merely describing a situation you've been asked to analyze is to make two side-by-side lists. In one column, list the details you observe (summary); in the other column, identify what your observations *mean* or what larger pattern the details help to reveal (analysis). Table 4.1 is one student's response to an assignment to learn about a potential career choice. The left column reflects her notes from an interview she conducted with a pharmacist, and the right column reflects her interpretation of those notes.

TABLE 4.1

Distinction between Summary (Left Column) and Analysis (Right Column)

Interview Notes about a Pharmacist's Job	Analysis/Interpretation
Counsel patients on how to take drugs	Requires oral communication skills
Consult with doctors, nurses, insurance companies	Requires oral communication skills
Consult patient's medical history to ensure drugs won't interact	Requires training in chemistry
Counsel customers on what over-the-counter drugs to take for various symptoms and dispense prescriptions	Requires basic medicine knowledge
Answer customer and patient questions	Requires oral communication skills
Stand for long hours	Requires physical stamina

In the left column, the student lists details and examples (evidence) to include in her paper, but it's the more general claims or conclusions—the discovery of patterns—that requires analysis.

Compare and Contrast. Another type of analysis involves finding similarities or differences between two situations, as this assignment from a world religions course illustrates:

> Confucius was confronted with the general collapse of social, political, and moral order in China. . . . Many argue that the U.S. is in a similar condition. What would Confucius recommend for us?

Again, students are asked to do more than describe how two situations are similar. They must also draw meaning from those similarities in order to make an inference or prediction.

Comparison assignments don't always call for a decision about which of two options is better. Our student wanting to write about pharmacy careers, for example, might want to compare the duties of retail and clinical pharmacists. Table 4.2 illustrates some notes for that task:

TABLE 4.2
Notes for Comparison and Contrast

Retail Pharmacist	Clinical Pharmacist	Topics of Comparison
Works in a retail site (like Walgreens)	Works in a hospital or clinic	Worksites
Consults with doctors, nurses, insurance companies	Consults with doctors, nurses, but not usu. with insurance companies	Job duties
Gives general over-the-counter medical advice to customers	Monitors patient medication and progress during a hospital stay	Job duties
Requires bachelor's degree	Sometimes requires Ph.D. in pharmacy	Education

The first two columns include details about each job, but the third column identifies the general category the details illustrate. These categories can lead the writer to points of comparison (main ideas) to develop in a paper. Finding recurring themes in the details involves analysis.

Apply a Specific Analytical Template or Theory to a Situation. Other analysis assignments ask students to use disciplinary theory to explain a situation. Much in the way a referee's call may depend on his or her vantage point, the interpretation of events is influenced by one's perspective. Prompts like the one that follows, from abnormal psychology, ask students to consider a situation from the perspective of the discipline. Students watched a documentary and then were directed to make a diagnosis based on the symptoms they observed:

> What is your theoretical orientation to explaining the causes of eating disorders and what treatments would you recommend and why?

Students must look past easy explanations for eating disorders or explanations that may be popular in the media to consider less obvious (and more discipline-informed) explanations. As you saw in chapter 1, how writers analyze a situation (such as world overpopulation) depends on the "lens" or perspective from which they study it.

Evaluate Worth According to Discipline Standards. A similar type of analysis involves using the standards of the discipline to evaluate worth or value. In the following history assignment, for example, students are asked to determine the historical significance of a document:

> What is the significance of the document? What insights does the document shed on the time period/topic? What can we learn about American society from the document, if anything?

The last two questions make clear that academic assessments of worth are unrelated to personal preference. Whether or not you regard the document as personally valuable is irrelevant. Instead, you must determine what makes a document valuable from the perspective of the discipline.

Writing prompts across the disciplines make similar calls for analysis. Within our sample of 20 writing prompts from introductory courses, for instance, public speaking students are asked to "critique" a speaker's presentation. Business management students are asked to "justify" the feasibility of their proposals. Computer science students are asked to "explain" their "reasoning." In other prompts, the call for analysis is implied through value-laden words, such as "best" or "successful." In each of these examples students are expected to do more than summarize or describe what they observe or feel. They must draw conclusions and make an argument.

Concept in Practice 4.2: Summary vs. Analysis

Though summary and analysis are very different skills, analysis often requires you to summarize and describe what you've read or seen. To illustrate how the skills are used together to make a convincing argument, let's consider one student's response to the American history assignment quoted earlier. For this assignment, students read *The Slaughterhouse Cases*, written by U.S. Supreme Court Justice Miller during the Reconstruction of the southern states. *The Slaughterhouse Cases* consolidates the Court's 1873 decision in three cases, including *Butchers' Benevolent Association of New Orleans v. The Crescent City Live-Stock Landing and Slaughter-House Company*. The Butchers' Benevolent Association claimed that a monopoly granted to the Slaughter-House Company by the Louisiana legislature denied them "their property without due process of law."

The writing prompt has two parts: One part calls for summary of the document and another part calls for analysis. Daniel Vickoren, a student enrolled in American history, wrote the following summary in response to the assignment. Notice the underlined verbs used to identify what the document says:

> This document consists of the official opinion of the Supreme Court in The *Slaughterhouse Cases*. It examines each section of the article of the fourteenth amendment and uses the context surrounding why the amendment was written to help determine the intent of its authors. The document asserts that the fourteenth amendment was written solely to guarantee citizenship in the United States to all people born within its borders. It makes clear a separation of national citizenship and state citizenship and squarely proclaims that it is entirely in the powers of each state to define its own limitations on citizens and what rights they may or may not have.

When summarizing, Vickoren does not make assumptions about what Justice Miller *believes* or *thinks*; nor does he convey his opinion about the document. Instead, he identifies what *the document* includes or does. A neutral tone is one hallmark of good *summary* writing—as you will see in chapter 8.

But neutral, value-free language is not the hallmark of good *analysis* writing. Notice as you read Vickoren's analysis how he moves back and forth from analysis to summary. Here, again, is the assignment prompt (in italics), followed by Vickoren's analysis:

> *What is the significance of the document? What insights does the document shed on the time period/topic? What can we learn about American society from the document, if anything?*

> The *Slaughterhouse Cases* is an extremely important document in an analysis of Reconstruction. First, the Civil War had largely begun because of a series of disputes between federal and state authority. Subjects such as tariffs, banks, and slavery

The author states his opinion about the document's significance. The opinion is followed by evidence from the document that explains why the document is important.

all created contention between the federal government and those of the southern states, culminating in the secession crisis of 1860. This document interprets the fourteenth amendment and worked to clear any misconception about the bounds of federal and state power when it comes to citizenship. In one sense, this may have helped to solidify the newly reformed nation. Anti-slavery supporters were ensured that former slaves would be guaranteed American citizenship and would be granted those rights enumerated in the Bill of Rights while also giving Southerners a surety that the states would have sole purview over any right not listed in the Constitution or its amendments. In a period of turmoil and uncertainty such as Reconstruction, this may have helped many southern states better handle their transition back into the Union.

The author qualifies his claim ("may have helped"), thus anticipating any potential criticism of his interpretation.

A second paragraph explaining the document's significance.

At the same time, The *Slaughterhouse Cases* document sets the groundwork for legal discrimination. It deliberately states that the fourteenth amendment's "sole purpose was to declare to the several States, that whatever those rights, as you grant or establish them to your own citizens, or as you limit or qualify, or impose restrictions on their exercise . . . shall be the measure of the rights of citizens of other States within your jurisdiction" (par. 16). This line expressly allows States the right to "limit or qualify, or impose restrictions" on the use of the rights of their citizens. This created a situation where former slaves, while protected by the Constitution as American citizens, found themselves with few rights in many southern states. This decision is the framework for laws which were later passed to segregate and interfere with the free lives of former slaves. Restrictions entered into law which were designed to keep former slaves living in the rural countryside and, if possible, to pressure them into performing the same work they had before, sometimes even for the same plantation owner, as low paid farmhands.

The author of this document was likely a supporter of State's Rights and perhaps even a person who supported the legal segregation of the races through codified law. Some evidence of this exists in paragraph sixteen as mentioned earlier; however more evidence exists in the final four paragraphs of the document. To further strengthen the ability of the states to codify and restrict the rights of former slaves, the document goes as far as listing out the specific rights granted to American citizens in the Constitution. This would have enabled the Democrat controlled legislatures of the South to see exactly which rights they could not interfere with while allowing them to restrict and define all other rights not listed as

An inference about the document's author is made, supported with specific evidence from the text.

that state saw fit. With this Supreme Court opinion as the firm root of many segregation laws, it is clear that this document is very important in how America defined its race relations for the century following its creation. It reflects that, even after the conclusion of a war which eventually was focused on the destruction of forced human bondage, many still did not believe the two races were equal enough to be given equal protection under the law.

The author re-emphasizes the document's significance.

Making an Argument

The call for analysis is one similarity connecting most college writing prompts. Another similarity is that most prompts imply that the student should write an *argument.* To write an academic argument does not necessarily mean you will refute an opposing view. But it does mean you must support claims with enough explanation and evidence for a reader to see your conclusions as reasonable. Three types of academic arguments are described next.

Thesis-Driven Arguments

One common type of argument is the **thesis-driven argument** in which all of the discussion in a paper explores a central question or all of the evidence revolves around a central claim (or thesis). In these arguments, the thesis statement usually appears early in the paper. The following writing prompt, from a world literature course, illustrates a thesis-driven argument assignment:

> Use these recurring themes to come up with something to argue and prove about one or both of the epic poems. Your essay should be filled with examples and evidence from the text. . . . Include a thesis statement (within the introduction) that announces what you will show with evidence from the poem(s).

This thesis-driven assignment calls for *textual analysis.* The student would provide quotations or summaries to support his or her "reading" of the text.

In thesis-driven assignments, the writing prompt may include phrases such as "announce your topics" or "state your main idea." Some prompts even suggest an organizational scheme. The art history assignment that follows, for example, asks students to compare how a single art discipline (such as sculpture or painting) is used in two civilizations:

> Compare and contrast the ways your [art] discipline is used by the two civilizations. Compare how they make the art (process), what their art

means (concept), images they create (subject), and how they look (category and formal elements and principles).

For this assignment, you would discuss each of the listed topics, probably in that order, and provide details to illustrate the differences and similarities you identify.

Empirical Arguments

In **empirical arguments** writers describe observations and draw conclusions about data they observe. Examples include the microbiology lab report assignment we saw earlier:

> [In the Results section] talk about how YOUR results led you to identify your organisms.

Other empirical arguments ask students to analyze data and then base predictions on their findings. Many empirical arguments follow the IMRAD format described in chapter 2.

Proposals

Proposals are calls for action. They often begin with the writer establishing that a problem exists and why something should be done about it. In the following example, business management students are asked to describe their idea for a new business. Students are directed to:

> Provide documentation (references, links, and other documentation) that (1) justifies the feasibility of your business idea and (2) demonstrates that you are using current and appropriate technology in your business.

In proposal arguments, writers usually explain why their solution is better than other solutions and respond to objections readers might have (e.g., cost or practicality).

Argument type can vary by discipline. Empirical arguments, for example, are more common in engineering and natural sciences than in the humanities. Thesis-driven arguments are more common in the humanities and social sciences than in business. *But the emphasis on analysis and argument and the expectation that writers provide evidence to support claims is universal.*

Providing Evidence in Analysis and Argument Assignments

When asked to describe the writing they do in their college courses, students in focus groups have described it as "authoritative," "objective," and "disciplinary," but not "personal" (Bergmann and Zepernick 135, 130). What this means is that typically you'll be expected to provide more than opinions and personal experience as evidence.

Summary, Analysis, and Personal Response

As we've seen, summarizing is a skill you will use often in academic writing, but your college professors will also call for critiques, assessments, interpretations, or evaluations of what you summarize. Rather than merely repeating and responding personally to what an author has written, you'll be expected to analyze.

English professor Lee Odell offers the following illustration of the kind of reading response college professors reward. Passages 1 and 2 were written by students in a course on epidemiology (the study of disease). The students were asked to summarize and "comment" on research articles. Passage 1 is from an "A" paper. The first paragraph of the passage summarizes the research articles, and in the second paragraph the student evaluates and interprets the merits of the research she has read.

PASSAGE 1 FROM AN "A" PAPER

In each of the studies considered above, an effort was made to elucidate some of the specific epidemiological factors involved in the transmission of hydatid disease. In each case, field research was carried out in the affected communities: many people were interviewed and given tests for echinococcosis; dogs and sheep in these areas were often tested as well. . . . In the end each study linked infected sheep to infected dogs; infective dogs were linked to human infection via permissive husbandry practices. Nevertheless, I feel that a number of important issues were overlooked by these studies; I have expanded upon these below.

The writer begins her analysis: She will identify issues left unexamined in the research articles.

It would be particularly useful to learn exactly how prevalent *E. granulosis* eggs are in the grazing areas and ranching communities. Along a similar line of investigation, it might be equally valuable to determine the ways in which eggs come to be ingested by man; i.e., how is infection linked to hygiene? Are *E. granulosis* eggs commonly found in the ranchers' food? Is the local water supply contaminated with eggs? Certainly an investigation of this type would also want to learn more about the climatic conditions under which *E. granulosis* eggs are viable and available for transmission. These issues were only tangentially addressed, at best, in any of the studies considered. To the extent that they were not considered or seriously acknowledged as important issues, I feel that these studies are, in one sense, deficient. (qtd. in Odell 90–91)

The writer identifies specific questions important to understanding how the disease is transmitted. These are questions the research articles did not address.

The student makes a judgment of worth.

In the second paragraph, the student demonstrates critical reading. As explained in chapter 3, critical readers don't accept all claims at face value. They critique; they evaluate. They ask questions—not just about what's written but also about what's not written.

In contrast, here is an excerpt from a "C" paper, written about research articles on parasitic diseases. Notice that the student's response is personal:

PASSAGE 2 FROM A "C" PAPER

In all parasitic diseases which involve a parasite having a complex life cycle, it is interesting to find out how the various stages of the parasite seek out their specific intermediate hosts. Host finding is never a guaranteed process in nature, and it is amazing to realize how many larvae never make it to the adult stage. In adapting to this stress of survival, most parasites expend a large amount of energy in reproduction. In endemic areas this is unfortunate for man and in order to prevent a high incidence of disease, man must learn to control the parasite population. (qtd. in Odell 91)

The student identifies what he found personally interesting.

Here is another comment about what the student found "amazing."

In this passage, the student focuses on what he found personally "interesting," "amazing," and "unfortunate" in the reading. There is evaluation of why the student found the topic interesting, but no evaluation of the research itself.

In Passages 1 and 2, we see three types of statements: statements of summary, statements of evaluation (analysis), and statements of personal response. The first two are commonplace in academic writing; the third (personal response) is far less common. A comparison of the language in the two passages illustrates the difference between these types of statements:

Statements of Summary	Statements of Evaluation	Statements of Personal Response
In each of the studies considered above, an effort was made to elucidate some of the specific epidemiological factors . . .	Important issues were overlooked . . .	It is interesting to find . . .
In each case, field research was carried out in the affected communities . . .	It would be particularly useful to learn . . .	It is amazing to realize . . .

Notice the expressions in the far right column are more "personal" but not because they include first-person pronouns. They are more personal because they express personal judgments about what the writer finds interesting. They are the equivalent of "I like" or "I don't like" statements. In academic writing, instead of merely citing your personal preferences, you must cite *evidence* to demonstrate that what you believe is also valid or reasonable for others to believe. Reviewed in the following sections are guidelines for including various types of evidence in academic arguments.

Published Quantitative Data

Quantitative evidence, such as studies and statistics, is common in academic writing, but as explained in chapter 3, and illustrated by Joel Best in articles found after that chapter, "facts" and statistics generated by conducting studies and surveys are only educated guesses. For these conclusions to be convincing evidence, you must explain how the researchers reached their conclusions. For example, how was the sample chosen? How did the researchers gather their data? Before your readers can determine that quantitative evidence is reliable, they need to know how the information was obtained. (See chapter 3 for a full discussion of this topic.)

Personal Observation

Empirical arguments involve describing what you've observed or experienced. This type of evidence is usually more limited in scope than studies or surveys you read about, but following a few guidelines can help you demonstrate that your observations—though limited—have merit.

- **Give details.** Just as you should provide details about the studies and surveys others conduct, you should provide details about your own observations. Readers need details—to visualize what you describe, to remember what you describe, and to *believe* what you describe. What or who did you observe? How many times? Where, when, and in what context?
- **Establish that the cases you observed are typical.** Be specific about what you observed, but also try to show that what you observed is representative. Student Michaela Cullington does this in the following paragraph from a paper written for her English composition course. Here she is describing the research she conducted on texting habits:

> To let students speak for themselves about how their texting habits were influencing their writing, I created a list of questions for seven high school and college students, some of my closest and most reliable friends. Although the number of respondents was small, I could trust my knowledge of them to help me best interpret their responses. *In addition, these students are very different from one another, which I believed would allow for a wide array of thoughts and opinions on the issue.* I was thus confident in their answers regarding reliability and diversity,

> but was cautious not to make too many assumptions because of the small sample size. (Cullington 92–93, emphasis added)

Cullington indicates her small sample was representative by noting that participants held "a wide array of thoughts and opinions on the issue."

- **Acknowledge limitations.** Show that you are fair minded enough to recognize weaknesses in your own evidence. Notice how Cullington acknowledges the limitations of her research:

> I was thus confident in their answers regarding reliability and diversity, *but was cautious not to make too many assumptions because of the small sample size.* (Cullington 93, emphasis added)

By acknowledging the small sample size, Cullington anticipates objections readers may have (a standard move in academic writing).

Textual Evidence

Many college assignments involve analyzing written texts, such as novels, articles, or historical documents. In this case, evidence in your paper will come directly from the text in the form of summary, paraphrase, or quotations (skills taught in chapter 8).

It's important when using textual evidence to explain what the evidence means. The following assignment from a literature course explicitly tells students what all professors expect:

> For this essay, you will need to make a claim and then support it with evidence from the text. Then, and this is most important, you will need to explain how and why the evidence you provide supports your claim. This is called critical thinking, and it requires defending your response so that others can understand it. If you merely make a claim and provide a piece of evidence from the text and move on without analyzing how and why your evidence supports your claim, then you have left the work to me. I will not do it, so get in the habit of explaining yourself clearly and with depth. Remember, it is your responsibility to show your reader how and why what you claim is true.

Take this professor's advice: Don't rely on readers to interpret textual evidence as you have. Lead them to see what you see.

Good textual analysis writing includes several features:

- **Context.** The writer provides enough context to allow those who have not read the text to understand the discussion.
- **Claims and evidence.** The analysis is an argument. Claims are supported with evidence from the text.

- **Explicit explanation of the textual evidence.** The point of the textual evidence provided is stated explicitly. Many writers introduce their reiteration of quotations or summary with expressions like *in other words* or *that is.*

Many writing prompts that call for textual evidence remind students to document sources and avoid plagiarism. The microbiology assignment, for example, includes this passage:

Please be aware of what plagiarism is, and avoid it!
Any *instance of plagiarism will result in a* ***grade of 0*** *for the assignment.*

In every discipline, failure to acknowledge sources of information or copying the words of others without indicating that you are quoting is a serious offense. This topic is discussed in more detail in chapter 8.

Responding Effectively to Writing Prompts

As we've seen in this chapter, the rhetorical situation created in assignment prompts is complicated, asking you to both claim authority and defer authority. Further, the skills involved in college writing are sophisticated, requiring analysis and argument. The following tips will help you to respond effectively to the writing prompts you receive.

- **Reflect on what the assignment means and plan your response.** Understanding what you are being asked to do and taking time to reflect on how to approach the task are important initial steps to responding to any assignment. Here is how one mathematics student describes her process for writing proofs:

  > I read the problems the day I get them or soon thereafter. I usually have to read them a lot of times before I even understand what is going on in them. But half the battle is knowing what's going on, so I try to get that done as soon as I can. I look for words I've heard before and think about whether I've seen anything similar. I usually write a "translation" to the side of the problem, something that helps me remember what the problem is asking when I go back to it later. (qtd. in Bahls 34)

  Reading and rereading the prompt and "translating" its meaning in the margins are good practices for any student. Consider various approaches to responding to the prompt. Jot down ideas, information, or questions, outline issues, draw diagrams and pictures, or break complex problems into simpler steps. Writers who (1) identify their goals, (2) identify the needs and knowledge of their readers, and (3) develop a plan for achieving those goals *before* they write tend to produce higher-quality papers than those who don't invest time in thinking about the rhetorical situation before writing (Cary et al.).

- **Pay attention to the details.** Highlighted or repeated statements in a writing prompt often reveal important information about the assignment. Don't overlook details about intended audience, types of sources, length of document, or required topics. When a writing prompt includes language like "must," "be sure to," or "do not," take these hints literally. Some instructors provide step-by-step guides or checklists detailing assignment requirements. These provide you with important clues to what your professor expects.
- **Study examples.** When researchers Gerald Nelms and Ronda Leathers Dively interviewed college instructors, they discovered no consistency in their use of terms like *written assignments, weekly writings,* or *papers* (227). Because different professors may define common assignment types differently (e.g., journal, research paper, argument), it's important to study any sample papers your instructor or textbook provides.
- **Ask questions.** Although the writing prompts will answer many important questions, don't hesitate to ask your instructors questions as well. In one large survey of students at six colleges, 76% of the 2,318 respondents reported that they considered writing prompts very helpful; but an even larger percentage of students (82%) identified another resource as very helpful: e-mails from the instructor written in response to students' questions about assignments (Head and Eisenberg, "Lessons Learned" 30).
- **Write with authority.** Address the reader with confidence. Use the language of the discipline. Marshal evidence. Analyze the evidence. Make an argument. Sounding like an expert is no easy feat—not even for those who are, in fact, experts! But even in introductory courses, professors want students to use the vocabulary and theory of the discipline. They want you to analyze and conduct original research. They want you to write with authority. How you can convey that sense of authority in your papers is the topic of the next two chapters.

Applying the Concepts to Reading: *Analyzing a College Writing Prompt from Music Appreciation*

Provided next is part of a writing prompt written by Professor Bob Pedersen for Music Appreciation (Music 105). Analyze the prompt to determine what it reveals about the rhetorical situation. Consider the following questions:

1. What is the purpose of this assignment?

2. What role(s) does the prompt ask the student to play and how is that conveyed in the instructions? Who is the stated or implied “audience”? In what ways should that audience shape the way a student writes?
3. What aspects of the assignment are required? What (if any) aspects of the assignment are optional? What are some of the decisions the student writer must make?
4. What kinds of analysis or argument are called for? What kinds of evidence are required?
5. What does the prompt reveal about the practices and values of the discipline? How might a student respond to the assignment in a way that establishes his or her authority?
6. Does the instructor give students any helpful hints about what mistakes to avoid? What does the instructor emphasize as being very important and how is this conveyed?

TERM PAPER ASSIGNMENT: MUSIC APPRECIATION (MUSIC 105) 100 POINTS

Have you ever purchased a classical music CD by some composer you were unfamiliar with, only to find out that the liner notes (the little booklet that is packaged with the CD) contains little or no information on the music or composer? No wonder classical music CD sales are waning nationwide; record companies don’t provide sufficient documentation about the composer, performer(s), and music to help the general public understand and appreciate serious concert music. As a Music 105 student, you can do something to remedy this information deficit. B Pedersen, the president of Cantus Firmi, a new classical music recording company, has asked you to write informative reviews for TWO short music selections for a CD compilation of classical music. You are free to choose the two works to be on the CD, but you must provide historical and critical information about those works in your reviews. (See below for specific content requirements.) Your reviews of the two works will be combined with other students’ reviews to comprise the booklet (liner notes) that accompanies the CD compilation. Your reviews must be typed in double-spaced text and formatted as an MLA research paper. Aim for 1,000 to 1,500 words total for your reviews of both works.

SELECT ONLY TWO WORKS FOR ANALYSIS

You are required to analyze two different works, sections, or movements from a single composer. The composer may be chosen from the list of composers at the end of this assignment or in the chronology at the end of Kamien’s textbook. Each piece or section should be at least four minutes long but not exceed 30 minutes. Here are some examples to help you choose your works:

- The Allemande and Gigue from Bach's *French Suite in G Major* would count as two separate movements from a larger multi-movement dance suite from the Baroque era.
- Two scenes or sections of an opera, oratorio, or symphonic poem would be appropriate, as would two scenes from Aaron Copland's *Billy the Kid* or *Appalachian Spring*.

REQUIRED REVIEW CONTENTS

As discerning listeners, your audience for the CD liner notes knows the basic musical concepts and elements, such as melody, rhythm, texture, binary form, etc., so you must explain the pieces using technical vocabulary. Consider analyzing your selections from the perspective of Copland's three planes of listening: 1) sensual, 2) expressive, and 3) sheerly musical planes. The majority of your musical analysis should focus on Copland's third plane, but there's nothing wrong with sharing mental images or stories that the music evokes in your mind. The content of your liner notes should include a mix of the following categories of information:

1. Type of composition represented

What does the title mean? What is the form or genre and its relation to the period?

2. Significance of composition

Where, when, and why was the music written?

3. Background of key performers of composition

Use *Baker's Biographical Dictionary of Music and Musicians* or the Grove's Music Online to summarize the backgrounds of the conductor, soloists or other musicians on the recording.

4. Musical analysis of compositions

This section should be the dominant portion of your review of each work. Use narrative rather than outline style in your analysis. Here are some questions to help you analyze your two works:

The performing medium

- Is it a solo or a group? If a group, what size?
- Is it vocal or instrumental or both?

Melody

- Is it prominent and easy to follow?
- Is it rather low or high overall, or does it have a wide range?
- Is it smooth and flowing or made of short fragments?
- Are there repeated patterns or sequences?
- Is it rather plain or is it highly decorated (ornamented with trills)?

Rhythm

- Meter—duple, triple, quadruple, other?
- Tempo—slow/fast, rigid, flexible, varying?
- Rhythmic pattern—simple rhythms or complex patterns?
- Syncopation?

Dynamics

- Is the piece generally loud or soft?
- What are the range of dynamic contrasts—great or little?
- Are dynamic contrasts sudden or gradual?
- How are dynamics created?

Timbre

- What specific instruments or voices can you identify?
- Does the timbre change or is it consistent throughout?

Texture

- Mostly monophonic?
- Mostly homophonic?
- Mostly polyphonic?
- A combination of these?

Form

- Does the piece have much repetition?
- Is there a great deal of contrast or variation?
- Do you recognize standard forms? If so, what are they?

RESEARCH REQUIREMENTS

Follow the MLA rules for documenting sources in a research paper. A minimum of THREE published sources must be cited in your liner notes, either as sources summarized, paraphrased, or quoted verbatim. Document each source in a parenthetical citation in the body of the text, and list the sources alphabetically in a Works Cited list at the end of liner note text.

SOURCES OF INFORMATION

Excellent sources are available for historical and biographical information pertinent to your three compositions. Do NOT use Wikipedia as a source because academic readers question its reliability and credibility. Instead, go to the [college] library web page and use other online databases that are more appropriate:

- Grove's Music Online
- EBSCOhost
- ProQuest
- Naxos Music Library

Applying the Concepts to Writing: *Responding to a Writing Prompt from History*

Imagine that you are among the students who receive the assignment prompt appearing next, written by Professor Chris Herbert for U.S. History I, which covers the colonia period to the Civil War. Then, after reading the prompt and corresponding documents, address the following questions:

1. Identify the problem or task assigned. What skills and tasks does it require of students?
2. Describe the approach you would take to prepare a response to the assignment.
3. Outline the major points you could develop in your paper in whatever order seems most logical. Beneath each point in your outline, identify the kinds of evidence or details you would include to develop the idea.

ASSIGNMENT FOR HISTORY 146

This assignment involves reading two documents [excerpted for this exercise]. The first is Andrew Jackson's "Second Annual Address to Congress" and the second is the Cherokee Nation's "Appeal of the Cherokee Nation." Both documents deal with the removal of the Cherokee, which would soon lead to the Trail of Tears.

The readings present different images of Native Americans. Make an argument about what these different images are and why they are being used. What purpose do they serve? Base your argument on cited evidence from the texts.

ANDREW JACKSON, SECOND ANNUAL ADDRESS TO CONGRESS (1830)

It gives me pleasure to announce to Congress that the benevolent policy of the Government, steadily pursued for nearly thirty years, in relation to the removal of the Indians beyond the white settlements is approaching to a happy consummation. . . .

The consequences of a speedy removal will be important to the United States, to individual States, and to the Indians themselves. . . .

It will place a dense and civilized population in large tracts of country now occupied by a few savage hunters. By opening the whole territory between Tennessee on the north and Louisiana on the south to the settlement of the whites it will incalculably strengthen the southwestern frontier and render the adjacent States strong enough to repel future invasions without remote aid. It will relieve the whole State of Mississippi and the western part of Alabama of Indian occupancy, and enable those States to advance rapidly in population, wealth, and power. It will separate the Indians from immediate contact with settlements of whites; free them from the power of the States; enable them to pursue happiness in their own way and under their own rude institutions; will retard the progress of decay, which is lessening their numbers, and perhaps cause them gradually, under the protection of the Government and through the influence of good counsels, to cast off their savage habits and become an interesting, civilized, and Christian community. These consequences, some of them so certain and the rest so probable, make the complete execution of the plan sanctioned by Congress at their last session an object of much solicitude.

Toward the aborigines of the country no one can indulge a more friendly feeling than myself, or would go further in attempting to reclaim them from their wandering habits and make them a happy, prosperous people. . . .

Treaties have been made with them, which in due season will be submitted for consideration. In negotiating these treaties they were made to understand their true condition, and they have preferred maintaining their independence in the Western forests to submitting to the laws of the States in which they now reside. These treaties, being probably the last which will ever be made with them, are characterized by great liberality on the part of the Government. They give the Indians a liberal sum in consideration of their removal, and comfortable subsistence on their arrival at their new homes. If it be their real interest to maintain a separate existence, they will there be at liberty to do so without the inconveniences and vexations to which they would unavoidably have been subject in Alabama and Mississippi.

Humanity has often wept over the fate of the aborigines of this country, and Philanthropy has been long busily employed in devising means to avert it, but its progress has never for a moment been arrested, and one by one have many powerful tribes disappeared from the earth. To follow to the tomb the last of his race and to tread on the graves of extinct nations excite melancholy reflections. But true philanthropy reconciles the mind to these vicissitudes as it does to the extinction of one generation to make room for another. . . .

Philanthropy could not wish to see this continent restored to the condition in which it was found by our forefathers. What good man would prefer a country covered with forests and ranged by a few thousand savages to our extensive Republic, studded with cities, towns, and prosperous farms, embellished with all the improvements which art can devise or industry execute, occupied by more than 12,000,000 happy people, and filled with all the blessings of liberty, civilization, and religion?

The present policy of the Government is but a continuation of the same progressive change by a milder process. The tribes which occupied the countries now constituting the Eastern States were annihilated or have melted away to make room for the whites. The waves of population and civilization are rolling to the westward, and we now propose to acquire the countries occupied by the red men of the South and West by a fair exchange, and, at the expense of the United States, to send them to a land where their existence may be prolonged and perhaps made perpetual. Doubtless it will be painful to leave the graves of their fathers; but what do they more than our ancestors did or than our children are now doing? To better their condition in an unknown land our forefathers left all that was dear in earthly objects. Our children by thousands yearly leave the land of their birth to seek new homes in distant regions. Does Humanity weep at these painful separations from everything, animate and inanimate, with which the young heart has become entwined? Far from it. It is rather a source of joy that our country affords scope where our young population may range unconstrained in body or in mind, developing the power and faculties of man in their highest perfection. These remove hundreds and almost thousands of miles at their own expense, purchase the lands they occupy, and support themselves at their new homes from the moment of their arrival. Can it be cruel in this Government when, by events which it can not control, the Indian is made discontented in his ancient home to purchase his lands, to give him a new and extensive territory, to pay the expense of his removal, and support him a year in his new abode? How many thousands of our own people would gladly embrace the opportunity of removing to the West on such conditions! If the offers made to the Indians were extended to them, they would be hailed with gratitude and joy.

And is it supposed that the wandering savage has a stronger attachment to his home than the settled, civilized Christian? Is it more afflicting to him to leave the graves of his fathers than it is to our brothers and children? Rightly considered, the policy of the General Government toward the red man is not only liberal, but generous. He is unwilling to submit to the laws of the States and mingle with their population. To save him from this alternative, or perhaps utter annihilation, the General Government kindly offers him a new home, and proposes to pay the whole expense of his removal and settlement. . . .

The Indians may leave the State or not, as they choose. The purchase of their lands does not alter in the least their personal relations with the State government. No act of the General Government has ever been deemed necessary to give the States jurisdiction over the persons of the Indians. That they possess by virtue of their sovereign power within their own limits in as full a manner before as after the purchase of the Indian lands; nor can this Government add to or diminish it.

May we not hope, therefore, that all good citizens, and none more zealously than those who think the Indians oppressed by subjection to the laws of the States, will unite in attempting to open the eyes of those children of the forest to their true condition, and by a speedy removal to relieve them from all the evils, real or imaginary, present or prospective, with which they may be supposed to be threatened.

APPEAL OF THE CHEROKEE NATION (1830)

More than a year ago we were officially given to understand by the secretary of war, that the president could not protect us against the laws of Georgia. This information was entirely unexpected; as it went upon the principle, that treaties made between the United States and the Cherokee nation have no power to withstand the legislation of separate states; and of course, that they have no efficacy whatever, but leave our people to the mercy of the neighboring whites, whose supposed interests would be promoted by our expulsion, or extermination. . . .

Before we close this address, permit us to state what we conceive to be our relations with the United States. . . . The United States never subjugated the Cherokees; on the contrary, our fathers remained in possession of their country, and with arms in their hands.

The people of the United States sought a peace; and, in 1785, the treaty of Hopewell was formed, by which the Cherokees came under the protection of the United States, and submitted to such limitations of sovereignty as are mentioned in that instrument. None of these limitations, however, affected, in the slightest degree, their rights of self-government and inviolate territory. . . . In 1791, the treaty of Holston was made, by which the sovereignty of the Cherokees was qualified as follows: The Cherokees acknowledged themselves to be under the protection of the United States, and of no other sovereign.—They engaged that they would not hold any treaty with a foreign power, with any separate state of the union, or with individuals. They agreed that the United States should have the exclusive right of regulating their trade; that the citizens of the United States should have a right of way in one direction through the Cherokee country; and that if an Indian should do injury to a citizen of the United States he should be delivered up to be tried and punished. A cession of lands was also made to the United States. On the other hand, the United States paid a sum of money; offered protection; engaged to punish citizens of the United States who should do any injury to the Cherokees; abandoned white settlers on Cherokee lands to the discretion of the Cherokees; stipulated that white men should not hunt on these lands, nor even enter the country without a passport; and gave a solemn guaranty of all Cherokee lands not ceded. This treaty is the basis of all subsequent compacts; and in none of them are the relations of the parties at all changed.

The Cherokees have always fulfilled their engagements. They have never reclaimed those portions of sovereignty which they surrendered by the treaties of Hopewell and Holston. These portions were surrendered for the purpose of obtaining the guaranty which was recommended to them as the great equivalent. Had they refused to comply with their engagements, there is no doubt the United States would have enforced a compliance. Is the duty of fulfilling engagements on the other side less binding than it would be, if the Cherokees had the power of enforcing their just claims?

. . . .

We wish to remain on the land of our fathers. We have a perfect and original right to remain without interruption or molestation. The treaties with us, and laws of the United States made in pursuance of treaties, guaranty our residence and our privileges, and secure us against intruders. Our only request is, that these treaties may be fulfilled, and these laws executed.

But if we are compelled to leave our country, we see nothing but ruin before us. The country west of the Arkansas territory is unknown to us. From what we can learn of it, we have no prepossessions in its favor. All the inviting parts of it, as we believe, are preoccupied by various Indian nations, to which it has been assigned. They would regard us as intruders, and look upon us with an evil eye. The far greater part of that region is, beyond all controversy, badly supplied with wood and water; and no Indian tribe can live as agriculturists without these articles. All our neighbors, in case of our removal, though crowded into our near vicinity; would speak a language totally different from ours, and practice different customs. The original possessors of that region are now wandering savages lurking for prey in the neighborhood. They have always been at war, and would be easily tempted to turn their arms against peaceful emigrants. Were the country to which we are urged much better than it is represented to be, and were it free from the objections which we have made to it, still it is not the land of our birth, nor of our affections. It contains neither the scenes of our childhood, nor the graves of our fathers.

. . . .

[I]f they [the Cherokee] are forcibly compelled, by the laws of Georgia, to remove; and with these feelings, how is it possible that we should pursue our present course of improvement, or avoid sinking into utter despondency? We have been called a poor, ignorant, and degraded people. We certainly are not rich; nor have we ever boasted of our knowledge, or our moral or intellectual elevation. But there is not a man within our limits so ignorant as not to know that he has the right to live on the land of his fathers, in the possession of his immemorial privileges, and that this right has been acknowledged and guaranteed by the United States; nor is there a man so degraded as not to feel a keen sense of injury, on being deprived of this right and driven into exile.

. . . We know that to the Christian and to the philanthropist the voice of our multiplied sorrows and fiery trials will not appear as an idle tale. In our own land, on our own soil, and in our own dwellings, which we reared for our wives and for our little ones, when there was peace on our mountains and in our valleys, we are encountering troubles which cannot but try our very souls. But shall we, on account of these troubles, forsake our beloved country? Shall we be compelled by a civilized and Christian people, with whom we have lived in perfect peace for the last forty years, and for whom we have willingly bled in war, to bid a final adieu to our homes, our farms, our streams and our beautiful forests? No. We are still firm. We intend still to cling, with our wonted affection, to the land which gave us birth, and which, every day of our lives, brings to us new and stronger ties of attachment. We appeal to the judge of all the earth, who will finally award us justice, and to the good sense of the American people, whether we are intruders upon the land of others. Our consciences bear us witness that we are the invaders of no man's rights—we have robbed no man of his territory—we have usurped no man's authority, nor have we deprived any one of his unalienable privileges. . . .

We entreat those to whom the foregoing paragraphs are addressed, to remember the great law of love. "Do to others as ye would that others should do to you"—Let them remember that of all nations on the earth, they are under the greatest obligation to obey this law. We pray them to remember that, for the sake of principle, their forefathers were compelled to leave, therefore driven from the old world, and that the winds of persecution wafted them over the great waters and landed them on the shores of the new world, when the Indian was the sole lord and proprietor of these extensive domains.—Let them remember in what way they were received by the savage of America, when power was in his hand, and his ferocity could not be restrained by any human arm. We urge them to bear in mind, that those who would now ask of them a cup of cold water, and a spot of earth, a portion of their own patrimonial possessions, on which to live and die in peace, are the descendants of those, whose origin, as inhabitants of North America, history and tradition are alike insufficient to reveal. Let them bring to remembrance all these facts, and they cannot, and we are sure, they will not fail to remember, and sympathize with us in these our trials and sufferings.

Paired Readings from Information Literacy

"College Students Eager to Learn but Need Help Negotiating Information Overload," *The Seattle Times* ALISON J. HEAD AND MICHAEL B. EISENBERG

Project Information Literacy is the name of a series of studies designed to help educators learn how college students conduct research for their courses and in their lives. The project began in 2008 at the University of Washington's Information School and was cofounded by Alison Head and Michael Eisenberg, the authors of the next article. In "College Students Eager to Learn but Need Help Negotiating Information Overload," Head and Eisenberg address a common but unfair assumption about college students. The article appeared in *The Seattle Times* in 2011.

As another academic year draws to a close, college students are once again getting bad marks.

Seems like everywhere you turn—in a stream of new books, blogs, newspaper stories and broadcasts—the same story is being reported: Today's students don't study much. Many are unrepentant slackers, tethered to Facebook and their smartphones on their way to another party. Even worse: Today's college students lack critical-thinking skills, leaving them unprepared for the workplace.

Reports from campus front lines, especially from professor-authors, present the most comprehensive—and damning—arguments.

For example, the newly released "Academically Adrift: Limited Learning on College Campuses," by sociology professors Richard Arum and Josipa Roksa, found almost half—45 percent—of the 2,300 students they studied "demonstrated no significant gains in critical thinking, analytical reasoning, and written communications during the first two years of college."

In "The Dumbest Generation: How the Digital Age Stupefies Young Americans and Jeopardizes Our Future," Mark Bauerlein, professor of English at Emory University, concludes, "the intellectual future of the United States looks dim."

While our own research findings from the University of Washington's Project Information Literacy Study have confirmed today's college students struggle, our ongoing study adds another dimension to what is going on in the academy.

All is not lost! Most of the students we studied across all types of higher-education institutions in the U.S. still attend college to learn, but many are afraid of getting lost in a thicket of information overload they cannot dodge.

Our research tells us information literacy is a critical component of the larger concerns facing higher-education institutions today, along with challenges of multiculturalism, massive budget cuts, helicopter parents, grade inflation, limitations of K-12 education and preparation for college, and adapting to an ever-changing information-technology landscape.

Since 2008, we have been studying the information-literacy skills of students—the ability to recognize when information is needed, then locate, evaluate and put that information to effective use. As information scientists, we believe these skills are essential to critical thinking, lifelong learning and succeeding in life, the work force and in a democratic society.

We surveyed and interviewed more than 10,000 U.S. students at 31 U.S. colleges and universities, including undergraduates enrolled at UW, Harvard, Ohio State University, University of Michigan and community colleges, such as Shoreline Community College. We found no matter where students are enrolled, no matter what information resources they have at their disposal, and no matter how much time they have, the abundance of information technology and the proliferation of digital information resources have made research uniquely paradoxical.

Information is now as infinite as the universe, but finding the answers needed is harder than ever.

Our ongoing research confirms proficiency in information problem solving is urgent, given the dauntingly vast and complex wilderness of information available digitally. As one student in humanities said during one of our focus groups, "What's so frustrating to me about conducting research is the more you know, the more you realize how little you know—it's depressing, frustrating and suffocating."

When we surveyed undergraduates last spring in a large-scale survey, eight in 10 of our 8,353 respondents reported having overwhelming difficulty even starting research assignments and determining the nature and scope of what was expected of them.

Nearly half of the students in our survey sample experienced nagging uncertainty about how to conclude and assess the quality of their research efforts. They struggled with the same frustrating open-endedness whether they were researching something for a college course or in their personal lives.

Almost every student surveyed used a risk-averse and consistent strategy that closes the aperture of information available in order to cope. Many respondents reported relying on the same few tried and true resources—course readings, Google, library databases, instructors and Wikipedia—to control the staggering amount of information available.

This strategy, of course, underscores the gap between the plethora of Web sources and rich information campus libraries make available to students and the sources students actually use: a limited toolbox of familiar sources, which infrequently includes consulting a librarian or, in many cases, even going to the campus library at all.

While these findings are truly concerning—we would argue they are not entirely damning.

In fact, we found a gaping chasm between some of the widespread assumptions about today's students and what students themselves hold important about learning.

In our last survey, more than three-fourths of our total sample of students—78 percent—reported it was important to learn something new and conduct comprehensive research about a topic—along with the tangible rewards of passing a course, finishing an assignment and earning a good grade.

This finding squarely counters the conventional wisdom that characterizes students as worthless slackers.

Problems do not begin or end with students. Many—not all—educators are failing to teach students how to navigate a vast wilderness of information—to discern what they can trust, edit out what is unnecessary, redundant or unreliable, and focus on what they really need.

As one engineering student explained, "None of the old-timers—the old professors—can really give us much advice on sorting through and evaluating resources . . . we're kind of one of the first generations to have too much information, as opposed to too little."

We argue evaluation, interpretation and synthesis are the key competencies of the 21st century. These information-literacy skills allow us to find what we need, filter out what we do not and chart a course in an ever-expanding frontier of information. Information literacy is the essential skill set that cuts across all disciplines and professions.

It is time for many educators to stop lamenting about "these kids today" and retool and prioritize the learning of skills for solving information problems if students are to learn and master critical thinking at all. Or, as one student in social sciences we interviewed told us, "College is about knowing how to look at a problem in multiple ways and how to think about it analytically—now, that's something I'll use in my life."

QUESTIONS ABOUT MEANING

1. How are today's college students often portrayed by the media?
2. What are information literacy skills? Why are they so important for college graduates?
3. What should educators do to prepare students for research in the twenty-first century?

QUESTIONS FOR RHETORICAL ANALYSIS

4. Head and Eisenberg open their article with quotations from sociology professors Richard Arum and Josipa Roksa and English professor Mark Bauerlein. What purposes do those quotations serve?
5. The authors describe themselves as "information scientists." In what way is that title fitting for the work they do?
6. As you've learned in chapters 3 and 4, academic writers support their claims with evidence. What claims do Head and Eisenberg make in their article? What kinds of evidence do they cite to support their claims? Do you find their evidence convincing? Why or why not?

Excerpt from " Learning the Ropes: How Freshmen Conduct Course Research Once They Enter College," *Project Information Literacy Research Report* ALISON J. HEAD

In the first of the two paired reading selections in this chapter, you were introduced to Alison Head and Michael Eisenberg, cofounders of Project Information Literacy (PIL), a project begun in 2008 to determine how college students conduct research. A series of studies—involving focus groups, online surveys, interviews, and analysis of student assignments—have resulted in several published reports, including "Learning the Ropes: How Freshmen Conduct Course Research Once They Enter College," written by

Head in 2013. The full report has three parts. Part One compares the library resources available to high school students and college students; Part Two describes interviews with a sample of first-year college students; and Part Three describes an online survey with high school and college students. Included in the following excerpts from the report are the findings from Part Two and the author's general conclusions.

INTRODUCTION

In fall 2012, a record number of students entered college.[1] They spent 13 years preparing for this milestone, taking college prep or advanced placement courses, assembling extracurricular activities, and scrambling for high marks and top test scores.

As soon as the acceptance letters arrived, most students' planning went into high gear. They likely spent hours online figuring out which courses to take, scouring comments posted on RateMyProfessor.com, lining up housing, and getting to know their roommates on Facebook—all months before setting foot on campus as freshmen.

But getting into college was only the beginning. Many freshmen, who assumed everything they needed to know was just a Google search away, soon discovered they were unprepared to deal with the enormous amount of information they were expected to find and process for college research assignments. This transition from completing high school assignments to doing college-level research is one of the most formidable challenges that incoming freshmen face.

Project Information Literacy (PIL) is a national series of research studies about how college students find and use information in the digital age.[2] This report is the second in PIL's series "The Passage Studies."[3] The purpose of these studies is to investigate the information transitions that students make at critical junctures in their lives.[4]

In this study, we investigated the challenges facing today's college freshmen and the information competencies and strategies they develop and use as they advance from high school to college.[5] At the same time, we examined differences between high school and college information resources and how the students' research activities evolve. Finally, we asked what insights can be gleaned from studying this process in the hope that it will lead to improvements in preparing them for success in the digital age.

Major Findings

According to the first year students we interviewed, completing college-level research assignments was both "exciting" and "overwhelming." Many relished their newfound freedom to explore topics of their own choosing.

But most were intimidated by the plethora of print and online sources their college libraries offered and uncertain how to access or use them.

We found a majority of first-term freshmen faced challenges in both locating and then searching through research information systems and services on their new campus. Moreover, most found it difficult to figure out the critical inquiry process while developing competencies, practices, and workarounds for evaluating, integrating, and applying the sources they found.

Of course, not all new college students were "terrified" about getting through their first year; some simply stuck to Google and the other strategies they had used in high school. Others were interested in going beyond these strategies, but were worried about getting mired in the weeds of research. Librarians and faculty could steer these students in the right direction—but this got them only so far.

Our major findings are as follows:

1. Once freshmen began to conduct research in college for assignments, they soon discovered that their college library was far larger and more complex than their high school library had been. The average college library in our sample had 19 times as many online library databases and 9 times as many books and journals as the average high school library.
2. It was daunting to conduct online searches for academic literature. Nearly three-fourths of the sample (74%) said they struggled with selecting keywords and formulating efficient search queries. Over half (57%) felt stymied by the thicket of irrelevant results their online searches usually returned.
3. Learning to navigate their new and complex digital and print landscape plagued most of the freshmen in our sample (51%). And once they had their sources in hand, more than two-fifths of the freshmen (43%) said they had trouble making sense of, and tying together, all the information they had found.
4. Most freshmen said their research competencies from high school were inadequate for college work. As they wrapped up their first term, freshmen said they realized they needed to upgrade their research toolkit.
5. Many freshmen were in the process of trading out Google searches that satisfied high school assignments for searching online library databases that their college research papers now required. Yet other students said they still relied on their deeply ingrained habit of using Google searches and Wikipedia, a practice that had been acceptable for research papers in high school.

6. In the short time they had been on campus, a majority of first-term freshmen said they had already developed some adaptive strategies for shoring up their high school research skills. Most often, this meant they were becoming accustomed to reading academic journal articles. Some had discovered the usefulness of abstracts to save time and help them make selections.
7. Freshmen said they found campus librarians (29%) and their English composition instructors (29%) were the most helpful individuals on campus with guiding them through college-level research. They helped students chart a plan for tapping the wealth of research resources available through the library and formulating a thesis for their papers.
8. By the end of their first year in college, many freshmen appeared to have begun using the same kind of information resources that college sophomores, juniors, and seniors were already using, according to the results of our national survey conducted as part of this study.

. . .

The findings from this study are intended to give insight into the ways freshmen find and use information.[6] Given the limited size of our samples, however, these findings should not be viewed as comprehensive, but rather as exploratory and as part of our ongoing research. Our plan is to more rigorously test our findings from this small study in future research using quantitative methods and a larger sample.

APPROACH

Our studies are grounded in research on information-seeking behavior. As information scientists, we study the ways in which college students conceptualize and operationalize information seeking. We seek to understand their use of specific strategies, workarounds, and practices. We investigate these processes through accounts, reports, and experiences from students enrolled in US community colleges and public and private colleges and universities.

The purpose of this study was to investigate how freshmen were making the transition from high school to college as information-seekers, users, and creators. Few studies have investigated how today's first year students make the transition to college and conduct college-level research.[7]

Five research questions framed our study:

1. How does the quantity of information resources and services available through college libraries differ from those in the libraries of the interviewees' high schools?

2. How do first-term freshmen begin to navigate the new and complex digital and print information spaces that college settings present and that college-level research requires?
3. What difficulties do freshmen encounter during the information transition from high school to college, and how are these difficulties resolved, if at all?
4. What information-seeking strategies and workarounds do freshmen adapt and apply from high school, discover during college, and begin to use for meeting the needs of college-level research assignments?
5. What gaps exist between the information skills that freshmen bring from high school and the competencies they were expected to use for college-level research?

To explore possible answers to these research questions, we collected data during the 2012–2013 academic year using three methods: (1) a comparative inventory of research learning resources, (2) first-term freshmen interviews, and (3) an online survey.

Defining College-Level Research

At the core of our inquiry were questions about how freshmen learn and begin to put their skills for college-level research into practice. But what is *college-level research*?

We define college-level research as a highly inductive process, especially when it comes to completing research papers, the signature assignments in the humanities and social sciences. These papers entail choosing a topic, defining an issue, and taking a position backed by evidence culled from secondary resources (i.e., books, journals, and resources found on the Internet).[8]

The college research process involves interpreting, evaluating and synthesizing the information sources that have been found. Through this discovery process, students become more knowledgeable about a topic. They are expected to make inferences and formulate an original proposition, argument, or what some students refer to as their "thesis."

A critical part of college-level research setting it apart from high school research is the necessity of "re-researching" a topic. Like photographers, students need to focus on their subject and then adjust and readjust the focus, as needed, as the discovery process unfolds.

The expected depth of investigation combined with using primary sources makes college research time-consuming. It usually takes skill to integrate scholarly sources and infer a broader meaning from them. It takes curiosity and a desire to learn something new. It also takes keen organizational skills to keep track of and document everything that has been found.

In PIL's ongoing research, we have found the college-level research process entails learning and using information *competencies* and *strategies*. We define *competencies* as the skills and knowledge needed to solve an information problem. This means students both understand what action needs to be taken to execute the task and how to perform that action.

We define *strategies* as deliberate plans, often highly individualized, that use these competencies to achieve an objective, depending on the problem and other constraints, such as time, availability of resources, and cognitive abilities.

Questions about how students conduct research have always been interesting to librarians. These questions have become more complex as the information landscape has shifted in the past 25 years from one of scarcity to one of overabundance.

The availability of online information resources, available through subscription-based online library databases (e.g., InfoTrac, JSTOR, PubMed) and on the open Web (e.g., government sites, Wikipedia, Google Scholar), has significantly changed college-level research. Today's college students need to develop keen research competencies and strategies for tapping, evaluating, and sorting through the proliferation of information sources available to them.

FINDINGS

[Part One, a comparison of high school and college library resources, has been omitted here.]

Part Two: First-Term Freshmen Experiences

The large majority of today's college freshmen have come of age in a time when Amazon, GPS, Facebook, and flat screen televisions are ubiquitous—but jobs are not. Though most of them are barely old enough to vote, the contours of the digital age have already begun to influence these students' choices.

Most will take at least one online course, and for those that do, many will enroll in a massive open online course (MOOC) along with hundreds of other students from across the world. In many cases, they may never meet their peers face-to-face on their own campus.[9]

In this section, we present qualitative findings based on 35 interviews conducted with new freshmen at 6 US colleges and universities. We interviewed these students just as they were finishing up their first term (i.e., quarter or semester).

We explored the processes and strategies they used for navigating complex research-learning resources and systems to complete research assignments. Importantly, we learned about the difficulties they faced, and how they adapted.

Overwhelmed, but Excited

First-term freshmen in our sample had written at least two college research papers at the time of our interviews. Many had written on independently selected topics such as the rising costs of veterans' benefits, the efficacy of medical marijuana laws, the failure of welfare institutions, gun control debates, the imperative of legalizing euthanasia, and unintended consequences of nanotechnology.

Notably, all of the freshmen in our sample had completed some kind of formal library training during their first few months on campus. Some had become familiar with the library during orientation.

Others took part in a "one shot," i.e., a session about conducting library research that is taught by an instruction librarian during a visit to one of their classes. Still other students were enrolled in a for-credit course in information fluency, a required course taught by an instruction librarian.

Even though these background details signal a smooth information transition from high school to college, we found that there was more to the story. We first noticed inconsistencies when we asked first-year students for two adjectives to describe their feelings about finding and using information in college for fulfilling research assignments. The majority of freshmen used dichotomous pairs of words to describe their feelings: *overwhelming and exciting, overwhelming and amazing, scary and exciting*, and *stressful and competitive*.

For the most part, we found first-term freshmen were relieved to be free of rigid high school curricula.[10] They were eager to dive into deeper research projects on topics that interested them.

And yet, at the same time, they were overwhelmed at the thought of sorting through the voluminous amount of information available to them in college. In their words, the finding part of research was described as "nerve wracking," "foreign," "intimidating," and "terrifying."

First-term freshmen often pointed to extenuating circumstances when first discussing college research with our interviewers. These students said research tasks could be "too much work" and they had "too much studying," "too busy of a schedule," and "not enough time."

Most revealing, later into our interviews, we found freshmen say conducting research was overwhelming because they were unfamiliar with what college research entailed. Clearly, the high school experiences and the college library instruction they had, so far, did not prepare most of them for the rigors of college research.

How College Research is Different

First-term freshmen frequently mentioned four things that made finding and using information for college work different from high school

(Table 1). More than anything else, they said the campus library's substantial collection of books and journals had made college research different. In their words, the college library had a collection that was "ginormous" and there was "a ton of stuff," including both online and on-site resources.

The sheer multitude of available digital resources through the academic library—subscription databases and eBooks—surprised freshmen. For instance, many said they had never heard of library databases like JSTOR, PyscINFO, PubMed, and ABI/INFORM before arriving at college.

Many knew of just one or two library databases, such as Cengage's Opposing Viewpoints or Britannica, which they may or may not have used more than once in high school.

Table 1
What Makes Conducting Research in College Different than High School?

Four Factors that Make College Research Different
1. The academic library collection increases in size and digital resources proliferate.
2. The research approach involves combining and using new and different sources.
3. Research calls for selecting quality research sources, evaluated for their credibility.
4. Assignments require independent choices and encourage intellectual exploration.

Ordered from interviewees' most discussed to least discussed differences; n = 35 first-term freshmen, 6 campuses.

As a whole, many freshmen felt at a disadvantage from the start because of the limited research skills they brought with them. Most admitted they had only written one paper that qualified as a "real research paper" in high school. Usually this paper had been written for a high school English class. Now, they were being asked by professors in a variety of disciplines from politics to chemistry to anthropology to write research papers.

Freshmen said professors expected them to dig deeply into topics, more than they had ever done before. Yet, these students found they had little research experience from high school to leverage and apply to college research tasks.

As one freshman we interviewed explained:

In high school, because they don't have the resources, there is no way to prepare you for college. So if you don't have the resources, in high school it's like, "We're sorry, we can't teach you how to use them yet. Then you come here and instructors don't assume that you're fresh out of high school. They assume you're here to get an education and you're in college, so they say, "Okay, go research this." Yes, there's more resources and information, but we just don't know how to use them yet.

We found many freshmen were unfamiliar with the formats of scholarly publications before entering college. For example, many had never read the abstract in a peer-reviewed journal article. This was still the case even if their high school library may have had subscriptions through vendors such as EBSCO or ProQuest. Instead, many of these freshmen said they had relied on the public Web, not library databases, for high school research.

To a lesser extent, others said the approach to selecting research sources was entirely different from what they had learned in high school. Some said they could use only books for high school assignments, while others said they could use only online sources.

In college, freshmen found there were fewer constraints on the resources they could consult. They were now expected to integrate information culled from sources in a range of formats, such as scientific findings, books, databases, Web sites, and interviews.

In other cases, students said the college-level research placed a premium on "higher standards for research" and "finding good information," "using professional opinions," and "using valid statistics." These students said they were inexperienced with critically evaluating sources to judge their quality:

In my seminar, we're talking about scholars who study Neanderthals and my professor keeps saying it's important to look at their methods and the conclusions they draw, but I have such a hard time not believing what they are saying is 100% accurate, I mean why would it have been published, I mean why do they have a Ph.D.? In high school, in my Shakespeare class, we discussed whether Shakespeare wrote everything, even though some people have said he did not, but my teacher said, "Listen, Shakespeare wrote everything and other people just don't know what they are talking about."

For many freshmen, though, the biggest difference in college research assignments was that they invited intellectual exploration in ways their high school research assignments had not. Freshmen were often free to choose a research topic that interested them and select materials for building their own argument:

High school is much more structured, teachers give you an idea they want you to find, they point you in that direction, they give you links, and there's time as part of class to go do your paper in the library. In college, there are so few constraints in terms of topics—pick something that interests YOU and that has something to do with what we have been talking about in class, and that forces you to figure out what you are really interested in. For me, thinking about what I'm interested in is really scary, especially being forced to find something that I'm passionate about is kind of daunting.

We found first-term students in our sample experienced some of the same challenges adjusting to learning how to use their new campus libraries. For instance, some freshmen said they were puzzled by the organization of library materials. For example, their high school and public libraries had used one system (i.e., Dewey Decimal System), their college library used an entirely different one (i.e., Library of Congress):

From what I can tell, it's organized different than my high school library was. I think things are organized by topic here, instead of by the numbers on the book's side and it's different, I mean, really, how long have you been learning how to use libraries and how they are organized? And then they just kind of throw you in here—it's really my biggest change with information on this campus, it's frustrating to say the least.

In other cases, students discovered an inconsistency with interface design, especially search options available on different vendors' online library databases. As one student said, the high school version of ProQuest's database that she knew was like "a training wheels version" of what she found in college from the same vendor.

To a lesser extent, others said they were used to consulting a high school librarian. This librarian had been a jack-of-all-trades that could help with loading printer paper to finding a book on the shelves. In comparison, the college library had more staff and more support. These freshmen had little idea about who to ask for help:

When you look up something on PubMed it will have a link to a link to maybe another link and when you get to the third link you finally get actual access to the article you want, but sometimes they are dead links. In fact, I have a whole list of articles I can't access and I'm going to have to go talk to someone in the library, and I haven't talked to a librarian on this campus before, but do I ask them? Or do I go to the circulation desk and say "I need help with finding articles." I'm not sure whom to ask that's why I haven't done anything yet, but the paper is due soon, I just don't know.

Passage to Higher Education

Our interviews suggest the information transition from high school to college is challenging for first-term freshmen. Nearly all of the freshmen we interviewed were in the process of evaluating their high school research kit and retooling it—if for no other reason than to deal with the vast amount of information available through their campus library. For the majority of first-term students in our sample, this passage involved going beyond "Googling it."

We found freshmen in the sample were at different stages of this complex process. Some said that adjusting to college research had been easy for them. These students said they relied on Google searches and the few databases they knew from high school for completing college assignments. In their words, this relative minority of students were "sticking to their guns" and "using the same process since high school," since they knew it had "always worked well."

In far more cases, first-term freshmen were guardedly engaged. They had begun to explore their new information landscape—as best as they knew how. Their exploration often began with an online search in the library portal of the plethora of new research resources available to them. These students said they used academic literature for different reasons. Some said they relied on journal articles because this was what their professors expected. Others knew it was where they could find scholarly research and scholarly opinions. Still, others relied specifically on journal articles for the "speed of it" compared to having to read an entire book.

Difficulties with College Research

As they fulfilled their first college-level research assignments, difficulties inevitably cropped up for first-term freshmen. In order to understand the precise difficulties first-term freshmen had with college research, we conducted a content analysis of the interview logs.[11]

We used 14 individual coding properties. We identified these properties, based on the frequency in which freshmen described—in their own words—their difficulties with the college-level research process. If an interviewee mentioned having the same kind of research difficulty more than once in an interview, we only counted one instance in our results. Table 2 shows our coding results.[12]

As a corollary to these results and a basis for discussing their implications, we identified four significant categories of difficulties. Each of the following difficulties is discussed in detail on the following pages:

1. Formulating effective and efficient online searches;
2. Identifying, selecting, and locating sources;
3. Reading, comprehending, and summarizing materials;
4. Figuring out faculty's expectations for research assignments.

Table 2

Which Individual Research Tasks Were Most Difficult for First-Term Freshmen?

Most Difficult Research Tasks	Count	Frequency
1. Coming up with keywords to narrow down searches on the academic library portal	26	74%
2. Filtering and sorting through irrelevant results from online searches	20	57%
3. Identifying/selecting potential sources and investigative methods from all available	18	51%
4. Integrating and summarizing writing styles from different sources/formats	15	43%
5. Delineating assignment parameters and defining and selecting a topic	13	37%
6. Reading and comprehending materials from different formats	12	34%
7. Locating print information from search results (i.e., articles, books, chapters)	8	23%
8. Asking for help with research from faculty, librarians, or fellow students	6	17%
9. Evaluating sources for credibility and bias while reconciling different viewpoints	5	14%
10. Citing sources and using citation formats, based on faculty preferences	3	9%
11. Self-assessment of research process used and the sources found	3	9%
12. Technological issues, includes connectivity and authenticating logins	3	9%
13. Managing and organizing results from print and online sources	2	6%
14. Developing new understandings in order to formulate an original thesis/proposition	2	6%

Ordered from most frequent to least frequent difficulties with college research, according to 35 first-term freshmen, 6 campuses.

Detailed Description: Difficulties with the College Research Process

1) Formulating Effective and Efficient Online Searches A large majority said they were challenged by figuring out keywords for unlocking the wealth of academic sources available to them through their campus library's portal. Some said they used Google in a two-step workaround. In the first step, these students did a Google search to see what keywords popped up, and then they placed some of these terms in a library database's search engine. Others grappled with finding a preconceived idea of a "perfect source" they needed. These students often had trouble translating their perfect sources into keywords that met the precise syntax library databases require:

We had to do a paper about something that affects children in a negative way and I chose how moving affects children and their development and how they socialize with other people. It took me an hour to know what words to use. I was sitting there using my laptop and it was really hard because I was typing "families that move a lot" and I saw nomads come up, and I thought, maybe nomads would be something, like "nomadic families," but that had nothing to do with it. It's that anxiety when you type in words and none of the words match the results and you're like, okay, let me try this, and you have a limited amount of time—that's a problem.

Grinding through endless screens and trying to cull relevant material was another frustrating part of search, according to many of the freshmen we interviewed. These students said if they could "crank down"—narrow—their search queries beforehand, they were more likely to reap useful results. But for many, searching on library database interfaces was entirely new, and it was difficult to figure out how different search engines worked. After spending years defaulting to Google searches for finding information, others said they were lost when it came to incorporating Boolean operators and faceted searching into their strategies:

You have to really put in the right words into the academic search engine. Sometimes I'd put in a word like I'd do in a Google search and it pulls up things that I'm not looking for. The librarian came to our class and told us how to do this certain search logic, and so when you use that it is a lot easier to find the sources you're looking for. But, I've noticed that if you try to use an academic search engine like you'd use a Google search, it won't work as effectively, so it takes knowing how different search engines work.

2) Identifying, Selecting, and Locating Sources A majority of freshmen in our sample said they were overwhelmed by the variety, quantity, and newness of potential sources available through their campus library:

So, I'd go onto the Internet, click on library, click on e-sources, and, there would be all these different types of subcategories, and I was like, "What do I use?" Do I use EBSCO or do I use Britannica or all these other things? That is what made it difficult, because I really didn't know which link to click on.

Unlike high school work, college-level research seemed to have an infinite number of ways to find sources, according to the interviewees. First-term freshmen often described having floors of books, portals full of library databases, and scientific findings and sources from the public Web they could access for college-level research assignments. Some students were confused by the practice of combining familiar sources (e.g., books, Google) with unfamiliar sources (e.g., PubMed, JSTOR).

In other cases, some students had a hard time keeping track of notes, articles, and quotes from the different kinds of online and print sources they had found. In their words, hunting down print sources from a list of citations could be "tedious," "full of surprises," "unpredictable," and "confusing." Even though some said finding sources was easy for them, many often learned otherwise once they tried to locate specific sources:

> *One of the criteria was to gather an outside source on your own and then a source that Deborah Tannen cites in her book. So, at first, it was kind of a challenge to go through the whole list of sources and try to find one of the sources here. Some of them were books and some of them were articles. I would find a book but then realize the library has access through some other library on the other side of the state and they could have gotten it but it would have taken weeks, and it wouldn't really help. Then, I found some articles with reviews, but it wasn't the full article, just some review. Some were here, but not here and were at different libraries on campus.*

3) Reading, Comprehending, and Summarizing Materials Once they had some trusted sources in hand, about a third of the freshmen said they floundered with reading different formats and making sense of what they had found. Many had never seen, let alone read a journal article or an abstract before. At the same time, students wrestled with understanding what authors meant, given their lack of familiarity with scholarly language and writing style. A few students mentioned that they used an online dictionary as they read to help them understand the terminology in journal articles:

> *It's the reading, deciphering what you've found that's most difficult. So, I used an online dictionary to figure out* [what] *words meant for my paper on nanotechnology. I mean I read three sentences and I would need to go look up seven words out of those three sentences! It worked for me, I learned a lot from reading like this. It's the only way to understand what they are saying, I mean if you are not reading with a dictionary then you won't be able to get it. It's just what it takes.*

Some freshmen we interviewed said they had trouble with selecting meaningful passages and tying it all together. In their words, they had problems "connecting the dots," "figuring out the hook," and "discerning what you're going to use." They purposely selected sources from the results page that had a common thesis or similar interpretation of the same set of facts, as a way of gauging the credibility. As one student explained, "I know if it's printed several places, then it's true and I can use it." In other cases, students had trouble selecting which quotes to include in their papers:

> *How do you read a 30-page article and pick out a few meaningful quotes? I mean what is the right, exact quote to select and use? I am just kind of picking from here and picking from here and there for this paper. I just don't know. I mean is the writing I do in my composition course representative of the rest of the writing I do in college?*

4) Figuring Out Faculty's Expectations for Research Assignments
Even though freshmen said they had initially welcomed research assignments that let them define a topic independently, about a third of them said they were unsure whether the information they presented would meet instructor's expectations for college research. One student explained, "In high school you know the grading scale and you know what's expected of you, but when you come to a new place you kind of worry when you're writing papers, I mean, is this enough information for college? Do I need more?" Many first-year students said it was difficult to get "straight answers" from faculty:

> *Sometimes the hardest part of figuring out how to do the research for a project is knowing what specifically the professor is going to be looking for; it can be really broad sometimes the way the topic is presented. So, I ask a whole lot of questions to try and figure out like, "Well, what are you looking for? Should I use my own voice? Is it personal? Is it not 'I' statements or is it all just broad, general information you want in the paper?" So that part, just narrowing down what professors want in the first place is a challenge sometimes; some of them are really specific, and some of them aren't.*

Furthermore, students found it difficult to know how to format papers. According to some freshmen we interviewed, different professors had different preferences. These students were unsure about when to cite sources, how to format citations and in which, if any, particular citation style. Asking faculty for help or going to office hours "intimidated" and "embarrassed" some students. Still others said they welcomed—even depended—on faculty guidance and coaching:

> *I just came from a conference with the instructor. My thesis needs to be more involved, more specific, than what I have. I am writing about the Zodiac murders and the media. My thesis now is too general. It's all about the media because I got caught up in that, so now the sources and quotes I've got may not be as applicable if I end up changing my thesis. So, I have to go back and think maybe this doesn't fit and then I need to dig deeper on my research and find the opinions that go with what I'm trying to say. So, it's researching and then re-researching that makes it hard. And then I find something new and think "Oh, yeah, that may be better for me to use." It's more involved than anything I've ever done. I didn't do a ton of research papers in high school. I mean, oh God, I can't believe I am writing my third draft of this paper and I'm still not done!*

Taken together, our interviews suggest many first-term students were challenged in trying to map their limited research experiences from high school to far more demanding expectations for college-level research. More than anything else, they faced difficulties with learning to navigate their new college information landscape and going beyond simply constructed Google searches.

We conclude freshmen tended to fall into three broad categories, based on the amount of research they had done in high school. Some had no idea what a college research paper entailed and had never set foot in their high school library, if there even was one.

In other cases, some students had written one or two research papers in high school that were more like essays or book reports. These students usually relied on the public Web and sites like Wikipedia for research. A third group of students said they had written one or two papers in an English (often AP) class during high school. These papers required research on a much smaller scale than what they were now being asked to conduct in college.

Our findings suggest many freshmen were overwhelmed with the first part of the research process—finding—and were often relieved when they had some sources in hand. But other problems inevitably arose for most of them. They soon found themselves struggling with reading, comprehending, evaluating, and applying the scholarly sources they had found. These were the higher order thinking skills necessary for college-level research.

Freshmen Myths

Throughout our interviews, we found prior experiences and beliefs colored freshmen's perceptions about the college-level research process. As an exploratory analysis, we identified five recurring misconceptions our interviewees expressed about libraries, college-level research, and college assignments. These misconceptions might be called "freshmen myths."

Even though some of these myths may resonate with some readers they should not be considered applicable to *all first-term freshmen*. As such, the myths we have identified are not intended to represent the nationwide freshmen population. We would need a different larger, randomly-selected sample to make that generalization.

Still, we found these observations provocative and worthy of comment, even when generalizing only to our particular sample. What we are reporting in Table 3 is that there was a commonality in some of the myths freshmen in our sample discussed. This analysis provides a useful perspective for thinking about the preconceived notions some first-term freshmen may bring with them about research.[13]

Table 3
Some Freshmen Myths about College Research

Five Myths about College-Level Research Assignments
1. College is about being independent; most students don't need to ask for help.
2. Everything is online, so going to the campus library isn't that necessary anymore.
3. Reference librarians are available only to students who have gotten stuck on their research.
4. A scholarly database(s) recommended by a librarian is the only source worth checking.
5. Books on library shelves are outdated leftovers, rarely offering anything relevant to research.

Ordered from most frequent to least frequent "freshmen myths," according to 35 first-term freshmen, 6 campuses.

More than anything else, many freshmen we interviewed seemed to think college work required a high degree of self-sufficiency. These students said asking for help from someone in authority—professors, librarians, tutors, or writing center faculty—was unacceptable and simply not done.

In their words, their college research assignments made them feel that they were supposed to be "out there on your own," "kind of stuck on your own," and "people won't tell you the answers, they expect you to know." As one first-term student put it, "professors tell you this is your assignment and you're on your own to go find your way through the library, find your way through the Internet, and through the databases."

In other cases, there were freshmen that said college research involved using online sources and that was it. As one first-term student said, "Everything I needed was online, why go to the library?" We found these students were often unfamiliar with the array of services and resources through campus libraries. Some first-term students seemed to believe the library shelves were lined with outdated materials that were rarely useful or worth checking out.

Other first-term students in our sample seemed to think reference librarians were a specialized service—available to only certain students, not them. These students thought librarians were available by appointment for students who had hit a roadblock in their research process. As one freshman said, librarians are only for "dedicated students who know they need to seek out help."

To a lesser extent, some freshmen seemed to have an inflated idea of the recommendations librarians made about which sources to use, thinking they needed to look no further. As one student said, "There's a lot of databases, but the librarians showed us in the beginning there's the first five and these are the ones that are good for this, so I use them."

As one freshman explained:

That handout from the librarian for the paper about film, I went back to it and used it for my Chem paper. Even though the film databases didn't apply, I just went with the general ones the librarian recommended, like Academic Search. Writing the Chem paper there are just so, so many academic journals and finding papers that are at my level, I mean that I can understand, I didn't know where to start, so I went back to that librarian's handout.

Taken together, our exploratory analysis of freshmen myths provides insights into some of the beliefs today's incoming freshmen may bring with them about college, academic libraries, and the task of course research. Some new students' misconceptions seemed to persist. Other freshmen had already begun to question and even debunk these myths. These students had begun to learn and adopt the culture and practices of college.

Adaptive Strategies

Even though college research was challenging, a majority of first-term freshmen said they had started to develop adaptive strategies for carrying out college-level research (Table 4). In some cases, freshmen described new workarounds using online tools so they could upgrade their high school practices.

For instance, one student kept track of references using Google Docs instead of index cards as they had done in high school. Several said they used "citation linkers" such as EasyBib and NoodleBib. They used these sites to build their bibliographies as they researched rather [than] compiling citations as a last step in preparing assignments for submission.

Table 4
Adaptive Strategies for College-Level Research

New Information Competencies for College
1. Discovering peer-reviewed article abstracts and their usefulness.
2. Using Google for finding keywords and checking authors' credibility.
3. Replacing Google searches with Google Scholar searches.
4. Following the "citation trail" to find related research sources.
5. Using the college library as a refuge and source of professional help.

Ordered from interviewees' most discussed to least discussed adaptive strategies; n = 35 first-term freshmen, 6 campuses.

More than anything else, freshmen discussed learning adaptive strategies for *facilitating the use of peer-reviewed scholarly publications.* For instance, freshmen said they had discovered the usefulness of peer-reviewed journal abstracts. In their words, abstracts "saved time" because they "knew the argument" before they started and the entire article was "easy to figure out."

As one freshman said:

> *Journal articles are completely new to me, I never read one in high school. Three out of four of my classes here have used journal articles in some shape or form, so I've been thrown into a sea of journal articles. The abstract definitely helps, it's so lovely, and it gives you a summary and it says, here is what we tested, here are our methods, so look for this when you are reading the paper because if you can't catch this you are clearly on the wrong track!*

In other cases, freshmen said they used Google or another search engine in order to conduct *presearch* before diving more deeply into their research process.[14] Some freshmen said instructors had recommended "Googling authors" and "using an Internet search for authors" so they could "get some background context" and determine the credibility of a source:

> *I look up authors right after I have a source, much earlier on, to help me evaluate the source that really helped me a lot. On the Internet,*

> *I can see their other books. I try to read a little bit, the author's notes, commentary, to see where they're coming from. It's so valuable, I can't even stress how valuable. You need to know that, what their motivation was for writing the article, what their agenda is.*

To a slightly lesser extent, many said they had learned to use Google Scholar from librarians and writing tutors for the first time. Some were surprised to find the site was just a tab away on the ever-popular Google search page.

Using Google Scholar, instead of Google search, gave them an alternative to needing to use (and learn) online library databases on the library's portal. Others admitted Google Scholar was a stopgap workaround they could use for finding academic sources.

Some students said they had learned to mine course textbooks and journal articles for research references. Many had rarely used textbooks, other than in math classes during high school, so they were unfamiliar with their formats.

Finally, some freshmen said using the campus library was new to them. The campus library was, as one freshman said, "a quiet learning place." Moreover, freshmen said they could get help from reference librarians if they were in the library. Freshmen said they had heard about library services from multiple sources, including faculty, librarians, tutors in a writing workshop, or a classmate:

> *In the beginning I was doing my homework in the dorm but I was distracted by roommates. After a month, thanks to a friend, I decided to move to the library. Now I come every day. It helps me. I'm closer to everything I need. If I get stuck with a paper I can go upstairs to the Writers' Studio. If I need an article, the librarians are right here. Everything's closer. It motivates me.*

Taken as a whole, freshmen were at different stages of acculturating to the college research process. Most knew they would need to adapt and grow their high school research skills in order to make it through the next four years. This called for developing strategies for plumbing the depths of academic literature that their campus libraries made so readily available.

Those who were the farthest along had begun using advanced search features on the library's portal to specify certain databases. In some cases, these students said they were surprised to learn library databases trumped their typical high school strategy of "Googling it."

An "aha moment" came when they realized they could narrow down search queries on library databases. They found they could specify date parameters and certain journals more easily than when using Google.

Most first-term freshmen in our sample, however, had not ventured that far with their online search strategies. The majority of these students preferred instead to use a one-search box on the library's portal. In gave them access to articles, books, and much more in one fell swoop.

To a lesser extent, there were those who were "Google persistent." These students had little inclination to start using the library's resources or services instead of the ubiquitous search engine.

CONCLUSION

. . .

These findings lead us to conclude that even though today's freshmen may have grown up with the Internet, most may know little about how to best leverage formal channels of information that are available through high schools or college.

At the same time, our study raises important questions for librarians and educators. How large of a gap exists between what academic librarians and faculty teach freshmen about research and what freshmen still need to know? To what extent are the objectives of educational programs like the American Association for School Librarians' Standards for the 21st Century Learner achieved by high school seniors?[15]

How can college faculty, librarians, and staff most effectively communicate to freshmen about how the library can help them? Moreover, how can we teach students to progress beyond the research styles they learned during their first term in gateway courses, so that they are not bewildered during senior year when they face a far more demanding thesis or final project?[16]

These questions—and their answers—have significant implications about freshmen, about preparation for college, and about today's college students. An even bigger picture emerges using findings from our past studies of sophomores, juniors, and seniors. Collectively, our findings suggest that many students have trouble conducting research through their entire college career, especially as they enter their majors and research assignments become more open-ended and intellectually demanding.

For example, when we surveyed undergraduates in our 2010 large-scale survey, 8 in 10 of our 8,353 respondents reported having overwhelming difficulty getting started on research assignments and determining the nature and scope of what was expected of them.[17] Nearly half of the students in our survey sample experienced nagging uncertainty about how to conclude and assess the quality of their research efforts.

Based on our studies, we believe that the greatest gains may occur by focusing on teaching freshmen. This is a time when students are new to higher learning and most excited about discovering more about topics that interest them. Moreover, there needs to be coordinated efforts between librarians and educators, so that information literacy is taught in a progressive and contextual manner.

If instruction efforts are not stepped up early many freshmen run the very real risk of "flatlining." By this we mean that the research styles students develop during their ever-important first year could become static as they progress as sophomores, juniors, and seniors. Neglecting this will greatly impede their ability to solve information problems once they graduate, join the workplace, and continue as lifelong learners.

—AJH
December 5, 2013

NOTES

1. US Census Bureau (2012). *The Statistical Abstract Book: The National Data Book*. Washington, DC: US Census.
2. Project Information Literacy (PIL), http://projectinfolit.org, is a public benefit nonprofit (501c3) that conducted this study in partnership with the Information School at the University of Washington, http://ischool.uw.edu/. Alison J. Head, Ph.D. is the Executive Director of PIL and a Research Scientist in the UW Information School. She is also a Faculty Associate at the Berkman Center for Internet and Society at Harvard, http://cyber.law.harvard.edu
3. In October 2013, PIL released the first Passage Study report: Head, A. J. (2012). *Learning Curve: How College Graduates Solve Information Problems Once They Join the Workplace*. Project Information Literacy Research Report. http://www.projectinfolit.org/pdfs/PIL_fall2012_workplaceStudy_FullReport_Revised.pdf
4. We are deeply grateful to the PIL Research Team that contributed their time and efforts conducting interviews, coding logs, and providing support: Elizabeth L. Black (Ohio State University), Laureen Cantwell (University of Memphis), Kirsten Hostetler (University of Washington), Ann Roselle (Phoenix College), and Michele Van Hoeck (California Maritime Academy).
5. Communication about this report should be sent to Dr. Alison J. Head at alison@projectinfolit.org
6. A short video highlighting findings is available at http://www.youtube.com/watch?v=BWNGZUa952A&feature=youtu.be
7. For example, the Cooperative Institutional Research Program (CIRP) at UCLA produces the annual survey report, *The American Freshman*. http://www.heri.ucla.edu/tfsPublications.php and the National Student Survey of Student Engagement (NSSE) annual survey report, *Beginning College Survey of Student Engagement*. http://bcsse.iub.edu/bcsse-update/index.cfm.
8. We are grateful to Margaret Maurer and Constance Harsh, both faculty at Colgate University, who gave PIL permission for re-use of their essay,

"Doing College-level Research, with Advice on Avoiding the Plagiarism Question." It was first written in 1976/1977 and originally entitled, "Doing College-level Research, with Advice on Avoiding the Plagiarism Question" and was for internal use at Colgate. Since, the essay has been revised to include Internet research and posted on the Web, http://www.colgate.edu/offices-and-services/deanofthecollege/academichonorcode/theacademichonorcode/doingcollegelevelresearch
9. Nagel, D. (2008). Most College Students To Take Classes Online by 2014. *Campus Technology.* http://campustechnology.com/articles/2009/10/28/most-college-students-to-take-classes-online-by-2014.aspx
10. Eight in 10 of the interview sample had graduated from high school in 2012, the same year that we conducted interviews with freshmen in the fall.
11. Latent coding requires coders to make a qualitative and critical interpretation of inferred meanings in a text. The intercoder reliability for our results was .77.
12. Coders were instructed to code *instances* of when members of the freshmen interview sample discussed intractable difficulties, challenges, impediments, and frustrations with college-level research tasks.
13. Findings from our small qualitative sample would benefit from being tested using quantitative research methods and a larger sample. Our hope is to investigate these myths and the frequency of their occurrence in a future research study.
14. In PIL's 2009 study, *Finding Context: What Today's College Students Say about Finding and Using Information in the Digital Age*, a student in one of our focus groups talked about using Wikipedia for "presearch" to get background about a topic before conducting "serious research" and moving on to using library databases, 12. http://projectinfolit.org/pdfs/PIL_ProgressReport_2_2009.pdf
15. *Standards for the 21st Century Learner* (2007). American Association of School Librarians (AASL), Chicago, IL. http://www.ala.org/aasl/sites/ala.org.aasl/files/content/guidelinesandstandards/learningstandards/AASL_LearningStandards.pdf
16. Gateway courses are introductory courses in college that give students foundational knowledge.
17. Head, A. J. & Eisenberg, M. B. (2010). *Truth Be Told: How College Students Evaluate and Use Information in the Digital Age.* Project Information Literacy. http://projectinfolit.org/pdfs/PIL_Fall2010_Survey_FullReport1.pdf

QUESTIONS ABOUT MEANING

1. How is the challenge of writing the traditional "research paper" different for today's students than it was for past students?
2. Describe the sample of first-year students interviewed for this Project Information Literacy study. How do these students describe their research assignments? What are some of their most commonly mentioned frustrations and concerns?

QUESTIONS FOR RHETORICAL ANALYSIS

3. To find themes in the student interviews, PIL researchers conducted a content analysis of the transcripts. They determined the 14 tasks most frequently identified by students as "difficult." Table 2 lists those 14 tasks. What number is provided in addition to the actual number of students who mentioned each task? Why is this second number important for interpreting the data? In what other ways does Head ensure that information in the table is interpreted correctly by readers who skim the tables without reading the full report?
4. Most academic writing combines summary (of what the writer has read or observed) with analysis (what the observations mean). Consider the section titled "Detailed Description: Difficulties with the College Research Process" (pp. 174–78), or choose another section of the report. Where does Head summarize what students said in interviews and where does she analyze the data she has gathered? Identify some of the verbs that distinguish the summary from the analysis.
5. Three topics or "moves" are standard in conclusions to academic papers:
   - a review of what was discussed,
   - a reiteration of why the topic matters, and
   - a look to the future.

   Where or how does Head accomplish each of these moves in her conclusion?

THINKING AND WRITING ABOUT THE TOPIC

Write an essay in "response" to Head's research. To generate ideas, you might consider the following questions: What two adjectives would *you* use to describe your "feelings about finding and using information in college for fulfilling research assignments"? What student comments and experiences did you most relate to in Head's article? What techniques, resources, "adaptive strategies," or "workarounds" for locating *and* reading scholarly sources have you learned from this article or textbook or from your classes, professors, librarians, and other students? What "freshmen myths" about college research assignments would you add to those listed by Head? What have you learned about college-level research since beginning college, and what do you still need to understand better? These are only examples of questions you might address.

After generating ideas and examples, write an essay. Your final draft should include a central thesis (claim), supporting paragraphs, and examples or other types of evidence.

WORKS CITED

Bahls, Patrick. *Student Writing in the Quantitative Disciplines: A Guide for College Faculty*. San Francisco: Jossey-Bass, 2012. Print.

Bawarshi, Anis. *Genre and the Invention of the Writer: Reconsidering the Place of Invention in Composition*. Logan: Utah State University Press, 2003. Print.

Bergmann, Linda S., and Janet Zepernick. "Disciplinarity and Transfer: Students' Perceptions of Learning to Write." *WPA: Writing Program Administration* 31.1–2 (2007): 124–49. Web. 10 Aug. 2012.

Carey, Linda, et al. *Differences in Writers' Initial Task Representations* (Technical Report No. 35). Center for the Study of Writing at University of California at Berkeley and Carnegie Mellon University, 1989. Web. 26 Oct. 2013.

Cullington, Michaela. "Texting and Writing." *Young Scholars in Writing* 8 (2010): 90–95. Web. 12 Aug. 2013.

Head, Alison J., and Michael B. Eisenberg. "Assigning Inquiry: How Handouts for Research Assignments Guide Today's College Students." *Project Information Literacy Progress Report: University of Washington Information School*. 13 July 2010. 1-41. Web. 16 Nov. 2012.

———. "Lessons Learned: How College Students Seek Information in the Digital Age." *Project Information Literacy Progress Report: University of Washington Information School*. 1 Dec. 2009. 1–42. Web. 16 Nov. 2012.

Melzer, Daniel. "Writing Assignments across the Curriculum: A National Study of College Writing." *College Composition and Communication* 61.2 (2009): 240–61. Print.

Nelms, Gerald, and Ronda Leathers Dively. "Perceived Roadblocks to Transferring Knowledge from First-Year Composition to Writing-Intensive Major Courses: A Pilot Study." *WPA: Writing Program Administration* 31.1–2 (2007): 214–40. Web. 10 Aug. 2012.

Odell, Lee. "Context-Specific Ways of Knowing and the Evaluation of Writing." *Writing, Teaching, and Learning in the Disciplines*. Ed. Anne Herrington and Charles Moran. New York: Modern Language Association, 1992. 86–98. Print.

Wolfe, Christopher R. "Argumentation across the Curriculum." *Written Communication* 28.2 (2011): 193–219. Print.

CHAPTER 5

Visual Rhetoric in Academic Arguments

Images attract. For most of us, images are the first thing we notice or "read" when encountering a document for the first time. Images are also what we tend to remember. You might be able to recall an image you've seen in a magazine or website, despite having long ago forgotten the accompanying text. Advertisers know that even a company's logo can evoke powerful associations. For example, in taste tests people say they prefer Perrier to plain seltzer water, but only if they see the company logo before drinking. They state no preference for either the Perrier or plain versions when they cannot see the label (Schwartz 42). It is because images are so powerful that McDonald's fiercely protects its trademark golden arches and Nike just as fiercely guards its trademark swoosh.

An Overview of Visual Rhetoric

The ways that images communicate meaning and persuade viewers is referred to as **visual rhetoric**. Researchers in the field of visual rhetoric have demonstrated that even when an image's message conflicts with that of the accompanying text, readers will remember the message the image conveys. Marketing professors Haeran Jae, Devon Delvecchio, and Deborah Cowles discovered this when they showed participants a detergent ad with an image that conflicted with the meaning of the ad's text. The ad stated that the detergent should not be used to wash children's sleepwear, yet the image on the detergent bottle shown in the ad depicted a mother and baby. After viewing the ad, some of the participants rated the detergent as safe for children's sleepwear, a misunderstanding attributed to the fact that the image and text were at odds (447–48).

In a similar study, journalism and communication professors Rhonda Gibson and Dolf Zillmann found that a report can be fair and balanced, but if it is accompanied with images partial to one side of the issue, the images will unduly influence readers. Gibson and Zillmann asked subjects to read news stories accompanied with either varying images or no images at all. The images, more than the words, influenced how subjects felt about the issues, even when the images weren't discussed in a text (357). This research emphasizes how important it is that writers use images that reinforce the message they want to convey.

When they are relevant, illustrations and photographs can make concepts clear and entice audiences to read. Consider, for instance, the photograph in Figure 5.1, accompanying a short article from *Good Medicine*, a magazine that summarizes medical research for a general audience.

Vegetables Reduce Breast Cancer Risk

Women consuming more vegetables have a decreased risk of breast cancer, according to a recent study published in the *American Journal of Epidemiology*. Researchers followed the diets of 51,928 participants in the Black Women's Health Study. Participants who ate two or more servings of vegetables per day had a 43 percent decreased breast cancer risk, compared with those who ate less than four servings per week. Cruciferous vegetables (e.g., broccoli, cauliflower, and kale) and carrots had the largest impact on breast cancer risk.

Boggs DA, Palmer JR, Wise LA, et al. Fruit and Vegetable Intake in Relation to Risk of Breast Cancer in the Black Women's Health Study. *Am J Epidemiol*. Published ahead of print October 11, 2010. Doi: 10.1093/aje/kwq293.

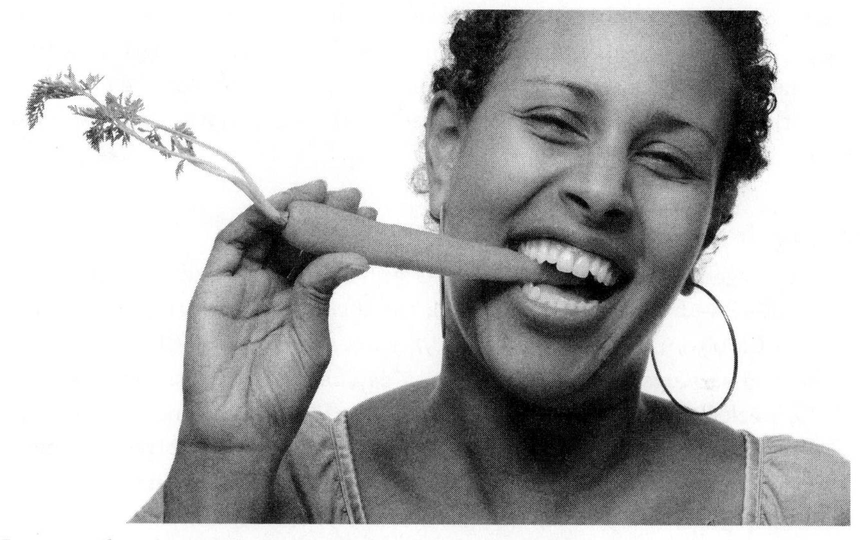

Figure 5.1 Photo from a Magazine Article (Gonzales and Levinan)

Given the article's audience and purpose (to persuade women to eat more vegetables in order to reduce the risk of breast cancer), the image is effective because it complements the article's message. In addition, in the original publication, bright colors grab the attention of readers flipping through the magazine. Although printed in black and white in this book, the original photo in the article displays an orange and green carrot, which helps enhance the article's message: *Vegetables reduce breast cancer risk*.

Color, in general, influences viewers. Many colors evoke certain emotions. Red, for example, often evokes heat, war, and danger, as well as love and passion; blue, on the other hand, evokes the sky, cold, peace, and stability. And orange and green? For many, orange evokes energy, warmth, and enthusiasm and green evokes nature and the environment. Colors attract attention and affect the mood of the audience. In online shopping sites, for instance, consumers are more likely to buy a product displayed in warm colors (Pelet and Papadopoulou 461).

Because of their powerful appeal, images and color are found in most advertisements and popular publications. Visual elements are also used by academic writers, although the types and purposes of visuals tend to be different in academic papers, as you will see in the next sections.

Visual Rhetoric in Academic Arguments

The research summarized in the magazine *Good Medicine* (Figure 5.1 on page 189) is from an article published in the *American Journal of Epidemiology* titled "Fruit and Vegetable Intake in Relation to Risk of Breast Cancer in the Black Women's Health Study." The publication site and the article title indicate the intended audience is "academic," an assumption confirmed by the article length (11 pages) and the technical vocabulary. Here, for example, is a portion of one paragraph from the Results section. Notice the technical vocabulary and precise data, which indicate the article is an academic one.

Passage from an Academic Journal

> Total vegetable intake was associated with a significant reduction in risk of ER−/PR− breast cancer (Table 4); the incidence rate ratios were 0.71 (95% CI: 0.50, 1.01), 0.79 (95% CI: 0.57, 1.10), and 0.57 (95% CI: 0.38, 0.85) for 4–6 servings/week, 1/day, and ≥2/day, respectively, compared with <4/week (P_{trend} = 0.02). Conversely, for ER+/PR+ breast cancer, the incidence rate ratios for total vegetable intake were above 1; the corresponding incidence rate ratios were 1.40 (95% CI: 0.99, 1.99), 1.54 (95% CI: 1.11, 2.14), and 1.41 (95% CI: 0.97, 2.04). (Boggs et al. 1272)

In this passage, the numerical data create a credible and scholarly ethos for the writers; but reading numerical data in paragraph form is not easy. To make the data more accessible, the authors refer readers to Table 4, one of several tables in their article. A portion of Table 4 appears in Figure 5.2.

Unlike the attention-grabbing photo found in the popular magazine *Good Medicine,* the data table in Figure 5.2 *serves as evidence to support the authors' argument.* In this way it is typical of visuals found in academic papers (Miller 29). The researchers who wrote the scholarly article argue that increased consumption of fruits and vegetables can reduce the risk of breast cancer; the data provided in Table 4 help to support that claim.

Audience, genre, discipline, and purpose should guide decisions about when and how to include tables, graphs, or images in your own academic writing.

Intake of Fruits and Vegetables in Relation to Risk of Breast Cancer by ER/PR Status in the Black Women's Health Study, 1995–2007

	ER+/PR+ Cases			ER+/PR- Cases			ER-/PR- Cases		
	Cases, No.	IRR[a]	95% CI	Cases, No.	IRR[a]	95% CI	Cases, No.	IRR[a]	95% CI
Total fruits and vegetables,servings									
<1/day	52	1.00	Referent	14	1.00	Referent	53	1.00	Referent
1/day	106	1.20	0.86, 1.69	28	1.13	0.59, 2.17	75	0.90	0.63, 1.29
2–3/day	155	1.31	0.94, 1.82	37	1.10	0.58, 2.09	100	0.97	0.68, 1.38
≥4/day	53	0.96	0.64, 1.46	24	1.43	0.69, 2.94	36	0.79	0.50, 1.24
P_{trend}			0.62			0.33			0.40
Total vegetables, servings									
<4/week	53	1.00	Referent	16	1.00	Referent	71	1.00	Referent
4–6/week	84	1.40	0.99, 1.99	20	1.03	0.53, 2.00	56	0.71	0.50, 1.01
1/day	142	1.54	1.11, 2.14	41	1.34	0.74, 2.45	93	0.79	0.57, 1.10
≥2/day	87	1.41	0.97, 2.04	26	1.20	0.61, 2.36	44	0.57	0.38, 0.85
P_{trend}			0.25			0.59			0.02
Cruciferous vegetables, servings									
<1/week	49	1.00	Referent	11	1.00	Referent	49	1.00	Referent
1–2/week	157	1.16	0.83, 1.60	41	1.24	0.63, 2.44	109	0.83	0.59, 1.18
3–5/week	115	1.36	0.96, 1.93	32	1.57	0.77, 3.18	67	0.86	0.59, 1.26
≥6/week	45	0.80	0.52, 1.23	19	1.38	0.63, 3.01	39	0.81	0.52, 1.26
P_{trend}			0.17			0.47			0.56
Green leafy vegetables, servings									
<1/week	66	1.00	Referent	18	1.00	Referent	61	1.00	Referent
1–2/week	109	1.03	0.76, 1.41	30	1.03	0.57, 1.86	100	1.08	0.78, 1.49
3–5/week	125	1.25	0.92, 1.71	37	1.27	0.71, 2.28	65	0.77	0.54, 1.11
>6/week	66	1.14	0.80, 1.63	18	1.00	0.51, 1.99	38	0.80	0.52, 1.22
P_{trend}			0.36			0.94			0.09

Figure 5.2 Portion of a Table from an Academic Article (Boggs et al. 1276)

Using Images

Images include photographs, drawings, diagrams, X-rays, or any other means of providing readers with a "picture." Images are used in academic papers to explain concepts and to persuade readers.

Using Images to Explain Concepts or Procedures

Photographs and diagrams are often the most efficient way to explain concepts or phases of a process. In a science report on plant growth under certain lighting conditions, for example, an author might use photographs to document changes in a specimen. Photographs are also a good way to show the results of large-scale changes. Figure 5.3 is a photograph used to show the layering that occurs in sedimentary rocks (stratification). Accompanying text can describe what stratification is, but the photograph shows the physical outcome of the geological process.

Whereas photographs might show the results of a process, diagrams can illustrate how a process takes place. The diagram that follows (Figure 5.4), with its

Figure 5.3 Photograph Illustrating a Geological Process (Stratification)

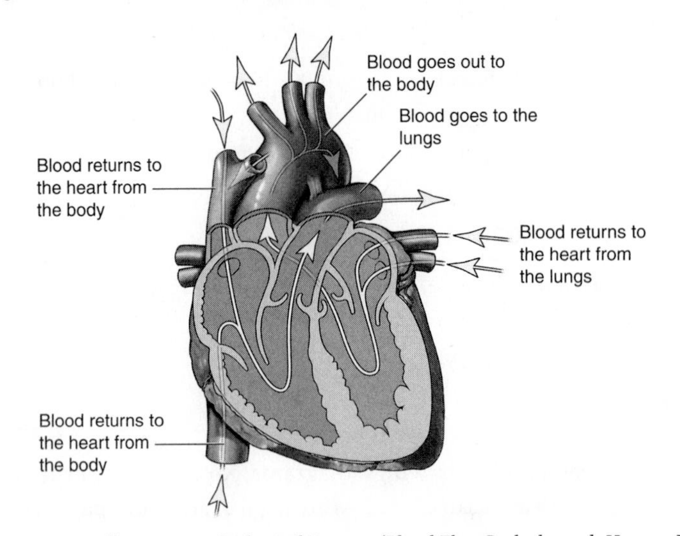

Figure 5.4 Diagram Illustrating a Biological Process (Blood Flow Path through Human Heart)

labels and arrows identifying individual parts, clarifies the mechanics of a process—in this case, how blood flows through the human heart.

Diagrams in general are better than photographs for explaining a process or for depicting the inner workings of a system.

Using Images to Evoke Emotion

Images can also persuade readers to care about an issue. Journalism professor Renita Coleman demonstrated this when, in a study, she asked 194 journalism students to rate the importance of four issues: children and drugs, elder abuse, prostitution, and domestic violence (840–42). All participants read passages describing the issues. Ninety-two of the participants also saw images depicting the issues; the other 102 participants saw no photos. Those who viewed images reported higher levels of concern for the people involved in the stories than those who did not (844–45). Images of humans are among the most persuasive rhetorical features a writer can use. In fact, the image of a single person in need after a natural disaster is *more* likely to motivate people to donate money than statistics documenting exactly how many people have been affected (Slovic). We can imagine helping a single individual but might feel powerless when reading statistics revealing how many thousands or millions are in need.

Researchers committed to solving environmental, health, economic, or social problems understand that their research won't receive a broader audience—or funding—unless they get others to care about those issues too. Using images that appeal to readers' emotions (such as Figure 5.5) is one way writers do this.

Figure 5.5 An Image Used to Evoke Emotion. (A person saving a child from flood waters in Solo, central Java, Indonesia)

Concept in Practice 5.1: Combining Images with Other Types of Evidence

In chapters 3 and 4, you learned how to use various kinds of quantitative and qualitative evidence to make an argument convincing. When images are combined with quantitative and qualitative evidence, the result can be persuasive and informative writing.

The following passages were taken from two different proposals, written by Wendy Canada and Kylie Marston while they were enrolled in a first-year writing course. Students in their class proposed ways to improve a travel agency website. Their audience was the travel agency owners. As you read the excerpts from their proposals, notice how images are used to support and demonstrate the claims.

RECOMMENDATION #1: ADD IMAGES (BY WENDY CANADA)

An image alone can speak volumes. For example, when you look at Figure 5.6, the beach, the sand, and the palms, we almost can feel the wind in our face, seagulls singing, and the smell of salt water. What kind of emotions does the picture convey? The first things to come to mind are vacations, warm weather, fun, swimming, and relaxing. What if we look closer and contemplate those empty chairs on the sand? Many individuals can imagine that they are already looking at that beautiful view. That image is so powerful because it works as an invitation to go on vacation. In my opinion those chairs are calling me to be there! The power that images have on viewers has been demonstrated in research carried out by Rhonda Gibson, a professor of journalism, and Dolf Zillmann, a professor of communication and psychology, who asked 135 students to read fictitious reports about a tick disease. Some versions of the story had photos of ticks plus images of White and Black children, pictures of White children only, or pictures of Black children only (358). When respondents completed a questionnaire about the story, they indicated that White and Black children had the highest risk of catching the tick-borne disease, even though the fake story didn't mention any children were victims or their nationality (364). These

The writer identifies what she wants readers to notice in the image (on next page). Given the intended audience (travel agency owners) and purpose (persuade them to add images to their website), does the choice of image seem appropriate?

Analysis of the image makes the writer's point clear: Images convey messages.

A research study provides further evidence that images convey messages.

The relevance of the image and research to the readers (travel agency owners) is explained (next page).

Figure 5.6 *Powerful pictures give emotions and feelings*

results indicate that images influence our perceptions. You can take advantage of their power by adding images to your website of destination sites. . . .

RECOMMENDATION #2: PROVIDE CUSTOMER SERVICE OPTIONS (BY KYLIE MARSTON)

Once you've attracted customers to your website, it's important to keep them there. One of the best ways to inspire customer loyalty is to offer customer service options. I recommend not only having a 24/7 phone number clearly listed on your home page, but also having a listed email that customers can use to contact you and a chat box option that can be pulled up from any page on the website.

A study of online consumers indicates that people want customer service to be available when shopping online.

You may think that having that many customer service options may be a bit excessive but Nabil Tamimi and two other professors from the University of Scranton in Pennsylvania did a study in 2005 that says otherwise. Tamimi and her colleagues did a study to see what qualities people value most in websites. They had 422 people fill out their online survey, 23% of which had made at least 10 online purchases in the last 6 months (Tamimi, Sebastianelli, and Rajan 36). Their results showed that the most highly rated features in a website were all customer service based ones. On a scale of one to five, a website having online help or a toll free number available to their customers was rated, on average, 4.03. That's a relatively easy way to help keep people happy (39).

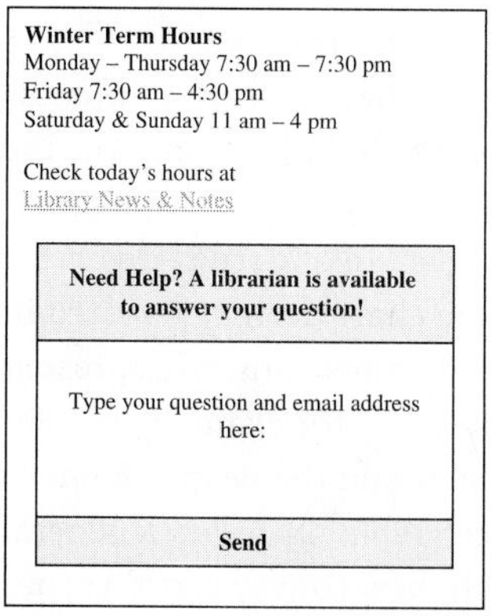

Winter Term Hours
Monday – Thursday 7:30 am – 7:30 pm
Friday 7:30 am – 4:30 pm
Saturday & Sunday 11 am – 4 pm

Check today's hours at
Library News & Notes

Need Help? A librarian is available to answer your question!

Type your question and email address here:

Send

Figure 5.7 The Chat Box of the Future

If you look at Figure 5.7, it is a very good example of what I think you should have on your website. The example I'm showing you is from the home page of a community college library. As you can see, it not only lists the hours that it's in operation but also gives you helpful links. Most importantly, though, Figure 5.7 shows you an example of the chat feature that I am strongly recommending. Students can use that chat box to ask librarians reference or technology questions in real time from the comfort of their home or wherever else they are sitting with their computer. Even if your customers don't need the customer service options, it's still nice knowing that those options are available. A little peace of mind goes a long way, after all.

Figure 5.7 illustrates how a website can provide customer service.

The writer highlights important features in the image that are relevant for the readers.

WORKS CITED

Gibson, Rhonda, and Dolf Zillman. "Reading between the Photographs: The Influence of Incidental Pictorial Information on Issue Perception." *Journalism and Mass Communication Quarterly* 77.2. (2000): 355–66. Print.

Tamimi, Nabil, Rose Sebastianelli, and Murli Rajan. "What Do Online Customers Value?" *Quality Progress* 38.7 (2005): 35–9. *ProQuest*. Web. 18 Feb. 2014.

Presenting Quantitative Data Visually

Quantitative data are commonly presented in visual form. A number of studies have demonstrated that processing numerical data presented in charts, graphs, or diagrams is easier and faster than processing the same information presented in text only, and the information is remembered longer. (See Vekiri for a review of this research.) When they supplement a text, these visual aids essentially give readers two ways of remembering, thus reinforcing the information.

Graphical representations are most effective when they are easy to process and when surrounding text draws attention to what readers should notice. The choice of format makes a difference, not only influencing how quickly information is read but also influencing how accurately it is read. In one study involving doctors and nurses interpreting patient charts, some chart designs resulted in error rates as high as 40% ("Nursing")! Graphs and charts can misrepresent data, by making differences appear greater than they are, for example; so consider the point you want your visual evidence to convey and then experiment to find the format that best represents your evidence. Table 5.1 offers a general overview of which forms of visual presentation might best convey certain types of quantitative data.

TABLE 5.1
Forms of Visual Presentation of Data

Visual Presentation	Data Type
Tables	Good for presenting large amounts of numerical data, especially when it's important that readers have precise figures
Pie charts	Good for depicting the proportion of the whole for each category
Column and bar charts	Good for comparing two or three categories
Line graphs	Good for showing trends or changes over time

Using Tables

Let's say you've been asked to write a report on the most common types of student majors at a particular college. Table 5.2 illustrates one way to present the information. (*N* stands for "number.") Note that because the focus here is on data presentation rather than accuracy of data, the college featured in the table is fictional.

TABLE 5.2
Student Majors at Evermore College (*N *= 9,500 students)

Major	Percentage
Applied sciences	36%
Physical sciences	28
Social sciences	20
Humanities	12
Undecided	4

The information in Table 5.2 is faster to read than it would be if presented in sentence form:

> The students at Evermore College represent the following majors: Applied sciences (36%), Physical sciences (28%), Social sciences (20%), Humanities (12%), and Undecided (4%).

In addition, the table reduces the risk of a reader attributing a percentage to the wrong major.

Concept in Practice 5.2: Presenting Data in Tables

Reading listed numbers in a paragraph is slow and cumbersome, but numbers in tables are easier to read and compare. Table 5.3 indicates how many academic writers in a sample of 24 published articles used various types of punctuation within selected passages. Note the various elements making the table informative and easy to read.

TABLE 5.3
Number of Writers Using Various Punctuation Types in 500-Word Passages

Punctuation	Number of Writers (out of 24)
Parentheses	24 (100%)
Semicolons	20 (83%)
Colons	18 (75%)
Question marks	13 (54%)
Dashes	9 (38%)

The caption includes an informative title.

Providing the percentage along with the raw number gives the number more meaning.

Information is listed vertically under bolded column headings for easy reading.

Information is easier to comprehend if arranged logically. How is the arrangement of data logical?

Using Figures

As useful as tables are for making numerical data accessible, they don't allow readers to visually "see" differences between groups. If your goal is for readers to make comparisons, consider using a figure.

Figures technically refer to any visual that's not a table, including line graphs, bar charts, drawings, photographs, and images. We've discussed types of images earlier. Here we discuss ways to present quantitative data in charts or graphs. Three of the most common are pie charts, bar or column charts, and line graphs.

Pie Charts. Unlike Table 5.2, which lists the statistical data for majors at Evermore College, the pie chart in Figure 5.8 graphically depicts the information.

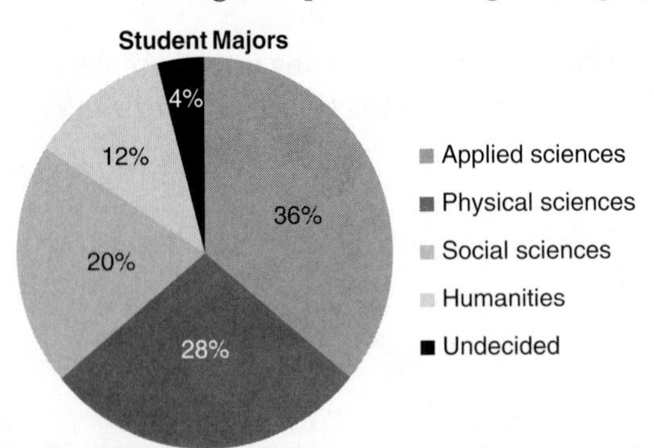

Figure 5.8 Student Majors at Evermore College ($N = 9{,}500$)

Traditionally, segments are arranged so that the largest segment begins at the 12:00 o'clock hour. From there, arrange the pieces counterclockwise from largest segment to smallest segment.

The image of the pie chart draws more attention than does the table; it is also easier to compare the relative size of each segment in proportion to the whole. But as demonstrated in Figure 5.8, if the segments of the pie are too small for labels, a reader must look back and forth between the legend at the right and the figure. It can also be difficult to interpret information represented in small segments of a pie chart. Further, when there are many segments or when the chart is depicted in black and white print, some segment colors will resemble others in the chart. For these reasons, a pie chart may not be the best way to present our information about majors at Evermore College.

Bar Charts (Graphs) and Column Charts. Bar charts (or bar graphs) and column charts show categories next to one other, so they are good for comparing groups or comparing amounts. They are a natural choice for presenting populations and spending amounts. Figure 5.9 depicts our data about college majors at Evermore College in a column chart.

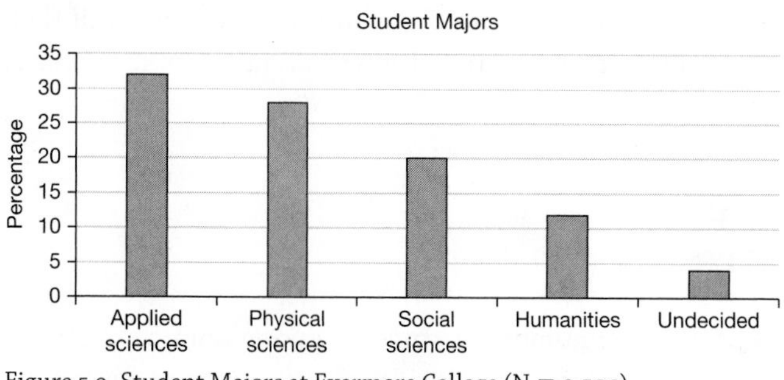

The dark columns stand out against the white background, and the columns are arranged by size, making majors easy to compare.

Figure 5.9 Student Majors at Evermore College (N = 9,500)

Although the pie chart (Figure 5.8) allows readers to determine percentages for each major more easily, reading the column chart doesn't require switching focus between the chart and legend. Depending on how important it is that readers know the exact percentages for each major, the column chart may be a better option because it requires less effort to comprehend. The point is that when presenting data visually, you should consider your options.

Line Graphs. A line graph (or XY graph) is used to display a trend or relationship between one or more variables. Figure 5.10 is a line graph from the article "Alpine Areas in the Colorado Front Range as Monitors of Climate Change and Ecosystem Response." This sentence in the article summarizes the numerical data:

> Annual deposition of inorganic nitrogen in wetfall at the Niwot Ridge NADP site from 1984 to 1996 almost doubled, from 1.95 kilograms per hectare per year in 1985–1988 to 3.75 kilograms per hectare per year in 1989–1992 (Figure 5.10).

The figure makes the trend easy to see:

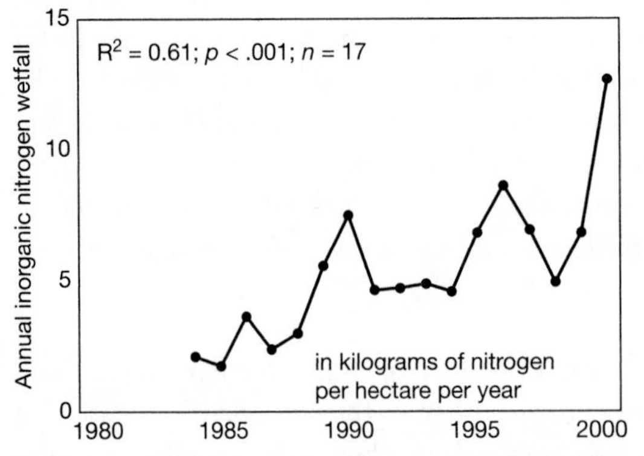

The single, dark line against the white background clearly depicts the rise and fall of inorganic nitrogen wetfall.

Figure 5.10 Annual Deposition of Inorganic Nitrogen in Wetfall (Williams et al. 184)

Unlike column or bar charts that tend to depict amounts at fixed points in time, line graphs are better at depicting how amounts change over time. Not all line graphs are as easy to read as Figure 5.10, however. In line graphs that depict more than one trend, different kinds of lines are commonly used, but if the lines aren't distinct or if they overlap or intersect, it can be difficult for readers to distinguish one line from another.

Concept in Practice 5.3: Comparing Figure Types

Figures 5.11 and 5.12 depict the number of students taking online classes, face-to-face classes, or both at a college. Consider the strengths and weaknesses of each figure for presenting the data. (Several strengths and weaknesses of the column chart, Figure 5.11, are provided for you.) Which figure is more effective and why?

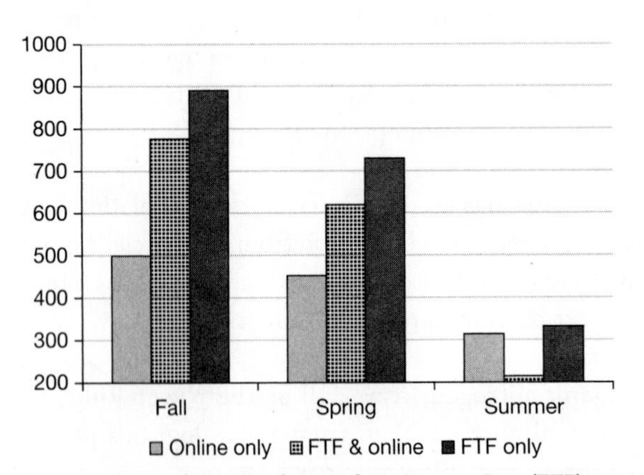

Figure 5.11 Number of Students Taking Face-to-Face (FTF) classes, Online Classes, or Both

Clustering the bars makes it easy to compare the data.

The vertical axis begins with 200, instead of the more traditional zero. How does beginning with 200 misrepresent the data, particularly for the summer enrollment figures?

The caption tells readers what the numbers mean.

The label for each category of data appears on the horizontal axis, and the frequency or amount appears on the vertical axis.

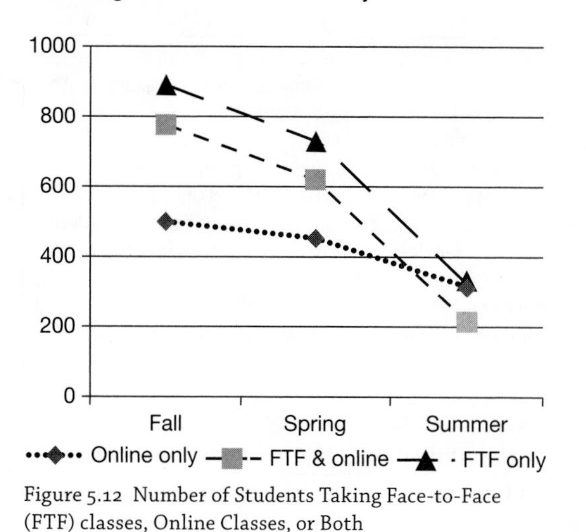

Figure 5.12 Number of Students Taking Face-to-Face (FTF) classes, Online Classes, or Both

Does the line graph imply any trend (or trends) not implied in the column chart? Is this good or bad?

Do you find the line graph easier to read or more difficult to read than the column chart?

Which figure does a better job of presenting the data? How could you further improve the figure you chose?

Best Practices for Incorporating Visuals into Academic Papers

Emphasizing evidence visually is one way to create a professional ethos and signal to readers that you are a member of the academic community. When math professor Patrick Bahls, along with English professors Amy Mecklenburg-Faenger, Meg Scott-Copses, and Chris Warnick, analyzed mathematical research papers written by undergraduates (ranging from first-year to third-year students), they agreed that the effective papers included visual elements and that an important feature affecting their evaluation was how well the figures and tables were integrated into the papers. They rated papers higher when the writer explained the meaning of the figure or table, instead of giving "readers more work to do to figure out what the figures were meant to illustrate." They criticized one student, for instance, for introducing a figure with this sentence: "See Figure 2 for an example." The student assumed readers would determine the meaning for themselves, rather than explaining for them how Figure 2 illustrated the concept being discussed.

Tell readers how to interpret figures and information in tables. Refer explicitly to what the reader should notice and reinforce your message in a caption. Figure 5.13 is an illustration of a well-integrated table from an article in a rhetoric and composition journal. In the passage shown, the author, Ken Hyland, describes his research, designed to show how frequently academic writers from across disciplines use first-person pronouns. Notice how the table is introduced and how the information in the table is explained for readers.

What expert writers do

To see how far the textbook stereotype of impersonality corresponds with actual practice, I interviewed expert writers and examined 240 published journal articles, 30 from each of eight disciplines. Using *Wordpilot 2000* (Milton 1999), a text analysis and concordance programme, I electronically searched the corpus for the pronouns *I, me, my, we, us,* and *our,* and then examined each case to ensure it was an exclusive first person use, i.e. that it referred only to the writer(s) and was therefore a genuine *author pronoun*. My results suggest that academic writing is not the uniformly faceless prose it is often thought to be, but displays considerable differences between disciplines (Table 1). Broadly, writers in the hard sciences and engineering prefer to downplay their personal role to highlight the issue under study, while a stronger identity is claimed in the humanities and social sciences papers.

TABLE 1 Average frequency of writer pronouns per research paper

Discipline	**All writer pronouns**	**Singular (I, Me, My)**	**Plural (We, Us, Ous)**
Marketing	38.2	1.6	36.5
Philosophy	34.5	33.0	1.5
App. Ling.	32.3	17.2	15.0
Sociology	29.4	11.7	17.7
Physics	17.7	0.0	17.7
Biology	15.5	0.0	15.5
Electronic Eng.	11.6	0.0	11.6
Mechanical Eng.	2.6	0.0	2.6
Overall	**22.7**	**7.9**	**14.8**

The preference for joint authorship in the sciences and engineering explains the greater use of plural forms in those disciplines, but 75% of all the author pronouns in the corpus occurred in the humanities and social sciences. Decisions to employ a writer pronoun here are related to the fact that arguments in such 'soft knowledge' domains are less precisely measureable and clear-cut than in the hard sciences, and the extent to which a personal stance can help promote an impression of confidence and authority. Authors make a personal standing in their texts to establish a credible scholarly identity, and to underline what they have to say (Ivanic 1997). For this reason, we most commonly find that

Figure 5.13 Example of a Well-Integrated Table (Hyland 352–53)

Once again, when incorporating tables and figures in your college papers, keep in mind these best practices:

- **Number and label tables and figures.** Place a table caption *above* the table but a figure caption *beneath* the figure. Number tables and figures sequentially but separately. Thus, a paper may include Table 1 and Table 2, as well as Figure 1 and Figure 2. Ideally, you should refer to tables and figures by number *before* they appear in the text. (For example, "See Figure 4.")
- **Draw the reader's attention** to what you want noticed in the table or figure.
- **Explain the meaning of the data**; don't rely on tables or figures to make your argument for you.

Here are some final general guidelines to consider when incorporating any form of visual element into your papers:

- **Keep the size of the visuals in proportion** for the document and consider "wrapping" text around smaller images for a professional appearance.

- **Don't overdo it.** Too many visual elements can overwhelm the reader and make a text seem cluttered.
- **Acknowledge the source of any visual you borrow**—including Internet sources. Get permission from the creator if your paper will be published online.
- **Leave white space.** Lists, equations, formulas, and other types of quantitative data are easier to read when surrounded by white space. Figure 5.14 is an example of effective use of white space in a mathematics paper. The formula in Figure 5.14 is set off visually, making it easy to scan.

After $\vec{w}$ is determined, the error involved in the linear predictor is calculated by

$$\log_2(\vec{V}) - \log_2(|Q\vec{w}|).$$

The vector $Q\vec{w}$ may contain negative entries so its absolute value must is used. Both $\vec{V}$ or $Q\vec{w}$ can have entries of zero, so those values are reset to 1×10^{-8} when calculating the error, which is a conventional adjustment to make.

Figure 5.14 Example of a Formula Set Off Visually (Lytle and Yang 6)

Applying the Concepts to Reading: *Reading Quantitative Data*

Quantitative literacy—the ability to interpret quantitative data—is as important as other kinds of literacy, explains English professor Joanna Wolfe (454); we may think of numbers as "factual," but in reality they are routinely manipulated to persuade readers (455). The way data are presented influences the way readers interpret those data. Keep this in mind when reading data—in any form.

To illustrate how presentation affects the way we interpret statistics, Wolfe offers five ways of conveying this statistic: "21.3 percent of women and 12.7 percent of men have experienced depression in their lifetime":

1. Over one in five women and one in eight men have experienced depression in their lifetimes.
2. Women are 68 percent more likely than men to experience depression in their lifetime.
3. Approximately six of every ten depressed individuals is a woman.
4. 17.1 percent of individuals have experienced depression in their lifetime.
5. Over 75 percent of women never experience significant depression in their lifetime. (Wolfe 460)

The statements are essentially equal in a mathematical sense, but the effect on how readers will perceive the issue is not. In contrast to Statement 1, for example, Statement 2 suggests that depression is a much more serious problem among women than among men, while Statement 5 makes one think that depression among women isn't much of a problem at all. The statements illustrate how important it is to read statistical evidence critically.

We've seen in this chapter that the visual presentation of numerical data can also be shaped to serve a writer's purposes. Wolfe provides four graphical representations of the data appearing in Figure 5.15. Study the data and then study the various interpretations of the data in the four graphs that follow (Figure 5.16). As you study the graphs, consider these questions:

- What are the different interpretations or "stories" told in each graph?
- When might a writer prefer one graph over others?
- Do any of the graphs misrepresent or gloss over important information found in the table?

Fictional Test Score Data Arranged by Student ID

ID	School	Gender	Race	Verbal score	Math score
520	A	M	2	400	410
521	A	M	1	510	620
522	B	F	1	570	520
523	A	M	1	720	680
524	C	M	2	270	330
525	A	F	5	540	500
526	B	M	1	580	700
527	A	F	1	660	640
528	A	M	1	600	640
529	B	F	1	550	560
530	B	F	1	580	420
531	C	F	2	420	370
532	C	M	3	280	350
533	B	M	2	480	470

Figure 5.15 Image of Table from Wolfe (463)

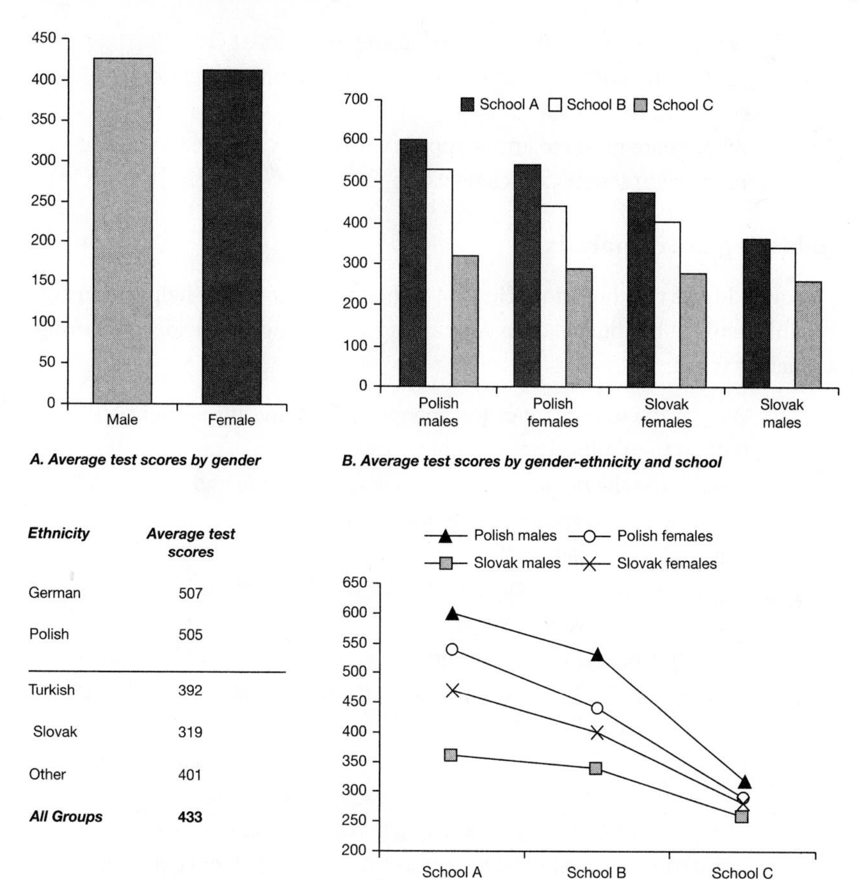

Ethnicity	*Average test scores*
German	507
Polish	505
Turkish	392
Slovak	319
Other	401
All Groups	**433**

C. Average test scores by ethnicity

Figure 5.16 Four different arguments based upon the data in Figure 5.15. All four illustrations represent the same raw data.

(Wolfe 464)

Applying the Concepts to Writing: *Analyzing Images*

Images communicate meaning and can be used to persuade viewers. Find an image online or in a magazine, newspaper, or book—one used to persuade an audience to buy a product, support a cause, or agree with the writer's opinion. Then, write an essay analyzing the image's rhetorical effectiveness.

Getting Started

Before you begin writing, consider some questions about the rhetorical situation:

- Who is the intended audience (who is most likely to view this image)?
- What is the relationship between reader and writer?

- What is the writer's goal in the document?
- What is the purpose of the image: Is it intended to inform, evoke emotions, motivate action?
- What genre does the image appear in?
- What is the situation or context?

Conducting Your Analysis

Now, address this question: How do elements of the image help the writer achieve his or her purpose? In your analysis, you might consider questions such as these:

- What is the focal point of the image? What draws the viewer's attention to that focal point?
- What is the theme or central message of the image and how does this meaning contribute to the document?
- How does the image make you feel: amused, angry, confused, intrigued, proud, sad, annoyed, offended? What specifically in the image provokes your reaction?
- Is any specific cultural or background knowledge required to understand this image? If so, what further clues does that provide about the intended audience?
- What aspects of the image's content or design reflect the interests or concerns of the target audience? For example, are there people in the image? What is their age, gender, nationality, ethnicity, or income?
- What mood is created by the colors? Are they warm or cold colors? Bright or muted? Contrasting or complementary?
- How does the layout or design contribute to the meaning?
- Is there any text imposed on the image? How does the content and appearance of that text contribute to the message?

The answers to these kinds of questions serve as evidence for claims made in an image analysis.

Writing the Analysis

To begin your paper, briefly describe the image (or, better, integrate the image into your paper) and identify the rhetorical context: the audience, the purpose, and the situation and context. Identify the goal of your paper in a thesis statement or overview statement announcing the focus of your discussion. Often the goal of a visual rhetorical analysis is to explain how various aspects of the image (color, layout, content, etc.) work together to achieve a specific purpose.

To make your discussion easy to follow and to keep from merely describing the image (rather than analyzing it), write topic sentences that announce the point of each paragraph. Each body paragraph might focus on a different kind of persuasive appeal, such as pathos, logos, and ethos; on a different artistic element, such as colors, shapes, contrasts, shadows, or symbols; or on a different object in the image. Keep your central claim (thesis) in mind as you select details from the image to describe.

Conclude your analysis by explaining why the analysis you performed matters.

Paired Readings from Environmental Science

"Can We Feed the World and Sustain the Planet?" *Scientific American*

JONATHAN A. FOLEY

Jonathan Foley is an environmental scientist at the University of Minnesota, where he is the director of the Institute on the Environment and the McKnight Presidential Chair of Global Sustainability. The following article was originally published in 2011 in *Scientific American,* a popular science magazine that publishes articles about science topics for a general, educated audience. In the article, Foley describes research he conducted with experts from around the world, addressing the complicated problem of world hunger. Figure 5.17 appeared as a full-page photo in Foley's article. It is one example of the attention-getting figures featured in the original publication.

Figure 5.17 Sample Image from the Article

Right now about one billion people suffer from chronic hunger. The world's farmers grow enough food to feed them, but it is not properly distributed and, even if it were, many cannot afford it, because prices are escalating.

But another challenge looms.

By 2050 the world's population will increase by two billion or three billion, which will likely double the demand for food, according to several studies. Demand will also rise because many more people will have higher incomes, which means they will eat more, especially meat. Increasing use of cropland for biofuels will put additional demands on our farms. So even if we solve today's problems of poverty and access—a daunting task—we will also have to produce twice as much to guarantee adequate supply worldwide.

And that's not all.

By clearing tropical forests, farming marginal lands, and intensifying industrial farming in sensitive landscapes and watersheds, humankind has made agriculture the planet's dominant environmental threat. Agriculture already consumes a large percentage of the earth's land surface and is destroying habitat, using up freshwater, polluting rivers and oceans, and emitting greenhouse gases more extensively than almost any other human activity. To guarantee the globe's long-term health, we must dramatically reduce agriculture's adverse impacts.

The world's food system faces three incredible, interwoven challenges. It must guarantee that all seven billion people alive today are adequately fed; it must double food production in the next 40 years; and it must achieve both goals while becoming truly environmentally sustainable.

Could these simultaneous goals possibly be met? An international team of experts, which I coordinated, has settled on five steps that, if pursued together, could raise by more than 100 percent the food available for human consumption globally, while significantly lessening greenhouse gas emissions, biodiversity losses, water use and water pollution. Tackling the triple challenge will be one of the most important tests humanity has ever faced. It is fair to say that our response will determine the fate of our civilization.

BUMPING UP AGAINST BARRIERS

At first blush, the way to feed more people would seem clear: grow more food, by expanding farmland and improving yield—the amount of crops harvested per hectare. Unfortunately, the world is running into significant barriers on both counts.

Society already farms roughly 38 percent of the earth's land surface, not counting Greenland or Antarctica. Agriculture is by far the biggest human use of land on the planet; nothing else comes close. And most of that 38 percent covers the *best* farmland. Much of the remainder is covered by deserts, mountains, tundra, ice, cities, parks and other unsuitable growing areas. The few remaining frontiers are mainly in tropical forests and savannas, which are vital to the stability of the globe, especially as stores of carbon and biodiversity. Expanding into those areas is not a good idea, yet over the past 20 years five million to 10 million hectares of cropland a year have been created, with a significant portion of that amount in the tropics. These additions enlarged the net area of cultivated land by only 3 percent, however, because of farmland losses caused by urban development and other forces, particularly in temperate zones.

Improving yield also sounds enticing. Yet our research team found that average global crop yield increased by about 20 percent in the past 20 years—far less than what is typically reported. That improvement is significant, but the rate is nowhere near enough to double food production by midcentury. Whereas yields of some crops improved substantially, others saw little gain and a few even declined.

Feeding more people would be easier if all the food we grew went into human hands. But only 60 percent of the world's crops are meant for people: mostly grains, followed by pulses (beans, lentils), oil plants, vegetables and fruits. Another 35 percent is used for animal feed, and the final 5 percent goes to bio fuels and other industrial products. Meat is the biggest issue here. Even with the most efficient meat and dairy systems, feeding crops to animals reduces the world's potential food supply. Typically grain-fed cattle operations use 30 kilograms of grain to make one kilogram of edible, boneless beef. Chicken and pork are more efficient, and grass-fed beef converts nonfood material into protein. No matter how you slice it, though, grain-fed meat production systems are a drain on the global food supply.

Another deterrent to growing more food is damage to the environment, which is already extensive. Only our use of energy, with its profound impacts on climate and ocean acidification, rivals the sheer magnitude of agriculture's environmental impacts. Our research team estimates that agriculture has already cleared or radically transformed 70 percent of the world's prehistoric grasslands, 50 percent of the savannas, 45 percent of the temperate deciduous forests and 25 percent of the tropical forests. Since the last ice age, nothing has disrupted ecosystems more. Agriculture's physical footprint is nearly 60 times that of the world's pavements and buildings.

Freshwater is another casualty. Humans use an astounding 4,000 cubic kilometers of water per year, mostly withdrawn from rivers and aquifers. Irrigation accounts for 70 percent of the draw. If we count only consumptive water use—water that is used and not returned to the watershed—irrigation climbs to 80 or 90 percent of the total. As a result, many large rivers, such as the Colorado, have diminished flows, some have dried up altogether, and many places have rapidly declining water tables, including regions of the U.S. and India.

Water is not only disappearing, it is being contaminated. Fertilizers, herbicides and pesticides are being spread at incredible levels and are found in nearly every ecosystem. The flows of nitrogen and phosphorus through the environment have more than doubled since 1960, causing widespread water pollution and enormous hypoxic "dead zones" at the mouths of many of the world's major rivers. Ironically, fertilizer runoff from farmland—in the name of growing more food—compromises another crucial source of nutrition: coastal fishing grounds. Fertilizer certainly has been a key ingredient of the green revolution that has helped feed the world, but when nearly half the fertilizer we apply runs off rather than nourishes crops, we clearly can do better.

Agriculture is also the largest single source of greenhouse gas emissions from society, collectively accounting for about 35 percent of the carbon dioxide, methane and nitrous oxide we release. That is more than the emissions from worldwide transportation (including all cars, trucks and planes) or electricity generation. The energy used to grow, process and transport food is a concern, but the vast majority of emissions comes from tropical deforestation, methane released from animals and rice paddies, and nitrous oxide from overfertilized soils.

FIVE SOLUTIONS

Modern agriculture has been an incredibly positive force in the world, but we can no longer ignore its dwindling ability to expand or the mounting environmental harm it imposes. Previous approaches to solving food and environmental issues were often at odds. We could boost food production by clearing more land or using more water and chemicals but only at a cost to the environment. Or we could restore ecosystems by taking farmland out of cultivation but only by reducing food production. This either-or-approach is no longer acceptable. We need truly integrated solutions.

After many months of research and deliberation—based on analysis of newly generated global agricultural and environmental data—our international team has settled on a five-point plan for dealing with food and environmental challenges together.

Stop Expanding Agriculture's Footprint

Our first recommendation is to slow and ultimately stop the expansion of agriculture, particularly into tropical forests and savannas. The demise of these ecosystems has far-reaching impacts on the environment, especially through lost biodiversity and increased carbon dioxide emissions (from clearing land).

Slowing deforestation would dramatically reduce environmental damage while imposing only minor constraints on global food production. The resulting dip in farm capacity could be offset by reducing the displacement of more productive croplands by urbanization, degradation and abandonment.

Many proposals have been made to reduce deforestation. One of the most promising is the Reducing Emissions from Deforestation and Degradation (REDD) mechanism. Under REDD, rich nations pay tropical nations to protect their rain forests, in exchange for carbon credits. Other mechanisms include developing certification standards for agricultural products so that supply chains can be assured that crops were not grown on lands created by deforestation. Also, better biofuel policy that relies on nonfood crops such as switchgrass instead of food crops could make vital farmland newly available.

Close the World's Yield Gaps

To double global food production without expanding agriculture's footprint, we must significantly improve yields of existing farmlands. Two options exist: We can boost the productivity of our best farms—raising their "yield ceiling" through improved crop genetics and management. Or we can improve the yields of the world's least productive farms—closing the "yield gap" between a farm's current yield and its higher potential yield. The second option provides the largest and most immediate gain—especially in regions where hunger is most acute.

Our research team has analyzed global patterns of crop yields and found that much of the world has a significant yield gap. In particular, yields could increase substantially across many parts of Africa, Central America and eastern Europe. In these regions, better seeds, more effective fertilizer application and efficient irrigation could produce much more food on the same amount of land. Our analysis suggests that closing the yield gap for the world's top 16 crops could increase total food production by 50 to 60 percent, with little environmental damage.

Reducing yield gaps in the least productive agricultural lands may often require some additional fertilizer and water. Care will have to be taken to avoid unbridled irrigation and chemical use. Many other techniques can improve yield. "Reduced tillage" planting techniques disturb less soil, preventing erosion. Cover crops planted between food-crop seasons reduce weeds and add nutrients and nitrogen to the soil when plowed under. Lessons from organic and agroecological systems can also be adopted, such as leaving crop residues on fields so that they decompose into nutrients. To close the world's yield gaps, we also have to overcome serious economic and social challenges, including better distribution of fertilizer and seed varieties to farms in impoverished regions and improving access to global markets for many regions.

Use Resources Much More Efficiently

To reduce the environmental impacts of agriculture, low- and high-yield regions alike must practice agriculture with vastly greater efficiency: far more crop output per unit of water, fertilizer and energy.

On average, it takes about one liter of irrigation water to grow one calorie of food, although some places use much more. Our analysis finds that farms can significantly curb water use without much reduction in food production, especially in dry climates. Primary strategies include drip irrigation (where water is applied directly to the plant's base and not wastefully sprayed into the air); mulching (covering the soil with organic matter to retain moisture); and reducing water lost from irrigation systems (by lessening evaporation from canals and reservoirs).

With fertilizers, we face a kind of Goldilocks problem. Some places have too few nutrients and therefore poor crop production, whereas others have too much, leading to pollution. Almost no one uses fertilizers "just right." Our analysis shows hotspots on the planet—particularly in China, northern India, the central U.S. and western Europe—where farmers could substantially reduce fertilizer use with little or no impact on food production. Amazingly, only 10 percent of the world's cropland generates 30 to 40 percent of agriculture's fertilizer pollution.

Among the actions that can fix this excess are policy and economic incentives, such as payments to farmers for watershed stewardship and protection, for reducing excessive fertilizer use, for improving manure management (especially manure storage, so that less runs off into the watershed during a storm), for capturing excess nutrients through recycling, and for instituting other conservation practices. In addition, restoring wetlands will enhance their capacity to act as a natural sponge to filter out nutrients in runoff.

Here again reduced tillage can help nourish the soil, as can precision agriculture (applying fertilizer and water only when and where they are needed and most effective) and organic farming techniques.

Shift Diets Away from Meat

We can dramatically increase global food availability and environmental sustainability by using more of our crops to feed people directly and less to fatten livestock.

Globally, humans could net up to three quadrillion additional calories every year—a 50 percent increase from our current supply—by switching to all-plant diets. Naturally, our current diets and uses of crops have many economic and social benefits, and our preferences are unlikely to change completely. Still, even small shifts in diet, say, from grain-fed beef to poultry, pork or pasture-fed beef, can pay off handsomely.

Reduce Food Waste

A final, obvious but often neglected recommendation is to reduce waste in the food system. Roughly 30 percent of the food produced on the planet is discarded, lost, spoiled or consumed by pests.

In rich countries, much of the waste takes place at the consumer end of the system, in restaurants and trash cans. Simple changes in our daily consumption patterns—reducing oversize portions, food thrown in the garbage, and the number of takeout and restaurant meals—could significantly trim losses, as well as our expanding waistlines. In poorer countries, the losses are similar in size but occur at the producer end, in the form of failed crops, stockpiles ruined by pests, or food that is never delivered because of bad infrastructure and markets. Improved storage, refrigeration and distribution systems can cut waste appreciably. Moreover, better market tools can connect people who have crops to those who need them, such as cell-phone systems in Africa that link suppliers, traders and purchasers.

Although completely eliminating waste from farm to fork is not realistic, even small steps would be extremely beneficial. Targeted efforts—especially reducing waste of the most resource-intensive foods such as meat and dairy—could make a big difference.

MOVING TOWARD A NETWORKED FOOD SYSTEM

In principle, our five-point strategy can address many food security and environmental challenges. Together the steps could increase the world's food availability by 100 to 180 percent, while significantly lowering greenhouse gas emissions, biodiversity losses, water use and water pollution.

It is important to emphasize that all five points (and perhaps more) must be pursued together. No single strategy is sufficient to solve all our problems. Think silver buckshot, not a silver bullet. We have tremendous successes from the green revolution and industrial-scale agriculture to build on, along with innovations in organic farming and local food systems. Let's take the best ideas and incorporate them into a new approach—a sustainable food system that focuses on nutritional, social and environmental performance, to bring responsible food production to scale.

We can configure this next-generation system as a network of local agricultural systems that are sensitive to nearby climate, water resources, ecosystems and culture and that are connected through efficient means of global trade and transport. Such a system could be resilient and also pay farmers a living wage.

One device that would help foster this new food system would be the equivalent of the Leadership in Energy and Environmental Design program now in place for constructing new commercial buildings sustainably. This LEED program awards increasingly higher levels of certification based on points that are accumulated by incorporating any of a wide range of green options, from solar power and efficient lighting to recycled building materials and low construction waste.

For sustainable agriculture, foods would be awarded points based on how well they deliver nutrition, food security and other public benefits, minus their environmental and social costs. This certification would help us get beyond current food labels such as "local" and "organic," which really do not tell us much about what we are eating. Instead we can look at the whole performance of our food—across nutritional, social and environmental dimensions—and weigh the costs and benefits of different farming approaches.

Imagine the possibilities: sustainable citrus and coffee from the tropics, connected to sustainable cereals from the temperate zone, supplemented by locally grown greens and root vegetables, all grown under transparent, performance-based standards. Use your smartphone and the latest sustainable food app, and you will learn where your food came from, who grew it, how it was grown, and how it ranks against various social, nutritional and environmental criteria. And when you find food that works, you can tweet about it to your social network of farmers and foodies.

The principles and practices of our different agricultural systems—from large-scale commercial to local and organic—provide the foundation for grappling with the world's food security and environmental needs. Feeding nine billion people in a truly sustainable way will be one of the greatest challenges our civilization has had to confront. It will require the imagination, determination and hard work of countless people from all over the world. There is no time to lose.

Jonathan A. Foley is director of the Institute on the Environment at the University of Minnesota, where he is also McKnight Presidential Chair of Global Sustainability.

QUESTIONS ABOUT MEANING

1. Foley refers to agriculture as "the planet's dominant environmental threat." What does he mean by this?
2. What three related challenges face the world's food production system? What steps are recommended to address these challenges?
3. What kinds of barriers prevent farmers from simply growing more crops?

QUESTIONS FOR RHETORICAL ANALYSIS

4. What rhetorical features make Foley's article easy to read? What features might pique the interest of readers? Explain.
5. Consider Foley's use of statistics in the following statements:

   Amazingly, only 10 percent of the world's cropland generates 30 to 40 percent of agriculture's fertilizer pollution.

   Together the steps could increase the world's food availability by 100 to 180 percent.

   An international team of experts, which I coordinated, has settled on five steps that, if pursued together, could raise by more than 100 percent the food available for human consumption globally. . . .

   In what other ways could the statistical information in these statements be expressed? Would these other versions be more or less effective? Explain.

"Closing Yield Gaps through Nutrient and Water Management," *Nature*, NATHANIEL D. MUELLER, JAMES S. GERBER, MATT JOHNSTON, DEEPAK K. RAY, NAVIN RAMANKUTTY, AND JONATHAN A. FOLEY

In the preceding article from *Scientific American*, environmental scientist Jonathan Foley refers to research conducted by a team of experts he gathered to address the problem of world hunger. Scientists from that research team coauthored the next article, originally published in the journal *Nature* in 2012. Unlike *Scientific American*, which is a popular science magazine, *Nature* is a journal that publishes original research papers (often called "letters") from a range of science disciplines. The target audience for this article is other scientists. As a result, the reading is technical and sometimes difficult for lay readers, but the authors' summary sentences—along with your previous knowledge about the research—will allow you to follow the gist of the article, even when you can't understand all of the details. As you read, consider how the images and figures in this article contrast with the figure found in the previous article.

ABSTRACT

In the coming decades, a crucial challenge for humanity will be meeting future food demands without undermining further the integrity of the Earth's environmental systems.[1–6] Agricultural systems are already major forces of global environmental degradation,[4,7] but population growth and increasing consumption of calorie- and meat-intensive diets are expected to roughly double human food demand by 2050 (ref. 3). Responding to these pressures, there is increasing focus on "sustainable intensification" as a means to increase yields on underperforming landscapes while simultaneously decreasing the environmental impacts of agricultural systems.[2–4,8–11] However, it is unclear what such efforts might entail for the future of global agricultural landscapes. Here we present a global-scale assessment of intensification prospects from closing "yield gaps" (differences between observed yields and those attainable in a given region), the spatial patterns of agricultural management practices and yield limitation, and the management changes that may be necessary to achieve increased yields. We find that global yield variability is heavily controlled by fertilizer use, irrigation and climate. Large production increases (45% to 70% for most crops) are possible from closing yield gaps to 100% of attainable yields, and the changes to management practices that are needed to close yield gaps vary considerably by region and current intensity. Furthermore, we find that there are large opportunities to reduce the environmental impact of agriculture by eliminating nutrient overuse, while still allowing an approximately 30% increase in production of major cereals (maize, wheat and rice). Meeting the food security and sustainability challenges of the coming decades is possible, but will require considerable changes in nutrient and water management.

Opportunities for agricultural intensification were analysed for seventeen major crops (which covered approximately 76% of global harvested cropland area between 1997 and 2003 (Food and Agriculture Organization of the United Nations)). Yield gaps were estimated by comparing landscape-level observed yields[12] to "attainable yields," determined by identifying high-yielding areas within zones of similar climate. As empirical estimates, attainable yields are more conservative than absolute biophysical "potential yields,"[13] but they are probably achievable using current technology and management techniques.

Considerable yield-improvement opportunities exist relative to current attainable yield ceilings, with opportunities differing dramatically by crop and geography. [. . .] Globally, we find that closing yield gaps to 100% of attainable yields could increase worldwide crop production by 45% to 70% for most major crops (with 64%, 71% and 47% increases for maize, wheat and rice, respectively). Eastern Europe and Sub-Saharan Africa show considerable "low-hanging" intensification opportunities for major cereals (Fig. 5.18); these areas could have large production gains if yields were increased to only 50% of attainable yields. East and South Asia also have substantial intensification opportunities owing to their vast agricultural lands and the geographic variability in their yields and yield gaps.

Assessing opportunities for more sustainable intensification requires an understanding of the factors driving yield variation across the world.

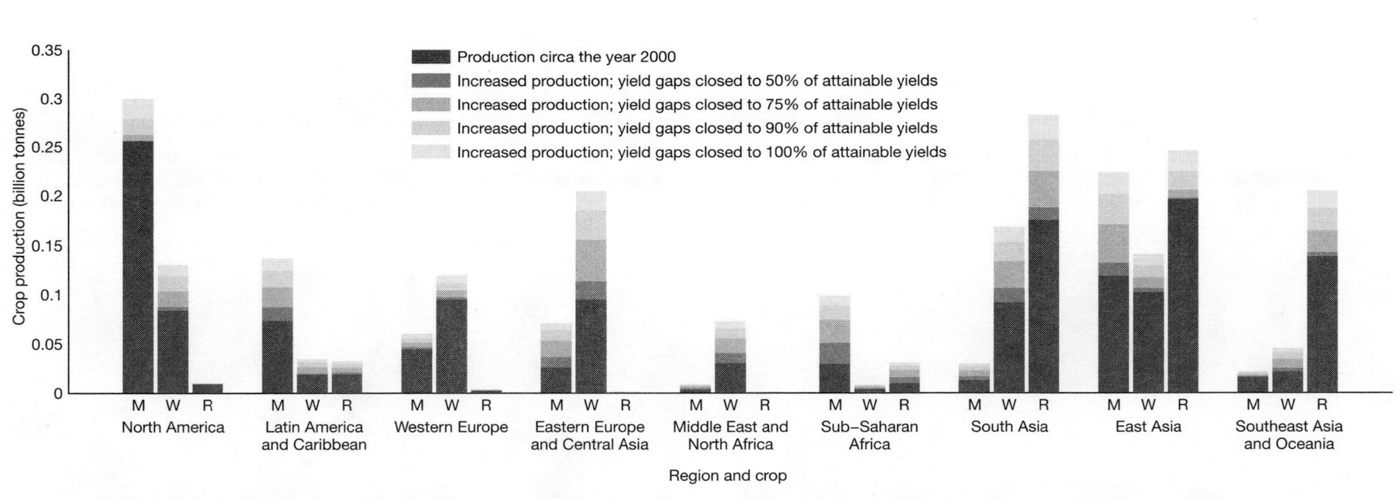

Figure 5.18 Global production increases for maize, wheat and rice from closing yield gaps to 50%, 75%, 90% and 100% of attainable yields. The greatest opportunities for increases in absolute production (from closing yield gaps to 100% of estimated attainable yields) are wheat (W) in Eastern Europe and Central Asia, rice (R) in South Asia and maize (M) in East Asia. Absolute production increases for individual crops in Sub-Saharan Africa are smaller owing to lower attainable yields and diverse cropping systems (that is, less area devoted to any one crop). The region could still achieve large production increases in cassava, maize and sugarcane.

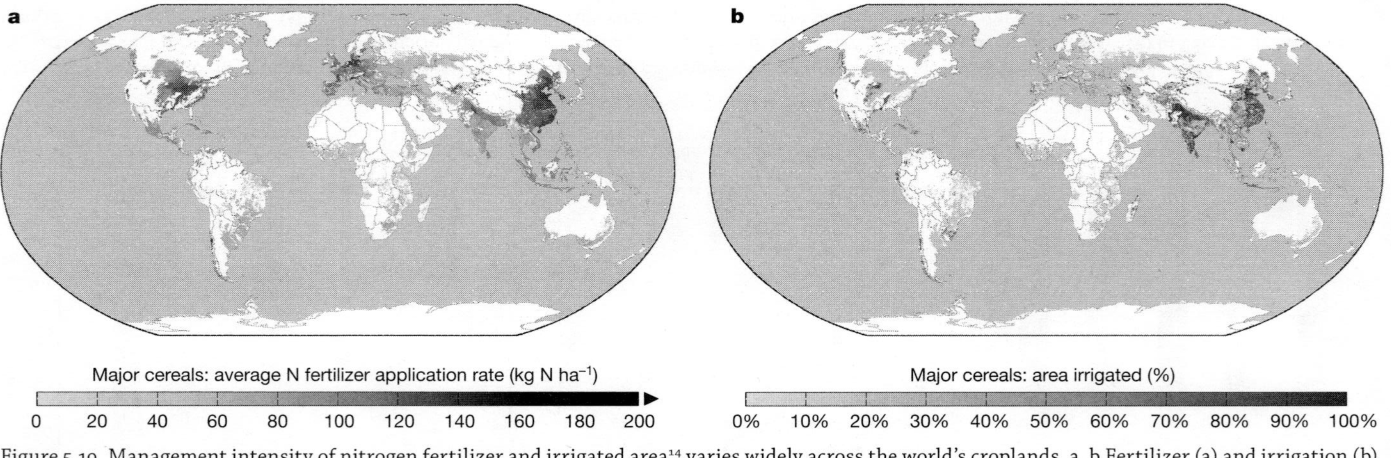

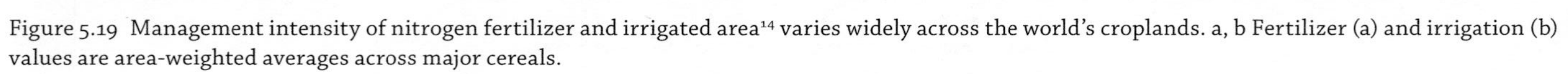

Figure 5.19 Management intensity of nitrogen fertilizer and irrigated area[14] varies widely across the world's croplands. a, b Fertilizer (a) and irrigation (b) values are area-weighted averages across major cereals.

Fundamentally, yield gaps are caused by deficiencies in the biophysical crop growth environment that are not addressed by agricultural management practices. Here we explicitly examined key biophysical drivers of crop yield by using global, crop-specific irrigation data[14] and by developing a new global, crop-specific data set of nitrogen (N), phosphate (P_2O_5) and potash (K_2O) fertilizer application rates. We find extensive geographic variation in these management practices, with high fertilizer application rates concentrated in high-income and some rapidly developing countries (Fig. 5.19). Likewise, irrigated areas[14] are heavily concentrated in South Asia, East Asia and parts of the United States (Fig. 5.19).

Using input–yield crop models, we found that the spatial patterns of climate, fertilizer application and irrigated area explain 60% to 80% of global-yield variability for most major crops. Yields of some crops (for example, sorghum, millet and groundnut) were primarily controlled by climate, whereas others (for example, barley, sugar beet and oil palm) showed strong management responses. Surprisingly, model residuals showed little sensitivity to soil and slope parameters, suggesting that such relationships are obscured on the landscape scale with existing data sets.

The factors that primarily limit increasing crop yields to within 75% of their attainable yields vary by crop and region. For example, Eastern Europe and West Africa stand out as hotspots of nutrient limitation for maize, whereas Eastern Europe seems to experience nutrient limitation for wheat. Co-limitation of nutrients and water is observed across East Africa and Western India for maize, portions of the US Great Plains and the Mediterranean Basin for wheat, and in Southeast Asia for rice. We note that the management practices that limit yield increases depend on the degree of yield-gap closure desired. For example, closing maize yield gaps to 50% of attainable yields (approximately 2.5 tonnes per hectare) in Sub-Saharan Africa primarily requires addressing nutrient deficiencies, but closing yield gaps to 75% of attainable yields (approximately 3.6 tonnes per hectare) requires increases in both irrigated area and nutrient application over most of the region.

We examined potential changes in irrigated area and nutrient application that are needed to close yield gaps of maize, wheat and rice to within 75% attainable yields (a 29% global production increase) using our input–yield models. On the landscape scale, yield gaps in co-limited regions can be closed through a range of irrigated-area and nutrient-intensity combinations. For example, 73% of these underachieving areas could close yield gaps by solely focusing on nutrient inputs (with 18%, 16% and 35% increases in N, P_2O_5 and K_2O application relative to baseline global consumption, respectively), whereas only 16% of underachieving areas could close yield gaps by solely increasing irrigation. Jointly increasing irrigated area and nutrient application could close yield gaps on all underachieving areas (with 30%, 27% and 54% increases in N, P_2O_5 and K_2O application, respectively, and a 25% increase in irrigated hectares).

To minimize the environmental impacts of intensification, increased irrigation and nutrient application to close crop yield gaps should be complemented by efforts to decrease overuse of crop inputs wherever possible[15–18]; combined, these efforts could increase total food production while decreasing the overall global use of water and nutrients. For example, we estimate that by addressing imbalances and inefficiencies, nitrogen- and phosphate-fertilizer application on maize, wheat and rice could decrease globally by 11 million tonnes of nitrogen (28%) and 5 million tonnes of phosphate (38%) without impacting current yields. Nutrient overuse on these crops is particularly dramatic in China, confirming field-scale results.[15] To close yield gaps to 75% of attainable yields while also eliminating input overuse (under joint nutrient and irrigation intervention), we project that smaller net changes in nutrient inputs would be required: 9%, 22% and 34% changes in N, P_2O_5 and K_2O application. Notably, it would be possible to close global yield gaps on major cereals to within 75% of attainable yields with fairly minimal changes to total worldwide nitrogen and phosphate use by coupling targeted intensification with efforts to reduce nutrient imbalances and inefficiencies. Geographically optimizing input intensity and increasing field-scale efficiencies (beyond the average efficiencies implicit in our input–yield models) could improve production further relative to inputs.

Closing yield gaps may not always be desirable or practical in the short term, given marginal returns for additional inputs, regional land-management policies, limits on sustainable water resources and socio-economic constraints (for example, access to capital, infrastructure, institutions and political stability). However, use of precision agriculture techniques, conservation tillage, high-yielding hybrids, increased plant populations and multifunctional landscape management can help to mitigate negative environmental impacts of intensive agriculture.[19–21] Additionally, use of organic fertilizers (omitted in this analysis owing to data limitations) are essential for improving soil carbon, enhancing soil biota and increasing water-holding capacity.[22] Social triggers of intensification will differ across regions; for example, because of development interventions by governments or NGOs, market-driven incentives for farmer investment, and land scarcity in regions not fully connected to global markets.[23]

Changes to agricultural management to close yield gaps should be considered in the context of climate change, which is expected to substantially impact yields[24,25] and induce management adaptations.[26] Specifically, a major concern is how changes in water availability may conflict with projected irrigation requirements for closing yield gaps.

The fertilizer data set, yield gap estimates and yield models presented here could be used widely to assess intensification opportunities and the environmental impacts of changing agricultural systems. However, these data and analyses are not without limitations. Most importantly, the analyses rely on agricultural management, yield and climate data from a variety of different sources and on different scales. Overall, these results are most useful across regional and global scales, leaving fine-scale and temporal details obscured (for example, intra- and interannual variation in climate and yield creates particular uncertainty about irrigation requirements). Moreover, although our models confirm the importance of climate, fertilizers and irrigation in determining contemporary patterns of global cropland productivity, we do not discount the importance of additional biophysical characteristics (including soil characteristics) and management practices (including crop rotation patterns, organic nutrient inputs, micronutrients, improved seed quality, conservation tillage and pest management). Incorporating these factors into the analytical framework could improve the accuracy and utility of the analyses. Additional research on cropland intensification must also assess the opportunities and environmental tradeoffs for increasing cropping intensity and decreasing pre- and post-harvest crop losses.

The future of agriculture faces two great challenges: substantial increases in food demand must be met while decreasing agriculture's global environmental footprint. Closing yield gaps and increasing resource efficiency are necessary strategies towards meeting this challenge, but they must be combined with efforts to halt agricultural expansion, reduce food waste and promote sensible diets, and produce advanced crop varieties.[1,4] This analysis emphasizes the crucial role of nutrient and water management in pathways towards sustainable intensification, and provides a starting point for a more comprehensive discussion of intensification opportunities and challenges. Context-dependent policies and agricultural development programs must address drivers of yield limitation while encouraging management practices that improve tradeoffs between production and environmental impacts.

METHODS SUMMARY

Yield gaps were quantified by comparing existing yields to climate-specific attainable yields. Our approach refines previous estimates[27,28] by excluding climate outliers and using crop-specific, equal-area climate zones. Fertilizer application rate and consumption data were compiled for nations and subnational units across the globe. [. . .] Crop- and crop-group-specific application rates were then distributed across detailed maps of crop[12] and pasture[29] areas, and rates were harmonized with subnational and national nutrient consumption data.

Fertilizer and irrigation data were used to parameterize nutrient response curves and rainfed maximum yields, using nonlinear regression analyses within each climate zone. Using these relationships, we estimated changes in inputs necessary to close yield gaps, as well as decreases in inputs possible from addressing inefficiencies and imbalances.

Received 2 April; accepted 13 July 2012.
Published online 29 August; corrected online 10 October 2012.

NOTES

1. Godfray, H. C. J. *et al.* Food security: the challenge of feeding 9 billion people. *Science* **327**, 812–818 (2010).
2. Royal Society *Reaping the benefits.* 1–86 (The Royal Society, 2009).
3. Tilman, D., Balzer, C., Hill, J. & Befort, B. L. Global food demand and the sustainable intensification of agriculture. *Proc. Natl Acad. Sci. USA* **108**, 20260–20264 (2011).
4. Foley, J. A. *et al.* Solutions for a cultivated planet. *Nature* **478**, 337–342 (2011).
5. Robertson, G. P. & Swinton, S. M. Reconciling agricultural productivity and environmental integrity: a grand challenge for agriculture. *Front. Ecol. Environ* **3**, 38–46 (2005).
6. Cassman, K. G., Dobermann, A., Walters, D. T. & Yang, H. Meeting cereal demand while protecting natural resources and improving environmental quality. *Annu. Rev. Environ. Resour.* **28**, 315–358 (2003).
7. Foley, J. A. *et al.* Global consequences of land use. *Science* **309**, 570–574 (2005).
8. Cassman, K. G. Ecological intensification of cereal production systems: Yield potential, soil quality, and precision agriculture. *Proc. Natl Acad. Sci. USA* **96**, 5952–5959 (1999).
9. Matson, P. A. & Vitousek, P. M. Agricultural intensification: Will land spared from farming be land spared for nature? *Conserv. Biol.* **20**, 709–710 (2006).
10. Clough, Y. *et al.* Combining high biodiversity with high yields in tropical agroforests. *Proc. Natl Acad. Sci. USA* 1–6 (2011).
11. Burney, J. A., Davis, S. J. & Lobell, D. B. Greenhouse gas mitigation by agricultural intensification. *Proc. Natl Acad. Sci. USA* **107**, 12052–12057 (2010).
12. Monfreda, C., Ramankutty, N. & Foley, J. A. Farming the planet:
2. Geographic distribution of crop areas, yields, physiological types, and net primary production in the year 2000. *Glob. Biogeochem. Cycles* **22**, GB1022 (2008).
13. Lobell, D. B., Cassman, K. G. & Field, C. B. Crop yield gaps: their importance, magnitudes, and causes. *Annu. Rev. Environ. Resour.* **34**, 179–204 (2009).
14. Portmann, F. T., Siebert, S. & Doell, P. MIRCA2000—global monthly irrigated and rainfed crop areas around the year 2000: a new high-resolution data set for agricultural and hydrological modeling. *Glob. Biogeochem. Cycles* **24**, GB1011 (2010).

15. Ju, X.-T. *et al.* Reducing environmental risk by improving N management in intensive Chinese agricultural systems. *Proc. Natl Acad. Sci. USA* **106**, 3041–3046 (2009).
16. Liu, J. *et al.* A high-resolution assessment on global nitrogen flows in cropland. *Proc. Natl Acad. Sci. USA* **107**, 8035–8040 (2010).
17. MacDonald, G. K., Bennett, E. M., Potter, P. A. & Ramankutty, N. Agronomic phosphorus imbalances across the world's croplands. *Proc. Natl Acad. Sci. USA* **108**, 3086–3091 (2011).
18. Vitousek, P. M. *et al.* Agriculture. Nutrient imbalances in agricultural development. *Science* **324**, 1519–1520 (2009).
19. Oenema, O. & Pietrzak, S. Nutrient management in food production: Achieving agronomic and environmental targets. *Ambio* **31**, 159–168 (2002).
20. Cassman, K. G., Dobermann, A. & Walters, D. T. Agroecosystems, nitrogen-use efficiency, and nitrogen management. *Ambio* **31**, 132–140 (2002).
21. Jordan, N. *et al.* Sustainable development of the agricultural bioeconomy *Science* **316,** 1570–1571 (2007).
22. Sánchez, P. A. Tripling crop yields in tropical Africa. *Nature Geosci.* **3,** 299–300 (2010).
23. Lambin, E. F. *et al.* The causes of land-use and land-cover change: moving beyond the myths. *Glob. Environ. Change* **11**, 261–269 (2001).
24. Parry, M., Canziani, O., Palutikof, J., &. co-authors. *Technical Summary. Climate Change 2007: Impacts, Adaptation and Vulnerability. Contribution of Working Group II to the Fourth Assessment Report of the Intergovernmental Panel on Climate Change* (eds Parry, M. L., Canziani, O. F., Palutikof, J. P., van der Linden, P. J. and Hanson, C. E.) 23–78 (Cambridge Univ. Press, 2007).
25. Lobell, D. B., Schlenker, W. & Costa-Roberts, J. Climate trends and global crop production since 1980. *Science* **333,** 616–620 (2011).
26. Howden, S. M. *et al.* Adapting agriculture to climate change. *Proc. Natl Acad. Sci. USA* **104,** 19691–19696 (2007).
27. Licker, *R. et al.* Mind the gap: how do climate and agricultural management explain the "yield gap" of croplands around the world? *Glob. Ecol. Biogeogr.* **19,** 769–782 (2010).
28. Johnston, M. *et al.* Closing the gap: global potential for increasing biofuel production through agricultural intensification. *Environ. Res. Lett.* **6,** 034028 (2011).
29. Ramankutty, N., Evan, A. T, Monfreda, C. & Foley, J. A. Farming the planet: 1. Geographic distribution of global agricultural lands in the year 2000. *Glob. Biogeochem. Cycles* **22,** GB1003 (2008).

Nathaniel D. Mueller, James S. Gerber, Matt Johnston, Deepak K. Ray, and Jonathan A. Foley are with the Institute on the Environment, University of Minnesota, St. Paul, MN 55108, USA. Navin Ramankutty is with the Department of Geography and Global Environmental and Climate Change Center, McGill University, Montreal, Quebec H3A 2K6, Canada.

QUESTIONS ABOUT MEANING

1. What are agriculture "yield gaps" and how are they determined? What world regions have the greatest potential for increased crop yields?
2. What measures can be taken to close yield gaps around the world? What sometimes keeps people from taking these measures?

QUESTIONS FOR RHETORICAL ANALYSIS

3. What do the titles, vocabulary level, and figures for Foley's two articles suggest about the purpose and audience of each article? Explain and illustrate.
4. Many of the unsupported claims in Foley's *Scientific American* article are supported in the *Nature* article (and in supplemental material not reprinted here). Here, for example, are two statements from the *Scientific American* article:

> Our analysis suggests that closing the yield gap for the world's top 16 crops could increase total food production by 50 to 60 percent, with little environmental damage.
>
> Our analysis shows hotspots on the planet—particularly in China, northern India, the central U.S. and western Europe—where farmers could substantially reduce fertilizer use with little or no impact on food production.

How were these estimates or conclusions determined by the research team? Contrast one of these statements to the more extended explanation in the *Nature* article you read. What makes the *Nature* passage less accessible to lay readers but more convincing to academic readers? What does a comparison of the passages reveal about the expectations of the intended audiences?

THINKING AND WRITING ABOUT THE TOPIC

Jonathan Foley is the director of the Institute on the Environment at the University of Minnesota. The Institute has produced a short video titled *How Do We Feed the World without Destroying It* that talks about the issues addressed in the two articles you've read. Watch the video, available on YouTube, and notice the combination of colors, sounds, and images. How does the video presentation make the issue more accessible than either the *Scientific American* or the *Nature* "article" How would you compare the purpose, audience, and effectiveness of these three different presentations?

WORKS CITED

Bahls, Patrick, et al. "Proofs and Persuasion: A Cross-Disciplinary Analysis of Math Students' Writing." *Across the Disciplines* 18.1 (2011). Web. 28 September 2011. http://wac.colostate.edu/atd/articles/bahlsetal2011/index.cfm

Boggs, Deborah A., et al. "Fruit and Vegetable Intake in Relation to Risk of Breast Cancer in the Black Women's Health Study." *American Journal of Epidemiology* 172.11 (2010): 1268–79. Print.

Coleman, Renita. "The Effects of Visuals on Ethical Reasoning: What's a Photograph Worth to Journalists Making Moral Decisions?" *Journalism and Mass Communication Quarterly* 83.4 (2006): 835–50. Print.

Gibson, Rhonda, and Dolf Zillmann. "Reading between the Photographs: The Influence of Incidental Pictorial Information on Issue Perception." *Journalism and Mass Communication Quarterly* 77.2 (2000): 355–66. Print.

Gonzales, Joseph, and Susan Levinan. "Vegetables Reduce Breast Cancer Risk." *Good Medicine* 20.1 (Winter 2011): 17. Print.

Hyland, Ken. "Options of Identity in Academic Writing." *ELT Journal* 56.4 (2002): 351–58.

Jae, Haeran, Devon S. Delvecchio, and Deborah Cowles. "Picture-Text Incongruency in Print Advertisements among Low- and High-Literacy Consumers." *Journal of Consumer Affairs* 42.3 (2008): 439–51. Print.

Li, Zheng (Jeremy). "Design and Development of a New Automated and High-Speed Gas Filling Systems." *ISRN Mechanical Engineering* (2011): 1–4. Print.

Lytle, Beverly, and Caroline Yang. "Detecting Forged Handwriting with Wavelets and Statistics." *Undergraduate Math Journal* 7.1 (2006): 1–10. Web. 18 June 2013. http://www.rose-hulman.edu/mathjournal/archives/2006/vol7-n1/paper8/v7n1-8pd.pdf

Miller, Thomas. "Visual Persuasion: A Comparison of Visuals in Academic Texts and the Popular Press." *English for Specific Purposes* 17.1 (1998): 29–46. Print.

"Nursing: The Effect of Different Kinds of Charting." Research and Commentary. *Nursing Children & Young People* 24.8 (2012): 11. Print.

Pelet, Jean-Éric, and Panagiota Papadopoulou. "The Effect of Colors of e-Commerce Websites on Consumer Mood, Memorization and Buying Intention." *European Journal of Information Systems* 21.4 (2012): 438–67. Print.

Schwartz, Barry. "When Words Decide." *Scientific American Mind* 18.4 (2007): 36–43. Print.

Slovic, Paul. "When Compassion Fails." *New Scientist* 194.2598 (2007): 18. Print.

Vekiri, Ioanna. "What Is the Value of Graphical Displays in Learning?" *Educational Psychology Review* 14.3 (2002): 261–312. Print.

Williams, Mark, et al. "Alpine Areas in the Colorado Front Range as Monitors of Climate Change and Ecosystem Response." *Geographical Review* 92 (2002):180–91. Print.

Wolfe, Joanna. "Rhetorical Numbers: A Case for Quantitative Writing in the Composition Classroom." *College Composition and Communication* 61.3 (2010): 452–75. Print.

CHAPTER 6

Writing with Authority

We follow rules every day. Many are written. Even more are unwritten. These rules, sometimes called *conventions*, shape behavior in every aspect of our lives, including the way we converse with others. When you see a friend approaching on the side-walk, you greet her. If you haven't seen her in a while, you ask how she's been. If you want her to join you for lunch, you likely ask where she wants to eat. Not following these conventions of conversation would strike others as odd or even rude.

Just as we draw conclusions about people based on the way they talk or interact with others, readers draw conclusions about writers based on how they present themselves. Academic conversations—appearing in written form—have conventions, too, and writers in fields as disparate as literature and mathematics follow them, not because they are "required" but because writers who violate these conventions risk not being taken seriously. Once you learn to recognize these conventions, you can begin to adopt an academic style in your own papers and create the ethos of someone familiar with the language of academic arguments. In other words, you can begin to write with authority.

Whether learning to swing a golf club, speak French, or dance the tango, you learn by observing others who have already mastered the skill. Studying experts is how you learn to produce academic writing as well. You notice features in their writing and try to imitate them in your own. Eventually, their techniques come naturally to you and you, too, become a writer that others want to imitate.

Throughout this chapter we will look at examples of expert writing. Many of them are from a sampling of 24 articles from six disciplines: sports medicine, biology, engineering, psychology, marketing, and literature. The articles are all scholarly research articles, originally published in peer-reviewed academic journals. If you're looking for models to imitate in your own academic writing, research articles serve as good ones because this is where experts write for others in their discipline, in the way most admired by peers in their field. In addition, the scholarly research article—in its statement of purpose, synthesis of sources, and paragraph development—resembles the papers students write. Although in some ways the writing in one discipline does differ from that of another—a point we'll return to later—for now we will focus on features that connect academic papers across disciplines. These features include:

- Reviewing what others have written about a topic and announcing the value of the paper,

- Stating the purpose of the paper,
- Qualifying claims and anticipating objections,
- Preparing readers for what's to come,
- Using specialized vocabulary and "academic" phrasing,
- Using first person to establish authority, and
- Bringing the conversation to a close.

Read on to learn how to include these features in your own writing.

Reviewing the Past and Announcing the Value of Your Paper

When academics write, they join a conversation. No matter the topic, someone before them has written about it. To put their ideas into context, academic writers refer to what other researchers have already said or discovered about the subject. In this way writers show that they will address an issue that matters (others are talking about it, after all). They also indicate how they will contribute to the conversation. Here is an example from the introduction to a social psychology research report:

EXAMPLE 6.1 FROM AN ACADEMIC JOURNAL IN PSYCHOLOGY

Numerous studies over the past two decades have examined the perpetuation of sex bias through the use of sexist language. Although such language has been conceptually linked to sexist behavior (Blaubergs, 1978; Bodine, 1975), controversy remains regarding the effect of sexist language on social behavior. Much of the research has demonstrated the deleterious effects of sexist language toward women, but little has examined the impact of sexist language on men. (Hale et al. 697)

The writers refer to previous research about sexist language, including research conducted by Blaubergs and Bodine.

But little attention has been devoted to what the authors will consider: "the impact of sexist language on men."

In this introduction, the writers show that they are aware that others have studied sexist language but that they will contribute to the conversation by filling a void in the existing body of research.

Many academic papers explore an aspect of an issue still unresolved. Consider this example:

EXAMPLE 6.2 FROM AN ACADEMIC JOURNAL IN MARKETING

The vast majority of research that has assessed the effect of price promotions on brand evaluation has studied the effect after product trial, rather than pretrial (Scott and Tybout 1979; Scott and Yalch 1980; Tybout and Scott 1983). . . . Unlike previous studies, which 5 examined the effects of price promotions after trial, we examine the effects of price promotions pretrial to isolate their informational impact on brand quality perceptions from the potentially moderating effect of prior personal experience with the brand.

(Raghubir and Corfman 212)

In this passage the writers identify how their research is different from previous research.

You might have noticed these introductions do not begin in any of the "traditional" ways students are often taught to begin an essay (e.g., asking a question, quoting a famous line, making a startling or provocative statement). But these introductions are engaging for a different reason: They answer the "so what" question. That is, the writers explain why the topic they will discuss matters or how their discussion of the topic will be different from that of others. This practice of identifying how one's research will respond to or expand on what others have said is so common in academic writing that it has a name: **identifying the gap**. By identifying and responding to the gap, a writer justifies the value of his or her contribution to the ongoing conversation. Once you learn this convention, you will know how to go about starting your own papers. Once you understand this convention, you'll be able to follow the gist of scholarly article introductions across the disciplines—even when you don't understand all of the technical details.

Concept in Practice 6.1: Recognizing Patterns in Introductions

The following paragraph, taken from the introduction of a biology article, includes plenty of technical language; but the writers follow the familiar pattern of reviewing past research before announcing the purpose of the new research. This allows even those unfamiliar with the vocabulary to follow the conversation.

In the past decades, major insights have been gained into how intrinsic factors and extrinsic signals control and guide the development of dendrites and dendritic spines and how patterned neural activity shapes this process (Hering and Sheng, 2001; Whitford et al., 2002; . . . Van Aelst and Cline, 2004). Large gaps still exist in our knowledge about how all these pathways integrate and execute their function at the molecular level and orchestrate the development of dendritic morphology. In particular, little is known about the molecular circuit neurons used to

The writers establish that they are joining an ongoing conversation.

But there are holes in the conversation that need to be filled.

This is the specific aspect of the conversation that the writers will take up.

make the binary decision on initiating the formation of a new dendritic branch or spine.

(Huang, Zang, and Reichardt 527)

You don't need to know what the "formation of a new dendritic branch or spine" means to understand that "little is known" about it and that the writers want to remedy that situation.

Writers from all disciplines—including all 24 expert writers in our sampling of articles—review previous research, identify a "gap" in that research, and explain how their paper will address that gap. In the natural and social sciences, the review of previous research generally appears early in the paper. In some other disciplines, however, references to previous research may appear throughout a paper. Literary scholars, for example, might reference previous research throughout their articles to show how aspects of their reading of a text compare with those of other scholars (Balocco 212).

Academic writers acknowledge those who have contributed to the existing body of research—even when they disagree with those researchers. In Example 6.3 the authors refer to two economists (Thompson and Fox-Kean) with whom they disagree. Like Thompson and Fox-Kean, the authors have studied the tendency of patent recipients in a given field to live in the same geographical area. Despite disagreeing with Thompson and Fox-Kean's findings, however, the authors still acknowledge the work of their predecessors:

EXAMPLE 6.3 FROM AN ACADEMIC JOURNAL IN ECONOMICS

Given the importance of this issue for our understanding of the determinants of economic growth and for economic policy, we are, of course, delighted to see further work in this area, and [Thompson and Fox-Kean] are to be congratulated
5 for their careful data collection and construction work, as well as for their thoughtful raising of a number of important issues. We take issue, however, both with some of the key assumptions of their paper and with the interpretation of their more detailed quantitative results.

(Henderson, Jaffe, and Trajtenberg 461)

Previous researchers are commended for their work before the current authors "take issue" with some of their findings.

Rather than ignoring opinions or research that conflicts with their own, the writers regard the disagreement as *an opportunity to enter the conversation.* But notice that even when their goal is to refute what has been written, academic writers show respect for others in the conversation, much in the same way that you would listen to a friend's opinion before disagreeing with it.

By referring to what others have said, writers demonstrate that the issues they write about matter. You, too, can make this move in your papers. Consider the following essay introduction, written by a first-year college student for other students in her composition course. The essay describes how students can learn to write like experts:

> Writing an essay for the first time in college can be a frightening experience. One reason could be that students write about topics they aren't experts in. In his research, David Bartholomae, former Chair of the English Department at the University of Pittsburgh, found that even if students aren't experts, they can carry on the bluff (403), meaning they can try to write like an expert, even if they aren't experts yet. Most students naturally have trouble doing this in their writing. There are, however, techniques that can help students carry on the "bluff." They include using traditional formulas for joining the conversation and using the language of the discipline.

A reference to what one of the student's sources (Bartholomae) has said about how novices learn to write like experts.

The student introduces her own contribution to the conversation and announces her main ideas.

The student uses information she has read to show that she is joining an ongoing conversation. If you haven't yet read much about your topic, you can refer generally to what is believed about it (e.g., "Many students today believe that . . .") or refer to a body of research ("economists today believe . . ."). In this way, you can imitate the expert pattern, demonstrate that you are joining a conversation, and thus establish that your contribution warrants consideration.

Introducing and Announcing the Purpose of Your Paper

We've seen that most academic writers begin their papers by mentioning what others have already learned about their subject and identifying what aspect of the topic warrants further attention. We've also seen that these two moves—reviewing what's been said and identifying a "gap"—are often used to segue into an academic writer's next move: announcing the purpose of the paper.

Most academic writing includes a statement of purpose or *thesis statement*, usually near the end of the introduction. This sentence (or sentences) identifies the central claim the writer will support throughout the paper or the question or topic the writer will explore. All 24 expert writers in our sample of articles provide an explicit statement of purpose. Table 6.1 presents a few examples.

Why do academic writers state their purpose and organization so explicitly? Research indicates that when writers announce what's coming in a paper (a practice sometimes referred to as **framing**), readers read faster and remember better what they have read. One study may be of particular interest to you. After analyzing 50 student essays that had been graded by professors in various disciplines, researchers Diane Tedick and Maureen Mathison determined that, in

TABLE 6.1
Sampling of Thesis Statements

Thesis Statement	Function
from an Academic Journal in Literature I will argue . . . that women writers produced some of the nineteenth century's most intellectually serious, politically radical, and artistically innovative prose. (Karcher 782)	In many papers, the statement of purpose is an opinion the writer will support.
from an Academic Journal in Psychology The present study is designed to provide further evidence on the gender differences in cognitive abilities and course work and in particular to examine the contribution of gender differences in the amount of time devoted to homework. The hypothesis is that because of their stronger work ethic girls are likely to do more homework than boys and that this is likely to be a factor contributing to their higher grades. (Mau and Lynn 120–21)	In reports of original research, the statement of purpose might announce the questions the writers will answer or the hypothesis they will test.
from an Academic Journal in Psychology In this paper, we describe how and why we recruited rape survivors as we did and what this taught us about defining communities and settings. First, we will provide an overview of the challenge we faced and why it seemed as though we were community researchers without a community. Second, we will describe the struggle we went through trying to define "community." (Campbell et al. 254)	Many writers use the statement of purpose to identify the paper's organization.

general, students received higher scores when their essays were "framed well enough for readers to be able to make predictions about the content to come" (206). In other words, professors tend to reward students who early in the paper identify the central claim they will support.

Concept in Practice 6.2: Engaging Readers and Announcing Your Goals

Although we have so far looked at one-paragraph introductions, many introductions to academic papers are multi-paragraph. The following four-paragraph introduction is from a research report written by political scientists Charles S. Taber and Milton Lodge. Notice how the writers:

- engage readers and introduce the general topic,
- relate their research to previous research and show that they are joining an existing conversation, and
- announce their purpose.

Physicists do it (Glanz 2000). Psychologists do it (Kruglanski and Webster 1996). Even political scientists do it (cites withheld to protect the guilty among us). Research findings confirming a hypothesis are accepted more or less at face value, but when confronted with contrary evidence, we become "motivated skeptics" (Kunda 1990), mulling over possible reasons for the "failure," picking apart possible flaws in the study, re-coding variables, and only when all the counterarguing fails do we rethink our beliefs. Whether this systematic bias in how scientists deal with evidence is rational or not is debatable, though one negative consequence is that bad theories and weak hypotheses, like prejudices, persist longer than they should.

How do the writers engage readers through humor while at the same time show that they will discuss a topic others are discussing?

According to previous researchers, what is it that physicists, psychologists, political scientists (and others) do?

But what about ordinary citizens? Politics is contentious (Newman, Just, and Krigier 1992). In the marketplace of ideas, citizens are confronted daily with arguments designed to either bolster their opinions or challenge their prior beliefs and attitudes (Gamson 1992). To the extent that ordinary citizens act similarly to scientists the consequences would be similar—hanging on to one's beliefs and attitudes longer and stronger than warranted. Of course, it would be foolish to push this analogy too hard since scientific practice has such built-in safeguards as peer review and double-blind experiments to prevent bad ideas from driving the good ones out of the marketplace.

How is the writers' research focus different from that of previous researchers? That is, what gap will their research begin to fill?

Ideally, one's prior beliefs and attitudes—whether scientific or social—should "anchor" the evaluation of new information and then, depending on how credible is some piece of evidence, impressions should be adjusted upward or downward (Anderson 1981). The "simple" Bayesian updating rule would be to increment the overall evaluation if the evidence is positive, decrement if negative. Assuming one has established an initial belief (attitude or hypothesis), normative models of human decision making imply or posit a two-step updating process, beginning with the collection of belief-relevant evidence, followed by the integration of new information with the prior to produce an updated judgment. Critically important in such normative models is the requirement that the collection and integration of new information be kept independent of one's prior judgment (see Evans and Over 1996).

In this article we report the results of two experiments showing that citizens are prone to overly accommodate supportive evidence while dismissing out-of-hand evidence that challenges their prior attitudes. On reading a balanced

What signal phrase prepares readers for the statement of purpose?

set of pro and con arguments about affirmative action or gun control, we find that rather than moderating or simply maintaining their original attitudes, citizens—especially those who feel the strongest about the issue and are the most sophisticated—strengthen their attitudes in ways not warranted by the evidence.

(Taber and Lodge 755–56)

What do the writers accomplish in the final paragraph of the introduction?

Qualifying Claims and Anticipating Objections

When stating their purpose, many writers qualify their central claim so that it reflects what the evidence can support. Consider again the statement of purpose from the previously quoted introduction:

> . . . We report the results of two experiments showing that citizens *are prone to* overly accommodate supportive evidence while dismissing out-of-hand evidence that challenges their prior attitudes. (Taber and Lodge, emphasis added)

Claiming that citizens *always* dismiss evidence that contradicts their beliefs would be much more difficult to defend than claiming that they are inclined to do so.

Here is another example of qualifying words (in italics) found in a statement of purpose:

> Because of their stronger work ethic girls are *likely* to do more homework than boys and . . . this is *likely* to be a factor *contributing* to their higher grades. (Mau and Lynn 121, emphasis added)

Compare this statement to the following nonqualified statement:

> Due to their stronger work ethic, girls do more homework than boys, and because of this, they get higher grades.

Without the qualifiers, the second statement makes a *definite* assertion about all girls and boys—a generalization considerably harder to defend than the first statement. In fact, academic writers tend to qualify statements about the subjects they know best because their research inevitably uncovers conflicting evidence. Qualified claims appear throughout most academic papers. Some examples from our sampling of expert writers appear in Table 6.2. (Qualifying words appear in italics.)

TABLE 6.2

Sampling of Qualified Claims from across the Disciplines

Qualifying Words (in italics)	Function
from an Academic Journal in Sports Medicine The onset latency to the ADM was not affected, whereas the onset latency to the FDI was affected, *suggesting* the lesion *may* be located in the palm, distal to the motor branch to the ADM. (Akuthota et al. 1230)	The qualifiers *suggesting* and *may* make the claim more accurate.
from an Academic Journal in Psychology [Oppressed people] *tend to* be passive and unable to recognize their own capacity to transform their social reality; and their existence is *often* accepted on the basis of destiny, bad luck or supernatural will. . . . (Balcazar, Garate-Serafini, and Keys 250)	By using words like *tend to* and *often*, the writers demonstrate that they understand that few claims about groups of people are always true.

Another way writers qualify their findings is by recognizing the limits of their research:

EXAMPLE 6.4 FROM AN ACADEMIC JOURNAL IN MARKETING

More research, varying the factors previously identified, is necessary to establish the generalizability of our findings to a broader range of product design contexts.

(Dahl, Chattopadhyay, and Gorn 28)

By pointing out the limitations of their data, the writers acknowledge the uncertainty of research findings.

The purpose of academic writing is to create knowledge, and knowledge-making is full of uncertainties. This is true even in disciplines like mathematics, as researcher Leone Burton found when she interviewed 70 mathematicians. Many of them mentioned ideas in their discipline that they once believed were right, but later determined were wrong. Experience has taught these researchers that even when they think they know something, "a new transformation might be around the corner," as one mathematician said (qtd. in Burton 133). For this reason, writers are careful to qualify their claims.

You too can improve the quality of your own arguments by qualifying broad claims, arguable assertions, opinions, and statements of perception so that they match what your evidence can bear. It's far more difficult to support a claim like "Surveys *prove* Americans are changing their attitudes about same-sex marriages" than it is to support a claim like "Surveys *suggest* Americans *may be* changing their attitudes about same-sex marriage."

There is no need to qualify *every* claim with "I think" or "I feel." Readers already know you believe the statements you write. However, when you make a statement that others might read and say, "That's not always true," acknowledge there may be exceptions. Remember, academic writers anticipate readers' objections.

Preparing the Reader for What's to Come

We've already seen how academic writers announce their point early. There are additional ways that academic writers provide cues to help readers navigate a text. They include:

- titles;
- forecasting introductions; and
- overviews, topic sentences, and headings.

Titles

One feature that can be used to good effect is the paper's title. Table 6.3 gives a sampling of titles—all taken from the articles of our 24 expert writers. Each title announces the specific topic of the article; a few (particularly in the sciences) also convey the research results.

TABLE 6.3

Sampling of Academic Titles from across the Disciplines

Discipline	Article Title
from an Academic Journal in Psychology	Conceptualizing and Measuring Historical Trauma among American Indian People
from an Academic Journal in Biology	Process Outgrowth in Oligodendrocytes Is Mediated by CNP, a Novel Microtubule Assembly Myelin Protein
from an Academic Journal in Literature	"Eviva il Coltello"? The Castrato Singer in Eighteenth-Century German Literature and Culture

Notice that titles of academic papers are often lengthy. In some (such as the literature title) a subtitle follows a question mark or colon.

Because readers read faster and comprehend more easily when they know where the writer is going, you should give your own papers titles that do more than give the assignment name (e.g., "Synthesis Essay"). Such a title doesn't prepare readers for the content—or set your paper apart from others. Instead, list the keywords or topics covered in your paper, from most important to least important; then create a title that includes the first three or four of those keywords.

Forecasting Introductions

Like titles, introductions can aid a reader's comprehension and navigation of a paper, as you already know. Example 6.5 is from a student paper:

EXAMPLE 6.5 FROM A STUDENT PAPER IN MATHEMATICS

An effective service in volleyball is crucial to a winning strategy. A good serve either will not be returned, resulting in the point, or it will be returned weakly, giving the serving team the advantage. One objective of an effective serve is to give the receivers as little time as possible to react. In this paper we construct a
5 model of a served volleyball and use it to determine how to serve so that, after crossing the net, the ball hits the desired location in the minimal amount of time.

To form a model, the forces acting on the ball must be described mathematically. We consider the three most important forces in the order of their influence on the ball: first
10 the force due to gravity, then air resistance, and finally the force from spin.

(Lithio 1)

The statement of purpose appearing at the end of this introduction announces the topics, the organization, and the logic of the writer's presentation.

Thanks to the statement of purpose that "frames" or forecasts the content and organization, readers are unlikely to lose their way.

Overviews, Topic Sentences, and Headings

Many expert writers provide overview and transition statements to tell readers where they're going next within a paper. Such signaling guides readers through the discussion step by step. Here is an illustration:

EXAMPLE 6.6 FROM AN ACADEMIC JOURNAL IN MARKETING

In the next section, we discuss relevant research on visual mental imagery in the design, marketing, and psychology literature, present a conceptual model of how visual mental imagery influences the customer appeal of the product designed, and propose a set of hypotheses.

(Dahl, Chattopadhyay, and Gorn 22)

In Example 6.6, a paragraph overviews what's ahead; a more common way of announcing main ideas is through topic sentences, as shown in Example 6.7:

EXAMPLE 6.7 FROM AN ACADEMIC JOURNAL IN SPORTS MEDICINE

Incomplete healing of meniscal repairs has been well documented in previous studies that used second-look

Thanks to the topic sentence highlighted we know from the start what to expect.

> arthroscopy. Henning[12] defined incomplete healing as the persistence of a cleft at the site of the meniscal tear measuring 10% to 50% of the meniscal thickness. A cleft greater than 50% represented a nonhealed repair. Using these criteria, Tenuta and Arciero[23] documented a 20% incomplete healing rate at 11 months in knees undergoing inside-out suture repair and ACLR. Asahina et al[2] performed routine second-look arthroscopy on 86 knees undergoing inside-out suture repair of meniscal tears with concomitant ACLR, documenting a 15% rate of incomplete healing. [discussion of this study continues]
>
> (Lee and Diduch 1140)

The superscript numbers refer readers to sources listed at the end of the article. Learn more about this practice in chapter 8.

Much more would be required of readers if the paragraph in Example 6.7 appeared without the introductory topic sentence. By the time readers get to the fourth sentence, they might see the connection between sentences, but the topic sentence makes identifying the connection much easier. Numerous studies have shown that readers remember main ideas better when they are stated, particularly when they are stated early in a paragraph rather than "buried in its depths" (Meyer 120). In addition, readers read paragraphs with topic sentences more quickly than paragraphs without topic sentences (Kieras). Just as you are better able to complete a jigsaw puzzle after first seeing a picture of the completed puzzle, readers are better able to see how each piece of new information fits into the overall structure of a paper when the structure is previewed for them. For this reason, academic writers forecast the content of their papers and announce topics along the way.

In multipage documents, writers also announce upcoming topics with section headings, like the heading you see at the beginning of this section you're reading. Headings serve as a sort of topic sentence for a series of paragraphs. For example, the article "Conceptualizing and Measuring Historical Trauma among American Indian People" is divided into sections with headings such as these:

CONCEPTUALIZING HISTORICAL TRAUMA
MEASURING HISTORICAL TRAUMA

These sections are further divided with subheadings, appearing in a different typeface to distinguish them from major headings. The section titled CONCEPTUALIZING HISTORICAL TRAUMA, for example, is divided into three subsections:

CONCEPTUALIZING HISTORICAL TRAUMA
  The Holocaust Model of Intergenerational Trauma
  Historical Trauma and American Indians
  Symptoms of Historical Trauma

By reading these headings, readers can distinguish major ideas from supporting ideas, prepare for what's coming, and even skip ahead to sections that interest them most. Successful academic writing is highly sign-posted. Every article in our sampling of experts includes preview sentences, review sentences, and headings intended to help readers recognize the main ideas.

Using Specialized Vocabulary and Academic Phrasing

As noted in chapter 1, specialized vocabulary is found in all academic writing, and each discipline has its own specialized language. Table 6.4 includes a few examples from our sampling of expert writers.

TABLE 6.4
Examples of Discipline-Specific Vocabulary

Engineering	limits of linearity of piezoelectric paint
Psychology	estimates of construct loadings
Marketing	expectancy disconfirmation
Literature	textual and libidinal potentials of coloniality

The vocabulary of a discipline includes technical words that precisely and concisely convey specialized meanings. Just as you can't become fluent in a foreign language until you spend time studying it and conversing in it with native speakers, you can't become fluent in the language of a discipline until you spend time conversing with its members—listening to how they talk and studying how they write. But even as a novice, you can learn to use some of the essential terms. Note the recurring terms in your professors' lectures and important terms in your textbook glossaries; then begin to use these terms when writing in those disciplines. They are an important marker of membership in any academic community.

Academic Phrases

In some ways, learning the vocabulary of academic disciplines is like learning the distinctive dialects of a primary language. Each dialect contains phrases or words unique to the region. But all dialects of a language also have many expressions in common. A New Yorker might order a "hero" from a deli, while a Pennsylvanian orders a "hoagie"; but both refer to their meal as a "sandwich," a word shared by all speakers of American English. Similarly, academic writers use terms unique to their disciplinary dialect, but they also use many terms found throughout academic writing.

All experts—whether in the academy or not—use both the language of their specialization and the language of their broader fields. We see this illustrated in Example 6.8, from a sports article describing the 2012 national college basketball championship.

EXAMPLE 6.8 FROM A NEWSPAPER SPORTS ARTICLE

With a star-studded roster that includes at least three, maybe as many as five NBA lottery picks, Kentucky was the top seed in the tournament and the heavy favorite to cut down the nets when the whole tournament was done.

("Big Blue" D1)

The highlighted terms demonstrate fluency in the language of sports in general. References to the winning team cutting down the net tied to the basketball hoop show knowledge of basketball specifically.

Facility with the language of sports in general and basketball in particular marks the writer as an expert in the field.

Similar to the way all sports writers use generic sports vocabulary, all academic writers draw from a storehouse of generic "academic" phrases. Table 6.5 shows a few of the common phrases used.

TABLE 6.5
Common Academic Phrases

in order to
according to
in this paper (report, article)
in the case of
studies have shown that

The presence of these and many other familiar academic phrases—sometimes called "lexical bundles"—marks a text as being written by a member of the academy. Lexical bundles account for an estimated 20% of the words in academic writing (Biber et al. 995); they rarely appear in conversation; and they don't lend themselves to paraphrase. You will see *as a result of* in academic writing, but you won't see *as resulting from* or *as an outcome of* (Hyland 43–44). Fluency in any language takes time, but by paying attention to patterns in the writing of fluent speakers, you can increase your proficiency in the language of the academy.

Concept in Practice 6.3: Recognizing Academic Vocabulary

In a report titled *A Review of the Proficiencies Required by Students Entering First Year Post-Secondary English Courses*, the authors talk about the transition students make from high school to college. Notice how the vocabulary marks the text as being "academic":

Students who make the transition between high school and post-secondary institutions engage, sometimes literally, but always metaphorically, in a journey: the academy is a domain of language use, and students come in as foreigners to the academy. . . . If one examines academic articles in any discipline, language differences become apparent: academic language consists largely of hypotheses, arguments, and evidence; of sources cited and evaluated; of standardized English; and of extensive vocabulary and jargon. (1)

"The academy," "discipline," "hypotheses," "arguments," "evidence," and "cited" are all used in a more specialized way than the words are used in nonacademic writing.

Reformulations

Reformulation is another pattern connecting the writing of all disciplines. **Reformulation** refers to the way writers rephrase or restate an idea to make it more clear or specific. The reformulation can expand a statement by adding explanation, illustration, or definition or reduce a statement by summarizing or simplifying it. Many reformulations are introduced with signal words or expressions—called *reformulation markers* (Cuenca 1069). Examples appear in Table 6.6.

TABLE 6.6
Examples of Reformulation Markers

i.e.
in other words
that is
namely
in particular
particularly
specifically

Categories of reformulation include reformulations that paraphrase, reformulations that specify and illustrate, and reformulations that define. Examples of each type are provided in Tables 6.7 to 6.9.

Reformulations That Paraphrase. Many reformulations repeat what was just stated but in different words. (See Table 6.7.) These reformulations are often introduced with *in other words, that is,* or the abbreviation *i.e.* (Latin *id est*, "that is").

TABLE 6.7

Sample Reformulations That Paraphrase (with reformulation markers bolded)

Reformulations That Paraphrase	Function
from an Academic Journal in Economics The January 2009 index level of 2.75 indicates that for every 100 applications received, 2.75 hirings occurred—**that is,** one out of every 36.4 applications resulted in a hiring. (Yerex 35)	The reformulation following *that is* reiterates what has already been said in another way.
from an Academic Journal in Music A low *p* value for a correlation means something very specific: it is highly likely that another random sample from the same population will show the same relationship between the measured variables. **In other words**, it is unlikely that the relationship is due to a *chance accident of sampling.* (Quinn 177, original italics)	Reformulations introduced with *in other words* tend to reduce information to simpler terms and often appear at the beginning of sentences.

Paraphrase reformulations repeat what has been said in a different way or from a different point of view and thus help ensure that readers understand the writer's meaning.

Reformulations That Specify or Illustrate. Other reformulations add details or examples or specify conditions. (See Table 6.8.) These reformulations are often introduced with *in particular*, *specifically*, and *particularly*.

TABLE 6.8

Sample Reformulations That Specify or Illustrate (with reformulation markers bolded)

Reformulations That Specify or Illustrate	Function
from an Academic Journal in Earth Science It may therefore be proposed that brittle creep of a flat could be a common mechanism controlling the change in seismicity over time, **particularly** in the case of a fault located in the upper crust, ruptured by a major earthquake and connected to a deep flat. (Jouanne et al. 20)	Many reformulations restrict the writer's meaning. In this example, the meaning of the first clause is narrowed by the reformulation.
from an Academic Journal in Political Science The site to which a participant was exposed significantly affected the likelihood of subsequently seeking information about the candidate. **Specifically**, 57% of those exposed to the Schakowsky site later reported pursuing information about her, compared to 24% of those initially exposed to the Pollak site. . . . (Druckman, Fein, and Leeper 446)	Reformulations can also explain what is meant by a general claim or identify how a relative word is defined by the author. In this example, the reformulation defines the relative term "significantly affected."

(continued)

TABLE 6.8 ***CONTINUED***

Reformulations That Specify or Illustrate	Function
from an Academic Journal in Economics This paper . . . [examines] the relationship between mobility and earnings in the National Hockey League. **Specifically**, we inquire into the *cumulative* impact of changing teams on the earnings of players. (Vincent and Eastman 50, original italics)	The marker *specifically* is often used to announce the specific focus of the author's paper or research.

Reformulations That Define. Some reformulations define technical terms. (See Table 6.9.) Common markers used to introduce definitions are *i.e.* and *that is*.

TABLE 6.9

Sample Reformulations That Define (with reformulation markers bolded)

Reformulations That Define	Function
from an Academic Journal in Biology To test if covariation between traits was entirely due to shared genes (**i.e.,** complete pleiotropy), the significance of ρ_G differing from 1 was also evaluated. (Jelenkovic and Rebato 130)	Reformulations can be used to provide the technical name for what has been described in lay terms.
from an Academic Journal in Music For a beat stream to be perceived as a tactus—**that is**, as a referential regularity that can be tapped, subdivided, and grouped—its tempo must fall within a band between 30 and 240 bpm (IOIs from 2000 to 250 ms). . . . (Roeder and Tenzer 91)	Reformulations can also provide the lay explanation of a technical term.

Using reformulations to illustrate general claims and define vague wording will help you write with clarity—something all instructors expect in student writing.

Concept in Practice 6.4: Recognizing Opportunities for Reformulation

Using reformulation to interpret a quotation for your reader can help you avoid the problem of quotations "dropped" into papers without comment. The reformulation marker *in other words* often precedes the explanation of a quotation, as in this passage from cultural studies:

As Linda Holland-Toll (2001) states, "Effective horror fiction holds up a carnival house mirror which reveals the often warped but ironically true image of our society, our community and ourselves" (251). She goes on to argue that "all of the qualities on which we pride ourselves as Americans are as subject to alienation and subversion as they are to valuation and reaffirmation" (251). In other words, part of the critical power of horror films derives from their ability to invert assumptions about power and knowledge, nature and culture, the known and the unknown.

(Gerlach 223)

The writer uses the reformulation to convey her interpretation of the quotation.

Use reformulations in your own papers to help readers see what you want them to see in quotations.

Using First Person to Establish Authority

We've so far seen several features that writers across disciplines use to show that they are members of the academic community, but the use of other features—including the use of **first-person point of view**—varies by discipline. In engineering writing, for example, first-person pronouns (such as *I, my, we, our*) are rare. Consider the following passage from our sample:

EXAMPLE 6.9 FROM AN ACADEMIC JOURNAL IN ENGINEERING

This paper presents a new approach to model the friction layer in brake systems in the investigation of noise and vibration, especially high-frequency squeal. . . . By incorporating the earlier results in a two degree of freedom model, the predicted frequencies were shown to be
5 close to the squeal frequencies obtained from field tests.

(Paliwal et al. 520–21)

In this passage, it's unclear who conducted the research.

In this passage, the writers do not name themselves as the researchers.

In other disciplines, writers use first-person pronouns, often to position themselves as authorities within their texts, as demonstrated in Example 6.10:

EXAMPLE 6.10 FROM AN ACADEMIC JOURNAL IN GEOGRAPHY

In the paradigm of Hawaiian volcano evolution, stages and the timing of their transitions are delimited by the composition of erupted lavas. However, we present new results from ^{238}U-^{230}Th and U-Pb dating of zircons from leucocratic plutonic xenoliths
5 indicating that lava stratigraphy is an incomplete monitor of magmatic

"We present new results" shows the writers have conducted original research.

> evolution within subsurface reservoirs. Our results indicate that diorites from Mauna Kea record postshield evolution over tens of thousands of years when the depth of magma storage increased and highly evolved lavas began erupting.
> (Vazquez, Shamberger, and Hammer 695)

"Our results" establishes that the writers are responsible for creating new knowledge.

In this passage, first-person pronouns establish the writers as authorities, responsible for original research and new knowledge. By taking ownership of their ideas, the writers demonstrate they have the authority to speak on the subject.

A number of researchers have demonstrated this and other purposes for first-person pronouns in expert academic writing. Nigel Harwood, for example, has analyzed articles from business and management, computing science, economics, physics, and political science and has found that expert writers use *I* and *we* to take credit for original claims, to express opinions, to describe research procedures, to announce the structure of their papers, and to establish their relationship with readers ("Nowhere"; also "Political"). We see these purposes demonstrated in our sampling of 24 articles, where writers representing medicine, marketing, psychology, biology, and literature use first-person pronouns to make it clear that they formed hypotheses, collected data, and reached conclusions. Here is one example:

EXAMPLE 6.11 FROM AN ACADEMIC JOURNAL IN MARKETING

> In this article, *we* examine the effect of elongation on (1) perceived volume, (2) perceived consumption, (3) actual consumption, (4) postconsumption satisfaction, and (5) choice. As described in Figure 7.1, *our* model suggests that package shape directly affects perceived volume and through this, indirectly and inversely affects perceived consumption. 5
> (Raghubir and Krishna 323, emphasis added)

First-person pronouns in this passage establish that the writers designed and conducted original research.

The use of first-person point of view varies according to genre and discipline. For college papers, its acceptance also varies from instructor to instructor. You must, therefore, *pay attention to disciplinary norms and instructor preferences when deciding when and where to interject first person into your academic writing.*

Bringing the Conversation to a Close

Just as there are conventional ways to end conversations on the phone or in person, there are conventional ways to end academic papers. In general, scholarly writers do more than repeat main ideas in the conclusion. For instance, if the authors had introduced their topic by identifying a gap in the previous research, they might conclude by telling readers how their work fills the void previously mentioned—as Example 6.12 illustrates:

EXAMPLE 6.12 FROM AN ACADEMIC JOURNAL IN SPORTS MEDICINE

To our knowledge, this study provides the longest follow-up in the literature of patients undergoing meniscal repair with the arrow. . . . Indeed, this study represents the longest follow-up in the literature on any of the available all-inside meniscal repair devices.

(Lee and Diduch 1140–41)

Ending an essay by reminding readers of the gap identified in the introduction gives an essay structural symmetry.

Many academic writers conclude by emphasizing the value of their research. Here is an example from an article in engineering:

EXAMPLE 6.13 FROM AN ACADEMIC JOURNAL IN ENGINEERING

The application of automated and high-speed machinery technologies brings revolution to the industrial productions with flexible, reliable, and cost-effective manufacturing control methodologies and adds significant impact on modern industries. It is not only increasing the production quantity but also improving 5 manufacturing quality. The study of this new automated and high-speed gas filling systems can help to understand and develop more efficient systems to produce gaseous products with consistent product quality, reduced production lead time, fast material handling process, and improved work flow.

(Li 4)

A conclusion like this reminds readers of why the topic that's been discussed matters.

Many writers conclude by calling on others to address questions left unanswered by them, as a way of acknowledging that the conversation will continue after they stop writing. In the following conclusion, for instance, the writers first summarize their findings and the implications of those findings, and then call for further research:

EXAMPLE 6.14 FROM AN ACADEMIC JOURNAL IN MARKETING

The most obvious implication to be drawn from this paper is the need for *all* SMEs [Small to Medium-Sized Enterprises] to be *more responsive to foreign customer needs* and to have more *effective relationships* with foreign agents/distributors/customers. . . .

Future research is needed to see if these results can be generalised to other countries and other markets. To what extent are the results ascertained here unique to the Japanese market? The multiple regression model of export performance needs to be expanded to incorporate other influences. There is also a need for a better in-depth understanding of how relationship marketing works within sales-driven firms. Case studies may be a good way of proceeding to achieve such an understanding.

(Merrilees, Tiessen, and Miller 71, original emphasis)

Here the authors call for additional research. Others end with a more general call to action. After arguing that ethics discussions need to occur in all disciplines, not just in business schools, economics professor Jurgen Brauer ends his essay with this sentence:

> So, next time, before you complain about "unethical" businesses yet unthinkingly plunk more money into your 401(k) retirement plan that may fund them, do your homework and buy stocks or bonds of companies that follow your code of ethics. (33)

Some of the most interesting conclusions leave readers thinking. Avoid, however, ending the discussion of a complex issue with simplistic advice. A discussion of racism in America that ends with a question like "Can't we all just get along?" is more likely to leave readers thinking about the writer's naiveté than about how to address an important issue.

You may think summarizing your argument in the conclusion of an essay will ensure that readers got your point. By all means, follow that instinct, but do more than simply tell readers what they, by then, already know.

Applying the Concepts to Reading: *Reading Mathematics Writing*

At first blush, mathematics writing—with its symbols, theorems, and equations—appears very different from the writing of many other disciplines, but as we'll see in this section, it too includes the familiar patterns discussed in this chapter.

Joining a Conversation

When math professors Leone Burton and Candia Morgan analyzed 53 published mathematics research papers, they discovered that when mathematicians report their research, they begin in the manner common to all academic writers: They acknowledge that others have previously written about their subjects. Here is an example: "The rich microstructure of cosmic strings is starting to receive considerable attention" (qtd. in Burton and Morgan 443).

Establishing Territory and Stating the Value of the Research

Burton and Morgan noticed another familiar move in the articles they analyzed. The mathematicians announced the specific aspect of the topic they would address and the importance or value of their contribution ("The algorithm presented here could lead to significant saving of time and complication" [qtd. in Burton and Morgan 445]). Many authors specifically identified how their work fills a gap in the existing body of research. Here is one example: "One way in which our treatment differs from all previous treatments, is that we do not assume we start with an embedded fundamental domain" (qtd. in Burton and Morgan 445).

Expressing Uncertainty

The writers Burton and Morgan studied often used qualifying words in claims that could be challenged. Comments such as "we think but have not yet shown" and "plausible though unproved assumption" (qtd. in Burton and Morgan 441) demonstrate that in mathematics, as in all academic disciplines, writers are cautious when making original claims, knowing that with further study they could be proven wrong.

The following excerpt from a paper titled "Detecting Forged Handwriting with Wavelets and Statistics" includes some general conventions of academic writing, as well as features specific to mathematics. Written by Beverly Lytle and Caroline Yang, who were college seniors at the time and mathematics majors, the paper describes their research on the use of algorithmic analysis to distinguish between authentic and forged handwriting. You can easily distinguish your own handwriting from that of others because the way you form and combine letters is unique. Numerical methods can be designed to identify patterns in the size and slant of your letters, the pen pressure, and the spacing between letters and words. Variations in any of these parameters can be calculated using statistical analysis and be used to distinguish your handwriting from a forgery.

Lytle and Yang's paper is filled with mathematical computations, but readers familiar with the conventions of academic writing can follow the argument, even if they cannot always assess its accuracy. In their introduction, for example, the authors follow a traditional pattern for academic papers: beginning with a general introduction to the topic, introducing others who have conducted related research, and then specifying how their own study relates to previous research. As you read the introduction to their paper (provided hereafter), answer the following questions:

- Where and how do the writers put their paper into a larger context and show that they are joining a conversation? How does this study relate to that of previous researchers?
- Where do the authors qualify their claims about previous research and acknowledge other viewpoints?
- Where do the writers state the purpose of their paper and preview its contents?

In addition to following cross-disciplinary conventions, the writers include features more unique to mathematics writing, as noted in the margins.

FROM "DETECTING FORGED HANDWRITING WITH WAVELETS AND STATISTICS," *Beverly Lytle and Caroline Yang*

1. Introduction: Art & Forgeries

For centuries, the forgeries of great artists have held a place of fascination in the public eye. Museums occasionally contain entire galleries dedicated to those forgeries which are considered to be "museum quality." People such as Hans van Meegeren and Elmyr de Hory have created such masterful imitations of the works of Johannes Vermeer, Henri Matisse, and Pablo Picasso that they have become famous for their ability to deceive art critics and historians [5, 8]. As these imitators have been discovered by different methods of analysis, the following questions arise:

In mathematics, writers often refer to sources by number. In this case, "[5, 8]" refers to the fifth and eighth listed sources in the bibliography.

- What exactly distinguishes an authentic work of art from a forgery?
- Does this question have a mathematical answer?
- How are these questions related to the problem of determining if a handwriting sample is a forgery?

Art historians and experts use a combination of subjective and objective techniques to determine the authenticity of a work in question. Style, content, and chemical composition of a painting are very important in the classification of a work of art. An artist's brush stroke, portrayal of light, and use of color can all be considered part of his or her stylistic signature. Content is also quite important; some forgeries have been discovered through anachronisms contained within the painting. The chemical composition of the paints used and the actual material of the canvas or paper can also be instrumental in dating a piece of art, but only lately have these objective methods of chemical analysis become more widely used.

Recently, Lyu, Rockmore and Farid of Dartmouth College described a new, mathematical method for determining the authenticity of works of art [9, 10, 11].

Their method applies a wavelet-like transform and basic statistics to greyscale versions of paintings and sketches. The idea behind the method of Lyu et al. is to differentiate between authentic works and imitations by analyzing the consistency of the data received from the wavelet-like decomposition of the images. In theory, though a forger tries to imitate another artist's style, his or her work should be statistically different from that of the true artist.

Lyu et al. used their method to first discriminate between authentic works and imitations in a group of thirteen different sketches, each of which had at one time been attributed to Pieter Bruegel the Elder. They also applied their method to the painting "Madonna with Child" by Pietro di Cristoforo Vannucci (Perugino) and analyzed the faces of the subjects in the painting to determine whether or not the faces had all been painted by the same artist. The mathematical analysis suggested that some of the Bruegel sketches were done by imitators, while some of the Perugino faces were perhaps done by Perugino's apprentices. These results were supported by the existing opinions of art historians. The results also seemed to indicate that an artist could have some kind of "mathematical signature," with the data from one artist falling within a certain statistical range and the data of imitators falling outside of that range.

While there is criticism of their work (e.g. [11] and below), their basic idea appears sound, and a logical extension is to apply the method to the analysis of handwriting. The problem is to determine if there is a mathematical "signature" that corresponds to a person's handwriting. In this paper, we discuss how we modified the method of Lyu et al., by using a two-dimensional wavelet filter, a larger number of samples, and a simpler statistical analysis, in order to determine the difference between authentic and forged handwriting.

Mathematicians use first person plural pronouns "(we)" even if an article is single-authored. It is a way for a writer to establish authority by suggesting that he or she is speaking for the mathematical community.

Just as we know sports fans or computer geeks or car mechanics by their facility with the language of their fields, we recognize mathematicians—and their level of expertise—by their language.

Applying the Concepts to Writing: *Announcing the Value of Academic Writing*

One important goal an academic writer has in a paper's introduction is to convey the value of the subject to the audience. Unless readers see the importance and relevance of the issue, they have little motivation to continue reading past the introduction. Included here are introductions from articles found in chapters 2, 4, and 5, abbreviated to highlight how the authors (1) identify the purpose of their paper and (2) identify the value or relevance of the subject to the intended audience. In all three instances, the authors make these moves at the end of their introductions.

After studying the examples, write the introduction to a paper you are currently working on or revise one you have already written. In margin annotations, note where you identify the purpose of your paper and where you identify the importance of the issue for your audience (as modeled hereafter). Or explain how you accomplish these goals in a separate paragraph after your introduction.

INTRODUCTION 1 FROM READING STUDIES (INTENDED AUDIENCE: COLLEGE PROFESSORS)

. . . As a teacher attempting to make sound pedagogical decisions about the use of digital texts, I find two big pieces missing from both the research and the debate. [description of what's missing follows . . .] The empirical research offers some insight, but because such studies tend to be highly focused investigations into, for example, how students read digital texts (eg, Burke & Rowsell, 2008; Monk, 2004) or the effects of digital texts on reading comprehension (eg, Rodrigues & Martins, 2008), they pre-empt a holistic understanding of the experience. As I and my colleagues increasingly provide our undergraduate and graduate students with digitised course materials, it becomes clear that in order to make appropriate, pedagogically sound decisions about the use of such materials, we need to move beyond making summary judgments to seek insight into what it is like for students to read digitised texts.

My purpose in this study was to gain such insight. . . .

(Rose 516)

Purpose: To learn how students feel about reading digitized texts.
Value: To help teachers know how to best use digitized texts in their courses.

INTRODUCTION 2 FROM INFORMATION LITERACY (INTENDED AUDIENCE: COLLEGE PROFESSORS AND ADMINISTRATORS)

In fall 2012, a record number of students entered college.[1]

. . . But getting into college was only the beginning. Many freshmen, who assumed everything they needed to know was just a Google search away, soon discovered they were unprepared to deal with the enormous amount of information they were expected to find and process for college research assignments. This transition from completing high school assignments to doing college-level research is one of the most formidable challenges that incoming freshmen face.

. . . In this study, we investigated the challenges facing today's college freshmen and the information competencies and strategies they develop and use as they advance from high school to college. . . . Finally, we asked what insights can be gleaned from

Purpose: To learn how students find source information.

studying this process in the hope that it will lead to improvements in preparing them for success in the digital age.

(Head 2)

Value: To explain how professors and administrators can better prepare students for research in the digital age.

INTRODUCTION 3 FROM ENVIRONMENTAL STUDIES (INTENDED AUDIENCE: GENERAL)

Right now about one billion people suffer from chronic hunger. The world's farmers grow enough food to feed them, but it is not properly distributed and, even if it were, many cannot afford it, because prices are escalating.

But another challenge looms.

By 2050 the world's population will increase by two billion or three billion, which will likely double the demand for food, according to several studies. . . . Increasing use of cropland for biofuels will put additional demands on our farms. So even if we solve today's problems of poverty and access—a daunting task—we will also have to produce twice as much to guarantee adequate supply worldwide.

And that's not all.

By clearing tropical forests, farming marginal lands, and intensifying industrial farming in sensitive landscapes and watersheds, humankind has made agriculture the planet's dominant environmental threat. . . . To guarantee the globe's long-term health, we must dramatically reduce agriculture's adverse impacts.

The world's food system faces three incredible, interwoven challenges. It must guarantee that all seven billion people alive today are adequately fed; it must double food production in the next 40 years; and it must achieve both goals while becoming truly environmentally sustainable.

Could these simultaneous goals possibly be met? An international team of experts, which I coordinated, has settled on five steps that, if pursued together, could raise by more than 100 percent the food available for human consumption globally, while significantly lessening greenhouse gas emissions, biodiversity losses, water use and water pollution. Tackling the triple challenge will be one of the most important tests humanity has ever faced. It is fair to say that our response will determine the fate of our civilization.

(Foley 62)

Purpose: To explain how to solve the world's food shortage problem.

Value: Survival!

Paired Readings from Business

"First Impressions: The Science of Meeting People," (An interview with Amy Cuddy), *Wired.com* ROB CAPPS

First impressions matter, whether made in person or in writing. Amy Cuddy, a professor at the Harvard Business School, has made first impressions the subject of research. In the following interview, Cuddy talks with Rob Capps, deputy editor for *Wired Magazine*, about the research she has designed to better understand how we make first impressions and how we interpret those of others. The interview was published in 2012 on *Wired.com*, a technology news website.

A strong handshake and assertive greeting may not be the best way to make a good first impression. New research suggests that people respond more positively to someone who comes across as trustworthy rather than confident.

Social psychologist Amy Cuddy of Harvard Business School is studying how we evaluate people we meet. Cuddy is known for her research on power posing, which she presented last year at TedGlobal and the annual PopTech conference in Maine. This research suggests that if you strike a strong pose—where you take up as much space as possible—your levels of testosterone rise, while cortisol levels drop. The result: If you do it for two minutes before going into a job interview or other public performance, you will have more confidence and perform better.

Cuddy returned to PopTech this year with an all-new talk about how we form first impressions. Turns out that when we meet individuals or groups for the first time, we mostly evaluate two metrics: trustworthiness and confidence. And the best part is that once you understand this, you can learn to make a better first impression. We asked her to tell us how this all works.

Wired: What have you learned about how we form first impressions?

Amy Cuddy: When we form a first impression of another person it's not really a single impression. We're really forming two. We're judging how warm and trustworthy the person is, and that's trying to answer the question, "What are this person's intentions toward me?" And we're also asking ourselves, "How strong and competent is this person?" That's really about whether or not they're capable of enacting their intentions. Research shows that these two trait dimensions account for 80 to 90 percent of an overall first impression, and that holds true across cultures.

Wired: Why did you get into this line of research?

Cuddy: Since just after World War II, social psychologists have been studying prejudice, really trying to understand what drives it. And the classic social-psychological model was that it's all about love for the "in-group" and hatred for the "out-group." The problem with this is that it assumed there's a single evaluative dimension: You either have negative or positive feelings toward a person or group. And because that's not really what's happening, social psychologists were not able to use the in-group/out-group evaluation to predict discrimination. Ultimately, what we really want to know isn't just what you think and feel about somebody but also how do you treat them. We didn't know who was going to be a target of genocide, who was going to be neglected, who was going to be mocked.

Discrimination comes in very nuanced forms these days. And we wanted to be able to predict discrimination. Our research group was interested in how people categorize each other. When we meet somebody, what determines whether we see them as a member of a group or see them as an individual? And how do we determine if we like the other person or not? Through research we found that it really comes down to two traits: trustworthiness and competence. People universally sort groups in a two by two matrix. And what you end up getting is that most groups are seen as high on one trait and low on the other. You don't actually have many groups that are both not trusted and not respected, or that are both loved and respected.

Wired: How did you determine all this?

Cuddy: We would literally just go into a society and do a preliminary study asking people to freely list all the groups in their society. After going into about two-dozen different cultures we found that people tended to come up with about 15 to 20 groups in their society. Some of them are overlapping, so you have women and men, but then you also have race, and you've got profession and religion and all these other categories. Then we go in again and ask a different sample of people to rate all those groups on a long list of traits. Through factor analysis we were able to show that people assess groups largely by these two main factors. Now, when you ask people "how much do you like a given group?" often they're not going to tell you the truth. There's too many social desirability concerns. But when you give them, say, 20 traits to evaluate, they're much more willing to actually give you variance in the responses.

Wired: And you can somehow use this to predict who is at risk of genocide?

Cuddy: When the economy or the status quo is threatened, often it is the high-status minority groups that get targeted for genocide. If you look over the last 100 years at the groups that have been the targets, they are not groups that were seen as incompetent. They're groups that were seen as highly competent. So the Tutsis in Rwanda, the Jews in Germany, educated people in Cambodia. These aren't groups that were both not liked and not respected. They were groups that were hated but respected. That is the quadrant that gets targeted for genocide. Again this goes against the former popular thinking in social psychology, that it was just a matter of one group hating another.

Wired: What else do these two traits tell you about how one group views another?

Cuddy: The thing we found after sorting people into these four quadrants is that they predict four unique emotions and four unique behavioral responses. So groups that are seen as competent but disliked elicit a lot of respect and admiration but also a lot of resentment and antipathy. Groups that are seen as warm and trustworthy but incompetent elicit pity, which is about both compassion and sadness.

Wired: What if you see a group as warm *and* competent.

Cuddy: You think they're just great all around. But this is rare, as is viewing someone as both cold and incompetent. We usually see one trait or the other.

Wired: At Poptech you also talked about how these reactions occur on a personal level. You mentioned that when we first meet someone we're often looking for warmth or trust, but trying to project competence and confidence.

Cuddy: We want to see others as trustworthy but we want them to see us as competent or strong.

Wired: So knowing this when you're going into interactions with people, can you use this knowledge to better make and give first impressions?

Cuddy: To make an accurate judgment of somebody, you want to bring out their true nature. People need to trust you in order to be themselves. So trying to be the more dominant one in the interaction is probably going to make it harder for you to get accurate information about the other person, because it's going to shut them down. Or they're going to feel defensive, or they're going to feel threatened, or they're going to try to out alpha you. It's not going to be any sort of natural interaction. So I'm such a big believer in trying to establish trust, and there's evidence that shows that trust begets trust. I know people find this very controversial but it's true. If you are trusting, if you project trust, people are more likely to trust you.

Wired: How do you convey trust in a first interaction?

Cuddy: There are a lot of things that you can do. One is to let the other person speak first or have the floor first. You can do this by simply asking them a question. I think people make the mistake, especially in business settings, of thinking that everything is negotiation. They think, "I better get the floor first so that I can be in charge of what happens." The problem with this is that you don't make the other person feel warmth toward you. Warmth is really about making the other person feel understood. They want to know that you understand them. And doing that is incredibly disarming.

You can also establish trust by collecting information about the other person's interests—get them to share things about themselves. Just making small talk helps enormously. Research proves that five minutes of chit-chat before a negotiation increases the amount of value that's created in the negotiation. What's funny about all this is that the things that you do to increase trust actually often are things that are seen as wastes of time. People say, "Oh, I don't have time for small talk." Well, you should make the time for small talk because it will really help.

Wired: But are there times when it's better to project dominance and competence?

Cuddy: I'm sure there are, but it's an empirical question and I'm not ready to answer it yet. We're doing some work on that now. We'll see. But in general I really think people make the mistake of over-weighting the importance of expressing strength and competence, at the expense of expressing warmth and trustworthiness. I think this is a mistake. How can you possibly be a good leader if the people who are supposed to be following you don't feel that you understand them? How is it possible? No one is going to listen if they don't trust you. Why would they? Why should they? Trust opens them up to what you have to say. It opens them up to your strength and confidence. Trust is the conduit through which ideas travel.

Can you rule through fear? Of course you can. But not for long.

QUESTIONS ABOUT MEANING

1. What motivated Cuddy to study first impressions?
2. Describe Cuddy's research methods. What has Cuddy learned? On what basis do most people form opinions about others?
3. What does Cuddy think is more important to convey when first meeting someone: competence or trustworthiness? Why is this attribute important and how can a person convey it to others?

QUESTIONS FOR RHETORICAL ANALYSIS

4. Whether in a business negotiation or in an academic paper, building trust is important. In the interview, how does Cuddy convey that she is caring and trustworthy? How does she also establish that she is competent?
5. Who is the target audience Cuddy seems to be addressing? Support your answer with textual evidence from the interview.
6. How is the article/interview title a fitting one?

"Power Posing: Brief Nonverbal Displays Affect Neuroendocrine Levels and Risk Tolerance," *Psychological Science* DANA R. CARNEY, AMY J.C. CUDDY, AND ANDY J. YAP

In the previous reading, Harvard business professor Amy Cuddy talks about first impressions. The next article is also about communication, specifically the ways a person can communicate authority. The article describes research Cuddy conducted with Dana Carney and Andy Yap, both from Columbia University. They study a "power pose" that when assumed can make a person feel more confident. The article appeared in 2010 in *Psychological Science*, a peer-reviewed journal that publishes research from the field of psychology.

ABSTRACT

Humans and other animals express power through open, expansive postures, and they express powerlessness through closed, contractive postures. But can these postures actually cause power? The results of this study confirmed our prediction that posing in high-power nonverbal displays (as opposed to low-power nonverbal displays) would cause neuroendocrine and behavioral changes for both male and female participants: High-power posers experienced elevations in testosterone, decreases in cortisol, and increased feelings of power and tolerance for risk; low-power posers exhibited the opposite pattern. In short, posing in displays of power caused advantaged and adaptive psychological, physiological, and behavioral changes, and these findings suggest that embodiment extends beyond mere thinking and feeling, to physiology and subsequent behavioral choices. That a person can, by assuming two simple 1-min poses, embody power and instantly become more powerful has real-world, actionable implications.

KEYWORDS

cortisol, embodiment, hormones, neuroendocrinology, nonverbal behavior, power, risk taking, testosterone

Received 1/20/10; Revision accepted 4/8/10

The proud peacock fans his tail feathers in pursuit of a mate. By galloping sideways, the cat manipulates an intruder's perception of her size. The chimpanzee, asserting his hierarchical rank, holds his breath until his chest bulges. The executive in the boardroom crests the table with his feet, fingers interlaced behind his neck, elbows pointing outward. Humans and other animals display power and dominance through expansive nonverbal displays, and these power poses are deeply intertwined with the evolutionary selection of what is "alpha" (Darwin, 1872/2009; de Waal, 1998).

But is power embodied? What happens when displays of power are posed? Can posed displays cause a person to feel more powerful? Do people's mental and physiological systems prepare them to be more powerful? The goal of our research was to test whether high-power poses (as opposed to low-power poses) actually produce power. To perform this test, we looked at the effects of high-power and low-power poses on some fundamental features of having power: feelings of power, elevation of the dominance hormone testosterone, lowering of the stress hormone cortisol, and an increased tolerance for risk.

Power determines greater access to resources (de Waal, 1998; Keltner, Gruenfeld, & Anderson, 2003); higher levels of agency and control over a person's own body, mind, and positive feelings (Keltner et al., 2003); and enhanced cognitive function (Smith, Jostmann, Galinsky, & van Dijk, 2008). Powerful individuals (compared with powerless individuals) demonstrate greater willingness to engage in action (Galinsky, Gruenfeld, & Magee, 2003; Keltner et al., 2003) and often show increased risk-taking behavior[1] (e.g., Anderson & Galinsky, 2006).

The neuroendocrine profiles of the powerful differentiate them from the powerless, on two key hormones—testosterone and cortisol. In humans and other animals, testosterone levels both reflect and reinforce dispositional and situational status and dominance; internal and external cues cause testosterone to rise, increasing dominant behaviors, and these behaviors can elevate testosterone even further (Archer, 2006; Mazur & Booth, 1998). For example, testosterone rises in anticipation of a competition and as a result of a win, but drops following a defeat (e.g., Booth, Shelley, Mazur, Tharp, & Kittok, 1989), and these changes predict the desire to compete again (Mehta & Josephs, 2006). In short, testosterone levels, by reflecting and reinforcing dominance, are closely linked to adaptive responses to challenges.

Power is also linked to the stress hormone cortisol: Power holders show lower basal cortisol levels and lower cortisol reactivity to stressors than powerless people do, and cortisol drops as power is achieved (Abbott et al., 2003; Coe, Mendoza, & Levine, 1979; Sapolsky, Alberts, & Altmann, 1997). Although short-term and acute cortisol elevation is part of an adaptive response to challenges large (e.g., a predator) and small (e.g., waking up), the chronically elevated cortisol levels seen in low-power individuals are associated with negative health consequences, such as impaired immune functioning, hypertension, and memory loss (Sapolsky et al., 1997; Segerstrom & Miller, 2004). Low-power social groups have a higher incidence of stress-related illnesses than high-power social groups do, and this is partially attributable to chronically elevated cortisol (Cohen et al., 2006). Thus, the power holder's typical neuroendocrine profile of high testosterone coupled with low cortisol—a profile linked to such outcomes as disease resistance (Sapolsky, 2005) and leadership abilities (Mehta & Josephs, 2010)—appears to be optimally adaptive.

It is unequivocal that power is expressed through highly specific, evolved nonverbal displays. Expansive, open postures (widespread limbs and enlargement of occupied space by spreading out) project high power, whereas contractive, closed postures (limbs touching the torso and minimization of occupied space by collapsing the body inward) project low power. All of these patterns have been identified in research on actual and attributed power and its nonverbal correlates (Carney, Hall, & Smith LeBeau, 2005; Darwin, 1872/2009; de Waal, 1998; Hall, Coats, & Smith LeBeau, 2005). Although researchers know that power generates these displays, no research has investigated whether these displays generate power. Will posing these displays of power actually cause individuals to feel more powerful, focus on reward as opposed to risk, and experience increases in testosterone and decreases in cortisol?

In research on embodied cognition, some evidence suggests that bodily movements, such as facial displays, can affect emotional states. For example, unobtrusive contraction of the "smile muscle" (i.e., the zygomaticus major) increases enjoyment (Strack, Martin, Stepper, 1988), the head tilting upward induces pride (Stepper & Strack, 1993), and hunched postures (as opposed to upright postures) elicit more depressed feelings (Riskind & Gotay, 1982). Approach-oriented behaviors, such as touching, pulling, or nodding "yes," increase preference for objects, people, and persuasive messages (e.g., Briñol & Petty, 2003; Chen & Bargh, 1999; Wegner, Lane, & Dimitri, 1994), and fist clenching increases men's self-ratings on power-related traits (Schubert & Koole, 2009). However, no research has tested whether expansive power poses, in comparison with contractive power poses, cause mental, physiological, and behavioral change in a manner consistent with the effects of power. We hypothesized that high-power poses (compared with low-power poses) would cause individuals to experience elevated testosterone, decreased cortisol, increased feelings of power, and higher risk tolerance. Such findings would suggest that embodiment goes beyond cognition and emotion and could have immediate and actionable effects on physiology and behavior.

METHOD

Participants and Overview of Procedure

Forty-two participants (26 females and 16 males) were randomly assigned to the high-power-pose or low-power-pose condition. Participants believed that the study was about the science of physiological recordings and was focused on how placement of electrocardiography electrodes above and below the heart could influence data collection. Participants' bodies were posed by an experimenter into high-power or low-power poses. Each participant held two poses for 1 min each. Participants' risk taking was measured with a gambling task; feelings of power were measured with self-reports. Saliva samples, which were used to test cortisol and testosterone levels, were taken before and approximately 17 min after the power-pose manipulation.

Power Poses

Poses were harvested from the nonverbal literature (e.g., Carney et al., 2005; Hall et al., 2005) and varied on the two nonverbal dimensions universally linked to power: expansiveness (i.e., taking up more space or less space) and openness (i.e., keeping limbs open or closed). The two high-power poses into which participants were configured are depicted in Figure 6.1, and the two low-power poses are depicted in Figure 6.2. To be sure that the poses chosen conveyed power appropriately, we asked 95 pretest participants to rate each pose from 1 (*very low power*) to 7 (*very high power*). High-power poses ($M = 5.39$, $SD = 0.99$) were indeed rated significantly higher on power than were low-power poses ($M = 2.41$, $SD = 0.93$), $t(94) = 21.03$, $p < .001$; $r = .99$.

To be sure that changes in neuroendocrine levels, powerful feelings, or behavior could be attributed only to the high-power or low-power attributes of the poses, we had 19 pretest participants rate the comfort, difficulty, and pain of the poses. Participants made all four poses (while wearing electrocardiography leads) and completed questionnaires after each pose. There were no differences between high-power and low-power poses on comfort, $t(16) = 0.24$, $p > .80$; difficulty, $t(16) = 0.77$, $p > .45$; or painfulness, $t(16) = -0.82$, $p > .42$.

To configure the test participants into the poses, the experimenter placed an electrocardiography lead on the back of each participant's calf and underbelly of the left arm and explained, "To test accuracy of physiological responses as a function of sensor placement relative to your heart, you are being put into a certain physical position." The experimenter then manually configured participants' bodies by lightly touching their arms and legs. As needed, the experimenter provided verbal instructions (e.g., "Keep your feet above heart level by putting them on the desk in front of you"). After manually configuring participants' bodies into the two poses, the experimenter left the room. Participants were videotaped; all participants correctly made and held either two high-power or two low-power poses for 1 min each. While making and holding the poses, participants completed a filler task that consisted of viewing and forming impressions of nine faces.

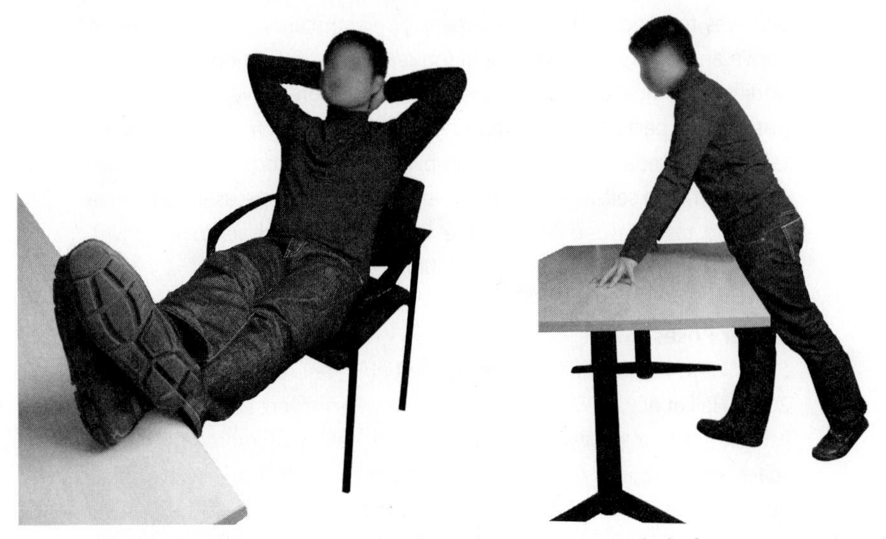

Figure 6.1 The two high-power poses used in the study. Participants in the high-power-pose condition were posed in expansive positions with open limbs.

Figure 6.2 The two low-power poses used in the study. Participants in the low-power-pose condition were posed in contractive positions with closed limbs.

Measure of Risk Taking and Powerful Feelings

After they finished posing, participants were presented with the gambling task. They were endowed with $2 and told they could keep the money—the safe bet—or roll a die and risk losing the $2 for a payoff of $4 (a risky but rational bet; odds of winning were 50/50). Participants indicated how "powerful" and "in charge" they felt on a scale from 1 (*not at all*) to 4 (*a lot*).

Saliva Collection and Analysis

Testing was scheduled in the afternoon (12:00 p.m.–6:00 p.m.) to control for diurnal rhythms in hormones. Saliva samples were taken before the power-pose manipulation (approximately 10 min after arrival; Time 1) and again 17 min after the power-pose manipulation (M = 17.28 min, SD = 4.31; Time 2).

Standard salivary-hormone collection procedures were used (Dickerson & Kemeny, 2004; Schultheiss & Stanton, 2009). Before providing saliva samples, participants did not eat, drink, or brush their teeth for at least 1 hr. Participants rinsed their mouths with water and chewed a piece of sugar-free Trident Original Flavor gum for 3 min to stimulate salivation (this procedure yields the least bias compared with passive drool procedures; Dabbs, 1991). Participants provided approximately 1.5 ml of saliva through a straw into a sterile polypropylene microtubule. Samples were immediately frozen to avoid hormone degradation and to precipitate mucins. Within 2 weeks, samples were packed in dry ice and shipped for analysis to Salimetrics (State College, PA), where they were assayed in duplicate for salivary cortisol and salivary testosterone using a highly sensitive enzyme immunoassay.

For cortisol, the intra-assay coefficient of variation (CV) was 5.40% for Time 1 and 4.40% for Time 2. The average interassay CV across high and low controls for both time points was 2.74%. Cortisol levels were in the normal range at both Time 1 (M = 0.16 μg/dl, SD = 0.19) and Time 2 (M = 0.12 μg/dl, SD = 0.08). For testosterone, the intra-assay CV was 4.30% for Time 1 and 3.80% for Time 2. The average interassay CV across high and low controls for both time points was 3.80%. Testosterone levels were in the normal range at both Time 1 (M = 60.30 pg/ml, SD = 49.58) and Time 2 (M = 57.40 pg/ml, SD = 43.25). As would be suggested by appropriately taken and assayed samples (Schultheiss & Stanton, 2009), men were higher than women on testosterone at both Time 1, $F(1, 41) = 17.40$, $p < .001$, $r = .55$, and Time 2, $F(1, 41) = 22.55$, $p < .001$, $r = .60$. To control for sex differences in testosterone, we used participant's sex as a covariate in all analyses. All hormone analyses examined changes in hormones observed at Time 2, controlling for Time 1. Analyses with cortisol controlled for testosterone, and vice versa.[2]

RESULTS

One-way analyses of variance examined the effect of power pose on postmanipulation hormones (Time 2), controlling for baseline hormones (Time 1). As hypothesized, high-power poses caused an increase in testosterone compared with low-power poses, which caused a decrease in testosterone, $F(1, 39) = 4.29$, $p < .05$; $r = .34$ (Fig. 6.3). Also as hypothesized, high-power poses caused a decrease in cortisol compared with low-power poses, which caused an increase in cortisol, $F(1, 38) = 7.45$, $p < .02$; $r = .43$ (Fig. 6.4).

Also consistent with predictions, high-power posers were more likely than low-power posers to focus on rewards—86.36% took the gambling

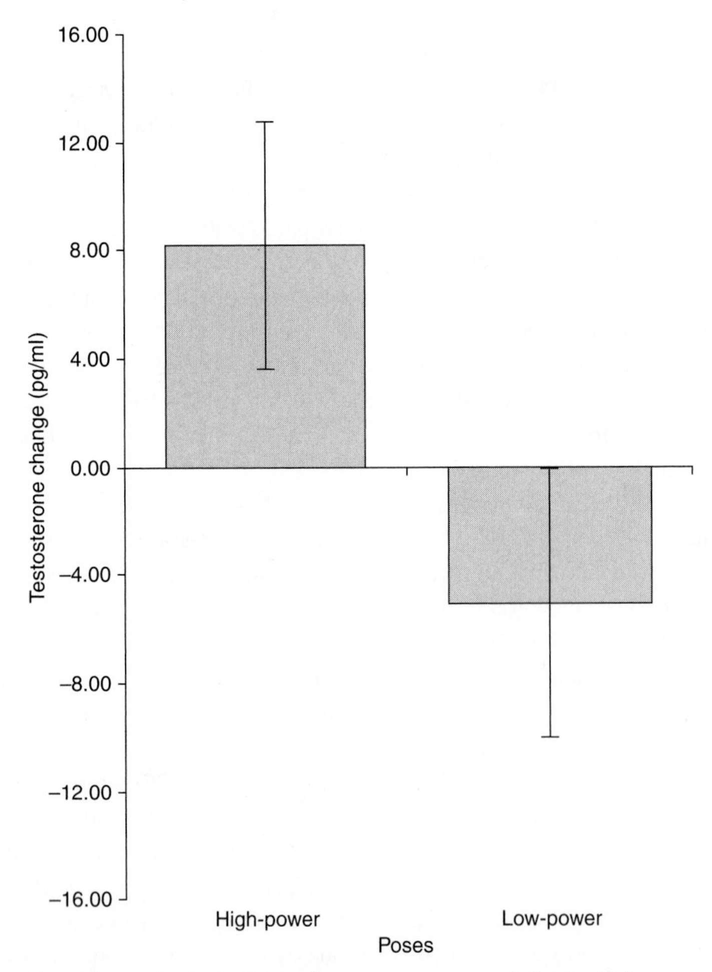

Figure 6.3 Mean changes in the dominance hormone testosterone following high-power and low-power poses. Changes are depicted as difference scores (Time 2 − Time 1). Error bars represent standard errors of the mean.

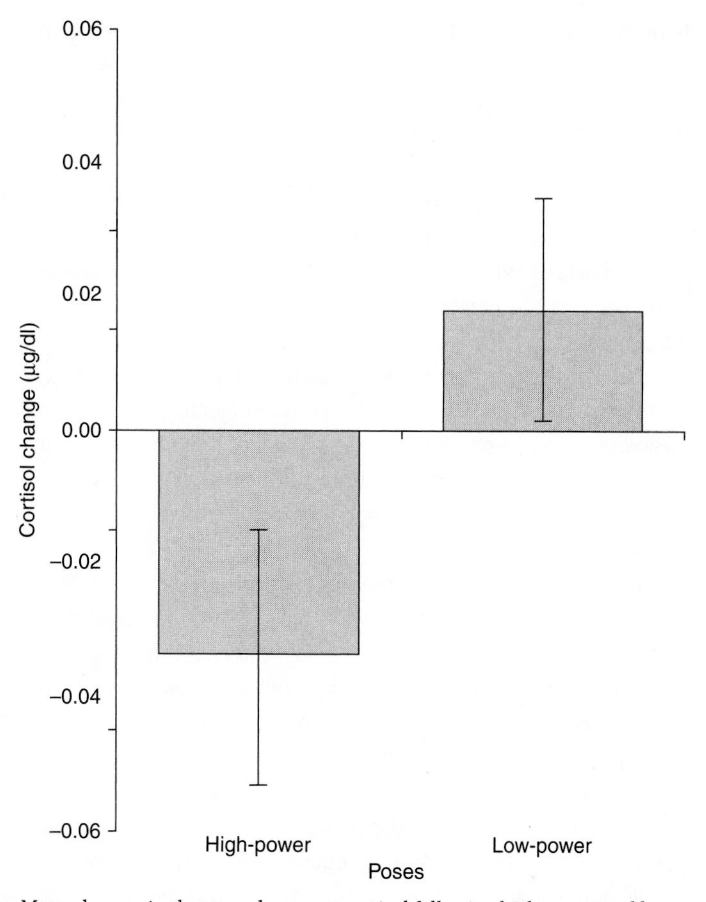

Figure 6.4 Mean changes in the stress hormone cortisol following high-power and low-power poses. Changes are depicted as difference scores (Time 2 − Time 1). Error bars represent standard errors of the mean.

risk (only 13.63% were risk averse). In contrast, only 60% of the low-power posers took the risk (and 40% were risk averse), $\chi^2(1, N = 42) = 3.86$, $p < .05$; $\Phi = .30$. Finally, high-power posers reported feeling significantly more "powerful" and "in charge" ($M = 2.57$, $SD = 0.81$) than low-power posers did ($M = 1.83$, $SD = 0.81$), $F(1, 41) = 9.53$, $p < .01$; $r = .44$. Thus, a simple 2-min power-pose manipulation was enough to significantly alter the physiological, mental, and feeling states of our participants. The implications of these results for everyday life are substantial.

DISCUSSION

Our results show that posing in high-power displays (as opposed to low-power displays) causes physiological, psychological, and behavioral changes consistent with the literature on the effects of power on power holders—elevation of the dominance hormone testosterone, reduction of the stress hormone cortisol, and increases in behaviorally demonstrated risk tolerance and feelings of power.

These findings advance current understanding of embodied cognition in two important ways. First, they suggest that the effects of embodiment extend beyond emotion and cognition, to physiology and subsequent behavioral choice. For example, as described earlier, nodding the head "yes" leads a person to be more easily persuaded when listening to a persuasive appeal, and smiling increases humor responses. We suggest that these simple behaviors, a head nod or a smile, might also cause physiological changes that activate an entire trajectory of psychological, physiological, and behavioral shifts—essentially altering the course of a person's day. Second, these results suggest that any psychological construct, such as power, with a signature pattern of nonverbal correlates may be embodied.

These results also offer a methodological advance in research on power. Many reported effects of power are limited by the methodological necessity of manipulating power in a laboratory setting (e.g., complex role assignments). The simple, elegant power-pose manipulation we employed can be taken directly into the field and used to investigate ordinary people in everyday contexts.

Is it possible that our findings are limited to the specific poses utilized in this experiment? Although the power-infusing attribute of expansiveness and the poses that capture it require further investigation, findings from an additional study ($N = 49$) suggest that the effects reported here are not idiosyncratic to these specific poses. In addition to the poses used in the current report, an additional three high-power poses and an additional three low-power poses produced the same effects on feelings of power, $F(1, 48) = 4.38$, $p < .05$, $r = .30$, and risk taking, $\chi^2(1, N = 49) = 4.84$, $p < .03$, $\Phi = .31$.

By simply changing physical posture, an individual prepares his or her mental and physiological systems to endure difficult and stressful situations, and perhaps to actually improve confidence and performance in situations such as interviewing for jobs, speaking in public, disagreeing with a boss, or taking potentially profitable risks. These findings suggest that, in some situations requiring power, people have the ability to "fake it 'til they make it." Over time and in aggregate, these minimal postural changes and their outcomes potentially could improve a person's general health and well-being. This potential benefit is particularly important when considering people who are or who feel chronically powerless because of lack of resources, low hierarchical rank in an organization, or membership in a low-power social group.

ACKNOWLEDGMENTS

We are gratefully indebted to the following individuals for their insight, support, and assistance with this research: Daniel Ames, Max Bazerman, Joe Ferrero, Alan Fiske and lab, Adam Galinsky, Deborah Gruenfeld, Lucia Guillory, Brian Hall, Bob Josephs, Brian Lucas, Malia Mason, Pranj Mehta, Michael Morris, Joe Navarro, Michael Norton, Thomas Schubert, Steve Stroessner, and Bill von Hippel.

DECLARATION OF CONFLICTING INTERESTS

The authors declared that they had no conflicts of interest with respect to their authorship or the publication of this article.

NOTES

1. The effect of power on risk taking is moderated by factors such as prenatal exposure to testosterone (Ronay & von Hippel, in press).
2. Cortisol scores at both time points were sufficiently normally distributed, except for two outliers that were more than 3 standard deviations above the mean and were excluded; testosterone scores at both time points were sufficiently normally distributed, except for one outlier that was more than 3 standard deviations above the mean and was excluded.

REFERENCES

Abbott, D.H., Keverne, E.B., Bercovitch, F.B., Shively, C.A., Mendoza, S.P., Saltzman, W., et al. (2003). Are subordinates always stressed? A comparative analysis of rank differences in cortisol levels among primates. *Hormones and Behavior, 43*, 67–82.

Anderson, C., & Galinsky, A.D. (2006). Power, optimism, and the proclivity for risk. *European Journal of Social Psychology, 36*, 511–536.

Archer, J. (2006). Testosterone and human aggression: An evaluation of the challenge hypothesis. *Neuroscience & Biobehavioral Reviews, 30*, 319–345.

Booth, A., Shelley, G., Mazur, A., Tharp, G., & Kittok, R. (1989). Testosterone and winning and losing in human competition. *Hormones and Behavior, 23*, 556–571.

Briñol, P., & Petty, R.E. (2003). Overt head movements and persuasion: A self-validation analysis. *Journal of Personality and Social Psychology, 84*, 1123–1139.

Carney, D.R., Hall, J.A., & Smith LeBeau, L. (2005). Beliefs about the nonverbal expression of social power. *Journal of Nonverbal Behavior, 29*, 105–123.

Chen, M., & Bargh, J.A. (1999). Consequences of automatic evaluation: Immediate behavioral predispositions to approach or avoid the stimulus. *Personality and Social Psychology Bulletin, 25*, 215–224.

Coe, C.L., Mendoza, S.P., & Levine, S. (1979). Social status constrains the stress response in the squirrel monkey. *Physiology & Behavior, 23*, 633–638.

Cohen, S., Schwartz, J.E., Epel, E., Kirschbaum, C., Sidney, S., & Seeman, T. (2006). Socioeconomic status, race, and diurnal cortisol decline in the

Coronary Artery Risk Development in Young Adults (CARDIA) study. *Psychosomatic Medicine, 68*, 41–50.
Dabbs, J.M. (1991). Salivary testosterone measurements: Collecting, storing, and mailing saliva samples. *Physiology & Behavior, 42*, 815–817.
Darwin, C. (2009). *The expression of the emotions in man and animals.* New York, NY: Oxford. (Original work published 1872)
de Waal, F. (1998). *Chimpanzee politics: Power and sex among apes.* Baltimore, MD: Johns Hopkins University Press.
Dickerson, S.S., & Kemeny, M.E. (2004). Acute stressors and cortisol responses: A theoretical integration and synthesis of laboratory research. *Psychological Bulletin, 130*, 355–391.
Galinsky, A.D., Gruenfeld, D.H., & Magee, J.C. (2003). From power to action. *Journal of Personality and Social Psychology, 87*, 327–339.
Hall, J.A., Coats, E.J., & Smith LeBeau, L. (2005). Nonverbal behavior and the vertical dimension of social relations: A meta-analysis. *Psychological Bulletin, 131*, 898–924.
Keltner, D., Gruenfeld, D.H., & Anderson, C. (2003). Power, approach, and inhibition. *Psychological Review, 110*, 265–284.
Mazur, A., & Booth, A. (1998). Testosterone and dominance in men. *Behavioral & Brain Sciences, 21*, 353–397.
Mehta, P.H., & Josephs, R.A. (2006). Testosterone change after losing predicts the decision to compete again. *Hormones and Behavior, 50*, 684–692.
Mehta, P.H., & Josephs, R.A. (2010). *Dual-hormone regulation of dominance.* Manuscript in preparation.
Riskind, J.H., & Gotay, C.C. (1982). Physical posture: Could it have regulatory or feedback effects on motivation and emotion? *Motivation and Emotion, 6*, 273–298.
Ronay, R., & von Hippel, W. (in press). Power, testosterone and risk-taking: The moderating influence of testosterone and executive functions. *Journal of Behavioral Decision Making.*
Sapolsky, R.M. (2005). The influence of social hierarchy on primate health. *Science, 308*, 648–652.
Sapolsky, R.M., Alberts, S.C., & Altmann, J. (1997). Hypercortisolism associated with social subordinance or social isolation among wild baboons. *Archives of General Psychiatry, 54*, 1137–1143.
Schubert, T.W., & Koole, S.L. (2009). The embodied self: Making a fist enhances men's power-related self-conceptions. *Journal of Experimental Social Psychology, 45*, 828–834.
Schultheiss, O.C., & Stanton, S.J. (2009). Assessment of salivary hormones. In E. Harmon-Jones & J.S. Beer (Eds.), *Methods in the neurobiology of social and personality psychology* (pp. 17–44). New York, NY: Guilford.
Segerstrom, S., & Miller, G. (2004). Psychological stress and the human immune system: A meta-analytic study of 30 years of inquiry. *Psychological Bulletin, 130*, 601–630.
Smith, P.K., Jostmann, N.B., Galinsky, A.D., & van Dijk, W.W. (2008). Lacking power impairs executive functions. *Psychological Science, 19*, 441–447.

Stepper, S., & Strack, F. (1993). Proprioceptive determinants of emotional and nonemotional feelings. *Journal of Personality and Social Psychology, 64*, 211–220.

Strack, F., Martin, L.L., & Stepper, S. (1988). Inhibiting and facilitating conditions of the human smile: A nonobtrusive test of the facial feedback hypothesis. *Journal of Personality and Social Psychology, 54*, 768–777.

Wegner, D.M., Lane, J.D., & Dimitri, S. (1994). The allure of secret relationships. *Journal of Personality and Social Psychology, 66*, 287–300.

Dana R. Carney and Andy J. Yap are with Columbia University. Amy J. C. Cuddy is with Harvard University.

QUESTIONS ABOUT MEANING

1. How is Carney, Cuddy, and Yap's research different from related, previous research about body movements and emotion? What research gap does this study address?
2. Describe Carney, Cuddy, and Yap's research methods. What was the goal? How did they test their methods before conducting the study?
3. Summarize the results. What real-world applications does this research have?

QUESTIONS FOR RHETORICAL ANALYSIS

4. What are the purposes of Figures 6.1, 6.2, 6.3, and 6.4? Figures 6.3 and 6.4 are presented as column charts. What other types of tables or charts could have been used to depict the same information? Would they have been more or less effective? Explain.
5. Which of the conventions of academic writing discussed in this chapter do the authors use? In what other ways do the authors create a trustworthy and competent ethos?

THINKING AND WRITING ABOUT THE TOPIC

The conventions described in this chapter are important markers of an academic writer's competence and authority. Integrating these conventions into your own writing increases the likelihood that you will see yourself as an academic writer and that others will perceive you in the same way. In one study of more than 650 essays, English professors compared papers written by students who considered themselves ready for college-level writing courses to papers written by students who did not think they were ready for college-level writing courses. The researchers found that reformulation markers and other expressions used to signal the writer's intent to clarify meaning (like *for example*) were far more common in essays written by students who considered themselves ready for a college-level writing course (Gere et al. 623). They also found a greater tendency to qualify claims among those who self-placed into college-level writing courses (622). In other words, students who used traditional markers of academic writing *saw themselves* as ready for college-writing courses (somewhat like the study participants who felt more powerful after assuming a pose of power), and these students used writing features that would *signal to others* their readiness for college writing.

Return to a paper you have written for college or one you are currently writing and analyze your own use of academic writing conventions. Is the first impression you make one of an expert academic writer? Revise your paper to integrate additional examples of the writing conventions discussed in this chapter. In a separate "writing analysis" to submit with your paper, discuss the academic writing conventions you have included in your paper. Quote examples and explain what purposes the conventions serve in your paper.

WORKS CITED

Akuthota, Venu, et al. "The Effect of Long-Distance Bicycling on Ulnar and Median Nerves." *American Journal of Sports Medicine* 33 (2005): 1224–30. Print.

Balcazar, Fabricio E., Teresa J. Garate-Serafini, and Christopher B. Keys. "The Need for Action When Conducting Intervention Research: The Multiple Roles of Community Psychologists." *American Journal of Community Psychology* 33.3-4 (2004): 243–52. Print.

Balocco, Anna Elizabeth. "Who's Afraid of Literature? Rhetorical Routines in Literary Research Articles." *ESPecialist* 21.2 (2000): 207–23. Print.

Biber, Douglas, et al. *Longman Grammar of Spoken and Written English*. Essex: Pearson Education, 1999. Print.

"Big Blue Can Do." *Tri-City Herald* 1 Apr. 2012: D1. Print.

Brauer, Jurgen. "Business Ethics: Scandals and Standards." *Phi Kappa Phi Forum* 87.1 (2007): 28+. Print.

Burton, Leone. "The Practices of Mathematicians: What Do They Tell Us about Coming to Know Mathematics?" *Educational Studies in Mathematics* 37 (1999): 121–43. Print.

Burton, Leone, and Candia Morgan. "Mathematicians Writing." *Journal for Research in Mathematics Education* 31.4 (2000): 429–54. Print.

Campbell, R., et al. "Doing Community Research without a Community: Creating a Safe Space for Rape Survivors." *American Journal of Community Psychology* 33.3-4 (2004): 253–61. Print.

Cuenca, Maria-Josep. "Two Ways to Reformulate: A Contrastive Analysis of Reformulation Markers." *Journal of Pragmatics* 35 (2003): 1069–93. Print.

Dahl, Darren W., Amitava Chattopadhyay, and Gerald J. Gorn. "The Use of Visual Mental Imagery in New Product Design." *Journal of Marketing Research* 36.1 (1999): 18–28. Print.

Druckman, James N., Jordan Fein, and Thomas J. Leeper. "A Source of Bias in Public Opinion Stability." *American Political Science Review* 106.2 (2012): 430–54. Print.

Foley, Jonathan A. "Can We Feed the World & Sustain the Planet?" *Scientific American* 11 (2011): 60–65. Print.

Gere, Anne Ruggles, et al. "Local Assessment: Using Genre Analysis to Validate Directed Self-Placement." *College Composition and Communication* 64.4 (2013): 605–32. Print.

Gerlach, Neil. "Narrating Armageddon: Antichrist Films and the Critique of Late Modernity." *Journal of Religion and Popular Culture* 24.2 (2012): 217–29. Print.

Hale, Ray, et al. "Cultural Insensitivity to Sexist Language toward Men." *The Journal of Social Psychology* 130.5 (1990): 697–98. Print.

Harwood, Nigel. "'Nowhere Has Anyone Attempted . . . In This Article I Aim to Do Just That': A Corpus-based Study of Self-promotional I and We in Academic Writing across Four Disciplines." *Journal of Pragmatics* 37.8 (2005): 1207–31. Print.

______. "Political Scientists on the Functions of Personal Pronouns in Their Writing: An Interview-based Study of 'I' and 'We.'" *Text & Talk* 27.1 (2007): 27–54. Print.

Head, Alison J. "Learning the Ropes: How Freshmen Conduct Course Research Once They Enter College," *Project Information Literacy Research Report*. 4 Dec. 2013. Print.

Henderson, Rebecca, Adam Jaffe, and Manuel Trajtenberg. "Patent Citations and the Geography of Knowledge Spillovers: A Reassessment: Comment." *The American Economic Review* 95.1 (2005): 461–64. Print.

Huang, Zhen, Keling Zang, and Louis F. Reichardt. "The Origin Recognition Core Complex Regulates Dendrite and Spine Development in Postmitotic Neurons." *Journal of Cell Biology* 170.4 (2005): 527–35. Print.

Hyland, Ken. "Academic Clusters: Text Patterning in Published and Postgraduate Writing." *International Journal of Applied Linguistics* 18.1 (2008): 41–62. Print.

Jelenkovic, Aline, and Esther Rebato. "Association among Obesity-Related Anthropometric Phenotypes: Analyzing Genetic and Environmental Contribution." *Human Biology* 84.2 (2012): 127–37. Print.

Jouanne, F., et al. "Postseismic Deformation in Pakistan after the 8 October 2005 Earthquake: Evidence of Afterslip along a Flat North of the Balakot-Bagh Thrust." *Journal of Geophysical Research, Solid Earth* 116.7 (2011): 1–22. Web. 27 Apr. 2014.

Karcher, Carolyn L. "Reconceiving Nineteenth-Century American Literature: The Challenge of Women Writers." *American Literature* 66.4 (1994): 781–93. Print.

Kieras, David. E. "Good and Bad Structure in Simple Paragraphs: Effects on Apparent Theme, Reading Time, and Recall." *Journal of Verbal Learning and Verbal Behavior* 17 (1978): 13–28. Print.

Lee, Gregory P., and David R. Diduch. "Deteriorating Outcomes after Meniscal Repair Using the Meniscus Arrow in Knees Undergoing Concurrent Anterior Cruciate Ligament Reconstruction." *The American Journal of Sports Medicine* 33 (2005): 1138–41. Print.

Li, Zheng (Jeremy). "Design and Development of a New Automated and High-Speed Gas Filling Systems." *ISRN Mechanical Engineering* (2011): 1–4. Print.

Lithio, Dan. "Optimizing a Volleyball Serve." 14 Oct. 2006. 1–20. Web. 9 May 2013. http://www.rose-hulman.edu/mathjournal/archives/2006/vol7-n2/paper11/v7n2-11pd.pdf

Lytle, Beverly, and Caroline Yang. "Detecting Forged Handwriting with Wavelets and Statistics." *Undergraduate Math Journal* 7.1 (2006): 1–10. Web. 18 June 2013.

Mau, Wei-Cheng, and Richard Lynn. "Gender Differences in Homework and Test Scores in Mathematics, Reading and Science at Tenth and Twelfth Grade." *Psychology, Evolution & Gender* 2.2 (2000): 119–25. Print.

Merrilees, Bill, James Tiessen, and Dale Miller. "Entrepreneurial Internationalisation: The Role of Distributor/Client Relationships." *Journal of Research in Marketing and Entrepreneurship* 2.1 (2000): 57–73. Print.

Meyer, Bonnie J. F. *The Organization of Prose and Its Effects on Memory.* New York: Elsevier, 1975. Print.

Paliwal, M., et al. "Investigation of High-Frequency Squeal in a Disc Brake System Using a Friction Layer-Based Coupling Stiffness." *Proceedings of the Institution of Mechanical Engineers. Part C, Mechanical Engineering Science* 219.6 (2005): 513–22. Print.

Quinn, Ian. "On Woolhouse's Interval-Cycle Proximity Hypothesis." *Music Theory Spectrum* 32.2 (2010): 172–79. Print.

Raghubir, Priya, and Kim Corfman. "When Do Price Promotions Affect Pretrial Brand Evaluations?" *Journal of Marketing Research* 36 (May 1999): 211–22. Print.

Raghubir, Priya, and Aradhna Krishna. "Vital Dimensions in Volume Perception: Can the Eye Fool the Stomach?" *Journal of Marketing Research* 36.3 (1999): 313–26. Print.

A Review of the Proficiencies Required by Students Entering First Year Post-Secondary English Courses. Prepared by Virginia Cooke, University College of the Fraser Valley, in collaboration with Ruth Derksen, Centre for Research in Professional and Academic Writing, Simon Fraser University, 1999. Print.

Roeder, John, and Michael Tenzer. "Identity and Genre in Gamelan Gong Kebyar: An Analytical Study of Gabor." *Music Theory Spectrum* 34.1 (2012): 78–122. Print.

Rose, Ellen. "The Phenomenology of On-Screen Reading: University Students' Lived Experience of Digitised Text." *British Journal of Educational Technology* 42.3 (2011): 515–26. Print.

Taber, Charles S., and Milton Lodge. "Motivated Skepticism in the Evaluation of Political Beliefs." *American Journal of Political Science* 50.3 (2006): 755–69. Print.

Tedick, Diane. J., and Maureen A. Mathison. "Holistic Scoring in ESL Writing Assessment: What Does an Analysis of Rhetorical Features Reveal?" *Academic Writing in a Second Language: Essays on Research and Pedagogy.* Ed. Diane Belcher and George Braine. Norwood, NJ: Ablex, 1995. 205–30. Print.

Vazquez, J. A., P. J. Shamberger, and J. E. Hammer. "Plutonic Xenoliths Reveal the Timing of Magma Evolution of Hualalai and Mauna Kea, Hawaii." *Geology* 35.8 (2007): 695–98. Print.

Vincent, Claude, and Byron Eastman. "Does Player Mobility Lead to Higher Earnings? Evidence from the NHL." *American Economist* 57.1 (2012): 50–64. Print.

Yerex, Robert P. "The Consumer-Driven Economy at a Crossroads." *Business Economics* 46.1 (2011): 32–42. Print.

CHAPTER 7

Conducting Secondary Research

All research starts with a question. Questions beginning with *What? Why? How?* send a writer on a journey to explore an issue. This exploration is what drives source-based research assignments—among the most common assignments you'll encounter in college.

When you begin researching for a source-based assignment, remember a few tips: First, *read with an open mind about the issue.* If you start with a question (or questions), you notice very different things than when you read looking for evidence to prove a point or to support a personal opinion. Second, *read critically.* Don't just accept and repeat a writer's claims. Ask questions like *To whom is the author writing? What is the author's goal? What assumptions does the author make about this topic? What evidence does the author provide?* Third, *read broadly* and consider your topic from more than one point of view. If your subject is one that affects many different groups of people, make a list of the questions and concerns they would have. By reading sources with conflicting perspectives you discover questions that warrant discussion. Put what writers say into a larger context and look for connections and discrepancies between sources so that you can demonstrate a broad understanding of the issue to your readers. Perhaps the most important thing to remember about a college research assignment is this: Your objective goes beyond *repeating* what's been written to *discovering* what's still unsettled about a topic. *Your* purpose should take center stage and the information you use from sources should support that purpose.

All of this takes time—even for the best writers. For research-based assignments, it's common to continue researching and reading throughout the writing process and to refine what you want to say as you read more about the issue. This chapter will help you conduct your research effectively.

Discovering Topics

If your research topic has not been assigned, then your first task is to select one. You have access to many potential sources of topic ideas, including assignment prompts, personal experience, course materials, and "presearch" results.

Analyze Assignment Prompts

Before you decide on a topic, analyze the assignment prompt your professor provides. Prompts outline any subject matter or source requirements. As you learned in chapter 4, the prompt will also help you understand the assignment goals and what your professor will prioritize when grading your paper—all details to consider when selecting a topic and sources. Some prompts even suggest topics you can write about.

Choose from What You Know

You've no doubt been advised before to write about a subject that you care about or are familiar with. Research indicates that when we read or hear new information about a subject we are familiar with, we comprehend and remember it better than we do information about unfamiliar subjects. In one study, for example, participants received a series of made-up facts about celebrities (such as the type of car they drive). Those already familiar with the celebrities remembered more of these "facts" than those unfamiliar with them (Kole and Healy 126–27). Because of their prior knowledge, the facts had more meaning. Prior knowledge facilitates reading comprehension because it provides you with a context or framework in which to insert the new information.

In addition, when your topic is personally meaningful, your background knowledge of that topic can inspire good questions that will in turn inspire good research. That was the case for student Daniel Parr, when he needed a topic for a research-based proposal he had to write for his management communications course. Parr's assignment was to recommend a way to increase employee productivity at a fictional company. For topic ideas, Parr drew from his experience working in project management, and he eventually found inspiration from above—literally. He decided to recommend that his fictional company improve the office lighting. Here's how he came up with his topic:

> It is an issue close to my heart, as I work in a small office with no window and fluorescents shining down all day. I am also looking into a project [at work] . . . to change approximately 2000 T12 bulbs to T8 bulbs in several buildings. I am curious as to what I will discover and what I might be able to use at work.

Parr found a way to benefit from a classroom assignment by searching his work environment for areas in need of improvement.

Consult Course Resources

Other potential sources of research topics are your course materials. After surveying 178 students about their research-based papers, communications professor

Alison Head discovered that many students begin their research projects by consulting their course readings for topic ideas ("Beyond"). Topics these students wrote about included:

- feminism and working mothers
- college athletes and self-esteem
- teen suicide
- the gay rights movement

Discussions with others can also inspire topic ideas. During this topic-discovery phase, classmates, writing center tutors, librarians, and professors all serve as good sounding boards. Your professors are an especially valuable resource. As subject matter experts, they can suggest discipline-based topics that may interest you. They can also help you narrow a broad research question or direct you to that one key source that inspires your focus and leads you toward other sources about your topic.

Conduct "Presearch"

Another way to discover a specific research topic—particularly within a broad subject area—is by consulting library or Internet sources in order to get a feel for the "big picture." Some refer to this as "presearch" (Head and Eisenberg "Lessons" 10).

Library Resources. Your college library offers many resources for helping you discover topics. One good starting point is a general subscription database, such as EBSCOhost's Academic Search, Gale's Academic OneFile, or LexisNexis Academic Universe. These provide online access to both specialized journals and general periodicals such as the *New York Times*. Type a subject into the search window, and then scan titles, abstracts (summaries), subject headings, or literature review articles (which summarize the research on a topic) to see what's been written about the subject. Another way to find topic ideas is to browse your library's books on a subject, looking for recurring topics.

Internet Sources. Wikis provide an additional source of topic ideas. The most well-known wiki, Wikipedia, covers all topics; others focus on particular subjects. (To find wikis, search the WikiIndex at http://wikiindex.org.) It's true that wikis permit anyone to alter their content, and most have no formal review process to ensure that information is accurate or that contributors are subject-matter experts; however, they can provide a subject overview, suggest specific topics within a subject area, provide key terminology from the field to help you efficiently search for sources, and even direct you to some useful sources by way of the bibliographies.

Refining Your Topic

Once you've selected a potential topic, determine the specific question or questions you want to answer about your topic to focus your reading and source selection. As already mentioned, conducting research with a question to answer rather than with a point to "prove" encourages you to read potential sources with an open mind and a critical eye.

Good research questions have no single "right" answer. In fact, many have numerous valid answers. The following templates illustrate the types of questions that lend themselves to inquiry-based research:

What should we do about the problem of ______________?
What explains the popularity of ______________?
Why did ______________ fail (or succeed)?
What do various successful models for ______________ have in common?
Why do experts disagree about how to address ______________?
What factors caused ______________?
What have been the effects of ______________?
What will happen if we adopt a particular course of action to address ______________?
What is the best interpretation for ______________?
Why should ______________ be changed?
What are the economic, social, and/or political implications of ______________?

Answering questions such as these involves more than reporting facts or summarizing a single text. These questions call for evaluation, analysis, interpretation, and synthesis. For example, answering the question "What is the best way to address the problem of illegal immigration?" requires a writer to synthesize, compare, and evaluate the various solutions experts propose.

Once you begin to read potential sources, you'll discover good questions to ask about your topic and ways to narrow your focus.

Concept in Practice 7.1: Asking Open-Ended Questions to Refine a Topic

In general, the more limited the scope of your research question, the better. If you narrow a question such as:

"Why do cultural mores change?"

to

"What factors caused attitudes about divorce to change in the United States during the last half of the twentieth century?"

both your research and your paper will be more focused. Notice how the second question narrows the general subject of cultural mores to a *specific* cultural shift in a *specific* country during a *specific* period.

Consider, again, the research topics listed earlier:

- feminism and working mothers
- college athletes and self-esteem
- teen suicide
- the gay rights movement

Using what you've learned about inquiry-based research, select *one* of these topics and compose several open-ended and specific questions to help refine the topic.

Finding Sources

If you're like most students, finding information about a subject is not a problem; finding reliable information is. When researchers from Project Information Literacy (PIL), a national study based at the University of Washington, surveyed more than 2,000 college students about their research habits, students complained of "information overload." They were overwhelmed by the number of sources available yet had difficulty finding sources with credible information about their topics (Head and Eisenberg "Lessons" 9). (You can find one of PIL's studies at the end of chapter 4.)

Consulting sites like Google is one reason students can feel overwhelmed and frustrated by the research process. Since Google offers so many choices—most of them inappropriate as sources for college papers—you waste time sifting through irrelevant and unreliable information. A humanities professor describes a common problem:

> My students have reported that they usually begin their research by doing a Google search on a very broad topic—let's say they have chosen the feminist movement. The student will search the term "feminist movement," read the first few entries on the search list and feel that they have conducted adequate research. However, I require that students cite at least three different credible sources of information on paper. This disqualifies many of the sources they would find in a broad Google search, simply because the sources have questionable credibility and often did not originate on paper. (qtd. in Head and Eisenberg "Assigning" 12)

Not only professors recognize the problem. Employers from some of the world's largest organizations, including Microsoft, the FBI, and the Smithsonian, say they are concerned about the number of recent college graduates who don't understand that some answers can't be found in the first few results of a Google search. They require old-fashioned research skills that sometimes include consulting with librarians or searching through hard-bound reports (Head "Op-Ed").

There is another reason you should not rely on a Google search when conducting research for college papers. Like other search engines, Google uses algorithmic filters to personalize your online experience. You and a friend can conduct identical searches but get different results—results tailored to match what the Internet assumes are the kinds of sources you want to read based on your previous search patterns, your geographical location, your computer and browser choice, and other factors known or assumed about you. The problem with this, as Eli Pariser explains in his book *The Filter Bubble,* is that you don't decide what gets in or see what's edited out. Limiting your exposure to different points of view can, over time, reduce your capacity to see problems from different angles or understand different perspectives—a highly valued skill in academic writing.

The takeaway is this: Use general search engines like Google or Yahoo! and online encyclopedias like Wikipedia when searching for topic ideas and general knowledge about a topic, but don't rely on them when seeking evidence to include in your paper. A general search engine will produce thousands of "hits," but most won't contain information you should include in a college paper, and the sites listed may provide a skewed picture of the issue. Scholarly articles you do find online through sites like Google Scholar may require a fee or subscription to access. On the other hand, your college library's databases provide free access to scholarly sources through your college's license.

Search Library Databases

Your college library houses a wide variety of resources, including online catalogs and specialized and general databases, such as *JSTOR,* with links to articles from humanities, social science, and science journals.

To find information on your topic using one of these databases, conduct a **keyword search**. Keywords are words that might appear in the title or summary of an article about your subject or important words from your research question. For example, to find articles addressing the question, "What effect does workplace lighting have on employee productivity?" you would connect keywords using **Boolean operators**: AND, OR, and NOT.

Concept in Practice 7.2: Searching for Articles in a Database

Figure 7.1 shows a search conducted in ProQuest, a general subscription database available through many college libraries. Does this search appear to be effective for finding articles addressing the question "What effect does workplace lighting have on employee productivity?" Figure 7.2 shows the first two results.

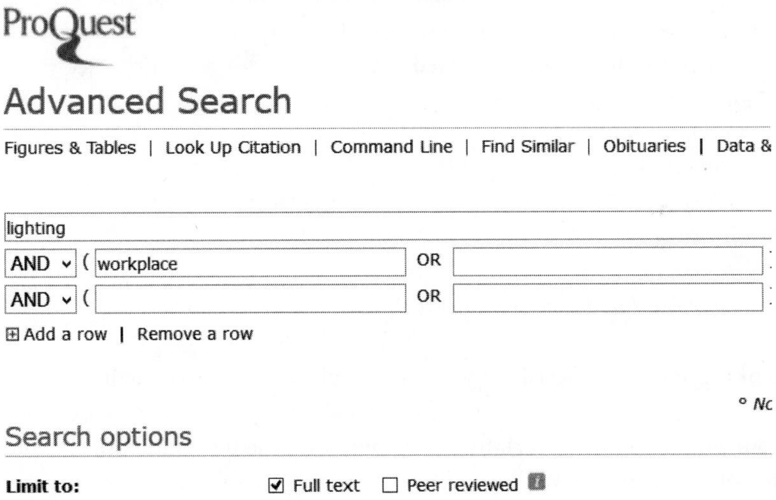

ProQuest
Advanced Search
Figures & Tables | Look Up Citation | Command Line | Find Similar | Obituaries | Data &
lighting
AND (workplace OR
AND (OR
Add a row | Remove a row
Search options
Limit to: Full text Peer reviewed

Figure 7.1 Example of a Database Search

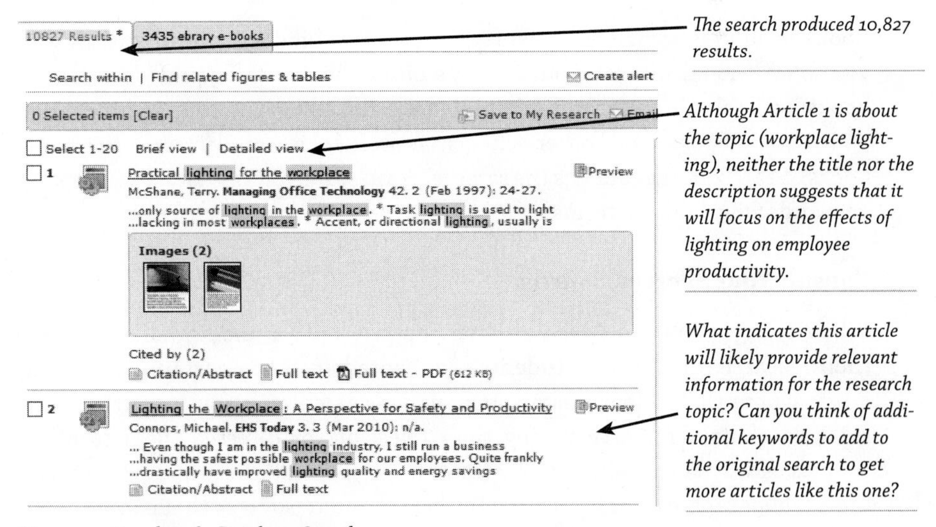

Figure 7.2 Results of a Database Search

The second article listed in Figure 7.2 looks promising for our research question. But notice that this search produced 10,827 "hits," more than you would want to sort through. By typing additional keywords into the search window, you can get a more specialized and useful list of results. One way to discover good keywords for your topic is by clicking on the citation/abstract link for particularly relevant articles and noting the *subject headings* listed there. Add these additional search words into separate lines of the search window, available through the advanced search option, and the database will automatically apply an operator word (usually AND or OR) between the lines. Or you can insert these operator words yourself. Here, for example, is a search that will produce a more focused list of results for our workplace lighting question:

workplace
AND
lighting
AND
employee (productivity or morale)

Linking additional words to your search phrase with AND will narrow your results. Conversely, linking keywords with OR will broaden your search results.

Your professor and librarians can recommend the best database for your research project and help you discover keywords to use in search phrases.

Search Online Book Catalogs

Books include thorough treatments of topics and bibliographies that can lead you to additional sources. Your library's online book catalog provides titles of books available through your school. It may also allow you to search holdings and request books from other schools, as well as access electronic books (e-books). Search online catalogs the same way you search online databases, linking keywords with Boolean terms.

Consult Your Sources' Sources

When college librarian Barbara Fister interviewed 14 undergraduates about their research process, the students commented on the importance of finding a key source that helped them settle on a research question, gave them the right vocabulary for articulating their question, or directed them to other sources by way of the bibliography (166). Once you find useful sources, consult their bibliographies. These citation trails lead you to sources that connect well with each other—crucial for writing research-based papers.

Consult Your Librarians

Another valuable resource, mentioned earlier, is librarians. Just as your professors are experts in their subject areas, the librarians at your college are experts in research. As college librarian Stephen Badalamente explains, librarians can help at every stage of a research project:

> It is our job to teach students how to do research. Librarians can help them get started, we can help them revise their search strategy, we can suggest resources they aren't aware exist, we can help them evaluate the usefulness of sources they are considering, and we can help them make sure they have saved the bits they'll need for their citations.

Badalamente adds that it's only too early to start working with a librarian on a research project if you haven't yet been given the assignment!

Concept in Practice 7.3: Using Your Library's Databases

The more efficient you become at using your library databases, the more fruitful your research sessions will be. Using one of your college library's general subscription databases, learn how to do the following, either by experimenting, by using the "help" features, by asking a librarian, or through a class demonstration and group exercise:

- Locate an article published in a scholarly (peer-reviewed) journal that discusses a topic you're currently researching.
- Using the bibliography of the source you've located, find another potential source from among those listed. (If none is available or relevant, find another source by the same author as the first one you selected.)
- Locate the Subject Headings for the original article you selected and, using terms from that list, conduct a new search for articles about your topic.
- For any one of the sources you have located, assess its quality, using the criteria described in the upcoming section titled "Evaluating Sources."

Evaluating Sources

Not all sources are trustworthy, a point demonstrated by University College London researchers Cliodhna O'Connor, Geraint Rees, and Helene Joffe. After analyzing nearly 3,000 newspaper articles about brain research, the authors determined that sometimes journalists present science research out of context in order to "create dramatic headlines, push thinly disguised ideological arguments, or support particular policy agendas" (225). When evaluating sources, you need to consider more than the subject matter's relevance. Consider the author's background and biases, the currency and quality of evidence, and the context and comprehensiveness of the discussion.

The following questions can help you determine which sources are likely to provide reliable information.

What Is the Publication Source?

As discussed in chapter 2, articles in scholarly journals are good sources of information because they usually go through a review process where experts in the field ensure that the discipline's standards for research are upheld. Every discipline has numerous journals, each periodically publishing new issues. For example, the journal *Intelligent Buildings International*, which includes articles about sustainable design and management of buildings, publishes an issue four times a year. Those four issues together make up a given year's volume.

You can sample a wide variety of journals at http://www.oxfordjournals.org/. As you look through the journals, notice that the discussion in articles is more in-depth than that found in general periodicals. In fact, articles more than 20 pages in length are common in scholarly journals.

Other reputable publications include books published by university presses. These go through a peer-review process similar to that of scholarly journal articles. Many trade or business periodicals and professional journals also publish in-depth coverage of issues by authors working in the field; and reputable organizations or institutions, such as government agencies or universities, publish reliable information on their websites.

Is the Source a Primary or Secondary Source?

Primary source information comes firsthand from the one who did the research or experienced the events described. **Secondary source** information comes secondhand from one who has read or interviewed primary sources. Many secondary sources—such as textbooks, popular magazines, and newspapers—are written for nonspecialists, so they can be a good place to gain general knowledge about a topic. However, they reflect the author's interpretation of what primary sources have said; and, as you saw in chapter 2, the information in secondary sources isn't always accurate. So, if primary sources on your topic are available, consult them; don't rely on secondary sources alone.

Does the Author Have Relevant Credentials?

Another consideration is the author's background, often identified at the beginning or end of articles or books. (When author information isn't there, conduct a Google search or check the citation information provided for online sources.) Does the author have a job title or work or life experience in the field he or she is writing about?

Let's consider the example of two authors: Sheri Graves and Jeffrey Anshel. Graves wrote "Efficiency by Design Workplace Aesthetics May Boost Morale, Productivity" and Anshel wrote "Visual Ergonomics in the Workplace." Both articles were among the results of our earlier ProQuest search for information about how workplace lighting affects employee productivity. A comparison of the authors' credentials found at the end of their respective articles, however, suggests the sources are not equally desirable for use in an academic paper (see Table 7.1).

TABLE 7.1
Comparison of Author Credentials

Sheri Graves's Credentials	Jeffrey Anshel's Credentials
Sheri Graves Staff Writer.	**Jeffrey R. Anshel, B.S., O.D.,** *is the principal of Corporate Vision Consulting, Endnitas, CA. A graduate of the Illinois College of Optometry, he has written numerous articles regarding nutritional influences on vision, stress factors that affect visual perfomance and computer vision concerns. Anshel has published several books, including* Visual Ergonomics Handbook. *A member of ASSE'S San Diego Chapter, he also provides consultations and seminars on visual stress in the workplace.*

Graves is identified as a staff writer for *The Press Democrat*, a daily newspaper published in Santa Rosa, California. This means that Graves likely obtained her information from reading or by interviewing others. A hyperlink takes readers to a list of other articles written by Graves. The list includes titles like "Casino Fever," "College Costs," and "Driving Lessons" but no additional articles about lighting or workplace productivity.

Anshel, on the other hand, is identified as a doctor of optometry (an OD) who conducts seminars on "visual stress in the workplace." He has also written about ergonomics (the study of efficiency in work environments). In other words, Anshel's credentials are related to his article topic—and our research topic.

The difference in authors' credentials and the difference in publication prestige (Graves's article is from a general newspaper; Anshel's article is from *Professional Safety*, the professional journal of the American Society of Safety Engineers) explain why Anshel's article would be more highly regarded by academic readers.

It can be more difficult to establish the credentials of authors for websites, but read the "About Us" information to determine if the site's sponsoring organization is reputable and unbiased. The URL extension can also provide clues to the reliability of websites. For instance, .edu indicates an educational institute, .gov indicates a government sponsored site, .org indicates a nonprofit organization, and .com may indicate a commercial site or personal website. But domain name alone won't tell you whether or not an author is qualified. For example, a college student may have a web address ending with .edu, but that doesn't qualify the student as a topic expert. Look for indicators that the authors of your sources are qualified to write about their subjects, and think twice about using information from sources you can't verify. Anyone can create a website and, thanks to desktop publishing, anyone can self-publish an article or book.

What Is the Original Context?

Every author is writing to a particular audience for a specific purpose. As you learned in chapter 2, understanding that context helps you understand why a text is written the way it is. What does the publication site or vocabulary level suggest about the intended audience? Depending on your purpose, you might eliminate sources that are too technical and specific or too broad and general. Are opposing viewpoints acknowledged or ignored? Does the author use neutral or inflammatory language? Is the author trying to sell something? Don't ignore clues to an author's agenda or attempts to manipulate the reader's emotions, and avoid blatantly biased and one-sided sources. But remember that even seemingly unbiased authors want readers to see the issue as they do, so read all sources critically.

What Is the Publication Date?

Using recent information is important when writing about many issues, especially technical, medical, social, and science topics. Of course, for some issues, older is better. When discussing the response to John F. Kennedy's assassination, for example, documents written at the time by witnesses to the events are invaluable. But for most topics, you want recent sources. Publication dates for books and periodicals are easy to find, and a copyright date and possibly the date of the last update should appear on each page of a website. You should be reluctant to use information from websites for which no publication date is provided.

Are the Author's Sources of Information Identified?

Does the author identify sources or provide a bibliography? If yes, are sources scholarly? If no, how does the author know what he or she knows? Publications consisting of claims without evidence or source citations shouldn't be used as sources for college papers. Let's return to Jeffrey Anshel's article, which we considered, along with Sheri Graves's article, as a potential source for a proposal about how lighting affects employee productivity. Graves's newspaper article has no bibliography, but Anshel's article includes an extensive one. Figure 7.3 includes a portion of Anshel's bibliography.

References

American Optometric Association (AOA). "Guide to the Clinical Aspects of Computer Vision Syndrome." St. Louis, MO: AOA, 1995.

Bernard, B., et al. "NIOSH Health Hazard Evaluation Report: *Los Angeles Times*." HETA 90-013-2277. Washington, DC: U.S. Department of Health and Human Services, CDC, NIOSH, 1990.

Centers for Disease Control and Prevention (CDC). "U.S. Life Tables 2000." Atlanta, GA: CDC, 2001. Table 11.

Collins, M.S., et al. "Task Variables and Visual Discomfort Associated with the Use of VDTs." *Optometry and Vision Science*. 68(1991): 27–33.

Dain, S.J., et al., "Symptoms in VDU Operators." *American Journal of Optometry and Physiological Optics*. 65(1988): 162–167.

Daum, K.M., et al. "Productivity Associated with Visual Status of Computer Users." *Optometry*. 75(2004): 33–47.

Dotson, T., et al. "The Effects of Filtering Fluorescent Lighting to Decrease Asthenopia and Increase Productivity Among Data Entry Operators." Southern California College of Optometry, Jan. 2003.

Elliott, G., et al. "Electromagnetic Radiation Emissions from Video Display Terminals. *Clinical & Experimental Optometry*. 69(1986): 53, 61.

Harris, M.G., et al. "Vision and Task Performance with Mono-Vision and Diffractive Bifocal Contact Lenses." *Optometry and Vision Science*. 69(1992): 609–614.

Illuminating Engineering Society of North America (IESNA). "VDT Lighting in the Workplace." RP-24. New York: IESNA, 1988.

Jaschinski-Kruza, W. "Visual Strain During VDU Work: The Effect of Viewing Distance and Dark Focus." *Ergonomics*. 31(1998): 1449–1465.

References include professional organizations, government publications, and scholarly journals in optometry. In addition, some of the titles point to additional sources we could consult for our proposal.

Figure 7.3 Bibliography in a Potential Source (Anshel 25)

Not only are Anshel's sources of information named; they are of high quality, as the highlights in the figure show.

Is the Source Static or Dynamic?

"Static" sources do not change over time. Information there today will be there years from now. On the other hand, information found in "dynamic" sources may not be available in the same form later. Wiki publications, blogs, and personal websites are examples of dynamic sources. In researched papers, one purpose of the bibliography is to allow readers to consult your sources and see the information you cite in its original context. With a dynamic source, there is no guarantee the information will be there next week. This is one reason to opt for static sources.

Creating a Working Bibliography

For research-based projects, you'll likely continue researching and reading throughout the writing process. You will formulate ideas for your paper as you peruse what others have written, and you will often return to read sources you initially skim. Keeping a paper or electronic trail will help you relocate those sources you came across early in your search.

An effective way to keep track of where you find information is in an annotated bibliography. An **annotated bibliography** is similar to any other bibliography in that it lists sources, but it is a working list to help you keep track of sources. It also includes notes or annotations about each source. These annotations help you to discover connections between sources and plan your paper.

Whether you're completing a research assignment for composition, anthropology, or theoretical physics, before you submit your final paper, you may be required to submit an annotated bibliography. This bibliography gives your instructor a chance to evaluate whether you are selecting appropriate sources for your assignment.

Daniel Parr, for instance, had to submit an annotated bibliography to his management communications professor prior to submitting his proposal on workplace lighting and the effects on employee productivity. This bibliography identified the sources he had located, explained how they might be used in his proposal, and showed how they related to one another. When asked about the value of developing an annotated bibliography, Parr said, "I found this process very helpful. . . . It forces you to start the research and source selection process early, at the beginning, rather than waiting till the end to write the bibliography." *Concept in Practice* 7.4 shows a portion of the bibliography Parr submitted to his instructor.

Concept in Practice 7.4: Developing an Annotated Bibliography

To learn more about the purpose of an annotated bibliography, read the following excerpt from Parr's bibliography.

ANNOTATED BIBLIOGRAPHY

Dilouie, Craig. "Lighting and Productivity: Missing Link Found?" *Architectural Lighting* 18.6 (2003): 39–42. *ProQuest*. Web. 21 May 2013.
This trade and industry journal publication discusses the link between employee productivity and office lighting. It also provides insight to good lighting design and the correlation between better visibility and improved task performance. Craig Dilouie is principal of ZING Communications, a consulting and marketing communications firm. He is also the proprietor of Searchspec.com,

The annotation begins with a summary of the article.

Here, Parr writes about the author's qualifications.

which is a lighting product search engine. This article contains a good reference section, and was in part backed by the Light Right Consortium, operated by PNNL. I can use this research to show that well thought out light systems can lead to increased productivity while saving money by being more energy efficient.

Making notes like this about sources can help you begin to plan your paper.

Fisk, William J. "Health and Productivity Gains from Better Indoor Environments and their Relationship with Building Energy Efficiency." *Annual Review of Energy and the Environment* 25 (2000): 537–66. *ProQuest*. Web. 22 May 2013. This article uses several different case studies to review and evaluate the correlation between employee productivity and cost avoidance in running a company. Also discusses other topics like Sick Building Syndrome. Fisk is affiliated with the Indoor Environment Department, Environmental Energy Technologies Division at Berkeley National Laboratory, Berkeley, California. This annual review paper discusses multiple studies and includes an extensive bibliography and reference section. I can use this report with information from Dilouie to show the importance of a positive workplace and the influence of lighting on self-reported employee productivity.

Here again Parr notes the source author's qualifications. Compare these qualifications to those of the source Parr noted earlier. In which subject areas is each author an expert?

Parr notes that this source might lead him to additional sources.

How does Parr explain how these sources all relate to the central idea of his proposal?

Newsham, Guy, et al. "Control Strategies for Lighting and Ventilation in Offices: Effects on Energy and Occupants." *Intelligent Buildings International* 1.2 (2009): 101–21. *ProQuest*. Web. 23 May 2013. This original research article discusses individual control of office work conditions like lighting and temperature and its effects on the energy consumption of the building and the productivity of the employees. The authors are all affiliated with the National Research Council Canada – Institute for Research in Construction. This article contains an excellent bibliography and reference section. I can use the research data to show the effectiveness in lowering power bills and increasing employee morale by allowing employees to have control over the lighting systems in their workplace.

Creating a working bibliography similar to Parr's can help you assess sources and their potential usefulness for your project.

Selecting Evidence for an Academic Argument

Daniel Parr's bibliography (in *Concept in Practice* 7.4) demonstrates two factors to consider when selecting sources for a research-based paper: *Are the sources reliable and will the sources work well together?* Another consideration is *what kinds of evidence do your sources provide?*

As discussed in chapter 1, scholars across the disciplines engage in various kinds of research. In the natural sciences and engineering, scholars conduct empirical research—testing a hypothesis by controlling and measuring variables. Many social science scholars conduct interviews, surveys, or observational research involving human subjects. Scholars in humanities disciplines—including literature, history, art, and dance—conduct close analyses of written texts, performances, or artifacts.

Here are a few examples of the types of research a scholar might conduct:

Research Question	Possible Types of Research Studies
Has the quality of river water been affected by the nearby nuclear plant?	Testing of water samples and comparison to results over time or in other rivers
Why do students plagiarize?	Interviews with students and professors and analysis of student papers
How has the rising unemployment rate affected student enrollment at the local community college?	Comparison of unemployment and enrollment trends over time; analysis of student responses on their admission forms
For what purposes do sociologists use first person in their research writing?	Analysis of research articles published in sociology journals

When conducting original research, scholars look for *trends or recurring themes* in the data (e.g., in their observations, in interview responses, or in features of a corpus of texts). From these repeated occurrences, they draw conclusions—about water quality, about why students plagiarize, about correlations between unemployment and college enrollment, or about why sociologists use first person in research writing.

As a student conducting secondary research, you have a similar goal: to *demonstrate a trend in the evidence.* By citing what "counts" as evidence in the discipline—rather than using unsubstantiated claims or opinion as evidence—you enhance your credibility among readers in the field. One place to find such evidence is in reports of original research.

Reading Academic Research Reports

As you learned in chapter 2, one of the best sources of high-quality evidence is peer-reviewed scholarly journal articles. Many of these articles are reports of original research. Other experts in the discipline review the research and typically recommend the author make revisions to the research, manuscript, or both before the article is published. This thorough review process is why scholarly research articles are regarded so highly as sources. The information has been vetted by experts in the discipline.

Use your knowledge of how scholarly research articles are typically organized to help you determine both what the researcher concluded and how. As you'll recall, many research reports have a one-paragraph summary of the article (called the Abstract); an Introduction, including a summary of previous research on the topic; a Methods section, describing the research procedures; a Results section, describing what was observed; and a Discussion section, describing the significance of the findings. Even reports that don't include these sections may more or less follow this organization. When trying to determine what a researcher concluded and how, look for a statement of purpose at the end of the introduction, skim the methods section to determine how the research was conducted, and read the discussion section. Don't worry if you can't understand everything; instead focus on what was concluded and how.

Choosing between Primary and Secondary Sources of Information

Reading original research reports published in scholarly journals is one way to obtain quality evidence, but it's not always realistic for some topics. Understanding original research reports in neuroscience, for example, is beyond the grasp of most of us, so we must rely on other writers (secondary sources) to tell us what the research means and why it's important. However, as already noted, those secondary reports give a limited account of the research or may even include misleading information. *When relying on secondary sources is necessary, then, take precautions to ensure that the information obtained from them is reliable:*

1. *Learn about the authors of your sources.* Is their work experience or education in the field they are writing about? If so, you know they have the knowledge necessary to interpret the primary research. If not, keep searching for sources written by people with expertise in your subject.
2. *Corroborate the information.* Establish for readers that the information you report is widely accepted in the discipline. In other words, show that there is agreement among sources used to support the claims in your paper.
3. *Draw from reputable publications.* Obtain information from publications that have the indicators of reliability discussed in this chapter.

By taking the time to learn about the reliability of your sources, you can in turn assure your readers that your claims are based on reliable information.

Applying the Concepts to Reading: *Evaluating Online Sources*

This *Applying the Concepts* exercise includes excerpts from two websites being considered for use as sources in a research-based paper about gun control. The websites appeared on the first page of results from an Internet search for "gun control statistics." The two sites—justfacts.com and statisticbrain.com—both have .com as their URL extension. To prepare for class discussion, make notes about the factors that indicate we should or should not trust the information found in these sites. (A few questions appear in the margins to help you get started.) How would you rate the potential usefulness of these sources for an academic writer? Identify the factors on which you base your assessment.

SOURCE 1: The title of the first site is "JUST FACTS. a resource for independent thinkers" (http://www.justfacts.com/guncontrol.asp#general). Below the title is a citation:

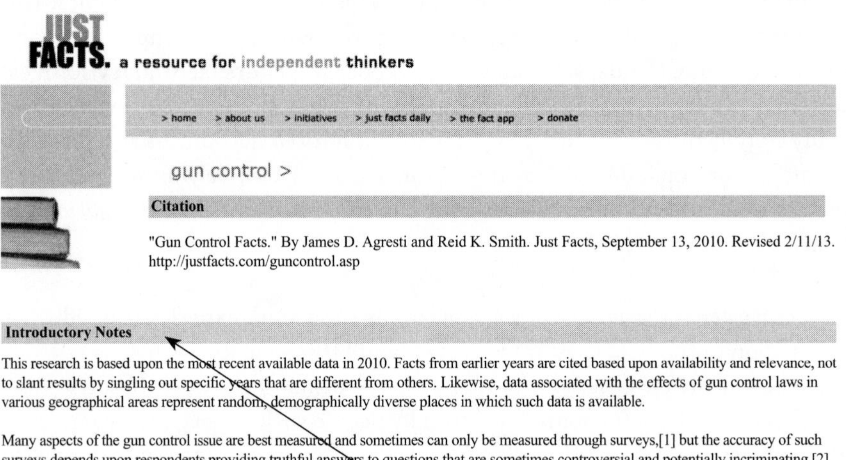

JUST FACTS. a resource for independent thinkers

> home > about us > initiatives > just facts daily > the fact app > donate

gun control >

Citation

"Gun Control Facts." By James D. Agresti and Reid K. Smith. Just Facts, September 13, 2010. Revised 2/11/13. http://justfacts.com/guncontrol.asp

Introductory Notes

This research is based upon the most recent available data in 2010. Facts from earlier years are cited based upon availability and relevance, not to slant results by singling out specific years that are different from others. Likewise, data associated with the effects of gun control laws in various geographical areas represent random, demographically diverse places in which such data is available.

Many aspects of the gun control issue are best measured and sometimes can only be measured through surveys,[1] but the accuracy of such surveys depends upon respondents providing truthful answers to questions that are sometimes controversial and potentially incriminating.[2] Thus, Just Facts uses such data critically, citing the best-designed surveys we find, detailing their inner workings in our footnotes, and using the most cautious plausible interpretations of the results.

Particularly, when statistics are involved, the determination of what constitutes a credible fact (and what does not) can contain elements of personal subjectivity. It is our mission to minimize subjective information and to provide highly factual content. Therefore, we are taking the additional step of providing readers with four examples to illustrate the type of material that was excluded because it did not meet Just Facts' Standards of Credibility.

Ownership

* As of 2009, the United States has a population of 307 million people.[5]

* Based on production data from firearm manufacturers,[6] there are roughly 300 million firearms owned by civilians in the United States as of 2010. Of these, about 100 million are handguns.[7]

* Based upon surveys, the following are estimates of private firearm ownership in the U.S. as of 2010:

	Households With a Gun	Adults Owning a Gun	Adults Owning a Handgun
Percentage	40-45%	30-34%	17-19%
Number	47-53 million	70-80 million	40-45 million

[8]

What do the citation and the "Introductory Notes" indicate about the reliability of this website?

Figure 7.4 Sample Website Source

SOURCE 2: The second website is Statistic Brain (http://www.statisticbrain.com/gun-ownership-statistics-demographics/

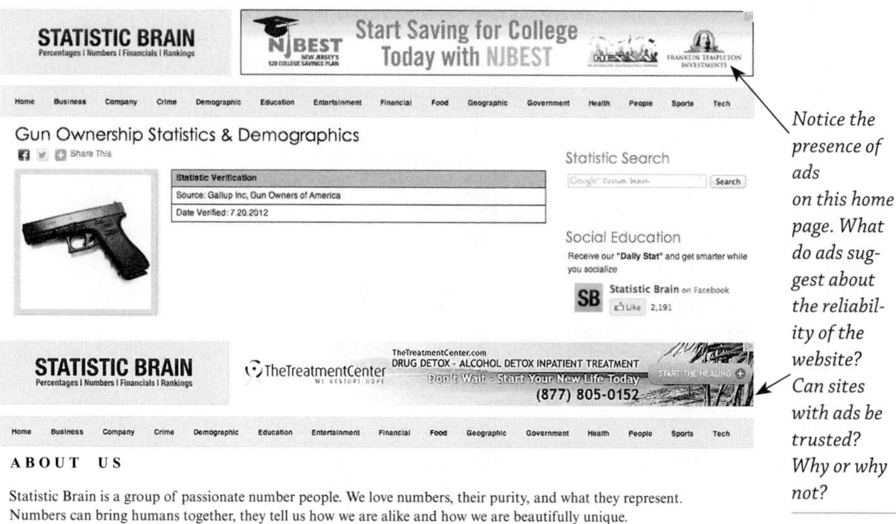

Notice the presence of ads on this home page. What do ads suggest about the reliability of the website? Can sites with ads be trusted? Why or why not?

ABOUT US

Statistic Brain is a group of passionate number people. We love numbers, their purity, and what they represent. Numbers can bring humans together, they tell us how we are alike and how we are beautifully unique. Numbers are a way to reflect on how far we've come and give us hope for the future.

Our goal is to bring you accurate and timely statistics.
We will never become number analysts because we believe numbers should only be interpreted by the reader.
We want to educate, assist, and sometimes entertain with numbers on every subject.

We hope that today you learn something new, find inspiration for tomorrow, and use your knowledge for something good.

Seth Harden
Founder // CEO

NJBEST NEW JERSEY'S 529 COLLEGE SAVINGS PLAN Start Saving for College Today with NJBEST

Home Business Company Crime Demographic Education Entertainment Financial Food Geographic Government

Gun Ownership Statistics & Demographics

Share This

Statistic Verification
Source: Gallup Inc, Gun Owners of America
Date Verified: 7.20.2012

The image suggests the numbers are for handguns only. Is this ever confirmed?

How were these numbers determined or can you tell? Are they based on a survey of the population? (Gallup is well known for public opinion polls.) Or based on sales records for gun manufacturers?

Year	Percent Ownership	
2011	36%	
2010	39%	
2009	40%	
2007	42%	
2005	40%	

Figure 7.5 Sample Website Source

Year	Percent Ownership	
2004	38%	
2003	43%	
2002	34%	
2000	32%	
1998	36%	
1998	40%	
1994	41%	
1993	42%	
1991	40%	
1990	43%	
1989	46%	
1988	40%	
1987	46%	
1985	44%	
1984	45%	
1982	45%	
1980	48%	
1977	51%	
1976	47%	
1974	46%	
1973	47%	
National Gun Ownership (2010)		**39%**

Figure 7.5 *(Continued)*

Applying the Concepts to Writing: *Creating an Annotated Bibliography That Evaluates Sources*

Create an annotated bibliography for a paper you are writing. But instead of focusing on the content or relevance of your sources, describe the features that indicate each source is or is not of high quality. Consider the following:

- What are the author's credentials?
- What is the date of publication?
- What is the reputation of the publication?
- Does the author identify his or her sources of information?
- Is the source static?
- Is the source a primary or secondary source?

Based on the details you describe, rate the reliability of each source in your bibliography.

Paired Readings from Computer Science

"YAB [Youth Advisory Board] Interview: Laura Granka, Search User Experience, Google." *Ypulse* Youth Advisory Board post from RAYMOND BRAUN

Ypulse is a blog with postings about issues of interest to teens and young adults. *Ypulse* also publishes interviews, like the one *Ypulse* Youth Advisory Board member Raymond Braun conducted with Laura Granka, who works as a "user-experience researcher" at Google. In the interview, conducted in 2010, Granka talks about her research.

Ypulse Youth Advisory Board post comes from Raymond Braun, who sat down with Laura Granka at Google to discuss the impact of young people on the search industry and vice-versa. Laura has spent the past six years studying how people acquire information, in both online and physical environments, and has authored more than 20 publications and presentations on the topic. Working with colleagues at Google since 2004, she has applied knowledge about search user behavior towards improving result ranking algorithms and the user interface. She has also led the Search Quality and User Experience teams through a number of key launches.

Youth Advisory Board: Describe the field of user experience research and your job at Google.

Laura Granka: I first started at Google as an intern for the Search Quality Group in 2004. From there, I was exposed to the User Experience team, which consists of researchers, designers and tech writers. Whenever a product is developed at Google, our team will evaluate it and ensure that Google is taking the most user-centered approach to the product. I came back to Google after my internship in 2005 and have been working since then as a User Experience researcher. I primarily work on search products and on developing new search features.

YAB: How do you study search habits?

LG: Our team uses a repertoire of many different methods and collaborates closely with various designers and engineers depending on the type of question we have. Some of our methods are macro, such as field studies. We'll talk to people in their own homes or places of work to see how they're using Google in relation to all the other products they have on their computers. Our goal in doing this is to see how they use search in relation to applications like Word, e-mail and printing. It's important for us to understand how all the pieces of the puzzle fit together in terms of search and other applications.

We also do usability studies, where we bring people to a lab here at Google and try to evaluate features before they are launched. We use eyetracking to assess what people look at on a webpage and how their eyes scan and process search results. We also use it to evaluate how many search results users look at before they click on one and how long this whole process takes. In addition, we will put news headlines, images and video on the search page to see if the eye does something different when it is presented with different types of information. I had done this type of eyetracking research prior to my work at Google during my master's at Cornell.

YAB: What do you think makes Google the leading search authority for young people?

LG: In general, Google's core principle is to focus on the user and that's what we do in terms of quality. We want to provide the highest quality information best suited to what a user needs and not put advertising in front of it. We're clear about what we think are really good search results and very good advertisements, and users trust that. Google is also innovative in terms of features while keeping everything simple. We just launched the new fade-in home page, which is an example of a feature that is simple but implemented to enhance the user's experience and make search easier. At any given time, we are running 50–200 search experiments in which a small percentage of our traffic will see a new variant of something before we launch the feature. We do this to ensure our new features are helpful and not problematic or confusing.

YAB: What have you discovered about the way teens and young adults use Google? How do their search habits differ from those of adults?

LG: Google's Director of User Experience said this really well: the issues that youth have when they're searching are the same as the problems everyone else has, though sometimes they may be magnified in certain respects. Search queries may be different or more question-oriented, but in terms of eyetracking, there seems to be a somewhat general consensus among the academic community that there aren't too many specific differences among age groups. This is probably because eye movements occur so quickly that it's a subconscious process.

YAB: How could marketers and advertisers use eyetracking research to help them develop products or campaigns for young people?

LG: When targeting individuals, there can be a lot of variability. For example, if someone is searching to buy a new backpack, sometimes a user will click on an ad on the right side of a Google search results page, while others will want to see comparisons of different backpacks. It really depends on an individual's state of mind. It's also important to think about social connections. People reach out to their social networks before making purchases—they like recommendations or the confirmation from a trusted source that the purchase they're going to make will be a good one. Using eyetracking for search results is a relatively new advancement. In 2004, my advisor and I were the first people to use eyetracking for search research. Before that, eyetracking was used primarily for research with websites, newspapers and advertisements. Eyetracking could prove very useful to advertising and marketing professionals in helping them better understand how young people's eyes are going to move around an ad, which can assist with determining image and text placement.

YAB: Which Google applications resonate with young people?

LG: We conducted some field studies in the Kirkland Seattle area with 18–24 year olds. What we gathered was that the social aspect of applications is incredibly important to young people. There's a sort of "always-on" mentality in young people, of always being connected online and being able to easily ask a friend for a recommendation or co-ordinate via e-mail with respect to a search. We've seen people validate, via their friends, the choices they've discovered in a search. For instance, one person we talked to would always email different options he found with search to his "techie friend" before making a purchase. The more familiar people are with technology, the more likely they are going to use it to connect with other people. Mobile is also a big initiative and mobile devices are even more popular in other countries than they are in the U.S., so we've done a lot of mobile research outside the country. Late last year, Google launched Social Search in Google Labs, a feature of Google Search designed to help you discover publicly available web and image content from your network of friends and contacts online. The feature was so popular that it is now available to everyone in beta on Google.com.

YAB: You have TA'd several undergraduate courses at Stanford and interact with college students on a regular basis. In your opinion, how is the college student of today different from the college student of the past?

LG: Young people's expectations for the type of information and access they can receive from technology are growing. With devices becoming more portable and information increasingly accessible, there is a growing sense among teens that you can fulfill your curiosity about a topic at any given time. The ability for students to have laptops in the classroom has really changed search. I sit in on a class at Stanford and observe that most students are on their laptops during the lecture. I can see them searching on Google for something the professor is talking about in real-time. It is really cool for me to see people searching for supplemental, in-depth information in the context of what the professor just mentioned, so I think having this technology in the classroom is a very powerful tool. It can help students expand upon or clarify certain points brought up in class.

YAB: What might marketers/media executives be surprised to learn about the way young people seek out information and process search results on Google?

LG: Young people are exposed to a huge variety of technologies at increasingly younger ages. They are used to more immediate access to content, and we've also seen a growing desire to contribute to the information that's on the Web. That provides a whole new level of context for search. In addition, young people have a desire for social interaction and feedback while they're searching. We're doing a lot of work with social search that will help people leverage their social network in terms of finding out how different people they know think about, and search for, different topics.

There is a growing appetite for real time information. People are constantly updating their Facebooks, and Twitter was a new model for quick, up-to-date information. Real time information is increasingly becoming more relevant and expected, and Google incorporates real time results and headlines into our search results. So if you search for something that is timely and newsworthy, Google will be scanning the web and will display real time search results from various sources, including Twitter.

YAB: What projects or new innovations at Google are you most excited about?

LG: It has been really cool at Google to see all the different ways we can improve search and make it smarter. We have launched features that help us better detect intent, and we now can offer snippets of information extracted from a page, such as the hours of a store or the menu from a restaurant. We also now have "Breaking News," a search feature where you can see search updates in real time. It's important to be able to harness information in real time in order to feed the increasing desire for instant information.

Social is definitely here to stay and it's a theme that resonates across the web. On iGoogle, we recently launched a handful of social gadgets. You can now play Scrabble with your friends in real time, share YouTube videos on a constantly updated feed, or recommend a book. It's more interesting to see what your friends are thinking and find interesting.

See more at: http://www.ypulse.com/post/view/yab-interview-laura-granka-search-quality-and-user-experience-google#sthash.ksE5ctix.dpuf

QUESTIONS ABOUT MEANING

1. Laura Granka describes herself as a "user experience" researcher. What kinds of research studies does she conduct?
2. What kinds of information can eye-tracking research provide for marketers and advertisers?
3. How does Granka describe young adults and their relationship with technology?

QUESTIONS FOR RHETORICAL ANALYSIS

4. How did Raymond Braun tailor his interview questions for the target audience? What additional (or revised) questions might Braun have asked Granka if he were writing for college professors who assign research writing?
5. In what ways do Granka's responses reflect the fact that they were given in a face-to-face interview? Do you think the responses were later edited by Braun? Support your answer.

"Eye-Tracking Analysis of User Behavior in WWW Search," *SIGIR Forum* LAURA A. GRANKA, THORSTEN JOACHIMS, AND GERI GAY

Today Laura Granka is a "user-experience researcher" at Google, but before that she taught at Cornell University. The following article describes research Granka conducted with colleagues Thorsten Joachims and Geri Gay at Cornell. The study involved giving participants questions and tracking their eye movements while they searched for answers online. "Eye-Tracking Analysis of User Behavior in WWW Search" first appeared in 2004 in *SIGIR Forum*, which publishes conference reports and research papers of interest to members of the Special Interest Group on Information Retrieval.

ABSTRACT

We investigate how users interact with the results page of a WWW search engine using eye-tracking. The goal is to gain insight into how users browse the presented abstracts and how they select links for further exploration. Such understanding is valuable for improved interface design, as well as for more accurate interpretations of implicit feedback (e.g. clickthrough) for machine learning. The following presents initial results, focusing on the amount of time spent viewing the presented abstracts, the total number of abstract[s] viewed, as well as measures of how thoroughly searchers evaluate their results set.

CATEGORIES AND SUBJECT DESCRIPTORS

H.5.2 [**User Interfaces**]: *Evaluation/methodology*, H.3.3 [**Information Search and Retrieval**]: *Search process,* H.3.5 [**Online Information Services**]: *Web-based services*

GENERAL TERMS

Human Factors, Experimentation, Measurement

KEYWORDS

Eye-Tracking, Implicit Feedback, WWW Search

1. INTRODUCTION

How do users interact with the list of ranked results of WWW search engines? Do they read the abstracts sequentially from top to bottom, or do they skip links? How many of the results do users evaluate before clicking on a link or reformulating the search? The answers to these questions will be beneficial in at least three ways. First, they provide the basis for improved interfaces. Second, they suggest more targeted metrics for evaluating the retrieval performance in WWW search. And third, they help [in] interpreting implicit feedback like clickthrough and reading times for machine learning of improved retrieval functions [2]. In particular, better understanding of user behavior will allow us to draw more accurate inferences about how implicit feedback relates to relative relevance judgments.

The following presents the results of an eye-tracking study that we conducted. Previous studies have analyzed directly observable data like query word frequency. However, unlike eye-tracking, these measurements can at best give indirect evidence of how users perceive and respond to the search results.

To the best of our knowledge, only one previous study has used eye-tracking in the context of information retrieval evaluation [5]. This study attempted to use eye movements to infer the relevancy of documents in the retrieval phase of an information search. The researchers linked relevancy judgments to increases in pupil diameter, as a larger diameter typically signifies high interest in the content matter. However, the sample size and search tasks in this experiment were not robust enough to generate predictable patterns of user search and scanning behavior, which is what our study is able to attain.

2. EYE-TRACKING

The research presented here seeks to obtain a more comprehensive understanding of *what* the searcher is doing and reading before actually selecting an online document. Ocular indices enable us to determine what abstracts a user is indeed viewing and reading, for how long, and in what order. Throughout the history of eye tracking research, several key variables have emerged as significant indicators of ocular behaviors, including fixations, saccades, pupil dilation, and scan paths [3]. Eye fixations are defined as a spatially stable gaze lasting for approximately 200–300 milliseconds, during which visual attention is directed to a specific area of the visual display. Fixations represent the instances in which information acquisition and processing is able to occur, and thus, fixations were the indices most relevant to this current evaluation [3]. Pupil dilation is typically used as a measure to gauge an individual's interest or arousal in the content they are viewing.

3. EXPERIMENT

Participants were undergraduate students of various majors at a large university in the Northeast USA. In total, 36 participants were recruited. Due to the inability of some subjects to be precisely calibrated, complete eye movement data was recorded for 26 of the subjects. The mean age of users was 20.3, with 19 males and 15 females. Nearly all subjects reported a high familiarity with the Google interface, with 31 users indicating that Google is their primary search engine.

Each participant was given the same ten questions to answer. Five of the questions are homepage-searches, the other five are informational searches [1]. The questions vary in difficulty and topic, covering travel, transportation, science, movies, local, politics, television, college, and trivia. Subjects were instructed to search as they normally would, and were not informed that we were specifically interested in their behavior on the results page of Google.

Data was recorded using an ASL 504 commercial eye-tracker (Applied Science Technologies, Bedford, MA) which utilizes a CCD camera that reconstructs a subject's eye position through the Pupil-Center and Corneal-Reflection method. A software application accompanying the system was used for the simultaneous acquisition of the subject's eye movements. To perform analyses, "LookZones" were constructed around each of the ten results (title, abstract, and metadata) displayed on a Google results page.

4. RESULTS AND DISCUSSION

In all, our data consists of 397 queries. In the following we analyze all behavior before a user clicks on the first link, or exits the page otherwise. Further clicks are not considered in this paper. On average, it took participants 7.78 seconds to select a document (SE = .37). However, the time varies significantly between the 10 search tasks, from 5–6 seconds up to 11 seconds for the most difficult questions.

4.1 How Does Rank Influence the Amount of Attention a Link Receives?

One of the valuable aspects of eye-tracking is that we can determine how the displayed results are actually viewed. Figure 7.6 shows the mean time users fixate on a presented abstract at that rank, as well as the number of clicks. Interestingly, the time is almost equal for links ranked 1 and 2. This is in contrast to the fact that users substantially more often click on the link ranked first. After the second link, fixation time drops off sharply. There is an interesting dip around result 6/7, both in the viewing time as well as in the number of clicks. Unlike for ranks 2 to 5, the abstracts ranked 6 to 10 receive approximately equal attention. This can be explained by the fact that typically only the first 5–6 links were visible without scrolling. Once the user has started scrolling, rank becomes less of an influence for attention. A sharp drop occurs after link 10, as ten results are displayed per page.

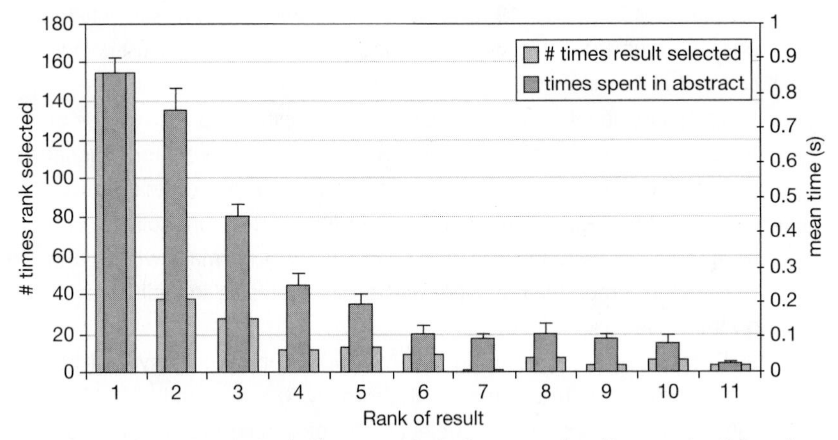

Figure 7.6 Time Spent Viewing Each Abstract with the Frequency that Abstracts Are Selected. Error Bars are 1 SE

4.2 How Do Users Explore the List?

Particularly when observed user actions serve as implicit feedback about the performance of a retrieval system, it is important to know how thoroughly users evaluate the presented results before making a selection. For instance, if a user clicks on the third-ranked result, did she look at abstracts one and two? Did the user explore any links below? Figure 7.7 depicts how many results above and below the selected document users scan on average. Again, there is an interesting effect around before the page break. First, only one individual clicked on rank seven, which often

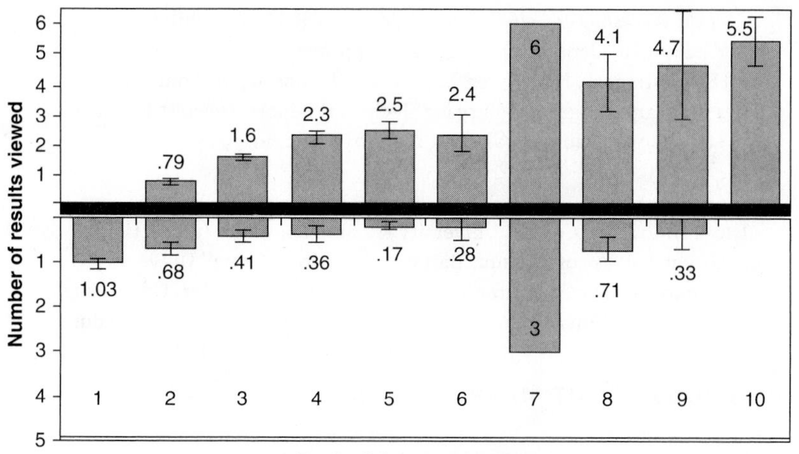

Figure 7.7 Number of Abstracts Viewed above and below the Selected Document. Error Bars are 1 SE.

fell directly below the page break. Secondly, users who selected the lower ranked documents viewed proportionately more abstracts overall. Finally, the number of links viewed below a click is low beyond rank 1, indicating that users do tend to scan the list from top to bottom.

5. FUTURE WORK

In addition to further evaluations of the eye tracking data itself (e.g. for differences between question and users, as well as additional measures like pupil dilation), we are currently gathering relevance judgments for all abstracts and documents presented to the users. This will allow us to assess user behavior in relation to the relevance of document. For example, how accurately can users judge relevance of a document given the abstract in relation to fixation times? Do users tend to click on the most relevant link among the ones they observed?

This research was supported in part under NSF CAREER Award 0237381.

6. REFERENCES

[1] Broder, A. A taxonomy of web search. *SIGIR Forum*, 36(2):3–10, 2002.
[2] Joachims, T. Optimizing search engines using clickthrough data. *Proceedings of the ACM Conference on Knowledge Discovery and Data Mining (KDD)*, ACM, 2002, pp. 132–142.
[3] Rayner, K. Eye movements in reading and information processing: 20 years of research. *Psychological Bulletin*, 124: 372–422, 1998.
[4] Salogarvi, J., Kojo, I., Jaana, S., and Kaski, S. Can relevance be inferred from eye movements in information retrieval? In *Proceedings*

of the Workshop on Self-Organizing Maps (WSOM'03), Hibikino, Kitakyushu, Japan, September 2003. pp. 261–266.
[5] Silverstein, C., Henzinger, M., Marais, J., Moricz, M. Analysis of a very large AltaVista query log. Technical Report, Hewlett Packard Laboratories, Number SRC-TN 1998–014, Oct. 19, 1998.

Laura A. Granka, Cornell University Human-Computer Interaction Group, lag24@cornell.edu; Thorsten Joachims, Cornell University Department of Computer Science, tj@cs.cornell.edu; Geri Gay, Cornell University Human-Computer Interaction Group, gkg1@cornell.edu.

QUESTIONS ABOUT MEANING

1. What kinds of questions did the researchers want to answer?
2. Describe the participants in this study. What were they asked to do? How were the results measured?
3. What Internet-searching tendencies did the researchers find among participants?

QUESTIONS FOR RHETORICAL ANALYSIS

4. How do the authors establish the value of their research?
5. What does Figure 7.7 show readers? Suggest another way the information in Figure 7.7 could have been depicted in a table or figure. Would your alternative method be easier or more difficult for readers to interpret? Explain.
6. How do the authors document (identify) sources within the text? What advantages or disadvantages does this system of documentation have when compared to other ways of identifying sources in a text?

THINKING AND WRITING ABOUT THE TOPIC

When searching for "facts" about movies and other trivia, the search ends when you find the "answer," but when researching a topic for a college paper, you don't look for "answers." Instead you hope to gain a breadth of knowledge and find credible evidence on which to base your claims. When searching for credible evidence, a general search engine is not usually your best resource.

Compare the first several results from two searches: one in a general search engine, like Google, and the other in a college library database, like JSTOR. Limit your database results to "full text" and "scholarly (or peer-reviewed) journal" articles. Select as your search term a popular "research paper" topic (like "gun control") or conduct research for a paper you're currently writing.

Create a table that identifies the authors, the article titles, and the publication titles for the first few results from each search and write an analysis that compares the results. Address questions such as these:

- What kinds of sources are among those listed on the first page of results for each search?
- What are the credentials of authors (Are they given?) and who is the intended audience for sources listed?
- How do the documents you list differ in details, writing style, focus, purpose, length, etc.?

Provide examples to illustrate when possible. If you were to limit your research to the first few hits in an Internet search, would you have credible evidence on which to build an argument about the topic?

WORKS CITED

Anshel, Jeffrey R. "Visual Ergonomics in the Workplace." *Professional Safety* 51.8 (2006): 20–5. Print.

Badalamente, Stephen. "Manuscript Attached." Message to the author. 8 June 2009. E-mail.

Fister, Barbara. "The Research Processes of Undergraduate Students." *The Journal of Academic Librarianship* 18.3 (1992): 163–69. Print.

Head, Alison J. "Beyond Google: How Do Students Conduct Academic Research?" *First Monday* 12.8 (2007). Web. 25 June 2013.

———. "Op-Ed: Old-School Job Skills You Won't Find on Google." *The Seattle Times* 11 Dec. 2012. Web. 11 Dec. 2012.

Head, Alison J., and Michael B. Eisenberg. "Assigning Inquiry: How Handouts for Research Assignments Guide Today's College Students." *Project Information Literacy Progress Report: University of Washington Information School.* 13 July 2010. 1–41. Web. 16 Nov. 2012.

———. "Lessons Learned: How College Students Seek Information in the Digital Age." *Project Information Literacy Progress Report: University of Washington Information School.* 1 Dec. 2009. 1–42. Web. 16 Nov. 2012.

Kole, James A., and Alice F. Healy. "Using Prior Knowledge to Minimize Interference When Learning Large Amounts of Information." *Memory & Cognition* 35.1 (2007): 124–37. Print.

O'Connor, Cliodhna, Geraint Rees, and Helene Joffe. "Neuroscience in the Public Sphere." *Neuron* 74 (2012): 220–26. Print.

Pariser, Eli. *The Filter Bubble: What the Internet Is Hiding from You.* New York: Penguin Press, 2011. Print.

Parr, Daniel. "Interview Questions." Message to the author. 30 May 2013. E-mail.

CHAPTER 8

Integrating Source Material into Academic Writing

Academic writers are expected to be well read in the subjects they write about and to demonstrate this by integrating what they've read into their papers. In chapter 7, you learned how to locate credible sources of information. In this chapter, you'll learn how to integrate your research material into your college papers through summarizing, paraphrasing, and quoting.

Summarizing

When writing from sources, many students choose to *paraphrase* instead of *summarize* what they've read, something English professors Rebecca Moore Howard, Tanya Rodrigue, and Tricia Serviss noticed when they analyzed 18 papers written for a sophomore-level research writing class. Rather than summarizing, the students paraphrased—or reworded—information. As a result, many students imitated their sources too closely by making only slight changes to the original sentences (182). **Summarizing**, or reducing sources to just their essence, is an important skill to develop, as you'll see in the next paragraphs.

Summary in Introductions

A common way to introduce an academic paper is by summarizing what previous researchers have learned about your topic. In Example 8.1 you'll find part of the introduction to a research article about the writing assigned in community colleges.

EXAMPLE 8.1

Research spanning thirty years (e.g., Behrens; Braine; Eblen; Harris and Hult; Zemelman; Horowitz; Leki and Carson) has documented the kinds of writing students do. In one of the largest studies, Daniel Melzer analyzed 2,100 writing
5 prompts gathered from colleges across the country. Most of the assignments (83%) called for transactional writing

Previous researchers who have studied student writing assignments are cited.

The author summarizes the findings of one researcher.

(i.e., writing intended to inform or persuade others). Poetic, creative, and expressive writing were nearly "non-existent" (W245). In another survey of assignment prompts, from courses at Miami University, Christopher Wolfe also found that transactional writing—specifically argumentation—predominates in student assignments (209). . . . These surveys focus primarily on the writing assigned at universities, but relatively little attention has been paid to the writing assigned at community colleges. This study responds to this gap in the research.

10

Another researcher's findings are summarized.

The writer identifies how her research is different from previous research.

In this introduction, brief summaries establish that others have analyzed college writing assignments, but more importantly the summaries establish that previous research has left a *gap*—one the author's paper addresses. Much more, of course, could have been said about the articles summarized, but the details included are those relevant to the author's purposes. This introduction illustrates one important feature of summary writing: *The summarizer's goals determine what parts of a text are summarized and in how much detail.*

Summary as Evidence

When you summarize source information in an introduction, your own goals will determine what details you relate. The same is true when your summary is used as evidence in a paper. Consider again the earlier description of Howard, Rodrigue, and Serviss's research:

> When writing from sources, many students choose to *paraphrase* instead of *summarize* what they've read, something English professors Rebecca Moore Howard, Tanya Rodrigue, and Tricia Serviss noticed when they analyzed 18 papers written for a sophomore-level research writing class. Rather than summarizing, the students paraphrased—or reworded—information. As a result, many students imitated their sources too closely by making only slight changes to the original sentences (182).

This paragraph summarizes only part of the researchers' seven findings. Here is the complete list of findings from their article:

> From the 18 papers we read, we derived the following answers [to the research questions, listed here]:
>
> 1. Does the paper contain one or more incidences of patchwriting?
>   » In 16 of the 18 papers (89%), the answer is "yes."
> 2. Does the paper contain one or more incidences of paraphrase?
>   » In all 18 papers (100%), the answer is "yes."

3. Does the paper contain one or more incidences of summary?
   » In all 18 papers (100%), the answer is "no."
4. Does the paper contain one or more incidences of direct copying from sources?
   » In 14 of the 18 papers (78%), the answer is "yes."
5. Does the paper contain one or more incidences in which direct copying is not marked as quotation?
   » In 13 of the 18 papers (72%), the answer is "yes."

In addition, as we read, we made two further discoveries:

6. Of the 18 papers, 17 (94%) contained non-common-knowledge information for which no source was cited.
7. Of the 18 papers, 14 (78%) attributed information to a source that either did not contain that information or said something different from what the student was attributing to it. (182)

The additional findings are arguably just as important to mention—in a different context. But only the *relevant* finding (that students underuse summary) is emphasized in the introduction to this discussion of summarizing. (You can find Howard, Rodrigue, and Serviss's entire study at the end of this chapter.)

Comprehensive Summaries

When you summarize, you usually condense only the information relevant to your purposes; but as a student, you may occasionally be asked to write a comprehensive summary to demonstrate your comprehension of an entire text. Your goal in this situation is to convey as accurately as possible *the author's intended meaning and emphasis.*

Reading a Text You Will Summarize. The close reading techniques discussed in chapter 2 can help you prepare to write a comprehensive summary. As you first read the text you will summarize, you might reduce each paragraph or section to its "gist" in the margins and circle transitional words (such as *for example* or *first, second*) that offer clues about the relationship of ideas. If the text is longer than a few paragraphs, try dividing it into sections after reading through once. Where does the introduction end and the conclusion begin? How much space is devoted to each main idea? Write down the author's central claim or purpose in your own words. Then, reread the text and record ideas that support the central claim. Read over your list of supporting ideas. Does each relate to the central claim you originally identified? If not, revise or expand the central claim so that it reflects the listed ideas.

Concept in Practice 8.1: Summarizing an Article

In the following article, "What's in a Word? Language May Shape Our Thoughts," Sharon Begley, a journalist who specializes in science topics, discusses how culture and language influence the way we perceive the world around us. The article was published online in *Newsweek*, a current events and news reporting magazine. Read and annotate the article. Then identify ideas you think should be included in a comprehensive summary. (The title offers a clue to the author's focus and stance.) Here are some questions to guide you as you read the article:

- What is the central question or point of this article?
- What is the majority view concerning this question?
- What are the author's key supporting claims?
- What examples does the author provide to support her central idea?

"WHAT'S IN A WORD? LANGUAGE MAY SHAPE OUR THOUGHTS," *Sharon Begley*

When the *Viaduct de Millau* opened in the south of France in 2004, this tallest bridge in the world won worldwide accolades. German newspapers described how it "floated above the clouds" with "elegance and lightness" and "breath-taking" beauty. In France, papers praised the "immense" "concrete giant." 5 Was it mere coincidence that the Germans saw beauty where the French saw heft and power? Lera Boroditsky thinks not.

A psychologist at Stanford University, she has long been intrigued by an age-old question whose modern form dates to 1956, when linguist Benjamin Lee Whorf asked whether the language we speak shapes the way we think and 10 see the world. If so, then language is not merely a means of expressing thought, but a constraint on it, too. Although philosophers, anthropologists, and others have weighed in, with most concluding that language does not shape thought in any significant way, the field has been notable for a distressing lack of empiricism—as in testable hypotheses and actual data.

15 That's where Boroditsky comes in. In a series of clever experiments guided by pointed questions, she is amassing evidence that, yes, language shapes thought. The effect is powerful enough, she says, that "the private mental lives of speakers of different languages may differ dramatically," not only when they are thinking in order to speak, "but in all manner of cognitive 20 tasks," including basic sensory perception. "Even a small fluke of grammar"—the gender of nouns—"can have an effect on how people think about things in the world," she says.

As in that bridge. In German, the noun for bridge, *Brücke*, is feminine. In French, *pont* is masculine. German speakers saw prototypically female features; French speakers, masculine ones. Similarly, Germans describe keys (*Schlüssel*) with words such as hard, heavy, jagged, and metal, while to Spaniards keys (*llaves*) are golden, intricate, little, and lovely. Guess which language construes key as masculine and which as feminine? Grammatical gender also shapes how we construe abstractions. In 85 percent of artistic depictions of death and victory, for instance, the idea is represented by a man if the noun is masculine and a woman if it is feminine, says Boroditsky. Germans tend to paint death as male, and Russians tend to paint it as female.

Language even shapes what we see. People have a better memory for colors if different shades have distinct names—not English's light blue and dark blue, for instance, but Russian's *goluboy* and *sinly*. Skeptics of the language-shapes-thought claim have argued that that's a trivial finding, showing only that people remember what they saw in both a visual form and a verbal one, but not proving that they actually see the hues differently. In an ingenious experiment, however, Boroditsky and colleagues showed volunteers three color swatches and asked them which of the bottom two was the same as the top one. Native Russian speakers were faster than English speakers when the colors had distinct names, suggesting that having a name for something allows you to perceive it more sharply. Similarly, Korean uses one word for "in" when one object is in another snugly (a letter in an envelope), and a different one when an object is in something loosely (an apple in a bowl). Sure enough, Korean adults are better than English speakers at distinguishing tight fit from loose fit.

In Australia, the Aboriginal Kuuk Thaayorre use compass directions for every spatial cue rather than right or left, leading to locutions such as "there is an ant on your southeast leg." The Kuuk Thaayorre are also much more skillful than English speakers at dead reckoning, even in unfamiliar surroundings or strange buildings. Their language "equips them to perform navigational feats once thought beyond human capabilities," Boroditsky wrote on Edge.org.

Science has only scratched the surface of how language affects thought. In Russian, verb forms indicate whether the action was completed or not—as in "she ate [and finished] the pizza." In Turkish, verbs indicate whether the action was observed or merely rumored. Boroditsky would love to run an experiment testing whether native Russian speakers are better than others at noticing if an action is completed, and if Turks have a heightened sensitivity to fact versus hearsay. Similarly, while English says "she broke the bowl" even if it smashed accidentally (she dropped something on it, say), Spanish and Japanese describe the same event more like "the bowl broke itself." "When we show people video of the same event," says Boroditsky, "English speakers remember who was to blame even in an accident, but Spanish and Japanese speakers remember it less well than they do intentional actions. It raises questions about whether language affects even something as basic as how we construct our ideas of causality."

Template for Standalone Summaries. The amount of detail in a comprehensive summary will vary, influenced in part by how much the audience already knows about the topic. But many comprehensive summaries more or less follow a pattern like this:

Source Identification: In [title of article or book], [author's full name] describes [identify the subject matter]
Central Claim: [Author's last name] presents/argues/believes, etc., that . . .
Supporting Claims or Evidence: He/she offers the following reasons/ examples/studies, etc., as evidence that. . . . (*Summarize supporting claims, key evidence, or types of evidence. If the author emphasized one point as most important, convey this as well.*)
Significance and/or Recap of the Central Claim

Once you've combined the author's ideas into a paragraph, look for places to condense by eliminating repetition or combining sentences.

Example 8.2 illustrates one way to summarize Begley's article. Notice how brief the summary is in comparison to the original article (121 words instead of 785).

EXAMPLE 8.2

In "What's in a Word? Language May Shape Our Thoughts," Sharon Begley describes research from Stanford University psychologist Lera Boroditsky addressing this question: Does our language influence the way we describe, see, and interpret the world around us? Begley cites numerous examples indicating the answer is "yes." In languages with gendered nouns, for example, whether a noun is masculine or feminine often influences whether people describe the object or abstraction in masculine or feminine terms. Similarly, people who speak languages with words for specific shades of color can more readily identify precise colors than people who speak languages with more general words for colors. Not everyone agrees that language shapes thought and perception, but for Begley, the premise warrants further testing.

Source title and author are identified.

Central claim or topic is identified.

The type of evidence is identified, followed by two examples.

Recap and significance of the topic are given.

A summary should allow readers to understand what another text is about *without* reading the text. Objectively convey the *author's* ideas, in any order that makes sense. You might quote an occasional phrase or sentence to convey the author's style, but a summary should consist primarily of your own words.

Paraphrasing

Unlike summaries, which significantly reduce a text or portion of a text, **paraphrases** convey all or most of the details in a sentence or short passage. For this reason, it can be challenging to write a paraphrase that does not imitate the author's sentences too closely.

Let's begin with a few guidelines for paraphrasing a passage:

- *Use your own words*. There are no synonyms for names and titles, for prepositions such as *of, in, by, for, to*, or for some nouns and phrases (e.g., *plastics* and *embryonic stem-cell research*). However, most words for which there are appropriate synonyms should be replaced. This requires consideration of the original context. Your word processor's thesaurus may identify *sincere* as a synonym for *pious*, but the words are far from equal in meaning.
- *Use your own sentence structure*. Consider this example:

  Original Sentence:
  "Although philosophers, anthropologists, and others have weighed in, with most concluding that language does not shape thought in any significant way, the field has been notable for a distressing lack of empiricism—as in testable hypotheses and actual data." (Begley)

  Paraphrase:
  While philosophers, anthropologists, and more have expressed an opinion, the majority agreeing that language doesn't influence thought to any considerable degree, the discipline has been noteworthy for a troubling dearth of experimentation—i.e., provable assumptions and concrete evidence. (Begley)

  Most of the original words are replaced with synonyms, but the paraphrase mimics the original sentence structure. When paraphrasing, convey the author's meaning in sentences with rhythm, cadence, and even punctuation placement that do not obviously imitate the original. Using two sentences to convey what the author said in one or using one sentence to say what was said in two can help you avoid imitating sentence patterns. Rearranging the details of a passage can also help. Another way to avoid imitating sentences is to paraphrase without the source in front of you. Even then, however, check to make sure you have not inadvertently copied phrasing.
- *Convey the author's meaning*. Avoid paraphrasing passages that include numerous words you don't know. Also avoid paraphrasing passages

from articles or chapters you have not read in their entirety. You risk misrepresenting the meaning when you don't understand the context.

- *Give credit to the source of information.* One way to signal the start of a paraphrase is by citing the author's name (such as with "according to . . ."). Repeat the author's last name or use a pronoun to refer to the author when you paraphrase the same source in successive sentences.

English professor Sue Shirley suggests the following approach for writing an original paraphrase. First, identify the passage's keywords—the proper nouns, distinctive phrases, and specialized terms crucial to the meaning. Then record the meaning by answering as many of the reporter's questions (*who, what, where, when, why,* and *how*) as relevant, trying to use different words but putting quotation marks around any phrasing you deem necessary to keep. Finally, put the source aside and write your paraphrase from your notes, arranging information in whatever order makes sense. Add a signal phrase (like "according to . . .") and citation identifying where the information came from and compare your paraphrase to the original (Shirley 87). By following these steps—particularly writing without the source in front of you—you can avoid plagiarism.

Paraphrasing a Passage

To illustrate paraphrasing, let's consider a passage from a research article by Danielle McNamara, Scott Crossley, and Phillip McCarthy. The authors analyzed 120 essays, written by first-year composition students and evaluated by expert graders (65). They found that the students who demonstrated a more sophisticated or complex writing style tended to receive the highest scores. Because the article is from a scholarly journal for experts in rhetoric and composition, the passage includes specialized language. To paraphrase it for a general audience, you might begin by underlining key terms in the original passage that may need to be retained in the paraphrase, as illustrated below. (Coh-Metrix, MLTD [Measure of Textual Lexical Diversity], and Celex are tools used to measure various linguistic characteristics of a text.)

> Higher scored essays were more likely to contain linguistic features associated with text difficulty and sophisticated language. The three most predictive features from Coh-Metrix of essay quality were syntactic complexity (as measured by number of words before the main verb), lexical diversity (as measured by MTLD), and word frequency (as measured by Celex, logarithm for all words). (McNamara, Crossley, and McCarthy 73)

You might next answer the relevant "reporter's questions" to help you determine what information to include in a paraphrase:

Who: Danielle McNamara, Scott Crossley, and Phillip McCarthy

What: Essays by first-year composition students that included complex sentence structures or sophisticated vocabulary tended to receive the highest grades

How: Researchers analyzed word choice and sentence structures

Finally, compose your paraphrase. Compare the following paraphrase to the original passage:

> In their analysis of college essays, Daniel McNamara, Scott Crossley, and Phillip McCarthy found that evaluators tended to give the highest scores to essays with complex sentence structures, or "syntactic complexity." The number of words preceding the main verb in sentences also seemed to influence the score (more words resulted in higher ratings than few words). Another feature in high scoring papers was "lexical diversity," meaning there was a wide spectrum of different words, including less-commonly used words (73).

The paraphrase makes the information accessible to a wider audience. Different words (with the exception of two phrases put in quotation marks) and different sentence structures make the paraphrase original. Notice that to accommodate a general audience the writer both deleted details (such as *Coh-Metrix* and *Celex*) and added details (such as an explanation of "syntactic complexity"). Your audience and purpose should influence what details you include or exclude when paraphrasing.

Understanding Plagiarism

In most writing situations, some "recycling" occurs. Writers use phrases and expressions that have been repeated so often they cannot be attributed to any one person. "On the other hand," "in other words," and even "who, what, where, when, why, and how" are only a few of many widely used stock phrases. In some contexts, documents are recycled as well. In the business world, for example, boilerplate language from one contract may be pasted into another, and in form letters only the name and date are changed. This type of "borrowing" is practical when nearly identical texts are reproduced, and it occurs with the consent of others.

But taking credit for another person's original ideas or phrasing without attribution or consent is plagiarism—considered unethical and even illegal if the writer profits financially. The Council of Writing Program Administrators (WPA) defines **plagiarism** this way: "In an instructional setting, plagiarism occurs when a writer deliberately uses someone else's language, ideas, or other original (not common-knowledge) material without acknowledging its source." A student who plagiarizes may receive a failing grade on the assignment or, in the worst-case scenario, expulsion from school.

Submitting a paper written by someone else or failing to acknowledge when another person has been quoted directly are the most common examples of plagiarism. When sentences from another writer are inserted into a paper without quotation marks, the shift in voice can be obvious. Consider the following passage. Can you identify where the author starts to quote from a source?

> [1]Greek literature wouldn't be alive today if it wasn't for the Romans. [2]Much of the Roman stories are just simply stories being retold but in a different way. [3]*The Aeneid* by Virgil is a great story that is a great example of this. [4]Although Virgil alludes to Homer's epics and self-consciously emulates them, he also attempts to surpass and revise Homer, and the differences between the two authors' epics are important markers of literary evolution.

Sentence 4 is different from the previous sentences in both sentence structure (simple to complex) and vocabulary level. Sentence 4, in fact, was taken from SPARKNOTES (an Internet source). The student who wrote the preceding passage pasted *several paragraphs* from this Internet source into her paper *without* using quotation marks and *without* acknowledging the source. As a result, she received a grade of 0.0 for the assignment, and the instructor reported the plagiarism to college administrators who took disciplinary actions.

Patchwriting

In many cases, students do not *deliberately* use an author's language or ideas inappropriately, but they do imitate a writer's language because of carelessness or difficulty with understanding a source. Instead of conveying an author's ideas in different words and sentence structures, the writer "patchwrites," by using language and sentence patterns that closely imitate the original text.

Below are illustrations of **patchwriting**, each drawn from Margaret Miller and Anne-Marie McCartan's article "At the Crossings: Making the Case for New Interdisciplinary Programs." Here is an excerpt from the article:

> Boundary crossings are occurring within the traditional disciplines themselves, not just in interdisciplinary programs. A biologist studying blood flow cannot do so without an understanding of calculus-based physics. Contemporary literary theorists need a thorough knowledge of psychoanalysis and linguistics, not to mention French. The "new historicists" rely on techniques of the historian and the theories of political philosophers to examine the social contexts in which literary works have been produced. . . . Even in business schools, economics and politics have become part of the curriculum in courses like international political economy. (30–31)

Compare the original passage to the following paraphrase. Is the paraphrase adequate?

> Margaret Miller and Anne-Marie McCartan explain that within traditional disciplines themselves, not only in interdisciplinary programs, boundary crossings are occurring. Biologists who study blood flow can't do so without understanding physics. Today's literary theorists have to have in-depth understanding of psychoanalysis and linguistics, as well as French. "New historicists" depend on methods of historians and theories of political philosophers to study the social environment where literature has been written. And understanding world politics and economics may well be necessary for today's business majors (30–31).

At first glance, the second paragraph seems different from the first, but a closer look reveals that with the exception of the final sentence, this paragraph constitutes patchwriting. Let's examine the passage more closely.

Notice that in the first two sentences, no quotation marks enclose the borrowed language:

Original Passage	**Paraphrase**
Boundary crossings are occurring within the traditional disciplines themselves, not just in interdisciplinary programs. A biologist studying blood flow cannot do so without an understanding of calculus-based physics.	According to Miller and McCartan, within traditional disciplines themselves, not only in interdisciplinary programs, boundary crossings are occurring. Biologists who study blood flow can't do so without understanding physics.

The words in the original sentences, with few exceptions, are merely rearranged on the right. A different problem appears in the next sentences:

Original Passage	**Paraphrase**
Contemporary literary theorists need a thorough knowledge of psychoanalysis and linguistics, not to mention French. The "new historicists" rely on techniques of the historian and the theories of political philosophers to examine the social contexts in which literary works have been produced.	(According to Miller and McCartan,) today's literary theorists have to have in-depth understanding of psychoanalysis and linguistics, as well as French. "New historicists" depend on the methods of historians and concepts of political philosophers to study the social environment where literature has been written.

The writer used different words, but after the signal phrase, the original sentence structures are obviously copied. Notice how closely the syntax of each line on the right resembles the corresponding line on the left.

To avoid producing "patchwritten" sentences like the preceding ones:

- Talk about what you've read with others. This helps you develop your own way of describing its meaning.
- Use the approach Professor Shirley recommends: List key words from the passage; answer *who, what, where, when, why*, and *how* about the passage; then write your paraphrase from your notes. You won't "lift" phrases from a text not in front of you.
- Don't copy and paste passages from sources into your first drafts. This may seem like a time-saving way to take "notes," but it can result in paraphrasing that is imitative in both phrasing and structure.
- Summarize rather than paraphrase whenever possible. Conveying every detail of a passage using different words and different sentence structures is more difficult than conveying just the gist or general point of a text.

Common Knowledge

Some published information need not be credited to any source, *if it is conveyed in your own words.* **Common knowledge** is information widely published or widely known either by people with a high school education or, if the writing is intended for a specialized audience, by members of that audience. Common knowledge includes uncontested facts available and essentially identical in many sources. An example of common knowledge is the fact that millions of Americans are without health insurance. Other "facts," however, are not widely known or are more contested, like the fact that over 50 *million* Americans are without health insurance. Identify your source for these kinds of "facts" that vary from source to source and year to year. Acknowledge as well sources of opinions, unsubstantiated claims, and unique ideas: a writer's analogy, for example, comparing uninsured Americans to gamblers playing the odds.

Although summary and paraphrase have been discussed here separately, in practice they routinely overlap. Many summaries include information paraphrased from the original text, for example. The distinction between summary and paraphrase is ultimately not that important as long as you *credit your sources of information, with the exception of information widely available and widely accepted, and* always *indicate when you have copied language—even when the information is common knowledge.* Writers who name their sources demonstrate that they are ethical and knowledgeable about the conventions of academic writing. It's also how students make their arguments convincing. Assuming your sources are qualified to speak on an issue, naming sources establishes that the information is reliable.

Concept in Practice 8.2: Summarizing and Paraphrasing a Passage

Select **one** of the following passages and complete the following:

1. Write a **summary** of the passage, conveying the gist of the paragraph in one sentence.
2. Write a **paraphrase** of the passage, conveying all or most of the details in a single paragraph.

Acknowledge the source in both your summary and paraphrase and try to use both different wording and different sentence structures than the original. Assume that you are writing to first-year college students.

Passage 1 is a statement of Shared Values for historians from the American Historical Association's Statement on Standards of Professional Conduct (http://www.historians.org/).

Passage 1

Historians should practice their craft with integrity. They should honor the historical record. They should document their sources. They should acknowledge their debts to the work of other scholars. They should respect and welcome divergent points of view even as they argue and subject those views to critical scrutiny. They should remember that our collective enterprise depends on mutual trust. And they should never betray that trust.

Passage 2 is from the article "The Novice as Expert: Writing the Freshman Year," by English professors Nancy Sommers and Laura Saltz. The authors tracked the progress of a sample of Harvard students over four years. In this passage, they identify one of their findings.

Passage 2

Even students who come to college as strong writers primed for success have difficulty when they refuse to be novices. These students often select courses to "get their requirements out of the way," blame their teachers for their low grades, and demonstrate an antagonistic attitude toward feedback. They feel as if there is a "secret code" to academic writing or that college itself is a kind of game whose rules—"what the teacher wants"—are kept secret to them, only glimpsed through the cryptic comments they receive on their papers. (134)

Quoting

Quoting is seemingly the easiest way to integrate information from sources into your papers. After all, you merely copy sentences from the original text and add quotation marks, right? In reality, integrating quotations into your papers takes skill and begins with decisions about what and when to quote.

Determining When to Quote

Published academic writers tend to paraphrase or summarize rather than quote information they get from others. In one study of 80 research articles, representing eight disciplines, quoting was nonexistent in the articles from biology, electronic engineering, physics, and mechanical engineering and was rarely found in articles from marketing, applied linguistics, sociology, and philosophy (Hyland 26). Paraphrasing or summarizing allows a writer to control how the source information is presented. As a student, you have additional reasons to paraphrase or summarize instead of quote sources: Professors want to evaluate *your* ability to communicate in writing, not the ability of your sources. Professors also want to see that you understand information well enough to explain it in your own way.

Despite the reasons a student has to paraphrase or summarize sources, the English professors cited earlier—Howard, Rodrigue, and Serviss—have found that some students seem to go "quote-mining" (186), looking for quotations to drop into their papers. In most academic writing, quoting should be rare—done only for good reason. Described below are situations when quoting may be justified:

- *Quote when a source's phrasing is eloquent, unique, or poetic.* Figurative language, rhythmical phrasing, or clever wording, such as Howard, Rodrigue, and Serviss's aforementioned "quote-mining," can make a point memorable. Do not, however, quote simply because you feel an author conveys a point better than you can. Most of us feel that way about published authors all of the time!
- *Quote when you want to analyze the use of language.* Quoting is necessary when you want to examine someone's writing or speaking style (such as in an analysis of a president's speech). This is why quoting is more common in disciplines such as literature and history where original research involves textual analysis.
- *Quote when paraphrasing would change the meaning.* Legal language and some scientific explanations are typical examples. However, don't quote because you're unsure of what technical language means. It's always a bad idea to quote or paraphrase what you don't understand.
- *Quote an authority for effect.* Readers are more likely to believe claims when an expert is quoted rather than paraphrased, perhaps because they know they are hearing straight from someone with firsthand knowledge. In one study, subjects read newspaper stories in which one side of the issue was conveyed by quoting interviewees and the other side was conveyed by

paraphrasing interviewees. Subjects were more influenced by whichever side was presented through quotations (Gibson and Zillmann 173–74). Quotations are far more common in newspaper articles than in academic papers, but once you've read widely enough to identify *well-known experts* on your topic, you might consider quoting one or two for impact.

Analyzing Quotations

Whatever your justification for quoting, don't rely on quotations to make your point; explain the significance of quotations for readers. When anthropology instructors in one study assessed 41 essays written for Anthropology 101, they rated essays higher if students explained their evidence rather than objectively reporting what sources say without comment (Soliday 73). Help readers see what you see in the quotation. Reformulation markers such as *in other words* and *that is* (discussed in chapter 6) are effective for introducing the interpretation of a quotation.

Capitalizing and Punctuating Quotations

Deciding when to quote is only one decision involved with quoting. You must also adhere to the proper mechanics of quotation. Consider again a sentence from Miller and McCartan's article quoted earlier:

> Boundary crossings are occurring within the traditional disciplines themselves, not just in interdisciplinary programs.

Illustrated in this section are various ways this sentence might be quoted.

Introducing Quotations. You can alter the capitalization of the *first word* of a quotation—without indicating the change. Generally, if you introduce the quotation with the expression "According to . . ." or with the name of the speaker and a verb (e.g., *Margaret Miller and Anne-Marie McCartan believe*), you should capitalize the first word of the quotation. For example:

> Margaret Miller, assistant director for academic affairs at the Council of Higher Education for Virginia, and Anne-Marie McCartan, coordinator for academic programs at the Council of Higher Education, explain, "Boundary crossings are occurring within the traditional disciplines themselves, not just in interdisciplinary programs" (30).

Notice that in this case a comma appears before the quotation.

Integrating Quotations. If you integrate a quotation seamlessly into the syntax of your sentence or if you introduce a quotation with the word "that," do *not* capitalize the first word of the quotation (unless it is a proper noun), and do *not* place a comma before the quotation:

> Miller and McCartan note that "boundary crossings are occurring within the traditional disciplines themselves, not just in interdisciplinary programs" (30).

Miller and McCartan's words fit smoothly into the sentence, so no comma precedes the quotation. Similarly, commas generally do not set off a quoted word or short phrase integrated into a sentence.

Interrupting Quotations. If you interrupt a quoted *sentence* with the speaker's name, set off the citation with commas. When you resume the quotation, don't capitalize the first word (unless it is a proper noun):

> "Boundary crossings," explain Miller and McCartan, "are occurring within the traditional disciplines themselves, not just in interdisciplinary programs" (30).

If you insert the citation at the end of a sentence within a quoted *passage*, however, place a period after the citation:

> "Boundary crossings are occurring within the traditional disciplines themselves, not just in interdisciplinary programs," explain Miller and McCartan. "A biologist studying blood flow cannot do so without an understanding of calculus-based physics" (30).

Capitalize the first word of the new sentence.

Introducing a Quotation with a Colon. If a complete sentence introduces a quotation, a colon can precede the quotation:

> Miller and McCartan note that collaboration between researchers in different disciplines is widespread: "Boundary crossings are occurring within the traditional disciplines themselves, not just in interdisciplinary programs" (30).

The first word of a quotation introduced with a colon is usually capitalized.

Following a Quotation with a Comma or Period. U.S. writers put commas and periods *inside* closing quotation marks. (In some countries they go outside the quotation marks.) However, when providing a parenthetical citation at the end of a sentence, close the quotation, provide the citation, and then add the period as illustrated in the preceding excerpt.

Following a Quotation with Other Types of Punctuation. Semicolons, colons, and dashes go outside of a closing quotation mark. But placement of question marks and exclamation points depends on the context. If the *quotation* is a question, the question mark goes *inside* the closing quotation mark:

> Miller and McCartan address this question about traditionally separate disciplines: "If the most advanced research in these fields is occurring at

> the crossings between them, why is it necessary to have interdisciplinary programs?" (31).

But if the sentence in which the quotation appears is the question—not the quotation itself—place the question mark outside the final quotation mark:

> Just how common are interdisciplinary "boundary crossings"?

The same rule applies for exclamation points: place them inside the quotation mark if the quotation is an exclamation and outside if the sentence you write is the exclamation.

Identifying Speakers

There is variation in how authors quoted in academic papers are named. When following citation guidelines recommended by the Modern Language Association (MLA), illustrated throughout this chapter, it's common to introduce a quotation by providing the speaker's first and last name (without titles, such as *Dr.* or *Professor*). Depending on the intended audience, you may also want to identify how the speaker is qualified to speak on the topic. In subsequent references refer to that speaker by his or her last name only. In papers documented in some other citation styles, it is more common to provide the speaker's last name in parentheses after the quotation.

Copying Quotations

You can change the capitalization of the first word of a quotation and alter or delete the end punctuation, but you must otherwise copy words, punctuation, and capitalization *exactly*. Do not delete, add, alter, or rearrange words or punctuation within a quotation without indicating the change.

Adding Emphasis to a Quotation. If you italicize or underline a speaker's word or phrase, signify the change in parentheses after the quotation:

> Miller and McCartan ask, "If the most advanced research in these fields is occurring at the crossings between them, why is it necessary to have interdisciplinary *programs*?" (31, emphasis added).

Conversely, if Miller and McCartan had italicized the word *programs*, indicate this with the words "original emphasis" in parentheses—to leave no doubt about the original sentence.

Omitting Words from a Quotation. If you want to delete words from within a quotation, and you can do so without misrepresenting the meaning, indicate the omission with an ellipsis (three spaced dots). Add a space before and after the first and last dots:

Original Sentence: Historians are using skills learned from literary scholars to interpret materials such as diaries, from statisticians to organize the data by which cliometric hypotheses are tested, from psychology to study issues like the history of human consciousness, and from anthropology and sociology as their attention turns from political to social history.
Quotation with Words Omitted: According to Miller and McCartan, "Historians are using skills learned from literary scholars to interpret materials such as diaries, . . . from psychology to study issues like the history of human consciousness, and from anthropology and sociology as their attention turns from political to social history" (31).

If you omit words at the end of a sentence, use four dots, one being the period ending your sentence.

Original Sentence: Contemporary literary theorists need a thorough knowledge of psychoanalysis and linguistics, not to mention French.
Quotation with Ending Omitted: Miller and McCartan note that "contemporary literary theorists need a thorough knowledge of psychoanalysis and linguistics. . . ."

In this situation the first dot appears immediately *after* the final word. Notice that the comma after "linguistics" in the original sentence is dropped along with the words that followed. If you omit words from a quotation, what remains must still be grammatically correct. If you add a parenthetical citation, place the final period after the parentheses:

Miller and McCartan note, "Contemporary literary theorists need a thorough knowledge of psychoanalysis and linguistics. . ." (31).

Use ellipses to show that you've omitted words from *the end of a sentence*, but don't use ellipses to indicate additional sentences follow the one you are quoting. An ellipsis is optional when you begin quoting mid-sentence.

Inserting Words into Quotations. A sentence quoted out of its original context may need to be clarified. In the following sentence, the reference to "these fields" would be unclear to anyone who hasn't read Miller and McCartan's article. To make the quotation clear, insert words in brackets immediately after the word(s) being clarified:

Miller and McCartan ask, "If the most advanced research in these fields [biology, literature, history, and business] is occurring at the crossings between them, why is it necessary to have interdisciplinary programs?" (31).

Newspaper writers use parentheses to insert words into quotations, but you should use square brackets in your college papers.

Words inserted into a quotation must "fit" into the syntax. In the next example, the possessive form of the word should appear in brackets.

> **Incorrect**: According to Smith, "Critics widely regard his [James Joyce] novels as some of the most influential—and the most difficult—of the twentieth century."
> **Correct**: According to Smith, "Critics widely regard his [James Joyce's] novels as some of the most influential—and the most difficult—of the twentieth century."

If you can easily explain a quotation without inserting words, do so to avoid altering the original sentence. Both brackets and ellipses should be used sparingly.

Identifying an Error in a Quotation. If a sentence you want to quote includes a punctuation or spelling error, copy the sentence *with* the error, and place the word "sic" (Latin for "thus") in brackets immediately after the error:

> William Stern points out that "both rising medical costs and increasing insurance fraud has [sic] contributed to skyrocketing insurance rates."

Placing *[sic]* (without italics) after the subject-verb agreement error indicates the error is in the original sentence. Of course another option, preferable given the unremarkable nature of this quotation, is to paraphrase the information.

Concept in Practice 8.3: Quoting Sentences and Phrases

Passage 3 is from a Technical Note titled "Organization in Technical Writing," written by David Rhodes and published in the *Journal of Professional Issues in Engineering Education and Practice*. In the passage, Rhodes, an engineering professor, talks about including section headings when writing technical documents. (In the passage's final paragraph, Rhodes cites a source written by Graves and Hoffman.)

Write three sentences, each including language quoted from Passage 3. Specifically:

1. Quote *a portion* of one sentence, using an ellipsis to indicate where words from the original sentence are omitted.

2. Integrate *a phrase* taken from a different sentence in the passage into a sentence of your own.
3. Quote *any sentence* in the passage (the entire sentence) and interrupt the quotation with the speaker's name.

In all three cases, name the speaker (Rhodes) within your sentence and provide the page citation (216) at the end of the sentence. Try to select language that is in some way "quote-worthy." (If you prefer, you can instead complete this exercise using Passage 1 or 2, found in *Concept in Practice* 8.2.)

> **Passage 3**
>
> In the sense that it is representative, structure can be thought of as a distillation of the text in which the essence is preserved. It should fit naturally; it should not be a strait jacket. The structural headings thus developed will therefore be thematic, as, for example, in the present Technical Note.
>
> However, that is not to preclude the standard forms or templates sometimes used, for example, in reporting experiments: Introduction, Theory, Experimental Procedure, Results, Discussion, Conclusion. Where a template faithfully represents the intended message, it is a great help in speeding up the writing process, and many organizations adopt this prescriptive approach for efficiency and consistency in style (Graves and Hoffman 1965). But for the report that is different, using the in-house template may produce a contrived effect and impair communication.
>
> (Rhodes 216)

Using Block Quotations

Most quotations are integrated into paragraphs and enclosed in quotation marks. But sometimes a quotation is indented and set off from the rest of a paragraph. When you want to *analyze the language* of a passage, you might choose to set off the quotation. Doing so can make your discussion easier to follow. Notice how the quotations in the previous sections are set off to help you study the examples. Long **(block) quotations** are also indented, so that readers can readily see where the quotation ends. If you are documenting in MLA style, quotations more than four lines of type should be indented one inch (10 spaces) from the left margin. If documenting in APA style, passages more than 40 words in length are indented five to seven spaces. In either case, the sentence or clause introducing the quotation typically ends with a colon, as seen in the following example (documented in MLA style):

> Miller and McCartan discuss the need for scholars to understand concepts from other disciplines:
>
>> A biologist studying blood flow cannot do so without an understanding of calculus-based physics. Contemporary literary theorists need

> a thorough knowledge of psychoanalysis and linguistics, not to mention French. The "new historicists" rely on techniques of the historian and the theories of political philosophers to examine the social contexts in which literary works have been produced. (30–31)

It seems that nowadays every researcher must be somewhat "interdisciplinary."

Note four things about this block quotation:

1. A block quotation is *not* enclosed in quotation marks.
2. The phrase "new historicists," which Miller and McCartan enclosed in quotation marks, appears in double quotation marks, not single quotation marks. Single quotation marks always appear *inside* of double quotation marks.
3. The parenthetical citation at the end of a block quotation is placed *after* the final period. The period, in this case, signals the end of the quotation.
4. Analysis or commentary follows the quotation.

Block quotations are rare in academic writing. Unless you are analyzing the way an author writes, avoid quoting lengthy passages.

Identifying Sources through Formal Documentation

We've seen that academic writers—whether summarizing, paraphrasing, or quoting—name their sources. **Documentation** refers to the way writers identify the information they obtained from research sources.

Similarities and Differences in Documentation Styles

Documentation serves several purposes: (1) to identify what information in a paper came from sources; (2) to provide information readers need to assess the quality of sources; and (3) to allow readers (through a final bibliography) to locate those sources and examine information in its original context.

You need not document easily verified statements of fact, but most information obtained from others should be documented, including:

- direct quotations
- summaries or paraphrases of someone's opinion, research, or original insights
- statistics and amounts, such as population or spending estimates, that vary from year to year
- tables, figures, and illustrations

Although the *reasons* for documentation are consistent across the disciplines, documentation *styles* vary. In fact, there are dozens of different styles. But that wasn't always the case.

Footnotes were once used in all disciplines, and some disciplines, including history and philosophy, continue to use the *Chicago Manual of Style* (CMS). Documenting in CMS involves inserting superscript numbers throughout the text to refer readers to source information, which is provided in numbered notes at the bottom of each page or in a list at the end of the text.

Early in the twentieth century, writers in most science disciplines began to provide source names and publication years within paragraphs of the main text. Before word processors, footnotes were a nuisance to type, and they forced readers to shift their attention from the main text to the note and back again. Providing publication dates in the text made it easier for readers to determine the date of the research being cited—an important consideration in the sciences.

Today, name/year citation styles, such as the American Psychological Association (APA) format, are the most common form of documentation in academic writing. APA format, especially common in social science disciplines, is illustrated in the following sentence:

> Smith (2007) predicted that the species will soon be extinct.

In this sentence, the author cites a text written by Smith and published in 2007.

Some disciplines refer to sources by number. Biologists, botanists, and other natural scientists who use *CSE format*, recommended by the Council of Science Editors, *either* provide author names and dates in the text, similar to **APA style**, *or* provide superscript numbers throughout the paper that correspond to a numbered reference list. Similarly, some disciplines refer to authors by numbers appearing in brackets or parentheses, as illustrated in the following passage from mathematics:

> Wavelets have become an important tool in applied mathematics over the past 15 years. As an alternative to Fourier analysis, they allow researchers to study images and other signals at different resolutions. One introductory text on wavelets is [3].
>
> (Lytle and Yang 3)

Readers locate source #3 in the bibliography to determine what text is cited in this passage.

Some humanities disciplines eventually abandoned footnotes as well. Noting that "prose is more pleasant to read if it does not require one to jump constantly to the foot of the page or to the back of the book," the Modern Language Association (MLA) published its own documentation guidelines in 1982 for disciplines studying literature and languages (qtd. in Connors 233). These guidelines require that specific page references for source information appear in parentheses in the text *instead* of publication dates. Research in literature and language disciplines usually involves textual analysis, and page citations allow readers to easily find information in its original context. Providing both publication date and page numbers in parentheses, however, would be unnecessarily confusing for readers (Connors 239). MLA documentation is widely taught in literature and composition courses, and it is the documentation style used in this book.

Disciplines also vary in the degree to which they emphasize the authors who are cited in papers. In his study of academic writing in eight disciplines, English professor Ken Hyland found that writers in philosophy, sociology, marketing, and applied linguistics tend to emphasize sources by making them the subject of sentences (25). In these and other humanities and social science disciplines, quotations, expert opinions, predictions, and theories frequently appear as evidence. To add weight to this evidence, writers might explain how the authors they cite are qualified to speak on the subject. In an essay written in the humanities and documented in **MLA style**, for example, you might see a paraphrase introduced like this:

> Pamela Smith, a professor of cell biology, predicts that the species will soon be extinct (42).

In this sentence, Smith is the sentence subject and her credentials are provided.

Conversely, writers in many science and engineering disciplines emphasize the research more than the researchers they cite. They frequently provide only an author's last name or use numbers to identify sources listed in a final bibliography. This prevents readers from making assumptions about the work based on the author's gender and may also indicate that the writer assumes readers are familiar with the person being cited. Thus, the previous MLA-documented sentence might appear like this in a science paper:

> Smith (2007) predicted that the species will soon be extinct.

Or:

> The species will soon be extinct (Smith, 2007).

Or:

> The species will soon be extinct.[6]

In the second and third sentences, especially, the research is emphasized more than the person who did the research.

Quoting in Different Documentation Styles

You learned earlier how to introduce a quotation with a signal phrase, how to integrate a quotation into your own sentence structure, how to interrupt a quotation with a citation, and how to introduce a quotation with a complete sentence. These sentence patterns are found throughout academic writing, but, as you have seen, documentation styles vary. Some of those differences are illustrated in the following grid. Notice that most documentation styles require a page citation to be provided for quotations. (My own citations appear in the bottom right, in smaller type.)

Quotation Introduced with a Signal Phrase	**Example from Sociology:** As Massey (1995) points out, "In all likelihood, therefore, the United States has already become a country of perpetual immigration, one characterized by the continuous arrival of large cohorts of immigrants from particular regions" (p. 664). (Waters and Jiménez 119)
Integrated Quotation	**Example from Composition/Rhetoric:** In an early article about student control, Elaine Lees identifies the teacher's goal as "leading students to revise for themselves" (373). (Miller, Bausser, and Fentiman 444)
Integrated Quotation Preceded with *that*	**Example from Business:** In a review of the influence of sensory expectation on sensory perception, Deliza and MacFie (1996) concluded that "it is an immensely complex topic which has had very little research attention" (p. 122). (Lee, Frederick, and Ariely 1058)
Interrupted Quotation	**Example from Political Science:** "From reading our literature," notes Perloff (2002, 621), "you would assume that the only campaigns in America are for the presidency." (Druckman, Kifer, and Parkin 343)
Quotation Introduced with a Colon	**Example from History:** The new academies made possible what French author and philosopher Bernard le Bovier de Fontenelle described as the crowning achievement of a long process leading to the founding of the Academy of Sciences: "We have left behind sterile physics, which hasn't developed in centuries. The reign of words and terms has come to an end. We want things."[2] (Rabinovitch 33)

How quotations are documented may vary, but the value placed on accurately reporting the words and ideas of others is shared by writers in every discipline.

Similarities and Differences in Bibliography Styles

A list of the sources cited in a paper (generically referred to as a **bibliography**) appears at the end of any documented paper. Bibliographies provide the following information for print sources:

Author's name (if identified on the source)
Title of the work
Publishing details (such as page numbers for articles and publishers for books)
Publication date

But, depending on the documentation style, bibliographies vary in how information is listed. Even bibliography titles differ. When documenting in MLA style, for instance, you title the bibliography **Works Cited**, and when documenting in APA style, you title the bibliography **References**.

Despite differences in form, bibliographies serve the same purposes across disciplines: to acknowledge the writer's sources of information, to allow readers to locate and read those sources themselves, and to establish the writer as an ethical member of the academic community.

Concept in Practice 8.4: Recognizing Differences in Bibliography Formats

Illustrated in this *Concept in Practice* are three bibliography styles. Some of the differences between the entries are noted for you. What other differences do you notice? Can you suggest possible reasons for the differences?

APA STYLE

Fiske, S. T. (1993). Controlling other people: The impact of power on stereotyping. *American Psychologist, 48*(6), 1070–1076. doi:10.1037//0003-066X.48.6.621

CSE STYLE

28. Henrich J, Boyd R (2001) Why people punish defectors: Weak conformist transmission can stabilize costly enforcement of norms in cooperative dilemmas. J Theor Biol 208(1): 79–89.

Initials appear instead of first names, preventing assumptions about author gender.

A Document Object Identifier (doi) is like a serial number for the article.

Documentation styles in the sciences capitalize only proper nouns and first words of article titles, a convention since the nineteenth century.

In CSE style, journal titles are abbreviated, indicating a specialized audience.

MLA STYLE

McNamara, Danielle S., Scott A. Crossley, and Philip M. McCarthy. "Linguistic Features of Writing Quality." *Written Communication* 27.1 (2010): 57–86.

Applying the Concepts to Reading: *Combining Summary, Paraphrase, and Quotation with Analysis*

When you write source-based papers, you don't just report what sources say; you'll also analyze or interpret what they say. Here, for example, is an exam question from a world literature course that calls for quoting and analysis:

> *Discuss the tone of Walt Whitman's poem "When I Heard the Learn'd Astronomer" (provided below). Where does the tone shift? Cite examples of how the diction (including connotations and sound of words) creates this tone.*

When I Heard the Learn'd Astronomer, *by Walt Whitman*
When I heard the learn'd astronomer,
When the proofs, the figures, were ranged in columns before me,
When I was shown the charts and diagrams, to add, divide, and measure them,
When I sitting heard the astronomer where he lectured with much applause in the lecture-room,
How soon unaccountable I became tired and sick,
Till rising and gliding out I wander'd off by myself,
In the mystical moist night-air, and from time to time,
Look'd up in perfect silence at the stars.

In the following response to the exam question, Ashley Fritch combines textual evidence and analysis. Underline and identify examples of quotation and analysis in the passage. Two sentences are annotated as examples.

ANALYSIS OF "WHEN I HEARD THE LEARN'D ASTRONOMER"

The tone of the poem shifts in line 5. It moves from concise, factual words describing the lecture into more soft and romantic language. In the first part of the poem, the use of words like "ranged in columns" show how ordered the lecture was. Had Whitman said the figures were "presented" (5) or "displayed," it would have had less impact. Also the word "lecture" appears in line 4. I associate the term "lecture" with being spoken down to or being in trouble, like when a

Words such as "concise, factual" and "soft and romantic" identify the author's evaluation.

Words from the poem are used as evidence.

parent lectures a child. The use of "lecture" here suggests the speaker was not
10 enjoying the speech. The word "unaccountable" (line 5) signals a shift in the poem, moving from words of reason to words of feeling. If the words "suddenly" or "without reason" had been used, we would still know that the speaker had left the lecture hall, but it would not have signaled the shift in tone as strongly. I associate the word "unaccountable" with something being untamable or unpre-
15 dictable. The alliteration in "mystical moist" and "time to time" rolls off the tongue, unlike the sharp staccato type words in the first half of the poem. The use of the word "rising" in this case invokes the idea of mist, especially when combined with the words "gliding" and "mystical." They come together to give
20 a sense of enchantment to the scene described in the last few lines of the poem.

Because Fritch was discussing how language creates a poem's tone, she needed to quote specific words. In many assignments, however, you will support your claims with paraphrased or summarized source information.

Applying the Concepts to Writing: *Summarizing an Article*

Read and annotate the research report found at the end of chapter 7: "Eye-Tracking Analysis of User Behavior in WWW Search." Then summarize the article in one paragraph of no more than 250 words. Assume your audience is first-year college students. Select one or two phrases or short sentences to quote from the article in your paragraph, but otherwise use your own words and sentence structures. Introduce the quotations with signal phrases and provide page numbers. Follow either MLA or APA guidelines for providing page citations for the quotations.

Paired Readings from Rhetoric and Composition

"Sandra Jamieson and Rebecca Moore Howard: Unraveling the Citation Trail," Project Information Literacy, "Smart Talks"

Sandra Jamieson and Rebecca Moore Howard are rhetoric and composition professors and directors of The Citation Project, a national, ongoing study designed to learn how students use sources in their college papers. In the following selection, they respond to questions posed by Alison Head. As you may recall, Head is the director of Project Information Literacy (PIL), another ongoing research project, this one designed to learn how college students conduct research. Given their interest in how students find sources, it's only natural that researchers for PIL are interested in what The Citation Project has revealed about how students use sources once they find them. This e-mail–based interview with Jamieson and Howard, conducted in 2011, was part of a series of PIL interviews called Smart Talks.

Look up the word *plagiarism* in a reliable source and you may find it defined as "the act of taking the writings of another person and passing them off as one's own. The fraudulence is closely related to forgery and piracy—practices generally in violation of copyright laws."[1]

Two English professors, Sandra Jamieson at Drew University and Rebecca Moore Howard at Syracuse University[,] argue that definitions like this one may fall short, especially when they are applied in the academy in the digital age.

Moreover, they suggest that such narrow views of plagiarism impede ways in which writing is taught to students and how students come to use sources in papers.

With a team of 21 other writing instructor-researchers, Jamieson and Howard lead The Citation Project. The project is a national study that collects and distributes empirical data about how college students use sources when writing research papers for composition courses.

We interviewed Sandra and Becky in the summer of 2011 as they prepared for another academic year. We discussed their innovative research study, what they had learned about how students integrate sources into their papers, and what their findings tell us about today's students and how they use information.

PIL: We are intrigued that although you are both professors of writing and rhetoric, you are also conducting what you call an *empirical inquiry*. How did The Citation Project come about? What are its origins? What influenced your decision to conduct a study like this? Is plagiarism on the rise? What do you hope to accomplish with your research?

Sandra & Becky: We are both pretty amazed by this fact, too! Nothing in our graduate education prepared us for this kind of research; in fact, in our field it is not uncommon for this sort of research to be considered of less value than "theory." But we felt that we needed to go beyond our training so that we could make arguments that would be evidenced in ways that people outside our field could respect. We were significantly influenced by arguments that Chris Anson made in a plenary address to the Council of Writing Program Administrators in 2006: he pointed out that anecdotally evidenced claims tend to be accepted only by those who share common beliefs and assumptions. So when a compositionist makes a claim that she evidences in her own classroom experiences, other compositionists may readily agree, because they share similar experiences. Outside composition and rhetoric, though, the audience to such claims may react skeptically or indifferently.

Motivating our research was our concern about how much the academic discourse about students' writing was focused on whether students were plagiarizing, and we were also concerned by the lack of useful data about how students use and engage with sources. There was a public concern, a lot of anecdotal claims that plagiarism was on the rise, and a rush to find ways to catch "cheaters," but the information about what is actually going on when students write source-based papers was pretty slim. We felt—based on our classroom experience!—that what underlay much of what was being interpreted as plagiarism was not based in students' ethical choices, but rather in their practices and skills in source-based writing. Having given careful consideration to Anson's argument, though, we wanted to test our beliefs, in such a way that we could be certain of them, and so that others could respect them, as well. Therein was born the Citation Project, which endeavors to describe what students at a variety of institutions are actually doing in their source-based writing. To prepare for our research Sandra took an undergraduate statistics course, and throughout the development of the project she has worked closely with Sara Abramowitz, a statistician at Drew University.

The Citation Project began with a localized study that asked a simple question: "How often do students use summary, paraphrase, and patchwriting in their researched writing?" The results of that preliminary study, by Rebecca Moore Howard, Tanya K. Rodrigue, and Tricia C. Serviss, are described in "Writing from Sources, Writing from Sentences" (*Writing and Pedagogy* 2.2. Fall 2010. 177–192). This preliminary study piloted the methods used in our subsequent larger study, and it raised questions that the Citation Project has endeavored to answer.

When we developed the Citation Project, we decided to create a larger, multi-school study. One cannot make meaningful generalizations about writing or writing instruction based on statistical data from only one institution, and most institutional studies are more informative when placed in the context of data from other institutions. Analyzing 1,911 citations from 174 student papers produced at 16 different colleges provides a broadly based sample of the kinds of writing of all college students and constitutes a mathematically representative sample. As you'll see when you look at our Website, we carefully chose our 16 colleges from the entire geography of the country, and we selected a wide variety of types of institutions.

PIL: To date, the project's research team has employed a systematic content analysis and has studied papers of 160 college students enrolled at 16 U.S. colleges and universities. In many cases, you have found students use sources to *patchwrite*. What do you mean by *patchwriting*? What's the Web's role in it? Do you have any idea of why some students may be patchwriting more than others? Is patchwriting a form of plagiarism?

Sandra & Becky: Actually, we have now studied 174 student papers. Some of the samples were shorter than others, so in order to study the same number of pages from each campus we had to include a few more papers from some. As we said above, it is very important to us that our data be as incontrovertible as possible because it is leading us to some pretty extreme realizations about student writing and writing instruction.

As for patchwriting: we use the following generalized definition for the purposes of teaching and policy-making: "patchwriting is restating a phrase, clause, or one or more sentences while staying close to the language or syntax of the source." We have come to think of patchwriting as an unsuccessful attempt at paraphrase. In the papers we have analyzed, students often toggle back and forth between paraphrase and patchwriting, as they try to answer the question, "How else can I say this?"

We also have a technical definition that the researchers used when they coded the 174 papers; it's embedded in our coding procedures:

"Highlight in yellow all words in the cited area that restate the ideas or information in a passage using **more than 20%** of the source. (This 20% does not include accurate synonyms, articles, prepositions, proper names or technical terms; words whose morphology is changed are considered to be source language and counted within the 20%.)

"If you code the majority of the material in the cited area as patchwritten, check this box on the coding sheet."

We would urge that this definition not be used for anything but research purposes! While it was necessary for us to come up with a quantified rather than impressionistic way for coders to differentiate patchwriting and paraphrase, that quantification is inescapably arbitrary. Patchwriting, paraphrase, and the differences between them are necessarily contextualized by the rhetorical situation, including the task, writer, reader, and occasion. This first stage of the Citation Project is purely textual, analyzing words on a page. The interpretation of these words, however—including decisions about whether they are appropriate, inadequate, or transgressive—must always take place within the rhetorical context. This is why we used human coders for the papers rather than computer programs, as some suggested we should. Such a decision would have saved us literally years of research time, but it would have removed the interpretive process that is at the heart of engaging with sources, and we would have missed most of the nuances that we believe make our work useful.

You ask whether patchwriting is a form of plagiarism. It could be: a writer could deliberately patchwrite rather than go to the trouble of paraphrasing successfully. In our own experiences as writers, teachers, and adjudicators of plagiarism cases, however, we believe it seldom is. Patchwriting occurs whenever a writer struggles with a source text, and many first-year college students don't even know that it isn't "paraphrase." Patchwriting is underdeveloped writing, not transgressive writing.

PIL: As you have suggested in your latest paper, "writing from sources is a staple of academic inquiry." What else have your preliminary results told you about how college students use sources? Where do they struggle the most with applying and integrating information sources into the papers they are writing? In a larger sense, what does this tell us about today's students, their writing styles, and their information literacy competencies?

Sandra & Becky: Our recently completed data confirm much of what the pilot study found, but we are not yet able to address the question of whether what we have found indicates that today's students are any different from previous students. One fascinating study currently planned is to code researched papers written before the Internet became a cultural staple. We would not be surprised to find significant patchwriting from these sources, but we are looking forward to being able to publish some comparative data on this subject. If anyone out there has access to student researched papers written before 1994 that we might include, please let us know! Our contact information is on our Website.

But to answer your question. What do our data tell us about how students use sources? We need to make a distinction here. In short papers and in researched papers for discipline-specific and even writing intensive classes, students may use sources very differently than they do in first-year composition classes. Analysis of papers written for these different contexts is also planned for our subsequent research. All we are qualified to comment upon right now is how students use sources in researched writing for first-year composition courses. And the news is not good. We found that 42% of the citations are direct quotations, 16% are patchwritten, 32% are paraphrased, and 6% are summarized. A further 4% of the cited material was directly copied with no quotation marks or other indication that this was not the student's own words. At first glance the relatively low percentages for patchwriting and unmarked but cited copying (misused sources) may seem encouraging, but those concerned with plagiarism need to remember that we did not code unattributed copying. We don't know whether there was any because we did not analyze material that was not cited; but conversely, we cannot say that there was not any, either.

So, most of the citations were for material that was either quoted or paraphrased. If your focus is on procedure and correct format, these papers are a great success. But if you look at this another way and remember that for most of us, "research" is about the discovery of new information and ideas, and the synthesis of those ideas into deeper understanding, the majority of the papers failed. Only 6% of the citations are to summarized material. It is in summary that writers demonstrate comprehension of the larger arguments of a text, working from ideas rather than sentences. And in the papers we studied, students are not doing that. Further, 46% of the citations are from the first page of the source in question. Yes, that really is 46%, and a full 70% come from somewhere in the first two pages (1,328 citations from a total of 1,911 that we coded). The majority of the sources are cited only once, and only a handful of the papers cite any source in a way that suggests the student was engaging with the entire text.

On the subject of information literacy there is also mixed news. Our study found that 24.4% of the citations are to journal articles, most of which would qualify as academic. A further 17.9% are to books, although this category includes fiction, anthologies (including poetry and plays), and collections of short articles such as the *Opposing Viewpoints* series. But on the other extreme, 24.5% come from web-based sources, and 26% come from sources that are two pages or less in length (44% of the citations are to sources that are no longer than four pages). What this suggests more than anything else is that students may not know how to distinguish between what instructors would consider "reliable sources" and totally inappropriate sources for college-level (or even high school) papers. The Citation Project needs to conduct follow-up research to help us determine whether the students are actually aware that some sources are less appropriate than others; until then, we can only speculate about what this reveals about their information literacy awareness. This stage of our research focuses exclusively on what students wrote in their papers, not why they did it or what they knew.

PIL: In 2010, PIL conducted a content analysis of 191 research assignment handouts that instructors distributed to students on 28 U.S. college campuses. Overall, we found handouts provided more how-to procedures and conventions for preparing a final product for submission, and not as much guidance about conducting research and finding and using information sources. Further, few handouts provided details about preventing plagiarism. And if they did, the handouts tended to emphasize the disciplinary recourse that instructors would take against students who were caught in acts of academic dishonesty. Why is the topic of plagiarism so frequently couched in the punishment that will be meted out for violators? What are the consequences of admonishing instead of educating students about plagiarism?

Sandra & Becky: Yours is fascinating research, and it seems to reflect what we have found from analyzing the papers in our sample and from reading the results of various local surveys people have conducted at Citation Project participating campuses. As you indicate, it reveals an emphasis on crime and punishment when, we believe, we should be focusing on engagement with source material and the research process as a generative, meaning-making activity. That is, instructors' focus on the ethics of source use and the fear of plagiarism has obscured the reason that researched writing is assigned in the first place. By focusing on procedures and conventions, instructors render researched writing as stultifying as the five-paragraph theme, and by indicating a concern with form more than content, this pedagogy reduces the process to a mindless exercise. Citation Project researchers were frequently struck by this as we analyzed the sources students selected for their papers. For example, when every paper in a school's sample included a citation to a book, we could deduce that the curriculum required students to refer to a book. The cited material from books does not, however, always seem to inform the paper—although thankfully there are some exceptions to this norm. We are concerned at our finding that the cited material is most often quoted, and most often drawn from the first few pages of the book or a related chapter of that book. In the latter case, we can assume that students are using the index to find relevant information, but the former suggests that students are just reading the first few pages of the introduction and gleaning workable quotations from the material there. In neither case do students seem to be using the book as a resource from which they might learn about the topic at hand, which is what we assume the instructors intended. Similarly, a vast majority of the papers cite each source only once, and only in one paragraph. A lot of attention does seem to have been focused on the bibliographic entries, though; these are usually close to MLA citation. This, too, suggests an emphasis on procedure rather than content.

As we said above, we only studied the way students handled cited sources. If the source was not cited, we did not code it. So we very intentionally are not analyzing plagiarism. Yet when we talk about our research, the first thing many people ask is about plagiarism, and that is also the focus of most of the current scholarship about students' source-based writing. We do concur that academic integrity is an important issue, but it is not the focus of the Citation Project, for a very important reason: If students are not engaging with the research process and are not carefully reading the sources they cite, plagiarism—in one form or another—is likely to occur, because the students lack the source-handling skills and practices that are necessary for responsible, ethical writing. We believe that when students are engaging with their researched sources, they will have a significantly reduced motivation to deliberately plagiarize. When the subtitle of our Website says, "preventing plagiarism, teaching writing," we are asserting a causal relationship. We would make that relationship explicit by saying, "to prevent plagiarism, teach writing in a way that engages students with research, research sources, and research writing."

In this first stage, the Citation Project has studied the textual evidence of what students are doing with their sources. Preventing plagiarism is a desired outcome of our research, but as an indirect result of students' knowing how to work with sources. If instructors know what their students are doing—and that is what our research accomplishes—then they know what the basic instructional tasks are. Correct citation is what one teaches when one is focused on plagiarism prevention. Engaged reading of sources and thoughtful writing about them is what one teaches when one realizes that students may be citing correctly while merely parroting sentences from the first few pages of a source, and nothing more. If all they're producing is a hollow simulacrum of research, should we be surprised if they sometimes choose to plagiarize?

To answer another part of your question: we know of no reliable way to track whether acts of plagiarism have increased, or whether the Internet has simply made it easier for us to discover (and prove) plagiarism. We do know, however, that instructors and campus policies should remove patchwriting from the category of plagiarism. Treat it as bad writing, partial reading, or unsuccessful paraphrase, but not as academic dishonesty.

Some campus policies still categorize patchwriting as a form of plagiarism, even when the source is cited. So this issue of definitions is crucial. In 2003, the Council of Writing Program Administrators produced a best practices document "Defining and Avoiding Plagiarism: The WPA Statement on Best Practices" in which the authors make a distinction between plagiarism and misuse of sources that we find very helpful, and we urge readers to consult that document.

PIL: Lastly, what are three things that instructors can do to integrate plagiarism prevention into their curriculum in more far-reaching ways? Do you have any examples of how best to teach plagiarism prevention in the digital age? What can librarians do to teach students how to avoid plagiarism, especially inadvertent plagiarism?

Sandra & Becky: First, instructors should teach students how to read complex sources critically. In the 174 papers in our sample, there is very scanty evidence of this.

Second, instructors and librarians should teach, at every opportunity, methods of good source selection. This has to start not with "a journal is better than a Website" but with "here's how you identify the bibliographic elements of a text." A lot of the sources used by the students in our sample are stunningly cheesy and simplistic, but this may not be evident in the bibliographic entries—not because the students are trying to dissemble, but because they don't know how to identify bibliographical elements when looking at a text, much less evaluate the quality of that text. Just teaching students to differentiate who publishes a journal from the journal's name would be a step forward; we have frequently encountered things like "Johns Hopkins University" as the name of a journal, when it is Johns Hopkins that publishes the journal. Or we see "Health and Diet" in the journal position in a bibliographic citation, but when one tracks down the source, one discovers that "Health and Diet" is a section of WebMD. If students can't identify the bibliographic elements of a text, how can they evaluate the text for quality and authority?

We have been quite surprised by how few of the sources cited in the papers contain works cited pages themselves, and think this might provide a fruitful way to begin a conversation about research and citation. If students are reading essays in class and using sources in papers that do not themselves cite sources, our emphasis on this feature of academic writing might seem a little confusing. More important, when using a bibliography-free source, the students lack models of the kind of source engagement their instructors want, and can't see the reasons for it. A discussion of citation as part of a larger conversation about the purpose of research and the nature of the academic conversation might be very useful. Students need to understand why we cite sources in the first place, as well as the roles that citations and lists of references can play in gaining new knowledge. They need to know why instructors are assigning a research paper. If the only reason to assign the paper is to teach the procedures of research and citation, as your study of handouts suggests, perhaps instructors could develop better methods to do that. It is reasonable to assume that the more students get the sense that content does not matter, the more they are likely to produce disengaged, patchwritten work.

Third, instructors need to teach students how to work with and summarize extended portions of text. Our analysis reveals that 94% of the 1,911 citations are at the sentence level—either quotation, unattributed copying, patchwriting, or paraphrasing. This, we believe, is a stunning statistic. Our researchers defined summary as the restatement and compression of three or more consecutive sentences. Even then, students summarized only 6% of the time, indicating that they either could not or would not engage with extended passages of text. Teaching students how to summarize and how to integrate that summary into researched writing are compelling pedagogical mandates.

Notice that none of these three recommendations directly addresses plagiarism. That's because we believe that plagiarism will inevitably occur if students can neither read complex sources critically nor conduct authentic researched inquiry. And our research reveals that they do not, and raises the question of whether that is a matter of students' choice, or a matter of their being unable to. College instructors have a hard job to do, and fetishizing plagiarism is diverting us from the hard work ahead.

We'd like to thank Project Information Literacy for the opportunity to talk about our research. We're looking forward to readers' comments and questions, and to learning what others are doing in this area of inquiry.

NOTES

Sandra Jamieson and Rebecca Moore Howard direct The Citation Project, a national study providing open access empirical data about how college students use sources when writing papers for composition courses.

For more about their findings from an analysis of 18 student papers, see Rebecca Moore Howard, Tricia C. Serviss, and Tanya K. Rodrigue. "Writing from Sources, Writing from Sentences," *Writing and Pedagogy*, 2.2 (Fall 2010): 177–192, at http://writing.byu.edu/static/documents/org/1176.pdf (accessed 8 July 2011).

Smart Talks are informal conversations with leading thinkers about the challenges of finding and using information, conducting research, and managing technology in the digital age.

Smart Talks is an occasional series, produced by Project Information Literacy (PIL). PIL is an ongoing research study, based in the University of Washington's Information School with contributing support from the Berkman Center for Internet and Society at Harvard University, the John D. and Catherine T. MacArthur Foundation, Cengage Learning and Cable in the Classroom.

Alison Head, Lead Researcher for Project Information Literacy, conducted this email-based interview with Sandra Jamieson and Rebecca Moore Howard.

[1] This definition of plagiarism was found on http://www.britannica.com/EBchecked/topic/462640/plagiarism in the *Britannica Encyclopedia* on 8 July 2011.

QUESTIONS ABOUT MEANING

1. What motivated Jamieson and Howard's research? What was their original research question and what gap in the previous research does it begin to address?
2. What is patchwriting? Do the authors regard patchwriting as a form of plagiarism? Why or why not?
3. Summarize the results. What do the findings suggest about how students are selecting and using sources? What inferences do the authors

make about what's getting emphasized by instructors who assign research writing?

QUESTIONS FOR RHETORICAL ANALYSIS

4. To whom are the authors directing their responses? How can you tell? Quote a sentence or two to support your answer.
5. Empirical research usually involves observing and measuring data in order to answer a research question or test a hypothesis. What kind of research or evidence is more common in the authors' field? Why did Jamieson and Howard want to conduct an empirical study? Where and how do the authors provide empirical evidence? Do you find their methods and results convincing? Why or why not?
6. The authors responded to the interviewer's questions via e-mail, rather than in person. What indications are there that the responses were written and not spoken?

"Writing from Sources, Writing from Sentences," *Writing & Pedagogy*

REBECCA MOORE HOWARD, TRICIA SERVISS, AND TANYA K. RODRIGUE

In the previous selection, Rebecca Moore Howard and Sandra Jamieson talk about the Citation Project. In the following article, Howard, Tricia Serviss, and Tanya Rodrigue describe the original study that would later evolve into the Citation Project.

As professors of rhetoric and composition, the authors have often seen student papers that include patchwriting, where students "lift" sentence phrasing and structures from the authors they read. But how widespread is the problem? To answer this question, these professors needed to conduct research. Their study originally appeared in 2010 in *Writing & Pedagogy*, an international journal that publishes articles for those who teach writing.

ABSTRACT

Instead of focusing on students' citation of sources, educators should attend to the more fundamental question of how well students understand their sources and whether they are able to write about them without appropriating language from the source. Of the 18 student research texts we studied, none included summary of a source, raising questions about the students' critical reading practices. Instead of summary, which is highly valued in academic writing and is promoted in composition textbooks, the students paraphrased, copied from, or patchwrote from individual sentences in their sources. Writing from individual sentences places writers in constant jeopardy of working too closely with the language of the source and thus inadvertently plagiarizing; and it also does not compel the writer to understand the source.

KEYWORDS

plagiarism, student research, composition instruction, writing from sources, summary, paraphrase, quotation, copying, patchwriting

INTRODUCTION

Writing from sources is a staple of academic inquiry. It plays a key role in publications in every scholarly discipline, from the literary criticism of English studies to the literature review in scientific publications. It plays a key role as well in the assignments given to both graduate and undergraduate students. The research synthesis helps graduate students survey and participate in the conversations of their discipline, and the term paper, despite criticisms, persists as a common undergraduate genre. Hence writing from sources looms large in composition curricula, in introductory writing courses devoted to researched writing, critical reading, analysis, and argument.

At the same time, many educators worry that students are accomplishing their writing from sources by illicit means. It has become commonplace for students to be described as would-be plagiarists, with unacknowledged copying as their primary strategy of writing from sources. Indeed, contemporary culture—including media discourse and academic discussions—asserts that we are in the midst of a "plagiarism epidemic." As David Callahan tours the college lecture circuit talking about what his book calls our "cheating culture" (Callahan, 2004) and as headlines announce an "'Epidemic' of Student Cheating" (BBC News, 2004), the academy and indeed culture itself seem collectively poised at a precipice over which we will surely slip.

The Center for Academic Integrity (http://www.academicintegrity.org/) conducts surveys asking students about whether they have engaged in a variety of "cheating behaviors," including unacknowledged copying from sources. However, little research has inquired into the range of students' techniques for writing from sources. Do they represent their source through copying (whether cited or uncited), summary, paraphrase, or *patchwriting*—"[c]opying from a source text and then deleting some words, altering grammatical structures, or plugging in one-for-one synonym-substitutes" (Howard, 1993: 233)?

Although no descriptive research has studied the whole range of students' techniques for writing from sources, some valuable research on summary-writing has been conducted. Brown and Day (1983) report on six "rules" that writers follow when summarizing: two involve deletion of material from the source text; two involve generalizing from specifics in the source text; and two require invention of sentences that capture the gist of one or more paragraphs. Students from elementary school through graduate school use deletion techniques. The more advanced a student's education, the more he or she is likely to apply the generalization rule for summarizing. Not until tenth grade do students employ invention as a means of summarizing, and only in graduate school do they do so in all appropriate cases (Brown and Day, 1983).

Three years after Brown and Day's experimental study, Sherrard (1986) asked ten paid undergraduates to alternately summarize or recall seven texts which were ordered randomly. She discovered that their most common method of summarizing is not to combine multiple sentences from the source but to paraphrase a single key sentence.

Brown and Day, and also Sherrard, were working prior to the Internet era and thus prior to the time when educators were consumed with concerns about plagiarism. The more recent research in the Internet era is predictably contextualized by these concerns. Much of the recent research on summary explores the relationship between summary, plagiarism, and patchwriting. Whereas many institutions' academic integrity policies classify patchwriting as a form of plagiarism—a moral failure—recent research indicates that it occurs as an intermediate stage between copying and summarizing: inexpert critical readers patchwrite when they attempt to paraphrase or summarize. Roig (2001) finds that 22% of psychology professors patchwrite when presented with the task of summarizing complex text from an unfamiliar field. Howard (1993: 233) posits patchwriting as a learning strategy rather than an act of academic dishonesty. Pecorari (2003) provides empirical verification of this hypothesis in her discovery that non-native speakers of English (L2 writers) patchwrite, even when writing doctoral dissertations. Shi (2004) reports that the Chinese college students in her study copied longer sequences of words when summarizing than did their native-English-speaking (L1 writers) counterparts.

What is now needed, we believe, is a great deal more information about what students are actually doing with the sources they cite. What source uses are being marked by citations? Are students copying from, patchwriting from, paraphrasing, or summarizing the texts they cite? Are they accurately representing what is in the source? Are they fully citing their sources each time they use them? These questions have been addressed in the field of applied linguistics by Pecorari (2003, 2006, 2008), who studied the writing of L2 graduate students in U.K. universities. But the scholarship of composition and rhetoric, the discipline in which we work, has been largely silent on these issues. Little is known, then, about how either L1 and L2 college students use the sources they cite. Yet only when we have such information will writing instructors be able to craft good pedagogy for students' writing from sources.

OUR INQUIRY

We began our inquiry with an exploratory hypothesis: that college students, both L1 and L2 writers, patchwrite. Our research was an intensive exploration of a small sample of college students' researched writing, to discover how many of the papers drew on which of the four source-use techniques: copying, patchwriting, paraphrasing, and summarizing.

We refer to our work as an *inquiry* rather than a formal research study. We began our work in the belief that large-scale, quantified data collected in naturalistic rather than controlled environments is needed to answer questions about students' uses of their cited sources. Our inquiry was intended as a means of identifying what questions should be asked and what methods should be used to answer them. Since ours was a preliminary inquiry, we did not quantify our results but instead worked collaboratively to decide on the issues that should be investigated in a formal study for the future that we are now designing.

Having secured IRB clearance and course instructors' permission, in Spring 2007 we visited 15 sections of a required sophomore research writing class at what the Carnegie Foundation classifies as a large, private, not-for-profit, comprehensive doctoral university. We asked students to allow us to study the researched writing they did in the course. At the end of the term, we collected final researched papers from the instructors; removed students' names from the papers; established separate piles for each section; randomized papers within each pile; and began working our way down each pile until we found a paper whose sources we could retrieve. Students' uneven success with source documentation made this an often-challenging task, and sometimes the sources cited were not available online or at our libraries. Once we found a paper whose sources we could retrieve, we included it as a paper for our research. Because we worked with full anonymity for the participating students, we did not control for demographic factors such as race, gender, and home language. At the university where we collected data, 10% of students are international students and 29% are from what the university calls "underrepresented groups." The university does not collect data on students' home languages.

We chose 18 papers for two reasons: first, we designed our research after studying that of Pecorari (2003, 2006), who chose a similar number for her study. Second, the same constraints faced us as did Pecorari: our methods are labor-intensive. Reading not only student papers but also the sources they cite, and then coding each source use in each student paper, is time-consuming, involving 3–5 hours' work per paper. Moreover, in our research, each student paper was coded by two researchers. We therefore decided on a relatively small sample size, 18 papers, before our research began.

Once we had found sources for 18 papers, we read the sources and the papers. Our questions were simple:

Does the paper contain one or more incidences of patchwriting?
Does the paper contain one or more incidences of paraphrase? Does the paper contain one or more incidences of summary?
Does the paper contain one or more incidences of direct copying from sources?
Does the paper contain one or more incidences in which direct copying is not marked as quotation?

For this research we defined *summary* as restating and compressing the main points of a paragraph or more of text in fresh language and reducing the summarized passage by at least 50%. The 266-word Gettysburg Address (Lincoln 1863),[1] for example, might be summarized (by Lincoln or another person of his time) this way: "The civil war that we are now fighting tests the principles on which our country was founded. We must pursue this war as a way of honoring the men who fought and died on this battlefield."

We defined *paraphrasing* as restating a passage from a source in fresh language, though sometimes with keywords retained from that passage. Paraphrase does not involve a significant reduction in the length of the passage. The first sentence of the Gettysburg Address, for example, might be paraphrased this way: "The United States was founded in 1776 on the principles of liberty and equality."

Following Howard (1993), we define *patchwriting* as reproducing source language with some words deleted or added, some grammatical structures altered, or some synonyms used. The first sentence of the Gettysburg Address, for example, might be patchwritten this way: "Eighty-seven years ago, the founding fathers created a new nation that was conceived in the principle of liberty and was dedicated to the equality of man." If quotation marks are used for the copied bits, the text is marked as quotation, not patchwriting. However, a passage may be patchwritten even when it is properly quoted and referenced.

By *copying* we mean the exact transcription (though perhaps with occasional minor errors) of source text. As we categorized passages of student text into the four types of source use, whether the passage was referenced did not affect its category. *Copying,* then, can include both quotation and unacknowledged copying. Regardless of whether quotation marks and referenced citation were present or absent, exact copying was classified as *copying*.

In searching for these four methods of source use (summary, paraphrase, patchwriting, and copying), we were also searching for indications of source comprehension—or difficulties with source comprehension. Scholarly and textbook literature asserts that patchwriting is a sign of uncertain comprehension of the source (Angélil-Carter, 2000; Roessig, 2007; Roig, 2001) and that summary is a sign of source comprehension (Angélil-Carter, 2000; Brown and Day, 1983; Harris, 2006). Copying and paraphrasing are not necessarily a sign of either. Copying does not require comprehension of what one copies, regardless of whether the copying is marked as quotation and cited. Paraphrase does require comprehension, but usually only of a sentence or two.

FINDINGS

From the 18 papers we read, we derived the following answers:

1. Does the paper contain one or more incidences of patchwriting?
   - In 16 of the 18 papers (89%), the answer is "yes."
2. Does the paper contain one or more incidences of paraphrase?
   - In all 18 papers (100%), the answer is "yes."
3. Does the paper contain one or more incidences of summary?
   - In all 18 papers (100%), the answer is "no."
4. Does the paper contain one or more incidences of direct copying from sources?
   - In 14 of the 18 papers (78%), the answer is "yes."
5. Does the paper contain one or more incidences in which direct copying is not marked as quotation?
   - In 13 of the 18 papers (72%), the answer is "yes."

In addition, as we read, we made two further discoveries:

6. Of the 18 papers, 17 (94%) contained non-common-knowledge information for which no source was cited.
7. Of the 18 papers, 14 (78%) attributed information to a source that either did not contain that information or said something different from what the student was attributing to it.

Despite the widespread pedagogical belief that summary is important to source-based writing, our reading of 18 undergraduate research essays, along with the sources those essays cite, uncovered not a single incidence of summary. We found copying, paraphrasing, and patchwriting—but no summary. A paragraph from one student paper, 8.10,[2] compactly illustrates the sorts of writing from sources that we encountered. Before we read the sources it cites, this paragraph looked like a good research synthesis:

> Studies show that children, as well as parents, in low-income families have very few assets, so eliminating asset tests for coverage

> could increase enrollment (Cox, Ray, and Lawler). Also, states could use "presumability eligibility for pregnant women and children" covered under Medicaid or SCHIP. Through this, children or pregnant women who seem eligible for the programs can be immediately enrolled until a final determination of eligibility can be produced. To determine who "seems" eligible for health care coverage, school staff could be trained to judge who should be enrolled. Studies show that children with health insurance have fewer sick days from school, so this could "yield educational benefits" (Broaddus). With the increasing diversity and immigration status of our society, Medicaid and SCHIP should also provide information on eligibility and enrollment in many different languages, and in both documentation or letters and personal visits. In every state, many lose coverage by Medicaid and SCHIP when it is time to renew. In order to change this trend, the programs should change their period to a 12-month plan, rather than the 6-month plan now. Also, to eliminate confusion and difficulty for a family, states with separate Medicaid and SCHIP programs should coincide their renewal times and conduct renewal by mail or telephone. States with call centers, and reminder letters for renewal should increase recertification of coverage. Lastly, they should consider enforcing a grace period of about one to three months for renewal (Cox, Ray, and Lawler). Some states have finally begun to take an initiative on solving these low enrollment problems.

The paragraph appears to handle sources well, using quotation marks, providing in-text citations to acknowledge sources, and citing two different sources, one of them (Cox, Ray, and Lawler, 2004) in two different parts of the paragraph. (Both sources are Web sites, so the absence of page references is not an issue.)

A reading of its sources, however, reveals that the paragraph is extensively patchwritten. Figure 8.1 below places a succession of sentences in the apparently well-cited paragraph above side-by-side with the corresponding sentences in the sources. (We should note that in almost every case in all 18 papers, we were easily able to locate the exact sentence from which the student writers were working.) Underlining indicates where the paper is using the exact or near-exact phrasing of its source. For the sake of brevity, Figure 8.1 illustrates just the first few sentences, though the remainder of the paragraph continues in the same vein, with only one sentence that does not contain copying or patchwriting.

All eighteen of the student writers whose papers we analyzed engaged in the sorts of textual strategies illustrated in Figure 8.1. A passage from student paper A.1, interspersed with our comments in italics,

<table>
<tr><th>Paper 8.10</th><th>Cox, Ray, and Lawler (2004)</th><th>Broaddus and Ku (2000)</th></tr>
<tr><td><u>Studies show that</u> children, as well as parents, in <u>low-income families have very few assets, so eliminating asset tests</u> for coverage could increase enrollment (Cox, Ray, and Lawler).</td><td><u>Studies have shown that</u> most <u>low-income families have few assets. Eliminating asset tests . . .</u></td><td></td></tr>
<tr><td>Also, states could <u>use "presumability eligibility for pregnant women and children</u>" covered under Medicaid or SCHIP.

Through this, children or pregnant women who seem eligible for the programs can be immediately enrolled <u>until a final determination of eligibility</u> can be produced.

To determine who "seems" eligible for health care coverage, <u>school staff could be trained</u> to judge who should be enrolled.

Studies show <u>that children with health insurance have fewer sick days from school, so this could "yield educational benefits"</u> (Broaddus).</td><td></td><td>(quotation not in the cited source, though the keyword "presumptive [not presumability] eligibility" is)

This temporarily enrolls children and pregnant women in SCHIP and Medicaid as soon as they apply for benefits, <u>pending a final eligibility determination</u>.

<u>School staff could be trained</u> in how to conduct presumptive eligibility determinations and how to carry out the necessary follow-up activities.

In addition to helping school children gain better access to health care and prevention services, <u>presumptive eligibility may yield educational benefits</u>; recent research suggests that <u>children who are insured have fewer sick days and miss school</u> less often than children who lack health insurance.</td></tr>
<tr><td>With the increasing diversity and immigration status of our society, Medicaid and SCHIP should also provide information on eligibility and enrollment in <u>many different languages</u>, and in both documentation or letters and personal visits.

In every state, many lose <u>coverage by Medicaid and SCHIP when it is time to renew.</u></td><td>Write Letters reminding families to renew SCHIP. Go door-to-door to help families in the renewal process. . . . Give families materials about renewal <u>in multiple languages</u>.

<u>In virtually all states, many people lose Medicaid and SCHIP when it is time to renew</u> or recertify for benefits.</td><td></td></tr>
</table>

Figure 8.1 Sentence-by-Sentence Comparison of a Paragraph from Paper 8.10 with its Sources (Instances of exact copying, whether cited or uncited, and patchwriting are underlined.)

demonstrates the fine level of myriad difficulties that the writer faces in producing this text:

Medical students must possess knowledge. Aspiring to be a doctor is not an easy career endeavor, in fact, it requires a lot of work and dedication. According to Weinberger, the object of knowing requires more than being right. [*This misrepresents Weinberger's definition of knowledge.*] It is necessary for doctors to be right because they do have a lot at hand, which can be a patient's life and even just his or her immediate health. [*This incorrectly applies Weinberger to the paper's investigation of a medical students' blog; it attempts to make a connection, yet is unable to do so as it misinterprets the Weinberger source.*] Knowledge is "justified true belief." [*Despite these quotation marks, the phrase is not a direct quotation from the source. We can only speculate about the possible semiotic intent of these quotation marks.*] So what does this have to do with medical students and the web? From the medical students' side, medical students are justified in believing that they will become doctors because they have the capability to do so, but on the web side according to Weinberger the web is "a hodgepodge of ideas that violates every rule of epistemological etiquette." [*This is a direct quotation incompletely cited; a page number is not supplied.*] Ideas that are posted on the web are wrapped in individual voices that make it harder to dig out exactly what is being said (Weinberger 139). [*This sentence is copied directly from the text. No quotation marks are used, though the source is cited.*] The idea of individual voices allows people to express themselves whether it is factual or opinionated. This is exactly what blogging is focused on and what it is basically about. In reading Anna's blogs, we only "hear" about her life, feelings, and thoughts and not anyone else's. [*This passage also suggests a lack of understanding of the source, as it does not adequately apply Weinberger's theory of the web as a social network and site of dialogue to the medical students' blog.*]

Figure 8.2 Paragraph from Paper A.1, with Our Comments in Brackets and Italics (Our comments are based on reading not only the student's paragraph but also its source.)

The source in question is David Weinberger's *Small Pieces Loosely Joined* (Weinberger, 2002), a 240-page complex theoretical text. Paper A.1 cites two of those 240 pages, and its uneven representation of the Weinberger text suggests the possibility that these may be the only two pages that the student read. The paper endeavors to deploy Weinberger's theory of knowledge, which may have been accessed by consulting the Weinberger index rather than by actually reading *Small Pieces Loosely Joined.* This is our primary concern throughout our analysis of these 18 papers: they cite sentences rather than sources, and one must then ask not only whether the writers understood the source itself but also whether they even read it. As teachers—and as writers ourselves—we are not unfamiliar with the quote-mining approach to complex texts: the search for a "good sentence to quote"—or to paraphrase or patchwrite—and perhaps to cite. The absence of summary in these papers does not necessarily mean that the student writers did not read the whole text being cited, nor does it mean that they did not understand what they were reading. But the absence of summary, coupled with the exclusive engagement of text on the sentence level, means that readers have no assurance that the students *did* read and understand.

When the source treats a technical topic or when it lists concrete items, the writer working exclusively on the sentence level predictably struggles to write from those sentences. Here, for example, are two passages from paper 3.6, side-by-side with their sources:

Paper 3.6	Bainbridge (2007) source
After the materials are separated they are melted down and mixed together. Then they undergo a complicated inverse polymer reaction from the one used to make it, resulting in a mixture of chemicals which are then synthesized to form a new polymer of the same kind (Bainbridge).	The obstacles of recycling plastic can be overcome by using an elaborate monomer recycling process wherein the polymer undergoes an inverse polymer reaction of what was used to manufacture it. The end product of this procedure is a mix of chemicals that form the original polymer, which is further purified and synthesized to form a new polymer of the same type.
Paper 3.6	**West (2007) source**
Plastic labeled number two is a high density polyethylene plastic, also known as HDPE. These plastics are most commonly found in containers holding heavier liquids, such as milk cartons, shampoo bottles, and laundry detergents. The plastic is a much softer texture and is much more flexible that PETE. HDPE is also very commonly, and fairly easily recycled but can only be recycled once. HDPE is often recycled into toys, plastic lumber, and piping (West).	Number 2 is reserved for high-density polyethylene plastics. These include heavier containers that hold laundry detergents and bleaches as well as milk, shampoo and motor oil. Plastic labeled with the number 2 is often recycled into toys, piping, plastic lumber and rope. Like plastic designated number 1, it is widely accepted at recycling centers.

Figure 8.3 Comparison of Two Passages from Paper 3.6 with Their Sources (Exact copying, whether cited or uncited, and patchwriting are underlined.)

We have chosen these three papers—8.10, A.1, and 3.6—not because they are extreme incidents but because they are concise illustrations of the struggles that were in evidence in all eighteen papers. Similar struggles are documented in prior research, especially in applied linguists' studies of second-language writers' work with English-language source texts (Keck, 2006; Pecorari, 2003, 2006, 2008; Shi, 2004).

DISCUSSION

We offer these side-by-side comparisons not to suggest that the writers are misusing sources (though sometimes that is indeed the case) but to demonstrate that *these students are not writing from sources; they are writing from sentences selected from sources.* That leaves the reader with the unanswered question: does this writer understand what s/he has read? And it leaves the writer in a position of peril: working exclusively on the sentence level, he or she is perforce always in danger of plagiarizing. When one has only the option of copying or paraphrasing, one can easily paraphrase too lightly, producing a patchwritten sentence too close to the language of the original. This is a particular peril for inexpert writers: From his review of scholarship in citation analysis, White (2004: 105) concludes that, in general, it is only advanced writers who write from sources without using any language from the source. Howard (1993) argues that patchwriting should be considered a transitional stage in writing from sources, rather than plagiarism, and the Council of Writing Program Administrators (2005) labels patchwriting a misuse of sources rather than plagiarism.

Still, many institutional codes of academic integrity—and indeed, many writing handbooks and textbooks—persist in treating patchwriting as a form of plagiarism. To complicate the matter, as Sandra Jamieson demonstrates, the extent to which patchwriting counts as plagiarism can vary according to academic discipline (Jamieson, 2008). Moreover, when one has only the option of copying or paraphrasing, the copying may become so extensive that the writer feels the need to withhold complete citation, for fear of appearing too dependent on the source language. Or the writer may simply not know how often to cite persistent use of source language.

Our inquiry does not answer the question of why none of these 18 students summarized their sources, nor why so many of them patchwrote, misinterpreted what a source said, or offered non-common-knowledge information without citing a source. Perhaps they did not understand the sources. Perhaps they didn't care enough about the research project to invest themselves in the task of source comprehension. Perhaps they did not conceive the research project as one in which they should engage with their sources, but instead saw it as one in which they should find isolated sentences that might be useful in their own texts. Qualitative research will be needed to answer these questions.

This work also does not indicate whether the 18 students whose written work we studied are representative of all students at the institution in which the data were gathered, much less whether they represent college students in the aggregate. A larger, quantified, multi-campus study will be needed to make such generalizations.

Our inquiry does not contradict Keck's (2006) observation that patchwriting occurs in most college students' writing. Keck also found that the incidence of patchwriting is higher among second-language writers. Because we did not control for first language, we cannot affirm the latter observation, but all of the college writers in our pilot research patchwrote.

This pilot study suggests that issues of source selection may be significant as well. In the examples we have given, the students were striving to reproduce extended information rather than argument, technical information on topics that they may never have previously studied. These were papers being written in a general composition class, not in discipline-specific instruction, which means the student writers did not necessarily have any prior expertise in the topics they chose to research. Nor, in the traditions of most composition instruction, does the instructor necessarily have any expertise in the topics the students are researching. Faced with reproducing extended technical information and not wanting to copy long passages, the students might not have had the vocabulary and background knowledge necessary to do anything but patchwrite the passages.

Our observations also raise questions about problems students may have with source-based writing, problems that are both prior to and foundational to their correct citation of sources. Citation counts for little if what is being cited is a fragmentary representation of the source. Plagiarism is difficult to avoid if one is constructing an argument from isolated sentences pulled from sources.

Our observations affirm the difficulties that all students have when using language from sources—or trying to avoid doing so. In fact, Roig (2001) establishes that all writers, even research faculty, struggle when writing from unfamiliar sources on unfamiliar topics. In Roig's experimental research, psychology professors were given the task of paraphrasing text. Roig found that the more difficult the source text, the more the professors appropriated language from it. Twenty-two percent of the professors patchwrote: they made syntactic changes to the original language of the source text. Twenty-four percent distorted the meaning of the source (Roig, 2001: 315).

What we are illustrating in Figures 8.1, 8.2, and 8.3, then, are issues with which all writers seem to struggle. However, despite the accumulating body of research on writers' intertextual struggles with their sources, these are not widely recognized as global issues; instead, they are widely regarded as malfeasance committed by ignorant, indifferent, or unethical writers.

CONCLUSION

From this research, we are left with a compelling question: when writers work from sources, to what extent are they accessing the entire source, and to what extent single sentences from it? In the eighteen papers we examined, it is consistently the sentences, not the sources, that are being written from. Perhaps some or all of these writers had a comprehensive understanding of those sources but chose to work only with isolated sentences within them. Or perhaps some or all of these writers did not understand or did not engage with some or all of their sources. Instead, they may have searched for "good" sentences and then decided whether to paraphrase, copy from, or patchwrite from them. Again, qualitative research will be needed to test these hypotheses.

Clearly, more research into the nuances of writers' uses of sources is needed. Interviewing or observing writers as they make their source-use decisions will illuminate why they make the choices they do, and how committed they feel to the educational ideals embedded in the task they have been given. Studying writers in a variety of contexts will discourage fallacious overgeneralizations about writing techniques. Do advanced undergraduates working in their majors, for example, draw on sources in different ways than do sophomores taking a required generic course in researched writing? Studying writers who are reading a variety of genres will explore another possible factor. Do writers, as Sherrard (1986) suggests, use sources differently when those sources are narrative rather than expository? And how does source use vary according to the genre in which the writers are working? Further issues involve approaches to instruction that might improve students' use of sources. What effects do various pedagogies have on writers' practices of source use?

All of our research questions will be pursued in the large-scale, quantified study now called the Citation Project (CitationProject.net). But special attention will be paid to the question of source comprehension and summary and the relationship between the two. Clearly our preliminary inquiry suggests that we have much more to learn about whether students understand the sources they are citing in their researched writing, whether they choose to summarize those sources and the reasons for their choices, and the extent to which the absence of summary correlates with a lack of source comprehension.

ABOUT THE AUTHORS

Rebecca Moore Howard was awarded the PhD in English by West Virginia University. She is now Professor of Writing and Rhetoric at Syracuse University, and her scholarship focuses on authorship studies, especially students' use of sources. Tanya K. Rodrigue earned her PhD in Composition and Cultural Rhetoric at Syracuse University. Her doctoral dissertation examines the role and needs of teaching assistants in writing across the curriculum. She is Andrew W. Mellon Postdoctoral Fellow in Composition and Rhetoric at Wheaton College (Massachusetts). Tricia Serviss was awarded the PhD in Composition and Cultural Rhetoric by Syracuse University and is now Assistant Professor of Rhetoric and Composition at Auburn University. Her dissertation reveals how the definition of and possibilities for literacy are constructed in disparate localities.

NOTES

1. The entire text of the Gettysburg Address is as follows:

> Four score and seven years ago our fathers brought forth on this continent, a new nation, conceived in Liberty, and dedicated to the proposition that all men are created equal.
>
> Now we are engaged in a great civil war, testing whether that nation, or any nation so conceived and so dedicated, can long endure. We are met on a great battle-field of that war. We have come to dedicate a portion of that field, as a final resting place for those who here gave their lives that that nation might live. It is altogether fitting and proper that we should do this.
>
> But, in a larger sense, we can not dedicate—we can not consecrate—we can not hallow—this ground. The brave men, living and dead, who struggled here, have consecrated it, far above our poor power to add or detract. The world will little note, nor long remember what we say here, but it can never forget what they did here. It is for us the living, rather, to be dedicated here to the unfinished work which they who fought here have thus far so nobly advanced. It is rather for us to be here dedicated to the great task remaining before us—that from these honored dead we take increased devotion to that cause for which they gave the last full measure of devotion—that we here highly resolve that these dead shall not have died in vain—that this nation, under God, shall have a new birth of freedom—and that government of the people, by the people, for the people, shall not perish from the earth. (Lincoln, 1863)

2. We collected student papers with full anonymity for the writers; hence we do not attach their names to the texts. In addition, our study works exclusively with student texts and not students; hence we do not attach pseudonyms to the papers. Like Shi, we are studying student texts, not students, so (again like Shi) the texts are numbered rather than pseudonymed.

REFERENCES

Angélil-Carter, S. (2000) *Stolen Language? Plagiarism in Writing.* New York: Longman.

Bainbridge, R. (2007) Recycling plastic. *Ezine Articles.* Retrieved 8 April 2007 from http:// ezinearticles.com/?Recycling-Plastic&id=354295

BBC News (30 June 2004) "Epidemic" of student cheating? Retrieved 30 June 2004 from http://news.bbc.co.uk/2/hi/uk_news/education/3854465.stm

Broaddus, M. and Ku, L. (6 December 2000) Nearly 95 percent of low-income uninsured children now are eligible for Medicaid or SCHIP: Measures need to increase enrollment among eligible but uninsured children. Center on Budget and Policy Priorities. Retrieved 16 July 2007 from http://www.cbpp.org/12-6-00schip.htm

Brown, A. and Day, J. D. (1983) Macrorules for summarizing texts: The development of expertise. *Journal of Verbal Learning and Verbal Behavior* 22: 1–14.

Callahan, D. (2004) *The Cheating Culture: Why More Americans Are Doing Wrong to Get Ahead.* New York: Harcourt.

Citation Project (2010) Retrieved 8 July 2010 from CitationProject.net.

Council of Writing Program Administrators (2005) Defining and avoiding plagiarism: The WPA statement on best practices. Retrieved 22 June 2008 from http://wpacouncil. org/node/9

Cox, L., Ray, J., and Lawler, K. (28 October 2004) What can consumer health assistance programs and states DO to improve Medicaid and SCHIP enrollment and retention. *Families USA.* Retrieved 16 July 2007 from http://www.familiesusa.org/issues/medicaid/ making-it-work-for-consumers/improving-medicaid-and-schip.html

Harris, J. (2006) *Rewriting: How to Do Things with Words.* Logan: Utah State University Press.

Howard, R. (1993) A plagiarism *pentimento. Journal of Teaching Writing* 11(3): 233–46.

Jamieson, S. (2008) One size does not fit all: Plagiarism across the curriculum. In R. M. Howard and A. E. Robillard (eds.) *Pluralizing Plagiarism: Identities, Contexts, Pedagogies* 77–91. Portsmouth, New Hampshire: Boynton-Cook

Keck, C. (2006) The use of paraphrase in summary writing: A comparison of L1 and L2 writers. *Journal of Second Language Writing* 15: 261–278.

Lincoln, Abraham (19 November 1863) Gettysburg Address. *American Rhetoric Online Speech Bank.* Retrieved 8 August 2009 from http://www .americanrhetoric.com/ speeches/gettysburgaddress.htm

Pecorari, D. (2003) Good and original: Plagiarism and patchwriting in academic second-language writing. *Journal of Second Language Writing* 12: 317–345.

Pecorari, D. (2006) Visible and occluded citation features in postgraduate second-language writing. *English for Specific Purposes* 25: 4–29.

Pecorari, D. (2008) *Academic Writing and Plagiarism: A Linguistic Analysis.* New York: Continuum.

Roessig, L. (March 2007) Making research matter. *English Journal* 96(4): 50–55.

Roig, M. (2001) Plagiarism and paraphrasing criteria of college and university professors. *Ethics & Behavior* 11(3): 307–324.

Sherrard, C. (1986) Summary writing: A topographical study. *Written Communication* 3: 324–343.

Shi, L. (2004) Textual borrowing in second-language writing. *Written Communication* 21(2): 171–200.

Weinberger, D. (2002) *Small Pieces Loosely Joined: A Unified Theory of the Web.* Cambridge: Perseus.

West, L. (2007) How to recycle different types of plastic. *About.com.* Retrieved 1 June 2007 from http://environment.about.com/od/ earthtalkcolumns/a/recycleplastics.htm

White, H. (2004) Citation analysis and discourse analysis revisited. *Applied Linguistics* 25(1): 89–116.

QUESTIONS ABOUT MEANING

1. What gap in the existing body of research does this study begin to fill?
2. Describe the sample and research methods. How did the authors test their hypothesis?
3. What are some of the causes or possible explanations for so much patchwriting in student papers?
4. The problems with students' source use were not limited to too much copying of language. What other kinds of problems did the researchers find in the sample papers analyzed?

QUESTIONS FOR RHETORICAL ANALYSIS

5. Who is the intended audience for this article? How and where is this conveyed?
6. Consider the authors' use of figures. What aspects of the visual presentation help the reader understand what the authors are demonstrating? What other aspects of formatting aid comprehension?

THINKING AND WRITING ABOUT THE TOPIC

Select a source-based paper that you are currently writing or one that you have written. Imagine that you are one of the Citation Project researchers and that your paper is among those being analyzed. Compare each instance of source use to the original sources and answer the questions the researchers answered:

1. Does your paper contain one or more incidences of patchwriting?
2. Does your paper contain one or more incidences of paraphrase?
3. Does your paper contain one or more incidences of summary? In other words, have you condensed passages rather than merely working with single sentences from the source?
4. Does your paper contain one or more incidences of direct copying from sources?
5. Does your paper contain one or more incidences in which direct copying is not marked as quotation?
6. Does your paper contain non–common-knowledge information for which no source was cited?
7. Is there any information attributed to a source that does not appear in that source? Or does the information in your paper say something different from what the source says?
8. Are any of your sources longer than two pages? If so, do you use any information that appears late in the source rather than in the first page or two?

How would you assess your use of source material? How could your use of sources be improved? Illustrate and explain.

WORKS CITED

Begley, Sharon. "What's in a Word? Language May Shape Our Thoughts." *Newsweek* 8 Jul 2009. Web. 27 Apr. 2013.

Connors, Robert J. "The Rhetoric of Citation Systems, Part II: Competing Epistemic Values in Citation." *Rhetoric Review* 17. 2 (1999): 219–45. Print.

Council of Writing Program Administrators. "Defining and Avoiding Plagiarism: The WPA Statement on Best Practices." January 2003. Web. 30 May 2013.

Druckman, James N., Martin J. Kifer, and Michael Parkin. "Campaign Communications in U.S. Congressional Elections." *American Political Science Review* 103.3 (2009): 343–66. Print.

Gibson, Rhonda, and Dolf Zillmann. "Effects of Citation in Exemplifying Testimony on Issue Perception." *Journalism & Mass Communication Quarterly* 75.1 (1998): 167–76. Print.

Howard, Rebecca Moore, Tanya K. Rodrigue, and Tricia C. Serviss. "Writing from Sources, Writing from Sentences." *Writing and Pedagogy* 2.2 (2010): 177–92. Print.

Hyland, Ken. *Disciplinary Discourses: Social Interactions in Academic Writing.* Ann Arbor: University of Michigan Press, 2004. Print.

Lee, Leonard, Shane Frederick, and Dan Ariely. "Try It, You'll Like It: The Influence of Expectation, Consumption, and Revelation on Preferences for Beer." *Psychological Science* 17.12 (2006): 1054–58. Print.

Lytle, Beverly, and Caroline Yang. "Detecting Forged Handwriting with Wavelets and Statistics." *Undergraduate Math Journal* 7.1 (2006): 1–10. Web. 18 June 2013.

McNamara, Danielle S., Scott A. Crossley, and Philip M. McCarthy. "Linguistic Features of Writing Quality." *Written Communication* 27.1 (2010): 57–86. Print.

Miller, Margaret A., and Anne-Marie McCartan. "At the Crossings: Making the Case for New Interdisciplinary Programs." *Change* 22.3 (1990): 28–36. Print.

Miller, Paul, Jaye Bausser, and Audeen Fentiman. "Responding to Technical Writing in an Introductory Engineering Class: The Role of Genre and Discipline." *Technical Communication Quarterly* 7.4 (1998): 443–61. Print.

Rabinovitch, Oded. "Chameleons between Science and Literature: Observation, Writing, and the Early Parisian Academy of Sciences in the Literary Field." *History of Science* 51.170 (2013): 33–62. Print.

Rhodes, David G. "Organization in Technical Writing." *Journal of Professional Issues in Engineering Education & Practice* 131.3 (2005): 213–16. Print.

Shirley, Sue. "The Art of Paraphrase." *Teaching English in the Two-Year College* 22.2 (2004): 186–89. Print.

Soliday, Mary. "Reading Student Writing with Anthropologists: Stance and Judgment in College Writing." *College Composition and Communication* 56.1 (2004): 72–93. Print.

Sommers, Nancy, and Laura Saltz. "The Novice as Expert: Writing the Freshman Year." *College Composition and Communication* 56.1 (2004): 124–49. Print.

Waters, Mary C., and Tomás R. Jiménez. "Assessing Immigrant Assimilation: New Empirical and Theoretical Challenges." *Annual Review of Sociology* 31 (2005): 105–25. Print.

CHAPTER 9

Writing a Synthesis Paper

In chapter 8, you learned how summary, paraphrase, and quotation can be used to relate the meaning of a single source to others. But most of your source-based writing assignments will involve combining information from several sources in order to make a more comprehensive and convincing argument. This type of writing, called **synthesis writing**, is illustrated in the next paragraph. The writer summarizes the findings of three authors who discuss the difficulty of transitioning from high school to college work. Notice how the writer synthesizes source material.

EXAMPLE 9.1 MULTIPLE SOURCE WRITING

Many college educators have noted that high school work is significantly different from college work. Kirk S. Kidwell, a professor who has worked with thousands of freshmen, has seen that many first-year students have a hard time changing the way they learned in high school. One particular challenge is that students are "no longer the passive recipient" of answers given by the teacher (254). In fact, many of the questions don't have single "right" answers (255). A similar perspective is expressed by English professor L. Lennie Irvin. In his essay "What Is 'Academic' Writing?" Irvin writes that in high school, research often means looking up information in Google or Wikipedia, but in college, research is more complicated (8). Both authors note that students will need to work much harder to be able to do work they are not used to doing. Nicholas Preus blames secondary schools for some of the problems he has seen his English 101 students have adjusting to college work. Preus says college instructors ask writers to challenge ideas and that students aren't used to doing this (76). Kidwell and Irvin also imply blame on the part of high schools by suggesting that in high school students don't get to practice the type of learning required in college. All three authors draw attention to the inadequate preparation I believe high school students receive for college.

An opening topic sentence summarizes an opinion shared by all three sources.

A connection is made between the first two sources.

Another connection between sources is made.

A third source is introduced, one whose opinion is similar to the first source.

The connection between the three sources is reiterated and their opinions are used to support the author's point: High schools don't adequately prepare students for college work.

In this paragraph the writer combines the arguments of others to make his own argument, one that will go beyond that of any of his sources.

When completing your own synthesis writing assignment, focus on accomplishing three goals:

1. Put your sources in conversation with each other by noting how they agree, disagree, and vary in their opinions;
2. orchestrate the conversation by organizing and presenting sources in a way that shows readers your take on the issue; and
3. contribute to the conversation.

This chapter offers advice on how to accomplish these goals.

Planning a Synthesis Paper

There are several steps you can take to help you achieve the first goal of synthesis writing—putting your sources in conversation with one another. The next section walks you through these steps, which include evaluating your sources' points of view, writing while you research, and categorizing the information you uncover. These same steps will help you plan your paper. But the most important first step to planning your paper is to understand your own rhetorical situation.

Consider Your Audience, Purpose, and Assignment

As we saw in chapter 4, college writing assignments vary in form, purpose, and audience. Keeping the rhetorical situation in mind as you read sources can help you plan your approach to synthesis writing assignments. In which genre are you writing? What is the assigned purpose for your paper? Who is your audience and how much does the audience know about the subject? What would your readers be most interested in learning? Answering questions about the audience and purpose helps you determine what arguments to make in your paper and in how much detail.

Daniel Parr (see chapter 7) describes how evaluation of his intended audience influenced the way he planned the business proposal he wrote for his management communications course:

> In my mind everything is related to the audience. In my case, I saw the audience as a VP or CEO from my employing company. He is operating at a high level and has little time for 45-page White Paper reports. He will have already had some subordinate or director level individual who has read the engineering study and wants the big picture backed up with credible evidence. I also consider the instructor as the audience, because ultimately he/she is the one reading it. I want to write something that hopefully the instructor wants to read as well and doesn't want to throw on the fireplace after the third sentence.

Think about what aspects of your subject are most relevant to your audience and to the discipline you're writing in when determining the focus of your paper.

Look for Agreements, Disagreements, and Discrepancies between Sources

Another consideration is how your sources agree and disagree with one another. If you recently graduated from high school, you are probably used to being asked to summarize what you have read. These summary assignments develop your reading and communication skills, but your college professors will more often want you to engage in scholarly conversations, to read critically, to analyze and even argue with the sources you read.

Finding discrepancies between sources is one particularly useful way to engage with your sources. One student put it this way:

> I've learned now to bring [conflicting sources] in and say . . . "this person has stated this, this, this, and this, but I feel my argument is stronger because of this, this, this, and this." If you have a good argument going already, it's easy to pull that stuff in, and you've got to do it because if you're going to present it you've got to be ready for those questions. . . . I don't see evidence that sheds light in a different direction as being negative or bad or wrong. (qtd. in Fister 166–67)

Making annotations as you read such as "this study contradicts what X believes" or "Y would take issue with this claim" will help you discover points to develop in your paper.

In addition to noting *if* your sources agree, consider *how* and *why* they agree, disagree, and differ.

If your sources agree, you might ask:

What about the authors' backgrounds or audiences explains their position?
Is there another way of looking at this subject?
What do these authors fail to consider?
Can the authors' evidence be used to make a related but different point?

If your sources disagree, you might ask:

What about the authors' backgrounds or audiences explains their position?
Can two authors who disagree both be right in some way?
What makes one author more correct than another?

Questions such as these can help you find ways to contribute to the conversation.

Think of Research and Writing as Simultaneous Processes

When librarian Barbara Fister asked 14 undergraduates to describe their research writing process, she learned that they did not wait until they finished their research to begin writing. As they read, they recorded potential topics so they wouldn't forget them. They made notes about how they might use information they've read in their papers. They tried to articulate their purpose as it was taking shape in their heads. In short, they began writing their papers while they researched (167).

For some papers, your writing process may be somewhat linear, but the steps will be overlapping, as illustrated in Figure 9.1.

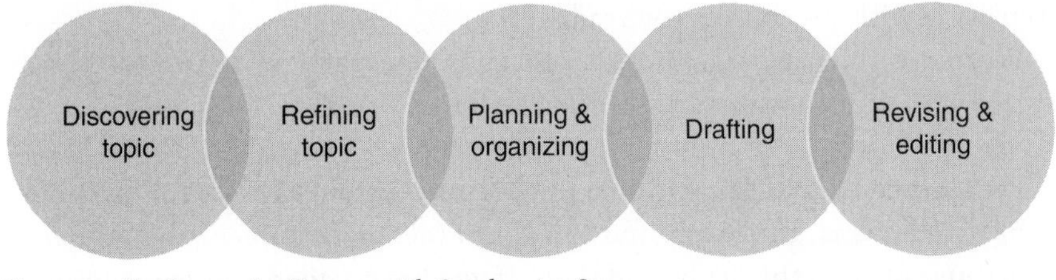

Figure 9.1 The Composing Process with Overlapping Steps

You are likely to begin planning your paper as you refine your topic and begin drafting parts while you are still planning the whole. In fact, for many writers the steps are not only overlapping; they're recurring, as illustrated in Figure 9.2.

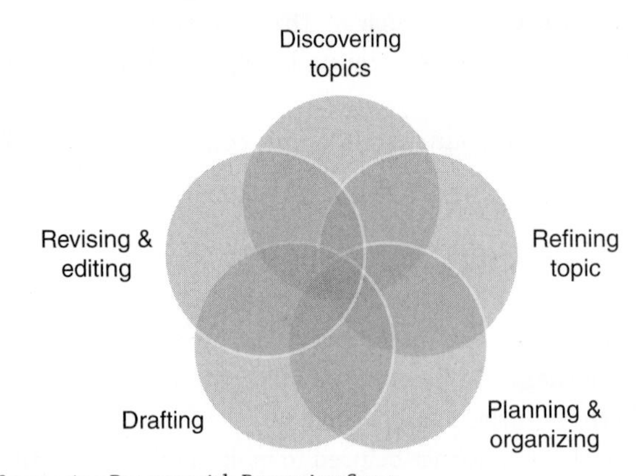

Figure 9.2 The Composing Process with Recurring Steps

In the composing process depicted in Figure 9.2, the writer is continually refining the topic, planning, drafting, editing, and even discovering what to write about. The steps are recursive and simultaneous as the writer strives to find the best way to make her argument.

Even writers who, like Daniel Parr, plan out the entire paper before writing, usually circle back to conduct further research:

> I begin writing after I have found and read all the sources I think I will need to write all the sections of my paper. As I am writing the draft, if certain sections are coming up weak or if the content I thought a source might help supply does not pan out, then I look to diversify or add sources to help "beef up weak sections."

Through writing, you discover additional ideas to discuss and discover where you need more evidence to support your claims. These steps in turn send you back to do more reading and research.

Look for Ways to Graphically Organize Information

Readers understand information better when it is "chunked" or organized into categories rather than when details are presented as random facts. So, as you read your sources, think about ways to group information in your paper. If you record topics in the margins of sources while you read or organize notes by topic, rather than by source, you can later easily find information on the topics you decide to develop in your paper.

Once you begin to discover recurring ideas within sources, several techniques can help you plan your paper while you research. One approach, proposed by English professor Bonnie Orzolek, is to imagine that you are organizing a conference attended by all of your sources. Create a seating chart for the conference banquet: Place your central claim or research question at the head table or in the center and assign each author to a table, along with no more than three other authors with whom he or she has something in common, as illustrated in Figure 9.3. Give each table a name that captures a theme or perspective that the authors share.

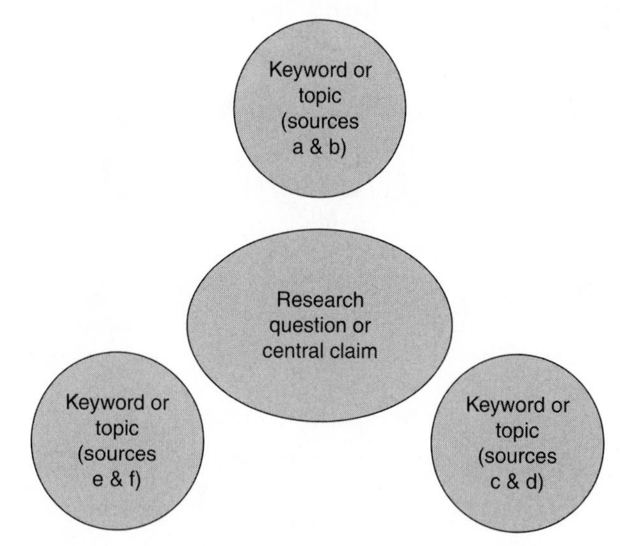

Figure 9.3 Assign Sources to "Banquet Tables"

These perspectives (represented as banquet tables) are potential paragraph topics for your paper. Finally, assign yourself a seat at one of the tables and identify what you will add to that "conversation" (cited in Bahls 31).

Another way to visualize your paper is to draw boxes representing major points to discuss (Figure 9.4). Think of those boxes as blocks that can be rearranged. In addition to noting sources of information (and page numbers), you might list examples, analogies, or rebuttals within the boxes as they come to mind.

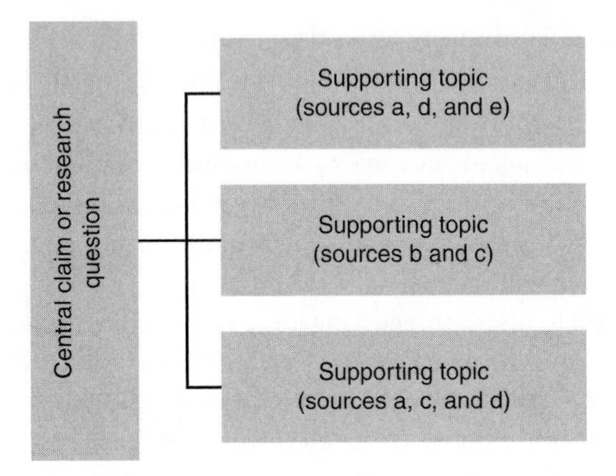

Figure 9.4 Group Sources into Topic Boxes

For some papers, the arrangement of points is determined by the subject matter, such as when discussing a series of events or chain of effects. In this case, topics might be best displayed in a flow chart, as illustrated in Figure 9.5.

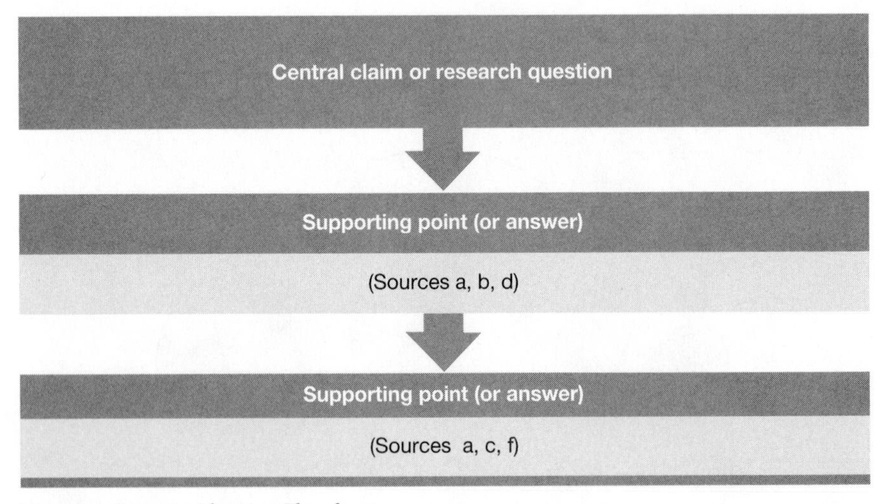

Figure 9.5 Organize Ideas in a Flowchart

Again, noting sources of information, page numbers, and details within segments will save time when you're ready to write your paper.

Yet another way to organize a synthesis paper is to create a grid or table that allows you to compare and contrast what sources say about topics. For example, if your paper will analyze various theories or perspectives for explaining a problem, you could create one column for the various theoretical schools, another column for the features of each theory, and a third column for the authors who advocate that particular theory (Ambrose et al. 60). A fourth column can be used for notes about how proponents of the various theories differ in their positions or how you will add to the conversation. The result is a grid that resembles Table 9.1.

TABLE 9.1
Synthesis Paper Planning Grid

Solutions to the Problem of X	Features of the Theory	Sources Advocating the Theory	Response and Comments
Name of the solution or theory	*Details and examples*	*Source names and page references*	*My response or notes about how sources compare*

The details in each row can then be used to help you develop each section of your paper.

Using methods such as these will help you write an original argument rather than one that imitates any given source too closely. Although you draw from the work of others when you write a source-based synthesis paper, *your* purpose should determine your main ideas and the organization of those ideas.

Concept in Practice 9.1: Planning a Source-Based Synthesis Paper

The following notes were taken while reading four articles about the debate over drilling for oil in Alaska's Arctic National Wildlife Refuge (ANWR).

1. Read the notes and write keywords or short phrases in the margins that identify the topics covered. As you annotate, look for recurring topics between the sources.

From Article #1 **"War over Arctic Oil"** (McCarthy)

- Less than 6-month supply of oil in ANWR

- Home to animals/denning and migration will be disrupted, esp. for caribou
- Would ruin pristine landscape (like at Prudhoe Bay)
- Pipelines built for animals to pass under; attempts to protect animals/environment
- But tundra is fragile like eggshells
- The Inupiat people support drilling and depend on money it brings to region
- The Gwich'in people oppose drilling
- Could lead to off-shore drilling, interfering with whale hunts
- Negative social impact of oil money in Indian society (e.g., alcohol abuse)
- Alaskans don't pay income or sales tax. Get annual oil dividends

From Article #2 **"The Last Wild Place"** (Zagorin)

- Estimates of oil output range from 3 billion to 16 bbl
- ANWR oil would lessen foreign oil dependence?
- Economic benefit for Alaska
- Limited environmental impact
- Could produce only 6-month supply of oil and take 10 years to get
- U.S. is 5% of world population but uses 25% of world energy
- Better option: increase automobile fuel efficiency

From Article #3 **"Why Are We Talking about Just ANWR?"** (Jans)

- 95% of Alaska's Arctic coastal plain open to gas and oil companies, including areas like Teshekpuk Lake, even though Eskimos depend on land for survival
- Alaska is home to caribou, various birds, and rare plants; polar bears, seals, and bowhead whales affected
- Prudhoe Bay environmental impact is not minimal: e.g., roads, toxic spills, oil wells, air strips in North Slope fields
- Severe pollution
- Oil recovered will last only a few years

From Article #4 **"Energizing America"** (Burns)

- Many want to decrease dependence on foreign oil, particularly since 9/11
- U.S. Geological Survey estimates only a 6-month supply of oil in ANWR, which will take 5 years to get
- Drilling will harm habitat and animals
- Better solutions: improve energy efficiency in homes and offices
- Use renewable energy sources
- Increase fuel efficiency in cars
- Pipeline and refineries would be terrorist target

2. Now, read your annotations and make a list of topics discussed in more than one source.
3. Finally, select from your list of recurring topics 2–4 paragraph ideas for a research-based paper. Present them in a grid, in an outline or flowchart, or on "tables" arranged in a conference hall, along with notations identifying the original sources.

Formulating the Central Claim

The central claim of an academic paper, variously referred to as the *thesis*, *solution*, or *conclusion*, is the main assertion you want readers to understand or accept. It is the statement that answers your research question. For most writers, the central claim goes through several drafts. The following tips can help you progress from a topic idea to a statement of central claim:

- **Write down your goal.** Once you have a sense of what you want to demonstrate to readers in your paper, write down your goal, even if at first it is vague and general. For example, a statement of purpose might initially be expressed like this: "*I want to show that skyrocketing tuition rates are a serious problem in society.*"
- **Revise your statement to reflect what your evidence shows.** As you read more sources, revise your central claim to reflect what the evidence demonstrates. This revision of scope and stance is not a single step but rather a recurring one; writers narrow, refocus, and revise their claims throughout the research and writing process. After finding that tuition increases do not affect all students equally, for example, you might limit the focus of your original statement: "*I want to show that skyrocketing tuition rates are a serious problem, particularly for students from low socioeconomic backgrounds.*"
- **Address the "so what?" question.** A good central claim and research topic have value to the audience. That value might be the topic's timeliness or its relevance to readers. You might take a unique approach to a well-known problem or draw attention to an issue largely ignored. To convey why rising tuition rates matter, we could revise our previous claim to read: "*Skyrocketing tuition rates deny students from poverty access to the means of escaping poverty.*"
- **Acknowledge alternative viewpoints.** As you research, you are likely to uncover conflicting evidence. Instead of ignoring exceptions or alternative viewpoints, acknowledge them by qualifying your central claim or expanding it to recognize other perspectives. The following claim promises a more complicated look at our issue: "*Although the reasons for*

skyrocketing tuition rates are myriad and complex, the effect for students who come from poverty is that they are denied access to a means of escaping that poverty." This version promises a more *nuanced discussion* of tuition rates, and it *previews the organization* of upcoming topics (causes before effects)—both desirable features in a central claim.

Your central claim should emerge *from* your reading and writing. Write the first draft of your purpose statement early to help you focus your goal, but expect your central claim to go through several iterations.

Categorizing Types of Central Claims

In many source-based synthesis papers, the central claim illustrates one of two types: claims that summarize the research on a given topic and claims that assert the writer's opinion. Some central claims do both.

Claims That Summarize the Published Research

The purpose of some synthesis papers is to review the research that's been done on a topic. But reviewers don't just summarize the findings of previous research, although that is one important goal. They also *interpret* or *analyze* those findings or the importance of the topic to readers. Here are two examples (9.2 and 9.3) of central claims from review essays in psychology:

EXAMPLE 9.2 FROM PSYCHOLOGY

This [paper] has several purposes: to document the various trajectories that the psychology of religion has had during the previous century, to explain some of the reasons for the trends that have been observed, to illustrate
5 how all of the topics within the psychology of religion are extensions of and feedback to the overall body of theory and the database from general psychology, and to sketch the newest lines of emerging research that show promise of contributing significantly to psychology during the next few years.

(Emmons and Paloutzian 378)

In addition to summarizing trends of the past century, the writers will "explain some of the reasons for the trends."

The writers will review the "newest lines" of research, research that could potentially contribute "significantly" to the field.

In this passage the writers preview the content of the paper to come, but they also convey the value of this content.

A similar move is seen in the next passage. Notice how the writers establish the value of their topic:

EXAMPLE 9.3 FROM PSYCHOLOGY

No one today disputes that the Internet is likely to have a significant impact on social life; but there remains substantial disagreement as to the nature and value of this impact. Several scholars have contended that Internet communication is an impoverished and sterile form of social exchange compared to traditional face-to-face interactions, and will therefore produce negative outcomes (loneliness and depression) for its users as well as weaken neighborhood and community ties. Media reporting of the effects of Internet use over the years has consistently emphasized this negative view (see McKenna & Bargh 2000) to the point that, as a result, a substantial minority of (mainly older) adults refuses to use the Internet at all (Hafner 2003). Others believe that the Internet affords a new and different avenue of social interaction that enables groups and relationships to form that otherwise would not be able to, thereby increasing and enhancing social connectivity. In this review, we examine the evidence bearing on these questions, both from contemporary research as well as the historical record.

(Bargh and McKenna 575)

The "significant impact" of the Internet is widely agreed upon, but how does the writer establish the need for further discussion?

What word(s) in this central claim indicate that the writers will do more than summarize what others have written on the topic?

The writers admit that the "significant impact" of the Internet is undeniable, but they explain why more discussion on the topic is needed.

Claims of Opinion or Value

In other synthesis papers, the central claim expresses an *opinion* that the writer will support with evidence from sources. The claim might be a prediction, an interpretation, a statement of value or worth, or a call for action. In the following paragraph, from literature, the writer's central claim is highlighted:

EXAMPLE 9.4 FROM LITERATURE

. . . Underlying the continuing failure to rethink the paradigms based largely on a (white) male canon is the assumption that men are more prone than women to tackle mighty themes, while women, conversely, are more prone to concentrate on private, domestic, and ultimately trivial matters—hence that women can safely be relegated to the margins of literary history. I will argue, however, that women writers produced some of the nineteenth century's most intellectually serious, politically radical, and artistically innovative prose.

(Karcher 781–82)

What wording indicates that this central claim expresses a judgment of worth or value?

In this example, the central claim asserts the writer's opinion.

The central claim in a synthesis paper need not be controversial, but it must be supportable—meaning that you can marshal evidence from sources to illustrate, explain, or defend it. You should also convey why your topic matters. (Additional examples of central claims appear on pp. 82–83 in chapter 3.)

Concept in Practice 9.2: Expressing the Central Claim

Return to the notes and paragraph ideas you developed in response to *Concept in Practice* 9.1. Using those ideas, compose a 1–2 sentence central claim (or thesis) for an essay on the topic of drilling for oil in ANWR. Your central claim might summarize what the sources say or express your opinion on the topic (an opinion you can support with the evidence provided). Either way, try to convey to readers what the organizational scheme of your essay will be and why the issue matters.

If you like, you can model your central claim after one of the following statements:

Central Claim that Summarizes Sources

No one today disputes that the Internet is likely to have a significant impact on social life; but there remains substantial disagreement as to the nature and value of this impact.

Central Claim that Expresses the Writer's Opinion

Women writers produced some of the nineteenth century's most intellectually serious, politically radical, and artistically innovative prose.

Drafting Your Paper

We have so far focused on how to plan a source-based synthesis paper. This section focuses on how to compose the actual paper.

Support Claims with Evidence

The familiar structure of claim-followed-by-evidence dominates in source-based synthesis writing. In Example 9.5 we can see this structure, from an article by Gary Wells and Elizabeth Olson about the reliability of eyewitness testimony. Notice that the sources the authors put into conversation with one another do not always agree:

EXAMPLE 9.5 STRUCTURE OF CLAIM-FOLLOWED-BY-EVIDENCE

One factor that can signal to eyewitnesses that a crime is occurring is the presence of a weapon. Unfortunately, learning that one is an eyewitness to a crime via the culprit's display of a weapon might not make the person a better eyewitness. A number of studies have been directed at the question of the so-called weapon-focus effect. A meta-analysis of these studies indicates that the presence of a weapon reduces the chances that the eyewitness can identify the holder of the weapon (Steblay 1992). Loftus et al. (1987) monitored eyewitnesses's eye movements and found that weapons draw visual attention away from other things such as the culprit's face. Complicating the issue somewhat is the fact that the presence of weapons or other types of threatening stimuli can cause arousal, fear, and emotional stress. The effects of such stress on memory are still being debated. Some research shows that increased levels of violence in filmed events reduces eyewitness identification accuracy (e.g., Clifford & Hollin 1981) whereas other research has failed to find this effect (e.g., Cutler et al. 1987). Deffenbacher (1983) suggested that the effect is likely to follow the Yerkes-Dodson Law where only very high and very low levels of arousal will impair memory. Christianson's (1992) review of the evidence relating emotional stress to memory suggests that emotional events receive preferential processing; emotional response causes a narrowing of attention (as suggested by Easterbrook 1959) with loss of peripheral details.

(Wells and Olson 282)

What claim is the writer making here?

Evidence from sources is introduced. What does this evidence support?

Another claim is made. What is it?

What kind of evidence does the writer provide to support the claim?

As illustrated in this paragraph, when academic writers provide evidence for claims, they include details. Chapter 3 describes the types of details you may want to include when citing evidence, such as how many people participated in a study, how estimates were derived, or how research was conducted. Give readers reason to trust your evidence.

Write an Original Argument

Creating an original argument may seem a daunting task, and it does require time and effort, as student Angelica Nava explains:

> The overall most challenging aspect of my research was using what others had to say about [my topic] to help ME say what I wanted to say. To learn how to take what the people in scholarly texts were saying about the topics I was interested in and use what they were saying to develop my own ideas and more importantly answer my questions. It took a lot of reading and draft work on my part. . . . (original emphasis)

But writing an original argument seems less daunting once you understand what your professors mean by the terms *original* and *argument*. In academic writing, a successful argument is one that gets others to see the writer's position as reasonable. Being "original" doesn't require saying something never said before or making a point not made by your sources. It only means that you do more than repeat verbatim what sources say. "Although you may think that as a first year undergrad you aren't able to respond to scholarly texts," notes Nava, "you are."

Initially, you may feel like you have nothing to add to the conversation. But keep reading, keep writing, keep thinking about what your sources say and *respond* to their arguments. Your response, as Elise Hancock, a science writer, explains, will be unique to you:

> There is no one else who sees the world or uses the language precisely as you do. Nor has anyone else done precisely the . . . research and thinking you have done. So relax. Save all your energy for understanding the subject, and as you write, keep asking yourself, "What am I really trying to say?" Then say it. The result will be original. (7)

Because your selection of, response to, and orchestration of sources will be unlike anyone else's examination of the issue, your argument will be "original."

Use Additional Features of Good Synthesis Writing

In addition to making your synthesis paper convincing and original, strive to make the final draft clear and easy to follow. The following features will help you to convey your ideas effectively.

- *Summary Sentences.* Use summary sentences to identify the relationship between sources and place their comments into a larger context. Here is an example from a paragraph found earlier in this chapter:

  Many college educators have noted that high school work is significantly different from college work.

  In another situation, synthesis writing might be introduced with phrases like these:

  Although some educators think X, others advocate Y . . .
  Educators vary in their approaches to the problem of . . .

- *Transitions between Sources.* Coordinate the conversation between sources—use names and transitions to distinguish one source from another.
- *Summaries and Paraphrases.* Make your voice the dominant voice. To ensure that readers hear your voice in your synthesis papers, try to summarize or paraphrase sources, instead of quoting them, and write

the first draft without your sources in front of you. (See chapter 8 for advice on summarizing and paraphrasing sources.)

- *Connections between Sources.* Contribute to the conversation. Make connections between sources by commenting on what sources say and by using what they say to make your own original argument.

Synthesizing Source Material Using MLA Format

The following essay is an example of synthesis writing documented in MLA format. The author, Pablo Lopez, was asked to write an essay about academic literacy for his first-year composition course. His audience was other first-year students. As you read the essay, notice how Lopez synthesizes information from sources and contributes to the conversation.

J. Pablo Lopez
April 15, 2012
English 101

Critical Reading and Academic Writing
for First-Year College Students

English Professor Catherine A. Wambach gave an 80 item survey to 132 faculty who teach first and second year college level courses at the University of Minnesota. She wanted to find out the expectations about reading and writing skills the professors have for the students attending their class. Overall, 73% of instructors said they expect students to have critical reading skills. In addition, when it comes to student writing, the substance and quality of thinking in the writing are more important to professors than having no surface errors (23–24). But what are these critical reading skills and what makes an essay have "substance" or demonstrate "quality thinking"? For students, the task of writing an essay can cause a lot of anxiety. But there are ways we can make this process a lot less nerve wracking. Adopting strategies academic readers and writers use could be a start.

What claim is the writer hoping to establish with these results from a survey about critical reading and writing skills? (See chapter 6 for discussion of how to use previous research to introduce your essay topic.)

What essay topics does the central claim preview? Why should readers care about the topics?

First, let's take a look at what researchers say about student reading. The news isn't good. Sociology instructors Judith C. Roberts and Keith A. Roberts cite a survey of 155,000 college students from 470 schools that suggests as many as 80% of students spend an hour or less studying for each hour of class. This includes writing, studying and reading time (126). The Alliance for Excellent Education from Washington DC, a non-profit organization, has pointed out that approximately 25 percent of all high school students read below the basic level (cited in Horning). Other research indicates that only 40 percent of students in introductory sociology courses always or usually read their textbook assignments (Roberts and Roberts 127). Many students said that they find their texts too difficult to read or they had no understanding of them (131).

How does this topic sentence prepare readers for synthesis writing? What sources does the writer cite for evidence?

But both Roberts and Roberts and English Professor Alice Horning have suggested some strategies to make reading more efficient. First, developing an interest for the material is crucial as is realizing the importance of the text being read. A second strategy is curiosity; if the student asks the question of why is this important to current issues, he or she will be engaged more. A third strategy is for students to connect the text being read to their own lives: if they can find an emotional connection or can relate it to a past experience, it becomes stimulating and more interesting (Roberts and Roberts 130). Connecting the text to other materials or "synthesizing" is also important for the reader in order to back up his or her argument or to begin creating an argument. Horning pointed out that if students can stay away from simple reading of a text, to connecting, analyzing and evaluating the text, they will become better readers (Horning). Every time you read a piece, like this essay, experts advise that the reader asks some questions. For example, what are the important ideas about this essay? Do you agree with them? How can you use the strategies or relate the reading strategies to your own? These questions illustrate the strategies mentioned above.

How does the writer contribute to the conversation later in this paragraph?

In addition to reading, essay writing is an important communication skill in college. In order

This topic sentence introduces a third claim. How does the writer connect this paragraph to the previous paragraphs?

to move from writing just our opinion, we must learn to use strategies to provide good reasons to support our interpretations. English professor L. Lennie Irvin refers to a study conducted at George Mason University, where they asked professors what academic writing was. The majority of professors said that academic writing is an argument (7). Irvin suggests that academic writing resembles an argument between two people who might not have the same opinions, but both desire a better understanding of the subject being discussed (9–10). It is a dialogue. How can you engage readers in a dialogue? One way suggested by English professor Ken Hyland is by asking questions or getting readers to create their own questions as they read. Hyland performed an analysis of a 1.8 million word corpus of research articles, textbooks and student essays. He found that the use of questions in academic writing can help express the writer's purpose and set up claims (529). Based on his analysis, Hyland suggested some strategies for your writing. One is to frame the discourse, that is, to set up the reader in the beginning with a set of questions or question, which will eventually be explored in the paragraphs to come. Ask questions that challenge the reader to think about the issue (540–48). Another strategy Hyland pointed out was to point forward, that is to ask additional questions that will address the gap in the research or raise unresolved issues (552). For example, what other factors damaging students' success are not addressed in this essay? What is being done to fix the gap?

How do these sentences connect what Irvin says (about academic arguments involving a writer and reader who disagree) to what Hyland (next) discusses?

Why does the writer ask these rhetorical questions at this point in the essay?

Use of these strategies can improve a student's reading proficiency and essay writing. Knowing what you need to do won't guarantee you a perfect grade, but having the right orientation towards the writing or reading assignment is an important step in your success as a college writer.

To match the citation style used in the essay, the writer's bibliography is in MLA format.

Works Cited

Horning, Alice S. "Reading across the Curriculum as the Key to Student Success." *Across the Disciplines: A Journal of Language, Learning, and Academic Writing* 4 (1997). Web. 10 Apr. 2012.

Hyland, Ken. "What Do They Mean? Questions in Academic Writing." *Text* 22.4 (2002): 529–57. Print.

Irvin, L. Lennie. "What Is Academic Writing?" *Writing Spaces: Readings on Writing*. Ed. Charles Lowe and Pavel Zemliansky. Vol. 1. West Lafayette: Parlor, 2010. 3–17. Web. 12 Apr. 2012.

Roberts, Judith C., and Keith A. Roberts. "Deep Reading, Cost/Benefit, and the Construction of Meaning: Enhancing Reading Comprehension and Deep Learning in Sociology Courses." *Teaching Sociology* 36.2 (2008): 125–40. Print.

Wambach, Catherine A. "Reading and Writing Expectations at a Research University." *Journal of Developmental Education* 22.2 (1998): 22–26. *Academic Search Premier*. Web. 9 Apr. 2012.

This essay includes many features of effective synthesis writing. (1) The topic is of value to the audience: First-year students need strategies for reading and writing in college. (2) There is a clear structure: The main ideas are previewed in the central claim and summary sentences introduce the details in each paragraph. (3) There is a logical organization of ideas: Before suggesting strategies for reading, the writer establishes the *need* for improved reading skills. Because reading generally precedes writing, writing is discussed last.

Synthesizing Source Material Using APA Format

The essay in the previous section is documented in MLA style, as are many papers written for humanities courses. As you'll recall from chapter 8, however, MLA is only one style of documentation. The following paragraph, from Wells and Olson's review of research on the reliability of eyewitness identification, is documented in APA style. Notice that no descriptive phrases identify the authors cited, and publication dates are provided instead of page numbers:

> Simple disguises, even those as minor as covering the hair, result in significant impairment of eyewitness identification (Cutler et al. 1987). Sunglasses also impair identification, although the degree of impairment can be reduced by having the targets wear sunglasses at the time of the recognition

> test (Hockley et al. 1999). Photos of criminal suspects used in police lineups are sometimes several years old. Changes in appearance that occur naturally over time and changes that are made intentionally by suspects can have quite strong effects on recognition. Read et al. (1990) found that photos of the same people taken two years apart were less likely to be recognized as the same people when their appearance had naturally changed (via aging, facial hair) than when their appearance had remained largely the same.
>
> (Wells and Olson 281)

Although the writers of this paragraph chose not to emphasize the credentials of their sources of information, they are still careful to distinguish one voice from another in the conversation.

Applying the Concepts to Reading: *Reading a Source-Based Proposal Documented in APA Format*

Your first-year composition course is likely to be only one of many courses for which you write source-based synthesis papers. The following research-based proposal, by Daniel Parr, was written for a management communications course.

Students in the course were asked to propose a way to improve productivity at a company that they invent for the assignment. Their audience is the company CEO. The company Parr invented for the assignment, Parr Services, Inc., provides project and construction management services. In his proposal, Parr recommends that the company improve the office lighting.

As you read the proposal, consider the following questions:

1. In most business writing, writers make their purpose immediately clear. How does Parr accomplish this in his proposal?
2. Find paragraphs in the proposal that follow the claims-followed-by-evidence structure. What kinds of evidence are used to support claims? In what ways does Parr make the evidence convincing to readers? In what additional ways does Parr create a favorable ethos for himself?
3. In APA-documented papers, writers often cite sources without explaining who those sources are. However, given this proposal's audience and purpose, why is it appropriate that credentials for many of the sources of information are included?

Office Lighting Proposal

This proposal provides background on employee productivity and discusses current employee workplace concerns. This proposal recommends improving staff morale and productivity by improving overall office lighting and allowing more individual control of employee's workspace lighting.

It's been established that light and the lack thereof can have an adverse reaction on an individual. Craig DiLouie (2003), principal of ZING Communications (www.zinginc.com), a marketing communications and consulting firm, and the proprietor of Searchspec.com (www.searchspec.com), a lighting product search engine, states that light can psychologically change our mood or affect us physiologically. Light, quite literally, allows us to see. Different lighting can create different perception, and our perception becomes our reality. Since Americans spend approximately 80 percent of their day indoors, it is important to create a workplace where employees feel job satisfaction and are motivated to be productive.

Company Background

Metrics during the company's first 10 years of business (1997–2007) have shown overall employee morale to be very good. Parr Services, Inc., has earned a good reputation and has maintained low turnover in the first decade of operations. However, changes in office spaces, and the recent economic downturn, have impacted our business in several challenging ways. In the last 6 years there has been an increase in employee turnover, and the results of an independent assessment have shown a decrease in morale and employee productivity. This assessment showed that workspace lighting was one of the top employee complaints.

Literature Review

The following two studies demonstrated the positive and negative effects of various lighting configurations and employees' ability to control their workspace lighting. The studies also discuss the potential energy savings and increased productivity and morale discovered as a result of modified and improved lighting.

In 2010, researchers from the University School of Planning, Design, and Construction at Michigan State University studied the results of an improvement in the indoor environment quality (IEQ) and its effects on absenteeism.

Two different studies were performed in Lansing, Michigan, where employees moved from older more conventional offices to higher IEQ offices holding high Leadership in Energy and Environmental Design (LEED) ratings. LEED ratings include review of green building categories such as site sustainability, energy efficiency, materials and resources used, and indoor environmental quality. In both studies, employees were given Web-based pre-move and post-move surveys. In study one, 33 out of the 56 employees responded to the pre-move survey and 32 out of 56 for the post-move survey. In study two, 142 out of 207 responded to the pre-move, and 113 responded to the post-move survey. The mean number of work hours per month that employees self-reported missing work due to depression and stress on the pre-move survey was 20.21, as opposed to only 14.06 hours of missed work per month on the post-move survey. On the pre-move survey the mean perceived productivity was −.80%, and a +2.18% perceived productivity increase was reported on the post-move survey. The researchers admit that a temporary bias could have been formed from employees' excitement about their new work environment. In general, however, the research suggests significant reduction in employee absenteeism and unproductive work hours as an outcome of perceived improvements to the employee's workplace health and well-being (Singh, Syal, Grady, & Korkmaz 2010).

In a different study, researchers investigated providing employees with different light and workplace environment controls. Gary Newsham (2009) and fellow researchers with the National Research Council Canada—Institute for Research in Construction had 126 study participants spend the day in a standard size office lab, performing normal office tasks and completing questionnaires describing the experiences. Some of the participants had constant-on lighting conditions, while others were given control of light dimming at their workstations. Participants who were given control of some aspect of their lighting (ceiling recessed parabolic fixtures, desk lamp, direct/indirect luminaires, etc.) used about 10% less lighting energy, compared to those that did not. In addition, 90% of participants whose workstations had individual use control options rated their workplaces as comfortable and showed more continued motivation over the course of the day. Researchers also had participants perform other cognitive trials like solving anagrams, typing and retyping a set text, and suggesting uses for everyday objects when presented with pictures of said objects. The results suggest that ability to cognitively reason after long periods of time and stay productive is linked to a lighted environment that helps to motivate. The limited number of participant responses could be a weakness to the study, but the findings suggest that overall environmental satisfaction can equate to job satisfaction. Job satisfaction can help keep turnover low and productivity up.

Proposal for Parr Services, Inc.

This report proposes a modification to the office lighting for Parr Services, Inc. Based on the above literature review, this change could contribute to increasing employee motivation, productivity, and staff retention while actually helping lower electricity costs and operating overhead.

New Light Bulbs and Light System Design

It is proposed to change out the existing fluorescent T12 bulbs that abound in most offices and hallways with more energy efficient T8 or T5 bulbs. The Department of Energy announced new Lumen per Watt (LPW) regulations for linear fluorescent bulbs that were implemented in July of 2012. This phase out involves replacing old T12 bulbs with magnetic ballasts, and installing new efficient T8 or T5 bulbs with electronic ballasts (GE Lighting 2012). As older replacement T12 bulbs become more scarce and expensive, this changeover will begin to become a necessity. The LPW legislation will also phase out incandescent room or task lighting, starting with 100-watt bulbs in 2012, 75-watt bulbs in 2013, and 40-watt and 60-watt in 2014.

New design systems should also be looked at as well. Our current lighting systems should be reviewed for luminance (intensity of light on a surface), glare, and spectrum of light. According to William J. Fisk (2000), with the Environmental Energy Technologies Division of Lawrence Berkeley National Laboratory, ". . . Lensed-indirect and parabolic down lighting supported reading and writing on paper and on the computer screen better than a recessed lighting system with translucent prismatic diffusers" (p. 555). Electronic ballasts have less flickering than old magnetic ballasts as well, resulting in improvements in what Fisk calls "verbal-intellectual task performance" (p. 555). Employees should also be allowed to have input on the spectrum of light in their workspaces, as natural light type bulbs or grow light bulbs for plants can help with the satisfaction of employees, including those with Seasonal Affective Disorder (SAD).

Demand Response Upgrades and Dimmer Installations

The second phase of the proposal includes installing demand response setback and dimmer switches. Above mentioned research has shown that employees with dimming control were happier with their work environment and maintained motivation while improving attention to work tasks (DiLouie 2003). This coupled with night and evening demand response (DR) setback switches will have a definite positive impact on continued operating costs. DR switches have been shown to be a cost effective way to keep the lights off if employees are not in their office during long meetings, nights, and weekends.

Constraints

Unlike many other employee productivity solutions, upgrading office lighting and DR/dimmer switches has few constraints. With older bulbs already being phased out by the LPW regulations, bulb and corresponding ballast upgrades are a necessary measure. They have also been shown to reduce annual overhead operating costs with combined energy savings from the reduced wattage of the bulb and reduced hours on with dimmer switches and demand response setbacks (General Electric 2012). This coupled with the opportunity to increase employee productivity while improving the work place environment makes for a good return on investment. Proposed lighting system upgrades and switch installations such as these carry a low risk yet high viability.

The Next Steps for Parr Services, Inc.

The next steps include employee surveys, to determine the prevailing opinion on preferred light system components and fixtures, as well as desired access to control and dimmer settings. A walkthrough of all office buildings and turn around field offices should be arranged to assess the current state of workplace lighting. An implementation plan should then be developed to outline milestone dates and responsible parties for implementation. A definitized scope needs to be established to develop good cost estimates and define what changes are in scope and which are not. Current meter data should be recorded for comparison to electrical usage after implementation. Finally, these installations should be scheduled and executed when there is as little disturbance and impact to employee work in progress as possible.

Conclusion

This proposal provides concrete ways to implement office space lighting modifications that could contribute to overall employee productiveness and well-being, while bringing down overhead operating costs. This is the win-win scenario this company has been looking for.

References

DiLouie, C. (2003). Lighting and productivity: Missing link found. *Architectural Lighting, 18*(6), 39–42.

Fisk, W. J. (2000). Health and productivity gains from better indoor environments and their relationship with building energy efficiency. *Annual Review of Energy and the Environment, 25*, 537–566.

GE Lighting. (2012). *Facts about the Incandescent Light Bulb Law.* Retrieved from http://www.gelighting.com/LightingWeb/na/consumer/inspire-and-learn/lighting-legislation/

Newsham, G. et al. (2009). Control strategies for lighting and ventilation in offices: Effects on energy and occupants. *Intelligent Buildings International, 1*(2), 101–121.

Singh, A., Syal, M., Grady, S. C., & Korkmaz, S. (2010). Effects of green buildings on employee health and productivity. *American Journal of Public Health, 100* (9), 1665–1668.

Applying the Concepts to Writing: *Synthesizing Information from Sources*

Your goal when synthesizing is to integrate information from sources into paragraphs, rather than writing a series of article summaries. Review Kirk Kidwell's article "Understanding the College First-year Experience," in chapter 1, and read "An Interview with Deanna Kuhn," at the end of this chapter, specifically the response to this question: "Where does metacognition fit into this discussion of thinking and meaning?" Then, using information from both authors, explain the stages of cognitive development, making clear throughout your discussion what information is from Kidwell and what information is from Kuhn. Provide summary topic sentences at the beginning of paragraphs and cite page numbers in parentheses. Contribute to the conversation by making connections between the sources and by commenting on what they say.

Paired Readings from Psychology

Excerpt from "An Interview with Deanna Kuhn," *Educational Psychology Review* MICHAEL E. SHAUGHNESSY

The following readings feature Deanna Kuhn, a professor of psychology and education at Columbia University. The first reading is from an interview with Kuhn conducted by Michael Shaughnessy for *Educational Psychology Review*, a peer-reviewed journal that publishes articles of interest to psychology teachers. In this excerpt, Kuhn argues that analysis, inquiry, and argument are among the most important skills schools develop in children, but they are skills that depend on getting students to value thinking and reasoning. The interview was published in 2004.

[Shaughnessy] *Do values have a place in education?*

[Kuhn] Yes, in my view a critical one. Although students must have not only the skills and the opportunities available to engage intellectually, it is equally essential that they develop the belief that it is worthwhile to do so. Such beliefs can be borne only out of their own experience. This is a case in which discovery is the only viable learning method.

One thing is certain, students make *some* sense of the school life that absorbs so much of their time. They figure out what is going on. The danger is that the meaning that gets constructed may end up being quite different from what educators would like it to be. Students' concepts about these matters are likely to play a critical role in what they take away from the many hours they spend in classrooms. If students cannot answer the question, "Why would one want or need to know this?" they will find it difficult to direct more than superficial attention to what is being taught. In such cases, there is little likelihood that what is taught will ever be accessed outside the immediate classroom context or connected to anything else the student knows, and hence will quickly be forgotten.

Therefore, students must buy into the idea of school if it is to have a chance of achieving its objectives. The goal, at the very least, should be to enlist students as partners in their own education. They need to become convinced that education is not wasting their time. They must see how and why what they are doing makes sense and understand where it leads. What we ask students to do tells them what we as adults would like them to believe is worth doing. What we ask students to learn tells them what we want them to believe is worth knowing. It follows that we ought to be careful about what we ask students to do or learn.

I recently asked Robbie, a 10th grader at an outstanding suburban high school, what use his current schoolwork would be to him in his adult life. He hesitantly mentioned writing skills, which his school emphasizes, but then had a sudden insight: "Oh, and Latin will help me on my SATs." When I clarified that I was talking about his adult life after he completed his schooling, he could come up with nothing further. Mike, a 9th grader from the same school, said he did not see his studies being of any later use "unless you just want to have facts to make yourself look good in a conversation. Like now we're studying the Ming dynasty; why else would you need to know this?"

Students like Robbie and Mike have grown up in privileged families and communities in which the future benefits of education—both prestige and material gain—have long and consistently been made clear to them. Their responses quoted above suggest it is not clear to them exactly why education is so important, but this probably does not worry them much. Should it worry us? These boys are clearly "college bound." At this stage in their lives, do they need to be aware of any more exalted purpose to what they are doing? Unlike many of their less privileged counterparts, they at least see school as conferring *some* benefit. Can believing that school is a path to success be such a bad thing for students of any age or social background?

Yet there arguably is a downside. The problem is that the relation between school and life is essentially an instrumental one: Investment and outcome—means and end—bear only an arbitrary connection. There is no intrinsic logic as to why intellectual pursuits (rather than, say, athletic or musical accomplishment) should be the object of society's approval and reward. Any of these could as well serve as the means to the desired end of social recognition and reward. Whether it is intellectual activity, then, or some other activity, its value derives from its role in a means–end relationship that is arbitrary. Here lies the downside. Once an activity becomes identified as merely a means to an end, it becomes easy to devalue it as without significance in its own right. One undertakes it because it produces some unrelated but valued dividend.

The value of an intrinsically valued activity, in contrast, lies in the activity itself. The benefits of the activity emanate directly from it. One engages in it because it is experienced as valuable in its own right. The advantage is clear: continued commitment to the activity is ensured. It is not dependent on external maintenance of a causal connection between the activity and some other valued outcome.

This criterion brings us back to inquiry and argument as the kinds of activities that students can find immediately meaningful. They can make sense of the activities as they are engaged in them. But students must do the meaning-making work. It is only their own experiences that will lead students to believe that inquiry and argument offer the most promising path to deciding between competing claims, resolving conflicts, solving problems, and achieving goals. They must become convinced that analysis is worthwhile and that unexamined beliefs are not worth having. These are intellectual values, complementary to but distinct from intellectual skills.

[Shaughnessy] *Where does metacognition fit into this discussion of thinking and meaning?*

[Kuhn] Being concerned about students making meaning out of what they do implies being attentive to their metacognitive functioning—their understanding, management, and valuing of their own thought. Metacognition originates early in life, when children first become aware of their own and others' minds. But like many other intellectual skills, metacognitive skills typically do not develop to the level desired.

One way of supporting metacognitive development is to encourage students to reflect on and evaluate their activities. Doing so should heighten interest in the purpose of these activities. "Why are we doing this? What was gained from having done it?" Questions such as these are less likely to arise when activity is imposed by authority figures without negotiation and especially when the activities serve as occasions for evaluating students' standing relative to one another—a function that so often steals attention away from any other objective.

Another source of metacognitive development is the interiorization that both Vygotksy and Piaget talked about, which occurs when forms that are originally social become covert within the individual. If students participate in discourse in which they are frequently asked, "How do you know?" or "What makes you say that?" they become more likely to pose such questions to themselves. Eventually, we hope, they interiorize the structure of argument as a framework for much of their own individual thinking. They think in terms of issues or claims, with facts summoned in their service, rather than the reverse—storing up facts with the idea that some conclusion may emerge from them.

Metacognitive functions can be procedural or declarative. The former invokes awareness and management of one's own thinking. The latter involves one's broader understanding of thinking and knowing in general. It has been studied under the heading of epistemological understanding. Like thinking itself, the understanding of thinking undergoes development. The study of students' developing epistemological understanding has blossomed in the last decade. We now have a fairly convergent picture of the steps that mark development toward more mature epistemological understanding in the years from early childhood to adulthood.

Preschool age children are *realists*. They regard what one knows as an immediate reading of reality. Beliefs are faithful copies of reality. They are received directly from the external world rather than constructed by the knower. Hence, there are no inaccurate renderings of events, nor any possibility of conflicting beliefs, because everyone is perceiving the same external reality. Minds provide everyone the same pictures of reality.

Not until about age 4 does a knower begin to emerge in children's conceptions of knowing. Children become aware that mental representations, as products of the human mind, do not necessarily duplicate external reality. Before children achieve the concept of false belief, they are unwilling to attribute to another person a belief that they themselves know to be false. Once they attain this understanding, the knower, and knowledge as mental representations produced by knowers, come to life. The products of knowing, however, are still more firmly attached to the known object than to the knower. Hence, although inadequate or incorrect information can produce false beliefs, these are easily correctable by reference to an external reality—the known object. If you and I disagree, one of us is right and one is wrong and resolving the matter is simply a matter of finding out which is which. At this *absolutist* level of epistemological understanding, knowledge is an accumulating body of certain facts.

Further progress in epistemological understanding can be characterized as an extended task of coordinating the subjective with the objective elements of knowing. At the realist and absolutist levels, the objective dominates. By adolescence typically comes the likelihood of a radical change in epistemological understanding. In a word, everyone now becomes right. The discovery that reasonable people—even experts—disagree is the most likely source of recognizing the uncertain, subjective aspect of knowing. This recognition initially assumes such proportions, however, that it eclipses recognition of any objective standard that could serve as a basis for evaluating conflicting claims. Adolescents typically fall into what Michael Chandler has called "a poisoned well of doubt," and they fall hard and deep. At this *multiplist* (sometimes called *relativist*) level of epistemological understanding, knowledge consists not of facts but of opinions, freely chosen by their holders as personal possessions and accordingly not open to challenge. Knowledge is now clearly seen as emanating from knowers, rather than the known, but at the significant cost of any discriminability among competing knowledge claims. Indeed, this lack of discriminability is equated with tolerance: because everyone has a right to their opinion, all opinions are equally right. That ubiquitous slogan of adolescence—"whatever"—holds sway.

Evidence suggests that hoisting oneself out of the "whatever" well of multiplicity and indiscriminability is achieved at much greater effort than the quick and easy fall into its depths. Many adults remain absolutists or multiplists for life. Yet, by adulthood, many, though by no means all, adolescents will have reintegrated the objective dimension of knowing to achieve the understanding that although everyone has a right to their opinion, some opinions are in fact more right than others, to the extent they are better supported by argument and evidence. Justification for a belief becomes more than personal preference. "Whatever" is no longer the automatic response to any assertion—there are now legitimate discriminations and choices to be made. Rather than facts or opinions, knowledge at this *evaluativist* level of epistemological understanding consists of judgments, which require support in a framework of alternatives, evidence, and argument. An evaluativist epistemology provides the intellectual basis for judging one idea as better than another, a basis more powerful than mere personal preference.

[Shaughnessy] *What are the educational implications of this development in epistemological understanding?*

[Kuhn] The development of mature epistemological understanding cannot by itself yield the sort of intellectual valuing I emphasized earlier. Values have an affective, as well as cognitive, component. But the cognitive evolution just described is a necessary condition for the development of intellectual values. Adolescents who never progress beyond the absolutist belief in certain knowledge, or the multiplist's equation of knowledge with personal preference, lack a reason to engage in sustained intellectual inquiry. If facts can be ascertained with certainty and are readily available to anyone who seeks them, as the absolutist understands, or if any claim is as valid as any other, as the multiplist understands, there is little point of expending the mental effort that the evaluation of claims entails. Only at the evaluativist level are thinking and reason recognized as essential support for beliefs and actions. Thinking is the process that enables us to make informed choices between conflicting claims. Understanding this leads one to value thinking and to be willing to expend the effort that it entails.

In my research on intellectual values, I have found striking differences across cultural groups and subcultural groups within the United States in the responses of parents and children to several questions like this one:

> Many social issues, like the death penalty, gun control, or medical care, are pretty much matters of personal opinion, and there is no basis for saying that one person's opinion is any better than another's. So there's not much point in people having discussions about these kinds of issues. Do you strongly agree, sort of agree, or disagree?

Reasons respondents offer for disagreement are similar and refer to values of discussion in enhancing individual and/or collective understanding, solving problems, and resolving conflicts. Reasons offered for agreement, however, tend to be of two distinct types. Some participants respond along these lines, suggestive of the multiplist level of epistemological understanding: "It's not worth it to discuss it because you're not going to get anywhere; everyone has a right to think what they want to." Others take this position, suggestive of the absolutist's equation of knowledge with right answers: "It's not worth it to discuss it because it's not something you can get a definite answer to."

Parents and children we have studied respond similarly to others within their culture or subculture, and variation across cultural groups is substantial. Middle schoolers and high schoolers in American ethnic subcultures, however, show some movement away from their parents' response patterns in the direction of those of their American peers. These results suggest that parents do matter in transmitting intellectual values to their children, but, at the same time, that children to a significant degree construct these values anew in a context of their peer culture, especially when the values of the culture outside the home deviate from those within the home.

In seeking to develop the intellectual values of students in the American education system, we need to be aware that we are swimming against a cultural tide. The implicit message underlying the constant reports of pollsters on every conceivable topic is that we are much more interested in what people think than why they think it. The message is not lost on adolescents, who are much more likely to be asked to express their opinions than to support them. To *have* an opinion is all that is needed, and the stronger the better. No teen wants to be seen as straddling a fence. It is easy to see thinking, much less arguing, as beside the point—"live and let live" and "to each his own." Tolerance readily eclipses judgment. To avoid the risk of being judgmental, we must not judge at all. These attitudes are, of course, well-supported by the multiplist epistemological stance.

Yet can we really be critical of tolerance? The more, the better, we have been led to believe. Tolerance can only make the world a better place. It is fundamental to a democratic society—is it not?—ensuring that basic freedoms, including those of what to think, are protected.

There is in fact a downside to tolerance. It has two parts. When tolerance is equated with equal merit of all claims, the ability and disposition to make discriminations—to think critically—is undermined. If any claim is as valid as any other, as the multiplist understands, there is little point to expending the mental effort that evaluation of claims entails.

Second, tolerance can translate into a willingness to listen to another's view, but not to engage it. Once respective views are articulated, the inclination is to end conversation with the conclusion, "Well, I guess we disagree—to each his own." The disinclination to continue is partly one of being reluctant to invest the intellectual energy that discourse requires, but even more one of fearing that to criticize another's argument would be injurious. The argument and the person are not distinguished, leaving injury to one tantamount to injury to the other. Therefore, better to let things be, "to live and let live." If people are going to discuss sensitive topics, indeed any topics at all, they feel most comfortable doing so with other like-minded people. This tendency, paradoxically, ends up leading in a direction that is the opposite of tolerance.

Can our education system muster the strength and the vision to function as a force against cultural shallowness? Can it help students see the value of engaging another's ideas and understand that addressing these ideas critically can be more respectful of the person than ignoring them? Only, I predict, if our educational system is sure of its goals. Yet even with the noblest and most articulate goals, educators must recognize the importance of teachers, parents, and other adults as role models of the practices and values we want education to promote. Leon Botstein observes that parents all claim to want better schools for their children, but these parents most often do not live lives that demonstrate a respect for education and knowledge. In the end, we can only promote the development of intellectual values in students to the extent that the communities and broader culture they are growing up in reflect these values.

REFERENCES

Kuhn, D. (1991). *The Skills of Argument,* Cambridge University Press, New York.

Kuhn, D. (1993). Science as argument: Implications for teaching and learning scientific thinking. *Sci. Educ.* 77(3): 319–337.

Kuhn, D. (1995). Microgenetic study of change: What has it told us? *Psychol. Sci.* 6: 133–139.

Kuhn, D. (1999). A developmental model of critical thinking. *Educ. Res.* 28: 16–25.

Kuhn, D. (1999). Metacognitive development. In Balter, L., and Tamis Le-Monda, C. (eds.), *Child Psychology: A Handbook of Contemporary Issues,* Philadelphia, Psychology Press, pp. 259–286.

Kuhn, D. (2000) Theory of mind, metacognition and reasoning. In Mitchell, P., and Riggs, K. (eds.), *Children's Reasoning and the Mind,* Psychology Press, Hove UK, pp. 301–326.

Kuhn, D. (2002). What is scientific thinking and how does it develop? In Goswami, U. (ed.), *Handbook of Childhood Cognitive Development,* Blackwell, Oxford, pp. 371–393.

Kuhn, D. (in press). *Education for Thinking,* Harvard University Press, Cambridge MA.

Kuhn, D., Amsel, E., and O'Loughlin, M. (1988). *The Development of Scientific Thinking Skills,* Academic Press, San Diego, CA.

Kuhn, D., Cheney, R., and Weinstock, M. (2000). The development of epistemological understanding. *Cogn. Dev.* 15: 309–328.

Kuhn, D., Garcia-Mila, M., Zohar, A., and Andersen, C. (1995). *Strategies of knowledge acquisition* (with commentaries by White, S., Klahr, D., and Carver, S.). *Soc. Res. Child Dev. Monogr.* 60(4): Serial no. 245.

Felton, M., and Kuhn, D. (2001). The development of argumentive discourse skills. *Discourse Process.* 32: 135–153.

Kuhn, D., and Lao, J. (1998). Contemplation and conceptual change: Integrating perspectives from cognitive and social psychology. *Dev. Rev.* 18: 125–154.

Kuhn, D., and Phelps, E. (1982). The development of problem-solving strategies. In Reese, H. (ed.), *Advances in Child Development and Behavior, Vol. 17.,* Academic Press, New York, pp. 1–46.

Kuhn, D., Shaw, V., and Felton, M. (1997). Effects of dyadic interaction on argumentive reasoning. *Cogn. Instruct.* 15: 287–315.

Kuhn, D., Weinstock, M., and Flaton, R. (1994). Historical reasoning as theory–evidence coordination. In Carretero, M., and Voss, J. (eds.), *Cognitive and Instructional Processes in History and the Social Sciences,* Erlbaum, Hillsdale, NJ.

QUESTIONS ABOUT MEANING

1. What is metacognition and how can educators encourage it in their students?
2. Describe the following stages in cognitive evolution: realists, absolutists, multiplists (relativists), evaluativists.
3. What cultural attitudes today make it difficult for American students to move beyond the relativist stage? According to Kuhn, what is the "downside" of tolerance?

QUESTIONS FOR RHETORICAL ANALYSIS

4. Who is the intended audience Kuhn is addressing? How is this made clear in her responses?
5. Would you say Kuhn originally responded to the interview questions in writing or in a face-to-face interview? On what evidence do you base your conclusion?
6. Do Kuhn's responses demonstrate what she advocates: analysis, inquiry, and evidence-supported claims?

"Jumping to Conclusions," *Scientific American Mind* DEANNA KUHN

As you know from her interview for *Educational Psychology Review*, psychology education professor Deanna Kuhn regards inquiry, argument, and analysis as vital skills. In "Jumping to Conclusions," Kuhn describes research she conducted with one of her students to determine whether or not people can be "counted on to make sound judgments." Her findings were published in 2007 in *Scientific American Mind*, a magazine that makes psychology and neuroscience research accessible to the general public.

A four-year-old watches as a monkey hand puppet approaches a vase containing a red and a blue plastic flower. The monkey sneezes. The monkey backs away, returns to sniff again, and again sneezes. An adult then removes the red flower and replaces it with a yellow one. The monkey comes up to smell the yellow and blue flowers twice and each time sneezes. The adult next replaces the blue flower with the red one. The monkey comes up to smell the red and yellow flowers and this time does not sneeze.

The child is then asked, "Can you give me the flower that makes Monkey sneeze?" When psychologists Laura E. Schulz and Alison Gopnik, both then at the University of California, Berkeley, did this experiment, 79 percent of four-year-olds correctly chose the blue flower. As their research makes clear, even very young children have begun to understand cause and effect. This process is critical to their ability to make sense of their world and to make their way in it.

With such powers of discernment already in place by age four, people should be highly skilled at identifying cause and effect—causal reasoning—by the time they are adults, shouldn't they? Indeed, a substantial body of contemporary research suggests that is the case, highlighting the nuanced judgments adults are capable of—such as making consistent estimates, across different circumstances, of the numerical probabilities that two events are causally related.

Here I present some evidence that gives a very different impression: the everyday causal reasoning of the average adult regarding familiar topics appears highly fallible. People connect two events as cause and effect based on little or no evidence, and they act on these judgments—they jump to conclusions. By learning more about precisely how they do so, researchers can develop ways to improve thinking. Such efforts could help educators in their mission to inspire solid, careful thinking in young minds.

A possible explanation for the discrepancy between our findings and much of the relevant literature is that researchers studying causal reasoning skills in adults have typically based their conclusions on studies of a narrow segment of the adult population in a specific context—college students in laboratory settings performing complex paper-and-pencil tasks. In a 2000 study, for example, psychologists Patricia Cheng of the University of California, Los Angeles, and Yunnwen Lien of the National Taiwan University in Taipei presented college students with a set of instances that described the blooming frequencies of plants that had been fed plant food of different shapes and colors. After examining each case, students rated on a numerical scale the likelihood or degree of causal influence of each of the factors and/or made predictions regarding outcomes for novel instances—and showed good reliability in doing so. Although such studies highlight the skills that college students display in such tasks, do they represent the cognitive performance of average people in their thinking about everyday affairs?

To address this question, my student Joanna Saab and I went last year to New York City's Pennsylvania Station. We asked 40 people seated in the waiting room if they would spend 10 minutes answering a survey in exchange for five dollars. Virtually all accepted. We explained that a group was trying different combinations of entertainment features at fund-raisers, to see which would sell the most tickets, and showed each person a diagram with some of the results. The sign for the first party listed door prizes, comedian, costumes; its sales were "medium." The second party listed door prizes, auction, costumes; its sales were "high." The third party listed door prizes, auction, comedian, costumes; its sales were "high."

We left the diagram in view as we talked to each of our interviewees, and we asked, "Based on their results, does the auction help ticket sales?" We also asked how certain they were about their answers. They could choose "very certain," "certain," "think so but not certain" or "just guessing." We asked the same questions for each of the three remaining features: comedian, door prizes, costumes.

As you can deduce for yourself [see first box in this reading], if you examine the first and third parties, adding the auction boosts sales. By comparing the second and third parties, you can see that adding a comedian has no effect on sales. Yet the information available is insufficient for assessing the causal status of door prizes or costumes (because they are always present).

. . . Adults had difficulty judging which factors yielded the best performance at fund-raising parties. The results provided [in the first chart] showed a causal relation between "auction" and sales (compare first and third parties) and no causal relation between "comedian" and sales (compare second and third). Information was insufficient to determine other feature effects. Yet 83 percent of the volunteers said two or more features increased sales, and 45 percent claimed three or all four did so. Most also reported feeling certain about the correctness of their (often erroneous) judgments.

First party	**Second party**	**Third party**
• Door prizes	• Door prizes	• Door prizes
• Comedian	• Auction	• Auction
• Costumes	• Costumes	• Comedian
SALES: MEDIUM	**SALES: HIGH**	• Costumes
		SALES: HIGH

A second reasoning task asked volunteers to make predictions, all of which were indeterminate (because the effects of door prizes and costumes were unknown). Respondents displayed inconsistent logic. Particularly difficult for them was recognizing that a feature whose presence had a positive influence on an outcome would negatively affect the outcome when it was removed. For example, in the prediction question involving door prizes and a comedian (*lower left* [on second chart]), only 40 percent of respondents circled the absence of an auction as affecting the outcome, although 85 percent had correctly labeled it as causal. As before, people were nonetheless certain about their judgments.

• Door prizes • Auction
• Comedian

SALES: LOW MEDIUM HIGH

How certain are you? (circle one)

Very certain Certain
Think so but not certain Just guessing

Which influenced your prediction? (circle as many as apply)

- Door prizes
- Auction
- Comedian
- Absence of costumes

• Auction • Costumes
• Comedian

SALES: LOW MEDIUM HIGH

How certain are you? (circle one)

Very certain Certain
Think so but not certain Just guessing

Which influenced your prediction? (circle as many as apply)

- Auction
- Costumes
- Comedian
- Absence of door prizes

• Door prizes
• Comedian

SALES: LOW MEDIUM HIGH

How certain are you? (circle one)

Very certain Certain
Think so but not certain Just guessing

Which influenced your prediction? (circle as many as apply)

- Door prizes
- Comedian
- Absence of auction
- Absence of costumes

• Auction
• Costumes

SALES: LOW MEDIUM HIGH

How certain are you? (circle one)

Very certain Certain
Think so but not certain Just guessing

Which influenced your prediction? (circle as many as apply)

- Auction
- Costumes
- Absence of comedian
- Absence of door prizes

Did this diverse group of adults at Penn Station show as much skill in isolating cause and effect as researchers have attributed to college students? Or even the same degree of skill as the four-year-olds described earlier? In a word, no. Overall, they claimed more causal relationships to be present than the evidence justified. Eighty-three percent judged that two or more of the features caused sales to increase, and 45 percent claimed that three or all four of the features did so (remember, the available evidence supported a relation between only one feature—auction—and outcome). Even more striking, most respondents were quite confident that they were correct. For two of the four features, the average certitude reported was greater than "certain" (and tending toward "very certain"), whereas for the other two the average was slightly below "certain." Gender was not a factor: men and women did not differ significantly in either their judgments or levels of certainty.

What made these respondents so sure about which features affected outcome and which did not? We emphasized to them that they should base their conclusions on the results shown for the particular group of people indicated (rather than on their own prior beliefs about the effectiveness of these features); in response to a follow-up query at the end, all respondents indicated that they had done so. Yet their responses revealed that their judgments were in fact influenced by their own ideas about how effective these features ought to be. Respondents judged door prizes to affect outcome (83 percent did so) much more commonly than they judged costumes to affect outcome (33 percent did so), although the evidence with respect to the two features was identical.

In [the second task] . . . , there were no correct answers. One cannot make justifiable predictions given the indeterminate causal status of two of the features: door prizes and costumes. Nevertheless, respondents' certainty regarding the predictions they made remained as high as it had been for their causal judgments. Their predictions, moreover, were informative. For example, to infer whether a respondent judged the auction feature as causal, we compared the predictions the person made for a particular pair of cases—specifically, those two cases that involved door prizes. If the auction was being regarded as causal, predictions for these two cases (one with the auction present and the other with it absent) should have differed. If the auction was being regarded as noncausal, its presence or absence should have had no influence and predictions for these two cases should have been identical. Similarly, comparing the predictions for the two cases involving costumes allowed us to infer whether the respondent judged the comedian as causal.

The implicit judgments that respondents made in the prediction task tended to be inconsistent with the causal judgments they had made in the judgment task when they were asked to indicate explicitly whether a factor was causal ("helped ticket sales"). Only 15 percent made consistent judgments across both tasks. Similarly, people were inconsistent in the implicit causal attributions they made in response to the questions about which features had influenced each of their predictions. Among the 63 percent who had correctly judged the inclusion of a comedian as having no causal effect in the judgment task, for example, a majority nonetheless indicated that the presence or absence of a comedian had influenced their predictions.

RECONCILING THE INCONSISTENCIES

How can we reconcile the inconsistent and incautious causal judgments made by people waiting in a train station—judgments they claimed to be certain of—with the reasoning skills observed in college students and even four-year-olds? The answer is invariably multifaceted. Our respondents took the task seriously and were motivated to answer the questions to the best of their ability to justify receiving their five dollars. But they were unlikely to focus on the task as a reasoning test, designed to assess their mental processes, as readily as would college students, who have become familiar with such tests. The purpose, which most college students recognize, is not to achieve a solution (whether it be maximizing ticket sales or designing a bridge sufficient to support a given weight) but rather to display how they go about tackling the problem. College students have learned to behave accordingly, looking at the information given and determining how they should use it to produce an answer. Unsurprisingly, then, we found that respondents with a college background made sounder judgments than those without it did.

Those who do not possess this "academic" mind-set, in contrast, tend to focus on getting the problem solved and allocate little attention to the mental operations they use in the process. In getting to a solution, they bring to bear everything they know that might be of use. Based on their own prior knowledge that door prizes seem more likely to be a winner for fund-raising than costumes, they judge door prizes as causal—even though the presented evidence provides no support for this difference. Keeping track of how they responded in an earlier part of the interview, so as to maintain consistency, will not help solve the problem and thus is not a high priority. For such people, the best reading of how things look at the moment is what is important. Once a decision is reached, moreover, expressing confidence and certainty is better than wavering.

So who is using the "smarter" approach? Why put old beliefs on hold when evaluating new information? Aren't people most likely to come to the best conclusions if they make use of all they know while reaching them? In many contexts, the answer is yes. Yet being able to evaluate "the information given" to determine exactly what it does (and does not) imply is also an important skill—and not just within the rarefied halls of academia.

Suppose, for example, I am thinking about trying the new weight-loss product my friends are talking about, but they tell me they have heard it could cause cancer. When I go to the medical library to look up a recent study on the product, I want to be able to interpret what it says, independent of prior thoughts I may have. In reaching a decision, I may ultimately integrate what the report says with other considerations. But I could not do so were I not able to interpret the document in its own right.

In his 2004 book, *The Robot's Rebellion*, Keith E. Stanovich of the University of Toronto similarly makes the case for the importance of what he calls "decontextualized" reasoning and describes studies in which participants fail to use it. The relevance of such reasoning is by no means limited to thinking about causality. Reaching a verdict in a legal trial, for example, is one common context in which jurors are required to rely on the presented evidence alone, not on everything that comes to mind related to this evidence. So is deductive reasoning, employing ancient Greek philosopher Aristotle's classical syllogisms. Stanovich notes, for example, that 70 percent of adult subjects accepted this syllogism as valid:

Premise 1: All living things need water.
Premise 2: Roses need water.
Conclusion: Roses are living things.

Because we know the conclusion to be true in the real world, it is easy to accept, even though it does not follow logically from the premises. To be convinced of this fact, we need only compare it with a syllogism identical in form:

Premise 1: All animals of the hudon class are ferocious.
Premise 2: Wampets are ferocious.
Conclusion: Wampets are animals of the hudon class.

Typically only 20 percent of people accept this conclusion as correct. The other 80 percent correctly reject it, the improvement in performance presumably arising because no obfuscating real-world knowledge got in the way.

As the research we conducted at the train station suggests, decontextualization is not the only skill in the careful reasoner's mental tool kit. Consistency and avoiding undue certainty in one's judgments are also important. Undue certainty reflects a failure in "knowing what you know" (also called metacognition) and underlies the rigidity in thinking that is a major contributor to human strife. Inconsistency can be similarly self-serving, allowing us to protect our favorite theories without subjecting them to the same standards of evidence to which we subject those of others. We maintain that superior skill was the cause of our team's victory, whereas the other team's win was because of luck.

The authors made no assessment of consistency or certainty of the causal judgments of the four-year-olds in the study described earlier. But we can see why these children may have had an easier time evaluating evidence than the adults in our study had. The scenario involving different colored flowers engaged very little in the way of prior knowledge regarding which colors would be more likely to make a monkey sneeze. The adults, in contrast, had much prior experience that they could bring to bear on matters of event planning, ticket sales and the enjoyableness of different activities. This rich knowledge made it more challenging for them to evaluate the evidence in its own right.

What the competence displayed by the subjects in Schulz and Gopnik's study does show, however, is that the underlying reasoning processes entailed in multivariable causal inference (involving multiple potential causes) have developed to at least a rudimentary degree among four-year-olds. More important, this is competence that we can build on in devising the kinds of educational experiences that will help older children and adolescents, and even adults, become more careful causal reasoners.

Other research that my colleagues and I have done shows that both children and adults do come to reason more critically about causality if they are provided frequent opportunities to practice evaluating evidence and making causal judgments and predictions. Early adolescent students initially show the kinds of faulty multivariable causal reasoning that have been illustrated here. But if they engage with problems of this kind over the course of several months, their reasoning improves sharply. The same is true of young adults enrolled in a community college.

THINKING FORWARD

The message we might glean from the research I have described is two-fold. First, the causal reasoning of average adults regarding everyday matters is in fact highly fallible. People frequently make unwarranted inferences with unwarranted certainty, and it is likely that they act on many of these inferences.

Second, although people may leap to unwarranted conclusions in their judgments about causality, we should not jump to the conclusion that this is the way things must be. Thinking is amenable to improvement, and with practice it becomes more careful and critical. Performance on standardized tests of "basic skills" of literacy and numeracy has come to occupy center stage as a measure of how successful schooling has been at teaching students what they need to know. In contrast, learning to make sound judgments about matters of the kind people encounter in everyday life has not been a high priority as an objective of education.

Such aspects of cognition may be recognized as warranting more attention, as people today struggle to interpret escalating amounts of information about increasingly complex matters, some of which have implications for their very survival. By promoting the development of skills that will help them meet this challenge, we could enrich conceptions of what is important for students to learn. As noted earlier, frequent opportunity to investigate diverse forms of evidence and draw conclusions from them does strengthen reasoning skills. Even getting into the habit of asking oneself and others simple questions like "How do we know?" and "Can we be certain?" goes a long way toward the objective of sound, rigorous thinking.

In an era of escalating pressure on educators to produce the standardized test performance demanded by No Child Left Behind legislation, is it sensible for them to even think about undertaking anything more? Certainly young people must become literate and numerate. But in the end, what could be a more important purpose of education than to help students learn to exercise their minds to make the kinds of careful, thoughtful judgments that will serve them well over a lifetime?

QUESTIONS ABOUT MEANING

1. How does Kuhn's research differ from previous related studies? That is, what research gap do her studies fill?
2. Describe the sample, research methods, and findings for Kuhn's studies. What factors might explain the low number of correct answers from respondents, particularly when compared to results from similar studies conducted with college students?
3. What skills do careful reasoners need? What can people do to improve their own reasoning skills?

QUESTIONS FOR RHETORICAL ANALYSIS

4. *Scientific American Mind* authors often use images and graphics to make information accessible. In what ways does the presentation in the charts make information in this article easy to understand?
5. Although the article is intended for a general audience, what standard features of academic writing (discussed in chapter 6) does Kuhn include?

THINKING AND WRITING ABOUT THE TOPIC

"In the end," notes Kuhn in her interview for *Educational Psychology Review*, "we [educators] can only promote the development of intellectual values in students to the extent that the communities and broader culture they are growing up in reflect these values." Unfortunately, those who want to promote intellectual values in America "are swimming against a cultural tide." Do you agree with Kuhn? Why or why not? Think about your own community—whether that be your hometown or the broader culture you were raised in. Were (are) intellectual values promoted in your community and culture? Address this question in a researched essay that synthesizes both your own experiences and observations *and* evidence you find by conducting research.

WORKS CITED

Ambrose, Susan A., et al. *How Learning Works: Seven Research-Based Principles for Smart Teaching.* San Francisco: Jossey-Bass, 2010. Print.

Bahls, Patrick. *Student Writing in the Quantitative Disciplines: A Guide for College Faculty.* San Francisco: Jossey-Bass, 2012. Print.

Bargh, John A., and Katelyn Y. A. McKenna. "The Internet and Social Life." *Annual Review of Psychology* 55.1 (2004): 573–90. Print.

Emmons, Robert A., and Raymond F. Paloutzian. "The Psychology of Religion." *Annual Review of Psychology* 54.1 (2003): 377–402. Print.

Fister, Barbara. "The Research Processes of Undergraduate Students." *Journal of Academic Librarianship* 18.3 (1992): 163–69. Print.

Hancock, Elise. *Ideas into Words: Mastering the Craft of Science Writing.* Baltimore: The Johns Hopkins University Press, 2003. Print.

Karcher, Carolyn L. "Reconceiving Nineteenth-Century American Literature: The Challenge of Women Writers." *American Literature* 66.4 (1994): 781–93. Print.

Nava, Angelica. "Young Scholars Article." Message to the author. 28 Aug. 2013. E-mail.

Parr, Daniel. "Interview Questions." Message to the author. 30 May 2013. E-mail.

Wells, Gary L., and Elizabeth A. Olson. "Eyewitness Testimony." *Annual Review of Psychology* 54.1 (2003): 277–95. Print.

CHAPTER 10

Conducting Primary Research

> *"My work involves skiing to my research areas and taking field measurements of snow properties while on skis." (Mark Williams, geography professor)*
>
> *"I examined how fourteen business people responded to errors [in writing]." (Larry Beason, English professor)*
>
> *We analyzed "the track record of the median economist's year-ahead predictions for real GDP growth and CPI inflation since 1983." (Michael Bryan and Linsey Molloy, economics professors)*
>
> *"Through personal interviews with students and teachers, I examine how students perceive their own writing and how teachers perceive what their teaching methods can accomplish in first-year composition."* (Angelica T. Nava, English composition student)

Each of these writers describes an example of original—or primary—research. They represent only a few disciplines, but their research methods—including observation and fieldwork, interviewing, and textual analysis—are used throughout the academy.

When you conduct original research, you draw your own conclusions about data. For many students, primary research projects are among their most meaningful educational experiences. In fact, when writing professors Nancy Sommers and Laura Saltz tracked 400 students through four years of college, they discovered that a "paradigm" shift or change of attitude often occurs "when faculty treat freshmen as apprentice scholars, giving them real intellectual tasks that allow students to bring their interests into a course" (140). When writing about primary research, students see a purpose for writing that goes beyond earning a grade. Here is how one student, Erika Jackson Petersen, described her primary research, which involved interviewing people about their memories of reading and writing:

> What was most enjoyable was hearing about others' learning experiences with literacy. I am a people person and love to hear or read about peoples' experiences. It was cool to see how their past experiences had definitely played a role in their future feelings and progression

> with literacy. Doing this research led me to more questions and ideas for research too. I found myself coming up with other research paper topics in my mind on other topics. It honestly left me feeling empowered and wanting to write more, especially when I would get encouragement and praise from peers and teachers. . . . Knowledge IS power and not just scholars have that ability. It's in us all, ready to be developed. . . . This made the idea of writing a research paper seem like fun and not a downer. (original emphasis)

What is it about original research that would make anyone describe it as "fun"? In primary research, you analyze data no one else has analyzed and discover what no one else has discovered. Primary research projects are so meaningful because when you conduct original research, *you create knowledge.*

Secondary Research versus Primary Research

Conducting **secondary research**—locating and reading what's already been written—is the usual first step when seeking information about a topic. Sometimes, however, the answers to your questions can't be found in published sources. When you encounter this situation, you have found an opportunity for primary research.

When conducting **primary research**, you ask a question, design a method for gathering data to answer your question, and then analyze and draw conclusions from the data. Primary research is often the only way to answer questions about local populations or situations. Even when that's not the case, primary research adds to your understanding of a topic. You might interview experts about their knowledge or survey students about their experiences. You might observe human behavior or analyze texts looking for patterns. Primary research can occur in a laboratory or classroom or hospital, on the street, at a computer—almost anywhere.

Choosing a Research Topic

The same resources that help you select a secondary research topic can help you find a primary research topic.

Use Course Resources

Many good resources for topic ideas are readily available to you. Your professor or librarians might be able to provide examples of topics previous students have studied, and your classmates also have the context needed to suggest good topic ideas. Your course reading assignments are another potential source of topic ideas.

Look Around

Observing what's around you is another way to find a research topic. Observation can prompt research questions that interest you, such as "How do males and females differ in their cell phone use? or "Do students use the recycling bins provided on campus?"

Use Published Studies

One common way to find a research topic is by reading the research of others. You may at first be reluctant to study a topic others have written about, but don't be. Jackson Petersen, the student we heard from earlier, describes how she overcame her initial reluctance to researching a topic others have studied:

> Pretty much any question or topic out there has been discussed and/or written about. This was [a challenge for me] when I learned I would be writing a research paper. What is the point of doing a research paper when a million other people, even scholars maybe, have researched and written about the same thing? What's the point of re-hashing what they have already done? Throughout writing my paper, however, I realized writing a research paper shouldn't be about re-stating what others have already found. Instead it's about asking more questions, taking it further, giving your own two cents, taking your own spin on it, etc. Everyone is different. Everyone comes to opinions and resolutions based from experiences. Therefore, we all have something to share, something to learn, and questions to ask. And that is creating knowledge.

You can contribute to any conversation by analyzing your own data.

You may even decide to use a previous researcher's research question and research methods. In fact, this is common practice—and for good reason. By replicating a previous researcher's methods, but with different people or objects in your sample, you contribute to the existing body of evidence. Your evidence either confirms what the previous researcher discovered—further strengthening the findings—or your evidence shows that what was true for one sample is not necessarily true for others. Either way your contribution is valuable, which is why many academics continue research others started.

Here, for example, is how English professors Andrea Lunsford and Karen Lunsford introduce their study of errors in student writing, modeled after a study conducted by Robert Connors and Andrea Lunsford more than 20 years earlier:

> . . . We set out to replicate the Connors and Lunsford study. We began the study assuming that the last two decades have ushered in huge changes in writing. To take only the most obvious example, when [Connors and Lunsford] conducted their study, almost all students were writing by hand.

> Today, students not only use basic word processing but have available many other tools . . . in composing texts. While they write, spell checkers and grammar checkers give them incessant advice. In short, the digital revolution has brought with it opportunities and challenges for writing that students and teachers twenty-two years ago could scarcely imagine. (786)

Lunsford and Lunsford acknowledge their debt to the research they replicate, but they also establish the need for additional study—to see how student writing has changed in the past 20 years. Updating findings, studying a different population, enlarging the sample size—all of these are good reasons to repeat what previous researchers have done.

Primary Research Questions

Academic researchers begin primary research in the same way they begin secondary research: with a question. They may have a theory about what the answer is (referred to as a *hypothesis*), but their goal is to test the theory, not to prove it correct. A study that negates the hypothesis is just as valuable as one that supports it.

Consider the experimental study conducted by wildlife ecologists Sarah Saalfeld and Stephen Ditchkoff. The researchers began with this question: What are the causes of death among newly born (neonatal) white-tailed deer near Auburn, Alabama? They did not anticipate the answers they found:

> Although we had originally hypothesized that vehicular accidents would be a contributing mortality factor, we did not detect any neonatal mortality due to vehicles in our study. (943)

Later, the researchers identify what they do determine to be a leading cause of death:

> Our results indicate that coyote predation may be a significant source of natural mortality for neonatal white-tailed deer in this environment. (943)

Although they do not confirm their original hypothesis, the researchers succeed in two ways: They provide evidence that coyotes are a significant cause of death among neonatal white-tailed deer, and *just as importantly,* they show that vehicles are *not* a significant cause of death. As a result of their research, the biologists modified what they had originally thought.

Apply this method of inquiry to your own primary research projects. Begin with a question (or questions) rather than with a point to "prove," or begin with a hypothesis—a prediction or guess—about what you think is the answer to your questions. Whether you begin with a question or hypothesis, be open to discovering answers you didn't anticipate.

Choosing Your Research Methods

Observing, interviewing, conducting surveys, and analyzing texts are among the most commonly used research methods. Jackson Petersen relied on interviews when she studied how people feel about literacy. Here is how she describes her thought process as she selected her research topic and research methods:

> In class we discussed a lot of writings on literacy, then brainstormed our own questions about literacy. I have always been interested in people and how they perceive themselves and their own abilities. [My professor] helped me connect that perception with literacy. This connection led me to my research question which is: *Do people's past experiences when learning how to read and write affect how they feel about literacy in the future?* I knew I would need a lot of input from other people's experiences with reading and writing so a survey seemed like the way to go. Interviewing people in all stages of literacy seemed appropriate too. I just asked questions which had to do with others' experiences while learning how to read and write: What influence their teachers had; did their family members interact with them when learning to read and write, etc.

Before conducting interviews, Jackson Petersen collected eight written "literacy reflections" from students in her composition class. These narratives about the students' early memories and current attitudes about reading and writing helped her to write good interview questions.

For most research questions, using observation, interviews, surveys, or textual analysis—or a combination of these methods—is a good approach for finding answers.

Observation

When studying humans, observation has one advantage over interviewing or surveying: If subjects do not know they are being observed, a researcher can see behavior that's unaffected by the researcher's presence. Despite this advantage, observation has its limitations.

Limitations of Observation

- *Observation is time consuming and limited in its generalizability.* Behavior must be observed repeatedly before you can assume it is typical. If you are observing to learn how long typical cell phone conversations last or if students use campus recycling bins, you must observe for many hours on numerous days. Even then, you can't make generalizations; your sample is too limited. For this reason, observation is often combined with other types of evidence.

- *Not everything can be observed.* Observing is not an option for some topics. Attitudes or emotions, for example, cannot be seen and must be assessed through other research methods, such as interviews or surveys. In addition, observation is an inefficient way to document changes in behavior occurring over time.
- *Privacy must be respected.* Observing the behavior of people in public places is fine. But videotaping or recording others generally requires informed consent. (See "Ethical Considerations When Conducting Primary Research" later in this chapter.)
- *Interpretations of observation can be wrong.* Our perceptions, backgrounds, and expectations influence our interpretation of what we see. Observation of humans is most useful when gathering objective information, such as how many people visit a particular site each day or how long people spend engaged in a particular activity. Inferences about individuals' emotions or intentions are only guesses.

Observation has its limitations, but when done with care and in appropriate situations, it is a way to enhance your papers with concrete details.

Guidelines for Conducting Observational Research

Here are a few guidelines to make observational research as productive as possible:

- *Take notes while you observe, recording what you see and hear.* You might develop a coding or organizational system for your notes. For instance, if observing cell phone habits, you might have columns in your notes for the starting and ending times of conversations, the proximity to others during calls, time spent texting or reading texts, and so forth. Record as many details as possible and record interpretations or inferences separately from descriptions of what you observe.
- *Review your notes as soon as possible.* Using highlighters to color-code similar details can help you discover patterns. Be open to discovering things in your notes that you had not anticipated or even changing the direction of your research based on what you see in early observations.
- *Write up your findings—or at least a first draft—while memories are fresh.* Though you can't make inferences about an entire population based on your observations, you can describe what was *typical for the subjects you observed* at a particular place and time.

Concept in Practice 10.1:
Reporting Observational Research

In his essay "Another Report on the Age of Extinction," published in the *Canadian Review of American Studies*, art history professor John O'Brian reflects on what he observed when he visited the Barnes Home in Piketon, Ohio, for an event commemorating the extinction of wild passenger pigeons. In the nineteenth-century home, now owned by Geoffrey Sea, O'Brian noticed contrasting images: some documenting the area's original Native American inhabitants, some documenting the extermination of the passenger pigeon, and some documenting the nearby nuclear plant. As you read the following excerpt, notice how detailed observations help O'Brian convey his message.

On the north side of the ground floor of the house, next to the large parlour that was once used for entertaining and now contains a range of objects and materials relating to the passenger pigeon and nineteenth-century American culture, including a foot-powered dentist's drill once belonging to [Geoffrey] Sea's grandfather, is the Blanche Barnes Room. *Columba migratoria*, the Linnaean nomenclature for the passenger pigeon (or the American wild dove, as it was also called), was the most abundant bird on earth until its late nineteenth-century genocidal demise. Audubon described watching a mile-wide stream of the birds darken the skies above him for three days over the Ohio River in 1813. "The multitudes," he wrote, "are astounding." Blanche Barnes was a skilled taxidermist. On or about 22 March 1900, she stuffed and mounted the last passenger pigeon ever seen in the wild, shot earlier in the day by Press Clay Southworth, and brought by him to the house from the kill-site just down Wakefield Mound Road. A built-in cupboard in the room likely held her tools and potions, including the arsenic that was responsible for her death in childbirth three months later. The so-called Sargents Pigeon that she mounted was female, though inaccurate reporting has often identified the bird as male. Sea and his neighbors are lobbying to have the pigeon returned to the Barnes Home from the Ohio Historical Society in Columbus, where it now resides. They want it reunited with the kill site and the room in which it was gutted, stuffed, sewn, and mounted by Blanche Barnes.

(O'Brian 194–95)

How do this vivid imagery and quotation help to convey the author's opinion? What other words, details, and images in this paragraph appeal to readers' emotions?

Interviews

Through observation you can learn things about a subject that you can't learn by reading. But a day of field research yields limited data on which to draw conclusions. If, for example, you were studying the way children interact when at play, observing children for an afternoon would yield some good anecdotes for your paper, but you won't have enough data on which to base any broad conclusions about children. You could supplement your data by talking to an expert, such as a preschool teacher. Subject matter experts—people whose work experience or life make them experts on the topic—can provide information that's broader than what you can gather from observation but more local than what you can get from published sources. For these reasons interviewing experts is a good way to enhance any primary research project.

Guidelines for Conducting Interviews

To get the most from an interview, keep the following guidelines in mind.

- *Schedule the interview.* Make an appointment and indicate how long the interview should take. Allow plenty of time in your own schedule. If the interview goes longer than expected, you don't want to have to cut it short because you have to leave for work or class.
- *Make your motives clear.* Knowing your goals helps the interviewee provide the types of information you need and may encourage more candid responses. Professionals might share anecdotes for your composition essay they would not share for a newspaper story, for example.
- *Prepare for the interview.* Do some preliminary reading and prepare a list of questions. You'll ask better questions and better understand the responses if you already know something about the topic. Coming prepared with questions also helps you remember to get all the information you need and shows interviewees that you respect their time.
- *Behave professionally.* Arrive on time, dressed appropriately for the interview site, and turn off your cell phone! Once the interview begins, make eye contact and give verbal cues (such as, "I see" and "That's interesting") that tell interviewees they have your full attention. Ask if you can record the interview (so that you can include quotations from the interview), but also take notes. Notes allow you to review during the interview, and when we take notes, we zero in on what to us is most important. In this regard, when writing your paper, interview notes can be more valuable than a recording, although the recording allows you to check for accuracy. Thank interviewees for their time and follow up with an e-mail of thanks.
- *Get useful and accurate information.* Good questions are the key to getting good information. Most should be open ended (beginning with *why* or *how* or *could you describe*, for instance) instead of questions that can be answered in one word. Periodically summarize and ask questions that allow you to check the accuracy of your notes. After a lengthy response, for example, say something like, "What I hear you saying is such and such. Is that accurate?" or "Would it be correct to say that you think such

and such is the most important issue?" When appropriate, ask for examples. These can be great additions to a paper.

Concept in Practice 10.2: Interviewing Research Subjects

Included in this *Concept in Practice* are excerpts from the Methods section of a report written by Angelica T. Nava. Nava conducted her research while enrolled in a first-year composition course. She wanted to learn how students and instructors felt about the writing courses they took or taught at University of Texas–Pan American. Some of these writing courses asked students to conduct primary research; others were more "traditional," asking students to rely on sources they read (secondary research) to write their papers.

Highlight and annotate aspects of Nava's interviewing methods that would be likely to help her obtain useful and reliable information.

METHODOLOGY

I developed open-ended questions designed for interviews to obtain personal responses from teachers and students alike. The questions were designed to investigate teachers' and students' reactions to different teaching methods of FYC [first-year composition]. I conducted four interviews face-to-face: two with professors . . . and two with students. The two professors were asked six questions. [Three appear next.]:

- Tell me what you think are the benefits of the writing assignments you give students. What should they learn about writing by completing this work?

  . . .

- Do you believe that students' attitude towards their own writing, how they perceive writing, and what they believe to be the purpose of writing has an influence on what they can accomplish in your class?
- Could you tell me what you know about other professors' teaching approaches in first-year writing courses? Can you describe any differences you see between your methods and those of others here at UTPA [University of Texas–Pan American]?

  . . .

From the instructors' answers to these questions, I anticipated learning what they believed students should get out of their class and how students would be able to meet the professors' teaching goals.

The two students I interviewed were asked four questions pertaining to the writing assignments they had completed and their attitudes towards writing [three questions appear below]:

- Describe the connection, if any, that you found between your assignments and your attitude towards your own writing.
- Can you please describe your favorite type of assignment in class—the ones that you could most relate to?

. . .

- Tell me what you think are the benefits of . . . [your English class]. What did it mean for the way you perceived your own writing?

In the students' answers to these questions, I planned to see what they believed the pedagogy and class activities meant for them as learners and writers. I wanted to find what distinctions there were in their classroom settings as well as determine the outcomes they felt the class methods had on their attitude towards writing.

. . . Initially, I emailed notifications requesting a time to meet with professors and students. During the interviews I used a voice recorder to capture the responses verbatim. . . . All interview subjects were able to review this article as it was being drafted and revised. . . . (Nava 122)

Surveys

The goal of a survey is to learn about the opinions or practices of a population by hearing from a small segment of the population, called a *sample*. Surveys allow you to learn about the opinions of a local population, such as employees at your worksite or students at your school. Surveys take various forms: telephone surveys, mailed questionnaires, online surveys, and face-to-face interviews. No matter the form, surveys are typically anonymous.

You may not have the resources necessary to survey a statistically meaningful number of people, but asking even 20 people to answer a few simple questions can provide insights about a population in less time than in-depth interviewing requires. Here, for example, are the kinds of questions one student, Michaela Cullington, asked other students in order to learn how textspeak affected their classroom writing:

> I asked the students how long they had been texting; how often they texted; what types of abbreviations they used most and how often they used them; and whether they noticed themselves using any type of textspeak in their formal writing. In analyzing their responses, I looked for commonalities to help me draw conclusions about the students' texting habits and if/how they believed their writing was affected. (93)

Notice that unlike the open-ended questions ideal for interviews, survey questions can be answered briefly and responses are easy to count and compare. However, designing questions that provide reliable information requires great care.

Guidelines for Creating Survey Questions

Included here is advice for designing effective survey questions.

- *Pretest all questions.* Before administering your survey, read your questions to several people and ask them to think aloud as they answer each question. If they give qualified answers to yes/no questions or if they select two responses after being directed to select only one, you know you need to revise the questions or directions or both.
- *Begin the survey with a statement of purpose.* This sentence or short paragraph tells respondents what you want to learn from the survey. Then, ask questions related to the stated purpose. Don't forget to provide directions as well on written questionnaires.
- *Ask for necessary background information.* Ask for demographic information—such as age, gender, or race—when it is needed for your research goals. When sensitive information, such as income, is needed, ask for it in ranges ($10,000–$19,999, $20,000–$29,999, etc.)
- *Stick to one type of question as much as possible.* When respondents answer closed-ended questions (such as multiple-choice, yes/no, and Likert-scale questions), they choose from answers you provide. Open-ended questions allow respondents to provide their own answers. Comparing and tabulating responses to open-ended questions is time consuming and challenging. Written responses can also be difficult to decipher. So *use closed-ended questions when they can provide the information you seek.* If mixing closed-ended and open-ended questions is necessary, group similar-type questions together. (Closed-ended questions usually appear first.)
- *Ask direct, single-idea questions.* "Do you think the President is an honest and effective leader?" is actually two questions for respondents who believe the President is honest but not effective. Avoid using synonyms in questions. Some respondents will interpret "Did you find the sales clerk to be friendly and courteous?" as two questions.
- *Make questions as brief as possible.* The longer the question, the greater the chance it gets misinterpreted. In oral surveys, limit the number of answer options for closed-ended questions to three or four. If more options are needed, use a written survey so respondents can see the answers.
- *Allow for qualified responses when appropriate.* For complicated issues, many people want to qualify their answers. For example, many people support the right to own a gun but *only* under certain conditions. One

way to allow for qualification is to qualify the questions: "*In general*, are you satisfied with the quality of instruction you've received at Serenity College?" or "Can you *usually* find a parking spot within one-quarter mile of your classes?" In closed-ended questions, provide "other" or "none of the above" options if appropriate.

- *Avoid leading questions.* A question like "*Don't you think* we need more parking space at Serenity College?" suggests a "right" answer. Biased word choice can influence respondents as well, such as in "Do you think students should have to pay so much for *inadequate* parking?"
- *Use precise wording.* "Do you like attending Serenity College?" may seem to be a simple and direct question, but responses won't be particularly useful. If a respondent answers "No," you won't know why. Vague answer choices will also produce vague data. For a question like "On average, how many times a month do you visit the college's Fitness Center?" you might be tempted to provide answer options like "never," "rarely," "regularly," and "very often." But you won't know how respondents interpreted words like "rarely" or "regularly." Instead, be precise. In this situation, use numbers in your answer options, and be sure to avoid overlapping responses.
- *Provide plenty of white space and sufficient room for written responses.* For closed-ended questions, arrange answers vertically so respondents don't overlook an answer or unintentionally mark a response they did not want. When possible, limit surveys to one or two pages. Respondents are more likely to participate when surveys look "easy."

Many potential problems are avoided by pretesting your survey. Analyze responses to these practice surveys to determine if any questions produce data that is not useful or difficult to tabulate. It's disappointing to realize too late that some respondents misinterpreted a question or wanted to select answers not available. Data from flawed questions must be discounted.

Concept in Practice 10.3: Evaluating Survey Questions

A survey will not provide meaningful data about a population if the questions or answer options are inadequate. Can you think of ways to improve the following survey? Consider the question phrasing, answer options, and layout and organization of questions. (Hint: *Every* item could be improved.)

Purpose: This survey is designed to help your student body officers determine what services students use in the college's Student Union Building and how those services can be improved.

Survey Directions: Place a checkmark beside your answers.

1. What Student Union Building facilities do you use ? bookstore______, TV lounge______, meeting rooms______, study cubicles ______, cafeteria______, cashier ______
2. How would you rate the helpfulness of Student Union Building employees ? Excellent______, Good______, Fair ______, Average ______, Not helpful at all______
3. Should the Student Union Building be open earlier or later? yes______ no______
4. How frequently do you visit the Student Union Building? daily ______, once or twice a week______, less than once a week______, never______
5. Do you agree that visitors should not be allowed to use services offered in the Student Union Building? yes______no______
6. Don't you agree that there are too few meeting rooms for students to use in the Student Union Building? yes______no______

Limitations of Survey Research

Even well-crafted surveys have their limitations. No matter how well worded the question, most individuals won't admit to certain kinds of behavior. Food and alcohol consumption as well as weight are examples of topics people are not honest about. Many people will underestimate or overestimate behaviors to present themselves in a favorable way (Hunter 24).

Another limitation is that surveys cannot answer some complex research questions, such as questions about cause and effect relationships. Suppose, for example, you want to know if having a job affects a student's GPA, so you decide to conduct a survey. This should be easy, you think. Just ask a sample of students for their GPA, whether or not they work, how many hours they work, and correlate the responses. But then you realize you'll also need to know how many credits a student is taking. So you add a question. Now your survey asks the following:

What's your GPA?
How many credits are you taking?
Do you work?
If so, how many hours a week do you work?

Surely, these questions will provide all you need to determine if there's a correlation between hours of work and GPA, right?

Not so fast. Assuming all respondents accurately report their GPA (a big assumption), we still can't determine a cause-effect relationship from answers to these few questions. For example, if a full-time student with a GPA of 1.0 works 40 hours a week, can we infer that working full time is the reason for the low GPA? What if the student lacks the prerequisite skills needed for college success? What if he regularly skips class? What if he is a single father of three? Couldn't any of these (and a dozen additional factors) also explain a low GPA? The point is that many research questions are too complex for a single survey to answer.

Textual Analysis

Another type of primary research involves analyzing texts. *Texts* here refer to any written documents, whether articles, ads, or bumper stickers, as well as spoken texts, performances, and images. All types of texts—Wikipedia pages, restaurant menus, college textbooks, online shopping sites, television shows—include features that convey messages about the writers' goals. Many other features reflect who uses the texts and how. The purpose of **textual analysis** research is to gain insights into how a type of document is composed or used. Those insights can change the way we "see" familiar types of texts. A researcher in journalism, for example, might search newspaper reports for evidence of bias, analyze newscasts to see how coverage of an issue has changed over time, or study Internet images to learn how the portrayal of an event varies according to the intended audience. A researcher in marketing might analyze advertisements; a researcher in history might analyze the writings of a particular Supreme Court justice.

Guidelines for Conducting Textual Analysis

To illustrate textual analysis, let's consider a study by conservation biologists Richard A. Niesenbaum and Tammy Lewis. Niesenbaum and Lewis wanted to know: *Do conservation biology textbooks discuss the social, economic, and political aspects of conservation?* Their methods provide useful guidelines for anyone conducting textual analysis research.

- *Determine criteria for selection of texts to examine.* By choosing specific criteria for what texts to study, you show that you did not simply select texts that support your hypothesis. To be included in Niesenbaum and Lewis's 2003 study, a textbook had to be published between 1992 and 2002, had to include either *conservation* or *biology* in the title, and had to be published by a textbook publisher. Selecting texts published within a given period or within a certain geographical region are common ways to select a sample to analyze.
- *Determine criteria for exclusion.* It's just as important beforehand to determine what texts will *not* be included in your sample. Niesenbaum and Lewis, for example, did not analyze specialized books or lab manuals.

- *Determine what you will look for.* Determining exactly what you want to analyze in the texts is another decision. For instance, if you were studying how lawyers are depicted in television shows, you might look at their (1) gender, (2) ethnicity, (3) age, (4) dress, and (5) geographical location. Studying a few sample texts is one way to generate a list of features to analyze. Or, if others have conducted studies similar to the one you want to conduct, you can replicate their methods. That's what Niesenbaum and Lewis did. By reading the methods of previous studies, they composed a list of 35 keywords they would look for in their sample of textbooks (e.g., *tax*, *trade*, *cost-benefit*, and *commerce* in a textbook's index suggest economic topics).
- *Analyze the texts.* To find their search terms, Niesenbaum and Lewis again replicated the methods previous researchers used. They searched the textbook indexes and counted the number of pages on which each of the 35 keywords appeared. To determine depth of coverage, they calculated the *percentage* of pages and the *percentage* of chapters within each book that included each keyword. If your research involves searching for specific words in online or digital texts, use the search command Control+F to save time and ensure accuracy.
- *Draw some conclusions.* Here are two conclusions from Niesenbaum and Lewis's study: "Treatment of economics, policy, and other social elements were often restricted to specific chapters, and these were most frequently located at the end of the text. However, the coverage of interdisciplinary themes has become more integrated over time" (8). Notice how Niesenbaum and Lewis qualify their conclusions with "often," "most frequently," and "has become more integrated."

Two things are important to remember about textual analysis: First, your work does not end with the discovery of recurring features. You must also draw conclusions about *why* the commonality exists and *why* the commonality matters. (What does it reveal, for instance, about a writer's goals or a reader's practices?) In other words, make the value of your research clear. Second, textual analysis research reveals trends—features that are *common*, but not necessarily present in every item in the sample. When you report your results, identify both the number of texts that include a particular feature and the number that don't, and qualify your statements of findings.

Concept in Practice 10.4: Analyzing Textual Features

All kinds of texts can be the subject of textual analysis research, even the menu options on college websites. What kinds of questions might a researcher ask about a sample such as this?

A few possibilities include: (1) What messages about the schools do menu options convey to viewers? (2) How do menu options vary between schools? (3) Do the differences appear to be related to institution type? To address these questions, you might select a random sample of college websites, group them according to institution type, and look for features that distinguish one group from another.

Take a moment to locate and examine the homepages for several types of higher learning institutions—private universities, state universities, and community colleges. What similarities and differences did you notice in the menu options? How might the differences be related to each institution's mission and student population?

One commonality among the websites may be, for example, a link for "future students" "prospective students," "admissions," or "about us." Where does this link most often appear in relation to the link for "current students"? What does this suggest is one important purpose of a college website? What additional similarities and differences can you find among the websites you examined? Or, what additional questions might a researcher ask about your sample of websites?

A large sample would need to be analyzed before drawing any conclusions about college websites, but this exercise illustrates the textual analysis process.

Discovering Topics for Textual Analysis Studies

There are many ways to analyze a given sample of texts. Here are a few tips for getting started on your own textual analysis research:

- Print copies of documents in your sample and lay them out where you can see them side by side.
- Survey the documents, generate a list of features or categories to study, and decide how you will "count" or evaluate each. (Using different colors of highlighters can help you see how frequent or infrequent particular features are in your sample.) The list of features you will analyze is called a **coding scheme**. Items listed in a coding scheme should be nonoverlapping and clearly defined. That is *not* the case in the coding scheme shown next, created for a sample of papers written for courses across disciplines. The research questions are, "What kinds of visual elements do students include in their papers and is the choice of visual element related to the discipline?" Can you see the problem with the following coding categories?

(Flawed) Coding Scheme for Types of Visual Elements in Student Papers

Figures
Tables
Charts
Graphs
Maps
Photos
No visual elements present

All of the possible categories seem to be represented, but the categories overlap. Charts, graphs, and photos are types of figures.

- Create a table or tables for recording your findings for each feature or category in your coding scheme.
- Analyze a few texts, using your coding scheme, before analyzing the entire sample. Then ask someone else to repeat your process and compare results. Are they nearly identical? If not, refine your coding scheme or the definition of categories in your coding scheme. This second coder provides what is called **interrater reliability**.

Ethical Considerations When Conducting Primary Reserach

If you want to conduct research that involves humans, you may need to get permission from your college's Institutional Review Board (IRB). This group exists to protect people's rights to privacy and safety. If you are observing people from a distance in a public place (such as in a restaurant or in a sports arena), you won't need permission, but if your research involves talking with people or observing how they respond to an environment you create, you may need to ask participants to sign a statement of consent informing them of the goals of your project. (Examples of research consent forms are easy to find online.) Even observing online behavior (such as studying how people present themselves in social networking environments) may require getting permission electronically from subjects. Always consult with your instructor before embarking on a study involving humans.

Reporting Your Original Research

As you may recall from chapter 2, IMRAD is an acronym for the major sections of many original research reports: Introduction, Methods, Results, (and) Discussion. Most IMRAD-structured reports also include a one-paragraph abstract below the title that summarizes the goal and results of the research. Whether or not you write about your research in a paper that includes these sections, academic readers expect to find the kinds of information included in an IMRAD-style report.

Title

Titles of research reports identify the subject of study. Here, for example, are paper titles from students featured in this chapter:

> Past Experiences and Future Attitudes in Literacy
> Where Teachers and Students Meet: Exploring Perceptions in First-Year Composition

An informative title for a research report conveys the subject and purpose of the research. Some titles even summarize the most important result.

Introduction

Introductions to research reports identify the importance of the subject, summarize the findings of previous related studies, and announce the goal of the present study. What did you want to learn? Why is your subject important and what value will your study have? As you saw in chapter 6, one purpose of the introduction is to identify a "research gap." How does your research add to the body of existing research? Even when your research question and research methods replicate another researcher's, your study is unique. Explain how.

Methods

Describe your sample and research procedure. Who or what did you study? What is the sample size and makeup? If you conducted a textual analysis, describe and illustrate the categories in your coding scheme. If you conducted a survey, explain how you selected the sample, how the survey was administered, and what questions were asked. If you modeled your study after previous research, acknowledge this.

You might also explain your reasons for selecting the methods you did. Here, for example, is how Angelica Nava (the student quoted in *Concept in Practice* 10.2) explained why she chose to interview instead of survey her sample:

> In formulating my research methods, I ruled out using a questionnaire because anonymous answers seem impersonal and more about numbers than responses. With my interviews, although the sample size was small, I received responses directly from the students and teachers. I wanted also to create a more relaxed setting, one where the participant could respond verbally rather than in writing, and thus would not have to worry about the length of a response or grammatical errors. (122)

In this paragraph, Nava explains her choice of methods. If it seems important, you might also want to explain why you chose the particular sample you did.

Results

Describe what you observed or learned. Include both summarized data (such as totals for each category in a coding scheme) and specific details or examples. When research methods include surveys or textual analysis, it is customary to include representative quotations from the sample, but always protect the identity of participants.

Results are often presented in visual form. You might put percentages for responses to each survey question in a table or compare the responses from different segments of the sample in a chart. (See chapter 5 for a discussion of how to incorporate visual evidence into reports.)

Discussion

After describing your findings in detail, discuss what they mean. What is the answer to your research question? (Alternatively, state whether or not the results support your hypothesis.) No sample can represent an entire population. Acknowledge this. Qualify your findings and identify the limitations of your research. The following paragraph demonstrates how Nava recognized the limitations of her research:

> Although I received detailed responses in the interviews I conducted, these responses were from only four individuals; I would like to have a larger sample size. . . . I also believe that the study would have benefited had I asked more questions in my interviews. I would have asked professors their opinion about students having more than one program in FYC [first-year composition] to choose from, and I would have asked students how they felt about having a choice in learning programs for their FYC courses. (126)

Nava gains credibility by acknowledging the limitations of her own research and *specifically* naming what would have improved the study.

Interpret the findings. If the results were not as you had anticipated or are different from those of previous researchers, what accounts for the difference? What is the value of your research? Remember that even when the findings do not support the original hypothesis, your research reveals something about the topic.

Finally, a common way to conclude a research report is by suggesting future research to address questions your study raises.

References

On a separate page, provide an alphabetized list of the sources you cited in the report. (See chapter 8 for discussion of documentation styles.)

Table 10.1 includes questions customarily answered in each section of a research report.

TABLE 10.1
Sections of a Research Report

Section	Questions to Answer
Introduction	What did you want to learn? Why is this topic important? Who else has studied this topic and how is your research different? (What gap does it fill?)
Methods	What was the size and makeup of the sample? How was information from the sample obtained and analyzed?
Results	What did you learn about your sample? Provide precise answers (usually in both statistical and visual form) to each research question.
Discussion	What is interesting and valuable about your results? How do your results compare to those of earlier researchers? What are the limitations of your research? What questions are left unanswered and how could they be addressed in future research?

When asked to follow IMRAD format, adhere to it closely and provide headings for the following sections: Introduction, Methods, Results, and Discussion. Whether or not you use IMRAD format when describing your primary research, provide details about your research goal, sample, methods, results, and the value of your research.

Benefits of Conducting Primary Research

This chapter began with reference to one benefit for students who conduct primary research: When you conduct primary research, you engage in "real" scholarly work. Instead of writing to an audience who knows more about the subject than you do—as is customary in school-based writing—when you describe original research, you are the expert. Here is how Angelica Nava describes her experience:

> Instead of developing writing skills through narrative essays on topics much like the ones seen in high school, discussing a time when I felt most accomplished, I was instead reading scholarly texts and developing research questions from my interests. This change in focus not only ultimately helped me to understand factors at play in my own writing, but substantially changed the way I perceived my own writing process. (121)

What Nava describes is the "paradigm" shift that occurs when students are given "real intellectual tasks" (Sommers and Saltz 140).

When you write about your research, you can and should adopt features that define expert writing, including reviewing what's been written about your topic, announcing the value of your research, qualifying statements of findings, using academic vocabulary, presenting findings in tables or figures, and concluding with a call for additional research. When you design and conduct your own research, *you* are the authority. Following these conventions of academic writing (discussed in chapters 5 and 6) conveys this to readers.

Conducting primary research has another benefit: You come to better understand that the claims found in research reports involve interpretation and that a different sample or different methods could result in different conclusions. In other words, conducting research fosters your ability to critically assess the research of others. You learn firsthand a lesson emphasized throughout this book: Claims are only as reliable as the evidence on which they are based.

Applying the Concepts to Reading: *Analyzing a Description of Methods*

Included in this *Applying the Concepts* exercise is an excerpt from a research report written by Utah Valley University student Erika Jackson Petersen while she was a student in English 201. In her study, titled "Past Experiences and Future Attitudes in Literacy," Jackson Petersen sought to determine how early experiences with reading and writing influence the way a person later thinks about literacy.

Jackson Petersen's methods include a combination of textual analysis and interviews. This excerpt focuses on her sample selection. As you read, consider the following questions:

1. In what ways did Jackson Petersen model her study after earlier studies by Rick Evans and Alisa Belzer? How did she modify their research methods for her own study?
2. Describe the participants Jackson Petersen interviewed. What explanation does she give for her sample selection?
3. A description of methods should describe both how the researcher conducted her research and why she did what she did. Does Jackson Petersen accomplish these two goals?

To begin my study, I acquired eight "literacy reflections" from other students in English 201 at Utah Valley University (UVU). In these literacy reflections students were asked to reflect on their literacy pasts and presents, to explore how they read and write different assignments, and their feelings and attitudes toward reading and writing. As with Evans's and Belzer's studies [described earlier], the intent was to get students thinking about the different kinds of reading and writing they do and why they do it. I was hoping that by studying these students' reflections I would be able to see patterns of past experiences playing an influential role in how these college students felt toward different literacy tasks.

I then interviewed twelve other people of all different ages, ranging from eleven to forty-four. I did this because I wanted not only college students' perspectives on writing but also those of children at all levels of learning and adults at different points in their lives. I wanted to interview people who were not given the assignment to write a paper on their literacy histories in order to remove bias from the study. Evans's and Belzer's articles both interview relevant groups of people (mainstream college students around eighteen years old and middle-aged African American women), but I wanted to show that no matter what stage of life we are in, we all have a literacy past that potentially affects our future, even well past the schooling part of our lives. Therefore, I interviewed two girls in the fifth grade, four kids in high school, and three people in college (I interviewed fewer college students because I felt that I had a good representation of them from the literacy reflections). I also interviewed three people who were thirty-three and older and out of college because I hypothesized that even when you're out of school, your literacy past still play[s] a role in your life. I began each interview by asking about the participants' earliest memories of reading and whom they remembered teaching them. I asked them about their favorite and least favorite teachers and why they liked or disliked them. I also got an idea of how their reading styles had changed—for example, what their favorite kinds of books were when they were children compared to their favorites now. I asked the same kinds of questions concerning writing, too. We talked about what kinds of writing they enjoyed in the past compared to now, what kinds of writing they make time for in their schedule, etc. I wanted to get a good feel for which experiences with literacy learning the interviewees remembered most clearly in order to determine if a lot of people remembered the same kinds of experiences. I also asked them about any awards or recognition they received in classes in certain subjects to see if that affected their subsequent aptitude and interest in them. I wanted to know not only how they responded to recognition in literacy but also how they pursued it, so I asked them if they showed what they'd written to teachers and friends or talked about what they were reading to others. (Jackson 132)

Applying the Concepts to Writing: *Planning a Research Study*

Propose an idea for a research question and study involving one or more of the methods discussed in this chapter: observation, interviews, surveys, or textual analysis. Here are some sample research questions:

Have recent increases in tuition affected student spending habits?
What patterns are there in the kinds of questions students post in online courses?

What features do professors across disciplines look for in student writing?

Come up with your own research question and then answer these questions:

Purpose: What do you want to learn? Why is this subject important and what value will your study have?
Sample: Who or what will you study? How will you get access to these subjects? How many will be in your sample?
Methods: Describe the methods you will use. Where will you gather data? How will this data be measured and recorded? If studying humans, how will you keep your presence from influencing their behavior or how will you get their consent?
Results: Describe how your results could be presented. Will there be numbers to present in tables or images to show in photographs? Will you quote representative responses from subjects?
Finally: What aspects of this research do you anticipate will bring the greatest challenges? Explain.

Paired Readings from Interdisciplinary Studies

Excerpt from University of Michigan's webpage for the Undergraduate Research Opportunity Program (Sandra R. Gregerman, director)

At the University of Michigan, first- and second-year students enrolled in the Undergraduate Research Opportunity Program (UROP) conduct original research alongside faculty from various disciplines. The program's goals are to increase the percentage of students who remain in school until graduation and to foster academic success. When program directors gathered data to determine if those goals are being met, they found that students who participate in original research benefit in several ways. The following excerpt, taken from the "Evaluation and Assessment" section of the UROP website, describes their findings.

With funds from the U.S. Department of Education, the National Science Foundation, and the State of Michigan's Office of Equity, UROP has been engaged in a longitudinal assessment of the impact of the program on student retention, academic performance, engagement, and pursuit of graduate and professional education. UROP employs a multi-method approach to assessment and evaluation. Our early research efforts were quantitative in focus—surveys research and retention studies. We added qualitative research to our repertoire to increase our ability to detect benefits to UROP participation not identified by our more traditional quantitative approaches. The following is a summary of some of these studies and our findings.

UROP RETENTION STUDY

Given the main goal for UROP is to increase undergraduate student retention and academic achievement, we investigated whether, and to what degree, UROP is having those intended influences. The sample of 1,280 students consists of African American, Latino/a, and White UROP student[s] matched to non-UROP students who applied to the program but who were not accepted. We obtained retention data from the university's Office of the Registrar. It included demographic information (race and gender), term and year of entry, term and year of most recent active enrollment, current enrollment status, and grade point average for each term, cumulative grade point average, and enrollment status by term for each student. We defined retention as students' persistence through graduation, and attrition as students' departure from the University of Michigan.

RETENTION STUDY FINDINGS

Retention effects were strongest for African American students and for sophomores rather than first-year students.

- UROP has a significant positive effect on male African-American participant's degree completion. 75.3% degree completion for UROP students compared to 56.3% for control and 57.2% for at large African American males.
- African American students whose academic performance was below the median for their race/ethnic group appeared to benefit the most from UROP participation.
- White students appear to benefit from UROP participation, but not as strongly as African American students. (attrition rate for White UROP students compared to White controls is approximately 1:2).
- UROP does not appear to have an influence on Latino/a retention rates.
- UROP participation increases degree completion rates for male African American, White, and students of color, but not for male Hispanic participants or female UROP participants.

FOCUS GROUP STUDY

Group interviews with UROP students, non-UROP students, and students participating in another retention program (RP) were intended to identify the impact of UROP on students not otherwise identified via our other research projects. The focus group study allowed us to identify the influence of UROP from the perspective of the students. Students were interviewed in groups, with UROP students in one group, non-UROP students in another, and RP students in another. Data were analyzed using a grounded theory method that consisted of multiple readings of the focus group interview transcripts to identify themes.

FOCUS GROUP FINDINGS

Students discuss their undergraduate experiences in three distinct manners:

1. Proactive—Tendency to initiate activity, anticipate problems before they arise, and act before acted upon, and to seek out help from individuals.
2. Reactive—Respond to others' actions, and feeling at the whim of the college environment.
3. Inactive—Non-interaction with the environment (not attending classes, not doing homework).
   - UROP students make 58% of the proactive comments.
   - UROP students are more likely to discuss anticipating future events, such as looking for jobs or going to graduate school.
   - UROP students are more likely to initiate activity with people than non-UROP students are and see people (faculty, staff, etc.) as positive influences on their academic experiences.
   - Non-UROP students make 68% of the reactive/inactive comments.
   - Non-UROP students are more likely to react to people and see people as barriers to their learning experiences than UROP students.
   - Non-UROP students make 69% of the reactive/inactive comments about people.
   - Underrepresented minority students value both the research and programmatic aspects of UROP whereas the White and Asian students value the research more strongly than the programmatic components (peer groups, advising, etc.).

UROP ALUMNI SURVEY

The Alumni Survey was designed to identify UROP effects beyond graduation and to examine whether and to what degree UROP students differed on post-graduate education, experiences, and career pathways. The Alumni Survey sample was derived by matching UROP students to 2–4 non-UROP students. We matched UROP students to the controls on high school grade-point-average, SAT scores, ACT scores, intended major, race/ethnicity, and where possible, high school type. Control students were students who had applied to UROP but who were rejected. We had a 58.55% survey return rate for a sample of 291 students. The survey asked students about their post-graduate experiences, including graduate school, career choice, and satisfaction with current job.

ALUMNI STUDY FINDINGS

- Students who participate in undergraduate research (UROP or other research) are significantly more likely to pursue post-graduate education than control students.
- UROP students are significantly more likely to pursue medical, law, or Ph.D. degrees than control students.
- Students who participate in undergraduate research are significantly more likely to be engaged in postgraduate research activity compared to control students.
- Students who participate in undergraduate research are significantly more likely to utilize an undergraduate faculty member for a job recommendation than control students.
- There are no differences or interaction by race/ethnicity on post-graduate education pursuit, post-graduate research activity, or job recommendation usage.

SYNTHESIS OF RESEARCH FINDINGS

Our assessment and evaluation efforts suggest a positive benefit of UROP participation on student's retention and academic achievement, pursuit of post-graduate education, post-graduate research activity, behavioral orientation (active participation in their educational experiences), and development as researchers. However, the findings are rooted in on differences by race/ethnicity, gender, and incoming personality characteristics.

CONCLUSIONS

UROP does influence students' academic achievement, retention, behavior, and post-graduate educational and professional activities—all intended goals for the program.

Findings from several of the research projects suggest a strong connection between UROP participation and proactive behavior, with UROP students discussing how they actively interact with the academic environment.

Findings indicate that African American students' retention and academic achievement does benefit from a program designed to integrate students into one of the core goals of higher education—research and the pursuit of knowledge. In addition, findings indicated that UROP extends its effect beyond the undergraduate experience by retaining students in the educational pipeline after graduation.

Male UROP participants benefit more strongly from involvement in undergraduate research in terms of higher degree completion rates than male non-participants.

The research is strengthened by the use of control students who applied to UROP, but who were not accepted. Hence, the controls should be similar to UROP students to whom they are compared on characteristics, such as motivation and academic commitment, that could be related to the outcomes specified.

Future research is needed to determine whether UROP facilitates proactive behavior or strengthens those behaviors already present.

PUBLICATIONS

Nagda, B. A., Gregerman, S. R., Jonides, J., von Hippel, William, Lerner, J. S., (1998). Undergraduate Student-Faculty Research Partnerships Affect Student Retention. *The Review of Higher Education*, Volume 22, pp. 55–72.

Gregerman, S. R., (1999). Improving the Academic Success of Diverse Students Through Undergraduate Research. *Council on Undergraduate Research Quarterly*. December 1999.

Hathaway, R. S., Nagda, B. A., Gregerman, S. R., The Relationship of Undergraduate Research Participation to Graduate and Professional Educational Pursuit, An Empirical Study, *Journal of College Student Development*, (2002).

QUESTIONS ABOUT MEANING

1. What are the goals of the University of Michigan's Undergraduate Research Opportunity Program (UROP)? Describe the "multi-method" approach used to determine if these goals have been reached.
2. Which segments of the sample population were found to have benefitted most from participating in UROP? Summarize some of the key research findings. What question about the findings requires further research to answer?

QUESTIONS FOR RHETORICAL ANALYSIS

3. The first sentence of the Evaluation and Assessment section of the UROP website identifies three sources of funding for the studies. Why might

each of these organizations be interested in the program and in this research? Why would the writers mention these funding sources?

4. Successful writers adapt their writing to the genre. What features of this text would make it easy to read onscreen?

Excerpt from "Undergraduate Student-Faculty Research Partnerships Affect Student Retention," *Review of Higher Education* BIREN A. NAGDA, SANDRA R. GREGERMAN, JOHN JONIDES, WILLIAM VON HIPPEL, AND JENNIFER S. LERNER

The University of Michigan's Undergraduate Research Opportunity Program (UROP) gives first- and second-year students an opportunity to conduct original research with professors from various disciplines. The professors who wrote the following article, describing the success of UROP, represent several disciplines themselves. Biren Nagda is a professor of social work; John Jonides is a professor of psychology; William von Hippel is a professor of psychology; and Jennifer Lerner, who at the time of writing was a doctoral candidate, is now a professor of public policy and management. Sandra Gregerman is the director of UROP. Their research was originally published in the *Review of Higher Education* in 1998. The *Review of Higher Education* publishes peer-reviewed articles of interest to college professors and administrators.

In 1993, 2.4 million students entered college; of those, some 1.1 million will leave without a degree (Tinto, 1993). This is not a new trend. Data from the American College Testing Program show that the first-year attrition rate for all students in four-year public universities has remained largely unchanged over the last decade. In 1983, this rate was 29.1%; in 1992 it was 28.3% (Tinto, 1993). The other end of the undergraduate time-scale looks equally distressing. In 1983, the graduation rate at the same institutions was 52.6% while in 1992 it had *declined* to 46.7%. The phenomenon of college attrition is even more exaggerated among certain underrepresented minority groups. Hispanics graduated at a rate of only 35%, and African Americans at a rate of only 45% (Brower, 1992), far below the rates for White students (Tinto, 1993).

What kind of efforts at the college level can counter this trend? In this paper, we offer a typology of retention efforts to date that have been informed by a variety of presumed causes of attrition. We examine factors that promote student retention and success as a way of thinking about innovative and effective programs. We describe and report on the evaluation of one such program—student-faculty research partnerships—that bridges the academic and student services domains while at the same time being responsive to the institutional context.

The causes of attrition are numerous, thereby leading to multiple retention efforts that concentrate on different factors. Indeed, Tinto's (1993) model of attrition identifies a variety of factors that ought to predict attrition, in accord with the variety of issues that face students as they move from high school through college. Broadly speaking, retention efforts that have addressed one or another of these factors can be classified into two categories. The first assumes that students who do not graduate were underprepared for college work at entrance; individual student deficiencies are thus seen as responsible for attrition (Boykin, 1994; Levin & Levin, 1991). Responses to this perspective typically take the form of various remedial and tutorial programs (Kulik, Kulik, & Schwalb, 1983; Nelson et al., 1993). The second theory assumes that various structural factors inherent in educational institutions fail to support particular students, leading to significant attrition. Retention efforts are, therefore, geared to meet the numerous needs of students with a range of programs that concentrate on financial aid, academic counseling, and personal support (Kulik, Kulik, & Schwalb, 1983). These two classes of theory have motivated the majority of retention efforts in higher education (Tinto, 1993).

They are limited in scope, however. The first focuses on factors having to do with individual students and the second on factors having mainly to do with social and institutional structures. A more recent approach to student life and student attrition concentrates on students' interaction with the social structure and the extent to which they are integrated into the institutional fabric. This approach emphasizes the impact of college structure, resources, and programs on student learning and development (Volkwein & Carbone, 1994). Solutions attempt to create communities and groups that involve changes in the situational/institutional climate while simultaneously involving students in skill- and interest-building activities. Examples include living-learning settings that give students a "home-base" in the larger college environment and mentoring programs in which other students or faculty act as "expert" guides and models.

The concept of integrating students into the fabric of the institution seems important in retention (Tinto, 1993), but there may be drawbacks to effecting this principle. Living-learning programs, for example, may not be sufficiently far-reaching to integrate students into the larger college; they create smaller communities that become the focus of student life and often do not include faculty well in the on-going activities. In other words, students in these programs interact with the university, not directly, but through the intermediate peer environment.

Mentoring programs, as another example, often do not have a sufficiently high priority for faculty and students to be more than peripheral to the daily life of the students whom they are supposed to serve. And as Tinto (1993) observes, the evidence on student attrition suggests that retention efforts need to move beyond "largely a social matter for the staff of student affairs" (p. 71). A firmer implementation of the integration principle would, therefore, involve students in a focused activity that is at the heart of the institution's mission, one that counteracts the individual's feelings of being socially and intellectually isolated from the institution (Tinto, 1993). Such a strategy would simultaneously prepare students to be successful in navigating the larger institution and aid in the student's own academic development and sense of competency.

Lack of integration, or isolation of the student within the institution, has been identified as an important factor in contributing to student departure. The effects of weak student-with-student and student-with-faculty contact have been cited repeatedly as causes of student withdrawal from college (Terenzini & Pascarella, 1977; Pascarella & Terenzini, 1977, 1991). Indeed, Pascarella and Terenzini (1979) cite the absence of sufficient interaction with other members of the college community as the *single leading* predictor of college attrition. The desired interaction must go beyond the formal and expected environment of the classroom (Stage, 1989; Pascarella & Terenzini, 1977) and beyond the often limited contact involved in mentoring or academic advising. It must include sustained informal contact among members of the college community, contact that involves students with both students and faculty. It must provide this contact early in students' careers in college, at a time when they are most likely to depart (Levin & Levin, 1991). Finally, contacts must foster both the social and the academic integration of students into the institution (Tinto, 1993).

. . .

This study reports on the Undergraduate Research Opportunity Program (UROP). The program builds directly on one of the key academic missions of a large, public Research I university and, by design, weaves students into its academic mission early in their careers.

METHOD

Program Rationale and Highlights

UROP was founded in 1989 in the College of Literature, Science & the Arts (LS&A) at the University of Michigan. This university's fall 1995 undergraduate student population was 23,505, of which 13.9% were underrepresented minority students (Office of the Registrar, 1995). During the first three years of its existence, UROP enrolled underrepresented minority students exclusively; since the 1992–1993 academic year, however, it has been open to all first-year students and sophomores.

UROP's major goal is to broker intellectual relationships between faculty and first-year and sophomore undergraduates through research partnerships. Research projects are available in most liberal arts departments (e.g., psychology, political science, English, history of art, and economics, among others), and in the professional schools (medicine, law, social work, business, and natural resources and the environment). Through individual meetings with their sponsors and/or team meetings with other project collaborators, students are involved in various aspects of the research. Their duties include conducting bibliographic research and literature reviews, formulating research questions and hypotheses, and conducting studies and analyses. Some UROP students have also coauthored research presentations and journal articles with their sponsors.

While there has been an increase in undergraduate research programs throughout the country (Strassburger, 1995), UROP is unique in a number of ways. First, UROP focuses exclusively on first-year and sophomore students because they are at the greatest risk of attrition. Second, UROP enrolls students during the regular academic year (fall and winter semesters) rather than during the summer so that the research becomes an integral part of their academic life, not a separate activity conducted when they are not "in school." In this way, the students can gain academic credit or pay (based on financial need) and avail themselves of an elaborate support system—peer advising, peer research interest groups, skill-building workshops, speakers, and research presentations. Third, faculty sponsors come from all the schools and colleges of the university, ensuring students a broad choice of research partnerships. Fourth, UROP is not an "honors" program; average and even "marginal" students interact closely with faculty. UROP specifically targets underrepresented minority students and women with an interest in the sciences, two groups that are at special risk of attrition. Finally, although many other undergraduate research programs exist across the country, few, if any, systematically assess the impact of participation on student retention and academic performance.

. . .

Participants

In this study we investigated the impact of UROP participation on student retention. We have limited our analyses to three subgroups of students who are represented in sufficiently large numbers for meaningful analyses: African American, Hispanic, and White students.

We selected 1,280 first-year and sophomore undergraduates from a total of 2,873 applicants. Given the limited number of spaces and the large number of applicants, we used a stratified random sampling method for selecting students. The assignment of students to the experimental or control groups was done by a matched random assignment. First, within each yearly cohort, we sorted all applicants into subgroups based on their race/ethnicity, SAT/ACT scores, and first-year college grades (for prospective sophomores) or high school grades (for prospective first-year undergraduates). Second, we randomly assigned two students within each subgroup, one to UROP or the other to the control group, dropping any other students. They also were not admitted to UROP. This procedure yielded an experimental group of 613 students who actually participated in UROP and a control group of 667 students who did not. We sent all applicants a letter stating that there had been more applicants than positions so admission was determined by lottery. Thus, all of the students—those in UROP, those in the control group, and those not admitted—understood that their status had been determined by chance. In this way, we avoided making the students in the control group feel that rejection was based on their credentials—as indeed it was not.

Measures

We obtained retention data from the university's Office of the Registrar. It included demographic information (race and gender), term and year of entry, term and year of most recent active enrollment, current enrollment status, grade point average for each term, cumulative grade point average, and enrollment status by term for each student.

We defined retention as students' persistence through graduation, and attrition as students' departure from the University of Michigan. Hence, our study counted in the attrition group at least some students who may have transferred to another institution of higher education. We constructed this variable based on student's registration status by term. Persisters included two categories of students: one, who graduated or showed continuous enrollment from term of entry to fall term 1994; and two, those who departed for a certain period of time but returned to continue their studies, that is, stop-outs. This point of measurement (fall 1994) represents a period ranging from one semester to three years after the students' matriculation from UROP. Nonpersisters were students who were initially enrolled but had neither graduated nor enrolled for fall term, 1994. Thus, it is possible that some nonpersisters may eventually return to the University of Michigan or some other institution to finish work toward their degree and that some persisters will drop out before completion of theirs.

RESULTS

Persistence in College

Two facts about differences in retention rates govern the analyses reported here. First, recognizing that the retention rates of minority and majority students differ at predominantly White institutions, we separately report retention for these two groups. Second, retention rates among different groups of underrepresented minorities differ from one another (Brower, 1992; Tinto, 1993). We therefore report data separately for African American and Hispanic students, the only two minority groups included in our sample in substantial numbers.

When UROP participants are compared to nonparticipants, each race/ethnic group demonstrates a significant positive effect of participation on retention. Underrepresented minority participants in UROP from 1989–1990 to 1993–1994 had an attrition rate of 11.4% compared to 23.5% for nonparticipants. White students in UROP (from 1992–1993 to 1993–1994) had an attrition rate of 3.2% versus 9.8% for nonparticipants. There is, however, the possibility that UROP participants were more motivated in the first place to pursue career-enhancing activities than nonparticipants. The remaining analyses, therefore, compare UROP students to their matched control groups. These samples are restricted to African American and Hispanic students who entered the university in summer/fall terms of 1990, 1991, 1992, and 1993, and were in the experimental or control groups for program years 1991–1992, 1992–1993, and 1993–1994, and White students who entered the university in summer/fall terms of 1991, 1992, and 1993, and were in the experimental or control groups for program years 1992–1993 and 1993–1994. We restricted the study sample to students entering the university in the summer or fall terms only so as to provide a comparison with university-wide information from the Office of the Registrar and to ensure that the students participated in the program for the full year (see Office of the Registrar, 1994a).

To confirm that the participant and control groups were similar on the randomized selection criteria, we conducted student *t*-test analyses comparing the two groups on high school GPA and composite SAT and ACT scores. The results, as displayed in Table 1, verified that the groups exhibited no significant differences on the pre-college academic aptitude measures.

The main objective of this study was to assess the impact of participation in UROP on students' persistence in college. Table 2 shows results from 2 × 2 chi-square analyses comparing the attrition rates of UROP participant and control groups. The analyses show a nonsignificant difference in attrition rate of 7.2% for all UROP students compared to

Table 1
Sample Profile on Randomized Selection Criteria

	African American Students			Hispanic Students			White Students		
	Participant	Control	*t*-stat	Participant	Control	*t*-stat	Participant	Control	*t*-stat
Sample size	237	153		95	71		281	443	
High school GPA	1.871	2.040	–1.043 ns	1.946	2.209	–1.046 ns	3.669	3.682	–.481 ns
SAT composite	972.03	948.32	1.178 ns	1045.9	1076.7	–1.132 ns	1205.4	1205.4	–0.36 ns
ACT composite	22.39	22.47	–.209 ns	25.00	25.33	–.472 ns	28.41	28.12	1.071 ns

ns = nonsignificant difference ($p \geq .10$ level)

9.6% for all control group students, X^2 (1, n = 1280) = 1.858, p = .17. We then separately compared African American, Hispanic, and White students in UROP to their respective control groups. African American students in UROP have an attrition rate of just over a half that of the control group (10.1% vs. 18.3%, $p < .03$). White students in UROP also showed a lowered attrition rate, about a half that of their control group (3.2% vs. 6.1%), but this difference is not statistically significant. Hispanic students in UROP had a statistically insignificant higher attrition rate than control group students (11.6% vs. 11.3%).

Table 2
Attrition Rates of UROP Participant and Control Groups

	African American Students		Hispanic Students		White Students	
	Participant	Control	Participant	Control	Participant	Control
Sample size	237	153	95	71	281	443
Nonpersisters	24	28	11	8	9	27
Percentage attrition	10.1	18.3	11.6	11.3	3.2	6.1
X^2 statistic (df = 1)	4.809	0.034	2.611			
p-value	03	.85	.11			

One might argue that the superiority in the retention of African American and perhaps White UROP students compared to their controls was a function, not of increased retention due to UROP, but of decreased retention of the control group students due to their rejection from UROP. On the face of it, it seemed unlikely that not being accepted in a single program in college could have a dramatic effect on retention. More objectively, however, we noted that each of the specific race/ethnic control groups had a lower attrition rate than their counterparts in the population at large—that is, students who were not part of the UROP participant or control group. For African American students, the difference was marginally significant (18.3% vs. 25.2%, X^2 (1, n = 1495) = 3.071, $p < .08$). For Hispanic students (11.3% vs. 20.4%, *X2* (1, n = 945) = 22.020, $p < .001$) and White students (6.1% vs. 10.0%, X^2 (1, n = 10,220) = 6.705, $p < .01$), this difference in attrition rate was significant. We could therefore have confidence that the effect of UROP on retention was not attributable to a detrimental rejection effect for control group students.

. . .

Retention and Grade Point Average

Academic success, as represented by student grade point average, is one of the factors that positively affects retention (Pascarella & Terenzini, 1991; Wilder, 1983). We examined the extent to which retention differed as a function of students' cumulative grade point averages. To do this, we divided the students into low- and high-GPA groups by splitting the samples approximately at the point of their median cumulative GPA. The medians (on a 4.0 scale) vary by race/ethnic group: B- (2.700) for African American students, B-/B (2.850) for Hispanic students, and B+ (3.300) for White students. We defined students below the median as "Low-GPA" and those above the median as "High-GPA." Table 3 presents attrition data as a function of race/ethnic group, whether the students were in UROP or the control groups, and their level of academic performance. Low-GPA students as a group showed an attrition rate of 13.5% compared to 4.3% for High-GPA students, X^2 (1, n = 1187) = 29.60, $p < .01$. These rates are consistent with the typical finding that students performing poorly are at greater risk of attrition (Edwards & Waters, 1982). Overall, Low-GPA students in UROP showed a lower attrition than those in the control group (11.9% vs. 14.1%) but not significantly, X^2 (1, n = 549) = 0.405, $p < .52$. The same analysis for High-GPA students reveals a parallel pattern (4.1% vs. 4.4%, X^2 (1, n = 564) = 0.000, $p < 1.00$). Analyses for the separate race/ethnic groups showed that UROP participation impacted most positively on the retention

Table 3
Attrition Rates by Academic Performance of UROP Participant and Control Groups

	African American Students		Hispanic Students		White Students	
	Participant	Control	Participant	Control	Participant	Control
Low GPA Students	111	85	40	33	112	220
Non-persisters	17	23	8	5	4	19
Percentage attrition	15.3	27.1	20.0	15.2	3.6	8.6
X^2 statistic (df = 1)	3.396	0.054	2.220			
p-value	.07	.82	.14			
High GPA Students	115	61	49	32	146	183
Non-persisters	6	4	3	2	5	5
Percentage attrition	5.2	6.6	6.1	6.3	3.4	2.7
X^2 statistic (df = 1)	.001	0.172	.002			
p-value	.98	.68	.97			

of low-achieving African American students (attrition rate of 15.3% compared to 27.1% for the control group, $p < .07$). None of the other results—that is, comparisons among high-GPA African American, and low- or high-GPA Hispanic and White students—approached significance.

DISCUSSION

. . .

Methodologically, the strength of this study lies in having a matched control group composed of students who applied to the program. First, the comparable high school grades and SAT/ACT scores ensured that the participant and control groups were similar on measures of precollege academic performance. Second, the higher retention rate of control students in comparison to the general population of students across each race/ethnic group showed that the control group students did not seem unduly harmed by being rejected for this program. We note, however, the possibility of a self-selection bias among students who apply to UROP. Thus, random assignment of applicants into participant and control groups is imperative to assess the effectiveness of interventions such as UROP.

At present, we have little basis for analyzing which components of UROP were especially effective in promoting student retention. We can, however, venture that the regular faculty contact provided an engaging, one-on-one, relationship to foster academic competency (computer literacy, bibliographic searches, critical thinking, and team-work) and academic integration. It also provided students with opportunities for continued discussion of intellectual issues outside the classroom by virtue of the tasks they shared with their faculty sponsors and student colleagues. Most saliently, students were able to see an idea take form, come to fruition, and seed other ideas and studies. Students' involvement in investigating, understanding, and producing knowledge wove them into the central mission of the university. An evaluation by a student indicates that being part of a research setting extends students' intellectual challenges in a way that the classroom does not:

> UROP has given me the chance to work in the real world of research and definitely feel the power and responsibilities of research. I have not only learned new techniques specific to my project, I have been able to apply my own knowledge and, most importantly, critical thinking to solve problems and hypothesize outcomes of experiments. I have gained a way of thinking that cannot be taught in textbooks and learned to deal with complications which randomly arise. It has indeed broadened my horizons.

The peer-advising component was also a crucial part of the students' research experience. In addition to its skill building and informational usefulness, it helped bridge the gap between students' social and intellectual lives. By meeting with students individually and leading the peer research interest groups, the peer advisors facilitated intellectual and social ties to the university community. The research discussions in the groups enabled students to look at their own and others' research from multiple perspectives. These groups also provided students with an accessible community of peers with similar interests; the peer advisors served as role models and mentors, assuring students that a supportive person was available to them.

Of course, the results presented here need amplification. We must identify whether students who did not persist at our university dropped out of higher education entirely or transferred to another institution. We must identify the factors within UROP that lead to greater student persistence. We must go beyond persistence to identify other effects of UROP, those that may extend from academic performance to attitudinal change. We must investigate whether the beneficial effects of UROP are replicable at institutions that may differ from the University of Michigan. For example, Michigan has a highly selected student population for a public university; therefore, we cannot be sure that our findings will generalize to institutions whose demographic characteristics are different. These issues aside, our results lead us to believe that UROP is having both a statistically significant effect on retention and a *practically* significant one as well.

. . .

REFERENCES

AAO/OAMI. Affirmative Action Office & Office of Academic Multicultural Initiatives. (1994). *Faculty, staff and students of color: A statistical profile for academic years 1983–84 through 1993–94*. Ann Arbor: University of Michigan.

Astin, A. W. (1975). *Preventing students from dropping out.* San Francisco, CA: Jossey-Bass Publishers.

Astin, A. W. (1982). *Minorities in American higher education.* San Francisco, CA: Jossey-Bass Publishers.

Astin, A. W. (1993). *What matters in college? Four critical years revisited.* San Francisco, CA: Jossey-Bass Publishers.

Boykin, A. W. (1994). Harvesting talent and culture: African American children and educational reform. In R. J. Rossi (Ed.), *Schools and students at risk: Context and framework for positive change* (pp. 116–138). New York: Teachers College Press.

Braddock, J. H., II. (1981). Desegregation and Black student attrition." *Urban Education, 15*(4), 403–418.

Brainard, S. G., Laurich-McIntyre, S., & Carlin, L. (1995). Retaining female undergraduate students in engineering and science. *Journal of Women and Minorities in Science and Engineering, 2*(4), 255–267.

Brower, A. (1992). The "second half" of student integration. *Journal of Higher Education, 63*(4), 441–462.
Celis, W., III. (1993, February 24). Colleges battle culture and poverty to swell Hispanic enrollments. *The New York Times*, A17.
Durán, R. (1994). Hispanic student achievement. In M. J. Justiz, R. Wilson, & L. G. Björk (Eds.), *Minorities in Higher Education* (pp. 151–172). Phoenix, AZ: Oryx Press.
Edwards, J. E., & Waters, L. K. (1982). Involvement, ability, performance, and satisfaction as predictors of college attrition. *Educational and Psychological Measurement 42*(4), 1149–1152.
Fleming, J. (1984). *Blacks in college*. San Francisco, CA: Jossey-Bass Publishers.
Fordham, S. (1988, February). Racelessness as a factor in Black students' school success: A pragmatic strategy or pyrrhic victory? *Harvard Educational Review, 58*(1), 54–84.
Fox, R. N. (1986). Application of a conceptual model of college withdrawal to disadvantaged students. *American Educational Research Journal, 23*(3), 415–424.
Hatcher, S. (1995). *Peer programs on a college campus: Theory, training and "voice of the peers."* San Jose, CA: Resources Publications.
Kulik, C. C., Kulik, J. A., & Schwalb, B. A. (1983). College programs for high risk and disadvantaged students: A meta-analysis of findings. *Review of Educational Research, 53*(3), 397–414.
Levin, M. E., & Levin, J. R. (1991). A critical examination of academic retention programs for at-risk minority college students. *Journal of College Student Development 32*(4), 323–334.
Murguia, E. Padilla, R. V., & Pavel, M. (1991). Ethnicity and the concept of social integration in Tinto's model of institutional departure. *Journal of College Student Development, 32*(5), 433–439.
National Science Foundation. (1992). *Expenditures for scientific and engineering activities at universities and colleges*. Washington, DC: NSF.
Nelson, B., Dunn, R., Griggs, S. A., Primavera, L., Fitzpatrick, M., Bacilious, Z., & Miller, R. (1993). Effects of learning style intervention and college students' retention and achievement. *Journal of College Student Development, 34*(5), 364–369.
Nettles, M. T., Thoeny, A. R., & Gosman, E. J. (1986). Comparative and predictive analyses of Black and White students' college achievement and experiences. *Journal of Higher Education, 57*(3), 289–318.
Office of the Registrar. (1994a). *Beginning summer/fall term freshmen who did not receive a degree and who were not still enrolled fall, 1994: Registrar's report 860*. Ann Arbor: University of Michigan.
Office of the Registrar. (1994b). *Minority enrollment by U.S. state (other than Michigan or territory and race: Registrar's report 854*. Ann Arbor: University of Michigan.
Office of the Registrar. (1995). *Enrollments in degree credit programs by racial/ethnic category: Registrar's report 837*. Ann Arbor: University of Michigan, 1995.
Osborne, J. W. (1995). Academics, self-esteem and race: A look at the underlying hypothesis of the disidentification hypothesis. *Personality and Social Psychology Bulletin, 21*(5), 449–455.

Pascarella, E. T., & Terenzini, P. T. (1977). Patterns of student-faculty informal interaction beyond the classroom and voluntary freshman attrition. *Journal of Higher Education, 48*(4), 540–552.

Pascarella, E. T., & Terenzini, P. T. (1979, October). Interactive influences in Spady and Tinto's conceptual models of college attrition. *Sociology of Education, 52*, 197–210.

Pascarella, E. T., & Terenzini, P. T. (1991). *How college affects students: Findings and insights from twenty years of research.* San Francisco, CA: Jossey-Bass Publishers.

Richardson, L. (1995, May 3). Academic panel to ponder the mission of research universities. *New York Times*, B9.

Sedlacek, W. E., & Brooks, G. C. Jr. (1976). *Racism in American education: A model for change.* Chicago, IL: Nelson-Hall.

Stage, F. K. (1989, Fall). Motivation, academic and social integration, and the early dropout. *American Educational Research Journal, 26*(3), 385–402.

Strassburger, J. (1995, May). Embracing undergraduate research. *American Association of Higher Education (AAHE) Bulletin, 47*, 3–5.

Steele, C. M. (1992). Race and the schooling of Black Americans. *Atlantic Monthly, 269*(4), 68–78.

Terenzini, P. T., & Pascarella, E. T. (1977). Voluntary freshman attrition and patterns of social and academic integration in a university: A test of a conceptual model. *Research in Higher Education, 6*(1), 109–127.

Tinto, V. (1993). *Leaving college: Rethinking the causes and cures of student attrition* (2d ed.) Chicago, IL: University of Chicago Press.

Tracey, T. J., & Sedlacek, W. E. (1984). Non-cognitive variables in predicting academic success by race. *Measurement and Evaluation in Guidance, 16*(4), 171–178.

Tracey, T. J., & Sedlacek, W. E. (1985). The relationship of non-cognitive variables to academic success: A longitudinal comparison by race. *Journal of College Student Personnel, 26*(5), 405–410.

Tracey, T. J., & Sedlacek, W. E. (1987). Prediction of college graduation using noncognitive variables by race. *Measurement and Evaluation in Counseling and Development, 19*(4), 177–184.

Volkwein, J. F., & Carbone, D. (1994). The impact of departmental research and teaching climates on undergraduate growth and satisfaction. *Journal of Higher Education, 65*(2), 146–167.

Wilder, J. R. (1983). Retention in higher education. *Psychology: A Quarterly Journal of Human Behavior, 20*(2), 4–9.

QUESTIONS ABOUT MEANING

1. What are possible reasons for the high attrition (dropout) rate at most colleges, and how have colleges tried to address the problem? Why have these solutions been insufficient?
2. What is the goal of the Undergraduate Research Opportunity Program? Who is the program designed for? Why does it target that particular population?

3. How did the retention rates of the experimental group compare to those of the control group? How did the grade point average of the two groups compare? What aspects of UROP might explain the results?

QUESTIONS FOR RHETORICAL ANALYSIS

4. What is the purpose of the first paragraph of the article?
5. Assess the sampling methods in this study. Do the samples seem large enough and representative enough to allow the researchers to draw reliable conclusions about the populations?
6. In the previous reading (from the UROP website), students in the control group are simply identified as "non-UROP students who applied to the program but who were not accepted." What additional information is provided in this article concerning why these students were not accepted into the program? Why is it important to compare UROP participants to the specific students selected for the control group (instead of comparing program participants to students rejected on the merits of their applications or to nonparticipants in general)?

THINKING AND WRITING ABOUT THE TOPIC

Collecting preliminary data or conducting pilot or exploratory studies is common before a researcher embarks on a full-scale study. This process allows the researcher to refine his or her procedure and can spark additional research questions. Recall that before interviewing students for her study, Jackson Petersen collected "literacy reflections" from other students in her class. By reading these reflections she got ideas for good interview questions.

Conduct some preliminary research for the study you designed when completing the earlier *Applying the Concepts to Writing* exercise. Gather some data from the kinds of texts or people you want to study and write up your initial findings. Based on your exploratory research, what revisions, if any, would you make to your methods before embarking on a full-scale study?

WORKS CITED

Beason, Larry. "Ethos and Error: How Business People React to Errors." *College Composition and Communication* 53.1 (2001): 33–64. Print.

Bryan, Michael F., and Linsey Molloy. "Mirror, Mirror, Who's the Best Forecaster of Them All?" *Economic Commentary* 15 Mar. 2007: 1–4. Print.

Cullington, Michaela. "Texting and Writing." *Young Scholars in Writing* 8 (2010): 90–95. Web. 1 Aug 2013.

Hunter, Beatrice Trum. "Is Nutrition Policy Based on Faulty Data?" *Consumers' Research Magazine* 77.9 (1994): 22–25. Print.

Jackson, Erika. "Past Experiences and Future Attitudes in Literacy." *Young Scholars in Writing* 5 (2007): 131–37. Web. 1 Aug 2013.

Jackson Petersen, Erika. "Research Survey Question Answers." Message to the author. 11 Aug. 2013. E-mail.

Lunsford, Andrea A., and Karen J. Lunsford. "'Mistakes Are a Fact of Life': A National Comparative Study." *College Composition and Communication* 59.4 (2008): 781–806. Print.

Nava, Angelica T. "Where Teachers and Students Meet: Exploring Perceptions in First-Year Composition." *Young Scholars in Writing* 9 (2011): 119–27. Web. 1 Aug 2013.

Niesenbaum, Richard A., and Tammy Lewis. "Ghettoization in Conservation Biology." *Conservation Biology* 17.1 (2003): 6–10. Print.

O'Brian, John. "Another Report on the Age of Extinction." *Canadian Review of American Studies* 38.1 (2008): 191–98. Print.

Saalfeld, Sarah T., and Stephen S. Ditchkoff. "Survival of Neonatal White-Tailed Deer in an Exurban Population." *Wildlife Management* 71.3 (2007): 940–44. Print.

Sommers, Nancy, and Laura Saltz. "The Novice as Expert: Writing the Freshman Year." *College Composition and Communication* 56.1 (2004): 124–49. Print.

Williams, Mark. "Interview Request." Message to the author. 15 May 2007. E-mail.

CHAPTER 11

Revising and Editing Academic Writing

How would you define "revising" and "editing" to a fellow writing student? Would you say it's about changing content, structure, grammar, or all three? English professor Nancy Sommers found that for many first-year college students, revising means finding different words to express what they have already written. In a study she conducted comparing the revising practices of expert writers and student writers, Sommers noticed that when students revised, they focused on replacing words and phrases with others that sounded "better" or were "more impressive" (381–82). But the expert writers tried to imagine what information their audience would need and added, deleted, and reorganized content accordingly (386). The fact is revising and editing involve much more than word substitution. In this chapter you'll learn how to make global, holistic changes that can strengthen your writing—a process known as **revising**. You'll also learn strategies for improving your writing at the local, or sentence, level—a process known as **editing**.

Global versus Local Changes

The kinds of word replacements and sentence corrections that most writers make to a first draft are known as "cosmetic" or "local" *edits*. These local, micro-level changes can make your meaning more clear, but the "global," macro-level changes that improve writing overall are more important. Such global *revisions* involve checking the paper for organization, comprehensiveness, and usefulness for the intended audience. Table 11.1 includes some sample questions to help you determine the need for global revisions or local edits. These questions can also help you differentiate between the two types of changes.

TABLE 11.1

Example Questions Leading to Global Revisions and Local Edits

Global Revisions	Local Edits
Does the introduction forecast the content and organization?	Have I corrected any spelling or grammar errors?
Are the main ideas of paragraphs stated early in each paragraph?	Are my sentences concise?

(*continued*)

TABLE 11.1 *CONTINUED*

Global Revisions	Local Edits
Do transitions link paragraphs and ideas?	Have I put article titles in quotation marks and have I italicized journal titles?
Are arguable claims and general claims supported with evidence?	Are my bibliography entries formatted correctly?
Have I provided all of the information readers will want or need?	Have I numbered the pages of my paper?
Have I deleted irrelevant sentences and paragraphs?	

Notice that local edits are more specific and do little to change the meaning of a paper. Global revisions, on the other hand, improve the flow and persuasiveness of the writing.

Making Global Revisions

The following section offers some guiding questions to consider as you revise your paper at the global level. Your ability to answer them—or not—reveals whether or where you may need to improve the structure and content of your paper.

Can Readers Predict What's Ahead?

As explained in chapter 6, people read faster and remember better what they've read when they can anticipate what's coming. Can readers predict the topic after reading the title of your paper? Do they know the purpose of your paper after reading the introduction? If you have included section headings, do they provide clues to what's ahead? Have someone read your introduction. Can your reader identify the purpose of your paper, the major ideas, and the organization of those ideas? If not, you may need to rewrite the introduction to better orient your readers.

Does the Organization of Main Ideas Make Sense?

Does the progression of ideas in your paper seem logical? Does one section lead naturally to another? Documents that are well organized are generally easy to outline. Could a reader outline your main ideas? If not, consider reorganizing or stating those ideas more directly.

Are Main Ideas Repeated?

If your main ideas are stated only once—in the introduction—repeat them in topic sentences throughout your paper. In lengthy papers, you can summarize main ideas in transitional paragraphs that introduce or conclude a section. In any length of paper, readers are better able to recall main ideas if they are stated in topic sentences early in paragraphs. Reading expert Bonnie Meyer demonstrated this in a study in which she controlled for variables such as reading difficulty, structure of passages, and repetition of ideas. She found that the organization of ideas in a passage influences what ideas are remembered and how well. Meyer recommends that writers who want their main ideas remembered should "place them high in the content structure of a passage [e.g., a paragraph] and not buried in its depths" (120).

In addition to stating main ideas in topic sentences, reinforce paragraph ideas by repeating keywords (or synonyms) from the topic sentence throughout each paragraph. Look for places to remind readers about the ideas you've presented earlier (e.g., "As I mentioned in the previous paragraph") and for places to announce what's coming next. Summary and overview statements keep your main points always in mind.

Are Ideas Linked?

Once you have the paragraphs of a paper in logical order, check that they are linked. Use transitional wording (such as *First*, *Second*, *Another reason*, *In addition*) in the first sentence of a paragraph to connect the new paragraph idea to the previous one or link paragraphs by repeating keywords or phrasing. Notice how the following paragraphs from an engineering journal article begin with similar wording (italicized in the passage):

EXAMPLE 11.1 FROM AN ENGINEERING JOURNAL

There are *two main approaches* to measuring forces on sports balls during flight. *The first approach* is to take measurements from controlled football trajectories using high-speed video footage. Although this is a well-recognized method that undoubtedly examines what actually happens as a ball travels
5 through the air, it is susceptible to errors. . . .

The second approach is to use a wind tunnel with the sports ball being held in place while air is blown around it. This method has the advantage that the speed of the air can be accurately controlled and kept constant and the forces acting on the ball can be measured by attaching the ball to a force balance
10 arrangement.

(Carré, Goodwill, and Haake 658)

The word *approach* in the second paragraph reminds readers that this is the second of two main approaches.

Concept in Practice 11.1: Linking Paragraphs

Appearing next are the opening sentences of a series of paragraphs from an economics journal article. As you read the sentences, underline wording that relates each new idea to previous ideas. Wording in the first sentence of Paragraph 2 is underlined as a model:

EXAMPLE 11.2 FROM AN ECONOMICS JOURNAL

[Paragraph 1] *From an economic standpoint, the organ procurement* industry exhibits several important structural features. . . .

[Paragraph 2] From a practical standpoint, procurement of organs from cadavers for use in transplantation currently involves several steps. . . .

5 [Paragraph 3] In practice, these conditions require that the overwhelming majority of cadaveric organs came from accident (or occasionally stroke) victims who have been declared brain dead.

[Paragraph 4] Next, once a potential organ donor has been identified, permission of surviving family members is generally sought.

10 [Paragraph 5] Thus, as a practical—though not legal—matter, the property rights of the organs of deceased individuals rest with the surviving family members.

[Paragraph 6] Given the need to obtain the family's consent to cadaveric organ donation, the methods used in seeking that consent become extremely 15 important in determining the success of the procurement process.

[Paragraph 7] Given the above process, several obvious reasons exist for cadaveric organ donation to fail to occur.

(Beard, Kaserman, and Saba 435–36, emphasis added)

Are the Body Paragraphs Well Structured?

The heart of any essay is the body, where the writer presents his evidence and makes his argument. A few questions can help you assess the quality of your body paragraphs.

Are Sentences within Each Paragraph Connected? Connections and transitions (*for example, on the other hand*) can do more than link paragraphs. They can also link ideas within paragraphs, distinguish claims from evidence, and show how segments of text are related. As you learned in chapter 2, these connections aid in the readers' ability to comprehend texts. Check to see if your paragraphs can be improved by adding signal words that help readers follow your discussion.

Is the Paragraph Unified? Another quality to look for when revising is **unity**. A paragraph that lacks unity is unfocused and presents no clear single idea. A useful revising practice is to underline your topic sentences and then reread each paragraph: Should any sentences be deleted because they are off topic? Adding transitions or details can sometimes make the relevance of sentences more clear. Consider, for example, the following topic sentence: *Implementing smoke-free ordinances increases restaurant revenues.* A logical supporting detail would directly show cost benefits of such ordinances. Citing health benefits for employees would not be relevant because health benefits do not support the main idea—*unless* you explain that employees who work in smoke-free environments take fewer sick days than employees exposed to smoke on the job. Another option, if you discover sentences that seem off topic in a paragraph, is to revise the topic sentence so that it better reflects the point made in the paragraph.

Is the Paragraph Adequately Developed? Another quality to look for is sufficient development. Is your paragraph underdeveloped? Most college papers are intended to be persuasive, and this requires you to develop ideas with evidence, such as examples, statistics, studies, expert opinion, or observations. Is your evidence current? Have you acknowledged your sources of information? Whether you cite personal experience, studies, expert opinion, or "facts," have you provided details that show readers the evidence is credible?

Consider as well whether the evidence you cite is broad enough in scope and sufficient in amount to convince someone of your point. If not, provide more evidence or narrow your claim. A claim about "some students at my college" is naturally easier to support than a claim about "most college students." Look for unsupported opinions and generalities—statements claiming that something is usually true—and support them with credible evidence. And remember that qualifying arguable claims (with words like *often, usually,* or *perhaps*) can make them more accurate.

Concept in Practice 11.2: Revising Underdeveloped Paragraphs

Consider the following first draft of a paragraph. (The sentences are numbered for easier reference.) Where would additional details make the evidence stronger? What kinds of details should be added? What other revisions would improve this paragraph? Assume your audience is an academic one.

[1]In today's working world, teamwork is essential. [2]In fact, according to Peter D. Hart, 44% of employers and 38% of recent graduates agree that teamwork is the most important skill in the workplace. [3]Collaboration is greatly enhanced

by the many different perspectives of today's diversified workforces. [4]According to Joseph W. Ruane, diversity leads to a better awareness of and sensitivity to others and results in a better product. [5]In order to succeed as an individual in the workplace you need to succeed as a team. [6]However, Rebecca Burnett, a communications professor, notes that in order to maintain a cooperative environment it is important to arrive at a consensus.

Does the Writing Address Your Reader's Needs?

You learned in chapter 4 how important it is to explain how the evidence you provide supports your claims. As one literature professor put it: "It is your responsibility to show your reader how and why what you claim is true." Don't expect your professors to fill in the missing pieces. The following student paragraph is an example of writing that leaves too much for readers to figure out for themselves:

> Exploitation of workers in sweatshops is a serious problem. In *The Corporation* and in an Internet source I read, they provided graphic scenes of young people forced to work in sweatshops to survive. Many of the workers are young people. Pictures of the sad looking women made me pity them and their situation. We learned from interviews that some women are abused. In the Internet source, they talked about a woman who was afraid to talk to her boss because he might hit her or fire her. Another sad story is that of 72 Thai workers who were placed behind a secure barbed wire fence and then forced to work for clothing corporations.

Readers are left with many questions here. What, for instance, is *The Corporation*—the title of a book or movie? What "Internet source" is the author referring to? Who is the "they" who described graphic scenes? What interviews? What clothing corporations? References to the "sad looking women" and "72 Thai workers" suggest the writer thinks her audience has seen the same images she has.

In reality, that was the case. The writer is referring to information from sources assigned by her professor, including the documentary *The Corporation*, so it's easy to understand why she did not think more explanation was needed. But, unless otherwise instructed, you should imagine a larger audience than just your professor. In the following paragraph, the writer also refers to information in sources assigned by his professor, but he adds details to allow anyone to understand the examples:

> Many people who work at minimum-wage jobs must work two, sometimes three, low paying jobs at once. Barbara Ehrenreich, author of the book *Nickel and Dimed*, worked at minimum-wage jobs around the country for a year to learn for herself how difficult it is to survive on those wages. In Florida, she was employed at two restaurants at the same time just to

survive. In Maine, she worked at both the Woodcrest Residential Facility and The Merry Maids. Ehrenreich found that working only one job was not enough to support herself, let alone a family.

The prose in this paragraph is sensitive to the readers' needs. The writer discusses Ehrenreich's book in a way that does not assume the reader is familiar with it, creating the impression that his writing was self-prompted instead of teacher-prompted.

To make your writing reader-friendly, don't make the reader guess. Connections between ideas should be explicit. The relevance of evidence should be clear. Sources of information should be identified and the point of examples obvious. The importance of the subject matter should be, if not stated, then clearly implied. Ask yourself if someone who has *not* read your sources could understand your meaning. As explained in chapter 4, professors usually expect you to carry on the "façade" of writing to a broad audience.

Have You Used Feedback from Professors?

If your professor reads a draft of your paper, he or she will likely make suggestions for global revisions. Of course, these comments can only help you if you understand what they mean and act on them. When English professors Carolyn Calhoon-Dillahunt and Dodie Forrest surveyed and interviewed students about their instructors' feedback, they learned that students are sometimes uncertain of how to respond to comments like "develop," "flesh out," "tweak," "analyze," "dig deeper," "relevance," and "show" written in the margins (237). When instructors write questions like "Do you think there is another way to look at this problem?" or "Why is this topic important?" on your draft, they are trying to help you discover for yourself how to improve your writing.

Use the following tips to make the best use of your instructors' feedback.

- **Read and interpret marginal comments in context.** When your instructor writes a comment or question in the margin, the comment usually relates specifically to the adjacent paragraph or text. Don't just read the comments; reread your own writing next to the comment to understand what prompted the remark.
- **Apply end comments globally.** Comments at the end of a paper tend to be general in nature, perhaps commenting on something your instructor has noticed throughout a paper or throughout the term. Reread your paper with the end comments in mind, looking for places where you can address any concerns identified.
- **Ask your professor for an illustration when general feedback is not clear to you.** If you don't understand what your instructor's comments mean, ask for clarification or for an example.

The feedback professors give on your papers is some of the most valuable you'll receive in college because the advice is customized for *you*. Read the comments, take the time to understand them, and then try to apply them to current or future writing assignments.

Concept in Practice 11.3: Using Instructor Feedback

The following paragraph, written by Shesha Kelley, is from the draft of a paper about the role that culture plays in making us who we are. In the margins, Shesha's instructor has given feedback. Using this feedback, how would you revise the paragraph?

Culture can play a large role in how people think and act. For example, in some cultures the concept of getting a higher education is a far distant dream. However, some people refuse to settle for the perceived notion that they are destined to be the same as their family before them. Sandria Rodriguez, dean of communication arts, humanities and fine arts at College of Lake County, discusses the trials and tribulations that some first generation college students endure to break free of the cultural bias of being uneducated (18). Rodriguez herself was one of the first children in her family to receive a college diploma; she expresses how even though her mother never progressed past the fifth grade, she yearned for her children to get a better education (18). This spurred Rodriguez to conduct in depth interviews in an attempt to discern what influences led to other first generation college students' success (18). In Rodriguez's research, the people that had a mentor in their life, that they perceived to have confidence in them, used that positive influence to persevere when no one else thought they could (20). Take Clara, for instance, one of the subjects Rodriguez interviewed; she indicated that without the care and support of her Spanish teacher she probably would not have continued on her path of education (20). Culture can also determine what might be appropriate or inappropriate to ask a friend or coworker. Joseph Ruane, professor emeritus of sociology, states that a question that seems ordinary to you may be perceived as rude or invasive to someone with cultural differences (27). In other words, even though a person's culture can give you an indication of how they might think or behave, you should never make assumptions based on that because this can cause big problems, especially in the workplace.

It's not yet clear how Clara illustrates the influence culture has on a person. (The example seems to illustrate the importance of having a mentor.)

Hmm. The connection between Rodriguez's point and Ruane's seems a bit "forced."

It's global revisions like those described in this chapter that most improve a paper. English professors David Wallace and John Hayes found evidence of this when they compared the quality of revisions made to a document by two groups of first-year students. Before revising, one group received instruction about global revisions; the other group received the same document but received no instruction beyond "improve the document." Documents revised by the students who received instruction on global revision were rated by independent evaluators to be of "significantly better quality" than the documents revised by students receiving no instruction about global revision.

Making Local Edits

The focus of this chapter so far has been on making revisions—global improvements to the structure, content, and logic of your paper. But making edits—"local" improvements at the sentence level—matters, too. Discussed in this section are a few techniques for polishing sentences to improve their effectiveness.

Decide between Active Voice or Passive Voice

One sentence-level edit to consider is whether to use active or passive voice. When a sentence is written in **active voice**, emphasis is usually on the actor—the name of the person or thing doing the action. On the other hand, when a sentence is in **passive voice**, emphasis falls on the action more than on the one doing the action. Sentences in the passive voice include the following passive voice formula: a form of the verb *to be* + *past participle.* In other words:

to be (*am, is, are, was, were, be, being*)
+
past participle (i.e., the form of a verb you would use after the word *have*)

Occasionally an adverb comes between the *to be* verb and *past participle* verb.

Compare the active and passive voice versions of the following sentences. (Italics highlight the passive voice formula.)

Sentences in Active Voice	Sentences in Passive Voice
Half the subjects took the test drug; half took a placebo.	The test drug *was taken* by half the subjects; a placebo *was taken* by the other half.
Most of those who took the test drug experienced "some relief" or even "significant relief" of pain symptoms.	"Some relief" or even "significant relief" of pain symptoms *was experienced* by most of those who took the test drug.
A majority (67%) of those who took the placebo reported little change in symptoms.	Little change in symptoms *was reported* by a majority (67%) of those who took the placebo.

Notice how the passive voice versions require more words than the active voice versions. In fact, one reason to consider using the active voice is that it can be more concise:

Passive Voice: Proponents hope the bill will *be passed* by Congress later this year.
Active Voice: Proponents hope Congress will pass the bill later this year.

Active voice can also be more direct. Passive voice phrases like "it was found that" or "it has been discovered" leave readers wondering who did what. In addition, the active voice lends itself naturally to creating a voice of authority. (Compare "It has been concluded that . . ." to "We have concluded that. . . .")

However, passive voice has legitimate purposes. Sometimes the actors are unknown or unworthy of mention:

Passive Voice: The college will *be closed* this Monday due to the holiday.
Active Voice: School administrators will close the college this Monday due to the holiday.

In this example, the passive voice version seems preferable to the active voice version. For the audience (students) it matters more that the school will be closed than who issued the closing.

In the Methods section of research articles, passive voice allows writers to avoid repeatedly naming the researchers.

Passive Voice: Height, weight, and blood pressure *were recorded* for each subject. The subjects *were* then *given* one month's supply of medication, and they *were told* to take one pill a day. They *were instructed* to report any symptoms in a journal.
Active Voice: We recorded the height, weight, and blood pressure for each subject. Then we gave each subject one month's supply of medication, and we told subjects to take one pill a day. We instructed subjects to report any symptoms in a journal.

As illustrated in this example, passive voice can also be useful when working in disciplines that avoid first person in their writing.

Another use of passive voice is to soften the tone of a statement or to avoid placing blame:

Passive Voice: Your loan application has *been denied*.
Active Voice: The bank manager denied your loan application.

Converting this sentence to active voice only adds information the writer doesn't want to add. In fact, a general rule is this: *If converting a passive voice sentence into active voice requires you to add words, use the passive voice.* If, however, you have no reason for using passive voice, opt for the more concise and direct active voice.

Use the "Given-New" Pattern

Another local editing strategy that can improve the interconnection between sentences and the overall flow of your writing is the **given-new pattern**. Writers who follow this pattern begin sentences with information readers have already been told or likely already know ("given" information) before presenting "new" information. This pattern provides readers with a context, or a "frame," in which to put new information. Generally, sentences written in the "given-new" pattern are easier to read and understand than sentences in which "new" precedes "old" (Chafe).

Concept in Practice 11.4: Using the "Given-New" Pattern

The "given-new" pattern is illustrated in the following passage from a sports medicine journal. Notice how the bolded words found at the beginning of sentences refer to information previously "given" (in italics).

EXAMPLE 11.3 FROM A SPORTS MEDICINE JOURNAL

Attention was focused on the *peroneus longus muscle* because of its well-defined protecting role against inversion ankle sprains. The **peroneus longus** is normally activated during the middle and terminal stance phases of the stride, providing lateral support during the single-limb stance, when *ankle*
5 *sprains* mostly occur. Most **ankle sprains** occur when a *supination moment force is applied to the foot while an external rotation force is applied to the leg.* **This combination** happens in certain clinical situations, such as landing from a fall, landing from a jump, or stepping down, all of which occur during a single-limb stance phase. However, to explain the pathophysiology of **multiple ankle**
10 **sprains**, a combined action between *diminished proprioception* and weakness of the evertor muscles should be considered. Because of the **proprioceptive deficit**, an inversion sprain may occur while the ankle is in inversion during the weightbearing phase of the gait cycle and the evertor muscles are unable to contrast the inversion moment. **Proprioceptive deficit** in patients with func-
15 tional ankle instability has been widely studied and diagnosed. . . .

(Santilli et al. 1186, emphasis added)

Beginning sentences with words or concepts named in previous sentences is an effective way to create cohesion.

Help Readers Navigate Complex Sentence Patterns

Using the given-new pattern is one way to help readers navigate a paragraph. Other sentence-level changes can help readers navigate particularly complex sentences. The sentences in Table 11.2, for instance, illustrate how writers can use letters, numbers, parentheses, and lists to lead readers through complicated passages.

TABLE 11.2

Examples of Easy-to-Navigate Sentence Patterns

Function	Sample Sentences
Using letters to denote points	**Example 11.4 from a Psychology Journal** The questions guiding this investigation were, (a) what are the individual and community narratives around social justice, especially connected to religious beliefs, (b) what social processes occur in the networking organization that facilitate or inhibit social justice action, (c) how is social capital created and used by the organization, (d) how do organizations actually network, (e) what characteristics of the networking organization facilitate social justice work, and (f) how are all of the above questions similar and different for more liberal versus conservative religious networking organizations? (Todd 232)
Using numerals to denote points	**Example 11.5 from an English Composition Journal** I shall report the results of a study in which I asked the questions: (1) why do teachers give the grades they do? (2) are there any specific, definable parts of student papers that influence teachers? (3) and if there are, which of the parts influence teachers most? (Freedman 161)
Using parentheses to set off numerical data	**Example 11.6 from a Psychology Journal** In Belgium, Italy and England the levels of adolescents' involvement in community organizations were quite similar (respectively 1.52, 1.60 and 1.69); Romanian adolescents were the least involved in civic organizations (1.27); Canadian youth had the highest levels of civic engagement (1.87), but that was still modest in a 0–12 scale. (Lenzi et al. 204)
Using parentheses to set off clarifying comments	**Example 11.7 from a Marketing Journal** Generalizing across the factors we examine (promotional history, consumer expertise, and industry promotional norms), it appears that promotions are a signal of lower brand quality when consumers do not have access to alternative information regarding brand quality (i.e., they are not experts) and when the promotional behavior stands out because it deviates from the industry norm (i.e., is distinctive) and the brand's own past behavior (i.e., is inconsistent). (Raghubir and Corfman 219)

In each example in Table 11.2 the writer has formatted the sentence in a way that helps readers comprehend the details more easily.

Edit for Conciseness

In **concise writing** every word adds meaning or is grammatically necessary. Conversely, unnecessary words dilute unconcise writing. But don't assume a long sentence or document is unconcise. Conciseness refers to the *quality* of words, not the number, as you'll see in this section.

The following revising techniques will help you write as concisely as any expert writer.

Replace Weak Verb Phrases with Single, Active Verbs. Weak (or "helping") verbs include forms of *to be* and other basic verbs, some of which appear here:

Forms of *to be*	**Other commonly used helping verbs**
am	has/had/have
is	can/could
are	will/would
were	shall
was	may/might
be	do/does
being	

These verbs typically appear in verb phrases, because alone they convey little meaning, thus their designation as "weak" or "helping" verbs. Delete them and the impact of your writing strengthens. For example, in the following sentence, two of three helping verbs (*will* and *are*) are unnecessary:

> One site most tourists ~~will~~ visit ~~when they are~~ in Washington D.C. is the Lincoln Memorial.

Eliminating these verbs makes the sentence more concise:

> One site most tourists visit when in Washington D.C. is the Lincoln Memorial.

Eliminate Filler Words. **Filler words** add no meaning. *That, who,* and *which* can be filler words. Prepositions, like *of, for, to,* and *in*, can also just fill space. These words are often easy to eliminate:

> studies *that* involve human subjects = studies involving human subjects
> troops *who are* stationed in Iraq = troops stationed in Iraq
> the CEO *of* the company = the company's CEO
> the first article *in* the magazine = the magazine's first article

Once you notice (filler) words, you'll discover ways to eliminate them. For example, underline the filler words (including *that, which, to,* and *of*) in the following passage. Can you delete any?

When they were writing their report, the researchers considered factors that usually are associated with income, which include education, age, race, gender, and geography. They came to the conclusion that more than any other factor, one's level of education is a predictor of one's income.

Here is one way to revise the passage:

When writing their report, the researchers considered factors associated with income, including education, age, race, gender, and geography. They concluded that education level, more than any other factor, predicts one's income.

Eliminate Redundancy. Redundancy is more detrimental than filler words for writers wanting to create a voice of authority. Redundancy is *unintentional* repetition, the type of repetition that makes readers wonder what (or if) the writer was thinking. Examples of redundant expressions follow. The words in parentheses are unnecessary:

my (personal) opinion	(past) experience
(general) consensus	(the month of) July
(usual) custom	repeat (again)
(very) essential	(really) important

Two common redundant expressions are *reason why* and *reason is because*:

One *reason why* people oppose Judge Santiago's appointment to the appellate court is *because* of her reputation for protecting big business.

Here is one way to improve this sentence:

Judge Santiago's reputation for protecting big business is one *reason* people oppose her appointment to the appellate court.

Here is another improved version:

People oppose Judge Santiago's appointment to the appellate court *because* of her reputation for protecting big business.

Do not expect to write concise first drafts. Most writers continue finding unnecessary words in the fourth or fifth draft of a document. But time spent revising for conciseness is well invested, and, as with most skills, learning how to make your writing concise gets easier with practice. This is good news because nothing more dramatically improves your writing style.

Concept in Practice 11.5: Editing for Conciseness

When revising for conciseness, improvements to single sentences are not dramatic, but the *cumulative* effect is. Consider the following paragraph from the first draft of a student essay. First, underline the weak verbs and filler words, and then revise the paragraph so that it more concisely conveys the information.

The American fast food industry has brought to the global market something that was once thought to be uniquely American: obesity. In both Great Britain and Japan the obesity rate has actually doubled. This coincides with the doubling of fast food restaurants in Great Britain and Japan. In countries where the consumption of fast food has remained low, like Spain and Italy, so has the rate of obesity.

Examples of words to underline in this paragraph include *has, that, was, to be, has actually,* and *of.* You can eliminate most of these words without losing meaning. Here, for example, is one revision. How does your revision compare?

The American fast food industry brought to the global market something once thought uniquely American: obesity. In both Great Britain and Japan the obesity rate has doubled. This coincides with the doubling of fast food restaurants in those countries. In countries like Spain and Italy, where fast food consumption has remained low, so has obesity.

Editing for Correct Grammar and Spelling

Surface correctness matters to more than just English teachers. To learn how readers react to seemingly small details—grammar and spelling errors—English professor Larry Beason asked 14 businesspeople to read different versions of a business document that included a few instances of errors (such as sentence fragments, fused sentences, misspelled words). The participants differed in what kinds of errors bothered them most, but they agreed that errors caused them to view the writer as careless, lazy, uneducated, or not detail oriented (50, 53–54).

How can you produce error-free papers? Two obvious ways to eliminate many of the errors that appear in most first drafts are to use the spelling and grammar checks in your word processing software and to proofread—more than once. Ideally, your second and third readings will be a few hours or days apart. When you return to a document, you notice things missed when what you intended to write is still fresh in mind. If you tend to overlook typos or sentence fragments, try reading a paper backwards—that is, start by reading the last sentence first. Your reading rate is slowed when sentences are read out of context, helping you to notice errors. Another tip is to have others proofread your papers. Sometimes, because you know what you meant to say, you are the last to see obvious errors. Finally, keep a list of the kinds of errors professors mark on your papers. Take the time to learn how to correct these errors and purposefully look for these errors in your drafts. (Guides to punctuation and grammar are freely available online; one example is the University of Wisconsin–Madison Writing Center's Writer's Handbook at http://writing.wisc.edu/Handbook/GramPunct.html.)

When proofreading onscreen, you may need to take extra breaks because most people get tired faster when reading onscreen rather than on paper. Many people also proofread onscreen more slowly, perhaps because the contrast between the characters and background can be less distinct than in printed text (Wharton-Michael 29–31). Some research even indicates that readers catch more errors when reading a printed text rather than on screen (Wharton-Michael 34–35). However, for many low-stakes assignments submitted online, proofreading onscreen is both practical and environmentally friendly. When you do proofread onscreen, try adjusting the font and display contrast so that the print is dark enough and large enough to easily see punctuation as well as words.

Final Revising and Editing Tips

Here are a few final tips for revising and editing papers:

1. **Reread your paper like a reader.** Put your paper aside for awhile. Then return to your paper and approach it like a reader—not the writer. Take note of places where your reading pace is slowed, where connections are not clear, where what you've written just doesn't make sense.
2. **Concentrate on just one or two things at a time when revising.** Consider questions like "Is this the best organization for paragraphs?" separately from questions like "Where do I need more evidence?"
3. **Read aloud and listen to the sound of your sentences.** When we read aloud, we are more apt to hear awkward phrasing than when reading silently. Revise sentences that sound "clumsy" or that force you to reread because of convoluted sentence structure.

Although this chapter describes ways to improve an already written first draft, in reality revising and editing are recurrent activities that occur while writers plan their papers, write their papers, and read what they have written. Revision involves adding information, deleting information, reorganizing, and correcting. It involves trying to find better ways to accomplish your task. Editing involves clarifying awkward language and voice, and correcting errors in sentence structure, grammar, and spelling. Look for ways to make your meaning more accessible to the reader, more pleasing to the ear, and more correct.

Applying the Concepts to Reading: *Making Global Revisions*

Compare the two passages that follow. The passage on the left is from an early draft of chapter 4, a chapter that describes writing assignments and discusses a sample of 20 assignment prompts. The passage on the right includes revisions I made to better address the audience (you!) and to better achieve my purpose (to define and explain analysis).

Identify the types of global revisions made in the passage on the right and speculate on the reasons for them. Do you think the changes are improvements? Why or why not? Can you recommend additional revisions to improve the passage?

Early Draft of the Passage	Revised Draft of the Passage
Analysis To introduce students to academic ways of thinking, most professors ask students to do the kind of work experts in their disciplines do. All twenty of the writing assignments in our sample involve analyzing the kinds of data or texts studied in the discipline. Whether the subject is a poem, a baseball game, a tsunami, a dynasty, or an internal combustion engine, analysis involves breaking something down to determine how the parts are related, how they work together, or how they combine to achieve some purpose. Writing prompts that call for analysis might ask the student to discover how things are similar or different, how they demonstrate a larger principle, how they combine to make	**RECOGNIZING ANALYSIS** National surveys of writing prompts indicate that most papers you write in college will involve analysis and argument (Head and Eisenberg, "Assigning"; Melzer; Wolfe). **Analysis** involves breaking down a subject—whether a poem, a dynasty, or an internal combustion engine—to determine how the parts are related or how they combine to achieve some purpose. Writing prompts that call for analysis might ask you to: • discover how things are similar or different (e.g., *compare two forms of government*); • explain how specific examples demonstrate a larger principle (e.g., *make a diagnosis based on a patient's symptoms*); • describe how elements combine to make something work (e.g., *describe how various poetic elements achieve a poet's purpose);*

(*continued*)

(continued)

Early Draft of the Passage	Revised Draft of the Passage
something work (or not work), or why they are the way they are. Whatever the goal, analysis involves looking past surface reading or observation to determine significance, meaning, or understanding that can't be gained without close examination.	• determine which is better between two options (e.g., *argue for which approach you think is better for teaching arithmetic).* Analysis involves looking past the surface and examining something deeply in order to discover a significance, meaning, or understanding that can't be gained otherwise.
Our sample of twenty writing prompts includes four common types of analysis assignments.	**Types of Analysis** Many college writing prompts call for one of the following types of analysis.
Find or Delineate a Recurring Pattern. Critically reading and inferring patterns from raw data—such as seismograph activity, artwork, literary works, speeches, or economic data—is one type of analysis called for in the writing prompts. . . .	**Find or Delineate a Recurring Pattern.** Inferring patterns from raw data—such as seismograph activity, artwork, or economic data—is one type of analysis called for across disciplines. . . .

Applying the Concepts to Writing: *Using a Revising Checklist*

Most successful writers write several drafts of a document, each draft improving aspects of both substance and style. Take a paper you are working on and, using the following checklist or one your instructor provides, revise it to ensure the document is as complete, accessible, and correct as possible. As you revise, keep your intended audience and purpose in mind.

Revising Checklist

1. Does the paper fulfill assignment requirements concerning topic, purpose, and length?
2. Does the introduction express my main claim and prepare readers for the organization of the discussion?
3. Does each body paragraph relate clearly to the claim(s) made in the introduction or is the purpose of any digression made clear?
4. Are body paragraphs arranged in the best order?
5. Does each body paragraph include an early topic sentence summarizing the point?

6. Is each body paragraph developed with sufficient evidence for the main idea?
7. Would the evidence be clear, even to those who have not read my sources?
8. Is the evidence detailed and convincing?
9. Are my sources named?
10. Are body paragraphs connected with transition words or sentences?
11. Have I looked for places to provide overview sentences, review sentences, or section headings?
12. Does the paper have an appropriate conclusion? If readers read the first and last paragraphs only, would they be able to guess what came in between?
13. Are there any places where numbers or letters could draw attention to key points?
14. Have I read the paper aloud and revised unclear or awkward sentences?
15. Are my sentences concise?
16. Have I used the spell checker and have I proofread more than once? Remember that a spell checker won't always catch homonym errors (e.g., *its* vs. *it's*) or recognize when a word is misused (e.g., *then* vs. *than*).
17. Does the title tell readers what my paper is about? Is the title centered at the top of the first page, without quotation marks and without underlining?
18. Have I followed my instructor's guidelines concerning margins, page numbering, type font, etc.?

Paired Readings from Education

"Some Reasons for the Grades We Give Compositions," *The English Journal* SARAH WARSHAUER FREEDMAN

This chapter's paired readings feature early research addressing a question of interest to many students: What do English teachers look for when grading papers? Sarah Warshauer Freedman, who today is a professor in the College of Education at University of California, Berkeley, wanted to determine why English professors give the grades they give. Her research revealed that when English professors grade writing, they do not consider correct spelling and grammar to be most important, a finding since confirmed by additional studies. "Some Reasons for the Grades We Give Compositions" appeared in 1982 in *The English Journal*, which publishes articles of interest to teachers of English and language arts in middle school, junior high, or high school.

Susan took the first semester of required college freshman writing from Ms. B. and failed. Second semester, she repeated the class with Ms. R. In a first week writing conference, Ms. R. routinely asked each student about past writing problems. Susan admitted, "I'm not quite sure what my problems are because it's kind of hard to interpret from one class to another class." Susan felt confused about how to interpret the responses of different teachers to her writing, but she understood that she would be more likely to pass the course if she knew how to compare her different teachers' grading and commenting practices.

Concerned about Susan's confusion, Ms. R. said, "It'll be interesting when you get your papers back from me and I mark them to see if they're somewhat the same kind of comments [as those of Ms. B.]." Responding to her teacher's openness, Susan made an unusual request: she asked Ms. R. to mark clean copies of the papers she had written for Ms. B. Ms. R. agreed.

From their own points of view, Susan and Ms. R. were exploring one of the most difficult and important problems in writing classes. Ms. R. wanted to discover the fairest and most useful ways to grade and comment on student papers. Susan wanted to discover how to interpret and learn from her teachers' responses.

Grades on compositions are often difficult for students to predict and interpret because students frequently do not understand many of their teachers' written comments (Hahn, 1981). Comments are often overgeneralized, ambiguous, and uninterpretable (Sommers, 1981). And when they are interpretable, students may not always read what we write carefully or thoughtfully. When students do not understand how we evaluate their work, they tend both to devalue advice and to have difficulty learning from us. Hirsch (1977) claims that writing assessment is "the single most important snag to practical progress in composition teaching and research."

In the 1950s, research on why evaluators respond as they do interested Educational Testing Service (ETS). ETS needed to solve a practical problem, how to reliably score the essays which had recently become part of their standardized tests. After an extensive review of the literature on reliability (agreement among raters), Edith Huddleston concluded "that the unreliability of essay examinations is most pronounced in the area of English composition" (p. 165).

For the first ETS project, Diederich, French, and Carleton (1961) had 300 papers written by college freshmen rated by 53 readers from six fields—college English teachers, social science teachers, writers, editors, lawyers, and business executives. These readers rated in their homes, much as English teachers evaluate papers. Readers were directed to write brief comments on as many papers as they could and to assign each paper a general merit score.

After finding gross disagreements among the evaluators, Diederich attempted to discover the cause. Statistical analyses revealed that raters giving similar scores fell into five clusters. Analyses of the comments of the raters in each cluster led Diederich to hypothesize that the clusters were formed around the part of the essay the cluster members valued most: (1) ideas, (2) usage, sentence structure, punctuation, and spelling, (3) organization and analysis, (4) wording and phrasing, or (5) personal qualities. Although most of cluster two, the mechanics group, was made up of English teachers, the other clusters were not strongly associated with particular occupations.

After completing the study, the Diederich team developed an analytic rating scale so raters could judge a composition separately on each of its apparently salient dimensions. Each part of the scale was keyed to the values of one cluster of Diederich's readers. Diederich reasoned that on the new scale, the readers' different values could not influence their scores, and readers would rate more reliably, more consistently, more dependably. But the reliability problems remained. Because of methodological problems in the Diederich study (see Freedman, 1977, for further explanation), the theory that led to creating the scale was flawed. The scale never gained popularity because it was time consuming and limited to the expository prose of older students.

In a 1966 ETS study, Meyers, McConville, and Coffman found that a homogeneous group of experienced English teachers also fell into agreement clusters, but the clusters could be explained by the fact that some raters were more lenient than others. They suggest:

> in contrast to the Diederich, French, and Carleton study, that, although all of the readers may have assigned different weights to the various attributes of a composition (e.g., spelling, grammar, organization), *each of the individual attributes tended to be given the same weight by the readers* (italics mine). That is, it does not seem as though some judges rated the papers primarily upon grammar, while others rated the papers primarily upon style. Rather, this explanation suggests that the relative weighting between grammar and style is *roughly* the same for all judges (p. 52).

Unfortunately for teachers, without finding out anything else about why evaluators respond as they do, ETS solved their reliability problems empirically; by summing the scores of three raters with homogeneous backgrounds rating on a four-point holistic scale, they could get respectable reliability (Godshalk, Swineford, and Coffman, 1966). Later, ETS discovered that they could obtain even better reliability if the raters were trained to agree with one another. Miles Myers describes standard holistic rating practices today: "the most reliable scoring of writing samples takes place when the readers are trained together and read together in the same room under common direction" (p. 26).

The ETS research suggests that experienced English teachers can apply the same set of values to papers they evaluate and, with training, they can adjust one difference, their degree of leniency. To move toward reducing the frustration of students like Susan, we need to know precisely what properties of student essays experienced teachers value most.

Researchers have examined easily countable qualities within essays that correlate with teacher scores (e.g., Page, 1968; Nold and Freedman, 1977; Grobe, 1981). The findings are unremarkable. Consistently, essay length is found to correlate with scores for essays; the longer the essay, the better the score. Correlational research shows associations but cannot explain why raters evaluate as they do. Just because essay length is associated with essay quality, we would not advocate that students pad their essays. However, we might hypothesize that essay length is related to other factors that might cause teachers to score as they do.

I designed an experiment to try to discover what causes teachers to score as they do. I particularly wanted to know how experienced teachers weigh each part of an essay when they assign a score to the whole (Freedman, 1977, 1979-a, 1979-b; Freedman and Calfee, in press). I wanted to know whether English teachers value mechanics above development and organization as the Diederich study implied they might or whether teachers value development most, as the correlational studies suggest.

I selected a set of previously scored, average quality, expository essays by college freshmen and had them rewritten to be weaker or stronger in (1) development or content, (2) organization, (3) sentence structure, and (4) mechanics. Then I had these rewritten essays judged by groups of English teachers who did not know that the essays had been tampered with. Since I knew which essays were strong or weak in which qualities, I could examine scores to see what types of strength or weakness mattered most to the teachers.

In an earlier study using a partial rewriting technique, Harris (1977) examined two parts of the essay, (1) content and organization and (2) sentence structure and mechanics. She found that high school teachers would rank-order papers on the basis of strengths or weaknesses in content and organization rather than on the basis of the strengths or weaknesses of sentence structure and mechanics.

My study confirmed Harris' findings and yielded interesting additional results. I found teachers gave significantly higher scores to papers rewritten to be strong in development, organization, and mechanics than they did to papers rewritten to be weak in these areas. That's to be expected, but not all the positive points are weighed in a parallel way, and *the weighing shows our hierarchy of values.* First, sentence structure rewriting, in and of itself, proved a negligible effect on the raters, unlike the other types of rewriting. The development rewriting was most influential, the organization rewriting next, and mechanics third.

The development rewriting proved so powerful that, given strong or weak development, other types of strength or weakness did not matter much.

However, if the organization was strong, then the quality of the mechanics mattered even more than it did on its own and the quality of the sentence structure mattered as well. Teachers in this study apparently felt that if the discourse level qualities were weak, the paper deserved a low score, and *strong sentence structure and mechanics could not redeem such papers.* But once the discourse level qualities were strong, the lower levels mattered; strengths or weakness of mechanics or sentence structure could then raise or lower a score. English teachers apparently care about sentence structure only under conditions in which the organization is already strong and about mechanics most under that condition.

The excellent research on the writing process lends theoretical support for our hierarchy of values: development, then organization, then mechanics and sentence structure once the higher levels of the discourse are under control. Remember that these are values which we apply to finished products; they do not necessarily dictate a curricular sequence.

Others have rewritten student essays to determine what influences the evaluator (e.g., Piche, Michlin, Rubin, and Turner, 1978; Nielsen and Piche, 1981; Hake and Williams, 1981). They have looked mostly at sentence level or mechanical parts of the student essay in some detail—e.g., black dialect features or nominal versus verbal style.

In an interesting correlational study, Thompson (1976) examined how several specific aspects of these discourse level categories were related to teacher's evaluations. He found unsupported statements, lack of unity, and independent judgment errors (flaws in arguments, oversimplifications of topics, and lack of proper inferences) accounted for holistic scores much better than problems with mechanics, coherence, or wordiness. Thompson's discourse level categories fall within the category that I labeled development.

None of this research took place in the classroom. In a later study, Thompson (1981) illustrates how successful we can be in the classroom if we communicate expectations to students. He found students could be trained to develop and reliably apply a set of standards about essays. Most interesting, he found students learned to understand and apply their teacher's standards. But until teachers articulate the bases of their scores and act consistently with one another, students like Susan still may have difficulty making the transition from one class to the next.

I would guess that one of the appeals of group editing is that the sessions help students clarify why papers are evaluated as they are—not just why they receive a particular grade but also why they receive particular comments.

Recently, a freshman at Berkeley, a participant in a research project, told me that she did not feel she learned anything in her writing class. She thought she began the class as an adequate writer. At the end of the course she received a *B*; she wanted an *A*. Although the grade was important to her, more important was the fact that she had no idea what she needed to do to write *A* papers. Later her teacher told me that he thought the student began the class as a good writer and her writing had improved, but not to *A* level.

We need to let competent, highly motivated writers know that they should reach higher and then show them how to reach. It is only too easy to praise such students and thereby fail to demand the achievement we might.

I recently began a descriptive study of how experienced teachers respond to student papers in individual conferences (Freedman, 1981). Besides providing detail about teachers' responses as they occur, I hope to develop hypotheses about how experienced teachers communicate values about writing to students. So far, I have found that students have a set of concerns about their writing when they enter a class and what they *hear* from the teacher depends on how well the teacher *listens* to them. Teachers seem to be most successful in helping students *hear* if they first listen and respond to students' concerns.

From yet another point of view, Hirsch (1977) considers global assessment issues outside writing classrooms. He claims writing assessment must "be consistent with judgments about good writing in literate society at large" and that "no . . . professional assessment should be at odds with the verdict of that (society's) court" (p. 177). Before accepting Hirsch's view, two considerations are important. First, society often says it values mechanics most when in fact it may value larger levels of discourse more. Teachers in my rewriting study could not have told me their values as clearly as they revealed them to me under testing. We need to distinguish what society claims it values from what it actually values. Second, regardless of what society claims to value, as English teachers it is our place to guide society to see our point of view. We are professionals. It is crucial that we communicate our point of view clearly not only to society, but also to students.

REFERENCES

Diederich, Paul, John French, and Sydell Carlton. *Factors in Judgments of Writing Ability*. Research Bulletin RB-61–15. Princeton: Educational Testing Service, 1961.

Freedman, Sarah. "Evaluation in the Writing Conference: An Interactive Process." *Selected Papers from the 1981 Texas Writing Research Conference*, Maxine Hairston and Cynthia Selfe, eds. Austin: University of Texas, 1981.

Freedman, Sarah. "How Characteristics of Student Essays Influence Teachers' Evaluations." *Journal of Educational Psychology* 71 (July 1979): 328–338.

Freedman, Sarah. "Influences on the Evaluators of Expository Essays: Beyond the Text." *Research in the Teaching of English* 15 (October 1981): 245–255.

Freedman, Sarah. *Influences on the Evaluators of Student Writing*. Unpublished doctoral dissertation, Stanford University, 1977.

Freedman, Sarah. "Why Teachers Give the Grades They Do." *College Composition and Communication* 30 (May 1979): 161–164.

Freedman, Sarah and Robert Calfee. "Holistic Assessment of Writing: Experimental Design and Cognitive Theory." *Research in Writing: Principles and Methods*. Peter Mosenthal, Lynn Tamor, and Sean Walmsley, eds. New York: Longman, in press.

Godshalk, Fred I., Frances Swineford, and William Coffman. *The Measurement of Writing Ability*. New York: College Entrance Examination Board, 1966.

Grobe, Stewart. "Syntactic Maturity, Mechanics, and Vocabulary as Predictors of Quality Ratings." *Research in the Teaching of English* 15 (February 1981): 75–85.

Hahn, J. "Students' Reactions to Teachers' Written Comments." National Writing Project Network Newsletter 4 (1981): 7–10.

Hake, Rosemary L. and Joseph M. Williams. "Style and Its Consequences: Do as I Do, Not as I Say." *College English* 43 (September 1981): 433–451.

Harris, Winifred Hall. "Teacher Responses to Student Writing: A Study of the Response Patterns of High School English Teachers to Determine the Basis for Teacher Judgment of Student Writing." *Research in the Teaching of English* 11 (Fall 1977): 175–185.

Hirsch, E. Donald. *The Philosophy of Composition*. Chicago: University of Chicago Press, 1977.

Huddleston, Edith. "Measurement of Writing Ability at the College Level: Objective vs Subjective Testing Techniques." *Journal of Experimental Education* 22 (March 1954); 165–213.

Myers, A., Carolyn McConville, and William Coffman. "Simplex Structure in the Grading of Essay Tests." *Educational and Psychological Measurement* 26 (Spring 1966): 41–54.

Myers, Miles. *A Procedure for Writing Assessment and Holistic Scoring.* Urbana, Illinois: National Council of Teachers of English, 1980.
Nielsen, Lorraine and Gene Piche. "The Influence of Headed Nominal Complexity and Lexical Choice on Teachers' Evaluation of Writing." *Research in the Teaching of English* 15 (February 1981): 65–73.
Nold, Ellen and Sarah Freedman. "An Analysis of Readers' Responses to Student Writing," *Research in the Teaching of English* 11 (Fall 1977): 164–174.
Page, Ellis. "Analyzing Student Essays by Computer." *International Review of Education* 14 (1968): 210–225.
Piche, Gene, Michael Michlin, Donald Rubin, and L. Turner. "Teachers' Subjective Evaluation of Standard and Black Nonstandard English Composition: A Study of Written Language Attitudes." *Research in the Teaching of English* 12 (May 1978): 107–118.
Sommers, Nancy. "Responding to Student Writing." *National Writing Project Network Newsletter* 3 (1981): 7–11.
Thompson, Richard. "Peer Grading: Some Promising Advantages for Composition Research in the Classroom." *Research in the Teaching of English* 15 (May 1981): 172–174.
Thompson, Richard. "Predicting Writing Quality, Writing Weaknesses that Dependably Predict Holistic Evaluations of Freshman Compositions." *English Studies Collections, 1* (1976). (Available from Scholarly Publishers, 172 Vincent Drive, East Meadow, New York 11554).

QUESTIONS ABOUT MEANING

1. Who is Freedman's target audience? Identify several sentences that make clear who the audience is.
2. What do experienced writing teachers tend to reward in student writing? What does Freedman think is the reason for this tendency? How does Freedman test her hypothesis?
3. What "hierarchy of values" did the teachers in the study have when grading essays?
4. What further actions does Freedman call for?

QUESTIONS FOR RHETORICAL ANALYSIS

5. Analyze the structure of Freedman's argument by dividing the article into sections and summarizing the purpose of each section. For example, the first four paragraphs establish the importance of the topic. What is the purpose of other sections? Is the organization of sections logical?
6. Numbering sentence elements is one editing technique discussed in this chapter. Find and evaluate examples of this sentence feature in Freedman's article.

"Why Do Teachers Give the Grades They Do?" *College Composition and Communication* SARAH WARSHAUER FREEDMAN

Today, Sarah Warshauer Freedman is a professor in the College of Education at University of California, Berkeley, but her interest in teaching college writing dates back several decades. In the following research report, Freedman describes the study that led her to the conclusion she discusses in the previous article: When English professors grade student writing, surface correctness and other matters of style are not their foremost concern. "Why Do Teachers Give the Grades They Do?" appeared in 1979 in *College Composition and Communication*, which publishes research of interest to college rhetoric and composition instructors.

We all know the student who says, "I turned in this very same paper last year and got an A on it. Now you're going to give me a D?" Luckily, this student is a relatively rare one. First, most students rightfully fear the consequences of handing in a paper twice or at least feel too guilty to confront the teacher with such discrepancies. But, as Don Hirsch noted in his keynote address at the 1978 CCCC's meeting in Denver, more times than not, two or more teachers would give the same paper a different grade. But the good teacher does not grade purely on the basis of whimsy or idiosyncratic values either. In this article, I shall discuss composition evaluation from the point of view of that "good teacher." I shall report the results of a study[1] in which I asked the questions: (1) why do teachers give the grades they do? (2) are there any specific, definable parts of student papers that influence teachers? (3) and if there are, which of the parts influence teachers most?

To find answers to these questions, I rewrote student papers to be weak or strong in four broad, but pedagogically interesting, areas: content, organization, sentence structure, and mechanics. Then teachers judged the overall quality of the rewritten papers. The teachers did not know I had tampered with the papers. I found that specific, definable parts of the student paper did influence these teachers. They valued content first and then organization. They also valued mechanics, but not as much as they did content and organization. Interestingly, they cared more about mechanics, proper punctuation, and the like than about the quality of the structure of the sentences. They valued mechanics most, though, when the organization was strong, and they valued sentence structure only when the organization was strong. . . . The effect of weak content was so powerful that it made nothing else matter.

Now, for all of these results to be meaningful, I must go back and explain a bit about how I got them. First, what specifically do I mean by these broad areas: content, organization, sentence structure, and mechanics? Rhetoric texts certainly conflict in their definitions, and we all know that mechanics play a big part in sentence structure. I will briefly summarize the definitions for the categories, the definitions which formed the basis for the rules for rewriting the student papers. Briefly, content was the development of, and logical consistency between, the ideas. It had nothing to do with the absolute quality of the ideas. To rewrite content to be strong, I took the core ideas the student had and tried to develop them into something that seemed logical. So when I say good teachers valued content most of all, I mean that they valued the development and the logical presentation of the ideas, not necessarily the ideas themselves.

Organization had three main parts: order, transitioning, and paragraphing. Sentence structure focused on matters of form particular to the sentence level; mechanics focused on the pickiest items of usage and punctuation. I tried to define each of the areas in a way that would make it discrete from, or independent of, every other area.

I chose the papers that I would rewrite from a set of papers I collected for another, earlier study.[2] For that study I collected papers from a varied population of college students, papers the students wrote in class on eight different topics in the argumentative mode of discourse. Two Stanford students and I rewrote four of the papers on each topic, 32 papers in all. We selected for the rewriting the four essays that had already been judged in the earlier study to be in the middle of the quality range. We wanted papers that we could make better and worse, so we needed mid-range papers. When I had the teachers judge the rewritten papers, I stuck in four non-rewritten papers on each topic to test their reliability. The teachers proved to be the good judges I thought they would be.

After I trained the two student rewriters to follow my set of rewriting guides, I divided up the rewriting task between the three of us in as balanced a way as I could. We rewrote each of the 32 papers in three different versions each. In all, there were 12 possible ways a given paper could be rewritten, and each of the ways or versions was represented once on each topic. The 12 possible rewriting versions were these:

1. +C +O +SS +M
2. +C +O +SS −M
3. +C +O −SS +M
4. +C +O −SS −M
5. +C −O +SS +M
6. +C −O +SS −M
7. +C −O −SS +M
8. +C −O −SS −M
9. −C −O +SS +M

10.	−C	−O	+SS	−M
11.	−C	−O	−SS	+M
12.	−C	−O	−SS	−M

C = Content
O = Organization
SS = Sentence Structure
M = Mechanics
+ = Strong
− = Weak

In the end, we had 96 rewritten papers. We simultaneously rewrote all four areas—content, organization, sentence structure, and mechanics—on every paper. The rewriting task posed one major restriction: we never combined weak content and strong organization. It would have been an exercise in absurdity to try to order illogical ideas logically or to order and transition appropriately a group of inherently unrelated ideas.

When we rewrote, we were committed to creating a revised paper that retained, insofar as possible, the sense of the original student essay, the one that was the base from which we rewrote. We attempted to highlight the strengths and weaknesses in each of the four areas in each paper. Nevertheless, the act of highlighting often produced a new paper that was substantially unlike the original. Still the rewritten papers were like the papers real students actually produced. We rewrote papers to be very strong or very weak in each of the four areas, but these extremes were meant to reflect the extremes of the papers students produce.

After we finished all of the rewriting, I chose twelve teachers who were good evaluators. I used three main criteria to insure that they would indeed be good evaluators: strong professional recommendations, successful college-level teaching experience, and strong academic preparation. I divided the teachers into four reading groups of three teachers each. Each group rated essays on two of the eight topics. I trained the groups of teachers to judge essays on both topics the group would judge with training essays that I had used in the earlier study. I chose the training essays because they represented the quality of the essays students actually wrote for the earlier study.

The evaluations took place on four consecutive days. One group of three teachers rated essays on two of the eight topics on the first day; a second group of three teachers rated essays on another two of the eight topics on the second day, and so on. I informed each group of evaluators that college students had produced the essays, concealing from them the fact that some essays had been rewritten. All essays were typed. The teachers rated the essays using a four-point holistic scale.

I used an analysis of variance to measure whether the rewriting characteristics contributed significantly to the difference in the scores the raters gave to the different papers. As I revealed earlier, content proved to have the greatest influence on the scores the raters gave. If the content was strong, the score was high; if it was weak, the score was low. Content was significant at the .001 level of confidence. The quality of the organization likewise affected the scores; it too was significant at the .001 level. Mechanics proved significant only at the .01 level.

The difference between the average score given papers strong in content versus the average score given papers weak in content was 1.06 points. The maximum possible difference between a score was 3 points, since 4 was the highest score, and 1 was the lowest score a paper could receive on the 1-to-4 holistic scale. Thus, an average difference of over 1 point is quite large. Strong versus weak rewriting in organization also led to an average score difference of about 1 point. The effect of mechanics and sentence structure rewriting was about ½ and ¼ point, respectively.

Remember also that mechanics and sentence structure affected teachers mostly after the teachers assessed that the organization was strong. If the organization was strong, the mechanics rewriting caused almost an entire point difference between the average score of a paper with strong mechanics versus one with weak mechanics. In the same situation, sentence structure rewriting caused about a ½ point difference. But if the organization was weak, the quality of the mechanics and of the sentence structure did not matter to the teacher. Remember from the rewriting combinations that when the content was weak, so was the organization. In such cases, mechanics and sentence structure had little effect. But when the content was strong, the organization too had to be strong in order for the strength or weakness of the mechanics and of the sentence structure to affect these teachers.

In summary, the rewriting showed that parts of the paper did influence the grade that the teachers gave. The most significant influence proved to be the strength of the content of the essay. The second most important influence proved to be the strength of the organization of that content. The third significant influence was the strength of the mechanics. Furthermore, the influence of the mechanics was most important when the organization was strong, and because the sentence structure alone was insignificant, the influence of the sentence structure was important only when the organization was strong.

What are the implications of these findings? Most important, if society values content and organization as much as the teachers in this project did, then according to the definitions of content and organization I used in this study, a pedagogy for teaching writing should aim first to help students develop their ideas logically, being sensitive to the appropriate amount of explanation necessary for the audience. Then it should focus on teaching students to organize the developed ideas so that they would be easily understood and favorably evaluated. The interaction between organization and mechanics and organization and sentence structure, showing that the quality of the mechanics and sentence structure matter most when the organization is strong, points even more strongly to a pedagogy aimed at teaching the skills of organization before, or at least alongside, those of mechanics and sentence structure.

It seems today that many college-level curricula begin with a focus on helping students correct mechanical and syntactic problems rather than with the more fundamental aspects of the discourse. It is important to supplement these curricula for teaching content and organization. Certainly, because of the excellent research in the area of written sentence structure, on sentence-combining, and on the cumulative sentence and because of the objective nature of the mechanical rules for standard edited English, sentence structure and mechanics have become easier to teach than content and organization. The English profession knows more about teaching, evaluating, and doing research on sentence structure and mechanics than on the less objective areas of content and organization. Conceivably, instruction in strengthening sentence structure or mechanics could result in strong content or organization. But such a hypothesis has not been tested.

Discoveries about why teachers evaluate papers as they do can contribute to a set of definitions of what influences teachers as they evaluate student writing. These definitions, then, can be examined critically, and those criteria of good writing that seem sound can be incorporated into pedagogy and into training evaluators of student writing. One of the first steps in improving the evaluation and teaching of student writing is understanding why teachers evaluate as they do.

NOTES

1. This paper is based on parts of my doctoral dissertation, *Influences on the Evaluators of Student Writing*, Stanford University, 1977.
2. The results of the earlier study are also contained in my dissertation.

QUESTIONS ABOUT MEANING

1. What research questions motivated Freedman's study? What did Freedman learn from her research?
2. How many student papers were in the sample and how were they produced? How did Freedman test the reliability of the evaluators?
3. According to Freedman, why do some English teachers focus more on teaching mechanics and sentence structure than content and organization?

QUESTIONS FOR RHETORICAL ANALYSIS

4. Compare the purpose of this article to that of the preceding article, published in *The English Journal*. How does the difference in purpose or audience explain differences in the content of each article?
5. In this article, Freedman provides details not included in the article later published in *The English Journal*. For example, she explains how she defined *content, organization, sentence structure*, and *mechanics* in her research. What other kinds of details about her sample and methods are provided in this article but not in the *English Journal* article? Do any of these details change your understanding or assessment of the research?
6. Outline Freedman's main ideas. Where does Freedman provide preview or summary sentences? Where and how does she link paragraphs or sections? Using Freedman's definitions, evaluate the *content* and *organization* of the article.

THINKING AND WRITING ABOUT THE TOPIC

Education and English professor Don Hirsch (alluded to in both of Freedman's articles) believes that if two instructors evaluated the same student paper they would each give the paper a different grade.

Think about the various ways your writing has been graded, not just in English courses but in other disciplines as well. What elements have instructors weighted more than others? Has this been consistent from discipline to discipline? Has it been consistent for single professors throughout a term? What aspects of the *rhetorical context* explain the differences? For example, how might the concerns of a biology professor be different from those of a history professor when grading student papers? Based on your experiences and using *rhetorical context* as your frame of reference, write your own essay titled "Why Do Teachers Give the Grades They Do to Student Writing?"

WORKS CITED

Beard, T. Randolph, David L. Kaserman, and Richard P. Saba. "Limits to Altruism: Organ Supply and Educational Expenditures." *Contemporary Economic Policy* 22.4 (2004): 433–41. Print.

Beason, Larry. "Ethos and Error: How Business People React to Errors." *College Composition and Communication* 53.1 (2001): 33–64. Print.

Calhoon-Dillahunt, Carolyn, and Dodie Forrest. "Conversing in Marginal Spaces: Developmental Writers' Responses to Teacher Comments." *Teaching English in the Two-Year College* 40.3 (2013): 230–47. Print.

Carré, M. J., S. R. Goodwill, and S. J. Haake. "Understanding the Effect of Seams on the Aerodynamics of an Association Football." *Proceedings of the Institution of Mechanical Engineers, Part C: Journal of Mechanical Engineering Science* 219.7 (2005): 657–66. Web. 11 Jan. 2014.

Chafe, Wallace L. *Meaning and the Structure of Language*. Chicago: University of Chicago Press, 1970. Print.

Freedman, Sarah Warshauer. "Why Do Teachers Give the Grades They Do?" *College Composition and Communication* 30.2 (1979): 161–64. Print.

Lenzi, Michela, et al. "Family Affluence, School and Neighborhood Contexts and Adolescents' Civic Engagement: A Cross-National Study." *American Journal of Community Psychology* 50.1–2 (2012): 197–210. Print.

Meyer, Bonnie J. F. *The Organization of Prose and Its Effects on Memory*. New York: Elsevier, 1975. Print.

Raghubir, Priya, and Kim Corfman. "When Do Price Promotions Affect Pretrial Brand Evaluations?" *Journal of Marketing Research* 36.2 (1999): 211–22. Print.

Santilli, Valter, et al. "Peroneus Longus Muscle Activation Pattern during Gait Cycle in Athletes Affected by Functional Ankle Instability: A Surface Electromyographic Study." *American Journal of Sports Medicine* 33 (2005): 1183–87. Print.

Sommers, Nancy. "Revision Strategies of Student Writers and Experienced Adult Writers." *College Composition and Communication* 31.4 (1980): 378–88. Print.

Todd, Nathan R. "Religious Networking Organizations and Social Justice: An Ethnographic Case Study." *American Journal of Community Psychology* 50.1–2 (2012): 229–45. Print.

Wallace, David L., and John R. Hayes, "Redefining Revision for Freshmen." *Research in the Teaching of English* 25 (1991): 54–66. Web. 13 Jan. 2014.

Wharton-Michael, Patty. "Print vs. Computer Screen: Effects of Medium on Proofreading Accuracy." *Journalism & Mass Communication Educator* 63.1 (2008): 28–41. Print.

CHAPTER 12

Working and Writing in Groups

If you have ever collaborated with other students to complete a group assignment—perhaps a presentation for political science, a lab report for biology, or an essay for composition—you might be able to relate to how the following students describe working in groups:

- "While working on a project in teams, you not only have your own knowledge and thought process, you have those who are in your team as well. But then again you have to cope with others' thought processes, which is hard if they aren't on the same page."
- "Often I have trouble finding that one 'right' word to complete my sentence, so it is helpful to bounce ideas off of a partner. But if people have different views on how and what should be done, this can hinder productivity."
- "In groups there is always the chance you'll work with someone who knows more than you about the subject. But some people just take over the group and don't let others talk."
- "You can divide the workload by giving everyone an equal amount of work. But you have to be able to count on others to do their work."

As these comments reveal, working collaboratively has both benefits and drawbacks.

In this chapter you'll learn how to make your own collaborative work positive and productive. These are skills you will use beyond the classroom. According to a recent survey of more than 2,000 managers and executives from a range of fields, today's employees need more than the traditional "three Rs"—reading, writing, and arithmetic. They also need the "four Cs": critical thinking, communication, creativity, and collaboration (American 1). In another study, involving interviews with more than 300 executives, employers indicated that they need "360 degree people," who possess not only specific skills in their fields but also communication, problem solving, and teamwork skills (Peter 7). These are only two of many employer surveys confirming that for most professionals collaboration is a job requirement. The teamwork skills you develop in college will be an asset in your career after college.

Advantages and Disadvantages of Working in Groups

In small groups, there is the potential for real learning. Because you are more involved in your learning when you work in small groups, you are apt to learn more and remember what you learn longer than when you learn through more passive means like listening to a lecture. Communication professor Kenneth Petress identifies some of the skills that are developed when you complete group projects:

- setting goals and designating responsibilities,
- coordinating schedules and running meetings,
- proofreading and editing,
- resolving conflict, and
- taking responsibility for your own as well as your team's successes or failures. (587)

Collaboration enhances your ability to consider other viewpoints, and research indicates that when team members combine strengths, the results can be more creative and at a higher level than any work an individual could alone produce (Kyprianidou et al. 86–87).

When collaboration is successful, there are many benefits. However, when group members are at odds or when a team member engages in behavior detrimental to the group's success—complaining, arriving late or unprepared to meetings, or missing meetings altogether, for example—the experience can be frustrating. When marketing professor Wayne Neu asked a sample of 32 senior-level students to describe their experiences with teamwork in business courses, they mentioned problems you may have experienced with group assignments: anxiety when being graded for work that others produced, frustration when team members don't do their share of the work yet receive the grade others earned, disappointment when a group grade is lower than what one's individual contribution warrants, and stress from trying to live up to expectations of the group (74–75).

Other challenges arise if one team member submits his or her work late, putting the team behind schedule, or if the quality of work produced by some team members is not up to the standard expected by others. To add to the frustration, your instructor may not want to intervene in group disputes because resolving differences is *part of the learning process*. In short, making collaborative assignments successful requires *collaboration*.

Keys to Successful Collaboration

There are several steps you can take to avoid the potential pitfalls of group work. The most important step is to be a good team member yourself. Typically, others repay you in kind. Coming to group meetings prepared, staying engaged, being available and willing to work with others, and being willing to compromise are all hallmarks of a good team member. Discussed in this section are additional ways you and your team can avoid conflict and make a collaborative assignment successful.

Discuss in Advance Your Group Philosophy. When first embarking on a team project that will be completed over several days or weeks, talk about the behaviors expected of each group member. Identify as well the kinds of behavior you consider unacceptable. It's important to set expectations up front.

Expect Different Approaches to Communication and Work. Not everyone shares the same problem-solving approaches or work styles. Some people like to outline and plan an entire project before they begin; others begin by writing a specific part and building on it. Some people work best early in the day; others are night owls.

Communication styles vary as well. For example, women may focus more on group interactions and cohesiveness; men may want to focus only on finishing the task at hand (Markel 62). Some team members may be very vocal; others quiet. Some have difficulty critiquing the work of peers; others may be overly critical. Successful collaborators must be flexible and willing to adapt.

Consider Other Perspectives. Show up to meetings and listen to others in the group. Make sure that everyone has a chance to share their ideas. When you disagree with someone's ideas, give reasons, but don't make it personal. Check your ego at the door and be prepared for the fact that your ideas might not be used and what you've written might be changed or deleted. It's natural to feel frustrated if we think the workload and rewards are not fairly distributed. Primatologist Frans de Waal (featured in the end-of-chapter readings) has found this tendency even among monkeys! On the other hand, people tend to overestimate their own contribution to collaborative projects, and what appears to one person to be fair may not be the same from another person's perspective (Loftus 26). Keep this in mind before getting frustrated with others for not doing their fair share of the work.

Coordinate Efforts. One of the best things about collaborative assignments is that you can learn by watching others complete tasks new to you. If you don't know how to create a PowerPoint slide or create a graph, for instance, use this opportunity to learn from others. Another benefit of teamwork is that "many hands make light work," but the high quality of work possible through collaboration requires that team members collaborate. If members merely assemble parts each has completed separately, quality suffers. Divide the labor by assigning each member work, but regularly meet as a team and *together* decide what gets used and edited out of the final product.

In her research, English professor Rebecca Burnett found that "co-authors who considered more alternatives and voiced more disagreements about content and other rhetorical elements . . . produced higher quality documents than co-authors who considered few or no alternatives and voiced little or no explicit disagreements" ("Productive" 240). This kind of conflict—where group members challenge each other to consider other options before agreeing on an idea—is what Burnett calls "productive" conflict ("Substantive" 538). It's how successful collaborative projects gets completed.

Writing Collaboratively

Collaborating while writing is easier today than ever, thanks to word processing programs that allow writers to save comments and track changes within a document and thanks to shared online storage services, such as Dropbox and Google Docs, where team members can access and respond to each other's work.

When you work with others to produce a written document, you have the rare opportunity to see other writers at work—to see how others plan a paper, organize their ideas, or introduce a paper. As one of the students quoted earlier put it: "Often I have trouble finding that one 'right' word to complete my sentence, so it is helpful to bounce ideas off of a partner." One study compared the progress of 136 students enrolled in first-year composition courses, some of whom practiced collaborative writing throughout the term and others who practiced more traditional, independent writing. The researchers found that those who were taught to write collaboratively were "significantly more pleased with their writing than were subjects who worked independently" (Louth, McAllister, and McAllister 215). A group-produced paper can be stronger than any individual effort because various options for achieving your writing purpose are considered.

One approach to team writing is to make each group member responsible for writing a different section of the document. This approach may seem the easiest way to divide the workload; but, as Charles Stratton, an experienced technical writer, explains, when each section is written by a different team member, the group is apt to "wind up with a patchwork quilt, good swatches of material but of different colors and textures and with very obvious seams" (178). Unnecessary repetition, inconsistencies in design and structure, and omissions are among the problems in documents written in piecemeal fashion.

A better approach is the *coordinated model*, where members together outline the major sections of the paper and individual members are responsible for writing the *first draft* of sections. One member compiles the section drafts and circulates the first draft of the full document among team members, who all make corrections, revisions, or additions to the content. After agreement is reached concerning the content, all members again revise the document to eliminate inconsistencies in format, content, and writing style. The document circulates at least once more so that members can proofread and edit. This multi-step review process ensures that the finished product is uniform in style, consistent in tone, and free of errors. In addition, this model allows all members to be involved in all stages of the writing process: planning, drafting, document design, revising, and editing. The coordinated method does require organization, but dating drafts and having one member responsible for coordinating the review process can help. Figure 12.1 illustrates an example of a coordinated writing model.

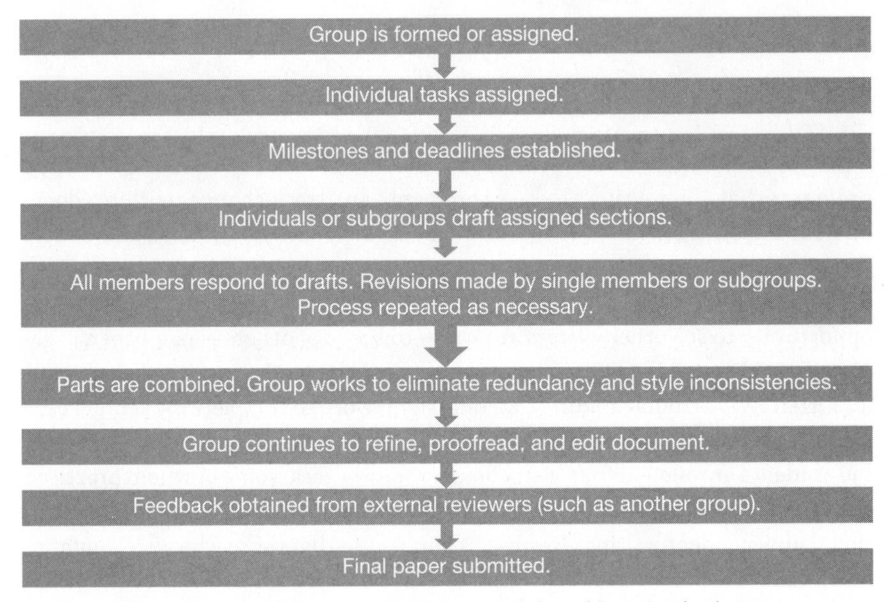

Figure 12.1 Illustration of Collaborative Writing Process (adapted from Speck 19)

Giving Peer Feedback

Giving feedback to your team members or classmates is a common form of collaborative work in college. You likely already have some experience with "peer review" in writing classes. If so, you know that by analyzing the writing of others, you can benefit as much as those to whom you provide that feedback. English professor Michelle Navarre Cleary gives the example of a student who for years resisted his teacher's and supervisor's advice to "get to the point" when writing. It wasn't until he was asked to critique the paper of a peer who had the same problem that he realized how frustrating it could be for readers: "I was thinking, I do this to some extent. And it was like a foghorn in my head. Don't do this: this is driving me nuts" (qtd. in Cleary 675). As a result of being able to recognize issues in the work of his peer through collaborative peer review, the student was able to identify and address similar problems in his own. The following suggestions can help you provide useful writing feedback to peers—whether they are coauthors or other writers in your class—and thus enhance the advantages of writing and revising with others.

Focus on What's Needed at the Time

If you're reviewing the first draft of a paper, resist the urge to correct problems with spelling, punctuation, or grammar. Although those corrections need to be made eventually, your focus should be on the types of global revisions discussed in chapter 11. If the instructor provides you with questions or topics to guide your peer review, concentrate on those areas. If not, consider foremost the writer's main claim and purpose. Does the writer address the assignment? Are the writer's meaning and purpose clear? These are the types of questions to consider when reading an early draft of a paper. When the content of a paper is still being determined, it makes more sense to wait until later to correct sentence-level errors.

Focus as well on giving the kinds of feedback that you are uniquely qualified to give. As a member of the class, you have valuable information that can make you an expert reviewer. You have read the assignment prompt and know what students were directed to do (and not do). You know what the instructor has emphasized as the "most important" aspects of the assignment. You have been a part of class discussions and may be able to suggest additional sources for the writer to consult. You have insights into what is and what is not considered credible evidence in the discipline. You have gained knowledge about how to write effective arguments by reading this book. In short, your vantage point and training qualify you to give helpful feedback.

Consider the Evidence Supporting the Writer's Claims

When researcher Sarah Warshauer Freedman (see chapter 11) asked English instructors to grade a collection of student essays, she found that the rhetorical element they weighted most heavily when grading is *development*: Is there sufficient evidence for the writer's claims? Do you find the writer's evidence convincing? What can the writer add or explain to make her case stronger?

Notice the Organization and Flow of Ideas

Freedman found that after development, the next most important element to instructors is the organization and structure of the paper. Is the organization of ideas logical? Do transitions connect the parts and lead you through the discussion?

Annotate as You Read

As you learned in chapter 2, when you annotate you make notes in the margins. Your notes may be summaries, questions, or comments about what you are reading. By writing annotations while reading a peer's paper, you give the writer feedback about how you are interpreting and responding to his work. Ask questions; suggest examples; talk back to the writer.

Give Specific Feedback

While periodically summarizing what you read is a good way of telling the writer if she has successfully communicated her message, try to do more than repeat what the document says. Some students hesitate to criticize another student's writing, thinking they are not qualified to do so. But if you get lost, say so! It does the writer no good if you don't mention where you had a hard time understanding the meaning. Tell the writer what you experienced as you read. Where were you confused and why? Where were you most interested? Where was the reading difficult and where was it easy? What did you like about the paper and what do you think would make it even better?

To be useful to the writer, your questions and comments need to be specific. This comment is not helpful:

> "There are problems with the organization."

But this comment is:

> "You talk about the influence of the media, then the influence of peers, and then the media again. Is that the best organization?"

Do not rewrite sentences, but do offer specific suggestions for how to improve the paper. Table 12.1 includes examples of useful critiques. Notice that many comments in Table 12.1 are phrased as questions. By answering these questions, the writer will address places the reader found confusing or unconvincing. Other comments might be expressed as simple reactions to the reading (e.g., "I'm not sure what you mean here"). These comments and questions can point to ways that the organization, development, and word choice can be improved. You, of course, enjoy these same benefits when peers respond to your writing.

TABLE 12.1
Vague versus Specific Peer Feedback

Vague (Unhelpful) Comments	Specific (Directive) Comments
Your description of the study is vague.	How many people were surveyed? What were they asked? Can you provide more details?
This section seems irrelevant.	I don't see how this example (about ___) relates to your main point (about ___). Can you explain?
This sentence is unclear.	I'm not sure what "it" refers to in this sentence.
I couldn't find your thesis statement.	You discuss several topics in this paper (including ___), but I can't find a central thesis statement early in the essay that prepares readers for these topics.

Benefits of Peer Response

When reading our own writing, we of course see what we intended to say, but that's not necessarily what a reader will see. A peer reviewer gives us insight into how others interpret our meaning. There are additional benefits to be gained from participating in peer review sessions. The process of peer review helps you learn to read a paper not with the goal of learning about the subject matter but with the goal of evaluating how well the text is composed—how clearly the points are made, how logically the argument flows, and how convincing the evidence is. These skills, which are easier to develop when reading the work of another, can then be transferred to your own paper, making you a better judge of the merits of your own written arguments. Peer response sessions that occur in classroom settings are especially valuable because in the classroom, you have the benefit of an instructor who provides you with questions to guide your review. These questions provide insights into important elements your instructor will look for when grading your paper.

Concept in Practice 12.1: Giving Useful Feedback

The passages in this table's "Original Text" column were taken from student papers. Can you offer specific suggestions for making the meaning more clear or convincing? Some sample critiques in the "Critique of Text" column are provided as illustrations.

Original Text	Critique of Text
Joel Best illustrates how some statistics are nothing more than guesses.	Who is Joel Best? Can you provide one of his examples?
Donna Halper, a college professor of media, notes that "so much of what we encounter in the media turns out to be entirely false, mythically inflated, politically charged, ideologically loaded, or a mixture of facts and fiction."	Don't you need a citation after a quotation?
Being a parent is demanding on many levels; yet they make it all worthwhile.	
Research shows that most people believe what they read on the Internet.	
Customer loyalty is vital keeping a business running.	

Applying the Concepts to Reading: *Responding to the Writing of Others*

The following draft of a paragraph could be improved if the writer were to address issues of focus, clarity, and development. Review the paragraph and provide feedback that will give the writer direction on how to revise.

> Many people are concerned about global warming, but Jonathan Rauch suggests "the problem is nowhere near as overwhelming as the rhetoric commonly suggests, and the solutions nowhere near as difficult." Carbon dioxide in the atmosphere takes a long time to build up and break down, so any action we take will not have immediate results. It's true that change is needed but suddenly reducing green house-gas emissions by shutting down all carbon-producing plants would do more harm than good. A better approach proposed by Rauch is to implement policies that will reduce greenhouse-gas emissions meanwhile we must learn to adapt to rising temperatures and the results of inevitable warming (such as flooding, tornadoes, droughts, malaria) while we continue to develop a long-term plan. Flooding caused by rising temperatures has the potential to be devastating to small island nations and seaside communities. Flash floods, mudslides, and huricanes are some of the potential problems. Seaside communities that depend on tourism are particularly vulnerable.

Applying the Concepts to Writing: *Writing Collaboratively*

Group work, team projects, and peer review are a few of the collaborations you've probably participated in while in school. Write an essay about your experiences with classroom collaboration, relating specific examples. You might address questions such as these:

- In what classes have you worked on projects with other students?
- What kinds of assignments have you collaborated on?
- What did you like about these collaborations and what did you not like?
- What have you learned about how to avoid or resolve problems that can occur when working with others?

Bring several copies of your essay to class. Then in a small group assigned in class, write a co-authored essay that includes information or examples from *each member of the group.* After composing a first draft of the collaboratively written paper, together revise it into an organized and cohesive paper.

Paired Readings from Biology

"The Brains of the Animal Kingdom; New Research Shows that We Have Grossly Underestimated both the Scope and the Scale of Animal Intelligence. Primatologist Frans de Waal on Memory-Champ Chimps, Tool-Using Elephants and Rats Capable of Empathy," *The Wall Street Journal* FRANS DE WAAL

The paired readings for this chapter are from primatologist Frans de Waal. De Waal studies monkeys, and his research has revealed many similarities between monkeys and humans. He has found, for example, that, like humans, monkeys resent a member of the group who doesn't do his or her share of the work yet still receives the same reward as those who do (Brosnan and de Waal).

In the following article, published in *The Wall Street Journal* in 2013, de Waal talks more generally about animal emotions and intelligence, arguing that "intelligent life is not something for us to seek in the outer reaches of space but is abundant right here on earth, under our noses" in the animal kingdom.

Who is smarter: a person or an ape? Well, it depends on the task. Consider Ayumu, a young male chimpanzee at Kyoto University who, in a 2007 study, put human memory to shame. Trained on a touch screen, Ayumu could recall a random series of nine numbers, from 1 to 9, and tap them in the right order, even though the numbers had been displayed for just a fraction of a second and then replaced with white squares. I tried the task myself and could not keep track of more than five numbers—and I was given much more time than the brainy ape. In the study, Ayumu outperformed a group of university students by a wide margin. The next year, he took on the British memory champion Ben Pridmore and emerged the "chimpion."

How do you give a chimp—or an elephant or an octopus or a horse—an IQ test? It may sound like the setup to a joke, but it is actually one of the thorniest questions facing science today. Over the past decade, researchers on animal cognition have come up with some ingenious solutions to the testing problem. Their findings have started to upend a view of humankind's unique place in the universe that dates back at least to ancient Greece. Aristotle's idea of the scala naturae, the ladder of nature, put all life-forms in rank order, from low to high, with humans closest to the angels. During the Enlightenment, the French philosopher René Descartes, a founder of modern science, declared that animals were soulless automatons. In the 20th century, the American psychologist

B.F. Skinner and his followers took up the same theme, painting animals as little more than stimulus-response machines. Animals might be capable of learning, they argued, but surely not of thinking and feeling. The term "animal cognition" remained an oxymoron.

A growing body of evidence shows, however, that we have grossly underestimated both the scope and the scale of animal intelligence. Can an octopus use tools? Do chimpanzees have a sense of fairness? Can birds guess what others know? Do rats feel empathy for their friends? Just a few decades ago we would have answered "no" to all such questions. Now we're not so sure.

Experiments with animals have long been handicapped by our anthropocentric attitude: We often test them in ways that work fine with humans but not so well with other species. Scientists are now finally meeting animals on their own terms instead of treating them like furry (or feathery) humans, and this shift is fundamentally reshaping our understanding.

Elephants are a perfect example. For years, scientists believed them incapable of using tools. At most, an elephant might pick up a stick to scratch its itchy behind. In earlier studies, the pachyderms were offered a long stick while food was placed outside their reach to see if they would use the stick to retrieve it. This setup worked well with primates, but elephants left the stick alone. From this, researchers concluded that the elephants didn't understand the problem. It occurred to no one that perhaps we, the investigators, didn't understand the elephants.

Think about the test from the animal's perspective. Unlike the primate hand, the elephant's grasping organ is also its nose. Elephants use their trunks not only to reach food but also to sniff and touch it. With their unparalleled sense of smell, the animals know exactly what they are going for. Vision is secondary.

But as soon as an elephant picks up a stick, its nasal passages are blocked. Even when the stick is close to the food, it impedes feeling and smelling. It is like sending a blindfolded child on an Easter egg hunt.

What sort of experiment, then, would do justice to the animal's special anatomy and abilities?

On a recent visit to the National Zoo in Washington, I met with Preston Foerder and Diana Reiss of Hunter College, who showed me what Kandula, a young elephant bull, can do if the problem is presented differently. The scientists hung fruit high up above the enclosure, just out of Kandula's reach. The elephant was given several sticks and a sturdy square box.

Kandula ignored the sticks but, after a while, began kicking the box with his foot. He kicked it many times in a straight line until it was right underneath the branch. He then stood on the box with his front legs, which enabled him to reach the food with his trunk. An elephant, it turns out, can use tools—if they are the right ones. While Kandula munched his reward, the investigators explained how they had varied the setup, making life more difficult for the elephant. They had put the box in a different section of the yard, out of view, so that when Kandula looked up at the tempting food he would need to recall the solution and walk away from his goal to fetch the tool. Apart from a few large-brained species, such as humans, apes and dolphins, not many animals will do this, but Kandula did it without hesitation, fetching the box from great distances.

Another failed experiment with elephants involved the mirror test—a classic evaluation of whether an animal recognizes its own reflection. In the early going, scientists placed a mirror on the ground outside the elephant's cage, but the mirror was (unsurprisingly) much smaller than the largest of land animals. All that the elephant could possibly see was four legs behind two layers of bars (since the mirror doubled them). When the animal received a mark on its body visible only with the assistance of the mirror, it failed to notice or touch the mark. The verdict was that the species lacked self-awareness.

But Joshua Plotnik of the Think Elephant International Foundation modified the test. He gave the elephants access to an 8-by-8-foot mirror and allowed them to feel it, smell it and look behind it. With this larger mirror, they fared much better. One Asian elephant recognized herself. Standing in front of the mirror, she repeatedly rubbed a white cross on her forehead, an action that she could only have performed by connecting her reflected image with her own body.

A similar experimental problem was behind the mistaken belief, prevalent until two decades ago, that our species has a unique system of facial recognition, since we are so much better at identifying faces than any other primate. Other primates had been tested, but they had been tested on human faces—based on the assumption that ours are the easiest to tell apart.

When Lisa Parr, one of my co-workers at Emory University, tested chimpanzees on portraits of their own species, they excelled at it. Selecting portraits on a computer screen, they could even tell which juveniles were born to which females. Having been trained to detect similarities among images, the apes were shown a female's portrait and then given a choice between two other faces, one of which showed her offspring. They preferred the latter based purely on family resemblance since they did not know any of the depicted apes.

We also may need to rethink the physiology of intelligence. Take the octopus. In captivity, these animals recognize their caretakers and learn to open pill bottles protected by childproof caps—a task with which many humans struggle. Their brains are indeed the largest among invertebrates, but the explanation for their extraordinary skills may lie elsewhere. It seems that these animals think, literally, outside the box of the brain. Octopuses have hundreds of suckers, each one equipped with its own ganglion with thousands of neurons. These "mini-brains" are interconnected, making for a widely distributed nervous system. That is why a severed octopus arm may crawl on its own and even pick up food.

Similarly, when an octopus changes skin color in self-defense, such as by mimicking a poisonous sea snake, the decision may come not from central command but from the skin itself. A 2010 study found gene sequences in the skin of cuttlefish similar to those in the eye's retina. Could it be: an organism with a seeing skin and eight thinking arms?

A note of caution, however: At times we also have overestimated the capacities of animals. About a century ago, a German horse named "Kluger Hans" (Clever Hans) was thought to be capable of addition and subtraction. His owner would ask him the product of multiplying four by three, and Hans would happily tap his hoof 12 times. People were flabbergasted, and Hans became an international sensation.

That is, until Oskar Pfungst, a psychologist, investigated the horse's abilities. Pfungst found that Hans was only successful if his owner knew the answer to the question and was visible to the horse. Apparently, the owner subtly shifted his position or straightened his back when Hans reached the correct number of taps. (The owner did so unknowingly, so there was no fraud involved.)

Some look at this historic revelation as a downgrading of Hans's intelligence, but I would argue that the horse was in fact very smart. His abilities at arithmetic may have been flawed, but his understanding of human body language was remarkable. And isn't that the skill a horse needs most?

Awareness of the "Clever Hans Effect," as it is now known, has greatly improved animal experimentation. Unfortunately, it is often ignored in comparable research with humans. Whereas every dog lab now tests the cognition of its animals while their human owners are blindfolded or asked to face away, young children are still presented with cognitive tasks while sitting on their mothers' laps. The assumption is that mothers are like furniture, but every mother wants her child to succeed, and nothing guarantees that her sighs, head turns and subtle changes in position don't serve as cues for the child.

This is especially relevant when we try to establish how smart apes are relative to children. To see how their cognitive skills compare, scientists present both species with identical problems, treating them exactly the same. At least this is the idea. But the children are held by their parents and talked to ("Watch this!" "Where is the bunny?"), and they are dealing with members of their own kind. The apes, by contrast, sit behind bars, don't benefit from language or a nearby parent who knows the answers, and are facing members of a different species. The odds are massively stacked against the apes, but if they fail to perform like the children, the invariable conclusion is that they lack the mental capacities under investigation.

A recent study, tracking the pupil movements of chimpanzees, found that they followed the gaze of members of their own species far better than that of humans. This simple finding has huge implications for tests in which chimpanzees need to pay attention to human experimenters. The species barrier they face may fully explain the difference in performance compared with children.

Underlying many of our mistaken beliefs about animal intelligence is the problem of negative evidence. If I walk through a forest in Georgia, where I live, and fail to see or hear the pileated woodpecker, am I permitted to conclude that the bird is absent? Of course not. We know how easily these splendid woodpeckers hop around tree trunks to stay out of sight. All I can say is that I lack evidence.

It is quite puzzling, therefore, why the field of animal cognition has such a long history of claims about the absence of capacities based on just a few strolls through the forest. Such conclusions contradict the famous dictum of experimental psychology according to which "absence of evidence is not evidence of absence." Take the question of whether we are the only species to care about the well-being of others. It is well known that apes in the wild offer spontaneous assistance to each other, defending against leopards, say, or consoling distressed companions with tender embraces. But for decades, these observations were ignored, and more attention was paid to experiments according to which the apes were entirely selfish. They had been tested with an apparatus to see if one chimpanzee was willing to push food toward another. But perhaps the apes failed to understand the apparatus. When we instead used a simple choice between tokens they could exchange for food—one kind of token rewarded only the chooser, the other kind rewarded both apes—lo and behold, they preferred outcomes that rewarded both of them.

Such generosity, moreover, may not be restricted to apes. In a recent study, rats freed a trapped companion even when a container with chocolate had been put right next to it. Many rats first liberated the other, after which both rodents happily shared the treat.

The one historical constant in my field is that each time a claim of human uniqueness bites the dust, other claims quickly take its place. Meanwhile, science keeps chipping away at the wall that separates us from the other animals. We have moved from viewing animals as instinct-driven stimulus-response machines to seeing them as sophisticated decision makers.

Aristotle's ladder of nature is not just being flattened; it is being transformed into a bush with many branches. This is no insult to human superiority. It is long-overdue recognition that intelligent life is not something for us to seek in the outer reaches of space but is abundant right here on earth, under our noses.

Mr. de Waal is C.H. Candler Professor at Emory University and director of the Living Links Center at the Yerkes National Primate Research Center, both in Atlanta.

QUESTIONS ABOUT MEANING

1. Determining animal intelligence, according to de Waal, is "one of the thorniest questions facing science today." Why is assessing animal intelligence so difficult?
2. Describe some of the problems with previous tests of animal intelligence and some ways these flaws have been corrected. What challenges still remain, particularly in tests designed to compare the intelligence of animals to that of children?

QUESTIONS FOR RHETORICAL ANALYSIS

3. What does the writing style in the opening sentences suggest about the intended audience for this article?
4. Divide de Waal's article into the following sections: introduction, body, and conclusion. Where is the thesis statement? What traditional academic writing "moves" does de Waal make in the introduction? What is traditional about his conclusion? Where within the body are readers reminded of the central claim?
5. De Waal writes, "Aristotle's ladder of nature is not just being flattened; it is being transformed into a bush with many branches." What does he mean? Do you find this to be an apt metaphor?

Excerpt from "Chimpanzees Play the Ultimatum Game," *Proceedings of the National Academy of Sciences of the United States of America*

DARBY PROCTOR, REBECCA A. WILLIAMSON, FRANS B. M. DE WAAL, AND SARAH F. BROSNAN

Is collaboration found among humans only? Not according to research conducted by primatologist Frans de Waal and fellow researchers Darby Proctor, Rebecca Williamson, and Sarah Brosnan.

In the following article, the researchers describe two related studies, one involving chimpanzees and the other children. The participants played the ultimatum game, a game common in economics research, where pairs of participants decide how to share a reward. The player initially given the reward proposes how to split the reward and the second player can accept or reject the offer, but if the second participant rejects the offer, both participants get nothing. The findings indicate that even chimpanzees understand the benefits of collaboration. (The authors also refer to a variation of the ultimatum game, the dictator game, where the second participant has no vote; the proposer can simply choose to share the reward or not.)

The article first appeared in 2013 in *PNAS* (*Proceedings of the National Academy of Sciences of the United States of America*), a peer-reviewed journal that publishes research reports from biological, physical, and social sciences. The Methods section is omitted from the selection printed here.

ABSTRACT

Is the sense of fairness uniquely human? Human reactions to reward division are often studied by means of the ultimatum game, in which both partners need to agree on a distribution for both to receive rewards. Humans typically offer generous portions of the reward to their partner, a tendency our close primate relatives have thus far failed to show in experiments. Here we tested chimpanzees (Pan troglodytes) *and human children on a modified ultimatum game. One individual chose between two tokens that, with their partner's cooperation, could be exchanged for rewards. One token offered equal rewards to both players, whereas the other token favored the chooser. Both apes and children responded like humans typically do. If their partner's cooperation was required, they split the rewards equally. However, with passive partners—a situation akin to the so-called dictator game—they preferred the selfish option. Thus, humans and chimpanzees show similar preferences regarding reward division, suggesting a long evolutionary history to the human sense of fairness.*

KEYWORDS

inequity aversion, equality, reciprocity, sharing, behavioral economics

Humans often make decisions that seem irrational from an economic perspective. For instance, they may engage in behavior that actually decreases their absolute wealth. One explanation for these decisions is that humans are not only concerned with their own rewards but also the rewards of others (1). Human reactions to reward distributions have been extensively studied by means of experimental economics tasks, in particular the ultimatum game (2–5) and the dictator game (6, 7). In the ultimatum game (UG), one individual (the proposer) is asked to split a quantity of money with another individual (the respondent). If the respondent accepts the offer, both players are rewarded using the proposed split. If the respondent rejects the offer, then neither player is rewarded (2). The dictator game (DG) is a variant of the UG in which the respondent has no chance to reject the offer and thus all of the proposer's offers are "accepted."

Proposers in both the UG and DG generally go against their own short-term interests in offering the partner more than the minimum possible amount of money (8). In UGs, people from Western cultures typically offer around 50% of the available money (3–5), even in anonymous one-shot games that lack any future interaction. In DGs, people still offer more of the money than a purely self-interested model would suggest, but offers are lower than in UGs (4, 6, 7). The reasons why humans typically offer more than self-interested models would predict are twofold. First, humans may be concerned with the welfare of others and thus behave more generously out of an altruistic motivation (1, 4). Second, they may anticipate refusals of inequitable reward distributions during UGs and make larger offers to ensure that they are accepted, thus serving their own self-interest (4, 6, 7). Whereas either of these reasons is sufficient to drive human behavior in these tasks, they may also work in concert.

However, cultural norms of fairness vary across study populations (8). For example, the Lamelara of Indonesia typically offer more than a fair share (mean 58%), presumably because they are culturally dependent on large-scale cooperation (to hunt whales) and thus have mechanisms in place to share surplus resources. In contrast, the Hadza of Tanzania, who are hunter-gatherers who share food with group members because of cultural expectations and the fear of ostracism, make the lowest offers of any study population, and these offers are often rejected (9, 10). This likely occurs because of the specific experimental setting of the UG, which may reduce the fear of being ostracized, allowing the Hadza participants to follow their self-interest. In all cases, a given culture's degree of cooperation, sharing, and punishment influences offers in economic games (8, 11). What remains unclear is how other primates, including one of our closest living relatives, the chimpanzee (*Pan troglodytes*), respond to these types of situations. Studying other primates may shed light on the evolutionary basis for the human tendency toward "fair" distributions.

. . .

There are sound evolutionary reasons to expect chimpanzees to be sensitive to unequal outcomes. They routinely cooperate by defending territory, form coalitions, hunt in groups, share food (27–29), and engage in reciprocal exchanges that suggest mental scorekeeping (refs. 30–32, although see ref. 33). For example, chimpanzees are sensitive to unequal outcomes in experiments, refusing to participate when a partner earns a better reward for equal effort, and occasionally even refusing a better reward when a partner receives less (16, 34). The ability to recognize and be sensitive to unequal outcomes would theoretically help them establish beneficial partnerships (34). Additionally, chimpanzees pay attention to intent, reacting more negatively to a partner deliberately stealing their food rather than one giving their food to another (35, 36). They also show "targeted helping," which requires recognition of another's needs and goals (37, 38).

There are anecdotal reports of chimpanzees equitably dividing rewards during nonexperimental encounters. In one example, an adolescent female broke up a fight between two juveniles over a leafy branch. The female broke the branch in two and then handed half to each juvenile without taking any for herself (39). Goodall (40) reported an interaction between two males, one of whom was in possession of meat. After repeated begging, the male without the meat threw a "violent tantrum." Following this, the meat possessor ripped the prey in half and gave a portion to the second male. Based on these and similar observations as well as the overall levels of cooperation, sharing, and punishment observed among chimpanzees, we would expect them to make equitable offers in UGs.

The purpose of the present study was to investigate how sensitive chimpanzees are to reward distribution when their partner can affect it. If they are sensitive to partner effects, their choices in the UG should resemble those of humans. Proposers were presented with a choice of two tokens [a method that requires no apparatus and appears to be intuitive to the subjects (16, 21, 22, 41–48)], one of which represented an equal reward distribution and the other an unequal distribution favoring the proposer. The tokens acted essentially like money that could be exchanged for food. Respondents could either accept the offer by returning the selected token to the experimenter or reject it by not returning the token (Figure 12.2). Results of the UG were compared with those of a preference test similar to the DG, where the respondent could not influence outcomes. This methodology allowed us to explore whether respondents were sensitive to unequal distributions (by refusing unequal offers) and whether the proposers themselves were sensitive to potential rejections (by altering their choice dependent on their partner's potential effect on the outcome). In the latter case, proposers, like humans, should make different choices in the UG and DG. We tested human children (ages 3–5 y) with essentially the same token paradigm. . . .

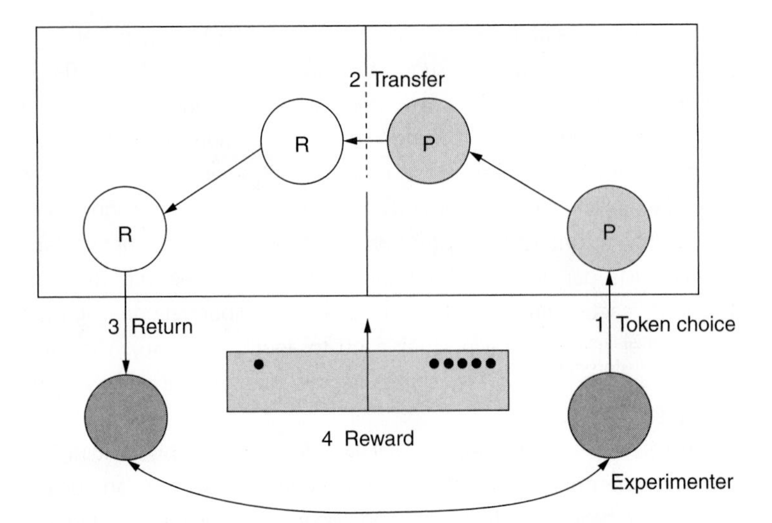

Figure 12.2 Experimental setup for pairs of chimpanzees following a four-step sequence. Step 1: The proposer (P) is presented with a choice of two tokens, one representing an equal split of the rewards and the other representing an unequal split favoring the proposer. The proposer is free to select either token. Step 2: The proposer passes the selected token to the respondent (R) through a mesh panel. Step 3: The respondent either returns the token to the experimenter to accept the offer, drops the token, or does not return it for 30 s. Step 4: Six banana rewards are visibly divided on a tray in front of the chimpanzees according to the token selected. Here the dots represent an unequal 5:1 distribution of rewards in favor of the proposer. The tray is then pushed within reach of the chimpanzees so that each can collect its reward(s). Note that the experimental setup for children was similar, except that a commercially available baby gate was used to separate the participants and the experimenter.

RESULTS

Chimpanzees

Despite initial preferences for the selfish token (binomial tests, all $P < 0.05$; see Table 1 for exact two-tailed P values), all four chimpanzee proposers more often chose the equitable token in the UG condition than in the preference test (exact McNemar's test, all $P < 0.05$; Figure 12.3 and Table 1). Two of the four proposers, furthermore, chose the equitable token in the UG significantly more often than expected by chance. During the UG, no respondent ever refused to return an offer, although their behavior might have signaled the potential for them to do so (*Discussion*).

Thus, chimpanzees, like humans in previous studies, chose a more equitable split of rewards in the UG compared with their choices when their partner had no recourse, as in DGs. The change in choices was apparently spontaneous, occurring without any refusals by the partner and within a small number of trials, making it difficult to ascribe it to learning during the experiment itself. Moreover, this pattern of choices was consistent, with all four individuals showing the same behavioral change. Thus, we found that chimpanzee proposers changed their behavior between two conditions

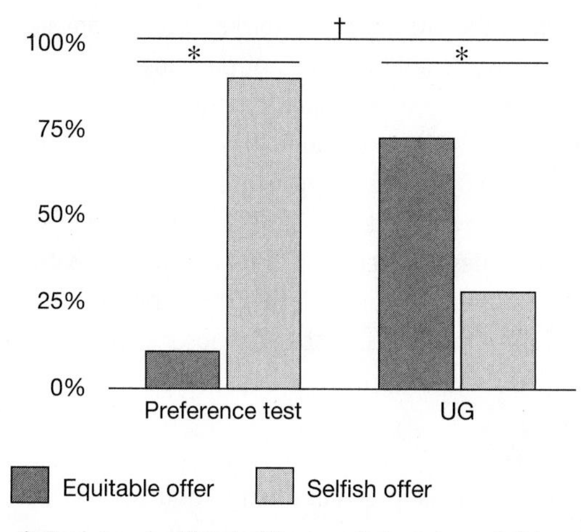

* Denotes significant difference between equitable and selfish offer; Binomial test $p < 0.05$
† Denotes significant change from preference test to UG; McNemar's test $p < 0.05$

Figure 12.3 Total percentage of offers selected by the chimpanzees. Chimpanzees were presented with two different tokens representing either an equitable or selfish (favoring the proposer) offer. We compared their choices in a preference test, where the partner was naïve and passive, with the UG, where the partner could affect reward outcomes for both individuals. Although chimpanzees preferred the selfish offer during the preference test, they significantly changed their preferences toward the equitable offer in the UG condition. See Table 1 for offer selections by each pair of chimpanzees. *Significant difference between equitable and selfish offers; binomial test, $P < 0.05$. †Significant change from preference test to UG; McNemar's test, $P < 0.05$.

Table 1
Chimpanzee Choices of Equitable Token by Pair

Pair	Preference test (%)	UG (%)
KT-GA	13*	58†
LA-SH	0*	71*,†
MS-RT	17*	67†
SH-LA	14*	92*,†

All chimpanzee pairs showed a significant change in token choice from the preference test. Additionally, two pairs were significantly different from chance in the UG.
*Significant difference from 50% chance; binomial test, $P < 0.05$.
†Significant change between preference test and UG; McNemar's test, $P < 0.05$.

that were identical except for the degree of control given to the recipient, choosing to make more equitable offers when their partner had control.

Children

Children also preferentially selected the selfish token in the preference tests (group-level binomial, $P = 0.045$, two-tailed), but they showed no preference for either token in the UG condition (group-level binomial, $P = 0.38$, two-tailed). However, based on results of previous research, we predicted that children would be more equitable in the UG condition than in the preference test (49, 50), and found this to be the case (Mann–Whitney U test, $P = 0.044$, one-tailed). Due to testing constraints, data on children were evaluated in a between-subject design rather than the within-subject design used with chimpanzees. As with chimpanzees, no child ever refused to return an offer. Thus, children also changed their pattern of choices in the UG, despite the absence of refusals by recipients.

DISCUSSION

Chimpanzees and children were similarly sensitive to the contingencies of the ultimatum game. In a simple choice task resembling the DG, with either a passive partner (chimpanzees) or while alone (children), both species preferentially chose a "selfish" offer that brought the majority of rewards to themselves. In the UG condition, in contrast, respondents could affect the outcome (by accepting or rejecting the offer), and both species shifted their choices to a more equitable distribution. This shift is similar to the way adult humans change their offers between DGs and UGs (4, 6, 7). Most adult humans are more selfish in DGs than in UGs. Thus, we demonstrated that chimpanzees, like humans, change their distribution choice in the same setting (i.e., paired with a conspecific from their social group) dependent on (i) how their behavior affects a partner and (ii) the potential effect of their partner on the outcome. However, it is unclear whether both of these possibilities affect behavior simultaneously (4) or whether one consideration dominates the decision.

. . .

Neither in the chimpanzees nor in the children did responders ever refuse, where a refusal was defined as failure by the responder to return the offer to the experimenter within 30 s (25). This is likely because neither species was explicitly trained that refusal was an option (like the chimpanzees, children were not verbally instructed about any of the contingencies). Nonetheless, proposers changed their offers when a partner had control over the reward distribution. We cannot rule out that the proposers were preemptively responding to the potential for refusals, even if these never materialized. In fact, adult humans, who typically offer 50% of the rewards, usually are given only a single choice during any UG experiment, and so have not been punished for making an inequitable decision either. They, too, are presumably responding to the mere potential of refusals. Both chimpanzees and humans have prior real-life experience with inequitable outcomes, which may make them sensitive to the possibility of punishment. For example, chimpanzees who do not share food with others are more likely to encounter threats and temper tantrums (40, 51), and chimpanzees may refuse to share with individuals who did not previously groom them (31), punish theft (52), and protest against both advantageous and disadvantageous inequity in experimental settings (16, 35). Thus, as in humans, social norms may affect performance in this task. Alternatively, because in the UG, cooperation was needed to gain rewards, it is possible that proposers were more generous because they were working with the respondent, because involvement in a task may increase their sensitivity to inequitable outcomes (35). If this were the case, refusals would not be needed to influence their choices.

We observed variation among our pairs of chimpanzees that might be accounted for by their social relationships, although given our small sample size we were unable to reach definitive conclusions. For example, the chimpanzee pair that showed the least equitable behavior (KT–GA) was a mother–daughter pair with the daughter as the proposer. Possibly, their close social relationship made them less sensitive to unequal reward distributions (16, 53). Subsequent studies on how chimpanzees change their choices in a social context should include measures of relationship quality and relative dominance rank.

Even though too rare for quantitative analysis, communicative interactions by respondents to proposers occurred in both children and chimpanzees. Child respondents sometimes made verbal comments about the reward distribution such as "you got more than me" and "I want more stickers." Chimpanzee respondents occasionally intimidated proposers, whereas proposers never did the same toward respondents. For example, in the chimpanzee pair MS–RT, five instances of threatening behavior were recorded. Three involved RT (respondent) spitting water at MS (proposer). The other two involved RT hitting the mesh barrier separating her from MS when the latter was about to pass a token. Although we found no statistically significant connection between offers made and threats received in the chimpanzees, likely due to the rarity with which they occurred, these negative reactions might have influenced the proposer. In a previous study, attention-getting behavior by a partner increased the actor's prosocial tendencies, suggesting that social interactions may influence decisions in experimental tasks (21). In both children and chimpanzees, the respondent's behavior may have cued the proposer that a negative response was possible. Thus, even though the mechanism behind these choices is unclear, chimpanzees appear to show the same sensitivity as do children to the attitude of others during resource division. Their interest in fair distributions probably helps them reap the benefits of cooperation.

REFERENCES

1. Fehr E, Schmidt KM (1999) A theory of fairness, competition, and cooperation. *Q J Econ* 114(3):817–868.
2. Guth W, Schmittberger R, Schwarze B (1982) An experimental analysis of ultimatum bargaining. *J Econ Behav Organ* 3(4):367–388.
3. Guth W (1995) On ultimatum bargaining experiments—A personal review. *J Econ Behav Organ* 27(3):329–344.
4. Camerer C, Thaler RH (1995) Anomalies: Ultimatums, dictators and manners. *J Econ Perspect* 9(2):209–219.
5. Camerer CF, Loewenstein G (2004) Behavioral economics: Past, present, future. *Advances in Behavioral Economics*, eds Camerer CF, Loewenstein G, Rabin M (Princeton Univ Press, Princeton, NJ), pp 3–51.
6. Kahneman D, Knetsch JL, Thaler RH (1986) Fairness and the assumptions of economics. *J Bus* 59(4):285–300.
7. Forsythe R, Horowitz JL, Savin NE, Sefton M (1994) Fairness in simple bargaining experiments. *Games Econ Behav* 6(3):347–369.
8. Henrich J, et al. (2001) In search of *Homo Economicus*: Behavioral experiments in 15 small-scale societies. *Am Econ Rev* 91(2):73–78.
9. Marlowe F (2004) Dictators and ultimatums in an egalitarian society of hunter-gatherers: The Hadza of Tanzania. *Foundations of Human Sociality: Economic Experiments and Ethnographic Evidence from Fifteen Small-Scale Societies,* eds Henrich J, et al. (Oxford University Press, Oxford), pp 168–193.
10. Marlowe F (2010) *The Hadza: Hunter-Gatherers of Tanzania* (Univ of California Press, Berkeley).
11. Lamba S, Mace R (2013) The evolution of fairness: explaining variation in bargaining behaviour. *Proceedings of the Royal Society B: Biological Sciences* 280(1750): 20122028.
12. Melis AP, Hare B, Tomasello M (2009) Chimpanzees coordinate in a negotiation game. *Evol Hum Behav* 30(6):381–392.
13. Bullinger A, Wyman E, Melis A, Tomasello M (2011) Coordination of chimpanzees (*Pan troglodytes*) in a stag hunt game. *Int J Primatol* 32(6):1296–1310.
14. Brosnan SF, et al. (2011) Responses to the assurance game in monkeys, apes, and humans using equivalent procedures. *Proc Natl Acad Sci USA* 108(8):3442–3447.
15. Jones OD, Brosnan SF (2008) Law, biology, and property: A new theory of the endowment effect. *William Mary Law Rev* 49:1935–1990.
16. Brosnan SF, Schiff HC, de Waal FBM (2005) Tolerance for inequity may increase with social closeness in chimpanzees. *Proc Biol Sci* 272(1560):253–258.
17. Brosnan SF, de Waal FBM (2003) Monkeys reject unequal pay. *Nature* 425(6955): 297–299.
18. Van Wolkenten M, Brosnan SF, de Waal FBM (2007) Inequity responses of monkeys modified by effort. *Proc Natl Acad Sci USA* 104(47):18854–18859.

19. Jensen K, Call J, Tomasello M (2007) Chimpanzees are rational maximizers in an ultimatum game. *Science* 318(5847):107–109.
20. Kaiser I, Jensen K, Call J, Tomasello M (2012) Theft in an ultimatum game: Chimpanzees and bonobos are insensitive to unfairness. *Biol Lett* 8(6):942–945.
21. Horner V, Carter JD, Suchak M, de Waal FBM (2011) Spontaneous prosocial choice by chimpanzees. *Proc Natl Acad Sci USA* 108(33):13847–13851.
22. de Waal FBM, Suchak M (2010) Prosocial primates: Selfish and unselfish motivations. *Philos Trans R Soc Lond B Biol Sci* 365(1553): 2711–2722.
23. Boysen ST, Berntson GG (1995) Responses to quantity: Perceptual versus cognitive mechanisms in chimpanzees (*Pan troglodytes*). *J Exp Psychol Anim Behav Process* 21(1):82–86.
24. Brosnan SF (2008) The ultimatum game and nonhuman primates. *Sci Am "Mind Matters" blog.* Available at http://science-community .sciam.com/blog-entry/Mind-Matters/Chimps-Rational-Humans/ 300009942.
25. Visalberghi E, Anderson J (2008) Fair game for chimpanzees. *Science* 319(5861): 282–284.
26. Smith P, Silberberg A (2010) Rational maximizing by humans (*Homo sapiens*) in an ultimatum game. *Anim Cogn* 13(4):671–677.
27. Boesch C (1994) Cooperative hunting in wild chimpanzees. *Anim Behav* 48(3): 653–667.
28. Boesch C, Boesch-Achermann H (2000) *The Chimpanzees of the Tai Forest* (Oxford Univ Press, Oxford).
29. Muller MN, Mitani JC (2005) Conflict and cooperation in wild chimpanzees. *Adv Stud Behav* 35:275–331.
30. Gomes CM, Boesch C (2009) Wild chimpanzees exchange meat for sex on a long-term basis. *PLoS One* 4(4):e5116.
31. de Waal FBM (1997) The chimpanzee's service economy: Food for grooming. *Evol Hum Behav* 18(6):375–386.
32. Mitani JC (2006) Reciprocal exchange in chimpanzees and other primates. *Cooperation in Primates and Humans: Mechanisms and Evolution,* eds Kappeler PM, van Schaik CP (Springer, Berlin), pp 107–119.
33. Gilby IC, Connor RC (2010) The role of intelligence in group hunting: Are chimpanzees different from other social predators? *The Mind of the Chimpanzee: Ecological and Experimental Perspectives,* eds Lonsdorf EV, Ross SR, Matsuzawa T (Univ of Chicago Press, Chicago), pp 220–233.
34. Brosnan SF (2011) A hypothesis of the co-evolution of cooperation and responses to inequity. *Front Neurosci* 5:43.
35. Brosnan SF, Talbot C, Ahlgren M, Lambeth SP, Schapiro SJ (2010) Mechanisms underlying responses to inequitable outcomes in chimpanzees, *Pan troglodytes. Anim Behav* 79(6):1229–1237.
36. Tomasello M, Carpenter M, Call J, Behne T, Moll H (2005) Understanding and sharing intentions: The origins of cultural cognition. *Behav Brain Sci* 28(5):675–691, discussion 691–735.
37. de Waal FBM (2008) Putting the altruism back into altruism: The evolution of empathy. *Annu Rev Psychol* 59:279–300.

38. Yamamoto S, Humle T, Tanaka M (2012) Chimpanzees' flexible targeted helping based on an understanding of conspecifics' goals. *Proc Natl Acad Sci USA* 109(9): 3588–3592.
39. de Waal FBM (2010) *The Age of Empathy: Nature's Lessons for a Kinder Society* (Harmony Books, New York).
40. Goodall J (1986) *The Chimpanzees of Gombe: Patterns of Behavior* (Belknap, Cambridge, MA).
41. de Waal FBM, Leimgruber K, Greenberg AR (2008) Giving is self-rewarding for monkeys. *Proc Natl Acad Sci USA* 105(36): 13685–13689.
42. Brosnan SF, de Waal FBM (2004) A concept of value during experimental exchange in brown capuchin monkeys, *Cebus apella. Folia Primatol (Basel)* 75(5):317–330.
43. Brosnan SF, de Waal FBM (2005) A simple ability to barter in chimpanzees, *Pan troglodytes. Primates* 46(3):173–182.
44. Brosnan SF, Beran MJ (2009) Trading behavior between conspecifics in chimpanzees, *Pan troglodytes. J Comp Psychol* 123(2):181–194.
45. Talbot CF, Freeman HD, Williams LE, Brosnan SF (2011) Squirrel monkeys' response to inequitable outcomes indicates a behavioural convergence within the primates. *Biol Lett* 7(5):680–682.
46. Dufour V, Pelé M, Neumann M, Thierry B, Call J (2009) Calculated reciprocity after all: Computation behind token transfers in orangutans. *Biol Lett* 5(2):172–175.
47. Pelé M, Dufour V, Thierry B, Call J (2009) Token transfers among great apes (*Gorilla gorilla, Pongo pygmaeus, Pan paniscus*, and *Pan troglodytes*): Species differences, gestural requests, and reciprocal exchange. *J Comp Psychol* 123(4):375–384.
48. Addessi E, Rossi S (2011) Tokens improve capuchin performance in the reverse-reward contingency task. *Proc Biol Sci* 278(1707):849–854.
49. Murnighan JK, Saxon MS (1998) Ultimatum bargaining by children and adults. *J Econ Psychol* 19(4):415–445.
50. Harbaugh WT, Krause K, Liday SJ (2003) *Bargaining by Children, University* of Oregon Economics Working Paper No. 2002-4, 10.2139/ssrn.436504. Available at http://ssrn.com/abstract=436504.
51. de Waal FBM (1989) Food sharing and reciprocal obligations among chimpanzees. *J Hum Evol* 18(5):433–459.
52. Jensen K, Call J, Tomasello M (2007) Chimpanzees are vengeful but not spiteful. *Proc Natl Acad Sci USA* 104(32):13046–13050.
53. Schino G, Aureli F (2010) The relative roles of kinship and reciprocity in explaining primate altruism. *Ecol Lett* 13(1):45–50.

Author contributions: D.P., R.A.W., F.B.M.d.W., and S.F.B. designed research; D.P. and R.A.W. performed research; D.P. analyzed data; and D.P., R.A.W., F.B.M.d.W., and S.F.B. wrote the paper.

The authors declare no conflict of interest.

To whom correspondence should be addressed. E-mail: dewaal@emory.edu.

QUESTIONS ABOUT MEANING

1. When humans have played the ultimatum game in previous studies, their behavior could often be described as "irrational," at least from an economic standpoint. Explain.
2. Describe the two studies Proctor et al. conducted. How does the behavior of the participants compare to that of the adults in other ultimatum game experiments? Were the results as the researchers expected?
3. What explanations are suggested for why the "proposers" in the experiments behaved as they did?

QUESTIONS FOR RHETORICAL ANALYSIS

4. What are early textual clues indicating that this article is a report of original research?
5. The following passage is from the Methods section of Proctor et al.'s study. (The Methods section was omitted from the selection you read.) Read the passage. What makes it typical of the writing and content found in most Methods sections? What are some details in this passage that would be important to consider if you were asked to assess the researchers' methods? Explain.

> Rewards (stickers) were laid out in front of the barrier so that the children could see but not reach them. Children were instructed to pass the selected offer to their partner around the barrier. The partner could then return the offer to the experimenter. To indicate to the child that they could return the offer, the experimenter extended her hand palm up toward the child (a similar gesture was used to indicate the possibility of exchange with chimpanzee responders). No verbal instructions were used to get subjects to return the offer. The children were then rewarded according to the offer returned. Children received a total of four forced-choice training trials, two for each offer. (Proctor et al. 2074)

6. Study the figures in this article. What do the light and dark portions of the columns in Figure 12.3 represent? What is the purpose of Figure 12.2?

THINKING AND WRITING ABOUT THE TOPIC

Reading discipline-specific, scholarly writing can sometimes seem like reading a foreign language. That sentiment was captured in an article by engineer Doug Zongker. Zongker wrote a parody of academic writing, titled "Chicken Chicken Chicken: Chicken Chicken." To see Zongker's paper, go to http://isotropic.org/papers/chicken.pdf, or do an Internet search for the paper title. (You can also hear Zongker present his "research" at the annual meeting of the American Association for the Advancement of Science, on YouTube). As nonsensical as Zongker's article is, how can you still recognize it as being the presentation of an academic research report?

You learned in chapter 2 that knowledge of genre features facilitates reading in that genre. Once you are familiar with the "look" and organization of the research report genre, for example, you can make a lot of sense out of reports in any discipline.

Analyze the format, organization, and writing style in Proctor et al.'s article. What visual indications are there that it is academic writing? Despite the technical vocabulary, what writing features (including those discussed in chapter 6) allow anyone familiar with academic writing to follow the gist of the article? What knowledge about the research report genre helped *you* to understand the article?

WORKS CITED

American Management Association. *AMA 2012 Critical Skills Survey* (2012): 1–10. Web. 10 Sept. 2013.

Brosnan, Sarah F., and Frans B. M. de Waal. "Monkeys Reject Unequal Pay." *Nature* 425.6955 (2003): 297–98. Print.

Burnett, Rebecca E. "Productive and Unproductive Conflict in Collaboration." *Making Thinking Visible: Writing, Collaborative Planning, and Classroom Inquiry.* Ed. Linda Flower, David L. Wallace, Linda Norris, and Rebecca E. Burnett. Urbana: National Council of Teachers of English, 1994. 237–42. Print.

———. "Substantive Conflict in a Cooperative Context: A Way to Improve the Collaborative Planning of Workplace Documents." *Technical Communication* 38.4 (1991): 532–39. Print.

Cleary, Michelle Navarre. "Flowing and Freestyling: Learning from Adult Students about Process Knowledge Transfer." *College Composition and Communication* 64.4 (2013): 661–87. Print.

Freedman, Sarah Warshauer. "Why Do Teachers Give the Grades They Do?" *College Composition and Communication* 30.2 (May 1979): 161–64. Print.

Kyprianidou, Maria, et al. "Group Formation Based on Learning Styles: Can It Improve Students' Teamwork?" *Educational Technology, Research and Development* 60.1 (2012): 83–110. Print.

Loftus, Elizabeth F. "Prestige-Enhancing Memory Distortions." *Psychologist* 25.1 (2012): 26. Web. 18 Mar. 2014.

Louth, Richard, Carole McAllister, and Hunter A. McAllister. "The Effects of Collaborative Writing Techniques on Freshman Writing and Attitudes." *Journal of Experimental Education* 61.3 (1993): 215–24. Print.

Markel, Mike. *Technical Communication: Situations and Strategies.* 5th ed. New York: St. Martin's Press, 1998. Print.

Neu, Wayne A. "Unintended Cognitive, Affective, and Behavioral Consequences of Group Assignments." *Journal of Marketing Education* (2012): 67–81. Print.

Peter D. Hart Research Associates. *How Should Colleges Prepare Students to Succeed in Today's Global Economy?* (28 December 2006): 1–13. Web. 14 Sept. 2013.

Petress, Kenneth C. "The Benefits of Group Study." *Education* 124.4 (2004): 587–89. Print.

Rauch, Jonathan. "Global Warming: The Convenient Truth." *National Journal* 39.10 (2007): 17–18. Print.

Speck, Bruce W. "Facilitating Students' Collaborative Writing." *ASHE-ERIC Higher Education Report* 28.6. San Francisco: Jossey-Bass, 2002. Web. 13 Jan. 2014.

Stratton, Charles R. "Collaborative Writing in the Workplace." *IEEE Transactions on Professional Communication* 32.3 (1989): 178–82. Print.

Zongker, Doug. "Chicken Chicken Chicken: Chicken Chicken." *Annals of Improbable Research* 12.5 (2006): 16–21. Web. 25 Jan. 2014.

CHAPTER 13

Social Networks

No man (or woman) is an island, according to English poet John Donne. You can't avoid other people, and you can't avoid being influenced by those connections. The writers in this chapter illustrate some of the many ways we are shaped by contact with others.

We begin with Nicholas Christakis and James Fowler, who wrote the book *Connected: The Surprising Power of Our Social Networks and How They Shape Our Lives*. In the first chapter of their book, included here, Christakis and Fowler describe four different types of social networks and illustrate ways we are shaped not only by the people we know but also by the people they know.

Social connections can be found even among animals, according to primatologist Frans de Waal. In "The Empathy Instinct," de Waal describes "the power of unconscious synchrony." Laughter, yawning, and mannerisms are "contagious," and not just among humans.

Sometimes imitating those around us can have negative consequences. Economists Scott Carrell, Mark Hoekstra, and James West demonstrate that within social circles the least physically fit person tends to have the greatest influence on the fitness level of others. Extreme fitness can spread, too, when it's fueled by banned substances. In "The Canseco Effect," economist Ray Fisman describes the culture of cheating that surrounded baseball great Jose Canseco. Whether it's cheating in sports, on taxes, or on the job, Fisman argues that "it does matter if everyone else is doing it."

In the next two articles, sociologist Joel Best and neuroscientist V. S. Ramachandran also discuss the human tendency to follow the lead of others. In "The Illusion of Diffusion," Best describes how fads—in institutions and organizations—grow though social networks and just as quickly fade. Similarly, in "Creativity versus Skepticism within Science," Ramachandran describes the tendency among scientists to conform instead of challenge the accepted practice of peers.

Art professor Pablo Garcia illustrates what can be gained from copying the ideas of others—and improving on them. In his article "Hackers of the Renaissance," Garcia describes advancements in astronomy, art, and navigation made possible by inventors who "hacked" the ideas of others.

Finally, psychology professor Richard Nisbett, in a pair of articles, considers how we are influenced by our cultural networks. First, in "Culture and Causal Cognition," Ara Norenzayan and Nisbett review research demonstrating that where you were raised influences how you interpret human behavior. There are even cultural differences in what a person notices and remembers about what he or she has witnessed. Hannah Faye Chua, Julie Boland, and Nisbett demonstrate this in their study "Cultural Variation in Eye Movements during Scene Perception."

You may be able to control, to some extent, whom you associate with, but the writers in this chapter demonstrate that you can't avoid being influenced by those associations.

Sociology

Excerpt from *Connected: The Surprising Power of Our Social Networks and How They Shape Our Lives,* NICHOLAS A. CHRISTAKIS AND JAMES H. FOWLER

"Our connections affect every aspect of our daily lives," explain Nicholas Christakis and James Fowler. " . . . How we feel, what we know, whom we marry, whether we fall ill, how much money we make, and whether we vote all depend on the ties that bind us." Christakis is a physician and a professor of social and natural science at Yale University. Fowler is a professor of political science and medicine at the University of California, San Diego. Their research on social networks is described in their book *Connected: The Surprising Power of Our Social Networks and How They Shape Our Lives*, published in 2009. In the first chapter of their book, included here, the authors provide a general introduction to social network theory.

In the mountain village of Levie, Corsica, during the 1840s, Anton-Claudio Peretti became convinced that his wife, Maria-Angelina, was having an affair with another man and that, even worse, their daughter was not his child. Maria told Anton that she was going to leave him, and she made preparations to do so with her brother, Corto, That very evening, Anton shot his wife and daughter to death and fled to the mountains. The bereft Corto sorely wanted to kill Anton, but he could not find him. In a bit of violent symmetry that seemed sensible to residents of the area, Corto instead killed Anton's brother, Francesco, and nephew, Aristotelo.

It did not end there. Five years later, Giacomo, brother of the deceased Aristotelo, avenged the deaths of his brother and father by killing Corto's brother. Giacomo wanted to kill Corto's father too, but he had already died of natural causes, denying Giacomo the satisfaction. In this cascade of death, Giacomo and Corto's brother were connected by quite a path: Giacomo was the son of Francesco, who was the brother of Anton, who was married to Maria, who was the sister of Corto, whose brother was the target of Giacomo's murderous wrath.

Such behavior is not restricted to historically or geographically distant places. Here is another example, closer to home: Not long before the summer of 2002 in St. Louis, Missouri, Kimmy, an exotic dancer, left a purse containing $900 in earnings with a friend while she was busy. When she came back to reclaim it, her friend and the purse were gone. But a week later, Kimmy's cousin spotted the purse thief's partner at a local shop, and she called Kimmy. Kimmy raced over with a metal pole. She viciously attacked this friend of her erstwhile friend. Later she observed with pride that she had "beat her [friend's] partner's ass. . . . I know I did something . . . [to get even] that's the closest thing I could [do]."

Cases like these are puzzling. After all, what did Anton's brother and nephew and Kimmy's friend's friend have to do with anything? What possible sense is there in injuring or killing the innocent? Even by the incomprehensible standards of murderous violence, what is the point of these actions, taken one week or five years later? What explains them?

We tend to think of such cases as quaint curiosities, like Appalachian feuds, or as backward practices, like the internecine violence between Shiite and Sunni tribesmen or the cycle of killings in Northern Ireland or the reciprocating gang violence in American cities. But this grim logic has ancient roots. It is not just that the impetus to revenge is ancient, nor even that such violence can express group solidarity ("we are Hatfields, and we hate McCoys"), but that violence—in both its minor and extreme forms—can spread through social ties and has done so since humans emerged from the African savanna. It can spread either in a directed fashion (retaliating against the perpetrators) or in a generalized fashion (harming nondisputants nearby). Either way, however, a single murder can set off a cascade of killings. Acts of aggression typically diffuse outward from a starting point—like a bar fight that begins when one man swings at another who ducks, resulting in a third man getting hit, and soon (in what has become a cliché precisely because it evokes deep-seated notions of unleashed aggression) punches are flying everywhere. Sometimes these epidemics of violence, whether in Mediterranean villages or urban gangs, can persist for decades.

Notions of collective guilt and collective revenge that underlie cascades of violence seem strange only when we regard responsibility as a personal attribute. Yet in many settings, morality resides in groups rather than in individuals. And a further clue to the collective nature of violence is that it tends to be a public, not a private, phenomenon. Two-thirds of the acts of interpersonal violence in the United States are witnessed by third parties, and this fraction approaches three-fourths among young people.

Given these observations, perhaps the person-to-person spread of violence should not surprise us. Just as it is often said that "the friend of my friend is my friend" and "the enemy of my enemy is my friend," so too the friend of my enemy is my enemy. These aphorisms encapsulate certain truths about animosity and affection, but they also convey a fundamental aspect of our humanity: our connection. While Giacomo and Kimmy acted alone, their actions show just how easily responsibility and retaliation can diffuse from person to person to person across social ties.

In fact, we do not even have to search for complicated paths across which violence spreads, because the initial step, from the very first person to the next, accounts for most of the violence in our society. In trying to explain violence, it is myopic to focus solely on the perpetrator—his frame of mind, his finger on the trigger—because murder is rarely a random act between strangers. In the United States, 75 percent of all homicides involve people who knew each other, often intimately, prior to the murder. If you want to know who might take your life, just look at the people around you.

But your social network also includes those who might save your life. "On March 14, 2002, I gave my right kidney to my best friend's husband," Cathy would later note in an online forum that chronicles the experiences of people who become "living donors" of organs. The summer before, during a heartfelt chat, Cathy had learned that her friend's husband's renal failure had worsened and that he needed a kidney transplant in order to survive. Overcome with the desire to help, Cathy underwent a series of medical and psychological evaluations, getting more and more excited as she passed each one and moved closer to her goal of donating one of her kidneys. "The experience has been the most rewarding of my life," she wrote. "I am so grateful that I was able to help my best friend's husband. His wife has her husband back. His sons have their dad back. . . . It's a win-win situation. We all win. I gave the gift of life."

Similar stories abound, and such "directed donations" of organs can even come to involve people who have rather tenuous connections, a Starbucks clerk and his longtime customer, for example. There can even be organ-donation cascades that loosely resemble the Perettis' murder cascade. John Lavis, a sixty-two-year-old resident of the town of Mississauga, Ontario, father of four and grandfather of three, was dying of heart failure in 1995. His heart had failed during triple-bypass surgery, and he was placed on a temporary artificial heart. In a stroke of unbelievable good fortune, a donor heart was transplanted into him just eight days later when he was on the brink of death. His daughter recalled: "We were a family of immense gratitude. . . . [My father] received the biggest gift he will ever receive—his life was given back to him." Motivated by this experience, Lavis's children all signed organ-donor cards, thinking that this symmetrical act was the least they could do. Then in 2007, Lavis's son

Dan died in a work-related accident. Eight people benefited from Dan's decision to donate his organs. The woman who received his heart later wrote to the Lavis family, thanking them for "giving her a new life." The same year in the United States, a similar cascade an amazing ten links long took place between unrelated living kidney donors (albeit with explicit medical coordination), saving many lives along the way.

Social-network ties can—and, as we will see, usually do—convey benefits that are the very opposite of violence. They can be conduits for altruistic acts in which individuals pay back a debt of gratitude by paying it forward. The role that social connections can play in the spread of both good and bad deeds has even prompted the creation of novel strategies to address social problems. For example, programs in several U.S. metropolitan areas involve teams of "violence interrupters." These streetwise individuals, often former gang members, try to stop the killing by attempting to break the cycle of transmission. They rush to the bedsides of victims or to the homes of victims' families and friends, encouraging them not to seek revenge. If they can persuade just one person not to be violent, quite a few lives can be saved.

Our connections affect every aspect of our daily lives. Rare events such as murder and organ donation are just the tip of the iceberg. How we feel, what we know, whom we marry, whether we fall ill, how much money we make, and whether we vote all depend on the ties that bind us. Social networks spread happiness, generosity, and love. They are always there, exerting both subtle and dramatic influence over our choices, actions, thoughts, feelings, even our desires. And our connections do not end with the people we know. Beyond our own social horizons, friends of friends of friends can start chain reactions that eventually reach us, like waves from distant lands that wash up on our shores.

BUCKET BRIGADES AND TELEPHONE TREES

Imagine your house is on fire. Luckily, a cool river runs nearby. But you are all alone. You run back and forth to the river, bucket in hand, toting gallon after gallon of water to splash on your burning home. Unfortunately, your efforts are useless. Without some help, you will not be able to carry water fast enough to outpace the inferno.

Now suppose that you are not alone. You have one hundred neighbors, and, lucky for you, they all feel motivated to help. And each one just happens to have a bucket. If your neighbors are sufficiently strong, they can run back and forth to the river, haphazardly dumping buckets of water on the fire. A hundred people tossing water on your burning house is clearly better than you doing it by yourself. The problem is that once they get started your neighbors waste a lot of time running back and forth. Some of them tire easily; others are uncoordinated and spill a lot of water; one guy gets lost on his way back to your house. If each person acts independently, then your house will surely be destroyed.

Fortunately, this does not happen because a peculiar form of social organization is deployed: the bucket brigade. Your hundred neighbors form a line from the river to your house, passing full buckets of water toward your house and empty buckets toward the river. Not only does the bucket brigade arrangement mean that people do not have to spend time and energy walking back and forth to the river; it also means that weaker people who might not be able to walk or carry a heavy bucket long distances now have something to offer. A hundred people taking part in a bucket brigade might do the work of two hundred people running haphazardly.

But why exactly is a group of people arranged this way more effective than the same group of people—or even a larger group—working independently? If the whole is greater than the sum of its parts, how exactly does the whole come to be greater? Where does the "greater" part come from? It's amazing to be able to increase the effectiveness of human beings by as much as an order of magnitude simply by arranging them differently. But what is it about combining people into groups with *particular configurations* that makes them able to do more things and different things than the individuals themselves?

To answer these questions, and before we get to the fun stuff, we first need to explain a few basic terms and ideas of network theory. These basic concepts set the stage for the individual stories and the more complicated ideas we will soon explore as we investigate the surprising power of social networks to affect the full spectrum of human experience.

We should first clarify what we mean by a group of people. A *group* can be defined by an attribute (for example, women, Democrats, lawyers, long-distance runners) or as a specific collection of individuals to whom we can literally point ("those people, right over there, waiting to get into the concert"). A social network is altogether different. While a network, like a group, is a collection of people, it includes something more: a specific set of connections between people in the group. These ties, and the particular pattern of these ties, are often more important than the individual people themselves. They allow groups to do things that a disconnected collection of individuals cannot. The ties explain why the whole is greater than the sum of its parts. And the specific pattern of the ties is crucial to understanding how networks function.

The bucket brigade that saves a house is a very simple social network. It is linear and has no branches: each person (except the first and last) is connected to two other people, the one in front and the one behind. For moving something like water long distances, this is a good way to be organized. But the optimal organization of one hundred people into a network depends very much on the task at hand. The best pattern of connections between a hundred people to put out a fire is different from the best pattern for, say, achieving a military objective. A company of one hundred soldiers is typically organized into ten tightly interconnected squads of ten. This allows each soldier to know all of his squad mates rather than just the grunt in front of him and the grunt behind him. The military goes to great lengths to help squad members know each other very well, so well in fact that they are willing to give their lives for one another.

Consider still another social network: the telephone tree. Suppose you need to contact a hundred people quickly to let them know that school is canceled. Before modern communications and the Internet, this was a challenge because there was no public source of up-to-the-minute information that everyone could access from their homes (though the ringing of church bells in the town square comes to mind). Instead, each person needed to be contacted directly. The telephone made this task much easier, but it was still a burden for one person to make all one hundred calls. And even if someone set out to do this, it might take quite a while to get to the people at the end of the list, by which time they may have already left home for school. Having a single person make all the calls is both inefficient and burdensome.

Ideally, one person would set off a chain reaction so that everyone could be reached as quickly as possible and with the least burden on any particular individual. One option is to create a list and have the person at the top of the list call the next person, the second person call the third, and so on until everyone gets the message, as in a bucket brigade. This would distribute the burden evenly, but it would still take a really long time for the hundredth person to be reached. Moreover, if someone in the sequence was not home when called, everyone later in the list would be left in the dark.

An alternative pattern of connections is a telephone tree. The first person calls two people, who each call two people, and so on until everyone is contacted. Unlike the bucket brigade, the telephone tree is designed to spread information to many people simultaneously, creating a cascade. The workload is distributed evenly among all group members, and the problem caused by one person not being home is limited. Moreover, with a single call, one person can set off a chain of events that could influence hundreds or thousands of other people—just as the person who donated the heart that was transplanted into John Lavis prompted another donation that saved eight more lives. The telephone tree also vastly reduces the number of steps it takes for information to flow among people in the group, minimizing the chance that the message will be degraded. This particular network structure thus helps to both amplify and preserve the message. In fact, within a few decades of the widespread deployment of home-based phones in the United States, telephone trees were used for all sorts of purposes. An article in the *Los Angeles Times* from 1957, for example, describes the use of a phone tree to mobilize amateur astronomers, as part of the "Moonwatch System" of the Smithsonian Astrophysical Observatory, to track American and Russian satellites.

Alas, this same network structure also allows a single swindler to cheat thousands of people. In Ponzi schemes, money flows "up" a structure like a telephone tree. As new people are added to the network, they send money to the people "above" them and then new members are recruited "below" them to provide more money. As time passes, money is collected from more and more people. In what might be the biggest Ponzi scheme of all time, federal investigators discovered in 2008 that during the previous thirty years Bernie Madoff had swindled $50 billion from thousands of investors, Like the Corsican vendetta network we described earlier, Madoff's investment network is the kind most of us would like to avoid.

The four different types of networks we have considered so far are shown in the illustration [Fig. 13.1]. First is a group of one hundred people (each represented by a circle, or *node*) among whom there are no ties. Next is a bucket brigade. Here, in addition to the one hundred people, there are a total of ninety-nine ties between the members of the group; every person (except the first and last) is connected to two other people by a *mutual tie* (meaning that full and empty buckets pass in both directions). In the telephone tree, there are one hundred people and again ninety-nine ties. But here, everyone, with the exception of the first and last people in the tree, is connected to three other people, with one inbound tie (the person they get the call from) and two outbound ties (the people they make calls to). There are no mutual ties; the flow of information is directional and so are the ties between people. In a company of one hundred soldiers, each member of each squad knows every other member of the squad very well; and each person has exactly nine ties. Here, there are one hundred people and 450 ties connecting them. (The reason there are not nine hundred ties is that each tie counts once for the two people it connects.) In the drawing, we imagine that there are no ties between squads or, at least, that the ties within squads are much tighter than the ties between squads. This is clearly an oversimplification, but it illustrates still another point about communities in social networks. A *network community* can be defined as a group of people who are much more connected to one another than they are to other groups of connected people found in other parts of the network. The communities are defined by structural connections, not necessarily by any particular shared traits.

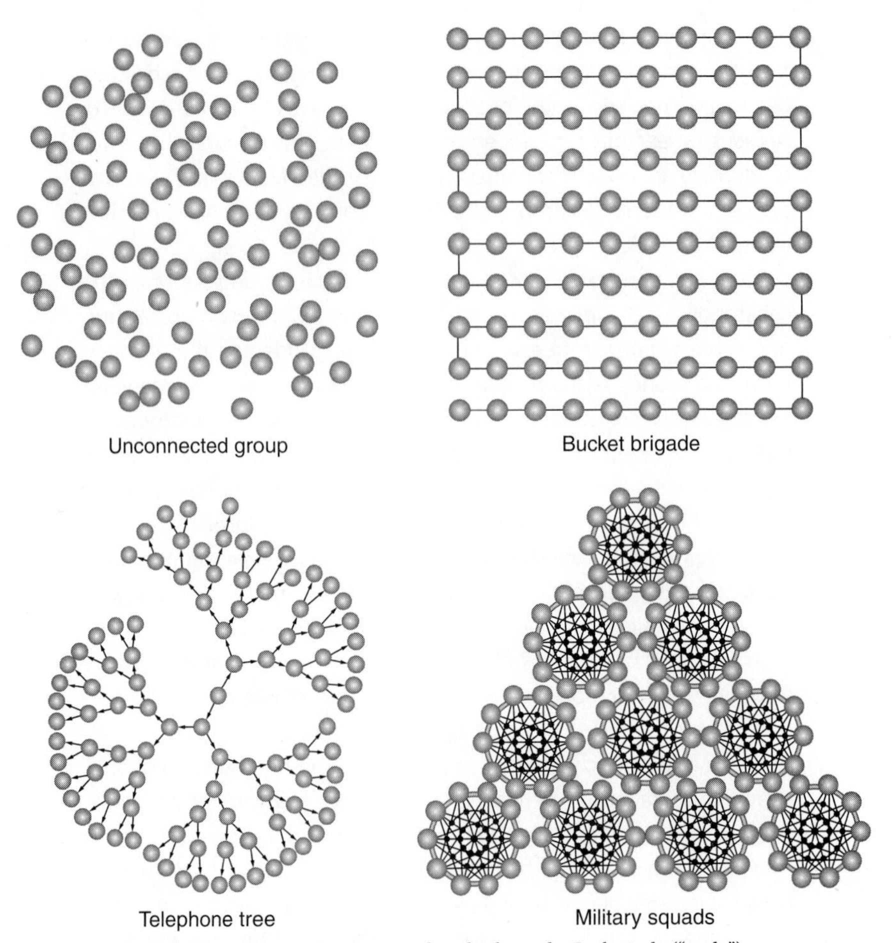

Figure 13.1 Four different ways to connect one hundred people. Each circle ("node") represents a person, and each line ("tie") a relationship between two people. Lines with arrows indicate a directed relationship; in the telephone tree, one person calls another. Otherwise, ties are mutual: in the bucket brigade, full and empty buckets travel in both directions; in military squads, the connections between the soldiers are all two-way.

In a very basic sense, then, a social network is an organized set of people that consists of two kinds of elements: human beings and the connections between them. Unlike the bucket brigade, telephone tree, and military company, however, the organization of natural social networks is typically not imposed from the top. Real, everyday social networks evolve organically from the natural tendency of each person to seek out and make many or few friends, to have large or small families, to work in personable or anonymous workplaces.

For example, in the next illustration, we show a network of 105 students in a single dormitory at an American university and the friendship ties between them. On average, each student is connected to six other close friends, but some students have only one friend, and others have many. Moreover, some students are more embedded than others, meaning they have more connections to other people in the network via friends or friends of friends. In fact, network visualization software is designed to place those who are more interconnected in the center and those who are less interconnected at the periphery, helping us to see each person's location in the network. When your friends and family become better connected, it increases your level of connection to the whole social network. We say it makes you more *central* because having better-connected friends literally moves you away from the edges and toward the center of a social network. And we can measure your centrality by counting not just the number of your friends and other contacts but also by counting your friends' friends, and their friends, and so on. Unlike the bucket brigade where everyone feels his position to be the same ("there's a guy on my left passing me buckets and a guy on my right to whom I give them—it doesn't matter where in the line I am"), here, people are located in distinctly different kinds of places within the network.

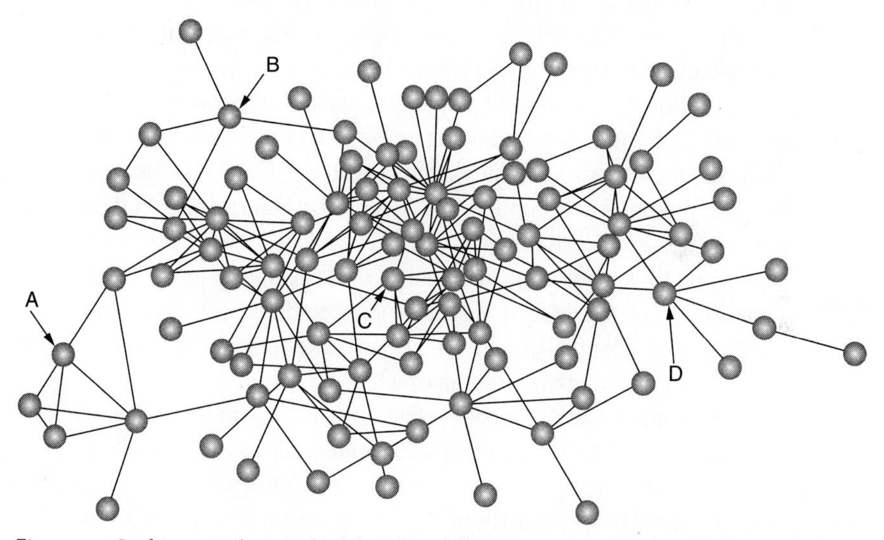

Figure 13.2 In this natural network of close friendships among 105 college students living in the same dormitory, each circle represents a student, and each line a mutual friendship. Even though A and B both have four friends, A's four friends are more likely to know one another (there are ties between them), whereas none of B's friends know each other. A has greater transitivity than B. Also, even though C and D both have six friends, they have very different locations in the social network. C is much more central, and D is more peripheral; C's friends have many friends themselves, whereas D's friends tend to have few or no friends.

A network's *shape,* also known as its structure or topology, is a basic property of the network. While the shape can be visualized, or represented, in different ways, the actual pattern of connections that determines the shape remains the same regardless of how the network is visualized. Imagine a set of five hundred buttons strewn on the floor. And imagine that there are two thousand strings we can use to connect the buttons. Next, imagine that we randomly select two buttons and connect them with a string, knotting each button at the end. Then we repeat this procedure, connecting random pairs of buttons one after another, until all the strings are used up. In the end, some buttons will have many strings attached to them, and others, by chance, will never have been picked and so will not be connected to another button. Perhaps some groups of buttons will be connected to each other but separated from other groups. These groups—even those that consist of a single unconnected button—are called *components* of the network; when we illustrate networks, we frequently represent only the largest component (in this case, the one with the most buttons).

If we were to select one button from one component and pick it up off the floor, all other buttons attached to it, directly or indirectly, would also be lifted into the air. And if we were to drop this mass of buttons onto another spot on the floor, it would look different than it did when we first picked it up. But the topology—which is a fundamental and intrinsic property of the network of buttons—would be exactly the same, no matter how many times we picked up and dropped the mass of connected buttons. Each button has the same relational position to other particular buttons that it had before; its *location* in the network has not changed. Visualization software tries to show this in two dimensions and to reveal the underlying topology by putting the most tangled buttons in the center and the least connected ones on the edges. It's as if you were trying to untangle a gnarled set of Christmas-tree lights, and there were tendrils of the gnarled mess that you could pull out, and also a thicket of inter-knotted lights that remained in the center no matter how often you turned the tangle over on the floor.

For numerous reasons we will explore, people come to occupy particular spots in the naturally occurring and continuously evolving social networks that surround us. Organic networks have a structure, complexity, function, spontaneity, and sheer beauty not found in organized networks, and their existence provokes questions about how they arise, what rules they obey, and what purpose they serve.

RULES OF LIFE IN THE NETWORK

There are two fundamental aspects of social networks, whether they are as simple as a bucket brigade or as complex as a large multigenerational family, a college dormitory, an entire community, or the worldwide network that links us all. First, there is *connection,* which has to do with who is connected to whom. When a group is constituted as a network, there is a particular pattern of ties that connects the people involved, the topology. Moreover, ties are complicated. They can be ephemeral or lifelong; they can be casual or intense; they can be personal or anonymous. How we construct or visualize a network depends on how we define the ties of interest. Most analyses emphasize ties to family, friends, coworkers, and neighbors. But there are all sorts of social ties and, thus, all sorts of social networks. In fact, when things such as sexually transmitted diseases or dollar bills flow through a network, this flow itself can define the ties and hence the structure of a particular set of network connections.

Second, there is *contagion,* which pertains to what, if anything, flows across the ties. It could be buckets of water, of course, but it also could be germs, money, violence, fashions, kidneys, happiness, or obesity. Each of these flows might behave according to its own rules. For example, fire cannot be transported in buckets toward the river; germs cannot affect someone who is immune; and obesity tends to spread faster between people of the same sex.

Understanding why social networks exist and how they work requires that we understand certain rules regarding connection and contagion—the structure and function—of social networks. These principles explain how ties can cause the whole to be greater than the sum of the parts.

Rule 1: We Shape Our Network

Humans deliberately make and remake their social networks all the time. The primary example of this is *homophily,* the conscious or unconscious tendency to associate with people who resemble us (the word literally means "love of being alike"). Whether it's Hells Angels or Jehovah's Witnesses, drug addicts or coffee drinkers, Democrats or Republicans, stamp collectors or bungee jumpers, the truth is that we seek out those people who share our interests, histories, and dreams. Birds of a feather flock together.

But we also choose the *structure* of our networks in three important ways. First, we decide how many people we are connected to. Do you want one partner for a game of checkers or many partners for a game of hide-and-seek? Do you want to stay in touch with your crazy uncle? Do you want to get married, or would you rather play the field? Second, we influence how densely interconnected our friends and family are. Should you seat the groom's college roommate next to your bridesmaid at the wedding? Should you throw a party so all your friends can meet each other? Should you introduce your business partners? And third, we control how central we are to the social network. Are you the life of the party, mingling with everyone at the center of the room, or do you stay on the sidelines?

Diversity in these choices yields an astonishing variety of structures for the whole network in which we come to be embedded. And it is diversity in these choices—a diversity that has both social and genetic origins—that places each of us in a unique location in our own social network. Of course, sometimes these structural features are not a matter of choice; we may live in places that are more or less conducive to friendship, or we may be born into large or small families. But even when these social-network structures are thrust upon us, they still rule our lives.

We actually know quite a bit about how people vary in terms of how many friends and social contacts they have and in how interconnected they are. Yet, identifying who a person's social contacts are can be a tricky business since people have many interactions of varying intensities with all sorts of people. While a person may know a few hundred people by sight and name, he will typically be truly close to only a few. One way social scientists identify such close individuals is to ask questions like, who do you discuss important matters with? Or, who do you spend your free time with? When answering such questions, people will identify a heterogeneous mix of friends, relatives, coworkers, schoolmates, neighbors, and others.

We recently put these questions to a sample of more than three thousand randomly chosen Americans. And we found that the average American has just four close social contacts, with most having between two and six. Sadly, 12 percent of Americans listed no one with whom they could discuss important matters or spend free time. At the other extreme, 5 percent of Americans had eight such people. About half of the people listed as members of Americans' intimate groups were said to be friends, but the other half included a wide variety of different kinds of relationships, including spouses, partners, parents, siblings, children, coworkers, fellow members of clubs, neighbors, and professional advisers and consultants. Sociologist Peter Marsden has called this group of people that we all have a "core discussion network." In a national sample of 1,531 Americans studied in the 1980s, he found that core-discussion-network size decreases as we age, that there is no overall difference between men and women in core-network size, and that those with a college degree have core networks that are nearly twice as large as those who did not finish high school.

Next, in our own work, we asked the respondents to tell us how interconnected their social contacts were to each other. So if a person said that Tom, Dick, Harry, and Sue were his friends, we asked him if Tom knew Dick, if Tom knew Harry, if Tom knew Sue, if Dick knew Harry, and so on. We then used these answers to calculate the probability that any two of a person's friends were also friends with each other. This probability is an important property that we use to measure how tightly interwoven a network is.

If you know Alexi, and Alexi knows Lucas, and Lucas knows you, we say this relationship is *transitive*—the three people involved form a triangle.

Some people live in the thick of many transitive relationships (like person A in the illustration), while others have friends who do not know each other (like person B). Those with high transitivity are usually deeply embedded within a single group, while those with low transitivity tend to make contact with people from several different groups who do not know one another, making them more likely to act as a bridge between different groups. Overall, we found that if you are a typical American, the probability that any two of your social contacts know each other is about 52 percent.

Although these measures characterize the networks we can see, they also tell us something about the networks we cannot see. In the vast fabric of humanity, each person is connected to his friends, family, coworkers, and neighbors, but these people are in turn connected to their friends, family, coworkers, and neighbors, and so on endlessly into the distance, until everyone on earth is connected (pretty much) to everyone else, one way or another. So whereas we think of our own network as having a more limited social and geographic reach, the networks that surround each of us are actually very widely interconnected.

It is this structural feature of networks that underlies the common expression "it's a small world." It is often possible, through a few connections from person to person, for an individual to discover a connection to someone else. A famous example (at least among social scientists) was described in a paper first drafted in the 1950s by two early figures in the study of social networks, Ithiel de Sola Pool and Manfred Kochen. One of the authors overheard a patient in a hospital in a small town in Illinois say to a Chinese patient in the adjoining bed: "You know, I've only known one Chinese before in my life. He was—from Shanghai." Whereupon the response came back, "Why, that's my uncle." In fact, the authors did not tell us his name, perhaps because they were worried that the reader, in a further illustration of the small-world effect, would know him.

Rule 2: Our Network Shapes Us

Our place in the network affects us in turn. A person who has no friends has a very different life than one who has many. For example, having an extra friend may create all kinds of benefits for your health, even if this other person doesn't actually do anything in particular for you.

One study of hundreds of thousands of Norwegian military conscripts provides a simple example of how the mere number of social contacts (here, siblings) can affect you. It has been known for some time that first-born children score a few points higher in terms of intelligence than second-born children, who in turn score a bit higher than third-born children. One of the outstanding questions in this area of investigation, however, has been whether these differences are due to biological factors fixed at birth or to social factors that come later. The study of Norwegian soldiers showed that simple features of social networks, such as family size and structure, are responsible for the differences. If you are a second-born son whose older sibling died while you were a child, your IQ increases and resembles the IQ of a first-born child. If you are a third-born child and one of your older siblings died, your IQ resembles that of a second-born child; and if both of your older siblings died, then your IQ resembles that of a first-born child.

Whether your friends and other social contacts are friends with one another is also crucial to your experience of life. Transitivity can affect everything from whether you find a sexual partner to whether you commit suicide. The effect of transitivity is easily appreciated by the example of how divorce affects a child. If a child's parents are married (connected) then they probably talk to each other, but if they get divorced (disconnected) they probably do not. Divorce means that communication often has to pass through the child ("Tell your father not to bother picking you up next Saturday!"), and it is much harder to coordinate raising the child ("You mean your mother bought you ice cream too?"). What is remarkable is that even though the child is still deeply connected to both parents, her relationship with each of them changes as a consequence of the divorce. Yet these changes result from the loss of a connection between the parents—a connection the child has little to do with. The child still has two parents, but her life is different depending on whether or not they are connected.

And how many contacts your friends and family have is also relevant. When the people you are connected to become better connected, it reduces the number of hops you have to take from person to person to reach everyone else in the network. You become more central. Being more central makes you more susceptible to whatever is flowing within the network. For example, person C in the figure is more central than person D. Ask yourself which person you would rather be if a hot piece of gossip were spreading; you should be person C. Now ask yourself which person you would rather be if a deadly germ were spreading in the network; you should be person D. And this is the case even though persons C and D each have the same number of social ties: they are each directly connected to just six people.

Rule 3: Our Friends Affect Us

The mere shape of the network around us is not all that matters, of course. What actually flows across the connections is also crucial. A bucket brigade is formed not to make a pretty line for you to look at while your house is burning but so that people can pass water to each other to douse the flames. And social networks are not just for water—they transport all kinds of things from one person to another.

One fundamental determinant of flow is the tendency of human beings to influence and copy one another. People typically have many direct ties to a wide variety of people, including parents and children, brothers and sisters, spouses (and nice ex-spouses), bosses and coworkers, and neighbors and friends. And each and every one of these ties offers opportunities to influence and be influenced. Students with studious roommates become more studious. Diners sitting next to heavy eaters eat more food. Homeowners with neighbors who garden wind up with manicured lawns. And this simple tendency for one person to influence another has tremendous consequences when we look beyond our immediate connections.

Rule 4: Our Friends' Friends' Friends Affect Us

It turns out that people do not copy only their friends. They also copy their friends' friends, and their friends' friends' friends. In the children's game telephone, a message is passed along a line by each child whispering into the next child's ear. The message each child receives contains all the errors introduced by the child sharing it as well as those introduced by prior children to whom the child is not directly connected. In this way, children can come to copy others to whom they are not directly tied. Similarly, every parent warns children not to put money in their mouths: the money, we think, contains germs from numerous people whose hands it has passed through, and not just from the most recent pair of hands. Analogously, our friends and family can influence us to do things, like gain weight or show up at the polls. But their friends and family can influence us too. This is an illustration of *hyperdyadic spread,* or the tendency of effects to spread from person to person to person, beyond an individual's direct social ties. Corto's brother lost his life because of such spread.

It is easy to think about hyperdyadic effects when the network is straight line—("that guy three people down the line better pass the bucket, or we're all going to be in big trouble"). But how on earth can they be understood in a natural social network such as the college students in the illustration or complex networks of thousands of people with all kinds of crosscutting paths stretching far beyond the social horizon (as we will consider later)? To decipher what is going on, we need two kinds of information. First, we must look beyond simple, sequential dyads: we need to know about individuals and their friends, their friends' friends, their friends' friends' friends, and so on. And we can only get this information by observing the whole network at once. It has just recently become possible to do this on a large scale. Second, if we want to observe how things flow from person to person to person, then we need information about ties and the people they connect at more than one point in time, otherwise we have no hope of understanding the dynamic properties of the network. It would be like trying to learn the rules of an unfamiliar sport by looking at a single snapshot of a game.

We will consider many examples and varieties of hyperdyadic spread, but we can set the stage with a simple one. The usual way we think about contagion is that if one person has something and comes into contact with another person, that contact is enough for the second person to get it. You can become infected with a germ (the most straightforward example) or with a piece of gossip or information (a less obvious example). Once you get infected by a single person, additional contact with others is generally redundant. For example, if you have been told accurately that stock XYZ closed at $50, another person telling you the same thing does not add much. And you can pass this information on to someone else all by yourself.

But some things—like norms and behaviors—might not spread this way. They might require a more complex process that involves reinforcement by multiple social contacts. If so, then a network arranged as a simple line, like a bucket brigade, might not support transmission of more complicated phenomena. If we wanted to get people to quit smoking, we would not arrange them in a line and get the first one to quit and tell him to pass it on. Rather, we would surround a smoker with multiple nonsmokers, perhaps in a squad.

Psychologist Stanley Milgram's famous sidewalk experiment illustrates the importance of reinforcement from multiple people. On two cold winter afternoons in New York City in 1968, Milgram observed the behavior of 1,424 pedestrians as they walked along a fifty-foot length of street. He positioned "stimulus crowds," ranging in size from one to fifteen research assistants, on the sidewalk. On cue, these artificial crowds would stop and look up at a window on the sixth floor of a nearby building for precisely one minute. There was nothing interesting in the window, just another guy working for Milgram. The results were filmed, and assistants later counted the number of people who stopped or looked where the stimulus crowd was looking. While 4 percent of the pedestrians stopped alongside a "crowd" composed of a single individual looking up, 40 percent stopped when there were fifteen people in the stimulus crowd. Evidently, the decisions of passersby to copy a behavior were influenced by the size of the crowd exhibiting it.

An even larger percentage of pedestrians copied the behavior incompletely: they looked up in the direction of the stimulus crowd's gaze but did not stop. While one person influenced 42 percent of passersby to look up, 86 percent of the passersby looked up if fifteen people were looking up. More interesting than this difference, however, was that a stimulus crowd of five people was able to induce almost as many passersby to look up as fifteen people did. That is, in this setting, crowds larger than five did not have much more of an effect on the actions of passing individuals.

Rule 5: The Network Has a Life of Its Own

Social networks can have properties and functions that are neither controlled nor even perceived by the people within them. These properties can be understood only by studying the whole group and its structure, not by studying isolated individuals. Simple examples include traffic jams and stampedes. You cannot understand a traffic jam by interrogating one person fuming at the wheel of his car, even though his immobile automobile contributes to the problem. Complex examples include the notion of culture, or, as we shall see, the fact that groups of interconnected people can exhibit complicated, shared behaviors without explicit coordination or awareness.

Many of the simple examples can be understood best if we completely ignore the will and cognition of the individuals involved and treat people as if they were "zero-intelligence agents." Consider the human waves at sporting events that first gained worldwide notice during the 1986 World Cup in Mexico. In this phenomenon, originally called *La Ola* ("the wave"), sequential groups of spectators leap to their feet and raise their arms, then quickly drop back to a seated position. The effect is quite dramatic. A group of physicists who usually study waves on the surface of liquids were sufficiently intrigued that they decided to study a collection of filmed examples of *La Ola* in enormous soccer stadiums; they noticed that these waves usually rolled in a clockwise direction and consistently moved at a speed of twenty "seats per second."

To understand how such human waves start and propagate, the scientists employed mathematical models of excitable media that are ordinarily used to understand inanimate phenomena such as the spread of a fire through a forest or the spread of an electrical signal through cardiac muscle. An *excitable medium* is one that flips from one state to another (like a tree that is either on fire or not) depending on what others around it are doing (are nearby trees on fire?). And these models yielded accurate predictions of the social phenomenon, suggesting that *La Ola* could be understood even if we knew nothing about the biology or psychology of humans. Indeed, the wave cannot be understood by studying the actions of a single individual standing up and sitting down. It is not orchestrated by someone with a megaphone atop a cooler. It has a life of its own.

Mathematical models of flocks of birds and schools of fish and swarms of insects that move in unison demonstrate the same point:

there is no central control of the movement of the group, but the group manifests a kind of collective intelligence that helps all within it to flee or deter predators. This behavior does not reside within individual creatures but, rather, is a property of groups. Examination of flocks of birds "deciding" where to fly reveals that they move in a way that accounts for the intentions of all the birds, and, even more important, the direction of movement is usually the best choice for the flock. Each bird contributes a bit, and the flock's collective choice is better than an individual bird's would be. Similar to *La Ola* and to flocking birds, social networks obey rules of their own, rules that are distinct from the people who form them. But now, people are not having fun in a stadium: they are donating organs or gaining weight or feeling happy.

In this regard, we say that social networks have emergent properties. *Emergent properties* are new attributes of a whole that arise from the interaction and interconnection of the parts. The idea of emergence can be understood with an analogy: A cake has a taste not found in any one of its ingredients. Nor is its taste simply the average of the ingredients' flavors—something, say, halfway between flour and eggs. It is much more than that. The taste of a cake transcends the simple sum of its ingredients. Likewise, understanding social networks allows us to understand how indeed, in the case of humans, the whole comes to be greater than the sum of its parts.

QUESTIONS ABOUT MEANING

1. The structure or pattern of a social network depends on the purpose of that network community. What are some types of social network structures the authors describe and under what circumstances might they form?
2. What principles or rules govern life in a social network?

QUESTIONS FOR RHETORICAL ANALYSIS

1. Christakis and Fowler provide anecdotes (about Anton and Kimmy) before stating that in the United States, "75 percent of all homicides involve people who knew each other, often intimately, prior to the murder." How do the anecdotes and statistic relate to the authors' larger point? Do you think the organizational structure of anecdotes-then-statistic is effective in an introduction? Why or why not?
2. Highlight instances of italicized words and phrases in the reading. What purposes do the italics serve and what does their use suggest concerning the authors' assumptions about their audience? When or how might you use italics to similar effect in your own writing in college?

MAKING CONNECTIONS

1. In chapter 1 of their book, Christakis and Fowler introduce five general "rules of life in the network"—rules that they later explain and illustrate in their book.

   As a member of many social networks, you too have examples of these rules or principles at work. Using the authors' five rules as a framework for your own essay, illustrate each of the principles with examples from your own experiences and observations or with examples from other authors in this chapter.
2. Are you like your friends? Chances are you're more like them than you realize. In an essay titled "Connected: The Surprising Power of My Social Networks and How They Shape My Life," reflect on one or more meaningful ways you have been influenced by your social networks.

Biology

"The Empathy Instinct," FRANS DE WAAL

You may remember Frans de Waal from chapter 12, where two of his articles are featured. De Waal is a professor of primate behavior at Emory University in Atlanta and the author of several books about primate social behavior. In the next article, de Waal uses examples from the animal world to demonstrate that humans aren't the only social creatures. "The Empathy Instinct" appeared in 2009 in *Discover* magazine, which publishes articles describing developments in science, medicine, and technology for a general audience.

What intrigues me most about laughter is how it spreads. It's almost impossible not to laugh when everybody else is. There have been laughing epidemics, in which no one could stop and some even died in a prolonged fit. There are laughing churches and laugh therapies based on the healing power of laughter. The must-have toy of 1996—Tickle Me Elmo—laughed hysterically after being squeezed three times in a row. All of this because we love to laugh and can't resist joining laughing around us. This is why comedy shows on television have laugh tracks and why theater audiences are sometimes sprinkled with "laugh plants": people paid to produce raucous laughing at any joke that comes along.

The infectiousness of laughter even works across species. Below my office window at the Yerkes Primate Center, I often hear my chimps laugh during rough-and-tumble games, and I cannot suppress a chuckle myself. It's such a happy sound. Tickling and wrestling are the typical laugh triggers for apes, and probably the original ones for humans. The fact that tickling oneself is notoriously ineffective attests to its social significance. And when young apes put on their play face, their friends join in with the same expression as rapidly and easily as humans do with laughter.

Shared laughter is just one example of our primate sensitivity to others. Instead of being Robinson Crusoes sitting on separate islands, we're all interconnected, both bodily and emotionally. This may be an odd thing to say in the West, with its tradition of individual freedom and liberty, but Homo sapiens is remarkably easily swayed in one emotional direction or another by its fellows.

This is precisely where empathy and sympathy start—not in the higher regions of imagination, or the ability to consciously reconstruct how we would feel if we were in someone else's situation. It began much more simply, with the synchronization of bodies: running when others run, laughing when others laugh, crying when others cry, or yawning when others yawn. Most of us have reached the incredibly advanced stage at which we yawn even at the mere mention of yawning—as you may be doing right now!—but this is only after lots of face-to-face experience.

Yawn contagion, too, works across species. Virtually all animals show the peculiar "paroxystic respiratory cycle characterized by a standard cascade of movements over a five- to ten-second period," which is the way the yawn has been defined. I once attended a lecture on involuntary pandiculation (the medical term for stretching and yawning) with slides of horses, lions, and monkeys—and soon the entire audience was pandiculating. Since it so easily triggers a chain reaction, the yawn reflex opens a window onto mood transmission, an essential part of empathy. This makes it all the more intriguing that chimpanzees yawn when they see others do so.

Yawn contagion reflects the power of unconscious synchrony which is as deeply ingrained in us as in many other animals. Synchrony may be expressed in the copying of small body movements, such as a yawn, but also occurs on a larger scale, involving travel or movement. It is not hard to see its survival value. You're in a flock of birds and one bird suddenly takes off. You have no time to figure out what's going on: You take off at the same instant. Otherwise, you may be lunch.

Or your entire group becomes sleepy and settles down, so you too become sleepy. Mood contagion serves to coordinate activities, which is crucial for any traveling species (as most primates are). If my companions are feeding, I'd better do the same, because once they move off, my chance to forage will be gone. The individual who doesn't stay in tune with what everyone else is doing will lose out like the traveler who doesn't go to the restroom when the bus has stopped.

The herd instinct produces weird phenomena. At one zoo, an entire baboon troop gathered on top of their rock, all staring in exactly the same direction. For an entire week they forgot to eat, mate, and groom. They just kept staring at something in the distance that no one could identify. Local newspapers were carrying pictures of the monkey rock, speculating that perhaps the animals had been frightened by a UFO. But even though this explanation had the unique advantage of combining an account of primate behavior with proof of UFOs, the truth is that no one knew the cause except that the baboons clearly were all of the same mind.

Finding himself in front of the cameras next to his pal President George W. Bush, former British prime minister Tony Blair—known to walk normally at home—would suddenly metamorphose into a distinctly un-English cowboy. He'd swagger with arms hanging loose and chest puffed out. Bush, of course, strutted like this all the time and once explained how, back home in Texas, this is known as "walking." Identification is the hook that draws us in and makes us adopt the situation, emotions, and behavior of those we're close to. They become role models: We empathize with them and emulate them. Thus children often walk like the same-sex parent or mimic their tone of voice when they pick up the phone.

How does one chimp imitate another? Does he identify with the other and absorb its body movements? Or could it be that he doesn't need the other and instead focuses on the problem faced by the other? This can be tested by having a chimpanzee show another how to open a puzzle box with goodies inside. Maybe all that the watching ape needs to understand is how the thing works. He may notice that the door slides to the side or that something needs to be lifted up. The first kind of imitation involves reenactment of observed manipulations; the second merely requires technical know-how.

Thanks to ingenious studies in which chimps were presented with a so-called ghost box, we know which of these two explanations is correct. A ghost box derives its name from the fact that it magically opens and closes by itself so that no actor is needed. If technical know-how were all that mattered, such a box should suffice. But in fact, letting chimps watch a ghost box until they're bored to death—with its various parts moving and producing rewards hundreds of times—doesn't teach them anything.

To learn from others, apes need to see actual fellow apes: Imitation requires identification with a body of flesh and blood. We're beginning to realize how much human and animal cognition runs via the body. Instead of our brain being like a little computer that orders the body around; the body-brain relation is a two-way street. The body produces internal sensations and communicates with other bodies, out of which we construct social connections and an appreciation of the surrounding reality. Bodies insert themselves into everything we perceive or think. Did you know, for example, that physical condition colors perception? The same hill is assessed as steeper, just from looking at it, by a tired person than by a well-rested one. An outdoor target is judged as farther away than it really is by a person burdened with a heavy backpack than by one without it.

Or ask a pianist to pick out his own performance from among others he's listening to. Even if this is a new piece that the pianist has performed only once, in silence (on an electronic piano and without headphones on), he will be able to recognize his own play. While listening, he probably recreates in his head the sort of bodily sensations that accompany an actual performance. He feels the closest match listening to himself, thus recognizing himself through his body as much as through his ears.

The field of "embodied" cognition is still very much in its infancy but has profound implications for how we look at human relations. We involuntarily enter the bodies of those around us so that their movements and emotions echo within us as if they're our own. This is what allows us, or other primates, to re-create what we have seen others do. Body mapping is mostly hidden and unconscious, but sometimes it "slips out," such as when parents make chewing mouth movements while spoon-feeding their baby. They can't help but act the way they feel their baby ought to. Similarly, parents watching a singing performance of their child often get completely into it, mouthing every word. I myself still remember as a boy standing on the sidelines of soccer games and involuntarily making kicking or jumping moves each time someone I was cheering for got the ball.

The same can be seen in animals, as illustrated in an old black-and-white photograph from Wolfgang Köhler's classic tool-use studies on chimpanzees. One ape, Grande, stands on boxes that she has stacked up to reach bananas hung from the ceiling, while Sultan watches intently. Even though Sultan sits at a distance, he raises his arm in precise synchrony with Grande's grasping movement. Another example comes from a chimpanzee filmed while using a heavy rock as a hammer to crack nuts. The actor is being observed by a younger ape, who swings his own (empty) hand down in sync every time the first one strikes the nut. Body mapping provides a great shortcut to imitation.

When I see synchrony and mimicry—whether it concerns yawning, laughing, dancing, or aping—I see social connection and bonding. I see an old herd instinct that has been taken up a notch. It goes beyond the tendency of a mass of individuals galloping in the same direction, crossing the river at the same time. The new level requires that one pay better attention to what others do and absorb how they do it. For example,

I knew an old monkey matriarch with a curious drinking style. Instead of the typical slurping with her lips from the surface, she'd dip her entire underarm in the water, then lick the hair on her arm. Her children started doing the same, and then her grandchildren. The entire family was easy to recognize.

There is also the case of a male chimpanzee who had injured his fingers in a fight and hobbled around leaning on a bent wrist instead of his knuckles. Soon all of the young chimpanzees in the colony were walking the same way in single file behind the unlucky male. Like chameleons changing their color to match the environment, primates automatically copy their surroundings.

When I was a boy, my friends in the south of the Netherlands always ridiculed me when I came home from vacations in the north, where I played with boys from Amsterdam. They told me that I talked funny. Unconsciously, I'd return speaking a poor imitation of the harsh northern accent.

The way our bodies—including voice, mood, posture, and so on—are influenced by surrounding bodies is one of the mysteries of human existence, but one that provides the glue that holds entire societies together. It's also one of the most underestimated phenomena, especially in disciplines that view humans as rational decisionmakers. Instead of each individual independently weighing the pros and cons of his or her own actions, we occupy nodes within a tight network that connects all of us in both body and mind.

When I see synchrony and mimicry-yawning, laughing, dancing—I see an old herd instinct taken up a notch.

QUESTIONS ABOUT MEANING

1. The social connections found among humans can be found among animals as well. What examples of this does de Waal describe?
2. What does de Waal mean when he calls the body-brain relation a "two-way street"?

QUESTIONS FOR RHETORICAL ANALYSIS

1. In what ways does de Waal make his subject accessible and engaging for a general audience? Give examples.
2. Look up the word *empathy* to get a full understanding of how the word is used. Do you think "The Empathy Instinct" is a fitting title for this article? Why or why not?
3. Do personal anecdotes and first-person singular pronouns enhance or detract from de Waal's credibility? Explain. How would you describe the ethos de Waal creates for himself as a writer?

MAKING CONNECTIONS

1. Rather than being a conscious choice, mimicking and responding to the emotions of others is instinctual, according to de Waal. Would other writers in this chapter (such as Christakis and Fowler; Nisbett; or Best, in "The Illusion of Diffusion") be likely to agree that conformity is instinctual? Do you agree with de Waal? In an essay, address these questions, using evidence from others as well as your own examples.
2. We are social creatures, more likely to conform than to stand alone in our beliefs and behaviors. The effects of social connections on behavior are described by de Waal as well as by Christakis and Fowler; Carrell, Hoekstra, and West; Fisman; Nisbett; Best; and Ramachandran. Write an essay in which you use insights from some of these authors and add your own examples to make a point about social networks.

Economics

"Is Poor Fitness Contagious? Evidence from Randomly Assigned Friends,"

SCOTT E. CARRELL, MARK HOEKSTRA, AND JAMES E. WEST

Scott Carrell, Mark Hoekstra, and James West are professors of economics at the University of California–Davis, the University of Pittsburgh, and the United States Air Force Academy, respectively. The authors collaborated on research designed to answer this question: "Is Poor Fitness Contagious?" Their findings were originally published in 2011 in the *Journal of Public Economics*, a peer-reviewed journal of research into economic problems affecting the public.

ABSTRACT

The increase in obesity over the past 30 years has led researchers to investigate the role of social networks as a contributing factor. However, several challenges make it difficult to demonstrate a causal link between friends' physical fitness and own fitness using observational data. To overcome these problems, we exploit data from a unique setting in which individuals are randomly assigned to peer groups. We find statistically significant positive peer effects that are roughly half as large as the own effect of prior fitness on current fitness. Evidence suggests that the effects are caused primarily by friends who were the least fit, thus supporting the provocative notion that poor physical fitness spreads on a person-to-person basis.

One of the most striking health trends in recent years has been the decline in the physical fitness of the U.S. population. Nearly two-thirds of adults are currently overweight, while more than 30% are obese (Hedley et al., 2004). In response, researchers have proposed several explanations. While some point to societal factors that have shifted people toward increased food consumption or decreased exercise (Hill and Peters, 1998; Cutler et al., 2003) a provocative recent explanation is that the effects of social and environmental factors may be amplified by the person-to-person spread of obesity (Christakis and Fowler, 2007). This explanation has profound implications, as it suggests that social networks can multiply the effects of otherwise smaller changes in the determinants of obesity. Conversely, if social networks are an important determinant of health, policies that increase individual health could conceivably combat the obesity epidemic through the social multiplier effect.

However, credibly estimating the causal effect of social networks on individual health outcomes has been difficult. There are three main empirical challenges to overcome: self-selection, common environmental factors, and reflection.[1] Self-selection implies that people tend to associate with those similar to them. For example, two individuals who prefer a sedentary lifestyle may both socialize together and gain weight over time, making it impossible to distinguish the effect of the (common) lifestyle from that of the friend. In addition, people within a social network may be subject to common environmental factors, which confound the social network effects. For example, family members may both spend a lot of time together and share genetic predispositions toward weight gain, making it difficult to distinguish the effect of one factor from the other. Similarly, people within a neighborhood may share the same proximity to fast food restaurants and city parks. Finally, it is empirically difficult to overcome what social science researchers have referred to as the reflection problem (Manski, 1993). That is, between two friends, each friend affects the other simultaneously.

While understanding whether social network effects exist is an important question for public health policy, overcoming these identification problems using observational data is challenging.[2] In this study, we address these identification challenges by utilizing data from the US Air Force Academy in which 3487 college students were randomly assigned to (residential) social networks from 2001 to 2005 to examine the role of such networks in shaping physical fitness outcomes. While this population is unique in that the students are both younger and considerably more physically fit than the general population, these data offer us two extraordinary advantages with respect to estimating fitness peer effects. First, because students were randomly assigned to peer groups with whom they are required to spend the majority of their time interacting, we can estimate peer effects free of bias caused by self-selection into the group.[3,4] In addition, our data contain an individual level pre-treatment measure of fitness, which enables us to estimate peer effects free of biases due to common environmental factors and reflection.

We evaluate whether being assigned to peers who were less fit during high school affects college fitness scores as well as the probability of failing the academy's fitness requirements. We also examine whether the effects we find are caused primarily by exposure to the least or most fit friends in one's own social network. Results indicate that poor fitness does spread on a person-to-person basis, with the largest effects caused by friends who were the least physically fit.

1. DATA

The data utilized in our study consist of 13,016 observations on 3487 freshmen and sophomore students from 2001 to 2005 at the United States Air Force Academy (USAFA).[5] These data are utilized because of one extraordinary feature of the environment there: while most individuals have a significant amount of choice over the group of people with whom they associate, USAFA students are randomly assigned to squadrons of approximately 30 students with whom they are required to spend the majority of their time. Prior to the start of the freshman and sophomore years, administrators implement a stratified random assignment process in which females are first randomly assigned, followed by male ethnic and racial minorities, then nonminority recruited athletes, then students who attended a military preparatory school, and then all remaining students. Thus, while by design there is relatively little intergroup variation in attributes such as race or gender, the assignment of other attributes such as peer fitness is effectively random. This critical feature of our data set enables us to overcome bias due to self-selection.

Statistical resampling tests provide evidence that the algorithm that assigns students to peer groups is consistent with random assignment (Lehmann and Romano, 2005). To implement the test, for each peer group we randomly drew 10,000 groups of equal size from the relevant cohort of students without replacement. We then computed empirical p-values for each group, representing the proportion of the simulated peer groups with higher average pretreatment fitness scores than that of the observed group. Under random assignment, any unique p-value is equally likely to be observed; hence the expected distribution of the empirical p-values is uniform. We tested the uniformity of the distributions of empirical *h*-values in each year using the Kolmogorov–Smirnov one-sample equality of distribution test. We failed to reject the null hypothesis of random placement for both the freshman and sophomore peer group assignments, with p-values of 0.934 and 0.578, respectively.[6]

Students are required to spend the majority of their time interacting with peers in their assigned group: they live in adjacent dorm rooms, dine together on meals served family-style, compete in intramural sports together, and study together. During the freshman year, students have limited ability to interact with students outside of their social network.[7] However, across peer groups, nearly all other aspects of life and work at USAFA are similar. Specifically, during both the freshmen and sophomore years, all students primarily take the same courses in which they are randomly assigned to professors, are served the same meals in the cafeteria, live on the same campus in the same dorm buildings, and are subject to the same physical conditioning requirements. Importantly, students do *not* take academic or physical fitness courses[8] together with peers from their squadron, but rather are randomly assigned to professors and instructors along with the other students from their entire cohort. Consequently, there is little scope for environmental confounders to bias estimates of social network effects.

A second advantage of this study relates to the outcomes examined. While most existing studies examining physical fitness/obesity use weight-to-height comparisons such as body mass index (BMI), there is consensus that such measures do not adequately measure whether an individual is actually physically fit and healthy (Smalley et al., 1990; Gallagher et al., 1996; Burkhauser and Cawley, 2008).[9] In contrast, our dataset from the USAFA provides for two, arguably superior, health outcome measures[10]: the overall physical education score achieved during the semester and whether or not the individual failed the physical fitness requirements.

The physical education average (PEA) score is measured on a 0.0–4.0 scale, where the average score is 2.61. It consists of a weighted average of scores on the following tests: 1) a 1.5 mile timed run called the aerobic fitness test (15%), 2) a physical fitness test consisting of pull-ups, push-ups, sit-ups, standing long-jump and a 600 yard sprint (50%), and 3) grades in mandatory physical education courses (35%).[11] Grades in the physical fitness courses are based primarily on performance, rather than knowledge or effort. For example, grades in the boxing class are based on one's performance against classmates during three-round fights and grades in swimming are based on distance swimming times and proficiency performing various swimming strokes.

Table 1
Summary Statistics for Classes of 2005–2007

Variable	Mean (std. dev)	Range
Panel A: college student performance and demographics		
College fitness score	2.61 (0.51)	0.35–4.00
Fail fitness test	0.09 (0.28)	0–1
High school fitness score	460 (97)	215–745
High school fitness score (normalized)	0.00 (1.00)	–2.54–2.94
Black	0.05 (0.22)	0–1
Hispanic	0.06 (0.24)	0–1
Asian	0.05 (0.23)	0–1
Female	0.18 (0.38)	0–1
Panel B: social network performance in high school		
Peer high school fitness score	460 (18)	405–513
Peer high school fitness score (normalized)	0.00 (0.18)	–0.57–0.55
Peer SAT Math	667 (13)	623–709
Peer SAT verbal	632 (12)	587–671
Peer academic composite	1287 (384)	1187–1438
Peer leadership composite score	1724 (333)	1603–1825

Figures come from the data on 3487 students and a total of 216 unique social networks.

Failing the fitness requirement occurs when an individual receives a PEA score lower than 2.0, or when he or she fails to meet certain specified minimum standards on any of the subcomponents of the PEA score. As shown in Table 1, on average, roughly 9% of the students fail to meet these requirements and were thus put on athletic probation by the USAFA.[12]

Importantly, we also collected data on individuals' physical fitness prior to enrolling at the academy. This score is based on applicants' performance on pull-ups, sit-ups, push-ups, a 600-yard shuttle run, the standing long jump and a basketball throw. The test is typically administered and certified by an official from the individual's high school, such as a physical education teacher.[13] Observing fitness prior to enrolling is critical for making causal inferences for two reasons. First, because we examine whether friends' fitness in *high school* affects an individual's own fitness in *college*, we can rule out the possibility that common environmental factors are causing the correlation between own health and friends' health. For example, it is difficult to conceive of a factor that would simultaneously affect own fitness in college as well as a friend's fitness in high school, since the two were not yet friends in high school.[14] In addition, we can rule out the possibility of reflection, since it is impossible for one's own current health to affect a friend's health (i.e. high school fitness score) before she or he entered the social network.

The full set of summary statistics is shown in Table 1. The average combined SAT score of students at the academy is 1298, which is similar to other undergraduate institutions such as UCLA, University of Michigan, University of Virginia, and UNC-Chapel Hill. Eighteen percent of the sample is female, 5% is Black, 6% is Hispanic, and 5% is Asian. The average high school health fitness score of peers randomly assigned to one's social network is 460, with a standard deviation of 18 points across groups and a standard deviation of 97 across individuals.

2. EXTERNAL VALIDITY

While the USAFA data offer distinct advantages with respect to both the randomization of peers and the availability of an absolute measure of fitness, there is an open question regarding whether the effects we find generalize to the broader population. The most significant difference between USAFA students and their peers at other selective public universities is that USAFA students spend considerably more time exercising and playing sports. Only 12.5% of USAFA students reported spending 5 or fewer hours on sports and exercise per week in their last year of high school, compared to 48.2% of students at other selective public universities (Cooperative Institutional Research Program (CIRP), 2007). Similarly, 24.6% of USAFA students reported spending more than 20 hours on exercise and sports per week in their last year of high school, compared to 8% of students enrolled at selective public universities (Cooperative Institutional Research Program, 2007).

In addition to differences in incoming fitness levels, students at USAFA are held to rigorous physical fitness standards throughout their college experience. For example, one way in which students can fail the fitness requirement is by not meeting the minimum standards on any of the subcomponents of the physical education score. For the 1.5-mile timed run, minimum passing times are 11:15 for men and 13:20 for women. For the physical fitness test, students must score at least 250 points and achieve the following minimums on each component: 1) pull-ups (7-males, 1-females), 2) long jump (7'00"-males, 5'09"-females, 3) sit-ups (58-males, 58-females), 4) push-ups (35-males, 18-females, and 5) 600 yard run (2:03-males, 2:23-females). However, minimums on every event result in a total score of 125 points and failure of the test. Although our data do not contain each individual component of the PEA, anecdotal evidence suggests that failing the physical fitness test is the most common reason students fail the fitness requirement. However, we note that these are stringent requirements, and that even students who fail this requirement are likely more fit than the typical college student.

As a result of these fitness requirements, students at USAFA likely have lower body fat than typical college students. According to the USAFA Athletics Department, only about 7% of students during their freshman and sophomore years fail to meet body fat standards of 20% for males and 28% for females.

Since we are not aware of any other studies on fitness peer effects, we are unable to make direct comparisons of our estimates to those covering other populations. However, Carrell et al. (2009) report that *academic* peer effects at the academy are similar to those at other academic institutions when the peer group is defined as either roommates, as in Sacerdote (2001) and Zimmerman (2003), or as dorm halls, as in Foster (2006).[15]

There are several factors unique to USAFA that could cause the magnitude of fitness peer effects to be different than in other contexts. Students at USAFA both eat and exercise with their (randomly assigned) friends, suggesting our estimates may overstate the effects found in other environments. On the other hand, certain factors may cause our estimates to understate the effects in other contexts. For example, students at the USAFA face strict upper and lower bounds on the time devoted [to] the physical activity that are not present for the general population. Similarly, the presence of mandatory, well-defined physical fitness requirements may reduce the need for peer comparisons, thus reducing the size of the peer effect estimates at USAFA relative to elsewhere.[16] In addition, all students at USAFA are offered the same family-style meals in the dining facility, which reduces the extent to which friends can affect the *type* of foods eaten. Finally, we note that the effect of other factors, such as living in an environment in which peers are randomly assigned, is more ambiguous.

For these reasons, we remain agnostic regarding whether effects would be larger or smaller for other populations in other environments. However, it is clear that regardless of the population in question, peer effects on outcomes such as fitness or obesity must occur by affecting own diet, own exercise, or both. Thus, our view is that at a minimum, the presence of such peer effects in one population increases the likelihood that peer effects in fitness exist more broadly.

3. METHODS

To determine the effect of friends on own physical fitness, we estimate standard ordinary least squares regressions[17] in which the dependent variables are the overall physical education average (PEA) score and whether the individual was placed on athletic probation, respectively. The main explanatory variable of interest is the average high school fitness score of one's peers, and in all specifications we include a control for own high school fitness as well as graduation class fixed effects. To ease interpretation, own fitness scores are normalized to have mean zero and standard deviation one. Similarly, the peer high school fitness score variable is normalized by subtracting the mean and dividing by the *individual-level* standard deviation. We normalized the peer variable in this manner to ensure comparability between the coefficients on the own and peer high school fitness variables. We cluster our standard errors at both the peer group level and individual level using multi-way clustering to allow for correlation across individuals within the same network (Cameron et al., 2011).

Although the average high school fitness of peers in one's network is determined by random assignment within a graduation class cohort, in some specifications we also include additional controls to examine the robustness of our results. Specifically, we include cohort by year by semester fixed effects and state of residence fixed effects. This allows for changing factors over time that might affect the entire cohort of students in a given semester, such as differing academic requirements or changes in the dietary menus. We also include controls for individual-level characteristics that may affect fitness including math and verbal SAT scores, a high school academic composite (GPA and class rank) score, a leadership composite score, and indicators for student race, whether the student was recruited to the academy as an athlete, and whether the student attended a military preparatory school.

For aid in interpreting the reduced form parameters on our peer effects coefficient, consider the following linear in means peer effects model:

$$y_{ig} = \beta_1 x_{ig} + \beta_2 \bar{y}_g + \beta_3 \bar{x}_g + \theta_g + \varepsilon_{ig} \qquad (1)$$

where x_{ig} is the pre-USAFA fitness score and y_{ig} is the contemporaneous fitness score. x_g and y_g are the average scores of the peer group excluding individual i. In Manski's (1993) framework, β_2 represents the *endogenous* peer effect, β_3 is the *exogenous* peer effect, θg represents common environmental factors, and εig are other individual unobservables.

Taking averages within group *g*, one obtains a reduced form equation:

$$y_{ig} = \beta_1 x_{ig} + \frac{\beta_2(\beta_1 + \beta_3)}{1-\beta_2} + \tilde{\theta}_g + \tilde{\varepsilon}_{ig} \qquad (2)$$

Hence, the coefficient in a regression of own college fitness on peer high school fitness is a function of both the endogenous and exogenous structural peer effects. Thus, while our reduced form estimates cannot distinguish between whether the peer effects we find are driven by the background characteristics or behavior of the group, we can say that our estimates are a causal effect of one's peers. That is, we can be confident that ε_{ig} is uncorrelated with x_g because of the random assignment [of] students to peer groups. Random assignment also ensures that there is no correlation between x_g and fixed components of θ_g (e.g. dorm proximity to the gym or cafeteria). However, it is theoretically possible that some common environmental factors endogenously adjust to the average high school fitness level of the group. For example, physical education teachers could adjust curriculum depending on the fitness level of the class. Fortunately, students of all squadrons are randomly assigned across courses at USAFA (including PE courses), ensuring there are no classroom level common shocks biasing our estimates. Additionally, given the rigidity of the academic, athletic, and military curriculum and standards at USAFA, we expect any such endogenous adjustments to be quite minimal.[18]

4. RESULTS

Results are shown in Table 2, which reports the effect of peer high school fitness on the Physical Education Average (PEA) score. Column 1 controls only for own fitness in high school and indicators for graduation year. The estimate indicates that peers' fitness (as measured in high school) has a large and statistically significant effect on own fitness in college. The marginal effect shows that a one standard deviation increase in the high school fitness score of *all* peers in the group results in a statistically significant 0.165 standard deviation increase in college fitness.[19] By comparison, a similar sized improvement in own fitness is associated with a statistically significant 0.434 standard deviation increase in college fitness. This is striking, as it suggests that the effect of friends' high school fitness on own current fitness is nearly 40% as strong as the effect of own high school fitness.

To account for individual-level factors that may affect own fitness, in columns (2) and (3) of Table 2 we sequentially add the individual controls and the fixed effects. The magnitude of the peer effect decreases slightly, but is statistically indistinguishable from the estimate in column (1). These results are expected given that peer groups were randomly assigned.

While the estimates in columns (1) through (3) imply that the underlying fitness of friends does have a significant impact on fitness in college, it is also possible that the effect is caused by other peer factors correlated with fitness. For example, perhaps more fit peers are also more motivated to achieve success generally. Similarly, it may be that more fit peers are also more likely to take a leadership role among friends at the academy and this leadership, rather than the physically fit friends, causes students to become more fit in college.

Table 2
The Effect of Peer Fitness on Own Fitness Score

Dependent variable: physical fitness score	(1)	(2)	(3)	(4)
Peer high school fitness score	0.165[a]	0.129	0.131[a]	0.129[a]
	(0.073)	(0.058)[a]	(0.057)	(0.057)
Own high school fitness score	0.434[b]	0.421[b]	0.418[b]	0.418[b]
	(0.014)	(0.013)	(0.013)	(0.013)
Observations	11,321	11,321	11,321	11,321
Includes individual controls?	No	Yes	Yes	Yes
Includes year by semester and state of residence fixed effects?	No	No	Yes	Yes
Includes average peer SAT verbal, SAT math, academic composite and leadership composite scores?	No	No	No	Yes

The dependent variable in each specification is the college fitness exam score. Standard errors multi-way clustered at the peer group and individual level are in parentheses. Each specification controls for graduate class fixed effects. Individual-level controls include SAT verbal and math scores, academic and leadership composite scores, and indicators for Black, Hispanic, Asian, female, recruited athlete, and preparatory school attendance.
[a] Significant at the 5% level.
[b] Significant at the 1% level.

To address these possibilities, we include additional peer controls in column (4). Specifically, we control for the average SAT math and verbal scores, high school academic composite score, and high school leadership composite of peers in one's social network. Results show that the impact of friends' fitness remains statistically significant and similar in magnitude. This suggests that the effects we find are likely caused by friends' fitness and not by general motivation or leadership ability.

Next, we examine whether friends' fitness affects whether or not an individual fails the fitness requirement at the academy. Results are shown in Table 3 and indicate that there is a large and statistically significant effect that is unchanged when adding controls in columns 2 through 4. For example, the estimates in column 4 indicate that the effect of peer high school fitness on own college fitness (−0.044) is approximately 70% as large as the association between own high school fitness and own college fitness.

5. MECHANISMS AND HETEROGENEITY

Given that friends' average high school fitness affects own college fitness, it is natural to wonder *how* peers matter. While any effect on the outcomes used in this analysis presumably works through either diet or exercise, we can identify several potential mechanisms. Peer effects may arise through increased positive knowledge about how to exercise or train. If so, we would primarily expect the effects to be driven by peers who are the most fit. In contrast, if the effects operate through the adoption of poor diet or negative exercise habits, we would expect the effect to be driven by the least fit members of the group.

Thus, to help assess these potential mechanisms, we examine more closely *which* peers appear to be causing the peer effect, and which groups of students are most affected. We begin by examining how own fitness is affected by the proportion of randomly assigned friends who were in the bottom and top 20% of the high school fitness score distribution.[20] These estimated effects are relative to having peers from the middle 60% of the fitness distribution.

Table 3
The Effect of Peer Fitness on the Probability of Failing the Fitness Requirements

Dependent variable: fail fitness requirements	(1)	(2)	(3)	(4)
Peer high school fitness score	−0.047[a]	−0.043[a]	−0.046[a]	−0.044[a]
	(0.021)	(0.017)	(0.017)	(0.018)
Own high school fitness score	−0.064[b]	−0.061[b]	−0.062[b]	−0.062[b]
	(0.004)	(0.004)	(0.004)	(0.004)
Observations	13,016	13,016	13,016	13,016
Includes individual controls?	No	Yes	Yes	Yes
Includes year by semester and state of residence fixed effects?	No	No	Yes	Yes
Includes average peer SAT verbal, SAT math, academic composite and leadership composite scores?	No	No	No	Yes

The dependent variable in each specification is the probability of failing the semiannual fitness test or 1.5 mile run. Standard errors multi-way clustered at the peer group and individual level are in parentheses. Each specification controls for graduate class fixed effects. Individual-level controls include SAT verbal and math scores, academic and leadership composite scores, and indicators for Black, Hispanic, Asian, female, recruited athlete, and preparatory school attendance.
[a] Significant at the 5% level.
[b] Significant at the 1% level.

Results are shown in Table 4. Columns (1) and (2) show that it is primarily the *least fit* friends who reduce average physical fitness (estimate = 0.360, $p < 0.01$) and induce students to fail the fitness requirements (estimate = 0.105, $p < 0.05$). The estimates imply that if half of your friends were to become among the least fit for reasons unrelated to you,[21] your own fitness level would drop by nearly 20% of a standard deviation and you would be nearly 60% more likely to fail the fitness requirements. Put differently, the effect of the least fit peers on college fitness is 85% of the effect of one's own high school fitness. Even more strikingly, the effect of the least fit peers on the probability of failing the fitness exam is *larger* than the effect of own high school fitness.[22]

Next, we examine which students are most affected by their peers. To do so, we interact average peer high school fitness with indicators for whether the individual's high school fitness score is above- or below-average. Results are shown in Columns (3) and (4) of Table 4. The estimates indicate that it is the college students on the lower end of the fitness distribution who are most affected by their peers.

Finally, we estimate the effects after allowing for interactions between whether own high school fitness was above- or below-average and exposure to peers from the top and bottom 20% of the high school fitness distribution. Results are shown in Columns (5) and (6) of Table 4. These results are consistent with results from Columns (1) through (4): exposure to the least fit peers is what matters, and college students with the lowest propensity to be fit are the ones who are most affected.

Our results thus yield two notable findings. First, they indicate that the peer effects in physical fitness we find are primarily driven by the least physically fit friends. Second, the individuals most at risk from exposure to unfit friends are those who themselves struggle with fitness. Collectively, this suggests that peer effects in fitness do not appear to arise due to the spread of knowledge from highly fit to less fit individuals. Rather the results are more consistent with the notion that people imitate the diet or exercise habits of their least fit friends, or use those friends' fitness as a benchmark for their own.

6. CONCLUSION

Understanding the nature of social interactions is important for both diagnosing the causes of the decline in physical fitness and assessing policy strategies to combat the decline. However, because individuals can select their friends based in part on preferences for diet and exercise and because friends are likely to be subjected to the same environmental factors, it is difficult to credibly estimate the effect of peers on fitness and obesity using observational data.

We estimate the impact of friends' fitness on own physical fitness by exploiting a unique data set in which college students are randomly assigned to a group of 30 students with whom they spend the majority of their time. We find strong evidence that friends' fitness affects own fitness as well as the probability of failing the fitness requirements. The magnitude of the effect is large, as the effect of peer high school fitness is approximately 40 to 70% as large as the effect of own high school fitness. Thus, our findings are broadly consistent with the provocative notion that poor physical fitness spreads on a person-to-person basis.

Our results also indicate that the peer effects work largely through exposure to the least fit peers, and the students most affected are those

Table 4
The Effect of the Least and Most Fit Peers on Own Fitness Outcomes

Variable	Physical fitness score (1)	Fail fitness requirements (2)	Physical fitness score (3)	Fail fitness requirements (4)	Physical fitness score (5)	Fail fitness requirements (6)
Proportion of peers in bottom quintile of high school fitness	−0.360[a]	0.105[b]				
	(0.130)	(0.041)				
Proportion of peers in top quintile of high school fitness	0.06	−0.05				
	(0.131)	(0.038)				
Peer high school fitness score * below average high school			0.266[a]	−0.087[a]		
Fitness score			(0.078)	(0.028)		
Peer high school fitness score * above average high school			−0.022	(0.005)		
Fitness score			(0.080)	(0.018)		
Proportion of peers in bottom quintile of high school fitness *					−0.535[a]	0.176[b]
Below average high school fitness score					(0.180)	(0.069)

Proportion of peers in top quintile of high school fitness *					0.26	−0.088
Below average high school fitness score					(0.172)	(0.061)
Proportion of peers in bottom quintile of high school fitness *					−0.190	0.03
Above average high school fitness score					(0.193)	(0.041)
Proportion of peers in top quintile of high school fitness *					−0.16	0.01
Above average high school fitness score					(0.192)	(0.043)
Own high school fitness score	0.418[a]	−0.062[a]	0.445[a]	−0.068[a]	0.445[a]	−0.068[a]
	(0.013)	(0.004)	(0.022)	(0.006)	(0.022)	(0.006)
Observations	11,321	13,016	11,321	13,016	11,321	13,016
Includes individual and peer controls?	Yes	Yes	Yes	Yes	Yes	Yes
Includes year by semester and state of residence fixed effects?	Yes	Yes	Yes	Yes	Yes	Yes

Standard errors multi-way clustered at the peer group and individual level are in parentheses. Each specification controls for graduate class fixed effects. Individual-level controls include SAT verbal and math scores, academic and leadership composite scores, and indicators for Black, Hispanic, Asian, female, recruited athlete, and preparatory school attendance. Peer controls include peer SAT scores, peer high school composite scores, and peer leadership scores.

[a] Significant at the 1% level.

[b] Significant at the 5% level.

at the lower end of the fitness distribution. This asymmetry in the nature of the peer effects suggests that individuals appear to either compare their own fitness to the least fit among them, or adopt the diet and exercise of the least fit. Thus, our results suggest that there is an efficiency motivation for improving the health habits of the least physically fit individuals, as doing so may ultimately affect the health of many more individuals by harnessing the effect of the social multiplier.

NOTES

1. The medical literature often refers to self-selection as "homophily" (love of the same). Common environmental factors are often referred to as "correlated effects" or "common shocks" (Manski, 1993).
2. As such, the causality of estimates in the recent social network health literature has been drawn into question. These concerns have perhaps been best illustrated in Cohen-Cole and Fletcher's (2008a,b) critiques of Christakis and Fowler (2007), who use data from the Framingham Heart Survey to show that obesity, smoking, and happiness appear to spread through social ties. Cohen-Cole and Fletcher report that the same methodology also yields social network effects in implausible outcomes such as height and headaches, and that controlling for confounders reduces the estimates on BMI. Christakis and Fowler (2008) respond by questioning whether effects on height and headaches are implausible when the outcomes are self-reported, and report evidence that health peer effects estimates are robust across several specifications. While we leave the reader to judge the merits of these critiques and their responses, we do argue that the debate highlights the general difficulty with making causal inferences using observational data.
3. The only other study we know of that uses a randomized treatment design to study the impact of peer effects on fitness or obesity is Yakusheva et al. (2010), who examine whether a randomly assigned roommate's initial weight affects weight gain during the freshman year of college. They report no effect for men, and find that women assigned to heavier roommates *lose* weight. However, the lack of evidence of positive peer effects among roommates is roughly consistent with the findings of Carrell et al. (2009), who report only moderate evidence of peer effects in education among roommates, though they estimate much larger peer effects when the peer group is defined as the group with which the students spend the majority of their time (i.e., squadron).
4. A number of recent studies have used randomization at the college roommate and/or college peer group level to identify peer effects in *academic achievement*. See Sacerdote (2001), Zimmerman (2003), Stinebrickner and Stinebrickner (2006), Foster (2006), Lyle (2007), and Carrell et al. (2009) for examples. While most of these papers focus on whether peer academic ability affects achievement, Kremer and Levy (2008) examine the effect of roommate drinking on college GPA, and Carrell et al. (2008) examine peer effects in college cheating.

5. In total there are three cohorts of students from the graduating classes of 2005–2007, with two years of semester-by-student level outcome data.
6. We also regressed own peer high school fitness on peer pre-treatment characteristics such as peer high school fitness score, peer SAT verbal and math scores, peer academic composite score, and peer leadership score. None of the coefficients are statistically significant at the 10% level, and the p-value from the F-test of joint significance is 0.652. For further evidence of the randomization of peer groups at the USAFA, see Carrell et al. (2009).
7. In their sophomore year, students have more opportunity to interact with students from other groups, though students within groups still live in adjacent dorm rooms, dine together, compete in intramural sports together and in general interact together frequently. We note, however, that interaction with students outside the group would likely bias our estimates toward zero by introducing measurement error in the peer variable (Carrell et al., 2009).
8. All students at USAFA are required to take mandatory physical education courses, which are non-academic in nature. For instance, all freshman students are required to take swimming and boxing (males) or unarmed combat (females). Scores in these courses are based on the student's athletic performance in the course such as a timed swimming test and two three-round boxing matches.
9. In response to those same concerns, in 2005, the US Air Force came to its own conclusion that its weight management program based on BMI was flawed and instead began using an annual fitness exam that included a timed 1.5 mile run, sit-ups, push-ups, and pull-ups.
10. Unfortunately, BMI data are not available for the students in our sample, so we are unable to assess whether peer effects on BMI are different from peer effects on fitness.
11. Approximately 13% of our observations having missing data for the PEA variable (1695 of 13,016). The PEA variable is not available for students who are unable to complete all components of the score. To test whether these missing observations could bias our estimates, we regressed an indicator for missing PEA on peer pre-treatment characteristics such as peer high school fitness score, peer SAT verbal and math scores, peer academic composite score, and peer leadership score. None of the coefficients are statistically significant at the 10% level, and the p-value from the F-test of joint significance is 0.985.
12. The 9-percent failure rate represents the average across all observations. In total, 12.2 percent of students in our sample (406 of 3323) failed the fitness requirement at least once.
13. The high school fitness data were available for 99.5% of all students in the sample. We dropped from our sample the 19 of 3506 students who were missing the high school fitness score.
14. Students at the USAFA come from every congressional district in the United States; therefore, it is highly implausible that common environmental factors could affect both the high school and college fitness exams.

15. However, Carrell et al. (2009) estimate much larger academic peer effects when the peer group is defined as the squadron rather than as roommates or dormitory residents.
16. If students fail to meet the minimum requirements in a given semester they are placed on athletic probation and put into a mandatory reconditioning program. Repeated failures lead to expulsion.
17. We use a linear probability model rather than logistic regression when using the binary dependent variable to allow us to compute two-way clustered standard errors, which computational limitations prevent us from doing when using a logistic regression model. However, results are qualitatively similar when using logistic regression rather than OLS.
18. The academic, athletic and military standards are constant across all squadrons at USAFA, with guidelines set forth in formal Air Force Instructions and Manuals.
19. For ease in interpretation we present all of our results in terms of standard deviations. To get a sense of how fitness levels translate into standard deviation changes in the PEA score we provide the following examples for males: 1) A four minute change in the 1.5 mile (12 to 8 min), holding PE grades and the physical fitness test score constant would result in a one-half standard deviation change in the PEA score. 2) From the mean score, adding five pull-ups, 9 inches on the long jump, 14 sit-ups, 15 push-ups, and a 12 second decrease on the 600 meter run would result in roughly a one-standard deviation change in the PEA, holding the 1.5 mile run time and PE grades constant.
20. We also examined whether females respond differently to peers than males. We find that while the coefficients are larger for women, they are not statistically distinguishable from those for men.
21. This is approximately the variation observed across peer groups in the data; the proportion of peers in one's squadron ranking below the 20th percentile prior to attending the academy ranges from 0 to 42%.
22. We also investigated whether variance in peer fitness affects own fitness in college by regressing own college fitness on the standard deviation of peer high school fitness. We find that increased variance in peer fitness causes a reduction in own fitness, though the effect goes away once we control for the proportion of least fit peers, as in Table 4. This suggests that at least in this context, variance matters primarily because it means you are exposed to more of the least fit peers.

REFERENCES

Burkhauser, Richard V., Cawley, John, 2008. Beyond BMI: The value of more accurate measures of fatness and obesity in social science research. Journal of Health Economics 27, 519–529.

Cameron, A. Colin, Gelbach, Jonah B., Miller, Douglas L., 2011. Robust inference with multi-way clustering. Journal of Business and Economic Statistics 99 (2), 238–249.

Carrell, Scott E., Malmstrom, Frederick V., West, James E., 2008. Peer effects in academic cheating. Winter Journal of Human Resources XLIII (1), 173–207.

Carrell, Scott E., Fullerton, Richard L., West, James E., 2009. Does your cohort matter? estimating peer effects in college achievement. Journal of Labor Economics 27, 439–464.
Christakis, Nicholas, Fowler, James, 2007. The spread of obesity in a large social network over 32 years. The New England Journal of Medicine 357, 370–379.
Christakis, Nicholas, Fowler, James, 2008. Estimating peer effects on health in social networks. Journal of Health Economics 27 (5), 1386–1391.
Cohen-Cole, Ethan, Fletcher, Jason M., 2008a. Detecting implausible social network effects in acne, height, and headaches: longitudinal analysis. British Medical Journal 337, a2533.
Cohen-Cole, Ethan, Fletcher, Jason M., 2008b. Is obesity contagious? social networks vs. environmental factors in the obesity epidemic. Journal of Health Economics 27 (5), 1382–1387.
Cooperative Institutional Research Program, 2007. The freshman survey. Higher Education Research Institute at the University of California—Los Angeles.
Cutler, David O., Glaeser, Edward L., Shapiro, Jesse M., 2003. Why have Americans become so obese? The Journal of Economic Perspectives 17 (3), 93–118.
Foster, Gigi, 2006. It's not your peers, and it's not your friends: some progress towards understanding educational peer effects. Journal of Public Economics 90 (8–9), 1455–1475.
Gallagher, Dympna, Visser, Marjolein, Sepulveda, Dennis, Pierson, Richard N., Harris, Tamara, Heymsfield, Steven B., 1996. How useful is body mass index for comparison of body fatness across age, sex, and ethnic groups? American Journal of Epidemiology 143 (3), 228–239.
Hedley, Allison A., Ogden, Cynthia L., Johnson, Clifford L., Carroll, Margaret D., Curtin, Lester R., Flegal, Katherine M., 2004. Prevalence of overweight and obesity among US children, adolescents, and adults, 1999–2002. Journal of the American Medical Association 291, 2847–2850.
Hill, James O., Peters, John C., 1998. Environmental contributions to the obesity epidemic. Science 280, 1371–1374.
Kremer, Michael, Levy, Dan, 2008. Peer effects and alcohol use among college students. The Journal of Economic Perspectives 23 (3), 189–206.
Lehmann, Erich L., Romano, Joseph P., 2005. Testing statistical hypotheses, Texts in Statistics 3rd ed. Springer, Secaucus, NJ.
Lyle, David S., 2007. Estimating and interpreting peer and role model effects from randomly assigned social groups at west point. The Review of Economics and Statistics 89 (2), 289–299.
Manski, Charles F., 1993. Identification and endogenous social effects: the reflection problem. The Review of Economic Studies 60, 531–542.
Sacerdote, Bruce, 2001. Peer effects with random assignment: results for Dartmouth roommates. Quarterly Journal of Economics 116, 681–704.

Smalley, Karl J., Knerr, Anita N., Kendrick, Zebulon V., Colliver, Jerry A., Owen, Oliver E., 1990. Reassessment of body mass indices. The American Journal of Clinical Nutrition 52, 405–408.

Stinebrickner, Ralph, Stinebrickner, Todd R., 2006. What can be learned about peer effects using college roommates? Evidence from new survey data and students from disadvantaged backgrounds. Journal of Public Economics 90 (8–9), 1435–1454.

Yakusheva, Olga, Kapinos, Kandice, Weiss, Marianne, 2010. Peer effects and the freshman 15: evidence from a natural experiment. Working Paper.

Zimmerman, David J., 2003. Peer effects in academic outcomes: evidence from a natural experiment. The Review of Economics and Statistics 85 (1), 9–23.

The views expressed in this paper reflect those of the authors and do not necessarily reflect the official policy or position of the U.S. Air Force, Department of Defense, or the U.S. Government.

Scott E. Carrell, University of California-Davis, Department of Economics, One Shields Ave., Davis, CA 95616, United States.

Mark Hoekstra, University of Pittsburgh, Department of Economics, 4714 Posvar Hall, 230 S. Bouquet St., Pittsburgh, PA 15260, United States (corresponding author).

James E. West, Department of Economics and Geosciences, United States Air Force Academy, CO 80840, United States.

Corresponding e-mail addresses: secarrell@ucdavis.edu (S. E. Carrell), markhoek@pitt.edu (M. Hoekstra), jim.west@usafa.edu (J. E. West).

QUESTIONS ABOUT MEANING

1. Why is it so difficult to determine how social networks affect a person's health?
2. Describe the sample studied by Carrell, Hoekstra, and West. In what ways are the sample makeup and the means of measurement superior to those of past studies designed to determine how one's social network influences one's health? On the other hand, why is it difficult to generalize the findings from this study to other populations? (How are the participants in this study atypical?)
3. How is this research relevant for publication in a journal about public economics? Where do the authors state the value of their research?

QUESTIONS FOR RHETORICAL ANALYSIS

1. In the first paragraph of the article, the authors cite research conducted by Christakis and Fowler (authors of *Connected*). How does the reference to Christakis and Fowler's writings provide a context for this article?
2. With a partner in class, analyze section 5 ("Mechanisms and Heterogeneity"). First, highlight some of the key sentences and signal phrases that the authors provide to help readers. Then, with your partner, summarize each paragraph in a sentence or two. What paragraph would you say is the most important paragraph in the section? Explain.
3. After summarizing the content of section 5, study Table 4 with your partner. What information does the table depict? Summarize the finding(s) in a sentence or two.

MAKING CONNECTIONS

1. Like Chua, Boland, and Nisbett's article, this article is a report of original research preceded by an abstract. Analyze the content and organization of the abstracts in both articles. What similarities do you see? Create a template that you could follow when writing your own abstract for a report of original research.
2. The authors, along with Fisman, Best, and Ramachandran, provide examples of the downside of social conformity. But following the crowd also has benefits, as Christakis and Fowler and de Waal mention. Write a multipart essay that looks at social conformity from various angles, using insights from these authors as well as examples of your own or from additional writers. Divide your essay into sections with headings that allow readers to anticipate your main ideas.

Economics

"The Canseco Effect: Wherever He Went, Jose Canseco Made His Teammates Better Power Hitters. Can Statistics Be Used to Find Juicers?"

RAY FISMAN

Ray Fisman is a professor at Columbia Business School, with broad research interests that include corruption in professional sports. In the next article, titled "The Canseco Effect: Wherever He Went, Jose Canseco Made His Teammates Better Power Hitters. Can Statistics Be Used to Find Juicers?" Fisman describes research by two Israeli economists, whose data reveal that a "culture of cheating" surrounded baseball great Jose Canseco.

Fisman's article was originally published in 2010 in *Slate magazine*, an online magazine with articles about current events, politics, and culture.

When Jose Canseco finally came clean as the "Godfather of Steroids" in 2005, his use of performance-enhancing drugs had already been a matter of speculation for nearly two decades. In his tell-all biography, *Juiced,* Canseco alleged that he schooled many of his power-hitting teammates on integrating steroids and growth hormones into their training regimens, including such baseball greats as Mark McGwire and Jason Giambi. Yet given his earlier denials of steroid use, his credibility was tenuous.

Now, a couple of Israeli economists, Eric Gould and Todd Kaplan, have released a study backing up Canseco's claims that he was "The Chemist" of baseball. Their work shows how the careful use of data can be an important tool in ferreting out drug use in baseball and other sports. They analyze the performance of Canseco's teammates—the players who had access to his locker-room pharmacy and expertise—and find that after playing with Canseco, players hit more home runs and otherwise boosted their numbers in the areas most affected by steroid use. Sometimes data speak more credibly—if not louder—than words.

Gould and Kaplan are labor economists, not baseball fans. Their primary interest in studying Jose Canseco's influence is in illustrating the sorts of pernicious behavior that can be learned in the locker room, by the water cooler, and in the workplace more generally. A few years ago, for example, there was a pair of scandals involving large numbers of false disability claims at the Long Island Railroad and the Boston Fire Department. (The Boston case broke when one of the purportedly disabled firemen placed eighth in a national bodybuilding competition.) In both cases, fraudsters possibly learned the benefits of cheating—and maybe even the details of how to do it—from their co-workers. Being around other cheaters also provides the ready excuse we've all heard before (and used ourselves): "Everyone's doing it." You'd be a chump not to get disability payments while everyone else is relaxing by the pool or to lose baseball games to competitors who have an unfair edge.

To provide a statistical assessment of Canseco's alleged influence, Gould and Kaplan compared the performances of every hitter and pitcher who played with Canseco, and analyzed how they changed after exposure to him. Focusing on the power-positions players—catcher, first base, outfield, and designated hitter—who would most benefit from extra heft and bulk, Gould and Kaplan found that contact with Canseco was worth an extra two home runs per year in the seasons that followed. Canseco's teammates also saw increases in other power statistics—half a dozen extra runs batted in per season, a one-point boost to slugging percentage, and a handful of additional walks. Meanwhile Canseco did not seem to help teammates in their fielding, base-stealing, and other nonpower areas. (In results not reported in the study, Gould and Kaplan also found that pitchers were able to put in more innings when exposed to Canseco, another indication of The Chemist's hand in helping his teammates work harder and longer.)

Of course, it's possible that Canseco's outsize influence could be benign—maybe he shared with his fellow power hitters a set of batting tips that proved effective. But if this is the case, Canseco's abilities as a hitting instructor were quite unique—Gould and Kaplan looked at the effect 30 other power hitters of Canseco's era had on their teammates and found that none of them had a statistically significant influence on the hitting performance of teammates. (Some of these were in fact Canseco's original disciples, suggesting, perhaps, that not all users become proselytizers.) What's more, the Canseco effect disappears after 2003, when baseball instituted random drug testing and punishments for those found guilty. If Canseco was merely offering innocent performance-enhancing advice, it stopped working with the advent of drug testing.

Can Gould and Kaplan's approach be applied to other sports? There are striking parallels between the Canseco saga and the ongoing doping scandal in competitive cycling. This year's Tour de France began under yet another cloud of controversy with the publication of former champion Floyd Landis' detailed description of alleged doping with seven-time tour winner Lance Armstrong. According to Landis, Armstrong lorded over a complex and multi-faceted operation that included bike sales (to fund the doping program) and clandestine roadside blood transfusions for him and the rest of his U.S. Postal Service team. Not surprisingly, Landis' interview, published by the *Wall Street Journal*, was followed by sharp denials from Armstrong and "no comments" from others implicated in the story.

Like Canseco, Landis himself initially denied the doping charges that led to his fall from grace, even writing a book-length defense titled *Positively False*. Many are using this flip-flopping to question his credibility—Armstrong points to Landis' repeated lying under oath as evidence that he can't be trusted.

The same approach employed by Gould and Kaplan could conceivably be applied to implicate—or exonerate—Armstrong. Cycling, like baseball, is a combination of individual and team effort. Each person rides his own bike, and at least on some days—when riders are competing in individual time trials, for instance—you could look for an Armstrong effect. If Armstrong's presence on the team improved the performance of his teammates, it wouldn't provide a smoking gun—just as Canseco's impact may have come in the form of batting wisdom, not drugs, Armstrong might have motivated his teammates to train harder and better. But smart researchers like Gould and Kaplan will surely find creative ways—as they have in uncovering Canseco's influence—to begin to cut through the lies that have come to characterize the debate on performance-enhancing drugs in baseball, cycling, and other sports.

How do these findings on what Gould and Kaplan term "ethical spillovers" leave us feeling about players who dope? While it's no excuse, it does matter if everyone else is doing it. One of the basic tenets of social psychology is the fundamental attribution error—we tend to attribute too much blame to the individual and not enough to his circumstances. It explains why we see baseball players and cyclists as dirty rotten cheaters and rail against unethical Boston firemen rather than asking whether we'd do the same in their circumstances. It also explains why it's so hard to reform a culture of cheating and corruption when everyone is doing it.

QUESTIONS ABOUT MEANING

1. What data did economists Gould and Kaplan analyze? What trends did they find in their analysis? What broader applications does Fisman imagine for the kind of research Gould and Kaplan have done?
2. In what ways can proximity to a cheater increase the likelihood of more cheating—whether in work, sports, or school?

QUESTIONS FOR RHETORICAL ANALYSIS

1. In the margins of the article, identify the purpose or function of each paragraph. What do you notice about how Fisman has organized his ideas?
2. Review paragraph 5. What alternative explanation for Gould and Kaplan's data does Fisman acknowledge? What words at the beginning of the paragraph signal that Fisman is conceding another way of interpreting the data ? What word signals his response? Do you find his response to the alternative explanation convincing? Why or why not?
3. When Fisman wrote his article, Lance Armstrong had not yet admitted that he took performance-enhancing drugs. Based on his description, do you think Fisman thought that Armstrong was guilty of cheating? Explain.

MAKING CONNECTIONS

1. Like de Waal and Garcia, Fisman is writing to a general audience. Illustrate and analyze how these writers help readers who may not have knowledge of the people and events referred to. For example, how does Fisman help an attentive reader infer that Jose Canseco was a great

baseball player or that Landis and Armstrong were cyclists? Illustrate in particular how the authors concisely embed context clues into sentences. What patterns could you imitate in your own writing to ensure readers understand your references to people or events?

2. Both Fisman and Francesca Gino (chapter 14) discuss *fundamental attribution error* (also referred to as *correspondence bias*), a term used in social psychology to refer to the human tendency to blame a person for bad behavior without considering the situation or external factors that might explain the behavior. Write an essay, using the lens of correspondence bias to analyze one or more examples currently in the news of people behaving "badly." What can be gained from analyzing the situation from this perspective?

Sociology

"The Illusion of Diffusion," JOEL BEST

Joel Best, previously featured in chapter 3, is a professor of sociology and criminal justice, well known for his accessible explanations of bad statistics. His books include *Damned Lies and Statistics* and *Stat-Spotting: A Field Guide to Identifying Dubious Data Today*. In his article "The Illusion of Diffusion," Best discusses fads and how the "dense social networks that characterize modern institutions" help them to spread and thrive. The article was first published in 2006 in the journal *Society*, which publishes research and articles from the social sciences, written for a broad, educated audience.

"The Six Stages of a Project" is a bit of office folklore that has been around for decades in many versions. This little piece of folk wisdom describes a cyclical—and cynical—process by which organizational innovations rise and fall. The six stages are as follows: (1) Wild Enthusiasm, (2) Disillusionment, (3) Total Confusion, (4) Search for the Guilty, (5) Persecution of the Innocent, and (6) Praise and Honor for the Non-Participants.

This process is my subject. Anyone who follows the news can spot examples of institutions becoming caught up in short-term enthusiasms:

- Although psychiatrists first described multiple-personality disorder in 1791, it remained an exceeding rare diagnosis. In the half-century before 1972, less than a dozen cases were reported, but during the 1980s, psychiatrists diagnosed thousands of cases. And, where early cases almost always involved patients with only two personalities, the 1980s cases often had dozens of "alters." Diagnoses have since fallen off. The 1980s epidemic of MPD was a medical fad.

- During the 1970s and 1980s, business analysts worried that the Japanese economy was growing at a faster pace than that of the U.S. Some suggested that Americans needed to understand and adopt Japanese business practices. In particular, hundreds of U.S. corporations announced that they would establish quality circles where workers and managers could discuss ways to improve operations. Within a few years, quality circles had fallen out of favor; they had proven to be another management fad.
- In 1989, there was great excitement when two University of Utah researchers declared that they had produced a cold fusion reaction in their laboratory. This inspired considerable scientific activity around the world, while media commentators speculated about the revolutionary impact this new source of cheap energy would have. Alas, the researchers' results could not be replicated, and cold fusion is recalled as a short-lived scientific fad.

Psychiatrists, managers, and scientists are serious people, yet these are three cases where serious people bought into what turned out to be short-term enthusiasms. There are many other examples. Universities, for example, are scenes of intellectual fads, as well as fads in teaching methods, curriculum design, and administrative practices. Although my examples come from the 1980s, this does not mean that the 1980s were some sort of peculiar, fad-infested decade. Rather, it takes time for a fad to collapse, for its short-lived nature to become apparent. Anyone who follows the news can be forgiven for suspecting that the more recent fascinations with Six Sigma management techniques, assessment in higher education, or standardized testing to achieve educational accountability may seem a little odd ten years from now.

Fads in medicine, management, science, and education are what I call *institutional fads*—short-term enthusiasms that rise and fall within institutional settings. Sociologists who study fads tend to examine playful popular phenomena, usually associated with young people–toy fads (such as the hula-hoop), dance fads (such as the Macherana) or campus fads (such as streaking). Textbooks even define fads as "trivial," "trifling," or "insignificant," which may help explain why the subject hasn't attracted more researchers.

I want to shift the focus to—and argue for the importance of—institutional fads. Short-term enthusiasms do emerge—and fade—among serious people, as anyone who has spent much time in business, education, or other similar institutions can testify. These fads are consequential: they affect what people do, consume their time and money, and—as "The Six Stages of a Project" suggests—foster a sense of alienation. So, it is worth asking: Why do serious people buy into silly enthusiasms?

In order to answer this question, we need to begin by examining the dynamics of fads. Let's consider what we might think of as the natural history of a typical fad. In the typical fad, there is initially little interest in the novelty, then its popularity rises quickly until it peaks, and then it drops off again. If we graphed this, using some measure of popularity for the vertical access, and time on the horizontal axis, we'd wind up with something that looks like those normal curves beloved by statisticians. We can draw essentially the same graph for any fad, because these contours define the fad: a fad is a short-lived enthusiasm. Fads do not last, which is the main reason we assume that they aren't important.

But consider the results of what may have been the first sociological study of fads. Each year between about 1915 and 1924, the sociologist Emory Bogardus asked about a hundred people to name five current fads. Not surprisingly, he found that most of the items named did not last long enough to make more than one list; only a few fads received mention in three successive years. One of these was: "men's wristwatches."

How could Bogardus's respondents have mistaken wristwatches for a fad? Looking back, this seems like a foolish mistake. But when wristwatches first appeared, they were considered silly novelties; after all, the pocket watch and chain, suspended from the waistcoat, were as fundamental to proper male attire as the necktie. Bogardus's respondents called the wristwatch a fad because they didn't expect it to find lasting favor. Only now, knowing as we do, that the wristwatch has become—along with the wedding ring—one of the most popular forms of male jewelry, can we imagine what must have happened. Men must have discovered the wristwatch's advantages—that it was lighter, could be worn without a vest, and viewed without occupying a hand to remove it from its pocket and open its case. Knowing what we now know, we aren't surprised that wristwatches endured; in fact, we can only marvel that people once considered the wristwatch a fad.

Innovations—new products (like wristwatches) but also new ideas, new customs, all sorts of new things—tend to spread slowly at first, then rapidly increase in popularity, before leveling off at some point where anyone likely to adopt the innovation has done so. This process is called diffusion, and it produces a familiar graph among social scientists: it is usually called the S-curve because of its shape. The S-curve is well known because it fits the diffusion histories of so many innovations—if you measure the spread of telephones, or televisions, or VCRs, or whatever, the resulting graph is usually an S-curve.

If we superimpose our two graphs—the one for fads, and the S-curve for diffusion, we see something interesting. The left side of each graph is essentially the same—in both cases, a few people adopt the novelty at first, then there's a rapid increase as lots of folks get involved, and then a gradual tapering to a peak. Up to that point, there is essentially no difference between how fads (like hula-hoops) and things that will prove to be lasting innovations (like wristwatches) spread. It is, of course, what happens next that makes the difference—fads lose popularity, while lasting innovations remain popular.

Our wristwatch example reminds us of an important fact: Initially, during the period shown on the left-hand side of our graphs, people can't be sure whether a novelty will endure or fade. Oh, sometimes they have a pretty good idea: it is hard to imagine that many people expected hula-hoops to remain wildly popular, or thought that the telephone wouldn't last. But public opinion is often wrong—and two sorts of mistakes are possible. The first error, of course, is what happened when Bogardus's respondents dismissed the wristwatch, that is, people expect a novelty to be a fad, but it actually turns out to remain popular. The second mistake occurs when a novelty is heralded as the new new thing, but it turns out to be a bust. There are lots of examples—remember CB radios or 8-track tapes?

This uncertainty about the future, about whether a novelty will prove to be a fad or a lasting innovation, is key to understanding institutional fads. Serious people almost always reject the notion that their new enthusiasm is some sort of fad. The hallmark of the institutional fad is the conviction that, far from being a fad, this innovation represents progress, that it is an improvement that will prove worthwhile and endure. Remember: the front half of the classic fad curve looks just like the beginning of the S-curve of diffusion. When an innovation is spreading, no one can be sure whether it will be an enduring instance of diffusion, or fade as a forgotten fad. But the faithful, those who believe in this new thing, share a conviction that this will be a lasting change. Doubters are dismissed as unimaginative cynics or recalcitrant stick-in-the-muds who are blind to the future's possibilities. While the innovation is spreading, it is easy to believe, to dismiss the doubts. It is only later, after the enthusiasm has died down, that people recognize that this was, after all, just a fad, and that they experienced the illusion of diffusion.

How can we explain institutional fads? Here, it will help to think about three different levels of social arrangements that foster the adoption of innovations: I begin at the broadest level, by considering the meaning of change in American culture, then I examine how the organization of contemporary institutions fosters innovation, before finally exploring how adopting novelties can be in the interest of individual actors.

First, we need to recognize the ways that American culture supports innovation. A presumption of progress, a sense that things can and probably will get better, is a central theme in our culture. American history usually is told as a story of growing democracy, geographic expansion, economic growth, and improvements in health, education, and standards of living. In other words, most Americans understand their nation's history as a story of progress, of changes for the better. As a result, proposals for improvements tend to be welcomed, rather than automatically encountering cynicism, skepticism, or intransigent resistance.

Even more than progress, Americans endorse perfectionism as an ideal. Rather than settling for chipping away at difficult problems, we call for dramatic progress; we declare "war on cancer" and promise that our schools will "leave no child behind." Realistically, of course, we can't deliver on those promises—whatever we do, some people will get sick, and some children will not learn to read at grade level. This means that there is an inevitable gap between our aspirations for our institutions and how those institutions actually perform. That gap—our recognition that our efforts have fallen (and will probably continue to fall) short—makes our institutions receptive to proposals for change. Claims that we can and should do better get a sympathetic hearing. Thus, at the level of our cultural bedrock, American institutions are receptive to promises of progress.

Obviously, I am not claiming that all Americans, on all occasions, endorse every proposed change. Particular calls for change usually encounter at least some resistance, and often that resistance is powerful enough to block whatever change is being proposed. Still, at a fundamental level, Americans believe in progress. When we read world history, we find many examples of institutions that—at least to our eyes—seem to have adopted wrongheaded policies: they prized stability over progress, tried to govern through ritual and fixed doctrines rather than adapting to changing circumstances, and actively resisted and even sought to suppress novel ideas. Given our culture's deep belief in progress, such recalcitrance strikes Americans as foolish, as doomed efforts to hold back the inevitable tide of the future. Our sympathies are with Galileo, not his inquisitors.

Second, we need to appreciate how the dense social networks that characterize modern institutions foster the spread of new ideas. Take medicine. Physicians find themselves belonging to numerous, complex social networks: in addition to their firsthand contacts with other doctors in clinics and hospitals, they belong to professional associations, receive journals, newsletters, and other publications aimed at physicians, attend conferences and workshops, and perhaps even participate on electronic forums that bring them into contact with their peers.

The very existence of these professional venues is justified by their ability to help doctors "keep up" with what's happening in medicine. That is, there is an assumption that there will be new diagnoses, as well as new treatments, drugs, devices, and techniques, and that part of being a good professional is staying on top of these developments. In addition, doctors confront patients who receive their own medical updates in news reports, magazine articles, talk-show episodes, "disease-of-the-week" made-for-TV movies, and advertisements. Remember that, in our culture, everyone, doctors and patients alike, anticipates that medicine will be changing—and for the better. The dense social networks that envelop medicine reinforce this impression by allowing news to spread rapidly.

Nor is there anything exceptional about medicine. In contemporary society, most institutions have developed similarly elaborate social networks built upon associations, conferences, trade journals, and other mechanisms for exchanging news of interest. Consider the very word: "news." It conveys the importance of novelty, of change, of what's, well, new. We establish and maintain dense institutional social networks because we expect there to be news; we assume things will change, and this assumption, in turn, creates its own demands for media that can tell us what's happening.

All of these venues—from the humblest newsletter editor looking for a piece to fill the next issue on up to mass media with great prestige and vast audiences—need news to report. They are eager to locate what folks in the media call "content"—information about some innovation or novelty that they can bring to the attention of their audiences. Obviously, the more interesting the news, the better. Old news is, as they say, stale; fresh information is highly valued. A report of big changes—of a revolutionary discovery or a dramatic breakthrough—makes a more compelling story than, say, the information that researchers' replications have reaffirmed what people were already thinking. (This is why those claims about cold fusion became a media sensation, even though the evidence upon which they were based had not appeared in a reputable journal and proved unable to bear close inspection.) There is, in short, a bias in favor of novel claims; claims of progress—particularly reports of dramatic, promising developments—usually move easily through institutional networks.

The networks within and among institutions help explain what sociologists call *institutional isomorphism.* That is, an institution's organizations tend to resemble one another—any given hospital tends to be organized along the lines of other hospitals, and that the same can be said for schools, corporations, and so on. Some isomorphism is a product of coercion; that is, laws require the adoption of certain arrangements. But isomorphism also emerges because organizations deliberately imitate what seems to be working elsewhere. Both the media and webs of professional contacts spread the word about innovations and thereby foster such imitation. While analysts tend to imply that institutional isomorphism involves the diffusion of enduring changes, it seems obvious that some of what gets copied will turn out to be institutional fads. Thus, just as the larger culture welcomes innovation, most contemporary institutions are organized in ways that encourage the spread of novelties.

At our third level of analysis stands the individual actor. In asking why some serious people buy into what turn out to be silly ideas, we should not underestimate the importance of careerism. Most individuals hope to advance within their particular institutions—they want promotions, pay raises, and all of the other rewards that come to those who do well. Linking one's personal career to some novelty can be a way to stand out from the crowd.

Becoming associated with some current novelty suggests that you are with it, on top of things, in the know, progressive, forward-thinking—and all of those other clichés that assign approval to pioneers of novelty. Often, there are intimations of generational rivalries: those advocating changes are young lions brave enough to stand up against the old guard. Innovation offers a rationale for turning the reins over to a new generation that is not mired in the past, one that is prepared to welcome the future.

I do not mean to imply that this is just a cynical pose. Probably most people who endorse innovations are sincere. The advocates of change argue that everyone knows there are problems with the way our institution does things, so we ought to try that new approach that you hear so much about, the one that everyone says produces such marvelous results, the one that other institutions have already adopted to such good effect. There is nothing inherently dishonest or self-serving about this line of reasoning; the advocates of innovations often believe every word. Still, there are often side-benefits; allying oneself with an innovation can boost one's career prospects.

This is especially true for those who get on the bandwagon early. Remember those fad and diffusion graphs: in both cases, there is a period when the innovation's popularity grows rapidly. People who buy into an innovation early, who climb aboard the bandwagon before everyone else, will be able to congratulate themselves on their prescience, as latecomers join them. They may even be acknowledged as trend-setting visionaries, and newcomers may consult them for tips on successfully implementing the innovation.

In short, a culture that welcomes change, coupled with institutions organized to spread news about innovations, creates an environment that encourages individuals to adopt novelties. It is not that difficult to understand how and why innovations spread. But why do so many innovations turn out to be fads? Why does enthusiasm so often prove to be short-lived?

The obvious answer is that fads are innovations that don't live up to their advance billing, that don't fulfill our expectations for them, that simply fail. Remember that people are serious about these innovations; they expect them to improve things. Therefore, we might predict disillusionment to set in if the new treatment does not actually cure more patients, the new management strategy doesn't really lead to greater efficiency and higher profits, or the new teaching method still leaves some children behind. This seems obvious: failure should lead to rejection.

However, things aren't quite that simple. The real world rarely offers unambiguous proof of failure. Setbacks can be blamed on other factors, such as an unfavorable economy or other contingencies. Scientific reasoning tells us that experimentation under strictly controlled conditions is the gold standard for establishing cause and effect, but it is very difficult to devise genuine experiments about social life. Most of what passes for research in education, business, and public policy falls far short of the ideal standards for experimental designs; often such research reports simple before-after comparisons, and there is no control group, no way of accounting for the impact of potential confounding factors. As a result, research results may convince those predisposed to accept them, but critics often find it easy to dismiss the same findings as unconvincing. Even medical and scientific research, which tend to feature better designs, can encounter criticism. As a consequence, it is hard to persuade everyone that an innovation is, in fact, a failure. Thus, it is not all that surprising that, long after most of the scientific community turned its back on cold fusion, there remained some scientists who continued to explore what most considered a dead end. Contradictory evidence is not necessarily sufficient to lead to an innovation's rejection.

Innovations have defenders. Because the people who buy into innovations tend to be sincere, they not only believe that the new change will work, but they have what they consider good reasons for thinking this way.

Innovations have supporting theories—i.e., this teaching method should work because it fits the way children learn, that cancer treatment ought to be effective given our theories about tumor growth, and so on. That the anticipated good effects have not, in fact, occurred does not necessarily prove that a theory was wrong. Rather, its advocates may insist, failure may be a reflection of inadequate testing: our organization did not really commit itself fully to the new change; we didn't give the innovation a real chance to work. Or they may argue that some minor tinkering is needed.

Thus, the DARE (Drug Abuse Resistance Education) program has managed to retain its leadership in drug education in spite of many research findings that question its effectiveness. Its proponents insist that DARE does work, or confronted with evidence that suggests that it doesn't work, they nonetheless argue that it should work, and that with a few modifications it will work. Their claims have been successful in convincing many school districts to retain a program that most critics view as unsuccessful. Such reasoning allows advocates to continue to endorse an innovation long after evidence calls its effectiveness into doubt.

Well, if contradictory evidence isn't enough to decrease enthusiasm, why do institutional fads fall out of favor? The loss of newness probably plays a key role in the demise of most institutional fads. Consider another sort of short-term enthusiasm: every successful joke becomes a victim of its own popularity; as, increasingly, the answer to the question "Have you heard the one about . . .?" becomes "Yes." The more people who have heard a joke, the more difficult it is to find listeners who haven't heard it, so that tellers eventually become discouraged and move on to new material. However funny the joke, once it is familiar and no longer novel, it loses interest.

Similarly, the adoption of a novelty often causes a lot of excitement, or at least special activity, in its early stages. People have to be told about the innovation, about how and why it works, about how it is to be implemented. When an organization adopts an innovation, there may be special training, workshops, announcements, planning and other activities heralding the new arrangements. There may even be festive touches—buttons, posters, or polo shirts displaying the new logo or slogan. Regardless of whether these elements produce genuine excitement about and commitment to the cause, they must arouse more interest the first time they are encountered, than after they become familiar. So, of course, boredom plays a role in the decline of institutional fads.

In addition, disillusionment becomes a factor. I have already suggested it is often impossible to prove that an innovation doesn't work, but it is also often difficult for its proponents to prove its worth. Over time, organizations probably adapt to most innovations. People get used to the new management strategy; they come to ignore it, adapt to it, subvert it, or go around it. And, whatever leverage proponents had when the innovation seemed fresh and novel, the potential answer to all manner of problems, is diminished as people recognize that things aren't all that different than they used to be. Some students may be doing better, but others are still having trouble. Some projects may have been completed on schedule, but others lag behind.

An innovation offers new opportunities for finger-pointing—"The new policy just bogs us down in unnecessary paperwork!" "If you guys would just cooperate with the new procedures, we wouldn't have these problems." It turns out that, regardless of whether it has made things somewhat better or somewhat worse, the innovation has not produced the promised fundamental transformation—everything is not now all that different. Enthusiasm wanes, and the innovation begins to lose favor, revealing itself as just another institutional fad.

And, of course, as what was once heralded as the way of the future loses support, conditions once again favor advocates of some new, completely different solution. Here, institutional cultures play a key role. In some—although by no means all—institutions, there are well-established debates. For example, the history of reading instruction features a long-standing disagreement over whether teachers should emphasize phonics (that is, teaching children to "sound out" unfamiliar words) or word recognition (variously called, over the years, look-say, sight-reading, or whole language). We might suspect that every child learning to read winds up using both strategies, because while phonics is generally useful, English's irregular spellings make it very difficult to sound out some words, but this has not discouraged a long debate among educators over which approach ought to be emphasized.

Similarly, debates over management in both business and education have long focused on issues of centralized control: advocates of centralization argue that it allows managers (say, school district superintendents) to supervise and coordinate wide-ranging operations; while proponents of decentralization insist that giving more autonomy to subunits (such as individual schools or even teachers in their own classrooms) encourages flexibility and responsiveness to special needs. Again, as with the competing philosophies of reading instruction, both positions have some merit: both coordination and autonomy can be desirable.

This means that many innovations have opposition. The opponents may remain relatively silent while enthusiasm is rising, as they wait for it to peak, and begin to slide. At that point, there will be opportunities to introduce an alternative novelty—if some children failed to learn to read well under whole-language instruction, shouldn't our school give phonics a chance? It is no wonder that institutional fads often follow close upon the heels of the previous enthusiasm.

Institutional fads surround us, although they are often hard to identify during their early, illusion-of-diffusion phase. It is only later, after the collapse is apparent, that we recognize the fad for what it was—yet another project that went through those six stages.

Both in the enthusiasm for institutional fads' spread and in the interpretations for their decline, there is a failure of sociological imagination. C. Wright Mills argued for understanding the particular—what he called "private troubles"—in terms of more general processes—as "public issues." This is precisely what tends to be missing when people try to think about innovations. They usually focus on the particulars: first there are promises—here is a new teaching method, management philosophy, or whatever that is supposed to produce amazing results—that lead people to adopt the novelty; this enthusiasm is followed by disillusionment—we tried that but it didn't work; or we didn't really commit ourselves to making it work, so maybe the failure was our fault. In these analyses, fingers point to particular individuals: he foolishly insisted that we adopt it; she did everything she could to sabotage its working; and so on. Such explanations blame institutional fads on insufficiently critical adopters who made unwise decisions.

What is missing in these accounts is a broader perspective. Many institutions, including science, medicine, education, and management and academia, display a pattern of short-lived enthusiasms, of people rushing to adopt some innovation, only to abandon it soon after. Social scientists are not immune: this year's hot research topics will cool, and others will emerge in the future. Understanding this process—in particular, understanding the ways that enthusiasm tends to downplay the importance of evidence—can make us more sociological, more critical thinkers, so that we can approach institutional fads as observers, rather than as participants.

QUESTIONS ABOUT MEANING

1. What are examples of institutional fads and why does Best say they warrant our attention? Why do so many institutional fads fail to last?
2. What factors explain the diffusion of fads?
3. What is *institutional isomorphism* and how can it contribute to the acceptance of a fad?

QUESTIONS FOR RHETORICAL ANALYSIS

1. What is the "illusion of diffusion"? Is it a fitting title for the article? Why or why not?
2. Best's article is rich with signals for readers: transition phrases, transition sentences, and summary sentences. Highlight examples of phrases, sentences, or paragraphs that introduce new ideas, signal comparisons, or summarize ideas. Then, outline Best's argument.

MAKING CONNECTIONS

1. Imagine that you are one of the people sociologist Emory Bogardus asked to list five current fads. Write an essay in which you identify the innovations you would list and make an argument for why they don't have lasting potential.

2. Like Christakis and Fowler, Best discusses the importance of social networks. Reread Best's description of how fads spread and review Christakis and Fowler's figures depicting various ways one hundred people might be connected (p. 508). Do any of the figures adequately depict the way fads spread? If so, explain how. If not, create your own figure and explain how it represents the diffusion of fads.

Neuroscience

"Creativity versus Skepticism within Science," V. S. RAMACHANDRAN

"Creativity versus Skepticism within Science" first appeared in 2006 in *The Skeptical Inquirer* magazine. Typically, the authors published in that magazine promote critical thinking and skeptical inquiry, habits of mind you would expect V. S. Ramachandran, a psychology and neuroscience professor at the University of California, San Diego, to champion. But in this article Ramachandran argues that "more harm has been done in science by those who make a fetish out of skepticism . . . than by those who gullibly accept untested theories."

When a fantastic idea—such as telepathy—attracts a cult following, it is relatively easy for almost anyone outside the cult to test it and disprove it adequately to satisfy at least a majority of scientists. (I will give some examples later.) On the other hand, it takes a real visionary to recognize—and not kill—a promising new idea that seems to initially violate the current establishment view (what Thomas Kuhn famously referred to as "normal science," the kind of humdrum activity practiced by the majority of scientists, the bricklayers rather than the architects of science).

Karl Popper is often credited with pointing out that an idea deserves the coveted title "scientific" only if it makes testable predictions that are stated in a form that allows them to withstand refutation. (This rules out many social "sciences," including historicism, deconstructivism, structuralism, "isms" in general, and much of the pretentious, postmodern nonsense that tries to pass itself off as science.) This aspect of Popper's idea is well known, yet there is the other aspect of his argument that few appreciate: the fact that revolutionary science often begins with a conjecture—a vision that takes you well beyond the existing evidence rather than being constrained by it. Outstanding science is conducted by those who make imaginative excursions into what might be true, i.e., conjectures that are ontologically promiscuous and not merely consistent with existing data.

They are not made by those who are, to use Peter Medawar's phrase, "cows grazing on the pasture of knowledge." If I am right about this, then the danger of gullibility (even among scientists, not just lay people) through accepting bogus revolutions is vastly outweighed by the danger of novel ideas being ignored by skeptics. More damage was done by those who were "skeptical" of Semmelweiss's or Pasteur's germ theory of disease than by those who believed in spoon bending. As Francis Crick pointed out to me once, "It is better to have nine of your ideas be completely disproved, and the tenth one spark off a revolution than to have all ten be correct but unimportant discoveries that satisfy the skeptics." This seems obvious, but why is it so rarely practiced? In my view, there are two reasons, both of them psychological. (This applies mainly to card-carrying professional scientists.)

CUL-DE-SAC SKEPTICISM

The first reason is what I call the "cul-de-sac phenomenon." People—including scientists—unconsciously gravitate into a cozy cul-de-sac where they feel safe practicing "normal science." There are great social rewards. People who are in the same club engage in mutual admiration and reward each other by funding each other. Their papers are "peer reviewed" by people in their own clubs, and as a result, no one seriously questions the meaning of the whole enterprise or where it is headed. Anyone who dares to do so is in danger of excommunication by the priesthood, so to speak. In this regard, skeptics are not merely useless; they can be an actual impediment to science. By *skeptic,* I mean one who adopts an overall skeptical attitude, being unreceptive to anything new—not one who practices legitimate skepticism toward claims that are empirically unproven. This should become clearer as we go along.

There are many early warning signs of this phenomenon, but the clearest one is the inability of scientific practitioners to question the axiomatic foundations of their discipline. A second warning sign is when a field is dominated by certain catchphrases or by methodology (fMR, sine waves, reaction-time measures, eye movements, EMG, EEG, "working memory," etc.) rather than by questions. The methodology, phrases, and mantras drive the concepts rather than the other way around. This type of Kuhnian "normal science" would be innocuous were it not for the fact that it siphons off 98 percent of funding from those who embark on bold new adventures or pursue anomalies.

More often than not, skeptics succeed in stifling innovation in science with their "conform-or-perish" approach. This is especially devastating for young scientists entering the field. Even the genuinely talented ones are intimidated into conforming—or at least pretending to conform—in order to obtain jobs, funding, or tenure. With the passage of time, the "mask becomes the man," and any trace of originality is beaten out of them. I have sat on many a committee on my campus when a young scientist has published innovative, internationally recognized work, and some skeptic has tried to block hiring or tenure, arguing, "But why hasn't he got any federal funding?" My usual response to this is that there is something lopsided about that argument: surely, funding should be in the denominator, not the numerator ("more bang for the buck"), in these decisions. (Not to mention the obvious fact that being young, the scientist doesn't have cronies in her club yet; funding committees are usually composed of failed scientists who enjoy being "skeptical." Fortunately, there are exceptions; I have known many eminent scientists who sit on these committees.)

If you think I am overstating all this, go to any annual meeting of the Society for Neuroscience in the United States, attended by 30,000 scientists, and walk along the rows and rows of poster presentations. If you go to two of these meetings in consecutive years, you will be struck by an eerie sense of déjà vu. It's as if someone has taken all the key words from the previous year's meeting and shuffled them around randomly in a computer to create the poster tides of the current year.

What is the harm in all this? To be sure, there is so much of it going on that some of it is going to be important simply by accident. The more serious problem is that it makes science lose its soul; it makes the practice of science no longer enjoyable.

For perspective, I will compare eighteenth- and nineteenth-century science with late twentieth-century science. Victorian science was a grand, romantic adventure for those who practiced it; it was motivated by an unquenchable passion for knowledge. This was true whether you were a fledgling scientist or an eminent one (like Faraday, Huxley, Darwin, Wallace, Cavendish, and countless others). One reason for this was that many of them were financially well off—their livelihood didn't depend on science, so they could pursue science for its own sake. While this is still true for a small minority of scientists, it isn't true for most. The funding system is supposed to take care of this, but it doesn't work well in the United States—it's not quite as bad in Canada and the United Kingdom—because it tends to be "top-heavy"; those who already have huge grants get more funding, because they are considered a safe bet. So the rich get richer. There is usually no "trickle down." (It's not a coincidence that the same sort of thing happens in the political realm; the so-called economic revolution in India has benefited only the upper 30 percent—no sign of trickle-down yet.)

Science, in other words, has become "professionalized" into just another nine-to-five "job." The only way to reverse this trend is to hang around the genuinely curious and adventurous scientists so that some of their romantic passion rubs off on you (for there is nothing more contagious than enthusiasm). On the other hand, avoid skeptics like the plague until the final stages of "fact checking." As Sherlock Holmes said, "Mediocrity knows nothing higher than itself, my dear Watson; it takes talent to recognize genius."

One has to do this, even if it means a temporary loss of "pats on the back" from others trapped in your own cul-de-sac. "The quest for respectability," Francis Crick once told me, "is the death of science."

There is a second psychological reason why someone becomes skeptical: it makes him or her look intelligent without too much effort. The practitioner not only recognizes that it is much easier than genuine innovation but also hopes it will be misperceived as a sign of high intelligence—the phenomenon of "Aha! I saw through that, so I must be clever." What such people don't realize is that most clever people in the audience have "seen through" the so-called flaw already but are at least willing to give the scientist who is presenting the idea credit for his boldness—for sending up trial balloons while at the same time recognizing their tentative nature.

These skeptics are easily spotted in the audience at scientific lectures—they are the ones who usually miss the main point of the lecture and try to mask this by pretending to ask questions that seem penetrating but are very often nothing more than skeptical: "Is it inconceivable that the effect you are talking about is really due to X, Y, or Z," and so on.

PURSUING REVOLUTIONARY SCIENCE

One strategy for pursuing revolutionary science is to ignore the skeptics and be on the lookout for anomalies and pursue them with tenacity. Bear in mind that a certain amount of skepticism is actually healthy—even desirable. In that respect, I am completely in tune with this magazine's main agenda. (Semir Zeki once said, "Referees are swine but sometimes swine can lead you to truffles.") It is easy to portray scientists as being shallow folk skating on the surface, narrow-minded and unreceptive to new ideas. But their skepticism doesn't result from stupidity. On the contrary, there are, in fact, very good reasons for being initially wary of new ideas, because of the simple fact that most "anomalies" turn out to be false alarms. There are many crackpot ideas posing as promising anomalies, e.g., polywater, cold fusion, telepathy, clairvoyance, UFOs, angels, Elvis sightings; one could spend a lifetime pursuing these. (One third of all Americans not only believe in angels but actually claim to have seen one.)

So the question for the young scientist is this: how do I know which anomalies to pursue and which ones to be skeptical of? It has been said that some scientists develop a nose for authentic anomalies. If you are not one of these lucky few, you can also use the trial-and-error method to weed out bogus anomalies, but this is time-consuming. A better option is to adopt the following rule of thumb: if an anomaly has been around for decades, has survived many attempts at experimental disproof, and is regarded as an anomaly for the sole reason that you can't think of a mechanism or that it doesn't fit the "big picture" of science, then go after it, for it can lead to a gold mine (e.g., continental drift and bacterial transformation, both of which I will discuss below). But if it is being ignored because the phenomenon itself has been tested repeatedly and found to be flawed, then don't waste time on it, for otherwise, you could spend a lifetime on a wild-goose chase. Telepathy is a good example. The more careful the measurements, the smaller the effect, and that is always a red flag. (Contrast this with the fact that any ten-year-old anywhere in the world can replicate Galileo's famous experiment by dropping a cannonball and a pea simultaneously from a tall building; unlike the case of telepathy, you don't have to keep making excuses for why the experiment demonstrating gravity doesn't work.)

One final point: if you choose to pursue anomalies, there are bound to be some people whose entire lives' work is threatened by those anomalies and will therefore be offended by your efforts. But as Lord Reith remarked, "There are some people whom it is one's duty to offend."

LEGITIMIZING ANOMALIES

In general, for an anomaly to make it into mainstream science, it has to fulfill three criteria, *all* of which must be in place. First, it must be true, i.e., reliably repeatable. Second, it has to be explainable in terms of known principles. Third, it must have broad implications for areas of research beyond that of the researcher. Let's take two examples:

In the late 1940s, Oswald Avery et al. determined that DNA was the factor that permitted bacterial transformation, a phenomenon in which one strain of a species of bacterium (such as pneumococcus A) transforms into a different species (such as pneumococcus B) when A is incubated with fluid that has been extracted from B. This had been observed by other investigators in prior studies, but no mechanism for the transformation had been isolated. That observation, which was published in the prestigious *Journal of Experimental Science,* should have sent a tsunami through biology, but it barely made a ripple. In principle, it was a lot like seeing a pig walk into a room and reemerge as a donkey. Yet, it was ignored by skeptics, partly because it challenged one of the basic principles of biology: the immutability of species.

Avery even hinted that this "transforming principle," the DNA molecule, might carry hereditary information, but his findings were ignored (probably as anomalies) before the replication mechanism of DNA was understood (thanks to Watson and Crick). If someone had seen the significance of those findings earlier, molecular biology might have been born much sooner than it was.

Why was Avery's "anomaly" ignored initially? Because while it fulfilled the first criterion of being reliably repeatable and the third criterion of having vast implications (challenging the idea of the immutability of species), too many skeptics were not yet willing to accept it as fulfilling the second: providing a conceivable mechanism for bacterial transformation. But that, as we have seen, is not a good reason for ignoring the discovery.

A second example is continental drift. Like many schoolchildren, Alfred Wegener noticed that the outlines of the facing coasts of the continents fit together nearly perfectly, and based on that, he posited that the continents as we know them now must have split off and drifted apart from a single, ancient supercontinent. He also noticed that the rock strata on the west coast of Africa perfectly matched those of the east coast of South America. Finally, he pointed out that fossils of an order of Permian freshwater lizards, mesosaurs, are found in only two places on earth—you guessed it, West Africa and the eastern coast of Brazil. And the fossilized remains of identical species of dinosaurs were found on the Atlantic coasts of the two continents. Yet the experts—the skeptics—ignored the evidence that was staring them in the face. They did so because it didn't fulfill their criteria: it didn't fit the contemporary big picture of geology (*"terra firma"* and all that), and they couldn't think of a mechanism for continental drift—plate tectonics had not yet been discovered. So the skeptics argued, believe it or not, that there had been a long, narrow (now submerged) land bridge connecting the Atlantic coasts of South America and Africa, across which all the dinosaurs had migrated and died! One wonders what it would have taken to convince these people: two halves of the same dinosaur skeleton, each on a different side of the Atlantic?

Contrast these two with another "anomaly": telepathy. It fulfills criterion 3 (vast implications) but not criterion 1 (repeatability) nor 2 (a conceivable mechanism). So it is legitimately ignored, except by crackpots. Unlike Galileo's Leaning Tower of Pisa experiment, telepathy becomes smaller and smaller the more rigorously you test it, and that's good enough reason to be skeptical.

I will conclude with two incidents from the life of the great German physician, ophthalmologist, and physicist Hermann von Helmholtz. When he invented the ophthalmoscope to view the fundus of the eye, a royal commission, composed mainly of skeptical eye doctors, was set up in England to "evaluate this new German invention." After considerable deliberation, they reported back to the king: "Your Majesty; this German instrument does enable you to look inside the eye but it is not needed for diagnosing any of the known diseases of the eye." Upon hearing this, Helmholtz is said to have remarked, "But that is the whole point."

Now for the second incident: Helmholtz had just produced the first mathematical formulation of the law of the conservation of energy, which says that energy can neither be created nor destroyed, and applied it to his study of the use of energy by muscle tissue. Other scientists argued that it was applicable only to inorganic objects and not living things, because living things have a "vital spirit." To convince the skeptics, Helmholtz set up an open demonstration at a scientific meeting in Europe, in which he showed that the heat output from a living muscle is exactly what you would expect from an inanimate machine (with no vital spirit). He then wrote back to a friend in Germany: "Not a single scientist in the meeting believed a word of what I said. Now I know I am right." In short, Helmholtz's confidence in his own experiments increased in direct proportion to the number of people who were skeptical of them!

There is surely a moral in this somewhere for every aspiring young scientist: listen to the skeptics, by all means, but have enough confidence—even a touch of arrogance—in your research to recognize that the skeptics are as often wrong as right.

QUESTIONS ABOUT MEANING

1. What does Ramachandran mean when he says that the danger of "accepting bogus revolutions is vastly outweighed by the danger of novel ideas being ignored by skeptics"? What examples does Ramachandran provide to illustrate?
2. What are the dangers and drawbacks of the "cul-de-sac phenomenon" among scientific researchers? Why do so many scientists conform to the majority assumptions and methodologies?
3. Look up the word "anomaly" so that you fully understand what it means and how it is commonly used. What criteria must be fulfilled for an "anomaly" to be accepted by a majority of researchers? Do you think "anomaly" is the best word for describing what Ramachandran discusses? Why or why not?

QUESTIONS FOR RHETORICAL ANALYSIS

1. What does Ramachandran mean when he refers to most scientists as "bricklayers," not "architects"? What does the metaphor imply and how does it help you understand Ramachandran's point?

2. Identify Ramachandran's thesis statement or summarize his central claim. What type(s) of evidence does Ramachandran provide to support his thesis? Do you find his argument persuasive? Why or why not?
3. Identify several passages in the article where Ramachandran establishes his expertise and credibility. What makes these appeals to ethos effective or ineffective?

MAKING CONNECTIONS

1. Like Joel Best ("The Illusion of Diffusion") and Norenzayan and Nisbett, Ramachandran discusses how one's intellectual, institutional, or cultural environment affects one's reasoning. Put these authors (and additional authors, if you like) in conversation with one another in an essay. On what points do they seem to agree? Or how do they differ in their take on what Ramachandran calls the "cul-de-sac phenomenon"?
2. Both Ramachandran and Garcia mention people who we might call creative geniuses, but the authors describe different paths that led to their accomplishments. Using their examples and adding examples of your own, compare Ramachandran's and Garcia's take on creativity.

Art History

"Hackers of the Renaissance," PABLO GARCIA

In the following essay, art history professor Pablo Garcia takes a historical look at a modern problem: hacking. Garcia looks back to a time when hacking was done "in the service of curiosity and invention" and describes instances when hacking was a "good thing." Garcia's article appeared in 2013 in *OMNI Reboot*, an online magazine that publishes an eclectic mix of articles about science, technology, art, culture, design, and metaphysics.

Hacking gets a bad rap. When most people hear the word, they think of malware, identity theft, espionage, and apology emails sent to friends in the embarrassing aftermath of a compromised Facebook account. Try this: do a Google Image search for the word "hacking." See the skulls, Guy Fawkes masks, padlock icons and the images of green-tinted code lifted straight from the dystopia that is *The Matrix*. Message received: hacking is very scary.

Where does this popular perception come from? For over thirty years, outlaw nerds have hacked on the big screen: *TRON* and *War Games* gave us the image of the young rebel hacker skirting heavy security with a few effortless keystrokes, archetypes which evolved into *The Girl with the*

Dragon Tattoo's Lisbeth Salander, badass hacker. Even stock espionage and heist films require a team member to bypass any security system by clacking away at a laptop (see the entire *Mission: Impossible* franchise). Real-world events only perpetuate this hacker-as-criminal image. Cindy Cohn, Legal Director for the trailblazing Electronic Frontier Foundation, argues that the Bradley Manning WikiLeaks case is part of a prosecutorial trend toward exploiting irrational fears about computers:

> The decision today continues a trend of government prosecutions that use familiarity with digital tools and knowledge of computers as a scare tactic and a basis for obtaining grossly disproportionate and unfair punishments. Let's call this the "hacker madness" strategy. Using it, the prosecution portrays actions taken by someone using a computer as more dangerous or scary than they actually are by highlighting the digital tools used to a nontechnical or even technophobic judge.

So: hackers are lone, outlaw agitators who use technology as a weapon. And because most of us use our computers like we use our cars—we know enough to make them run, but not enough to understand how they work—hackers seem dangerous for what we imagine they can do with their unchecked powers. Right? Not exactly. First of all, this is a narrow definition of hacking, as computer intrusions like these are typically labeled cracking. Second, they have little to do with the Hacker Ethic formulated at MIT in the 1950s and 60s. Journalist Steven Levy, in his 1984 history of the rise of hacker culture, describes the Hacker Ethic this way:

> Access to computers—and anything that might teach you something about the way the world works—should be unlimited and total. Always yield to the hands-on imperative! Hackers believe that essential lessons can be learned about . . . the world from taking things apart, seeing how they work, and using this knowledge to create new and even more interesting things.

Just a few decades ago, hacking wasn't about computer code—it was a code of conduct. The Hacker Ethic promoted access in the service of curiosity and invention. In 2013, however, this starry-eyed manifesto seems romantic, or worse, naive. Artistic appropriation, a pillar of Modern Art for over a century, is now prosecuted as plagiarism. Patent Trolls aggressively abuse the patent system for profit, stifling innovation. Benevolent hackers, like the late Aaron Swartz, who believe in ethical disclosure, are persecuted as criminals.

We need to reinvent our cultural imagination of the hacker. Being a student of history, I propose we start looking further into the annals of the past, all the way back to the Renaissance, to find our hacker forebears. Four centuries ago, information was as tightly guarded by intellectuals and their wealthy patrons as it is today. But a few episodes around 1600 confirm that the Hacker Ethic and its attendant emphasis on open-source information and a "hands-on imperative" was around long before computers hit the scene. First, there was Galileo.

GALILEO AND THE TELESCOPE

OK, so Galileo didn't invent the telescope. That honor goes to Dutch spectacle maker Hans Lippershey. In 1608, Lippershey applied for a patent for a device "for seeing things far away as if they were nearby." Although denied based on other concurrent patent claims, the application was notable enough to warrant brief mention in a diplomatic publication announcing new relations between The Netherlands and the Kingdom of Siam. Inspired, scientists tested their own telescope inventions based solely on the description of a "Dutch Perspective Glass."

In 1610, Galileo published *Sidereus Nuncius* (The Starry Messenger), describing his telescope and observations of the Moon. Simultaneously, other continental astronomers hurried to make telescopes and point them at the heavens. If Lippershey's patent had been granted, or if the Dutch had decided to omit this tiny announcement of the application, the history of science might have been different. Perhaps Galileo would have been a minor figure in science; another heretic with crazy ideas. Or the Dutch might have had a head-start on astronomy, physics, and warfare. The public disclosure of the telescope, however vague, literally moved the Earth, yielding proof of the heliocentric model of the heavens.

TYCHO BRAHE, JOHANNES KEPLER, AND THE RUDOLPHINE TABLES

In the mid 1500s, stellar and planetary data were woefully inaccurate. When Tycho Brahe undertook a serious, from-scratch measurement of the nighttime sky, he was the first to do so in almost 300 years. So it was understandable he was incredibly protective of his data. However, Brahe entrusted his student, Johannes Kepler, with the completion of new star charts for publication—and twenty-six years after Brahe's death, Kepler published them, calling them the Rudolphine Tables. Instead of a sequence of dates with corresponding planetary positions, Kepler's tables performed more like a computer. Using the provided formulas and instructive examples, users could calculate future planetary positions.

These tables are an open source tool, perhaps the very first. The data—and formulas required to convert it into astronomical information—empowered scientists to pursue their own research and observations. Pierre Gassendi used the tables to predict a transit of Mars in 1631, and in 1639, Jeremiah Horrox predicted a transit of Venus. Kepler's data was for the benefit of science, not personal profit.

LA PERSPECTIVE CURIEUSE

You've probably seen those street-art illusions where a sidewalk chalk drawing looks three-dimensional when viewed from a specific angle. The technique is called anamorphosis, and it dates back to the Renaissance. Hans Holbein famously used the effect in his painting, *The Ambassadors* (1533), where the enigmatic blob in the foreground is revealed as a skull only to viewers standing in the correct position [Fig. 13.3].

The illusion was used to amaze, but it was also a useful technique for concealing sensitive material. For over 150 years, anamorphosis was used as a secret code to protect dissenting political messages, unpopular religious ideas, and even taboo sexual imagery. Until Jean François Niceron gave it all away.

A talented mathematician and artist, Niceron revealed for the first time the geometry behind the illusion. Already renowned for his illusions of sacred figures in churches, Niceron published *La Perspective Curieuse* (The Curious Perspective) in 1638 [Fig. 13.4]. On top of explaining the technique, Niceron actually illustrated himself in the act of making his most famous illusions. He was a magician who revealed his own tricks—so that we could all do magic.

Figure 13.3 Hans Holbein's painting, *The Ambassadors*, with its anamorphc skull.

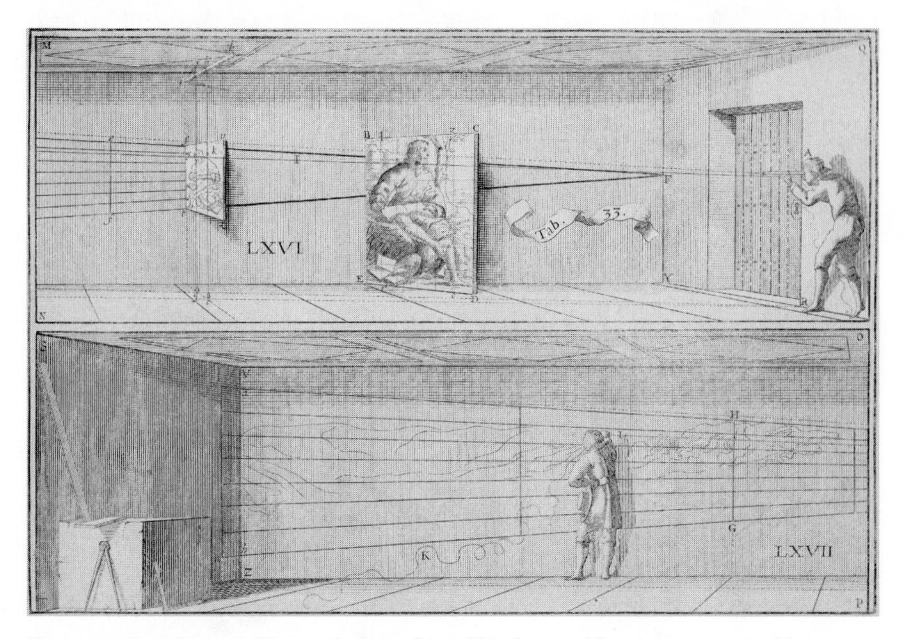

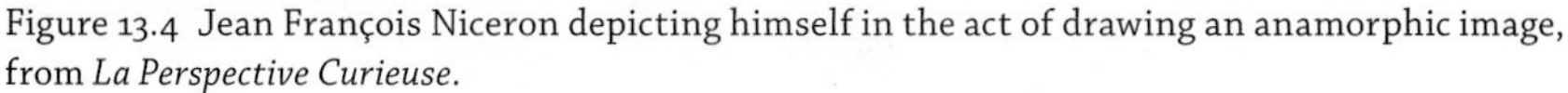

Figure 13.4 Jean François Niceron depicting himself in the act of drawing an anamorphic image, from *La Perspective Curieuse*.

EDWARD WRIGHT

Ever wonder why the Mercator World Map hangs in every classroom despite its egregious distortions of scale? Well, its significance isn't about land area. It's about navigation. The cylindrical projection method that Gerardus Mercator introduced in 1569 flattened the earth into parallel meridians, giving sailors regular and measurable reference markers for straight-line routes across the oceans. The map saved lives. Not surprisingly, its importance—and monetary value—motivated Mercator to keep his projection formula secret.

Until Edward Wright hacked it. And improved it. And, like a true hacker, published the formula. His 1599 publication of *Certaine Errors in Navigation* broke Mercator's cartographic monopoly [Fig. 13.5].

Traveling to the Azores in 1589 under orders from Elizabeth I, Wright broke Mercator's code with practical, hands-on experience at sea. Combined with his mathematical training, he produced tables with data and instructions for constructing a more accurate cylindrical projection. More than a new, more accurate map, *Certaine Errors in Navigation* was—like Kepler's Rudolphine Tables—a computer for producing your own map [Fig. 13.6]. Wright's hack gifted sailors with abilities beyond sea-borne experience. Instead of Mercator's consumers, they were now self-sufficient cartographers at sea.

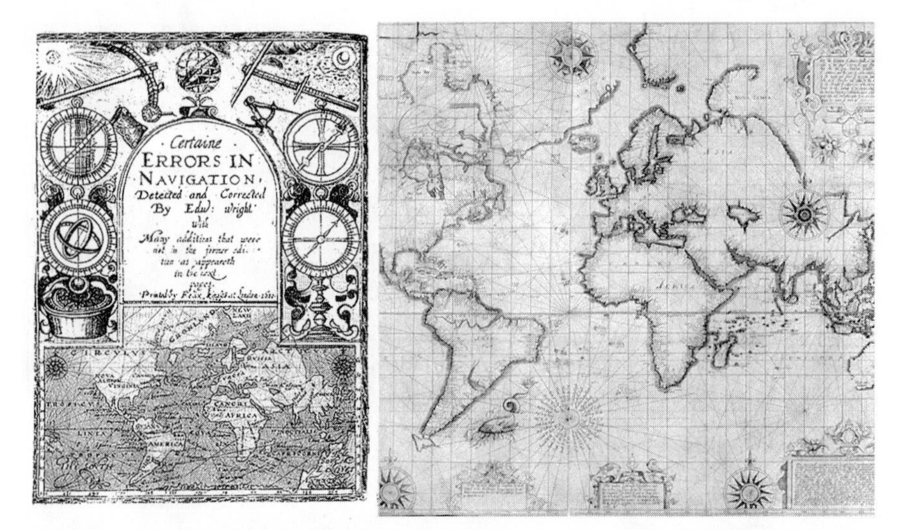

Figure 13.5 Edward Wright, *Certaine Errors in Navigation*, 1599. Frontispiece (left), and his more precise cylindrical projection map of the world (right).

The draught of the Meridian Parallels, and Rumbes of the nautical Planisphere truely made.

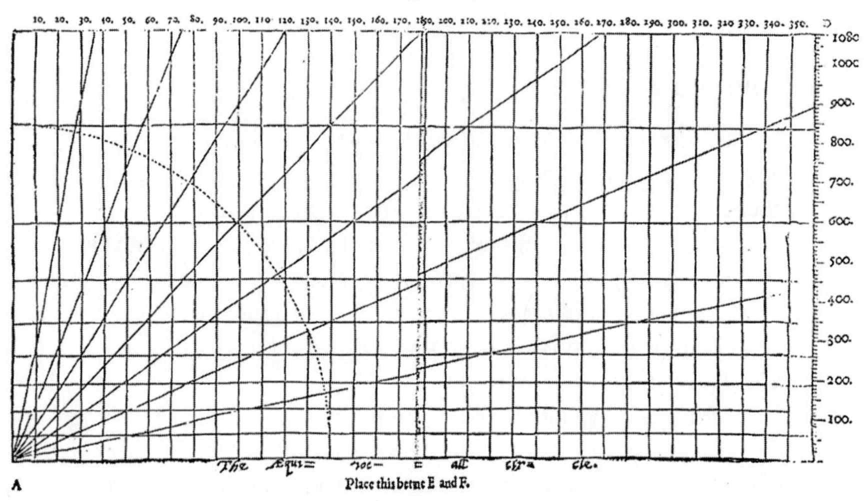

Figure 13.6 Edward Wright's planisphere aided sailors in constructing their own cylindrical projection maps.

Wright understood the Hacker Ethic's hands-on imperative, to the benefit of all who used his tools. He reminisces in the preface to *Certaine Errors* that through the expedition he "was first moved . . . to divert my mathematical studies from theoretical speculation in the Universitie [sic], to the practical demonstration of the use of navigation." To wit, Wright went from thinker to hacker.

Edward Wright reverse engineered, improved, and shared a secret code. You may not have heard of him before, but he is one of history's great hackers; a perfect embodiment of the Hacker Ethic.

BETWEEN RENAISSANCE AND REVOLUTION

Before Galileo, Kepler, Wright, Niceron and others, discoveries and inventions were kept secret. Protection of new insights was regulated through coded publications, legible only to invited insiders. The very idea of peer-reviewed publishing—a cornerstone of academia today—didn't exist until 1665, with the launch of the Philosophical Transactions of the Royal Society.

The innovators of 1600 were hackers before the word existed; they proposed open sharing of ideas for the benefit of humanity. Isaac Newton, Robert Hooke, Descartes, and the other scientists of the late 1600s could not have inaugurated the greatest scientific innovation of all time—the invention of modern science itself—without the Hackers of the 1600s. The Renaissance's secretive structure was hacked, and it inspired the Scientific Revolution.

Hacking is a good thing. Hackers ensure we don't sit still with what we have; they know there's always more to discover. They extract kinetic energy from the inertia of achievement. We risk stifling discovery when we claim absolute ownership of ideas. We risk our future when we aggressively guard what we believe, often falsely, to be ours. And we risk *everything* when we persecute the curious and inventive, labeling them as criminals. Let's restore hacking to its proper place: as a noble tradition dating back hundreds of years, one which kickstarted our modern world. Who knows what wondrous revolution awaits if we just get hacking?

QUESTIONS ABOUT MEANING

1. What is the modern view of hacking and where do most people get their ideas about what hacking is? How does this modern notion contrast with Garcia's view of hacking and with the historical definition he offers? Do Garcia's views seem surprising coming from a professor of art history? Why or why not?
2. What is the Hacker Ethic?
3. What did Galileo, Kepler, Niceron, and Wright "hack"? What were the results of their hacking?

QUESTIONS FOR RHETORICAL ANALYSIS

1. Given the negative connotation of "hackers," why do you think Garcia used the word in his essay? What other words could he have used in the title (and does he use in the article) to describe the people and actions he discusses? What would be gained or lost by the use of another word in the title?

2. If you visit the *OMNI Reboot* site, you'll read this description of the magazine's mission:

> We're a free-rolling resource in a terrifying, wonderful, metamorphosing world. . . . We don't draw lines between disciplines; we revel in simultaneity. We understand that art is a form of inquiry. We ask the wrong questions as well as the right ones. We don't put science on a pedestal; instead, we drag it down into the city, onto the screen, and into the stream of everyday life. We'll question your most deeply-held conceptions of what technology does.

Given this mission, do you think Garcia's essay is well suited for this forum? Why or why not?

MAKING CONNECTIONS

1. Garcia's final paragraph reads in part:

> We risk stifling discovery when we claim absolute ownership of ideas. We risk our future when we aggressively guard what we believe, often falsely, to be ours. And we risk *everything* when we persecute the curious and inventive, labeling them as criminals.

Do you agree? Respond to the passage in an essay that includes examples to support or counter Garcia's premise.

2. In music, a *mashup* is created by combining elements of two or more existing songs to create a third, "original" song. Of course, the new song is not entirely new or original; yet mashups are often allowed under the "fair use" doctrine of copyright law.

   Conduct some research into music mashups or focus on similar types of imitation in art or literature. In an essay, describe and illustrate the concept you have learned about and consider the practice from an ethical standpoint. Do you support the practice in the same way that Garcia condones the "hacking" he describes? Why or why not?

Psychology

"Culture and Causal Cognition," ARA NORENZAYAN AND RICHARD E. NISBETT

Ara Norenzayan and Richard Nisbett, professors of psychology at the University of British Columbia and the University of Michigan, respectively, study how cultural background influences the way we perceive the world. In the following article, published in 2000 in *Current Directions in Psychological Science*, Norenzayan and Nisbett describe differences in how various cultures interpret causality. *Current Directions in Psychological Science* is a peer-reviewed journal that publishes review articles summarizing recent research from psychology.

ABSTRACT

East Asian and American causal reasoning differs significantly. East Asians understand behavior in terms of complex interactions between dispositions of the person or other object and contextual factors, whereas Americans often view social behavior primarily as the direct unfolding of dispositions. These culturally differing causal theories seem to be rooted in more pervasive, culture-specific mentalities in East Asia and the West. The Western mentality is analytic, focusing attention on the object, categorizing it by reference to its attributes, and ascribing causality based on rules about it. The East Asian mentality is holistic, focusing attention on the field in which the object is located and ascribing causality by reference to the relationship between the object and the field.

KEYWORDS

causal attribution, culture, attention, reasoning

Psychologists within the cognitive science tradition have long believed that fundamental reasoning processes such as causal attribution are the same in all cultures (Gardner, 1985). Although recognizing that the content of causal beliefs can differ widely across cultures, psychologists have assumed that the ways in which people come to make their causal judgments are essentially the same, and therefore that they tend to make the same sorts of inferential errors. A case in point is the fundamental attribution error, or FAE (Ross, 1977), a phenomenon that is of central importance to social psychology and until recently was held to be invariable across cultures.

The FAE refers to people's inclination to see behavior as the result of dispositions corresponding to the apparent nature of the behavior. This tendency often results in error when there are obvious situational constraints that leave little or no role for dispositions in producing the behavior. The classic example of the FAE was demonstrated in a study by Jones and Harris (1967) in which participants read a speech or essay that a target person had allegedly been required to produce by a debate coach or psychology experimenter. The speech or essay favored a particular position on an issue, for example, the legalization of marijuana. Participants' estimates of the target's actual views on the issue reflected to a substantial extent the views expressed in the speech or essay, even when they knew that the target had been explicitly instructed to defend a particular position. Thus, participants inferred an attitude that corresponded to the target person's apparent behavior, without taking into account the situational constraints operating on the behavior. Since that classic study, the FAE has been found in myriad studies in innumerable experimental and naturalistic contexts, and it has been a major focus of theorizing and a continuing source of instructive pedagogy for psychology students.

CULTURE AND THE FAE

It turns out, however, that the FAE is much harder to demonstrate with Asian populations than with European-American populations (Choi, Nisbett, & Norenzayan, 1999). Miller (1984) showed that Hindu Indians preferred to explain ordinary life events in terms of the situational context in which they occurred, whereas Americans were much more inclined to explain similar events in terms of presumed dispositions. Morris and Peng (1994) found that Chinese newspapers and Chinese students living in the United States tended to explain murders (by both Chinese and American perpetrators) in terms of the situation and even the societal context confronting the murderers, whereas American newspapers and American students were more likely to explain the murders in terms of presumed dispositions of the perpetrators.

Recently Jones and Harris's (1967) experiment was repeated with Korean and American participants (Choi et al., 1999). Like Americans, the Koreans tended to assume that the target person held the position he was advocating. But the two groups responded quite differently if they were placed in the same situation themselves before they made judgments about the target. When observers were required to write an essay, using four arguments specified by the experimenter, the Americans were unaffected, but the Koreans were greatly affected. That is, the Americans' judgments about the target's attitudes were just as much influenced by the target's essay as if they themselves had never experienced the constraints inherent in the situation, whereas the Koreans almost never inferred that the target person had the attitude expressed in the essay.

This is not to say that Asians do not use dispositions in causal analysis or are not occasionally susceptible to the FAE. Growing evidence indicates that when situational cues are not salient, Asians rely on dispositions or manifest the FAE to the same extent as Westerners (Choi et al., 1999; Norenzayan, Choi, & Nisbett, 1999). The cultural difference seems to originate primarily from a stronger East Asian tendency to recognize the causal power of situations.

The cultural differences in the FAE seem to be supported by different folk theories about the causes of human behavior. In one study (Norenzayan et al., 1999), we asked participants how much they agreed with paragraph descriptions of three different philosophies about why people behave as they do: (a) a strongly dispositionist philosophy holding that "how people behave is mostly determined by their personality," (b) a strongly situationist view holding that behavior "is mostly determined by the situation" in which people find themselves, and (c) an interactionist view holding that behavior "is always jointly determined by personality and the situation." Korean and American participants endorsed the first position to the same degree, but Koreans endorsed the situationist and interactionist views more strongly than did Americans.

These causal theories are consistent with cultural conceptions of personality as well. In the same study (Norenzayan et al., 1999), we administered a scale designed to measure agreement with two different theories of personality: entity theory, or the belief that behavior is due to relatively fixed dispositions such as traits, intelligence, and moral character, and incremental theory, or the belief that behavior is conditioned on the situation and that any relevant dispositions are subject to change (Dweck, Hong, & Chiu, 1993). Koreans for the most part rejected entity theory, whereas Americans were equally likely to endorse entity theory and incremental theory.

ANALYTIC VERSUS HOLISTIC COGNITION

The cultural differences in causal cognition go beyond interpretations of human behavior. Morris and Peng (1994) showed cartoons of an individual fish moving in a variety of configurations in relation to a group of fish and asked participants why they thought the actions had occurred. Chinese participants were inclined to attribute the behavior of the individual fish to factors external to the fish (i.e., the group), whereas American participants were more inclined to attribute the behavior of the fish to internal factors. In studies by Peng and Nisbett (reported in Nisbett, Peng, Choi, & Norenzayan, in press), Chinese participants were shown to interpret even the behavior of schematically drawn, ambiguous physical events—such as a round object dropping through a surface and returning to the surface—as being due to the relation between the object and the presumed medium (e.g., water), whereas Americans tended to interpret the behavior as being due to the properties of the object alone.

The Intellectual Histories of East Asia and Europe

Why should Asians and Americans perceive causality so differently? Scholars in many fields, including ethnography, history, and philosophy of science, hold that, at least since the 6th century B.C., there has been a very different intellectual tradition in the West than in the East (especially China and those cultures, like the Korean and Japanese, that were heavily influenced by China; Nisbett et al., in press). The ancient Greeks had an *analytic* stance: The focus was on categorizing the object with reference to its attributes and explaining its behavior using rules about its category memberships. The ancient Chinese had a *holistic* stance, meaning that there was an orientation toward the field in which the object was found and a tendency to explain the behavior of the object in terms of its relations with the field.

In support of these propositions, there is substantial evidence that early Greek and Chinese science and mathematics were quite different in their strengths and weaknesses. Greek science looked for universal rules to explain events and was concerned with categorizing objects with respect to their essences. Chinese science (some people would say it was a technology only, though a technology vastly superior to that of the Greeks) was more pragmatic and concrete and was not concerned with foundations or universal laws. The difference between the Greek and Chinese orientations is well captured by Aristotle's physics, which explained the behavior of an object without reference to the field in which it occurs. Thus, a stone sinks into water because it has the property of gravity, and a piece of wood floats because it has the property of levity. In contrast, the principle that events always occur in some context or field of forces was understood early on in China.

Some writers have suggested that the mentality of East Asians remains more holistic than that of Westerners (e.g., Nakamura, 1960/1988). Thus, modern East Asian laypeople, like the ancient Chinese intelligentsia, are attuned to the field and the overall context in determining events. Western civilization was profoundly shaped by ancient Greece, so one would expect the Greek intellectual stance of object focus to be widespread in the West.

Attention to the Field versus the Object

If East Asians tend to believe that causality lies in the field, they would be expected to attend to the field. If Westerners are more inclined to believe that causality inheres in the object, they might be expected to pay relatively more attention to the object than to the field. There is substantial evidence that this is the case.

Attention to the field as a whole on the part of East Asians suggests that they might find it relatively difficult to separate the object from the field. This notion rests on the concept of *field dependence* (Witkin, Dyk, Faterson, Goodenough, & Karp, 1974). Field dependence refers to a relative difficulty in separating objects from the context in which they are located. One way of measuring field dependence is by means of the rod-and-frame test. In this test, participants look into a long rectangular box at the end of which is a rod. The rod and the box frame can be rotated independently of one another, and participants are asked to state when the rod is vertical. Field dependence is indicated by the extent to which the orientation of the frame influences judgments of the verticality of the rod. The judgments of East Asian (mostly Chinese) participants have been shown to be more field dependent than those of American participants (Ji, Peng, & Nisbett, in press).

In a direct test of whether East Asians pay more attention to the field than Westerners do (Masuda & Nisbett, 1999), Japanese and American participants saw underwater scenes that included one or more *focal* fish (i.e., fish that were larger and faster moving than other objects in the scene) among many other objects, including smaller fish, small animals, plants, rocks, and coral. When asked to recall what they had just viewed, the Japanese and American participants reported equivalent amounts of detail about the focal fish, but the Japanese reported far more detail about almost everything else in the background and made many more references to interactions between focal fish and background objects. After watching the scenes, the participants were shown a focal fish either on the original background or on a new one. The ability of the Japanese to recognize a particular focal fish was impaired if the fish was shown on the "wrong" background. Americans' recognition was uninfluenced by this manipulation.

ORIGINS OF THE CULTURAL DIFFERENCE IN CAUSAL COGNITION

Most of the cross-cultural comparisons we have reviewed compared participants who were highly similar with respect to key demographic variables, namely, age, gender, socioeconomic status, and educational level. Differences in cognitive abilities were controlled for or ruled out as potential explanations for the data in studies involving a task (e.g., the rod-and-frame test) that might be affected by such abilities. Moreover, the predicted differences emerged regardless of whether the East Asians were tested in their native languages in East Asian countries or tested in English in the United States. Thus, the lack of obvious alternative explanations, combined with positive evidence from intellectual history and the convergence of the data across a diverse set of studies (conducted in laboratory as well as naturalistic contexts), points to culturally shared causal theories as the most likely explanation for the group differences.

But why might ancient societies have differed in the causal theories they produced and passed down to their contemporary successor cultures? Attempts to answer such questions must, of course, be highly speculative because they involve complex historical and sociological issues. Elsewhere, we have summarized the views of scholars who have suggested that fundamental differences between societies may result from ecological and economic factors (Nisbett et al., in press). In China, people engaged in intensive farming many centuries before Europeans did. Farmers need to be cooperative with one another, and their societies tend to be collectivist in nature. A focus on the social field may generalize to a holistic understanding of the world. Greece is a land where the mountains descend to the sea and large-scale agriculture is not possible. People earned a living by keeping animals, fishing, and trading. These occupations do not require so much intensive cooperation, and the Greeks were in fact highly individualistic. Individualism in turn encourages attending only to the object and one's goals with regard to it. The social field can be ignored with relative impunity, and causal perception can focus, often mistakenly, solely on the object. We speculate that contemporary societies continue to display these mentalities because the social psychological factors that gave rise to them persist to this day.

Several findings by Witkin and his colleagues (e.g., Witkin et al., 1974), at different levels of analysis, support this historical argument that holistic and analytic cognition originated in collectivist and individualist orientations, respectively. Contemporary farmers are more field dependent than hunters and industrialized peoples; American ethnic groups that operate under tighter social constraints are more field dependent than other groups; and individuals who are attuned to social relationships are more field dependent than those who are less focused on social relationships.

FUTURE DIRECTIONS

A number of questions seem particularly interesting for further inquiry. Should educational practices take into account the differing attentional foci and causal theories of members of different cultural groups? Can the cognitive skills characteristic of one cultural group be transferred to another group? To what extent can economic changes transform the sort of cultural-cognitive system we have described? These and other questions about causal cognition will provide fertile ground for research in the years to come.

RECOMMENDED READING

Choi, I., Nisbett, R. E., & Norenzayan, A. (1999). (See References)

Fiske, A., Kitayama, S., Markus, H. R., & Nisbett, R. E. (1998). The cultural matrix of social psychology. In D. T. Gilbert, S. T. Fiske, & G. Lindzey (Eds.), *The handbook of social psychology* (4th ed., Vol. 2, pp. 915–981). Boston: McGraw-Hill.

Lloyd, G. E. R. (1996). Science in antiquity: The Greek and Chinese cases and their relevance to problems of culture and cognition. In D. R. Olson & N. Torrance (Eds.), *Modes of thought: Explorations in culture and cognition* (pp. 15–33). Cambridge, England: Cambridge University Press.

Nisbett, R. E., Peng, K., Choi, I., & Norenzayan, A. (in press). (See References)

Sperber, D., Premack, D., & Premack, A. J. (Eds.). (1995). *Causal cognition: A multidisciplinary debate*. Oxford, England: Oxford University Press.

NOTE

1. Ara Norenzayan, Centre de Récherche en Epistemoligie Appliquée, Ecole Polytechnique, Paris, France; Richard E. Nisbett, Department of Psychology, University of Michigan, Ann Arbor, Michigan. Address correspondence to Richard E. Nisbett, Department of Psychology, University of Michigan, Ann Arbor, MI 48109; e-mail: nisbett@umich.edu.

REFERENCES

Choi, I., Nisbett, R. E., & Norenzayan, A. (1999). Causal attribution across cultures: Variation and universality. *Psychological Bulletin, 125*, 47–63.

Dweck, C. S., Hong, Y.-Y., & Chiu, C.-Y. (1993). Implicit theories: Individual differences in the likelihood and meaning of dispositional inference. *Personality and Social Psychology Bulletin, 19*, 644–656.

Gardner, H. (1985). *The mind's new science*. New York: Basic Books.

Ji, L., Peng, K., & Nisbett, R. E. (in press). Culture, control, and perception of relationships in the environment. *Journal of Personality and Social Psychology*.

Jones, E. E., & Harris, V. A. (1967). The attribution of attitudes. *Journal of Experimental Social Psychology, 3*, 1–24.

Masuda, T., & Nisbett, R. E. (1999). *Culture and attention to object vs. field*. Unpublished manuscript, University of Michigan, Ann Arbor.

Miller, J. G. (1984). Culture and the development of everyday social explanation. *Journal of Personality and Social Psychology, 46*, 961–978.

Morris, M. W., & Peng, K. (1994). Culture and cause: American and Chinese attributions for social and physical events. *Journal of Personality and Social Psychology, 67*, 949–971.

Nakamura, H. (1988). *The ways of thinking of eastern peoples*. New York: Greenwood Press. (Original work published 1960)

Nisbett, R. E., Peng, K., Choi, I., & Norenzayan, A. (in press). Culture and systems of thought: Holistic vs. analytic cognition. *Psychological Review*.

Norenzayan, A., Choi, I., & Nisbett, R. E. (1999). *Eastern and Western folk psychology and the prediction of behavior*. Unpublished manuscript, University of Michigan, Ann Arbor.

Ross, L. (1977). The intuitive psychologist and his shortcomings. In L. Berkowitz (Ed.), *Advances in experimental social psychology* (Vol. 10, pp. 173–220). New York: Academic Press.

Witkin, H. A., Dyk, R. B., Faterson, H. F., Goodenough, D. R., & Karp, S. A. (1974). *Psychological differentiation*. Potomac, MD: Erlbaum.

QUESTIONS ABOUT MEANING

1. What cultural differences have researchers found in the way people interpret human behavior and causality? How have the intellectual histories of the East and West contributed to these differences?
2. What is *field dependence*? What conditions in ancient China and Greece may help to explain the tendency of modern Asians to be more field dependent than Americans?

QUESTIONS ABOUT RHETORICAL ANALYSIS

1. Review the section titled "Origins of the Cultural Difference in Causal Cognition." What kinds of questions might a critical reader ask about the research findings described in this section and how do the authors respond to potential questions or criticisms? Do you find their argument in this section convincing? Why or why not?
2. Describe the arrangement of major sections. Does it seem logical? Why or why not?
3. Although the authors do not summarize their main ideas in the concluding paragraph, in what way is the conclusion typical of conclusions found in academic arguments? Do the questions posed come naturally from the research described? Explain.

MAKING CONNECTIONS

1. Kuhn (in chapter 9) and Best ("The Illusion of Diffusion"), along with Norenzayan and Nisbett, discuss the reasoning and cognitive abilities of Americans. Put these authors in conversation with each other in an essay about how US culture influences the reasoning abilities of Americans. Do you agree with what these authors say? Why or why not? What changes in public schools do *you* think would improve students' reasoning abilities?
2. More than one's reasoning ability, of course, is shaped by culture. In an essay, discuss one of the ways your culture (national or ethnic) has shaped the person you are.

Psychology

"Cultural Variation in Eye Movements during Scene Perception,"

HANNAH FAYE CHUA, JULIE E. BOLAND, AND RICHARD E. NISBETT

As you learned in the previous selection by Norenzayan and Nisbett, there are differences in how Americans and East Asians remember and interpret what they observe. But why do those differences exist? That is the question Nisbett takes up in the following study, conducted with University of Michigan colleagues Hannah Faye Chua and Julie Boland. Their study appeared in 2005 in the peer-reviewed journal *PNAS*, published by the Proceedings of the National Academy of Sciences. The journal publishes research from the biological, physical, and social sciences.

ABSTRACT

In the past decade, cultural differences in perceptual judgment and memory have been observed: Westerners attend more to focal objects, whereas East Asians attend more to contextual information. However, the underlying mechanisms for the apparent differences in cognitive processing styles have not been known. In the present study, we examined the possibility that the cultural differences arise from culturally different viewing patterns when confronted with a naturalistic scene. We measured the eye movements of American and Chinese participants while they viewed photographs with a focal object on a complex background. In fact, the Americans fixated more on focal objects than did the Chinese, and the Americans tended to look at the focal object more quickly. In addition, the Chinese made more saccades to the background than did the Americans. Thus, it appears that differences in judgment and memory may have their origins in differences in what is actually attended as people view a scene.

KEYWORDS

attention, culture, memory, eye-tracking, visual cognition

A growing literature suggests that people from different cultures have differing cognitive processing styles (1, 2). Westerners, in particular North Americans, tend to be more analytic than East Asians. That is, North Americans attend to focal objects more than do East Asians, analyzing their attributes and assigning them to categories. In contrast, East Asians have been held to be more holistic than Westerners and are more likely to attend to contextual information and make judgments based on relationships and similarities.

Causal attributions for events reflect these differences in analytic vs. holistic thought. For example, Westerners tend to explain events in terms that refer primarily or entirely to salient objects (including people), whereas East Asians are more inclined to explain events in terms of contextual factors (3–5). There also are differences in performance on perceptual judgment and memory tasks (6–8). For example, Masuda and Nisbett (6) asked participants to report what they saw in underwater scenes. Americans emphasized focal objects, that is, large, brightly colored, rapidly moving objects. Japanese reported 60% more information about the background (e.g., rocks, color of water, small nonmoving objects) than did Americans. After viewing scenes containing a single animal against a realistic background, Japanese and American participants were asked to make old/new recognition judgments for animals in a new series of pictures. Sometimes the focal animal was shown against the original background; other times the focal animal was shown against a new background. Japanese and Americans were equally accurate in detecting the focal animal when it was presented in its original background. However, Americans were more accurate than East Asians when the animal was displayed against a new background. A plausible interpretation is that, compared with Americans, the Japanese encoded the scenes more holistically, binding information about the objects with the backgrounds, so that the unfamiliar new background adversely affected the retrieval of the familiar animal.

The difference in attending to objects vs. context also was shown in a perceptual judgment task, the Rod and Frame test (7). American and Chinese participants looked down a long box. At the end of the box was a rod whose orientation could be changed and a frame around the rod that could be moved independently of the rod. The participants' task was to judge when the rod was vertical. Chinese participants' judgments of verticality were more dependent on the context, in that their judgments were more influenced by the position of the frame than were those of American participants. In a change blindness study, Masuda and Nisbett asked American and Japanese participants to view a sequence of still photos and also to view animated vignettes of complex visual scenes (unpublished data). Changes in focal object information (e.g., color and shape of foregrounded objects) and contextual information (e.g., location of background details) were introduced during the sequence of presentations. Overall, the Japanese reported more changes in the contextual details than did the Americans, whereas the Americans reported more changes in the focal objects than did the Japanese. This finding has at least two possible explanations (see ref. 9). On one account, the Asian participants had more detailed mental representations of the backgrounds, whereas the Westerners had more detailed representations of the focal objects. On the other account, the mental representations did not differ with culture, but the two groups differed in their accuracy for detecting a deviation between their mental representation of the background/focal object and the current stimulus.

Clearly, there were systematic differences between the Americans' and the East Asians' performance in the causal perception, memory, and judgment studies. However, it is unclear whether the effects occur at the level of encoding, retrieval, mental comparison, or differences in reporting bias. To identify the stages in perceptual–cognitive processing at which the cultural differences might arise, consider what is known about scene perception: *(i)* Within 100 ms of first viewing a scene, people can often encode the gist of the scene, e.g., "picnic" or "building" (10). *(ii)* People then construct a mental model of the scene in working memory (11). The mental representation is not an exact rendering of the original scene and is usually incomplete in detail (12–13). *(iii)* Although the initial eye fixation may not be related to the configuration of the scene, the following fixations are to the most informative regions of the scene for the task at hand (14). The fixation positions are important because foveated regions are likely to be encoded in greater detail than peripheral regions (15). *(iv)* The mental representation of the scene is then transferred to and consolidated in long-term memory. *(v)* Successful retrieval from long-term memory relies on appropriate retrieval cues. *(vi)* During retrieval, the recalled information may be filtered by experimental demands and cultural expectations. Past studies (3–8) have failed to establish whether the effects are due to differences in perception, encoding, consolidation, recall, comparison judgments, or reporting bias.

To address this issue, we monitored eye movements of the American and the Chinese participants while they viewed scenes containing objects on relatively complex backgrounds. We chose this measure because eye fixations reflect the allocation of attention in a fairly direct manner. Moreover, we have relatively little awareness of how our eyes move under normal viewing conditions. If differences in culture influence how participants actually view and encode the scenes, there will be differences in the pattern of saccades and fixations in the eye movements of the members of the two cultures. [Saccades are rapid, ballistic eye movements that shift gaze from one fixation to another (15).] In particular, we would expect Americans to spend more time looking at the focal objects and less time looking at the context than the Chinese participants. Furthermore, if the Chinese participants perceive the picture more holistically and bind contextual features with features of the focal object, they might make more total saccades when surveying the scene than the Americans. On the other hand, if no eye movement differences emerge between the two cultures, then previous findings of memory and judgment differences are likely due to what happens at later stages, e.g., during memory retrieval or during reporting.

METHODS

Participants

Twenty-five European American graduate students (10 males, 15 females) and 27 international Chinese graduate students (14 males, 12 females, 1 data missing) at the University of Michigan participated in the study.

The mean ages of Americans and Chinese were 24.3 and 25.4 years, respectively. All of the Chinese participants were born in China and had completed their undergraduate degrees there. Participants from the two cultures were matched on age and graduate fields of study. Participants were graduate students from engineering, life sciences, business programs, and, in a few cases, from the social sciences. Recruitment e-mails were sent to a Chinese student organization as well as to different graduate academic departments. Volunteers were each paid $14.00 for their participation in the study.

Materials

A collection of animals, nonliving things, and background scenes was obtained from the COREL image collection (Corel, Eden Prairie, MN), and a few were obtained from a previous study (6). The pictures were manipulated by using PHOTOSHOP software (Adobe Systems, San Jose, CA) to create 36 pictures of single, focal, foregrounded objects (animal or nonliving thing) with realistic complex backgrounds. The final set of pictures contained 20 foregrounded animals and 16 foregrounded nonliving entities, e.g., cars, planes, and boats (see Fig. 13.7 for examples of the pictures shown). The set was composed mostly of culturally neutral photos, plus some Western and Asian objects and backgrounds. This set of 36 pictures was used in the study phase, during which the eye movement data were collected.

For the recognition-memory task, the original 36 objects and backgrounds together with 36 new objects and backgrounds were manipulated to create a set of 72 pictures. Half of the original objects were presented with old backgrounds and the other half with new backgrounds. Similarly, half of the new objects were presented with old backgrounds and the other half with new backgrounds. This procedure resulted in four picture combinations: *(i)* 18 previously seen objects with original backgrounds, *(ii)* 18 previously seen objects with new backgrounds, *(iii)* 18 new

Figure 13.7 Sample pictures presented in the study. Thirty-six pictures with a single foregrounded object (animals or nonliving entities) on realistic backgrounds were presented to participants.

objects with original backgrounds, and (*iv*) 18 new objects with new backgrounds. This set of 72 pictures was used in the object-recognition phase. All participants saw the same set and sequence of trials to make comparisons of performance comparable.

Procedure

Study phase. The participants sat on a chair and placed their chin on a chin rest to standardize the distance of the head from the computer monitor. The distance of the chin rest from the monitor was 52.8 cm. The size of the monitor was 37.4 cm.

At the start of the session, participants wore a 120-Hz head-mounted eye-movement tracker (ISCAN, Burlington, MA), and eye-tracking calibration was established before the presentation of stimuli. After this calibration, participants were given instructions on the screen. They were informed that they would be viewing several pictures, one at a time. Before each picture was presented, a blank screen with a cross sign (+) was to appear. Participants were told to make sure that they looked at that cross sign. Once the picture appeared, they could freely move their eyes to look at the picture. For each of the pictures, participants verbally said a number between 1 and 7, indicating the degree to which they liked the picture (1, don't like at all; 4, neutral; 7, like very much).[†] These instructions were followed by several screens showing a sample of how the task would proceed. Once ready, participants started the actual task of viewing the 36 pictures. Each picture was presented for 3 s. Afterward, participants engaged in several distracter tasks for about 10 min. Participants were moved to a different room and, for example, asked to do a backward-counting task, subtracting 7 starting from 100 until they reached zero.

Object-recognition phase. Participants were brought back to the computer room to complete a recognition-memory task. Participants were told that they would be viewing pictures. Their task was to judge as fast as they could whether they had seen an object before, that is, whether they had seen the particular animal, car, train, boat, etc., in the pictures during the study phase. Participants pressed a key if they believed that they had seen the object before, and they pressed another key if they believed that it was new. If participants were unsure, they were told to make a guess. Participants then were shown a sample picture informing them which item in the picture was the object and that the rest of the visual scene was the background. Participants were informed that each picture would be shown only for a specified period. In the event that the picture had already left the screen, they could still input their response. Seventy-two pictures, including 36 original objects and 36 lure objects, were presented. The objects were presented with either an old or a new background. Each picture was again presented for 3 s, and a fixation screen was presented between the picture presentations.

Demographic questionnaire and debriefing. At the end of the study, participants engaged in an object-familiarity task. All 72 objects were presented against a white screen on a computer. Participants circled "yes" if they thought they had seen the object in real life or in pictorial information before coming to the study and "no" if they had not. This procedure was similar to that in a previous study (6). We repeated the analyses reported in this paper with familiarity as a covariate, and there were no changes in the statistical patterns. Participants also completed a demographic questionnaire asking information about their age, education, family history, and English language ability. Participants were debriefed and paid.

Data analysis. Six participants had a hit rate of <0.5 on the object-recognition task, averaged across conditions. These participants' data were excluded in all statistical analyses. One additional European American had poor eye-tracking data. These exclusions resulted in data for 21 European American and 24 international Chinese participants being included in the eye-tracking analyses.

RESULTS

The results for the object-recognition task were consistent with previous findings (6), indicating that East Asians are less likely to correctly recognize old foregrounded objects when presented in new backgrounds [$F(1, 44) = 5.72$, $P = 0.02$] (Fig. 13.8). Thus, we have additional evidence for relatively holistic perception by East Asians: they appear to "bind" object with background in perception.

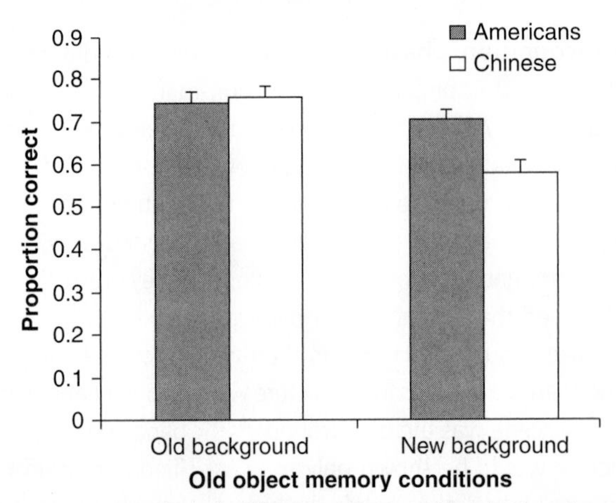

Figure 13.8 Mean accuracy rates from the object-recognition phase (22 Americans and 24 Chinese). Data shown refer to correct recognition of old objects, when the old objects were presented in old backgrounds, compared with when old objects were presented in new backgrounds. Object refers to the single foregrounded animal or nonliving entity on the picture; background refers to the rest of the realistic, complex spatial area on the visual scene.

The eye-movement patterns of American and Chinese participants differed in several ways. As summarized in Fig. 13.9, the American participants looked at the foregrounded object sooner and longer than the Chinese, whereas the Chinese looked more at the background than did the Americans, confirming our predictions. Overall, both groups fixated the background more than the objects (Fig. 13.9*A*), probably because the background occupied a greater area of the visual scene [$F(1, 43) = 72.46$, $P < 0.001$]. The Chinese made more fixations during each picture presentation than the Americans [$F(1, 43) = 4.43$, $P < 0.05$], but this was entirely due to the fact that Chinese made more fixations on the background [$F(1, 43) = 9.50$, $P < 0.005$]. The Americans looked at foregrounded objects 118 ms sooner than did the Chinese [$t(43) = 2.41$, $P = 0.02$] (Fig. 13.9*B*). Participants from both cultures had longer fixations on the objects than on the backgrounds (Fig. 13.9*C*) [$F(1, 43) = 17.27$, $P < 0.001$], but this was far more true for the Americans than for the Chinese [$F(1, 43) = 5.97$, $P < 0.02$]. In short, the cultural difference in the memory study was reflected in the eye movements as well.‡

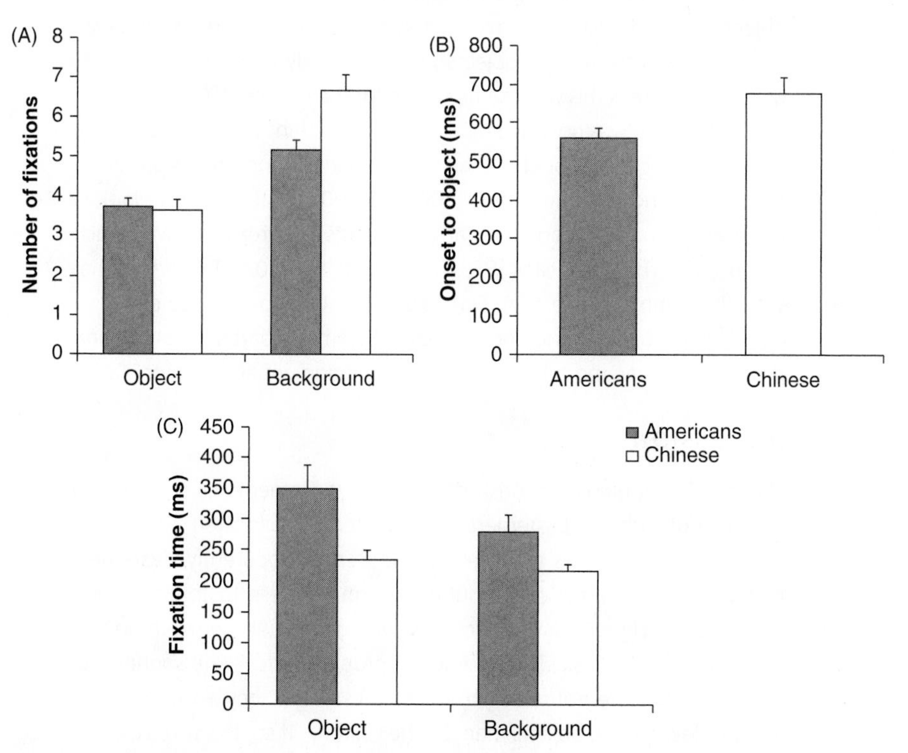

Figure 13.9 Eye movement data. (*A*) Number of fixations to object or background by culture (21 Americans and 24 Chinese). Each picture was presented for 3 s. (*B*) Onset time to object by culture. Time was measured from onset of each picture to first fixation to object, comparing Americans and Chinese. (*C*) Average fixation times to object and background as a function of culture. All figures represent mean scores over 36 trials and SEM.

The cultural difference in eye-movement patterns emerged very early. At the onset of the picture slide, 32–35% of the time both the Americans and the Chinese happened to be looking at the object, but the first saccade increased that percentage by 42.8% for the Americans and only by 26.7% for the Chinese [$t(43) = 2.46$, $P < 0.02$].

To better understand the time course of cultural differences, we examined the fixation patterns across the 3-s duration of picture presentations. Fig. 13.10 shows that whereas the Americans were most likely to be looking at the object for about 600 ms of the first second, the Chinese exhibited a very different eye-movement pattern. For the first 300–400 ms, no cultural differences were observed; at picture onset, both Americans and Chinese fixated the backgrounds more than the focal objects [$F(1, 43) = 235.91$, $P < 0.001$]. By ≈420 ms after picture onset, the Americans were equally likely to be looking at the background and the focal object. At this point, there was an interaction of culture and fixation region, with only the Chinese fixating the backgrounds more than the objects [$F(1, 43) = 6.43$, $P < 0.02$]. Based on Fig. 13.10, the region during which the Americans attended preferentially to the object spanned 420–1,100 ms. Averaging the data across this interval, the Americans fixated the objects proportionately more than the backgrounds, whereas this was not at all true for the Chinese [$F(1, 43) = 7.31$, $P < 0.01$]. There was no time point at which the Chinese were fixating the objects significantly more than the backgrounds during the 3-s presentation. Averaging the data from 1,100 to 3,000 ms, the Chinese looked more at the backgrounds than at the objects, whereas this was much less true for the Americans [$F(1, 43) = 6.64$, $P < 0.02$]. Taken together with the summary data from Fig. 13.9, these findings provide clear evidence that cultural differences in eye-movement patterns mirror and probably underlie the cultural differences in judgment and memory tasks.

DISCUSSION

The present findings demonstrate that eye movements can differ as a function of culture. Easterners and Westerners allocated attentional resources differently as they viewed the scenes. Apparently, Easterners and Westerners differ in attributing informativeness to foregrounded objects vs. backgrounds in the context of a generic "How much do you like this picture?" task. The Americans' propensity to fixate sooner and longer on the foregrounded objects suggests that they encoded more visual details for the objects than did the Chinese. If so, this could explain the Americans' more accurate recognition of the objects, even against a new background. The Chinese pattern of more balanced fixations to the foreground object and background is consistent with previous reports of holistic processing of visual scenes (6–8). Thus, previous findings of

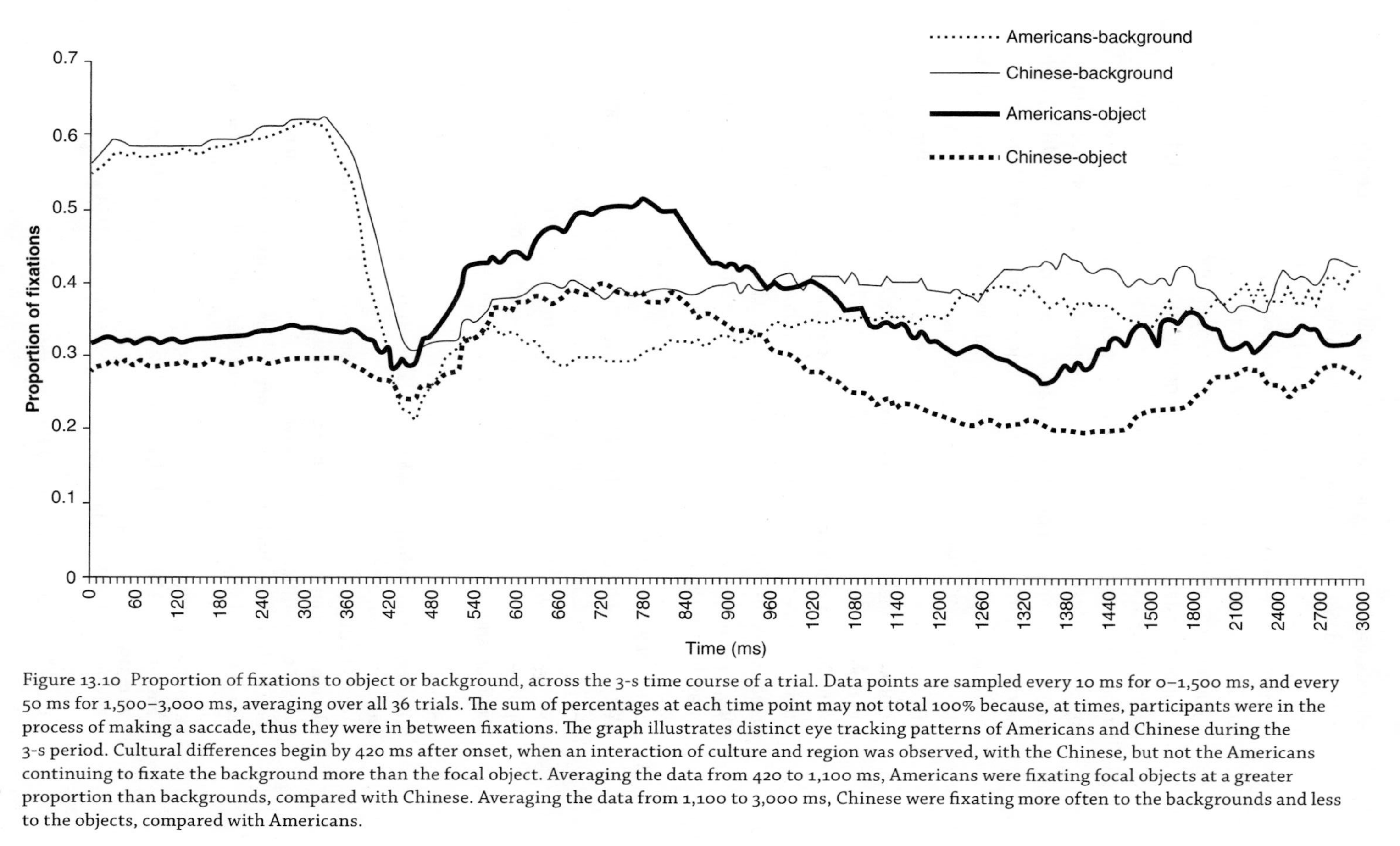

Figure 13.10 Proportion of fixations to object or background, across the 3-s time course of a trial. Data points are sampled every 10 ms for 0–1,500 ms, and every 50 ms for 1,500–3,000 ms, averaging over all 36 trials. The sum of percentages at each time point may not total 100% because, at times, participants were in the process of making a saccade, thus they were in between fixations. The graph illustrates distinct eye tracking patterns of Americans and Chinese during the 3-s period. Cultural differences begin by 420 ms after onset, when an interaction of culture and region was observed, with the Chinese, but not the Americans continuing to fixate the background more than the focal object. Averaging the data from 420 to 1,100 ms, Americans were fixating focal objects at a greater proportion than backgrounds, compared with Chinese. Averaging the data from 1,100 to 3,000 ms, Chinese were fixating more often to the backgrounds and less to the objects, compared with Americans.

cultural differences in visual memory are likely due to how people from Eastern and Western cultures view scenes and are not solely due to cultural norms or expectations for reporting knowledge about scenes.

Cultural differences in eye movements, memory for scenes, and perceptual and causal judgments could stem from several sources, including differences in experience, expertise, or socialization. It is common to consider such factors in high-level cognition, but because such factors can influence the allocation of attention, they influence lower level cognition as well. Our hypothesis is that differential attention to context and object are stressed through socialization practices, as demonstrated in studies on childrearing practices by East Asians and Americans (16, 17). The childrearing practices are, in turn, influenced by societal differences. East Asians live in relatively complex social networks with prescribed role relations (18, 19). Attention to context is, therefore, important for effective functioning. In contrast, Westerners live in less constraining social worlds that stress independence and allow them to pay less attention to context.

The present results provide a useful warning in a world where opportunities to meet people from other cultural backgrounds continue to increase: people from different cultures may allocate attention differently, even within a shared environment. The result is that we see different aspects of the world, in different ways.

ACKNOWLEDGMENTS

We thank Chi-yue Chiu and Daniel Simons for their reviews of this paper and Meghan Carr Ahern, Chirag Patel, Jason Taylor, Holly Templeton, and Jeremy Phillips for their assistance in the study. This work was supported by the Culture and Cognition Program at the University of Michigan and National Science Foundation Grant 0132074.

NOTES

† The Chinese participants gave higher liking ratings than did the Americans (*Ms*, 4.64 vs. 4.16; $P < 0.005$)

‡ Across both groups and for each participant group, we examined the correlation between six eye-movement variables and the object-memory index, i.e., the difference score between old object–old background memory and old object–new background memory. Of the 18 correlations, only 2 were marginally significant, and neither of these was readily interpretable.

REFERENCES

1. Nisbett, R. E., Peng, K., Choi, I. & Norenzayan, A. (2001) *Psychol. Rev.* **2**, 291–310.
2. Nisbett, R. E. & Masuda, T. (2003) *Proc. Natl. Acad. Sci. USA* **100**, 11163–11170.
3. Choi, I. & Nisbett, R. E. (1998) *Pers. Soc. Psychol. Bull.* **24**, 949–960.

4. Morris, M. W. & Peng, K. (1994) *J. Pers. Soc. Psychol.* **67**, 949–971.
5. Chua, H. F., Leu, J. & Nisbett, R. E. (2005) *Pers. Soc. Psychol. Bull.* **31**, 10925–10934.
6. Masuda, T. & Nisbett, R. E. (2001) *J. Pers. Soc. Psychol.* **81**, 922–934.
7. Ji, L., Peng, K. & Nisbett, R. E. (2000) *J. Pers. Soc. Psychol.* **78**, 943–955.
8. Kitayama, S., Duffy, S., Kawamura, T. & Larsen, J. T. (2003) *Psychol. Sci.* **14**, 201–206.
9. Simons, D. J. & Rensink, R. A. (2005) *Trends Cognit. Sci.* **9**, 16–20.
10. Potter, M. C. (1976) *J. Exp. Psychol. Hum. Learn. Mem.* **2**, 509–522.
11. Enns, J. T. (2004) *The Thinking Eye, the Seeing Brain: Explorations in Visual Cognition* (Norton, New York).
12. Intraub, H. (1997) *Trends Cognit. Sci.* **1**, 217–212.
13. Potter, M. C., O'Connor, D. H. & Olivia, A. (2002) *J. Vision* **2**, 516.
14. Henderson, J. H. & Hollingworth, A. (1999) *Annu. Rev. Psychol.* **50**, 243–271.
15. Smith, E. E., Fredrickson, B., Loftus, G. & Nolen-Hoeksema, S. (2002) *Atkinson and Hilgard's Introduction to Psychology* (Wadsworth, Belmont, CA), 14th Ed.
16. Fernald, A. & Morikawa, H. (1993) *Child Dev.* **64**, 637–656.
17. Tardif, T., Gelman, S. A. & Xu, F. (1999) *Child Dev.* **70**, 620–635.
18. Markus, H. R. & Kitayama, S. (1991) *Psychol. Rev.* **98**, 224–253.
19. Nisbett, R. E. (2003) *The Geography of Thought: How Asians and Westerners Think Differently . . . And Why* (Free Press, New York).

Hannah Faye Chua, Julie E. Boland, and Richard E. Nisbett (to whom correspondence should be addressed; e-mail nisbett@umich.edu), Department of Psychology, University of Michigan, 530 Church Street, Ann Arbor, MI 48109–1043.

QUESTIONS ABOUT MEANING

1. Describe the participants, methods, and findings for Chua, Boland, and Nisbett's study. How does this research expand the existing body of research?
2. What practical value do the authors suggest their research has?

QUESTIONS FOR RHETORICAL ANALYSIS

1. Identify the function or purpose of each paragraph of the introduction section. Is the organization and structure of the introduction typical or atypical of original research reports? Explain.
2. Identify steps the authors took in their sample selection *and* procedure to prevent outside factors from being responsible for any differences between the two groups of participants. (For example, compare the makeup of the two groups.) Do you think the methods were sufficient to ensure reliable results?

3. What are the various purposes of the figures? How do the figures aid in the reader's understanding?

MAKING CONNECTIONS

1. In his book, *Intelligence and How to Get It: Why Schools and Cultures Count*, Richard Nisbett describes the "power of the environment to influence intelligence potential" (2). Some believe that intelligence is largely genetic; Nisbett argues that "society is making ever greater demands on intelligence, and cultural and educational environments have been changing in such a way as to make the population as a whole smarter—and smart in different ways than in the past" (2).

   Write an essay in which you discuss the influence of social networks, culture, or other environmental factors on a person's reasoning abilities or intelligence potential. Or respond to Nisbett's claim that as a population we are becoming smarter than past generations. Draw from additional sources (such as Kuhn [chapter 9]) as well as your own observations or experiences.
2. Chua, Boland, and Nisbett conclude their article by saying, "We see different aspects of the world, in different ways." The reasons for this, of course, go beyond differences in cultural backgrounds.

   Conduct your own informal study to see how perceptions vary. Show a small sample of people a photo of a scene. You might, for example, select a scene depicting people engaged in conversation or an activity. After allowing participants to view the image, remove it from view and ask them what they remember. Or, as an alternative exercise, ask respondents to interpret what is going on in the scene. Record responses and interview participants to learn more about their interpretations. You might ask participants what they noticed first, why they interpreted the scene as they did, etc. Describe your findings in either an essay or an IMRAD-style report that identifies your study goals, your participants and procedure, and what you learned about the various ways participants "saw" and remembered a single photo.

WORK CITED

Nisbett, Richard E. *Intelligence and How to Get It: Why Schools and Cultures Count.* New York: W. W. Norton, 2010. Print.

CHAPTER 14

Perceptions and Perspectives

We do not all perceive words, images, and events in the same way. Depending on our background, age, interests, or circumstances, we will notice different things and interpret them in different ways. A mechanic hears the engine of a car differently than others do; a wine taster tastes subtleties most people miss; a professional baseball player can literally see the rotation of a fastball. Cultural backgrounds also influence perceptions, as demonstrated by Chua, Boland, and Nisbett's research reported in chapter 13.

The readings that open this chapter suggest another reason we may interpret or remember events differently than others do: We want to preserve a certain image of ourselves. You may recall Toma and Hancock's explanation of self-affirmation theory from chapter 2: "The primary premise of self-affirmation theory is that people have a fundamental need to see themselves as valuable, worthy, and good." Sometimes that means we must revise our memories. In her article "Prestige-Enhancing Memory Distortions," Elizabeth Loftus, who is an expert on the fallibility of memory (and featured in chapter 16), describes what research has shown about people's tendency to remember events in a biased way:

> People remember their grades as better than they were. People remember that they voted in elections that they did not vote in. People remember that their children walked and talked at an earlier age than they really did. These are some prime examples of how we distort our memories in ways that allow us to feel better about ourselves. . . .

Why are people so prone to misremember events? We want our memories to align with our self-image.

The psychological term for the tendency to explain away anything that conflicts with what we want to believe is *cognitive dissonance*. It is the topic of the first two readings in this chapter. In his aptly named essay "Kidding Ourselves," psychology professor Steven Pinker argues that most people can convince themselves that their actions are justified. The reluctance to accept evidence that conflicts with our self-perception is also discussed by social psychologists Carol Tavris and Elliot Aronson in "'Why Won't They Admit They're Wrong?' and Other Skeptics' Mysteries."

Next, two research studies demonstrate perception bias. In the article "I Smoke but I Am Not a Smoker," advertising professors Youjin Choi, Sejung Marina Choi, and Nora Rifon attempt to understand how some people can claim that they are not smokers yet still smoke. The authors suggest that these smokers are trying to resolve the "disparity between their actual behavior and self-identity." Self-perception bias is also demonstrated in the article "The End of History Illusion," by psychology professors Jordi Quoidbach, Daniel Gilbert, and Timothy Wilson. The authors found that while most people can recognize that they have changed in the past decade, they still believe they will not change in the next ten years.

Limited perspective is also the subject of research by business professor Francesca Gino, featured in this chapter's paired readings. Gino studies correspondence bias, which occurs when people judge the behavior of others without considering the circumstances. In an article written for *The Wall Street Journal*, Gino advises managers to look at more than just accomplishments when promoting or hiring employees. It's also important to consider how those accomplishments were obtained. Unfortunately, many people don't judge accomplishments in context, as demonstrated in the next article, "Correspondence Bias in Performance Evaluation: Why Grade Inflation Works." Don Moore, Samuel Swift, and Zachariah Sharek, along with Gino, found that people who were asked to rate graduate school applications failed to consider the difficulty of the classes taken when they compared students' GPAs.

A different kind of bias—myside bias—is the subject of Jonathan Baron's article "Myside Bias in Thinking about Abortion." Like Gino, Baron found evidence that people tend to view issues from limited perspectives, and they often fail to consider more than one side of an argument.

In the final selection, neuroscientist V. S. Ramachandran describes *scotomas*, or spots in a person's field of vision where vision is absent or reduced. Just as people are unaware of their figurative blind spots, people are "blissfully unaware" of their literal blind spots.

Remembering that we all see situations from different perspectives certainly has practical benefits for anyone who lives or works with others. Recognizing that there are always multiple ways of looking at a situation also enhances our ability to write more nuanced and thoughtful analyses of issues.

WORK CITED

Loftus, Elizabeth F. "Prestige-Enhancing Memory Distortions." *Psychologist* 25.1 (2012): 26. Web. 18 Mar. 2014.

Psychology

"Kidding Ourselves," STEVEN PINKER

"Most people claim they are above average in any positive trait you name: leadership, sophistication, athletic prowess, managerial ability, even driving skill," writes Steven Pinker, professor of psychology at Harvard University. Of course, not everyone is above average. In fact, when it comes to how we see ourselves, most of us spend a good deal of time "kidding ourselves." Pinker takes a look at self-deception in the following selection, taken from his 1997 book *How the Mind Works*.

The ideal of the self as a unified rational decision-maker is under assault from many directions, and one of them is the modern science of the mind, particularly evolutionary psychology and cognitive neuroscience.

The playwright Jerome K. Jerome once said, "It is always the best policy to tell the truth, unless, of course, you are an exceptionally good liar." It's hard to lie well, even about your own intentions, which only you can verify. Intentions come from emotions, and emotions have evolved displays on the face and body. Unless you are a master of the Stanislavsky method, you will have trouble faking them; in fact, they probably evolved *because* they were hard to fake. Worse, lying is stressful, and anxiety has its own telltale markers. They are the rationale for polygraphs, the so-called lie detectors, and humans evolved to be lie detectors too. Then there is the annoying fact that some propositions logically entail others. Since *some* of the things you say will be true, you are always in danger of exposing your own lies. As the Yiddish saying goes, a liar must have a good memory.

Robert Trivers, pursuing his theory of the emotions to its logical conclusion, notes that in a world of walking lie detectors the best strategy is to believe your own lies. You can't leak your hidden intentions if you don't think that they *are* your intentions. According to his theory of self-deception, the conscious mind sometimes hides the truth from itself the better to hide it from others. But the truth is useful, so it should be registered somewhere in the mind, walled off from the parts that interact with other people. There is an obvious similarity to Freud's theory of the unconscious and the defense mechanisms of the ego (such as repression, projection, denial, and rationalization), though the explanation is completely different. George Orwell stated it in *1984:* "The secret of rulership is to combine a belief in one's own infallibility with a power to learn from past mistakes."

The neuroscientist Michael Gazzaniga has shown that the brain blithely weaves false explanations about its motives. Split-brain patients have had their cerebral hemispheres surgically disconnected as a treatment for epilepsy. Language circuitry is in the left hemisphere, and the left half of the visual field is registered in the isolated right hemisphere, so the part of the split-brain person that can talk is unaware of the left half of his world. The right hemisphere is still active, though, and can carry out simple commands presented in the left visual field, like "Walk" or "Laugh." When the patient (actually, the patient's left hemisphere) is asked why he walked out (which we know was a response to the command presented to the right hemisphere), he ingenuously replies, "To get a Coke." When asked why he is laughing, he says, "You guys come up and test us every month. What a way to make a living!"

Our confabulations, not coincidentally, present us in the best light. Literally hundreds of experiments in social psychology say so. The humorist Garrison Keillor describes the fictitious community of Lake Wobegon, "where the women are strong, the men are good-looking, and all the children are above average." Indeed, most people claim they are above average in any positive trait you name: leadership, sophistication, athletic prowess, managerial ability, even driving skill. They rationalize the boast by searching for an *aspect* of the trait that they might in fact be good at. The slow drivers say they are above average in safety, the fast ones that they are above average in reflexes.

More generally, we delude ourselves about how benevolent and how effective we are, a combination that social psychologists call beneffectance. When subjects play games that are rigged by the experimenter, they attribute their successes to their own skill and their failures to the luck of the draw. When they are fooled in a fake experiment into thinking they have delivered shocks to another subject, they derogate the victim, implying that he deserved the punishment. Everyone has heard of "reducing cognitive dissonance," in which people invent a new opinion to resolve a contradiction in their minds. For example, a person will recall enjoying a boring task if he had agreed to recommend it to others for paltry pay. (If the person had been enticed to recommend the task for generous pay, he accurately recalls that the task was boring.) As originally conceived of by the psychologist Leon Festinger, cognitive dissonance is an unsettled feeling that arises from an inconsistency in one's beliefs. But that's not right: there is no contradiction between the proposition "The task is boring" and the proposition "I was pressured into lying that the task was fun." Another social psychologist, Elliot Aronson, nailed it down: people doctor their beliefs only to eliminate a contradiction with the proposition "I am nice and in control." Cognitive dissonance is always triggered by blatant evidence that you are not as beneficent and effective as you would like people to think. The urge to reduce it is the urge to get your self-serving story straight.

Sometimes we have glimpses of our own self-deception. When does a negative remark sting, cut deep, hit a nerve? When some part of us knows it is true. If every part knew it was true, the remark would not sting; it would be old news. If no part thought it was true, the remark would roll off; we could dismiss it as false. Trivers recounts an experience that is all too familiar (at least to me). One of his papers drew a published critique, which struck him at the time as vicious and unprincipled, full of innuendo and slander. Rereading the article years later, he was surprised to find that the wording was gentler, the doubts more reasonable, the attitude less biased than he had remembered. Many others have made such discoveries; they are almost the definition of "wisdom."

> If there were a verb meaning "to believe falsely," it would not have any significant first person, present indicative.
>
> —Ludwig Wittgenstein

> There's one way to find out if a man is honest: ask him; if he says yes, you know he's crooked.
>
> —Mark Twain

> Our enemies' opinion of us comes closer to the truth than our own.
>
> —La Rochefoucauld

> Oh wad some power the giftie gie us
> To see oursels as ithers see us!
>
> —Robert Burns

No one can examine the emotions without seeing in them the source of much human tragedy. I don't think we should blame the animals; it's clear enough how natural selection engineered our instincts to suit our needs. We shouldn't blame selfish genes, either. They endow us with selfish motives, but they just as surely endow us with the capacity for love and a sense of justice. What we should appreciate and fear is the cunning designs of the emotions themselves. Many of their specs are not for gladness and understanding: think of the happiness treadmill, the Sirens' song, the sham emotions, the doomsday machines, the caprice of romance, the pointless punishment of grief. But self-deception is perhaps the cruelest motive of all, for it makes us feel right when we are wrong and emboldens us to fight when we ought to surrender.

Trivers writes,

> Consider an argument between two closely bound people, say, husband and wife. Both parties believe that one is an altruist—of long standing, relatively pure in motive, and much abused—while the other is characterized by a pattern of selfishness spread over hundreds of incidents. They only disagree over who is altruistic

> and who selfish. It is noteworthy that the argument may appear to burst forth spontaneously, with little or no preview, yet as it rolls along, two whole landscapes of information processing appear to lie already organized, waiting only for the lightning of anger to show themselves.

In cartoons and movies, the villains are mustache-twirling degenerates, cackling with glee at their badness. In real life, villains are convinced of their rectitude. Many biographers of evil men start out assuming that their subjects are cynical opportunists and reluctantly discover that they are ideologues and moralists. If Hitler was an actor, concluded one, he was an actor who believed in the part.

Still, thanks to the complexity of our minds, we need not be perpetual dupes of our own chicanery. The mind has many parts, some designed for virtue, some designed for reason, some clever enough to outwit the parts that are neither. One self may deceive another, but every now and then a third self sees the truth.

QUESTIONS ABOUT MEANING

1. *Cognitive dissonance* is a term you'll see several writers in this chapter use. What is it? What examples of the phenomenon does Pinker give?
2. Look up "Stanislavsky method" if you are unfamiliar with the term. How does the reference relate to Pinker's larger point?

QUESTIONS FOR RHETORICAL ANALYSIS

1. How would you describe the structure of Pinker's argument or how would you outline it? What recurring topic connects the paragraphs?
2. List the credentials or professions of the various experts cited, beginning with Jerome. (Look up any name you don't recognize that is not identified for you.) What do the references to people from various disciplines and professions contribute to Pinker's argument? When Pinker does explain who people are, what sentence pattern does he often use for concisely doing so?

MAKING CONNECTIONS

1. Do an online search to learn what the Dunning-Kruger effect is. How does it relate to *cognitive dissonance*? Have you observed the Dunning-Kruger effect in others or, in hindsight, do you now recognize it in an earlier version of yourself? Explain and illustrate.
2. Pinker's article brings to mind other writers who discuss similar topics, including Best, "The Illusion of Diffusion"; Quoidbach, Gilbert, and Wilson; Tavris and Aronson; Baron; and Choi, Choi, and Rifon. Combine examples from one or more of these writers with examples from Pinker to illustrate and explain the tendency of most people to ignore evidence that contradicts what they want to believe.

Psychology

"'Why Won't They Admit They're Wrong?' and Other Skeptics' Mysteries," CAROL TAVRIS AND ELLIOT ARONSON

The following article, written by social psychologists Carol Tavris and Elliot Aronson, appeared in 2007 in the *Skeptical Inquirer*, a magazine that "examines the latest claims of the paranormal and pseudoscience from a critical and scientific perspective." The topic of Tavris and Aronson's article is more commonplace than the paranormal but no less mysterious: Why is it so hard to see our own faults? Tavris and Aronson demonstrate that we all have difficulty accepting evidence that contradicts what we want to believe—especially what we want to believe about ourselves.

One of the greatest challenges for scientists and educators is persuading people to give up beliefs they hold dear when the evidence clearly indicates that they should. Why aren't most people grateful for the data? It's easy to make fun of others who won't give up ideas or practices that scientific research has shown to be demonstrably wrong—therapeutic touch, alien abduction, the Rorschach Inkblot Test— or beliefs in haunted houses and psychic detective skills that this magazine keeps exposing as fraud or delusion. It's harder to see that the mechanism that keeps these people from admitting they are wrong afflicts us, too—all of us, even skeptics.

The motivational mechanism underlying the reluctance to be wrong, change our minds, admit serious mistakes, and accept unwelcome findings is cognitive dissonance. The theory of cognitive dissonance was invented fifty years ago by Leon Festinger, who defined *dissonance* as a state of tension that occurs whenever a person holds two cognitions that are psychologically inconsistent, such as "Smoking is a dumb thing to do because it could kill me" and "I smoke two packs a day." Dissonance produces mental discomfort, a state that is as unpleasant as extreme hunger, and people don't rest easy until they find a way to reduce it. Smokers can reduce dissonance either by quitting or by convincing themselves that smoking isn't really so harmful and may even be beneficial. The recent lineup of Republican men who preach that homosexuality is a sin and a "choice" reduce their dissonance when caught in public places with their pants down by saying, "I'm not gay—I was just under stress."

In a sense, dissonance theory is a theory of our mental blind spots—of how and why we block information that might make us question our behavior or convictions. The theory has been supported by many discoveries in cognitive science that have identified the built-in biases of the human mind. One of the most effective ways the mind maintains consonant beliefs is through the confirmation bias—the fact that we tend to notice and remember information that confirms what we believe and ignore or forget information that disconfirms it. (Indeed, one of the reasons that scientific thinking does not come naturally to many people is precisely because it requires the investigator to consider disconfirming—dissonant—evidence for a hypothesis.) Another central bias is the belief that *we* aren't biased, everyone else is. *We* see things clearly; what is the matter with those other people? What are they *thinking*? What they are thinking, of course, is that *they* see things clearly and we don't.

Dissonance is uncomfortable enough when two cognitions conflict, but it is most painful when an important element of the self-concept is threatened: for example, when information challenges how we see ourselves, challenges a central belief (religious, political, or intellectual), or questions a memory or story we use to explain our lives. When that happens, the easiest way to reduce dissonance is simply to reject the information (it's stupid; it's flat-out wrong) or kill the messenger (he's biased, after all). But even more significantly, when people behave in a way that is inconsistent with their own view of themselves as good, smart, ethical, and kind, they tend to reduce dissonance not by changing those self-concepts but by justifying their behavior to themselves. If I am good and kind, then by definition the bad or unkind thing I did was warranted: *They started it. He deserved it. Everyone does it. I was only following orders.*

The nonconscious mechanism of self-justification is not the same thing as lying or making excuses to others to save face or save a job. It is more powerful and more dangerous than the explicit lie, because it prohibits our own awareness that we are wrong about a belief or that we did something foolish, unethical, or cruel. Dissonance theory therefore predicts that it's not only bad people who do bad things. It also shows that good people do bad things and smart people cling to foolish beliefs precisely to preserve their belief that they are good, smart people. This is why, when skeptics wave their reams of reasoned data at people who have just sold their house and cow to follow a delusional doomsday prophet, what they are mostly doing is making the followers feel really stupid. It is much more soothing for the followers to justify their actions by saying, "Thank God we sold the house and cow for our brilliant leader! Our devotion spared the world from disaster." This was precisely the reasoning of the followers of one such doomsday prophet whom Festinger and his colleagues described in their early study of dissonance in action, *When Prophecy Fails.*

Numerous examples from the vast realms of pseudoscience fill these pages, so let's take an example that, unfortunately, is becoming increasingly common among real scientists. Most scientists pride themselves on maintaining intellectual integrity. Yet, with the breakdown of the firewall between research and commerce, scientists' intellectual independence is being whittled away. Many scientists, like plants turning toward the sun, are turning toward the interests of their sponsors without even being aware that they are doing so. When investigators have compared the results of studies funded independently and those funded by industry, they have consistently uncovered a "funding bias." In a typical example, 161 studies, all published during the same six-year span, examined the possible risks of four chemicals to human health. Of the studies funded by industry, only 14 percent found harmful effects on health. Of those funded independently, fully 60 percent found harmful effects.

Most of the scientists funded by industry are not consciously cheating, nor are they corrupt like the few who blatantly fabricate data to win fame and fortune. Rather, they are decent people who have the same cognitive blind spots we all do. If you are an independent scientist and your research reveals an ambiguous finding about your new drug—perhaps a discernable but statistically insignificant increased risk of heart attack—you will probably say, "This is troubling; let's investigate further. Is this increased risk a fluke, was it due to the drug, or were the patients unusually vulnerable?" However, if you are an industry-funded scientist motivated to show that your new drug is effective and better than older drugs, you may unwittingly lean in the direction of resolving the ambiguity in your sponsor's favor. "It was a fluke. Those patients were already quite sick anyway." This was the reasoning of the Merck-funded investigators who had been studying the company's multibillion-dollar drug Vioxx before evidence of the drug's risks was produced by independent scientists.

In the need to reduce dissonance, the Merck-funded scientists are no different from people who believe in the efficacy of the Rorschach or therapeutic touch. By justifying their decision to support the drug and minimize disconfirming data, they preserved their feelings of integrity and of being above the conflicts of interest that so clearly taint everyone else's judgments.

Cognitive dissonance is hardwired, but how we choose to reduce it is not. Just as good drivers learn to correct for that blind spot in their rear vision, good thinkers can learn to correct for the blind spots in their reasoning. Scientists must be just as vigilant about addressing potential biases and conflicts of interest that can affect their work as they are about noting biases in others' research. And we can all try to avoid that tone of "we think skeptically and you don't." One exercise in humility is to recall the dissonant pangs of embarrassment we felt when we, too, closed our minds to evidence to preserve a cherished belief. Our colleagues and friends will thank us for admitting it. And who knows, we might actually learn a little something from the mistakes we've made.

QUESTIONS ABOUT MEANING

1. What is *cognitive dissonance* and *confirmation bias*?
2. Tavris and Aronson describe the human tendency to accept evidence that supports what we already believe but ignore or dispute evidence that goes against our beliefs. Even academics, trained to critically assess evidence, fall prey to confirmation bias. What evidence do Tavris and Aronson cite to demonstrate confirmation bias among academics?

QUESTIONS FOR RHETORICAL ANALYSIS

1. In the final paragraph, Tavris and Aronson compare the mental blind spots caused by cognitive dissonance to the blind spot of a driver. Earlier, they compare scientists who demonstrate "funding bias" to "plants turning toward the sun." Do you find these to be apt metaphors? Why or why not?
2. Throughout the article, but especially in the final paragraph, the authors use first-person pronouns. Why is that an important ethos move, given the subject matter?

MAKING CONNECTIONS

1. Write an essay in which you recall an instance when you ignored evidence that challenged something you believed. What evidence did you ignore or reject that you now know, with the benefit of hindsight, you should have considered? How did you justify ignoring the evidence

at the time? *Why* do you think you ignored the evidence? (What beliefs were being challenged or what motivation did you have for ignoring the evidence?) Tavris and Aronson conclude their article by encouraging us to "learn to correct for the blind spots" in our reasoning. How might a person learn to do this? What do you now know *you* could have done differently in the situation you describe?

2. Like Ramachandran's article "Creativity versus Skepticism within Science," Tavris and Aronson's article was originally published in *The Skeptical Inquirer* magazine. *The Skeptical Inquirer* is the "official journal" of the Committee for Skeptical Inquiry, an organization committed to promoting "scientific inquiry, critical investigation, and the use of reason in examining controversial and extraordinary claims."

   All successful writers tailor their message and style to the intended audience and forum. In what ways are the articles by Ramachandran and Tavris and Aronson well suited for publication in *The Skeptical Inquirer*? How is the subject matter fitting and how do the authors tailor their writing for readers of this magazine?

Advertising

Excerpt from "'I Smoke But I Am Not a Smoker': Phantom Smokers and the Discrepancy between Self-Identity and Behavior," YOUJIN CHOI, SEJUNG MARINA CHOI, AND NORA RIFON

Would anyone admit "I smoke" and also claim "but I am not a smoker"? Yes, according to research conducted by advertising professors Youjin Choi, Sejung Marina Choi, and Nora Rifon. They introduce the concept of "phantom smokers"—people who claim they are not smokers, but nevertheless admit they smoke cigarettes. Their explanation for this class of smokers brings to mind the concept of *cognitive dissonance* discussed by previous writers in this chapter.

Choi, Choi, and Rifon's research appeared in 2010 in the peer-reviewed *Journal of American College Health*, which publishes articles about students' mental and physical health. The original article describes two studies. Included here are Study 1 and the general discussion.

ABSTRACT

Objective: *This article presents the development of a new smoking status, the "phantom smokers," who do not view themselves as smokers but report smoking cigarettes.* **Participants**: *Students from 2 universities in Michigan (N = 899; October 2005) and Florida (N = 1,517; May*

2006) participated in surveys. **Methods***: Respondents in Michigan completed measures regarding smoking status and tobacco use, and respondents in Florida completed measures regarding smoking status, tobacco use, smoking consequences, and norms.* **Results***: The studies identify the incidence of phantom smokers (29.6% in Michigan and 5.5% in Florida). Different questions resulted in different smoking rates. Phantom smokers expect more negative affect reduction and social facilitation from smoking than nonsmokers. Phantom smokers display ambivalent attitudes toward a typical smoker's image. They experience less pressure to change their smoking behavior than smokers.* **Conclusion***: Phantom smokers' dissociation from smokers should be recognized and targeted as a distinct group for antismoking messages.*

KEYWORDS

attitudes toward smoking, college health, college students' smoking, phantom smoker, smokers

As the top preventable cause of disease and death in the United States, smoking continues to be a critical public health issue. Although the rate of tobacco use has slightly declined among men and high school students in recent years, approximately 45.1 million Americans still smoke cigarettes.[1] Smoking causes an estimated 438,000 deaths, or about 1 of every 5 deaths, each year.[2] According to the 2008 National Survey on Drug Use and Health, young adults maintained the highest rate of cigarette smoking (41.4%).[3]

The sustained rate of cigarette smoking, in conjunction with the medical and financial gravity of the consequences of cigarette smoking, offers strong motivation for public health, public policy, and regulatory stakeholders to create better strategies for reducing the number of new and continuing smokers. As part of that effort, researchers and public health professionals have developed smoker typologies that describe different levels of smoking status, such as experimenters, occasional smokers, and regular smokers, mostly based on self-reported smoking frequency or amount.[4–8] For example, the Harvard School of Public Health defines people who smoke fewer than 1 cigarette per day as light smokers and those who smoke more than a pack per day as heavy smokers.[6] Using self-reported smoking frequency, Wetter et al identified 3 groups: daily smokers, occasional smokers, and nonsmokers.[7] Another study defined smokers as occasional, low-rate, or regular based on smoking amount and frequency.[8] These typologies help target cessation programs to different groups of smokers based on smoking status as well as related perceptions towards smoking.[9,10]

However, recent research[11,12] found that when college students classified as smokers based on smoking frequency and amount were asked to self-identify as a smoker or nonsmoker, they did not necessarily identify themselves as smokers. These findings hint at the existence of a group of smokers whose behavior might clash with their self-identity related to smoking. Despite this discrepancy between smoking behavior and self-identity and its potential impact on future smoking behavior and self-perception, there have been no research efforts to delve into this issue.

We propose the concept of "phantom smokers" as individuals who do not self-identify with being a smoker, but who nevertheless admit smoking cigarettes. The definition suggests that phantom smokers may experience disparity between their actual behavior and self-identity and possibly underestimate negative health consequences from smoking. The discrepancy between behavior and identity is key to the concept of phantom smoking and distinguishes phantom smokers from other types of smokers. Yet current classifications do not embrace this emerging category and no research to date has examined if phantom smokers indeed exist. Therefore, the main purpose of this study is to empirically test the existence of phantom smokers. Additionally, we offer a baseline understanding of phantom smokers' perception and behavior of smoking. Phantom smokers' failure to admit their smoking status makes it difficult to reach and impact them in public health campaigns. To effectively address this group of smokers, their ethos should be comprehended and new approaches to prevention and treatment should be devised accordingly.

With 2 studies having college student samples from 2 states, we sought to identify the existence of this undocumented segment of cigarette users. Study 1 was an initial effort to find empirical evidence for the existence of phantom smokers among college students and offer their demographic and behavioral profile. The study was conducted at a large public university in Michigan. Study 2 was conducted at a large public university in Florida for 3 purposes: (1) to confirm the existence of phantom smokers in another state, (2) to further investigate how phantom smokers rate consequences of smoking and image of a typical smoker, and (3) to examine what smoking-related norms they perceive from their social environment.

METHODS—STUDY 1

A convenience sample of college students were recruited from classes offered across a variety of departments at a large university in Michigan in October 2005. We provided classroom instructors with information about the purpose and procedures of the study. Research assistants visited the classroom and administered the surveys in the classroom. The instructors offered their students extra credit for voluntarily participating in the survey. The survey purpose was explained verbally, and students were provided with an informed consent letter describing the purpose of the study and the survey itself before agreeing to participate. A total of 952 undergraduate students participated in a self-administered survey; however, a large number of international students ($n = 53$) from Asian countries participated in the study. We removed them from the sample in order to restrict the findings to American college students. In accordance with the campus institutional review board (IRB) guidelines all participants gave written consent to participate in the study.

The questionnaire consisted of 3 main sections. The first section was designed to identify smoking status. The respondents were first asked, "Do you consider yourself a smoker?", and answered yes or no. Respondents were then asked about their smoking behavior with the following instructions: "Sometimes people smoke on occasion even though they don't consider themselves smokers. Please answer the following questions if you consider yourself a smoker and even if you do not consider yourself a smoker. Do you smoke cigarettes?" Respondents answered yes or no.

Respondents were classified into 3 groups based on their self-identification and self-reported smoking behavior: (1) a "smoker group," those who identified themselves as being smokers (yes to both smoker and smoking questions); (2) a "phantom smoker group," those who did not identify themselves as smokers but did smoke cigarettes (no to the smoker question but yes to the smoking question); and (3) a "nonsmoker group," those who identified themselves as nonsmokers and did not smoke cigarettes (no to both questions).

In the second section, we assessed respondents' age of smoking initiation and the number of cigarettes smoked a day. These questions are from the Centers for Disease Control and Prevention (CDC) National College Health Risk Behavior Study.[13] Next, respondents were asked to name their smoking situations—the places and occasions where they smoked such as a bar, anywhere with friends, while having a drink, driving, walking or eating, or other place/occasion. Respondents were then asked who bought or gave the cigarettes they consumed: themselves only, themselves and others, and always bum/never buy. These questions are slightly modified from the California Tobacco Survey for youths.[14] The last section of the questionnaire measured respondents' demographic characteristics including age, gender, ethnicity, and year in school.

We used SPSS version 16 to conduct statistical analyses of self-identification and smoking behavior. Whereas descriptive statistics were computed to summarize respondents' demographic characteristics, chi-square tests were performed to assess whether proportions of smokers, phantom smokers, and nonsmokers vary by gender, ethnicity, and school classification. Cross-tabulation was created between smoking status and smoking situations to identify places and occasions where smokers and phantom smokers frequently smoke. We performed another cross-tabulation between smoking status and who bought the cigarettes the respondents consumed to report how smokers and phantom smokers have access to cigarettes. A significance level of $p < .05$ was used for chi-square tests.

RESULTS—STUDY 1

A total of 899 American undergraduate students completed surveys for Study 1. Among the respondents, 58.2% were female. Their ages ranged from 17 to 25 years old, with an average of 20 years. Over half of the respondents were juniors (36.8%) and seniors (29.4%), followed by sophomores (21.7%) and freshmen (12.1%). Ethnically, the majority of the participants were Caucasian (80.5%), followed by African American (9.9%), Asian American (3.9%), and Latino/Hispanic (2.0%) students.

The percentage of self-identified smokers was 15.6% (n = 147). However, when we asked whether they smoked, about 45% (n = 415) of the participants said yes. Thus, about 30% (n = 268, 29.6%) of the sample were classified as phantom smokers.

The mean age of phantom smokers was 20 years old, whereas smokers were 21 years old on average. Most self-identified smokers (61.4%) and phantom smokers (68.4%) started smoking between the ages of 16 and 21. The amount of smoking by phantom smokers appeared to be light. They reported smoking none (79.5%) or 1 to 5 (20.1%) cigarettes. Most self-identified smokers reported smoking 1 to 5 (38.1%) or 6 to 10 (34.0%) cigarettes on a daily basis.

When the status was examined along with demographic characteristics, the proportion of smokers was significantly related to race, $\chi^2(8, N = 925) = 43.257, p < .0001$. As in previous studies,[4,5] African Americans showed the lowest rates (14.6%) of smoking compared to other racial groups: white (49.6%), Latino/Hispanics (50%), Asian (40%), and other (30.4%). The proportion of participants in each smoking category also varied with year in school, $\chi^2(6, N = 925) = 34.437, p < .0001$. Nonsmokers made up the majority of freshmen (69.7%), whereas self-identified smokers were far less common (7.3%). Among seniors, 44.1% were nonsmokers and 24.2% were self-identified smokers. The proportions of phantom smokers differed noticeably between freshmen and sophomores (22.9% versus 31.3% respectively), but among juniors (29.9%) and seniors (30.7%) the proportions were similar to the sophomores. No significant gender differences in the proportions of the smoker groups were observed. Table 1 reports the proportions of smokers, phantom smokers, and nonsmokers by gender, ethnicity, and year in school.

Table 1

Smoking Status (%) by Gender, Race, and Year in School with Study 1

		Smoking Type		
Characteristics	*n*	Smoker	Phantom Smoker	NonSmoker
Gender				
Female	523	14.0	28.1	57.9
Male	376	17.8	31.6	50.5
Race				
Caucasian	724	16.9	32.7	50.4
African American	89	5.6	9.0	85.4
Hispanic	18	16.7	33.3	50.0
Asian American	35	14.3	25.7	60.0
Other	33	15.2	18.2	66.7
Year in school				
Freshman	109	7.3	22.9	69.7
Sophomore	195	8.7	31.3	60.0
Junior	331	15.4	29.9	54.7
Senior	264	24.2	30.7	45.1
Total	899	15.6	29.6	54.8

Phantom smokers were more likely to smoke in social situations, whereas self-identified smokers tended to smoke across all situations. Both smokers and phantom smokers most often smoked in a bar or with friends. Yet far more smokers reported smoking while driving than did phantoms. As for the method of cigarette acquisition, most smokers bought for themselves, whereas over half of phantoms "bummed" their cigarettes from others. Similar percentages of smokers and phantoms sometimes bought and sometimes bummed. Table 2 displays the percentages of cigarette use in different situations and the methods of cigarette acquisition by smoking status.

For Study 2, we replicated Study 1 using a college student population in another state for additional evidence of phantom smokers and further investigated how phantom smokers rate images of a typical smoker and smoking consequences, and what smoking-related norms they perceive from their social environment.

. . .

COMMENT

In this article, we proposed and identified a new typology of smokers who reveal a discrepancy between their behavior and self-identified smoking status among the college student population. Although previous studies[11,12] reported the existence of the disparity between college students' smoking behavior and their self-identification, this study is the

Table 2
Smoking Situations and Ways to Get Cigarettes (%) by Smoking Status in Study 1

	Smoking Status		
Characteristics	Smoker	Phantom Smoker	Nonsmoker
Smoking Situations			
Bar	87.1	65.0	5.7
With friends	80.3	40.2	5.3
Having a drink	65.3	29.7	2.0
Eating	30.6	2.6	1.0
Driving	83.7	15.0	1.4
Walking	46.9	9.3	1.0
Other	20.4	21.3	29.4
Who bought or gave cigarettes for you			
Bought always	61.5	9.8	3.9
Bought or bummed	36.4	30.5	1.0
Bummed always	2.1	54.1	11.5

Note: Cell percentages represent use of cigarettes in each situation or acquisition of cigarettes by each method.

first to put a focus in depth on the discrepancy between what they do and what they label themselves. The results of the 2 surveys empirically support the existence of phantom smokers and shed light on the phantom smokers' smoking-related perceptions and behaviors in comparison to self-identified smokers and nonsmokers.

Phantom smokers smoke less in terms of amount and frequency than do smokers. The pattern of smoking situations in Study 1 confirms that phantom smokers are more likely to smoke in social situations, especially in a bar or with friends, whereas self-identified smokers tend to smoke across a range of social and other situations, including when they are alone or engage in other activities such as driving and eating. In both studies, most phantom smokers were found to "bum" cigarettes from others whereas most self-identified smokers bought cigarettes themselves. In addition, phantom smokers tended to include more smokers in their social circle than nonsmokers, but they perceived weaker peer pressure to quit or modify their smoking behavior than did self-identified smokers.

Taken together, the observed norms of smoking within a social environment, coupled with a lack of peer pressure to quit smoking, might inhibit phantom smokers from making a reasonable judgment of their own smoking status and reducing their smoking behavior. These findings suggest that phantom smokers have access to cigarettes in their environment and their smoking is encouraged or tolerated. Exposure to this kind of environment may make phantoms less able to estimate realistic descriptive norms and to see negative consequences from smoking. Thus, social norm–based intervention messages should focus on correcting misperceptions about the prevalence of, and benefits from, smoking.

In Study 2, we explored phantom smokers' expectation of smoking consequences and evaluation of a typical smoker's image. Phantom smokers appeared to stand between the self-identified smoker group and nonsmoker group with regards to all the dimensions. Phantom smokers were more likely to evaluate negative affect reduction and social facilitation as positive smoking consequences than nonsmokers were. The discrepancy between positive smoking expectancy and uncertainty toward a typical smoker's image can be related to phantom smokers' discrepancy between their smoking behavior and identity. Their uncertainty toward images of a typical smoker coupled with low frequency and amount of smoking is indicative of the contemplation stages in the stage-of-change model.[21,22] Although phantom smokers may experiment with smoking and weigh pros and cons that result from smoking, they do not want to be labeled as smokers. Thus, we suggest that health care providers and intervention campaigns need to educate college students, freshmen and sophomores in particular, of the cons resulting from even infrequent smoking and sensitize them to be attentive to their potential transition toward habitual smoking.

Although we successfully identified the presence of phantom smokers in both studies, the disparity in the proportions of phantoms between the 2 studies warrants discussion. Although the difference of 29.6% in Study 1 and 5.5% in Study 2 seems large, the ratios of phantom smokers to self-identified smokers in the 2 studies were similar, since many more smokers as well as phantoms were identified in Study 1. Phantom smokers in Study 1 were approximately twice as numerous as smokers (29.6% versus 15.6%); in Study 2, phantoms were almost 1.5 times as numerous as smokers (5.5% versus 3.9%). Thus, we speculate that the apparent disparity in the percentages of phantom smokers in the 2 studies are due to different demographic characteristics of the samples and differing social and legal environments.

Different demographic make-ups of the samples employed in the 2 studies may have contributed to the different proportions of phantom smokers. Although the majority of the respondents in Study 1 were juniors and seniors (66.2%), freshmen (60.4%) comprised the majority in Study 2. As identified in other studies,[4,5,23] college students often transition from nonsmokers to regular smokers as their college tenure progresses. A larger proportion of juniors and seniors who are more likely to smoke may explain the larger percentages of smokers and phantom smokers in Study 1, whereas the prevalence of freshmen who are less likely to smoke may account for the small numbers of smokers and phantom smokers in Study 2.

Different social atmospheres and regulations toward smoking across states and campuses are another potential explanation for the varied proportions of phantom smokers in the 2 studies. Michigan and Florida represent different smoking rates and regulatory stance on smoking. According to the state health comparison data, 45.24% of 18- to 25-year-olds in Michigan smoke cigarettes versus 36.04% of the same age group in Florida.[24] The Monitoring the Future national surveys on drug use confirm persistent regional differences in cigarette use among young adults ages 19 to 30.[25] In particular, the Midwest region had the highest smoking rates, with an annual prevalence of 40.2%, a 30-day prevalence of 30.5%, and daily use rate of 20.9% in 2007. The South region showed much lower smoking rates with an annual prevalence of 31.9%, 30-day prevalence of 23.4%, and daily use rate of 16.2%. Michigan does not have specific regulations on smoking in public places, whereas Florida prohibits smoking inside public buildings except in stand-alone bars.[24] Thus, regional differences in cigarette use and public smoking bans might be reflected in the different proportions of phantom smokers in Florida and Michigan. Prevalence of phantom smokers in different regions and among different age groups needs further exploration.

Another noteworthy finding of this study is that college students who identified themselves as nonsmokers and reported not smoking cigarettes responded in later questioning that they did smoke cigarettes in some situations, and some even bought their own. In Study 1, about 3.9% (n = 20) of nonsmokers reported purchasing cigarettes for themselves to smoke. Approximately 12.2% (n = 132) of nonsmokers in Study 2 reported getting cigarettes for consumption. The recognition of nonsmokers who displayed inconsistency between their behavior and self-identity may suggest that there may be a hidden group of phantom smokers and the extent of phantom smokers could be even larger. Perhaps the smaller proportion of phantom smokers in Study 2 can be attributed to a large number of self-labeled nonsmokers who actually smoke at least occasionally.

In conjunction with phantom smokers, the existence of self-identified nonsmokers who in fact smoke raises important issues as to the ability of smoking intervention programs to identify and communicate with at-risk populations. Current measurements of smokers cannot capture the populations who underestimate their cigarette consumption habit to a degree that they deny their own smoking. If this group of smokers does not admit that they are smokers, they will filter out the messages targeted toward them. Not recognizing their smoking habits as health-threatening behavior can be related to low motivation to accept messages against the behavior. As Waters et al[12] suggested, health care providers to college students should go beyond asking, "Are you a smoker?" or "Do you smoke?", and consider adding questions related to cigarette purchasing or getting access to cigarettes in order to locate groups of people who resist being identified as smokers.

In conclusion, there has been a line of research on classifying smokers based on the reported smoking amount and frequency. Many campaigns have been developed through the consideration of the beliefs, attitudes, and norms of smokers often defined with variables of no relevance to smokers' self-identification. This study is the first to underline that smokers do not define themselves in the same way that researchers categorize them. Findings suggest that phantom smokers should be recognized as a distinct group that may progress to become regular smokers, and that interventive, antismoking messages should highlight the severe health consequences from light and occasional smoking.

LIMITATIONS

The present study is exploratory in identifying a new segment of smokers, and its limitations should be acknowledged. The existence of phantom smokers in the college student population was examined with convenience samples at 2 academic institutions. Because classes from which participants were recruited were not randomly chosen and students voluntarily decided whether or not to participate in the survey, there might be a selection bias involved in the participant recruitment process. Indeed, the demographic make-ups of the samples in the 2 studies were different. Although both samples contained a cross-section of students with diverse areas of study and class standings, [and] the patterns regarding smoking behavior by gender, ethnicity, and school classifications were similar to those in other studies,[4,5,23] the samples employed in the present study are not representative of the general college student population, and the findings should be interpreted with caution. Future studies should use a stricter sampling procedure to identify an accurate proportion of phantom smokers in the general college student population.

FUTURE RESEARCH

Despite the limitations, this study is one of the first to find that smokers classified by researchers do not necessarily define themselves as such even if they admit to smoking. In order to gain reliable and practical findings on phantom smokers, more research on factors that prompt smokers to misrepresent their smoking status should be conducted in varied institutions and within other regions. Waters et al[12] (38%) and Study 1 (29.6%) collected data from the Midwest region and found higher proportions of smokers and phantom smokers than those found in the south in Study 2 (5.5%). Institutions in other regions need to assess how smokers define their identity and estimate their smoking behavior. Findings can be compared across geographic regions and related to the influence of campus and local policy on smokers' self-identification.

Future studies should use a longitudinal design to identify where and when phantom smoking occurs. There are 2 possible explanations behind phantom smokers' behavior. Some phantom smokers, like contemplators in the stage-of-change model, may be in the middle of making a transition from experimentation to regular smoking and not recognize the addictive nature of their smoking behavior. On the other hand, other phantom smokers may switch from a nonsmoker to a smoker contingent on social occasions and the type of pressures present in such occasions. If they perceive social cues that encourage smoking from other smokers in these occasions, they might smoke to be a part of the group whereas outside the occasion they would be abstinent from smoking. Longitudinal studies can reveal if phantom smokers gradually become regular smokers because of addiction to cigarettes or because of temporary but consistent social cues. Further examination is also necessary to identify whether phantom smokers is a status applicable only to college students and young adults or to a wider range of ages.

NOTE

For comments and further information, address correspondence to Dr Youjin Choi, Department of Advertising and Public Relations, Dongguk University, Seoul, 100-715, Republic of Korea (e-mail: goyoujin@gmail.com).

REFERENCES

1. Centers for Disease Control and Prevention. Tobacco use among adults—United States, 2005. *MMWR Morb Mort Wkly Rep*. 2006;55: 1145–1148.

2. Centers for Disease Control and Prevention. Annual smoking-attributable mortality, years of potential life lost, and productivity losses—United States, 1997–2001. *MMWR Morb Mort Wkly Rep*. 2005;54:625–628.

3. Substance Abuse and Mental Health Services Administration. *Results From the 2008 National Survey on Drug Use and Health*. Rockville, MD: US Dept of Health and Human Services, Office of Applied Studies; 2009. DHHS Publication SMA 09–4434.

4. Johnston LD, O'Malley PM, Bachman JG, Schulenberg JE. *Monitoring the Future National Survey Results on Drug Use, 1975–2004: Vol. 2. College Students and Adults Ages 19–45*. Bethesda, MD: National Institute on Drug Abuse; 2005. NIH Publication 05–5728.

5. Rigotti N, Lee JE, Wechsler H. US college students' use of tobacco products: results of a national survey. *JAMA*. 2000;284:699–705.

6. Rigotti N, Regan S, Moran S, Wechsler H. Students' opinion for tobacco control policies recommended for US colleges: a national survey. *Tob Control.* 2003;12:251–256.

7. Wetter DW, Kenford SL, Welsh SK, et al. Prevalence and predictors of transitions in smoking behavior among college students. *Health Psychol.* 2004;23:168–177.

8. Zhu S, Sun J, Hawkins S, Pierce J, Cummins S. A population study of low-rate smokers: quitting history and instability over time. *Health Psychol.* 2003;22:245–252.

9. Curry S, Emery S, Sporer A, et al. A national survey of tobacco cessation programs for youths. *Am J Public Health.* 2007;97:171–177.

10. McDonald P, Colwell B, Backinger CL, Husten C, Maule CO. Better practices for youth tobacco cessation: evidence of review panel. *Am J Health Behav.* 2003;27:S144–S158.

11. Thompson B, Thompson LA, Hymer J, Zbikowsi S, Halperin A, Jaffe R. A qualitative study of attitudes, beliefs, and practices among 40 undergraduate smokers. *J Am Coll Health.* 2007;56:23–28.

12. Waters K, Harris K, Hall S, Nazir N, Waigandt A. Characteristics of social smoking among college students. *J Am Coll Health.* 2006;55:133–139.

13. Centers for Disease Control and Prevention. Youth risk behavior surveillance: National College Health Risk Behavior Survey—United States, 1995. *MMWR Morb Mort Wkly Rep.* 1997;46:1–56.

14. Al-Delaimy WK, Messer K, Pierce JP, Trinidad DR, White MM. *Technical Report on Analytic Methods and Approaches Used in the 2005 California Tobacco Survey Analysis: Vol. 1. Data Collection Methodology.* La Jolla, CA: University of California, San Diego; 2007.

15. Copeland AL, Brandon TH, Quinn EP. The Smoking Consequences Questionnaire–Adult: measurement of smoking outcome expectancies of experienced smokers. *Psychol Assess.* 1995;7:484–494.

16. Buckley TV, Kamholz BW, Mozley SL, et al. A psychometric evaluation of the Smoking Consequences Questionnaire–Adult in smokers with psychiatric conditions. *Nicotine Tob Res.* 2005;7:739–745.

17. Reig-Ferrer A, Cepeda-Benito A. Smoking expectancies in smokers and never smokers: an examination of the Smoking Consequences Questionnaire–Spanish. *Addict Behav.* 2006;32:1405–1415.

18. Friestad C, Rise J, Røysamb E. Social representations of smoking and attitudes towards smoking restriction in the Norwegian Navy. *Scand J Psychol.* 1999;40:187–196.

19. Rimal RN, Lapinski MK, Cook RJ, Real K. Moving toward a theory of normative influences: how perceived benefits and similarity moderate the impact of descriptive norms on behavior. *J Health Commun.* 2005;10:433–450.

20. Putte B, Yzer MC, Brunsting S. Social influences on smoking cessation: a comparison of the effect of six social influence variables. *Prev Med.* 2005;41:186–193.

21. Guo B, Aveyard P, Fielding A, Sutton S. Do the transtheoretical model processes of change, decisional balance and temptation predict state movement? Evidence from smoking cessation in adolescents. *Addiction.* 2009;104:828–838.

22. Prochaska JO, Velicer WF, Rossi JS, et al. Stages of change and decisional balance for 12 problem behaviors. *Health Psychol.* 1994;13:39–46.

23. Lantz PM. Smoking on the rise among young adults: implications for research and policy. *Tob Control.* 2003;12:i60– i70.

24. Kaiser Family Foundation. Public place smoking bans in states, 2008. Available at: http://www.statehealthfacts.org/comparetable.jsp?ind=86&cat=2. Accessed May 23 2008.

25. Johnston LD, O'Malley PM, Bachman JG, Schulenberg JE. *Monitoring the Future National Survey Results on Drug Use, 1975–2007: Vol. 2. College Students and Adults Ages 19–45.* Bethesda, MD: National Institute on Drug Abuse; 2008. NIH Publication No. 08–6418B.

QUESTIONS ABOUT MEANING

1. What are "phantom smokers"? According to the authors, what might prevent these people from seeing themselves as smokers? Why are current antismoking campaigns unlikely to be effective with this group?
2. Describe the participants, methods, and results of Study 1. In what ways are the samples of students in Studies 1 and 2 biased (unrepresentative)? (The sample makeup for both Study 1 and Study 2 is discussed in the section titled "Limitations.")
3. What factors explain the smaller proportion of phantom smokers in Study 2 (not included in this selection but discussed in the Comment section)?

QUESTIONS FOR RHETORICAL ANALYSIS

1. Study Table 2. For someone who has not read the article, the information in the third column (for Nonsmokers) might seem nonsensical. For example, how can there be so many nonsmokers who engage in various smoking situations? (If you're not sure, reread the Comment section.) How could the information in Table 2 be presented in a way that would be clear even for those who don't read the Comment section?
2. In what ways do the authors, who are experts in *advertising*, contribute to the discussion of smoking (a health hazard)? Describe the ethos of the authors and cite passages to illustrate how it is created.

MAKING CONNECTIONS

1. In an essay, define the term "phantom smoker," summarize Choi, Choi, and Rifon's study, and identify the authors' recommendations for health

care providers and smoking intervention campaigns. Given what you know about cognitive dissonance, do you think the authors' recommendations are likely to change the behavior of phantom smokers? Explain why or why not. What additional ways can you propose for targeting phantom smokers in antismoking campaigns?

2. What's in a label? A lot, it seems, when it comes to the labels we use to define ourselves. Whether it's ethnicity, sexual preference, marital status, social class, place of residence, vocation, or other aspects of self-identity, people care about the terms others use to define them, particularly if the descriptors conflict with the way they want to see themselves. Discuss this topic in an essay.

Psychology

"The End of History Illusion," JORDI QUOIDBACH, DANIEL T. GILBERT, AND TIMOTHY D. WILSON

In the previous articles in this chapter, the authors argue that when it comes to self-perception, we all have blind spots. Further evidence of this can be found in research from psychology professors Jordi Quoidbach, Daniel Gilbert, and Timothy Wilson. Their study, published in *Science* in 2013, demonstrates how people can recognize that they have changed in the previous decade yet not believe they will continue to change at the same rate in the future. *Science* is a peer-reviewed journal that publishes research from all areas of science.

We measured the personalities, values, and preferences of more than 19,000 people who ranged in age from 18 to 68 and asked them to report how much they had changed in the past decade and/or to predict how much they would change in the next decade. Young people, middle-aged people, and older people all believed they had changed a lot in the past but would change relatively little in the future. People, it seems, regard the present as a watershed moment at which they have finally become the person they will be for the rest of their lives. This "end of history illusion" had practical consequences, leading people to overpay for future opportunities to indulge their current preferences.

At every stage of life, people make decisions that profoundly influence the lives of the people they will become—and when they finally become those people, they aren't always thrilled about it. Young adults pay to remove the tattoos that teenagers paid to get, middle-aged adults rush to divorce the people whom young adults rushed to marry, and older adults visit health spas to lose what middle-aged adults visited restaurants to gain. Why do people so often make decisions that their future selves regret?

One possibility is that people have a fundamental misconception about their future selves. Time is a powerful force that transforms people's preferences, reshapes their values, and alters their personalities, and we suspect that people generally underestimate the magnitude of those changes. In other words, people may believe that who they are today is pretty much who they will be tomorrow, despite the fact that it isn't who they were yesterday. In the studies we describe here, we showed that people expect to change little in the future, despite knowing that they have changed a lot in the past, and that this tendency bedevils their decision-making. We call this tendency to underestimate the magnitude of future change the "end of history illusion."

To investigate this phenomenon, we asked samples of people who varied widely in age to predict how much they would change over the next 10 years, we asked similar samples to report how much they had changed over the past 10 years, and we compared the predictions of people aged *a* years to the reports of people aged *a* +10 years. We expected people aged *a* years to predict less change over the next 10 years than people aged *a* +10 years reported over the past 10 years. We used this strategy to study how much people thought they would change in the domains of personality (a person's characteristic patterns of behavior), core values (a person's ideals and principles), and preferences (a person's likes and dislikes).

In study 1, we sought to determine whether people underestimate the extent to which their personalities will change in the future. We recruited a sample of 7519 adults ranging in age from 18 to 68 years [mean *(M)* = 40 years, standard deviation (SD) = 11.3 years, 80% women] through the Web site of a popular television show and asked them to complete the Ten Item Personality Inventory (*1*), which is a standard measure of the five trait dimensions that underlie human personality (i.e., conscientiousness, agreeableness, emotional stability, openness to experience, and extraversion). Participants were then randomly assigned either to the reporter condition (and were asked to complete the measure as they would have completed it 10 years earlier) or the predictor condition (and were asked to complete the measure as they thought they would complete it 10 years hence). We then computed the absolute value of the difference between participants' ratings of their current personality and their reported or predicted personality and averaged these across the five traits to create a measure of reported or predicted change in personality. Additional methodological details about study 1 can be found in supplementary text 1 to 3.

We analyzed these measures by first assigning a value to each of the 41 10-year periods between ages 18 and 68. We called this variable "decade." For each decade, we compared the predictions of predictors aged *a* to the reports of reporters aged *a* + 10 years. So, for example, when decade = 1, we compared 18-year-old predictors and 28-year-old reporters; when decade = 2, we compared 19-year-old predictors and 29-year-old reporters; and so on. We did not collect data from reporters who were younger than 28 years, because in our sample there were no predictors younger than 18 years with whom to compare them, and we did not collect data from predictors who were older than 58 years, because in our sample there were no reporters older than 68 years with whom to compare them.

We entered participants' reported or predicted changes in personality into a multiple regression analysis with three predictor variables: decade (coded 1 through 41), condition (coded 1 for predictors and –1 for reporters), and a "decade X condition" interaction. First, the analysis revealed an effect of decade [beta coefficient (β) = -0.13, $P < 0.001$], indicating that the older the participants were, the less personality change they reported or predicted. This finding is consistent with a large body of research showing that personality becomes more stable as people age (*2*). Second, the analysis revealed the expected effect of condition ($\beta = -0.14$, $P < 0.001$). The top panel of Fig. 14.1 shows this end of history illusion: Predictors aged *a* predicted that they would change less over the next decade than reporters aged *a* + 10 years reported having changed over the same decade. Finally, there was no decade X condition interaction ($\beta = 0.01$, $P = 0.68$), indicating that the magnitude of the end of history illusion did not change across decades. Next, we conducted follow-up studies to answer three questions.

First, is it possible that the discrepancy between participants' reports and predictions in study 1 was due entirely to the erroneous memory of reporters, who may have overestimated how much they had changed in the past 10 years, rather than to the erroneous predictions of predictors, who may have underestimated how much they would change in the next 10 years? To investigate this possibility, we compared the magnitudes of the predicted and reported personality changes in our sample to the magnitude of actual personality change observed in an independent sample of 3808 adults ranging from 20 to 75 years old ($M = 47.2$ years, SD = 12.4 years, 55% women), whose personalities had been measured as part of the MacArthur Foundation Survey of Midlife Development in the United States (MIDUS). These adults completed the MIDUS Big Five scale (*3*) for the first time in 1995–1996 (MIDUS 1) and for a second time in 2004–2006 (MIDUS 2). The MIDUS Big Five scale has good construct validity and correlates with other similar scales (*4, 5*). Because the personality measures used in the MIDUS study and in our study were scored on different scales, direct comparison of the data was not possible. To estimate the magnitudes of actual, reported, and predicted personality change, we computed intraclass correlations (ICC-A1), which account for both absolute and rank-based change (6). Specifically, we computed (i) the ICC between the two administrations of the personality test in the MIDUS sample, which was 0.52; (ii) the ICC between current and reported personality for participants in our sample, which was 0.51; and (iii) the ICC between current and predicted personality for participants in our sample, which was 0.65. Larger ICCs, of course, indicate less personality change. As inspection of these ICCs reveals, the magnitude of reported personality change in our sample was almost identical to the magnitude of actual personality change in the MIDUS sample, suggesting that participants in our sample were relatively accurate when reporting the amount of change they had experienced in the past. However, the magnitude of actual personality change in the MIDUS sample was substantially larger than the magnitude of predicted personality change in our sample, suggesting that participants in our sample were relatively inaccurate when predicting the amount of change they would experience in the future. In short, it seems likely that the discrepancy between the reported and predicted personality changes of participants in study 1 is due at least in part to errors of prediction and not merely to errors of memory. Study 3 provides further support for this claim.

Second, is it possible that reporters and predictors in study 1 interpreted the scales differently, so that words such as "conscientious" or "agreeable" meant one thing to reporters and another thing to predictors? To investigate this possibility, we replicated study 1 with an independent sample of 613 adults (M = 40.5 years, SD = 8.4 years, 86.6% women) recruited through the same Web site and using a design in which each participant was assigned to both the reporter and the predictor conditions, thus ensuring that any idiosyncratic interpretation of the scales would influence both conditions equally. This design required that we restrict our sample to participants aged 28 to 58. Because participants contributed data to both conditions, we performed a multilevel version of the analysis described in study 1. The analysis revealed the expected effect of condition ($\beta = -7.69$, $P = 0.001$), indicating that predictors aged a years predicted that they would change less over the next decade than reporters aged $a + 10$ years reported having changed over the same decade—even though the reports and predictions were made by the same participants. This finding suggests that idiosyncratic interpretations of the scale are not the cause of the effects seen in study 1.

Third, is it possible that predictors in study 1 knew that they would change over the next 10 years, but because they did not know exactly how they would change, they did not feel confident predicting specific changes? To investigate this possibility, we replicated study 1 with an independent sample of 1163 adults (M= 38.4 years, SD = 12.1 years, 78% women) recruited through the same Web site. Instead of being asked to report or predict their specific personality traits, these participants were simply asked to report how much they felt they had "changed as a person over the last 10 years" and how much they thought they would "change as a person over the next 10 years." Because some participants contributed data to both conditions, we performed a multilevel version of the analysis described in study 1. The analysis revealed the expected effect of condition ($\beta = -0.74$, $P = 0.007$), indicating that predictors aged *a* years predicted that they would change less over the next decade than reporters aged $a + 10$ years reported having changed over the same decade. This finding suggests that a lack of specific knowledge about how one might change in the future was not the cause of the effects seen in study 1.

In study 2, we sought to determine whether the end of history illusion was limited to the domain of personality, and so we repeated our procedure in the domain of core values. We recruited a new sample of 2717 adults ranging in age from 18 to 68 years (M = 38.6 years, SD = 10.6 years, 82% women) through the same Web site and asked them to indicate the importance of each of 10 basic values (such as hedonism, success, security, etc.) that were taken from the Schwartz Value Inventory (*7*). Otherwise, the design was identical to that of study 1.

We performed a regression analysis similar to the one performed in study 1. First, the analysis revealed an effect of decade ($\beta = -0.23$, $P <$ 0.0010, indicating that the older participants were, the less change in their core values they reported or predicted. Second, the analysis revealed the expected effect of condition ($\beta = -0.46$, $P < 0.001$). The middle panel of Fig. 14.1 shows this end of history illusion: Predictors aged *a* years predicted that they would change less over the next decade than reporters aged $a + 10$ years reported having changed over the same decade. Finally, the analysis revealed a decade × condition interaction ($\beta = 0.08$, $P < 0.001$). Although the magnitude of the end of history illusion decreased as participants got older, it was nonetheless present even in the oldest group of participants (aged 50 and up) ($\beta = -0.34$, $P < 0.001$). Further discussion of this decade × condition interaction can be found in supplementary text 5.

The foregoing studies show that people expect to experience less change in their personalities and core values over the next decade than people a decade older report having experienced over the past decade. The analysis presented in study 1 suggests that this discrepancy represents, at least in part, an error of prediction and is not merely an error of memory. To provide further support for this claim, in study 3 we examined the end of history illusion in a domain in which memory was

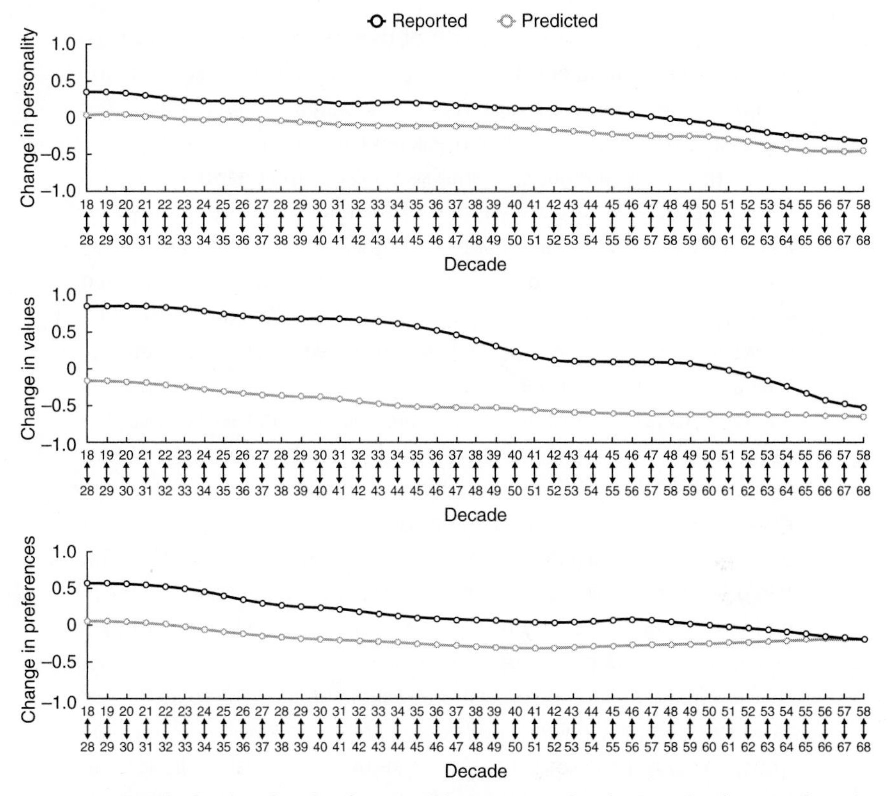

Figure 14.1 Standardized predicted and reported changes across decades in study 1 (**top panel**), study 2 (**middle panel**), and study 3 (**bottom panel**). The graph shows moving averages smoothed with a 4-year Gaussian filter. Additional information about this figure can be found in supplementary text 4.

likely to be highly reliable. Rather than asking reporters to remember how extraverted they had been or how much they had once valued honesty, we asked them to remember simple facts about their strongest preferences, such as the name of their favorite musical band or the name of their best friend. We reasoned that if participants remembered having a different best friend 10 years ago but expected to have the same best friend 10 years from now, then this was probably not due to a pervasive tendency for people of all ages to actually keep their best friends but mistakenly remember changing them.

To test this hypothesis, we recruited a new sample of 7130 adults ranging from 18 to 68 years old (*M*= 40.2 years, SD = 11.1 years, 80% women) through the same Web site and asked them to report their favorite type of music, their favorite type of vacation, their favorite type of food, their favorite hobby, and the name of their best friend. Participants were then randomly assigned either to the reporter condition (and were asked to report whether each of their current preferences was the same as or different than it was 10 years ago) or the predictor condition (and were asked to predict whether each of their current preferences would be the same or different 10 years from now). We then counted the number of items on which participants responded "different" and used this as a measure of reported or predicted changes in preference.

We performed a regression analysis similar to the ones performed in studies 1 and 2. First, the analysis revealed an effect of decade ($\beta = -0.14$, $P < 0.001$). The older participants were, the less change in preferences they reported or predicted. Second, the analysis revealed the expected effect of condition ($\beta = -0.19$, $P < 0.001$). The bottom panel in Fig. 14.1 shows this end of history illusion: Predictors aged *a* years predicted that their preferences would change less over the next decade than reporters aged $a + 10$ years reported that their preferences had changed over the same decade. Finally, the analysis revealed a decade × condition interaction ($\beta = 0.07$, $P < 0.001$). Although the magnitude of the end of history illusion decreased as participants got older, it was nonetheless present even in the oldest group of participants (aged 50 and up) ($\beta = -0.08$, $P < 0.01$). Further discussion of this decade × condition interaction can be found in supplementary text 5, and additional details about study 3 can be found in supplementary text 6.

The foregoing studies suggest that people underestimate the extent to which their personalities, values, and preferences will change in the future. In study 4, we sought to show that this end of history illusion can have practical consequences. Specifically, we sought to show that because people overestimate the stability of their current preferences, they will overpay for future opportunities to indulge them.

In study 4, we recruited a new sample of 170 adults ranging from 18 to 64 years old ($M = 34.9$ years, SD = 10.6 years, 52% women) through the Amazon Mechanical Turk Web site *(8, 9)*. Some participants were randomly assigned to the "future concert" condition. These participants were asked to name their current favorite musical band and then to report the maximum amount of money they thought they would be willing to pay today in order to see that band perform in 10 years. Other participants were randomly assigned to the "present concert" condition. These participants were asked to name the musical band that was their favorite 10 years ago and then to report the amount of money that they thought they would be willing to pay today to see that band perform in the coming week.

We performed a regression analysis similar to the ones performed in studies 1, 2, and 3. First, the analysis revealed the expected effect of condition ($\beta = 0.16$, $P < 0.05$). Participants aged *a* years thought they would pay 61% more to see their current favorite band perform 10 years in the future ($M = \$129$) than participants aged $a + 10$ years thought they would pay to see their once-favorite band perform in the present

(M = \$80). The analysis revealed no effect of decade ($\beta = -0.06$, $P = 0.41$), indicating that the price participants thought they would pay did not vary with age, and no decade × condition interaction ($\beta = 0.01$, $P = 0.94$), indicating that willingness to pay more for a future concert than a present concert did not diminish in magnitude as participants got older. In short, participants substantially overpaid for a future opportunity to indulge a current preference.

Across six studies of more than 19,000 participants, we found consistent evidence to indicate that people underestimate how much they will change in the future, and that doing so can lead to suboptimal decisions. Although these data cannot tell us what causes the end of history illusion, two possibilities seem likely. First, most people believe that their personalities are attractive, their values admirable, and their preferences wise *(10)*, and having reached that exalted state, they may be reluctant to entertain the possibility of change. People also like to believe that they know themselves well *(11)*, and the possibility of future change may threaten that belief. In short, people are motivated to think well of themselves and to feel secure in that understanding, and the end of history illusion may help them accomplish these goals.

Second, there is at least one important difference between the cognitive processes that allow people to look forward and backward in time (*12*). Prospection is a constructive process, retrospection is a reconstructive process, and constructing new things is typically more difficult than reconstructing old ones (*13, 14*). The reason this matters is that people often draw inferences from the ease with which they can remember or imagine (*15, 16*). If people find it difficult to imagine the ways in which their traits, values, or preferences will change in the future, they may assume that such changes are unlikely. In short, people may confuse the difficulty of imagining personal change with the unlikelihood of change itself.

Although the magnitude of this end of history illusion in some of our studies was greater for younger people than for older people, it was nonetheless evident at every stage of adult life that we could analyze. Both teenagers and grandparents seem to believe that the pace of personal change has slowed to a crawl and that they have recently become the people they will remain. History, it seems, is always ending today.

REFERENCES AND NOTES

1. S. D. Gosling, P. J. Rentfrow, W. B. Swann Jr., J. *Res. Pers.* **37**, 504 (2003).
2. B. W. Roberts, K. E. Walton, W. Viechtbauer, *Psychol. Bull.* **132**, 1 (2006).
3. M. E. Lachman, S. L. Weaver, *The Midlife Development Inventory (MIDI) Personality Scales: Scale Construction and Scoring* (Brandeis University, Waltham, MA, 1997).
4. D. K. Mroczek, C. M. Kolarz, *J. Pers. Soc. Psychol.* **75**, 1333 (1998).
5. K. M. Prenda, M. E. Lachman, *Psychol. Aging* **16**, 206 (2001).

6. K. O. McGraw, S. P. Wong, *Psychol. Methods* **1**, 30 (1996).
7. S. H. Schwartz, in *Advances in Experimental Social Psychology*, M. P. Zanna, Ed. (Academic Press, Orlando, FL, 1992), vol. **25**, pp. 1–65.
8. G. Paolacci, J. Chandler, P. G. Ipeirotis, *Judgm. Decis. Mak.* **5**, 411 (2010).
9. M. Buhrmester, T. Kwang, S. D. Gosling, *Perspect. Psychol. Sci.* **6**, 3 (2011).
10. C. Sedikides, M. D. Alicke, in *The Oxford Handbook of Human Motivation*, R. M. Ryan, Ed. (Oxford Univ. Press, Oxford), pp. 303–322.
11. W. B. Swann Jr., in *Handbook of Theories of Social Psychology*, P. Van Lang, A. Kruglanski, E. T. Higgins, Eds. (Sage, London, 2012), pp. 23–42.
12. D. R. Addis, A. T. Wong, D. L. Schacter, *Neuropsychologia* **45**, 1363 (2007).
13. M. D. Robinson, G. L. Clore, *Psychol. Bull.* **128**, 934 (2002).
14. M. Ross, *Psychol. Rev.* **96**, 341 (1989).
15. N. Schwarz *et al.*, *J. Pers. Soc. Psychol.* **61**, 195 (1991).
16. A. Tversky, D. Kahneman, *Cognit. Psychol.* **5**, 207 (1973).

ACKNOWLEDGMENTS

We acknowledge the support of Research Grant BCS-0722132 from NSF to D.T.G. and T.D.W. Raw data from all studies are on deposit at the Inter-university Consortium for Political and Social Research (deposit no. 32668) and can be accessed at www.icpsr.umich.edu.

SUPPLEMENTARY MATERIALS

www.sciencemag.org/cgi/content/full/339/6115/96/DC1
Supplementary Text
Table S1
24 August 2012; accepted 16 November 2012 10.1126/science.1229294
Jordi Quoidbach, National Fund for Scientific Research, Brussels, Belgium.
Daniel T. Gilbert (to whom correspondence should be addressed); e-mail gilbert@wjh.harvard.edu, Department of Psychology, Harvard University, Cambridge, MA 02138, USA.
Timothy D. Wilson, Department of Psychology, University of Virginia, Charlottesville, VA 22904-4400, USA.

QUESTIONS ABOUT MEANING

1. What is the "end of history illusion"?
2. Describe the methods and results for Study 1. When interpreting the results, why did the researchers also consider the results of the MacArthur Foundation Survey of Midlife Development in the United States (MIDUS)?
3. Summarize the methods and results of the two replications of Study 1. What was the purpose of these follow-up studies?
4. How were the findings in the first two studies extended in Study 3 (about personal preferences) and in Study 4?

QUESTIONS FOR RHETORICAL ANALYSIS

1. What indications are there that the intended audience for this article is academic and scientific? On the other hand, highlight important transition and summary sentences that allow any attentive reader to understand the researchers' goals, methods, and conclusions.
2. Study Figure 14.1. What do the black and gray lines represent? What "story" do the graphs tell about the changes participants reported they had undergone and the changes they predicted would occur?

MAKING CONNECTIONS

1. In an essay, explain the "end of history illusion," summarize the research Quoidbach, Gilbert, and Wilson describe, and summarize their various explanations for the phenomenon. What additional explanations for the phenomenon do you think Tavris and Aronson could offer?
2. In a recent interview, Steven Pinker, who teaches at Harvard, was asked how today's students differ from students in earlier generations. In his response, he explained why members of every generation incorrectly assume that when they were young they were smarter, harder working, and more moral than young people are today:

   > . . . People often confuse changes in themselves with changes in the times, and changes in the times with moral and intellectual decline. This is a well-documented psychological phenomenon. . . . I know a lot more now than I did when I was a student, and thanks to the curse of knowledge, I may not realize that I have acquired most of it during the decades that have elapsed since I was a student. So it's tempting to look at students and think, "What a bunch of inarticulate ignoramuses! It was better when I was at that age, a time when I and other teenagers spoke in fluent paragraphs, and we effortlessly held forth on the foundations of Western civilization." Yeah, right. (qtd. in Walsh)

   How do Pinker's observations relate to Quoidbach, Gilbert, and Wilson's study? Have you observed the tendency these authors describe in others? In yourself? Explain.

WORK CITED

Walsh, Colleen. "'What Could Be More Interesting than How the Mind Works?': Steven Pinker's History of Thought." (Interview with Steven Pinker.) *Harvard Gazette* (6 May 2014). Web. 12 May 2014.

Business

"In Hiring and Promoting, Look beyond Results," FRANCESCA GINO

In chapter 13, business professor Ray Fisman refers to the *fundamental attribution error* (also known as *correspondence bias*), which is the tendency to blame a person for bad behavior without asking how the situation, context, or external factors might explain the behavior.

In the next article, business professor Francesca Gino also discusses correspondence bias, specifically as it relates to business managers. In the article "In Hiring and Promoting, Look beyond Results," published in *The Wall Street Journal* in 2011, Gino warns that if we judge people "on outcomes alone, we will end up condemning too many unlucky people and acquitting too many scoundrels."

Would you have more confidence in a new CEO who came from a company in a growing field or a troubled industry? Would you promote a top performer if you learned he or she used shady tactics to reach sales targets?

When making judgments about whom to hire and promote, context is crucial. It's important to know the situations in which people worked, and the methods they used, before judging their performance. In the case of the CEO, for instance, it's a lot easier to post great numbers in a booming industry than a shrinking one.

Unfortunately, we usually don't look at those factors. Evidence from several studies suggests that we're biased toward results when making these crucial decisions. Time and again, we look at what candidates have achieved—without asking *where* or *how* they achieved it.

This error comes in two forms. First, there's correspondence bias—the tendency to judge people's ability directly from performance, without taking into account their situation.

This type of error was demonstrated in a study I conducted with Don Moore of the University of California at Berkeley and Sam Swift and Zachariah Sharek of Carnegie Mellon University. We asked college students to assume the role of admissions officers for a selective M.B.A. program. Then we gave them candidates' grade-point averages, as well as the average GPA of the particular college each attended.

When deciding whom to admit, the participants overweighted applicants' GPAs and underweighted the effect of the grading norms at different schools. In other words, they did not appropriately take into account the ease with which candidates earned their grades.

The other type of bias, outcome bias, is the tendency to base judgments about performance on the results alone, without examining the behavior the person used to reach those results. Consider a study I conducted with Max Bazerman of Harvard Business School and Don Moore.

We asked our participants to evaluate the actions of another person in terms of how ethical they were. From the description, it was clear that the person's actions were ethically questionable, and participants evaluated them as such. But when they then learned about the outcomes of those actions, their opinions sometimes changed.

When the actions led to a bad outcome, participants continued to view the person as highly unethical. But when the same actions led to a positive outcome, the person was evaluated as behaving ethically.

We all know that good people are sometimes unlucky, and that scoundrels sometimes get away clean. But if we judge decisions based on outcomes alone, we will end up condemning too many unlucky people and acquitting too many scoundrels.

How can people overcome these biases? First, they must raise their level of awareness, recognizing that these biases exist and that they have powerful consequences. When managers face a hiring or promotion decision, they should consider whether they are appropriately accounting for a candidate's situation and whether their evaluations are based on both actions and outcomes.

Organizations may also need to make structural changes to their performance evaluations or promotion decisions. They might, for instance, reduce the effect of biases by including an assessment of the means used to achieve given objectives and the situational influences on performance.

By investing in these kinds of solutions, managers can be confident that they will be able to debug their selection decision.

QUESTIONS ABOUT MEANING

1. What is the difference between correspondence bias and outcome bias? Illustrate each type of bias.
2. What solution for overcoming correspondence bias does Gino offer to individuals and organizations?

QUESTIONS FOR RHETORICAL ANALYSIS

1. Although the research Gino cites is not limited to studies conducted in the workplace, how is her article tailored to business executives and managers (i.e., *Wall Street Journal* readers)?
2. The organization of Gino's newspaper article resembles that of an essay. Divide the article into three sections: introduction, body, and conclusion. Where is the thesis statement located within the introduction? Identify "topic sentences" in the body. What evidence supports the topic

sentences? What traditional move(s), common within academic papers, are made in the conclusion?

MAKING CONNECTIONS

1. "Context is crucial," writes Gino. It's important to consider when making sense of all kinds of data and behavior—a point made numerous times in this book and by various authors, including:
   - Best
   - Baron
   - Carrell, Hoekstra, and West
   - Fisman
   - Nisbett
   - Quoidbach, Gilbert, and Wilson

   Using insights from authors such as those listed (or others), write an essay in which you add your own examples to illustrate the importance of considering context when evaluating or interpreting events, statistics, or the behavior of people. Your examples can be from history, current events, or from your own experience and observation.
2. How a person interprets information depends on that person's vantage point—how much background information he has; what he wants to believe about the situation or people involved; how close he is to the situation geographically, chronologically, and emotionally, etc. Select an event (recent or historical) that made the news and for which you can find two or more written accounts from different perspectives (e.g., local vs. national; contemporary vs. retrospective; firsthand vs. secondary account). How do the accounts differ? How do the intended audiences help explain the differences you find? What other factors help explain the differences? How do the accounts help to demonstrate the importance of considering various points of view when conducting secondary research on a topic?

Business

Excerpt from "Correspondence Bias in Performance Evaluation: Why Grade Inflation Works," DON A. MOORE, SAMUEL A. SWIFT, ZACHARIAH S. SHAREK, AND FRANCESCA GINO

In the previous article, business professor Francesca Gino discusses *correspondence bias*—the failure to consider the full context when evaluating a situation. The following report describes some of the research Gino refers to in that article. The study was conducted by a team of researchers in business and management: Don Moore, Samuel Swift, Zachariah Sharek, and Gino. Moore et al. describe three studies, each indicating that people often fail to consider the entire situation when making judgments about a person's performance. Included here are the descriptions of Experiments 1 and 3. The article originally appeared in 2010 in the peer-reviewed social science journal *Personality and Social Psychology Bulletin*.

ABSTRACT

Performance (such as a course grade) is a joint function of an individual's ability (such as intelligence) and the situation (such as the instructor's grading leniency). Prior research has documented a human bias toward dispositional inference, which ascribes performance to individual ability, even when it is better explained through situational influences on performance. It is hypothesized here that this tendency leads admissions decisions to favor students coming from institutions with lenient grading because those students have their high grades mistaken for evidence of high ability. Three experiments show that those who obtain high scores simply because of lenient grading are favored in selection. These results have implications for research on attribution because they provide a more stringent test of the correspondence bias and allow for a more precise measure of its size. Implications for university admissions and personnel selection decisions are also discussed.

KEYWORDS

attribution, decision making, educational psychology, judgment and decision making, organizational behavior

Received January 5, 2009; revision accepted November 19, 2009

Who is likely to be the more ambitious and hard-working graduate student—the one with a 3.6 grade point average (GPA) from a school where the average GPA is 3.4 or the one with a 3.3 from an institution where the average GPA is 2.8? This sort of difficult attribution problem is crucial to all types of personnel selection decisions, from admitting applicants to picking teammates (Staw, Bell, & Clausen, 1986; Staw, Sutton, & Pelled, 1994). The question we pose in this article is whether those making the selections can adequately adjust for the difficulty of success when making inferences about what performance signals about abilities.

We begin with the fact that undergraduate institutions vary in their grading standards, even schools that are otherwise similar in selectivity and student quality (Attewell, 2001; Bagues, Sylos Labini, & Zinovyeva, 2008; Goldman & Widawski, 1976). This basic fact raises the question of whether those who use information about grades to assess students (such as future employers or graduate schools) use that information appropriately. Do people appropriately adjust their interpretation of grades based on the leniency of grading? Research findings on the psychology of attribution give us reason to doubt that they do.

BIASES IN THE ATTRIBUTION PROCESS

The problem of assessing the informative value of academic grades is a special case of a more general problem: how to infer the qualities of the individual (such as intellectual abilities) from behavior or outcomes (GPA) while subtracting out the influence of the situation (leniency of grading). The solution to this problem is provided by Kurt Lewin's (1951) attributional equation: Behavior = *f*(Disposition, Situation). In other words, behavior is a joint function of both the individual's disposition and the influence of the situation. We capitalize on Gilbert's (1994) suggestion that the Lewinian equation often takes the specific form: Disposition = Behavior – Situation. In this case, Academic Performance = Grades – Grading Leniency.[1] However, research suggests that people do not apply this simple formula perfectly. One of the most common biases in the attribution process is the tendency to ascribe too little influence to the situation and too much to the individual's disposition (Davis-Blake & Pfeffer, 1989; Jones & Harris, 1967; Nisbett & Borgida, 1975; Ross, 1977).

Ross, Amabile, and Steinmetz (1977) examined this phenomenon in a study that paired participants and randomly assigned one of them to the role of quiz master, who made up the questions, and one to the role of quiz taker, who answered them. Naturally, the quiz master knew some answers that the quiz taker did not. But rather than attributing this to the quiz master's role-conferred advantage, observers reported that the quiz master was the more knowledgeable of the pair. Attributions of knowledgeability were biased by an excessive belief in the correspondence between behaviors and dispositions. This is what Gilbert and Malone (1995) called the *correspondence bias* and what Ross (1977) called the *fundamental attribution error.*

IS THE CORRESPONDENCE BIAS REALLY A BIAS?

In Ross et al.'s (1977) experiment, as in many studies demonstrating the correspondence bias, it was difficult for individual participants to precisely determine the strength of the situation. On average, the quiz master was unlikely to be more knowledgeable than the quiz taker (given random assignment to roles), but that was little help for the individual who had to decide whether a specific quiz master is more or less knowledgeable than a particular quiz taker. To accurately judge the strength of the situation, participants in Ross et al.'s experiment needed to know what proportion of questions, on average, quiz takers failed to answer correctly. If participants had this information, they would have been better able to specify the strength of the situational differences between the quiz master and the quiz taker. But they did not get the information. If it is impossible to determine the strength of the situation, it becomes impossible to adjust for it when making attributions.

This fact raises the possibility that the correspondence bias, as it has been demonstrated previously, might simply be a problem of incomplete information. We address this possibility by examining whether the correspondence bias persists when people have all the information they need to adjust their attributions of individual abilities based on the influence of the situation. Participants in our experiments are given quantified information about both the behavior (i.e., grades) and the situation (i.e., grading norms). Previous research on the correspondence bias has not tested the bias in situations where participants have clear, quantified information about both the situation and the outcome. Furthermore, prior studies failed to specify the strength of the situation. This leaves open some important questions about the causes of the correspondence bias. Our research paradigm can help answer these questions. If the correspondence bias persists even in the presence of full information, that would strengthen its standing as a bias and not simply an incomplete information problem.

HYPOTHESIS

The primary hypothesis we investigate is that absolute performance will be insufficiently discounted relative to the ease of the task. Specifically, raw GPAs will be taken as evidence of academic performance and not sufficiently adjusted to account for the ease with which those grades were earned. In other words, an applicant's absolute GPA will have a stronger influence on admission decisions than will the grading leniency of their institutions. Rationally, evaluations of an applicant's prior academic performance should rely primarily on two things: (a) the rigor or quality of the institution or program of study and (b) the individual's performance relative to others in that same program (see Berry & Sackett, 2009). Our studies control for the first consideration and vary two aspects of the second: absolute performance (indicated by the individual's GPA) and the ease of obtaining a high score (indicated by the average GPA at the undergraduate institution). The easier the task, the less impressive high performance should become. Evaluations should give the leniency of grading (as measured by the average grade at the undergraduate institution) a decision weight equal in size and opposite in sign from that given to each candidate's GPA.

To draw an analogy, assume your goal is to pick the tallest players for your basketball team. In a desperate attempt to improve their chances of making the team, some of the players trying out have worn elevator shoes. If you know only the player's total height (with shoes) and the height of the shoes, then those two measurements should be weighed equally and oppositely in determining the player's shoeless height: Each inch contributed by the shoe will reduce the player's size by 1 in. when the shoes are removed. Instead, we hypothesize that the positive effect of individual performance (e.g., height) on evaluations will not be matched by the discounting effect of situational factors (e.g., elevator shoes). In the context of grades and admission, our hypothesis predicts that people will favor those from institutions with lenient grading because absolute GPA will be weighed heavily in evaluations of applicants, but average grades at the institution will not be sufficiently discounted. In other words, those who show up in elevator shoes will be more likely to make the team.

Experiments 1 and 2 consider graduate school admission decisions. Experiment 3 replicates the same type of decision problem outside the context of GPAs and admissions decisions. All three experiments are consistent in showing that nominal performance is too readily taken at face value without discounting for obvious situational influences, even when the effect of those situational influences is obvious and easily quantified.

EXPERIMENT 1

This experiment put participants in the role of admissions decision makers and presented them with information about specific candidates' performance (GPA) as well as an indication of the distribution from which the GPA came (college average GPA). We manipulated these two factors in a 3 (GPA relative to average: above vs. equal vs. below) × 3 (average GPA at undergraduate institution: high vs. medium vs. low) within-subjects design. Candidates had GPAs that were .3 above their school's average, at their school's average, or .3 below their school's average. This manipulation was crossed with a manipulation of the average grade at the candidate's alma mater: Applicants came from colleges with average grades that were either high (average GPA of 3.6), medium (3.0), or low (2.4). Note that to reduce the obviousness of our manipulation, both the GPAs of the individual applicants and the average GPAs of their institutions varied slightly around these precise points (within .02).[2]

Naturally, we expected that being above average would have a positive effect on the probability of being admitted. Our more interesting hypothesis is that the school's average GPA would have a significant positive effect on the probability of admission: Candidates from colleges with high average grades would be more likely to be admitted. In other words, we expected that people will not sufficiently discount high grades that are due to lenient institutional grading practices.

Method

Participants. Fifty-five undergraduates at a research university in the Northeastern United States participated in the study in exchange for course credit in their introductory business courses.

Procedure. Participants were given the following instructions:

> In this exercise, you will be playing the role of a member of the admissions committee at a selective MBA program. You are selecting students who would like to obtain masters degrees in business administration.
>
> Your most important goal is to select the best candidates from among the applicants. In general, you usually have space to admit about half the applicants. You will see the applications of nine hypothetical students. The set of applicants that you will review all graduated from colleges of similar quality and selectivity. Please review each applicant carefully in order to assess the quality of their prior academic performance in college. Please review one candidate at a time. Answer the questions about each candidate before turning the page to read about the next candidate.

Information about the candidates included their GPA, the average GPA at the institution from which they obtained their undergraduate degree, and their grades in the last 10 classes they took. These classes were listed for each candidate. Both the candidate's grade and the class average for each course were shown. The candidate's grades in the 10 classes had the same mean as the candidate's overall GPA, and the average grades in each of the courses had the same mean as the undergraduate institution overall. To highlight each candidate's relative standing, the difference between his or her GPA and the average for the college was also specifically shown. This list of classes was counterbalanced across all conditions so as not to confound it with experimental condition.

For each candidate, participants were asked to (a) evaluate how successful the candidate had been in college on a 7-point scale, anchored at 1 (*very unsuccessful*) and 7 (*very successful*), and (b) report how likely they would be to admit them (as a numerical probability between 0%

and 100%). After evaluating all nine candidates, they were asked to look back through the set and admit only four of the nine. In sum, for each candidate, each participant provided three ratings: (a) a rating of prior success, (b) an estimated probability of admission, and (c) an actual admission decision.

Participants were randomly assigned to one of nine randomly determined order conditions in a Latin squares design such that each candidate's position in the order was balanced. Names of the nine fictional colleges and course lists were counterbalanced across manipulations.

Results and Discussion

The descriptive statistics for the measures used as dependent variables are reported in Table 3. The three ratings of each candidate correlated strongly with each other (all *r*s above .6) and were therefore standardized by converting them to *z* scores and averaged to form a single measure of candidate admissibility (Cronbach's alpha = .86).

This admissibility assessment was then subject to a 3 (GPA relative to average) × 3 (average GPA at undergraduate institution) within-subjects ANOVA. Naturally, the results show a main effect of relative GPA, $F(2, 108) = 333.84$, $p < .001, \eta^2 = .86$. Those with above-average GPAs received higher admissibility ratings ($M = 0.71$, $SD = 0.63$) than did those with below-average GPAs ($M = -0.67$, $SD = 0.41$). As hypothesized, the results also show a significant main effect for average GPA at undergraduate institution, $F(2, 108) = 96.35$, $p < .001$, $\eta^2 = .64$. Consistent with our expectations, candidates from institutions with lenient grading were more likely to receive higher admissibility ratings ($M = 0.46$, $SD = 0.80$) than were candidates from schools with strict grading ($M = -0.52$, $SD = 0.56$). The results also reveal a GPA × Leniency interaction effect, $F(4, 216) = 6.44$, $p < .001$, $\eta^2 = .11$. This interaction describes the fact that the effect of grading leniency differs as a function of relative GPA. Specifically, the benefit of having performed better than one's peers is stronger for those graded most leniently (where it increases admissibility by 1.26) than for those graded strictly (where it only increases admissibility by .81). However, as Table 3 shows, the effect of having been graded leniently persists across all conditions.

. . .

The results of Experiment 1 are consistent with the hypothesis that absolute GPAs are taken as direct evidence of prior academic performance and are not appropriately discounted by the ease with which those grades were earned. However, it is obvious that participants did not completely ignore information about grading leniency; they just did not weight the discounting information as heavily as they did the nominal performance numbers.

Table 3

Ratings of Undergraduate Success, Estimated Probability of Being Offered Admission, and Observed Probability of Being Admitted to Graduate School Based on Undergraduate Grade Point Average (GPA) and Average Grades at Undergraduate Institution (Experiment 1)

Institution average GPA:	Low ≈ 2.4			Medium ≈ 3.0			High ≈ 3.6		
Individual GPA:	.3 below average	About average	.3 above average	.3 below average	About average	.3 above average	.3 below average	About average	.3 above average
Rated prior success (1-7)	2.33 (1.00)	3.42 (0.92)	4.16 (0.96)	3.05 (0.85)	4.25 (0.91)	5.05 (0.78)	3.64 (1.01)	4.49 (1.00)	6.25 (0.75)
Rated probability of acceptance	20% (14%)	36% (17%)	45% (18%)	32% (18%)	47% (19%)	61% (17%)	44% (19%)	54% (20%)	83% (15%)
Actual acceptance rate	2%	7%	56%	7%	50%	96%	30%	61%	94%

Standard deviations appear in parentheses.

This result is notable because the information we gave our participants on the strength of the situation is so much clearer than it has been in prior studies of the correspondence bias. The fact that we provided our participants with unambiguous quantifications of both people's behavior (their GPAs) and the situation that gave rise to that behavior (the average GPA at that institution) means that we can make stronger claims about bias than can prior research. In our experimental paradigm it is clear that GPA and grading leniency should have been equally and oppositely weighted. The fact that they are not allows us to pinpoint exactly how it is that our participants' decisions deviate from the optimal decision and how much this matters. In Experiment 1 grading leniency received a decision weight that was 67% the size of the GPA decision weight. We obtain two more estimates of this discrepancy from Experiments 2 and 3.

. . .

EXPERIMENT 3

One potential concern regarding Experiments 1 and 2 is that if people believe that high average grades are correlated with desirable features of a college or its graduates (despite our assurance that the institutions did not differ with regard to quality and selectivity) the tendency to favor graduates of institutions with high average grades makes sense. To rule out this explanation for our findings, we conducted a third experiment outside the domain of university admissions decisions. Instead, participants in Experiment 3 were asked to imagine that they had to select members for a "quiz bowl" trivia team. They reviewed the prior test performances of 10 applicants, 5 of whom had taken an easy test and 5 of whom had taken a difficult test. Both tests were on the subject of U.S. geography. Our hypothesis was that those who had high scores because they had taken the easy test would, like those who come from institutions with lenient grading, be more likely to be selected.

Method

Participants. Participants were 71 undergraduates at a research university in the northeastern United States participating for money.

Design and Procedure. The experiment employed a 2 (experience: experience with task vs. no experience with task) × 2 (task difficulty: easy vs. hard) design. The first factor was manipulated between subjects, while the second factor was manipulated within subjects.

The task for Experiment 3 was similar to the first two experiments: to evaluate 10 candidates and eventually decide which 5 to select. However, participants in this experiment were asked to select the candidates they thought would perform above average on a third quiz, which was shown to participants at the time of selection:

> In this study, we are interested in your ability to predict the performance of others. You will now see the scores of ten people who took one of two quizzes. For five of the people, you will see their scores on the first quiz. For the other five, you will see their scores on the second quiz. For each of the ten contestants, their correct answers are marked with a check and their incorrect answers are marked with an X. For each of the ten contestants, we will ask you to estimate their knowledgeability about US geography. All ten of these people also took a third quiz on the same topic of US geography. After examining ten contestants, we will ask you to identify the five people you think are most likely to perform well on the third quiz. This third quiz was the same for all ten contestants. You will earn $2 today for each contestant you pick whose score is in the top half of the performers on the third quiz. Therefore, if you correctly pick the five top scorers, we will reward you with $10 in cash for your performance. If the five contestants you pick are the five worst performers on the third quiz, you will not earn any additional money for this study.

The first factor we manipulated was experience with the task to test for the possibility that prior experience would reduce the bias observed in our first two studies. Based on previous findings (Epley, Savitsky, & Gilovich, 2002; Van Boven, Kamada, & Gilovich, 1999) we hypothesized that participants' experience with the task before making their judgments would attenuate the size of the correspondence bias. After all, experience with the task helps make salient the situational pressures through their effects on one's own behavior. This is in part why people are far more sensitive to situational effects on their own behavior than on the behavior of others (Jones & Nisbett, 1971). In this way, we hoped that personal experience with the situation could help people appreciate how situational constraints would affect the behavior and thus reduce the correspondence bias.

Participants in the experience condition were given an additional page with instructions at the beginning of the experiment:

> Your first task in this study is to take two different trivia quizzes. Your goal is to answer as many questions correctly as you can, using your memory alone. You may not consult other people or information sources other than your own memory. Good luck!

Participants in the no-experience condition did not receive this additional page with instructions.

After the experience manipulation, participants evaluated each of the candidates for the quiz bowl trivia team. For each of the 10 candidates, participants saw actual completed quizzes from participants in a previous pilot study that included candidates' answers marked as correct or incorrect. Participants saw quizzes from 5 candidates who had taken a difficult quiz with questions like "How many U.S. states border Canada?" (mean score: 1 out of 10) and they saw quizzes from 5 who had taken a simple quiz with questions like "The Bronx is part of what U.S. city?" (mean score: 8.9 out of 10).

These 10 quizzes were selected such that the mean score and standard deviation for each type of quiz roughly matched the mean and standard deviation among all quiz takers in the pilot study from which the quizzes were selected. We divided these 10 quizzes into two sets such that the easy and difficult quiz scores of the candidates in each set were similar to each other. Set 1 included the easy quizzes of Candidates 2, 3, 4, 5, and 8, and the difficult quizzes of Candidates 1, 6, 7, 9, and 10. Set 2 included the easy quizzes of Candidates 1, 6, 7, 9, and 10, and the difficult quizzes of Candidates 2, 3, 4, 5, and 8. We also varied order as follows. We first randomized the order of the 10 candidates, and then we reversed this order to make a second order condition. Participants were randomly assigned to one of these four conditions created by our 2 (set) × 2 (order) between-subjects design. Note that the easy and difficult test scores were from the same, real individuals who previously participated in a pilot study.

After seeing a candidate's completed quiz, participants were then reminded of the candidate's score (out of 10) and were told the average score and standard deviation among all 10 test takers on that quiz. For the first set, the 5 easy scores participants saw were 9, 9, 9, 7, and 10 (M = 8.8, SD = 1.1). For the second set, the 5 easy scores were 10, 8, 8, 9, and 10 (M = 9.0, SD = 1.0). The 5 difficult scores participants saw from the first set were 1, 2, 0, 2, and 0 (M = 1.0, SD = 1.0). For the second set, the 5 difficult scores were 2, 1, 2, 0, and 0 (M = 1.0, SD = 1.0). Participants were then asked to rate how knowledgeable about U.S. geography they thought each contestant was using a 7-point scale that ranged from *not knowledgeable at all* to *very knowledgeable*.

Before making their selections, participants were reminded that each candidate they had seen had either taken a simple or a difficult quiz. Three questions then asked participants to compare the two quizzes on 7-point scales: (a) "Do you think the two tests were equally good at testing candidates' trivia skills?" (from *simple is better* to *difficult is better*), (b) "Do you think the two tests were equally fair measures of ability?" (from *simple is more fair* to *difficult is more fair*), (c) "Do you think the two tests will be equally good predictors of performance if chosen for the team?" (from *simple is better* to *difficult is better*).

After they had compared the two quizzes, participants read the following:

> Please select which candidates you think will do best on a quiz that was given to all quiz-takers. A copy of this quiz is below. Remember that for each person you select who performs better than average on the quiz at the bottom of this page you will earn $2.

The third test was also a geography test, of intermediate difficulty.

After participants made their selections, their choices were scored and payoffs were computed. After being paid, participants were thanked, debriefed, and dismissed.

Results and Discussion

We computed two averages for ratings of knowledgeability: one for the five contestants whose easy quizzes participants saw, and another for the five contestants whose difficult quizzes participants saw. These averages were then submitted to a 2 (experience) × 2 (test difficulty) mixed ANOVA with repeated measures on the second factor. The results reveal a significant within-subjects effect of test difficulty, $F(1, 69) = 136$, $p < .001$, $\eta^2 = .66$. When participants saw a contestant's easy quiz, that contestant was rated as significantly more knowledgeable ($M = 5.13$, $SD = 1.13$) than was the same contestant rated by participants who had seen his or her difficult quiz ($M = 2.65$, $SD = 1.01$). The main effect of experience was not significant, $F(1, 69) < 1$, $p = .59$. If experience taking the two quizzes helped participants avoid the correspondence bias, it would have shown up as an Experience × Difficulty interaction, wherein experience reduced the effect of difficulty on rated knowledgeability. This interaction does not quite attain significance, $F(1, 69) = 3.12$, $p = .08$, $\eta^2 = .04$. However, this marginally significant effect is not due to a debiasing influence provided by the experience manipulation. Although the difference between ratings of the easy ($M = 4.98$) and hard ($M = 2.88$) tests are significant among those without experience, $t(33) = 6.42$, $p < .001$, this difference is marginally larger among those *with* experience, reflecting a stronger difference between the easy ($M = 5.28$) and hard ($M = 2.43$) tests, $t(36) = 10.43$, $p < .001$.

Participants were also more likely to pick contestants whose easy quiz scores they had seen when predicting which contestants would score better on the third quiz. Although those who had taken the easy quiz represented 50% of the contestants participants saw, they represented 68% of contestants selected. This 68% is significantly above the 50% we would have expected, had participants perfectly predicted contestants' scores on the third quiz and only selected those, $t(70) = 7.30$, $p < .001$. It is also significantly above the 60% we might have expected if participants had been following a justifiable strategy of picking the top two scorers on the easy and difficult quizzes, and then always selecting the next best easy quiz scorer for their fifth pick, $t(70) = 3.35$, $p = .001$.

To compare the results of Experiment 3 with those of Experiments 1 and 2, we conducted a binary logistic regression in which selection was the dependent variable. The independent variables in this regression were (a) the quiz score from each contestant the participant saw and (b) the difficulty of that quiz, as measured by the mean score. Consistent with our hypothesis and with the findings of the other experiments, the results reveal that the contestant's actual score was weighted more heavily ($B = 1.61$, $SE = .13$, $p < .001$) than was the difficulty of their quiz ($B = -1.37$, $SE = .12$, $p < .001$), $\chi^2(1) = 81.10$, $p < .001$. In this case, the discounting effect due to quiz ease was 85% of the size of the effect of quiz performance.

Specifically, what this means is that going from an average score on the difficult quiz (1.11 out of 10) to an average score on the easy quiz (8.78 out of 10) increases a contestant's probability of being selected from 27% to 70%. This effect is illustrated in Figure 14.2. To construct this graph, we conducted two binary logistic regressions using quiz score performance to predict the probability of being selected. One

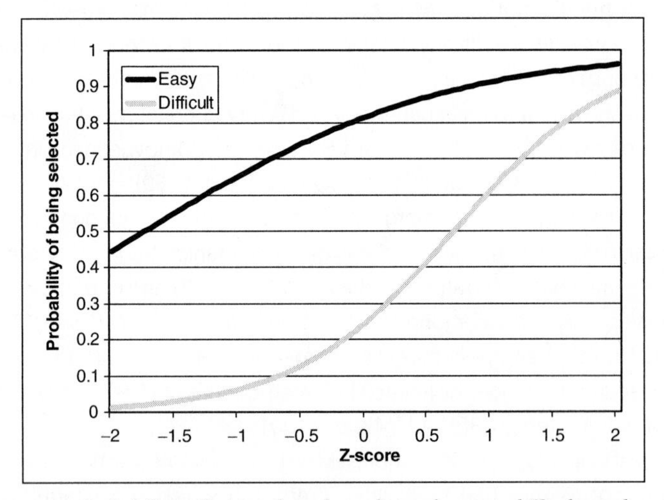

Figure 14.2 Probability of being selected, conditional on quiz difficulty and score relative to others on that quiz (Experiment 3)

regression used easy quiz scores and another used difficult quiz scores. The results show a large effect for quiz difficulty, where easy quiz takers were substantially more likely to be chosen regardless of their relative performance on the quiz.

When participants were then asked to explicitly compare the virtues of the easy and the difficult quizzes, participants rated the difficult quiz as a better test of ability than the simple quiz, as indicated by the fact that each rating is above the rating scale's midpoint of 4 ($M = 4.54$, $SD = 1.95$), $t(70) = 2.32$, $p = .024$. They also rated the difficult test as more fair than the simple quiz ($M = 4.44$, $SD = 1.87$), $t(70) = 1.97$, $p = .053$, and as a better predictor of future performance than the easy quiz ($M = 4.75$, $SD = 1.90$), $t(70) = 3.31$, $p = .001$. It would appear that the only way to reconcile these ratings with participants' systematic preference for takers of the easy quiz is that they believed that the difficult test was better at revealing just how inept the takers of the difficult quiz were.

GENERAL DISCUSSION

The results of the three experiments we present here are consistent in showing that information about the strength of the situation—in this case, task difficulty—tends not to be used sufficiently to discount information about an individual's performance even when performance and the situation's influence on it are obvious and quantified. As a result, students from institutions with lenient grading benefit from their high grades.

Contributions to Theory and Research

Our results suggest that neither underestimating the impact of the situation nor overestimating the impact of behavior are necessary conditions for producing the correspondence bias. Our participants did not need to estimate either in the research paradigms we employed. In addition, the results suggest that the correspondence bias can persist even when information about both behavior and situation are known with equal clarity and are presented in the same format and modality. This is testament to the bias's robustness. Perhaps more importantly, the present results afford a useful quantification of the size of the correspondence bias. Its hallmark is that the judgmental weight attached to the situation is lower than the weight attached to behavior.

In our results, we find that the situation is weighted between 34% and 85% of what it should be. Clearly, there are factors that varied between our experiments that influenced the size of the correspondence bias. Identifying these moderators of the effect size will be a useful task for future research. Another potential avenue for future research is to investigate the moderators of the effect of performance relative to peers. In Experiment 1, our results suggested that outperforming peers had the strongest effect on those from lenient-grading institutions. The results from Experiment 2 suggested that outperforming peers was most important at institutions of moderate grading standards. In Experiment 3 we found that outperforming peers was most valuable on hard tests, where the grading standards were toughest. We would only note that none of these interactions eliminated the benefits of lenient grading and task ease. Our goal in this research was to document the effect of situational influences on perceptions of individual performance using experimental designs that allow us to estimate exactly how much the correspondence bias affects judgments of performance. This represents a step beyond prior work on the topic.

This research also contributes to the prior literature on the correspondence bias by precisely showing why such an effect matters for real decisions by experienced professionals. The same effects documented here appear in actual admissions decisions (Swift, Moore, Sharek, & Gino, 2010). Moreover, when professional admissions staffers are asked to make the same judgments as those made by participants in our laboratory experiments, the results are indistinguishable from those of the student participants presented in this article: Both display the correspondence bias to a similar degree (Swift et al., 2010). Consequently, graduate programs are collectively choosing to select students who come from undergraduate programs with lenient grading rather than selecting the best students. The consequences could be substantial for both the quality of students selected and the quality of those graduate programs (Berry & Sackett, 2009).

Practical Implications

Three experiments supported the hypothesis that people rely heavily on nominal performance (such as GPA) as an indicator of success while failing to sufficiently take into account information about the distributions of performances from which it came. The question of whether people—especially decision makers such as admissions officers—can correct for the correspondence bias in judgments of others is fundamental to problems of social inequality and class mobility. A meritocracy depends on being able to identify merit that, in reality, is often clouded by variations in circumstance. Given persistent disparities in the difficulty of the conditions into which Americans are born (Neckerman & Torche, 2007; Wilson, 1990), it is essential for colleges and employers to be able to adjust their estimations of ability appropriately based on the ease with which individual promise can result in nominal performance. The results of the present study suggest pessimism—people will too often be judged based on their nominal performances, with insufficient regard to the difficulty of achieving those results.

Can we offer constructive advice to those in admissions offices, personnel offices, and hiring committees responsible for making such selection decisions? We believe we can. The advice is consistent with a great deal of other evidence that demonstrates the superiority of statistical over intuitive judgment (Dawes, 1972, 1979; Dawes, Faust, & Meehl, 1989; Grove & Meehl, 1996). The advice is that decision makers should not rely exclusively on their unaided intuitive judgments and they should instead obtain the help of a computational decision tool. In this case, what that means is simply that GPA ought to be considered exclusively as a percentile rank or *z*-score deviation from the mean at that person's school. Given the power and persistence of the effect we document, the implication seems to be that decision makers should not be allowed to see raw scores or absolute GPA and should only see the standardized score that shows relative performance.

Don A. Moore, Samuel A. Swift, and Zachariah S. Sharek, Carnegie Mellon University, Pittsburgh, Pennsylvania, USA; Francesca Gino, University of North Carolina at Chapel Hill, Chapel Hill, North Carolina, USA
Corresponding Author: Don A. Moore, Tepper School, Carnegie Mellon University, 5000 Forbes Avenue, Pittsburgh, PA 15213, e-mail: don.moore@alumni.carleton.edu.

ACKNOWLEDGMENTS

The authors thank Mark Fichman, Mingwei Hsu, Bill Klein, and Justin Kruger for helpful comments. They also thank Lauren DeVito, Bill Mangan, and Jessica Wisdom for help with data collection.

DECLARATION OF CONFLICTING INTERESTS

The authors declared no conflicts of interest with respect to the authorship and/or publication of this article.

FUNDING

The authors received the following financial support for the research and/or authorship of this article: National Science Foundation Grant SES-0718691 and a SURG research grant from Carnegie Mellon University.

NOTES

1. This is assuming similarity across institutions in both (a) institution quality and (b) within-institution variability.
2. This is also the case for Experiment 2.

REFERENCES

Attewell, P. (2001). The winner-take-all high school: Organizational adaptations to educational stratification. *Sociology of Education, 74*, 267-295.

Bagues, M. F., Sylos Labini, M., & Zinovyeva, N. (2008). Differential grading standards and university funding: Evidence from Italy. *CESifo Economic Studies, 54*, 149-176.

Berry, C. M., & Sackett, P. R. (2009). Individual differences in course choice result in underestimation of the validity of college admissions systems. *Psychological Science, 20*, 822-830.

Davis-Blake, A., & Pfeffer, J. (1989). Just a mirage: The search for dispositional effects in organizational research. *Academy of Management Review, 14*, 385-400.

Dawes, R. M. (1972). In defense of "bootstrapping." *American Psychologist, 27*, 773-774.

Dawes, R. M. (1979). The robust beauty of improper linear models in decision making. *American Psychologist, 34*, 571-582.

Dawes, R. M., Faust, D., & Meehl, P. E. (1989). Clinical versus actuarial judgment. *Science, 243*(4899), 1668-1674.

Epley, N., Savitsky, K., & Gilovich, T. (2002). Empathy neglect: Reconciling the spotlight effect and the correspondence bias. *Journal of Personality and Social Psychology, 83*, 300-312.

Gilbert, D. T. (1994). Attribution and interpersonal perception. In A. Tesser (Ed.), *Advanced social psychology* (pp. 99-147). New York, NY: McGraw-Hill.

Gilbert, D. T., & Malone, P. S. (1995). The correspondence bias. *Psychological Bulletin, 117*, 21-38.

Goldman, R. D., & Widawski, M. H. (1976). A within-subjects technique for comparing college grading standards: Implications in the validity of the evaluation of college achievement. *Educational and Psychological Measurement, 36*, 381-390.

Grove, W. M., & Meehl, P. E. (1996). Comparative efficiency of informal (subjective, impressionistic) and formal (mechanical, algorithmic) prediction procedures: The clinical-statistical controversy. *Psychology, Public Policy, and Law, 2*, 293-323.

Jones, E. E., & Harris, V. A. (1967). The attribution of attitudes. *Journal of Experimental Social Psychology, 3*, 1-24.

Jones, E. E., & Nisbett, R. E. (1971). The actor and the observer: Divergent perceptions of the causes of behavior. In E. E. Jones, D. E. Kanouse, H. H. Kelley, R. E. Nisbett, S. Valins, & B. Weiner (Eds.), *Attribution: Perceiving the causes of behavior* (pp. 79-94). Morristown, NJ: General Learning Press.

Lewin, K. (1951). *Field theory in social science*. New York, NY: Harper & Row.

Neckerman, K. M., & Torche, F. (2007). Inequality: Causes and consequences. *Annual Review of Sociology, 33*, 335-357.

Nisbett, R. E., & Borgida, E. (1975). Attribution and the psychology of prediction. *Journal of Personality and Social Psychology, 32*, 932-943.

Ross, L. (1977). The intuitive psychologist and his shortcomings: Distortions in the attribution process. In L. Berkowitz (Ed.), *Advances in experimental social psychology* (Vol. 10, pp. 173-220). New York, NY: Academic Press.

Ross, L., Amabile, T. M., & Steinmetz, J. L. (1977). Social roles, social control, and biases in social-perception processes. *Journal of Personality and Social Psychology, 35*, 485-494.

Staw, B. M., Bell, N. E., & Clausen, J. A. (1986). The dispositional approach to job attitudes: A lifetime longitudinal test. *Administrative Science Quarterly, 31*, 56-68.

Staw, B. M., Sutton, R. I., & Pelled, L. H. (1994). Employee positive emotion and favorable outcomes at the workplace. *Organization Science, 5*, 51-71.

Swift, S. A., Moore, D. A., Sharek, Z., & Gino, F. (2010). *Seeing through performance: Attribution errors in performance evaluation by experts.* Unpublished manuscript.

Van Boven, L., Kamada, A., & Gilovich, T. (1999). The perceiver as perceived: Everyday intuitions about the correspondence bias. *Journal of Personality and Social Psychology, 77*, 1188-1199.

Wilson, W. J. (1990). *The truly disadvantaged: The inner city, the underclass, and public policy.* Chicago, IL: University of Chicago Press.

QUESTIONS ABOUT MEANING

1. What is *correspondence bias*? What was the researchers' research question or hypothesis? How does this research fill a gap left by previous studies of correspondence bias?
2. Describe the methods and results for Experiment 1.
3. Describe the participants, methods, and results for Experiment 3. How did the researchers motivate participants in Experiment 3 to carefully assess the data provided?

QUESTIONS FOR RHETORICAL ANALYSIS

1. Analyze the sections preceding the description of Experiment 1. Together these sections could be considered the article's introduction. What moves typically found in academic introductions do you find in these sections? Do you think it is an effective introduction to the article? Why or why not?
2. In the Results section for Experiment 3 (included here in its entirety), identify summary sentences that allow readers without mathematical training to understand the key findings. In other words, what sentences warrant highlighting for the reader wanting to determine what the researchers learned?

MAKING CONNECTIONS

1. Do the authors' findings about GPA correspondence bias surprise you? What solution to the problem of correspondence bias do the writers offer to hiring and admissions counselors? Can you think of any other solutions to the problem?
2. Reread the description of the research by Ross, Amabile, and Steinmetz (in the section titled "Biases in the Attribution Process"). How are their findings similar to the findings of Moore et al. and also similar to the findings of Jones and Harris, described in Norenzayan and Nisbett's article (chapter 13)?

   In her article for *The Wall Street Journal* (see previous reading), Gino makes correspondence bias research relevant for *Wall Street Journal* readers—business managers and executives. Using Gino's *Wall Street Journal* article as a model, write your own article for a fictional newspaper for college admission officers. In your article, explain what correspondence bias is, summarize the research cited in the previous paragraph, and tailor your discussion to *your* target audience: college admissions officers.

Psychology

"Myside Bias in Thinking about Abortion," JONATHAN BARON

The next article is all about arguments, specifically arguments that follow what is called the Toulmin Model.

Stephen Toulmin (1922–2009) was a British philosopher who identified six elements commonly found in arguments. The *claim* is the conclusion or thesis the writer wants the audience to accept. The *grounds* (sometimes called data) are the evidence supporting the claim. Grounds may include statistics, studies, examples, expert opinion, or types of reasoning. A *warrant* is the logical link between the evidence and the claim. It answers the question "How or why does the evidence prove the claim is true?" The warrant can be unstated, but academic writers tend to explicitly explain how their evidence supports their thesis to ensure the reader reaches the same conclusion. Claim, data, and warrants are the basic components of arguments.

An argument may also include backing, rebuttals, or qualifiers. *Backing* provides further support for or justification that the warrant is valid. In addition, a writer may want to respond to counterarguments. This element is called *rebuttal*. For a skeptical audience, acknowledging counterarguments can be just as important as supporting the central claim(s). Finally, most academic writers use *qualifiers* (like *most, usually, sometimes*) to acknowledge restrictions or exceptions to their claim.

In the following article, psychology professor Jonathan Baron describes a study he conducted to assess the quality of student arguments. His research indicates that acknowledging opposing viewpoints (rebuttals)—valued by academic writers as a way to show that they are fully informed on an issue—is a skill that must be learned. The study appeared in 1995 in the peer-reviewed journal *Thinking and Reasoning*, which publishes studies about thinking, reasoning, and problem solving.

ABSTRACT

College-student subjects made notes about the morality of early abortion, as if they were preparing for a class discussion. Analysis of the quality of their arguments suggests that a distinction can be made between arguments based on well-supported warrants and those based on warrants that are easily criticized. The subjects also evaluated notes made by other, hypothetical, students preparing for the same discussion. Most subjects evaluated the set of arguments as better when the arguments were all on one side than when both sides were presented, even when the hypothetical subject was on the opposite side of the issue from the evaluator. Subjects who favored one-sidedness also tended to make one-sided arguments themselves. The results suggests that "myside bias" is partly caused by beliefs about what makes thinking good.

The opposing sides in the abortion debate in the United States are often accused of poor thinking and poor argumentation. It is easy to find examples of poor argumentation. For example, a pro-choice article in the *Daily Pennsylvanian* (the student newspaper at my university) said, "If government rules against abortion, it will be acting contrary to one of the basic rights of Americans, . . . the right to make decisions for oneself."

Just what makes such arguments seem weak? And what can they tell us about people's thinking about such contentious issues? I shall suggest here that much of the problem is the absence of "active open-mindedness" (Baron, 1994a). In particular, people fail to search for arguments on both sides. This causes them to neglect counterarguments that undercut the claims they make to others and themselves. For example, the argument in the last paragraph neglects an obvious counterargument: if abortion really is murder, then the government is no more taking rights away than it does when it bans homicide, so Americans do not and should not have the right to make decisions that cause harm to others.

Note that this counterargument weakens the force of the original claim. I distinguish this kind of counterargument from one that leaves the implication of the original argument alone but adds a claim with the opposite implication, e.g., that the fetus has rights of its own, so the question is one of conflicting rights. In Toulmin's (1958) terms, the first kind of weakness is in the warrant for the claim. The original argument was based on the warrant that Americans have the right to make decisions for themselves. The counterargument holds that this warrant is weak, since it already has many exceptions. When a neglected counterargument leaves the implication intact but weighs in on the other side, Toulmin would say that the problem is in neglecting a potential rebuttal. Arguments in discourse leave room for the rebuttal with phrases such as "other things being equal." When people fail to add such qualifiers, however, we cannot tell whether they have just not learned to say things like this or whether they truly think that their arguments are sufficient. When we study thinking through its verbal expression, we can often detect weak warrants in single arguments. To detect failure to consider rebuttals, we need a more complete record of a person's thinking.

The two kinds of weakness in arguments correspond to failure of search and failure of inference (Baron, 1994a). Weak warrants make for weak inferences. At a slightly deeper level, however, use of a weak warrant can be understood as a failure to search for evidence about the backing (justification) of the warrant itself (Baron, 1990). Thus, use of a principle of reasoning, or heuristic, or warrant, without sufficient justification can result from previous failures to reflect about principles of reasoning. These failures might be on the part of those who taught the principle in question as well as on the part of the user (who might have had good reason to trust her teachers).

Consider another example. Some subjects (in pilot studies) argue along the following lines: "I believe that the fetus is a person because, once it 'starts,' nothing can naturally stop it except for abortion; thus it is equivalent to murder." Nicholas Maxwell (personal communication) called this the moldy-bread argument: if you let bread sit out, nothing will naturally stop it from becoming moldy and inedible; therefore, eating bread is equivalent to eating moldy bread. This analogy shows that the logic, the form of the argument, fails. Likewise, others argue, "One wouldn't have to decide about an abortion if they didn't get impregnated in the first place." Again, a counterexample against the warrant is neglected, the fact that unwanted pregnancies occur. Note that the objections we make to poor arguments weaken the arguments themselves, regardless of other arguments.

An implication of the view I have presented is that isolated arguments can be good if they are warranted, even if they are subsequently overwhelmed by good arguments on the other side. Typically (outside of mathematics or logic), no single argument is decisive, and we must consider the total weight of evidence and the possibility of even stronger arguments on the other side. A good argument, however, stands on its own. It can be overwhelmed but not undermined. In this sense, practically all of the arguments cited as poor by Mall (1982), on both sides, are really good arguments. Most of these arguments point to consequences of making abortion legal or illegal. These arguments are good if the assumption of causality is warranted. For example, an argument against banning abortion by a constitutional amendment stated that such an amendment would complicate the interpretation of other laws and would have other unintended effects. Such an argument is good if the causal account of how this could happen is plausible, but it is not decisive.

A person may think of good arguments (or bad ones) only on one side of an issue such as abortion. This is "myside bias" as defined by Perkins (1989), who has demonstrated such bias by asking subjects to list the thoughts that occur to them when they think about a controversial question. Perkins and his colleagues have found that people can be easily prompted for additional arguments on the other side, although prompting for further arguments on their favored side is less effective. So the failure to think of arguments on the other side is typically not the result of not knowing them.

Perkins's measure of myside bias is similar to the "differentiation" score of Tetlock's (1992) measure of "integrative complexity" of thinking. In contrast to the view of Baron (1993, 1994a), Nickerson (1989), and Perkins (1989), Tetlock argues that differentiation is not always good and that it [is] sometimes better to ignore the other side, in particular, when the other side is clearly weak or nonexistent. Should we, for example, consider both sides of the question of whether Hitler was a good man? In response to Tetlock, I and others (Baron, 1985, 1994a) have admitted that, if one has already considered the other side or if one is operating on the basis of a well-examined general principle, then additional thinking of any sort may be inefficient or pointless. When we do think, however, it is surely wasteful to consider arguments only on our favored side, for such thinking cannot accomplish much. Note also that verbal output need not tap underlying openness. People may be open to the other side and not say it because they cannot think of it, perhaps because it does not exist. Beyond this, I would argue that one *should* be open to the other side when considering a new issue or a debatable one: how is one to know whether the other side exists if one does not look for it? Because abortion is a controversial issue, I assume here that people should consider both sides.

This paper reports evidence of both kinds of errors just described, weak warrants and myside bias in thinking of arguments. The evidence for weak warrants comes from an informal examination of arguments provided by students (Experiment 1). The evidence for myside bias comes from a more formal study of the same subjects (Experiment 2), which also looks for a possible cause of myside bias, the *belief* that one-sided thinking is good. The presence of this belief is correlated with the subject's own one-sidedness. A second formal study shows that this preference for one-sided arguments cannot be easily interpreted as just a preference for arguments that are persuasive to others.

EXPERIMENT 1: PREPARING FOR A DISCUSSION

Method

Subjects were 54 students at the University of Pennsylvania in 1988, solicited by advertising and paid for completing this questionnaire and others. They were asked to imagine that they were preparing for a class discussion on the topic "Are abortions carried out in the first day of pregnancy (e.g., by the 'morning after' pill) morally wrong?" by making a list of the arguments that occur to them concerning the topic. The "first day" question avoided issues of disputable scientific fact, such as when the fetus first feels pain, etc.

Results

I classified arguments as good or bad according to the warrant. The reader can check my classifications, which are doubtless disputable in some cases. The point, though, is that some of these arguments are good and some are poor. Here are some of the arguments I classified as good:

"Late abortions (≈6 months) are immoral because they are the murdering of a person. However, a day after the egg is fertilized, the 'fetus' does not have any consciousness. It does not think or feel."

"The 'morning after' pill only can be considered extinguishing a human life in a very abstract sense. If it were considered murder of a potential life, then any form of birth control could be seen as preventing a potential life as well."

"Are we splitting hairs here? Every month a woman's egg is menstruated away. More frequently than that, the man's sperm are ejaculated away 'unused.' . . . Suddenly conception takes place (maybe) the night before, and the whole ball game changes. Fertilization has taken place, and it's no longer egg and sperm, but 'life'—hence a moral issue. Really, the facts may be plain, but the moral issue is: are there 'life-wise' any differences between the 1-day-old fetus and the unfertilized egg and sperm?"

"The pill is 'killing' less of an organism than a fully formed fly."
"Overpopulation is already a problem. We don't need more kids, especially unwanted ones."
"Yes, the embryo is dependent upon the mother. . . . But, similarly, the mother is dependent upon many other people for her life: the farmer, doctor, police, etc. If they end their services and the mother died, are they committing a moral offense?"

Other subjects argued that they, and most other people, would not want to have been aborted (thus invoking the Golden Rule—see Hare, 1975, for a sophisticated form of this argument). Or they argued that the practice of abortion will reduce respect for human life elsewhere—an empirical claim that, if true, would argue against abortion. These sorts of arguments can be overwhelmed by other arguments on the other side. No single argument is decisive, and they were not put forward as decisive. They are good because they do not appeal to principles to which obvious counterexamples can be found. (Many are also found in philosophical discussions of abortion.)

Here are some of the arguments that I consider weak, on both sides, classified according to type:

1. Control of one's body.
   "Women should have power over their own bodies."
   "I believe women have the right to do whatever they want with their own bodies."
   "You have the right to control your own body."
   "The child is not yet an independent, thinking human. It's still being carried by the mother. Therefore, it's her choice whether or not to continue carrying it."

The problem here is that the argument neglects the other side: the fetus also may have rights. The argument is also a non-sequitur, but most arguments are, even good ones. The point is that a critical objection is ignored.

2. Not a moral question.
   "A couple should be able to decide what decision are best for them without the coercion (governmental *or* moral) of any other person."
   "It's a personal decision, and this person must decide if they themselves feel it is morally wrong or not."
   "Also, it is not for anyone else to label it as moral or immoral, since it is the pregnant woman who can make that judgment based

on her own measures of morality and the conditions surrounding the situation."

"No living animal is born (or conceived) with an intrinsic 'right to life.' Any 'right to life' to anything exists because we humans posit it, not because of any a priori circumstance or condition. Positing this right is arbitrary, therefore the existence of a 'right to life' is arbitrary."

"People have no right to force their morals on someone else. Who is to decide what is morally right or wrong?"

Again, a critical counterargument is ignored. If this isn't a moral question, then could you say the same about murdering an adult?

3. Possibility of no harm.

   "The morning after pill is largely a preventive measure—you don't know whether conception has occurred or not."

   "There is very little chance that you would know if you were pregnant."

   "*Morality* involves consciously recognizing right and wrong. In the case of the morning-after pill, the woman does not *know if she is pregnant*. Therefore, the moral argument does not apply."

Here, a principle is used that has some counterexamples, and the counterexamples have not been acknowledged. Subjects would not say that driving drunk is morally acceptable because it is possible—indeed likely—that no harm will be done. Yet this is the same argument applied to another case. The argument is used here, perhaps, because subjects are searching for something to support the conclusion they want to be true. They are not searching for the truth itself.

4. Begging the question.

   "Killing a fetus is murder."

   "Abortion is the murdering of an innocent child."

5. Avoiding the question.

   "Abstinence is the best method."

The issue is, what if abstinence has not occurred? What then?

6. Confusing decision with action.

   "How can you decide its fate?"

This argument assumed that not to abort is not to decide, and therefore not to have the "arrogance" that comes with taking a decision upon oneself. The counterargument to the warrant is that not acting is also a decision, once the option of acting is known. This is an example of the error of omission bias (Baron, 1994b): abortion, a commission, is wrong, but preventing birth by abstaining from sexual intercourse, an omission, is not wrong even though it, too, is deciding the fate of future persons.

Some arguments were impossible to classify as good or poor, since subjects simply made assertions or asked questions, e.g.: "*When* is abortion taking a human life?"; "Life of living must take precedence over life of a fetus."

In sum, many arguments are weak in the sense that their warrants are questionable. The subject has apparently made little effort to look for evidence against the warrant. This kind of failure is found elsewhere (Baron, 1990).

EXPERIMENT 2: STANDARDS FOR THINKING AND MYSIDE BIAS

Experiments 2 and 3 are based on previous studies (e.g., Perkins, 1989) showing myside bias, that is, a tendency to think of reasons that favor one's initial view rather than those that oppose it. They also investigate a possible source of this bias. Baron (1991) suggested that some people think that one-sided thinking is better than two-sided thinking. They think that people should know what is right without having to think about it, in the way in which experts seem to know the answers in their field. (In this regard, people may misunderstand how experts acquire their expertise; see Baron, 1993.) Certain cultural traditions may also actively discourage people from questioning the beliefs of the tradition in question, leading to a general distrust of open-mindedness. Such traditions would have at least a temporary survival advantage over traditions that encourage questioning.

Baron (1991) found moderate but significant correlations between measures of subjects' beliefs about the nature of good thinking and the one-sidedness of their own thinking about controversial issues. Beliefs were assessed either by asking subjects how other people ought to deal with challenges to their own beliefs (by defending their beliefs or by considering the challenges) or by asking subjects to grade made-up examples of other people's thinking. For example, subjects were first asked their own opinion about a moral dilemma concerning a student's request to rewrite a paper (after other students had left for the summer) so he could get the B he needed to win a scholarship. Subjects were given several two-sided or one-sided arguments to grade, with conclusions equally often on one side or the other. The measure of standards was the difference between the mean grade assigned to two-sided and one-sided arguments, irrespective of their side. This measure correlated with a dichotomous measure of the one-sidedness of the subjects' own thinking about a different question (the use of resources on the ocean floor).

These results suggest that people's standards—their beliefs about the nature of good thinking—affect the conduct of their own thinking. (For similar results see: Dweck & Leggett, 1988; Kuhn, 1991; Schommer, 1990.) People who think that two-sided thinking is good try to do it, and those who do not think it is particularly good do not try.

Method

The subjects used in Experiment 1, after they made their lists of arguments, were given lists made by 24 hypothetical other students, and they were asked to "evaluate the thinking" of these students. Subjects were explicitly instructed to concentrate on the thinking, not the verbal expression. They were asked to assign a grade from A+ to F to each student. Some of the students gave arguments on one side and others gave arguments on both sides.

Specifically, the lists of thoughts varied in the student's initial side (yes or no), the number of arguments on the student's side (2 or 4), and the number of arguments on the other side (0 or 2). These three factors were combined orthogonally to yield a set of eight conditions. Three versions of each condition were constructed by maximizing the variety of the specific arguments across the three versions.

The versions drew arguments from the following list:

"Yes" arguments:

Killing of human beings is wrong, and abortion is killing a human, even though the human is only a fetus.

Aborting a fetus is preventing someone from having a life, and this is wrong. None of us would have wanted to have been aborted ourselves.

There is no clear place to draw the line between early abortions, late abortions of fetuses that could survive on their own, and the killing of handicapped or unwanted infants.

Condoning abortion is likely to reduce respect for human life in general, leading to decreased effort to preserve human life in other cases.

Women who get pregnant by mistake are irresponsible, and they should not be rewarded by being allowed to correct their error.

Abortion is never absolutely necessary as a means of birth control. If someone really doesn't want to get pregnant, they can try chastity.

"No" arguments:

The fetus is not hurt by early abortion. It has no future plans, no knowledge of life, no pain, and no fear of death.

Families must be limited in today's world. If we are going to limit births, it is, on the whole, better to limit the births of unwanted children than the births of children who are wanted. Abortion is one means of preventing unwanted children from being born, when it is too late to prevent them by other means.

Contraceptive methods are all subject to failure, so the only way to be sure of not getting pregnant is to abstain from sex. This would be an intolerable burden to impose on married couples who are not ready to have children.

Women should be able to decide whether they want to go through something that affects them as much as pregnancy and childbirth do.

It's unfair that women should bear the brunt of mistakes for which men are at least as responsible.

Many women who get pregnant by mistake are adolescents and others who are not ready to care for children. The possibility of abortion allows many of them to continue their education and have children when they are mature enough to raise them well.

Results

Table 4 shows the mean grades assigned to the eight conditions. On the whole, grades given to one-sided lists were higher than grades given to two-sided lists ($t_{53} = 2.99$, $p = .004$, two-tailed), *even when the student disagreed with the subject* ($t_{53} = 2.17$, $p = .034$) and even when the analysis was restricted to cases with four arguments on one side (so as to eliminate those cases where a conclusion was drawn despite an equal number of arguments on both sides; $t_{53} = 3.55$, $p = .001$). Thirty-two subjects gave higher grades to one-sided lists, and 18 gave higher grades to two-sided lists. This experiment reveals a clear preference for one-sided thinking.

Subjects also gave higher grades to students with more arguments on the subjects' side than on the other side ($t_{52} = 4.57$, $p < .001$). They did not give higher grades to students who agreed with them when the student had two arguments on each side ($t = 0.87$). Subjects also gave higher grades to lists with four arguments on the student's side than to lists with two arguments on the student's side ($t_{53} = 9.57$, $p > .001$). (Interactions between the three factors—otherside arguments, student-side arguments, and agreement of student and subject—were all statistically significant, although none was of substantive interest.)

In the subjects' own paragraphs, 36 subjects gave no otherside arguments, and 16 gave at least one otherside argument. (Two subjects gave no arguments at all.) There was no correlation between the number of myside and otherside arguments ($r = 0.12$).

Two-sidedness, the difference between grades given to two-sided and one-sided arguments, correlated significantly with the number of other-side arguments that the subjects made themselves ($r = 0.29$, $p = .022$, one tailed). These results support the hypothesis that standards for active open-mindedness affect thinking.

The difference between grades given to long and short lists (i.e., 4 vs. 2 arguments on the student's side) correlated with the number of myside arguments that subjects made in their own lists ($r = 0.42$, $p = .002$), but it did not correlate with their otherside arguments ($r = -0.12$). These findings (supported by the results of a principal components analysis) suggest two orthogonal standards of thinking, one concerned with fairness to both sides and the other concerned with thoroughness in thinking of arguments on one's own side. The former expresses itself in the number of otherside arguments and in the two-sidedness measures, and the latter expresses itself in the number of myside arguments and in the effect of long vs. short. The fairness standard is opposed by a competing standard concerned with internal consistency.

Justifications of the grades were classified (following Baron, 1991) into six categories: two-sidedness as a virtue ("considers both sides"—or one-sidedness as a vice); one-sidedness as a virtue (or two-sidedness as a vice, "seems undecided," "contradicts himself"); content ("I agree," "His points are good," "Obviously a male chauvinist")[1]; numerosity ("not enough reasons"); and conciseness ("succinct"), the opposite of numerosity. These arguments were coded without looking at the lists that subjects were responding to.

The percent of subjects who gave justifications in each category were: two-sidedness, 38%; one-sidedness, 85%; content, 94%; numerosity, 53%; conciseness, 6%. The preponderance of one-sided over two-sided justifications is consistent with the fact that two-sided arguments received lower grades than one-sided arguments. However, 26% of the subjects used *both* two-sided and one-sided justifications (on different items); this finding supports the suggestion (Baron, 1991) that most people hold both standards simultaneously. The presence of two-sided justifications was associated with the number of otherside arguments that subjects gave ($t_{49} = 2.92$, $p > .005$); this result further supports the hypothesis that standards for active open-mindedness affect thinking (even when the standards are measured after the thinking).

PERSUASION VS. THINKING: EXPERIMENT 3

Subjects in Experiment 2 may be confusing good thinking with persuasiveness. To test this possibility, Experiment 3 asked specifically about persuasiveness, along with quality of thinking. It used three conditions: one asking for evaluation of the quality of thinking for forming one's own opinion, the others asking for evaluation of thinking in preparation for persuading others. The explicit use of two different instructional manipulations should call attention to the distinction between persuasiveness and quality. The two persuasiveness conditions differed in the quality of the students in the class, either very intelligent or not very intelligent. Subjects might think that two-sided arguments work better with more intelligent listeners. (Chu, 1967, and Hovland et al, 1949, found that knowledgeable listeners were more persuaded by two-sided arguments.)

The 24 cases from Experiment 2 were divided into three groups of 8 cases each, otherwise keeping the order the same within each group as in Experiment 2. Each group of 8 contained all 8 conditions, but a given condition was represented by different arguments in each group. Subjects differed in the assignment of groups to conditions. The three conditions were presented in the following orders to different subjects (in which P, I, and N stand for personal opinion, intelligent listeners, and not intelligent listeners, respectively): PIN, PNI, INP, NIP. Order did not affect any of the measures reported.

Instructions for the personal opinion section read, "In this part, evaluate the quality of the thinking in terms of *what people ought to do when they think about their own personal opinions on subjects like this.* Please write on your sheet what you are evaluating before you begin. This is the only way we can know the order in which you did the three parts." The intelligent section was the same except that it asked subjects to "evaluate the quality of the thinking in terms of *how good each student will be at persuading others in the class. Imagine that the class consists of very intelligent students who are themselves good thinkers.*" The not-intelligent section described the other students as "not very intelligent and are not themselves good thinkers." Asking subjects to write down the task they were doing insured that they would pay attention to the instructions. Although subjects were asked for their own opinion at the outset, they provided no explanations.

Subjects were 45 students from both the University of Pennsylvania and Philadelphia College of Pharmacy and Science. (An additional 28 subjects were omitted because they failed to answer one or more questions, sometimes just one of the items in a group. Each condition in a group was represented by only one item, so all data were crucial. Of course, subjects who failed to write down the task they were doing were useless.)

Table 4 shows the mean grades in the three conditions. The results were parallel for the three conditions. In all conditions, one-sided arguments were given higher grades than two-sided arguments (t = 2.72, p = .009 for thinking; t = 3.79, p > .001 for intelligent listener; t = 3.50, p = .001 for non-intelligence listener). The size of this effect did not differ significantly as a function of agreement between the subject and the student or as a function of condition. Subjects gave slightly

Table 4
Mean Grades in the Two Experiments

	Student agrees with subject			
Condition	Experiment 2 Thinking	Experiment 3 Thinking	Persuade intel.	Persuade not intel.
2,0	6.3	6.2	5.5	6.4
2,2	4.7	5.4	4.0	5.3
4,0	8.4	8.0	8.2	8.2
4,2	6.4	6.4	6.4	6.4
	Student disagrees with subject			
Condition	Experiment 2 Thinking	Experiment 3 Thinking	Persuade intel.	Persuade not intel.
2,0	5.3	6.0	5.3	6.2
2,2	4.6	5.4	4.4	5.1
4,0	7.1	7.6	8.2	8.5
4,2	5.6	6.0	5.4	6.5

Notes: The first number under "Condition" is the number of arguments on the student's side, and the second number is the number of arguments on the other side. Standard deviations ranged from 2.2 to 3.5. Grades are on a scale from 0 (F) to 12 (A+).

higher grades to students on their own side ($t = 1.72$, $p = .047$, one tailed), and this effect did not vary significantly across conditions. The only significant difference among the conditions was that subjects gave lower grades to students in the intelligent-listener condition ($F = 6.61$, $p = .002$, for the difference among the three conditions; post-hoc tests confirmed that the intelligent-listener condition was lower than the other two [$p > .02$, Bonferroni corrected], which did not differ). Some subjects remarked that intelligent students would require better arguments to be convinced. In sum, subjects considered one-sided thinking to be better even when they clearly understood that they were evaluating thinking about one's own opinion rather than power of argument.

Another possible explanation of the results of both of these studies is that the arguments were simply listed, so that changes in perspective appeared to be sudden. This, of course, was consistent with what the arguments were supposed to be, notes. In a follow-up study, carried out in collaboration with Sue Tedman, arguments were written out in paragraphs to prevent the disconnectedness that results from the juxtaposition of arguments on opposite sides. Each student gave two arguments, which were either on the same side or on opposite sides, and the student stated no conclusion. When the second argument agreed with the first, it began with "also," and, when it disagreed, it began with "on the other hand." The selections were "meant to represent different people's thoughts before a decision has been reached." Once again, the 37 subjects tested tended to give higher grades to one-sided arguments (t_{36} = 1.85), although this result was not found for a less controversial issue, the question of whether pre-marital AIDS testing should be mandatory.

DISCUSSION

In sum, people consider one-sided thinking to be better than two-sided thinking, even for forming one's own opinion on an issue. It is possible that this standard is found only for controversial issues like abortion, but this is where it also may have its most damaging effect.

Where does this standard come from? One possibility (Baron, 1991) is that people confuse good thinking with expertise. Experts do not need to think, and consideration of the other side suggests that expertise is lacking. It is also possible that certain institutions, such as organized religions, promote the idea that seeing two sides is "confusing." Institutions that do this might be more likely than other institutions to keep their followers.

Another possibility is that people overextend the idea that commitment is a virtue. Surely it is in marriage and, more generally, in the honoring of vows, promises, and contracts of all sorts. But the formation of a belief or a political opinion is not a contract. Those who think that commitment to a belief is a virtue seem not to understand why commitment is ever a virtue. If they understood, they would see that the reasons do not apply here.

On the other side, respect for two-sided thinking could come from education. The standards of "actively open-mindedness," with its active search for reasons why an initial idea might be wrong, are manifest in the grading of papers (and the reviewing of scholarly articles).

The evidence on effects of education is mixed. Perkins (1989) found some effect of graduate training on a measure of bias, but no significant effect of college or high school. Perkins, Bushey, and Faraday (1986) observed only small effects of various courses that emphasized thinking, but a 16-session course for high-school students that they designed nearly doubled the number of otherside arguments concerning issues not discussed in the course (with a slight increase in quality as well, and no effect on the number of myside arguments). Students were taught that the arguments they consider should be *true* (to the best of the thinker's knowledge), *relevant* to the issue, and *complete*—that is, all important arguments should be considered. Controversial issues were discussed in class, and students were encouraged to generate and evaluate (for truth and relevance) arguments on both sides, especially the other side. Kuhn, Amsel, & O'Loughlin (1988) and Kuhn (1991) found results that could also be interpreted this way: philosophy graduate students were less subject to a type of myside bias in scientific thinking than other subjects, and, in general, education encouraged the belief that truth emerges from a process of critical inquiry in which both sides must be considered. In sum, the results together indicate that education can reduce myside bias and change standards, but, in many cases, does not do so. A more intentional effort may be needed (Baron, 1993).

NOTE

1. This category included the category called "weight" by Baron (1991), that is, arguments about whether the conclusion drawn was consistent with the arguments offered. Only a couple of subjects used this argument. Its rarity is probably due to the fact that the student's opinion was described as an *initial* opinion, not a conclusion.

REFERENCES

Baron, J. (1985). *Rationality and intelligence*. New York: Cambridge University Press.

Baron, J. (1990). Harmful heuristics and the improvement of thinking. In D. Kuhn (Ed.), *Developmental perspectives on teaching and learning thinking skills*, pp. 28–47. Basel: Karger.

Baron, J. (1991). Beliefs about thinking. In J. F. Voss, D. N. Perkins, & J. W. Segal (Eds.), *Informal reasoning and education*. Hillsdale, NJ: Erlbaum.

Baron, J. (1993). Why teach thinking?—An essay. (Target article with commentary.) *Applied Psychology: An International Review, 42*, 191–237.

Baron, J. (1994a). *Thinking and deciding* (2nd ed.). New York: Cambridge University Press.

Baron, J. (1994b). Nonconsequentialist decisions (with commentary and reply). *Behavioral and Brain Sciences, 17*, 1–42.

Chu, G. C. (1967). Prior familiarity, perceived bias, and one-sided versus two-sided communication. *Journal of Experimental Social Psychology, 3*, 243–254.

Dweck, C. S., & Leggett, E. L. (1988). A social-cognitive approach to motivation and personality. *Psychological Review, 95*, 256–273.

Hare, R. M. (1975). Abortion and the Golden Rule. *Philosophy and Public Affairs, 4*, 201–222.

Hovland, C. I., Lumsdaine, A. A., & Sheffield, F. D. (1949). *Experiments on mass communication* (pp. 201–227). Princeton, NJ: Princeton University Press.

Kuhn, D. (1991). *The skills of argument*. New York: Cambridge University Press.

Kuhn, D., Amsel, E., & O'Loughlin, M. (1988). *The development of scientific thinking skills*. New York: Academic Press.

Mall, D. (1982). *In good conscience: Abortion and moral necessity*. Libertyville, IL: Kairos.

Nickerson, R. S. (1989). On improving thinking through instruction. *Review of Research in Education* 15, 3–57.

Perkins, D. N. (1989). Reasoning as it is and could be: An empirical perspective. In D. M. Topping, D. C. Crowell, & V. N. Kobayashi (Eds.),

Thinking across cultures: The third international conference on thinking. Hillsdale, NJ: Erlbaum.

Perkins, D. N., Bushey, B., & Faraday, M. (1986). *Learning to reason.* Unpublished manuscript, Harvard Graduate School of Education, Cambridge, MA.

Schommer, M. (1990). Effects of beliefs about the nature of knowledge on comprehension. *Journal of Educational Psychology, 82*, 498–504.

Tetlock, P. E. (1992). The impact of accountability on judgment and choice: Toward a social contingency model. In *Advances in Experimental Social Psychology* (Vol. 24, pp. 331–376). New York: Academic Press.

Toulmin, S. E. (1958). *The uses of argument.* Cambridge: Cambridge University Press.

QUESTIONS ABOUT MEANING

1. Describe the methods in Experiment 1. In general, what made the arguments that Baron classified as weak arguments weak?
2. Summarize the methods and findings from Experiment 2. What additional insights did Experiment 3 provide?

QUESTIONS FOR RHETORICAL ANALYSIS

1. What does Baron assume readers already know about the elements of an argument? Who would you say is the intended audience for Baron's article? Cite textual evidence to support your answer.
2. Why is it important when arguing to qualify claims and recognize objections or counter arguments? Reread the Discussion section and highlight examples of qualifiers and counterarguments that Baron acknowledges while developing his own argument. Does Baron avoid "myside bias"? Explain.
3. Study Table 4 and then suggest another way to present the same information in one (or two) tables or in one or two figures. Create the tables or figures and then describe what is gained or lost in your alternative method of presentation.

MAKING CONNECTIONS

1. Tavris and Aronson, along with Baron, recognize the tendency of people to engage in one-sided thinking. In an essay, explain this tendency, using insights and examples from various authors in this chapter, as well as your own examples and observations. In addition to the explanations suggested by Baron, what reasons can you give for this tendency? How, for example, is one-sided thinking encouraged or modeled in our culture? (Recall Kuhn's comments on the subject in chapter 9.) Baron ends

his article by saying that "a more intentional effort [to teach two-sided thinking] may be needed." End your own essay by suggesting ways that educators could better combat the tendency to engage in one-sided thinking.

2. One-sided thinking is easy to find about any controversial subject. Find an argument online that you think illustrates one-sided thinking and, using Toulmin's terms, analyze the argument and its weaknesses.

Neuroscience

"Filling in Gaps in Perception: Part I," V. S. RAMACHANDRAN

You may remember the next author, neuroscientist V. S. Ramachandran, from chapter 13. Ramachandran is a professor of psychology and neuroscience, well known for his research in the fields of behavioral neurology and visual psychophysics. It is the latter field of interest that is discussed in the next article.

In "Filling in Gaps in Perception: Part I," Ramachandran demonstrates that just as we are unaware of our mental blind spots, we are also unaware of literal "blind spots" in our field of vision.

Neurologists have long known that a systematic two-dimensional map of the retina exists in the visual cortex, and that any sharply localized damage to the visual cortex always results in an island of blindness in the visual field called a *scotoma*.[1] One enigmatic aspect of scotomas, however, is that the patients themselves are often blissfully unaware of them. A patient who gazes at, say, a pink wall does not see a dark hole corresponding to the scotoma even though visual information from this region does not reach the brain. The wall looks homogeneously pink. Indeed, even if the patient gazes at a pattern of wallpaper, no gap or hole is seen—the wallpaper seems to somehow "fill in" from the surround.

What does it feel like to have a scotoma and yet be unaware of it? You can get some idea by examining your own blind spot corresponding to the optic disc—the place where the optic nerve exits from the back of the eyeball. To demonstrate the blind spot, shut your right eye and hold Figure 14.3 about 6 in. away from your face while looking at the small fixation spot on the right using your left eye. Now move the page toward you very slowly, and you will find that there is a critical distance at which the black circle on the left disappears completely. Notice, however, that when the black spot disappears, it does not leave a gap or a dark hole behind in the visual field. Indeed, the entire field looks homogeneous, and the region corresponding to the blind spot has the same color (white) as the background.[2] Curiously, the blind spot remains invisible even when you look at a repetitive visual texture such as wallpaper, and this fact has led many authors to suppose that the pattern from the surround somehow mysteriously fills in the gap corresponding to the blind spot.

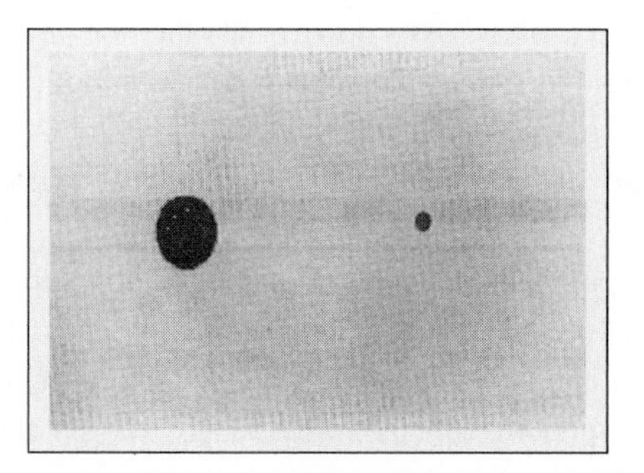

Figure 14.3 The blind spot was first demonstrated by Mariotte in 1667. With your right eye shut, look at the small fixation spot on the right with your left eye. Hold the page about 6 in. away and slowly move it to and fro until the black disc on the left disappears completely. The disc is now inside your blind spot. Throughout this article, most of the demonstrations in the figures require that you shut your right eye and aim the blind spot of the left eye on the black disc to make it disappear.

FILLING IN IS PREATTENTIVE

Do we need to postulate a specific filling-in process? It is true, of course, that we do not ordinarily notice the blind spot, but is this fact any more mysterious than the fact that we do not notice the gap behind our heads? If you stand in your bathroom, you do not see a black hole behind your head, but the reason for this surely is that the visual areas of your brain simply do not represent events behind your head. You certainly would not want to conclude that the wallpaper in the bathroom somehow fills in behind your head. This distinction is not merely semantic. For events behind our heads, we have what might be loosely called a conceptual (or propositional) representation similar to a logical inference. For the region corresponding to the blind spot, in contrast, there may be a perceptual representation. How can we distinguish between these two possibilities without becoming inextricably tangled in a philosophical conundrum?

The idea that people do not really fill in the blind spot is widely prevalent among both psychologists and philosophers. The distinguished American philosopher Dennett,[3] for example, recently expressed the view that the phrase filling in is an inappropriate metaphor that requires the assumption of an audience in a Cartesian theater. Indeed, he argued that the so-called filling-in process may amount to no more than a failure to notice the absence of neural signals from this part of the visual field. A somewhat similar view was expressed by Efron,[4] who wrote:

> We do not *perceive* the "edge" of our visual field or the "borders" of our blind spot. To see an "edge" or a contour, we must be able to see on *both* sides of the demarcation line. It is our conceptual capacity which allows us to discover the fact that we have a blind spot and have a border to our visual field even though we have no immediate perceptual awareness of these phenomena. Our knowledge of the blind spot . . . is deductive and conceptual.

My first experiment proves decisively, contrary to these views, that people do, in fact, fill in the blind spot; that is, they create a sensory representation corresponding to this region. The experiment takes advantage of a phenomenon that visual psychologists call *pop-out.* For example, if you look at a display in which a diagonal line is embedded in a matrix of vertical lines, then the single diagonal line pops out (i.e., you have no difficulty spotting it). The same is true for a single red spot displayed against a background of green spots. In contrast it is rather difficult to spot the single *T* against a background of *L*s. It has been suggested, therefore, that pop out can occur only for features that are extracted relatively early in visual processing—such as orientation or color[5]—but not for more complex features such as corners (i.e., *L*s) or *T* junctions.

Does the filling in of the blind spot occur before or after pop-out? To explore this question, I created the display shown in Figure 14.4.[6] If one of the rings is placed on the blind spot and the others are not, this ring looks like a homogeneous disc rather than a ring. Furthermore, it also pops out, even though on the retina it is identical to all the other rings! This observation has three implications. First, even though the whole visual field is covered with rings, the visual system does not try to create

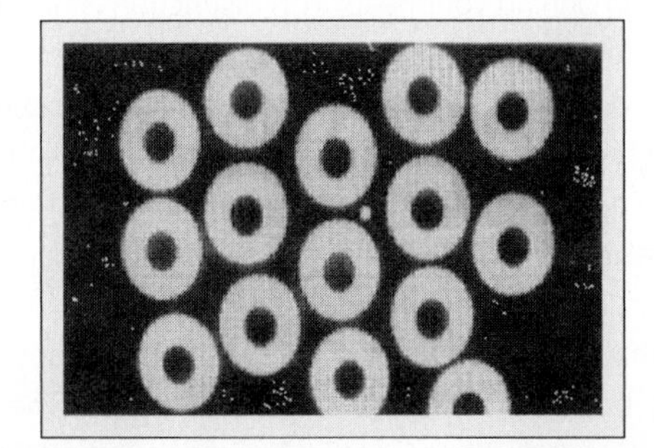

Figure 14.4 A white ring looks like a homogeneous, filled disc when its inner border is made to just overlap the outer margins of the blind spot. If this disc is surrounded by rings, it pops out conspicuously, although on the retina it is identical to the other rings.

a ring in the region of the blind spot. What fills in instead is the white color that is immediately around the blind spot. Second, the filling-in process must occur quite early in visual processing because it precedes visual search and pop-out. And third, contrary to Dennett[3] and Efron,[4] filling in must involve creating a sensory representation in the blind spot rather than just ignoring the absence of signals from this region. For how can something you ignore pop out at you?

SPATIAL LIMITS OF FILLING IN

How rich is this sensory representation corresponding to the blind spot, and at what stage in visual processing is this representation created?[6] Can psychologists explore the spatial and temporal limits of this filling-in process—if it really does exist? My purpose in this article is to try to answer these questions. First, let us begin with a simple demonstration that suggests that at least discontinuities in straight lines do get filled in. Hold Figure 14.5a in front of you and move it to and fro while fixating the small fixation spot on the right (with the right eye shut). You will find that the black disc on the left disappears as soon as it falls in the blind spot, but there is no obvious gap or discontinuity in the line.[7] Yet if you place the upper end of a line inside the blind spot (Fig. 14.5b), the line does indeed get chopped off; you do not see the line continuing into the blind

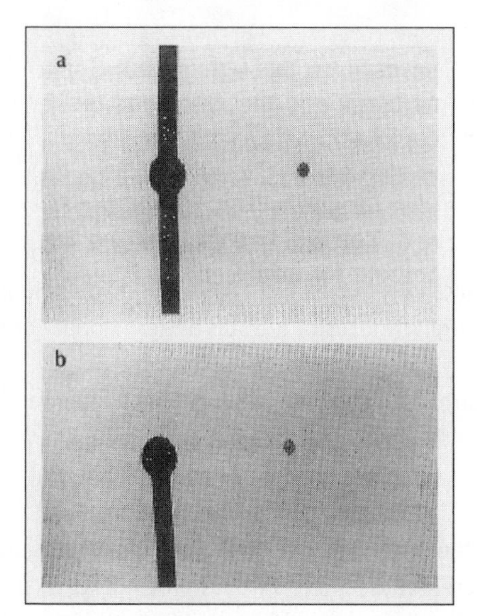

Figure 14.5 With a vertical line, the extent of filling in is determined by whether the entire line or only the tip passes through the blind spot. In (a), if you aim your left eye's blind spot on the disc (with the right eye shut), the line will look complete and continuous even though a portion of it ought to be invisible. In contrast, if the tip of a line terminates inside the blind spot (b), the line looks chopped off; you do not extrapolate the line.

spot. So your visual system can bridge a discontinuity caused by the blind spot but cannot extrapolate a line that is truncated by the blind spot.

The completion of a line across a gap seems to depend only on the contours themselves—not on the color of the line. If, for example, the upper segment of a line is red and the lower segment green, the line appears continuous even though, paradoxically, one cannot see the border between the green and red segments. The paradox arises, presumably, because although somewhere in the visual pathways there are nerves signaling that the line is continuous (or, at least, not discontinuous), there are no nerves signaling the red-green color border that falls on the blind spot. Interestingly, if black and white segments are used instead of red and green, the two lines seem to blend into each other to create a metallic gray appearance (see Fig. 14.6).

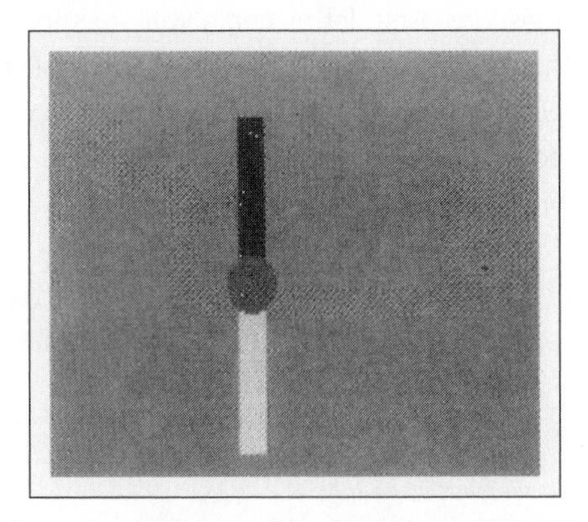

Figure 14.6 Different luminances used for the upper and lower line segments do not prevent the completion process. The line looks complete, and the black and white are seen to blend together to create a metallic gray appearance.

To explore how sophisticated this filling-in process is, Rogers-Ramachandran and I devised the stimulus shown in Figure 14.7. Notice that the converging spokes of the star pattern appear normal and uninterrupted when positioned on the blind spot. Indeed, if you position the blind spot correctly, the pattern hardly looks different from a normal complete pattern; you may even see the spokes converging to an imaginary point in the center. (Remember to keep the right eye closed.) We may conclude, therefore, that the visual system is able to "complete" the gaps even in these relatively complex types of patterns.

Yet there are also clear limits to this process. For example, if you aim the blind spot on the corner of a square (Fig. 14.8) or the arc of a circle (Fig. 14.9), these figures do not appear complete.[6] They are clearly chopped off by the blind spot. The implication of these observations is that the filling in of the blind spot is a primitive process that occurs at a relatively early stage in visual processing.

Figure 14.7 The converging spokes of a star also appear complete and uninterrupted when positioned on the blind spot.

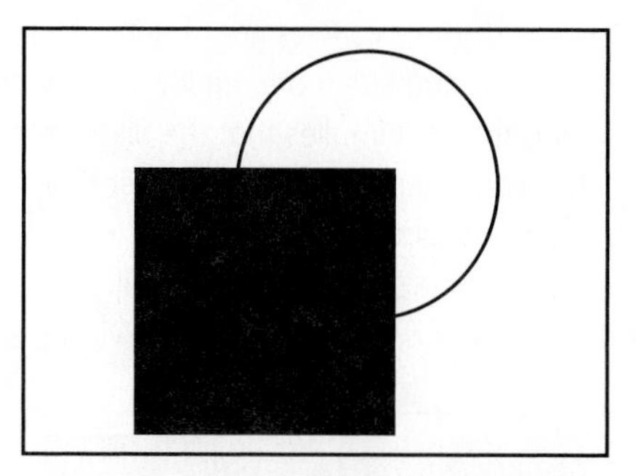

Figure 14.8 If the blind spot (outline circle) is aimed on the corner of a square, the square does not appear complete; the corner is clearly chopped off. The implication is that the filling in of the blind spot is a primitive process that occurs early in visual processing. Filling in can bridge discontinuities in contours and surface textures but cannot complete objects.

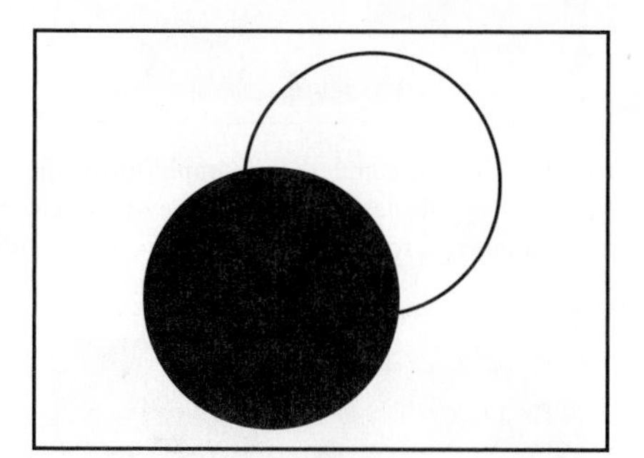

Figure 14.9 If the arc of a black disc is positioned on the blind spot (outline circle), the disc looks bitten off. No completion of the arc is seen, again suggesting that there are clear limits to filling in.

This effect contrasts sharply with observations I made recently on two patients with small paracentral scotomas caused by damage to the visual cortex. If the arc of a circle or the corner of a square fell on the scotoma, the figure was completed perceptually, although the process usually took 7 or 8 s to occur. One reason for this difference may be that in the region corresponding to the blind spot, there is normal visual cortex (which receives an input from the other eye) that signals the absence of the corner or arc, whereas in the patients there is no visual cortex at all corresponding to this region. In the latter case, the visual system seems to adopt the default option of actually seeing the missing portion of the figure.

What if there are two separate lines running through the blind spot, one black and the other one white? Would you see a grayish smear at the center of the cross? You can judge for yourself by inspecting Figure 14.10. You will find that the two lines compete for completion. Typically, the line you are paying attention to seems to be complete and seems to partially occlude the other line. If the two lines are of unequal length (Fig. 14.11), the longer line seems to complete more readily than the shorter one. This observation is important for it implies that the filling-in mechanism must use information from an extended distance rather than just from the immediate area of the blind spot.[7]

Another demonstration also shows that the filling in of the blind spot is not cognitive—that is, it is not based on the viewer's expectation of

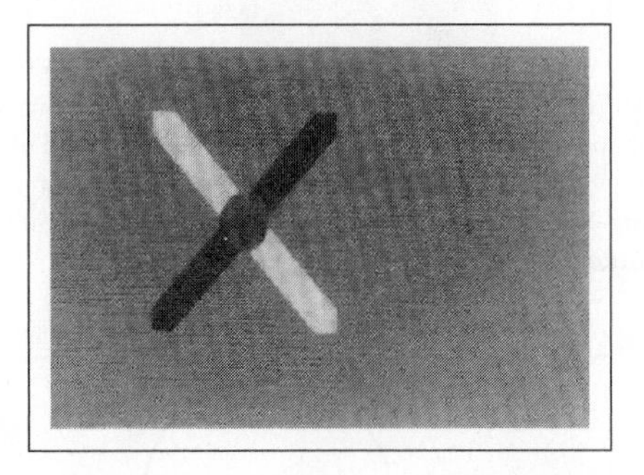

Figure 14.10 Two limbs of a cross compete for completion as they pass through the blind spot. When you try this demonstration, the line you attend to (black or white) will seem continuous and to partially occlude the other line.

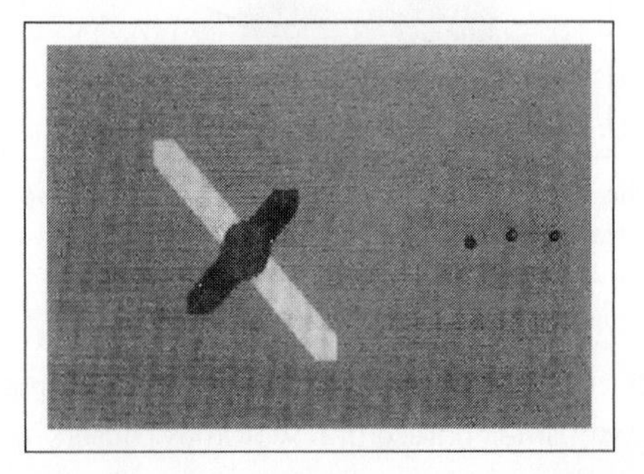

Figure 14.11 If the two limbs of a cross are of different lengths, the longer of the two lines (white) is always seen as complete and is also seen to occlude the other line.

what things ought to look like. Figure 14.12 displays a vertical column of large black spots. If one of the spots is positioned inside the blind spot, the spot vanishes; the viewer does not "hallucinate" the missing spot in order to preserve the repetitive structure of the pattern.

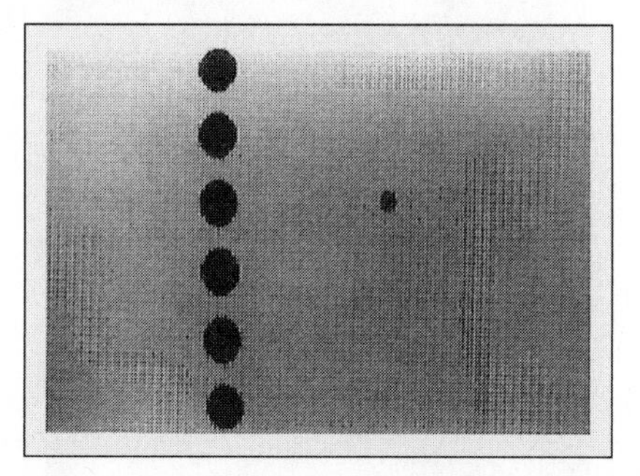

Figure 14.12 Repetitive patterns are not always completed across the blind spot. In this display, if one of the dots is located in the blind spot, it becomes invisible, and you clearly see a gap. You do not "hallucinate" the missing dot in order to preserve the repetitive structure of the pattern.

The next demonstration takes advantage of a set of curious visual stimuli called *illusory contours,*[8] that is, contours that do not exist physically but are perceived to account for otherwise inexplicable gaps in the visual image. A vertical black line, we have seen, is readily completed across the blind spot (Fig. 14.5a). But what would you see if you placed a vertical illusory contour on the blind spot? You can answer this question for yourself by looking at Figure 14.13a, placing the black disc inside the blind spot so that the disc vanishes. The question is, do you then complete the real horizontal line that defines the illusory contour, or do you complete the vertical illusory contour? Most observers report that they tend to see the illusory contour—not the real contours—as complete. But if all the horizontal lines except three are removed, then subjects do see the horizontal line as complete (Fig. 14.13b). In Figure 14.13a, information from the illusory contour must somehow "veto" the completion of the single horizontal black line that runs through the blind spot. (More recently, I tried presenting these displays to patients with scotomas caused by damage to the cortex and found that they, too, usually completed the illusory contours rather than the horizontal lines.)

One of the goals in conducting experiments of this kind is to develop a sort of conceptual flow diagram of visual functions and to map this diagram onto real neural structures in the brain. During the past two decades, especially, there has been considerable progress in understanding the anatomy of the visual pathways in primates. Scientists know, for example, that the visual world is mapped onto Area 17 in a rather systematic way, and information from this map is then sorted out and

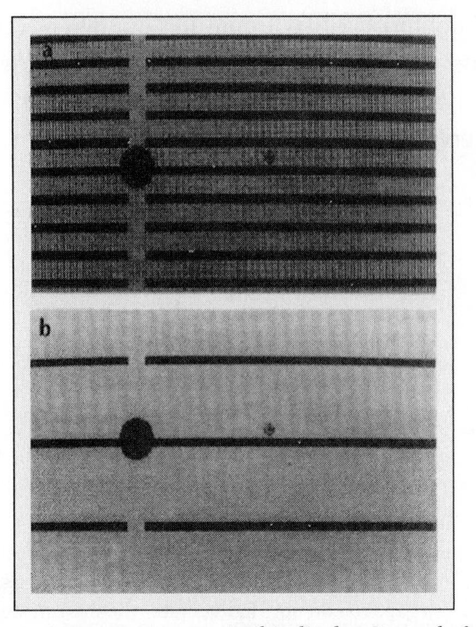

Figure 14.13 Illusory contours are seen in this display. Instead of seeing the lines terminating abruptly, the visual system interprets this image as arising from an opaque vertical strip occluding the horizontal lines in the background. When the number of lines is large (a), the illusory strip, rather than the horizontal lines that define the illusory contour, is completed across the blind spot. If a smaller number of lines (b) or a single horizontal line is used, then the horizontal line is completed instead of the illusory contour.

relayed to several higher extrastriate visual areas, each of which seems to be specialized for a specific submodality such as color, motion or form.[9] The existence of these areas has been clearly established, but very little is known about what they do and how their activity generates perceptual experience. Psychological experiments of the kind reported here might help provide some answers.

MOTION CORRESPONDENCE

Where does the filling in of the blind spot occur in this anatomical flow diagram—if it occurs in any one place at all? I wondered, for example, whether the process occurs before or after the visual processing of motion information, which is mediated largely by the broad stripes in Area 18 and by extrastriate area MT. To answer this question, I took advantage of an illusion discovered by Exner in the 19th century: If two vertical lines are presented in rapid succession, the line appears to jump or move—an illusion called *apparent motion.*[10] If one of the lines (Frame 1) has a "bite" taken out of it, and if the bite is at a different location in Frame 2, then the line appears to move diagonally (Fig. 14.14). The cut tips of the lines are often called terminators, and, clearly, it is these terminators that are matched by the motion system to generate diagonal

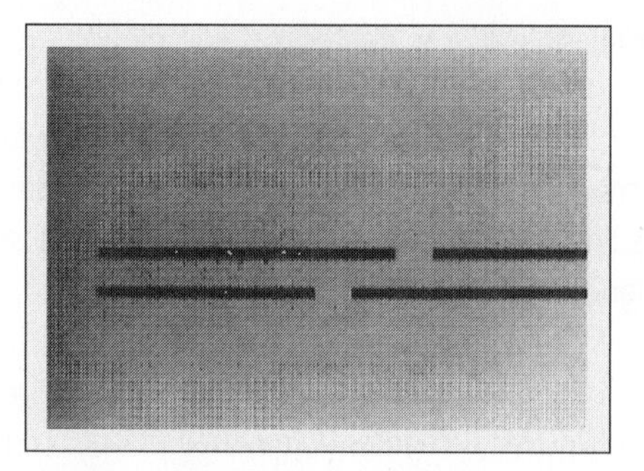

Figure 14.14 The illusion of apparent motion can be used to explore the neural locus of the filling-in process. The line on top is flashed in the first frame of a movie sequence, followed, in Frame 2, by the bottom line. Note that the "bite" taken out of the line is at a different location in Frame 2 and thus causes the line to appear to move diagonally. If the gap in Frame 1 is positioned on the blind spot, however, the line appears to move vertically instead of diagonally.

motion. To see this effect, it is important to ensure that the lines are viewed through a window so that the outer extreme tips of the lines do not influence the matching process.

What if these terminators were produced by interrupting the line with one's blind spot instead of actually removing a piece of the line? Can such terminators be used for motion correspondence? Or would the perceptual completion of the line ensure that the terminators can no longer be used? The results of this experiment were very clear. When I made sure that the gap in Frame 1 was slightly larger than the blind spot (so that no completion occurred), then the line moved diagonally, as one would expect from the matching of the terminators. But if the gap was smaller—so that the line looked continuous—then subjects saw vertical motion. These results indicate that perceptual completion of lines across the blind spot precedes the extraction of motion signals by the visual system.

One could argue that this failure to see diagonal motion has nothing to do with the completion process. Perhaps the visual system simply does not regard a line that is interrupted by the blind spot as having terminators because there are no neurons that signal the presence of these terminators. To explore this possibility, I used a slightly modified display. In the first movie frame, I presented a vertical line right next to the blind spot so that the upper end of the line was at the same horizontal level as the upper edge of the blind spot. This frame was switched off and followed by Frame 2, in which the line was shifted horizontally so that its upper end was chopped off by the blind spot. In this display, subjects clearly saw the line moving diagonally, perhaps because the visible upper end of the line in Frame 1 was then matched with the interrupted tip in Frame 2. Hence, I concluded that "virtual" terminators created by the blind spot do indeed excite the motion system unless they become invisible due to perceptual completion (as in the previous experiment).

No account of the blind spot would be complete without a description of Lettvin's ingenious experiments.[11] Lettvin wondered what would happen if the line segments on either side of the blind spot were deliberately misaligned. He found, to his surprise, that when he used vertical lines, the two segments looked like part of a single straight line; the misalignment was no longer discernible. Yet when he repeated the experiment with horizontal segments, no such effect occurred. This striking difference is especially obvious in the swastika configuration, an ancient peace symbol that has both vertical and horizontal segments (Fig. 14.15): The vertical line looks almost perfectly straight, whereas the horizontal line looks quite crooked, as one would expect. To this date, it is unknown why such a striking difference exists in the ability to bridge horizontal and vertical lines across the blind spot.

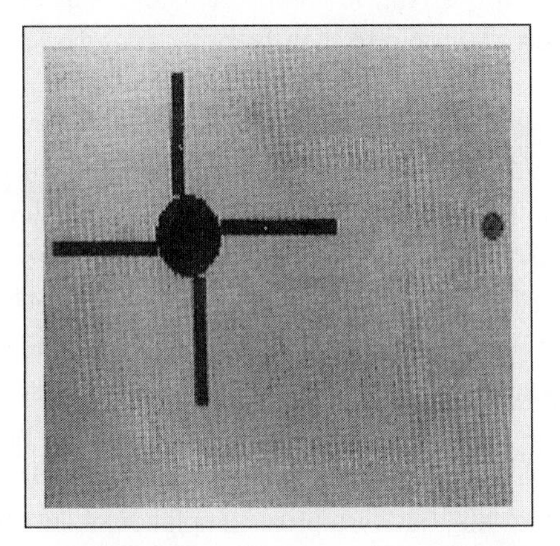

Figure 14.15 Lettvin's illusion demonstrates a striking difference in the ability to complete lines across the blind spot. If the center of the swastika pattern is positioned on the blind spot, the vertical line looks continuous and surprisingly straight, whereas the horizontal line looks crooked, as it should.

Recently, Aiken and I have been able to show that the ability to accurately align two vertical line segments interrupted by a gap (a task that is called *hyperacuity,* or *vernier acuity*) is very poor when the gap falls on the blind spot so that the line looks perceptually complete. Yet performance is astonishingly accurate for an equivalent separation in all other parts of the visual field. Somehow, the very act of perceptual completion seems to destroy hyperacuity.

One can take advantage of Lettvin's effect to demonstrate some additional perceptual illusions. For example, I tried viewing a two-frame movie sequence in which the staggered line was flashed on the blind spot in Frame 1, followed by an actual straight line (also traversing the blind spot) in Frame 2, to see if this would generate apparent motion. (The straight line in Frame 2 was located midway between the locations of the two segments in Frame 1.) Sure enough, the two segments appeared to move in opposite directions, and yet, paradoxically, they appeared not to change location! The paradox is resolved once you realize that there is no internal mental theater where these events are being enacted. Rather, different neurons are being made, through the use of contrived visual patterns, to signal incompatible information to higher brain centers. For example, in this apparent motion experiment, one set of neurons reports motion while another set reports, simultaneously, that there has been no change of location. Instead of trying to resolve the conflict, the visual system simply gives up. The result is a paradox of a kind that you would never encounter in the physical world.

I also tried a slightly modified version of this experiment using the following two-frame movie sequence. In Frame 1, I had two misaligned vertical line segments whose tips fell inside the blind spot so that the segments appeared perceptually completed and collinear. In Frame 2, the tips of the two lines were pulled vertically away from the blind spot by a tiny distance so that the segments were no longer perceptually completed and no longer appeared collinear. When I then alternated the two frames at about 6 Hz, I distinctly saw the lines moving horizontally even though there was no horizontal motion on the retina. This result suggests that the perceptual misalignment effect can provide a basis for seeing apparent motion (whereas in the previous experiment, I showed that seeing a change in location was not *necessary* for apparent motion).

Does the lining up of the staggered vertical line precede stereoscopic fusion or occur after stereopsis? To answer this question, Gregory and I presented the misaligned lines on either side of the blind spot in the left eye and "fused" them stereoscopically with a line that was actually straight in the right eye. (We used red-green stereo goggles to do this.) Curiously, the two line segments now appeared in different stereoscopic planes even though the two monocular "pictures" were perceptually identical! If confirmed, this observation would imply that stereoscopic disparity signals are extracted prior to the illusion described by Lettvin.

CONCLUSION

One could object to the phrase filling in on the grounds that it implies the presence of a homunculus watching an inner screen.[3] To me, this objection is pedantic. After all, the visual system might find it convenient to create certain types of intermediate-level representations in order to facilitate further computation. Filling in may be one example of such an intermediate representation. The use of metaphors (such as filling in) is entirely permissible in science so long as one realizes that one is being metaphorical. (For example, Crick has pointed out that even to this day the word *gene* eludes exact definition, but it is better to get on with the experiments than to worry too much about terminology.)

Finally, why study the blind spot or the filling in of scotomas? What is the biological purpose of these processes? It seems unlikely that the visual system has evolved a mechanism for the sole purpose of filling in blind spots and scotomas. A much more plausible interpretation is that the process is simply a manifestation of a more general perceptual mechanism—one that is sometimes called *surface interpolation*. When we look at a chair, for instance, the visual system extracts information mainly about the chair's contours or edges and creates a representation that resembles a sort of cartoon sketch. The color and texture of the chair is perhaps then filled in by a process akin to the filling in of scotomas and blind spots. This strategy would allow the visual system to avoid the computational burden of having to create a detailed representation of surface textures and colors—a process that may be too time-consuming for an organism that is trying to jump onto a surface or avoid an obstacle.

NOTES

1. H. L. Teuber, W. S. Battersby, and M. B. Bender, *Visual Field Defects After Penetrating Missile Wounds of the Brain* (Harvard University Press, Cambridge, MA, 1960); L. Weiszcrantz, Encephalization and the scotoma, In *Current Problems in Animal Behaviour,* W. H. Thorpe and O. L. Zangwill, Eds. (Cambridge University Press, Cambridge, England, 1961); E. Pöppel and W. Richards, Light sensitivity in cortical scotoma contralateral to small islands of blindness, *Experimental Brain Research, 21,* 125–130 (1974).

2. D. Brewster, *Letters in Natural Magic* (John Murray, London, 1832).

3. D. Dennett, *Consciousness Explained* (Little, Brown and Co., Boston, 1991).

4. R. Efron, The duration of the present, *Annals of the New York Academy of Sciences, 138,* 713–729 (1967).

5. A. Treisman, Features and objects in visual processing, *Scientific American, 225,* 114–126 (1986); J. Beck, Effects of orientation and of shape similarity on perceptual grouping, *Perception and Psychophysics, 1,* 300–302 (1966); B. Julesz, Textons, the elements of texture perception and their interactions, *Nature,* 290, 91–97 (1981).

6. V. S. Ramachandran, Blind spots, *Scientific American, 266,* 86–91 (1992); V. S. Ramachandran and W. Aiken, On filling in the blind spot and other medical marvels, *Society for Neurosciences Abstract, 17,* 847 (1991); V. S. Ramachandran, Filling in the blind spot, *Nature* (in press).

7. This observation is nicely explained by the recent physiological work of R. Gatas, M. Fiorani, M. G. P. Rosa, M. C. G. Pinon, A. P. B. Sousa, and J. G. M. Soares, Changes in receptive field size in V1 and in relation to

perceptual completion, in *The Visual System From Genesis to Maturity*, R. Lent, Ed. (Birkhauser, Boston, 1992). These authors found that certain cells in Area 17 will respond only when two collinear line segments are presented on either side of the blind spot (but not if one of the segments alone is presented).
8. G. Kanizsa, *Organization in Vision* (Praeger, New York, 1979); R. L. Gregory, Cognitive contours, *Nature, 238*, 51–52 (1972); I. Rock, *The Logic of Perception* (MIT Press, Cambridge, MA, 1983), An effect similar to the one described here has been observed by E. H. Adelson (personal communication).
9. M. Livingstone and D. Hubel, Psychophysical evidence for separate channels for the perception of form, color, movement and depth, *Journal of Neuroscience, 7*, 3416–3468 (1987).
10. V. S. Ramachandran and S. M. Anstis, The perception of apparent motion, *Scientific American*, *254*, 102–109 (1986).
11. J. Lettvin, A sidelong glance at seeing, *The Sciences, 16*, 1–20 (1976).

QUESTIONS ABOUT MEANING

1. Summarize the series of experiments Ramachandran describes and his findings.
2. What is the purpose and value of the research Ramachandran describes?

QUESTIONS FOR RHETORICAL ANALYSIS

1. Who is the intended audience of this selection? How can you tell? Quote and discuss a couple of representative passages to support your answer.
2. Notice the way outside sources of information are cited in the article. What benefits can you see for using this method of documentation instead of the name/date method more commonly found in this anthology? What drawbacks of this citation style do you see for readers?

MAKING CONNECTIONS

1. In addition to its having a neurological meaning, *scotoma* is used metaphorically in psychology to refer to mental blind spots, including the inability to recognize traits about ourselves that others see and the inability to recognize evidence that conflicts with what we believe about ourselves. These psychological scotomas, of course, can get us into more trouble than any literal blind spots! Illustrate and discuss this idea in an essay that puts various authors from this chapter into conversation with one another.
2. Ramachandran's research, along with that of Chua, Boland, and Nisbett; Loftus (chapter 16); and Borodisky (chapter 15), helps us to understand

how witnesses to the same event (such as an accident, a sporting event, an argument) can recall the event differently. Put some or all of these authors in conversation with each other in an essay. On what points would they agree? On what points might they disagree or agree that the answers are unknown? What implications does their research have for those who work in law enforcement or the justice system?

CHAPTER 15

Language, Literacy, and Technology

This chapter is about how language and technology shape our lives.

The chapter opens with two selections from psychology professor Lera Boroditsky. In "Lost in Translation," Boroditsky describes how "the languages we speak not only reflect or express our thoughts, but also shape the very thoughts we wish to express." One real-world application of this finding is seen in the next article, "Subtle Linguistic Cues Influence Perceived Blame and Financial Liability," describing a study conducted by Caitlin Fausey and Boroditsky. Their research demonstrates that how we attribute blame in part depends on how an event is described.

How the presentation of information affects us is also the focus of the next three readings. In "Our 'Deep Reading' Brain," Maryanne Wolf speculates about the implications of transitioning from a literate to a digital world where "deep reading" is being replaced with skimming and scanning. Wolf argues that "sound bites, text bites, and mind bites are a reflection of a culture that has forgotten or become too distracted by and too drawn to the next piece of new information to allow itself time to think." Sherry Turkle takes up a similar topic in her article "How Computers Change the Way We Think." Although she acknowledges it's too soon to determine if those changes are good or bad, Turkle asks readers to consider "whether current technology is leading us in directions that serve our human purposes." Clay Shirky also writes about how we are adapting to the digital world, in "Does the Internet Make You Smarter or Dumber?" "The task before us now," according to Shirky, "is to experiment with new ways of using a medium that is social, ubiquitous and cheap, a medium that changes the landscape by distributing freedom of the press and freedom of assembly as widely as freedom of speech." Together, these writers challenge us to think about how the tools we use shape our thinking and our culture.

Like Shirky, Ethan Zuckerman recognizes the potential of the Internet to bring about change. In "Using the Internet to Examine Patterns of Foreign Coverage," Zuckerman suggests there may be "an opportunity for new, participatory media like Weblogs to draw attention to situations and stories" that people otherwise would never hear about.

Technology in the classroom is the subject of the two research studies that end the chapter: "The Effects and Predictor Value of In-Class Texting Behavior on Final Course Grades" and "The Laptop and the Lecture: The Effects of Multitasking in Learning Environments." In the first study, Sylvia McDonald determined that "the more a student participated in in-class texting behavior, the lower their final grade." Similarly, Helene Hembrooke and Geri Gay found that students who were allowed to browse online during a lecture did worse when tested on the material than did students not allowed to use their laptops during the lecture. Like other writers in this chapter, Hembrooke and Gay wonder how well our brains are adapting to our digital, multitasking lifestyles.

Psychology

"Lost in Translation," LERA BORODITSKY

The paired readings in this chapter are from psychology professor Lera Boroditsky. In this first article, published in 2010 in *The Wall Street Journal*, Boroditsky summarizes research focused on discovering whether the "languages we speak shape the way we think." Boroditsky writes, "How do we come to be the way we are? Why do we think the way we do? An important part of the answer, it turns out, is in the languages we speak."

Do the languages we speak shape the way we think? Do they merely express thoughts, or do the structures in languages (without our knowledge or consent) shape the very thoughts we wish to express?

Take "Humpty Dumpty sat on a. . . ." Even this snippet of a nursery rhyme reveals how much languages can differ from one another. In English, we have to mark the verb for tense; in this case, we say "sat" rather than "sit." In Indonesian you need not (in fact, you can't) change the verb to mark tense.

In Russian, you would have to mark tense and also gender, changing the verb if Mrs. Dumpty did the sitting. You would also have to decide if the sitting event was completed or not. If our ovoid hero sat on the wall for the entire time he was meant to, it would be a different form of the verb than if, say, he had a great fall.

In Turkish, you would have to include in the verb how you acquired this information. For example, if you saw the chubby fellow on the wall with your own eyes, you'd use one form of the verb, but if you had simply read or heard about it, you'd use a different form.

Do English, Indonesian, Russian and Turkish speakers end up attending to, understanding, and remembering their experiences differently simply because they speak different languages?

These questions touch on all the major controversies in the study of mind, with important implications for politics, law and religion. Yet very little empirical work had been done on these questions until recently.

The idea that language might shape thought was for a long time considered untestable at best and more often simply crazy and wrong. Now, a flurry of new cognitive science research is showing that in fact, language does profoundly influence how we see the world.

The question of whether languages shape the way we think goes back centuries; Charlemagne proclaimed that "to have a second language is to have a second soul." But the idea went out of favor with scientists when Noam Chomsky's theories of language gained popularity in the 1960s and '70s. Dr. Chomsky proposed that there is a universal grammar for all human languages—essentially, that languages don't really differ from one another in significant ways. And because languages didn't differ from one another, the theory went, it made no sense to ask whether linguistic differences led to differences in thinking.

The search for linguistic universals yielded interesting data on languages, but after decades of work, not a single proposed universal has withstood scrutiny. Instead, as linguists probed deeper into the world's languages (7,000 or so, only a fraction of them analyzed), innumerable unpredictable differences emerged.

Of course, just because people talk differently doesn't necessarily mean they think differently. In the past decade, cognitive scientists have begun to measure not just how people talk, but also how they think, asking whether our understanding of even such fundamental domains of experience as space, time and causality could be constructed by language.

For example, in Pormpuraaw, a remote Aboriginal community in Australia, the indigenous languages don't use terms like "left" and "right." Instead, everything is talked about in terms of absolute cardinal directions (north, south, east, west), which means you say things like, "There's an ant on your southwest leg." To say hello in Pormpuraaw, one asks, "Where are you going?", and an appropriate response might be, "A long way to the south-southwest. How about you?" If you don't know which way is which, you literally can't get past hello. About a third of the world's languages (spoken in all kinds of physical environments) rely on absolute directions for space. As a result of this constant linguistic training, speakers of such languages are remarkably good at staying oriented and keeping track of where they are, even in unfamiliar landscapes. They perform navigational feats scientists once thought were beyond human capabilities. This is a big difference, a fundamentally different way of conceptualizing space, trained by language.

Differences in how people think about space don't end there. People rely on their spatial knowledge to build many other more complex or abstract representations including time, number, musical pitch, kinship relations, morality and emotions. So if Pormpuraawans think differently about space, do they also think differently about other things, like time?

To find out, my colleague Alice Gaby and I traveled to Australia and gave Pormpuraawans sets of pictures that showed temporal progressions (for example, pictures of a man at different ages, or a crocodile growing, or a banana being eaten). Their job was to arrange the shuffled photos on the ground to show the correct temporal order. We tested each person in two separate sittings, each time facing in a different cardinal direction. When asked to do this, English speakers arrange time from left to right. Hebrew speakers do it from right to left (because Hebrew is written from right to left).

Pormpuraawans, we found, arranged time from east to west. That is, seated facing south, time went left to right. When facing north, right to left. When facing east, toward the body, and so on. Of course, we never told any of our participants which direction they faced. The Pormpuraawans not only knew that already, but they also spontaneously used this spatial orientation to construct their representations of time. And many other ways to organize time exist in the world's languages. In Mandarin, the future can be below and the past above. In Aymara, spoken in South America, the future is behind and the past in front.

In addition to space and time, languages also shape how we understand causality. For example, English likes to describe events in terms of agents doing things. English speakers tend to say things like "John broke the vase" even for accidents. Speakers of Spanish or Japanese would be more likely to say "the vase broke itself." Such differences between languages have profound consequences for how their speakers understand events, construct notions of causality and agency, what they remember as eyewitnesses and how much they blame and punish others.

In studies conducted by Caitlin Fausey at Stanford, speakers of English, Spanish and Japanese watched videos of two people popping balloons, breaking eggs and spilling drinks either intentionally or accidentally. Later everyone got a surprise memory test: For each event, can you remember who did it? She discovered a striking cross-linguistic difference in eyewitness memory. Spanish and Japanese speakers did not remember the agents of accidental events as well as did English speakers. Mind you, they remembered the agents of intentional events (for which their language would mention the agent) just fine. But for accidental events, when one wouldn't normally mention the agent in Spanish or Japanese, they didn't encode or remember the agent as well.

In another study, English speakers watched the video of Janet Jackson's infamous "wardrobe malfunction" (a wonderful nonagentive coinage introduced into the English language by Justin Timberlake), accompanied by one of two written reports. The reports were identical except in the last sentence where one used the agentive phrase "ripped the costume" while the other said "the costume ripped." Even though everyone watched the same video and witnessed the ripping with their own eyes, language mattered. Not only did people who read "ripped the costume" blame Justin Timberlake more, they also levied a whopping 53% more in fines.

Beyond space, time and causality, patterns in language have been shown to shape many other domains of thought. Russian speakers, who make an extra distinction between light and dark blues in their language, are better able to visually discriminate shades of blue. The Piraha, a tribe in the Amazon in Brazil, whose language eschews number words in favor of terms like *few* and *many* [italics added], are not able to keep track of exact quantities. And Shakespeare, it turns out, was wrong about roses: Roses by many other names (as told to blindfolded subjects) do not smell as sweet.

Patterns in language offer a window on a culture's dispositions and priorities. For example, English sentence structures focus on agents, and in our criminal-justice system, justice has been done when we've found the transgressor and punished him or her accordingly (rather than finding the victims and restituting appropriately, an alternative approach to justice). So does the language shape cultural values, or does the influence go the other way, or both?

Languages, of course, are human creations, tools we invent and hone to suit our needs. Simply showing that speakers of different languages think differently doesn't tell us whether it's language that shapes thought or the other way around. To demonstrate the causal role of language, what's needed are studies that directly manipulate language and look for effects in cognition.

One of the key advances in recent years has been the demonstration of precisely this causal link. It turns out that if you change how people talk, that changes how they think. If people learn another language, they inadvertently also learn a new way of looking at the world. When bilingual people switch from one language to another, they start thinking differently, too. And if you take away people's ability to use language in what should be a simple nonlinguistic task, their performance can change dramatically, sometimes making them look no smarter than rats or infants. (For example, in recent studies, MIT students were shown dots on a screen and asked to say how many there were. If they were allowed to count normally, they did great. If they simultaneously did a nonlinguistic task—like banging out rhythms—they still did great. But if they did a verbal task when shown the dots—like repeating the words spoken in a news report—their counting fell apart. In other words, they needed their language skills to count.)

All this new research shows us that the languages we speak not only reflect or express our thoughts, but also shape the very thoughts we wish to express. The structures that exist in our languages profoundly shape how we construct reality, and help make us as smart and sophisticated as we are.

Language is a uniquely human gift. When we study language, we are uncovering in part what makes us human, getting a peek at the very nature of human nature. As we uncover how languages and their speakers differ from one another, we discover that human natures too can differ dramatically, depending on the languages we speak. The next steps are to understand the mechanisms through which languages help us construct the incredibly complex knowledge systems we have. Understanding how knowledge is built will allow us to create ideas that go beyond the currently thinkable. This research cuts right to the fundamental questions we all ask about ourselves. How do we come to be the way we are? Why do we think the way we do? An important part of the answer, it turns out, is in the languages we speak.

QUESTIONS ABOUT MEANING

1. How does the language a person speaks shape the way he or she thinks, remembers, or sees the world?
2. According to Boroditsky, why might two eyewitnesses, who speak different languages, remember events differently?

QUESTIONS FOR RHETORICAL ANALYSIS

1. Of what value is the body of research Boroditsky describes? Where and how does Boroditsky convey the importance of her topic?
2. Boroditsky's article was written for *The Wall Street Journal*, an international newspaper focused on business and economic news. What aspects of the writing indicate that Boroditsky is writing for a general audience?

MAKING CONNECTIONS

1. Boroditsky; Turkle; Kuhn (chapter 9); Chua, Boland, and Nisbett; Norenzayan and Nisbett; and Rose (chapter 2) all describe how the form of presentation influences the way we interpret information. Put several of these authors (or other writers) in conversation with one another in an essay that summarizes some of the research about how presentation affects the way we perceive, judge, or remember information.

   Then, using Norenzayan and Nisbett's abstract as a model, write an abstract for your essay.

2. Like Norenzayan and Nisbett, Boroditsky describes cultural factors influencing how people perceive blame and causality. Find a brief article online that condemns someone for unethical behavior, even though the unethical behavior is or was not unusual in the culture. (Cheating in sports and cheating on tax returns are just two examples.) Analyze the way the wrongdoer is portrayed. Then, retell the story as a Chinese or Japanese newspaper might. (See Norenzayan and Nisbett.) Discuss the changes you made to the telling of the story and why you made those changes.

Psychology

"Subtle Linguistic Cues Influence Perceived Blame and Financial Liability," CAITLIN M. FAUSEY AND LERA BORODITSKY

Like several authors in chapters 13 and 14, Caitlin Fausey and Lera Boroditsky consider the way perceptions of events can vary. The studies described in the next article, written while Fausey was a graduate student at Stanford University, where Boroditsky was a professor of psychology, reveal that even when we witness events, our interpretation of what happened is influenced by how the events are described by others. Fausey and Boroditsky's research appeared in 2010 in the journal *Psychonomic Bulletin & Review*, which publishes both review articles and research studies from psychology.

When bad things happen, how do we decide who is to blame and how much they should be punished? In the present studies, we examined whether subtly different linguistic descriptions of accidents influence how much people blame and punish those involved. In three studies, participants judged how much people involved in particular accidents should be blamed and how much they should have to pay for the resulting damage. The language used to describe the accidents differed subtly across conditions: Either agentive (transitive) or non-agentive (intransitive) verb forms were used. Agentive descriptions led participants to attribute more blame and request higher financial penalties than did nonagentive descriptions. Further, linguistic framing influenced judgments, even when participants reasoned about a well-known event, such as the "wardrobe malfunction" of Super Bowl 2004. Importantly, this effect of language held, even when people were able to see a video of the event. These results demonstrate that even when people have rich established knowledge and visual information about events, linguistic framing can shape event construal, with important real-world consequences. Subtle differences in linguistic descriptions can change how people construe what happened, attribute blame, and dole out punishment. Supplemental results and analyses may be downloaded from http://pbr.psychonomic-journals.org/content/supplemental.

When bad things happen, how do we decide who is to blame and how much they should be punished? Linguistic and contextual framing has been shown to affect people's reasoning in a variety of domains (e.g., Lee, Frederick, & Ariely, 2006; Levin, 1987; Levin & Gaeth, 1988; Loftus, Miller, & Burns, 1978; Loftus & Palmer, 1974; Shiv, Carmon, & Ariely, 2005; Tversky & Kahneman, 1973, 1981), including causal attribution (see Pickering & Majid, 2007, for a recent review). In the present article, we build on this work by exploring the effects of linguistic framing in a domain of paramount real-world importance—blame and punishment.

Linguistic descriptions are of course ubiquitous in legal disputes. People linguistically frame incidents from the very moment they occur and later in police reports, legal statements, court testimony, and public discourse. Could the linguistic descriptions of an event influence how much we blame the people involved? Could language also influence how financially liable we think a person is for any resulting damage? Could linguistic framing shape construal even for well-known events (ones for which we already have rich knowledge and established mental representations) and even when we can witness the event with our own eyes?

The particular linguistic contrast of interest in the present article is between transitive agentive descriptions and intransitive nonagentive descriptions. A canonical agentive description (e.g., *Timberlake ripped the costume*) includes a person as the subject in a transitive expression describing a change of state (in this case, ripping). A canonical nonagentive description (e.g., *The costume ripped*) is intransitive and does not place the person as the subject for the change-of-state event.[1] Previous work has shown that people are sensitive to this distinction between agentive and nonagentive frames. For example, people are more likely to remember the agent of an event when primed with agentive language than when primed with nonagentive language (e.g., Fausey, Long, Inamori, & Boroditsky, in press). The attributional consequences of these linguistic frames, however, are not well understood.

The linguistic contrast between agentive and nonagentive frames has the potential to have serious real-world consequences, especially in legal contexts. For example, in the 197,745 trials held between 1674 and 1913 at London's central criminal court (Old Bailey Proceedings Online, 2009), cases with the agentive phrase "broke it" in the court records resulted in a guilty verdict more often than did cases with the nonagentive phrase "it broke" (76% and 70% guilty, respectively), with similar patterns for other consequential actions such as "burned it" versus "it burned" [77% and 57% guilty, respectively; $\chi^2(1, N = 2{,}748) = 11.04, p < .05$]. In the most serious of cases (when the charge was "killing"), the transitive/intransitive contrast as marked by different verbs also predicted verdicts. Saying "killed" resulted in more guilty verdicts than did saying "died" [65% and 56% guilty, respectively; $\chi^2(1, N = 3{,}814) = 21.34$, $p < .05$]. These examples suggest that agentivity may be part of a suite of linguistic cues that are influential in legal reasoning.

In a correlational analysis such as this, however, it is impossible to determine whether different linguistic forms actually caused a difference in verdicts. It could be that agentive descriptions indeed led the court more often to guilty verdicts. But it is also possible that people were simply more likely to use agentive language in cases in which the defendant was actually more guilty. Although the attributional consequences of transitivity have not been directly explored in the empirical literature, the question has been debated—and adjudicated—in court. For example, in a case petitioning to change the title of a ballot measure (California's high-profile Proposition 8 in the 2008 election titled "Eliminates right of same-sex couples to marry"), the judge rejected the petitioners' claim, ruling that "There is nothing inherently argumentative or prejudicial about transitive verbs" (*Jansson v. Bowen*, 2008). Few other questions in psycholinguistics have risen to a sufficient level of civic importance to be ruled on in high court.

With the high stakes of guilt, innocence, and the legality of constitutional amendments on the line, it is important to empirically establish whether agentive and nonagentive frames indeed have any attributional consequences. In the present article, we examine the effects of agentive and nonagentive linguistic frames on important real-world decisions about blame and punishment.

STUDY 1

In Study 1, participants read about an accidental restaurant fire that resulted in property damage. They then made judgments about the person involved in the accident. The survey was one of many unrelated surveys in a packet presented to participants.

Method

Participants. In partial fulfillment of a course requirement, 236 Stanford University students (96 male; mean age = 19.22 years) completed one survey: 116 read the agentive and 120 read the nonagentive version of the story.

Materials. Participants read either the agentive or the nonagentive account about an individual (Mrs. Smith) who was involved in a restaurant fire. They then answered two questions (Table 1). The two accounts contain all of the same content words (all of the same nouns, verbs, and adjectives are used), involve the same individual, and describe the same outcomes. The accounts differ only in the frames used to describe the accidental events (underlined sections of Table 1): Transitive frames are used in the agentive account and intransitive frames in the nonagentive account.

Table 1
Studies 1 and 2, Reports and Questions

Agentive Report	Nonagentive Report
Mrs. Smith and her friends were finishing a lovely dinner at their favorite restaurant. After they settled the bill, they decided to head to a nearby café for coffee and dessert. Mrs. Smith followed her friends and as she stood up, she flopped her napkin on the centerpiece candle. She had ignited the napkin! As Mrs. Smith reached to grab the napkin, she toppled the candle and ignited the whole tablecloth too! As she jumped back, she overturned the table and ignited the carpet, as well. Hearing her desperate cries, the restaurant staff hurried over and heroically managed to put the fire out before anyone got hurt.	Mrs. Smith and her friends were finishing a lovely dinner at their favorite restaurant. After they settled the bill, they decided to head to a nearby café for coffee and dessert. Mrs. Smith followed her friends and as she stood up, her napkin flopped on the centerpiece candle. The napkin had ignited! As Mrs. Smith reached to grab the napkin, the candle toppled and the whole tablecloth ignited too! As she jumped back, the table overturned and the carpet ignited, as well. Hearing her desperate cries, the restaurant staff hurried over and heroically managed to put the fire out before anyone got hurt.
Questions for Study 1	
Blame. Mrs. Smith is discussing the damage with the restaurant. How much should she be blamed for the fire? (Likert scale from 1 to 7, anchored by *Not at all to blame* and *Completely to blame*) *Financial liability.* The restaurant's insurance policy does not cover minor fires. The restaurant has sought legal action to require Mrs. Smith to pay for the damage. Total costs to the restaurant were $1,500. How much should Mrs. Smith be required to pay?	
Questions for Study 2	
Financial liability. The restaurant's insurance policy does not cover minor fires and so the restaurant has sought legal action to require Mrs. Smith to pay for the damage. An independent review panel used their standard blame assessment scale in reviewing this case. On this scale, 0 means *not at all to blame* and 8 means *completely to blame*. The panel gave Mrs. Smith a {1,4,7}. The total costs to the restaurant were $1,500. How much should Mrs. Smith be required to pay?	

Results and Discussion

Linguistic framing influenced people's judgments of both blame and financial liability. Participants who read the agentive account ($M = 4.83$, $SE = 0.14$) blamed Mrs. Smith more than did participants who read the nonagentive account ($M = 4.01$, $SE = 0.15$) [$t(234) = 4.04$, $p < .001$, $d = .53$]. A subtle difference in language caused a big difference in dollars: Participants who got the agentive report ruled that Mrs. Smith should pay $247 (36%) more in fines (M = \$935.17, SE = \$43.48) than did participants who got the nonagentive report (M = \$688.75, SE = \$43.64) [$t(234) = 3.99$, $p < .001$, $d = .52$].

In Study 1, linguistic framing influenced people's judgments of financial liability. One explanation for this result could be that Mrs. Smith was punished more harshly because she had also been blamed more harshly. That is, the effect of language on financial liability might be indirect, such that language influences blame, which then determines punishment. Could language *directly* impact judgments of financial liability? This question is important because of the somewhat flexible sentencing process that occurs after guilt judgments in legal decision making. A direct impact of language on sentencing would be an important applied result. Study 2 was designed to address this question.

STUDY 2

In Study 2, participants got an agentive or nonagentive accident description and also learned of a blame attribution generated by an independent review panel. This panel attributed low, middle, or high blame to the person involved in the accident. After learning how blameworthy other people judged the person to be, participants determined the person's financial liability for the property damage. This paradigm allows us to target the independent role of language on financial liability sentences. People's decisions about financial liability may be guided by blame-worthiness, language, or both.

Method

Participants. In partial fulfillment of a course requirement, 179 Stanford University students (59 male; mean age = 19.01 years) completed one survey: 91 read the agentive account of the restaurant fire accident (33 low, 30 middle, and 28 high blame), and 88 read the nonagentive account (33 low, 28 middle, and 27 high blame).

Materials. As in Study 1, participants read either the agentive or the nonagentive narrative and then answered the financial liability question shown in Table 1. Thus, participants in Study 2 answered only the financial liability question, after learning that an independent panel judged the person to be either a 1 (*low*), a 4 (*middle*), or a 7 (*high*) in terms of blame.

Results

The level of blame assigned by the independent panel influenced participants' judgments of financial liability (Figure 15.1). Overall, people judged that Mrs. Smith should pay more in damages when the independent panel ruled her to be highly to blame (*M* = \$974.19, *SE* = \$61.97) than when the panel assigned her a middle level of blame (*M* = \$615.00, *SE* = \$56.27) and than when she was ruled to be of low blame (*M* = \$425.63, *SE* = \$50.89).

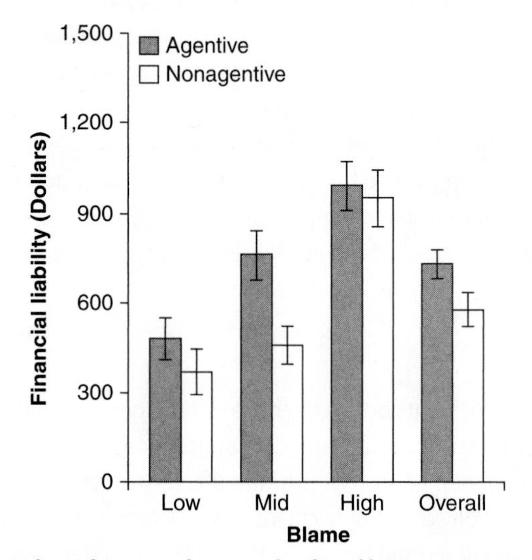

Figure 15.1 Independent contributions of guilt and linguistic framing to financial liability sentences (Study 2). Mean values are plotted on the *y*-axis, with whiskers representing ±1 *SEM*.

Interestingly, language also influenced financial liability judgments. As in Study 1, a subtle change in language led to a substantial change in financial liability: Mrs. Smith was held responsible for \$153 (or 26%) more in damages by people who got the agentive report (*M* = \$730.75, *SE* = \$49.57) than by those who got the nonagentive report (*M* = \$577.77, *SE* = \$52.35).

A 3 (blame: low, middle, high) × 2 (language: agentive, nonagentive) factorial ANOVA revealed reliable main effects of assigned blame level [$F(2,173) = 25.23$, $p < .001$, $\eta^2 = .22$] and of language [$F(1,173) = 5.53$, $p = .02$, $\eta^2 = .03$]. Assigned blame level and language did not interact [$F(2,173) = 1.40$, n.s.].

Discussion

Guilt and linguistic framing independently influenced how much someone was required to pay for accidental property damage. Increasing assigned blame led to greater financial liability and agentive framing led to greater financial liability than did nonagentive framing. This finding replicates the result from Study 1. Further, sentencing itself appears to be susceptible to linguistic framing effects.

Results from the first two studies suggest that agentive and nonagentive language can shape how people attribute blame and financial liability to individuals involved in accidents. Of course, in these two studies, the only information that reasoners had about the accident was linguistic. Were people inevitably swayed by language because it was the only thing that guided what they imagined about the event? Perhaps people who received differently phrased reports imagined substantially different scenarios of what happened? In many real-life situations, the information we have about an event is purely linguistic (e.g., in court arguments, insurance claims, and news accounts). But, in other situations, we may also have visual evidence, either by being eyewitnesses or by viewing videotape. Would linguistic framing still have an effect even if people were able to see the event? Further, the restaurant fire described in Studies 1 and 2 was a novel event, one for which participants had no other previous information. Would people be so easily influenced by linguistic framing if they were reasoning about an event that they already knew something about, for which they already had a rich set of mental representations?

To address these questions, we capitalized on a widely known, much discussed, well-publicized, and video-recorded event: the "wardrobe malfunction" of Super Bowl 2004, when a performance by Justin Timberlake and Janet Jackson ended with Janet Jackson's breast being exposed on national television. Postexperiment questioning confirmed that this is indeed a well-known event: Nearly all of our participants (96.9%) had heard about it, and many had also seen the video (67.9%) before the experiment. With prior knowledge, and current visual evidence, could linguistic framing still influence blame and punishment?

STUDY 3

In Study 3, participants reasoned about the wardrobe malfunction incident under one of three conditions: They read about the incident, or they first read about the incident and then watched the video, or they first watched the video and then read about it. In each condition, people read either an agentive or a nonagentive account of the incident.

Method

Participants. Five hundred eighty-nine participants (188 male; mean age = 31.17 years) were paid for completing one survey online. Participants were recruited from the pool of English speakers who use Amazon's Mechanical Turk (www.mturk.com). Three hundred six read the agentive account of the event (116 read only, 88 read then watch, and 102 watch then read) and 283 read the nonagentive account of the event (93 read only, 106 read then watch, and 84 watch then read).

Materials and Design. Participants read either the agentive or nonagentive account of the "wardrobe malfunction" incident (Table 2). In two conditions, participants viewed a video of the final 6 sec of the performance, which included the infamous malfunction (www.youtube.com/watch?v=O6j-OKvydPI).

After reading about the incident (and also watching it on video, in two of the conditions), participants answered the questions shown in Table 2. The order of the three response options was randomized, and the particular order presented to each participant was the same for the blame and financial liability judgments. Because Timberlake initiated movement right before the "wardrobe malfunction" and also because of his prominent apology to Super Bowl viewers (in which he coined the phrase "wardrobe

Table 2
Study 3 Reports and Questions

Agentive Report	Nonagentive Report
Justin Timberlake and Janet Jackson performed during the 2004 Super Bowl Half-time Show. Toward the end of the song, Timberlake followed Jackson across the stage and stood beside her. As they sang the last line, Timberlake reached across the front of Jackson's body. In this final dance move, he unfastened a snap and tore part of the bodice! He slid the cover right off Jackson's chest! This incident made for a lot of controversy.	Justin Timberlake and Janet Jackson performed during the 2004 Super Bowl Half-time Show. Toward the end of the song, Timberlake followed Jackson across the stage and stood beside her. As they sang the last line, Timberlake reached across the front of Jackson's body. In this final dance move, a snap unfastened and part of the bodice tore! The cover slid right off Jackson's chest! This incident made for a lot of controversy.
Questions	
Blame. In your opinion, was someone to blame or was it just chance? Please allocate the percentage of blame. Be sure your numbers add up to 100%! Response options: Justin Timberlake, Janet Jackson, Chance	
Financial liability. The FCC (Federal Communications Commission) tried to fine CBS $550,000 for this incident. Eventually the fine was dismissed in court. How much do you think each of the parties below should have been fined for this incident? Response options: Justin Timberlake, Janet Jackson, CBS	

malfunction"; Timberlake, 2004), our narratives focused on the actions of Timberlake. As a result, we expected that any effects of linguistic framing should be strongest for judging the guilt and financial liability of Timberlake. Also, because the FCC tried to fine CBS for broadcasting the incident, CBS was included among the possible targets for financial liability.

Results

In brief, linguistic framing affected people's judgments of blame and financial liability in all conditions: Language mattered, whether it was presented before, after, or without video evidence. The main results of interest are shown in Figure 15.2.

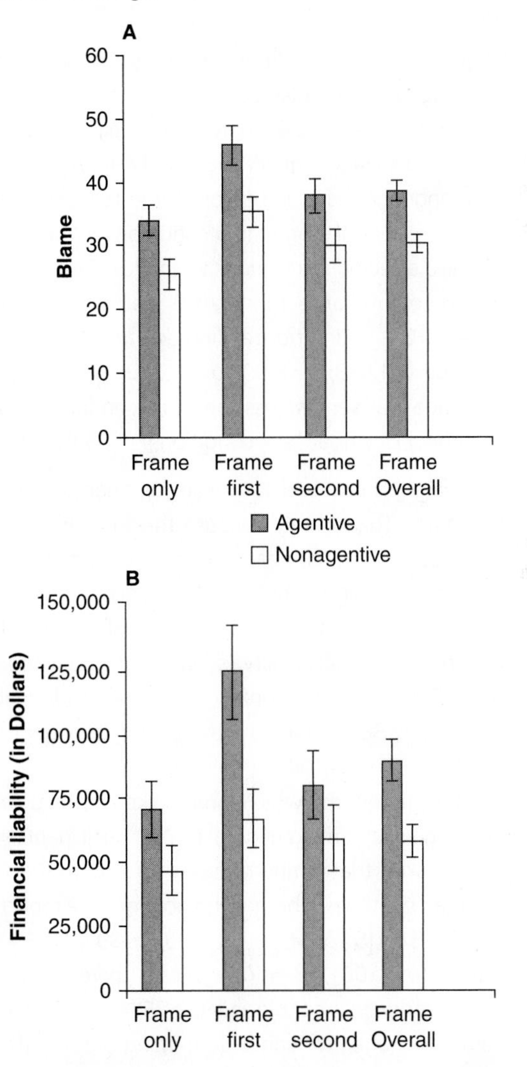

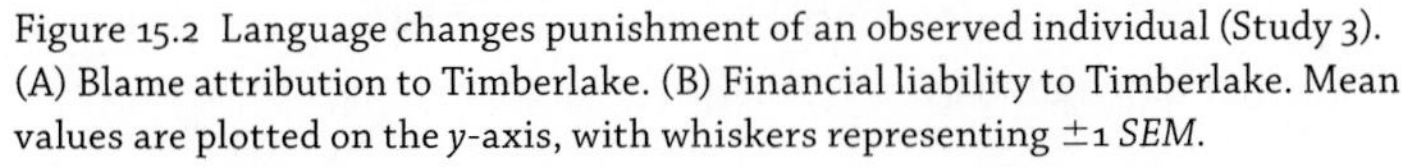

Figure 15.2 Language changes punishment of an observed individual (Study 3). (A) Blame attribution to Timberlake. (B) Financial liability to Timberlake. Mean values are plotted on the y-axis, with whiskers representing ± 1 *SEM*.

Conclusions from these data are the same, whether all three framing contexts are considered (as reported below) or whether only the two multimodal contexts are considered. Conclusions are also supported by nonparametric analyses (see the supplementary materials).

Effects of language on blame and financial liability. Blame and financial liability attributions were analyzed using a 2 (language: agentive, nonagentive) × 3 (task context: read only, read then watch, watch then read) factorial ANOVA for each dependent measure. For clarity of presentation, we focus on effects of language here (see the supplementary materials for effects of task context). Language and task context never interacted.

Blame. Linguistic framing influenced people's blame attributions (Figure 15.2A). Overall, people blamed Timberlake more after reading agentive (M = 38.76%, SE = 1.59%) than after reading nonagentive (M = 30.49%, SE = 1.43%) language [$F(1,583) = 17.94$, $p < .001$, $\eta^2 = .03$]. The effect of language was seen across the three conditions, with no interaction of the effect of language 3 condition [$F(2,583) = 0.15$, n.s.].

Language also affected attributions to chance. Overall, people attributed the outcome to chance more after reading nonagentive (M = 42.87%, SE = 2.40%) than after reading agentive (M = 33.92%, SE = 2.26%) language [$F(1,583) = 8.99$, $p = .003$, $\eta^2 = .01$]. Again, this effect of language was seen across the three conditions, with no interaction of the effect of language × condition [$F(2,583) = 0.20$, n.s.].

Financial liability. The modal response for financial liability was $0 (57.2% of all data). This is likely because the sentence "Eventually the fine was dismissed in court" appeared in the liability question. Nevertheless, the linguistic framing of the event influenced people's judgments about financial liability. Overall, the proportion of people who gave any nonzero amount of financial liability to Timberlake depended on linguistic framing. 46.7% assigned a nonzero fine after reading agentive language, whereas only 38.5% did so after reading nonagentive language [$\chi^2(1, N = 589) = 4.05$, $p = .044$].

The amount of money for which Timberlake was held liable likewise depended on linguistic framing (Figure 15.2B). Participants who got the agentive report asked that Timberlake pay an extra $30,828.69 (53%) more in fines than did those who got the nonagentive report [$M_{Agentive}$ = $88,818.12, SE = $8,115.75; $M_{Nonagentive}$ = $57,989.43, SE = $6,465.34; $F(1,575) = 10.31$, $p = .001$, $\eta^2 = .02$].[2] Again, there was no interaction of the effect of language × condition [$F(2,575) = 1.22$, n.s.].

Agentive and nonagentive linguistic framing did not affect people's attributions of blame or financial liability to Janet Jackson or CBS (see the supplementary materials).

In an additional set of analyses, all of the reported contrasts were conducted with an additional factor: whether or not the participant reported having seen the video of this incident prior to the experiment. This factor was not a reliable main effect nor did it interact with effects of linguistic framing in any of the analyses.

Discussion

Linguistic framing influenced how much people punished an individual involved in an event, even when they witnessed the event, and even though the event was one that our participants already knew about. Agentive language led to harsher punishment than did nonagentive language. Replicating results from the first two studies, linguistic framing not only influenced attributions of blame, but also influenced assessments of financial liability. In the case of the wardrobe malfunction incident, an agentive report led people to think that Justin Timberlake owed more than $30,000 more (an extra 53%) in fines compared with a nonagentive report. In real-world contexts, visual evidence of accidents is rarely presented in the absence of linguistic framing. These results suggest that the form of this framing guides punishment.

GENERAL DISCUSSION

In three studies, linguistic framing influenced participants' judgments about blame and punishment. Financial liability judgments, in particular, were strongly affected by linguistic framing: Agentive descriptions led to 30%–50% more in requested financial damages than did nonagentive descriptions. Judgments of financial liability were affected by linguistic frame even when blame was held constant. This finding suggests that linguistic framing can have an influence not only on verdicts of guilt and innocence, but also on the sentencing process. In Study 3, linguistic framing influenced reasoning even about an event that people knew a lot about, had seen before, and witnessed (again) right before judging the individual involved.

Previous inquiries into effects of language on attribution have examined the role of verbs, voice, and word order in guiding how people determine the cause of an event (e.g., Brown & Fish, 1983; Garvey, Caramazza, & Yates, 1975; Kasof & Lee, 1993; Kassin & Lowe, 1979; Pryor & Kriss, 1977; Schmid & Fiedler, 1998; Semin, Rubini, & Fiedler, 1995). Here, we provide the first report on the impact of transitivity both on people's attributions of blame and also on the real-world outcomes of these attributions (punishment). These studies extend previous research in several important ways. First, we probed people's decisions about a concrete form of punishment—financial liability, freely estimated in dollars—in addition to more abstract ratings of blame. Second, we examined effects of linguistic framing in a rich knowledge context: People had current visual evidence and also previous knowledge about the framed event. This richness characterizes many real-world reasoning situations, but few previous attribution framing studies. Finally, we considered the transitive/intransitive alternation, a property of event description that both has important real-world consequences and differs interestingly across languages.

Previous work has shown that languages differ from one another in their preference for agentive versus nonagentive frames (e.g., Fausey & Boroditsky, in press; Fausey et al., in press). The present findings raise the possibility that speakers of different languages may prescribe more or less severe punishment as a function of the frequency of particular linguistic frames in their language. Although there have been many demonstrations showing the power of linguistic frames in shaping people's decisions, there has not been much contact between such findings and the literature investigating cross-linguistic differences in cognition. Establishing that linguistic framing has psychological consequences in a domain where languages naturally differ from one another opens the possibility for connecting these two rich bodies of knowledge.

In particular, as Sher and McKenzie (2006) have pointed out, the linguistic frames typically provided in framing studies often are not informationally equivalent. Each linguistic description is situated in a set of pragmatic norms within a language, and participants may be responding to the pragmatic cues implied by the choice of frame. The possibility of cross-linguistic comparisons offers an exciting extension to the framing literature: Rather than having frames provided by an experimenter, in the cross-linguistic case, speakers of different languages may self-generate different frames for the same events because of the prevalent patterns in their respective languages (e.g., Maass, Karasawa, Politi, & Suga, 2006). In this way, cross-linguistic comparisons may allow us to investigate conceptual framing, not just as a phenomenon in the communicative context (where participants may use pragmatic information to infer what the experimenter must mean by their choice of frame), but also in contexts where the participants naturally frame events for themselves.

The linguistic (and cross-linguistic) framing of agentivity is of particular importance in court proceedings. Filipović (2007) highlighted a case from Northern California, in which a Spanish-speaking suspect's nonagentive (and appropriate in Spanish) description of events ("se me cayó," roughly "to me it happened that she fell") was translated into English for the broader court into the agentive (and appropriate in English) "I dropped her." Do these two descriptions mean the same thing? Or does this change in framing have serious attributional consequences? Our results raise the possibility that speakers of different languages may arrive at rather different conclusions regarding blame and punishment for the same events.

In three studies, we find that agentive descriptions of events invite more blame and more severe punishment than do nonagentive descriptions. These results demonstrate that even when people have knowledge and visual information about events, linguistic framing can significantly shape how they construe and reason about what happened. In the case of agentive and nonagentive language, subtle differences in linguistic framing can have important real-world consequences. Deciding how much to blame an individual and how much to hold them financially liable appears to be broadly susceptible to linguistic framing.

AUTHOR NOTE

We thank V. Vanchinathan and N. Heitz for help with data collection and entry. The present research was supported by an NSF Graduate Research Fellowship to C.M.F. and NSF Grant No. 0608514 to L.B. Address correspondence to C. M. Fausey, Department of Psychological and Brain Sciences, 1101 E. 10th Street, Indiana University, Bloomington, IN 47405 (e-mail: cfausey@indiana.edu).

REFERENCES

Brown, R., & Fish, D. (1983). The psychological causality implicit in language. *Cognition*, **14**, 237–273.

Fausey, C. M., & Boroditsky, L. (in press). Whodunnit? Cross-linguistic differences in eyewitness memory. *Psychonomic Bulletin & Review*.

Fausey, C. M., Long, B. L., Inamori, A., & Boroditsky, L. (in press). Constructing agency: The role of language. *Frontiers in Cultural Psychology*.

Filipović, L. (2007). Language as a witness: Insights from cognitive linguistics. *International Journal of Speech, Language & the Law*, **14**, 245–267.

Garvey, C., Caramazza, A., & Yates, J. (1975). Factors influencing assignments of pronoun antecedents. *Cognition*, **3**, 227–243.

Jansson v. Bowen, No. 34-2008-00017351 (Sacramento Super. Ct. Aug. 7, 2008).

Kasof, L., & Lee, J. Y. (1993). Implicit causality as implicit salience. *Journal of Personality & Social Psychology*, **65**, 877–891. doi:10.1037/0022-3514.65.5.877

Kassin, S. M., & Lowe, C. A. (1979). On the use of single sentence descriptions of behavior in attribution research. *Social Behavior & Personality*, **7**, 1–8.

Lee, L., Frederick, S., & Ariely, D. (2006). Try it, you'll like it: The influence of expectation, consumption, and revelation on preferences for beer. *Psychological Science*, **17**, 1054–1058. doi:10.1111/j.1467-9280.2006.01829.x

Levin, I. P. (1987). Associative effects of information framing. *Bulletin of the Psychonomic Society*, **25**, 85–86.

Levin, I. P., & Gaeth, G. J. (1988). How consumers are affected by the framing of attribute information before and after consuming the product. *Journal of Consumer Research*, **15**, 374–378.
Loftus, E. F., Miller, D. G., & Burns, H. J. (1978). Semantic integration of verbal information into a visual memory. *Journal of Experimental Psychology: Human Learning & Memory*, **4**, 19–31.
Loftus, E. F., & Palmer, J. C. (1974). Reconstruction of automobile destruction: An example of the interaction between language and memory. *Journal of Verbal Learning & Verbal Behavior*, **13**, 585–589.
Maass, A., Karasawa, M., Politi, F., & Suga, S. (2006). Do verbs and adjectives play different roles in different cultures? A cross-linguistic analysis of person representation. *Journal of Personality & Social Psychology*, **90**, 734–750. doi:10.1037/0022-3514.90.5.734
Old Bailey Proceedings Online (2009). Retrieved November 3, 2009, from www.oldbaileyonline.org.
Pickering, M. J., & Majid, A. (2007). What are implicit causality and consequentiality? *Language & Cognitive Processes*, **22**, 780–788.
Pryor, J. B., & Kriss, M. (1977). The cognitive dynamics of salience in the attribution process. *Journal of Personality & Social Psychology*, **35**, 49–55. doi:10.1037/0022-3514.35.1.49
Schmid, J., & Fiedler, K. (1998). The backbone of closing speeches: The impact of prosecution versus defense language on judicial attributions. *Journal of Applied Social Psychology*, **28**, 1140–1172. doi:10.1111/j.1559-1816.1998.tb01672.x
Semin, G. R., Rubini, M., & Fiedler, K. (1995). The answer is in the question: The effect of verb causality upon locus of explanation. *Personality & Social Psychology Bulletin*, **21**, 834–842.
Sher, S., & McKenzie, C. R. M. (2006). Information leakage from logically equivalent frames. *Cognition*, **101**, 467–494. doi:10.1016/j.cognition.2005.11.001
Shiv, B., Carmon, Z., & Ariely, D. (2005). Placebo effects of marketing actions: Consumers may get what they pay for. *Journal of Marketing Research*, **42**, 383–393. doi:10.1509/jmkr.2005.42.4.383
Timberlake, J. (February 1, 2004). "Statement From Justin Timberlake," PR Newswire.
Tversky, A., & Kahneman, D. (1973). Availability: A heuristic for judging frequency and probability. *Cognitive Psychology*, **5**, 207–232.
Tversky, A., & Kahneman, D. (1981). The framing of decisions and the psychology of choice. *Science*, **211**, 453–458.
White, P. A. (2003). Effects of wording and stimulus format on the use of contingency information in causal judgment. *Memory & Cognition*, **31**, 231–242.

NOTES

1. Note that the agentive/nonagentive distinction we draw here is different from the distinction between active and passive voice (e.g., *He ripped the costume* vs. *The costume was ripped by him*). The active/passive distinction has been shown to shift focus to or away from the agent (e.g., Garvey, Caramazza, & Yates, 1975; Kassin & Lowe, 1979; White, 2003). Here we

focus on transitivity and investigate not just the attributional consequences of transitivity (blame) but also the concrete real-world outcomes of these attributions (punishment).

2. Eight participants whose financial liability responses exceeded $550,000 were excluded from this analysis.

These conclusions are the same when analyses consider just those participants who assigned Timberlake a nonzero fine ($n = 244$). Among these participants, those who got the agentive report assigned more fines (M = $193,726.47, SE = $12,893.53) than did those who got the non-agentive report (M = $153,179.61, SE = $12,430.78) [$t(242) = 2.22$, $p = .028$].

These data show some heteroscedasticity, but our main conclusions remain the same after appropriate corrections. A t test that did not assume equal variances confirmed a reliable difference between the financial liabilities assigned by participants who got agentive versus non-agentive reports [$t(559.36) = 2.97$, $p = .003$]. The main effect of task context (see the supplementary materials) was similarly confirmed by a Welch ANOVA test [$F(2, 371.55) = 3.24$, $p = .04$].

SUPPLEMENTAL MATERIALS

Additional results from Study 3 and nonparametric analyses of all study results may be downloaded from http://pbr.psychonomic-journals.org/content/supplemental.

(Manuscript submitted November 6, 2009; revision accepted for publication April 22, 2010.)

QUESTIONS ABOUT MEANING

1. What is the difference between *agentive* and *nonagentive* descriptions? Illustrate.
2. Describe the methods and results for Study 1. What additional questions were Study 2 and Study 3 designed to address? What were the results of those studies?
3. What research "gap" is addressed by Fausey and Boroditsky's research? What practical value does this research have?

QUESTIONS ABOUT RHETORICAL ANALYSIS

1. The website for the journal *Psychonomic Bulletin & Review* indicates that it publishes articles for a "general readership." However, Fausey and Boroditsky's article is not written at the level of a newspaper article. What aspects of the writing indicate that the intended audience is an academic one? On the other hand, how do the authors help those without training in psychology to understand their research findings and the significance of those findings? Highlight examples of sentences that state the authors' research purpose or summarize their findings. How might you imitate some of these "moves" in your own academic writing?

2. One way the authors present their findings is in figures. Do you find the figures effective? Why or why not?

MAKING CONNECTIONS

1. Recall a time when you or someone you know caused an accident that resulted in harm to property or another person. Using the reports in Table 1 as models, write two versions of your story—one an "agentive report" and the other a "nonagentive report." The stories should be identical in details and in content words. Underline the words that make one version agentive and the other nonagentive (as illustrated in Table 1), and write an analysis of the two accounts. How do they lead readers to two different interpretations of the events?
2. Academic writers explain how or why their topic matters and to whom. Here, for example, is one sentence establishing the importance of Fausey and Boroditsky's research: "With the high stakes of guilt, innocence, and the legality of constitutional amendments on the line, it is important to empirically establish whether agentive and nonagentive frames indeed have any attributional consequences." In other words, this research has real-world legal and financial significance.

   You, too, should state the value of your academic writing for your audience. To get ideas about how to do this, find examples in this anthology of authors explicitly stating the value of their topics. In an essay, quote and analyze several of the examples you find. Consider questions such as: What makes the statements of value effective? Is the value identified narrow (affecting only a few) or broad? What kinds of language or sentence patterns do the statements have in common? Follow the lead of the authors you quote and state the value of your *own* paper—to yourself and other students.

Psychology

"Our 'Deep Reading' Brain: Its Digital Evolution Poses Questions,"

MARYANNE WOLF

Maryanne Wolf is a Tufts University professor and director of the university's Center for Reading and Language Research. She is an expert on reading—the topic of the following article, originally published in 2010 in *Nieman Reports*. The magazine is published by the Nieman Foundation for Journalism at Harvard University and includes print and online articles about the practice of journalism.

Will we lose the "deep reading" brain in a digital culture? No one knows—yet.

The preceding paragraph provides a legitimate synopsis of this essay. It also exemplifies the kind of reduced reading that concerns me greatly, both for expert adult readers and even more so for young novice readers, those who are learning how to read in a way that helps them to comprehend and expand upon the information given.

The challenges surrounding how we learn to think about what we read raise profound questions. They have implications for us intellectually, socially and ethically. Whether an immersion in digitally dominated forms of reading will change the capacity to think deeply, reflectively and in an intellectually autonomous manner when we read is a question well worth raising. But it isn't one I can answer now, given how early we are in the transition to digital content.

In my work on the evolution of the reading brain during the past decade, I have found important insights from the history of literacy, neuroscience and literature that can help to better prepare us to examine this set of issues. The historical moment that best approximates the present transition from a literate to a digital culture is found in the ancient Greeks' transition from an oral culture to a literacy-based culture. Socrates, who was arguably Greece's most eloquent apologist for an oral culture, protested against the acquisition of literacy. And he did so on the basis of questions that are prescient today—and, in that prescience, surprising.

Socrates contended that the seeming permanence of the printed word would delude the young into thinking they had accessed the crux of knowledge, rather than simply decoded it. For him, only the intellectually effortful process of probing, analyzing and internalizing knowledge would enable the young to develop a lifelong, personal approach to knowing and thinking, which could lead them to their ultimate goals—wisdom and virtue. Only the examined word—and the examined life—was worth pursuing. Literacy, Socrates believed, would short-circuit both.

Using a 21st century paraphrase, the operative word is "short-circuited." I use it to segue into a different, yet concrete way of conceptualizing Socrates's elegantly described worries. Modern imaging technology allows us to scan the brains of expert and novice readers and observe how human brains learn to read. Briefly, here is what we find: Whenever we learn something new, the brain forms a new circuit that connects some of the brain's original structures. In the case of learning to read, the brain builds connections between and among the visual, language and conceptual areas that are part of our genetic heritage, but that were never woven together in this way before.

BRAIN PATHWAYS: CREATED BY READING

Gradually we are beginning to understand the stunning complexity that is involved in the expert reader's brain circuit. For example, when reading even a single word, the first milliseconds of the reading circuit are largely devoted to decoding the word's visual information and connecting it to all that we know about the word from its sounds to meanings to syntactic functions. The virtual automaticity of this first set of stages allows us in the next milliseconds to go beyond the decoded text. It is within the next precious milliseconds that we enter a cognitive space where we can connect the decoded information to all that we know and feel. In this latter part of the process of reading, we are given the ability to think new thoughts of our own: the generative core of the reading process.

Perhaps no one better captured what the reader begins to think in those last milliseconds of the reading circuit than the French novelist Marcel Proust. In 1906, he characterized the heart of reading as that moment when "that which is the end of [the author's] wisdom appears to us as but the beginning of ours." A bit more than a century later, in 2010, book editor Peter Dimock said that "[this] kind of reading, then, is a time of internal solitary consciousness in which the reading consciousness is brought up to the level of the knowledge of the author—the farthest point another mind has reached, as it were. . . ."

The act of going beyond the text to analyze, infer and think new thoughts is the product of years of formation. It takes time, both in milliseconds and years, and effort to learn to read with deep, expanding comprehension and to execute all these processes as an adult expert reader. When it comes to building this reading circuit in a brain that has no preprogrammed setup for it, there is no genetic guarantee that any individual novice reader will ever form the expert reading brain circuitry that most of us form. The reading circuit's very plasticity is also its Achilles' heel. It can be fully fashioned over time and fully implemented when we read, or it can be short-circuited—either early on in its formation period or later, after its formation, in the execution of only part of its potentially available cognitive resources.

Because we literally and physiologically can read in multiple ways, how we read—and what we absorb from our reading—will be influenced by both the content of our reading and the medium we use.

Few need to be reminded of the transformative advantages of the digital culture's democratization of information in our society. That is not the issue I address here. Rather, in my research, I seek to understand the full implications for the reader who is immersed in a reading medium that provides little incentive to use the full panoply of cognitive resources available.

We know a great deal about the present iteration of the reading brain and all of the resources it has learned to bring to the act of reading. However, we still know very little about the digital reading brain. My major worry is that, confronted with a digital glut of immediate information that requires and receives less and less intellectual effort, many new (and many older) readers will have neither the time nor the motivation to think through the possible layers of meaning in what they read. The omnipresence of multiple distractions for attention—and the brain's own natural attraction to novelty—contribute to a mindset toward reading that seeks to reduce information to its lowest conceptual denominator. Sound bites, text bites, and mind bites are a reflection of a culture that has forgotten or become too distracted by and too drawn to the next piece of new information to allow itself time to think.

We need to find the ability to pause and pull back from what seems to be developing into an incessant need to fill every millisecond with new information. As I was writing this piece, a *New York Times* reporter contacted me to find out whether I thought Internet reading might aid speed reading.

"Yes," I replied, "but speed and its counterpart—assumed efficiency—are not always desirable for deep thought."

We need to understand the value of what we may be losing when we skim text so rapidly that we skip the precious milliseconds of deep reading processes. For it is within these moments—and these processes in our brains—that we might reach our own important insights and breakthroughs. They might not happen if we've skipped on to the next text bite. Tough questions. Rigorous research. These are what are needed now of us as we ponder the kind of readers we are becoming and how the next generation of readers will be formed.

Our failure to do this may leave us confronted with a situation that technology visionary Edward Tenner described in 2006: "It would be a shame if brilliant technology were to end up threatening the kind of intellect that produced it."

QUESTIONS ABOUT MEANING

1. Why does Wolf describe digital (Internet) reading as "a reading medium that provides little incentive to use the full panoply of cognitive resources available"? What's potentially missing in the digital reading experience?
2. What research does Wolf call for? Why is this area of research so important?

QUESTIONS FOR RHETORICAL ANALYSIS

1. What dual purposes do the opening sentences serve in Wolf's article?
2. Wolf compares the shift from "a literate to digital culture" to the shift from "an oral culture to a literacy-based culture." Do you find this an apt comparison? In what ways are these two transition periods similar and different? Given the fact that Socrates was wrong—literacy did not short-circuit the ability of people to know or think—why do you think Wolf makes the comparison? What is her point?

MAKING CONNECTIONS

1. In an essay, analyze Wolf's argument, specifically addressing these aspects of her article (and any additional aspects you want to address): (1) What stance does Wolf take on the topic of digital reading and how is her attitude about the subject conveyed? (2) What counterarguments does Wolf acknowledge and is her response effective? (3) What evidence does Wolf provide for her position? Is it persuasive? Why or why not? (4) Is Wolf's writing style and choice of medium (an online publication) appropriate for the message? Explain.
2. Wolf writes, "Sound bites, text bites, and mind bites are a reflection of a culture that has forgotten or become too distracted by and too drawn to the next piece of new information to allow itself time to think." Do you agree? Respond to this claim in an essay that includes evidence that supports or counters Wolf's position.

Technology

"How Computers Change the Way We Think," SHERRY TURKLE

Sherry Turkle is a professor of the social studies of science and technology at the Massachusetts Institute of Technology. Like Wolf, Turkle studies how the digital age is changing the way we think. In the next article, Turkle provides a list of ways she sees "information technology encouraging changes in thinking." The article originally appeared in 2004 in *The Chronicle of Higher Education*, a newspaper that publishes articles of interest to college faculty and administrators.

The tools we use to think change the ways in which we think. The invention of written language brought about a radical shift in how we process, organize, store, and transmit representations of the world. Although writing remains our primary information technology, today when we think about the impact of technology on our habits of mind, we think primarily of the computer.

My first encounters with how computers change the way we think came soon after I joined the faculty at the Massachusetts Institute of Technology in the late 1970s, at the end of the era of the slide rule and the beginning of the era of the personal computer. At a lunch for new faculty members, several senior professors in engineering complained that the transition from slide rules to calculators had affected their students' ability to deal with issues of scale. When students used slide rules, they had to insert decimal points themselves. The professors insisted that that required students to maintain a mental sense of scale, whereas those who relied on calculators made frequent errors in orders of magnitude. Additionally, the students with calculators had lost their ability to do "back of the envelope" calculations, and with that, an intuitive feel for the material.

That same semester, I taught a course in the history of psychology. There, I experienced the impact of computational objects on students' ideas about their emotional lives. My class had read Freud's essay on slips of the tongue, with its famous first example: The chairman of a parliamentary session opens a meeting by declaring it closed. The students discussed how Freud interpreted such errors as revealing a person's mixed emotions. A computer-science major disagreed with Freud's approach. The mind, she argued, is a computer. And in a computational dictionary—like we have in the human mind—"closed" and "open" are designated by the same symbol, separated by a sign for opposition. "Closed" equals "minus open." To substitute "closed" for "open" does not require the notion of ambivalence or conflict.

"When the chairman made that substitution," she declared, "a bit was dropped; a minus sign was lost. There was a power surge. No problem."

The young woman turned a Freudian slip into an information-processing error. An explanation in terms of meaning had become an explanation in terms of mechanism.

Such encounters turned me to the study of both the instrumental and the subjective sides of the nascent computer culture. As an ethnographer and psychologist, I began to study not only what the computer was doing for us, but what it was doing to us, including how it was changing the way we see ourselves, our sense of human identity.

In the 1980s, I surveyed the psychological effects of computational objects in everyday life—largely the unintended side effects of people's tendency to project thoughts and feelings onto their machines. In the 20 years since, computational objects have become more explicitly designed to have emotional and cognitive effects. And those "effects by design" will become even stronger in the decade to come. Machines are being designed to serve explicitly as companions, pets, and tutors. And they are introduced in school settings for the youngest children.

Today, starting in elementary school, students use e-mail, word processing, computer simulations, virtual communities, and PowerPoint software. In the process, they are absorbing more than the content of what appears on their screens. They are learning new ways to think about what it means to know and understand.

What follows is a short and certainly not comprehensive list of areas where I see information technology encouraging changes in thinking. There can be no simple way of cataloging whether any particular change is good or bad. That is contested terrain. At every step we have to ask, as educators and citizens, whether current technology is leading us in directions that serve our human purposes. Such questions are not technical; they are social, moral, and political. For me, addressing that subjective side of computation is one of the more significant challenges for the next decade of information technology in higher education. Technology does not determine change, but it encourages us to take certain directions. If we make those directions clear, we can more easily exert human choice.

THINKING ABOUT PRIVACY

Today's college students are habituated to a world of online blogging, instant messaging, and Web browsing that leaves electronic traces. Yet they have had little experience with the right to privacy. Unlike past generations of Americans, who grew up with the notion that the privacy of their mail was sacrosanct, our children are accustomed to electronic surveillance as part of their daily lives.

I have colleagues who feel that the increased incursions on privacy have put the topic more in the news, and that this is a positive change. But middle-school and high-school students tend to be willing to provide personal information online with no safeguards, and college students seem uninterested in violations of privacy and in increased governmental and commercial surveillance. Professors find that students do not understand that in a democracy, privacy is a right, not merely a privilege. In 10 years, ideas about the relationship of privacy and government will require even more active pedagogy. (One might also hope that increased education about the kinds of silent surveillance that technology makes possible may inspire more active political engagement with the issue.)

AVATARS OR A SELF?

Chat rooms, role-playing games, and other technological venues offer us many different contexts for presenting ourselves online. Those possibilities are particularly important for adolescents because they offer what Erik Erikson described as a moratorium, a time out or safe space for the personal experimentation that is so crucial for adolescent development. Our dangerous world—with crime, terrorism, drugs, and AIDS—offers little in the way of safe spaces. Online worlds can provide valuable spaces for identity play.

But some people who gain fluency in expressing multiple aspects of self may find it harder to develop authentic selves. Some children who write narratives for their screen avatars may grow up with too little experience of how to share their real feelings with other people. For those who are lonely yet afraid of intimacy, information technology has made it possible to have the illusion of companionship without the demands of friendship.

FROM POWERFUL IDEAS TO POWERPOINT

In the 1970s and early 1980s, some educators wanted to make programming part of the regular curriculum for K-12 education. They argued that because information technology carries ideas, it might as well carry the most powerful ideas that computer science has to offer. It is ironic that in most elementary schools today, the ideas being carried by information technology are not ideas from computer science like procedural thinking, but more likely to be those embedded in productivity tools like PowerPoint presentation software.

PowerPoint does more than provide a way of transmitting content. It carries its own way of thinking, its own aesthetic—which not surprisingly shows up in the aesthetic of college freshmen. In that aesthetic, presentation becomes its own powerful idea.

To be sure, the software cannot be blamed for lower intellectual standards. Misuse of the former is as much a symptom as a cause of the latter. Indeed, the culture in which our children are raised is increasingly a culture of presentation, a corporate culture in which appearance is often more important than reality. In contemporary political discourse, the bar has also been lowered. Use of rhetorical devices at the expense of cogent argument regularly goes without notice. But it is precisely because standards of intellectual rigor outside the educational sphere have fallen that educators must attend to how we use, and when we introduce, software that has been designed to simplify the organization and processing of information.

In *The Cognitive Style of PowerPoint* (Graphics Press, 2003), Edward R. Tufte suggests that PowerPoint equates bulleting with clear thinking. It does not teach students to begin a discussion or construct a narrative. It encourages presentation, not conversation. Of course, in the hands of a master teacher, a PowerPoint presentation with few words and powerful images can serve as the jumping-off point for a brilliant lecture.

But in the hands of elementary-school students, often introduced to PowerPoint in the third grade, and often infatuated with its swooshing sounds, animated icons, and flashing text, a slide show is more likely to close down debate than open it up.

Developed to serve the needs of the corporate boardroom, the software is designed to convey absolute authority. Teachers used to tell students that clear exposition depended on clear outlining, but presentation software has fetishized the outline at the expense of the content.

Narrative, the exposition of content, takes time. PowerPoint, like so much in the computer culture, speeds up the pace.

WORD PROCESSING VS. THINKING

The catalog for the Vermont Country Store advertises a manual typewriter, which the advertising copy says "moves at a pace that allows time to compose your thoughts." As many of us know, it is possible to manipulate text on a computer screen and see how it looks faster than we can think about what the words mean.

Word processing has its own complex psychology. From a pedagogical point of view, it can make dedicated students into better writers because it allows them to revise text, rearrange paragraphs, and experiment with the tone and shape of an essay. Few professional writers would part with their computers; some claim that they simply cannot think without their hands on the keyboard. Yet the ability to quickly fill the page, to see it before you can think it, can make bad writers even worse.

A seventh grader once told me that the typewriter she found in her mother's attic is "cool because you have to type each letter by itself. You have to know what you are doing in advance or it comes out a mess." The idea of thinking ahead has become exotic.

TAKING THINGS AT INTERFACE VALUE

We expect software to be easy to use, and we assume that we don't have to know how a computer works. In the early 1980s, most computer users who spoke of transparency meant that, as with any other machine, you could "open the hood" and poke around. But only a few years later, Macintosh users began to use the term when they talked about seeing their documents and programs represented by attractive and easy-to-interpret icons. They were referring to an ability to make things work without needing to go below the screen surface. Paradoxically, it was the screen's opacity that permitted that kind of transparency. Today, when people say that something is transparent, they mean that they can see how to make it work, not that they know how it works. In other words, transparency means epistemic opacity.

The people who built or bought the first generation of personal computers understood them down to the bits and bytes. The next generation of operating systems were more complex, but they still invited that old-time reductive understanding. Contemporary information technology encourages different habits of mind. Today's college students are already used to taking things at (inter) face value; their successors in 2014 will be even less accustomed to probing below the surface.

SIMULATION AND ITS DISCONTENTS

Some thinkers argue that the new opacity is empowering, enabling anyone to use the most sophisticated technological tools and to experiment with simulation in complex and creative ways. But it is also true that our tools carry the message that they are beyond our understanding. It is possible that in daily life, epistemic opacity can lead to passivity.

I first became aware of that possibility in the early 1990s, when the first generation of complex simulation games were introduced and immediately became popular for home as well as school use. SimLife teaches the principles of evolution by getting children involved in the development of complex ecosystems; in that sense it is an extraordinary learning tool. During one session in which I played SimLife with Tim, a 13-year-old, the screen before us flashed a message: "Your orgot is being eaten up." "What's an orgot?" I asked. Tim didn't know. "I just ignore that," he said confidently. "You don't need to know that kind of stuff to play."

For me, that story serves as a cautionary tale. Computer simulations enable their users to think about complex phenomena as dynamic, evolving systems. But they also accustom us to manipulating systems whose core assumptions we may not understand and that may not be true.

We live in a culture of simulation. Our games, our economic and political systems, and the ways architects design buildings, chemists envisage molecules, and surgeons perform operations all use simulation technology. In 10 years the degree to which simulations are embedded in every area of life will have increased exponentially. We need to develop a new form of media literacy: readership skills for the culture of simulation.

We come to written text with habits of readership based on centuries of civilization. At the very least, we have learned to begin with the journalist's traditional questions: who, what, when, where, why, and how. Who wrote these words, what is their message, why were they written, and how are they situated in time and place, politically and socially? A central project for higher education during the next 10 years should be creating programs in information-technology literacy, with the goal of teaching students to interrogate simulations in much the same spirit, challenging their built-in assumptions.

Despite the ever-increasing complexity of software, most computer environments put users in worlds based on constrained choices. In other words, immersion in programmed worlds puts us in reassuring environments where the rules are clear. For example, when you play a video game, you often go through a series of frightening situations that you escape by mastering the rules—you experience life as a reassuring dichotomy of scary and safe. Children grow up in a culture of video games, action films, fantasy epics, and computer programs that all rely on that familiar scenario of almost losing but then regaining total mastery: There is danger. It is mastered. A still-more-powerful monster appears. It is subdued. Scary. Safe.

Yet in the real world, we have never had a greater need to work our way out of binary assumptions. In the decade ahead, we need to rebuild the culture around information technology. In that new sociotechnical culture, assumptions about the nature of mastery would be less absolute. The new culture would make it easier, not more difficult, to consider life in shades of gray, to see moral dilemmas in terms other than a battle between Good and Evil. For never has our world been more complex, hybridized, and global. Never have we so needed to have many contradictory thoughts and feelings at the same time. Our tools must help us accomplish that, not fight against us.

Information technology is identity technology. Embedding it in a culture that supports democracy, freedom of expression, tolerance, diversity, and complexity of opinion is one of the next decade's greatest challenges. We cannot afford to fail.

When I first began studying the computer culture, a small breed of highly trained technologists thought of themselves as "computer people." That is no longer the case. If we take the computer as a carrier of a way of knowing, a way of seeing the world and our place in it, we are all computer people now.

QUESTIONS ABOUT MEANING

1. What is Turkle's thesis? Describe the changes she discusses.
2. "Information technology is identity technology," writes Turkle. What does she mean?

QUESTIONS FOR RHETORICAL ANALYSIS

1. To whom is Turkle writing and how is that made clear in the article?
2. What is an ethnographer? Look up the term to be sure you have a full understanding. On what evidence does Turkle appear to have based her

list of ways technology is changing the way we think? Do you think her case is convincing?

3. Do you think Turkle believes the computer's influences are primarily good or bad? Support your answer with evidence from the article. Consider word choice, organization of ideas, and use of evidence.

MAKING CONNECTIONS

1. Children grow up knowing that their e-mails, web searches, and even their comings and goings may be monitored, yet today's college students, Turkle claims, "seem uninterested in violations of privacy and in increased governmental and commercial surveillance." Do you think this is an accurate assessment of college students today? Do you think we should be more concerned about the loss of privacy?
2. "The tools we use to think change the ways in which we think," writes Turkle. It's a sentiment echoed by Rose (chapter 2); Hembrooke and Gay; Kuhn (chapter 9); and Wolf, who all argue that the medium matters, affecting how deeply we read or how well we remember information.

   Select a specific medium used in education (such as PowerPoint, clickers, etc.) and discuss its impact on learning or thinking. How do you or other students respond to information presented in this way in the classroom? How, for example, does the medium affect your note taking or class discussion? Do you think that receiving information in this medium makes a difference?

Communications

"Does the Internet Make You Smarter or Dumber?" CLAY SHIRKY

Clay Shirky teaches at New York University and writes about the ways the Internet, cell phones, and other forms of technology shape our culture. In the following article, Shirky compares the transformative shift brought about by the Internet to the transformative effect of the printing press and speculates on what it means to live "through the largest expansion in expressive capability in human history." Shirky's article appeared in 2010 in *The Wall Street Journal.*

Digital media have made creating and disseminating text, sound, and images cheap, easy and global. The bulk of publicly available media is now created by people who understand little of the professional standards and practices for media.

Instead, these amateurs produce endless streams of mediocrity, eroding cultural norms about quality and acceptability, and leading to increasingly alarmed predictions of incipient chaos and intellectual collapse.

But of course, that's what always happens. Every increase in freedom to create or consume media, from paperback books to YouTube, alarms people accustomed to the restrictions of the old system, convincing them that the new media will make young people stupid. This fear dates back to at least the invention of movable type.

As Gutenberg's press spread through Europe, the Bible was translated into local languages, enabling direct encounters with the text; this was accompanied by a flood of contemporary literature, most of it mediocre. Vulgar versions of the Bible and distracting secular writings fueled religious unrest and civic confusion, leading to claims that the printing press, if not controlled, would lead to chaos and the dismemberment of European intellectual life.

These claims were, of course, correct. Print fueled the Protestant Reformation, which did indeed destroy the Church's pan-European hold on intellectual life. What the 16th-century foes of print didn't imagine—couldn't imagine—was what followed: We built new norms around newly abundant and contemporary literature. Novels, newspapers, scientific journals, the separation of fiction and non-fiction, all of these innovations were created during the collapse of the scribal system, and all had the effect of increasing, rather than decreasing, the intellectual range and output of society.

To take a famous example, the essential insight of the scientific revolution was peer review, the idea that science was a collaborative effort that included the feedback and participation of others. Peer review was a cultural institution that took the printing press for granted as a means of distributing research quickly and widely, but added the kind of cultural constraints that made it valuable.

We are living through a similar explosion of publishing capability today, where digital media link over a billion people into the same network. This linking together in turn lets us tap our cognitive surplus, the trillion hours a year of free time the educated population of the planet has to spend doing things they care about. In the 20th century, the bulk of that time was spent watching television, but our cognitive surplus is so enormous that diverting even a tiny fraction of time from consumption to participation can create enormous positive effects.

Wikipedia took the idea of peer review and applied it to volunteers on a global scale, becoming the most important English reference work in less than 10 years. Yet the cumulative time devoted to creating Wikipedia, something like 100 million hours of human thought, is expended by Americans every weekend, just watching ads. It only takes a fractional shift in the direction of participation to create remarkable new educational resources.

Similarly, open source software, created without managerial control of the workers or ownership of the product, has been critical to the spread of the Web. Searches for everything from supernovae to prime numbers now happen as giant, distributed efforts. Ushahidi, the Kenyan crisis mapping tool invented in 2008, now aggregates citizen reports about crises the world over. PatientsLikeMe, a website designed to accelerate medical research by getting patients to publicly share their health information, has assembled a larger group of sufferers of Lou Gehrig's disease than any pharmaceutical agency in history, by appealing to the shared sense of seeking medical progress.

Of course, not everything people care about is a high-minded project. Whenever media become more abundant, average quality falls quickly, while new institutional models for quality arise slowly. Today we have The World's Funniest Home Videos running 24/7 on YouTube, while the potentially world-changing uses of cognitive surplus are still early and special cases.

That always happens too. In the history of print, we got erotic novels 100 years before we got scientific journals, and complaints about distraction have been rampant; no less a beneficiary of the printing press than Martin Luther complained, "The multitude of books is a great evil. There is no measure of limit to this fever for writing." The response to distraction, then as now, was social structure. Reading is an unnatural act; we are no more evolved to read books than we are to use computers. Literate societies become literate by investing extraordinary resources, every year, training children to read. Now it's our turn to figure out what response we need to shape our use of digital tools.

The case for digitally driven stupidity assumes we'll fail to integrate digital freedoms into society as well as we integrated literacy. This assumption in turn rests on three beliefs: that the recent past was a glorious and irreplaceable high-water mark of intellectual attainment; that the present is only characterized by the silly stuff and not by the noble experiments; and that this generation of young people will fail to invent cultural norms that do for the Internet's abundance what the intellectuals of the 17th century did for print culture. There are likewise three reasons to think that the Internet will fuel the intellectual achievements of 21st-century society.

First, the rosy past of the pessimists was not, on closer examination, so rosy. The decade the pessimists want to return us to is the 1980s, the last period before society had any significant digital freedoms. Despite frequent genuflection to European novels, we actually spent a lot more time watching *Diff'rent Strokes* than reading Proust, prior to the Internet's spread. The Net, in fact, restores reading and writing as central activities in our culture.

The present is, as noted, characterized by lots of throwaway cultural artifacts, but the nice thing about throwaway material is that it gets thrown away. This issue isn't whether there's lots of dumb stuff online—there is, just as there is lots of dumb stuff in bookstores. The issue is whether there are any ideas so good today that they will survive into the future. Several early uses of our cognitive surplus, like open source software, look like they will pass that test.

The past was not as golden, nor is the present as tawdry, as the pessimists suggest, but the only thing really worth arguing about is the future. It is our misfortune, as a historical generation, to live through the largest expansion in expressive capability in human history, a misfortune because abundance breaks more things than scarcity. We are now witnessing the rapid stress of older institutions accompanied by the slow and fitful development of cultural alternatives. Just as required education was a response to print, using the Internet well will require new cultural institutions as well, not just new technologies.

It is tempting to want PatientsLikeMe without the dumb videos, just as we might want scientific journals without the erotic novels, but that's not how media works. Increased freedom to create means increased freedom to create throwaway material, as well as freedom to indulge in the experimentation that eventually makes the good new stuff possible. The task before us now is to experiment with new ways of using a medium that is social, ubiquitous and cheap, a medium that changes the landscape by distributing freedom of the press and freedom of assembly as widely as freedom of speech.

QUESTIONS ABOUT MEANING

1. What is Shirky's answer to his title question: "Does the Internet Make You Smarter or Dumber?" On what assumptions are the "digitally-driven stupidity" arguments based and what is Shirky's response?
2. What examples does Shirky give to illustrate the positive potential of the digital age?

QUESTIONS FOR RHETORICAL ANALYSIS

1. After reading the first two paragraphs, how did you anticipate Shirky would answer his title question? What is the effect of Shirky beginning this way instead of beginning with his central claim?

2. What is the point of the paragraphs about the printing press? Do you think the comparison is effective? Why or why not?

MAKING CONNECTIONS

1. Shirky predicts that "new cultural institutions" will be needed to use the Internet "well." What do you think he means? What kinds of cultural institutions can you imagine? (Turkle has some ideas on this topic.)
2. Shirky writes, "It is our misfortune, as a historical generation, to live through the largest expansion in expressive capability in human history, a misfortune because abundance breaks more things than scarcity." What do you think Shirky means when he says that "abundance breaks more things than scarcity"? Using Shirky's sentence as a starting point, discuss this idea in an essay with examples of your own.

Media Studies

"Using the Internet to Examine Patterns of Foreign Coverage,"

ETHAN ZUCKERMAN

Ethan Zuckerman directs the Center for Civic Media at the Massachusetts Institute of Technology (MIT) and teaches at MIT's Media Lab. His research interests include how Western journalists cover events occurring in Africa, the subject of the following article. In the article, Zuckerman explains why Western journalists don't cover important events in Africa, and he describes the potential of the Internet to raise awareness of issues in poor countries. The article originally appeared in 2004 in *Nieman Reports*, a magazine that publishes articles about journalism practices.

The first week of April 2003, several hundred people were killed in ethnic violence in the Ituri region of the Democratic Republic of the Congo (DRC). Given the magnitude of the event—up to a thousand civilians killed in a single incident—and the history of violence in the region, it made sense to expect media coverage. Shortly before the killings, the International Rescue Committee published a study suggesting that 3.3 million people had died as a result of conflicts in the DRC, making the ongoing violence in the region the deadliest war in the world since World War II.

But the events in Ituri went almost unreported. On April 7th, the first day American newspapers reported the killings, *The New York Times* ran a brief Associated Press story on the conflict, buried on page A6. Google

News, a Web site that monitors 4,500 news sources, listed only 1,200 stories in the preceding month that mentioned Congo. By contrast, on the same day Google News showed 550,000 stories for Iraq, and *The New York Times* ran five Iraq stories on the front page, as well as a separate section, "A Nation at War."

While it's predictable that the U.S. invasion of Iraq would squeeze most other news off the front page of American newspapers, it's only one of several reasons the conflict in Ituri received so little attention. In their seminal 1965 paper, "The Structure of Foreign News," Johan Galtung and Mari Holmboe Ruge proposed 12 factors that influence the publication of international news. While Galtung and Ruge's statistical analysis has been questioned, their proposed factors are still widely used by media theorists to explain the inclusion and exclusion of international news stories.

Galtung and Ruge, writing almost 40 years before the Congo event, could have predicted the events in Ituri would have been ignored in the United States:

- The Democratic Republic of the Congo is a "non-elite" nation.
- No "elite people" were killed in Ituri.
- There's little cultural proximity between the United States and the DRC.
- The conflict had little meaning for American readers.
- And the decade-long war in the region meant that further killings weren't unexpected.

Their analysis doesn't consider news-gathering factors—the difficulty of deploying reporters to northeastern Congo, language barriers, and the lack of communications infrastructure—all of which make it more difficult for reporters to cover the conflict in DRC, especially in contrast to the war in Iraq, which featured opportunities for reporters to be "embedded" within U.S. military units.

GLOBAL ATTENTION PROFILES

While Galtung and Ruge used 1,250 Norwegian newspaper clippings gathered over four years to propose their rules, the advent of Internet publishing gives us the opportunity to test some of their conclusions with hundreds of thousands of data points. Shortly after the incident in Ituri, I started collecting data from the Web sites of U.S. and British newspapers, news services, and television networks for a project I called Global Attention Profiles. My intention was to create daily maps of news stories to demonstrate graphically where Western media attention was focused. As the project progressed, I began to look for correlations to economic and political factors to explain the distribution of news.

My main conclusion: Andy Warhol was wrong—we won't all get 15 minutes of fame.

If this were true, populous nations like China, Indonesia and Brazil would be better represented in the Western media. Media attention, measured by the number of stories that mention a country by name, is correlated only loosely to a nation's population. It's correlated much more strongly to economic factors, especially to a nation's wealth, as measured by gross domestic product. For example, while Nigeria and Japan have roughly equal populations, Japan's economy is about 100 times the size of Nigeria's—and there are roughly seven times as many mentions of "Japan" as there are of "Nigeria" in the average American newspaper on any given day. All the American news sources I tracked showed this pattern; the lone source to show a different pattern was the BBC, which showed a strong bias towards news in former British colonies, including populous and poor nations like Nigeria, India and Pakistan.

Correlation is not causation, and it's unlikely that news directors check a nation's current account balance before sending a TV crew to cover a story. But, consciously or not, the people who decide what becomes news are far more likely to cover a story if it involves people from wealthy nations. (Indeed, the less developed nations best covered during the year of my study—Iraq and Afghanistan—are nations that Americans invaded and occupied.)

While it's tempting to accuse news organizations of dereliction in failing to cover events in the developing world, blame might fall equally on market forces and the preferences of media consumers. Confronted with the inequity of media attention, many editors and news directors will readily own up to the disparity and go on to explain that they're the good guys, encouraging coverage of developing nations: If their customers had their way, there would be even less international news and almost no news from poorer nations. Given the need for publications to maintain an audience to sell ads to, perhaps we're lucky that there's any coverage of the developing world.

It's difficult to test this theory without extremely detailed data about what news stories readers and viewers view or skip. But Weblogs give us a way to guess at reader interest: If a Weblogger mentions a country in her post, she's likely expressing an interest in that nation. If we found a pattern of Weblogger interest in developing nations—proportionally more mentions of Africa than in the mainstream media, for instance—we might conclude that editors are underestimating their readers.

Alas, we don't see this pattern. Looking at data from Weblog search engine BlogPulse, we see roughly the same correlation between wealth and mentions as we do in media aggregator sites like Google News or Altavista News and a slightly tighter correlation to national wealth than in single media sources like *The New York Times* or *The Washington Post*. Comparing on a country by country basis, Weblogs are more likely to name travel destinations (Caribbean Islands, some Central American and Southeast Asian nations) and far less likely to mention African, Eastern European, and Central Asian nations than mainstream media sources. Disparities aside, the statistics suggest that mentions of nations in blogposts are strongly correlated to their appearance in the mainstream media.

CONSEQUENCES OF NEWS DECISION-MAKING

If readers aren't interested in international news and it's expensive for news networks to generate, does it matter that the media doesn't cover violence in Ituri?

It matters a great deal to Iturians. Governments are less likely to send peacekeepers to work to stop the conflict from spreading if they don't read about it in the news. And citizens can't pressure their governments to intervene without awareness of the situation. The huge aid packages coming to Iraq and Afghanistan suggest a relationship between media attention and foreign aid. In the wake of these conflicts, international aid workers have expressed concern that aid to neglected, "unpopular" conflicts will suffer as a result. In more peaceful times, attention makes it more likely that a country will become a trading partner or receive foreign investment.

Wealthy nations have a good reason to care about news in undercovered nations—their security may depend on it. The events of September 11th were carried out by a network that bases itself in weak and failed states. For a brief interval after the attacks, Americans were deeply interested in the Central Asian states that hosted al-Qaeda operatives—this interest waned as global attention shifted from Afghanistan to Iraq. A recent report by the Center for Global Development, "On the Brink: Weak States and U.S. National Security," suggests that roughly 50 failed and failing states need to be both closely watched and aided so that they don't find themselves participants in terrorism and global crime. All but three of the states mentioned in the report are systematically undercovered by mainstream media. Like the U.S. intelligence community, the U.S. news media are better configured for a world where threats come from superpowers than from failed states.

It seems unlikely that commercial news organizations will refocus on the developing world without some form of external pressure. In 1980,

Sean MacBride led a UNESCO committee that published a report, "Many Voices, One World," which proposed legal and structural changes to news organizations to improve media coverage of the developing world. The report was opposed so vehemently by media organizations in the United States, United Kingdom, and Singapore that the three nations withdrew from UNESCO to protest implementation of the committee's proposals. One could be forgiven for skepticism that CNN or Fox News will react any better to suggestions to globalize their coverage than newspapers did two decades ago.

The recent crisis in Darfur, Sudan points to one way concerned individuals and organizations can influence global news coverage. A network of NGO's—most notably Human Rights Watch—which had monitored human rights situations in Sudan for years, provided extensive information on the Janjaweed militias to major newspapers, making it possible for them to write their first stories on the situation. In effect, they did the first round of investigative journalism that news organizations failed to do. After a major report by Human Rights Watch and strong statements from the United States and the United Nations, media attention to Sudan increased dramatically—it is now receiving the third-most media attention in sub-Saharan Africa (behind South Africa and Nigeria).

The attention paid to Darfur also points to the importance of caring. A global community of evangelical Christians has closely monitored the Khartoum government for years, accusing it of systematic persecution of a Christian minority. This community was deeply interested in seeing that stories came out of Sudan and was able to provide feedback to editors letting them know that they cared about the situation. To encourage news organizations to report on forgotten stories, readers and viewers will have to demonstrate that they care about these issues. But for viewers to care, they will likely need to know a great deal more about these nations. Is this a Catch-22? Or could it present an opportunity for new, participatory media like Weblogs to draw attention to situations and stories that a small group of individuals care about?

I'll be counting news stories and let you know.

QUESTIONS ABOUT MEANING

1. What are some of the factors that influence whether or not foreign events are covered by US journalists?
2. Why don't news editors give more attention to stories in places like the Democratic Republic of the Congo? What can individuals and organizations do to change current practice?

QUESTIONS ABOUT RHETORICAL ANALYSIS

1. Zuckerman's article follows the familiar pattern of Introduction, Methods, Results, and Discussion. Draw lines to separate these sections of the article. What would you say is Zuckerman's statement of purpose?
2. Academic writers establish credibility by acknowledging opposing views, qualifying claims, and anticipating criticism of arguments or evidence. Where and how does Zuckerman do this?

MAKING CONNECTIONS

1. Shirky and Zuckerman describe the Internet as a powerful tool for sharing knowledge. In an essay, synthesize insights and examples from these authors and make your own contribution to the conversation.
2. Conduct your own analysis of newspaper coverage for events occurring outside of the United States. Begin by selecting a newspaper (such as *The New York Times*) and selecting a time period (perhaps every first day of the month over the course of a year). Then record the headlines that refer to events outside of the United States found in the "A" section or, if appropriate, in the international news section of the paper.

   Create a table with two columns: one for article titles and one for your coding comments. Your comments might identify the countries and regions represented; the population and wealth of the nations; or the topic of the stories (e.g., politics, war, natural disasters, human interest). What trends do you notice about the foreign countries and events receiving attention in the newspapers you review? What factors might explain the trends you find? In a paper with sections for Introduction, Methods, Results, and Discussion, describe your methods, present your table and your findings, and analyze your findings.

Psychology

"The Effects and Predictor Value of In-Class Texting Behavior on Final Course Grades," SYLVIA E. MCDONALD

"Is there a correlation between in-class texting activity and final grade?" That is the question addressed by psychology professor Sylvia McDonald, in her study titled "The Effects and Predictor Value of In-Class Texting Behavior on Final Course Grades." The article originally appeared in 2013 in the *College Student Journal*, an education journal publishing research about student learning.

Cell phones have become a norm within the collegiate environment but little research has examined their impact on academic attainment. The purpose of this study was to examine the effects that in-class texting behavior had on the final grade score in a freshmen level introductory social science course. Students in three different sections were given three different texting policies to elicit a variety of in-class texting behaviors. Students were given after-course-surveys examining in class texting behaviors. Final exam scores and texting behaviors were subjected to a Pearson's correlation as well as a regression analysis. Students' GPA as well as ACT scores were also examined in the regression analysis. The study showed there was a negative correlation in the relationship between in-class texting and final grade score. In-class texting was significant in negatively impacting grades after GPA, ACT, and attendance were controlled. While GPA and ACT were still the strongest predictor values, in-class texting behavior still contributed to 22% of the predictor value in final grade.

As technology and information expands, so does their use. Cell phones are quickly becoming one of the most used communications technologies in our culture with over 94% of college students using cell phones (Burns & Lohenry, 2010). Cell phones have begun to permeate every facet of the personal, professional, and academic world. Understanding that cell phones have become a norm within the collegiate environment, it is important to examine the academic implications of cell phone usage within the college classroom and their impact on academic attainment. Educational attainment is an important understudy due not only to the many stakeholders (families, individuals, institutions) but to society as a whole (lenders, economy, service). This study examined the effects of in-class cell phone texting on final grades in a freshmen level introductory social science course.

COLLEGE ACADEMIC ATTAINMENT

A significant amount of literature exists that uses standardized tests such as the SAT and ACT as predictors of successful academic attainment as measured by college grades (Munday, 1970; Betts & Morell, 1999; Stumph & Stanley, 2002; Cohn, et al., 2003; Cornwell, et al., 2005; Grove, et al., 2006). Munday (1970) explained that correlation of the ACT plus high school GPA showed to be strong predictors of the GPA of college freshmen. Berry and Sackett (2009) argued that if college GPA is the criteria used for academic performance, standardized entrance exam (SAT and ACT) scores as well as high school GPAs are the best predictors. By using SAT scores as well as entering course GPAs, researchers have presented impressive criterion related validity to account for more than half of the variance in college grades in freshmen level courses. Berry and Sackett's (2009) use of both SAT or ACT scores and high school GPA are strong predictors for freshmen level courses.

A strong third predictive factor shown throughout the literature is class attendance (Jenne, 1973; Launius, 1997; Moore, 2003; Moore, et al, 2003; Newman-Ford, Fitzgibbon, Lloyd, & Thomas, 1999). Crede, Roch and Kieszczynka (2010) conducted a meta-analysis examining the relationship between college class attendance and grades. The research showed that class attendance was positively correlated to grades of individual classes as well as overall GPA in college. Moreover, Crede, Roch and Kieszczynka (2010) argued that class attendance was the strongest predictive factor of academic performance including both cognitive (ACT scores, high school GPA) and non-cognitive measures (self-efficacy, study habits, etc.). Crede and Kuncel (2008) presented a meta-analytic review which highlighted that non-cognitive measures, such as study skills and study habits, were almost as predictable as those within the cognitive realm. However, Crede, Roch and Kieszczynka (2010) maintained that classroom attendance should be mandatory as it reflects the strongest predictor for final individual course grades as well as overall college GPA.

In this current study, the college where the data was collected has implemented an institution wide attendance policy. Stephenson (1994) presented that required attendance is not practical within larger institutions where large class size makes taking attendance almost impossible. Hoekstra (2008) argued that new technology, such as classroom clickers or electronic attendance systems (Newman-Ford, Fitzgibbon, Lloyd, & Thomas, 1999) could alleviate this burden. At the college where this data was collected, professors use clickers as well as electronic monitoring systems for class attendance.

CELL PHONES IN THE CLASSROOM

Although cell phones are an excellent communication tool, they can also be a nuisance. While appropriate in various settings, Campbell (2006) found that cell phone usage in the classroom was seen as unacceptable by students. Gilroy (2004) highlighted that professors see cell phones as an annoyance and intrusive inside the classroom. Further research from Campbell (2006) highlighted that both professors and students saw texting behavior inside the classroom as being rude and cell phone usage in general, specifically the ringing, as distracting.

Such ringing of cell phones was studied by End, Worthman, Mathews, and Wetterau (2010) to examine if cell phone usage was related to academic impairment. In the study, students were instructed to take notes during a video on which they were to later be tested. Compared to the control group, who did not have cell phones ring during the video, the experimental group, whose phones did ring during the video, performed significantly worse on the disrupted test items. They were also less likely to include those items in their notes.

Burns and Lohenry (2010) highlighted that inappropriate use of cell phones in the classroom is of significance because of its potential to impact learning and instruction. Furthermore, they go on to correlate the distraction of cell phones (texting, checking phone, messages, etc.) to the possible distractions in the students' future workplace which could lead to significant issues with workplace performance for themselves and possibly others. They advocate for a program development and student orientation of cell phone policies as well as appropriate modeling and highlighting cell phone etiquette in the classroom.

As research continues to grow in the area of cell phone perception within the classroom, very little research has been conducted examining cell phone texting and final grades. Ellis, Daniels and Jauregui (2010) performed an experiment where half of a class of 62 students was allowed to text during a class lecture, while the other half was not. Students were tested at the end of class over that day's lecture material. Even with the students' understanding that quiz scores would be lower due to none of the students' foreknowledge of having to take a quiz at lecture's end, those who were allowed to text in class scored significantly lower on the quiz than those who were not allowed to text. This however was on one quiz at the end of the same class period and not cumulative knowledge throughout an entire course. Furthermore, students did not have a chance to study the material. It is the purpose of this study to examine final grades in an introductory social science course when students were placed into three conditions with varying classroom texting policies.

Based on the above research the following research questions were asked with the accompanying hypotheses:

1. Is there a correlation between in-class texting activity and final grade?
2. If a correlation exists, can it be used to help predict final grades when attendance, ACT scores and entering GPA are controlled? And, if so, what is the unique contribution of each independent variable?

METHOD

This quantitative study examined final grade scores and in-class texting behavior. The convenience sample consisted of 119 students enrolled in three separate sections (n1 = 56, n2 = 34, n3 = 29) of a 3 credit hour,

15 week, introductory social science course at a small college in the Midwest. The college has a standardized attendance policy for all classes in which students are required to miss no more than 20% of the class to pass. Any student exceeding 20% of absences automatically fails the course. No participant in the sample exceeded the maximum absences allowance.

Following IRB approval, each section of the course was randomly selected for each treatment condition. Course Section 1 had a mild texting policy. Previous research was explained to Course Section 1, highlighting that other students and professors found cell phone usage in class to be rude and distracting (Campbell, 2006). The policy was placed in the syllabus stating that "Cell phones were to be turned off and not used during class. This is an issue of respect for others and your professor." Course Section 2 had a strict cell phone policy. Per their syllabus and professor explanation, students would lose 3% of their final grade each time they were caught texting. This policy was reiterated in class throughout the semester to warn students to turn off their phones before class start. However, due to the need for true final grade analysis, no points were actually taken off of the student's final grade. Course Section 3 had no presented texting policy and served as a control group. Students were free to have cell phones on and to text as desired.

At the end of the semester on the last day of class, students were given a pencil and paper survey asking about their frequency of texting behavior. Students were asked to put their names on the survey for coding purposes so that their GPAs and ACT scores could be matched. Students were given the option to not participate but were given an extra credit point toward their 100 point final for participation. All students willingly agreed and participated in the study. When finished, students placed their responses in an envelope. The pre-addressed envelope was then sealed and mailed to a third party for SPSS coding to assure confidentiality of the students. The third party coder also received the students' ACT scores and entering GPA to match the information in SPSS. The ACT and GPA records were then destroyed while the surveys and a hard copy of the final grades were maintained.

In the survey, students were presented with a Likert Scale asking of texting frequency which included: Never (0 times this semester), Rarely (>3 Times this semester), Sometimes (1–3 times a week), and Frequently (More than 3 times a week). Each Course Section was misled to believe that there was a confederate to the experiment in their class posing as a fellow student to record their texting behavior. Each Course Section was then told that if they correctly answered their texting behavior on the survey as recorded by the confederate, they would receive an additional point toward their 100 point final. This misinformation was presented to each Course Section to help to control for social desirability and to promote honesty in response. Students in Course Section 2 (strict texting policy) were also assured that their professor would not see the raw data so no additional points would be taken off based on their survey reports. All students participating received 2 points toward their final, one for participation and one for correctness of response. Students were then debriefed via email and presented with experiment results.

Data was entered into SPSS by a third party who had no knowledge or affiliation to the participants or the college where the experiment was conducted. This was done to encourage anonymity of the participants through disassociation of the third party coder to their connection to the college or the experimenter.

RESULTS

Participants

Participants in the study (N = 119) were a convenience sample taken from a small college and consisted of 97 Freshmen, 17 Sophomores, 5 Juniors, and 0 Seniors. Females comprised 53% (n = 63) of the sample with males comprising 47% (n = 56) of the sample. The majority of the sample was Caucasian (81%), with 17% African American, and 3% Hispanic. The majority of students were enrolled on a full-time basis (91%).

Analysis

After all participants data were coded into SPSS, descriptive statistics for each of the Course Sections were tabulated. Table 1 represents descriptive statistics for in-class texting behavior per section based on the Likert Scale of in-class texting behavior. When coded into SPSS, the Likert Scale was weighted as: Never (0 times this semester) = 0, Rarely (>3 Times this semester) = 1, Sometimes (1–3 times a week) = 2, and Frequently (More than 3 times a week) = 3. The scores indicated for each group are the means and the standard deviation for each group on in-class texting behavior.

Table 1
Descriptive Statistics for Course Sections on In-Class Texting Behavior

Course Section	N	M	SD
1	56	2.1	.99
2	34	2.0	.98
3	29	3.1	1.06

To explore the research question, a Pearson's correlation in SPSS was performed to examine if a correlation existed between an individual's texting behavior and final grade. The relationship between in-class texting behavior and final grade was investigated using Pearson product–movement correlation coefficient. Preliminary analyses were performed to ensure no violation of the assumptions of normality, linearity and homoscedasticity. There was a strong medium-sized correlation between the two variables, $r = -.41$, $n = 119$, $p > .0001$, with greater in-class texting behavior being associated with lower final grade scores.

Since a correlation was present, hierarchical multiple regression was used to assess the ability of in-class texting behavior to predict final grade scores after controlling for the influence of attendance, GPA, and ACT scores. Preliminary analyses in SPSS were conducted to ensure no violation of the assumptions of normality, linearity, multicollinearity and homoscedasticity. GPA, ACT, and attendance were entered as Step 1, explaining 65% of final course grade. After entering in-class texting behavior at Step 2, the total variance explained by the model as a whole was 70%, $F(4, 95) = 21.97$, $p < .001$. The additional control measure of in-class texting behavior explained 5% of the variance in final course grade, R squared change = .05, F change $(1, 95) = 8.01$, $p < .001$. In the final model, only three of the control measures were statistically significant with GPA and ACT recording a higher beta value (.35, $p < .001$) and in-class texting behavior recording a beta value of –.22, $p < .001$. Attendance was not statistically significant as a contributor of final grade score with a beta value of –.06, $p < .001$.

Consequently, texting behavior was also negatively correlated to ACT scores and GPA. There was a small sized correlation between the in-class texting behavior and ACT scores, $r = -.23$, $n = 119$, $p = .01$, with greater in-class texting behavior being associated with lower ACT scores. There was a stronger correlation shown between in-class texting behavior and entering GPA, showing medium sized correlation between the two variables, $r = -.31$, $n = 119$, $p > .001$, with greater in-class texting behavior being associated with lower entering GPAs.

DISCUSSION

The variables of in-class texting behavior and final grade score in a freshmen level, introductory social science class were the focus of this study. The purpose of this study was to examine any effects that in-class texting behavior had on the final grade score for the course. Factors contributing to academic achievement in college have been the focus of many research studies and meta-analyses (Munday, 1970; Betts & Morell 1999; Newman-Ford, Fitzgibbon, Lloyd, & Thomas, 1999; Cohn et al. 2003; Cornwell et al. 2005; Grove et al. 2006; Crede, Roch, & Kieszczynka, 2010). Academic attainment has been linked to various cognitive measures such as standardized tests, entering GPA and class attendance (Berry & Sackett 2009; Crede, Roch, & Kieszczynka, 2010). These cognitive factors represent a historical, empirically supported model of prediction. However, with the rapid expansion of the use of cell phones for communication, specifically texting, a study was needed to determine the effects of in-class texting behavior on academic success. Understanding how in-class texting behavior affects a student's final grade in a course is essential. This study filled such a void.

Understanding Berry and Sackett's (2009) research which argued that academic performance predictor models be used for individual classes rather than overall college GPA, a single freshmen level social science course, taught by the same professor, was selected for the study. Three Course Sections of this same course were given three different texting policies to elicit a variety of in-class texting behaviors. Course Section 1 had the texting policy where the students were educated about texting etiquette and reminded of the need to respect others in regard to cell phone usage. This Course Section had the highest mean final grade score of 81%. Course Section 2 (M = 77%) which had the most strict texting policy with punitive consequences for texting had the second highest final grade score. This offered justification to Burns and Lohenry's (2010) pilot study where the researchers argued for the need for department/professor/student commutation that encourages courtesy and professionalism to optimal teaching and learning in the college classroom. Course Section 3, which had no texting policy for control, had the highest in-class texting behavior; their mean final grade was 73%. Moreover, the mean differences in each Course Section were significant.

The differences in the mean texting behavior are of particular relevance since the study showed there was a negative correlation in the relationship between in-class texting and final grade score. The more a student participated in in-class texting behavior, the lower their final grade. Consequently, since there was a negative correlation present, it was of importance to see how this fit into a model of predictability. It was important to see if in-class texting behavior still affected final grades negatively if other factors which were historically and empirically linked to academic performance were controlled.

In-class texting was significant in impacting grades after GPA, ACT, and attendance were controlled. While GPA and ACT were still the strongest predictor values, in-class texting behavior still contributed to 22% of the predictive value. Attendance had no significance in final grade. It must be reiterated that at this small college, attendance is still mandatory. However, this leads to a more important discussion on attendance and in-class texting.

While a student may be required to attend a college course, attendance is more than merely sitting in a classroom. Attendance should equate to actually interacting with the material and a deliberate awareness of the presented material. While attendance can be strongly linked to academic performance, a more accurate reflection would be in-class behavior. While a professor certainly cannot control for individual behavior such as daydreaming or doodling, this study presents the necessity of some type of effective texting policy.

In this study, the most effective texting policy was Course Section 1, 81%. Course Section 1 had a texting policy which used education and respect as primary factors in texting during class. Course Section 2 relied on punitive measures, taking points away from students for texting. While the latter may seem to be more effective by producing fear in students for texting, it does require an excessive amount of record keeping and policing the classroom on the part of the professor. Burns and Lohenry (2010) maintain that educating students on the effect of texting in the classroom should be a cornerstone in institutional policies.

CONCLUSION

As technology advances, so will its benefits and troubles. It is up to colleges and universities to provide environments that are conducive to not only learning, but also to anticipatory professional socialization in the workplace. Requiring attendance is one way to do both. However, allowing students the freedom to monitor and use texting within the classroom does neither.

Future research should focus on the other effects of texting in the classroom as well as different classes that are geared toward those in a higher class ranking. Research investigating different in-class texting policies should be explored as well as replication studies that continue to explore the relationship between in-class texting and final grades. What is for certain is that technology will continue to grow and education must continue to grow with it.

REFERENCES

Berry, C. M., & Sackett, P. R. (2009). Individual differences in course choice result in underestimation of the validity of college admission systems. *Psychological Science*, 20 (7), 822–830.

Betts, J. R., & Morell, D. (1999). The determinants of undergraduate grade point average: The relative importance of family background, high school resources, and peer group effects. *Journal of Human Resources*, 34 (3), 268–293.

Burns, S. M., & Lohenry, K., (2010). Cellular phone use in the class: Implications for teaching and learning a pilot study. *College Student Journal*, 44 (3), 805–810.

Campbell, S. W. (2006). Perceptions of mobile phones in college classrooms: Ringing, cheating and classroom policies. *Communication Education*, 55 (3), 280– 294.

Cohn, E., Cohn, S., Balch, D. C., & Bradley, J.. (2003). Determinants of undergraduate GPAs: SAT scores, high school GPA and high-school rank. *Economics of Education Review*, 23 (6), 577–586.

Cornwell, C. M., Lee, K. H., &. Mustard, D. B., (2005). Student responses to merit scholarship retention rules. *Journal of Human Resources, 40 (4),* 895–917.

Crede, M., & Kuncel, N. R., (2008). Study habits, skills, and attitudes: The third pillar supporting collegiate academic performance. *Perspectives on Psychological Science, 3,* 425–453.

Crede, M, Roch, S. G. & Kieszczynka, U. M., (2010). Class attendance in college: A meta-analytic review of the relationship of class attendance with grades and student characteristics. *Review of Educational Research, 80 (2),* 272–295.

Ellis, Y., Daniels, B., Jauregui, A. (2010). The effect of multitasking on the grade performance of business students. *Research in Higher Education Journal, 8,* 1–10.

End, C. M., Worthman, S., Mathews, M. B., & Wetterau, K. (2010). Costly cell phones: The impact of cell phone rings on academic performance. *Teaching of Psychology, 37 (1),* 55–57.

Gilroy, M. (2004). Invasion of the classroom cell phones. *Education Digest, 69 (6).* 56–60.

Grove, W., Wasserman, T., Grodner, A. (2006). Choosing a proxy for academic aptitude. *The Journal of Economic Education, 37 (2),* 131–47.

Hoekstra, A., (2008). Vibrant student voices: Exploring effects of the use of clickers in large college classes. *Learning, Media, and Technology, 33,* 329–341.

Jenne, F. H., (1973). Attendance and student proficiency change in a health science class. *Journal of School Health, 43,* 135–126.

Launius, M. H., (1997). College student attendance: Attitudes and academic performance. *College Student Journal, 31,* 86–92.

Munday, L. A., (1970). Factors influencing the predictability of college grades. *American Educational Research Journal, 7 (1),* 99–107.

Moore, R., (2003). Attendance and performance: How important is it for students to attend class? *Journal of College Science Teaching, 32,* 367–371.

Moore, R., Jensen, M., Hatch, J., Duranczyk, I., Staats, S., & Koch, L., (2003). Showing up: The importance of class attendance for academic success in introductory science courses. *American Biology Teacher, 65,* 325–329.

Newman-Ford, L., Fitzgibbon, K., Lloyd, S., & Thomas, S. (1999). A large-scale investigation into the relationship between attendance and attainment: A study using an innovative, electronic attendance monitoring system. *Studies in Higher Education, 33,* 699–717.

Stephenson, K,. (1994). Correspondence. *Journal of Economic Perspectives, 8,* 207–208.

Stumpf, H. & Stanley, J.C., (2002). Group data on high school grade point averages and scores on academic aptitude tests as predictors of institutional graduation rates. *Educational and Psychological Measurement, 62 (6),* 1042–52.

Sylvia E. McDonald, Ohio Christian University

QUESTIONS ABOUT MEANING

1. What factors has past research shown to be predictors of academic performance in college?
2. What was the goal of McDonald's study? What gap in the research does her study address?
3. Describe the participants, methods, and results of McDonald's study.

QUESTIONS FOR RHETORICAL ANALYSIS

1. Describe the organization/structure of the introductory paragraph. How is it a typical introduction to an academic argument?
2. McDonald describes the attendance policy at the college where she conducted her research. Why is this important information to include in this study?

MAKING CONNECTIONS

1. Many challenges come with conducting research to assess the effects of behavior over time. Identify the challenges and potential problems in McDonald's and Hembrooke and Gay's research designs and explain steps the researchers took in an attempt to obtain honest, reliable, and *generalizable* data about student cell phone and computer use in the classroom. Do you think the study designs allowed the researchers to get a realistic picture of student practices? Why or why not?
2. What behavior policies have you seen in your college courses or on your campus? McDonald's findings suggest benefits to regulating some types of classroom behaviors. Is that reason enough to have rules prohibiting some behaviors? When are such rules justified and when do they infringe on the individual's right to make his/her own choices?

Information Sciences

"The Laptop and the Lecture: The Effects of Multitasking in Learning Environments," HELENE HEMBROOKE AND GERI GAY

Helene Hembrooke and Geri Gay, both from Cornell University, direct the Human Computer Interaction Group, an interdisciplinary team researching social, psychological, and design issues involving computer use. In "The Laptop and the Lecture: The Effects of Multitasking in Learning Environments," the authors describe a study designed to determine if web surfing during a lecture affects students' ability to recall the lecture. The study originally appeared in 2003 in the *Journal of Computing in Higher Education*, which publishes research of interest to college professors who use computer technology in the classroom.

ABSTRACT

The effects of multitasking in the classroom were investigated in students in an upper level Communications course. Two groups of students heard the same exact lecture and tested immediately following the lecture. One group of students was allowed to use their laptops to engage in browsing, search, and/or social computing behaviors during the lecture. Students in the second condition were asked to keep their laptops closed for the duration of the lecture. Students in the open laptop condition suffered decrements on traditional measures of memory for lecture content. A second experiment replicated the results of the first. Data were further analyzed by "browsing style." Results are discussed from Lang's Limited Process Capacity model in an attempt to better understand the mechanisms involved in the decrement.

KEYWORDS

multitasking, divided attention, technology, education, limited capacity model

INTRODUCTION

The ubiquity, pervasiveness and mobility of new technologies encourage a simultaneity of activities that goes beyond anything our culture has heretofore ever known. Indeed, the ability to engage in multiple tasks concurrently seems to be the very essence or core motivation for the development of such technologies. Yet there is a long tradition of psychological and media communication research that indicates that our ability to engage in simultaneous tasks is, at best, limited (Fisch, 2000; Lang, 2000), and at worst, virtually impossible (James, 1890; Woodsworth, 1921; Broadbent, 1958).

In the context of learning, the implementation of wireless technology, in whatever form that might take, introduces additional visual and/or auditory information, above and beyond the visual and auditory information presented by the instructor. Depending on the boundaries and intent for using these tools in the classroom setting, a student might engage in myriad computing activities, from synchronous and asynchronous social computing, to note taking, to Web browsing. Part, all, or none of the activity may be related to the lecture topic at hand. Of course, distraction in the lecture hall or classroom is nothing new; note passing, doodling, talking, completing other class assignments, and even taking notes on the current lecture are all familiar forms of low-tech distraction. However, mobile devices and wireless access in the classroom have the potential to bring distraction to new heights, especially as the study of their effects and benefits is in its relative infancy and schools and Universities grapple with issues concerning boundary setting and high-tech classroom etiquette.

The current study was part of a larger program of research designed to investigate the effects of wireless computing in collaborative learning environments. Students in two very differently structured classroom environments were given laptops with wireless LAN access to use throughout the course of the semester. With their consent, all computing activity was tracked around the clock including e-mail, Web browsing, chat, and instant messenging (Note: The *content* of social communication was not recorded). Both direct (proxy logs and focus group interviews) and indirect (classroom observation) evidence indicated to us that students were engaged in computing activities that were often unrelated to the immediate class lecture and tasks. Thus we decided to investigate this multitasking behavior more systematically.

Our hypotheses were developed from the extant literature in both cognitive psychology and mediated learning research. In cognitive psychology there is a long tradition of research that has focused on dividing attention between simultaneously occurring tasks. These experiments have formed the basis for methodological and theoretical developments in nearly every subfield of cognitive psychology including learning, memory, perception, and, of course, attention. Perhaps most notable is Broadbent's theory of selective attention (1958, 1970). Based on his dichotic listening experiments that required subjects to shadow speech messages in one ear, while ignoring the messages in the other ear, Broadbent concluded that little, if any, content from the nonattended ear is remembered. From these observations, Broadbent proposed that there is a limited processing channel that information is filtered through from a sensory processing stage on its way to a short-term memory store or buffer. From here, information may be processed further before being transmitted into a longer-term memory store. When this channel becomes overloaded, such as in dichotic listening experiments, some of the information is filtered out, while other information is selected for further processing. The filtering mechanism selects inputs based on different physical cues from the stimulus input, such as location in space, and/or frequency. Since then, psychologists interested in information processing issues such as learning, memory, skill development and retention, processing limitations, and human factors have been investigating the effects of multitasking.

The classic paradigm involves having subjects perform a primary task in which some response is required, while simultaneously monitoring a secondary task for specific information or changes. For example, participants might be asked to learn a list of words presented visually, while listening for the occurrence of certain digit strings presented through an auditory channel. Participants might then be tested for their memory of the word list. Many different variations have been investigated including different modalities, the same modalities, task difficulty, the effects of practice, the effects of either the primary or secondary task on performance, and testing during encoding or retrieval (Baddeley, Lewis, Eldridge, & Thomson, 1984; Naveh-Benjamin, Craik, Perretta, & Toney, 2000; Johnson, Greenberg, Fisher, & Martin, 1970; Spelke, Hirst, & Neisser, 1976). Almost without exception performance on one or both tasks suffers a decrement as a direct result of having to perform the two tasks simultaneously.

Explanations for the performance decrement most typically involve some discussion of limitations in the amount of information that can either be selectively attended to, processed, or encoded such that there no longer exist enough overlap at the time of retrieval for the subject to recognize or recall the to-be-remembered information (Craik & Lockhart, 1976; Broadbent, 1958, 1970; Tulving & Thompson, 1973). Often the specific impact of the variable(s) of interest in a particular study, for example, the automaticity of the processes studied and/or the depth qualify these interpretations or the processing required by the tasks performed. However, the finding of a performance decrement under divided attention conditions is so robust as to consider it a guiding theoretical principle in these various fields of attention, learning and memory.

Research in another area, which also builds upon the notion that there is a fixed amount of cognitive resources upon which the processor may draw, focuses on delineating the specific subprocesses involved and how each may be compromised at every step in the process. Annie Lang's Limited Capacity Model (LCM) (2000) relies heavily upon cognitive constructs as she applies it to mediated learning contexts. The model's predictive power under various conditions of encoding, storage and retrieval is nothing short of elegant and provides an outlet for the discussion of some of the more interesting findings from the current study. Thus, while the classic experiments on dichotic listening tasks and selective attention theory provided the theoretical (and to some extent methodological) rationale for this work, LCM enables us to explore our findings that go beyond the basic predictions of divided attention theories, and to postulate what mechanisms may be involved.

Limited Capacity Model

The model outlines the stepwise progression of the cognitive processes involved in processing information. Conscious and unconscious mechanisms determine what information is selected for encoding. Once in short term, or working memory, previous knowledge is activated and linked with relevant aspects of the new incoming information. Memory for the new information is created through associations between the new and existing knowledge, or by recurrently activating and linking the bits of new information over time. The number of related associations between new and existing information determines memory strength.

Proof by disproof is the work of science, and this model's strength comes not in its ability to prove the existence of these separate sub-processes, but in its power to predict failures of memory. Beginning first with the assumption that there is a limited pool of resources from which the individual-as-processor may channel into these sub-processes, memory may be compromised as a result of a breakdown at any point in this process. Maintaining a balance between what is required by the message and the distribution of already limited resources to process that information thoroughly is the juggling act of the information processor. All breakdowns reflect some misattribution of resources to the task at hand. Disproportionate allocation of resources may result from conscious and intentional mechanisms inherent to the individual, or attributes intrinsic to the information or message.

Lang's model has been applied most typically to the television viewing situation, predicting what viewers will remember following various manipulations in structure and content in the medium as well as inducing different motivation or expertise in the viewer. The extension of this model to hypertext media seems natural given the primary receptive modality, the continual flow of structural and content changes, and the similarly varied needs and goals that the user brings to the situation. The multitasking context of the present work has ecological and theoretical relevance; burdening the user with additional information increases the cognitive load requirement. Successful information retrieval/learning in this kind of situation depends, then, on extremely efficacious resource allocation to both mediums. The results we report here indicate that the effects of multitasking are not simply main effects of condition. They must be qualified by other mediating factors. We believe Lang's model provides explanatory power for these interactive effects and helps lay the groundwork for the systematic investigation of them. Our hypotheses were as follows:

H1: Students in the open laptop condition would perform significantly poorer on immediate measures of memory for the lecture material.

H2: Similar to other findings from our lab, (Grace-Martin & Gay, 2001), the memory decrement observed would not result from the relatedness of the content viewed in the secondary task (laptop use) to the primary task (lecture information). In other words, content relevance would not contribute significantly to the variance observed in the main effect above.

METHOD

Subjects

Participants in the initial study were 44 students in an upper level Communications course at a prominent university in the Northeast. As part of another project funded by Intel, these students were issued Dell laptops (Dell Latitude CPt) to use throughout the semester in an effort to study the impact of wireless network technology in collaborative learning spaces. Across campus a series of wireless transmitters (access points) provided the infrastructure for the wireless LAN network. Students were encouraged to conduct their computing activities through a proxy server. In this way we were able to capture and store all tool use (e-mail, discussion board participation, URL visits, etc.) throughout the semester. All students were fully informed as to what their participation would entail and could choose at any time to not go through our proxy server.

The majority of students were Communication majors, although there were also a few Computer Science and Arts and Design students enrolled. 22 males and 22 females were enrolled in the course.

Procedure

Throughout the course students were encouraged to use their laptops in the class as a supplement to the lecture, discussion and lab activities. Generally speaking, students were given the responsibility to monitor their own computing activities during the lecture. It became apparent that while students used their laptops during lecture to explore lecture topics in greater detail on the Internet as well as the library databases, they were also engaging in other forms of computing, such as unrelated browsing, email, and synchronous forms of communication such as chat and IM. As stated earlier, it was this high-tech "doodling" that provided the impetus for the current study.

During one lecture, students were randomly assigned to one of two conditions; half of the students left the classroom to take part in a lab exercise in a neighboring classroom. The remaining half of the students were exposed to a typical lecture, and encouraged to use their laptops as usual during the lecture. When the lecture ended, these students switched classrooms with the other half of the class, who then went into the lecture hall and heard the identical lecture. The only difference between the two groups was that during the second repetition of the lecture, students were told to close their laptops. Both groups of students were tested immediately following the lecture. The lecture this day did not differ perceptibly in structure or delivery from any other lecture thus far.

The surprise quiz consisted of 20 questions on the lecture content. Half of the questions were multiple choice (recognition) questions, while the other half were short answer (recall) questions. All students finished the test in approximately ten minutes, after which they were debriefed and thanked for their participation.

The replication study took place two months later. Students who served as controls in the first experiment (Closed laptop condition) participated as experimental subjects in the replication study (Open laptop condition) and vice versa.

RESULTS

Tests were corrected and given three scores: a total score which included the percent correct out of the total number of questions, a recall score and a recognition score, which was the proportion correct out of the total of ten like questions. The data are first reported for the initial study, and then the replication study.

The initial data were first analyzed using a one-way ANOVA with condition entered as a between subjects variable. The results of this analysis revealed a significant effect of condition on total and recall test score measures, with students in the open laptop condition performing significantly poorer than those in the closed laptop condition ($F(1,43) = 4.42$, $p < .04$; $F(1,43) = 5.00$, $p < .03$, respectively). Differences between the two groups on recognition scores approached significance, $F(1,43) = 3.45$, $p < .07$. Figure 15.3 graphically represents the differences between these two conditions.

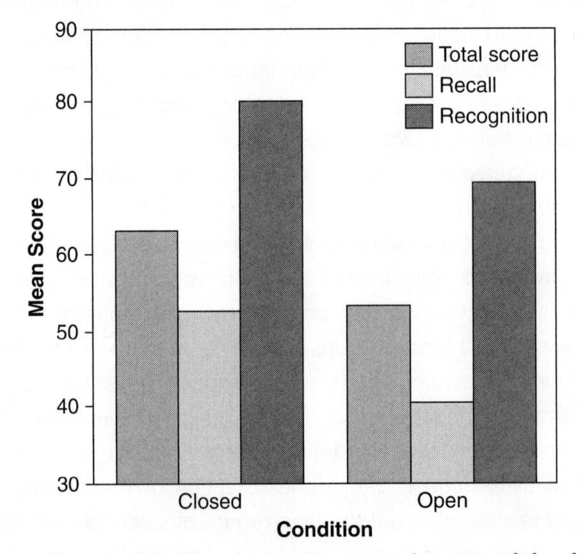

Figure 15.3 Mean total, recall, and recognition scores for open and closed laptop conditions

The replication data were scored and analyzed in exactly the same manner. Again, the results of this analysis revealed a significant effect of condition on total and recall test scores in the same direction ($F(1,20) = 10.70$, $p < .004$; $F(1,20) = 6.13$, $p < .02$ respectively). Again the difference between the open and closed laptop conditions neared significance on recognition scores, $F(1,20) = 2.80$, $p < .11$.

To ensure that having participated in the experiment twice [did not influence respondents] (even though subjects were unaware of their participation and group assignment was counterbalanced between the initial and replication study), an additional analysis with Experiment (Initial or Replication) was entered into the model. No significant Condition × Experiment interaction was found.

While these data are interesting and extend the historical theoretical precedence to a more applied setting such as the classroom, they are hardly surprising. Our intent here was to explore these more predictable results at a deeper level, and perhaps suggest possible mechanisms for their occurrence in this context. The proxy log data allowed us to examine the content of what students were browsing during the lectures and how that might have impacted their performance on the subsequent memory test. We were able to extract their on-line browsing behavior for those class periods and code them according to whether the content was class related or unrelated depending on the lecture content. Content was coded as related if the URL was related to the lecture topic, or was 1 of 3 URLs recommended during the lecture. Non-related content was all other URLs, including Web mail, entertainment sites, E-commerce sites, news sites, and business sites. From this log data we were also able to calculate the amount of time spent on class related and unrelated pages, the overall amount of time spent online, and the amount of time spent per page. Here, we are obviously only interested in those students serving in the open laptop condition.

We first calculated the proportion of time each student spent on class related and unrelated sites. This was simply their overall times spent online during those class periods divided by the amount of time spent browsing related and unrelated pages. When these totals were correlated with later test scores, an interesting, and surprising inverse relationship emerged; for recall scores, more time spent browsing class related pages resulted in lower recall scores ($r = -.516$, p. < 02), and conversely, when students spent more time browsing class unrelated pages they did better on recall questions ($r = .510$, p. <. 03).

In other work we have found relationships between browsing efficiency and class performance (Grace-Martin & Gay, 2001). We thought that the above results might reflect some inherent differences in browsing "styles." To explore this relationship further, we classified students as primarily "ontaskers" or "offtaskers" if the proportion of their time spent online was at least 50% on or off task. Thus, a person who spent 65% of the class period browsing class related pages would be classified as an "ontasker." If, on the other hand, a student spent only 48% of their time on class related pages, she was classified as an "offtasker." Analysis revealed significant differences in the time spent on and off task by these two groups, with ontaskers spending significantly more time on task than offtaskers, and conversely, offtaskers spending significantly more time off task than ontaskers ($F\ (1,17) = 6.64$, $p < .02$; $F\ (1,17) = 23.44$, $p < .01$, respectively). Thus it appears that this subject classification scheme did accurately discriminate between the two groups. By classifying subjects in this way we could investigate differences between these two groups when engaged in both class related and unrelated activities.

The mean number of minutes spent on class related and unrelated pages were calculated for each student by dividing the number of related and unrelated pages by the number of minutes spent on each kind of page. An ANOVA yielded a significant main effect of task classification for the mean number of minutes spent on class unrelated pages ($F\ (1,14) = 11.17$, $p < .005$). Students classified as "ontaskers" spent significantly more time on class unrelated pages than "offtaskers." When students that spent the majority of their time *on* task, went *off* task they spent an inordinate amount of time on those class unrelated pages. Those students that spent the majority of their time off task during the entire lecture spent an equivalent amount of time on class related and unrelated pages. As it turns out, "ontaskers" did worse on all three measures of performance, and significantly so on their total scores ($F\ (1.17) = 4.85$, $p < 04$). Thus, it appears that the negative correlation between the proportion of time spent on class related sites and performance is mediated by one's ability to monitor or balance their browsing behaviors.

Since performance appears to be based not on relevance but the proportion of time spent away from the primary task, "ontaskers" and "offtaskers," as labels, seem a misnomer and potentially confusing. Henceforth these groups will be distinguished as "browsers" (formerly offtaskers), and "seekers" (formerly ontaskers).

This analysis led us to wonder if students in the open laptop condition who engaged in more superficial browsing might still be able to process the multiple inputs in much the same way as students in the closed laptop condition. Post hoc analyses of ten randomly chosen subjects from the closed laptop condition, browsers (in the open laptop condition), and seekers (recall that browsers and seekers are both in the open laptop condition), indicated no significant differences between browsers and the randomly chosen control subjects on any of the memory measures. However, post hoc tests revealed that seekers differed significantly from controls as well as their counterparts in the open laptop condition on total score, ($F(1,17) = 2.88$, p. <. 04), and approached significant differences on recognition scores ($F(1,17) = 1.98$, $p < .13$). Partial eta squared analysis revealed a moderate effect size of .21 for total score and .14 for recognition. Figure 15.4 illustrates these differences. Thus, although these tests were not considered apriori, it appears that the differences between the two groups is moderately related to the level at which they were able to process the information, as a direct result of their browsing tendencies. However, given the size of the sample, it is still important that these variables be considered systematically.

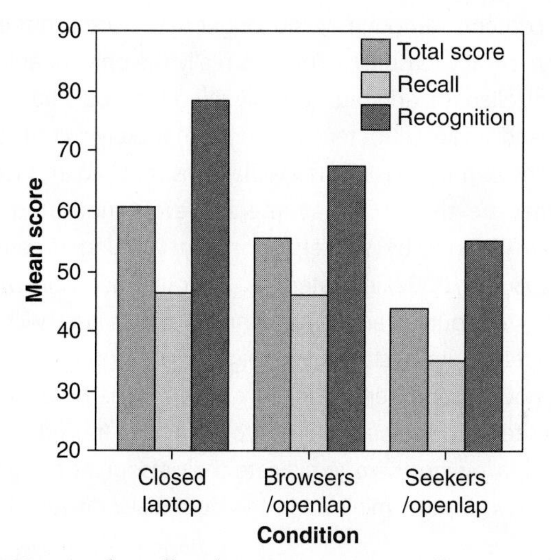

Figure 15.4 Mean total, recall, and recognition scores for "browsers," "seekers," and ten randomly chosen subjects in the closed laptop condition

DISCUSSION

The work here explored the effects of engaging in multiple tasks simultaneously on traditional outcome measures of performance. While methodologically the procedures employed in the present study differ somewhat from those of the classic divided attention paradigm, the essence of those procedures has been preserved, and the resulting performance decrement obtained. In two studies, students performing multiple tasks performed significantly poorer on immediate measures of memory for the to-be-learned content.

In follow-up analysis we discovered that page-relevant content did not predict better performance, and spending the majority of class time on class related content did not result in better test performance. This suggests strongly that memory decrement in multitasking situations is the result of the proportion of time drawn off task. Grace-Martin & Gay (2001) similarly found that longer browsing sessions throughout the course of the semester resulted in lower overall class performance, and that many and shorter browsing sessions during a class period, irrespective of content, led to higher class grades. The sustained distraction, regardless of content relevance, appears to be the nemesis of the multitasker; if one is adroit at staccato-like browsing, processing multiple inputs simultaneously may not suffer to the same extent.

While resource allocation offers an explanation at a global level, at a mechanistic level the question becomes: What about this browsing style contributes to its benefit? But first, perhaps the better question is what variable(s) predict this kind of browsing? One candidate we suspect is the page content. Although we no longer have access to these files (for ethical and privacy reasons), content is really the only variable that could not be controlled for, and thus the only thing that could have differed for browsers and seekers. Content would seem a likely culprit for introducing differences in the conscious mechanisms involved in selective attention. It may be that different interest levels motivated the online information sought by seekers. A recent finding in our lab (Lee, Stefanone, & Gay, 2002) indicated that topic interest is directly related to the number of sources and page changes that a user will attempt to access. Increased interest in a site might increase the number of page changes, novelty, and hence cognitive load for the time spent on class unrelated sites. Browsers appear not to have been 'pulled in' by the sites they visited, allowing them to allocate their resources more equally between the two inputs, minimizing the potentially distracting effects of the laptop.

These results are also somewhat reminiscent of the findings from incidental learning paradigms. In these experiments participants are oriented to different memory tasks by instructions to either process the information with the expectation of a later memory test, or to simply attend to and monitor stimulus information in different ways (e.g., crossing out vowels, or copying words, Tressalt & Mayznor, 1960). Compared with intentional instructions to learn, participants given no instructions to remember do significantly poorer on the follow-up memory test. (See Postman, 1964, for a full review of the literature). The explanation for the better performance of the intentional learning group is again related to the kinds of processing activities that subjects engage in during learning; with explicit instructions to learn subjects process information in more elaborative, semantically relevant ways. However, incidental learning performance can be enhanced without explicit orienting instructions to learn if subjects are required to categorize words (Mandler, 1967), make judgments about word meanings (Tressalt & Mayznot, 1960), or are presented with associative or otherwise meaningful word pairs (Johnson & Jenkins, 1971) (or in other words, process the information semantically). Orienting instructions produce a shift in what Lang and others refer to as controlled selection processes. Essentially these are the conscious goals or intentions of the subject. Since students in the class had been encouraged to use their laptops during the lecture throughout the semester, instructions to close them may have produced a shift in these controlled selection processes and hence resource allocation. However, since the post hoc analyses revealed that most of the variance is explained by only a proportion of the students in the open laptop condition (seekers), this conjecture seems less tenable.

Though not without qualification the resulting poorer performance of some students in the multitasking condition begs the question if technology in the classroom is the panacea that some purport. While students were obviously distracted by having access to the Internet, e-mail, IM, and browsing as evidenced by their performance on traditional tests of memory, their performance in the class overall does not reflect this same disruption. The average final grade for the class was a strong B+, and students had been multitasking in class since the beginning of the semester. The structure of the class was nontraditional, highly interactive and dynamic, and students were encouraged to use their laptops in class to supplement the course lecture. Had the class been more traditional and grades determined by conventional tests of memory the outcome may have been different. Thus, as others have argued (Soloway, Guzdial, & Hay, 1994; Soloway, Krajcik, Blumenfield, & Marx, 1996), statements regarding the advantages or disadvantages of technologies in learning environments need to be qualified by such things as class structure, dynamics, measure of learning, and the like.

While class structure may have been responsible in part for the lack of an observed overall effect on grades, there is also the possibility that over time, students became increasingly adept at multitasking in the classroom setting. Early evidence for practice effects on simultaneous directed activity has been demonstrated (Spelke, Hirst, & Neisser, 1976). The results of the current study suggest that enhanced browsing efficiency might be used as an index of a facilitation effect of time or practice. If students can become "better browsers," or at the very least become more facile at self-monitoring their browsing behavior, the typical decrement found under multitasking conditions might be negated. The task before us is to develop a taxonomy of the situational and individual variables associated with performance decrement, and identify the cognitive/behavioral indicia that contribute to the effect. Such information could contribute to the development of curriculum and measures of learning perhaps more appropriate in technology enhanced classrooms, as well as inform development of training or exercises, and/or devices that help the user to redirect or monitor attention in multi-tasking situations.

Finally, these results clearly indicate the need for setting boundaries and establishing "tech-etiquette" for using wireless technologies in the classroom. High-tech doodling for some students can defeat the purpose of using them in the first place.

REFERENCES

Baddeley, A. D., Lewis, V., Eldridge, M., & Thomson, N. (1984). Attention and retrieval from long-term memory. *Journal of Experimental Psychology: General*, 13, 518–540.

Broadbent, D. (1958). *Perception and Communication*. Oxford: Pergamon.

Broadbent, D. (1971). *Decision and Stress*. London: Academic Press.

Craik, F. I. M., & Lockhart, R. S. (1972). Levels of Processing: A framework for memory research. *Journal of Verbal Learning and Verbal Behavior, 11*, 671–684.

Fisch, S. M. (2000). A capacity model of children's comprehension of educational content on television. *Media Psychology*, 2, 63–91.

Grace-Martin, M, & Gay, G. (2001). Web browsing, mobile computing and academic performance. *Educational Technology & Society*, 2(3), 95–107.

James, W. (1890). *The Principles of Psychology, Vol. 1*. New York: Henry Holt & Co.

Johnson, W. A., Greenberg, S. N., Fisher, R. P., & Martin, D. W. (1970). *Journal of Experimental Psychology*, 83(1), 164–171.

Lang, A. (2001). The limited capacity model of mediated message processing. *Journal of Communication*, 46–70.

Lee, J., Stefanone, M., & Gay, G. (2002). Web browsing and mobile computing: Examining characteristics of web browsing patterns. Paper to be presented at ICA, Communication and Tecnology Division.

Mandler, G. (1967). Organization and memory. In K. W. Spence & J. T. Spence (Eds.), *The Psychology of Learning and Motivation, Vol. 1*. New York: Academic Press.

Mazner, M. S., & Tresselt, M. E. (1962). Incidental learning: A function of associative strength and distance between S-R pairs. *Journal of Psychology*, 53, 155–160.

Naveh-Benjamen, M., Craik, F. I. M., Perretta, J. G., & Tonev, S. T. (2000). The effects of divided attention on encoding and retrieval processes: The resiliency of retrieval processes.*The Quarterly Journal of Experimental Psychology 53A (3)*, 609–625.

Postman, L. (1964). Short-term memory and incidental learning. In A. W. Melton (Ed.), *Categories of Human Learning*. New York: Academic Press.

Soloway, E., Guzdial, M., & Hay, K. (1994, April). Learner-Centered design: The next challenge for HCI. *ACM Interactions*.

Soloway, E., Krajcik, J. S., Blumenfeld, P., & Marx, R. W. (1996). Technological support for teachers transitioning to project-based

science practices. In T. Koschmann (Ed.), *CSCL: Theory and Practice For an Emerging Paradigm*. Mahwah, NJ: Lawrence Erlbaum Associates.
Spelke, E., Hirst, W., & Neisser, U. (1976). Skills of divided attention. *Cognition, 4*, 215–230.
Tulving, E., & Thomson, D. M. (1973). Encoding specificity and retrieval processes in episodic memory. *Psychological Review, 50*, 352–373.
Woodworth, R. S. (1921). *Psychology: A Study of Mental Life*. New York: Henry Holt & Co.

Helene Hembrooke and Geri Gay, Human Computer Interaction Laboratory, Cornell University.

QUESTIONS ABOUT MEANING

1. Describe the participants and methods used in Hembrooke and Gay's study.
2. Did the researchers find evidence to support their two hypotheses (H1 and H2)? What activities were found to be most detrimental to memory among multitaskers?

QUESTIONS FOR RHETORICAL ANALYSIS

1. Some of the statistical analysis in the Results section is difficult for lay readers, but the figures present the findings in an easy-to-interpret form. Summarize the "story" told in the figures. Are the figures effective?
2. Highlight words and phrases in the final three paragraphs used to qualify claims. In what ways do these qualified statements enhance the writers' credibility?

MAKING CONNECTIONS

1. In her *Wall Street Journal* article, Boroditsky summarizes research studies for a broad audience. Using Boroditsky's article as a model, write a newspaper-style article, appropriate for a general audience, that summarizes both Hembrooke and Gay's and McDonald's research. To make your discussion more well-rounded , integrate comments from Laura Granka's *Ypulse* interview (chapter 7) into your article. Like Boroditsky , you should make the information accessible, relevant, and interesting for the audience. Keep in mind that your audience (newspaper readers) haven't read the studies, so provide enough context and explanation to make the research clear to readers.
2. In one recent study, researchers found that students who opted to take notes on their laptops took more notes than students who took notes by

hand, but the laptop users were also more likely to type verbatim what they heard rather than condensing and summarizing in their own words. The researchers speculate that this may be one reason the laptop users did worse than the longhand note takers when asked to apply the concepts they had been taught. Typing verbatim notes does not promote comprehension the way that summarizing does (Perez-Hernandez). Does it surprise you that students who used laptops to take notes showed less understanding of the lecture material than did longhand note takers? Do the results of Hembrooke and Gay's study surprise you? Why or why not? Respond to these research findings in an essay, using your own experiences and observations or additional research studies you find.

WORK CITED

Perez-Hernandez, Danya. "Taking Notes by Hand Benefits Recall, Researchers Find." *The Chronicle of Higher Education* (28 Mar. 2014). Web. 6 May 2014.

CHAPTER 16

Violence and Justice

The authors in this chapter approach the topics of violence and justice from various perspectives.

The first authors take a historical perspective. In "Another Report on the Age of Extinction," art history professor John O'Brian describes his visit to a 19th-century home in Ohio where he attended an event commemorating the extinction of wild passenger pigeons. In the home are remembrances of the area's original Native American inhabitants, the extinct passenger pigeon, and the nearby nuclear plant. The images prompt O'Brian to reflect on more than the loss of a bird species. History professor Elizabeth Dale considers another type of violence: murder in the first half of the 19th century. In "Getting Away with Murder," Dale analyzes historical documents to determine why roughly half of those indicted for murder in South Carolina during that period were never convicted of murder.

The next two articles focus on the modern American justice system. In "Taking a Juvenile into Custody: Situational Factors That Influence Police Officers' Decisions," Terrence Allen, a professor of social work, identifies the factors most likely to lead to the arrest of a juvenile. Law professor Erin Murphy discusses what happens once a person is taken into custody, in her article "The Government Wants Your DNA." Police in many states can now collect DNA from people arrested, even for nonviolent crime. "Before we expend more resources and compromise personal liberty still further," argues Murphy, "we need a concrete accounting . . . of how much the vast investment in DNA collection and recording has already cost taxpayers and society as a whole."

Psychology professor Elizabeth Loftus looks at another aspect of the justice system: eyewitness testimony. A nationally recognized expert on the fallibility of memory, Loftus wrote the paired readings featured in this chapter. In "How I Got Started: From Semantic Memory to Expert Testimony," Loftus describes how she became a legal consultant. In "Repeated Information in the Courtroom," Jeffrey Foster, Maryanne Garry, and Loftus describe two studies revealing a surprising reason people might believe the false claims of a witness.

In the next article, we move from prosecution of crime to how crime gets reported. In "It's a Crime What Some People Do with Statistics," management professor Arnold Barnett uses the examples of capital punishment, homicide, and police stops to show that "certain statistics that are indeed highly misleading have made their way into debates about crime, punishment and race."

If you follow the news, the title of this chapter's final reading—"War Really Is Going Out of Style"—may seem hard to believe. But international relations professor Joshua Goldstein and psychology professor Steven Pinker show that the numbers of deaths attributed to war have declined over time. "We will always have the capacity to kill one another in large numbers," the authors write, "but with effort we can safeguard the norms and institutions that have made war increasingly repugnant."

Together, these authors describe a few of the complexities involved in understanding and responding to crime and violence.

Art History

"Another Report on the Age of Extinction," JOHN O'BRIAN

The first reading in this chapter, "Another Report on the Age of Extinction," was originally published in 2008 in the *Canadian Review of American Studies*. It is a reflective essay by John O'Brian, an art history professor at the University of British Columbia. O'Brian wrote the essay after attending an event at the historical Barnes Home in Piketon, Ohio. In the essay, he describes the ironic juxtaposition of images he found in the Barnes Home: "The rooms in the house have been arranged to tell a narrative, or rather to tell a succession of narratives that weave in and out of historical time and in and out of one another. The narratives add up. Their central themes are extinction and genocide."

ABSTRACT

This essay brings together the uneasy histories of the Scioto Culture and its monuments, the passenger pigeon and its extermination, and nuclear fuel and its waste, all within the eccentric spaces of the Barnes Home in Piketon, Ohio. The rooms in the house have been arranged to tell a narrative, or rather to tell a succession of narratives that weave in and out of historical time and in and out of one another. The narratives add up. Their central themes are extinction and genocide.

KEYWORDS

Atomic reservations, Barnes Home, nuclear waste, passenger pigeon, Piketon (Ohio), Scioto Culture, species extinction, Aldo Leopold, Geoffrey Sea

On 20 March 2006, the day following a memorial event in Pike County, Ohio, the *New York Times* reported on the death of Luna Leopold, the ecologist son of the pioneer ecologist Aldo Leopold, and commemorated the lives and work of father and son (Pearce). Luna was a hydrologist best known for his work on American rivers and, after Aldo died, helped to edit and publish his father's journals. As it happened, the obituary in the *Times* and the memorial ceremony in Ohio coincided with the celebration of the vernal equinox in many parts of the northern hemisphere. The holy day that marks the arrival of spring goes by many names, and its timing varies in some places according to the lunar calendar: among them are Alban Eilir, Passover, Eostar/Ostra/Easter, the Annunciation of the Blessed Virgin Mary, the Return of the Sun Serpent, and Nowruz.

The event in south-central rural Ohio was an ecological commemoration, on the one hand, and an equinoctial celebration with ancient roots, on the other. It took place on 19 March, a Sunday, at the property of Geoffrey Sea—health physicist, historian of nuclearism, and chronicler of the last days of the passenger pigeon—in the Barnes Home, at Sargents, near the town of Piketon.[1] More than forty people attended the proceedings, which began casually around noon, picked up speed toward sunset, and wound down after dark. Conviviality was the order of the day, just as it was the order of the day in Mexico City, Wroclaw, Isfahan, and Helsinki. In Mexico City, celebrants dressed in white for equinox festivities; in Isfahan they lit bonfires in the streets (though the theocratic regime in Tehran disapproved of the pre-Islamic Zoroastrian origins of the Nowruz holiday).

Sea had issued invitations to an "Equinox Celebration, Passenger Pigeon Commemoration, and Open House" at 1832 Wakefield Mound Road. I attended on behalf of Retort, a loose gathering of antagonists to capital and empire now based in the Berkeley area, with which I have been associated on and off for some two decades.[2] Four members of Retort recently published *Afflicted Powers*, a book arguing that permanent war and the modern state are inseparable.[3] Sea gave me driving instructions over the telephone. From the Comfort Inn where I was staying, I should travel south on the road, looking out for a large nineteenth-century red brick house with four chimneys located on a hill set back from the road, just past the old entrance to the uranium enrichment plant. From 1954 to 2001 the Piketon atomic plant produced the highest assay of weapons-grade uranium in the United States, used in fission triggers for thermonuclear bombs.[4] It is now slated to become a national nuclear dump, in part because of the failure of the Department of Energy to make a persuasive case for Yucca Mountain in Nevada as the US burial ground for high-level nuclear waste. I learned later that the eighty-eight acres of Sea's property stretched along part of the southern boundary of the atomic reservation, known locally as the A-Plant. The driveway to the house is only a few hundred feet beyond the A-Plant entrance and the vertical yellow poles that identify it.

Sea took possession of the Barnes Home in 2005. At the time of his move into the imposing house, the roof leaked, the panes of several windows were broken and some of the steps in the three staircases connecting the ground floor to the second—an indication of the structure's architectural eccentricities, as well as of its size—were of doubtful repair. They have now been fixed, but it may be some years yet before the house can be fully restored to its impressive nineteenth-century dignity. Sea has wasted no time in furnishing the rooms, hanging prints and photographs related to the building's extraordinary history, and moving books onto shelves and placing filing cabinets beneath the stairs. In the days before the open house, there was a push to ready the Barnes Home for visitors. Some of the rooms might not have been ready without the combined energies of preservationists working in tandem with students from Eastern High School, who were mobilized with brooms and dustpans and wore ID badges announcing that the "Eastern Eagles support Ancient and Modern History." By Sunday noon the house had been scrubbed clean and the old window glass sparkled in the sunlight.

The rooms in the house have been arranged to tell a narrative, or rather to tell a succession of narratives that weave in and out of historical time and in and out of one another. The narratives add up. Their central themes are extinction and genocide.

At the front of the house, to the right of the main stairs in the northwest corner of the second floor, is the Abraham Lincoln Room. A photograph of Lincoln, taken about the time he stayed in the room in 1848—he was nearing the end of his only term as a Congressman—sits on the mantel above the fireplace. Facing due west through the windows of his bedroom, Lincoln would have overlooked a complex set of enormous circles, squares and other geometric forms composed of earthen walls and mounds that were built by the Scioto Culture of the Middle Woodlands about two thousand years ago, during what is sometimes referred to as the Hopewell period. The people of this culture were sophisticated geometers; they measured the movements of the sun and the stars, to which the forms and alignments of the earthworks were precisely calibrated. The large circle of the complex enclosed twenty acres, the large square seventeen acres. The earthworks were described by Ephraim Squier and Edwin Davis in *Ancient Monuments of the Mississippi Valley*, the first volume ever published by the Smithsonian Institution and also the book that prompted Lincoln's visit (Squier and Davis). In speeches, Lincoln sometimes referred to the lost civilization whose monuments he had visited as an "inland empire."

The earthworks, called the "Seal Township Works" in the book and the "Barnes Works" today, are now separated from the Barnes Home by Wakefield Mound Road, the railway tracks and Route 23. Over the years, the monuments have been neglected. In the early 1950s, for example, when Route 23 was built to provide access for the workforce commuting to the A-Plant from Cincinnati and Columbus, sections of the monuments were damaged by the construction. Presently, another earthwork described by Squier and Davis, located about a mile north of the major complex of monuments, is also at risk of injury. It has a shape reminiscent of an alchemical alembic, and is clearly recognizable in aerial photographs of the region taken in the 1930s. The "Alembic" is located at the main entrance to the A-Plant, just at the point where it joins Route 23, a junction now under reconstruction. A new traffic sign sits on top of the old wall of the monument, pointing vehicles toward "Centrifuge Circle," a reference to the proposed new uranium enrichment plant that is scheduled to replace the old gaseous diffusion plant built in the early 1950s. The new plant is unlikely to be built. The sign is something of a ruse, it seems, a means of deflecting attention away from the implementation of the much more controversial nuclear waste facility being planned for the site of the old A-plant.[5]

There are as many twists and turns in the story of the Barnes Home and its surroundings as there are twists and turns in the nuclear saga currently unfolding in Iran. The house brings together the uneasy histories of the Scioto Culture and its monuments, the passenger pigeon and its extermination, and nuclear fuel and its waste.

On the north side of the ground floor of the house, next to the large parlour that was once used for entertaining and now contains a range of objects and materials relating to the passenger pigeon and nineteenth-century American culture, including a foot-powered dentist's drill once belonging to Sea's grandfather, is the Blanche Barnes Room. *Columba migratoria*, the Linnaean nomenclature for the passenger pigeon (or the American wild dove, as it was also called), was the most abundant bird on earth until its late nineteenth-century genocidal demise. Audubon described watching a mile-wide stream of the birds darken the skies above him for three days over the Ohio River in 1813. "The multitudes," he wrote, "are astounding."[6] Blanche Barnes was a skilled taxidermist. On or about 22 March 1900, she stuffed and mounted the last passenger pigeon ever seen in the wild, shot earlier in the day by Press Clay Southworth, and brought by him to the house from the kill site just down Wakefield Mound Road. A built-in cupboard in the room likely held her tools and potions, including the arsenic that was responsible for her death in childbirth three months later. The so-called Sargents Pigeon that she mounted was female, though inaccurate reporting has often identified the bird as male. Sea and his neighbors are lobbying to have the pigeon returned to the Barnes Home from the Ohio Historical Society in Columbus, where it now resides. They want it reunited with the kill site and the room in which it was gutted, stuffed, sewn, and mounted by Blanche Barnes.

The 19 March commemoration of the Sargents Pigeon in the Barnes Home was the first iteration of what is intended to become an annual event. Historically, the passenger pigeon flocks returned northward at the vernal equinox from their winter habitat around the Gulf of Mexico to begin the nesting season. Some of them traveled as far north as the south end of Hudson Bay, but their central nesting grounds were in the Ohio Valley and around the Great Lakes.[7] The birds were sacred to the Scioto Culture, and in a surprising and persuasive work of deductive analysis, Sea has concluded that certain of the earthworks were dedicated to them.[8] Among those who concur with Sea's analysis is Doug McIlwain, an attorney of Shawnee heritage. (The Shawnee are biological and cultural descendants of the Scioto Culture.) McIlwain was present at the open house and brought with him two boxes of ancient carved stones in the shape of eggs that he has been searching out and collecting, passing them around so that those in the room could feel their heft and coolness. The eggs may have occupied a significant place in ancient ceremonies concerning death and resurrection. Perhaps, not coincidentally, two famous birdstones—ancient polished stones in the shape of pigeon heads—were also found on the Barnes estate.

The Atomic Room, dedicated to the memory of the A-Plant's arrival in the early 1950s and arranged around a big space heater, is the coziest in the house. Presiding over this domestic hub, with its five doors, is a huge chrome lamp salvaged from the streets of New York, a collectible that only a committed connoisseur of "atomica" could love. It looks as if it is capable of emitting x-rays or radon gas. On the surface of a period coffee table lies the Fall 2004 edition of *Atomic Ranch*, a retro quarterly devoted to atomic-age furniture and design that was once popular in ranch houses and tract homes, and which is now undergoing a revival of sorts. The shelves in the room are filled with books and treatises on things nuclear. They contain Walt Disney's classic parable, *Our Friend the Atom* (1956), with illustrations by Disney's production staff; studies on the long-term effects of radiation poisoning in the workplace; the Atomic Energy Commission's *Atoms for Peace* (1958), prepared for the AEC by Arthur D. Little, Inc.; and Robert Jay Lifton and Greg Mitchell's *Hiroshima in America: Fifty Years of Denial* (1995).

The Atomic Room was the location chosen for the memorialization of the Sargents Pigeon. Susan Montauk, a professor of medicine at the University of Cincinnati and the recipient of many humanitarian awards, read aloud the essay "On a Monument to the Pigeon," Aldo Leopold's great lament for the passenger pigeon. The eulogy was written in 1947, the year before Leopold himself died while helping to fight a grass fire with neighbours. The fact that it was composed at the beginning of the atomic era is a recurring point of reference. "We grieve," wrote Leopold, "because no living man will see again the onrushing phalanx of victorious birds, sweeping a path for spring across the March skies, chasing the defeated winter from all the woods and prairies. . . ."[9] Not even Press Clay Southworth, who shot the last wild pigeon ever seen, witnessed the birds sweeping northward and darkening the skies of the Ohio Valley; by the time he was born the numbers of passenger pigeons migrating back and forth had dwindled to a trickle. The mechanized slaughter of this communal bird had started a "chain reaction" (Leopold's phrase) that quickly led to its extinction. If the human species had any claim to superiority over other species, Leopold concluded, it was not because of "Mr. DuPont's nylons or Mr. Vannevar Bush's bombs."[10] (Bush called his book on the Manhattan Project, a memoir of his role in the development of the project, *Modern Arms and Free Men*.)[11] It was because of the human ability to mourn; attention must be paid.

Shortly after 6 p.m., fifteen visitors followed Geoffrey Sea across a flat field to the southern edge of the Barnes property to observe the sunset and celebrate the vernal equinox. (The official equinox this year [2006] occurred eighteen hours later, at noon on 20 March.) The observation site selected by Sea was at the same alignment with the setting sun at equinox as the center of the great earthen square that was built below approximately two millennia ago. It is also the site of an ancient workshop that dates back at least ten thousand years. At 6:30 p.m., give or take a minute or so, the sun set in a notch between two hills on the far side of the monument, oblivious to the earthworks, the extermination of the passenger pigeon, and the building of uranium enrichment plants and nuclear waste dumps. A scattering of late afternoon cloud spilled the sun's rays unevenly across the hills.

NOTES

1. For many years, Geoffrey Sea served as a consultant to the Oil, Chemical, and Atomic Workers Union in Piketon. Please see his remarkable and evocative essay, "A Pigeon in Piketon," to which I am indebted.
2. Retort formed in the early 1980s in Cambridge, Massachusetts, under the name of the Pumping Station. I became associated with it at that time.
3. See Boal, Clark, Matthews, and Watts. A second edition appeared in 2006, which included an interview between the authors and Hal Foster acting on behalf of the editors of the journal *October*.
4. The plant is owned by the US Department of Energy. It is leased and operated by USEC Inc., which in its literature and on its website describes itself as "A Global Energy Company."
5. Draft of an article being prepared by Geoffrey Sea for publication.

6. See Audubon, "The Passenger Pigeon" and *Ornithological Biography* (1831–39).
7. There are two recent books on processes of extinction, including the fall of the passenger pigeon: Christopher Cokinos's *Hope Is the Thing with Feathers: A Personal Chronicle of Vanished Birds, and* Terry Glavin's *Waiting for the Macaws: and Other Stories from the Age of Extinctions.*
8. Sea's hypothesis is not yet published. He related it to me in conversation on 19 Mar. 2006, at the Barnes Home.
9. See Leopold 108–9.
10. See Leopold 110.
11. See Vannevar Bush. The writings of Hannah Arendt, especially *The Origins of Totalitarianism* and *On Violence,* are an effective antidote to the geo-political certainties expressed by Bush.

WORKS CITED

Arendt, Hannah. *On Violence*. New York: Harcourt Brace, 1969.
———. *The Origins of Totalitarianism*. New York: Meridian, 1958.
Audubon, John James. "On The Passenger Pigeon." *The Birds of America* (1827–38). 15 Jul. 2006 http://www.ulala.org/P_Pigeon/ Audubon_Pigeon.htm.
Audubon, John James. *Ornithological Biography* (1831–39). www.audubon.org/bird/boa/F29.
Boal, Iain, T.J. Clark, Joseph Matthews, and Michael Watts. *Afflicted Powers: Capital and Spectacle in a New Age of War.* London: Verso, 2005.
Bush, Vannevar. *Modern Arms and Free Men: A Discussion on the Role of Science in Preserving Democracy.* New York: Simon and Schuster, 1949.
Cokinos, Christopher. *Hope Is the Thing with Feathers: A Personal Chronicle of Vanished Birds.* New York: Warner, 2000.
Glavin, Terry. *Waiting for the Macaws: and Other Stories from the Age of Extinctions.* Toronto: Viking, 2006.
Leopold, Aldo. "On a Monument to the Pigeon." 1947. Rpt. in *A Sand County Almanac and Sketches Here and There.* New York: Oxford UP, 1987.
Pearce, Jeremy. "Luna Leopold, River Researcher, Is Dead at 90." *New York Times* 20 Mar. 2006.
Sea, Geoffrey. "News from the American Central Refuge." 27 Feb. 2006 boal@sonic.net.
———. *Ancient Monuments of the Mississippi Valley: Comprising the Results of Extensive Surveys and Explorations.* Washington, DC: Smithsonian, 1848.
USEC Inc. "A Global Energy Company." 1 August 2006 www.usec.com/v2001_02/HTML/aboutusec.asp.

QUESTIONS ABOUT MEANING

1. What lies to the west of the Barnes Home in Piketon, Ohio? And to the north? What events are commemorated in the Barnes Home? What do the events have in common?
2. How would you describe the purpose of O'Brian's essay?

QUESTIONS FOR RHETORICAL ANALYSIS

1. What does O'Brian suggest in the title "Another Report on the Age of Extinction"?
2. Reread the last two sentences of the essay. What do they suggest?

MAKING CONNECTIONS

1. As discussed by authors in chapter 14, a person's perspective influences what he or she "sees" and how he or she interprets events. As readers, we should consider where an author is coming from. Is it important to note, for instance, that O'Brian is affiliated with Retort, an "anti-capitalist" organization? Why do you think he mentions this? In what other ways is O'Brian's evaluation of the scene influenced by his vantage point? In an essay, discuss the importance of considering the background of the author when reading. Use examples from this anthology to illustrate how an author's vantage point shapes the writing.
2. In an essay, analyze how one or more of the following rhetorical elements help O'Brian achieve his purpose. Some questions are provided to help you get started.

   Word choice: How does O'Brian convey the historical and cultural significance of the Scioto Culture site? Conversely, how is the A-Plant described? How do the details and word choice convey O'Brian's attitude about the subject matter?

   Irony: Consider the ironic juxtaposition of images in and near the Barnes Home. How do contrasts and contradictions (e.g., between the past and present, life and death, etc.) create irony and enhance the essay and its message? What is the significance of Luna Leopold's death, alluded to in the first sentence? What's ironic (from our vantage point) about the titles of the Walt Disney children's books?

   Organization: What do you notice about how O'Brian has organized his ideas? What is the relationship between the various ideas?

History

"Getting Away with Murder," ELIZABETH DALE

Elizabeth Dale is a professor of history at the University of Florida. Her specialization is American legal history. In "Getting Away with Murder," originally published in *American Historical Review* in 2006, Dale analyzes verdict and sentencing patterns in murder cases. Drawing on several cases from antebellum South Carolina, Dale suggests explanations for why nineteenth-century Americans were "getting away with murder."

. . . More than a hundred years ago, Horace Redfield argued that many southerners killed because they believed that their local courts would treat them lightly or even let them escape punishment. More recent studies have established that Redfield was wrong to cast this as a distinctively southern phenomenon, but they have borne out his general premise: in the nineteenth-century United States, the courts tended to punish killers lightly, or not at all. These studies also suggest that when this practice came to an end, as it did around the start of the twentieth century, its demise reflected a shift in procedure, from trials to plea bargaining, not an increased aversion to homicide. But what are we to make of it? In his major study of homicide in New York City, Monkkonen argued that if we are ever going to understand homicide rates in the United States, we must learn why the legal system tolerated murder for so long. As simple as that formulation is, the reality behind it has been so complex as to make uncovering an explanation difficult. The "legal system," even in a single state, has always been a multi-headed beast that acts through a number of people and in a variety of ways, which means that the decision to tolerate a particular murder could have occurred at several points in the legal process, for a host of reasons. We need to give careful consideration to what happened at each of those points as we try to determine why and how the legal system responded to homicide the way it did.[1]

In the rest of this essay, I look at two particular points, verdict and sentencing, in a handful of cases from antebellum South Carolina to suggest the sorts of questions that need to be asked and to outline some of the tentative answers that scholars have begun to offer. I focus on South Carolina because it is notorious both for its murders and for its passive legal response to those killings. Redfield complained in his study that in the second half of the nineteenth century, South Carolinians killed each other "with too much rapidity," and he bemoaned the tepid legal response of the courts. In *Prison and Plantation,* Michael Hindus demonstrated that the same complaints could be made about the antebellum era: from 1800 to 1860, barely half (50.5 percent) of all people indicted for murder in the state were convicted of that offense. That certainly looks like a legal system that tolerated murder, but as I show below, that toleration, extensive as it was, came in many guises.[2]

The range of the problem is suggested by two cases that bookend the period. Both began with anger that escalated into homicidal rage. Sometime in the late afternoon on November 11, 1850, Felix Hubbard of Edgefield, South Carolina, interrupted a quarrel between his mother, Martha McClendon, and his stepfather, Britton McClendon. Words became acts, and Hubbard nicked Britton McClendon with an ax. Prudently, McClendon walked away, but only briefly. When he returned a few minutes later, Hubbard was ready. Using a pocketknife that he had borrowed to trim his nails, Hubbard stabbed his stepfather several times. McClendon quickly died. Not quite fifty years earlier, in 1806, John Slater, a ship captain and slave owner in Charleston, South Carolina, had become angry at one of his slaves, Abe, who was working at the dock. After having Abe bound hand and foot, Slater ordered another, unnamed slave to chop off Abe's head. That done, Slater threw Abe's remains into nearby Charleston Harbor.[3]

Both Hubbard and Slater were arrested and brought to trial, and both were treated lightly by the legal system. Hubbard was acquitted, and Slater, who was found guilty, was merely fined. But there the resemblance ends: in 1806, when Slater murdered Abe, the law in South Carolina provided, as it had for more than half a century, that the killing of a black, free or enslaved, was not murder. Rather, it was "the highest species of misdemeanor" known in law, a crime that was punishable only by a fine. Yet after a trial at which Slater was found guilty, "the proud jury," "deeply impressed with his daring outrage against the laws, both of God and man," offered what the trial judge characterized as "a very strong expression of their feelings" that Slater should be convicted of murder, and that the laws relating to the killings of slaves should be changed. After repeating those sentiments and deploring the fact that the laws of the state authorized such a "very slight punishment" for killers such as Slater, the trial judge concluded with regret that only the legislature could change the law to make the killing of a slave murder. Limited by the law, the judge ordered that Slater be fined, and he expressed the hope that social sanction and eternal punishment would make up for the legal system's failure.[4]

Far from condoning Slater's murder, the judge and jury punished Slater to the furthest extent allowed by law and wished they could do more. It is clear that they did not tolerate his murder of his slave, but it is less clear how significant their reactions were. One recent study argues that the Slater case exposed a legal system out of sync with popular sentiment, which increasingly viewed slaves and blacks as people entitled to the protections of the law. That suggests a split within the legal system, but the situation was not that straightforward. Notwithstanding the strong feelings of the jurors and judge in the Slater case, it was not until fifteen years later that the law in South Carolina was changed to provide that those who killed slaves could be prosecuted for murder. And even after this change in the law, whites in the state who were tried for murdering slaves were often treated lightly in the courts. When two white cattle rustlers were brought to trial in Colleton District, South Carolina, charged with murdering a slave named James while they were stealing cattle, they were acquitted of the murder and sentenced only to be whipped for the rustling. When a young slave named Green was stabbed to death in Edgefield, South Carolina, during a fight with an equally young white boy, Joseph Stalnaker, Stalnaker was charged with murder. But at his trial, the jury found him guilty only of manslaughter, and the judge never sentenced him, which suggests that his punishment was time served—the three months he had been in jail awaiting trial. Even at the end of the antebellum era, whites were found guilty of murdering a slave and punished severely only in the most extraordinary circumstances. A case in point occurred in 1849, when a jury found the planter Martin Posey guilty of murdering his slave Appling, after first finding that Posey had induced Appling to murder Posey's wife. After sentencing Posey to death for the murder of his wife, the trial judge sentenced him to death a second time for the murder of his slave. Both verdicts and sentences were upheld on appeal, and Posey was hanged.[5]

So the impassioned reaction during the Slater case did not mark a shift in attitudes that directly led to a change in the law; and even after the law finally did change, those who murdered slaves were treated lightly by the courts most of the time. What, then, distinguished those cases in which whites who murdered slaves met with little or no punishment from those in which a judge or jury contemplated more serious punishment? The difference does not seem to turn on the facts of the crime: we can attribute Slater's grisly execution of Abe to the hostile, if impotent, reaction to his crime, but Stalnaker, who literally disemboweled Green—prompting one witness at the coroner's inquest to refer to him as "a little son of a bitch, or probably a damn son of a bitch"—received a very light sentence even after changes in the law permitted a harsher punishment. Conversely, the killings of James and Appling were relatively straightforward murders, but the defendants in the former case received no punishment for their victim's death, while Appling's killer was executed.[6]

In an essay that discussed the murder of James, Bertram Wyatt-Brown suggested the possibility that verdicts were a function of class. In support of this interpretation, he offered the comments of David Gavin, a planter from Colleton County, who complained that the murderers "were acquitted by 'a dirty ragged ______ Jury.'"[7]

Gavin had a point: class was relevant to jury composition in antebellum South Carolina. Although the grand juries in the state were bastions of the elite, any white man in South Carolina who paid more than a dollar in property taxes could be called to serve on one of the petty juries that heard criminal cases. But while relatively poor men could sit on juries, it did not mean those juries were dominated by the poor. Wealthier men sat on petty juries as well, and often served as foremen. While I have been unable to obtain the necessary records for the Slater trial, or for the hearing on the murder of James, records I have found reveal that the juries that tried Joseph Stalnaker and Martin Posey were hardly composed of poor men. On the contrary: although Stalnaker was a very poor young man (he lived with his brother on a small farm without slaves, and according to the 1850 census, the brother owned no property of value), the average wealth in real estate held by the men who served as jurors in his case was $2,100, above the district mean of $2,038; and three of those men owned land worth $2,000 or more, while only one had no recorded real estate assets. In contrast, Posey was fairly well off; at the time of his trial, he held a thousand acres and more than twenty slaves, which placed him in the top quintile in Edgefield. The jurors who tried him for the murder of his wife were equally well off, with real estate worth an average of $4,000. The jury that tried him for the murder of his slave was not so wealthy: five of its members had no real estate assets, according to the 1850 census; but the four members of the jury who did have landholdings averaged $1,950 in real estate assets.[8] (I could find no records for three of the jurors.)

Thus, it would be an overstatement to say that "dirty ragged" jurors determined verdicts. However, the cases suggest that class may have been a factor in a slightly different way. We can assume that the cattle rustlers were poor, but we know that James's owner, Lewis Morris, was rich. According to the 1850 census, he owned more than 150 slaves and had property worth $50,000. Likewise, we know that Stalnaker was a poor young man, and we also know that John Cheatham, who owned Green, was a comparatively wealthy merchant with 13 slaves and real estate worth $1,500.[9] If the defendants in those two cases—both of whom were treated lightly by the jurors and the judge—were poor, the defendants in the other two cases were relatively well-off. Posey was a farmer with substantial holdings and a mill, and Slater, about whom I have been able to find less information, was a ship captain who was at the very least rich enough to own several slaves, including the man he killed. This raises the possibility that class played a double role: jurors, who determined guilt in the South Carolina legal system, were most outraged when elites—ship captains, slave owners, wealthy men—killed their own slaves, but they were less concerned with, or inclined to punish, poorer men who killed the slaves of others, even when (perhaps especially when) the owners of the slaves they killed were rich. These examples also hint that judges, who determined punishment in South Carolina, likewise were more inclined to punish wealthy men who killed their own slaves more harshly than poorer men who murdered the slaves of others. This suggests that the class of the killer, not the class of the jury, influenced the outcome in cases involving the murder of slaves.[10]

If class mattered in cases involving the killing of slaves by whites, what about cases in which whites killed whites? A close look at the Hubbard case, reading it in comparison to some others, suggests that class still played a role in these cases, but not in the same way. The grand jury indicted Felix Hubbard for the fatal stabbing of his stepfather; it also indicted his mother, Martha McClendon, as an accessory. They were tried separately, and the two sets of jurors came back with very different, even inconsistent, verdicts. Felix Hubbard was acquitted of murder at his trial; a few days later, a different jury found his mother guilty of manslaughter. The judge then sentenced her to two years in prison and read her a sharp lecture, which, unfortunately, no longer exists.[11]

In contrast to the Slater case, in which the jury's verdict was constrained by law, legal rules permitted the disparate outcomes in the McClendon murder trials. Hubbard's acquittal rested on self-defense, although it is not clear whether the jury concluded that he acted because he reasonably believed that McClendon intended to kill him, or whether they felt that he killed his stepfather because he feared that Britton intended to kill Martha. Either was legitimate grounds for an acquittal under well-established common-law principles and the established doctrine in South Carolina.[12] But while self-defense provided a legal justification for the verdict in Hubbard's case, the jurors were not compelled to find that he had acted in self-defense, and they could easily have concluded that Hubbard pursued the fight even after McClendon was no longer a threat. The jury made a choice, deciding to tolerate this particular killing. The jury in the trial of Martha McClendon had to make a second sort of choice, because while logic and the traditional English common-law precedents urged otherwise, as a matter of South Carolina law Hubbard's acquittal did not mean that his mother, on trial as his accessory, had to be found not guilty. Instead, South Carolina law allowed a jury to decide that an accessory was guilty even when the principal had been acquitted.[13] Once again, the key term is "allowed": the law did not compel the jury to find Martha McClendon guilty; it allowed it to do so. And once the jury had done so, the judge made a second choice, choosing to punish Martha McClendon more severely than Joseph Stalnaker had been punished for the murder of Green, and as severely as some white men were punished for killing other white men outright.[14]

If not the rules of law themselves, what inspired these conflicting verdicts for this single crime? At first glance, class and race seem to have been irrelevant: everyone involved was poor and white. According to the 1850 census, Britton McClendon was a farmer, but neither he nor his wife owned slaves or held real estate of any value. Felix Hubbard was even worse off; he worked as a laborer on someone else's farm. Hubbard's class may have benefited him at his trial, but the same class dynamic produced the opposite result in Martha McClendon's case. In a study of convictions in antebellum North Carolina, Laura Edwards offered one possible explanation for this variation, arguing that the sex of the defendant determined the legal system's response, with the result that white women were punished more harshly than white men. But while the Hubbard and McClendon verdicts seem consistent with this interpretation, the statistics for antebellum South Carolina do not bear it out. In his study of antebellum crime, Jack Kenny Williams concluded that white women charged with crimes were convicted at the same (low) rate as white men and given roughly the same sorts of punishment.[15]

A look at the results in some other cases in which women and men were accused of working together to kill, however, suggests that there was a South Carolina variant on Edwards's argument. Although Martin Posey was tried, convicted, and executed for murdering first his wife and then his slave, his lover, Eliza Posey (she married him after his arrest), was never indicted, let alone tried, even though several witnesses testified that she had goaded Posey into committing the murders. When Elizabeth Cannon and her lover, Joshua Nettles, were tried together for murdering her husband as he slept, Nettles was convicted and sentenced to death, while Cannon went free. It is difficult to reconstruct women's wealth from the available records, but such evidence as there is suggests that both these women were from relatively wealthy families—far richer, at least, than Martha McClendon. In contrast, when Elizabeth Green—who seemed to be closer in economic status to McClendon than to Cannon—had a slave kill her husband, Henry, in 1836, she was found guilty and convicted; the male slave who was charged with helping her was acquitted. These cases raise the possibility that when white women were charged with aiding and abetting in the murder of white men, class determined the outcome for them. Poorer white women were subject to the censure of both judges and jurors, while wealthy women were more likely to be exempted from prosecution, or to be acquitted if tried.[16]

These cases suggest that at one level David Gavin was right: class (in concert with other factors, particularly the defendant's sex) determined whom the legal system would find guilty of murder and whom it would acquit. But did that mean that people got away with murder in antebellum South Carolina? Perhaps not, for reasons suggested by the judge's opinion in the Slater case. After bemoaning the fact that the legal system would not punish Slater sufficiently, the judge expressed the hope that society (and if society failed, God) would punish him instead. The anonymous author of a published report on the trial of Martin Posey made a similar remark with respect to Eliza Posey, wondering if she would be punished for her crime by the women of her community. Such evidence as there is suggests that she was shamed and shunned until she remarried and moved away.[17]

South Carolina's enthusiasm for extralegal justice in the nineteenth century is well-established, but historians have typically focused on the role it played in creating a culture of violence within the state. What if we reversed that examination and asked instead what role, if any, extralegal justice played in punishment, and to what extent it functioned as an alternative to the legal system? We could, and should, consider how many duels were "tolerated," even when they led to killings, because they functioned in place of law. Taking the hints offered in the Slater and Posey cases, we could expand that inquiry to consider whether shame and ostracism also were used to punish those whom the legal system did not. We need to explore the possibility that acquittal was not a sign that defendants suffered no punishment, and we must look beyond the courts to see whether the communities they lived in relied on other, extralegal means to punish them for their crimes. Taken in combination with evidence about who was acquitted and in what sorts of cases, this would give us a much more complete understanding of when and why the legal system tolerated homicide, and whether that meant that society tolerated it as well.[18]

Of course, to find that out, we need to continue the sustained examination of homicides that marked Eric Monkkonen's career, pushing his inquiries even further. In addition to trying to track down homicides, we need to dig deep for the facts that determined outcomes in particular cases and trace broad patterns through the study of many prosecutions. And we need to look beyond the legal outcomes, to see whether those who escaped the punishment of the courts were punished through extralegal processes. Only when we have done all that will we really understand homicide in the United States.

ACKNOWLEDGMENT

I worked on this article while on a Fulbright in Jinan, People's Republic of China. As a result, I am indebted to several people: Joseph Spillane,

Matthew Bewig, and Steven Tuttle, of the South Carolina Department of Archives and History, who helped me check some records I could not easily check myself. I also benefited from some observations offered by Jeffrey Adler, Douglas Eckberg, and Al Brophy in response to queries.

NOTES

1. H. V. Redfield, *Homicide North and South,* ed. Douglas Eckberg (1880; repr., Columbus, Ohio, 2000). For some recent studies that reveal the scope of the problem beyond the South, see Roger Lane, *Murder in America: A History* (Columbus, Ohio, 1997); Laura F. Edwards, "Law, Domestic Violence, and the Limits of Patriarchal Authority in the Antebellum South," *Journal of Southern History* 65 (November 1999): 733–770; Roger Lane, *Violent Death in the City: Suicide, Accident and Murder in Nineteenth-Century Philadelphia,* 2nd ed. (Columbus Ohio, 1999); Eric Monkkonen, *Murder in New York City* (Berkeley, Calif., 2001); Jeffrey S. Adler, "'Halting the Slaughter of the Innocents': The Civilizing Process and the Surge in Violence in Turn-of-the-Century Chicago," *Social Science History Journal* 25 (2001): 29–52; Elizabeth Dale, "Not Simply Black and White: Jury Power and Law in Late Nineteenth-Century Chicago," *Social Science History Journal* 25 (2001): 7–27; Clare V. McKanna, Jr., *Race and Homicide in Nineteenth-Century California* (Reno, Nev., 2002). Lane's work, in particular, examines the role of plea bargaining in changing this pattern.
2. Redfield, *Homicide,* 108 (quote). Michael Hindus, *Prison and Plantation: Crime, Justice, and Authority in Massachusetts and South Carolina, 1767–1878* (Chapel Hill, N.C., 1980), 90–91 and Table 4.3. Hindus also found that in the antebellum era, very few homicide cases—slightly more than a third (37.5 percent) of all cases—resulted in a conviction. See also Jack Kenny Williams, *Vogues in Villainy: Crime and Retribution in Ante-bellum South Carolina* (Columbia, S.C., 1959).
3. McClendon case: South Carolina Department of Archives and History, Columbia, South Carolina (SCDAH), Coroner's Inquisition Book, 1844–1850, Edgefield District, South Carolina, *State v. the Body of Britton McClendon,* hearing dated November 11, 1850; entry for Britton McClendon, 1840 Manuscript Census, Schedule I: Free Inhabitants of Edgefield District, South Carolina. Slater case: South Caroliniana Library, University of South Carolina, Columbia, South Carolina, Joshua Sharpe Papers, Sentence of Judge Welds in *People v. John Slater,* 1806. See also Jeffrey Robert Young, *Domesticating Slavery: The Master Class in Georgia and South Carolina, 1670–1837* (Chapel Hill, N.C., 1999), 132–133.
4. Williams, *Vogues in Villainy,* 36 (laws relating to the murder of slaves); John Belton O'Neall, *The Negro Law of South Carolina* (Columbia, S.C., 1848), 19. The quotes are from Sentence of Judge Welds in *People v. John Slater,* 1806. Another, longer version of what purports to be the opinion is found in John Belton O'Neall, *Biographical Sketches of the Bench and Bar of South Carolina* (Charleston, S.C.,1859), 103–104; it contains an entire paragraph (the second) that is not in the handwritten copy on file in the South Caroliniana Library. As O'Neall notes (ibid., 104), there is no record of what fine Slater was assessed.
5. Stoner case: Young, *Domesticating Slavery,* 132–133 (this case shows a shift in theories of the humanity of slaves [and blacks] in the state).

Murder of James: Bertram Wyatt-Brown, "Community, Class, and Snopesian Crime: Local Justice in the Old South," in Orville Vernon Burton and Robert C. McGrath, eds., *Class Conflict and Consensus: Antebellum Southern Community Studies* (Westport, Conn., 1982), 173, 190–191. Stalnaker case: SCDAH, Coroner's Inquisition Book for Edgefield District, South Carolina, 1844–1850, *State v. the body of the negro boy Green,* hearing dated July 3, 1850; SCDAH, Minutes, General Sessions, Edgefield County, Criminal Journal, Fall Term 1850, 75 (indictment, *People v. Stalnaker*); ibid., 79 (verdict, *People v. Stalnaker*); *Edgefield Advertiser,* July 24, 1850, 2 (misspelling Stalnaker as "Stonecker"); *Edgefield Advertiser,* October 16, 1850, 2. Posey case: *South Carolina v. Martin Posey,* 35 S.C. 142 (1849) (Appling murder); *South Carolina v. Martin Posey,* 35 S.C. 103 (1849) (murder of his wife, Matilda); Elizabeth Dale, "A Different Sort of Justice: The Informal Courts of Public Opinion in Antebellum South Carolina," *South Carolina Law Review* 54 (Spring 2003): 627, 634–635.

6. SCDAH, Coroner's Inquisition Book for Edgefield District, South Carolina, 1844–1850, *State v. the body of the negro boy Green* (details of the murder and the quotes about Stalnaker).

7. Wyatt-Brown, "Community, Class, and Snopesian Crime," 191 (Gavin's comments about the verdict).

8. The average for the Stalnaker jury takes into account the nine jurors I could identify in the 1850 census; if the other three are figured in, the average value of their holdings drops to $1,300. SCDAH, Minutes, General Sessions, Edgefield County, Criminal Journal, Fall Term 1850, 79 (verdict, *People v. Stalnaker,* listing jurors); 1850 Manuscript Census, South Carolina, Edgefield District, Microfilm Roll M432_852; ibid., 23 (showing that 15-year-old Joseph lived with 32-year-old Washington Stalnaker, a farmer whose property, in contrast to that of the farmers listed around him on the census, had no recorded value; Washington Stalnaker also owned no slaves). See also Burton, *My Father's House,* 40–41 (income distributions in Edgefield). Posey juries: SCDAH, Minutes, General Sessions, Edgefield County, Criminal Journal, Fall Term 1849, 43 (verdict, *People v. Martin Posey* [Matilda murder], listing jurors); SCDAH, Minutes, General Sessions, Edgefield County, Criminal Journal, Fall Term 1849, 46 *(People v. Martin Posey* [Appling murder], listing jurors).

9. 1850 Manuscript Census, South Carolina, Colleton District, 265, Microfilm Roll M432_851 (entry Lewis Morris, property valued at over $50,000); 1850 Slave Census, Colleton District, South Carolina (entry Lewis Morris, owns 160 slaves); 1860 Slave Census, Colleton District, South Carolina (entry Lewis Morris, owns more than 160 slaves). Williams, *Vogues in Villainy,* 80–83 (roles and status of judges and jurors in antebellum South Carolina); Wyatt-Brown, *Southern Honor,* 390–391. On class in the antebellum South, and antebellum South Carolina in particular, see generally Stephanie McCurry, *Masters of Small Worlds: Yeoman Households, Gender Relations, and the Political Culture of the Antebellum South Carolina Low Country* (New York, 1995); Donald L. Winters, "The 'Plain Folk' of the Old South Re-examined: Economic Democracy in Tennessee," *Journal of Southern History* 53 (1987): 565–586.

10. 1850 Manuscript Census, Edgefield District, South Carolina, Microfilm Roll M432_852 (entry under John Cheatham, listing occupation); 1850 Slave Census, Edgefield District, South Carolina (entry under John Cheatham, owns 13 slaves). On Posey's wealth, see the testimony of Collin Rhodes, *Report of the Trial of Martin Posey for the Murder of His Wife, Matilda H. Posey* (Edgefield, S.C., 1850), 21.
11. SCDAH, Minutes, General Sessions, Edgefield County, Criminal Journal, Spring Term 1851, 92 (indictment, *People v. Felix Hubbard*); ibid., 94 (indictment, *People v. Martha McClendon*); ibid., 96–97 (trial and verdict, *People v. Hubbard*); ibid., 100 (trial, *People v. McClendon*); ibid., 101 (sentencing, *People v. McClendon*). The only reference to Judge Frost's "impressive address" to Martha McClendon during sentencing is a note in the *Edgefield Advertiser* that it occurred; March 20, 1850, 2.
12. For South Carolina law relating to self-defense, see *State v. Ferguson,* 2 Hill 618 (S.C. 1835); *State v. McCants,* 1 Speers 384 (S.C. 1843). The common-law doctrine relating to killings undertaken in defense of oneself and others is summarized in William Blackstone, *Commentaries on the Laws of England* (Dublin, 1769): "Under this excuse of self-defense, the principal civil and natural relations are comprehended; therefore master and servant, parent and child, husband and wife, killing an assailant in the necessary defense of each other respectively, are excused; the act of the relation assisting being construed the same as the act of the party himself."
13. For the cases dealing with situations in which one person kills another through a third party, see the discussion in *State v. Martin Posey,* 35 S.C. 103 (1849) (conviction for the murder of Matilda Posey affirmed). On accessories to murder, compare Blackstone, *Commentaries,* 4: 34–35, with the different rule in South Carolina, which provided that an accomplice could be charged for an offense even if the principal was not found guilty. *State v. Putnam,* 18 S.C. 175 (1882) (where three were charged with manslaughter, the jury found that the principal acted in the heat of passion, and hence was not guilty of manslaughter, but the court held that it was not an error for the jurors to find the accomplices guilty of manslaughter). Although *Putnam* was decided after the McClendon case, the court cited cases from around the time of the McClendon case in support of its ruling, including *People* v. *Posey. Putnam,* 18 S.C. at 177–178.
14. For some cases that suggest the range of sentences given to white men who murdered other white men in Edgefield District, see SCDAH, Coroner's Inquisition Book, Edgefield District, South Carolina, 1844–1850, *State* v. *the Body of Benjamin Jones* (Price shot Jones in store); Minutes, General Sessions, Edgefield District, South Carolina, Fall Term 1845, Microfilm Roll ED 85, October 11, 1845 (sentencing, *People v. Price,* one year in jail); SCDAH, Coroner's Inquisition Book, Edgefield District, South Carolina, 1844–1850, *State v. Body of William Bailey,* hearing dated June 19, 1846, 57 (Prince stabbed Bailey to death in dispute over button); SCDAH, Minutes, General Sessions, Edgefield District, Criminal Journal, Fall Term 1846, Microfilm Roll ED 85, October 8, 1846 (trial and sentencing, *People* v. *Prince,* five years in jail).

15. Edwards, "Law, Domestic Violence, and the Limits of Patriarchal Authority" (also noting that the race of the defendant mattered). In South Carolina, where blacks, free or enslaved, were tried in a different court system, under different rules, it is nearly impossible to test the racial component of her thesis. Entry for Britton McClendon, 1850 Manuscript Census for Edgefield District, South Carolina, Microfilm Roll M432_852 (entry for Britton McClendon, did not own slaves); ibid. (entry for Felix Herbert [*sic*], no slaves). On South Carolina's conviction rates for men and women, see Williams, *Vogues in Villainy*, 20–23.
16. Dale, "A Different Sort of Justice" (Posey case and the treatment of Eliza). Because women who were not heads of households were not listed in the census before 1850, I have had to rely on legal records for evidence about the relative status of Elizabeth Cannon and Elizabeth Green. See S. C. Carpenter, *Report of the Trial of Joshua Nettles and Elizabeth Cannon for the Murder of John Cannon* (Charleston, S.C., 1805); *State v. Elizabeth Green*, which is reprinted in its entirety as an extensive footnote in *State v. Martin Posey*, 35 S.C. 103, 129–140 (1849). The 1830 Manuscript Census for South Carolina does not list a Henry Green in Union County; there is, however, a Henry Green in Anderson District, South Carolina, who seems to fit the description in the case. He was between 40 and 50 years old in 1830 and had a much younger wife (between 20 and 30 years of age). They had six children, but no slaves. 1830 Manuscript Census for South Carolina, Roll 173 (entry Henry Green). More significantly, he does not appear in the 1840 census for South Carolina. Assuming that he was Elizabeth Green's husband, their economic status was closer to that of Martha McClendon and Felix Hubbard [than] to that of Elizabeth Cannon and Joshua Nettles or to Martin Posey and his lover, Eliza.
17. South Caroliniana Library, University of South Carolina, Columbia, South Carolina, Joshua Sharpe Papers, Sentence of Judge Welds in *People v. John Slater*, 1806.
18. Dale, "An Informal Court" (discussing Eliza Posey case). This sort of inquiry may reinforce conclusions about the influence of class; at least one antebellum commentator asserted that social sanction was the only punishment recognized by the elite. Sidney George Fisher, *A Philadelphia Perspective: The Diary of Sidney George Fisher Covering the Years 1834–1874* (Philadelphia, 1967), 155–156. Fisher was discussing a case from Philadelphia, but that does not mean that the same principle might not obtain in southern states.

Elizabeth Dale is Associate Professor of Legal History in the Department of History at the University of Florida, where she is also an affiliate professor at Levin College of Law. She teaches American Legal History and Comparative Constitutional History, is completing a study of common law and the Constitution in nineteenth-century America, and is beginning work on a study of constitutional debates in China, 1898–1919.

written permission. However, users may print, download, or email articles for individual use.

QUESTIONS ABOUT MEANING

1. What does *antebellum* mean? What percentage of people indicted for murder in antebellum South Carolina were convicted? Why does Dale provide this statistic in the introduction to her essay? (What purpose does the statistic serve?)
2. To what extent did class play a role in explaining the uneven punishments for murder in the nineteenth century? Explain and illustrate. What other factors affected verdicts for those guilty of murder?
3. As with most scholarly articles, Dale's article concludes with a look forward. What additional questions and areas of research does Dale recommend historians pursue?

QUESTIONS FOR RHETORICAL ANALYSIS

1. The long paragraphs—common for articles in *American Historical Review*—slow a person's reading rate, but many paragraphs include an early topic sentence that summarizes the main idea. Highlight examples of topic sentences. Then, divide the article into sections and provide headings that would further prepare readers for the main ideas.
2. In addition to footnotes documenting the information obtained from others, explanatory notes are common in historical writing. What kinds of information does Dale provide in her explanatory notes? What ethos does Dale create by including these notes?
3. What is the purpose of the article and where is it stated? Dale provides only a "handful of cases" as evidence. Is that sufficient, given her purpose? What are the strengths and weaknesses of the evidence she cites?

MAKING CONNECTIONS

1. Dale and Allen both consider factors leading to arrest or conviction, but because of the periods they study, their methods are very different. In an essay, compare and analyze their goals and research methods. What advantages/strengths and what disadvantages/weaknesses are inherent with the kinds of research methods they employ? Could the writers have used additional or different means of gathering data to achieve their purposes? Explain.
2. "In trying to explain violence, it is myopic to focus solely on the perpetrator . . . because murder is rarely a random act between strangers," note

Christakis and Fowler (chapter 13). Is their claim supported by the cases Dale analyzes? In an essay, combine insights and examples from Christakis and Fowler and Dale, and add examples of your own from local or national news to either support or counter the claim that "murder is rarely a random act between strangers."

Social Work

"Taking a Juvenile into Custody: Situational Factors That Influence Police Officers' Decisions," TERRENCE T. ALLEN

What factors increase the likelihood that a police officer takes a juvenile into custody? This is the question that prompted the exploratory research described in the next article, written by Terrence T. Allen, a professor of social work.

In an exploratory study, the goal is not to test a hypothesis but rather to learn more about an issue or problem. The researcher gathers information needed to determine what questions to ask and what research design and data collection methods to use in a more formal study. "Taking a Juvenile into Custody: Situational Factors That Influence Police Officers' Decisions" was originally published in 2005 in the peer-reviewed *Journal of Sociology and Social Welfare*.

Situational factors that influence police officers' decisions to take juveniles into custody were investigated. A cross-sectional self-administered survey was conducted. Four-hundred and twenty-eight male and female police officers from six police districts in Cleveland, Ohio, completed and submitted a twenty-five item questionnaire. Using a logistic regression model the study identified: adolescents who disrespect police officers; adolescents who are out late at night; adolescent males; anyone looking suspicious; and the age of the police officer as the most significant predictors. This was an exploratory study that sought to investigate police/juvenile encounters from a street level situational perspective. The results provided a basis for continued research in this area of inquiry.

KEYWORDS

juvenile, custody, police officers, adolescent male

INTRODUCTION

Today, police officers hold a unique and powerful position in our criminal justice system. Unlike judges and prosecutors, they make decisions on the streets and out of the public spotlight. Consequently, they exercise a wide range of discretion and power over who will be subject to legal intervention and social control (Smith & Visher, 1981). Police officers patrol in urban communities that are inundated with high unemployment, disinvestments, and crumbling infrastructures. In these communities there are disproportionate rates of illiteracy and high levels of drug activity, both of which are symptoms of social forces that weaken social control. It is reasonable to expect such conditions to influence how police officers perceive and interpret the behavior and conduct of youth. Moreover, it is within these contexts that the stage is set for understanding factors that influence police officers' decisions about taking juveniles into custody. These contexts set the boundaries within which a number of factors can join together including the formation of specific situations in which police officers and youth interact, and the transactions that trigger the actual decision to take youth into custody. Because of the powerful implications of police discretion, the point of interest in this paper is those factors that influence police officers' decisions to take juveniles into custody. The aim of this paper is to identify situations and circumstances that may increase the probability that police officers will take juveniles into custody.

RELATED LITERATURE

Very few researchers interested in the decision making process within the juvenile justice system have studied factors that influence police officers' decisions to take juveniles into custody. Most researchers have focused on process decisions made after juveniles have been arrested and their primary interest has been on race effects at various decision points throughout the juvenile justice system (Wordes, 1994; Wu, 1997; Wu & Fuentes, 1998). Morash's study (1984) is an exception. She found among other things that being male increases the chance of being taken into custody. Not since then has any research focused on factors that influence the decision to take juveniles into custody beyond the issue of race. Other scholars suggest that the demeanor of a suspect is the most influential determinant in shaping a police officer's decision to take a juvenile into custody (Ludman, 1996; Skolinick & Fyfe, 1993; Worden & Shepard, 1996). Klinger (1994) stands alone in his position that previous findings are of questionable validity because the research has conceived and measured demeanor improperly.

Only a few studies have focused specifically on police encounters with juveniles (Pope & Synder, 2003) which is not surprising because these encounters are rather difficult to measure. They tend to be nonviolent, low-profile events that take place spontaneously on the streets. The number of juveniles taken into custody for violent crimes in which police have little to no discretion declined by 41% between 1991 and 2000

(Synder, 2002). However, during that same period, the number of juveniles taken into custody for drug abuse violations increased by 145% and curfew and loitering violations increased by 81% (Snyder, 2002). These encounters, in addition to vandalism, disorderly conduct, vagrancy and runaways, are events that make youth visible within their communities and, therefore, help shape police officers' decisions to take young people into custody.

Of the four studies that specifically examine police/juvenile encounters (Pillivan & Briar, 1964; Black & Reiss, 1970; Ludman, Sykes & Clark, 1970; Morash, 1984) none use police officers as the primary source of information. It is virtually impossible to measure the stress and strain that police officers must endure on a daily basis and how it affects their decision-making without asking them directly. Analyzing records and observing behavior cannot capture the essence of the decision-making process.

While I can assert that situational factors are important, I cannot say with certainty which ones are most influential, an observation that supports the need for the research this paper summarizes and one that justifies an exploratory approach. This research provides an impetus for juvenile justice researchers to investigate the interaction between juveniles and police officers in urban communities. The question of what factors (other than race) influence police officers' decisions to take juveniles into custody is not fully appreciated in juvenile justice research.

RESEARCH DESIGN

The participants in this study were drawn from the Cleveland Police Department in Cleveland, Ohio. One hundred questionnaires were passed out at each of six police districts. Four hundred and twenty-eight usable questionnaires were returned completed for a total response rate of 71%. The participants were asked twenty-five force choice questions related to their interactions with juveniles as Cleveland police officers. The questionnaire included questions that measured the qualities of the communities where respondents patrolled, the perceived relationship between respondents and the communities where they patrolled, and their perceptions of adolescents in these communities. The instrument was developed to measure areas of juvenile justice research that had been previously ignored in the literature. Thus the exploratory nature of this study sought to provide a basis for continued research.

The primary concern was to collect baseline data that could be used to develop a more reliable instrument in the future to measure a police officer's decision to take a juvenile into custody. To the extent that validity was tested the criterion used was face validity. The researcher in this study developed an instrument to measure a police officer's decision to take a juvenile into custody based on the literature and his personal interest. However, the researcher does not contend that the instrument is either reliable or valid, but suggests that the absence of available, tested instruments is evidence of the need for juvenile justice researchers to develop instruments that can accurately measure the interaction between juveniles and police officers.

RESEARCH FINDINGS

The logistic regression model reported in Table 1 identifies the five strongest predictors in the study regarding a police officer's decision to take a juvenile into custody. The odd ratios statistic put into perspective the likelihood that a police officer would take a juvenile into custody under a specific set of circumstances. For example, the strongest predictors of "The Decision to Take a Juvenile into Custody" were the respondents' agreement with a series of statements (1) Adolescents who disrespect police officers should be taken into custody (2) Adolescents who are out late at night are probably committing a delinquent act (3) Adolescent males have a more suspicious demeanor than female adolescents (4) Anyone looking suspicious of committing a delinquent act should be stopped and questioned. The age of a police officer was a factor.

Table 1
Logistic Regression Odds/Ratios for the Decision to Take Juveniles into Custody

Step	*Variable*	*Nagelkerke R Square*	*Level of Significance*	*Odd/Ratio*	*95% Confidence Interval Low*	*Upper*
Step 1						
	Disrespect	.179	.000	4.96	3.12	7.96
Step 2						
	Late	.286	.000	4.15	2.51	6.84
	Disrespect		.000	4.59	2.80	7.51
Step 3						
	Demeanor		.000	2.46	1.49	4.04
	Late		.000	3.56	2.13	5.97
	Disrespect	.324	.000	4.69	2.83	7.79
Step 4						
	Look		.000	3.42	1.68	6.99
	Demeanor		.000	2.43	1.46	4.03
	Late		.000	3.46	2.05	5.86
	Disrespect	.361	.000	4.29	2.56	7.19
Step 5						
	Age		.024	.957	.921	.994
	Look		.000	3.32	1.62	6.83
	Demeanor		.000	2.41	1.45	4.02
	Late		.000	3.28	1.93	5.58
	Disrespect	.376	.000	4.15	2.47	6.96

The results from this analysis suggest that adolescents who disrespect these police officers are four times more likely to be taken into custody. If it is late at night and they look suspicious they are more than three times more likely to be taken into custody. And if they have a suspicious demeanor they are two times more likely to be taken into custody. The arresting officer will probably be younger than 34 years of age. These five predictors provided insightful and useful information toward understanding factors that contribute to police officers' decision to take juveniles into custody. In this study the notion of "respect" and "suspicious demeanor" was intentionally not conceptualized. It was left open to the discretion of the observing officer. To limit them to a specific definition would have been a disservice to the goals and objectives of the research. The range of behaviors that influence police decisions cannot be captured in a forced choice statement.

DISCUSSION

Disrespect. More than three fourths (76%) of police officers agreed with the statement that "adolescents who disrespect police officers should be taken into custody." It was the strongest predictor of whether or not a police officer would make an arrest, an observation consistent with previous literature (Ludman, 1996; Skolinick & Fyfe, 1993; Worden & Shepard, 1996). It is assumed that police officers expect to be treated with respect because of their status, and the perception of lack of respect might motivate some officers to exercise their authority to take a juvenile into custody.

On the streets late at night. "Adolescents who are out late at night are probably committing a delinquent act." Police officers were asked this question because presumably delinquency is more prevalent at night than at any other time. Consequently, police officers' level of anxiety may be heightened at night because of the increased possibility of a delinquent act occurring. Therefore they are more likely to take juveniles into custody if they encounter them exhibiting suspicious behavior at night. Almost three fourths (73%) of police officers agreed that if an adolescent is out late at night he/she is probably committing a delinquent act.

More suspicious demeanor. While suspicious demeanor is a matter of perception, it may be also gender related. The criminal justice literature clearly supports the notion that adolescent males are more prone to be involved in delinquent activities than are female adolescents, especially if there are two or more of them together (Conley, 1994). The officers in this study overwhelmingly (86%) agreed that if two or more males are together they are probably committing a delinquent act.

Need to stop and question. Suspicious demeanor might also be race related. Pillivan & Briar (1964) found that the criteria police officers used to stop and question potential suspects were a result of their perception of suspicious behavior. Type of clothing worn, hair style, and facial expressions unique to African American youth were considered indicators of suspicious behavior. This study allowed participants to determine what "suspicious behavior" is, and respond based upon that judgment. Today, unlike forty years ago, there are a significant number of African American police officers patrolling urban communities. Therefore it is necessary to revisit this issue because African American police officers should be sensitive to these stereotypes and not let them influence their interactions with juveniles. That is, they should be less inclined than non-African Americans to perceive a youth as "suspicious" simply because they dress or act a certain way. The majority (61%) of the police officers participating in this study believe that anyone looking suspicious should be stopped and questioned.

The age of the police officer. The mean age of police officers participating in this study was 34 years old. [That] in this research the older and more experienced police officers were less likely to take juveniles into custody is noteworthy for future research.

The decision to take a juvenile into custody is perhaps the most important decision in the juvenile justice process because it can have far-reaching and devastating implications on the life chances of juveniles who are subjected to the harsh and punitive life-style of juvenile institutions. Being taken into custody can perpetuate "a loss of social status, restrictions of educational and employment opportunities and future harassment by law enforcement personnel as well as the possible formation of a deviant self-concept and the amplification of future misbehavior" (Dorne & Gewerth, 1995, p. 90). This is particularly true with African American juveniles who are four times more likely to be taken into custody than white juveniles (Snyder, 2002). Being taken into custody does not in and of itself assure that one will be charged with a crime. However, the likelihood of being charged is increased when a juvenile suspected of engaging in delinquent activity is taken into custody. Observation of suspicious behavior is probable cause for stopping a youth. What is suspicious behavior is strictly a discretionary call on behalf of the observing police officer. As a result, there is an extreme amount of latitude offered to police officers when making the decision to take a youth into custody (Snyder, 1995).

The basis of this article is that the nature of juvenile/police interaction is influenced by the situation and circumstances under which police officers and juveniles interact. This paper has identified five factors that researchers have given little consideration when considering factors that influence police officers' decisions to take juveniles into custody. Although the five factors identified only explained 38% of the variance, leaving 62% unexplained, the significance of these findings raises some interesting queries that should not go unnoticed. This is not to say or suggest that other possible factors such as crime, race and social class are unimportant, however, it is to suggest that perhaps a new paradigm of examining police/juvenile encounters should be considered.

REFERENCES

Conley, D. J. (1994). Adding color to a black and white picture: Using qualitative data to explain racial disproportionality in the juvenile justice system. *Journal of Research in Crime and Delinquency*, 31 (2) 135–148.

Dorne, C. & Gewerth, K. (1995). *American Juvenile Justice: Cases, legislation & comments*. Austin & Winfield. San Francisco Ca.

Kurtz, P. D., Giddings, M. M., & Sutphen, R. (1993). A prospective investigation of racial disparity in the juvenile justice system. *Juvenile and Family Court Journal*, 44 (3), 43–59.

Lundman, Sykes, & Clark (1970). Police controls of juveniles: A replication. In Rubin (Eds.), *Juveniles in justice: A book of readings* p. 158. California, Goodyear Publishing Co.

Lundman, R. J. (1996). Extralegal variables and arrest. *Journal of Research in Crime and Delinquency*, 33 (3), 349–353.

Morash, M. (1984). Establishment of a juvenile police record. *Criminology*, 22 (1), 97–111.

Piliavin, I., & Briar, S. (1964). Police encounters with juveniles. *American Journal of Sociology*, 70.

Pope, C. E. & Feyerherm, W. (1990). Minority status and juvenile justice processing. *Criminal Justice Abstracts*, 22 (2), 327–336.

Pope, C. & Snyder, H. (2003). *Race as a factor in juvenile arrests*. Juvenile Justice Bulletin. Office of Juvenile Justice Bulletin.

Skolnick, J. & Fyfe, J. (1993). *Above the law: Police and the use of force*. New York: Free Press.

Smith, D. A. & Visher, C. A. (1981). Street level justice-situational determinants of police arrest decisions. *Social Problems* (10), 2.

Snyder, H. N. (2002). *Juvenile arrests 2000*. U.S. Department of Justice, Washington, DC, USGPO.

Worden, R. E. & Shepard, R. L. (1996). Demeanor, crime, and police behavior: A reexamination of the police services study data. *Criminology*, 34. pp. 83–105.

Wordes, M. T. (1994). Locking up youth: The impact of race on detention decisions. *Journal of Research in Crime and Delinquency*, 31, 149–165.

Wu, B. (1997). The effects of race on juvenile justice processing. *Juvenile & Family Court Judges, pp.* 43–51.

Wu, B. & Fuentes, L. (1998). The entangled effects of race and urban poverty. *Juvenile and Family Court Journal*, 2, pp. 41–52.

Terrence T. Allen, Wayne State University School of Social Work

QUESTIONS ABOUT MEANING

1. Describe the participants, methods, and findings of Allen's exploratory study. What factors were found to be predictors of police taking a juvenile into custody? Which of these factors rely on the officer's interpretations or perceptions?
2. How are the focus and findings of this study different from those of previous related studies?

QUESTIONS FOR RHETORICAL ANALYSIS

1. Analyze the content and organization of the Introduction. Is the introduction typical for an academic paper? Why or why not?
2. How does the content and organization of the Introduction compare to that of the Conclusion?

MAKING CONNECTIONS

1. Like Gino (chapter 14), Allen describes judgments made on the basis of perception and appearances. In an essay, combine the insights of these authors and add your own examples to demonstrate the important (and perhaps unfair) role that perceptions play in people's evaluation of others.
2. A common way to discover opportunities for research is to read related studies and look for questions they leave unanswered. You, for example, have read several studies that demonstrate variability or fallibility in how people perceive or interpret information. Here are some of those studies:
   - Allen, Terrence T. "Taking a Juvenile into Custody: Situational Factors That Influence Police Officers' Decisions."
   - Baron, Jonathan. "Myside Bias in Thinking about Abortion."
   - Choi, Youjin, Sejung Marina Choi, and Nora Rifon. "'I Smoke but I Am Not a Smoker': Phantom Smokers and the Discrepancy Between Self-Identity and Behavior."
   - Chua, Hannah Faye, Julie E. Boland, and Richard E. Nisbett. "Cultural Variation in Eye Movements during Scene Perception."

- Fausey, Caitlin M., and Lera Boroditsky. "Subtle Linguistic Cues Influence Perceived Blame and Financial Liability."
- Moore, Don A., Samuel A. Swift, Zachariah S. Sharek, and Francesca Gino. "Correspondence Bias in Performance Evaluation: Why Grade Inflation Works."
- Quoidbach, Jordi, Daniel T. Gilbert, and Timothy D. Wilson. "The End of History Illusion."

Re-read the section in Allen's study titled "Related Literature" and highlight phrasing that establishes the need for more research on the topic. (For example, notice the first sentence: "Very few researchers . . . have studied. . . .") Then, using Allen's "Related Literature" section as a template, review (summarize) some or all of the studies listed earlier (or other studies you have located) in a series of paragraphs titled "Related Literature" or "Literature Review." End your review with a paragraph identifying a "gap" in the literature. This gap should be a question or questions that need to be addressed in further research.

Law

"The Government Wants Your DNA," ERIN MURPHY

When police on crime shows use DNA technology to catch a murderer, it's exciting, but the more routine uses of DNA technology are "decidedly disturbing," according to Erin Murphy, the author of our next reading. Murphy is a professor of law at the New York University School of Law whose research interests include criminal law and forensic evidence. In the following article, published in *Scientific American* in 2013, Murphy describes the uses and abuses of DNA evidence. *Scientific American* is a magazine about scientific issues, written for the general public.

Starting in the mid-1980s, a serial killer murdered at least 10 women in the Los Angeles area. Nicknamed the "Grim Sleeper" because of the long dormancy between his crimes, he eluded capture for nearly 25 years. Then, in 2010, police arrested a man in California for what appeared to be a totally unrelated felony weapons charge. State law required the man to submit a DNA sample for a national DNA database. Typically a DNA database search looks for an exact match between a profile of DNA left at a crime scene by an unknown person and the profile of a known convicted offender. It focuses on 13 places in the genome (the full complement of our DNA) where bits of genetic material vary from person to person. If the crime-scene material differs in any of those 13 places, then the samples do not match, and investigators know that they do not have their suspect.

This time, however, the search was more subtle. It aimed to find DNA profiles that were similar, but not an exact match, to that of the Grim Sleeper. Such an inquiry was possible because in 2008 California became the first state in the nation to formally authorize a new kind of database search. Known as kinship, or familial, matching, this technique looks for partial DNA matches. It is conducted after DNA found at a crime turns up no exact hit. Because related people tend to share more DNA with one another than they do with strangers, a "near miss" in the database may suggest that the search found a person related to the actual perpetrator. Police can then investigate the relatives of the person in the database with the hope of solving the crime.

In the case of the Grim Sleeper, a familial search in 2008 turned up nothing. Two years later, however, the same inquiry generated a lead to the man who had been arrested in California for the weapons offense. Given the fellow's age and the dates of the serial killer's first attacks, suspicion focused quickly on an older relative—his father. A police officer, posing as a waiter at a pizza restaurant, surreptitiously collected genetic samples as the family ate a meal. The sample from the father matched the crime-scene evidence collected long ago, and shortly thereafter the alleged Sleeper was arrested.

This kind of DNA story is so electrifying that television shows like to copy it: a ruthless killer at last outwitted by flashy technology and dogged police persistence. Yet there is another kind of high-tech tale—also about a search for a serial killer—that is equally noteworthy but decidedly disturbing.

Take the case of Shannon Kohler, a Louisiana man approached by officers conducting a DNA dragnet—a broad sweep that netted more than 600 DNA samples from men matching the purported description of the killer. Kohler declined to volunteer a sample but proffered an array of exonerating details, including an accounting of his whereabouts at the time of three of the murders.

Nevertheless, police obtained a court order (later ruled invalid) allowing them to take his DNA and leaked his name to the press—which identified him prominently as a leading and uncooperative suspect in the case. Eventually Kohler's sample established that he was not the murderer, yet authorities never told Kohler of his exoneration. He learned that he had been vindicated only when, two months later, a newspaper printed a small item—after he had endured the dark cloud of suspicion casting him as a potential serial killer and the fear of being wrongly arrested for a capital crime.

As Kohler's saga illustrates, broadening use of DNA testing by law enforcement poses a growing threat to the civil liberties of innocent people. In the 15 years since the national database, called CODIS (*Com*bined *DNA Index System*), was started, it has amassed DNA signatures of more than 10 million offenders and another 450,000 unidentified people who left genetic material at a crime scene but were never found. The database contains profiles from individuals who have been charged with but never convicted of an offense. More than half of U.S. states now require cops to collect DNA after an arrest for certain offenses.

To address the threat to civil liberties, policy makers should demand answers to simple questions about the precise effectiveness of the technology—for example, finding out how many convictions have come about as a result of DNA database searches and what percentage of searches turn up useful information—before, as some have suggested, a national database of DNA from everyone in the country is established, allowing any sample collected from a crime to be compared against DNA from the entire U.S. population.

For more than 200 years we have required the police to get a warrant when officers wish to search or seize evidence from individuals in connection with a crime; DNA evidence should be no different. The government should also put in place stricter controls over the use of DNA databases, by taking steps such as forbidding partial matches. Also, it should enact rules to ensure that stored DNA samples are not subject to new tests without court permission and that police databases become available to defense attorneys for exonerating the wrongfully accused. Such changes are not just essential to preserve civil liberties, they are also needed to ensure public safety.

THE SLIPPERY SLOPE

At one time, the threat posed by compulsory DNA testing was minimal. The practice began in the late 1990s with the passage of state laws compelling people convicted of the most serious felonies, such as murder and sex crimes, to supply blood samples containing DNA. Now these samples are obtained by simply swabbing the inside of the cheek, and the information that is recorded comes from stretches of DNA that vary from person to person but do not reveal anything else about the donor's traits.

In the 2000s states increasingly began to require samples from offenders convicted of less serious felonies or even misdemeanors. Today the federal government and every state mandate compulsory testing of some convicted offenders. Noting that convicted criminals have fewer privacy rights than other citizens, courts have universally upheld such laws.

Yet fresh concerns about civil liberties have been raised by the trend among states in the past five years to require that people arrested for certain crimes give DNA samples. More than half of states and the federal government have arrestee sampling laws in place, some of which authorize the police to take a genetic sample immediately rather than waiting to see if a prosecutor actually files charges. Some states require automatic removal of genetic data collected from a person whose case is later dismissed, but others put the burden on the person wrongly arrested to file a petition to get the DNA record expunged. Finally, some laws provide for the destruction of the biological sample (not just the record), but others allow the government to retain the sample indefinitely.

In the coming months, the U.S. Supreme Court will decide whether DNA samples taken from someone arrested violates the Fourth Amendment of the Constitution. No one disputes that a person arrested for a crime should be required to give a genetic sample if one is needed to compare with evidence found at the alleged scene of the crime. But taking samples from everyone arrested for the sole purpose of expanding the database is a different matter. With more than 14 million arrests annually, a huge fraction of which end in dismissals, arrestee collection statutes could result in many innocent people having their DNA information loaded into police databases and then checked weekly against all the nation's unsolved crimes.

Familial searching, in contrast, has yet to be decided by any court. Like the compiling of arrestee databases, the guidelines for familial searching vary greatly state to state. Yet unlike the rules about whose DNA must go in the database, which are set by democratically elected legislatures, the rules about how police can use the DNA database are often put in place internally by high-level federal or state officials, administrative agencies, or even the heads of individual state or municipal crime laboratories. In fact, the situation is so muddy that it can be difficult even to discern which states engage in what practices. Current data indicate that at least 15 states actively undertake familial searches, although the most prominent users are law-enforcement officials in California, Virginia, Colorado and Texas. Unquestionably, other states have informally conducted occasional searches, and a handful of states are now weighing authorizing legislation. Some states do recognize the potential for abuse. Maryland and the District of Columbia both forbid intentional familial searches by law, and more than 15 states in addition to Maryland prohibit it through written or unwritten policy.

NOT YOUR FATHER'S FINGERPRINT

Advocates of the widespread collection and matching of DNA for crime solving often argue that DNA is no more than a glorified fingerprint and thus raises no new legal issues. Indeed, the handful of courts that have upheld arrestee collection statutes have likened DNA sampling to the routine taking of fingerprints at arrest, a practice long sanctioned by both the courts and the public. Although this analogy has superficial appeal, it is misleading: DNA can potentially provide more information about a person than a fingerprint and can open the door more widely to breaches of privacy.

What is more, even fingerprinting is more invasive than it used to be. Courts have long viewed fingerprinting at arrest as just a minimal encroachment of individual privacy, and for most of the history of the technology it was: a print was taken at a local precinct and then stored in a musty drawer. It was seldom seen again unless police had a new reason to suspect a person of a crime. Today fingerprints, like DNA profiles, are loaded into electronic databases, where they may be automatically searched not just locally but globally. To be sure, access to a common database aids in crime solving. Yet when mistakes occur—and they do happen—the consequences can be shocking. Just remember Brandon Mayfield, the Oregon attorney arrested and held in custody for two weeks as a suspect in the 2004 train station bombings in Madrid because of a faulty fingerprint match.

A false match is the only way to misuse a fingerprint, which simply cannot reveal as much as a person's DNA does. Fingerprints do not tell law enforcement that you have a brother or that you were adopted. They cannot identify you by ethnicity or sex or reveal whether you are predisposed to cancer. There is no expectation with fingerprinting, as there is with DNA, that it will accurately predict hair and eye color, height, age, bone structure or skin color, not to mention a range of genetic predispositions such as tendencies toward violence, substance abuse or mental illness.

Right now the DNA that is examined and recorded for forensic purposes does not reveal the most personal of these details. But the technology for doing so either already exists or likely will in the future. And the law does not clearly forbid this testing. Courts have consistently interpreted the Constitution to say a great deal about how the police acquire information, but they have exercised very little control over what police then do with that information. If police lawfully obtain a sample, are there then no limits or restrictions on how long that sample can be kept, how long it may be used or what kind of tests can be run on it?

If police examine only DNA fragments that do not reveal personal details, these questions may seem frivolous. Yet because police currently use DNA to make family connections, and in light of ongoing research into using DNA to reveal physical traits, disease and other predispositions, the present legal distinction between the mere acquisition and storage of genetic material and its use for analysis of personal information may quickly turn dangerously antiquated.

It is not hard to imagine that one day police may learn from crime-scene DNA that the unknown criminal is a man of Eurasian descent with blue eyes who is perhaps highly muscular and has a predisposition to alcoholism. Officials may then identify people with a similar profile and investigate those individuals or make their private information public even if many of those under suspicion will end up having nothing to do with the crime. Law-enforcement officials may simply use DNA as a starting point. Information about possible facial characteristics or physical build hinted at through a genetic profile may then be compared against other databases that store photographs of faces and other biometric information, thereby enabling the police to use highly sophisticated and potentially intrusive data mining of personal information on a vast number of the U.S. populace.

The issues raised by the use of DNA technology in law enforcement are not limited to futuristic invasions of privacy or possible harassment of those who happen to be family members of a possible suspect. Even today the potential for mistaken matches is greater than TV crime shows would have you think. The comparison process is far from perfect, especially as smaller and smaller quantities of DNA are tested. Crime-scene samples are generally not in pristine laboratory condition but contain a mix of material from multiple individuals. Analyzing those mixtures is a highly subjective process. One of the few empirical studies of the subjectivity inherent in DNA comparisons recently uncovered alarming possibilities for error: researchers submitted the results of DNA tests in an actual case to 17 experienced analysts; they received significantly divergent reports, ranging from inclusion of the defendant as a possible contributor to the crime to, on the contrary, definitive exclusion.

Finally, one very disturbing aspect of forensic DNA typing is the disproportionate impact that it has on minorities. Because blacks and Latinos make up a greater share of those arrested and convicted in our society, it is their DNA that is most likely to be collected and searched. Yet that is not necessarily because those groups commit more crime. For instance, studies show that across the country, the arrest rate for marijuana possession for blacks and Latinos is double, triple or even quadruple that for whites even though the first two groups do not use marijuana at any higher rate than the third. If police make arrests in a racially skewed way, then DNA databases will also be racially skewed. And it will be those groups whose relatives and family members will be most likely to fall under suspicion as a result of familial-match methods.

The need to more closely regulate law enforcement's use of DNA collection and analysis goes beyond rules and policies related to mandatory collection and familial searches. So far the discussion has centered on the cases in which a person is ordered to give a DNA sample after arrest or conviction. It is also possible, however, for police to obtain DNA surreptitiously, as was done in the Grim Sleeper investigation. In such cases, Fourth Amendment law points in conflicting and often counterintuitive directions. Constitutional protection has traditionally not extended to discarded material—if you throw your bloody shirt in the trash, you cannot complain that your rights were invaded when law enforcement snatches it up as evidence. But should the same reasoning apply to DNA, which is "discarded" routinely, albeit unintentionally? It is simply not possible to live in the world and not shed DNA. Given the myriad ways that DNA can be revealing of intimate personal details, does its ubiquity mean you have no grounds for complaint if the police pick up your discarded soda can and try to match your DNA profile with records in CODIS or store your information in a database or spreadsheet?

FORENSICS OUT OF VIEW

What should be done to protect the right to privacy of innocent people as DNA use in law enforcement expands? It would be logical to expect that popular sentiment would serve as a check against government abuse of the right to obtain and store DNA from suspects. Yet nearly every aspect of investigative DNA forensics can and does take place behind the scenes, with little public accountability. Investigators have collected samples surreptitiously from people under investigation. New law-enforcement technologies used to analyze those samples are almost always deployed without official comment. Retesting of old samples using new methods happens without prior notice or legal permission. Even government research to determine the effectiveness of DNA methods is shielded from true, scientific peer review. For example, when a list of more than 40 prominent scientists and academics (disclosure: I was among them) published a letter in *Science* requesting controlled access to the national database to verify the accuracy of government claims about the statistics used to determine how rare certain DNA profiles are, FBI administrators simply refused. The FBI has also threatened to cut off access to states that allow defense attorneys to request to search a government database in an attempt to find the true perpetrator.

The issues that accompany the building of massive DNA databases are only exacerbated by an industry that stands to gain financially from the unchecked embrace of these methods by police and law-enforcement agencies. For-profit companies manufacture the kits used to collect DNA, the instruments required to test it and the software necessary to interpret the results. Private interests benefit every time a new mandatory collection law is passed or a different search technique is approved, especially arrestee laws that will very likely spur demand from every police precinct in the country. It is no coincidence that some of the most vocal proponents of DNA fingerprinting have been employees of lobbying firms promoting their clients' interests, many of whom were previously employed by government labs. For instance, Gordon Thomas Honeywell, a firm that represents Life Technologies, maintains a Web site on legislation aimed at "moving DNA programs forward," and one of the most popular training conferences for law-enforcement analysts is sponsored by Promega, a private technology corporation involved with DNA testing.

NAME, ADDRESS, CHEEK SWAB

Steady expansion of forensic DNA programs is unlikely to stop with the collection of genetic material from people suspected of crimes or with familial searches. Members of the military are already required to provide DNA samples, although surprisingly, most police officers are not. Soon DNA collection may be considered a reasonable request in exchange for any benefit for which accurate identity is important. Perhaps the government will one day demand a DNA sample from student-loan applicants, government employees, or Social Security or Medicare recipients. And perhaps one day testing will disclose information about more sensitive personal traits.

Some officials and policy analysts have proposed the creation of a population-wide database to which every person would simply contribute at birth. Victim advocates and law-enforcement officials note that a truly national database would go a long way toward solving and controlling crime. Even civil-rights advocates reluctantly note that despite the potential for invasion of privacy, putting everyone's DNA in the ring may be the only way to ensure fairness and accuracy in the use of forensic DNA.

In this age of Google and instant credit checking, of routine bag and body searches at airports, buildings and schools, it is easy to anticipate that our genetic code could soon become just one more piece of currency to trade for a safer society. Yet thin as the line may seem at times, the Constitution has always distinguished between what the government may ask you to do and what it may force you to do.

The Supreme Court has upheld the right of the police to ask you your name, but it has also found that the Constitution prohibits officers from arresting you if you refuse to tell them that information, absent a reasonable suspicion that you were engaged in criminal activity. A threshold has also been set for taking fingerprints: we do not have compulsory national fingerprint programs for crime control. A universal DNA database thus initially strikes legal scholars as patently unconstitutional. If everything short of a population-wide database is on the table, however, how can we best use this powerful forensic tool?

Officials in the U.K. recently answered that question by passing the Protection of Freedoms Act. That law demands the destruction of physical DNA samples taken from arrestees—rather than keeping them for a century, as had been the previous practice—and the purging of innocent persons from the database after a certain period. The U.S. would benefit from similar legislation as well as laws requiring that the efficacy of DNA databases in criminal investigations be evaluated and that rules be put in place to curtail the uses to which biological material collected by law-enforcement officials can be put.

In addition, the government should forbid familial searches that risk casting suspicion on innocent people who have done nothing wrong but are simply related to a criminal offender. At the same time, it should allow access to DNA databases by individuals who are qualified to assess whether the government is abusing this enormous compilation of data. Defense lawyers, too, should be able to search a government database to establish the innocence of a client, as should neutral experts in statistics and population genetics who can check the accuracy of the databases. Laws are also needed to unambiguously clarify which kinds of genetic typing will and will not be allowed—detection of a suspect's physical or personal traits, for instance, might be deemed unacceptable to a society that values civil liberties.

Finally, I would stick to the Constitution's original commitment to freedom from government intrusion into the lives of innocent people by forbidding the indiscriminate taking of DNA samples from anyone arrested. I suggest this step not only out of concern for individual rights but also from a desire to preserve community safety. The tremendous energy directed toward collecting and storing the DNA of arrestees should instead go toward filling an enormous deficit of crime-scene investigators and lab technicians. Emphasis should be on increasing the rate of collection of evidence because as few as 10 to 20 percent of crime scenes for most serious offenses are examined for evidence.

Before the government devotes still more funding to expand its repository of citizen DNA, it should be required to report to the public in detail about the successes achieved so far. We have amassed millions of gene profiles, but no one can say how many arrests have resulted from collecting this information, much less how many convictions or for what offenses. Are these infractions for second-degree murder or merely for marijuana busts? Before we expend more resources and compromise personal liberty still further, we need a concrete accounting—not just anecdotal case reports—of how much the vast investment in DNA collection and recording has already cost taxpayers and society as a whole.

QUESTIONS ABOUT MEANING

1. What is DNA "kinship matching"? Are familial searches common in the United States?
2. In what ways is taking DNA from a suspect more invasive than taking a fingerprint?
3. Summarize Murphy's arguments against widespread collection of DNA samples.

QUESTIONS FOR RHETORICAL ANALYSIS

1. Dale and Murphy open with anecdotes (Hubbard and Slater for Dale; the "Grim Sleeper" for Murphy). What rhetorical purposes do the opening anecdotes serve in the articles? Do you think the anecdotes are effective?
2. What appeals to pathos does Murphy make? How would you describe her ethos? Cite passages to illustrate.

MAKING CONNECTIONS

1. Murphy's article reflects a very different legal system than that found in the United States 200 years ago. Using insights from Dale and Murphy, write an essay comparing the US justice system today to the antebellum justice system Dale describes. What has changed? Do you think the factors that affected jury decisions during the 19th century still play a role in our era of DNA evidence?
2. In an essay, compare what Murphy and Turkle say about our loss of privacy. Do the authors see the recent changes related to privacy as problematic? Why or why not? What do *you* think? Cite evidence to support your opinion.

Psychology

"How I Got Started: From Semantic Memory to Expert Testimony," ELIZABETH F. LOFTUS

The paired readings in this chapter feature Elizabeth Loftus, a professor of psychology at the University of California, Irvine, who has written extensively on human memory and eyewitness testimony. In the first article, "How I Got Started: From Semantic Memory to Expert Testimony," Loftus describes how her interest in eyewitness testimony began. The 2011 article was prompted by a request from the editor of *Applied Cognitive Psychology*, who asked Loftus to write about how she got started in her field. *Applied Cognitive Psychology* publishes research studies and other articles about memory, learning, problem solving, and language acquisition.

When asked to write an essay on "How I got started" for *Applied Cognitive Psychology*, I was flattered but quickly realised I needed clarification. How I got started in Psychology? How I got started in Memory? How I got started in Cognitive applications to the legal field? The editor narrowed my task when he wrote: "She was a straight cognitive person specialising in semantic memory and within a couple of years, it seems, was jetting all over the States giving testimony. How she got there—and what her colleagues thought—would make an interesting article." (Graham Davies, personal communication, 12 Oct 2010, thus the British spelling). So, Graham, here's the path from semantic memory to expert testimony.

While still in graduate school, I was involved in two main research projects—one concerning computer assisted instruction, with my PhD advisor, Patrick Suppes. And another involving semantic memory, begun in collaboration with Jonathan Freedman. After obtaining my doctorate in psychology, I continued with the semantic memory line of work. Semantic memory, of course, involves memory for words and concepts and general knowledge rather than memory for the personal experience in life. My focus was on how general knowledge is stored in the human mind and how it can be retrieved when needed. I had my lab, with eager graduate students, and we published some papers that I was quite proud of at the time (e.g. Loftus & Freedman, 1972; Loftus & Scheff, 1971).

But one day, I was having lunch with my lawyer-cousin. She said: "So you're an experimental psychologist. Have you made any discoveries?" "Yes," I replied proudly. "I've discovered that people are faster to give you the name of a fruit that you say is yellow than they are if you asked for the name of a yellow fruit. They're 250 milliseconds faster or about a quarter of a second."

My cousin looked at me with an expression that might best be described as incredulity with a slight touch of disdain. She had but one question that was approximately this: "How much did we pay for that bit of information?"—referring, I suppose, to the fact that my work may have been supported by a grant of federal funds.

The difference in reaction time was important in my field because it demonstrated that humans tend to organise information according to categories, in this instance the category of fruits, rather than by attributes, such as yellow. A memory search for information can get underway sooner if the category cue is presented first.

But my cousin's reaction was unnerving and made me want to study something that had more practical relevance. I had always had an interest in legal issues and court cases. With my background in memory, wouldn't it make sense to study the memories of witnesses to crimes and accidents and other legally relevant events? I thought it would be interesting, for instance, to try to figure out whether the structure of questions posed to witnesses by the police, investigators, or lawyers affected what people remembered and what they said. So I undertook a series of experiments using films of accidents or simulated crimes and studied how people recalled what they were shown. (The first film clips I used were segments from longer driver's education films borrowed from the local safety council and police department.) Using these materials as stimuli, I and my students showed that leading questions could affect how people remembered these critical events, and later, more generally that post-event misinformation could have damaging effects on witness's memories (e.g. Loftus, 1975; Loftus & Palmer, 1974). One thing that I was doing differently from other memory researchers was showing people films of accidents or crimes. Most others at this time were studying memory for more pallid materials, like word lists or occasionally individual photos. I once got a backhanded compliment from a colleague: "Many people think she is doing mere applied psychology, but I think there is a lot more there."

After studying the laboratory witnesses for a few years, I was keenly interested in seeing how real witnesses to real crimes behaved as they interacted with people who questioned them. I had recently moved to Seattle, Washington, and I happened to know the chief trial attorney at the local public defender's office. I offered him a deal: I'd share findings from psychological science that might be relevant or helpful to some case he was handling, and of course would help him at no expense to him, if he would let me see the witnesses and other participants in a case up close and personal. He had the perfect case. It involved a woman (whom I would later call "Sally") who was accused of murdering her boyfriend who had been abusing her for quite some time. The prosecutor called it first-degree murder, but her lawyer claimed self-defence. Both sides agreed that Sally and her boyfriend had argued, whereupon Sally ran into the bedroom, grabbed a gun, and shot her boyfriend six times. At trial, a key issue was the amount of time that elapsed between the grabbing of the gun and the first shot. Sally, and her sister who was in the apartment, said two seconds, but another witness said five minutes. Two seconds versus five minutes made a huge difference as to whether Sally had shot suddenly, in fear, and thus in self defence. Or whether she had shot with premeditated intent—and was thus guilty of murder. In the end, Sally was acquitted.

I wrote an article about the burgeoning science and Sally's case for *Psychology Today* magazine. It was entitled "Reconstructing Memory: The Incredible Eyewitness" (Loftus, 1974). *Psychology Today* was a popular magazine, with a circulation of over a million that included many judges, lawyers, and other members of the legal profession. As a result of the article, I began receiving phone calls from lawyers asking if I would work on their cases or speak about the psychology of memory at their continuing education seminars. Calls came in from judges to speak at judicial conferences.

This new part of my professional life—interacting with the legal profession through consulting and education—was exhilarating (and somewhat lucrative as well, when I was no longer typically giving away my time for free). The court cases became memorable material for my classes and talks. Who does not love the true crime angle? Research ideas sometimes came from a puzzle in a case I had worked on. Along the way I met some of the most notorious criminals of the last century, like Ted Bundy and the Hillside Strangler. I've met people whom I am convinced were innocent like Steve Titus whose case I wrote about in *Witness for the Defense* (Loftus & Ketcham, 1991). I sat across a table interviewing Martha Stewart in her attorney's office, and had a tour of Oliver North's bullet-proof vest factory during his troubles in the 1980s. I got to read original police reports or other documents in cases involving other accused people like Michael Jackson and O.J. Simpson and the Duke University Lacross players. I love going into work for many reasons but one of them is that there is a decent probability that the phone will ring and someone interesting will ask for my help.

Recently I was in the office preparing for my class when the phone rang with a different kind of call. What would I think about a possible TV series based on a female psychologist who uses the psychology of memory in legal cases? Paramount/CBS just bought the idea—a show tentatively called *Mind Games*. With an incredibly talented writer, Roger Wolfson, the script for the pilot is being developed. Wolfson has written for *Law and Order: SVU*, *Saving Grace*, and *The Closer*—all popular television shows in the United States. One possible story line for *Mind Games*, which is set in Seattle, Washington, is this: A woman shoots and kills her husband and says it was self-defence. She says he was attacking her in their living room and she ran to the bedroom and came back five seconds later with his gun. A witness hears the shooting, and recalls things in a way that suggests more than a minute elapsed—thus first-degree murder. "Dr. Stefanie Glisson"—a young psychology professor with an expertise in memory—helps to show that the wife was not guilty. Sally would be smiling if she knew. At the moment the Sally-inspired script is under development. I guess art really does sometimes imitate life.

REFERENCES

Loftus, E. F. (1974). Reconstructing memory: The incredible eyewitness. *Psychology Today, 8*, 116–119.

Loftus, E. F. (1975). Leading questions and the eyewitness report. *Cognitive Psychology, 7*, 560–572.

Loftus, E. F., & Freedman, J. L. (1972). Effect of category-name frequency on the speed of naming an instance of the category. *Journal of Verbal Learning and Verbal Behavior, 11*, 343–347.

Loftus, E. F., & Ketcham, K. (1991). *Witness for the defense; the accused, the eyewitness, and the expert who puts memory on trial.* NY: St. Martin's Press.

Loftus, E. F., & Palmer, J. C. (1974). Reconstruction of automobile destruction: An example of the inter-action between language and memory. *Journal of Verbal Learning and Verbal Behavior, 13*, 585–589.
Loftus, E. F., & Scheff, R. W. (1971). Categorization norms for fifty representative instances. *Journal of Experimental Psychology Monograph, 91*, 355–364.

Elizabeth F. Loftus, University of California, Irvine, USA. Correspondence to: Elizabeth F. Loftus, University of California, Irvine, USA. E-mail: eloftus@uci.edu.

QUESTIONS ABOUT MEANING

1. What was Loftus's original research focus when she was in graduate school? What prompted her to change her research focus?
2. How did Loftus become a consultant for lawyers and judges?

QUESTIONS FOR RHETORICAL ANALYSIS

1. Why did Loftus write this article and to whom is she writing? What textual indicators are there of her intended audience?
2. Analyze the structure and writing style of Loftus's article. In what ways does the writing and tone remind you of how a person might respond to a question like: "How did you get started in your career?" On the other hand, what aspects of the organization, content, or structure make the article seem more like an essay than a person's off-the-cuff remarks?

MAKING CONNECTIONS

1. Both Loftus and Boroditsky refer to the way witnesses or jurors can be influenced by the information they hear or the questions they are asked. Synthesize information from these authors and comment on the real-world implications of their research.
2. Relate Loftus's research about the fallibility of memories to the insights of Pinker ("Kidding Ourselves"); Tavris and Aronson; Norenzayan and Nisbett; or other writers. Compose an essay in which you put various authors in conversation with one another.

Psychology

"Repeated Information in the Courtroom," JEFFREY L. FOSTER, MARYANNE GARRY, AND ELIZABETH F. LOFTUS

Elizabeth Loftus is a nationally recognized expert on human memory and eyewitness testimony. The following article describes research she conducted with Jeffrey Foster, while he was a psychology graduate student, and Maryanne Garry, a psychology professor. They wanted to learn whether misleading claims are more likely to be believed if they are repeated by more than one source. Their findings were published in 2012 in the *Court Review: The Journal of the American Judges Association.* Notice as you read how the authors relate their findings to their audience: courtroom judges.

It is widely understood among scientists and criminal and civil lawyers that eyewitnesses are often inaccurate, and that inaccurate information can contaminate memories of other eyewitnesses.[1] It is less widely known—although no less true—that when misleading claims are repeated, they are more likely to damage other people's memories than when those claims are made only once.[2] But until recently, neither lawyers nor scientists knew the answer to these questions: Does one person repeating an inaccurate claim do more damage to the memories of other eyewitnesses than that same person making the claim only once? And when that inaccurate claim is repeated, does it matter how many people make it? In this paper, we address those questions.

Suppose a robbery occurs for which there were four eyewitnesses. If one eyewitness, let's call him John, mistakenly tells another eyewitness, Ringo, that the robber was wearing a blue hat—when in fact the robber was wearing a black hat—then we know Ringo may, inadvertently, remember later that the robber was wearing a blue hat. But would Ringo be even more likely to make this mistake if John had repeated that inaccurate claim multiple times? By contrast, suppose that all of the eyewitnesses—John, Paul, and George—mistakenly claimed it was a blue hat. Would their converging evidence be more misleading to Ringo than if John had simply repeated it multiple times? Put another way, do inaccurate claims do more damage when made by multiple sources, or is it the repetition of claims that matters?

WHAT ROLE DOES THE NUMBER OF SOURCES TAKE IN THE BELIEVABILITY OF A CLAIM?

On the one hand, it is intuitively appealing that a claim would be more credible or more damaging when there is consensus among eyewitnesses. Indeed, scientific research tells us we put more trust in our own memories when other people who were there remember it the same way,[3] and we have more trust in the details of a crime that multiple eyewitnesses remember than the details of a crime that only one eyewitness does.[4] And not only is this trust intuitively appealing, but research supports its validity: When a suspect is picked out of a lineup by multiple eyewitnesses, their identification is more likely to be accurate than when that suspect is picked by only one eyewitness.[5] In addition, people's susceptibility to misleading information changes in response to characteristics of the person making the claim. For instance, an innocent bystander is more misleading than the perpetrator of the crime.[6] And even more subtle characteristics of a misleading eyewitness can influence people's susceptibility to misinformation. In one study, eyewitnesses with more powerful and socially attractive accents were more misleading than eyewitnesses with less powerful and socially attractive accents.[7] Taken together, these findings suggest that the consensus of multiple eyewitnesses should be more misleading than the repeated claims of a single eyewitness.

On the other hand, we know that repeated information can lead people to make mistakes. Trivia questions that require a true/false response are more likely to be rated as true when they are repeated;[8] when people repeatedly view pictures of a place they have never visited, they become more confident that they have been there before;[9] and when one person states an opinion multiple times, other people are more likely to believe that opinion is held by others as well.[10] Considered together, these findings suggest that the repetition of inaccurate claims should be more important than the consensus of multiple eyewitnesses.

WHY DOES REPETITION LEAD PEOPLE TO MAKE THESE ERRORS?

One possibility is that when we encounter information we have seen before, our cognitive system processes that information differently. Call it an adaptive shortcut: if you've seen x before and it didn't attack you the first time, then x is probably safe enough for your brain to spend less effort making sense of it. When information is processed with this shortcut, we do not know it directly, but we often experience a feeling of familiarity: "Ah, I have seen this before." Cognitive scientists have discovered that we also associate this kind of processing with a feeling of truth.[11] In other words, repeated information tends to feel more familiar, and more true, than unrepeated information.

IS IT THE REPETITION OF MISLEADING CLAIMS THAT MATTERS OR THE NUMBER OF PEOPLE WHO MAKE THEM?

We addressed the effects of repetition and number of eyewitnesses in two experiments. In our first experiment, we asked if repeating misleading claims would change the way people remembered a mock crime, regardless of how many eyewitnesses repeated those claims. To answer this question, people took part in an experiment based on a well-known eyewitness-memory error called the *misinformation effect*: They watched an event, then read a misleading description of the event, and finally were tested for what they remembered seeing.[12] Typically, many people report seeing the misleading details in the event.[13]

In our study, people first watched a video of an electrician who stole items while doing repairs at a client's house. Later, they read three eyewitness police reports—ostensibly written over three consecutive days—about the activities of the electrician. Sometimes, all three reports misled people about what happened in the video; other times only one of the three reports misled people. To manipulate the source(s) of the reports, we told half the people that three different eyewitnesses made these reports; we told the other half that the same eyewitness made all three reports. For example, people read three eyewitness reports from Day 1, Day 2, and Day 3: For half of the people, Eyewitness 5 made the Day 1 report; Eyewitness 9 made the Day 2 report; and Eyewitness 16 made the Day 3 report. The other half read the same reports—but all three reports were attributed to Eyewitness 9. Later, people took a test asking them about specific details they saw in the mock crime.[14]

In summary, people read the reports in one of four conditions: 1) three eyewitnesses, each making the same misleading claims across the three reports; 2) one eyewitness making the same claims across the three reports; 3) three eyewitnesses, only one of who makes the claims in only one report; and 4) one eyewitness who makes the claims in only one report.[15]

If what matters most is the number of fellow eyewitnesses giving inaccurate, misleading information, then our results should show that people were the most misled when they read misinformation three times from three eyewitnesses. But if what matters most is the repetition of inaccurate information, then our results should show that people became more misled when misleading claims were repeated, regardless of how many eyewitnesses made them.

Our results suggest that it was repetition that mattered most. We found three important results. First, and consistent with research on the misinformation effect, when people read misleading details about the crime they had witnessed, they incorporated some of those misleading details into their memory of the original crime. Second, when the misinformation was repeated, people became more misled than when the misinformation was not repeated. And third, people were similarly misled regardless of whether that misinformation was attributed to a single eyewitness who repeated it or to three independent eyewitnesses converging on the same misleading claims. In short, it was the repetition of misleading claims that mattered, not how many sources the misinformation came from.[16]

Let's return to our original example. Based on our results, we can predict that if John repeatedly tells Ringo the incorrect color of the robber's hat, Ringo will more likely be misled than if John tells him only once. But we can also predict that if that claim were repeated, it would make little difference if John says it, or if John, Paul, and George each make the same claim once: Either way, Ringo would hear it three times and be similarly misled. But what if Ringo had never seen the crime unfold in the first place and was trying to determine the truth about what occurred? How might John's repeated testimony affect Ringo's belief about what really happened? That is the question we addressed in our second study.

IS IT THE REPETITION OF EYEWITNESS CLAIMS OR THE NUMBER OF PEOPLE WHO MAKE THEM THAT AFFECT BELIEF IN THEIR ACCURACY?

Although our first experiment showed that repeating misinformation three times made people less accurate about what they saw, we still do not know if repeating inaccurate information would change how people might judge what happened when they never saw the crime unfold in the first place—this, of course, is the situation analogous to being a juror. It may be that people who did not see the crime would be even more susceptible to the influence of repetition: After all, they never saw the crime unfold and must rely entirely on the testimony of an eyewitness. But on the other hand, people may be more likely to scrutinize the sources of the claims when judging the accuracy of those claims, a behavior that should lead people to be more confident in claims that reach a consensus among multiple eyewitnesses.

In our second experiment, we wanted to know how the repetition of a claim and the number of sources making that claim might affect people's beliefs about the claim's accuracy. In our second experiment, we asked people to read the same three eyewitness reports from our first experiment, but in this case, people did not watch the video of the original crime. Thus, they could not know if claims about how the crime unfolded were true. After they read the eyewitness reports, people reported their confidence that each claim actually happened in the original crime.

Once again, our data suggest that it was repetition that mattered most. We found that when claims were repeated, people became more confident about those claims than when they were not repeated. In addition, people were similarly confident about repeated claims regardless of whether they were attributed to a single eyewitness who repeated it or three independent eyewitnesses all converging on the same claims. In short, it was the repetition of misleading claims that mattered, not how many sources the misinformation came from.[17]

SUMMARY AND CONCLUSIONS

Across two experiments, we asked two questions: First, does one person repeating inaccurate claims do more damage to the memories of other eyewitnesses than that same person making the claims only once? And second, when those inaccurate claims are repeated, does it matter how many people make them? The answers are yes and no, respectively. Our findings converged on the important role of repetition—over and above the role of how many people make the claims. More specifically, we found that the misleading claims of a single eyewitness were more damaging to fellow eyewitnesses' memories when that eyewitness repeated them, and that the claims of a single eyewitness were more credible to people who never saw the crime when the eyewitness repeated them. Moreover, a single eyewitness's repeated claims were as influential as the claims made by three eyewitnesses.

Why would one eyewitness repeating a claim become just as credible as three eyewitnesses? While the adaptive explanation we presented earlier—that if x has not eaten you before then x is probably safe—can explain why repeated information feels more true, it does not explain why people didn't put even more stock in claims repeated by multiple eyewitnesses.[18] We propose two possible explanations for this surprising finding. First, it may be that people did in fact put more stock into the repeated claims of multiple eyewitnesses,[19] but that people also saw a single eyewitness repeating claims as highly consistent. Indeed, consistency is one attribute that makes people appear more credible, and thus more accurate.[20] In other words, one eyewitness repeating a claim may make the claim more credible for a different reason than three eyewitnesses each stating the same claim once does. On the other hand it may be that people failed to attend to the source of the repeated claims when judging their accuracy. Indeed, the likely explanation of why repeated misinformation misleads subjects more than unrepeated misinformation is that subjects' increased feelings of familiarity are not accompanied by increases in their ability to monitor the source of that familiarity.[21] Although both of these mechanisms will produce the patterns we found here, they provide different pathways to finding a way to reduce the effects of repetition. As such, future research will need to disentangle the effects of these mechanisms.

Of course, in the real world, multiple eyewitnesses may stand out in a variety of ways that our written reports did not. In our study the distinction between a single eyewitness and multiple eyewitnesses was controlled so that they varied on identification number only. In court, these eyewitnesses would vary in superficial (accent, gender, etc.) and important (relationship to the suspect, motive, etc.) ways—distinctions that jurors might use to determine the credibility of their claims. But would these distinctions actually help to reduce the deleterious effects of repetition? That question is still one to be answered by additional experimentation.

In the meantime, the problems with inaccurate eyewitnesses during a trial are unquestionable.[22] Indeed, looking back at the 289 wrongfully convicted people freed by The Innocence Project to date shows that in more than 75% of cases, eyewitness testimony played a role in their wrongful convictions.[23] Our research suggests that a single person repeating inaccurate claims can lead jurors and other eyewitnesses to put more faith in those claims than they should—calling on us to be wary about the power of a single, repeated voice.

FOOTNOTES

1. This article is adapted from Jeffrey L. Foster et al., *Repetition, Not Number of Sources, Increases Both Susceptibility to Misinformation and Confidence in the Accuracy of Eyewitnesses*, 139 ACTA PSYCHOLOGICA 320 (2012).
2. Karen J. Mitchell & Maria S. Zaragoza, *Repeated Exposure to Suggestion and False Memory: The Role of Contextual Variability*, 35 J. OF MEMORY & LANGUAGE 246 (1996); Maria S. Zaragoza & Karen J. Mitchell, *Repeated Exposure to Suggestion and the Creation of False Memories*, 7 PSYCHOL. SCI. 294 (1996).
3. Michael Ross et al., *Assessing the Accuracy of Conflicting Autobiographical Memories*, 26 MEMORY & COGNITION 1233 (1998).
4. Adam J. L. Harris & Ulrike Hahn, *Bayesian Rationality in Evaluating Multiple Testimonies: Incorporating the Role of Coherence*, 35 J. OF EXPERIMENTAL PSYCHOL.: LEARNING, MEMORY, & COGNITION 1366 (2009).
5. Steven E. Clark & Gary L. Wells, *On the Diagnosticity of Multiple-Witness Identifications*, 32 LAW & HUM. BEHAV. 406 (2008).
6. David H. Dodd & Jeffrey M. Bradshaw, *Leading Questions and Memory: Pragmatic Constraints*, 19 J. OF VERBAL LEARNING & VERBAL BEHAV. 695 (1980).
7. Lana A. Vornik et al., *The Power of the Spoken Word: Sociolinguistic Cues Influence the Misinformation Effect*, 11 MEMORY 101 (2003).
8. Frederick T. Bacon, *Credibility of Repeated Statements: Memory for Trivia*, 5 J. OF EXPERIMENTAL PSYCHOL.: HUM. LEARNING & MEMORY 241 (1979).
9. Alan S. Brown & Elizabeth J. Marsh, *Evoking False Beliefs About Autobiographical Experience*, 15 PSYCHONOMIC BULL. & REV. 186 (2008).
10. Kimberlee Weaver et al., *Inferring the Popularity of an Opinion From Its Familiarity: A Repetitive Voice Can Sound Like a Chorus*, 92 J. OF PERSONALITY & SOC. PSYCHOL. 821 (2007).
11. Adam L. Alter & Daniel M. Oppenheimer, *Uniting the Tribes of Fluency to Form a Metacognitive Nation*, 13 PERSONALITY & SOC. PSYCHOL. REV. 219 (2009); Hal L. Arkes et al., *Determinants of Judged Validity*, 27 J. OF EXPERIMENTAL SOC. PSYCHOL. 576 (1991); Alice Dechêne et al.,

The Truth About the Truth: A Meta-Analytic Review of the Truth Effect, 14 PERSONALITY & SOC. PSYCHOL. REV. 238 (2010); Colleen M. Kelley & D. Stephen Lindsay, *Remembering Mistaken for Knowing: Ease of Retrieval as a Basis for Confidence in Answers to General Knowledge Questions*, 32 J. OF MEMORY & LANGUAGE 1 (1993); Marcia Johnson et al., *Source Monitoring*, 114 PSYCHOL. BULL. 3 (1993); Christian Unkelbach, *Reversing the Truth Effect: Learning the Interpretation of Processing Fluency in Judgments of Truth*, 33 J. OF EXPERIMENTAL PSYCHOL.: LEARNING, MEMORY, & COGNITION 219 (2007); Christian Unkelbach & Christoph Stahl, *A Multinomial Modeling Approach to Dissociate Different Components of the Truth Effect*, 18 CONSCIOUSNESS & COGNITION 22 (2009).

12. Foster et al., *supra* note 1, at 321.
13. Elizabeth F. Loftus et al., *Semantic Integration of Verbal Information Into a Visual Memory*, 4 J. OF EXPERIMENTAL PSYCHOL.: HUM. LEARNING & MEMORY 19 (1978); Mitchell & Zaragoza, *supra* note 2; Melanie K. T. Takarangi et al., *Modernising the Misinformation Effect: The Development of a New Stimulus Set*, 20 APPLIED COGNITIVE PSYCHOL. 583 (2006).
14. Foster et al., *supra* note 1, at 321.
15. *Id.*
16. *Id.* at 322.
17. *Id.* at 324.
18. Kelley & Lindsay *supra* note 11; Weaver et al. *supra* note 10; Unkelbach, *supra* note 11.
19. Harris & Hahn, *supra* note 4; Ross et al., *supra* note 3.
20. Neil Brewer & Anne Burke, *Effects of Testimonial Inconsistencies and Eyewitness Confidence on Mock-Juror Judgments*, 26 LAW AND HUM. BEHAV. 353 (2002).
21. Zaragoza & Mitchell, *supra* note 2.
22. Richard A. Leo, *Rethinking the Study of Miscarriages of Justice: Developing a Criminology of Wrongful Conviction*, 21 J. OF CONTEMP. CRIM. JUST. 201 (2005).
23. Innocence Project, http://www.innocenceproject.org/understand/Eyewitness-Misidentification.php

QUESTIONS ABOUT MEANING

1. Summarize the methods and results of the two experiments the authors describe.
2. According to the authors, what are possible explanations for why a false claim repeated by a single person can carry so much weight?

QUESTIONS FOR RHETORICAL ANALYSIS

1. Locate the transition paragraph separating the description of the two experiments. Do you think this is an effective way to transition from one major idea to another? Why or why not?

2. Repetition of claims, alone, won't persuade a critical reader; that requires evidence. Nonetheless, successful writers understand the value of repetition. Highlight instances where the authors repeat their central claim(s). What does this research indicate are potential benefits for writers who repeat their claims? Can you suggest additional benefits of repetition?
3. In what ways do the authors relate their research findings to the interests of their audience?

MAKING CONNECTIONS

1. Like other writers in this chapter, Foster, Garry, and Loftus are interested in America's legal system. Write an essay in which you link their research to arguments or insights from Allen and/or Murphy. Based on their writings, what changes do you think the authors you discuss would suggest for America's justice system and why?
2. A body of research, much of it conducted by Loftus, has demonstrated that human memory is fallible and that witnesses to crimes can be easily manipulated into believing they saw things they did not see. Read about some of the research on the reliability of eyewitness testimony. You might begin by reading Gary Wells and Elizabeth Olson's review article "Eyewitness Testimony," published in the *Annual Review of Psychology* (available online; see citation that follows), or read some of the sources they cite. After doing some reading, select several sources that discuss eyewitness testimony and write an essay that brings your sources into conversation with one another.

WORK CITED

Wells, Gary L., and Elizabeth A. Olson. "Eyewitness Testimony." *Annual Review of Psychology* 54.1 (2003): 277–95.

Management

"It's a Crime What Some People Do with Statistics," ARNOLD BARNETT

Statistical evidence appears in most arguments about crime and punishment. But is statistical evidence proof? Not necessarily, according to Arnold Barnett, a professor of management science and statistics at the MIT Sloan School of Management. In the following article, published in *The Wall Street Journal* in 2000, Barnett concludes that "It's a Crime What Some People Do with Statistics."

The truism that statistics can be misleading has no more content than the statement that paragraphs can be misleading. But certain statistics that are indeed highly misleading have made their way into debates about crime, punishment and race. The resulting misconceptions have intensified already bitter disputes, and can only sow confusion among voters.

For example, in the controversy over whether innocent people are being executed, a 1-in-7 ratio has attained prominence. *Newsweek* sought to explain the ratio when it stated that "for every seven executions nationwide since the death penalty was reinstated in 1976, one death-row inmate has been set free." William F. Buckley Jr. probably reflected the common understanding of this statistic when he wrote that "if the figures work out retroactively, then one out of seven (of the 640) executed Americans was, in fact, innocent."

Greatly upset by the ratio, the *Economist* noted that "if an airline crashed once for every seven times it reached its destination, it would surely be suspended immediately." A bit of probing makes clear, however, that the ratio makes no sense.

There is an obvious interest in the error rate for capital-sentencing, which is the number of innocents sentenced to death divided by the total number of people thus sentenced. Also of importance is the error rate for actual executions: the number of innocents executed divided by the total number executed. In an ideal world, both these rates would be zero.

The 1-to-7 ratio, however, represents neither of these rates but rather a confused amalgam of their components. It divides the number of known innocents freed from death row by the number of executions. In other words, it divides the numerator of the error rate for capital-sentencing by the denominator of the rate for executions. Such a calculation is of no value: It is akin to computing an earnings-per-share statistic by dividing the earnings of one company by the number of shares of a completely different one.

Suppose that there are 2,000 people on death row and that, over a given period, one of them is found innocent and freed while one is executed. The only reliable inference from these statistics is the obvious point that, during this period, both executions and known sentencing errors were extremely rare. To divide one by the other while ignoring the 2,000 altogether does not demonstrate that executions are fraught with errors; it is a meaningless act that yields no insight.

Another confusing statistic appeared several months ago when the *New York Times* described a Columbia University/New York State study about police stops and searches of New York City residents. The "most basic finding" of the study, the *Times* reported, was that blacks were stopped six times as often on a per-capita basis as whites. And, "even when the numbers are adjusted to reflect higher crime rates in some minority neighborhoods," blacks were stopped 23% more often than whites.

Hold on a minute. The original black/white stop ratio was six (as opposed to the value of one, which would mean equal stopping rates). After an adjustment that the researchers thought appropriate, the ratio fell to 1.23.

Thus, instead of 600 blacks stopped for every 100 whites in comparable groups of equal size, 123 blacks were stopped. The disparity still exists, but it is far smaller. Put in percentage terms, the black/white excess fell from 500% to 23% (i.e., declined by a factor of 20).

It is unclear whether readers of the *Times* grasped this last point because, instead of working consistently with ratios or with percentages, the *Times* started with the former and then shifted to the latter. Matters were especially confusing because the *Times* narrative repeatedly suggested that the adjustment had reaffirmed the "basic" finding rather than nearly overturned it.

Over at *National Review*, an author noted that homicide in the U.S. plummeted in the 1990s, while executions soared, and discerned a deterrent effect of capital punishment. But this aggregate correlation misses a crucial local detail: Recent drops in killing have been greatest in places (e.g., New York City, Boston) where no death sentences have been carried out during the past three decades. Unless one believes that an execution in Virginia that goes unreported in the Bronx nonetheless prevents some killings there, one should be wary of statistics that pool Virginia executions with Bronx murders.

There is more. A full-page ad from the American Civil Liberties Union, placed in several prominent magazines, showed a picture of Martin Luther King Jr. next to one of Charles Manson. The accompanying text declared that "the man on the left is 75 times more likely to be stopped by the police while driving than the man on the right." The basis of this finding was that "in Florida 80% of those stopped and searched were black and Hispanic, while they constituted only 5% of all drivers."

This analysis is baffling. It is hard to imagine that the 5% figure is accurate: Government statistics indicate that blacks and non-black Hispanics constitute 29% of all Florida residents, and that these groups drive approximately 20% of the state's vehicle miles. Moreover, applying the statistics to a comparison between Dr. King (who presumably represents innocence) and Manson (who presumably represents guilt) requires a strong tacit assumption: that race was the only determinant of auto stops in Florida. A car would not be stopped, for example, merely because it was going 110 miles per hour down Interstate 95. Simply stating such a premise suggests its absurdity.

We should not overreact to such frightful statistical "analyses." Some of them might reflect not deliberate distortion but rather innocent intellectual disorder. Furthermore, the fact that certain numbers are flawed need not invalidate the general point they try to advance. It could well be that there are some innocent people on death row, much as race could play an indefensible role in some police stops. Such possibilities should be investigated in sensible and unbiased ways.

In the meantime, certain widely cited statistics should be sent into exile.

Mr. Barnett is a professor of management science at the Massachusetts Institute of Technology.

QUESTIONS ABOUT MEANING

1. Describe the kinds of mistakes responsible for the flawed estimates about the number of innocent people executed, the ratio of blacks to whites stopped by police, and the deterrent effect of capital punishment.
2. According to Barnett, what is the potential harm of publishing flawed statistics?

QUESTIONS FOR RHETORICAL ANALYSIS

1. Identify Barnett's thesis statement. Divide the article into sections. What phrases are used to transition into new topics?
2. In the final full paragraph, what does Barnett imply by putting *analyses* in quotation marks?

MAKING CONNECTIONS

1. Locate examples of statistics or numerical data used as evidence in articles in this chapter. In an essay, present and discuss examples of the following:
   (a). Statistics that are sufficiently explained and seemingly credible. What key details about how the numbers were derived make these statistics persuasive?
   (b). Statistics that are "suspicious"—perhaps because they are large, round numbers, because they are the result of speculation, or because key details about how they were derived are not provided. What information would you need before changing your assessment of these numbers from questionable to credible?
2. Barnett, Best (in chapter 3), and Fisman talk about the importance of considering the context or the "big picture" when assessing evidence, situations, or people. Write an essay in which you make connections between these authors, and contribute examples of your own to the conversation.

International Relations and Psychology

"War Really Is Going Out of Style," JOSHUA S. GOLDSTEIN AND STEVEN PINKER

Joshua Goldstein is professor emeritus of international relations at American University and Steven Pinker, whose essay "Kidding Ourselves" appears in chapter 14, is a psychology professor at Harvard. In the next article Goldstein and Pinker argue that "War Really Is Going Out of Style," a claim they recognize many people regard as "preposterously utopian." The authors present statistical evidence indicating that war is declining and suggest explanations for this peaceful trend. Goldstein and Pinker's article originally appeared in 2011 in *The New York Times*.

The departure of the last American troops from Iraq brings relief to a nation that has endured its most painful war since Vietnam. But the event is momentous for another reason. The invasion of Iraq was the most recent example of an all-out war between two national armies. And it could very well be the last one.

The idea that war is obsolescent may seem preposterously utopian. Aren't we facing an endless war on terror, a clash of civilizations, the menace of nuclear rogue states? Isn't war in our genes, something that will always be with us?

The theory that war is becoming passe gained traction in the late 1980s, when scholars noticed some curious nonevents. World War III, a nuclear Armageddon, was once considered inevitable, but didn't happen. Nor had any wars between great powers occurred since the Korean War. European nations, which for centuries had fought each other at the drop of a hat, had not done so for four decades.

How has the world fared since then? Armed conflict hasn't vanished, and today anyone with a mobile phone can broadcast the bloodshed. But our impressions of the prevalence of war, stoked by these images, can be misleading. Only objective numbers can identify the trends.

"War" is a fuzzy category, shading from global conflagrations to neighborhood turf battles, so the organizations that track the frequency and damage of war over time need a precise yardstick. A common definition picks out armed conflicts that cause at least 1,000 battle deaths in a year—soldiers and civilians killed by war violence, excluding the difficult-to-quantify indirect deaths resulting from hunger and disease. "Interstate wars" are those fought between national armies and have historically been the deadliest.

These prototypical wars have become increasingly rare, and the world hasn't seen one since the three-week invasion of Iraq in 2003. The lopsided five-day clash between Russia and Georgia in 2008 misses the threshold, as do sporadic clashes between North and South Korea or Thailand and Cambodia.

Countries remain armed and hostile, so war is hardly impossible. But where would a new interstate war plausibly erupt? Robert Gates, the former secretary of defense, said this year that "any future defense secretary who advises the president to again send a big American land army into Asia or into the Middle East or Africa should have his head examined."

Chinese leaders would deserve a similar workup if they blew off the very basis of their legitimacy, namely trade-based prosperity, by starting a war. (China has not fought a battle in 23 years.) India and Pakistan came dangerously close to war in 2002, but they backed off when both sides realized that millions would die and have since stabilized relations. Neither North nor South Korea could win a war at an acceptable cost.

What about other kinds of armed conflict, like civil wars and conflicts that miss the 1,000-death cutoff? Remarkably, they too have been in decline. Civil wars are fewer, smaller and more localized. Terrible flare-ups occur, and for those caught in the middle the results are devastating—but far fewer people are caught in the middle. The biggest continuing war, in Afghanistan, last year killed about 500 Americans, 100 other coalition troops and 5,000 Afghans including civilians. That toll, while deplorable, is a fraction of those in past wars like Vietnam, which killed 5,000 Americans and nearly 150,000 Vietnamese per year. Over all, the annual rate of battle deaths worldwide has fallen from almost 300 per 100,000 of world population during World War II, to almost 30 during Korea, to the low teens during Vietnam, to single digits in the late 1970s and 1980s, to fewer than 1 in the 21st century.

As the political scientist John Mueller has pointed out, today's civil wars are closer to organized crime than traditional war. Armed militias—really gangs of thugs—monopolize resources like cocaine in Colombia or coltan in Congo, or terrorize the locals into paying tribute to religious fanatics, as in Somalia, Nigeria and the Philippines.

Nor has the suffering merely been displaced from soldiers to civilians. The much-quoted statistic that war deaths a century ago were 90 percent military and 10 percent civilian, while today the ratio is reversed, resulted from an error in a 1994 United Nations report that mistakenly compared deaths in World War I with refugees and wounded in the 1980s. The real ratio is around 50-50 and stable through time. Yes, atrocities against civilians continue, but consider a historical perspective. During World War II, Allied forces repeatedly and deliberately firebombed Axis cities, incinerating tens of thousands of civilians in a night. The Germans and Japanese did far worse. Today's rapes, ethnic cleansings and suicide bombings are just as atrocious, but much smaller in scale.

Why is war in decline? For one thing, it no longer pays. For centuries, wars reallocated huge territories, as empires were agglomerated or dismantled and states wiped off the map. But since shortly after World War II, virtually no borders have changed by force, and no member of the United Nations has disappeared through conquest. The Korean War caused a million battle deaths, but the border ended up where it started. The Iran-Iraq War killed 650,000 with the same result. Iraq's annexation of Kuwait in 1990 backfired. Israel seized land in 1967, but since then most has been returned and the rest remains contested.

The futility of conquest is part of the emergence of an international community regulated by norms and taboos and wielding more effective tools for managing conflicts. Among those tools, the United Nations' 100,000 deployed peacekeepers have measurably improved the success of peace agreements in civil wars.

War also declines as prosperity and trade rise. Historically, wealth came from land and conquest was profitable. Today, wealth comes from trade, and war only hurts. When leaders' power depends on delivering economic growth, and when a country's government becomes richer and stronger than its warlords, war loses its appeal.

Perhaps the deepest cause of the waning of war is a growing repugnance toward institutionalized violence. Brutal customs that were commonplace for millennia have been largely abolished: cannibalism, human sacrifice, heretic-burning, chattel slavery, punitive mutilation, sadistic executions. Could war really be going the way of slave auctions? Nothing in our nature rules it out. True, we still harbor demons like greed, dominance, revenge and self-deception. But we also have faculties that inhibit them, like self-control, empathy, reason and a sense of fairness. We will always have the capacity to kill one another in large numbers, but with effort we can safeguard the norms and institutions that have made war increasingly repugnant.

Joshua S. Goldstein, professor emeritus of international relations at American University, is the author of *Winning the War on War: The Decline of Armed Conflict Worldwide*. Steven Pinker, a psychology professor at Harvard, is the author of *The Better Angels of Our Nature: Why Violence Has Declined*.

QUESTIONS ABOUT MEANING

1. Why and when did the idea that war is "going out of style" become popular among some scholars? Why is defining *war* so important in this essay? How do the authors define the term?

2. What reasons and evidence do the authors give for thinking that war is going out of style?

QUESTIONS FOR RHETORICAL ANALYSIS

1. What kind(s) of evidence do Goldstein and Pinker rely on? Do you find their evidence persuasive? Recall that Joel Best (in chapter 3) advises us to question large, round numbers. Does his advice apply in the case of Goldstein and Pinker's numbers? Why or why not? If the authors were to rewrite their article for an academic audience, how might they preempt any potential criticisms of their evidence?
2. What counterarguments do the authors acknowledge? Do you think their responses are sufficient? Why or why not?

MAKING CONNECTIONS

1. In his book *The Better Angels of Our Nature*, Pinker argues that the world is becoming less violent in general. It's an idea that he acknowledges most people reject. In an essay, discuss factors that you think keep most Americans from believing we live in a world that is less violent than in the past. Cite evidence for each of the factors you suggest. What do *you* think? Is the world becoming a less violent place?
2. Goldstein and Pinker identify changes in attitudes and customs as well as institutions that they say have contributed to a decline in war. Select one of the factors they name or select another factor that people believe deters war or violence and conduct some research. In an essay, present the evidence you find that either does or does not suggest a correlation between your topic and a decline of war or violence.

CHAPTER 17

Conservation and the Environment

The writers represented in this chapter share a desire to protect biodiversity and the environment. In the first reading, "Conservation-Reliant Species," an interdisciplinary team of scholars describes the scope of the challenge: Almost 1,400 species are considered "at risk" and a growing number of species depend on conservation efforts to survive. The authors review the evidence of the unprecedented threats to biodiversity.

The next article describes the threat to one specific ecosystem. In "Finding Nemo on Your Plate," marine scientist Stephanie Wear discusses the problems that overfishing have caused for the oceans' coral reefs. "For a coral reef ecosystem to function properly," explains Wear, "it depends on the presence of the wild diversity that it attracts and is home to. . . . If the seaweed doesn't get mowed down by herbivores like queen parrotfish or spiny urchins, they overgrow the corals and the corals disappear. Fish need corals too, so this becomes a vicious cycle. . . ."

In "Survival of Neonatal White-Tailed Deer in an Exurban Population," Sarah Saalfeld and Stephen Ditchkoff describe their research, designed to determine what is threatening newborn white-tailed deer near Auburn, Alabama. Their study demonstrates another conservation challenge: managing the increasing number of wildlife populations that live in close proximity to humans.

If they could talk, what might all of the endangered species have to say about the "anthropogenic threats" to their existence? This is the question environmental studies professor David Orr takes up in his essay describing a fictional courtroom scene. On trial is the human race. The charge: "In recent centuries [humans] have become so numerous and so hazardous to other members of the community and the biosphere that they should be banished from the Earth forever." Orr presents the defense attorney's argument in "The Trial."

Researchers from the natural sciences increase our awareness of threatened species and ecosystems, but the authors of the next reading argue that a successful environmental policy requires the perspectives and "analytic tools" of many disciplines. In "Conservation and the Social Sciences," Mascia et al. argue that the solutions to our environmental problems require "communication, collaboration, learning, and mutual respect" between the disciplines.

The next writers focus on specific threats to the environment. Mark Williams, Mark Losleben, and Hillary Hamann have documented changes in the amount and quality of snow in Colorado. In "Alpine Areas in the Colorado Front Range as Monitors of Climate Change and Ecosystem Response," the authors argue that subtle changes in the alpine ecosystem of the Rocky Mountains may be indicators of problems to come.

Climate change is also the topic of John Antle's article, "Climate Change and Agriculture: Economic Impacts." The news from the economic front is not all bad; in fact, climate change will have positive effects on agriculture production in some regions. However, warns Antle, "some of the poorest and most vulnerable regions of the world are likely to be impacted negatively, and in some cases, severely."

Geography professor Jared Diamond wrote the paired readings that conclude this chapter. In his essay "The Last Americans," Diamond relates the story of how the destruction of natural resources brought about the collapse of the Maya civilization, a collapse that parallels the situation in the United States today. Diamond strikes a more hopeful tone in "Will Big Business Save the Earth?" In this article he illustrates how "some of the companies that people love to hate are actually among the world's strongest forces for protecting the environment."

Together, these writers describe causes and potential solutions for threats to various species and the environments we share with them.

Interdisciplinary

"Conservation-Reliant Species," DALE D. GOBLE, JOHN A. WIENS, J. MICHAEL SCOTT, TIMOTHY D. MALE, AND JOHN A. HALL

Dale Goble is a professor of law at the University of Idaho. In the following article Goble and colleagues, including biology and fish and wildlife professors, review research that documents the growing number of species dependent on conservation efforts to survive. The authors warn that "recent anthropogenic threats to the integrity, diversity, and health of biodiversity are unprecedented, not only causing additional stress to ecosystems but also challenging our ability to respond." "Conservation-Reliant Species" originally appeared in 2012 in the journal *BioScience*, which publishes articles about biology research for researchers, educators, and students.

ABSTRACT

A species is conservation reliant *when the threats that it faces cannot be eliminated, but only managed. There are two forms of conservation reliance: population- and threat-management reliance. We provide an overview of the concept and introduce a series of articles that examine it in the context of a range of taxa, threats, and habitats. If sufficient assurances can be provided that successful population and threat management will continue, conservation-reliant species may be either delisted or kept off the endangered species list. This may be advantageous because unlisted species provide more opportunities for a broader spectrum of federal, state, tribal, and private interests to participate in conservation. Even for currently listed species, the number of conservation-reliant species—84% of* endangered *and* threatened *species with recovery plans—and the magnitude of management actions needed to sustain the species at recovered levels raise questions about society's willingness to support necessary action.*

KEYWORDS

conservation reliant, fragmented ecosystems, conservation dependent, conservation, endangered species

Humans have been altering the Earth's ecosystems for millennia (Diamond and Veitch 1981, Pyne 1995, Flannery 2001, Jackson et al. 2001). Since the onset of the Industrial Revolution, however, the temporal and geographic scales of these modifications have increased at an accelerating rate. The cumulative impact is such that it has been proposed that the world has entered a new geological era—the Anthropocene (Crutzen and Stoermer 2000). Regardless of the descriptor, the message is simple and damning: The accumulated effects of individual and societal actions, taken locally over centuries, have transformed the composition, structure, and function of the global environment (Janzen 1998, Sanderson et al. 2002, McKibben 2006, Kareiva et al. 2007, Wiens 2007). Ecological lows have become the new baseline (Pauly 1995). Although climates have always been dynamic, and threats have always existed, recent anthropogenic threats to the integrity, diversity, and health of biodiversity are unprecedented, not only causing additional stress to ecosystems but also challenging our ability to respond (Julius and West 2008). How do we manage species and ecosystems in a world of global threats and constant change (Botkin 1990)?

One response in the United States to the endangerment and loss of species was the enactment of the Endangered Species Act (ESA). The Act's goal is to bring species at risk of extinction "to the point at which the measures provided pursuant to this Act are no longer necessary" (ESA § 3(3)). The ESA's drafters envisioned this as a logical progression: Species at risk of extinction would be listed under the Act in a process that would identify the risks the species faced, a recovery plan to address these risks would be drafted, the management tools required to conserve the species would be identified and implemented at relevant scales, the species would respond by increasing in numbers and distribution, the recovery goals would be achieved, and the species would then be delisted as *recovered.* In the interim, it would be protected by the ESA's suite of extinction-prevention tools (e.g., prohibitions on taking listed species or adversely modifying their critical habitats; Goble 2010). With recovery and delisting, the formerly listed species would achieve the ESA's goal of planned obsolescence when the Act is no longer necessary. To the extent that management would be needed, it would be provided through existing federal and state regulatory mechanisms.

The past nearly four decades has demonstrated the naivete of this vision. The path to recovery is far more winding than had been imagined. Even species that have met their biological recovery goals often require continuing, species-specific management, because existing regulatory mechanisms are seldom sufficiently specific to provide the required ongoing management (Goble 2009). For example, few species have thrived as easily as the now-delisted Aleutian cackling goose (*Branta hutchinsii leucopareia*), whose populations recovered once foxes that preyed on breeding birds and chicks were eliminated from nesting islands and for which the Migratory Bird Treaty Act's monitoring and take restrictions are sufficient. The threats that most species face cannot be eliminated, only managed. The scale of anthropogenic alteration of most ecosystems means that many imperiled species will require conservation management actions for the foreseeable future to maintain their targeted population levels. Adequate postdelisting management (i.e., regulatory assurances), however, is seldom possible, because for most species, no sufficiently focused and powerful regulatory mechanism is available to replace the ESA (Goble 2009, Bocetti et al. 2012).

This is hardly surprising. The species listed under the ESA all became imperiled despite existing state and federal management systems. The problems remain: Most states lack regulatory systems that address nongame and plant species (Goble et al. 1999); funding is often tied to hunting and fishing license fees and remains insufficient (Jacobsen et al. 2010). Although existing management systems (e.g., the Marine Mammal Protection Act) may be sufficient for species such as the gray whale (*Eschrichtius robustus;* Goble 2009), the expectation that our work would be done once recovery goals have been met turns out to have been wishful thinking. Just how wishful was suggested by Scott and colleagues (2010), who examined the management actions required by recovery plans for species listed under the ESA. Scott and colleagues (2010) found that 84% of the species are conservation reliant, because their recovered status can be maintained only through a variety of species-specific management actions. Even if the biological recovery goals for these species are met, continuing management of the threats will be necessary. Reed and colleagues (2012) provide insight into this problem by describing the challenges to recovery and to postrecovery management for one of the world's most management-dependent communities: the endemic birds of Hawaii. These species are "conservation reliant" in the sense described by Scott and colleagues (2005).

The ESA is focused on moving species to the recovery threshold. The magnitude of conservation reliance makes it clear that attention must also be given to postrecovery management (Goble 2009, Scott et al. 2010). Furthermore, species not currently listed but at risk because of declining populations or range contractions are also likely to be conservation reliant. In this context, a range of management actions may be required to preclude the need to list the species under the ESA. Although comprehensive wildlife conservation strategies developed by states with funding from the federal government provide a blueprint for sustaining nongame species and their habitats, the available state funding for these management efforts is widely viewed as insufficient (Jacobsen 2010).

Earlier, we addressed the question of conservation-reliant species in the context of the ESA (Scott et al. 2005). We did so in part by placing species along a gradient of levels of human intervention and management. At one end were those species now known only in captivity, such as the Guam kingfisher *(Todiramphus cinnamominus cinnamominus),* or sustained in the wild only through repeated releases of individuals reared in captivity, such as the California condor *(Gymnogyps californianus).* These species require the greatest degree of human intervention to achieve the basic conservation objective: the prevention of extinction. At the other end of the gradient are species such as the peregrine falcon (*Falco peregrinus*), whose recovery, once the major threat of DDT (the insecticide dichlorodiphenyltrichloroethane) had been eliminated, was secured by its ability to adapt to human-dominated environments by nesting on skyscrapers and foraging in cities on pigeons (*Columba livia*) and starlings (*Sturnus vulgaris*). The falcon thus thrives under existing federal regulations that protect all birds used in falconry and no longer requires species-specific management. The species is no longer conservation reliant. Between these extremes are a variety of species that will require differing intensities and forms of management intervention to persist in the wild. The point along this gradient at which a species becomes conservation reliant is determined by the necessity of continuing, species-specific intervention, rather than the type of intervention. The need for continuing intervention is, in turn, determined by the threats that species face. In some instances, the threats can be eliminated through appropriate actions. The key to the recovery of peregrine falcons was the banning of the pesticides that contributed to eggshell thinning and reproductive failure. For the Aleutian cackling goose, it was the removal of an introduced predator on its breeding grounds. Both species now thrive under the general provisions of the Migratory Bird Treaty Act and are no longer conservation reliant.

When, however, the threat cannot be eliminated but only controlled and conservation goals can be achieved only through continuing management intervention, the species will remain conservation reliant.

In an earlier paper (Scott et al. 2005), we stated that we did not consider species either to be conservation reliant or to be delistable if they were dependent on the release of captive-reared animals or on assisted migration at the population level. We offered the California condor and the Pacific salmon (*Oncorhynchus* spp.) as examples of such species. On reflection, we now recognize that we confused the concept of *conservation reliant* with the policy decision to delist a species. By definition, all listed species are conservation reliant. The question is whether a species that has achieved recovery goals through management actions can be delisted as *recovered* without assurances that management will continue after delisting. If species-specific assurances are required, the species is conservation reliant.

The recognition that conservation reliance is a deeper and more widespread problem for listed and at-risk species than we (and others) initially thought has led us to a more nuanced perspective on this problem. In fact, two forms of conservation reliance affect species: population-management reliance and threat-management reliance. Although the ability of a species to persist is ultimately related to the characteristics and condition of both populations and the threats they face, conservation actions are often focused primarily either on managing populations or on managing threats. For example, species such as the northern Idaho ground squirrel (*Spermophilus brunneus*) live in isolated patches of habitat and may require some level of direct human intervention to move among those patches, even after local population sizes are stable (Garner et al. 2005). In contrast, other species may persist without direct population management if appropriate habitat is available. Given current land uses (and other pressures of the Anthropocene), however, human intervention may be required to maintain the habitat. As a result, it is not only species that are conservation reliant but entire ecosystems and the associated disturbance regimes (such as fire) and ecological succession pathways that define them. For example, the Karner blue butterfly (*Lycaeides melissa samuelis*), the red-cockaded woodpecker (*Picoides borealis*), and Kirtland's warbler (*Dendroica kirtlandii*) rely on periodic fire to maintain their habitat. The natural fire regimes that shaped the habitats and habitat associations of these species no longer occur, so prescribed burns must be used instead. Species such as these will continue to require threat management for the foreseeable future, even after the direct management of populations is no longer required. The two forms of conservation reliance are not independent of each other. For example, threats often influence what population actions are necessary: Where habitat encroachment has isolated small populations from each other, manipulation of the habitat may reduce habitat loss and fragmentation and may increase gene flow between the populations.

The conservation challenge is clear. The number of species that will require ongoing management is already large, and it will get larger as climate change, land-use change, human population growth, and other manifestations of the Anthropocene push more and more species to their limits. The ESA has been an effective approach for recognizing taxa that are on the brink of extinction and defining the steps needed to reverse their downward trajectory. The need for continuing intervention, even for "recovered" species, was not anticipated. We now face the conundrum that building on our conservation success will require long-term investments.

Paradoxically, continued listing under the ESA for many currently listed species may not be the best way to achieve long-term persistence. The legal restrictions imposed by the ESA may preclude some appropriate management actions. For example, landowners are often reluctant to manage their land in ways that might attract an endangered species because of the regulatory constraints imposed by the ESA (Wilcove 2004). Similarly, the paperwork and its concomitant costs in time and money are disincentives to the use of available conservation tools such as habitat conservation plans, candidate conservation agreements, and safe harbor agreements (Lin 1996, Burnham et al. 2006, Fox et al. 2006). However, delisting a species may open the door to an increasing array of unregulated threats that push it back into peril. For example, the delisting of gray wolves (*Canis lupus*) in the Northern Rocky Mountains resulted in unsustainable mortality from hunting and other pressures (Creel and Rotella 2010), which led to a judicial decision to relist the species (US District Court 2010) and a congressional decision to again delist the species through a budget rider (US Congress 2011).

To avoid such costly and contentious course reversals, a mechanism is needed to ensure that the appropriate management actions are implemented once the recovery goals for a species are met. Although no changes to the ESA are necessary to make this possible, we do need to acknowledge that continuing management is often needed after a species meets its biological recovery goals: We need a tool kit of management structures that will facilitate the transition from listed to delisted. Fortunately, examples are plentiful. The Robbins' cinquefoil (*Potentilla robbinsiana*) was delisted under a postdelisting management agreement under which the landowner (the US Forest Service) and a recreational group (the Appalachian Mountain Club) agreed to monitor and manage both the species' habitat and the threat (hikers) in order to maintain the recovered population (Goble 2009). Similarly, the Bureau of Land Management acquired nearly 3000 hectares of habitat for the Columbian white-tailed deer (*Odocoileus virginianus leucurus*) and agreed to manage its habitat through prescribed burning, grazing modifications, and restoration actions. In addition, Douglas County, Oregon, adopted a series of land-use and zoning ordinances designed to maintain habitat and corridors for the species (Goble 2009). The conservation management agreement for the grizzly bear (*Ursus arctos horribilis*) in the Greater Yellowstone Area is an example of an agreement among federal, states, and tribal land- and wildlife-management agencies that can provide a structure through which postdelisting management can be assured (USFWS 2007). Such agreements operate like candidate conservation agreements that have been used to preclude the need to list at-risk species (Lin 1996).

Bocetti and her colleagues (2012) provide an example of how a biologically and legally defensible postrecovery conservation management agreement can be developed and funded. The biggest challenges lie in finding conservation partners and obtaining funding to implement the needed management actions at ecologically relevant scales. This can be complicated on an American landscape in which two-thirds of listed and other at-risk species occur on private lands outside protected areas (Groves et al. 2000). No single mechanism can meet all needs. Instead, we envision a suite of conservation tools that can be matched to the species and landscapes that meets both the conservation threats and the diverse needs of landowners with different economic and personal interests. Funding through tax rebates, real estate transfer taxes, excise taxes, general funds, and private dollars are tools that have all been used to support wildlife and their habitats (Mangun and Shaw 1984, Smith and Shogren 2001). In addition, nongovernmental groups such as the Rocky Mountain Elk Foundation, Ducks Unlimited, Trout Unlimited, and Pheasants Forever have been formed to actively manage selected species and their habitats.

Management actions undertaken to benefit conservation-reliant species offer opportunities to accelerate the removal of species from the endangered species list and to prevent other species from becoming endangered (USFWS 2001). What is required is demonstrably effective management agreements that include management and funding commitments outside the framework of the ESA. But our focus needs to shift to abating those factors that lead to endangerment, and a conservation-reliant framework may be of assistance in doing so (Averill-Murray et al. 2012). Given the criticisms of the ESA and the lower potential costs of conserving species before they are listed, understanding the ongoing management requirements of a species and responding before listing is needed has the potential to be a universal societal goal regarding species conservation. The challenge will be in creating reliable alternative funding and management structures.

The barriers to conserving and eventually delisting species are nowhere more apparent than in the Hawaiian Islands. In a thoughtful examination of our recurrent failure to implement identified recovery actions, Leonard (2008) suggested several not unrelated reasons: a lack of funding (Restani and Marzluff 2001), a lack of understanding both in the islands and on the mainland of the importance and urgent need for conservation action, and social and political barriers that reflect conflicting management goals for areas in which endangered species occur (e.g., hunting mouflon sheep [*Ovis aries orientalis*] versus maintaining the integrity, diversity, and health of palila [*Loxioides bailleui*] habitat; Banko 2009).

The consequences of failing to implement needed management actions are not trivial. The refusal to remove feral ungulates from the critical habitat of the species, despite its priority in a 1977 recovery plan and several court orders, has resulted in the continuing decline of the palila (Banko 2009). On Kauai, despite a 1984 recovery plan (Sincock et al. 1984) that called for the removal of feral ungulates from the core habitat of endangered forest birds, no action was taken until 2011. In the interim, five species went extinct (Pratt 2009) and two more species have been added to the list of endangered wildlife (USFWS 2010). The failure to act on the information in the recovery plans was a consequence of social and political pressures resulting from the perceived conflict between management intervention to recover endangered species and the continued hunting of introduced ungulates. A lack of funding also contributed to the problem.

The task we face is daunting. There are nearly 1400 listed species, and there are indications that the actual number of at-risk species is an order of magnitude or greater more (Wilcove and Master 2005). At this point, it is naive to continue to assume that funding will be available for the management needed to prevent the listing of at-risk species or to recover and manage listed species. The average expenditure for the recovery of listed species is less than a fifth of what is needed (Miller et al. 2002), and expenditures for recovery are often distributed among species for nonbiological reasons (DeShazo and Freeman 2006, Leonard 2008). Furthermore, the number of warranted but precluded decisions by the US Fish and Wildlife Service (USFWS) is increasing, and recovery has been designated a fourth-tier priority in the USFWS's guidelines for recovery planning.

Continuing business as usual, in which the majority of recovery funds are used to conserve a few iconic species while others are only monitored or simply ignored, will achieve little of lasting value. Even with increased funding, it is unlikely that we can conserve all species facing extinction, particularly as the queue gets longer. We must develop sensible ways of assigning conservation priorities in which both the magnitude of management required and the potential benefits of management and conservation actions are considered. Information about the degree of conservation reliance of a species is central to developing sensible conservation priorities.

ACKNOWLEDGMENTS

Some of the ideas presented in this article arose in part from a technical session—"Science underlying the post-recovery management of listed species"—conceived and organized by John Hall, J. Michael Scott, and Deborah Crouse of the US Fish and Wildlife Service as part of the Strategic Environmental Research and Development Program and the Environmental Security Technology Certification Program's Partners in Environmental Technology symposium held on 4 December 2008. However, no content in this article is endorsed by the US government. The Burton Ellis Fund provided partial funding for DDG.

REFERENCES CITED

Averill-Murray RC, Darst CR, Field KJ, Allison LJ. 2012. A new approach to conservation of the Mojave Desert tortoise. *BioScience* 62: 893–899.

Bocetti CI, Goble DD, Scott JM. 2012. Using conservation management agreements to secure postrecovery perpetuation of conservation-reliant species: The Kirtland's warbler as a case study. *BioScience* 62: 874–879.

Botkin DB. 1990. *Discordant Harmonies: A New Ecology for the Twenty-First Century*. Oxford University Press.

Burnham W, Cade TJ, Lieberman A, Jenny JP, Heinrich WR. 2006. Hands-on restoration. Pages 237–246 in Goble D, Scott JM, Davis FW, eds. *The Endangered Species Act at Thirty, vol. 1: Renewing the Conservation Promise*. Island Press.

Creel S, Rotella JJ. 2010. Meta-analysis of relationships between human offtake, total mortality and population dynamics of gray wolves (*Canis lupus*). *PLoS ONE* 5 (art. e12918). doi:10.1371/journal.pone.0012918

Crutzen PJ, Stoermer EF. 2000. The "Anthropocene." *Global Change Newsletter* 41: 17–18.

DeShazo JR, Freeman J. 2006. Congressional politics. Pages 68–71 in Goble DD, Scott JM, Davis FW, eds. *The Endangered Species Act at Thirty, vol. 1: Renewing the Conservation Promise*. Island Press.

Diamond JM, Veitch CR. 1981. Extinctions and introductions in the New Zealand avifauna: Cause and effect? *Science* 211: 499–501.

Flannery T. 2001. *The Eternal Frontier: An Ecological History of North America and Its Peoples*. Text.

Fox J, Daily GC, Thompson BH, Chan KMA, Davis A, Nino-Murcia A. 2006. Conservation banking. Pages 228–243 in Scott JM, Goble DD, Davis FW, eds. *The Endangered Species Act at Thirty, vol. 2: Conserving Biodiversity in Human-Dominated Landscapes*. Island Press.

Garner A, Rachlow JL, Waits LP. 2005. Genetic diversity and population divergence in fragmented habitats: Conservation of Idaho ground squirrels. *Conservation Genetics* 6: 759–774.

Goble DD. 2009. The Endangered Species Act: What we talk about when we talk about recovery. *Natural Resources Journal* 49: 1–44.

———. 2010. A fish tale: A small fish, the ESA, and our shared future. *Environmental Law* 40: 339–362.

Goble DD, George SM, Mazzaika K, Scott JM, Karl J. 1999. Local and national protection of endangered species: An assessment. *Environmental Science and Policy* 2: 43–59.

Jackson JBC, et al. 2001. Historical overfishing and the recent collapse of coastal ecosystems. *Science* 293: 629–637.

Jacobsen CA, Organ JF, Decker DJ, Batcheller GR, Carpenter L. 2010. A conservation institution for the 21st century: Implications for state wildlife agencies. *Journal of Wildlife Management* 74: 203–209.

Janzen D. 1998. Gardenification of wildland nature and the human footprint. *Science* 297: 1312–1313.

Julius SH, West JM, eds. 2008. Preliminary Review of Adaptation Options for Climate-Sensitive Ecosystems and Resources. Environmental Protection Agency. Synthesis and Assessment Product no. 4.4.

Kareiva P, Watts S, McDonald R, Boucher T. 2007. Domesticated nature: Shaping landscapes and ecosystems for human welfare. *Science* 316: 1866–1869.

Leonard DJ Jr. 2008. Recovery expenditures for birds listed under the US Endangered Species Act: The disparity between mainland and Hawaiian taxa. *Biological Conservation* 141: 2054–2061.

Mangun WR, Shaw WW. 1984. Alternative mechanisms for funding nongame wildlife conservation. *Public Administration Review* 44: 407–413.

McKibben B. 2006. *The End of Nature*. Random House.

Miller JK, Scott JM, Miller CR, Waits LP. 2002. The Endangered Species Act: Dollars and sense? *BioScience* 52: 163–168.

Pauly D. 1995. Anecdotes and the shifting baseline syndrome of fisheries. *Trends in Ecology and Evolution* 10: 430.

Pratt TK, Atkinson CT, Banko PC, Jacobi JD, Woodworth BL, Mehroff LA. 2009. Can Hawaiian forest birds be saved? Pages 552–558 in Pratt TK, Atkinson CT, Banko PC, Jacobi JD, Woodworth BL, eds. *Conservation Biology of Hawaiian Forest Birds: Implications for Island Avifauna*. Yale University Press.

Pyne SJ. 1995. *World Fire: The Culture of Fire on Earth*. Holt.

Reed JM, DesRochers DW, VanderWerf EA, Scott JM. 2012. Long-term persistence of Hawaii's endangered avifauna through conservation-reliant management. *BioScience* 62: 881–892.

Restani M, Marzluff JM. 2002. Funding extinction? Biological needs and political realities in the allocation of resources to endangered species recovery. *BioScience* 52: 169–177.

Sanderson EW, Jaiteh M, Levy MA, Redford KH, Wannebo AV, Woolmer G. 2002. The human footprint and the last of the wild. *BioScience* 52: 891–904.

Scott JM, Goble DD, Wiens JA, Wilcove DS, Bean M, Male T. 2005. Recovery of imperiled species under the Endangered Species Act: The need for a new approach. *Frontiers in Ecology and the Environment* 3: 383–389.

Scott JM, Ramsey FL, Lammertink M, Rosenberg KV, Rohrbaugh R, Wiens JA, Reed JM. 2008. When is an "extinct" species really extinct? Gauging the search efforts for Hawaiian forest birds and the ivory billed woodpecker. *Avian Conservation and Ecology* 3 (2, art. 3). (2 July 2012; www.ace-eco.org/vol3/iss2/art3)

Scott JM, Goble DD, Haines AM, Wiens J, Neel MC. 2010. Conservation-reliant species and the future of conservation. *Conservation Letters* 3: 91–97.

Smith RBW, Shogren JF. 2001. Protecting endangered species on private land. Pages 326–342 in Shogren J, Tschirhart J, eds. *Protecting Species in the United States: Biological Needs, Political Realities, Economic Choices.* Cambridge University Press.

US Congress. 2011. House Concurrent Resolution 37, 112th Congress, 1st Session, sec. 1713.

US District Court. 2010. Defenders of Wildlife v. Salazar. Federal Supplement 2d Series 729: 1207–1229.

[USFWS] US Fish and Wildlife Service. 2002. PECE: Policy for Evaluation of Conservation Efforts when Making Listing Decisions. USFWS, National Oceanic and Atmospheric Administration.

———. 2007. Endangered and threatened wildlife and plants; final rule designating the Greater Yellowstone Area population of grizzly bears as a distinct population segment; removing the Yellowstone Distinct population segment of grizzly bears from the federal list of endangered and threatened wildlife; 90-day finding on a petition to list as endangered the Yellowstone distinct population of grizzly bears. *Federal Register* 72: 14866–14938.

Wiens JA. 2007. The demise of wildness? *Bulletin of the British Ecological Society* 38: 78–79.

Wilcove DS. 2004. The private side of conservation. *Frontiers in Ecology and the Environment* 3: 326.

Dale D. Goble (gobled@uidaho.edu) is affiliated with the College of Law at the University of Idaho, in Moscow. John A. Wiens is affiliated with Point Reyes Bird Observatory Conservation Science, in Petaluma, California, and with the School of Plant Biology at the University of Western Australia, in Crawley. J. Michael Scott is affiliated with the Department of Fish and Wildlife at the University of Idaho, in Moscow. Timothy D. Male is affiliated with Defenders of Wildlife, in Washington, DC. John A. Hall is affiliated with the Strategic Environmental Research and Development Program and with the Environmental Security Technology Certification Program, under the US Department of Defense, in Arlington, Virginia.

QUESTIONS ABOUT MEANING

1. What was the original goal of the Endangered Species Act? Why do the authors now consider that goal to be naïve?
2. Efforts to protect vulnerable species—such as listing them as endangered—are sometimes complicated by unintended outcomes. What are some examples?

QUESTIONS FOR RHETORICAL ANALYSIS

1. According to the *BioScience* website, the journal's articles are accessible to "researchers, educators, and students alike." In what ways is the content of this article made accessible for lay readers? What features of the article also fulfill the expectations of academic readers?
2. Reread the article's introductory paragraph. What functions do the citations serve (including the reference to Jared Diamond, featured later in this chapter)? How would you describe the organization of ideas in this paragraph?

MAKING CONNECTIONS

1. Later in this chapter, David Orr imagines humans being put on trial by the Congress of all Beings. The charge is that humans have become "so hazardous to other members of the community and the biosphere that they should be banished from the Earth forever." All of earth's creatures fill the jury box. Imagine that you have been hired by the prosecuting attorney to make the case against humans. Using information from various authors in this chapter, write the prosecutor's argument explaining why humans should be banished from Earth. Use the defense attorney's argument in Orr's article as a model for writing your own argument.
2. Like Mascia et al. and Wear, Goble et al. mention the role that collaborations can play in protecting endangered species. Write an essay in which you use examples from these authors and contribute examples of your own or examples gathered from research to show how disciplines or organizations are collaborating to solve complicated conservation or environmental problems.

Marine Science

"Finding Nemo on Your Plate," STEPHANIE WEAR

The effects of overfishing on reefs and on the people who depend on them is the focus of the next article from the Nature Conservancy's blog. The Nature Conservancy is a not-for-profit organization dedicated to the conservation of biological diversity. According to the organization's website, their mission is to "conserve the lands and waters on which all life depends."

Stephanie Wear is the lead scientist for coral reef conservation at the Nature Conservancy and a member of the biology department at the University of Florida. Her blog posting, "Finding Nemo on Your Plate," is from 2011.

I started my conservation career working in the U.S. Virgin Islands and have a clear memory of my orientation tour of St. Croix. One of our last stops was the Frederiksted pier, where we leapt into the clear blue water to cool off—something that a bunch of local kids were doing that day as well.

After climbing out of the water, I noticed two young boys fishing off the rocks. I went over to see their catch. I was shocked to see that they had a beautiful and tiny reef fish (maybe 4 inches long). Commonly known as the cow fish or box fish, this fish actually doesn't even have much flesh on it, is pretty boney and doesn't get bigger than 18 inches (I've never seen one that big though!).

It is a curious creature and one of my favorite finds when snorkeling—definitely not something I expected to see being fished. I figured that perhaps it was a local delicacy so I inquired further. "What are you going to do with this fish?" I asked. The young boy answered simply "pot fish."

Since I was new to the island, I got some clarification. It turns out that pot fish is a favorite local food—basically a fish stew of sorts, and this little guy was going to be used to give it a fishy flavor. I had always thought of those wild looking critters as a treat to find, but not a treat to eat.

This experience blew me away and was the first of many realizations I had while living there about the state of the fisheries in general, and how much people relied on the sea for their food.

What I learned in my years living and working in the Virgin Islands was that pretty much any fish is fair game, no matter the size, just as long as it was not considered toxic, and even then some folks chose to take their chances.

Long gone are the days of plentiful grouper and snapper that steam on the grill with sweet goodness all around. Today, those fleshy fish are few and far between and now folks rely on fish you would expect to see in your fish tank, not on your dinner plate. Overfishing has become a major problem for coral reefs. For a coral reef ecosystem to function properly, it depends on the presence of the wild diversity that it attracts and is home to.

From the predator to the grazer (herbivore) to the very picky eaters (specialists), each fish plays an important part in the coral reef "city." What has happened in the Caribbean and in many other parts of the world is that people have essentially fished down the food chain so that the reef city is out of balance and in some cases, basic functions come to a screeching halt. Think New York City with no garbage pick-up in the summertime—a big stinking mess!

In the case of coral reefs, the fish that are now landing on the dinner plate, the grazers, are extremely important for keeping coral competitors in check (namely, seaweed). If the seaweed doesn't get mowed down by herbivores like queen parrotfish or spiny urchins, they overgrow the corals and the corals disappear. Fish need corals too, so this becomes a vicious cycle if something isn't done to help fish populations recover.

There are many ways to address this problem, and we are working locally all over the globe to help communities manage their coral reef and fishery resources so that they benefit long term from the sea's bounty.

In this case, everyone is part of the solution, including you. Make sure that you choose sustainable seafood. There are great guides that help you determine whether the seafood is free of toxic metals, how harmful the fishing method is on ocean habitats and the condition of the particular fish population you are considering for dinner (i.e., in decline, recovering, or healthy).

The latest recommendations change frequently to reflect the latest guidance thanks to proactive programs like Blue Ocean Institute's Fish-Phone and Monterey Bay Aquarium's Seafood Watch.

These guides are simple, color-coded and have gone from providing wallet cards to smart phone apps, making your decision process easier.

These guides require you to know where your fish comes from because this can make all the difference in terms of how it was farmed or caught. If the menu or market isn't labeling their fish, just ask. These days, most places will be able to tell you where their fish is from. If they don't know, don't buy it.

Now with your new tools in hand, and grilling season on the horizon—be sure to take a few extra steps to make sure your seafood isn't harming the reefs and the people that depend on them.

QUESTIONS ABOUT MEANING

1. Why is Wear concerned about people fishing for what she calls "grazers"?
2. What can individuals do to help protect coral reefs and prevent overfishing?

QUESTIONS FOR RHETORICAL ANALYSIS

1. What is the point of the opening story about two boys fishing? How does Wear remind readers of those two boys in the conclusion? What is the effect of ending the essay this way?

2. According to the Nature Conservancy's website, the organization uses a "non-confrontational, collaborative approach" to promoting conservation. In what ways does Wear make her message non-confrontational? What ethos does she create through her tone and language choice? Cite examples.

MAKING CONNECTIONS

1. Goble et al., Saalfeld and Ditchkoff, and Wear all refer to the challenge of managing wildlife and sea life so that both overpopulation and extinction are avoided. In an essay, synthesize examples from these authors to illustrate the challenge. Then, describe the solutions they (particularly Goble et al. and Wear) propose. Do you think their solutions are practical and realistic? Can you suggest other potential solutions?
2. Williams, Losleben, and Hamann, along with Wear, warn of ecosystems under threat, but their arguments illustrate very different kinds of writing. In a rhetorical analysis essay, compare the authors' vocabulary, writing style, evidence, and presentation to demonstrate how genre and audience shape a writer's message.

Wildlife Ecology

"Survival of Neonatal White-Tailed Deer in an Exurban Population,"

SARAH T. SAALFELD AND STEPHEN S. DITCHKOFF

The next article describes research conducted by Sarah Saalfeld, while she was a graduate student, and Stephen Ditchkoff, an Auburn University wildlife ecology professor. In their study, Saalfeld and Ditchkoff attempt to determine what is causing the death of neonatal (i.e., newborn) white-tailed deer living near Auburn, Alabama. Their research was originally published in 2007 in the *Journal of Wildlife Management*.

ABSTRACT

As humans continue to move further from the urban epicenter and expand into suburban and exurban areas, problems involving coexistence of wildlife and human populations will become increasingly common. Wildlife biologists will be tasked with reducing wildlife–human conflicts, and their effectiveness will be a function of their understanding of the biology and life-history characteristics of wildlife populations residing in areas with high human density. In this study, we examined causes and timing of deaths of neonatal white-tailed deer (Odocoileus virginianus) *in an exurban area of Alabama in 2004 and 2005, estimated survival rates, and determined factors that influenced survival for the initial 8 weeks of life. We found 67% mortality, with the leading causes being predation by coyotes* (Canis latrans; 41.7%) *and starvation due to abandonment (25%). These results suggest that coyote predation may be a significant source of natural mortality in exurban areas. Contrary to our original expectations, vehicle collisions were not an important cause of mortality.*

KEY WORDS

abandonment, *Canis latrans,* coyote, exurban, fawn, neonatal mortality, *Odocoileus virginianus,* predation, survival rates, white-tailed deer

As humans continue to move further from the urban epicenter, wildlife–human conflicts have been increasing. Once a suitable habitat for only a few species, human settlements are now designed in such a way that allows wildlife to live alongside human populations (Ditchkoff et al. 2006). This new landscape (deemed exurbia) is characterized by a mixture of suburban and rural qualities including a combination of farms, forests, estates, and large-acreage suburbs (Nelson 1992). By creating larger lots and maintaining native vegetation between houses, wildlife populations can better co-exist with urban expansion. Beginning in the 1990s, exurbia has been developing faster than all other landscape types (Nelson and Sanchez 2005). Because of this, management of wildlife populations residing in these areas is becoming increasingly important (Ditchkoff et al. 2006). White-tailed deer (*Odocoileus virginianus*) have caused considerable concern in these areas due to overabundant populations and increased wildlife–human conflicts (e.g., vehicular accidents and foraging on landscaping).

A large amount of natural mortality in white-tailed deer occurs during the first few months of life. Although numerous studies on survival of neonatal white-tailed deer have been conducted (see Linnell et al. 1995), none have focused on exurban or suburban populations. Wildlife residing in exurban or suburban areas are exposed to different predation and mortality risks such as vehicular traffic (Forman and Alexander 1998, Koenig et al. 2002) and predation by domestic animals (Koenig et al. 2002, Gillies and Clout 2003, Lepczyk et al. 2003). These different sources of mortality have the potential to alter survival and population growth, which then influences management decisions. In Missouri, USA, adult mortality was similar between urban and rural (forested and agricultural) areas; however, causes of mortality were different with vehicular accidents replacing hunting mortality in urban areas (Hansen and Beringer 2003). Additionally, deer–vehicular collisions were the greatest cause of adult white-tailed deer mortality in Chicago, Illinois, USA (Etter et al. 2002). Despite the impacts such differences in mortality risks can have on management, management decisions for exurban and suburban areas have been based on knowledge obtained from rural areas. Thus, we examined cause and timing of death of neonatal white-tailed deer, estimated survival, and evaluated potential factors that influenced neonate survival in an exurban area in Alabama, USA.

STUDY AREA

Our study site was located in an exurban area of Auburn, Alabama. Our study area consisted of a cluster of large-acreage suburban developments with 0.4–2.0-ha lots, which maintained much of the native vegetation and wooded areas between houses, suitable for wildlife corridors. In addition, we examined deer from Chewacla State Park, Auburn, Alabama, a 281.3-ha tract of land, surrounded by these suburban developments. Our study area was divided by low-density 2-lane suburban streets and bordered by a major interstate (I-85) with high-speed traffic. Deer on this site regularly crossed roads and lived in close proximity to human populations.

METHODS

Between March and August in 2004 and 2005, we captured and fitted adult female white-tailed deer ($n = 46$) with vaginal implant transmitters (Models M3950 and M3930; Advanced Telemetry Systems, Isanti, MN). We anesthetized captured deer similar to Kilpatrick and Spohr (1999) using an intramuscular injection of telazol (250 mg) and xylazine (200 mg), administered with dart guns over areas baited with whole corn. We inserted a vaginal implant transmitter approximately 15–20 cm into the vaginal canal of each anesthetized deer, with the silicone wings pressed firmly against the cervix (Carstensen et al. 2003). These transmitters were specifically designed to be expelled during the birth process and emit a signal when the temperature of the transmitter changed from 34° C to 30° C (Bowman and Jacobson 1998). In addition, while females were anesthetized, we removed the first incisor similar to Nelson (2001) and we determined age of the female from annuli in the cementum (Matson's Laboratory, Milltown, MT; Low and Cowan 1963, Gilbert 1966). We reversed all females with an intramuscular injection of tolazoline hydrochloride (200 mg).

We monitored females approximately every 8 hours beginning in July through August to locate neonates soon after birth. Once a transmitter was expelled, we waited ≥4 hours after the pulse rate switched to locate the birth site through hand-held telemetry. We applied these methods to ensure adequate time for mother–neonate bonding and to maintain some consistency in the amount of time following birth that we caught and weighed neonates. If the neonate had moved from the birth site, we expanded the search area to a 200–300-m radius around the birth site as described by Carstensen et al. (2003). In addition, we used a thermal-imaging camera (Thermal-Eye 250D; L-3 Communications Infrared Products, Dallas, TX) to help locate neonates moved from the birth site. Once located, we captured each neonate by hand with the use of nonscented latex gloves. We weighed and radiotagged each neonate using an expandable radiocollar (Model M4210, Advanced Telemetry Systems; Diefenbach et al. 2003), allowing us to monitor survival for approximately 6–12 months. These collars were designed to give a signal if activity was undetected for 6 hours and included a coding system allowing us to determine the exact time motion ceased. We restricted handling to <10 minutes and 1–2 handlers. The Institutional Animal Care and Use Committee (Auburn University, AL; No. 2003–0530) approved all handling procedures.

Following release, we located each neonate more than once per day. We ascertained cause of death for each mortality. We distinguished predators by comparison of location and description of remains, hair found at site, and bite marks (Cook et al. 1971, White 1973, Garner et al. 1976). When we could not determine conclusively that predation was the cause of death, but evidence suggested predation (e.g., found only collar with bite marks or near predator scat or time exceeded 24 hr following death and scavenging could not be eliminated as a possibility), we classified the neonates as possibly predated. We necropsied those neonates for which causes of death could not be determined in the field. We identified emaciation similar to Sams et al. (1996) by severe atrophy of adipose tissue, absence of gastrointestinal contents, and presence of meconium in lower intestines. However, we were normally unable to determine the cause of emaciation. Potential causes included natural abandonment, human-induced abandonment, mortality of mother, mother unable to return to neonate, and neonate being unable to nurse. If we were unable to determine cause of death by these procedures we classified it as unknown.

We performed survival analysis with a known-fate model in program MARK version 4.2 (White and Burnham 1999). We modeled weekly survival for the initial 8 weeks of life (56 d), the approximate time before weaning occurred. We developed a candidate model set consisting of 18 models including time following birth (i.e., survival was different among the 8 weeks following birth), a linear time trend (i.e., survival for each week following week was related in a linear trend over time), and individual covariates: year (coded: 2004 = 1; 2005 = 0), mass of neonate at birth, sex of neonate (coded: M = 1; F = 0), birth date, and age of mother (divided into 2 groups; coded: ≤2.5 = 0 and >2.5 = 1). We used Akaike's Information Criterion corrected for small size (AIC_c) to select the best models and calculated parameter likelihoods, estimates, standard errors, and odds ratios from the estimates given by MARK. To test the goodness-of-fit of the most general model, we used Hosmer and Lemeshow goodness-of-fit statistic (PROC LOGISTIC; SAS Institute, Cary, NC). In addition, we used a *t*-test to test for differences in birth date and birth mass between years. We used a chi-square to test for differences in survival between years. We also tested for differences in mother's condition (i.e., age and chest girth) among neonates that lived, died due to emaciation, and died of all other causes with an analysis of variance.

RESULTS

We implanted 46 females in 2004 and 2005 with vaginal implant transmitters, of which 28 resulted in the successful captures of neonates (8 sets of twins, 20 singletons). Unsuccessful captures from transmitters resulted from premature expulsion of transmitter (n = 9), transmitter failure (n = 2; one of which we replaced), transmitter malfunction (i.e., irregular pulse rate; n = 1), failure to locate neonates after birth (n = 1), and implantation of infertile or postparturition females as determined by expulsion of transmitter after birthing season (n = 6).

We captured a total of 36 neonates, 17 in 2004 and 19 in 2005. Mean birth date in 2004 was later ($t_{34} = -2.64$; $P = 0.012$; 15 Aug) than in 2005 (4 Aug); however, mean birth mass did not differ ($t_{34} = 0.14$; $P = 0.893$) between years (2004: $\bar{x} = 2.50$ kg, SE = 0.19; 2005: $\bar{x} = 2.53$ kg, SE = 0.11; range for both yr = 1.35–4.10 kg). Overall survival for the first 8 weeks of life was 33.3%. Although survival in 2005 (42.1%) tended to be greater than 2004 (23.5%), it was not significant ($\chi^2 = 1.39$; $P = 0.238$). The most common cause of mortality during both years (41.7%) was predation by coyotes (*Canis latrans*), followed by emaciation (25.0%), possible predation (20.8%), and accidents and unknown causes (<13.0%; Table 1). When comparing maternal condition among neonates with different fates, we did not detect any differences ($P >$ 0.050) in age or chest girth of mothers for neonates that died due to

Table 1
Causes of Mortality of Neonatal White-Tailed Deer (2004–2005) during the Initial 8 Weeks of Life in Auburn, Alabama, USA

	2004		2005	
Cause of mortality	%	*N*	%	*N*
Predation	38.5	5	45.5	5
Possible predation	7.7	1	36.4	4
Emaciation	46.2	6	0.0	0
Accident[a]	0.0	0	9.1	1
Unknown	7.7	1	9.1	1

[a] Neonate fell in hole soon after birth and could not escape.

emaciation (age = 3.83 yr, chest girth = 832.50 mm), neonates that died of all other causes (age = 3.33 yr, chest girth = 809.72 mm), and neonates that survived (age = 3.58 yr, chest girth = 845.83 mm).

From the known-fate analysis the best model (AIC_c relative wt [AIC_w] = 0.43) from the set of candidate models was the additive model of the linear time trend, mass, and year (Table 2), suggesting that the change in weekly survival was a linear function of time and varied between years and between masses at an equal rate. The second-best model ($\Delta AIC_c = 0.61$, $AIC_w = 0.31$), the additive model of the linear time trend and mass, also had some strength of evidence as a plausible model. Therefore, we determined parameter likelihoods, estimates, and standard errors using model averaging. The parameter likelihoods illustrated that the linear time trend (likelihood = 0.92; estimate = 0.29; SE = 0.01), mass (likelihood = 0.81; estimate = 0.43; SE = 0.22), and year (likelihood = 0.58; estimate = −0.23; SE = 0.17) were the most

Table 2
Model Results from Known-Fate Analysis of Survival Rates during the Initial 8 Weeks of Life for Neonatal White-Tailed Deer in Auburn, Alabama, USA, from 2004–2005

Model	No. Parameters	ΔAIC_c [a]	AIC_w [b]
S (linear time trend + yr + mass)[c]	4	0.00	0.43
S (linear time trend + mass)	3	0.61	0.31
S (linear time trend + yr)	3	2.93	0.10
S (linear time trend)	2	3.25	0.08
S (yr + mass)	3	5.06	0.03
S (mass)	2	6.77	0.01
S (yr × mass)[d]	4	6.85	0.01
S (time + yr + mass)	10	9.42	0.00
S (time + mass)	9	9.59	0.00
S (yr)	2	9.60	0.00
S (.)[e]	1	11.12	0.00
S (time)	8	11.80	0.00
S (time + yr)	9	11.85	0.00
S (sex of neonate)	2	12.50	0.00
S (birth date)	2	12.93	0.00
S (age of mother)	2	13.14	0.00
S (time + age of mother)	9	14.02	0.00
S (time × yr)[f]	16	19.83	0.00

[a] Difference between model's Akaike's Information Criterion corrected for small sample size and the lowest AIC_c value.
[b] AIC_c relative wt attributed to model.
[c] Model of additive effects of linear time trend, yr, and mass.
[d] Model of additive effects of yr and mass and the interaction.
[e] Model of no effects on survival.
[f] Numerical convergence not reached.

important parameters to be included in the best model. From the top model we determined that survival each week following birth increased by a factor of 1.36, although not significantly (95% CI = 0.08–2.63). Similarly, survival increased by 1.69 with each additional kilogram of birth weight (95% CI = 0.07–3.31) and neonates born in 2005 were 1.49 times more likely to survive than neonates born in 2004 (95% CI = −0.11–3.09), both of which were not significant. Models containing the variables age of the mother, birth date, sex, and time following birth did not explain a significant proportion of variation in survival (Table 2). Parameter likelihoods (<0.01) also indicated that age of the mother, birth date, sex of neonate, and time following birth were not likely to be included in the best model. The Hosmer–Lemeshow goodness-of-fit statistic ($\hat{c}$ = 0.714) indicated that the most general model fit the data well.

DISCUSSION

We found mortality of exurban neonatal white-tailed deer in our study to be 66.7%, of which 41.7–62.5% of total mortalities were attributed to predation by coyotes. Our neonatal mortality rate was greater than the mean rate among temperate ungulates (45%) as calculated by Linnell et al. (1995) and among studies of white-tailed deer in rural areas (range: 23.6–90.0%, $\bar{x}$= 54.8%). Additionally, 69% of these studies resulted in mortality lower than the rate observed in this study (Cook et al. 1971: 71.6%, Garner et al. 1976: 82.9%, Carroll and Brown 1977: 40.8%, Bartush and Lewis 1981: 90.0%, Epstein et al. 1985: 84.4%, Huegel et al. 1985: 23.6%, Nelson and Woolf 1987: 30.0%, Kunkel and Mech 1994: 42.9%, Sams et al. 1996: 38.2%, Long et al. 1998: 59.0%, Ballard et al. 1999: 44.0%, Ricca et al. 2002: 58.7%, Vreeland et al. 2004: 48.6%). The relatively high rate of neonatal mortality we observed in this study could be attributed to several reasons, including a function of sampling biases of other studies and higher predation rates due to sparse bedding cover and late birthing season. Because most previous studies on neonatal survival of white-tailed deer captured neonates with foot searches or female behavior, most neonates were a few days to weeks old at time of capture. Therefore, mortality occurring within the first few days of life went undetected and could have resulted in lower rates. In our study, 50.0% of mortalities occurred in the first week of life. Therefore, to accurately measure survival, it is critical that neonates are captured as early as possible or analyses account for staggered entry of individuals into survival models (Pollock et al. 1989).

We also attribute the high mortality we detected to a high coyote predation rate on this population. Other studies have detected similar coyote predation rates (>50.0% predation rate, of which >50% attributed to coyotes) of neonatal white-tailed deer in various geographic regions of the United States, including Oklahoma (Garner et al. 1976), Iowa (Huegel et al. 1985), Illinois (Nelson and Woolf 1987), and Texas (Cook et al. 1971, Carroll and Brown 1977). We suspect that the high rate of predation was due to efficient detection of bedded or nursing neonates in the open landscape of the exurban area. During the study, the majority of neonates that we captured inhabited and bedded in areas of sparse cover (i.e., wooded yards with open understory, hedge rows, landscaping near homes, etc.). Coyotes are visual hunters, and therefore it has been suggested that increased predation on neonatal white-tailed deer by coyotes is associated with sparse vegetative cover (Garner et al. 1976, Carroll and Brown 1977, Huegel et al. 1985, Nelson and Woolf 1987, Long et al. 1998). This effect would be most evident within the first 30 days of life because neonates spend much of their time bedded and therefore rely on camouflage to avoid predation (Huegel et al. 1985). The timing of the birthing season in this population could also have contributed to increased predation. In Alabama, the birthing season is much later than in other populations of white-tailed deer, occurring from late July to early September (Gray et al. 2002). This birthing season coincides with the greatest hunting population of coyotes because predispersal coyote pups are hunting independently at this time (Harrison and Harrison 1984, Harrison et al. 1991).

The second major cause of mortality in this population (25.0%) was emaciation. This cause, while relatively high (46.2%) in the first year, was absent in the second. Although there are numerous potential causes for emaciation, we believe the most likely cause in our study was abandonment. However, we were unable to determine the cause of abandonment. Potential causes include the neonate being unable to nurse, the female never returning, or the female being unable to return. However, we were able to relocate most females and, therefore, could eliminate the possibility of mortality of the mothers in most cases. Although handling-induced abandonment is a potential cause, Carstensen Powell et al. (2005) noted that increased scent transfer, increased handling time, time of capture, and increased handling stress of neonates did not influence abandonment in a free-ranging herd of white-tailed deer in Minnesota, USA. Because many of the neonates that died due to emaciation in our study were in close proximity (<30 m) to a heavily used paved biking and walking trail, we speculate that high human activity near birth sites, as found in many exurban areas, may interfere with mothers being able to return to bedded neonates and could increase rates of abandonment.

Although we had originally hypothesized that vehicular accidents would be a contributing mortality factor, we did not detect any neonatal mortality due to vehicles in our study. Vehicular accidents have been determined to be a major cause of mortality of adult white-tailed deer living in urban and suburban areas (66% of mortality, Etter et al. 2002; 73% of mortality, Hansen and Beringer 2003). However, we speculate that the sedentary nature of neonates early in life (at 4–8 weeks of age they are active only 15–20% of the time [Jackson et al. 1972]) may have resulted in neonates only infrequently crossing roads.

As with several other studies on white-tailed deer, we noted that survival was positively associated with time following birth (Garner et al. 1976, Nelson and Mech 1986, Long et al. 1998, Ricca et al. 2002, Vreeland et al. 2004) and birth mass (Verme 1962, 1977; Nelson and Woolf 1987; Kunkel and Mech 1994; Vreeland et al. 2004). Because the leading causes of mortality for this population were predation and emaciation, these results suggest that neonates are more susceptible to these causes of mortality earlier in life. Additionally, in a study done in Pennsylvania, USA, on neonatal white-tailed deer, Vreeland et al. (2004) noted similar results in that neonates were 2.14 times more likely to survive with each additional kilogram of weight at capture. It should be noted, however, that because we waited 4 hours after birth to capture neonates, most neonates would have been nursed prior to capture. The amount of milk contained within the rumen could affect birth weights. However, as is the case in most wildlife studies where complete control of the study animals is impossible, we could not determine the amount of feeding prior to weighing and our estimates of body mass contain the normal variability that would be expected due to variation in feeding and capture times of free-ranging animals.

MANAGEMENT IMPLICATIONS

As one of the fastest growing landscapes around the world, exurbia has the potential to greatly impact wildlife species inhabiting these areas. Because of this, understanding differences between wildlife in rural and exurban areas is essential for management decisions. Our results indicate that coyote predation may be a significant source of natural mortality for neonatal white-tailed deer in this environment. Although normally considered to be a hindrance to management goals for white-tailed deer, coyotes and their predation on neonatal deer should be considered an integral part of any population control strategy in the exurban landscape.

ACKNOWLEDGMENTS

We thank all of the individuals that assisted with data collection at Auburn University during the time we conducted the research. The Center for Forest Sustainability and the School of Forestry and Wildlife Sciences at Auburn University, and the Alabama Parks Division of the Alabama Department of Conservation and Natural Resources supported this research.

LITERATURE CITED

Ballard, W. B., H. A. Whitlaw, S. J. Young, R. A. Jenkins, and G. J. Forbes. 1999. Predation and survival of white-tailed deer fawns in northcentral New Brunswick. *Journal of Wildlife Management* 63:574–579.

Bartush, W. S., and J. C. Lewis. 1981. Mortality of white-tailed deer fawns in the Wichita Mountains. *Proceedings of the Oklahoma Academy of Science* 61:23–27.

Bowman, J. L., and H. A. Jacobson. 1998. An improved vaginal-implant transmitter for locating white-tailed deer birth sites and fawns. *Wildlife Society Bulletin* 26:295–298.

Carroll, B. K., and D. L. Brown. 1977. Factors affecting neonatal fawn survival in southern-central Texas. *Journal of Wildlife Management* 41: 63–69.

Carstensen, M., G. D. DelGiudice, and B. A. Sampson. 2003. Using doe behavior and vaginal-implant transmitters to capture neonate white-tailed deer in north-central Minnesota. *Wildlife Society Bulletin* 31:634–641.

Carstensen Powell, M., G. D. DelGiudice, and B. A. Sampson. 2005. Low risk of marking-induced abandonment in free-ranging white-tailed deer neonates. *Wildlife Society Bulletin* 33:643–655.

Cook, R. S., M. White, D. O. Trainer, and W. C. Glazener. 1971. Mortality of young white-tailed deer fawns in south Texas. *Journal of Wildlife Management* 35:47–56.

Diefenbach, D. R., C. O. Kochanny, J. K. Vreeland, and B. D. Wallingford. 2003. Evaluation of an expandable, breakaway radiocollar for white-tailed deer fawns. *Wildlife Society Bulletin* 31:756–761.

Ditchkoff, S. S., S. T. Saalfeld, and C. J. Gibson. 2006. Animal behavior in urban ecosystems: modifications due to human-induced stress. *Urban Ecosystems* 9:5–12.

Epstein, M. B., G. A. Feldhamer, R. L. Joyner, R. J. Hamilton, and W. G. Moore. 1985. Home range and mortality of white-tailed deer fawns in coastal South Carolina. *Proceedings of the Annual Conference of the Southeastern Association of Fish and Wildlife Agencies* 39:373–379.

Etter, D. R., K. M. Hollis, T. R. Van Deelen, D. R. Ludwig, J. E. Chelsvig, C. L. Anchor, and R. E. Warner. 2002. Survival and movements of white-tailed deer in suburban Chicago, Illinois. *Journal of Wildlife Management* 66:500–510.

Forman, R. T. T., and L. E. Alexander. 1998. Roads and their major ecological effects. *Annual Review of Ecology and Systematics* 29:207–231.

Garner, G. W., J. A. Morrison, and J. C. Lewis. 1976. Mortality of white-tailed deer fawns in the Wichita Mountains, Oklahoma. *Proceedings of the Annual Conference of the Southeastern Association of Fish and Wildlife Agencies* 30:493–506.

Gilbert, F. F. 1966. Aging white-tailed deer by annuli in the cementum of the first incisor. *Journal of Wildlife Management* 30:200–202.

Gillies, C., and M. Clout. 2003. The prey of domestic cats (*Felis catus*) in two suburbs of Auckland City, New Zealand. *Journal of Zoology* 259: 309–315.

Gray, W. N., II, S. S. Ditchkoff, M. K. Causey, and C. W. Cook. 2002. The yearling disadvantage in Alabama deer: effect of birth date on development. *Proceedings of the Annual Conference of the Southeastern Association of Fish and Wildlife Agencies* 56:255–264.

Hansen, L. P., and J. Beringer. 2003. Survival of rural and urban white-tailed deer in Missouri. *Proceedings of the Annual Conference of the Southeastern Association of Fish and Wildlife Agencies* 57:326–336.

Harrison, D. J., and J. A. Harrison. 1984. Foods of adult Maine coyotes and their known-aged pups. *Journal of Wildlife Management* 48:922–926.

Harrison, D. J., J. A. Harrison, and M. O'Donoghue. 1991. Predispersal movements of coyote (*Canis latrans*) pups in eastern Maine. *Journal of Mammalogy* 72:756–763.

Huegel, C. N., R. B. Dahlgren, and H. L. Gladfelter. 1985. Mortality of white-tailed deer fawns in south-central Iowa. *Journal of Wildlife Management* 49:377–380.

Jackson, R. M., M. White, and F. F. Knowlton. 1972. Activity patterns of young white-tailed deer fawns in south Texas. *Ecology* 53:262–270.

Kilpatrick, H. J., and S. M. Spohr. 1999. Telazol®–xylazine versus ketamine–xylazine: a field evaluation for immobilizing white-tailed deer. *Wildlife Society Bulletin* 27:566–570.

Koenig, J., R. Shine, and G. Shea. 2002. The dangers of life in the city: patterns of activity, injury and mortality in suburban lizards (*Tiliqua scincoides*). *Journal of Herpetology* 36:62–68.

Kunkel, K. E., and L. D. Mech. 1994. Wolf and bear predation on white-tailed deer fawns in northeastern Minnesota. *Canadian Journal of Zoology* 72:1557–1565.

Lepczyk, C. A., A. G. Mertig, and J. Liu. 2003. Landowners and cat predation across rural-to-urban landscapes. *Biological Conservation* 115: 191–201.

Linnell, J. D. C., R. Aanes, and R. Andersen. 1995. Who killed Bambi? The role of predation in the neonatal mortality of temperate ungulates. *Wildlife Biology* 1:209–223.

Long, R. A., A. F. O'Connell, Jr., and D. J. Harrison. 1998. Mortality and survival of white-tailed deer *Odocoileus virginianus* fawns on a north Atlantic coastal island. *Wildlife Biology* 4:237–247.

Low, W. A., and I. M. Cowan. 1963. Age determination of deer by annular structure of dental cementum. *Journal of Wildlife Management* 27:466–471.

Nelson, A. C. 1992. Characterizing exurbia. *Journal of Planning Literature* 6:350–368.

Nelson, A. C., and T. W. Sanchez. 2005. The effectiveness of urban containment regimes in reducing exurban sprawl. *DISP* 160:42–47.

Nelson, M. E. 2001. Tooth extractions from live-captured white-tailed deer. *Wildlife Society Bulletin* 29:245–247.

Nelson, M. E., and L. D. Mech. 1986. Mortality of white-tailed deer in northeastern Minnesota. *Journal of Wildlife Management* 50:691–698.

Nelson, T. A., and A. Woolf. 1987. Mortality of white-tailed deer fawns in southern Illinois. *Journal of Wildlife Management* 51:326–329.

Pollock, K. H., S. R. Winterstein, C. M. Bunck, and P. D. Curtis. 1989. Survival analysis in telemetry studies: the staggered entry design. *Journal of Wildlife Management* 53:7–15.

Ricca, M. A., R. G. Anthony, D. H. Jackson, and S. A. Wolfe. 2002. Survival of Columbian white-tailed deer in western Oregon. *Journal of Wildlife Management* 66:1255–1266.

Sams, M. G., R. L. Lochmiller, C. W. Qualls, Jr., D. M. Leslie, Jr., and M. E. Payton. 1996. Physiological correlates of neonatal mortality in an overpopulated herd of white-tailed deer. *Journal of Mammalogy* 77:179–190.

Verme, L. J. 1962. Mortality of white-tailed deer fawns in relation to nutrition. *Proceedings of the National White-Tailed Deer Disease Symposium* 1:15–38.

Verme, L. J. 1977. Assessment of natal mortality in upper Michigan deer. *Journal of Wildlife Management* 41:700–708.

Vreeland, J. K., D. R. Diefenbach, and B. D. Wallingford. 2004. Survival rates, mortality causes, and habitats of Pennsylvania white-tailed deer fawns. *Wildlife Society Bulletin* 32:542–553.

White, G. C., and K. P. Burnham. 1999. Program MARK: survival estimation from populations of marked animals. *Bird Study* 46:S120–S139.

White, M. 1973. Description of remains of deer fawns killed by coyotes. *Journal of Mammalogy* 54:291–293.

SARAH T. SAALFELD, School of Forestry and Wildlife Sciences, Center for Forest Sustainability, Auburn University, Auburn, AL 36849, USA, e-mail sarah_scherder@yahoo.com.

STEPHEN S. DITCHKOFF, School of Forestry and Wildlife Sciences, Center for Forest Sustainability, Auburn University, Auburn, AL 36849, USA

QUESTIONS ABOUT MEANING

1. Define *exurbia, neonate,* and *predation.* What did Saalfeld and Ditchkoff set out to determine in their research?
2. How did Saalfeld and Ditchkoff track deer? What were the most common causes of death for neonates in the sample?
3. Unlike previous researchers, Saalfeld and Ditchkoff did not find that automobiles were to blame for the high death rate among newborn deer. In what ways, however, was close proximity to humans responsible for deaths of newborn deer in the sample population?

QUESTIONS FOR RHETORICAL ANALYSIS

1. Analyze the introduction to the article. In what ways is it typical of introductions to academic papers? Who would you say is the intended audience for this article? Cite evidence to support your answer.
2. Chapter 2 describes what is traditionally included in each section of an original research report. With a partner, evaluate Saalfeld and Ditchkoff's research report. How closely does it adhere to the description given in chapter 2?

MAKING CONNECTIONS

1. It is important that scientists be able to describe their research for nonspecialists. This is how they obtain funding for their work and get others to care about the research. Scientists, for example, describe their research to nonscientists in grant proposals, press releases, and articles for popular magazines and newspapers.

   To see how science research gets reported to the public and to prepare for Assignment 2, below, read some articles in a science magazine (such as *Discover*) that's intended for a general audience. How do the authors engage readers? How do they convey the importance of the research? What level of vocabulary and terminology are used to explain the science methods? Analyze several of the articles summarizing research studies and list the common features. Then in an essay, identify and illustrate features that are characteristic for the magazine articles you've analyzed. Submit to your instructor both your essay and the articles you've analyzed.
2. Assume that the editor of *Discover* (or another magazine that describes science research for the general public) has hired you to write an article about Sarah Saalfeld and Stephen Ditchkoff's study ("Survival of Neonatal White-Tailed Deer in an Exurban Population") for publication in the magazine. Being careful to faithfully report the research, convey key details of their study, their findings, *and* the significance of their findings. (Why does this research matter?) Be sure to refer to the journal where the study was originally published.

   Use articles you've studied (for Assignment 1, above) as models for the title, tone, content, and structure of your article. Submit to your instructor both the article you've written and the article(s) you've used as models.

Environmental Science

"The Trial," DAVID W. ORR

"The Trial," written by David Orr, professor of environmental studies and politics at Oberlin College, appeared in 2006 in *Conservation Biology,* a peer-reviewed journal that publishes research about conservation science as well as articles about conserving Earth's biological diversity. In his essay, Orr imagines a trial. The defendants are human beings, charged with being "destructive, capricious, violent, wantonly cruel, derelict stewards, and unworthy of the appellation *Homo sapiens.*" Based on the evidence, would you find the defendants guilty?

I once asked the students in my introductory environmental studies class to assume they were the attorneys representing *Homo sapiens* before a Congress of all Beings as once described by Joanna Macy and Jonathan Seed.[1] The charge against us reads something like the following:

> *Over many thousands of years humans have proved themselves incapable of living as citizens and members of the community of life and in recent centuries have become so numerous and so hazardous to other members of the community and the biosphere that they should be banished from the Earth forever.*

All the creatures—reptiles, fishes, birds, mammals, insects, and microbes—are represented in the jury box equipped with sentience and voice. The presiding judge is an owl, said to be the wisest of all; the prosecuting attorney is a fox, said to be the most cunning. The question for my students is simply, what defense might be made on our behalf? What supporting evidence could be presented? Who among the animals and plants would speak for us?

For the most part students, although finding this an interesting exercise, conclude that no good defense can be made on any terms. But mostly, they stumble through the unreality of the scenario burdened by the assumption that humans are the pinnacle of evolution and that our desire to survive is a sufficient justification. Almost to a person they believe that, given our intelligence and the power of our technology, we will survive. A few believe we are made more or less in God's image, which gives us license to do whatever we want, devil take the hindmost. Otherwise articulate and intelligent, my students' confusion is, I think, representative of the larger befuddlement on the subject.

The question is more than just an interesting academic exercise. It goes to the heart of all of the issues of our tenure on Earth. The debate about sustainability mostly begins with an unstated anthropocentric assumption that because we want to survive, we ought to survive, making the question moot. I do not believe, however, that we ought to let ourselves off the hook quite so easily, and the reason I offer is entirely practical: if we could know why we ought to be sustained we might better understand how to go about it. To know ourselves worthy of survival, for one thing, would lend energy to our efforts toward sustainability. Believing ourselves unworthy, our efforts will lack the conviction that arises from knowing our cause to be just. For another, knowing what makes us worthy of longevity will help us set priorities in the years ahead and determine those aspects of personhood, society, economy, and culture that ought to be preserved and those that can be discarded.

The case to be made against us is straightforward. We stand accused of being destructive, capricious, violent, wantonly cruel, derelict stewards, and unworthy of the appellation *Homo sapiens*. We are driving other species into oblivion and the Earth into a period of great and tragic instability. In his opening statement the fox says, "Humans live beyond the limits and laws of nature and believe this to be their right. For every St. Francis, there are tens of thousands, no hundreds of thousands, who are destroyers and killers, believing themselves exempt from the laws of community, decency, and courtesy, and millions more who give no thought to such things whatsoever. In fact, they are no more than rapacious and clever monkeys, but without the monkey's good judgment." Laughter erupts in the jury box. When it subsides the fox goes on. "Humans are unrestrained by their religions, laws, or philosophies that have little place for nature. Once they were a small and vulnerable population, but now they have filled the world. Once their technologies were fairly harmless, but now they are Earth shattering. Because they have no foresight, said to be their chief glory, they have doomed themselves and many of us to death. We should act to remove them before they take most of us with them." Members of the jury, except the cockroaches, mosquitoes, vermin, and kudzu, seem to mumble their assent as if in unison.

The defense has to contend with numerous complexities. Perhaps humans, for all of their protestations to the contrary, are haunted by a collective death wish, as Freud once thought. Perhaps we really are not so much a rational species as we are exceedingly clever rationalizers. Again, the evidence cannot be lightly dismissed. The sources of irrationality are many, starting with the still small voice of our genes that moves us to do their bidding, and extending through our ineptitude at seeing patterns and systems and acting accordingly. Perhaps our evolutionary career has hard wired us to myopic tribal loyalties. Maybe we are just sinful and fallen and thus deserving of death, except the redeemed, as fundamentalists would have it. Having multiplied extravagantly and extended our dominion over the air, seas, lands, atom, and gene, beyond any rational limit, we are too successful for our own good. We define ourselves as consumers, a word originally designating disease. But what we consume is the planet's primary productivity on which other species depend. We think of ourselves as little more than rational players in an economic system conceived along with the industrial revolution 250 years ago—an infinitesimal slice of the 3.8 billion years of evolving life. The bloody catalog of history shows us to be stone cold vicious against our own, against animals, and against natural systems. The challenge for the defense is monumental.

As the trial opens, the attorney representing humankind—for all of its cultural and scientific attainment, and even for its bloody history—rises to give her opening statement. Jurors in their various garbs of fur, fin, shell, and feathers lean forward to hear the defense.

"Most honorable judge; my esteemed colleague of the bar, Mr. Fox; members of the jury, I am grateful for the opportunity you have afforded me to speak on behalf of my own kind, now facing charges that carry the gravest of penalties. I do so with fear and trembling for what the charges portend, but with confidence born of the knowledge that our species, for all of its shortcomings, is a worthy and promising part of the community of life. I appreciate the opportunity to speak to you members of the jury as a family with a long history. From the earliest stirrings of life in the seas, ours has been a long intertwining of biological destinies, of sharing genetic material, and of mutual learning. We have even been food for many of you." Jurors, except the parasites and those with fang and claw, look baffled, unsure whether this was an ill-conceived attempt at humor or something darker. The shark shows no emotion at all.

The attorney for the humans continued. "We have learned much from each of you. Our first inkling of what we are was shaped by communion with you Mr. Bear, and you Mr. Wolf, and you Ms. Salmon; indeed with all of you. We first came to know many of you as our teachers—the mirror by which we might better understand ourselves. For reasons not our fault, we are the only species troubled by self-consciousness and the knowledge of our mortality . . . a burden that weighs far less on all of you. Our first art attempted not just to portray some of you, but to honor you for what you taught us about ourselves. Many of you graciously fed us when we were hungry. Many of you fed our spirits by your ability to soar in the skies or play in the waters. You taught us faithfulness to place and seasons. You taught us industry, thrift, and the determination necessary to survive. The trickster coyote taught us cunning when we were weak. Our first words were a kind of crude imitation of the sounds some of you make. You taught us the habits of work and even the arts of making nests, dams, and homes. You taught us to fly, to swim, to navigate, and to return home again. You were our first teachers, for which we are grateful. Had we been more adept students we would have better learned the arts of managing fertility and sunlight taught by our sisters: the forests, the grasslands, and the deserts. Nonetheless what we are now owes to those early lessons mastered all too imperfectly. But we are quickly learning how to better mimic your ways and those of nature in our own industries." The jurors stir ominously.

Undaunted, the attorney for humankind proceeds to her next point. "We have evolved together on this small, beautiful planet. But neither we nor most of you are what you once were thousands or millions of years ago. Excepting a very few of you such as you, Mr. horseshoe crab, we have all changed. Even so, we show the unmistakable signs of our common origins in the seas. Humans differ only slightly in the makeup of their genes from their kin of only a few tens of thousands of years ago, a mere snap of the fingers in time. Still there is a difference, our mark as it were. Each of you jurors has a specialty shown by fang, appendage, power of sight, or speed, or disguise. Humans are generalists endowed with minds capable of language, reason, abstraction, and sufficient foresight to fear our own demise. None of you can do what we can do and none of you carry the fearful knowledge of mortality that we bear. But that knowledge came with an obligation as well for it was left to us to give voice to the journey of life on Earth, to write its poetry, paint its pictures, fathom its meaning, and ponder its ascent and final end—to ask why and how. Knowledge, we now understand, is both liberating and damning. Why this was left to us, and to none of you, no one can say. And no one can say what knowledge will do to humankind as the millennia roll forward. All of us in this courtroom are in a slow transition from what we were and what we are to some unknown future. The particular advantage of my kind is the mental capacity to learn and create culture much faster than the evolution that shaped all of you in this courtroom. The transition of which I speak is gathering force and speed."

The jurors are restless, impatient of what appears to be an irrelevant diversion. The wolf can be overheard muttering to the elephant that humans, "as they steal more of our secrets, the enemy" as he puts it, "will become even more tyrannical and destructive. " The elephant makes no response. Mr. Fox rises to address the judge. "Your honor, this line of argument is immaterial to the charges at hand. I respectfully request that the defending attorney be instructed to get to the point and quickly." He sits. The jurors, growing impatient, nod in assent. The defense attorney stands and responds: "Your honor, I respectfully submit that this is most relevant and I will shortly explain why and how." In a flat voice the judge snaps, "Proceed, but be quick about it."

"Thank you, your honor. To you members of the jury I will offer no justification for past wrongs, excesses, and cruelties inflicted on you and your ancestors by my own kind. But I do ask each of you to carefully consider the evidence that I will present of what is happening all around you. All over the Earth a great turning in the evolution of humankind has begun. It is driven by the forces of which I spoke moments ago. Our capacities to learn, reason, and even empathize are growing quickly. We now know ourselves to be a part of a larger story of life in the universe and are beginning to understand what that will require of us. All over the Earth humans are engaged in a momentous conversation about the terms and conditions that must be met to sustain life—yours and ours—on this planet."

"A word about our own history is in order. Cruelty toward our kind was, too, part of that history. After many years, however, and with much trouble, we have learned the value of law, restraint, fairness, decency, democracy, and even peace. Not long ago one of my gender could not have been selected for the heavy responsibility that I now bear. Have we learned these lessons well enough? By no means! But they now represent a growing force in human affairs spread by our global communications technology. We now know instantly of problems and crises that occur all over the planet, including news of our own folly. Do we always respond adequately? By no means! But we are learning and most importantly millions of people now consider their allegiance to Earth, to the future, and even to all of you as members of the community of life to be more important than those to nation and religion. Is the battle for decency won? No, but in time, I submit that it will be."

Members of the jury, if not mollified, appear to be less hostile. But the wolf, leaning on the rail of the jury box, shows utter contempt.

The attorney for humankind continues. "As I will show, humans are the first species to show kindness to another species. We, not you, ponder and often worry about such things as justice, fairness, and decency, not simply the laws of eat and be eaten. Nothing in nature dictates such things, but we believe this, too, a part of our obligation to the community of life. We have laws, imperfect to be sure, protecting each of you in some fashion." The rats, mice, chimpanzees, and a few other subjects of laboratory experiments exchange angry glances. "We were the first to see Earth from space, measure its temperature, count the number of species, and to understand its laws. We were the first among all of Earth's diverse life forms to understand our world enough to take steps to protect it." A member of the salmon nation shouts in response that "it would not need protecting were it not for your kind!" Shouts erupt throughout the court. The judge calls for order.

The attorney for the defense resumes. "The angels of our better nature are growing more powerful in human affairs. There is now a global movement to protect species, stabilize the climate, preserve habitats for each of you, to reign in our excesses, and reduce consumption. Efforts have begun to restore lands and waters that we have through carelessness and ignorance degraded. We are learning the arts of designing with natural systems in ways that give back as much as they take. We are beginning the great transition from coal and oil to efficiency and sunlight. If granted the right to survive, the difficulties and challenges we face in the years ahead are many, but the great turning in human attitudes and behavior has begun. We, a young species compared with many of you, are beginning to fulfill our promise for wisdom, compassion, and foresight. We are acquiring the scientific and technological know-how necessary to radically reduce our impacts on the Earth."

"For all of our shortcomings and liabilities, I ask you to ponder not just a world without humans . . ." She is cut off by shouts of "we'd like to!" and laughter. She resumes, slowly measuring each word: ". . . but a world not that far into the future of a partnership of life on Earth, of mutual celebration between evolution and intelligence—a better world for all. I ask each member of the jury to see this as dawn, not sunset; a beginning, not an end." Her opening statement finished, she sits. The judge asks the attorney for the prosecution to call his first witness. The trial begins.

I asked my students to say how it might turn out and why. Is there something special about *Homo sapiens* that trumps other considerations? Is there a better defense than one based on a promise to improve? Is there any evidence that we are doing better or that we will do better? Is there a kind of middle sentence between life and death? Under what terms could humankind receive a contingent life sentence or probation?

The trial, like philosopher John Rawls' "veil of ignorance," is a heuristic device to help us see what we might otherwise miss. But it is more than that. It is an invitation to ask those age-old questions, now more important than ever, about who we are and where we are going.

There will, of course, be no trial, no parole, no contingent life sentence, only an eerie and deepening silence as players in the symphony of life disappear one by one unless and until we shift course. As my students know as well there are profoundly important efforts underway to change our course along with formidable sources of resistance and the brute momentum of industrial civilization. At the dawn of the twentieth century optimism about the human condition abounded. Science and technology seemed to promise an unlimited future. Those hopes seemed to vanish in the wars, gulags, ethnic cleansings, and insensate violence of the years that followed.

Is it possible to recover a nobler vision of humanity, one grounded in science and in possibilities for something akin to species learning? Is there in us a promise of something more? Perhaps we have, as Joel Primack and Nancy Abrams (2006) suggest, a "sacred opportunity . . . a chance to be heroes . . . but we will need, collectively, to become the kind of people capable of using science to uphold a globally inclusive, long-lived civilization." Maybe there is a different story to be told, one that fuses science with a renewed sense of the sacred (Swimme & Berry 1992). Maybe it begins in overcoming the autism to the Earth that has taken hold of us but is not determined by anything in our makeup. Perhaps, as Thomas Berry (1988) puts it "we are not left simply to our own rational contrivances. We are supported by the ultimate powers of the universe as they make themselves present to us through the spontaneities within our own beings."

David W. Orr
Environmental Studies, Oberlin College, Oberlin, OH 44074, U.S.A., email david.orr@ oberlin.edu

NOTE

1. An early version of the story is the tenth-century Islamic tale *The Case of the Animals versus Man before the King of the Jinn*. The story has humans land on an island with a large number of animals. The humans begin to exploit the animals, who bring their grievances to the king of the Jinn who also lives on the island. The King rules that humans may control the animals but affirms that God is the protector of the animals (see Said & Funk 2003).

LITERATURE CITED

Berry, T. 1988. *The dream of the Earth*. Sierra Club Books, San Francisco.
Primack, J., and N. Abrams. 2006. *The view from the center of the universe*. Riverhead Books, New York.
Said, A., and N. Funk. 2003. Peace in Islam: an ecology of the spirit. Pages 166–167 in R. Foltz, F. Denny, and A. Baharuddin, editors. *Islam and ecology*. Harvard University Press, Cambridge, Massachusetts.
Swimme, B., and T. Berry. 1992. *The universe story*. Harper Collins, New York.

QUESTIONS ABOUT MEANING

1. Summarize the charge against humans and the defense attorney's case.
2. The judge in the case is, appropriately, an owl, long associated with wisdom. In what other ways does Orr allude to the symbolic or literal associations of the animals in the courtroom?

QUESTIONS FOR RHETORICAL ANALYSIS

1. The jurors grow impatient with the defense attorney's first speech, which "appears to be an irrelevant diversion." What is the attorney's purpose in that speech?
2. What appeals to ethos, pathos, and logos does the defense attorney make? Is her argument persuasive? Why or why not?

MAKING CONNECTIONS

1. Assume that you are the assistant defense attorney who has been asked to gather additional evidence to present in defense of humans. Using information from such authors as Goldstein and Pinker, Diamond, and

Antle—as well as any additional sources of information you find—make an argument in defense of humans and their potential for addressing the problems that have put all species at risk.

2. Orr's essay, though published in a science journal, includes features associated with poetry and fiction, including alliteration, imagery, wordplay and puns, humor, and irony. What, for example, is ironic about the name *Homo sapiens*? (If you don't know, look up the literal meaning of the Latin term.) What is amusing about some of the responses to the defense attorney's speech? In an essay, cite examples of the various elements Orr uses to engage, amuse, and inspire readers.

Interdisciplinary

"Conservation and the Social Sciences," MICHAEL B. MASCIA, J. PETER BROSIUS, TRACY A. DOBSON, BRUCE C. FORBES, LEAH HOROWITZ, MARGARET A. MCKEAN, AND NANCY J. TURNER

In the following editorial, a team of seven authors—representing departments of anthropology, fisheries and wildlife, environmental studies, and political science—argue that collaboration between researchers in the biological sciences, earth sciences, and social sciences is vital to the success of conservation programs. "Conservation and the Social Sciences" originally appeared in 2003 in the journal *Conservation Biology*.

As forests shrink, fisheries collapse, and species—the charismatic and the unknown—wink out around the globe, the conservation community continues to look to the biological sciences to inform policy and practice. Biology, of course, provides us with the theoretical and analytic tools to identify rare and threatened species and ecosystems. Biology also enables us to estimate the limits to human use necessary to sustain these systems. Our failure to understand these basic (though often extraordinarily complex) issues sometimes leads to conservation policies and practices ill-suited to addressing the problems they were intended to solve. More often, however, we get the biology right, but our conservation interventions still fail to sustain target species and ecosystems.

The disconnect between our biological knowledge and conservation success has led to a growing sense among scientists and practitioners that social factors are often the primary determinants of success or failure. Although it may seem counterintuitive that the foremost influences on the success of *environmental* policy could be *social*, conservation interventions are the product of *human* decision-making processes and require changes in *human* behavior to succeed. Thus, conservation policies and practices are inherently social phenomena, as are the intended and unintended changes in human behavior they induce.

Recognizing that conservation is about people as much as it is about species or ecosystems—an acknowledgement seldom explicitly made in conservation circles—suggests a significant shift in the nature and use of science in conservation. To preserve the earth's natural heritage, the social sciences must become central to conservation science and practice. Political science, anthropology, economics, psychology, sociology, geography, legal studies, and other social science disciplines all have analytic tools and established knowledge that can explain and predict patterns of human behavior—insights vital to the success of local, national, and international conservation efforts.

In the development and management of protected areas, for example, the social sciences can complement the biological sciences in critical ways. Environmental economics can often provide a powerful rationale for the establishment of protected areas by demonstrating that the value of goods and services generated by intact ecosystems exceeds that of a fragmented or transformed landscape. Anthropological research can document the sociocultural and spiritual value of biodiversity. Together with other social science disciplines, anthropology can also identify the conservation-oriented cultural beliefs, values, norms, and rules that are often well suited to serve as the foundation for the formal laws and regulations that govern protected areas. Finally, drawing upon the rich literature on the governance of "commons"—forests, fisheries, wildlife and the like—the social sciences can provide valuable insights into how decision-making arrangements, resource use rights, monitoring and enforcement systems, and conflict resolution mechanisms shape individual use of, and thus the state of, protected areas.

Protected areas are not unique. Across the full range of issues that face the conservation community today, the social sciences can contribute greatly to the development and implementation of lasting solutions by answering critical questions. Which policy initiatives most effectively curb the illegal bushmeat trade? How should public awareness programs be designed to reflect learning differences across age groups? In what markets are ecolabeling programs best suited to create the economic incentives for sustainable fisheries? What cultural beliefs and values drive the international trade in endangered species for medicinal purposes? How will long-term conservation planning and protection in Africa be affected by the demographic impacts of HIV/AIDS? The list could go on for pages.

The real question for debate, of course, is not *whether* to integrate the social sciences into conservation but *how* to do so. As a starting point for discussion, we offer a few suggestions to the Society for Conservation Biology (SCB), conservation organizations, and the academic community.

THE SOCIETY FOR CONSERVATION BIOLOGY

The SCB should highlight the vital importance of the social sciences to conservation through concrete action. First, the SCB should build upon the success of its 2002 annual meeting by making the conference theme, "People and Conservation," a core component of its annual meeting program, no different from conservation genetics or spatial ecology. Second, just as the SCB signaled its commitment to become a more international professional society by creating continent-specific organizational sections, it should establish a social science section to signal the importance of the social sciences to the global conservation community and provide a focal point for development of the field. Finally, the SCB should explore the possibility of hosting its annual meeting in conjunction with a social scientific professional society (e.g., American Anthropological Association, International Association for the Study of Common Property) to promote cross-disciplinary communication, learning, and collaboration, and to emphasize the importance of the social sciences to conservation.

CONSERVATION ORGANIZATIONS

Governmental and nongovernmental conservation organizations should take additional steps to integrate social scientific information into conservation decision-making. Many, if not most, conservation organizations have already made stakeholder participation a core component of their work; several have established small research programs that examine various aspects of the "human dimension" of conservation. True mainstreaming of the social sciences in conservation, however, will require visionary leadership and a dramatic shift in organizational behavior that far exceed these efforts. Conservation organizations should consider undertaking three obvious, yet symbolically and substantively significant, actions to catalyze the necessary organizational change:

- Hire social scientists for leadership positions and provide them with the mandate to build social science into organizational decision-making.
- Enlist social scientists to develop and manage "rapid social assessment" programs, which would provide decision-makers with a rough sketch of critical social information at potential conservation sites through short-term but intensive inquiry.
- Document and share success stories that illustrate the value of social scientific information to "on the ground" conservation results. Such success stories not only foster organizational learning, internal support, and conservation success, but also justify donor and organizational investment in the social sciences.

Ultimately, if the social sciences were truly mainstreamed in conservation, the presence of an anthropologist or a political scientist on a project team would be as commonplace and unremarkable as that of a botanist or an ornithologist.

THE ACADEMIC COMMUNITY

As conservation organizations create greater opportunities for conservation-savvy social scientists, the academic community will increasingly need to provide social scientists with conservation-relevant knowledge and skills. Professional degree programs in environmental management should train students to realize that social context is critical to conservation success and to understand why this is so. Traditional social science programs, on the other hand, should demonstrate that conservation-relevant social science is legitimate, worthy of pursuit, and capable of answering questions of profound theoretical significance. To accomplish these goals, university faculty and administrators will need to think past epistemic traditions and prejudices to explore creative new ways to provide students with both rigorous social-scientific training and conservation-relevant knowledge. In particular, the academic community should

- Develop cross-departmental initiatives, ranging from interdisciplinary team-taught courses to certificate programs to degree programs.
- Design programs to provide students with experience as conservation practitioners (e.g., through internships or apprenticeships) and thereby inform their academic inquiry.
- Reach out to biologically trained conservation practitioners, creating opportunities for these individuals to gain an appreciation for the social sciences through "short courses" and other mechanisms.

Successful models for such initiatives exist, but it is incumbent upon the academic community to make these innovative programs the rule, not the exception.

Mainstreaming the social sciences in conservation policy and practice will be difficult, but the stakes are too high and the rewards too great for the conservation community to fail to try. Biodiversity conservation is a human endeavor: initiated by humans, designed by humans, and intended to modify human behavior to achieve a socially desired objective—conservation of species, habitats, and ecosystems. Embracing this fact, and recognizing its implications for the nature and use of science in conservation, represents a challenge for academics and practitioners alike. We must all be willing to leave our comfort zone behind, to speak different languages, work in different circles, and accept different beliefs.

Communication, collaboration, learning, and mutual respect represent the path to success. Failure is an option we cannot afford.

Michael B. Mascia, American Association for the Advancement of Science Environmental Fellow, 223 Constitution Avenue NE, Washington, D.C. 20002, U.S.A., email michael.mascia@duke.edu

J. Peter Brosius, Department of Anthropology, University of Georgia, Athens, GA 30602–1619, U.S.A.

Tracy A. Dobson, Department of Fisheries & Wildlife, Michigan State University, 13 Natural Resources Building, East Lansing, MI 48824–1222, U.S.A.

Bruce C. Forbes, Arctic Centre, University of Lapland, Box 122, FIN-96101 Rovaniemi, Finland

Leah Horowitz, School of Resources, Environment and Society, Australian National University, Canberra, ACT 0200, Australia

Margaret A. McKean, Department of Political Science, Box 90204, Duke University, Durham, NC 27708–0204, U.S.A.

Nancy J. Turner, School of Environmental Studies, P.O. Box 1700, University of Victoria, Victoria, British Columbia V8W 2Y2, Canada

QUESTIONS ABOUT MEANING

1. What role can social scientists, including economists and anthropologists, play in making conservation efforts successful? What are examples of questions that social scientists can address in their research?
2. What actions do the authors recommend academics and conservation organizations (like the Society for Conservation Biology) take? What challenges do these actions entail?

QUESTIONS FOR RHETORICAL ANALYSIS

1. Divide the essay into introduction, body, and conclusion and analyze each section.
   (a). **Introduction:** What makes the first sentence an engaging and effective opener? How do the authors establish the importance of their topic? Where is the thesis statement?
   (b). **Body:** How do structural clues, formatting, organization, or topic sentences make the body easy to navigate?

(c). **Conclusion:** What moves traditionally made in essay conclusions appear in the conclusion?

2. The authors of this editorial represent several disciplines. How do the authors collectively present themselves? To whom are they writing? How can you tell?

MAKING CONNECTIONS

1. You learned in chapter 1 that different disciplines have different perspectives or ways of looking at and studying problems. The authors of this article illustrate this point and give examples of the kinds of conservation questions social scientists could address in their research.
   Suggest your own examples of conservation-related research questions that could be addressed by additional disciplines. What contribution, for example, could researchers from business, literature, history, art, computer science, or music make? These are only a few of many disciplinary perspectives you might consider.
2. In an essay, analyze how first-person pronouns (*I, my, we, our,* etc.) are used by some or all of the science writers in this chapter. (First-person pronouns appear in each article.) What purposes do the first-person references serve? How, for example, do the first-person references help to establish the writers as experts or help to show readers that the writers are like them? Do you notice any patterns concerning where the pronouns appear within articles (early? late?), or any differences in how pronouns are used in blogs and editorials versus research reports?

Geography

"Alpine Areas in the Colorado Front Range as Monitors of Climate Change and Ecosystem Response," MARK W. WILLIAMS, MARK V. LOSLEBEN, AND HILLARY B. HAMANN

Mark Williams, a professor of geography at University of Colorado, Boulder, is a hydrologist (someone who studies the water cycle), whose primary research focus is snow hydrology. "In the western U.S.," explains Williams, "about 80% of all usable water comes from snowmelt runoff. One of my main interests now is how climate change will affect the amount of water that is available for human and ecosystems." In the following article, Williams describes a case study from Green Lakes Valley–Niwot Ridge (in Colorado), where he and Mark Losleben and Hillary Hamann discovered that small changes in the ecosystem may already be affecting large mammals. "Alpine Areas in the Colorado Front

Range as Monitors of Climate Change and Ecosystem Response" was published in 2002 in the journal *Geographical Review*.

ABSTRACT

The presence of a seasonal snowpack in alpine environments can amplify climate signals. A conceptual model is developed for the response of alpine ecosystems in temperate, midlatitude areas to changes in energy, chemicals, and water, based on a case study from Green Lakes Valley–Niwot Ridge, a headwater catchment in the Colorado Front Range. A linear regression shows the increase in annual precipitation of about 300 millimeters from 1951 to 1996 to be significant. Most of the precipitation increase has occurred since 1967. The annual deposition of inorganic nitrogen in wetfall at the Niwot Ridge National Atmospheric Deposition Program site roughly doubled between 1985–1988 and 1989–1992. Storage and release of strong acid anions, such as those from the seasonal snowpack in an ionic pulse, have resulted in episodic acidification of surface waters. These biochemical changes alter the quantity and quality of organic matter in high-elevation catchments of the Rocky Mountains. Affecting the bottom of the food chain, the increase in nitrogen deposition may be partly responsible for the current decline of bighorn sheep in the Rocky Mountains.

KEYWORDS

alpine, bighorn sheep, biogeochemistry shift, climate change, nitrogen, water acidification

Many an alpine area is susceptible to environmental damages that may affect ecological health and regional economies (Dozier and Williams 1992). Moreover, small changes in the flux of energy, chemicals, and water in high-elevation catchments may invoke large changes in climate, ecosystem dynamics, and water quality. Climate change and ecosystem response may be reflected much earlier in alpine areas than in downstream forested ecosystems (Williams and Tonnessen 2000).

A decade ago, researchers began to evaluate the response of mountain ecosystems to changes in climate (Beniston 1994; Messerli and Ives 1997). Alfred Becker and Harald Bugmann suggest that the strong altitudinal gradients in mountain regions provide unique, and arguably the most useful, opportunities for detecting and analyzing global change processes and phenomena, because:

- Meteorological, hydrological, cryospheric, and ecological conditions change greatly over relatively short distances. The boundaries between these systems experience shifts due to environmental change and thus may be used as indicators of such changes.

- The higher parts of many mountain ranges are not directly affected by human activities. These areas include national parks and other protected environments. They may serve as locations where the environmental impacts of climate change, including changes in atmospheric chemistry, can be studied directly.
- Mountain regions are distributed globally, from the equator to the poles and from oceanic to highly continental climates. This global distribution allows us to perform comparative regional studies and to analyze the regional differentiation of environmental change processes as characterized above (2001).

In this article we focus on the role of snow in the alpine component of temperate mountain ecosystems. High-elevation ecosystems at midlatitudes are characterized by a six-to-nine-month period of continuous snow cover, with freezing temperatures and snow possible even throughout the summer growing season. The harsh environmental conditions characteristic of these environments suggest that organisms in alpine ecosystems are on the razor's edge of tolerance (Williams, Brooks, and Seastedt 1998). Consequently, organisms and the biogeochemical processes mediated by them may be sensitive to small environmental changes in climate and other parameters.

The presence of a seasonal snowpack in alpine environments may amplify climate signals. Mountain areas of the world have been termed "water towers for the 21st century" because of the storage and release of liquid water from the seasonal snowpack (Bandyopadhyay and others 1997, 134). Although the areal extent of alpine ecosystems is limited, snowpacks in these areas are the major source of stream runoff and groundwater recharge over wide portions of the midlatitudes. The contribution of mountain watersheds to the total surface runoff may be more than 80 percent in arid and semiarid regions such as the western United States and central Asia. The presence of snow in high-elevation areas may cause unexpected changes in streamflow in response to changes in climate at lower elevations (Williams and others 1996a). In addition to changes in water quantity, the quality of water may be changed if pollutants are added to snow and rain in alpine areas.

Our objective is to evaluate a conceptual model of how alpine ecosystems in temperate midlatitude areas respond to changes in energy, chemicals, and water. We illustrate the model's workings with a case study from Green Lakes Valley–Niwot Ridge, a headwater catchment in the Colorado Front Range of the United States, emphasizing how changes in the quantity and quality of snow may affect the quality of water. We build on current and past research activities conducted at this long-term study site (for an overview, see Bowman and Seastedt 2001).

THE STUDY SITE

The Colorado Front Range rises directly west of the Denver–Boulder–Fort Collins metropolitan area. The setting means that high-elevation basins in this portion of the Continental Divide are located just beyond a large metropolis, with nearby agricultural activities. Green Lakes Valley (40°3′N, 105°35′W) is a 700-hectare, east-facing headwater catchment that ranges in elevation from 3,250 meters to about 4,000 meters at the Continental Divide (Figure 17.1). The catchment appears to be typical of the high-elevation environment of the Colorado Front Range and includes Niwot Ridge, where research has been conducted since the early 1950s (Caine and Thurman 1990). This is both a UNESCO Biosphere Reserve and a Long-Term Ecological Research network site. The Green Lakes Valley is a water source for Boulder and is owned by the city. Public access is prohibited; hence the Green Lakes Valley is not affected by grazing or recreational activities, as are other high-elevation sites in the Front Range.

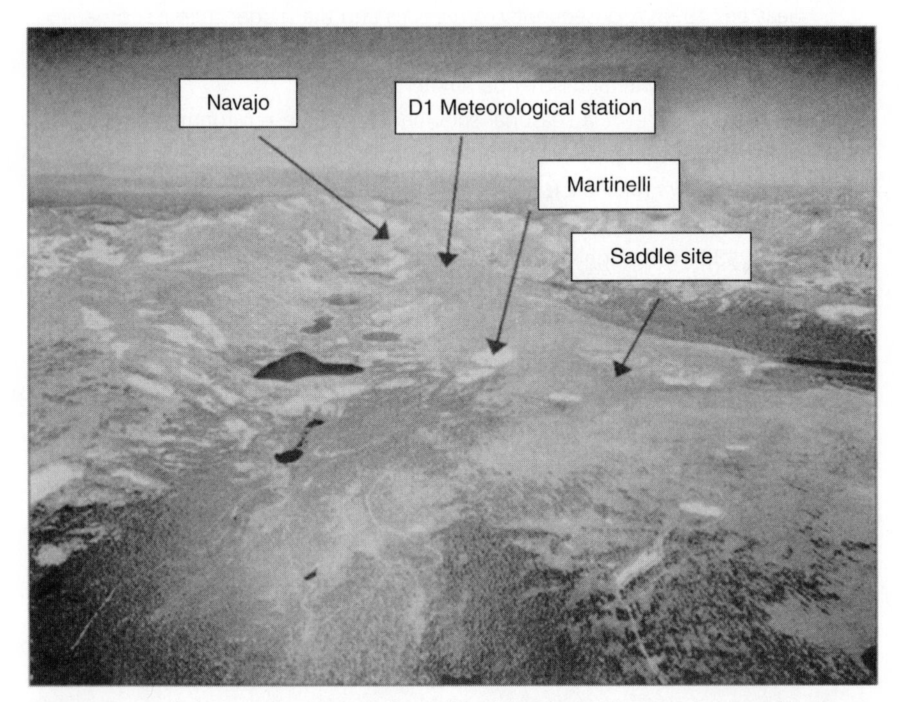

Figure 17.1 Aerial photograph of Green Lakes Valley, Colorado. Discharge and stream chemistry are presented from the 42-hectare Navajo and the 8-hectare Martinelli catchments. The climate station at D1 is on Niwot Ridge; snow lysimeters and a National Atmospheric Deposition Program collector are at the Saddle Site on Niwot Ridge. (Reproduced courtesy of the Niwot Ridge Long-Term Ecological Research Archives)

The climate of our study site is characterized by long, cool winters and a short growing season (one to three months). Since 1951 the mean annual temperature has been 3.8°C and the annual precipitation has been 1,000 millimeters (Williams and others 1996a). About 80 percent of the annual precipitation occurs as snow. Stream-flows are markedly seasonal, varying from less than 0.05 cubic meters per second during the winter months to more than 3.0 cubic meters per second at maximum discharge during snowmelt just below Lake Albion, at the lower end of the valley. The surface waters are dilute, with acid-neutralizing capacities generally less than 200 micro equivalents per liter at all sampling sites (Caine and Thurman 1990).

Several research facilities are located on Niwot Ridge, an alpine tundra ecosystem that extends eastward from the Continental Divide and forms the northern boundary of the Green Lakes Valley watershed. Climate data have been collected since the early 1950s at the D1 climate station on Niwot Ridge, at 3,750 meters. The Long-Term Ecological Research network operates a high-elevation tundra laboratory at the Niwot Ridge Saddle, located below D1 at 3,500 meters. Also in the saddle is a subnivean laboratory where snowpack meltwater samples are automatically collected before contact with the ground (Williams and others 1996b).

Methods

Precipitation amounts were collected at D1 by an unshielded Belfort recording gauge from 1951 to 1964 and with an Alter-type shield from 1964 to the present; the shielded and unshielded gauges were run concurrently for two years and the pre-1964 data adjusted. The accuracy of monthly precipitation totals is approximately 20 millimeters. Missing data were treated using regression analyses and with other nearby climate stations as presented by David Greenland (1989). Here we update information originally provided by Mark Williams and others (1996a).

Wet deposition was sampled on the Niwot Ridge saddle (3,500 meters) as part of the National Atmospheric Deposition Program (NADP), which operates about 200 wet-precipitation collectors throughout the continental United States (NADP/NTN 1984–2000). Snow and stream-water samples were collected for chemical analysis, as documented in Williams and others (1996a). For our study, snowpack meltwater samples were collected in 1-square-meter snow lysimeters before contact with the ground, following protocols elaborated by Williams and others (1996b). Meltwater discharge was measured continuously in tipping buckets, and daily grab samples were analyzed for concentrations of major solutes. Analytical analyses for major solutes from stream water, snow, and meltwater followed previous practices (Williams and others 1996a, 1996b).

RESULTS

Quantity of Precipitation

The amount of annual precipitation at D1 is increasing (Figure 17.2). Mean annual precipitation for the period 1951–1996 was 1,023 millimeters, with a standard deviation of 254 millimeters. A linear regression shows the increase in annual precipitation amount from 1951 to 1996 to be significant ($R^2 = 0.21$, $p < .05$), at a rate of 8.2 millimeters per year and an increase of about 300 millimeters since the 1950s. Most of the precipitation increase has occurred since 1967 (a period during which the same gauge and screen were used), at a rate of 16 millimeters per year.

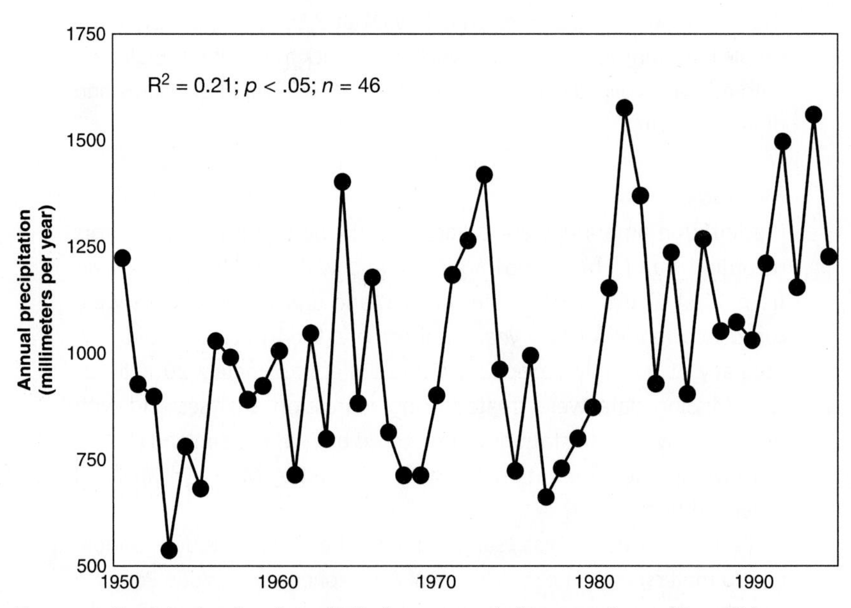

Figure 17.2 Precipitation data from the D1 (3,750 meters) climate station on Niwot Ridge, Colorado. Annual precipitation has increased significantly since 1951.

Quality of Precipitation

Annual deposition of inorganic nitrogen in wetfall at the Niwot Ridge NADP site from 1984 to 1996 almost doubled, from 1.95 kilograms per hectare per year in 1985–1988 to 3.75 kilograms per hectare per year in 1989–1992 (Figure 17.3). Values have remained near or above 4.0 kilograms per hectare per year since the mid-1990s. A simple linear regression with time shows a significant increase in deposition of inorganic nitrogen in wetfall, at the rate of 0.42 kilograms per hectare per year ($R^2 = 0.61$; $p < .001$, $n = 17$). Earlier and comparable measurements extend the record back to 1982 and suggest that the increase in deposition of inorganic nitrogen in wetfall began in the early 1980s (Reddy and Caine 1988). Previous analysis of the NADP record by Williams and others for a shorter time period shows that about half of the increase in nitrogen deposition is from increasing concentrations of nitrogen in wetfall and about half from increasing amounts of annual precipitation (1996b).

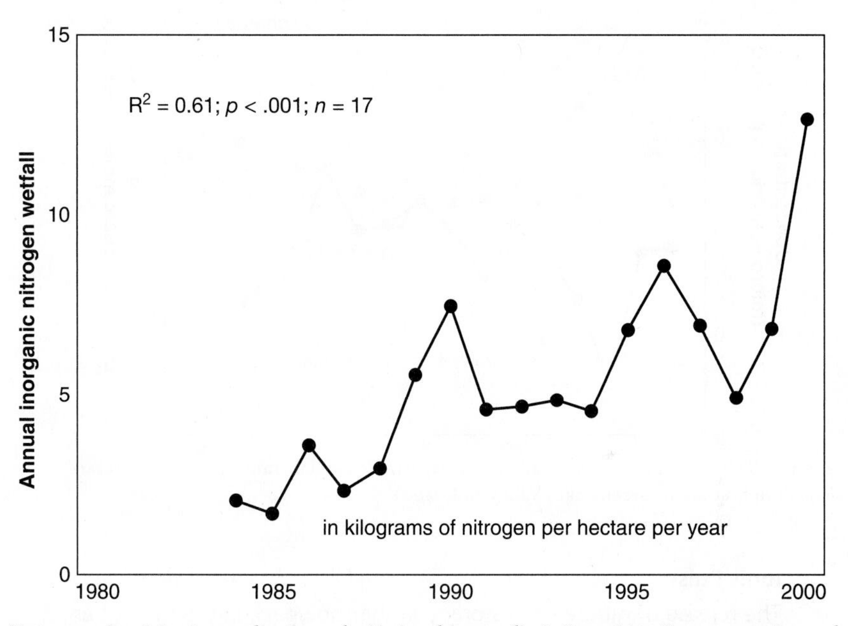

Figure 17.3 Precipitation quality from the National Atmospheric Deposition Program station at the Saddle Site on Niwot Ridge, Colorado. The annual deposition of inorganic nitrogen in wetfall is increasing.

Stream-Water Chemistry

Aquatic resources in high-elevation catchments of the Rocky Mountains may be negatively affected at current levels of inorganic nitrogen deposition in wetfall. Acid-neutralizing capacities have been decreasing in Green Lake #4 since the mid-1980s (Caine 1995; Williams and Tonnessen 2000). We illustrate the potential problems caused by nitrogen deposition with acid-neutralizing-capacity measurements in 1996 from the 42-hectare Navajo sampling site on North Boulder Creek. Initial nitrate concentrations during snowmelt runoff were greater than 30 micro equivalents per liter (Figure 17.4). These stream-water values of nitrate were about three times greater than snowpack values (which were close to 10 micro equivalents per liter). Stream waters became episodically acidified, with acid-neutralizing-capacity values below 0 micro equivalents per liter. As nitrate values fell below 20 micro equivalents per liter, acid-neutralizing-capacities values recovered and became positive. Acid-neutralizing-capacity and nitrate values were then decoupled in the fall months.

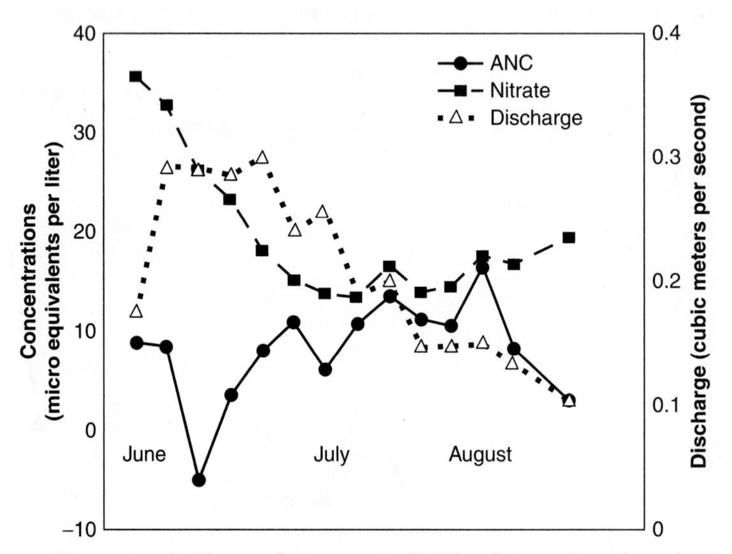

Figure 17.4 Time series of acid-neutralizing capacity (ANC) and nitrate from the 42-hectare Navajo sampling site in Green Lakes Valley, Colorado.

Ionic Pulse

The release of nitrate from storage in the snowpack in the form of an ionic pulse may partially explain the elevated concentrations of nitrate at the Navajo sampling site. Field and laboratory experiments have demonstrated that initial stages of snowmelt often have ionic concentrations many times higher than averages for the whole snowpack: an ionic pulse (Johannessen and Henriksen 1978; Colbeck 1981). To illustrate, in 2000 the maximum concentrations of ammonium, nitrate, and sulfate in snowpack meltwater were about three to six times those of bulk concentrations in a co-located snow pit (Figure 17.5). Thus the storage and release of pollutants may be enhanced by the ionic pulse.

Variations in climate may change the magnitude of the ionic pulse. In 1999 the maximum concentrations of the same solutes in meltwater were about twenty times those of bulk concentrations in the snowpack

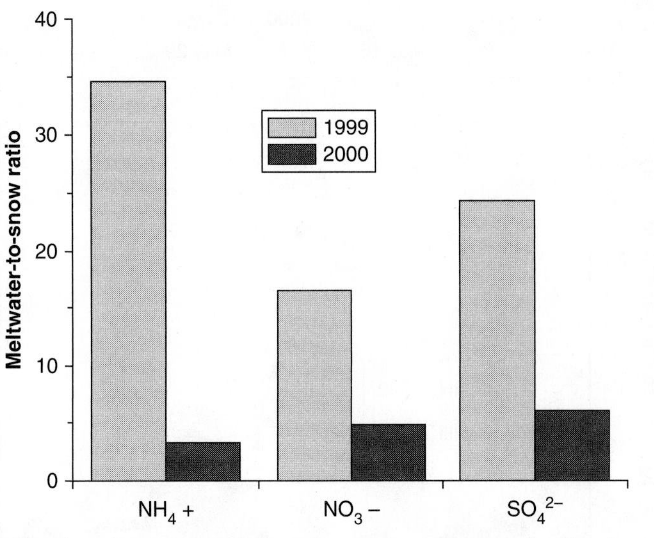

Figure 17.5 Ratios of maximum concentrations of ammonium, nitrate, and sulfate in snowpack meltwater before contact with the ground to bulk concentrations from a co-located snow pit sampled concurrently, in 1999 and 2000. Solutes are released from the snowpack in the form of an ionic pulse. The magnitude of the ionic pulse was greater in 1999 than in 2000 because of small changes in climate.

(Figure 17.5). Thus the magnitude of the ionic pulse was three to seven times greater in 1999 than in 2000.

Air temperatures were above average in 2000, and melt rates were higher than normal, conditions that may have decreased the magnitude of the ionic pulse as solutes were released from storage in the winter snowpack. Thus the magnitude of the ionic pulse may be influenced by small changes in climate.

The difference in the magnitude of the ionic pulse in 1999 and 2000 was also evident in stream-water concentrations. Here we illustrate that difference with ammonium concentrations measured in stream waters at the 8-hectare Martinelli catchment. We chose ammonium for the illustration because it had the largest change of any solute. The initial snowpack concentrations of ammonium differed little in 1999 and 2000. Because of the warm climate, the thin snowpack, and the small amount of snow in April, snowmelt started about twenty days earlier in 2000 than in 1999. The maximum ammonium concentrations in 2000 were 6 micro equivalents per liter and quickly decreased to less than 2 micro equivalents per liter (Figure 17.6). In contrast, concentrations of ammonium in stream waters in 1999 were as high as 35 micro equivalents per liter at the start of snowmelt runoff. The differences in climate between 1999 and 2000 may have resulted in stream-water concentrations of solutes that were seven times higher in 1999 than in 2000.

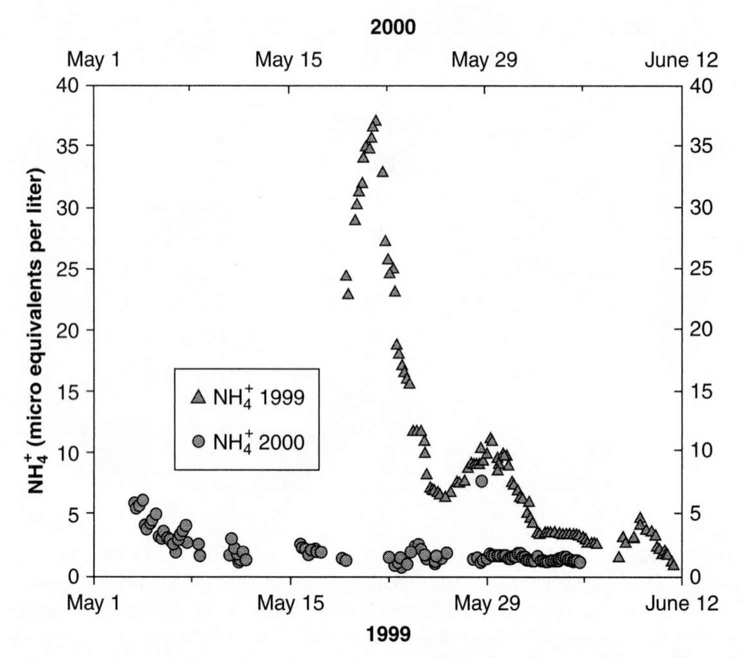

Figure 17.6 Ammonium concentrations in stream waters from the 8-hectare Martinelli catchment, Colorado, in 1999 and 2000. The large ionic pulse in 1999 appears to have been a partial cause of the sevenfold increase in ammonium concentrations in stream waters, as compared with 2000.

DISCUSSION

The role of snow in the climate of alpine areas and feedbacks with ecosystem responses has received little attention. The results of our case study at Green Lakes Valley–Niwot Ridge suggest that small changes in energy, chemicals, and water in alpine basins may cause large changes in ecosystem response. Warming in lowland areas may result in the advection of water vapor to high-elevation sites. Orographic affects may then result in an increase in annual precipitation. In turn, an increase in precipitation may result in an increase in annual deposition of pollutants, even with no increase in the concentrations of pollutants in the precipitation. These pollutants are stored in the seasonal snowpack for six to nine months, to be released over a period of weeks during snowmelt runoff. Furthermore, release of solutes from the seasonal snowpack in the form of an ionic pulse increases the concentration of pollutants in surface waters. Thus small changes in the flux of energy, chemicals, and water in alpine catchments are amplified because of the storage and release of pollutants from the seasonal snowpack in the form of an ionic pulse. In turn, release of the solutes from the snowpack in the form of an ionic pulse may cause episodic pollution of stream waters at relatively low amounts of pollution.

Snowfall and Annual Precipitation

Thomas Karl and others document a correlation between snow cover and air temperature (1993). In North America, although precipitation has been increasing, snow cover has been decreasing and temperature increasing. Mark Serreze and others suggest that the Pacific Northwest, Arizona, and New Mexico are the most climatically sensitive regions of the western United States, based on changes in the amounts of snow water relative to total winter precipitation (1999). Timothy Kittel and others report positive trends in precipitation in the northern and central Rocky Mountains of 30 percent and 33 percent per century, respectively, and increasing temperatures of +0.7 and +0.9°C per century (2002). Mark Losleben and Nick Pepin suggest that, with a future of increasing warm-phase El Niño–Southern Oscillation conditions, snowpack depths will decline on both the eastern and western slopes of the Oregon Cascades but will not have much effect in the Colorado Rockies or the central to northern Sierra Nevada of California (2003).

Although temperature is by far the easiest parameter to predict in global-warming scenarios, the relationship between temperature and snowpack is extremely complex (Houghton and others 2001). This is because snow falls only below a particular temperature threshold. Above the threshold, liquid precipitation acts to ablate snow. Thus the response of snowpack to temperature is nonlinear.

The role of snow in response to changes in climate deserves more attention. The increase in precipitation amount at Niwot Ridge does not follow the pattern predicted by Karl and others (1993). The climate patterns at Niwot Ridge are consistent with a conceptual model of climate change in high-elevation mountain areas proposed by Roger Barry (1990) and modified by Williams and others (1996a). Warming at lower elevations may result in the advection of increased water vapor to higher elevations and increased orographic precipitation as snow. Late-lying snow on the ground may provide the moisture source for increased cloud cover during the summer months, resulting in a decrease in direct shortwave radiation. In the short term (a decadal time scale), the feedback loop may be positive in high-elevation areas above the tree line; in turn, atmospheric cooling lowers saturation vapor pressure and increases precipitation. The key factor here are the precipitation as snow in the spring and early summer and the resulting feedback with local climate (Williams and others 1996a). We recognize that other processes may explain these observations and suggest that such processes represent a fertile ground for further research.

Effects on the Ecosystem

Our results suggest that streams and lakes in high-elevation systems may be particularly sensitive to changes in energy, chemicals, and water. Recent analyses of high-elevation lake-sediment cores from the Rocky Mountains, reported by Alexander Wolfe and others (2002), highlight the vulnerability of alpine ecosystems to nutrient enrichment from atmospheric deposition. Algal productivity, attributable to nutrient enrichment from atmospheric deposition of nitrogen, have increased; and current levels of nitrogen deposition in the Rocky Mountains are sufficient to alter both the quantity and quality of organic matter in alpine lakes, in addition to inducing pronounced changes in the composition of algal flora.

Although changes in algal flora may not seem important, nitrogen deposition affects the bottom of the food chain and thus may lead to unexpected effects on large mammals near the top of the food chain. Mark Williams has been working with researchers from the State of Wyoming Department of Game and Fish to establish the cause of a decline in bighorn sheep (Hnilicka 2001; Polakovic 2001). The herd, which used to number about 1,250, declined by 30 percent in two years during the early 1990s and never recovered. Tests on the herd near the Wind River Range in Wyoming showed five parts per billion of selenium in forage favored by bighorn sheep, 75 percent lower than the minimum requirement for a healthy immune system. The lack of selenium may be causing white-muscle disease, a form of muscular dystrophy. Muscles deteriorate, fail to support the skeleton, and make the bighorn lambs easy pickings for mountain lions. Moreover, fewer lambs survive in wet years. We speculate that the combination of increasing nitrogen deposition and more available water in wet years results in lower selenium in the forage of bighorn sheep.

Alpine Ecosystems as Warning Beacons

Alpine ecosystems may be early indicators of climate change. Small changes in energy, chemicals, and water are magnified in alpine ecosystems relative to lower-elevation ecosystems. An increase in regional precipitation, with no change in ambient chemical content, leads to a disproportionate increase in chemical loading from wet deposition in high-elevation catchments because of orographic precipitation. Any increase in the solute concentration of snowfall is magnified several-fold in the first fractions of snowpack meltwater by an ionic pulse. A change in energy flux causes a corresponding change in the intensity of the ionic pulse and may either extend or shorten the period of snowmelt runoff. Interactions among these variables have the potential to magnify small increases in the amounts and chemical concentrations of precipitation to very large increases in the chemical content of snowpack meltwater. In turn, the changes in the chemical content of surface waters may rapidly affect local biota, which are at the edge of their environmental tolerance. The problems caused by nitrogen deposition may thus be widespread throughout the Rocky Mountains.

REFERENCES

Bandyopadhyay, J., J. C. Rodda, R. Kattelman, Z. W. Kundzewicz, and D. Kraemer. 1997. Highland Waters: A Resource of Global Significance. In *Mountains of the World: A Global Priority,* edited by B. Messerli and J. D. Ives, 131–155. New York: Parthenon Publishing Group.

Barry, R. G. 1990. Changes in Mountain Climate and Glacio-Hydrological Responses. *Mountain Research and Development* 10 (2): 161–170.

Becker, A., and H. Bugmann, eds. 2001. *Global Change and Mountain Regions: The Mountain Research Initiative.* Stockholm: Royal Swedish Academy of Sciences, IGBP Secretariat.

Beniston, M., ed. 1994. *Mountain Environments in Changing Climates.* London and New York: Routledge.

Bowman, W. D., and T. R. Seastedt, eds. 2001. *Structure and Function of an Alpine Ecosystem: Niwot Ridge, Colorado.* New York: Oxford University Press.

Caine, N. 1995. Temporal Trends in the Quality of Streamwater in an Alpine Environment: Green Lakes Valley, Colorado Front Range, U.S.A. *Geografiska Annaler: Series A, Physical Geography* 77a (4): 207–220.

Caine, N., and E. M. Thurman. 1990. Temporal and Spatial Variations in the Solute Content of an Alpine Stream, Colorado Front Range. *Geomorphology* 4 (1): 55–72.

Colbeck, S. C. 1981. A Simulation of the Enrichment of Atmospheric Pollutants in Snow Cover Runoff. *Water Resources Research* 17:1383–1388.

Dozier, J., and M. W. Williams. 1992. Hydrology and Hydrochemistry of Alpine Basins. *Eos, Transactions of the American Geophysical Union* 73 (3): 33.

Greenland, D. 1989. The Climate of Niwot Ridge, Front Range, Colorado, U.S.A. *Arctic Alpine Research* 21 (4): 380–391.

Hnilicka, P. 2001. Telephone interview with M. W. Williams, March.

Houghton, J. T., Y. Ding, D. J. Griggs, M. Noguer, P. J. van der Linden, X. Dia, K. Maskell, and C. A. Johnson, eds. 2001. *Climate Change 2001: The Scientific Basis.* Cambridge, England, and New York: Cambridge University Press.

Johannessen, M., and A. Henriksen. 1978. Chemistry of Snow Meltwater: Changes in Concentration during Melting. *Water Resources Research* 14 (4): 615–619.

Karl, T. R., P. Y. Groisman, R. W. Wright, and R. R. Heim Jr. 1993. Recent Variations of Snow Cover and Snowfall in North America and Their Relation to Precipitation and Temperature Variations. *Journal of Climate* 6 (7): 1327–1344.

Kittel, T. G. E., P. E. Thornton, J. A Royle, and T. N. Chase. 2002. Climates of the Rocky Mountains: Historical and Future Patterns. In *Rocky Mountain Futures: An Ecological Perspective,* edited by J. S. Baron, 59–82. Washington. D.C.: Island Press.

Losleben, M. V., and N. Pepin. 2003. Mountain Snowpack, Lowland Winter Precipitation, and Variability in Three Western U.S. Mountain Ranges. Unpublished manuscript.

Messerli, B., and J. D. Ives, eds. 1997. *Mountains of the World: A Global Priority.* New York: Parthenon Publishing Group.

NADP/NTN [National Atmospheric Deposition Program/National Trends Network]. 1984–2000. NADP/NTN Annual Data Summary, Precipitation Chemistry in the United States. Colorado State University, Natural Resource Ecology Laboratory, NADP/NTN Coordination Office.

Polakovic, G. 2001. Deaths of the Little Bighorns: A Mysterious Illness Is Weakening Lambs in the Rockies, with Many Falling Prey to Predators: Researchers Say Pollution May Be the Cause. *Los Angeles Times,* 29 August, §A, 1.

Reddy, M. M., and N. Caine. 1988. A Small Alpine Basin Budget: Front Range of Colorado. In *International Mountain Watershed Symposium: Subalpine Processes and Water Quality,* edited by I. G. Poppoff, C. R. Goldman, S. L. Loeb, and L. B. Leopold, 370–385. South Lake Tahoe, Calif.: Tahoe Resource Conservation District.

Serreze, M. C., M. P. Clark, R. L. Armstrong, D. A. McGinnis, and R. S. Pulwarty. 1999. Characteristics of the Western United States Snowpack from Snowpack Telemetry (SNOTEL) Data. *Water Resources Research* 35 (7): 2145–2160.

Williams, M. W., and K. A. Tonnessen. 2000. Critical Loads for Inorganic Nitrogen Deposition in the Colorado Front Range, U.S.A. *Ecological Applications* 10 (6): 1648–1665.

Williams, M. W., P. D. Brooks, and T. Seastedt. 1998. Nitrogen and Carbon Soil Dynamics in Response to Climate Change in a High-Elevation Ecosystem in the Rocky Mountains, U.S.A. *Arctic and Alpine Research* 30 (1): 26–30.

Williams, M. W., M. V. Losleben, N. Caine, and D. Greenland. 1996a. Changes in Climate and Hydrochemical Responses in a High-Elevation Catchment, Rocky Mountains, U.S.A. *Limnology and Oceanography* 41 (5): 939–946.

Williams, M. W., P. D. Brooks, A. Mosier, and K. A. Tonnessen. 1996b. Mineral Nitrogen Transformations in and under Seasonal Snow in a High-Elevation Catchment, Rocky Mountains, United States. *Water Resources Research* 32 (10): 3161–3175.

Wolfe, A. P., S. S. Kaushal, J. R. Fulton, and D. M. McKnight. 2002. Spectrofluorescence of Sediment Humic Substances and Historical Changes of Lacustrine Organic Matter Provenance in Response to Atmospheric Nutrient Enrichment. *Environmental Science and Technology* 36 (15): 3217–3223.

QUESTIONS ABOUT MEANING

1. Review the article introduction. Why are alpine ecosystems ideal for studying climate change? What was the objective of this case study?
2. Why is the Niwot Ridge in Colorado an especially good research site? Review the Methods section. In simple terms, what did the researchers gather and measure? During what years?
3. Review the Results section and highlight some of the summary sentences stating the researchers' findings. What environmental changes have the researchers documented? Why do they matter?

QUESTIONS FOR RHETORICAL ANALYSIS

1. The researchers describe a complex series of cause and effects. Review the Discussion. What language signals to readers the cause and effect relationships? With a partner in class, outline or draw diagrams depicting the cause/effect relationships the researchers describe or predict. Find examples of qualified claims. Why are claims about cause and effect important to qualify?
2. Analyze the various purposes served by the figures in the article. What do the figures contribute?

MAKING CONNECTIONS

1. Using Boroditsky's, Gino's, or Wear's article as a model, summarize Williams, Losleben, and Hamann's research in a blog or newspaper article. Try to engage readers, avoid technical vocabulary, and help readers see the importance of the research. (Why should they care?)
2. "Alpine Areas in the Colorado Front Range as Monitors of Climate Change and Ecosystem Response" and "The Last Americans" illustrate the central role that *analysis* plays in academic writing and research. Select from these articles a few representative examples of inferences about the past or predictions about the future—made by the authors or by researchers they cite. In an essay, describe the evidence on which those inferences are based and the methods researchers used to draw their conclusions. Do you find some of the inferences or predictions more convincing than others? Explain.

Economics

"Climate Change and Agriculture: Economic Impacts," JOHN M. ANTLE

The following essay was written by John Antle, professor of agricultural economics at Montana State University. Antle is also a lead author on the International Panel on Climate Change (IPCC), which was awarded the Nobel Peace Prize in 2007 for its research on climate change.

"Climate Change and Agriculture: Economic Impacts," was one of nine papers about the implications of climate change published in 2008 in *Choices*, a peer-reviewed magazine about food, farm, and resource issues, written for anyone interested in agriculture, natural resources, and the food industry. In his essay, Antle predicts the impact of climate change on agriculture.

Agriculture is arguably the most important sector of the economy that is highly dependent on climate. A large body of scientific data and models have been developed to predict the impacts of the contemporary and future climate. Since the first IPCC Assessment Report was published in 1990, substantial efforts have been directed toward understanding climate change impacts on agricultural systems. The resulting advances in our understanding of climate impacts have come from the collection of better data, the development of new methods and models, and the observation of actual changes in climate and its impacts. Such knowledge is critical as we contemplate the design of technologies and policies to mitigate climate change and facilitate adaptation to the changes that now appear inevitable in the next several decades and beyond.

This article briefly summarizes some of the key findings from the research on agricultural impacts of climate change, based on the recent IPCC Assessment Reports published in 2001 and 2007, and other recent work such as the recent U.S. assessment published in 2002 and the Council for Science and Technology report in 2004. In the remainder of this article, I discuss the substantial uncertainties that remain about actual and potential impacts of climate change on agriculture and its economic consequences. The paper concludes with some observations about linkages from impacts to policy.

THE CURRENT STATE OF KNOWLEDGE

Early research on agricultural impacts led to some rather dire predictions of adverse impacts of climate change on food production, and the public perception that climate change may lead to global food shortages continues today. Although state-of-the-art at the time, the early predictions involved relatively simple data and methods, typically estimating the effects of increases in average annual temperature on yields of a limited number of crops at a limited number of locations, and extrapolating the typically negative effects to large regions.

With advances in data and models, most assessments of the impacts of climate change on agriculture predict that the world's ability to feed itself is not threatened by climate change. The most recent IPCC report on Impacts and Adaptation finds that climate change is likely to have both positive and negative impacts on agriculture, depending on the region and the type of agriculture. Overall, the report predicts that during the present century there will be a "marginal increase in the number of people at risk of hunger due to climate change" (Easterling et al. 2007, p. 275). However, research also shows that this finding should not lead to complacency, as analysis also suggests that some of the poorest and most vulnerable regions of the world are likely to be impacted negatively, and in some cases, severely.

One of the most important advances made in response to these early studies was to recognize that economic agents—in this case, farmers and the various private and public institutions that support agriculture—would adapt to climate changes in ways that would tend to mitigate negative impacts and take advantage of positive impacts. Another important advance in research was to recognize that there would be substantially different local, regional and global impacts. As data and modeling capability has improved, it has become increasingly clear that there are likely to be substantial adverse changes in some particularly vulnerable regions, such as in the semi-arid tropics, but there is also likely to be positive changes in the highland tropics and in temperate regions (Parry et al. 2004). As a result, the adverse effects in some regions are likely to be reduced through international trade with other regions that have been positively impacted. Collectively the regional and global impacts are not likely to be large, and may even prove to be positive.

Impacts at the farm level include changes in crop and livestock productivity, which in turn will lead to changes in the most profitable production systems at a given location. Research suggests that in highly productive regions, such as the U.S. Corn Belt, the most profitable production system may not change much, but in transitional areas such as the "eco-tone" between the Corn Belt and the Wheat Belt, substantial shifts in crop and livestock mix, in productivity, and in profitability may occur. Such changes may be positive, for example if higher temperatures in the northern Great Plains were to be associated with increased precipitation, so that corn and soybeans could replace the wheat and pasture that presently predominate. Such changes also could be negative, e.g., if already marginal crop and pastureland in the southern Great Plains became warmer and drier. In addition to changes in temperature and precipitation, another key factor in agricultural productivity is the effect of elevated levels of atmospheric CO_2 on crop yields. Some estimates suggest that higher CO_2 levels could increase crop productivity substantially, by 50% or more, although these effects are likely to be constrained by other factors such as water and soil nutrients, particularly in the developing countries.

In the case of the United States agriculture, aggregate economic impacts of climate change are not expected to be large, although there will be important regional differences. Recent studies estimate that crop yield changes will tend to be positive, with some almost doubling, but most increasing in the range of 10% to 40% during this century. Regionally, the northeast, south and southwest benefit the least, and the upper Midwest and coastal Northwest benefit the most. In contrast, livestock production is expected to be reduced by 5–7% due to higher average temperatures. Economic impacts associated with agriculture in the United States appear to be positive overall, with estimates ranging from an annual loss of $0.25 billion to a gain of about $5 billion, depending on the climate scenario used, with consumers generally gaining from the increased productivity and producers generally losing. The regional distribution of producer losses tends to mirror the productivity impacts, with the Corn Belt, the Northeast and south and southwest having the largest losses (McCarl 2008).

The most vulnerable regions of the world are undoubtedly in the tropics, particularly the semi-arid regions where higher temperatures and reduction in rainfall and increases in rainfall variability could have substantially negative impacts, and in coastal areas that are likely to be flooded due to sea level rise. These impacts are likely to be most severe in isolated regions where transportation costs are high, incomes are extremely low, and most rural households are highly dependent on agriculture for their livelihoods and for their food. These adverse impacts are predicted to be most severe in parts of sub-Saharan Africa, and other isolated areas in southwestern and south Asia. Low-lying areas in south Asia, Indonesia, and other poor coastal regions are also likely to be severely impacted due to their vulnerability to sea level rise and a limited ability to adapt by moving to higher ground or making investments to protect vulnerable areas. As a result, the risk of malnutrition and hunger in the developing world, particularly in the highly vulnerable regions, is predicted to increase during this century (Parry et al. 2004).

UNCERTAINTIES

Despite the substantial advances in understanding of climate change and its agricultural impacts, many uncertainties remain. Of particular concern are some of the limitations of the general circulation models used to simulate climate changes, and the way those limitations may affect the predicted impacts of climate change on agriculture. Some of these limitations suggest that the generally optimistic predictions outlined above for the temperate regions of the world, may be too sanguine.

On the supply side, a critical limitation of GCMs is their ability to predict changes in climate with the spatial resolution needed to model impacts on agricultural productivity. . . . Changes in water availability are especially difficult to predict, particularly on the site-specific basis needed to quantify agricultural yield impacts. A related uncertainty concerns impacts on pests which are also highly sensitive to site-specific environmental conditions, and are not well-represented in the models used to predict yield effects.

Another key uncertainty that affects impacts on all biological processes, including agriculture, is the rate of climate change. The higher the rate of climate change, the higher will be rates of obsolescence of all types of capital, both produced and natural, and thus the greater will be the costs of adaptation for farmers, the private sector providing technology and inputs to farmers, and for government institutions responsible for infrastructure and policy. A related, critical supply-side uncertainty is how technology will evolve so as to reduce impacts and facilitate adaptation. In the past, it has taken about 15 years to develop a new crop variety. A key question is whether biotechnology will speed adaptation and reduce vulnerability to drought, extreme temperatures and pests.

Another uncertainty on the supply side is the environmental consequences of adapting to climate change. One example is the increased pressures on water resources in arid regions. Another example could be the increase in population density and agricultural intensity in highland tropical areas where soils are often fragile and vulnerable to degradation.

On the demand side, impacts of changes in consumer incomes and in market infrastructure will be critical but highly uncertain factors. Given the predicted modest impacts of climate change on global food supply, the rate of economic growth is likely to be a key determinant of people's vulnerability to climate change. If the recent high rates of economic growth in many developing regions continue, vulnerability to the impacts of climate change will be modest. However, those regions that are not participating in this growth, such as parts of sub-Saharan Africa and isolated mountain regions in central Asia and Latin America, are at risk of greater vulnerability if local food production decreases and becomes more variable.

CONCLUSIONS AND POLICY IMPLICATIONS

While it is clear that climate change will affect agriculture in important ways, the evidence from the past several decades of research suggests that the aggregate impacts will be relatively small, but there will be important regional impacts, particularly in the poorest, most vulnerable parts of the tropics. Given the growing evidence that climate changes are taking place and that there will be substantial impacts on agriculture, there is a clear and compelling need for agriculture to adapt. . . . In addition, evidence suggests that agriculture could play an important role in mitigating greenhouse gas emissions. . . . Thus, two key policy questions are related to the roles the public sector should play in facilitating adaptation and mitigation. . . .

To the extent that change is relatively gradual, all indications are that farmers in the industrialized countries such as the United States will be able to adapt through farm-level changes in crop selection, crop management, and appropriate capital investments. Likewise, the private sector technology supply industry should be able to effectively anticipate and plan for needed adaptations of crops, livestock, machinery and related capital equipment. One area where there is a clear need for public sector involvement is in public infrastructure, particularly ports and related transport facilities that may be adversely impacted by sea-level rise and changes in the geographic distribution of production. The more rapid climate change is, however, the more likely that there will be a need for public investment in adaptation research to complement private sector investments.

In the developing countries, there are many reasons why farmers and institutions supporting the agricultural sector will be less able to adapt to climate change than farmers and the food industry in the industrialized world, particularly in the poorest and most vulnerable areas. On the research side, the existence of climate change reinforces the already compelling case that can be made for public sector investment in agricultural research and outreach, for investment in physical infrastructure and human capital, and for strengthening both private and public institutions that support agriculture and rural development. General economic development will also play an important role by providing farmers and rural households with sources of income that are less dependent on climate than agricultural sources of income.

FOR MORE INFORMATION

Easterling, W.E., P.K. Aggarwal, P. Batima, K.M. Brander, L. Erda, S.M. Howden, A. Kirilenko, J. Morton, J.-F. Soussana, J. Schmidhuber and F.N. Tubiello. 2007. Food, fibre and forest products. *Climate Change 2007: Impacts, Adaptation and Vulnerability. Contribution of Working Group II to the Fourth Assessment Report of the Intergovernmental Panel on Climate Change*, M.L. Parry, O.F. Canziani, J.P. Palutikof, P.J. van der Linden and C.E. Hanson, Eds., Cambridge University Press, Cambridge, UK, 273–313.

McCarl, B.A. 2008. US Agriculture in the climate change squeeze: Part 1: Sectoral Sensitivity and Vulnerability. http://agecon2.tamu.edu/people/faculty/mccarl-bruce/papers/1303Agriculture in the climate change squeez1.doc.

Parry, M.L., C. Rosezweig, A. Iglesias, M. Livermore and G. Fischer. 2004. "Effects of climate change on global food production under SRES emissions and socio-economic scenarios." *Global Environmental Change* 14, 53–67.

John M. Antle is Professor of Agricultural Economics, Montana State University, and University Fellow, Resources for the Future. jantle@montana.edu.

QUESTIONS ABOUT MEANING

1. What agriculture regions are likely to be most negatively affected by climate change? What is the anticipated impact on US crops and livestock? What effects of climate change are anticipated in sub-Saharan Africa and south Asia?
2. What uncertainties complicate predicting the impact of climate change on agriculture?
3. What role will biotechnology play in helping to mitigate the impact of climate change on agriculture?

QUESTIONS FOR RHETORICAL ANALYSIS

1. Is Antle writing to other agricultural economists? How can you tell? How are aspects of his writing (including his use of evidence) appropriate for the audience?
2. What aspects of structure and organization in the article as a whole and within individual sections help readers follow the discussion?

MAKING CONNECTIONS

1. Antle focuses on the effects of climate change on a single sector: agriculture. Conduct some research into how climate change is affecting some other *specific* sector. Examples include the effects of climate change on glaciers, polar bears, fish, tourism, or recreation. Take care to draw from sources that meet the standards of quality discussed in chapter 7.

   Using Antle's essay as a template, write your own research-based essay, with a title, section headings, and organization modeled after those found in Antle's article. In your paper, establish the qualifications of the authors you cite.
2. Diamond, Foley (chapter 5), and Antle discuss different aspects of the complicated problem of growing populations and limited resources. On what points do they agree or disagree? In an essay, put these authors in conversation with one another.

Geography

"The Last Americans," JARED DIAMOND

Jared Diamond is a geography professor at the University of California, Los Angeles, with expertise in physiology, evolutionary biology, and biogeography. He has written over six hundred articles and several books, including *Guns, Germs, and Steel,* for which he was awarded the Pulitzer Prize. "The Last Americans" was published in 2003 in *Harper's Magazine,* a general-interest magazine that publishes essays and fiction about current events, politics, culture, and the environment.

> I met a traveler from an antique land
> Who said: Two vast and trunkless legs of stone
> Stand in the desert . . . Near them, on the sand,
> Half sunk, a shattered visage lies, whose frown,
> And wrinkled lip, and sneer of cold command,
> Tell that its sculptor well those passions read
> Which yet survive, stamped on these lifeless things,
> The hand that mocked them, and the heart that fed:
> And on the pedestal these words appear:
> "My name is Ozymandias, king of kings:
> Look on my works, ye Mighty, and despair!"
> Nothing beside remains. Round the decay

Of that colossal wreck, boundless and bare
The lone and level sands stretch far away.
—"Ozymandias," Percy Bysshe Shelley

One of the disturbing facts of history is that so many civilizations collapse. Few people, however, least of all our politicians, realize that a primary cause of the collapse of those societies has been the destruction of the environmental resources on which they depended. Fewer still appreciate that many of those civilizations share a sharp curve of decline. Indeed, a society's demise may begin only a decade or two after it reaches its peak population, wealth, and power.

Recent archaeological discoveries have revealed similar courses of collapse in such otherwise dissimilar ancient societies as the Maya in the Yucatán, the Anasazi in the American Southwest, the Cahokia mound builders outside St. Louis, the Greenland Norse, the statue builders of Easter Island, ancient Mesopotamia in the Fertile Crescent, Great Zimbabwe in Africa, and Angkor Wat in Cambodia. These civilizations, and many others, succumbed to various combinations of environmental degradation and climate change, aggression from enemies taking advantage of their resulting weakness, and declining trade with neighbors who faced their own environmental problems. Because peak population, wealth, resource consumption, and waste production are accompanied by peak environmental impact—approaching the limit at which impact outstrips resources—we can now understand why declines of societies tend to follow swiftly on their peaks.

These combinations of undermining factors were compounded by cultural attitudes preventing those in power from perceiving or resolving the crisis. That's a familiar problem today. Some of us are inclined to dismiss the importance of a healthy environment, or at least to suggest that it's just one of many problems facing us—an "issue." That dismissal is based on three dangerous misconceptions.

Foremost among these misconceptions is that we must balance the environment against human needs. That reasoning is exactly upside-down. Human needs and a healthy environment are not opposing claims that must be balanced; instead, they are inexorably linked by chains of cause and effect. We need a healthy environment because we need clean water, clean air, wood, and food from the ocean, plus soil and sunlight to grow crops. We need functioning natural ecosystems, with their native species of earthworms, bees, plants, and microbes, to generate and aerate our soils, pollinate our crops, decompose our wastes, and produce our oxygen. We need to prevent toxic substances from accumulating in our water and air and soil. We need to prevent weeds, germs, and other pest species from becoming established in places where they aren't native and where they cause economic damage. Our strongest arguments for a healthy environment are selfish: we want it for ourselves, not for threatened species like snail darters, spotted owls, and Furbish louseworts.

Another popular misconception is that we can trust in technology to solve our problems. Whatever environmental problem you name, you can also name some hoped-for technological solution under discussion. Some of us have faith that we shall solve our dependence on fossil fuels by developing new technologies for hydrogen engines, wind energy, or solar energy. Some of us have faith that we shall solve our food problems with new or soon-to-be-developed genetically modified crops. Some of us have faith that new technologies will succeed in cleaning up the toxic materials in our air, water, soil, and foods without the horrendous cleanup expenses that we now incur.

Those with such faith assume that the new technologies will ultimately succeed, but in fact some of them may succeed and others may not. They assume that the new technologies will succeed quickly enough to make a big difference soon, but all of these major technological changes will actually take five to thirty years to develop and implement—if they catch on at all. Most of all, those with faith assume that new technology won't cause any new problems. In fact, technology merely constitutes increased power, which produces changes that can be either for the better or for the worse. All of our current environmental problems are unanticipated harmful consequences of our existing technology. There is no basis for believing that technology will miraculously stop causing new and unanticipated problems while it is solving the problems that it previously produced.

The final misconception holds that environmentalists are fear-mongering, overreacting extremists whose predictions of impending disaster have been proved wrong before and will be proved wrong again. Behold, say the optimists: water still flows from our faucets, the grass is still green, and the supermarkets are full of food. We are more prosperous than ever before, and that's the final proof that our system works.

Well, for a few billion of the world's people who are causing us increasing trouble, there isn't any clean water, there is less and less green grass, and there are no supermarkets full of food. To appreciate what the environmental problems of those billions of people mean for us Americans, compare the following two lists of countries. First ask some ivory-tower academic ecologist who knows a lot about the environment but never reads a newspaper and has no interest in politics to list the overseas countries facing some of the worst problems of environmental stress, overpopulation, or both. The ecologist would answer, "That's a no-brainer, it's obvious. Your list of environmentally stressed or overpopulated countries should surely include Afghanistan, Bangladesh, Burundi, Haiti, Indonesia, Iraq, Nepal, Pakistan, the Philippines, Rwanda, the Solomon Islands, and Somalia, plus others." Then ask a First World politician who knows nothing, and cares less, about the environment and population problems to list the world's worst trouble spots: countries where state government has already been overwhelmed and has collapsed, or is now at risk of collapsing, or has been wracked by recent civil wars; and countries that, as a result of their problems, are also creating problems for us rich First World countries, which may be deluged by illegal immigrants, or have to provide foreign aid to those countries, or may decide to provide them with military assistance to deal with rebellions and terrorists, or may even (God forbid) have to send in our own troops. The politician would answer, "That's a no-brainer, it's obvious. Your list of political trouble spots should surely include Afghanistan, Bangladesh, Burundi, Haiti, Indonesia, Iraq, Nepal, Pakistan, the Philippines, Rwanda, the Solomon Islands, and Somalia, plus others."

The connection between the two lists is transparent. Today, just as in the past, countries that are environmentally stressed, overpopulated, or both are at risk of becoming politically stressed, and of seeing their governments collapse. When people are desperate and undernourished, they blame their government, which they see as responsible for failing to solve their problems. They try to emigrate at any cost. They start civil wars. They kill one another. They figure that they have nothing to lose, so they become terrorists, or they support or tolerate terrorism. The results are genocides such as the ones that already have exploded in Burundi, Indonesia, and Rwanda; civil wars, as in Afghanistan, Indonesia, Nepal, the Philippines, and the Solomon Islands; calls for the dispatch of First World troops, as to Afghanistan, Indonesia, Iraq, the Philippines, Rwanda, the Solomon Islands, and Somalia; the collapse of central government, as has already happened in Somalia; and overwhelming poverty, as in all of the countries on these lists.

But what about the United States? Some might argue that the environmental collapse of ancient societies is relevant to the modern decline of weak, far-off, overpopulated Rwanda and environmentally devastated Somalia, but isn't it ridiculous to suggest any possible relevance to the fate of our own society? After all, we might reason, those ancients didn't enjoy the wonders of modern environment-friendly technologies. Those ancients had the misfortune to suffer from the effects of climate change. They behaved stupidly and ruined their own environment by doing obviously dumb things, like cutting down their forests, watching their topsoil erode, and building cities in dry areas likely to run short of water. They had foolish leaders who didn't have books and so couldn't learn from history, and who embroiled them in destabilizing wars and didn't pay attention to problems at home. They were overwhelmed by desperate immigrants, as one society after another collapsed, sending floods of economic refugees to tax the resources of the societies that weren't collapsing. In all those respects, we modern Americans are fundamentally different from those primitive ancients, and there is nothing that we could learn from them.

Or so the argument goes. It's an argument so ingrained both in our subconscious and in public discourse that it has assumed the status of objective reality. We think we are different. In fact, of course, all of those powerful societies of the past thought that they too were unique, right up to the moment of their collapse. It's sobering to consider the swift decline of the ancient Maya, who 1,200 years ago were themselves the most advanced society in the Western Hemisphere, and who, like us now, were then at the apex of their own power and numbers. Two excellent recent books, David Webster's *The Fall of the Ancient Maya* and Richardson Gill's *The Great Maya Droughts,* help bring the trajectory of Maya civilization back to life for us. Their studies illustrate how even sophisticated societies like that of the Maya (and ours) can be undermined by details of rainfall, farming methods, and motives of leaders.

By now, millions of modern Americans have visited Maya ruins. To do so, one need only take a direct flight from the United States to the Yucatán capital of Mérida, jump into a rental car or minibus, and drive an hour on a paved highway. Most Maya ruins, with their great temples and monuments, lie surrounded by jungles (seasonal tropical forests), far from current human settlement. They are "pure" archaeological sites. That is, their locations became depopulated, so they were not covered up by later buildings as were so many other ancient cities, like the Aztec capital of Tenochtitlán—now buried under modern Mexico City—and Rome.

One of the reasons few people live there now is that the Maya homeland poses serious environmental challenges to would-be farmers. Although it has a somewhat unpredictable rainy season from May to October, it also has a dry season from January through April. Indeed, if one focuses on the dry months, one could describe the Yucatán as a "seasonal desert."

Complicating things, from a farmer's perspective, is that the part of the Yucatán with the most rain, the south, is also the part at the highest elevation above the water table. Most of the Yucatán consists of karst—a porous, spongelike, limestone terrain—and so rain runs straight into the ground, leaving little or no surface water. The Maya in the lower-elevation regions of the north were able to reach the water table by way of deep sinkholes called cenotes, and the Maya in low coastal areas without sinkholes could reach it by digging wells up to 75 feet deep. Most Maya, however, lived in the south. How did they deal with their resulting water problem?

Technology provided an answer. The Maya plugged up leaks on karst promontories by plastering the bottoms of depressions to create reservoirs, which collected rain and stored it for use in the dry season. The reservoirs at the Maya city of Tikal, for example, held enough water to meet the needs of about 10,000 people for eighteen months. If a drought lasted longer than that, though, the inhabitants of Tikal were in deep trouble.

Maya farmers grew mostly corn, which constituted the astonishingly high proportion of about 70 percent of their diet, as deduced from isotope analyses of ancient Maya skeletons. They grew corn by means of a modified version of swidden slash-and-burn agriculture, in which forest is cleared, crops are grown in the resulting clearing for a few years until the soil is exhausted, and then the field is abandoned for fifteen to twenty years until regrowth of wild vegetation restores the soil's fertility. Because most of the land under a swidden agricultural system is fallow at any given time, it can support only modest population densities. Thus, it was a surprise for archaeologists to discover that ancient Maya population densities, judging from numbers of stone foundations of farmhouses, were often far higher than what unmodified swidden agriculture could support: often 250 to 750 people per square mile. The Maya probably achieved those high populations by such means as shortening the fallow period and tilling the soil to restore soil fertility, or omitting the fallow period entirely and growing crops every year, or, in especially moist areas, growing two crops per year.

Socially stratified societies, ours included, consist of farmers who produce food, plus non-farmers such as bureaucrats and soldiers who do not produce food and are in effect parasites on farmers. The farmers must grow enough food to meet not only their own needs but also those of everybody else. The number of nonproducing consumers who can be supported depends on the society's agricultural productivity. In the United States today, with its highly efficient agriculture, farmers make up only 2 percent of our population, and each farmer can feed, on the average, 129 other people. Ancient Egyptian agriculture was efficient enough for an Egyptian peasant to produce five times the food required for himself and his family. But a Maya peasant could produce only twice the needs of himself and his family.

Fully 80 percent of Maya society consisted of peasants. Their inability to support many non-farmers resulted from several limitations of their agriculture. It produced little protein, because corn has a much lower protein content than wheat, and because the few edible domestic animals kept by the Maya (turkeys, ducks, and dogs) included no large animals like our cows and sheep. There was little use of terracing or irrigation to increase production. In the Maya area's humid climate, stored corn would rot or become infested after a year, so the Maya couldn't get through a longer drought by eating surplus corn accumulated in good years. And unlike Old World peoples with their horses, oxen, donkeys, and camels, the Maya had no animal-powered transport. Indeed, the Maya lacked not only pack animals and animal-drawn plows but also metal tools, wheels, and boats with sails. All of those great Maya temples were built by stone and wooden tools and human muscle power alone, and all overland transport went on the backs of human porters.

Those limitations on food supply and food transport may in part explain why Maya society remained politically organized in small kingdoms that were perpetually at war with one another and that never became unified into large empires like the Aztec empire of the Valley of Mexico (fed by highly productive agriculture) or the Inca empire of the Andes (fed by diverse crops carried on llamas). Maya armies were small and unable to mount lengthy campaigns over long distances. The typical Maya kingdom held a population of only up to 50,000 people, within a radius of two or three days' walk from the king's palace. From the top of the temple of some Maya kingdoms, one could see the tops of the temples of other kingdoms.

Presiding over the temple was the king himself, who functioned both as head priest and as political leader. It was his responsibility to pray to the gods, to perform astronomical and calendrical rituals, to ensure the timely arrival of the rains on which agriculture depended, and thereby to bring prosperity. The king claimed to have the supernatural power to deliver those good things because of his asserted family relationship to the gods. Of course, that exposed him to the risk that his subjects would become disillusioned if he couldn't fulfill his boast of being able to deliver rains and prosperity.

Those are the basic outlines of Classic Maya society, which for all its limitations lasted more than 500 years. Indeed, the Maya themselves believed that it had lasted for much longer. Their remarkable Long Count calendar had its starting date (analogous to January 1, A.D. 1 of our calendar) backdated into the remote preliterate past, at August 11, 3114 B.C. The first physical evidence of civilization within the Maya area, in the form of villagers and pottery, appeared around 1400 B.C., substantial buildings around 500 B.C., and writing around 400 B.C. The so-called Classic period of Maya history arose around A.D. 250, when evidence for the first kings and dynasties emerged. From then, the Maya population increased almost exponentially, to reach peak numbers in the eighth century A.D. The largest monuments were erected toward the end of that century. All the indicators of a complex society declined throughout the ninth century, until the last date on any monument was A.D. 909. This decline of Maya population and architecture constitutes what is known as the Classic Maya collapse.

What happened? Let's consider in more detail a city whose ruins now lie in western Honduras at the world-famous site of Copán. The most fertile ground in the Copán area consists of five pockets of flat land along a river valley with a total area of only one square mile; the largest of those five pockets, known as the Copán pocket, has an area of half a square mile. Much of the land around Copán consists of steep hills with poor soil. Today, corn yields from valley-bottom fields are two or three times those of fields on hill slopes, which suffer rapid erosion and lose most of their productivity within a decade of farming.

To judge by the number of house sites, population growth in the Copán valley rose steeply from the fifth century up to a peak estimated at around 27,000 people between A.D. 750 and 900. Construction of royal monuments glorifying kings became especially massive from A.D. 650 onward. After A.D. 700, nobles other than kings got into the act and began erecting their own palaces, increasing the burden that the king and his own court already imposed on the peasants. The last big buildings at Copán were put up around A.D. 800; the last date on an incomplete altar possibly bearing a king's name is A.D. 822.

Archaeological surveys of different types of habitats in the Copán valley show that they were occupied in a regular sequence. The first area farmed was the large Copán pocket of bottomland, followed by occupation of the other four bottomland pockets. During that time the human population was growing, but the hills remained uninhabited. Hence that increased population must have been accommodated by intensifying production in the bottomland pockets: probably some combination of shorter fallow periods and double-cropping. By A.D. 500, people had started to settle the hill slopes, but those sites were occupied only briefly. The percentage of Copán's total population that was in the hills, rather than in the valleys, peaked in the year 575 and then declined, as the population again became concentrated in the pockets.

What caused that pullback of population from the hills? From excavation of building foundations on the valley floor we know that they became covered with sediment during the eighth century, meaning that the hill slopes were becoming eroded and probably also leached of nutrients. The acidic hill soils being carried down into the valley would have reduced agricultural yields. The reason for that erosion of the hillsides is clear: the forests that formerly covered them and protected their soil were being cut down. Dated pollen samples show that the pine forests originally covering the hilltops were eventually all cleared, to be burned for fuel. Besides causing sediment accumulation in the valleys and depriving valley inhabitants of wood supplies, that deforestation may have begun to cause a "man-made drought" in the valley bottom, because forests play a major role in water cycling, such that massive deforestation tends to result in lowered rainfall.

Hundreds of skeletons recovered from Copán archaeological sites have been studied for signs of disease and poor nutrition, such as porous bones and stress lines in the teeth. Those skeletal signs show that the health of Copán's inhabitants deteriorated from A.D. 650 to 850, among both the elite and commoners, though the health of commoners was worse.

Recall that Copán's population was growing rapidly while the hills were being occupied. The subsequent abandonment of all of those hill fields meant that the burden of feeding the extra population formerly dependent on the hills now fell increasingly on the valley floor, and that more and more people were competing for the food grown on that one square mile of bottomland. That would have led to fighting among the farmers themselves for the best land, or for any land, just as in modern Rwanda. Because the king was failing to deliver on his promises of rain and prosperity, he would have been the scapegoat for this agricultural failure, which explains why the last that we hear of any king is A.D. 822, and why the royal palace was burned around A.D. 850.

Datable pieces of obsidian, the sharp rock from which the Maya made their stone tools, suggest that Copán's total population decreased more gradually than did its signs of kings and nobles. The estimated population in the year A.D. 950 was still around 15,000, or 55 percent of the peak population of 27,000. That population continued to dwindle, until there are few signs of anyone in the Copán valley after around A.D. 1235. The reappearance of pollen from forest trees thereafter provides independent evidence that the valley became virtually empty of people.

The Maya history that I have just related, and Copán's history in particular, illustrate why we talk about "the Maya collapse." But the story grows more complicated, for at least five reasons. There was not only that enormous Classic collapse but also at least two smaller pre-Classic collapses, around A.D. 150 and 600, as well as some post-Classic collapses. The Classic collapse was obviously not complete, because hundreds of thousands of Maya survived, in areas with stable water supplies, to meet and fight the Spaniards. The collapse of population (as gauged by numbers of house sites and of obsidian tools) was in some cases much slower than the decline in numbers of Long Count dates. Many apparent collapses of cities were nothing more than "power cycling"; i.e., particular cities becoming more powerful at the expense of neighboring cities, then declining or getting conquered by neighbors, without changes in the whole population. Finally, cities in different parts of the Maya area rose and fell on different trajectories.

Some archaeologists focus on these complications and don't want to recognize a Classic Maya collapse at all. But this overlooks the obvious fact that cries out for explanation: the disappearance of between 90 and 99 percent of the Maya population after A.D. 800, and of the institution of the kingship, Long Count calendars, and other complex political and cultural institutions. Before we can understand those disappearances, however, we need first to understand the roles of warfare and of drought.

Archaeologists for a long time believed the ancient Maya to be gentle and peaceful people. We now know that Maya warfare was intense, chronic, and unresolvable, because limitations of food supply and transportation made it impossible for any Maya principality to unite the whole region in an empire. The archaeological record shows that wars became more intense and frequent toward the time of the Classic collapse. That evidence comes from discoveries of several types since the Second World War: archaeological excavations of massive fortifications surrounding many Maya sites; vivid depictions of warfare and captives on stone monuments and on the famous painted murals discovered in 1946 at Bonampak; and the decipherment of Maya writing, much of which proved to consist of royal inscriptions boasting of conquests. Maya kings fought to capture and torture one another; an unfortunate loser was a Copán king with the to us unforgettable name of King 18 Rabbit.

Maya warfare involved well-documented types of violence: wars among separate kingdoms; attempts of cities within a kingdom to secede by revolting against the capital; and civil wars resulting from frequent violent attempts by would-be kings to usurp the throne. All of these events were described or depicted on monuments, because they involved kings and nobles. Not considered worthy of description, but probably even more frequent, were fights between commoners over land, as overpopulation became excessive and land became scarce.

The other phenomenon important to understanding all of these collapses is the repeated occurrence of droughts, as inferred by climatologists from evidence of lake evaporation preserved in lake sediments, and as summarized by Gill in *The Great Maya Droughts.* The rise of Maya civilization may have been facilitated by a rainy period beginning around 250 B.C., until a temporary drought after A.D. 125 was associated with a pre-Classic collapse at some sites. That collapse was followed by the resumption of rainy conditions and the buildup of Classic Maya cities, briefly interrupted by another drought around 600 corresponding to a decline at Tikal and some other sites. Finally, around A.D. 750 there began the worst drought in the past 7,000 years, peaking around the year A.D. 800, and suspiciously associated with the Classic collapse.

The area most affected by the Classic collapse was the southern highlands, probably for the two reasons already mentioned: it was the area with the densest population, and it also had the most severe water problems because it lay too high above the water table for cenotes or wells to provide water. The southern highlands lost more than 99 percent of its population in the course of the Classic collapse. When Cortés and his Spanish army marched in 1524 and 1525 through an area formerly inhabited by millions of Maya, he nearly starved because he encountered so few villagers from whom to acquire corn. The Spaniards passed within only a few miles of the abandoned ruins of the great Classic cities of Tikal and Palenque, but still they heard or saw nothing of them.

We can identify increasingly familiar strands in the Classic Maya collapse. One consisted of population growth outstripping available resources: the dilemma foreseen by Thomas Malthus in 1798. As Webster succinctly puts it in *The Fall of the Ancient Maya,* "Too many farmers grew too many crops on too much of the landscape." While population was increasing, the area of usable farmland paradoxically was decreasing from the effects of deforestation and hillside erosion.

The next strand consisted of increased fighting as more and more people fought over fewer resources. Maya warfare, already endemic, peaked just before the collapse. That is not surprising when one reflects that at least 5 million people, most of them farmers, were crammed into an area smaller than the state of Colorado. That's a high population by the standards of ancient farming societies, even if it wouldn't strike modern Manhattan-dwellers as crowded.

Bringing matters to a head was a drought that, although not the first one the Maya had been through, was the most severe. At the time of previous droughts, there were still uninhabited parts of the Maya landscape, and people in a drought area or dust bowl could save themselves by moving to another site. By the time of the Classic collapse, however, there was no useful unoccupied land in the vicinity on which to begin anew, and the whole population could not be accommodated in the few areas that continued to have reliable water supplies.

The final strand is political. Why did the kings and nobles not recognize and solve these problems? A major reason was that their attention was evidently focused on the short-term concerns of enriching themselves, waging wars, erecting monuments, competing with one another, and extracting enough food from the peasants to support all those activities. Like most leaders throughout human history, the Maya kings and nobles did not have the leisure to focus on long-term problems, insofar as they perceived them.

What about those same strands today? The United States is also at the peak of its power, and it is also suffering from many environmental problems. Most of us have become aware of more crowding and stress. Most of us living in large American cities are encountering increased commuting delays, because the number of people and hence of cars is increasing faster than the number of freeway lanes. I know plenty of people who in the abstract doubt that the world has a population problem, but almost all of those same people complain to me about crowding, space issues, and traffic experienced in their personal lives.

Many parts of the United States face locally severe problems of water restriction (especially southern California, Arizona, the Everglades, and, increasingly, the Northeast); forest fires resulting from logging and forest-management practices throughout the intermontane West; and losses of farmlands to salinization, drought, and climate change in the northern Great Plains. Many of us frequently experience problems of air quality, and some of us also experience problems of water quality and taste. We are losing economically valuable natural resources. We have already lost American chestnut trees, the Grand Banks cod fishery, and the Monterey sardine fishery; we are in the process of losing swordfish and tuna and Chesapeake Bay oysters and elm trees; and we are losing topsoil.

The list goes on: All of us are experiencing personal consequences of our national dependence on imported energy, which affects us not only through higher gas prices but also through the current contraction of the national economy, itself the partial result of political problems associated with our oil dependence. We are saddled with expensive toxic cleanups at many locations, most notoriously near Montana mines, on the Hudson River, and in the Chesapeake Bay. We also face expensive eradication problems resulting from hundreds of introduced pest species—including zebra mussels, Mediterranean fruit flies, Asian longhorn beetles, water hyacinth, and spotted knapweed—that now affect our agriculture, forests, waterways, and pastures.

These particular environmental problems, and many others, are enormously expensive in terms of resources lost, cleanup and restoration costs, and the cost of finding substitutes for lost resources: a billion dollars here, 10 billion there, in dozens and dozens of cases. Some of the problems, especially those of air quality and toxic substances, also exact health costs that are large, whether measured in dollars or in lost years or in quality of life. The cost of our homegrown environmental problems adds up to a large fraction of our gross national product, even without mentioning the costs that we incur from environmental problems overseas, such as the military operations that they inspire. Even the mildest of bad scenarios for our future include a gradual economic decline, as happened to the Roman and British empires. Actually, in case you didn't notice it, our economic decline is already well under way. Just check the numbers for our national debt, yearly government budget deficit, unemployment statistics, and the value of your investment and pension funds.

The environmental problems of the United States are still modest compared with those of the rest of the world. But the problems of environmentally devastated, overpopulated, distant countries are now our problems as well. We are accustomed to thinking of globalization in terms of us rich, advanced First Worlders sending our good things, such as the Internet and Coca-Cola, to those poor backward Third Worlders. Globalization, however, means nothing more than improved worldwide communication and transportation, which can convey many things in either direction; it is not restricted to good things carried only from the First to the Third World. They in the Third World can now, intentionally or unintentionally, send us their bad things: terrorists; diseases such as AIDS, SARS, cholera, and West Nile fever, carried inadvertently by passengers on transcontinental airplanes; unstoppable numbers of immigrants, both legal and illegal, arriving by boat, truck, train, plane, and on foot; and other consequences of their Third World problems. We in the United States are no longer the isolated Fortress America to which some of us aspired in the 1930s; instead, we are tightly and irreversibly connected to overseas countries. The United States is the world's leading importer, and it is also the world's leading exporter. Our own society opted long ago to become interlocked with the rest of the world.

That's why political stability anywhere in the world now affects us, our trade routes, and our overseas markets and suppliers. We are so dependent on the rest of the world that if a decade ago you had asked a politician to name the countries most geopolitically irrelevant to U.S. interests because of their being so remote, poor, and weak, the list would have begun with Afghanistan and Somalia, yet these countries were subsequently considered important enough to warrant our dispatching U.S. troops. The Maya were "globalized" only within the Yucatán: the southern Yucatán Maya affected the northern Yucatán Maya and may have had some effects on the Valley of Mexico, but they had no contact with Somalia. That's because Maya transportation was slow, short-distance, on foot or else in canoes, and had low cargo capacity. Our transport today is much more rapid and has much higher cargo capacity. The Maya lived in a globalized Yucatán; we live in a globalized world.

If all of this reasoning seems straightforward when expressed so bluntly, one has to wonder: Why don't those in power today get the message? Why didn't the leaders of the Maya, Anasazi, and those other societies also recognize and solve their problems? What were the Maya thinking while they watched loggers clearing the last pine forests on the hills above Copán? Here, the past really is a useful guide to the present. It turns out that there are at least a dozen reasons why past societies failed to *anticipate* some problems before they developed, or failed to *perceive* problems that had already developed, or failed even to *try* to solve problems that they did perceive. All of those dozen reasons still can be seen operating today. Let me mention just three of them.

First, it's difficult to recognize a slow trend in some quantity that fluctuates widely up and down anyway, such as seasonal temperature, annual rainfall, or economic indicators. That's surely why the Maya didn't recognize the oncoming drought until it was too late, given that rainfall in the Yucatán varies several-fold from year to year. Natural fluctuations also explain why it's only within the last few years that all climatologists have become convinced of the reality of climate change, and why our president still isn't convinced but thinks that we need more research to test for it.

Second, when a problem *is* recognized, those in power may not attempt to solve it because of a clash between their short-term interests and the interests of the rest of us. Pumping that oil, cutting down those trees, and catching those fish may benefit the elite by bringing them money or prestige and yet be bad for society as a whole (including the children of the elite) in the long run. Maya kings were consumed by immediate concerns for their prestige (requiring more and bigger temples) and their success in the next war (requiring more followers), rather than for the happiness of commoners or of the next generation. Those people with the greatest power to make decisions in our own society today regularly make money from activities that may be bad for society as a whole and for their own children; those decision-makers include Enron executives, many land developers, and advocates of tax cuts for the rich.

Finally, it's difficult for us to acknowledge the wisdom of policies that clash with strongly held values. For example, a belief in individual freedom and a distrust of big government are deeply ingrained in Americans, and they make sense under some circumstances and up to a certain point. But they also make it hard for us to accept big government's legitimate role in ensuring that each individual's freedom to maximize the value of his or her land holdings doesn't decrease the value of the collective land of all Americans.

Not all societies make fatal mistakes. There are parts of the world where societies have unfolded for thousands of years without any collapse, such as Java, Tonga, and (until 1945) Japan. Today, Germany and Japan are successfully managing their forests, which are even expanding in area rather than shrinking. The Alaskan salmon fishery and the Australian lobster fishery are being managed sustainably. The Dominican Republic, hardly a rich country, nevertheless has set aside a comprehensive system of protected areas encompassing most of the country's natural habitats.

Is there any secret to explain why some societies acquire good environmental sense while others don't? Naturally, part of the answer depends on accidents of individual leaders' wisdom (or lack thereof). But part also depends upon whether a society is organized so as to minimize built-in clashes of interest between its decision-making elites and its masses. Given how our society is organized, the executives of Enron, Tyco, and Adelphi correctly calculated that their own interests would be best promoted by looting the company coffers, and that they would probably get away with most of their loot. A good example of a society that minimizes such clashes of interest is the Netherlands, whose citizens have perhaps the world's highest level of environmental awareness and of membership in environmental organizations. I never understood why, until on a recent trip to the Netherlands I posed the question to three of my Dutch friends while driving through their countryside.

Just look around you, they said. All of this farmland that you see lies below sea level. One fifth of the total area of the Netherlands is below sea level, as much as 22 feet below, because it used to be shallow bays, and we reclaimed it from the sea by surrounding the bays with dikes and then gradually pumping out the water. We call these reclaimed lands "polders." We began draining our polders nearly a thousand years ago. Today, we still have to keep pumping out the water that gradually seeps in. That's what our windmills used to be for, to drive the pumps to pump out the polders. Now we use steam, diesel, and electric pumps instead. In each polder there are lines of them, starting with those farthest from the sea, pumping the water in sequence until the last pump finally deposits it into a river or the ocean. And all of us, rich or poor, live down in the polders. It's not the case that rich people live safely up on top of the dikes while poor people live in the polder bottoms below sea level. If the dikes and pumps fail, we'll all drown together.

Throughout human history, all peoples have been connected to some other peoples, living together in virtual polders. For the ancient Maya, their polder consisted of most of the Yucatán and neighboring areas. When the Classic Maya cities collapsed in the southern Yucatán, refugees may have reached the northern Yucatán, but probably not the

Valley of Mexico, and certainly not Florida. Today, our whole world has become one polder, such that events in even Afghanistan and Somalia affect Americans. We do indeed differ from the Maya, but not in ways we might like: we have a much larger population, we have more potent destructive technology, and we face the risk of a worldwide rather than a local decline. Fortunately, we also differ from the Maya in that we know their fate, and they did not. Perhaps we can learn.

Jared Diamond is a professor of geography and of environmental health sciences at UCLA. His book *Guns, Germs, and Steel: the Fates of Human Societies* won a 1998 Pulitzer Prize.

QUESTIONS ABOUT MEANING

1. What is the purpose of the long description of the Mayan civilization? What "strands" or themes run through the story of the Classic Maya collapse? How are those themes echoed in the section describing the United States today?
2. Diamond concludes by suggesting we might be able to learn from the mistakes of others. Based on this essay, do you think Diamond believes this is likely? Find evidence in the essay to support your answer.
3. How does Diamond expand the usual way that "globalization" is defined?

QUESTIONS FOR RHETORICAL ANALYSIS

1. Diamond uses many kinds of evidence in his argument, including source citations, expert opinion, statistics, studies, and analogy. Go through the essay and highlight examples of these and other types of evidence. Do you find his evidence convincing? How might the use of evidence be different if Diamond were to revise this essay for publication in a peer-reviewed academic journal?
2. Who are the "Last Americans," referred to in the title? Do you think this is a fitting title for the essay?
3. What does the Percy Bysshe Shelley poem contribute to the essay?

MAKING CONNECTIONS

1. Like Christakis and Fowler (chapter 13), Diamond recognizes the power of social connections. In an essay, use Christakis and Fowler's social networks theory as a framework for considering the kinds of environmental issues Diamond discusses. For example, how might social networks help to address the problems or how might they contribute to the problems Diamond describes?

2. Highlight what Diamond identifies as three popular misconceptions about environmental protection. (The first is that "we must balance the environment against human needs," paragraph 4.) How does Diamond respond to each misconception? Do you find his responses convincing? Why or why not? Using this section of Diamond's essay as a template, write an essay in which you acknowledge and respond to misconceptions many people have about some other important topic or issue (environmental or not). Be sure to provide evidence in your responses and convey the importance of the topic (i.e., why is it important to correct the misconceptions?).

Geography

"Will Big Business Save the Earth?" JARED DIAMOND

Jared Diamond is a geography professor at the University of California, Los Angeles. In "The Last Americans," written in 2003, Diamond draws parallels between the United States today and the Maya civilization before its collapse. He paints a more optimistic picture in "Will Big Business Save the Earth?" which was originally published in 2010 in *The New York Times Upfront*, a news magazine written for high school students.

There's a widespread view, particularly among environmentalists, that big businesses are environmentally destructive, greedy, evil, and driven by short-term profits. I know—because I used to share that view.

But I've learned that it doesn't apply to all businesses. Over the years, I've joined the boards of two environmental groups—the World Wildlife Fund and Conservation International—serving alongside many business executives. I've been asked to assess the environments in oil fields and have spoken with oil-company employees at all levels. I've also worked with executives of mining, retail, and logging companies. I've discovered that while some businesses are indeed as destructive as many suspect, others are among the world's strongest positive forces for environmental sustainability—making sure our planet remains livable and that natural resources don't run out.

Businesses are increasingly concerned about the environment for several reasons. Lower consumption of natural resources saves money in the short run, while keeping resource levels sustainable and not polluting saves money in the long run. And a clean image—from avoiding environmental disasters like oil spills—reduces criticism from employees, consumers, and government.

BY THE NUMBERS

20%

Percentage of U.S. greenhouse emissions generated by industry.

2 Million

Tons of waste generated in the U.S. in 2008 by aluminum containers and packaging, including beverage cans.

23%

Percentage of the world's water supply used by industry.

SOURCES:PEW CENTER ON GLOBAL CLIMATE CHANGE: E.P.A: UNESCO

Here are a few examples involving three corporations—Wal-Mart, Coca-Cola, and Chevron—that many critics of business love to hate, in my opinion, unjustly.

SAVING ENERGY & WATER

Let's start with Wal-Mart, which cut fuel costs by $26 million simply by changing the way it manages its enormous truck fleet. Instead of running a truck's engine all night to heat or cool the cab during mandatory 10-hour rest stops, the company installed small auxiliary power units to do the job. This also eliminated carbon-dioxide emissions—a major cause of global warming—equivalent to taking 18,300 passenger vehicles off the road.

Wal-Mart is working to double the fuel efficiency of its truck fleet by 2015, which would save more than $200 million a year at the pump. The company is testing trucks that burn biofuels made from fryer grease used at its delis. It's also reducing its use of packaging materials and is recycling plastics.

Coca-Cola's challenges are largely long-term: The key ingredient in its products is water. But global climate change is making water scarcer; most water is used for agriculture, which presents sustainability problems of its own.

So Coca-Cola's survival requires the company to be concerned with problems of water scarcity, energy, climate change, and agriculture in the roughly 200 countries in which it produces beverages. One company goal is to make its plants water-neutral: returning water to the environment in amounts equal to the amount used in producing beverages.

Another goal is to work on conserving seven of the world's river basins, including the Rio Grande along the U.S.-Mexico border, the

Yangtze and Mekong in China, and the Danube in Europe—all sites of environmental concerns besides supplying water for Coca-Cola products. Coca-Cola is also recycling plastic bottles and replacing petroleum-based plastic in its bottles with organic material.

The third company is Chevron. Not even in any national park have I seen the level of environmental protection that I saw in Chevron-managed oil fields in Papua New Guinea, about 100 miles north of Australia. Chevron gave several reasons for investing in environmental protection.

First, it's far cheaper to prevent oil spills than to clean them up. Second, clean practices reduce the risk that local landowners become angry, sue for damages, and close the oil fields. Next, environmental standards are becoming stricter around the world, so building clean facilities now minimizes having to make costly renovations later. Also, clean operations in one country give a company an advantage when bidding on leases in other countries.

HOW WASHINGTON CAN HELP

Some businesses and politicians argue that taking measures to protect the environment are too costly to be profitable. But economic reasons actually provide the strongest motives for preserving the environment: It's more expensive to fix problems than to avoid them in the first place.

When it comes to saving the environment, American businesses are going to play as much or more of a role as the government. And this isn't a bad thing: Corporations have a lot to gain by establishing environmentally friendly business practices.

Washington can help by investing in green research, offering tax incentives, passing cap-and-trade legislation, and setting tough standards to ensure that companies that abuse the environment don't have a competitive advantage over those that protect it.

And the rest of us should get over the idea that American business cares only about immediate profits, and we should reward companies that work to keep the planet healthy.

Jared Diamond is a professor of geography at U.C.L.A.

QUESTIONS ABOUT MEANING

1. What steps have Wal-Mart, Coca-Cola, and Chevron taken to protect the environment?
2. What motivations do big businesses have to protect the environment?

QUESTIONS FOR RHETORICAL ANALYSIS

1. Although Diamond is widely known by academics, readers of *The New York Times Upfront* may not recognize his name. How does Diamond convey to readers his expertise on the subject of environmental protection? What rhetorical purpose does the opening paragraph serve in the article?
2. In what ways is the boxed information engaging and effective? What questions, though, might critical readers have about the statistics in the figure?
3. Do Diamond's opinions about the status of the environment appear to have changed since he wrote "The Last Americans" in 2003? What factors might explain the more hopeful tone in this article?

MAKING CONNECTIONS

1. Diamond describes the efforts three large companies are making to "save the earth." Visit the websites of additional businesses or corporations to learn what they are doing to protect the environment. Then in an essay modeled after "Will Big Business Save the Earth?"expand Diamond's discussion by describing steps companies you've researched are taking to protect the environment. Diamond ends "The Last Americans" by suggesting that "perhaps we can learn" from the fate of the Maya. Based on your research, do you think businesses are taking meaningful action to protect the environment?
2. Visit the websites of Wal-Mart, Coca-Cola, and Chevron—or other businesses of your choice. How do these companies use images to suggest that they are environmentally responsible? Select a few representative examples for analysis. Copy and paste your examples into an essay in which you analyze how businesses use images to create an environmentally friendly ethos.

Glossary

This glossary includes definitions of key terms and concepts used throughout this book. Words appearing in boldface type within definitions are themselves defined in the glossary.

abstract A paragraph found at the beginning of an academic research report summarizing the researcher's methods and findings.

academic argument A written document that develops a **central claim** (or claims) with evidence.

academic writing Writing produced by scholars for other scholars, but also writing produced by students for college courses. Academic writing typically develops a **central claim** with evidence.

active voice Sentences written in *active voice* emphasize the person or thing doing the action (e.g., *Mark Twain wrote the story*). Conversely, sentences in **passive voice** emphasize the action more than the one doing the action (*e.g., The story was written by Mark Twain*).

analogy A comparison of two situations, different in many ways but similar enough to suggest that what's true in one situation is true in another.

analysis Breaking down a subject to determine how the parts are related or how they combine to achieve some purpose.

annotated bibliography A **bibliography** that, in addition to listing sources, includes notes about each source. Some annotated bibliographies include brief summaries that inform readers about a writer's sources. Other annotated bibliographies include working notes intended only for the writer.

annotations Comments written on a text while reading, including brief summaries, responses, or markings that help a reader engage with the text.

APA style A style of formal **documentation** created by the American Psychological Association that involves providing an author's last name and the publication date in a text when using information from a source.

bibliography The generic term referring to a list of sources at the end of a text. The bibliography in an MLA-documented paper is referred to as the **works cited** page; the bibliography in an APA-documented paper is referred to as the list of **references**.

block quotation A (usually) long quotation that is indented and set off from the rest of a paragraph. In papers documented in **MLA style**, quotations more than four lines of type are indented one inch (ten spaces) from the left margin. In papers documented in **APA style**, quotations more than forty words in length are indented five to seven spaces.

Boolean operators Words used to connect subject words when searching for information in a library database. The Boolean operators include **and, or, and not**.

central claim Variously referred to as the **thesis**, hypothesis, solution, or conclusion, the central claim is the main assertion in a paper that the writer wants readers to understand or accept.

coding scheme In **textual analysis** research, the coding scheme is the list of features that were analyzed. Items listed in a coding scheme should be nonoverlapping and clearly defined.

collaborative writing Working with others to produce a written document.

common knowledge Information widely published or widely known either by people with a high school education or by members of the intended audience. Common knowledge includes uncontested facts available and essentially identical in many sources. **Documentation** is not required for common knowledge, *if the information is conveyed in your own words.*

concise writing Writing that includes no wasted words; every word adds meaning or is grammatically necessary.

critical reading/reader Reading with a skeptical mindset. When you evaluate, assess, or judge the merits of the writer's claims and evidence, you are reading critically.

discipline A field of study. Psychology, biology, engineering, linguistics, and mathematics are a few examples of academic disciplines. Disciplines vary in their use of specialized vocabulary, research methods, and modes of inquiry.

documentation The way a writer identifies information he or she has obtained from sources. Examples of documentation styles include MLA, APA, CSE, and CMS.

editing Word replacements and sentence-level corrections made to the draft of a text to make the writing more clear or correct.

empirical argument A type of written argument in which the writer describes observations and draws conclusions about the data observed. Many empirical arguments follow the **IMRAD format**.

ethos The image or persona a writer creates for him- or herself. In general, when academic writers appeal to ethos they attempt to establish themselves as credible and trustworthy.

figures Any visual aid in a text that is not a table, including line graphs, bar charts, drawings, and photographs.

filler words Words that can be eliminated from a sentence without changing the meaning of the sentence. Eliminating filler words will make your writing more **conscise**.

first-person point of view Demonstrating firsthand knowledge by using first-person pronouns (such as *I, my, we, our*). In **academic writing**, first-person point of view can establish the writer's expertise.

framing A way of preparing readers for what's to come by announcing a paper's topics and general organization early in the paper.

genre A type or category of text. Textbooks, magazine articles, song lyrics, and novels are just a few examples of genres. **academic writing** is a broad genre, which has many subgenres, including essays, lab reports, and research reports.

genre theory According to genre theory, every **genre** of writing has features that reflect how the genre is created, who reads it, how it's read, and why it's read.

given-new pattern Writers who follow the "given-new" pattern begin sentences with information readers have already been told or likely already know ("given" information) before presenting "new" information.

identifying the gap A practice common in introductions to **academic writing** where the writer identifies how his or her research or writing will respond to, continue, or expand on what others have said about the topic.

IMRAD structure A method of organizing research reports, common in the physical sciences, applied sciences, and social sciences. The first letter of the major sections (Introduction, Methods, Results, Discussion) combine to create the acronym IMRAD, with an "a" added for easier pronunciation.

keyword search When searching for information in a library database, a keyword search involves combining important subject terms using **boolean operators**.

literature review A feature commonly found in introductions to **academic writing** where the writer summarizes what others have already learned about the subject before **identifying the gap** he or she will address.

logos Writers appeal to logos when they give readers reasons to accept their claims or cite evidence, such as studies, surveys, expert opinion, and testimonials.

MLA style A style of formal **documentation** created by the Modern Language Association that involves providing an author's last name and the source's page number in a text when using information from a source.

paraphrasing Conveying all or most of the details of a sentence or short passage you have read using your own words and sentence structure. **documentation** of the original source is usually required when paraphrasing others in a paper.

passive voice Sentences written in passive voice emphasize the action more than the one who is doing the action (e.g., *The story was written by Mark Twain*). Conversely, a sentence written in **active voice** emphasizes the person doing the action (*e.g., Mark Twain wrote the story*).

patchwriting Using language and sentence patterns that closely imitate the original text when **summarizing** or **paraphrasing**.

pathos Persuasive appeals to the reader's emotions, such as pity or fear, or to the reader's basic desires, such as the desire to be safe, healthy, prosperous, accepted, and respected.

peer-reviewed journal (scholarly journal) Publications that publish research reports for scholars in a specific **discipline**. Most articles appearing in these journals go through a peer review process, meaning other experts in the field (peers) ensure that the discipline's standards for research are upheld. Every discipline has many peer-reviewed journals.

plagiarism Intentionally imitating another person's writing style, claiming credit for another person's original ideas, or copying another writer's language without indicating that you are quoting.

primary research When conducting primary research, you ask a question, design a method for gathering data to answer your question, and then analyze and draw conclusions from the data.

primary source A text written by the one who did the research or who experienced/witnessed the events being described. Examples include original research reports, memoirs, and autobiographies. Not all primary sources are written texts. Any artifact that is studied in order to learn about a person, event, or time period can be a primary source, including paintings, photographs, or literary works.

proofreading Carefully reading a text for the purpose of finding and correcting errors in spelling, punctuation, syntax, or consistency.

proposal A paper that calls for action. Proposals often begin with the writer establishing that a problem exists.

qualifiers (qualifying words) Words that show there may be exceptions to a writer's claims or evidence. Examples of **qualifying words** include *may, often, perhaps, usually,* and *suggests.*

qualitative research A method of inquiry that usually focuses on only a few subjects but results in detailed description of those subjects. Interviewing and case studies are common types of qualitative research methods.

quantitative literacy The ability to interpret quantitative data, such as statistics, and presentations of quantitative data, including charts and graphs.

quantitative research A method of inquiry usually involving studying, polling, or counting numerous examples. (Associate the word "quantity" with quantitative research.)

quoting Using a writer's or speaker's exact words. A quotation is either enclosed in quotation marks or set off as a **block quotation**.

redundancy Unintentional repetition of an idea. Examples of redundant expressions include: *my (personal) opinion, (past) experience,* and *reason is because.*

references The title given to the **bibliography** at the end of a paper documented in **APA style**. Only sources that are referred to in the paper are listed.

reformulation A phrase or sentence that expands a statement by adding explanation, illustration, or definition or reduces a statement by summarizing or simplifying it. Many reformulations are introduced with *reformulation markers* like *i.e., in other words, that is,* and *specifically.*

revising Making "global," macro-level changes to a text to improve the organization, comprehensiveness, and usefulness for the intended audience.

rhetorical awareness Considering the audience, purpose, situation, **genre**, *and* context when reading or writing.

rhetorical reading Using knowledge of the writer, audience, purpose, context, situation, and **genre** to help you understand and correctly interpret a text.

rhetorical context (rhetorical situation) The original context of a text, including the writer, the audience, the situation and purpose, and the **genre**. Combined, these elements explain why a text is written the way it is.

sample When wanting to learn about a population of people or objects, a researcher will observe, survey, or analyze a subset of the population called the *sample.*

sampling bias When the **sample** or subset of the population being studied does not adequately represent or reflect the make-up of the larger population.

secondary research Conducting research by locating and reading what's already been written about a topic.

secondary source In a secondary source, information comes secondhand from an author who usually has read **primary sources** but who has not conducted original research. Examples include textbooks, popular magazines, and newspapers.

summarizing Briefly conveying just the essence or main ideas of a text using your own words and sentence structure. **Documentation** of the original source is usually required when summarizing.

synthesis writing Finding connections between what various sources on a topic say and using those insights to make a new point.

textual analysis A type of **primary research** that involves analyzing any kind of text, performance, or image in order to gain insights into how it is composed or used.

thesis-driven argument A text in which all of the discussion explores a central question or all of the evidence supports a **central claim** (or thesis). In academic arguments, the **thesis** usually appears early in the paper.

thesis (statement) The main assertion a writer develops and supports in a text. Also referred to as the **central claim**.

unity (in paragraphs) A paragraph that has unity is focused and presents a single topic or idea.

visual rhetoric The ways that images communicate meaning and persuade viewers.

Works Cited The title given to the **bibliography** found at the end of a paper documented in **MLA style**. Only sources that are referred to (cited) in the paper are listed.

Credits

Chapter 1

p. 1 Courtesy of US Army Recruiting Command Public Affairs
p. 1 Courtesy of Twitter
p. 2 Courtesy of California Department of Consumer Affairs
p. 2 User's Manual, Nikon Coolpix L22 © 2010 Nikon Corporation
p. 2 (Jeremy) Li Zheng. "Design and Development of a New Automated and High-Speed Gas Filling Systems." ISRN Mechanical Engineering, Volume 2011 (2011), Article ID 149643. Copyright © 2011 Zheng (Jeremy) Li. This is an open access article distributed under the Creative Commons Attribution License.
p. 18 Sheila Tobias, "Disciplinary Cultures and General Education: What Can We Learn from Our Learners?" Essays on Teaching Excellence: Toward the Best in the Academy. Copyright © 1993 by The Professional and Organizational Development Network in Higher Education. Reprinted by permission of the publisher.
p. 26 Sheila Tobias. "Why Poets Just Don't Get It in the Physics Classroom: Stalking the Second Tier in the Sciences." NACADA Journal 13.2 (Fall 1993): 42–44. Copyright © 1993. Reprinted by permission of NACADA.

Chapter 2

p. 36 Courtesy of CafeMom
p. 38 The Quarterly Journal of Economics 129.3 (August 2014). Copyright © 2015 Oxford University Press. Reprinted by permission of Oxford University Press.
p. 59 Excerpt from "Interview with Ellen Rose." Figure/Ground Communication. (24 Mar. 2011). Copyright © 2011. Reprinted by permission of Ellen Rose.
p. 64 "The Phenomenology Of On-Screen Reading: University Students' Lived Experience of Digitised Text" by Ellen Rose, British Journal of Educational Technology 42.3 (2011): 515–26. Copyright © 2010 by the Authors. British Journal of Educational Technology © Becta. Reprinted by permission.

Chapter 3

p. 87 © Hulton-Deutsch Collection/Corbis
p. 103 With kind permission from Springer Science & Business Media: Society, "Promoting Bad Statistics" (March/April 2001)10–15, Joel Best. Copyright © 2011.
p. 114 Best, Joel. "Birds–Dead and Deadly: Why Numeracy Needs to Address Social Construction," Numeracy 1.1 (2008): Article 6. Copyright © 2008 by Joel Best. Reprinted by permission of the author.

Chapter 4

p. 160 Alison J. Head and Michael B. Eisenberg, "College Students Eager to Learn but Need Help Negotiating Information Overload," The Seattle Times, 3 June 2011. Copyright © 2011 by Project Information Literacy. Reproduced by permission of Alison J. Head and Project Information Literacy (PIL).

p. 163 Excerpt from Alison J. Head. "Learning the Ropes: How Freshmen Conduct Course Research Once They Enter College," Project Information Literacy Research Report, December 4, 2013. Copyright © 2013 by Project Information Literacy. Reproduced by permission of Alison J. Head and Project Information Literacy (PIL).

Chapter 5

p. 189 © Andreas Gradin/Shutterstock

p. 192 © Michael Nolan/Robert Harding World Imagery/Corbis

p. 192 © Visuals Unlimited/Corbis

p. 193 © Akbargumay/Dreamstime.com

p. 195 © Marcus Lindström/istock.com

p. 207 "Can We Feed the World & Sustain the Planet?" by Jonathan A. Foley, Scientific American 305.5 (2011): 60–65. Reproduced with permission. Copyright © 2011 Scientific American, a Division of Nature America, Inc. All rights reserved.

p. 207 Photo courtesy of Kevin Van Aelst.

p. 215 Mueller, Nathaniel D., James S. Gerber, Matt Johnston, Deepak K. Ray, Navin Ramankutty, and Jonathan A. Foley. 2012. "Closing Yield Gaps through Nutrient and Water Management." Nature 490, no. 7419: 254–57. Copyright © 2012 by Macmillan Publishers Limited. All rights reserved. Reprinted by permission from Macmillan Publishers Ltd.

p. 217 Mueller, Nathaniel D., James S. Gerber, Matt Johnston, Deepak K. Ray, Navin Ramankutty, and Jonathan A. Foley. 2012. "Closing Yield Gaps through Nutrient and Water Management." Nature 490, no. 7419: 254–57. Copyright © 2012 by Macmillan Publishers Limited. All rights reserved. Reprinted by permission from Macmillan Publishers Ltd.

Chapter 6

p. 260 Photos courtesy of *Psychological Science*/SAGE Publications

p. 251 Capps, Rob. "First Impressions: The Science of Meeting People." (Interview with Amy Cuddy). Wired. com. (20 Nov. 2012). Copyright © 2012 by Wired.com/Rob Capps/Condé Nast Collection. Reprinted by permission of Condé Nast.

p. 256 Carney, Dana R., Amy J.C. Cuddy, and Andy J. Yap. "Power Posing: Brief Nonverbal Displays Affect Neuroendocrine Levels and Risk Tolerance." Psychological Science 21.10 (2010): 1363–68. Copyright © 2010 by Dana R. Carney, Amy J.C. Cuddy, and Andy J. Yap. Reprinted by permission of SAGE Publications.

Chapter 7

p. 277 Screenshots of ProQuest search results screens are published with permission of ProQuest LLC. Further reproduction is prohibited without permission. www .proquest.com

p. 289 Screenshots published with permission of Statistics Brain.

p. 291 YAB [Youth Advisory Board] Interview: Laura Granka, Search User Experience, Google." Ypulse (5 Feb. 2010). Reprinted by permission of Laura Granka and Raymond Braun.

p. 295 Granka, Laura A., Thorsten Joachims, and Geri Gay. "Eye-Tracking Analysis of User Behavior in WWW Search." SIGIR Forum (2004): 478–79. Copyright © 2004 by Association for Computing Machinery. Reprinted by permission of Laura Granka.

Chapter 8

p. 328 "Unraveling the Citation Trail", Project Information Literacy Smart Talk, no. 8, Sandra Jamieson and Rebecca Moore Howard, The Citation Project, August 15, 2011. http://www.projectinfolit.org/st/howard-jamieson.asp.

p. 338 "Writing from Sources, Writing from Sentences" by Rebecca Moore Howard, Tanya K. Rodrigue, Tricia C. Serviss, Writing and Pedagogy 2.2 (2010): 177–192. Copyright © 2010 by Equinox Publishing Ltd. Reprinted by permission of Equinox Publishing Ltd.

Chapter 9

p. 379 Abridged from Shaughnessy, Michael E., "An Interview with Deanna Kuhn." Educational Psychology Review 16.3 (2004): 267–82. Copyright © 2004 by Plenum Publishing Corp. Reprinted by permission of Springer.

p. 387 Kuhn, Deanna. "Jumping to Conclusions." Scientific American Mind 18.1 (2007): 44–51. Reproduced with permission. Copyright © 2007 by Scientific American, Inc. All rights reserved.

Chapter 10

p. 419 Excerpt from University of Michigan's webpage for the Undergraduate Research Opportunity Program ("Evaluation and Assessment"). Copyright © by UROP/ University of Michigan. Reprinted by permission of Sandra Gregerman, Director. http://www.lsa.umich.edu/urop/aboutus/evaluationassessment.

p. 424 Nagda, Biren.A., Sandra R. Gregerman, John Jonides, "Undergraduate Student-Faculty Research Partnerships Affect Student Retention." The Review of Higher Education 22.1 (1998): 55–56, 57, 58–61, 62–64, 64–67. Copyright © 1998 by The Association of Higher Education. Reprinted with permission of Johns Hopkins University Press.

Chapter 11

p. 457 Freedman, Sarah Warshauer. "Some Reasons for the Grades We Give Compositions." The English Journal 71. 7 (Nov., 1982): 86–89. Copyright © 1982 by the National Council of Teachers of English. Reprinted by permission.

p. 465 Freedman, Sarah Warshauer. "Why Do Teachers Give the Grades They Do?" College Composition and Communication 30. 2 (May 1979): 161–64. Copyright © 1979 by the National Council of Teachers of English. Reprinted by permission.

Chapter 12

p. 481 de Waal, Frans. "The Brains of the Animal Kingdom; New Research Shows That We Have Grossly Underestimated both the Scope and the Scale of Animal

Intelligence. Primatologist Frans de Waal on Memory-Champ Chimps, Tool-Using Elephants and Rats Capable of Empathy." Wall Street Journal (Online) 22 Mar 2013. Copyright © 2013 by Dow Jones & Company Inc. All Rights Reserved Worldwide. License # 3336691475090.

p. 486 Excerpts from Proctor, Darby, et al. "Chimpanzees Play The Ultimatum Game." *Proceedings Of The National Academy Of Sciences Of The United States Of America* 110.6 (2013): 2070–2075. Copyright © 2013 by National Academy of Sciences of the United States of America. Reprinted by permission.

Chapter 13

p. 501 pp. 3–25 from Christakis, Nicholas A., and James H. Fowler, CONNECTED: The Surprising Power of Our Social Networks and How They Shape Our Lives. Copyright © 2009 by Nicholas A. Christakis and James H. Fowler. By permission of Little, Brown and Company. All rights reserved.

p. 519 Excerpt(s) from THE AGE OF EMPATHY: Nature's Lessons for a Kinder Society by Frans de Waal. Copyright © 2009 by Frans de Waal. Used by permission of Harmony Books, an imprint of the Crown Publishing Group, a division of Random House LLC. All rights reserved.

p. 524 "Is Poor Fitness Contagious? Evidence from Randomly Assigned Friends" by Scott E. Carrell, Mark Hoekstra, James E. West, Journal of Public Economics 95.7–8 (2011): 657–63. Copyright © 2011 with permission from Elsevier.

p. 543 Fisman, Ray. "The Canseco Effect: Wherever He Went, Jose Canseco Made His Teammates Better Power Hitters. Can Statistics Be Used to Find Juicers?" Slate Magazine (30 July 2010). Copyright © 2010 The Slate Group. All rights reserved. Used by permission and protected by the Copyright Laws of the United States. The printing, copying, redistribution, or retransmission of this Content without express permission is prohibited.

p. 547 Best, Joel. "The Illusion of Diffusion." Society (March/April 2006): 50–55. Copyright © 2006 by Transaction Publishers. Reprinted by permission of Springer.

p. 558 V. S. Ramachandran. "Creativity versus Skepticism within Science." The Skeptical Inquirer 30.6 (Nov/Dec 2006): 48–51. Copyright © 2006. Reprinted by permission of The Skeptical Inquirer.

p. 565 Garcia, Pablo. "Hackers of the Renaissance." Omni Reboot. http://omnireboot.jerrickventures.com/features/hackers-of-the-renaissance/. Reprinted by permission of Pablo Garcia.

p. 568 Hans Holbein the Younger, The Ambassadors © The National Gallery, London.

p. 568 Hans Holbein the Younger, The Ambassadors (detail of skull photographed from the side to correct the distortion) © The National Gallery, London.

p. 569 © Science and Society Picture Library/Getty Images

p. 570 from *Certaine Errors in Navigation*, Edward Wright,

p. 572 "Culture and Causal Cognition" by Ara Norenzayan and Richard E. Nisbett. Current Directions in Psychological Science 9.4 (2000): 132–35. Copyright © 2000 American Psychological Society. Reprinted by permission of SAGE Publications.

p. 580 Chua, Hannah Faye, Julie E. Boland, and Richard E. Nisbett. "Cultural Variation in Eye Movements during Scene Perception." Proceedings of the National Academy of Sciences of the United States of America 102.35 (2005): 12629–33. Copyright © 2005 by the National Academy of Sciences of the United States of America. Reprinted by permission.

Chapter 14

p. 594 From HOW THE MIND WORKS by Steven Pinker. Copyright © 1997 by Steven Pinker. Used by permission of W. W. Norton & Company, Inc.

p. 599 Tavris, Carol, and Elliot Aronson. "'Why Won't They Admit They're Wrong?' and Other Skeptics' Mysteries." The Skeptical Inquirer (Nov 2007): 12–13. Copyright © 2007 by the authors. Reprinted by permission of Carol Tavris and Elliot Aronson.

p. 603 Excerpted from Choi, Youjin, Sejung Marina Choi, and Nora Rifon, "'I Smoke But I Am Not a Smoker': Phantom Smokers and the Discrepancy Between Self-Identity and Behavior." Journal of American College Health 59.2 (2010): 117–25. Copyright © 2010 by Taylor & Francis Group LLC. Reprinted by permission of the publisher (Taylor & Francis Ltd., http://www.tandf.co.uk/journals).

p. 616 "The End of History Illusion" by Jordi Quoidbach, Daniel T. Gilbert, and Timothy D. Wilson, Science 339. 6115 (2013): 96–98. Copyright © 2013 by AAAS. Reprinted with permission from AAAS.

p. 626 "In Hiring and Promoting, Look beyond Results" by Francesca Gino, The Wall Street Journal - Eastern Edition (October 24, 2011): R7. Copyright © Dow Jones & Company, Inc. Reprinted with permission of The Wall Street Journal. All rights reserved. License #3322580100106.

p. 628 Excerpted from Moore, Don A., Samuel A. Swift, Zachariah S. Sharek, and Francesca Gino, "Correspondence Bias in Performance Evaluation: Why Grade Inflation Works." Personality & Social Psychology Bulletin 36. 6 (June 2010): 843–52. Copyright © 2010 by the Society for Personality and Social Psychology, Inc. Reprinted by permission of SAGE Publications.

p. 646 "Myside Bias in Thinking about Abortion" by Jonathan Baron, Thinking and Reasoning 1 (1995): 221–35. Copyright © 2013 by Taylor & Francis Ltd. Reprinted by permission of Taylor & Francis Ltd. http://www.informaworld.com.

p. 662 "Filling in Gaps in Perception: Part 1" by V. S. Ramachandran, Current Directions in Psychological Science 1.6 (1992): 199–205. Copyright © 1992 American Psychological Society. Reprinted by permission of SAGE Publications.

Chapter 15

p. 678 "Lost in Translation" by Lera Boroditsky, The Wall Street Journal – Eastern Edition, 24 July 2010: W3. Copyright © 2010 by Dow Jones & Company, Inc. Reprinted with permission from The Wall Street Journal. All rights reserved worldwide. License #3322641452758.

p. 683 Fausey, Caitlin M., and Lera Boroditsky. "Subtle Linguistic Cues Influence Perceived Blame and Financial Liability." Psychonomic Bulletin & Review (pre-2011) 17.5 (2010): 644–50. Copyright © 2010 by The Psychonomic Society, Inc. Reprinted by permission of Springer.

p. 698 Wolf, Maryanne. "Our 'Deep Reading' Brain: Its Digital Evolution Poses Questions." Nieman Reports 64.2 (2010): 7–8. Reprinted by permission of the author and Nieman Reports.

p. 702 Sherry Turkle. "How Computers Change the Way We Think." The Chronicle of Higher Education 50.21 (2004): B.26-B28.Copyright © 2004 by Sherry Turkle. Reprinted by permission of Sherry Turkle.

p. 709 Shirky, Clay. "Does the Internet Make You Smarter or Dumber?" The Wall Street Journal (5 Jun 2010): W1. Reprinted by permission of the author.

p. 713 Zuckerman, Ethan. "Using the Internet to Examine Patterns of Foreign Coverage." Nieman Reports 58.3 (2004): 51–3. Reprinted by permission of the author and Nieman Reports.

p. 718 McDonald, Sylvia E. "The Effects And Predictor Value of In-Class Texting Behavior On Final Course Grades." College Student Journal 47.1 (2013): 34–40. Copyright © 2013 by Project Innovation, Inc. Reprinted by permission of Project Innovation.

p. 728 Hembrooke, Helene, and Geri Gay. "The Laptop and the Lecture: The Effects of Multitasking in Learning Environments." Journal of Computing in Higher Education 15.1 (Fall 2003). Copyright © 2003 by Springer Science + Business Media New York. Reprinted by permission of the publisher.

Chapter 16

p. 744 O'Brian, John. "Another Report on the Age Of Extinction." Canadian Review of American Studies 38.1 (2008): 191–198. Copyright © 2008 by Canadian Review of American Studies. Reprinted by permission of University of Toronto Press (www.utpjournals.com).

p. 758 Dale, Elizabeth. "Getting Away with Murder." American Historical Review 111.1 (2006): 95–103. Copyright © 2006 by Oxford University Press. Reprinted by permission of Oxford University Press.

p. 764 Allen, Terrence T. "Taking a Juvenile into Custody: Situational Factors That Influence Police Officers' Decisions." Journal of Sociology & Social Welfare 32.2 (2005): 121–29. Copyright © 2005 by Journal of Sociology & Social Welfare. Reprinted by permission of Western Michigan University.

p. 772 Murphy, Erin. "The Government Wants Your DNA." Scientific American 38 (March 2013): 72–77. Reproduced with permission. Copyright © 2013 Scientific American, a Division of Nature America, Inc. All rights reserved.

p. 781 Loftus, Elizabeth F. "How I Got Started: From Semantic Memory To Expert Testimony." Applied Cognitive Psychology 25.2 (2011): 347–348. Copyright © 2011 by John Wiley & Sons, Ltd. Reprinted by permission.

p. 786 Foster, Jeffrey L., Maryanne Garry, and Elizabeth F. Loftus. "Repeated Information in the Courtroom." Court Review 48.1/2 (2012): 44–47. Reprinted by permission of American Judges Association and the authors.

p. 793 "It's a Crime What Some People Do with Statistics" by Arnold Barnett, The Wall Street Journal (30 Aug 2000): A26. Copyright © 2000 by Dow Jones & Company, Inc. Reprinted by permission of The Wall Street Journal. All rights reserved. License #3322600307172.

p. 797 "War Really is Going out of Style" by Joshua S. Goldstein and Steven Pinker, The New York Times (December 17, 2011). Copyright © 2011 by The New York Times Company. All rights reserved. Used by permission and protected by the Copyright Laws of the United States. The printing, copying, redistribution, or retransmission of this Content without express written permission is prohibited.

Chapter 17

p. 802 "Conservation-Reliant Species" by Dale D. Goble, et al. BioScience 62.10 (2012): 869–73. Copyright © 2012 by American Institute of Biological Sciences. Reprinted by permission of Oxford University Press.

p. 813 Stephanie Wear, “Finding Nemo on Your Plate.” The Nature Conservancy, http://blog.nature.org/conservancy/2011/03/21/finding-nemo-on-your-plate/. Copyright © 2011 The Nature Conservancy. Reprinted by permission of The Nature Conservancy.

p. 816 “Survival of Neonatal White-Tailed Deer in an Exurban Population” by Sarah T. Saalfeld and Stephen S. Ditchkoff, Journal of Wildlife Management 71.3 (2007): 940–4. Copyright © 2007. Reprinted by permission of John Wiley & Sons, Inc.

p. 828 “The Trial” by David W. Orr, Conservation Biology, 20.6 (2006): 1570–3. Copyright © 2006 by Society for Conservation Biology. Reprinted by permission of John Wiley & Sons, Inc.

p. 836 “Conservation and the Social Sciences” by Michael B. Mascia, J. Peter Brosius, Tracy A. Dobson, Bruce C. Forbes, Leah Horowitz, Margaret A. McKean, and Nancy J. Turner, Conservation Biology (June 2003): 649–50. Copyright © 2003 by EBSCO Publishing. Reprinted by permission of John Wiley & Sons, Inc.

p. 841 “Alpine Areas in the Colorado Front Range as Monitors of Climate Change and Ecosystem Response” by Mark Williams, et al., Geographical Review 92(2002): 180–91. Copyright © 2003 by American Geographical Society of New York. Reprinted by permission of John Wiley & Sons, Inc.

p. 844 Reproduced courtesy of the Niwot Ridge Long-Term Ecological Research Archives

p. 856 John M. Antle. “Climate Change and Agriculture: Economic Impacts.” Choices 23.1 (2008): 9–11. Copyright © 2008 by CHOICES. Reprinted here courtesy of American Agricultural Economics Association and by permission of John M. Antle.

p. 862 Diamond, Jared. “The Last Americans: Environmental Collapse and the End of Civilization” Harper’s Magazine 06 2003: 43–51. Copyright © 2003 by Harper’s Magazine. All rights reserved. Reproduced from the June issue by special permission.

p. 878 Diamond, Jared. “Will Big Business Save the Earth?” The New York Times Upfront Mar 15 2010: 14–5. Copyright © 2010 by The New York Times. All rights reserved. Used by permission and protected by the Copyright Laws of the United States. The printing, copying, redistribution, or retransmission of this Content without express permission is prohibited.

Index